microeconomics

➤ R. Glenn Hubbard

Columbia University

➤ Anthony Patrick O'Brien

Lehigh University

PEARSON

Prentice
Hall

Upper Saddle River, New Jersey 07458

Library of Congress Cataloging-in-Publication Data

Hubbard, R. Glenn.
    Microeconomics / R. Glenn Hubbard, Anthony Patrick O'Brien.
      p. cm.
    Includes bibliographical references and index.
    ISBN 0-13-034826-0
    1. Microeconomics.   I. O'Brien, Anthony Patrick.   II. Title.
    HB172.H83 2006
    338.5—dc22

2005014958

Executive Editor: David Alexander
Developmental Editor: Lena Buonanno
Executive Marketing Manager:
Sharon M. Koch
Marketing Development Manager:
Kathleen McLellan
Director, Key Markets: David Theisen
Editorial Director: Jeff Shelstad
Acquisitions Editor: Jon Axelrod
Project Manager, Editorial:
Francesca Calogero
Editorial Assistant: Michael Dittamo
Director of Development: Steve Deitmer
Media Project Manager: Peter Snell
Media Product Development Manager:
Nancy Welcher
Director of Marketing: Eric Frank
Marketing Assistant: Tina Panagiotou
Director of Market Development:
Annie Todd
Associate Director, Production Editorial:
Judy Leale
Senior Managing Editor: Cynthia Regan
Production Editor: Michael Reynolds
Permissions Supervisor: Charles Morris
Production Manager, Manufacturing:
Arnold Vila

Creative Director: Maria Lange
Art Director: Pat Smythe
Interior Design: Liz Harasymczuk
Cover Design: Pat Smythe
Illustrator, Interior: ElectraGraphics, Inc.
Infographics: Ray Cruz
Director, Image Resource Center:
Melinda Reo
Manager, Rights and Permissions:
Zina Arabia
Manager: Visual Research: Beth Brenzel
**Manager, Cover Visual Research &
Permissions:** Karen Sanatar
Image Permission Coordinator:
Cynthia Vincenti
Photo Researcher: Diane Austin
Manager, Print Production:
Christy Mahon
Print Production Liaison: Suzanne Duda
**Composition/Full-Service Project
Management:** Carlisle Publishers Services
Printer/Binder: Courier
Cover Printer: Phoenix Color
Typeface: 10.5/12 Minion

Credits and acknowledgments borrowed from other sources and reproduced, with permission, in this textbook appear on appropriate page C-1.

Pearson Education LTD.
Pearson Education Singapore, Pte. Ltd
Pearson Education, Canada, Ltd
Pearson Education–Japan

Pearson Education Australia PTY, Limited
Pearson Education North Asia Ltd
Pearson Educación de Mexico, S.A. de C.V.
Pearson Education Malaysia, Pte. Ltd

10 9 8 7 6 5 4 3 2 1
ISBN 0-13-034826-0

PEARSON
Prentice
Hall

For Constance, Raph, and Will

——R. Glenn Hubbard

To my mother and the memory of my father

——Anthony Patrick O'Brien

Authorship

Glenn Hubbard policymaker, professor, and researcher. R. Glenn Hubbard is the Dean and Russell L. Carson Professor of Finance and Economics in the Graduate School of Business at Columbia University and Professor of Economics in Columbia's Faculty of Arts and Sciences. He is also a research associate of the National Bureau of Economic Research and a director of Automatic Data Processing, Black Rock Closed-End Funds, Dex Media, Duke Realty, KKR Financial Corporation, and Ripplewood Holdings. He received his Ph.D. in economics from Harvard University in 1983. From 2001–2003, he served as Chairman of the White House Council of Economic Advisers, and from 1991–1993, he was Deputy Assistant Secretary of the U.S. Treasury Department. Glenn Hubbard's fields of specialization are public economics, financial markets and institutions, corporate finance, macroeconomics, industrial organization, and public policy. He is the author of more than 90 articles in leading journals, including the *American Economic Review, Journal of Finance, Journal of Financial Economics, Journal of Political Economy, Journal of Public Economics, Quarterly Journal of Economics, RAND Journal of Economics,* and *Review of Economics and Statistics.* His research has been supported by grants from the National Science Foundation, the National Bureau of Economic Research, and numerous private foundations.

Tony O'Brien award-winning professor and researcher. Anthony Patrick O'Brien is a professor of economics at Lehigh University. He received his Ph.D. from the University of California, Berkeley, in 1987. He has taught principles of economics for more than 15 years, in both large sections and small honors classes. He received the Lehigh University Award for Distinguished Teaching. He was formerly the director of the Diamond Center for Economic Education and was named a Dana Foundation Faculty Fellow and Lehigh Class of 1961 Professor of Economics. He has been a visiting professor at the University of California, Santa Barbara, and the Graduate School of Industrial Administration at Carnegie Mellon University. Anthony O'Brien's research has dealt with such issues as the evolution of the U.S. automobile industry, the sources of U.S. economic competitiveness, the development of U.S. trade policy, the causes of the Great Depression, and the causes of black–white income differences. His research has been published in leading journals, including the *American Economic Review,* the *Quarterly Journal of Economics,* the *Journal of Money, Credit, and Banking, Industrial Relations,* and the *Journal of Economic History.* His research has been supported by grants from government agencies and private foundations. In addition to teaching and writing, Anthony O'Brien also serves on the editorial board of the *Journal of Socio-economics.*

Contextual Learning

We are convinced that students learn to apply economic principles best if they are taught in a familiar context. Whether they open an art studio, do social work, trade on Wall Street, work for the government, or tend bar, students must understand the economic forces behind their work. And though business students will have many opportunities to see economic principles in action in various courses, liberal arts students may not. We therefore use many diverse, real-world business and policy examples to illustrate economic concepts and to develop educated consumers, voters, and citizens.

Here are several chapters that demonstrate our approach:

Chapter 4, "Economic Efficiency, Government Price Setting, and Taxes"

We use the concepts of consumer surplus and producer surplus to measure the economic effects of price ceilings and price floors as they relate to the familiar examples of rental properties and the minimum wage. We revisit consumer surplus and producer surplus in three additional chapters. In Chapter 8, "Comparative Advantage and the Gains from International Trade," we analyze government policies that affect trade. In Chapter 14, "Monopoly and Antitrust Policy," we examine the effect of market power on economic efficiency. In Chapter 15, "Pricing Strategy," we examine the effect of firm pricing policy on economic efficiency.

Chapter 5, "Externalities, Environmental Policy, and Public Goods"

To pique interest and expose students to policy issues early in the course, we cover current topics such as air pollution and global warming and the two approaches to dealing with them, command and control approach and tradeable emissions allowances. We also cover the Coase theorem and explain how private bargaining leads to economic efficiency in a market with an externality.

Chapter 7, "Firms, the Stock Market, and Corporate Governance"

We look at the firm, how it is organized, how it raises funds, and the information it provides to investors. We also illustrate how in a market system entrepreneurs meet consumer wants and efficiently organize production. To explore how government policy affects business, we cover the WorldCom and Enron business scandals and the objectives of the 2002 Sarbanes-Oxley Act.

Chapter 8, "Comparative Advantage and International Trade"

We return to comparative advantage, which we introduced in Chapter 2, to discuss outsourcing, globalization, and trade. We also analyze the economic effects of trade policies.

Modern Organization

Chapter 12, "Monopolistic Competition: The Competitive Model in a More Realistic Setting"

We devote a full chapter to monopolistic competition prior to covering oligopoly and monopoly. Although many instructors cover monopolistic competition very briefly or dispense with it entirely, we think it is an overlooked tool for reinforcing the basic message of how markets work in a context that is much more familiar to students than are the agricultural examples that dominate other discussions of perfect competition. We use the monopolistic competition model to introduce the downward-sloping demand curve material usually introduced in the monopoly chapter. This helps students grasp the important point that nearly all firms—not just monopolies—face downward-sloping demand curves. Covering monopolistic competition directly after perfect competition also allows for the early discussion of topics such as brand management and the sources of competitive success. Nevertheless, we wrote the chapters so that professors who prefer to cover monopoly (Chapter 14) directly after perfect competition (Chapter 11) can do so without loss of continuity.

Chapter 13, "Oligopoly: Firms in Less Competitive Markets"

We use game theory to analyze competition among oligopolists. Game theory helps students understand how companies with market power make strategic decisions in many competitive situations. We use familiar companies such as Wal-Mart, Target, Coca-Cola, PepsiCo, and Dell in our game theory applications.

Chapter 15, "Pricing Strategy"

We explore how firms attempt to maximize profit. Students encounter pricing strategies everywhere—when they buy a movie ticket, book a flight for spring break, or research book prices online. We use these relevant, familiar examples to illustrate how companies use such pricing strategies as price discrimination, cost-plus pricing, and two-part tariffs.

Chapter 17, "The Economics of Information"

We explore the important fact that consumers, firms, and governments must make decisions on the basis of incomplete information. Students face uncertainty and make decisions with incomplete information every day in the used car market, labor market, and health insurance market. We help students analyze these familiar situations and explore the perspective of the consumer and firm. We also apply the concepts of adverse selection and moral hazard to financial markets.

Business Applications

When George Lucas was asked why he made *Star Wars,* he replied, "It's the kind of movie I like to see, but no one seemed to be making them. So, I decided to make one." We realized that no one seemed to be writing the kind of textbook we wanted to use in our classes. So, after years of supplementing texts with fresh, lively, real-world examples from newspapers, magazines, and professional journals, we decided to write an economics text that delivered complete economics coverage with many real-world business examples. Our goal was to keep our classes "widget free."

We believe the course is a success if students can apply what they have learned in both personal and business settings, and if they have developed the analytical skills to understand what they read in print. That's why we explain economic concepts by using many real-world business examples and applications. Here are a few examples:

How do firms like **Home Depot** respond to a growing Hispanic market?

Did **Abercrombie and Fitch** narrow its target market too much?

How can firms compete with **Wal-Mart**?

Each CHAPTER-OPENING CASE sets a real-world context for learning, sparks students' interest in economics, and gives the chapter a unifying theme.

Each chapter opener covers a real-world situation faced by companies such as Coca-Cola, Walt Disney, and the New York Mets. The company is integrated in the narrative, graphs, and pedagogical features of the chapter. Many of the chapter openers focus on the role of the entrepreneur in developing new products and bringing them to the market. Here are a few examples of topics we explore:

Why do firms like **3Com** outsource to China?

What is **BMW**'s strategy for growth?

Why was the **Google** IPO so successful, and how can we track the stock?

How does **Starbucks** grow through product differentiation?

How Hewlett-Packard Manages the Demand for Printers

➤ In early 2005 the board of directors at Hewlett-Packard (H-P) ousted chief executive officer Carly Fiorina and replaced her with Mark Hurd, then the chief executive officer of NCR Corporation. What happened?.

Carly Fiorina had been a business celebrity for many years. In July 1999 she became H-P's chief executive officer, which made her the first woman to head one of the 100 largest firms in the United States. In 2002, she brought about the largest merger of two technology firms in U.S. history when H-P purchased Compaq Computer Corporation. By

with Compaq had failed to improve H-P's performance in the personal computer market.

Printers, and not personal computers, are H-P's most successful product. Although printers account for only about 30 percent of the firm's sales, they account for 70 percent of its profits. In fact, as *An Inside Look* at the end of this chapter discusses, to increase the demand for printers the firm is willing to sell its personal computers at low prices.

Hewlett-Packard's success, like that of any firm, depends on its ability

example, Carly Fiorina announced that sales of H-P printers had declined sharply in the first half of that year compared to the first half of 2000. Two events caused this decline: First, many individuals and small businesses unexpectedly decided not to upgrade their existing computers to faster and more powerful machines. Pur[...] are a key part of [...] ers. Second, t[...] moved into rece[...] incomes of ma[...] reducing the pr[...] nesses. Fiorina[...]

Policy Examples

***AN INSIDE LOOK* shows students how to apply the concepts of a chapter to the analysis of a newspaper article.**

Reading the newspaper and other periodicals is an important part of understanding the current business climate. At the end of each chapter, a two-page periodical feature consists of an excerpt of an article, analysis of the article, graph(s), and critical thinking questions.

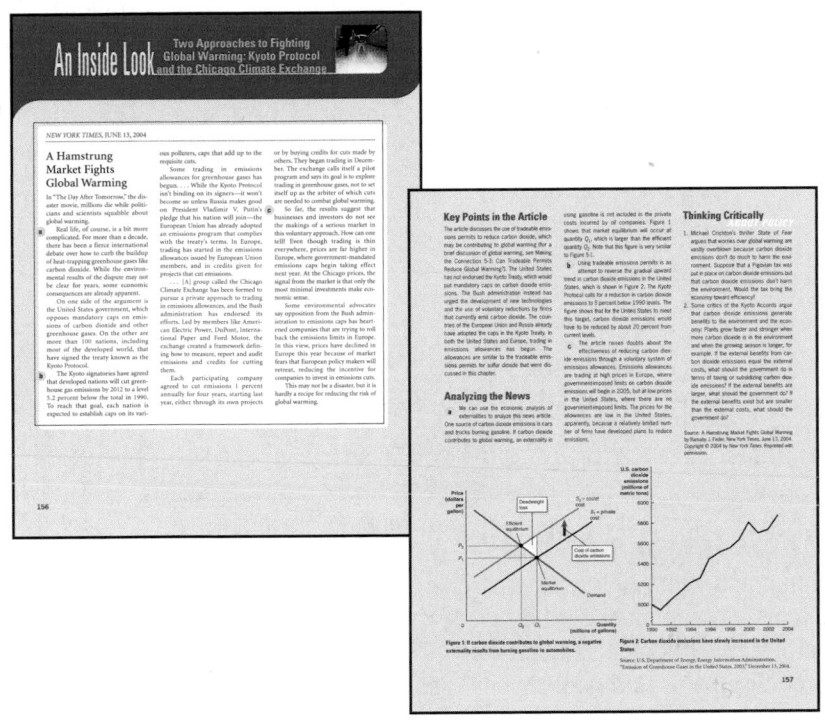

***MAKING THE CONNECTION* between concepts and the real world.**

In each chapter, between two and four "Making the Connection" features present relevant, stimulating, and provocative news stories, primarily about business.

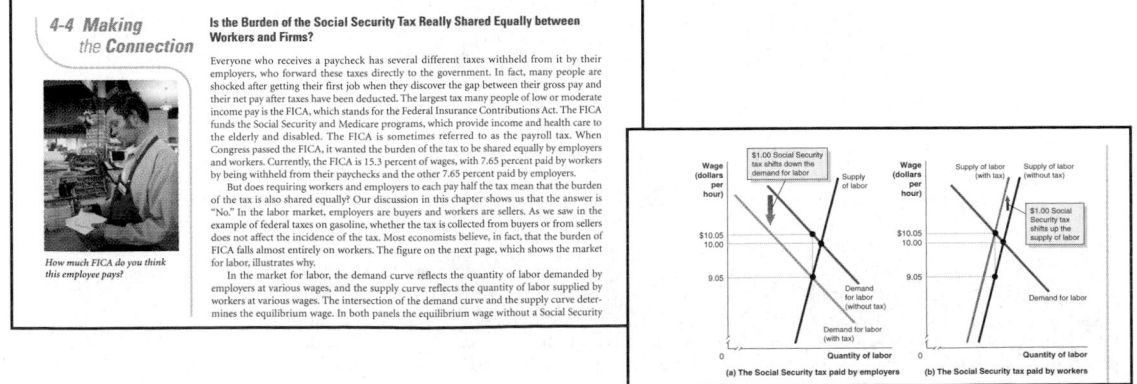

Solved Problems

SOLVED PROBLEMS offer a hands-on approach to learning.

As we all know, many students have great difficulty handling applied economics problems. We help students overcome this hurdle by including two or three worked-out problems tied to select chapter-opening learning objectives and the associated quantitative information. Our goals are to keep students focused on the main ideas of each chapter and to give students a model of how to solve an economic problem by breaking it down step by step. There are additional exercises in the end-of-chapter materials tied to every Solved Problem.

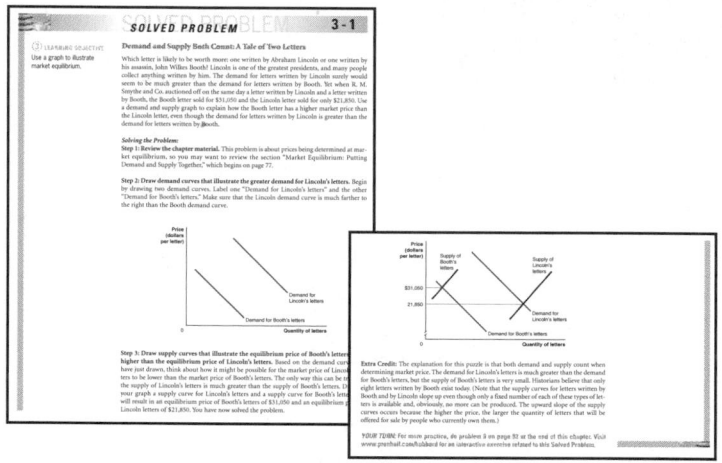

Don't Let This Happen To You!

We know from many years of teaching which concepts students find most difficult. Each chapter contains a box feature alerting students to the most common pitfalls in that chapter's material. We test the students' understanding by following up with a related question in the end-of-chapter "Problems and Applications" section.

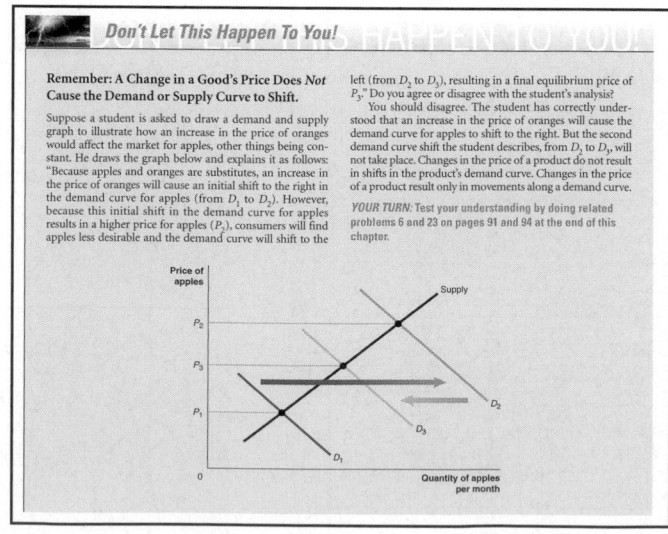

Graphs and Summary Tables

Graphs

Graphs are an indispensable part of the principles of economics course but are a major stumbling block for many students. Every chapter (except Chapter 1) includes end-of-chapter problems that require students to draw, read, and interpret graphs. Interactive graphing exercises can be found on the book's supporting Web site. We use four devices to help students read and interpret graphs:

1. Captions
2. Boxed Notes
3. Color-Coded Curves

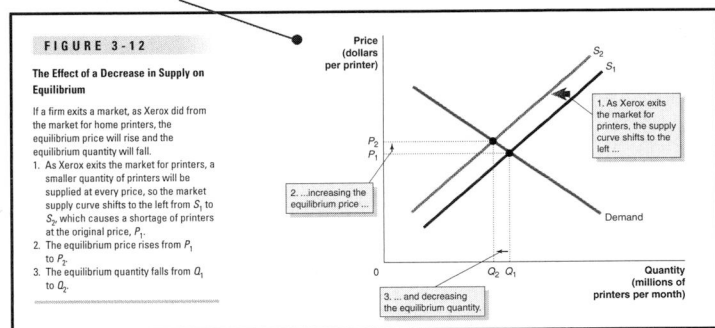

4. Summary Tables with Graphs

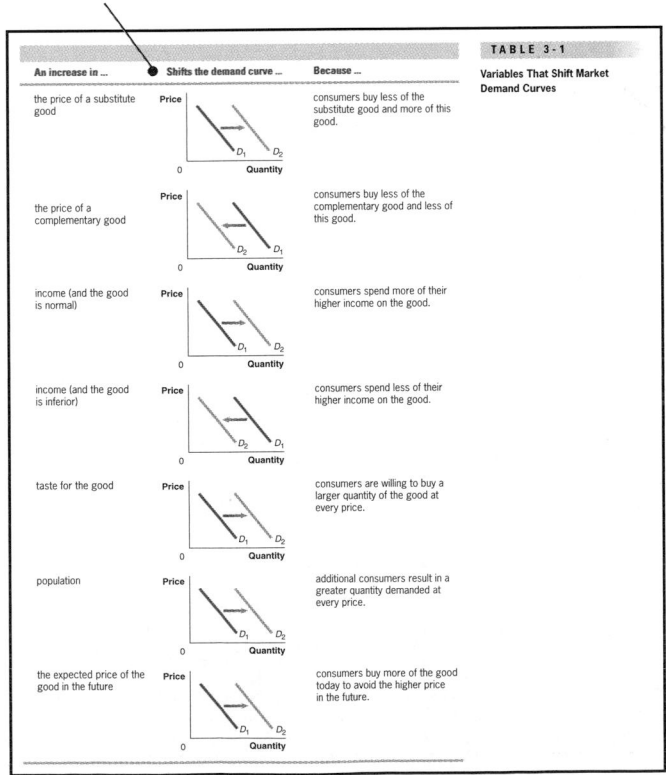

Integrated Resources

Integrated Resources

The authors and Prentice Hall have worked together to integrate all text, print, and media resources to make teaching and learning easier.

Integration Benefits Students and Instructors

All textbooks have supporting resources, but not all textbooks have supporting resources that are seamlessly integrated with each other and the text. One of the driving forces behind the development of this resource package is our belief that concepts are grasped more easily in a familiar setting. That's why we decided to integrate the features of the text with the print and media resources for both students and instructors. And we did more than "integrate." We also enhanced the lecture materials by including additional examples in the Instructor's Manual.

Everything works together for a unified, efficient teaching and learning experience. Here's one example:

On this page is a "Solved Problem" that appears in the text. The facing page shows you how we integrate that Solved Problem—as well as the "Don't Let This Happen To You!" feature—in the end-of-chapter problems. Additional Solved Problems appear in the Instructor's Manual and Study Guide. See the pages that follow for more about supplements.

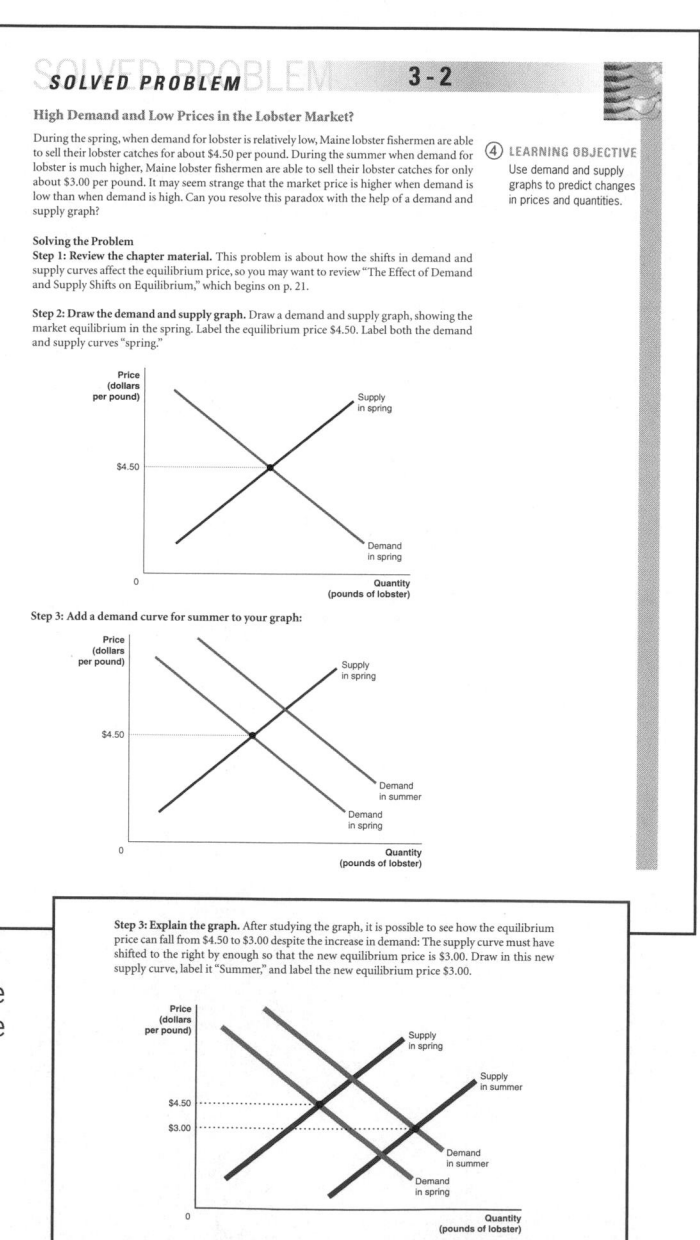

SOLVED PROBLEM 3-2

High Demand and Low Prices in the Lobster Market?

During the spring, when demand for lobster is relatively low, Maine lobster fishermen are able to sell their lobster catches for about $4.50 per pound. During the summer when demand for lobster is much higher, Maine lobster fishermen are able to sell their lobster catches for only about $3.00 per pound. It may seem strange that the market price is higher when demand is low than when demand is high. Can you resolve this paradox with the help of a demand and supply graph?

④ LEARNING OBJECTIVE
Use demand and supply graphs to predict changes in prices and quantities.

Solving the Problem
Step 1: Review the chapter material. This problem is about how the shifts in demand and supply curves affect the equilibrium price, so you may want to review "The Effect of Demand and Supply Shifts on Equilibrium," which begins on p. 21.

Step 2: Draw the demand and supply graph. Draw a demand and supply graph, showing the market equilibrium in the spring. Label the equilibrium price $4.50. Label both the demand and supply curves "spring."

Step 3: Add a demand curve for summer to your graph:

Step 3: Explain the graph. After studying the graph, it is possible to see how the equilibrium price can fall from $4.50 to $3.00 despite the increase in demand: The supply curve must have shifted to the right by enough so that the new equilibrium price is $3.00. Draw in this new supply curve, label it "Summer," and label the new equilibrium price $3.00.

Integrated Resources

Solved Problems appear in the chapters. Additional Solved Problems appear in following areas:

- **end-of-chapter Problems and Applications section**

- **instructor's manual**

- **PowerPoint slides**

- **print study guide**

- **test item file**

- **interactive study guide**

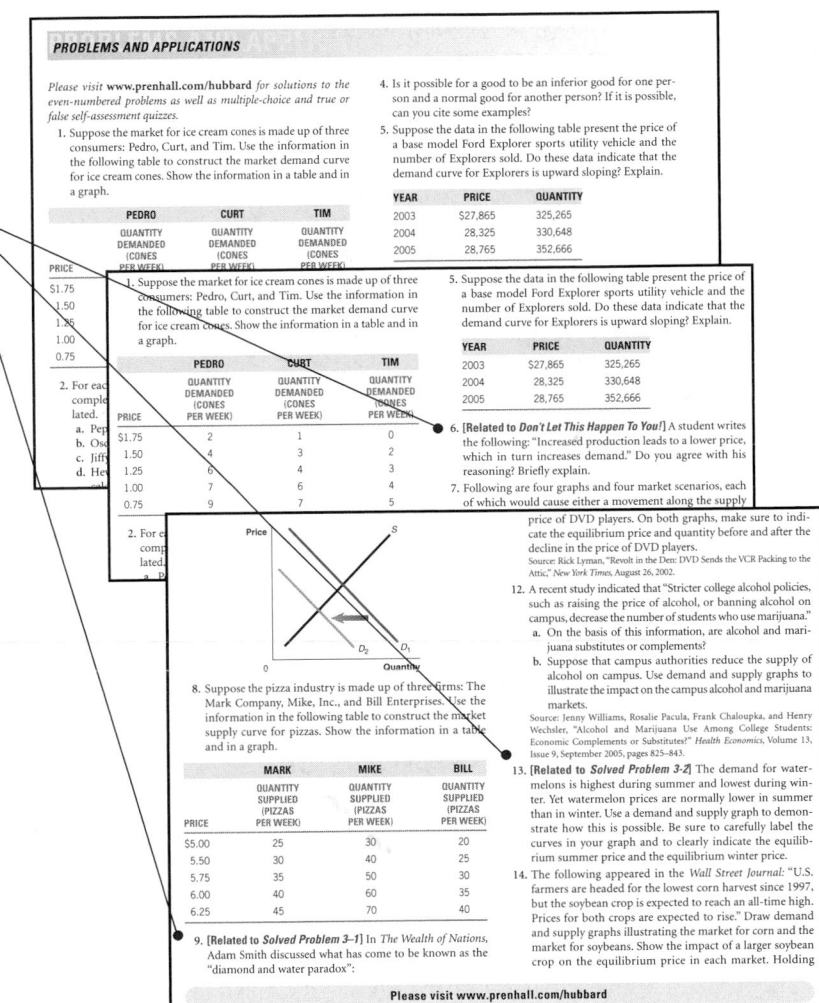

Supplements

Resources for the Instructor
Instructor's Manual
Prepared by Edward Scahill of Scranton University, the Instructor's Manual includes chapter-by-chapter summaries, learning objectives, extended examples and class exercises, teaching outlines incorporating key terms and definitions, teaching tips, topics for class discussion, *new* Solved Problems, and solutions to all review questions and problems in the book. The Instructor's Manual is available in print and for download from the Instructor's Resource Center.

Test Banks
Prentice Hall has prepared two test banks to accompany the text. *Each* test bank includes 2,000 multiple-choice questions, true/false, short answer, and graphing questions.

TestGen
This computerized package allows instructors to customize, save, and generate classroom tests. The test program permits instructors to edit, add, or delete questions from the test banks; edit existing graphics and create new graphics; analyze test results; and organize a database of tests and student results. This software allows for extensive flexibility and ease of use. It provides many options for organizing and displaying tests, along with search and sort features. The software and the test banks can be downloaded from the Instructor's Resource Center (**www.prenhall.com/hubbard**).

Acetates
All figures and tables from the text are reproduced and provided as full-page, four-color acetates.

PowerPoint Lecture Presentation
There are three sets of PowerPoint® slides for professors to use prepared by Fernando and Yvonn Quijano:

1. A comprehensive set of PowerPoint® slides that can be used by instructors for class presentations or by students for lecture preview or review. The presentation includes all the graphs, tables, and equations in the textbook. It displays figures in step-by-step, automated mode, using a single click per slide.
2. A simplified version of the comprehensive PowerPoint® slides containing an outline of the topics covered in the text for professors and instructors to enhance by using their own teaching material.
3. A comprehensive set of PowerPoint® slides with CRS (Classroom Response Systems) questions built in so instructors can incorporate CRS "clickers" into their classroom lectures. For more information on Prentice Hall's partnership with CRS systems, see the facing page.

Instructors may download these PowerPoint® presentations from the Instructor's Resource Center (www.prenhall.com/hubbard).

Instructor's Resource CD-ROM
The Instructor's Resource CD-ROM contains all faculty and student resources that support this text. Instructors have the ability to access and edit the Instructor's Manual, Test Banks, and PowerPoint® presentations. By simply clicking on a chapter or searching for a keyword, faculty can access an interactive library of resources. Faculty can pick and choose from the various supplements and export them to their hard drive.

Supplements

Classroom Response Systems

Classroom Responses Systems (CRS) is an exciting new wireless polling technology that makes large and small classrooms even more interactive because it enables instructors to pose questions to their students, record results, and display those results instantly. Students can answer questions easily using compact remote-control transmitters. Prentice Hall has partnerships with leading classroom response systems providers and can show you everything you need to know about setting up and using a CRS system. We'll provide the classroom hardware, text-specific PowerPoint® slides, software, and support, and we'll also show you how your students can benefit! Learn more at **www.prenhall.com/crs.**

Blackboard and WebCT Course Content.

Prentice Hall offers fully customizable course content for the Bb and WebCT Course Management Systems.

Resources for the Student
Study Guide

The comprehensive study guide reinforces the textbook and provides students with the following:

- A chapter summary
- Learning tips
- Section-by-section review of the concepts presented
- Discussion of each Learning Objective
- Discussion and further explanation of the "Making the Connections," Solved Problems, and "Don't Let This Happen To You!" boxes in each section
- An additional Solved Problem for each one that exists in the text (with solutions)
- Additional applications and exercises

Companion Web Site.

This free Web site, **www.prenhall.com/hubbard**, gives students access to select solutions to end-of-chapter problems, additional Solved Problems, interactive study guides, economics updates, student PowerPoint® slides, and many other resources to promote success in the principles of economics course.

PowerPoint® Slides

For student use as a study aide or note-taking guide, these PowerPoint® slides, prepared by Fernando and Yvonn Quijano, may be downloaded from the companion Web site at **www.prenhall.com/hubbard**. The slides include:

- All graphs, tables, and equations in the text
- Figures in step-by-step, automated mode, using a single click per slide
- End-of-chapter key terms with hyperlinks to relevant slides

SafariX WebBooks

SafariX WebBooks (online versions of the printed texts) will be available for students to purchase in lieu of a standard print text, without any modifications needed to how the instructor or professor teaches the course.

Learn more at **www.prenhall.com/safariX**.

Problem Solving for Students.

Automatically graded assignments (and the ability to get the highest possible grade by reworking the same assignments with new problems) motivate students to solve a lot more problems.

Instant feedback, including detailed tutorial instruction (complete solutions, step-by-step explanations, links to book material, etc.), provides instant gratification and immediate learning.

Graphing tools and questions integrated into assignments enable students to manipulate and even draw graphs that are automatically graded.

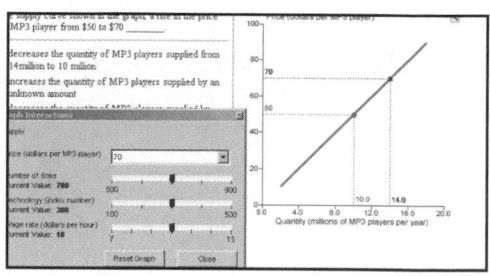

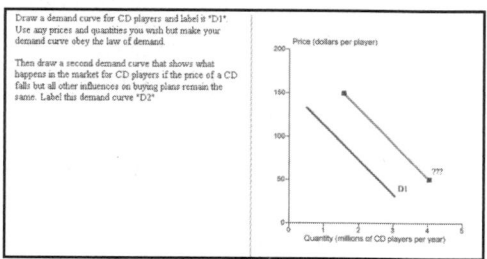

Solving Problems for Professors.

Easily create, assign, and automatically grade homework, quizzes, and tests.

Assign problems and exercises based on the actual end-of-chapter materials in the text book. Many have algorithmic versions for variety and extra practice.

Track students' progress through one easy-to-view, automatically populated grade book.

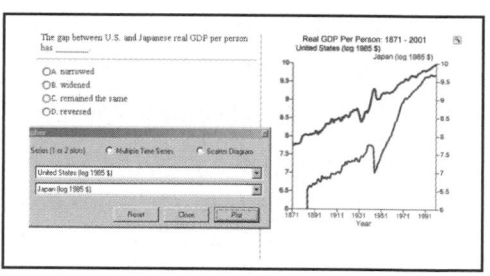

Get supplementary problems and teaching resources (like test banks and lecture slides) all in one place.

These features, plus personalized study plans for students, full e-text options, practice tests, eStudy guides, and more, are all available in...

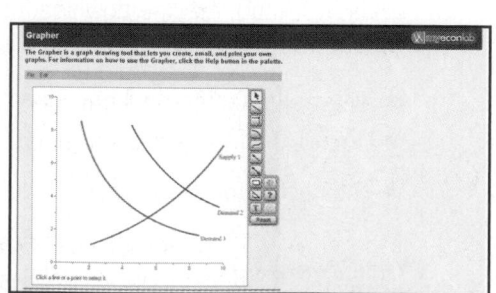

Class Testers, Accuracy Reviewers, and Consultants

Acknowledgements

No principles of economics text can be written without the help of many people.

Class Testers

We are grateful to both the professors who class tested manuscript and their students for providing clear-cut recommendations on how to make chapters interesting, relevant, and comprehensive.

Charles A. Bennett, Gannon University

Anne E. Bresnock, University of California–Los Angeles and California State Polytechnic University–Pomona

John Eastwood, Northern Arizona University

David Eaton, Murray State University

Paul Elgatian, St. Ambrose University

Patricia A. Freeman, Jackson State University

Frank Gunter, Lehigh University

Ahmed Ispahani, University of LaVerne

Brendan Kennelly, Lehigh University and National University of Ireland–Galway

Linda Childs-Leatherbury, Lincoln University, Pennsylvania

Ernest Massie, Franklin University

Carol McDonough, University of Massachusetts–Lowell

Shah Mehrabi, Montgomery College

Sharon Ryan, University of Missouri–Columbia

Bruce G. Webb, Gordon College

Madelyn Young, Converse College

Accuracy Review Board

Our accuracy checkers did a particularly painstaking and thorough job of helping us proof the graphs, equations, and features of the book in page proof stages. We are grateful for their time and commitment to the book:

Kelly H. Blanchard, Purdue University

Travis Hayes, University of Tennessee–Chattanooga

Anisul M. Islam, University of Houston–Downtown

James A. Moreno, Blinn College

Edward Scahill, University of Scranton

Robert Whaples, Wake Forest University

Consultant Board

We received guidance at several critical junctures from a dedicated Consultant Board. We relied on the Board for input on content, figure treatment, and design.

Susan Dadres, Southern Methodist University

Harry Ellis, Jr., University of North Texas

Robert Godby, University of Wyoming

William L. Goffe, State University of New York–Oswego

Donn M. Johnson, Quinnipiac College

Mark Karscig, Central Missouri State University

Jenny Minier, University of Kentucky

Nicholas Noble, Miami University

Matthew Rafferty, Quinnipiac College

Helen Roberts, University of Illinois–Chicago

Robert Rosenman, Washington State University

Joseph M. Santos, South Dakota State University

Martin C. Spechler, Indiana University–Purdue University–Indianapolis

Robert Whaples, Wake Forest University

Reviewers

Reviewers

The guidance and recommendations of the following professors helped us shape the manuscript over the course of three years. We extend special thanks to Robert Whaples of Wake Forest University and Lee Craig of North Carolina State University for reviewing and preparing some of the review questions and problems and applications that appear at the ends of chapters.

ALABAMA Harold W. Elder, University of Alabama–Tuscaloosa • James L. Swofford, University of Southern Alabama **ARIZONA** Doug Conway, Mesa Community College • John Eastwood, Northern Arizona University • Price Fishback, University of Arizona **CALIFORNIA** Renatte Adler, San Diego State University • Robert Bise, Orange Coast Community College • Victor Brajer, California State University–Fullerton • Anne E. Bresnock, University of California–Los Angeles and California State Polytechnic University–Pomona • James G. Devine, Loyola Marymount University • Roger Frantz, San Diego State University • Andrew Gill, California State University–Fullerton • Steve Hamilton, California Polytechnic State University–Fullerton • Ahmed Ispahani, University of LaVerne • Philip King, San Francisco State University • Don Leet, California State University–Fresno • Kristen Monaco, California State University–Long Beach • Michael J. Potepan, San Francisco State University • Ratha Ramoo, Diablo Valley College • Frederica Shockley, Chico State University • Rodney B. Swanson, University of California–Los Angeles • Kristin A. Van Gaasbeck, California State University–Sacramento • Anthony Zambelli, Cuyamaca College **COLORADO** Nancy Jianakoplos, Colorado State University • Jay Kaplan, University of Colorado–Boulder • Stephen Weiler, Colorado State University **CONNECTICUT** Donn M. Johnson, Quinnipiac College • Judith Mills, Southern Connecticut State University • Matthew Rafferty, Quinnipiac College **DELAWARE** Fatma Abdel-Raouf, Goldey-Beacom College • Andrew T. Hill, University of Delaware **FLORIDA** Herm Baine, Broward Community College–Central • Martine Duchatelet, Barry University • Hadley Hartman, Santa Fe Community College • Richard Hawkins, University of West Florida • Augustine Nelson, University of Miami • Jamie Ortiz, Florida Atlantic University • Robert Pennington, University of Central Florida • Jerry Schwartz, Broward Community College–North • William Stronge, Florida Atlantic University **IOWA** Terry Alexander, Iowa State University • Paul Elgatian, St. Ambrose University **ILLINOIS** James Bruehler, Eastern Illinois University • Louis Cain, Loyola University Chicago and Northwestern University • Rik Hafer, Southern Illinois University–Edwardsville • Helen Roberts, University of Illinois–Chicago • Eric Schulz, Northwestern University • Neil T. Skaggs, Illinois State University • Laurie Wolff, Southern Illinois University–Carbondale **INDIANA** Kelly Blanchard, Purdue University • Thomas Gresik, University of Notre Dame • Fred Herschede, Indiana University–South Bend • James K. Self, Indiana University–Bloomington • Esther-Mirjam Sent, University of Notre Dame • Martin C. Spechler, Indiana University–Purdue University–Indianapolis **KANSAS** Jodi Messer Pelkowski, Wichita State University • Josh Rosenbloom, University of Kansas **KENTUCKY** Tom Cate, Northern Kentucky University • David Eaton, Murray State University • Robert Gillette, University of Kentucky • Hak Youn Kim, Western Kentucky University • Jenny Minier, University of Kentucky • John Vahaly, University of Louisville **LOUISIANA** Wesley A. Payne, Delgado Community College **MASSACHUSETTS** William L. Casey, Jr., Babson College • Todd Idson, Boston University • Anthony Laramie, Merrimack College • Carol McDonough, University of Massachusetts–Lowell • William O'Brien, Worcester State College • Gregory H. Wassall, Northeastern University • Bruce G. Webb, Gordon College **MARYLAND** Kathleen A. Carroll, University of Maryland–Baltimore County • Shah Mehrabi, Montgomery College • David Mitch, University of Maryland–Baltimore County • John Neri, University of Maryland • Henry Terrell, University of Maryland **MICHIGAN** John Nader, Grand

Reviewers

Valley State University • Robert J. Rossana, Wayne State University • Mark Wheeler, Western Michigan University **MISSOURI** Jo Durr, Southwest Missouri State University • Julie H. Gallaway, Southwest Missouri State University • Mark Karscig, Central Missouri State University • Sharon Ryan, University of Missouri–Columbia • Ben Young, University of Missouri–Kansas City **MISSISSIPPI** Patricia A. Freeman, Jackson State University **NEBRASKA** Craig MacPhee, University of Nebraska–Lincoln • Mark E. Wohar, University of Nebraska–Omaha **NEW JERSEY** Len Anyanwu, Union County College • Maharukh Bhiladwalla, Rutgers University–New Brunswick • Gary Gigliotti, Rutgers University–New Brunswick • John Graham, Rutgers University–Newark • Berch Haroian, William Paterson University • Paul Harris, Camden County College **NEW MEXICO** Donald Coes, University of New Mexico **NEW YORK** William L. Goffe, State University of New York–Oswego • Wayne A. Grove, LeMoyne College • Christopher Inya, Monroe Community College • Mary Lesser, Iona College • Leonie Stone, State University of New York–Geneseo • Jogindar S. Uppal, State University of New York–Albany **NORTH CAROLINA** Lee A. Craig, North Carolina State University • Kathleen Dorsainvil, Winston-Salem State University • Marc Fusaro, East Carolina University • Peter Schuhmann, University of North Carolina–Wilmington • Carol Stivender, University of North Carolina–Charlotte • Robert Whaples, Wake Forest University **OHIO** John P. Blair, Wright State University • Darlene DeVera, Miami University • Ernest Massie, Franklin University • Nicholas Noble, Miami University • Rochelle Ruffer, Youngstown State University • Melissa Thomasson, Miami University • Sourushe Zandvakili, University of Cincinnati **OREGON** Bill Burrows, Lane Community College • Tom Carroll, Central Oregon Community College • Larry Singell, University of Oregon **PENNSYLVANIA** Gustavo Barboza, Mercyhurst College • Charles A. Bennett, Gannon University • Howard Bodenhorn, Lafayette College • Milica Bookman, St. Joseph's University • Robert Brooker, Gannon University • Linda Childs-Leatherbury, Lincoln University • Satyajit Ghosh, University of Scranton • Mehdi Haririan, Bloomsburg University • Brendan Kennelly, Lehigh University • Iordanis Petsas, University of Scranton • Edward Scahill, University of Scranton • Sandra Trejos, Clarion University • Peter Zaleski, Villanova University **SOUTH CAROLINA** Calvin Blackwell, College of Charleston • Chad Turner, Clemson University • Madelyn Young, Converse College **SOUTH DAKOTA** Joseph M. Santos, South Dakota State University • Jason Zimmerman, South Dakota State University **TENNESSEE** Bichaka Fayissa, Middle Tennessee State University • Travis Hayes, University of Tennessee–Chattanooga • Christopher C. Klein, Middle Tennessee State University **TEXAS** Rashid Al-Hmoud, Texas Tech University • Mike Cohick, Collin County Community College • Susan Dadres, Southern Methodist University • Harry Ellis, Jr., University of North Texas • Nicholas Feltovich, University of Houston–Main • Charles Harold Fifield, Baylor University • Richard Gosselin, Houston Community College–Central • James W. Henderson, Baylor University • Ansul Islam, University of Houston–Downtown • Kathy Kelly, University of Texas–Arlington • Thomas Kemp, Tarrant County College–Northwest • Akbar Marvasti, University of Houston–Downtown • Carl Montano, Lamar University • James Moreno, Blinn College • John Pisciotta, Baylor University • Sara Saderion, Houston Community College–Southwest **UTAH** Aric Krause, Westminster College **VIRGINIA** Lee A. Coppock, University of Virginia • Carrie Meyer, George Mason University • James Roberts, Tidewater Community College–Virginia Beach • Sarah Stafford, The College of William & Mary • Michelle Vachris, Christopher Newport University • James Wetzel, Virginia Commonwealth University **WASHINGTON** Robert Rosenman, Washington State University **WISCONSIN** • Pascal Ngoboka, University of Wisconsin–River Falls • Kevin Quinn, St. Norbert College • John R. Stoll, University of Wisconsin–Green Bay **WYOMING** Robert Godby, University of Wyoming

A Word of Thanks . . .

We benefited greatly from the dedication and professionalism of the Prentice Hall team. Executive Editor David Alexander's energy and support were indispensable. David helped mold the presentation and provided words of encouragement whenever our energy flagged. Developmental Editor Lena Buonanno worked tirelessly to ensure this text was as good as it could be. We are literally astonished at the amount of time, energy, and unfailing good humor she brought to this project. Director of Key Markets David Theisen provided invaluable insight into how best to structure a principles text. His advice helped shape nearly every chapter. Executive Marketing Manager Sharon Koch and Marketing Development Manager Kathleen McLellan helped develop a unique and innovative marketing plan. Steve Deitmer, Director of Development, brought sound judgement to the many decisions required to create this book. Mike Reynolds, Pat Smythe, and Maria Lange turned our manuscript pages into a beautiful published book. Photo researcher Diane Austin located photographs that captured the essence of key concepts.

A good part of the burden of a project of this magnitude is borne by our families. We appreciate the patience, support, and encouragement of our wives and children. We extend special thanks to Constance Hubbard for her diligent reading of page proofs.

BRIEF CONTENTS

CONTENTS

Part 3: Firms in the Domestic and International Economies

Part 5: Market Structure and Firm Strategy

Part 6: Markets for Factors of Production

Part 7: Information, Taxes, and the Distribution of Income

FLEXIBILITY CHART

The following chart helps you organize your syllabus based on your teaching preferences and objectives:

Core	Policy	Optional
CHAPTER 1: Economics: Foundations and Models *Uses the debate of outsourcing to discuss the role of models in economic analysis.*	**CHAPTER 4:** Economic Efficiency, Government Price Setting, and Taxes	**CHAPTER 1: APPENDIX:** Using Graphs and Formulas
CHAPTER 2: Trade-offs, Comparative Advantage, and the Market System *Includes coverage of the role of the entrepreneur, property rights, and the legal system in a market system.*	**CHAPTER 5:** Externalities, Environmental Policy and Public Goods *This chapter may be delayed until after Chapter 14.*	**CHAPTER 4 APPENDIX:** Quantitative Demand and Supply Analysis *Provides a quantitative analysis of rent control.*
CHAPTER 3: Where Prices Come From: The Interaction of Demand and Supply	**CHAPTER 18:** The Tax System and the Distribution of Income	**CHAPTER 7:** Firms, the Stock Market, and Corporate Governance *Unique chapter that includes coverage of the Sarbanes-Oxley Act.*
CHAPTER 6: Elasticity: The Responsiveness of Demand and Supply	**BONUS WEB SITE CHAPTER:** Microeconomics Issues for Business *Visit www.prenhall.com/hubbard for continually updated coverage of economic issues that relate to both consumers and firms.*	**CHAPTER 7 APPENDIX:** Tools to Analyze Firms' Financial Information *Covers present value and financial statements.*
CHAPTER 8: Comparative Advantage and the Gains from International Trade *This chapter may be delayed until after Chapter 16.*		**CHAPTER 8 APPENDIX:** Multinational Firms *Covers the benefits and challenges of operating overseas businesses.*
CHAPTER 10: Technology, Production, and Costs		**CHAPTER 9:** Consumer Behavior and Behavioral Economics *Covers utility theory and unique coverage of social influences on behavior and network externalities.*
CHAPTER 11: Firms in Perfectly Competitive Markets		**CHAPTER 9 APPENDIX:** Using Indifference Curves and Budget Lines to Understand Consumer Behavior *Complete and intuitive coverage for those instructors who prefer to cover indifference curves rather than utility theory.*
CHAPTER 12: Monopolistic Competition: The Competitive Model in a More Realistic Setting		**CHAPTER 10 APPENDIX:** Isoquants and Isocosts *Provides a formal analysis of how firms choose the combination of inputs to produce a given level of output.*
CHAPTER 13: Oligopoly: Firms in Less Competitive Markets *Includes full coverage of game theory and unique coverage of Porter's Five Forces Model of Competition.*		**CHAPTER 15:** Pricing Strategy *Unique chapter that covers price discrimination, cost-plus pricing, and two-part tariffs.*
CHAPTER 14: Monopoly and Antitrust Policy *This chapter may be covered after Chapter 11.*		**BONUS WEB SITE CHAPTER:** Microeconomics Issues for Business *Visit www.prenhall.com/hubbard for continually updated coverage of economic issues that relate to both consumers and firms.*
CHAPTER 16: The Markets for Labor and Other Factors of Production *Covers all factors of production in one chapter and includes coverage of discrimination, unions, compensating differentials, and personnel economics.*		
CHAPTER 17: The Economics of Information *Covers asymmetric information and moral hazard.*		

microeconomics

chapter

one

Economics:
Foundations and Models

What Happens When U.S. Firms Move to China?

➤ You have probably seen the words "Made in China" on a variety of the products you own, including running shoes, clothing, towels, and sheets. It may not be surprising that relatively simple products are manufactured in China, where workers receive much lower wages than in the United States. Until recently, though, most people would not have expected sophisticated, high-technology products to be designed and manufactured in China. That is why an announcement by Massachusetts-based 3Com Corporation in late 2004 was so surprising. 3Com is a leading high-technology firm with 2,000 employees and annual sales of $700 million. The firm introduced a new network switch for corporate computer systems that not only was manu-

factured in China but had been designed by Chinese engineers.

3Com's price for the switch was $183,000. 3Com's even larger rival, Cisco Systems—which is based in San Jose, California, with 34,000 employees and annual sales of more than $30 billion—charged $245,000 for a comparable switch, designed and manufactured in the United States. The difference in price showed that even when producing some high-technology goods, it was cheaper for U.S. firms to operate in China. Because the salaries of engineers are so much lower in China, 3Com was able to use four times as many engineers to design its switch, which it claimed had twice the capacity of Cisco's switch. The cost to manufacture the switch was also much lower in

China, where the average factory worker earns only $0.64 per hour, including benefits, compared with about $22.00 per hour earned by the average factory worker in the United States.

Many U.S., Japanese, and European firms have been moving the production of goods and services to other countries. This process of firms producing goods and services outside of their home country is called *outsourcing* (sometimes also referred to as *off-shoring*). U.S. firms have been outsourcing for decades, but some of the recently outsourced jobs require high skill levels, as was true of the jobs 3Com moved from the United States to China. To cite another example that has received much publicity, Dun & Bradstreet (now known as D&B), a

After studying this chapter, you should be able to:

LEARNING OBJECTIVES

① Discuss these three important economic ideas: *People are rational. People respond to incentives. Optimal decisions are made at the margin.*

② Discuss how an economy answers these questions: *What* goods and services will be produced? *How* will the goods and services be produced? *Who* will receive the goods and services?

③ Understand the role of models in economic analysis.

④ Distinguish between microeconomics and macroeconomics.

⑤ Become familiar with important economic terms.

business information firm founded in New York in 1841, has begun purchasing much of its software engineering services from a firm in Bangalore, India, because Indian software engineers typically receive salaries 75 percent lower than do software engineers in the United States.

Articles on outsourcing appear frequently in business magazines and the financial pages of newspapers, and the issue has also been the subject of heated debate among political commentators, policymakers, and presidential candidates. The focus of the debate has been the question: "Has outsourcing been good or bad for the U.S. economy?" This question is one of many that cannot be answered without using economics. In this chapter, and the remainder of this book, we will see how economics helps in answering important questions about outsourcing, as well as many other issues. Economics provides us with tools for understanding why outsourcing has increased, why some firms are more likely to move production to other countries, and what the effects of outsourcing will be on the wages of U.S. workers, the profits of U.S. firms, and the overall ability of the U.S. economy to produce more and better goods and services. *An Inside Look* on page 16 discusses the effects of economic growth in China on jobs and wages in the United States and Europe.

Source: Pete Engardio and Dexter Roberts, "The China Price," *Business Week*, December 6, 2004.

In this book, we use economics to answer questions such as the following:

➤ How are the prices of goods and services determined?

➤ How does pollution affect the economy, and how should government policy deal with these effects?

➤ Why do firms engage in international trade, and how do government policies affect international trade?

➤ Why does government control the prices of some goods and services, and what are the effects of those controls?

Economists do not always agree on the answers to every question. In fact, as we will see, economists engage in lively debates on some issues. Economics is a dynamic field in which new questions are constantly arising, and new methods of analyzing and answering those questions are being developed.

All the questions we discuss in this book reflect a basic fact of life: People must make choices as they try to attain their goals. The choices reflect the trade-offs people face because we live in a world of **scarcity,** which means that although our wants are unlimited, the resources available to fulfill those wants are limited. You might like to have a 60-inch plasma television in every room of your home, but unless you are a close relative of Bill Gates, you probably lack the money to purchase them. Every day you must make choices about how to spend your limited income on the many goods and services available. The finite amount of time available to you also limits your ability to attain your goals. If you spend an hour studying for your economics midterm, you have one less hour available to study for your history midterm. Firms and the government are in the same situation you are: They have limited resources available to them as they attempt to attain their goals. **Economics** is the study of the choices consumers, business managers, and government officials make to attain their goals, given their scarce resources.

We begin this chapter by discussing three important economic ideas that we will return to many times in the book: *People are rational. People respond to incentives. Optimal decisions are made at the margin.* Then we consider the three fundamental questions that any economy must answer: *What* goods and services will be produced? *How* will the goods and services be produced? *Who* will receive the goods and services? Next we consider the role of *economic models* in helping us to analyze the many issues presented throughout this book. **Economic models** are simplified versions of reality used to analyze real-world economic situations. Later in this chapter, we explore why economists use models and how they construct them. Finally, we discuss the difference between microeconomics and macroeconomics, and we preview some important economic terms.

Scarcity The situation in which unlimited wants exceed the limited resources available to fulfill those wants.

Economics The study of the choices people make to attain their goals, given their scarce resources.

Economic model Simplified versions of reality used to analyze real-world economic situations.

Building a Foundation: Economics and Individual Decisions

As you try to achieve your goals, whether they are buying a new computer or finding a part-time job, you will interact with other people in *markets*. A **market** is a group of buyers and sellers of a good or service and the institution or arrangement by which they come together to trade. Most of economics involves analyzing what happens in markets. Throughout this book, as we study how people make choices and interact in markets, we will return to three important ideas:

1. People are rational.
2. People respond to economic incentives.
3. Optimal decisions are made at the margin.

① **LEARNING OBJECTIVE**
Discuss these three important economic ideas: *People are rational. People respond to incentives. Optimal decisions are made at the margin.*

Market   A group of buyers and sellers of a good or service and the institution or arrangement by which they come together to trade

People Are Rational

Economists generally assume that people are rational. This assumption does *not* mean that economists believe everyone knows everything or always makes the "best" decision. It does mean that economists assume that consumers and firms use all available information as they act to achieve their goals. Rational individuals weigh the benefits and costs of each action, and they choose an action only if the benefits outweigh the costs. For example, if Microsoft charges a price of $239 for a copy of Windows, economists assume that the managers at Microsoft have estimated that a price of $239 will earn Microsoft the most profit. The managers may be wrong; perhaps a price of $265 would be more profitable, but economists assume that the managers at Microsoft have acted rationally on the basis of the information available to them in choosing the price. Of course, not everyone behaves rationally all the time. Still, the assumption of rational behavior is very useful in explaining most of the choices that people make.

People Respond to Economic Incentives

Human beings act from a variety of motives, including religious belief, envy, and compassion. Economists emphasize that consumers and firms consistently respond to *economic* incentives. This fact may seem obvious, but it is often overlooked. For example, according to an article in the *Wall Street Journal*, the FBI couldn't understand why banks were not taking steps to improve security in the face of an increase in robberies: "FBI officials suggest that banks place uniformed, armed guards outside their doors and install bullet-resistant plastic, known as a 'bandit barrier,' in front of teller windows." FBI officials were surprised that few banks took their advice. But the article also reported that installing bullet-resistant plastic costs $10,000 to $20,000 and a well-trained security guard receives $50,000 per year in salary and benefits. The average loss in a bank robbery is only about $1,200. The economic incentive to banks is clear: It is less costly to put up with bank robberies than to take additional security measures. That banks respond as they do to the threat of robberies may be surprising to the FBI—but not to economists.

Optimal Decisions Are Made at the Margin

Some decisions are "all or nothing": An entrepreneur decides whether or not to open a new restaurant. She either starts the new restaurant or she doesn't. You decide whether to enter graduate school or to take a job. You either enter graduate school or you don't. But most decisions in life are not all or nothing. Instead, most decisions involve doing a little more or a little less. If you are trying to decrease your spending and increase your saving, the decision is not really a choice between saving every dollar you earn or spending it all. The choice is actually between buying a café mocha at Starbucks every day or cutting back to three times per week.

Economists use the word *marginal* to mean an extra or additional benefit or cost of a decision. Should you watch another hour of TV or spend that hour studying? The *marginal benefit* (or, in symbols, *MB*) of watching more TV is the additional enjoyment you receive. The *marginal cost* (or *MC*) is the lower grade you receive from having studied a little less. Should Apple Computer produce an additional 300,000 iPods? Firms receive *revenue* from selling goods. Apple's marginal benefit is the additional revenue it receives from selling 300,000 more iPods. Apple's marginal cost is the additional cost—for wages, parts, and so forth—of producing 300,000 more iPods. *Economists reason that the optimal decision is to continue any activity up to the point where the marginal benefit equals the marginal cost—in symbols, where* MB = MC. Often we apply this rule without consciously thinking about it. Usually you will know whether the additional enjoyment from watching a television program is worth the additional cost involved in not spending that hour studying, without giving it a lot of thought. In business situations, however, firms often have to make careful calculations to determine, for example, whether the additional revenue received from increasing production is greater or less than the additional cost of the production. Economists refer to analysis that involves comparing marginal benefits and marginal costs as **marginal analysis.**

Marginal analysis Analysis that involves comparing marginal benefits and marginal costs.

In each chapter of this book, you will see a special feature entitled "Solved Problem." This feature will increase your understanding of the material by leading you through the steps of solving an applied economic problem. After reading the problem, you can test your understanding by working the related problems that appear at the end of the chapter, on the Web site (www.prenhall.com/hubbard), and in the study guide that accompanies this book.

SOLVED PROBLEM   1-1

(1) LEARNING OBJECTIVE

Discuss these three important economic ideas: *People are rational. People respond to incentives. Optimal decisions are made at the margin.*

Apple Computer Makes a Decision at the Margin

Suppose Apple is currently selling 3,000,000 iPods per year. Managers at Apple are considering whether to raise production to 3,300,000 iPods per year. One manager argues, "Increasing production from 3,000,000 to 3,300,000 is a good idea because we will make a total profit of $100 million if we produce 3,300,000." Do you agree with her reasoning? What, if any, additional information do you need to decide whether Apple should produce the additional 300,000 iPods?

Solving the Problem:

Step 1: Review the chapter material. The problem is about making decisions, so you may want to review the section "Optimal Decisions Are Made at the Margin," which begins on page 5. Remember to think "marginal" whenever you see the word "additional" in economics.

Step 2: Explain whether you agree with the manager's reasoning. We have seen that any activity should be continued to the point where the marginal benefit is equal to the marginal cost. In this case, that involves continuing to produce iPods up to the point where the additional revenue Apple receives from selling more iPods is equal to the marginal cost of producing them. The Apple manager has not done a marginal analysis, so you should not agree with her reasoning. Her statement about the *total* profit of producing 3,300,000 iPods is not relevant to the decision whether or not to produce the last 300,000 iPods.

Step 3: Explain what additional information you need. You will need additional information to make a correct decision. You will need to know the additional revenue Apple would earn from selling 300,000 more iPods and the additional cost of producing them.

YOUR TURN: Test your understanding by doing related problems 4, 5, and 6 on page 19 at the end of this chapter. Visit www.prenhall.com/hubbard for an interactive exercise related to this Solved Problem.

The Economic Problem That Every Society Must Solve

We have already noted the important fact that we live in a world of scarcity. As a result, any society faces the economic problem that it has only a limited amount of economic resources—such as workers, machines, and natural resources—and therefore can produce only a limited amount of goods and services. Therefore, society faces **trade-offs:** Producing more of one good or service means producing less of another good or service. Trade-offs force society to make choices, particularly when answering the following three fundamental questions:

1. *What* goods and services will be produced?
2. *How* will the goods and services be produced?
3. *Who* will receive the goods and services produced?

Throughout this book, we will return to these questions many times. For now, we can briefly introduce each question.

What Goods and Services Will Be Produced?

How will society decide whether to produce more economics textbooks or more DVD players? More day care facilities or more football stadiums? Of course, "society" does not make decisions; only individuals make decisions. The answer to the question of what will be produced is determined by the choices made by consumers, firms, and the government. Every day you help to decide which goods and services will be produced when you choose to buy an iPod rather than a DVD player, or a café mocha rather than a chai tea. Similarly, Apple must choose whether to devote its scarce resources to making more iPods or more iBook laptop computers. The federal government must also choose whether to spend more of its limited budget on breast cancer research or on homeland security. In each case, consumers, firms, and the government face the problem of scarcity by trading off one good for another.

How Will the Goods and Services Be Produced?

Firms choose how to produce the goods and services they sell. In many cases, firms face a trade-off between using more workers or using more machines. For example, a local service station has to choose whether to provide car repair services using more diagnostic computers and fewer auto mechanics or more auto mechanics and fewer diagnostic computers. Similarly, movie studios have to choose whether to produce animated films using highly skilled animators to draw them by hand or fewer animators and more computers. In deciding whether to move production offshore to China, firms are often choosing between a production method in the United States that uses fewer workers and more machines or a production method in China that uses more workers and fewer machines.

Who Will Receive the Goods and Services Produced?

In the United States, who receives the goods and services produced depends largely on how income is distributed. Those individuals with the highest income have the ability to buy the most goods and services. Often, people are willing to give up some of their income—and, therefore, some of their ability to purchase goods and services—by donating to charities to increase the incomes of poorer people. In 2004, Americans donated $241 billion to charity, or an average donation of $2,100 for each household in the country. An important policy question, however, is whether the government should intervene to make the distribution of income more equal. Such intervention already occurs in the United States, because people with higher incomes pay a larger fraction of their incomes in taxes and because the government makes payments to people with low incomes. There is disagreement over whether the current attempts to redistribute income are sufficient or whether there should be more or less redistribution.

② **LEARNING OBJECTIVE**

Discuss how an economy answers these questions: *What* goods and services will be produced? *How* will the goods and services be produced? *Who* will receive the goods and services?

Trade-off The idea that because of scarcity, producing more of one good or service means producing less of another good or service.

Centrally planned economy An economy in which the government decides how economic resources will be allocated.

Market economy An economy in which the decisions of households and firms interacting in markets allocate economic resources.

Centrally Planned Economies versus Market Economies

Societies organize their economies in two main ways to answer the three questions of what, how, and who. A society can have a **centrally planned economy** in which the government decides how economic resources will be allocated. Or a society can have a **market economy** in which the decisions of households and firms interacting in markets allocate economic resources.

From 1917 to 1991, the most important centrally planned economy in the world was that of the Soviet Union, which was established when V. I. Lenin and his Communist Party staged a revolution and took over the Russian Empire. In the Soviet Union, the government decided what goods to produce, how to produce them, and who would receive them. Government employees managed factories and stores. The objective of these managers was to follow the government's orders, rather than to satisfy the wants of consumers. Centrally planned economies like the Soviet Union have not been successful in producing low-cost, high-quality goods and services. As a result, the standard of living of the average person in a centrally planned economy tends to be quite low. All centrally planned economies have also been political dictatorships. Dissatisfaction with low living standards and political repression finally led to the collapse of the Soviet Union in 1991. Today, only a few small countries, such as Cuba and North Korea, still have completely centrally planned economies.

All the high-income democracies, such as the United States, Canada, Japan, and the countries of Western Europe, are market economies. Market economies rely primarily on privately owned firms to produce goods and services and to decide how to produce them. Markets, rather than the government, determine who receives the goods and services produced. In a market economy, firms must produce goods and services that meet the wants of consumers, or the firms will go out of business. In that sense, it is ultimately consumers who decide what goods and services will be produced. Because firms in a market economy compete to offer the highest-quality products at the lowest price, they are under pressure to use the lowest-cost methods of production. For example, in the past 10 years some U.S. firms, particularly in the electronics and furniture industries, have been under pressure to reduce their costs to meet those of Chinese firms.

In a market economy, the income of an individual is determined by the payments he receives for what he has to sell. If he is a civil engineer and firms are willing to pay a salary of \$85,000 per year for engineers with his training and skills, that is the amount of income he will have to purchase goods and services. If the engineer also owns a house that he rents out, his income will be even higher. One of the attractive features of markets is that they reward hard work. Generally, the more extensive the training a person has received and the longer the hours the person works, the higher the person's income will be. Of course, luck—both good and bad—also plays a role here, as elsewhere in life. We can conclude that market economies answer the question "Who receives the goods and services produced?" with the answer "Those who are most willing and able to buy them."

The Modern "Mixed" Economy

In the nineteenth and early twentieth centuries, the U.S. government engaged in relatively little regulation of markets for goods and services. Beginning in the middle of the twentieth century, government intervention in the economy dramatically increased in the United States and other market economies. This increase was primarily caused by the high rates of unemployment and business bankruptcies during the Great Depression of the 1930s. Some government intervention was also intended to raise the incomes of the elderly, the sick, and people with limited skills. For example, in the 1930s, the United States established the Social Security system, which provides government payments to retired and disabled workers, and minimum wage legislation, which sets a floor on the wages employers can pay in many occupations. In more recent years, government intervention in the economy has also expanded to meet such goals as protection of the environment and the promotion of civil rights.

Some economists argue that the extent of government intervention makes it no longer accurate to refer to the U.S., Canadian, Japanese, and Western European economies as market economies. Instead, they should be referred to as *mixed economies.* In a **mixed economy,** most economic decisions result from the interaction of buyers and sellers in markets, but the government plays a significant role in the allocation of resources. As we will see in later chapters, economists continue to debate the role government should play in a market economy.

One of the most important developments in the international economy in recent years has been the movement of China from being a centrally planned economy to being a more mixed economy. The Chinese economy had suffered decades of economic stagnation following the takeover of the government by Mao Zedong and the Communist Party in 1949. Although China remains a political dictatorship, production of most goods and services is now determined in the market, rather than by the government. The result has been rapid economic growth that in the near future may lead to total production of goods and services in China surpassing total production in the United States.

Mixed economy An economy in which most economic decisions result from the interaction of buyers and sellers in markets, but in which the government plays a significant role in the allocation of resources.

Efficiency and Equity

Market economies tend to be more efficient than centrally planned economies. There are two types of efficiency: *productive efficiency* and *allocative efficiency.* **Productive efficiency** occurs when a good or service is produced at the lowest possible cost. **Allocative efficiency** occurs when production reflects consumer preferences. Markets tend to be efficient because they promote competition and facilitate *voluntary exchange.* **Voluntary exchange** refers to the situation in which both the buyer and seller of a product are made better off by the transaction. We know that the buyer and seller are both made better off, because otherwise the buyer would not have agreed to buy the product or the seller would not have agreed to sell it. Productive efficiency is achieved when competition among firms in markets forces the firms to produce goods and services at the lowest cost. Allocative efficiency is achieved when the combination of competition among firms and voluntary exchange between firms and consumers results in firms producing the mix of goods and services that consumers prefer most. Competition will force firms to continue producing and selling goods and services as long as the additional benefit to consumers is greater than the additional cost of production. In this way, the mix of goods and services produced will reflect consumer preferences.

Productive efficiency The situation in which a good or service is produced at the lowest possible cost.

Allocative efficiency A state of the economy in which production reflects consumer preferences; in particular, every good or service is produced up to the point where the last unit provides a marginal benefit to consumers equal to the marginal cost of producing it.

Voluntary exchange The situation that occurs in markets when both the buyer and seller of a product are made better off by the transaction.

Although markets promote efficiency, they don't guarantee it. Inefficiency can arise from various sources. To begin with, it may take some time to achieve an efficient outcome. When DVD players were introduced, for example, productive efficiency was not achieved instantly. It took several years for firms to discover the lowest-cost method of producing this good. As we will discuss in Chapter 4, governments sometimes reduce efficiency by interfering with voluntary exchange in markets. For example, many governments limit the imports of some goods from foreign countries. This limitation reduces efficiency by keeping goods from being produced at the lowest cost. The production of some goods damages the environment. In this case, government intervention can increase efficiency, because without such intervention firms may ignore the costs of environmental damage, and thereby fail to produce the goods at the lowest possible cost.

Just because an economic outcome is efficient does not necessarily mean that society finds it desirable. Many people prefer economic outcomes that they consider fair or equitable, even if these outcomes are less efficient. **Equity** is harder to define than efficiency, but it usually involves a fair distribution of economic benefits. For some people, equity involves a more equal distribution of economic benefits than would result from an emphasis on efficiency alone. For example, some people support taxing people with higher incomes to provide the funds for programs that aid the poor. Although equity may be increased by reducing the incomes of high-income people and increasing the incomes of the poor, efficiency may be reduced. People have less incentive to open new businesses, to supply labor, and to save if the government takes a significant

Equity The fair distribution of economic benefits.

amount of the income they earn from working or saving. The result is that fewer goods and services are produced and less saving takes place. As this example illustrates, *there is often a trade-off between efficiency and equity*. In this case, the total amount of goods and services produced falls, although the distribution of the income to buy those goods and services is made more equal. Government policymakers often confront this trade-off.

Economic Models

Economists rely on economic theories or *models* (the words "theory" and "model" are used interchangeably) to analyze real-world issues, such as the economic effects of outsourcing. As mentioned earlier, economic models are simplified versions of reality used to analyze real-world economic situations. Economists are certainly not alone in relying on models: An engineer may use a computer model of a bridge to help test whether it will withstand high winds, or a biologist may make a physical model of a nucleic acid to better understand its properties. One purpose of economic models is to make economic ideas sufficiently explicit and concrete to be used for decision making by individuals, firms, or the government. For example, we will see in Chapter 3 that the model of demand and supply is a simplified version of how the prices of products are determined by the interactions among buyers and sellers in markets.

Economists use economic models to answer questions. For example, consider the question from the opening of this chapter: Has outsourcing been good or bad for the U.S. economy? For a complicated question such as the effects of outsourcing, economists often use several models to examine different aspects of the issue. For example, a model of how wages are determined might be used to analyze how outsourcing affects wages in particular industries. A model of international trade might be used to analyze how outsourcing affects income growth in the countries involved. Sometimes economists use an existing model to analyze an issue, but in other cases economists must develop a new model. To develop a model, economists generally follow these steps:

1. Decide on the assumptions to be used in developing the model.
2. Formulate a testable hypothesis.
3. Use economic data to test the hypothesis.
4. Revise the model if it fails to explain well the economic data.
5. Retain the revised model to help answer similar economic questions in the future.

The Role of Assumptions in Economic Models

Any model is based on making assumptions because models have to be simplified to be useful. We cannot analyze an economic issue unless we reduce its complexity. For example, economic models make *behavioral assumptions* about the motives of consumers and firms. Economists assume that consumers will buy those goods and services that will maximize their well-being or their satisfaction. Similarly, economists assume that firms act to maximize their profits. These assumptions are simplifications because they do not describe the motives of every consumer and every firm. How can we know if the assumptions in a model are too simplified or too limiting? We discover this when we form hypotheses based on these assumptions and test these hypotheses using real-world information.

Forming and Testing Hypotheses in Economic Models

A *hypothesis* in an economic model is a statement that may be either correct or incorrect about an *economic variable*. An **economic variable** is something measurable that can have different values, such as the wages paid to software programmers. An example of a hypothesis in an economic model is the statement that outsourcing by U.S. firms reduces wages paid to software programmers in the United States. An economic hypoth-

Economic variable Something measurable that can have different values, such as the wages of software programmers.

esis is usually about a *causal relationship;* in this case, the hypothesis states that outsourcing causes, or leads to, lower wages for software programmers.

Before accepting a hypothesis, we must test it. To test a hypothesis we must analyze statistics on the relevant economic variables. In this case, we must gather statistics on the wages paid to software programmers, and perhaps on other variables as well. Testing a hypothesis can be tricky. For example, showing that the wages paid to software programmers fell at a time when outsourcing was increasing would not be enough to demonstrate that outsourcing *caused* the wage fall. Just because two things are *correlated*—that is, they happen at the same time—does not mean that one caused the other. For example, suppose that the number of workers trained as software engineers greatly increased at the same time that outsourcing was increasing. In that case, the fall in wages paid to software engineers might have been caused by the increased competition among workers for these jobs, rather than by the effects of relocating programming jobs from the United States to India or China. Over a period of time, many economic variables will be changing, which complicates testing hypotheses. In fact, when economists disagree about a hypothesis, such as the effect of outsourcing on wages, it is often because of disagreements over interpreting the statistical analysis used to test the hypothesis.

Note that hypotheses must be statements that could in principle turn out to be incorrect. Statements such as "Outsourcing is good" or "Outsourcing is bad" are value judgments, rather than hypotheses, because it is not possible to disprove them.

Economists accept and use an economic model if it leads to hypotheses that are confirmed by statistical analysis. In many cases, the acceptance is tentative, however, pending the gathering of new data or further statistical analysis. In fact, economists often refer to a hypothesis having been "not rejected," rather than being "accepted," by statistical analysis. But what if statistical analysis clearly rejects a hypothesis? For example, what if the model leads to a hypothesis that outsourcing by U.S. firms lowers wages of U.S. software programmers, but this hypothesis is rejected by the data? In that case, the model must be reconsidered. It may be that an assumption used in the model was too simplified or too limiting. For example, perhaps the model we used to determine the effect of outsourcing on wages paid to software programmers assumed that software programmers in China and India had the same training and experience as software programmers in the United States. If, in fact, U.S. software programmers have more training and experience than Chinese and Indian programmers, this difference may explain why our hypothesis was rejected by the economic statistics.

The process of developing models, testing hypotheses, and revising models occurs not just in economics but also in disciplines such as physics, chemistry, and biology. It is often referred to as the *scientific method*. Economics is a *social science* because it applies the scientific method to the study of the interactions among individuals.

In each chapter, the feature entitled "Making the Connection" discusses a business news story, or other application, related to the chapter material. Read Making the Connection 1-1 for two viewpoints about outsourcing.

When Economists Disagree: A Debate over Outsourcing

1-1 Making the Connection

There is an old saying in the newspaper business that it's not news when a dog bites a man, but it is news when a man bites a dog. In 2004, many newspapers ran a "man bites dog" story concerning economics.

Most economists believe that international trade—including the trade that results when firms move production offshore—increases economic efficiency and raises incomes. It was news, then, when MIT economist Paul Samuelson, a winner of the Nobel Prize in Economics, wrote an article in the *Journal of Economic Perspectives* questioning whether incomes in the United States will be higher as a result of the outsourcing of jobs to India and China. Samuelson presented a model of the effects of outsourcing that can be illustrated with the following hypothetical case: Suppose a bank in New York has been using a company in South Dakota to handle its telephone customer service. It then switches to using a company in Bangalore, India that pays its workers much lower wages. Samuelson argued that even when the workers fired by the

Does outsourcing by U.S. firms raise or lower incomes in the United States?

South Dakota firm eventually find new jobs, these may pay lower wages. If outsourcing becomes widespread enough, Samuelson argued, it may result in a significant decline in U.S. incomes.

Many economists objected to Samuelson's argument. One economist who wrote a rebuttal to Samuelson was Jagdish Bhagwati, a former student of Samuelson's and a professor of economics at Columbia University. Bhagwati argued that in Samuelson's example the wages of South Dakota call center workers were reduced by outsourcing, but the costs to the bank were also reduced, which would allow the bank to reduce the prices it charged its customers. In Bhagwati's model, these gains to consumers from lower prices more than offset the loss to workers from lower wages, so the United States experiences a net gain from outsourcing. Samuelson argued, though, that if the United States exports the product—in this case banking services—to other countries, the lower price hurts the exporting firms. In that case, the United States might still be hurt by outsourcing.

This brief summary does not do full justice to the models of Samuelson and Bhagwati, which are too complicated for us to cover in this chapter. We can, however, discuss the sources of the disagreement between these two economists. We have seen that economists sometimes differ about the assumptions that should be used in building a model. That is not the case here: Samuelson and Bhagwati basically agree on the model and the assumptions to be used. Instead, they disagree over how to interpret the relevant economic statistics. Bhagwati argues that the number of U.S. jobs moving to other countries has been relatively small, amounting to about 1 percent of the jobs created in the U.S. economy each year. He also argues that the jobs lost to outsourcing tend to be low-wage jobs, such as telephone customer service or data entry, and are likely to be replaced by higher-wage jobs. Samuelson argues that the impact of outsourcing is greater than Bhagwati believes, and he is less optimistic that newly created jobs in the United States will pay higher wages than the jobs lost to outsourcing.

The debate between Samuelson and Bhagwati demonstrates that economics is an evolving discipline. New models are continually being introduced, and new hypotheses are being formulated and tested. We can expect the debate over the economic impact of outsourcing to continue to be lively.

Sources: Paul A. Samuelson, "Where Ricardo and Mill Rebut and Confirm Arguments of Mainstream Economists Supporting Globalization," *Journal of Economic Perspectives,* Vol. 18, No. 3, Summer 2004, pp. 135–146; Jagdish Bhagwati, Arvind Panagariya, and T. N. Srinivasan, "The Muddles Over Outsourcing," *Journal of Economic Perspectives,* Vol. 18, No. 4, Fall 2004, pp. 93–114; and Steve Lohr, "An Elder Challenges Outsourcing's Orthodoxy," *New York Times,* September 9, 2004, p. C1.

Normative and Positive Analysis

Throughout this book as we build economic models and use them to answer questions, we need to bear in mind the distinction between *positive analysis* and *normative analysis.*

Positive analysis is concerned with *what is* and **normative analysis** is concerned with *what ought to be.* Economics is about positive analysis, which measures the costs and benefits of different courses of action.

We can use the federal government's minimum wage law to compare positive and normative analysis. In 2005 under this law, it was illegal for an employer to hire a worker at a wage less than $5.15 per hour. Without the minimum wage law, some firms and some workers would voluntarily agree to a lower wage. Because of the minimum wage law, some workers have difficulty finding jobs and some firms end up paying more for labor than they otherwise would have. A positive analysis of the federal minimum wage law uses an economic model to estimate how many workers have lost their jobs because of the law, its impact on the costs and profits of businesses, and the gains to workers receiving the minimum wage. After economists complete this positive analysis, the decision as to whether the minimum wage law is a good idea or a bad idea is a normative one and depends on how people assess the trade-off involved. Supporters of the law believe that the losses to employers and to workers who are unemployed as a result of the law are more than offset by the gains to those workers who receive higher wages than they would have without the law. Opponents of the law believe the losses are greater than the gains. The assessment by any individual would depend, in part, on that person's values and political views. The positive analysis provided by an economist would play a role in the decision but can't by itself decide the issue one way or the other.

In each chapter you will see a "Don't Let This Happen To You!" box like the one below. The goal of these boxes is to alert you to common pitfalls in thinking about economic ideas. After reading the box, test your understanding by working the related problem that appears at the end of the chapter.

Positive analysis Analysis concerned with what is.

Normative analysis Analysis concerned with what ought to be.

Microeconomics and Macroeconomics

Economic models can be used to analyze decision making in many areas. We group some of these areas together as *microeconomics* and others as *macroeconomics*. **Microeconomics** is the study of how households and firms make choices, how they interact in markets, and how the government attempts to influence their choices. Microeconomic issues include explaining how consumers react to changes in product prices and how firms decide what prices to charge. Microeconomics also involves policy issues, such as analyzing the most efficient way to reduce teenage smoking, analyzing the costs and

 LEARNING OBJECTIVE
Distinguish between microeconomics and macroeconomics.

Microeconomics The study of how households and firms make choices, how they interact in markets, and how the government attempts to influence their choices.

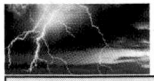 *Don't Let This Happen To You!*

Don't Confuse Positive Analysis with Normative Analysis

"Economic analysis has shown that the minimum wage law is a bad idea because it causes unemployment." Is this statement accurate? As of 2005, the federal minimum wage law prevents employers from hiring workers at a wage of less than $5.15 per hour. This wage is higher than some employers are willing to pay some workers. If there were no minimum wage law, some workers who currently cannot find any firm willing to hire them at $5.15 per hour would be able to find employment at a lower wage. Therefore, positive economic analysis indicates that the minimum wage law causes unemployment (although economists disagree about how much unemployment is caused by the minimum wage). *But,*

those workers who still have jobs benefit from the minimum wage because they are paid a higher wage than they otherwise would be. In other words, the minimum wage law creates both losers (the workers who become unemployed and the firms that have to pay higher wages) and winners (the workers who receive higher wages).

Do the gains to the winners more than offset the losses to the losers? The answer to that question involves normative analysis. Positive economic analysis can only show the consequences of a particular policy; it cannot tell us whether the policy is "good" or "bad." So, the statement at the beginning of this box is inaccurate.

YOUR TURN: Test your understanding by doing related problem 16 on page 20 at the end of this chapter.

Macroeconomics The study of the economy as a whole, including topics such as inflation, unemployment, and economic growth.

benefits of approving the sale of a new prescription drug, and analyzing the most efficient way to reduce air pollution.

Macroeconomics is the study of the economy as a whole, including topics such as inflation, unemployment, and economic growth. Macroeconomic issues include explaining why economies experience periods of recession and increasing unemployment and why over the long run some economies have grown much faster than others. Macroeconomics also involves policy issues, such as whether government intervention is capable of reducing the severity of recessions.

The division between microeconomics and macroeconomics is not hard and fast. Many economic situations have *both* a microeconomic and a macroeconomic aspect. For example, the level of total investment by firms in new machinery and equipment helps to determine how rapidly the economy grows—which is a macroeconomic issue. But to understand how much new machinery and equipment firms decide to purchase, we have to analyze the incentives individual firms face—which is a microeconomic issue.

⑤ **LEARNING OBJECTIVE**

Become familiar with important economic terms.

A Preview of Important Economic Terms

In the following chapters you will encounter certain important terms again and again. Becoming familiar with these terms is a necessary step in learning economics. Here we provide a brief introduction to some of these terms. We will discuss them all in greater depth in later chapters:

➤ *Entrepreneur.* An entrepreneur is someone who operates a business. In a market system it is entrepreneurs who decide what goods and services to produce and how to produce them. An entrepreneur starting a new business puts his or her own funds at risk. If an entrepreneur is wrong about what consumers want or about the best way to produce goods and services, the entrepreneur's funds can be lost. This is not an unusual occurrence: In the United States, about half of new businesses close within four years. Without entrepreneurs willing to assume the risk of starting and operating businesses, economic progress would be impossible in a market system.

➤ *Innovation.* There is a distinction between an *invention* and *innovation*. An invention is the development of a new good or a new process for making a good. An innovation is the practical application of an invention. (Innovation also may be used more broadly to refer to any significant improvement in a good or in the means of producing a good.) Much time often passes between the appearance of a new idea and its development to the point where it can be widely used. For example, the Wright Brothers first achieved self-propelled flight at Kitty Hawk, North Carolina, in 1903, but the Wright Brothers' plane was very crude, and it wasn't until the introduction of the DC-3 by Douglas Aircraft in 1936 that regularly scheduled intercity airline flights became common in the United States. Similarly, the first digital electronic computer—the ENIAC—was developed in 1945, but the first IBM personal computer was not introduced until 1981 and widespread use of computers did not have a significant effect on the productivity of American business until the 1990s.

➤ *Technology.* A firm's technology is the processes it uses to produce goods and services. In the economic sense, a firm's technology depends on many factors, such as the skill of its managers, the training of its workers, and the speed and efficiency of its machinery and equipment.

➤ *Firm, company, or business.* A firm is an organization that produces a good or service for profit. Economists use the words "firm," "company," and "business" interchangeably.

➤ *Goods.* Goods are tangible merchandise, such as books, computers, or DVD players.

➤ *Services.* Services are activities done for others, such as providing haircuts or investment advice.

➤ *Revenue.* A firm's revenue is the total amount received for selling a good or service. It is calculated by multiplying the price per unit by the number of units sold.

➤ *Opportunity cost.*   The concept of opportunity cost is one of the most important in economics. The opportunity cost of any activity is the highest-valued alternative that must be given up to engage in that activity. Consider the example of an entrepreneur who could receive a salary of $80,000 per year working as a manager at a firm but opens her own firm instead. In that case, the opportunity cost of her entrepreneurial services to her own firm is $80,000, even though she does not pay herself an explicit salary.

➤ *Profit.*   A firm's profit is the difference between its revenue and its costs. Economists distinguish between *accounting profit* and *economic profit*. Accounting profit excludes the cost of some economic resources that the firm does not pay for explicitly. Economic profit includes the opportunity cost of all resources used by the firm. When we refer to profit in this book, we mean economic profit. It is important not to confuse *profit* with *revenue.*

➤ *Household.*   A household consists of all persons occupying a home. Households are suppliers of factors of production—particularly labor—used by firms to make goods and services. Households also demand goods and services produced by firms and governments.

➤ *Factors of production or economic resources.*   Firms use factors of production to produce goods and services. The main factors of production are labor, capital, human capital, natural resources—including land—and entrepreneurial ability. Households earn income by supplying the factors of production to firms.

➤ *Capital.*   The word "capital" can refer to *financial capital* or to *physical capital.* Financial capital includes stocks and bonds issued by firms, bank accounts, and holdings of money. In economics, though, "capital" refers to physical capital, which includes manufactured goods that are used to produce other goods and services. Examples of physical capital are computers, factory buildings, machine tools, warehouses, and trucks. The total amount of physical capital available in a country is referred to as the country's *capital stock.*

➤ *Human capital.*   Human capital refers to the accumulated training and skills that workers possess. For example, workers with a college education generally have more skills and are more productive than workers who have only a high school degree.

Conclusion

The best way to think of economics is as a group of useful ideas about how individuals make choices. Economists have put these ideas into practice by developing economic models. Consumers, business managers, and government officials use these models every day to help them make choices. In this book, we explore many key economic models and give examples of how they can be applied in the real world.

Most students taking an introductory economics course do not major in economics or become professional economists. Whatever your major may be, the economic principles you will learn in this book will improve your ability to make choices in many aspects of your life. These principles will also improve your understanding of how decisions are made in business and government.

Reading the newspaper and other periodicals is an important part of understanding the current business climate and learning how to apply economic concepts to a variety of real-world events. At the end of each chapter, you will see a two-page periodical feature entitled *An Inside Look*. This feature consists of an excerpt of an article that relates to the company we introduced at the start of the chapter and also to the concepts we have discussed throughout the chapter. A summary and analysis and supporting graphs highlight the economic key points of the article. Test your understanding by answering the *Thinking Critically* questions. Read *An Inside Look* on the next page to learn why some economists argue that fears about outsourcing to China are unjustified.

ECONOMIST, SEPTEMBER 30, 2004

The Halo Effect

"WHAT you cannot avoid, welcome," says an old Chinese proverb. The world would be wise to bear that in mind in its dealings with China. The country's global integration will have a bigger impact on the world economy than that of any previous emerging economy. Fortunately, though, it will be mostly a force for good, boosting overall prosperity.

China's ascent will affect the outside world more than Japan's did in its time. . . .

The idea that China may become the world's biggest economy, with an enormous army of cheap workers, fills many in the rich western world with dread. Yet China's combination of rapid growth, vast size and openness could deliver a big boost to incomes outside China as well as at home. Rather like America when it entered the world economy in the late 19th century, China will be giving a huge boost to both global demand and supply. . . .

a Jobs will be lost in manufacturing in the developed world, but new jobs will be created, largely because most of the money that China earns from exports is being spent on imports from rich economies. Sustained growth in income and jobs relies on a continuous shift of resources to higher-value industries. A frozen job market with no hiring or firing would be in nobody's interest.

Individual countries can maximise their gains from Chinese integration and minimise their losses by making their own economies more flexible, increasing mobility between sectors and improving education. A study by the McKinsey Global Institute looked at what happened to workers who lost their jobs because of firms moving their production to low-wage countries such as China or India. McKinsey estimates that in America 70% of them find new work within six months, but in Germany only 40% do, partly because of a generous benefit system as well as strict hiring and firing laws. . . .

b In flexible labour markets, many of the workers who lose their jobs will eventually be re-employed in more productive industries. It is ironic, therefore, that American politicians and businessmen have been complaining most loudly about China stealing their country's jobs. With its flexible economy, America should adjust more easily than Europe. Fears about the threat from China stem from a series of widely held myths.

American business lobbies and trade unions claim that offshoring has cost their country [3 million] manufacturing jobs in the past three years. But most of those job losses were likelier to have been caused by the recession or by labour-saving IT investment. . . .

Moreover, even if outsourcing does export jobs to China, part of the income created there flows back as increased demand for American goods and services. Work by Matthew Slaughter, an economist at the Tuck School of Business at Dartmouth College, finds that outsourcing also creates new jobs back home for engineers, finance and marketing experts to supply services or hi-tech components to foreign affiliates. In a study of 2,500 American multinational firms in the ten years to 2001, Mr. Slaughter found that the number of jobs in their foreign subsidiaries rose by 2.9 [million], but in America itself by as much as 5.5 [million]. Moreover, these firms' domestic employment increased faster than jobs in purely domestic firms. . . .

c Fears that Chinese exports are growing at the expense of other countries are based on a fixed-lump-of-trade fallacy. In fact, trade is a positive-sum game: the more participants there are, the more opportunities arise, allowing countries to produce more with the same amount of labour and to obtain goods and services more cheaply. China's expansion will hugely add to those opportunities.

Key Points in the Article

This article discusses the effect of economic growth in China on jobs and wages in the United States and Europe. The article notes that many people fear that a rapid growth in China will reduce incomes and economic growth in the United States and Europe. The article argues these fears are unjustified. It also provides advice on the types of policies countries should pursue to increase their gains from China's integration into the world economy.

Analyzing the News

a Figure 1 shows that for several countries, including the United States, China has become an increasingly important market for exports. We noted previously in this chapter that markets tend to be efficient because they involve *voluntary exchange*. With voluntary exchange both the buyer and the seller are made better off. This insight applies to international trade between the United States and China as much as to domestic trade within the United States. One strength of a market system is that it facilitates shifting of resources from declining industries to expanding industries, as noted in the article.

b Making the Connection 1-1 presented the debate between economists Paul Samuelson and Jagdish Bhagwati over whether outsourcing has helped or hurt the U.S. economy. One key aspect of the debate concerned whether workers who lose their jobs because of outsourcing are eventually likely to find comparable or better jobs. The article makes the argument that when labor markets are flexible—meaning that there are few restrictions on workers moving between jobs—it is more likely that displaced workers will find good replacement jobs.

c We have seen in this chapter that economists use models to analyze economic issues such as the effects of outsourcing. One advantage of economic models is that they make explicit the assumptions that are being made. Models also generate hypotheses that can be tested against the real world. According to the article, people who fear that an increase in exports from China must come at the expense of other countries also are using a model, but it is a model that is not explicitly stated. The article refers to this model as the "fixed-lump-of-trade fallacy." We know the model is a fallacy because the evidence shows that many countries can increase their exports at the same time.

Thinking Critically

1. The article argues that outsourcing to China will make the global economy and the U.S. economy more prosperous and efficient. What impact does the article suggest outsourcing will have on equity?
2. What evidence from the article suggests that positive analysis of the impact of outsourcing will be difficult, even among people using the same economic model?

Source: "The Halo Effect: How China's Expansion Will Affect Jobs and Growth Elsewhere," *Economist*, September 30, 2004. © 2004 The Economist Newspaper Ltd. All rights reserved. Reprinted with permission. Further reproduction prohibited. www.economist.com

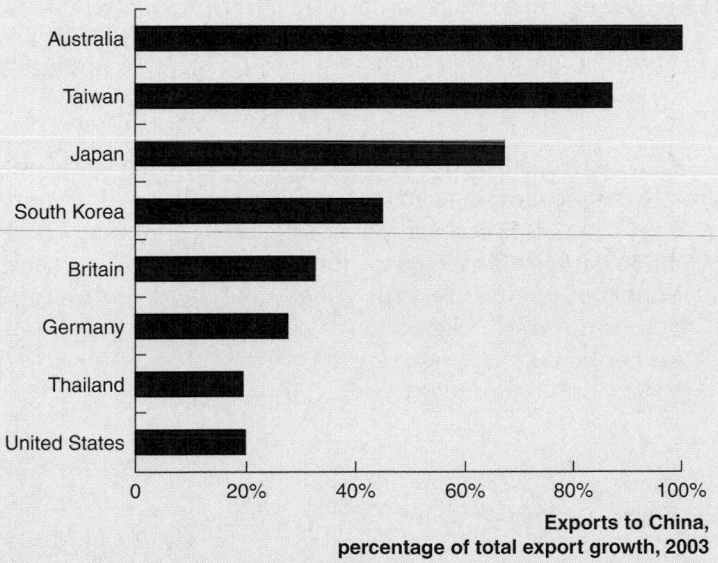

Exports to China,
percentage of total export growth, 2003

Figure 1: Many countries, including the United States, have experienced rapidly increasing exports to China.

Source: Thomson Datastream: national statistics.

SUMMARY

LEARNING OBJECTIVE ① Discuss these three important economic ideas: People are rational. People respond to incentives. Optimal decisions are made at the margin. Economists assume people are rational in the sense that consumers and firms use all available information as they take actions intended to achieve their goals. Rational individuals weigh the benefits and costs of each action, and choose an action only if the benefits outweigh the costs. Although people act from a variety of motives, ample evidence indicates that they respond to economic incentives. Economists use the word "marginal" to mean extra or additional. The optimal decision is to continue any activity up to the point where the marginal benefit equals the marginal cost.

LEARNING OBJECTIVE ② Discuss how an economy answers these questions: *What* goods and services will be produced? *How* will the goods and services be produced? *Who* will receive the goods and services? The choices of consumers, firms, and governments determine what goods and services will be produced. Firms choose how to produce the goods and services they sell. In the United States, who receives the goods and services produced depends largely on how income is distributed in the marketplace. In a centrally planned economy, most economic decisions are made by the government. In a market economy, most economic decisions are made by consumers and firms. Most economies, including that of the United States, are mixed economies in which most economic decisions are made by consumers and firms, but in which the government also plays a significant role. There are two types of efficiency: *productive efficiency* and *allocative efficiency*. Productive efficiency occurs when a good or service is produced at the lowest possible cost. Allocative efficiency occurs when production reflects consumer preferences. *Equity* is harder to define than efficiency,

but it usually involves a fair distribution of economic benefits. Government policymakers often face a trade-off between equity and efficiency.

LEARNING OBJECTIVE ③ Understand the role of models in economic analysis. Economists rely on economic models when they apply economic ideas to real-world problems. *Economic models* are simplified versions of reality used to analyze real-world economic situations. Economists accept and use an economic model if it leads to hypotheses that are confirmed by statistical analysis. In many cases, the acceptance is tentative, however, pending the gathering of new data or further statistical analysis. Economics is a *social science* because it applies the scientific method to the study of the interactions among individuals. Economics is concerned with positive analysis rather than normative analysis. Positive analysis is concerned with what is. Normative analysis is concerned with what ought to be.

LEARNING OBJECTIVE ④ Distinguish between microeconomics and macroeconomics. *Microeconomics* is the study of how households and firms make choices, how they interact in markets, and how the government attempts to influence their choices. *Macroeconomics* is the study of the economy as a whole, including topics such as inflation, unemployment, and economic growth.

LEARNING OBJECTIVE ⑤ Become familiar with important economic terms. Becoming familiar with important terms is a necessary step to learn economics. These important economic terms include capital, entrepreneur, factors of production, firm, goods, household, human capital, innovation, opportunity cost, profit, revenue, and technology.

KEY TERMS

Allocative efficiency 9	Economics 4	Market economy 8	Productive efficiency 9
Centrally planned economy 8	Equity 9	Microeconomics 13	Scarcity 4
Economic model 4	Macroeconomics 14	Mixed economy 9	Trade-off 7
Economic variable 10	Marginal analysis 6	Normative analysis 13	Voluntary exchange 9
	Market 5	Positive analysis 13	

REVIEW QUESTIONS

1. What is scarcity? Why is scarcity central to the study of economics?

2. Briefly discuss each of the following economic ideas: People are rational. People respond to incentives. Optimal decisions are made at the margin.

3. What are the three economic questions that every society must answer? Briefly discuss the differences in how centrally planned, market, and mixed economies answer these questions.

4. What is the difference between productive efficiency and allocative efficiency?

5. What is the difference between efficiency and equity? Why do government policymakers often face a trade-off between efficiency and equity?

6. Why do economists use models? How are economic data used to test models?

7. Describe the five steps by which economists arrive at a useful economic model.

8. What is the difference between normative analysis and positive analysis? Is economics concerned mainly with normative analysis or mainly with positive analysis? Briefly explain.

9. Briefly discuss the difference between microeconomics and macroeconomics.

PROBLEMS AND APPLICATIONS

Please visit **www.prenhall.com/hubbard** *for solutions to the even-numbered problems as well as multiple-choice and true or false self-assessment quizzes.*

1. In a column in the *Wall Street Journal,* Robert McTeer Jr., former president of the Federal Reserve Bank of Dallas, wrote, "My take on training in economics is that it becomes increasingly valuable as you move up the career ladder. I can't think of a better major for corporate CEO's [chief executive officers], congressmen or American presidents." Why might studying economics be particularly good preparation for being the top manager of a corporation or a leader in government?
Source: Robert D. McTeer Jr., "The Dismal Science? Hardly!" *Wall Street Journal,* June 4, 2003.

2. Does Bill Gates, the richest person in the world, face scarcity? Does everyone? Are there any exceptions?

3. Do you agree or disagree with the following assertion: "The problem with economics is that it assumes consumers and firms always make the correct decision. But we know everyone's human, and we all make mistakes."

4. **[Related to *Solved Problem 1-1*]** Suppose Dell is currently selling 250,000 Pentium 4 laptops per month. A manager at Dell argues, "The last 10,000 laptops we produced increased our revenue by $8.5 million and our costs by $8.9 million. However, because we are making a substantial total profit of $25 million from producing 250,000 laptops, I think we are producing the optimal number of laptops." Briefly explain whether you agree with the manager's reasoning.

5. **[Related to *Solved Problem 1-1*]** Two students are discussing Solved Problem 1-1.
Joe: "I think the key additional information you need to know in deciding whether to produce 300,000 more iPods is the amount of profit you currently are making while producing 3,000,000. Then you can compare the profit earned from selling 3,300,000 iPods with the profit earned from selling 3,000,000. This information is more important than the additional revenue and additional cost of the last 300,000 iPods produced."
Jill: "Actually, Joe, knowing how much profits change when you sell 300,000 more iPods is exactly the same as knowing the additional revenue and the additional cost."
Briefly evaluate their arguments.

6. **[Related to *Solved Problem 1-1*]** Late in the semester a friend tells you, "I was going to drop my psychology course so I could concentrate on my other courses, but I had already put so much time into the course that I decided not to drop it." What do you think of your friend's reasoning? Would it make a difference to your answer if your friend has to pass the psychology course at some point to graduate? Briefly explain.

7. In the first six months of 2003, branches of Commerce Bank in New York City were robbed 14 times. The New York City Police recommended steps the bank could take to deter robberies, including the installation of plastic barriers called "bandit barriers." The police were surprised the bank did not take their advice. According to a deputy

commissioner of police, "Commerce does very little of what we recommend. They've told our detectives they have no interest in ever putting in the barriers." Wouldn't Commerce Bank have a strong incentive to install bandit barriers to deter robberies? Why, then, wouldn't they do it?

Source: Dan Barry, "Friendly Bank Makes It Easy for Robbers," *New York Times*, July 5, 2003.

8. In 1838, the U.S. Army was given the job of moving the Cherokees, Creeks, Choctaws, and Seminoles from the eastern United States to Oklahoma. Contractors were given $65 per person (about $1,270 in today's money) to provide food and medicine for the Indians during the 1,000-mile forced march. Many of the contractors provided scanty food portions, bad meat, and no medicine. As a result, approximately one-quarter of these Indians perished along the way. How could the incentives have been changed so that the death rates would have been lower?

9. Suppose an economist develops an economic model and finds that "it works great in theory, but it fails in practice." What should the economist do next?

10. Dr. Strangelove's theory is that the price of mushrooms is determined by the activity of subatomic particles that exist in another universe parallel to ours. When the subatomic particles are emitted in profusion, the price of mushrooms is high. When subatomic particle emissions are low, the price of mushrooms also is low. How would you go about testing Dr. Strangelove's theory? Discuss whether or not this theory is useful.

11. Would you expect the new and better machinery and equipment to be adopted more rapidly in a market economy or in a centrally planned economy? Briefly explain.

12. Centrally planned economies have been less efficient than market economies.
    a. Has this happened by chance or is there some underlying reason?
    b. If market economies are more economically efficient than centrally planned economies, would there ever be a reason to prefer having a centrally planned economy rather than a market economy?

13. Thomas Sowell, an economist at the Hoover Institution at Stanford University, has written that "All economic systems not only provide people with goods and services, but also restrict or prevent them from getting as much of these goods and services as they wish."

    Why is it necessary for all economic systems to do this? How does a market system prevent people from getting as many goods and services as they wish?

    Source: Thomas Sowell, *Applied Economics: Thinking Beyond Stage One*, New York: Basic Books, 2004, p. 16.

14. Suppose that your local police department recovers 100 tickets to a big NASCAR race in a drug raid. It decides to distribute these to residents and announces that tickets will be given away at 10 A.M., Monday morning at City Hall.
    a. What groups of people will be most likely to try to get the tickets? Think of specific examples and then generalize.
    b. What is the opportunity cost of distributing the tickets this way?
    c. Productive efficiency occurs when a good or service (such as the distribution of tickets) is produced at the lowest possible cost. Is this an efficient way to distribute the tickets? If possible, think of a more efficient method of distributing the tickets.
    d. Is this an equitable way to distribute the tickets? Explain.

15. Many large firms have begun outsourcing work to China.
    a. Why have they done this?
    b. Is outsourcing work to low-wage Chinese workers a risk-free proposition for large firms?

16. [Related to *Don't Let This Happen To You!*] Explain which of the following statements represent positive analysis and which represent normative analysis:
    a. A 50-cent-per-pack tax on cigarettes will reduce smoking by teenagers by 12 percent.
    b. The federal government should spend more on AIDS research.
    c. Rising paper prices will increase textbook prices.
    d. The price of coffee at Starbucks is too high.

17. Briefly explain whether each of the following is primarily a microeconomic issue or a macroeconomic issue:
    a. The effect of higher cigarette taxes on the quantity of cigarettes sold
    b. The effect of higher income taxes on the total amount of consumer spending
    c. The reasons for the economies of East Asian countries growing faster than the economies of sub-Saharan African countries
    d. The reasons for low rates of profit in the airline industry

18. The American Bar Association has proposed a law that would prohibit anyone except lawyers from giving legal advice. Under the proposal, income tax preparers, real estate agents, hospitals, labor unions, and anyone else who offered legal advice would be penalized. One critic of the proposal argued that the proposal would protect attorneys more than it would protect consumers.
    a. How might the proposal protect consumers?
    b. Why did the critic of the proposal argue that it would protect attorneys more than it would protect consumers?
    c. Briefly discuss whether you consider the proposed law to be a good idea.

    Source: Adam Liptak, "U.S. Opposes Proposal to Limit Who May Give Legal Advice," *New York Times*, February 3, 2003.

Using Graphs and Formulas

Graphs are used to illustrate key economics ideas. Graphs appear not just in economics textbooks but also in newspaper and magazine articles that discuss business and economic ideas. Why the heavy use of graphs? Because they serve two useful purposes: (1) They simplify economic ideas, and (2) They make the ideas more concrete so they can be applied to real-world problems. Economic and business issues can be complicated, but a graph can help cut through complications and highlight the key relationships needed to understand a business issue. In that sense, a graph can be like a street map.

For example, suppose you take a bus to New York City to see the Empire State Building. After arriving at the Port Authority Bus Terminal, you will probably use a map similar to the one shown below to find your way to the Empire State Building.

Maps are very familiar to just about everyone, so we don't usually think of them as being simplified versions of reality, but they are. This map does not show much more than the streets in this part of New York City and some of the most important buildings. The names, addresses, and telephone numbers of the people who live and work in the area aren't given. Almost none of the stores and buildings those people work and live in are shown either. It doesn't tell you which streets allow curbside parking and which don't. In fact, the map tells you almost nothing about the messy reality of life in this section of New York City, except how the streets are laid out, which is the essential information you need to get from the Port Authority to the Empire State Building.

Think about someone who says, "I know how to get around in the city, but I just can't figure out how to read a map." It certainly is possible to find your destination in a city without a map, but it's a lot easier with one. The same is true of using graphs in economics. It is possible to arrive at a solution to a real-world problem in economics and business without using graphs, but it is usually a lot easier if you do use them.

Often the difficulty students have with graphs and formulas is just a lack of familiarity. With practice, all the graphs and formulas in this text will become familiar to you. Once you are familiar with them, you will be able to use them to analyze problems that would otherwise seem very difficult. What follows is a brief review of how graphs and formulas are used.

Graphs of One Variable

Figure 1A-1 displays values for *market shares* in the U.S. automobile market using two common types of graphs. Market shares show the percentage of industry sales accounted for by different firms. In this case, the information is for groups of firms: the "Big Three"—Ford, General Motors, and DiamlerChrysler—as well as Japanese firms, European firms, and Korean firms. Panel (a) displays the information on market shares as a *bar graph,* where the market share of each group of firms is represented by the height of its bar. Panel (b) displays the same information as a *pie chart,* with the market share of each group of firms represented by the size of its slice of the pie.

Information on economic variables is also often displayed in *time-series graphs.* Time-series graphs are displayed on a coordinate grid. In a coordinate grid we can measure the value of one variable along the vertical axis (or *y*-axis), and the value of another variable along the horizontal axis (or *x*-axis). The point where the vertical axis intersects the horizontal axis is called the *origin.* At the origin the value of both variables is zero. The points on a coordinate grid represent values of the two variables. In Figure 1A-2 we measure the number of automobiles and trucks sold worldwide by the Ford Motor Company on the vertical axis, and we measure time on the horizontal axis. In time-series graphs, the height of the line at each date shows the value of the variable measured on the vertical axis. Both panels of Figure 1A-2 show Ford's worldwide sales during each year from 1999 to 2003. The difference between panel (a) and panel (b)

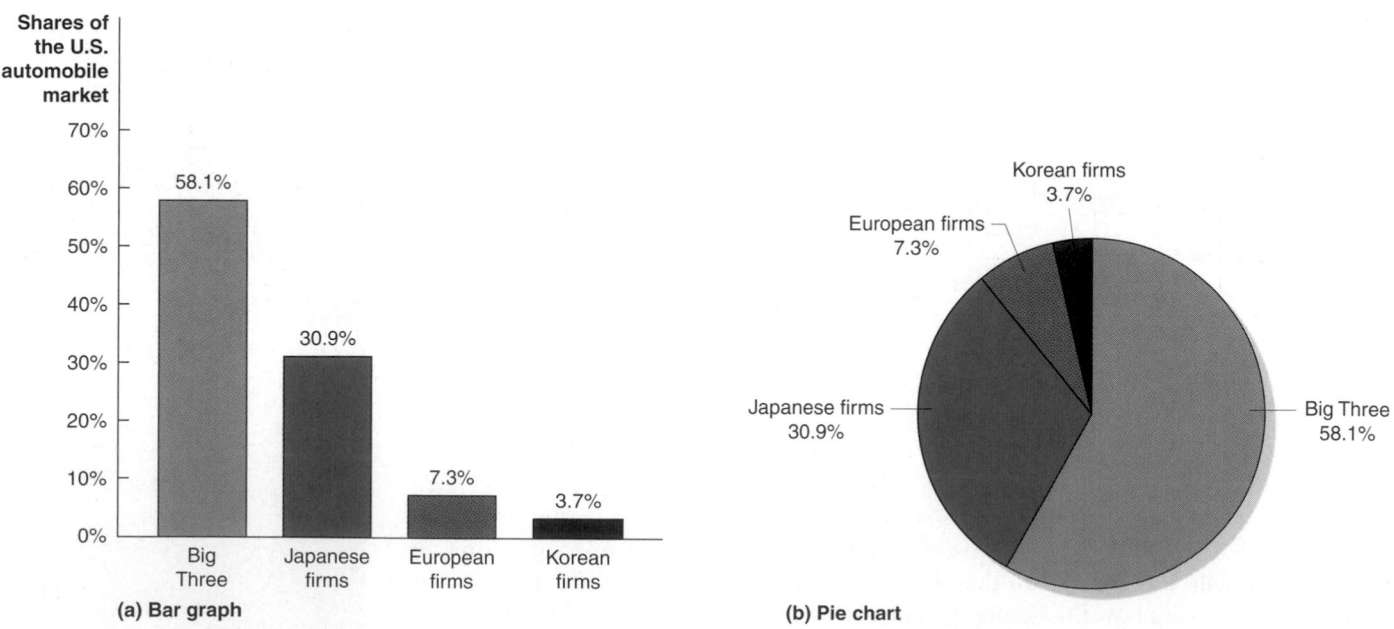

FIGURE 1A-1   **Bar Graphs and Pie Charts**

Values for an economic variable are often displayed as a bar graph or as a pie chart. In this case, panel (a) shows market share data for the U.S. automobile industry as a *bar graph,* where the market share of each group of firms is represented by the height of its bar. Panel (b) displays the same information as a *pie chart,* with the market share of each group of firms represented by the size of its slice of the pie.

Source: Ann Keeton, "December U.S. Auto Rise; GM's Decline," *Wall Street Journal,* January 5, 2005, p. A2.

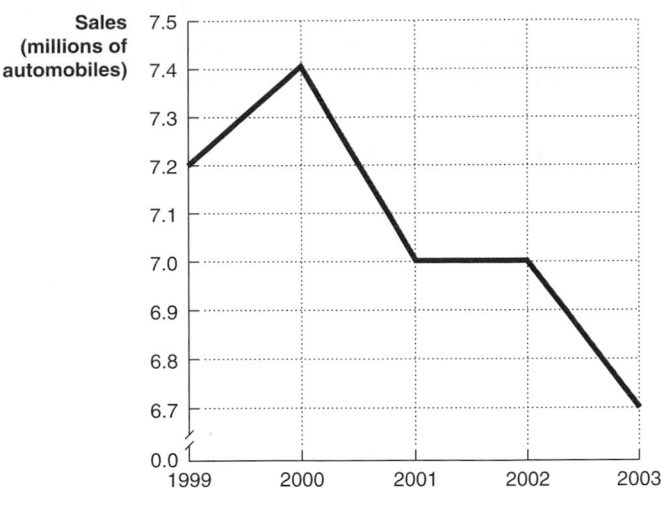

(a) Time-series graph with truncated scale

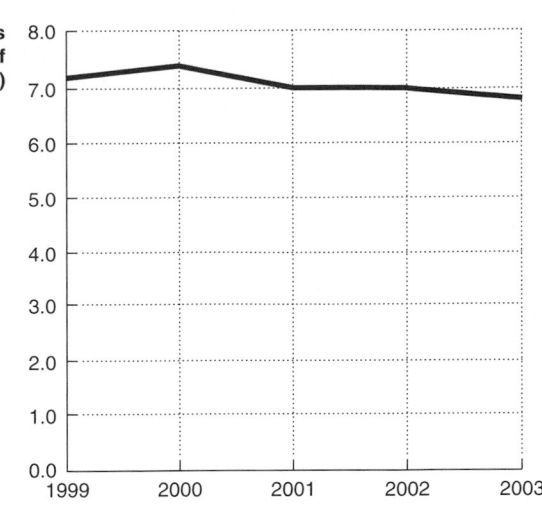

(b) Time-series graph where the scale is
not truncated

FIGURE 1A-2   **Time-Series Graphs**

Both panels present time-series graphs of Ford Motor Company's worldwide sales during each year from 1999 to 2003. Panel (a) has a truncated scale on the vertical axis, while panel (b) does not. As a result, the fluctuations in Ford's sales appear smaller in panel (b) than in panel (a).

Source: Ford Motor Company, *Annual Report*, various years.

illustrates the importance of the scale used in a time-series graph. In panel (a), the scale on the vertical axis is truncated, which means that it does not start with zero. The slashes (//) near the bottom of the axis indicate that the scale is truncated. In panel (b), the scale is not truncated. In panel (b) the fluctuations in Ford's sales appear smaller than in panel (a). (Technically, the horizontal axis is also truncated because we start with the year 1999, not the year 0.)

Graphs of Two Variables

We often use graphs to show the relationship between two variables. For example, suppose you are interested in the relationship between the price of a pepperoni pizza and the quantity of pizzas sold per week in the small town of Bryan, Texas. A graph showing the relationship between the price of a good and the quantity of the good demanded at each price is called a *demand curve*. (As we will discuss later, in drawing a demand curve for a good we have to hold constant any variables other than price that might affect the willingness of consumers to buy the good.) Figure 1A-3 shows the data you have collected on price and quantity. The figure shows a two-dimensional grid on which we measure the price of pizza along the *y*-axis and the quantity of pizza sold per week along the *x*-axis. Each point on the grid represents one of the price and quantity combinations listed in the table. We can connect the points to form the demand curve for pizza in Bryan, Texas. Notice that the scales on both axes in the graph are truncated. In this case, truncating the axes allows the graph to illustrate more clearly the relationship between price and quantity by excluding low prices and quantities.

Slopes of Lines

Once you have plotted the data in Figure 1A-3, you may be interested in how much the quantity of pizza sold increases as the price decreases. The *slope* of a line tells us how

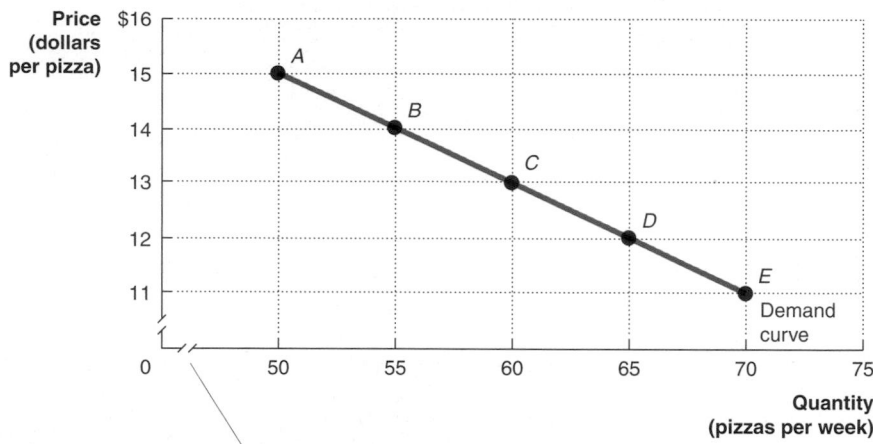

Price (dollars per pizza)	Quantity (pizzas per week)	Points
$15	50	A
14	55	B
13	60	C
12	65	D
11	70	E

As you learned in Figure 1A-2, the slashes (//) indicate the scales on the axes are truncated, which means that numbers are omitted: On the horizontal axis numbers jump from 0 to 50, and on the vertical axis numbers jump from 0 to 11.

much the variable we are measuring on the *y*-axis changes as the variable we are measuring on the *x*-axis changes. We can use the Greek letter delta (Δ) to stand for the change in a variable. The slope is sometimes referred to as the rise over the run. So, we have several ways of expressing slope:

$$\text{Slope} = \frac{\text{Change in value on the vertical axis}}{\text{Change in value on the horizontal axis}} = \frac{\Delta y}{\Delta x} = \frac{\text{Rise}}{\text{Run}}.$$

Figure 1A-4 reproduces the graph from Figure 1A-3. Because the slope of a straight line is the same at any point, we can use any two points in the figure to calculate the slope of the line. For example, when the price of pizza decreases from $14 to $12, the quantity of pizza sold increases from 55 per week to 65 per week. Therefore, the slope is:

$$\text{Slope} = \frac{\Delta \text{Price of pizza}}{\Delta \text{Quantity of pizza}} = \frac{(\$12 - \$14)}{(65 - 55)} = \frac{-2}{10} = -0.2.$$

The slope of this line gives us some insight into how responsive consumers in Bryan, Texas are to changes in the price of pizza. The larger the value of the slope (ignoring the negative sign), the steeper the line will be, which indicates that not many additional pizzas are sold when the price falls. The smaller the value of the slope, the flatter the line will be, which indicates a greater increase in pizzas sold when the price falls.

Taking Into Account More Than Two Variables on a Graph

The demand curve graph in Figure 1A-4 shows the relationship between the price of pizza and the quantity of pizza sold, but we know that the quantity of any good sold depends on more than just the price of the good. For example, the quantity of pizza sold in a given week in Bryan, Texas can be affected by such other variables as the price of hamburgers, whether an advertising campaign by local pizza parlors has begun that week, and so on. Allowing the values of any other variables to change will cause the position of the demand curve in the graph to change.

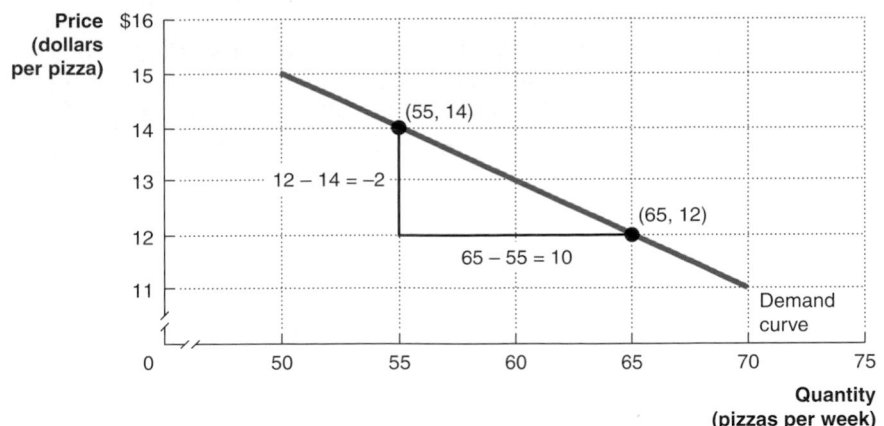

FIGURE 1A-4

Calculating the Slope of a Line

We can calculate the slope of a line as the change in the value of the variable on the y-axis divided by the change in the value of the variable on the x-axis. Because the slope of a straight line is constant, we can use any two points in the figure to calculate the slope of the line. For example, when the price of pizza decreases from $14 to $12, the quantity of pizza demanded increases from 55 per week to 65 per week. So, the slope of this line equals -2 divided by 10, or -0.2.

Suppose, for example, that the demand curve in Figure 1A-4 was drawn holding the price of hamburgers constant at $1.50. If the price of hamburgers rises to $2.00, then some consumers will switch from buying hamburgers to buying pizza, and more pizzas will be sold at every price. The result on the graph will be to shift the line representing the demand curve to the right. Similarly, if the price of hamburgers falls from $1.50 to $1.00, some consumers will switch from buying pizza to buying hamburgers, and fewer pizzas will be sold at every price. The result on the graph will be to shift the line representing the demand curve to the left.

The table in Figure 1A-5 shows the effect of a change in the price of hamburgers on the quantity of pizza demanded. For example, suppose at first we are on the line labeled *Demand curve₁*. If the price of pizza is $14 (point *A*), an increase in the price of hamburgers from $1.50 to $2.00 increases the quantity of pizza demanded from 55 to 60 per

	Quantity (pizzas per week)		
Price (dollars per pizza)	When the Price of Hamburgers = $1.00	When the Price of Hamburgers = $1.50	When the Price of Hamburgers = $2.00
$15	45	50	55
14	50	55	60
13	55	60	65
12	60	65	70
11	65	70	75

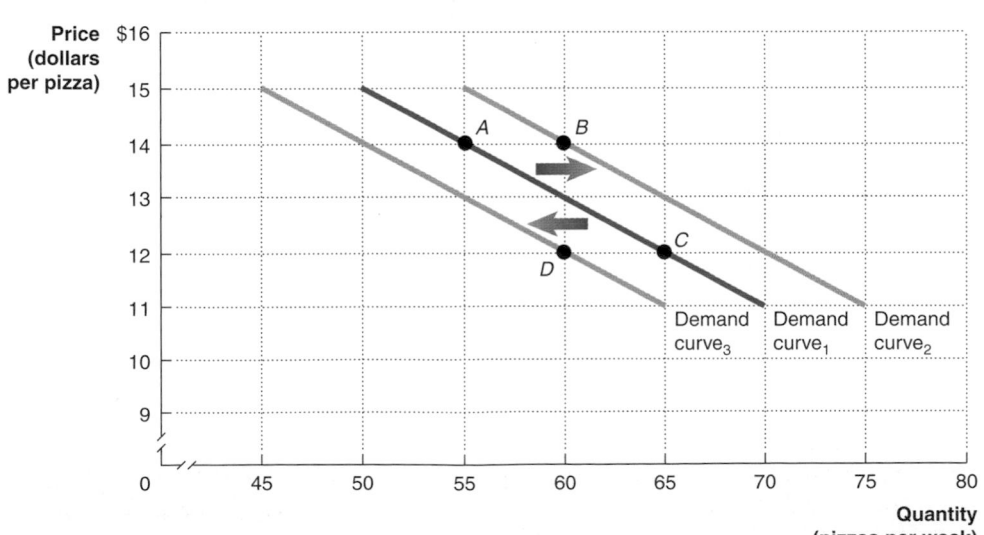

FIGURE 1A-5

Showing Three Variables on a Graph

The demand curve for pizza shows the relationship between the price of pizzas and the quantity of pizza demanded, *holding constant other factors that might affect the willingness of consumers to buy pizza*. If the price of pizza is $14 (point *A*), an increase in the price of hamburgers from $1.50 to $2.00 increases the quantity of pizza demanded from 55 to 60 per week (point *B*) and shifts us to Demand curve₂. Or, if we start on Demand curve₁ and the price of pizza is $12 (point *C*), a decrease in the price of hamburgers from $1.50 to $1.00 decreases the quantity of pizza demanded from 65 to 60 per week (point *D*), and shifts us to *Demand curve₃*.

week (point *B*), and shifts us to *Demand curve₂*. Or, if we start on *Demand curve₁* and the price of pizza is $12 (point *C*), a decrease in the price of hamburgers from $1.50 to $1.00 decreases the quantity of pizza demanded from 65 to 60 per week (point *D*) and shifts us to *Demand curve₃*. By shifting the demand curve, we have taken into account the effect of changes in the value of a third variable—the price of hamburgers. We will use this technique of shifting curves to allow for the effects of additional variables many times in this book.

Positive and Negative Relationships

We can use graphs to show the relationships between any two variables. Sometimes the relationship between the variables is *negative,* meaning that as one variable increases in value the other variable decreases in value. This was the case with the price of pizza and the quantity of pizza demanded. The relationship between two variables can also be *positive,* meaning that the values of both variables increase together. This positive co-movement is the case, for example, with the level of total income—or *disposable personal income*— received by households in the United States and the level of total *consumption spending,* which is spending by households on all types of goods and services, apart from houses. The table in Figure 1A-6 shows the values for income and consumption spending for the years 2001–2004 (the values are in billions of dollars). The graph plots the data from the table, with national income measured along the horizontal axis and consumption spending measured along the vertical axis. Notice that the four points do not all fall exactly on the line. This is often the case with real-world data. To examine the relationship between two variables, economists often use the straight line that best fits the data.

Slopes of Nonlinear Curves

The relationship between some economic variables cannot be represented accurately by a straight line. For example, panel (a) of Figure 1A-7 shows the hypothetical relationship between Apple's total cost of producing iPods and the quantity of iPods produced. The relationship is curved, rather than linear. In this case, the cost of production is increasing at an increasing rate, which often happens in manufacturing. Put a different way, as we move up the curve, its slope becomes larger. To see this effect, first remember that we calculate the slope of a curve by dividing the change in the variable on the *y*-axis by the

---

FIGURE 1A-6

Graphing the Positive Relationship between Income and Consumption

In a positive relationship between two economic variables, as one variable increases, the other variable also increases. This figure shows the positive relationship between disposable personal income and consumption spending. As disposable personal income in the United States has increased, so has consumption spending.

Source: U.S. Department of Commerce, Bureau of Economic Analysis.

Year	Disposable Personal Income (billions of dollars)	Consumption Spending (billions of dollars)
2001	$7,486	$7,055
2002	7,827	7,376
2003	8,159	7,760
2004	8,632	8,229

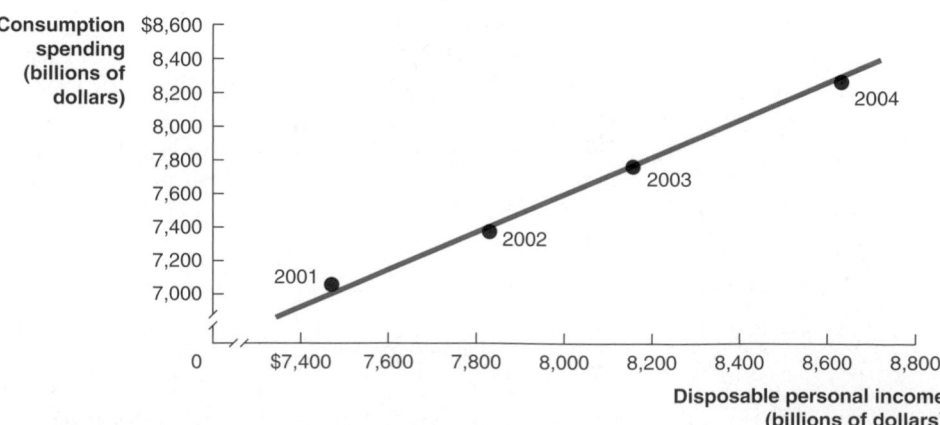

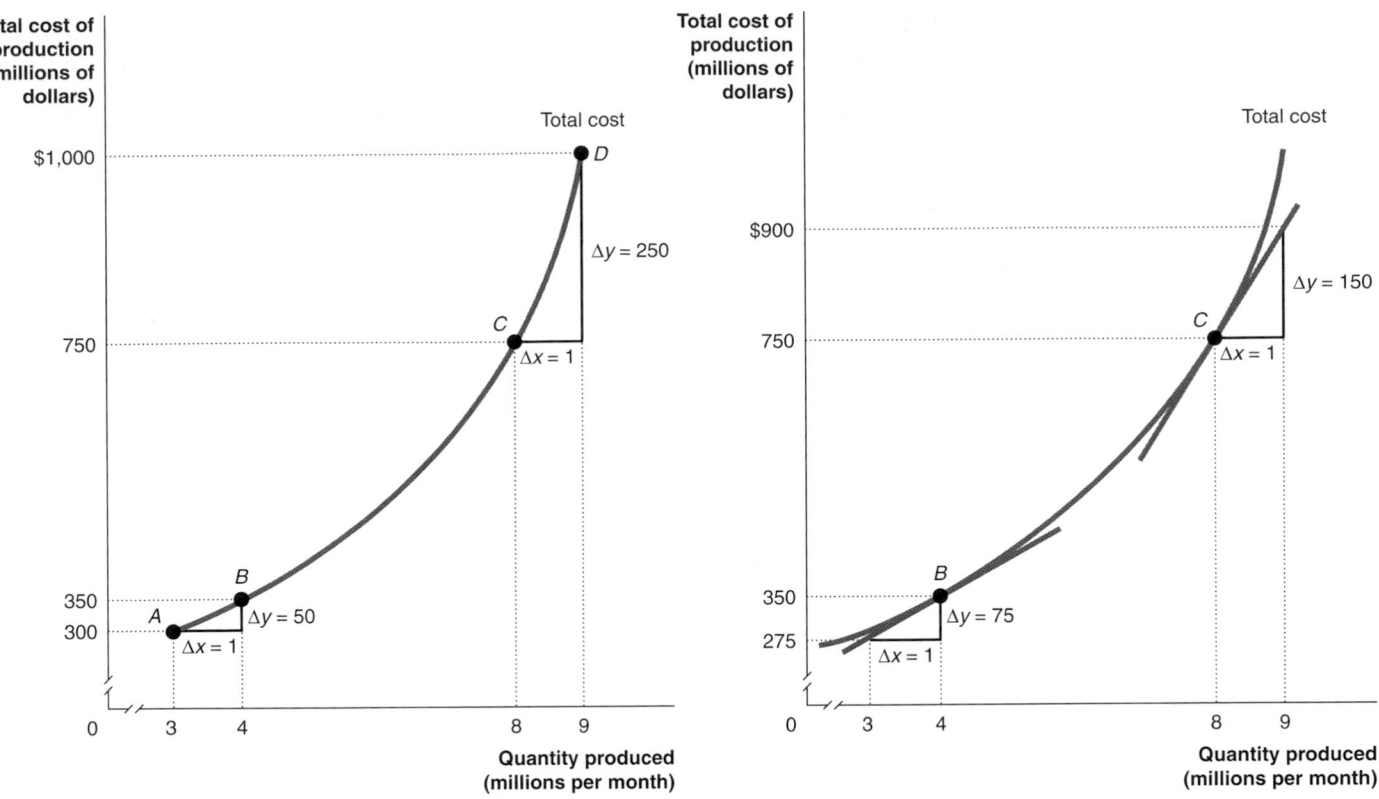

(a) The slope of a nonlinear curve is not constant

(b) The slope of a nonlinear curve is measured by the slope of the tangent line

FIGURE 1A-7   The Slope of a Nonlinear Curve

The relationship between the quantity of iPods produced and the total cost of production is curved, rather than linear. In panel (a), in moving from point *A* to point *B*, the quantity produced increases by 1 million iPods, while the total cost of production increases by $50 million. Farther up the curve, as we move from point *C* to point *D*, the change in quantity is the same—1 million iPods—but the change in the total cost of production is now much larger: $250 million.

Because the change in the *y* variable has increased, while the change in the *x* variable has remained the same, we know that the slope has increased. In panel (b), we measure the slope of the cuve at a particular point by the slope of the tangent line. The slope of the tangent line at point *B* is 75, and the slope of the tangent line at point *C* is 150.

change in the variable on the *x*-axis. In moving from point *A* to point *B*, the quantity produced increases by 1 million iPods, while the total cost of production increases by $50 million. Farther up the curve, as we move from point *C* to point *D*, the change in quantity is the same—1 million iPods—but the change in the total cost of production is now much larger: $250 million. Because the change in the *y* variable has increased, while the change in the *x* variable has remained the same, we know that the slope has increased.

To measure the slope of a nonlinear curve at a particular point, we must measure the slope of the *tangent line* to the curve at that point. A tangent line will only touch the curve at that point. We can measure the slope of the tangent line just as we would the slope of any straight line. In panel (b), the tangent line at point *B* has a slope equal to

$$\frac{\Delta \text{Cost}}{\Delta \text{Quantity}} = \frac{75}{1} = 75.$$

The tangent line at point *C* has a slope equal to

$$\frac{\Delta \text{Cost}}{\Delta \text{Quantity}} = \frac{150}{1} = 150.$$

Once again we see that the slope of the curve is larger at point *C* than at point *B*.

Formulas

We have just seen that graphs are an important economic tool. In this section, we will review several useful formulas and show how to use them to summarize data and to calculate important relationships.

Formula for a Percentage Change

One important formula is the *percentage change.* The percentage change is the change in some economic variable, usually from one period to the next, expressed as a percentage. An important macroeconomic measure is the real *Gross Domestic Product* or GDP. GDP is the value of all the final goods and services produced in a country during a year. "Real" GDP is corrected for the effects of inflation. When economists say that the U.S. economy grew 4.4 percent during 2004, they mean that real GDP was 4.4 percent higher in 2004 than it was in 2003. The formula for making this calculation is:

$$\left(\frac{GDP_{2004} - GDP_{2003}}{GDP_{2003}} \right) \times 100$$

or, more generally for any two periods:

$$Percentage\ change = \left(\frac{Value\ in\ the\ second\ period - Value\ in\ the\ first\ period}{Value\ in\ the\ first\ period} \right) \times 100.$$

In this case, real GDP was \$10,381 billion in 2003 and \$10,842 billion in 2004. So, the growth rate of the U.S. economy during 2004 was:

$$\left(\frac{\$10,842 - \$10,381}{\$10,381} \right) \times 100 = 4.4\%.$$

Notice that it didn't matter that in using the formula we ignored the fact that GDP is measured in billions of dollars. In fact, when calculating percentage changes, *the units don't matter.* The percentage increase from \$10,381 billion to \$10,842 billion is exactly the same as the percentage increase from \$10,381 to \$10,842.

Formulas for the Areas of a Rectangle and a Triangle

Areas that form rectangles and triangles on graphs can have important economic meaning. For example, Figure 1A-8 shows the demand curve for Pepsi. Suppose that the price is currently \$2.00 and that 125,000 bottles of Pepsi are sold at that price. A firm's *total revenue* is equal to the amount it receives from selling its product, or the price times the quantity sold. In this case, total revenue will equal \$2.00 per bottle times 125,000 bottles, or \$250,000.

FIGURE 1A-8

Showing a Firm's Total Revenue on a Graph

The area of a rectangle is equal to its base multiplied by its height. Total revenue is equal to price multiplied by quantity. Here, total revenue is equal to the price of \$2.00 per bottle times 125,000 bottles, or \$250,000. The area of the green-shaded rectangle shows the firm's total revenue.

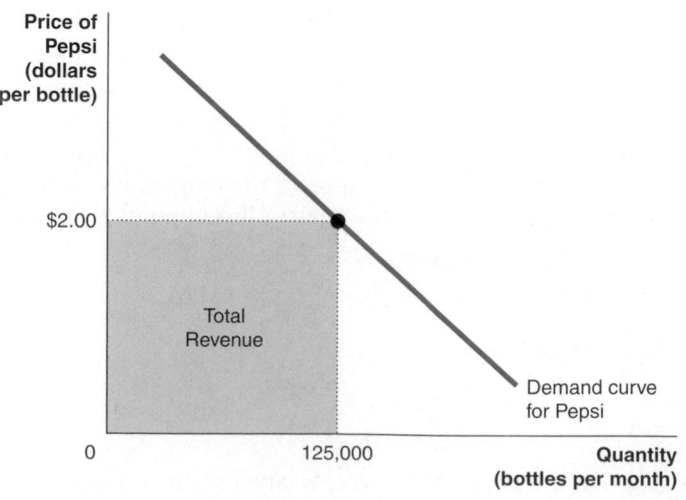

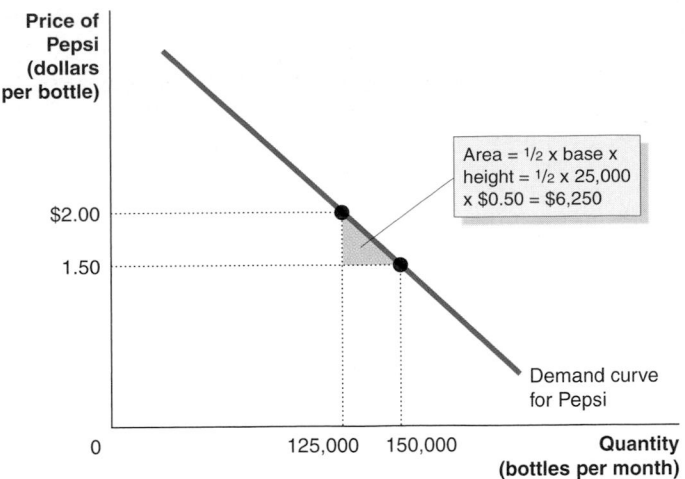

FIGURE 1A-9

The Area of a Triangle

The area of a triangle is equal to ½ multiplied by its base multiplied by its height. The area of the blue-shaded triangle has a base equal to 150,000 − 125,000, or 25,000 and a height equal to $2.00 − $1.50, or $0.50. Therefore, its area equals ½ × 25,000 × $0.50, or $6,250.

The formula for the area of a rectangle is:

$$\text{Area of a rectangle} = \text{base} \times \text{height}.$$

In Figure 1A-8, the green-shaded rectangle also represents the firm's total revenue because its area is given by the base of 125,000 bottles multiplied by the price of $2.00 per bottle.

We will see in later chapters that areas that are triangles can also have economic significance. The formula for the area of a triangle is:

$$\text{Area of a triangle} = \tfrac{1}{2} \times \text{base} \times \text{height}.$$

The blue-shaded area in Figure 1A-9 is a triangle. The base equals 150,000 − 125,000, or 25,000. Its height equals $2.00 − $1.50, or $0.50. Therefore its area equals ½ × 25,000 × $0.50, or $6,250. Notice that the blue area is only a triangle if the demand curve is a straight line, or linear. Not all demand curves are linear. However, the formula for the area of a triangle will usually still give us a good approximation, even if the demand curve is not linear.

Summary of Using Formulas

You will encounter several other formulas in this book. Whenever you must use a formula, you should follow these steps:

1. Make sure you understand the economic concept that the formula represents.
2. Make sure that you are using the correct formula for the problem you are solving.
3. Make sure that the number you calculate using the formula is economically reasonable. For example, if you are using a formula to calculate a firm's revenue and your answer is a negative number, you know you made a mistake somewhere.

PROBLEMS AND APPLICATIONS

Please visit **www.prenhall.com/hubbard** *for solutions to the even-numbered problems as well as multiple-choice and true or false self-assessment quizzes.*

1. The following table gives the relationship between the price of custard pies and the number of pies Jacob buys per week.

PRICE	QUANTITY OF PIES	WEEK
$3.00	6	July 2
2.00	7	July 9
5.00	4	July 16
6.00	3	July 23
1.00	8	July 30
4.00	5	August 6

a. Is the relationship between the price of pies and the number of pies Jacob buys a positive relationship or a negative relationship?
b. Plot the data from the table on a graph similar to Figure 1A-3. Draw a straight line that best fits the points.
c. Calculate the slope of the line.

2. The following table gives information on the quantity of lemonade demanded on sunny and overcast days. Plot the data from the table on a graph similar to Figure 1A-5. Draw two straight lines representing the two demand curves—one for sunny days, the other for overcast days.

PRICE (DOLLARS PER GLASS)	QUANTITY (GLASSES OF LEMONADE PER DAY)	WEATHER
$0.80	30	Sunny
0.80	10	Overcast
0.70	40	Sunny
0.70	20	Overcast
0.60	50	Sunny
0.60	30	Overcast
0.50	60	Sunny
0.50	40	Overcast

3. Using the information in Figure 1A-2, calculate the percentage change in auto sales from one year to the next. Between which years did sales fall at the fastest rate?

4. Real GDP in 1981 was $5,292 billion. Real GDP in 1982 was $5,189 billion. What was the percentage change in real GDP from 1981 to 1982? What do economists call the percentage change in real GDP from one year to the next?

5. Assume the demand curve for Pepsi passes through the following two points:

PRICE PER BOTTLE OF PEPSI	NUMBER OF BOTTLES OF PEPSI SOLD
$2.50	100,000
1.25	200,000

a. Draw a graph with a linear demand curve that passes through these two points.
b. Show on the graph the areas representing total revenue at each price. Give the value for total revenue at each price.

6. What is the area of the blue triangle shown in the following figure?

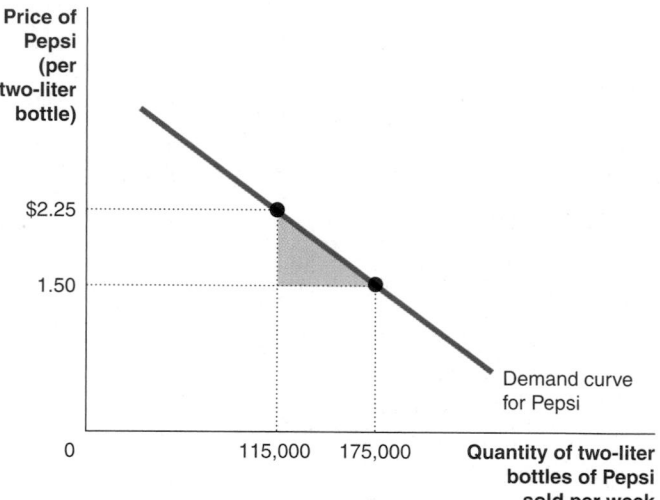

chapter

two

Trade-offs, Comparative Advantage, and the Market System

Managers Making Choices at BMW

➤ When you think of cars that combine fine engineering, high performance, and cutting-edge styling, you are likely to think of BMW. The Bayerische Motoren Werke, or Bavarian Motor Works, was founded in Germany in 1916 as a company devoted to manufacturing aircraft engines. In the early 1920s, BMW began to make motorcycles. In 1928 it produced its first car. Today, BMW employs nearly 100,000 workers in 23 factories in 15 countries to produce eight car models. In 2004, it had worldwide sales of about $70 billion.

To compete in the automobile market, the managers of BMW must make many strategic decisions, such as whether to introduce a new car model. In 2004, for example, BMW introduced the 1-Series, a hatchback that is significantly smaller than most other BMW models. Some BMW managers had opposed developing the 1-Series because they believed that it was inconsistent with the company's image of producing more expensive, higher-performance models. But other managers argued that the company needed a model that would appeal to younger drivers and could compete with the Volkswagen Golf and the Audi A3. Another strategic decision faced by BMW's managers is where to focus their advertising. In the late 1990s, for example, some of BMW's managers opposed advertising in China because they were skeptical about the country's sales potential. Other managers, however, argued that rising incomes were rapidly increasing the size of the Chinese market. BMW decided to advertise in China, and by 2004 it had become the company's eighth-largest market.

Over the years, BMW's managers have also faced the strategic decision of whether to concentrate production in factories in Germany or to build new factories in its overseas markets. Keeping production in Germany makes it easier for BMW's managers to supervise production and to employ German workers, who generally have high levels of technical training. Building factories in other countries, however, has two benefits. First, the lower wages paid to workers in other countries reduce the

LEARNING OBJECTIVES

After studying this chapter, you should be able to:

① Use a production possibilities frontier to analyze opportunity costs and trade-offs.

② Understand comparative advantage and explain how it is the basis for trade.

③ Explain the basic idea of how a market system works.

cost of manufacturing vehicles. Second, BMW can reduce political friction by producing vehicles in the same country in which they sell them. In 2003, BMW opened a plant at Shenyang, in northeast China, to build its 3-Series and 5-Series cars. Previously, in 1995, BMW opened a U.S. factory in Spartanburg, South Carolina, which currently produces the Z4 roadster and X5 sports utility vehicle (SUV).

Managers also face smaller scale—or tactical—business decisions. For instance, for many years, BMW used two workers to attach the gearbox to the engine in each car. In 2002, an alternative method of attaching the gearbox using a robot, rather than workers, was developed.

In choosing which method to use, managers at BMW faced a trade-off because the robot method had a higher cost, but installed the gearbox in exactly the correct position, which reduces engine noise when the car is driven. Ultimately, the managers decided to adopt the robot method. A similar type of tactical business decision must be made in scheduling production at BMW's Spartanburg, South Carolina, plant. The plant produces both the Z4 and the X5 models, and a decision must be made each month as to the quantity of each model that should be produced. *An Inside Look* on page 54 discusses a similar decision BMW has to make at its Munich, Germany, plant.

Scarcity The situation in which
unlimited wants exceed the limited
resources available to fulfill those
wants.

➤ In a market system, managers at most firms must make decisions like those
made by BMW's managers. The decisions managers face reflect the key fact of economic life: **Scarcity** *requires trade-offs.* Scarcity exists because we have unlimited
wants but only limited resources available to fulfill those wants. Goods and services
are scarce. So, too, are the economic resources, or *factors of production*—
workers, capital, natural resources, and entrepreneurial ability—used to make them.
Your time is scarce, which means you face trade-offs: If you spend an hour studying
for an economics exam, you have one less hour to spend studying for a psychology
exam or going to the movies. If your university decides to use some of its scarce
budget funds to buy new computers for the computer labs, those funds will not be
available to buy new books for the library or to resurface the student parking lot. If
BMW decides to devote some of the scarce workers and machinery in its Spartanburg assembly plant to producing more Z4 roadsters, those resources will not be
available to produce more X5 SUVs.

Many of the decisions of households and firms are made in markets. One key
activity that takes place in markets is trade. By engaging in trade, people can raise
their standard of living. Trade involves the decisions of millions of households and
firms spread around the world. In this chapter, we provide an overview of how the
market system coordinates the independent decisions of these millions of households and firms. We begin our analysis of the economic consequences of scarcity
and the working of the market system by introducing an important economic model:
the *production possibilities frontier.*

① **LEARNING OBJECTIVE**
Use a production possibilities
frontier to analyze opportunity
costs and trade-offs.

Production possibilities frontier A
curve showing the maximum
attainable combinations of two
products that may be produced with
available resources.

Production Possibilities Frontiers and Real-World Trade-offs

As we saw in the opening to this chapter, BMW operates an automobile factory in Spartanburg, South Carolina, where it assembles Z4 roadsters and X5 sports utility vehicles.
Because the firm's resources—workers, machinery, materials, and entrepreneurial
skills—are limited, BMW faces a trade-off: Resources devoted to producing Z4s are not
available for producing X5s, and vice versa. Chapter 1 explained that economic models
can be useful in analyzing many questions. We can use a simple model called the
production possibilities frontier to analyze the trade-offs BMW faces in its Spartanburg
plant. A **production possibilities frontier** is a curve showing the maximum attainable
combinations of two products that may be produced with available resources. In BMW's
case, the two products are Z4 roadsters and X5 sports utility vehicles, and the resources
are BMW's workers, materials, robots, and other machinery.

Graphing the Production Possibilities Frontier

Figure 2-1 uses a production possibilities frontier to illustrate the trade-offs facing
BMW. The numbers from the table are plotted in the graph. The line in the graph is
BMW's production possibilities frontier. If BMW uses all its resources to produce roadsters, it can produce 800 per day—point *A* at one end of the production possibilities
frontier. If BMW uses all its resources to produce SUVs, it can produce 800 per day—
point *E* at the other end of the production possibilities frontier. If BMW devotes
resources to producing both vehicles, it could be at a point like *B*, where it produces 600
roadsters and 200 SUVs.

BMW's Production Choices at Its Spartanburg Plant		
Choice	Quantity of Roadsters Produced	Quantity of SUVs Produced
A	800	0
B	600	200
C	400	400
D	200	600
E	0	800

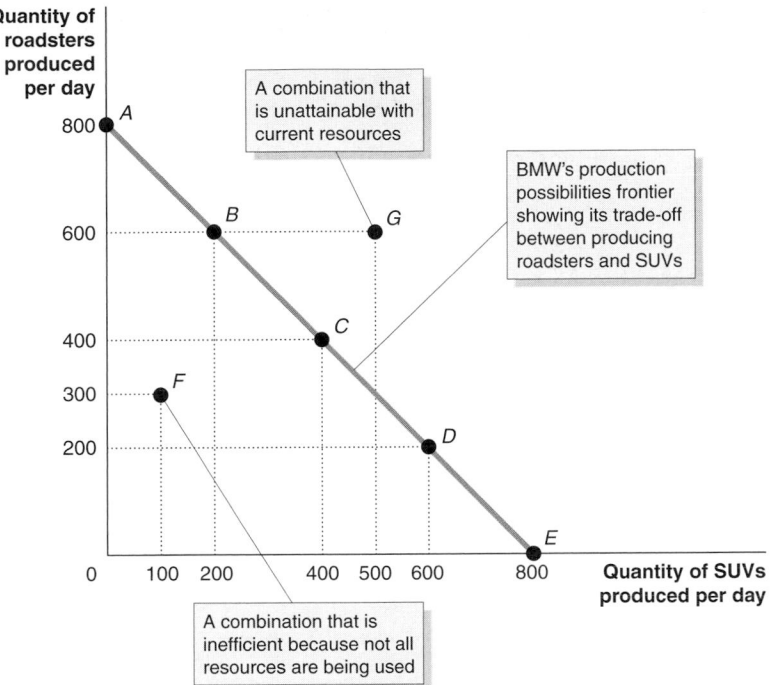

A combination that is unattainable with current resources

BMW's production possibilities frontier showing its trade-off between producing roadsters and SUVs

A combination that is inefficient because not all resources are being used

FIGURE 2-1

BMW's Production Possibilities Frontier

BMW faces a trade-off: To build one more roadster, it must build one less SUV. The production possibilities frontier illustrates the trade-off BMW faces. Combinations on the production possibilities frontier—like points *A, B, C, D,* and *E*—are *technically efficient* because the maximum output is being obtained from the available resources. Combinations inside the frontier—like point *F*—are *inefficient* because some resources are not being used. Combinations outside the frontier—like point *G*—are *unattainable* with current resources.

All the combinations either on the frontier—like *A, B, C, D,* and *E*—or inside the frontier—like point *F*—are *attainable* with the resources available. Combinations on the frontier are *efficient* because all available resources are being fully utilized, and the fewest possible resources are being used to produce a given amount of output. Combinations inside the frontier—like point *F*—are *inefficient* because maximum output is not being obtained from the available resources—perhaps because the assembly line is not operating at capacity. BMW might like to be beyond the frontier—at a point like *G* where it would be producing 600 roadsters and 500 SUVs—but points beyond the production possibilities frontier are *unattainable* given the firm's current resources. To produce the combination at *G*, BMW would need more machines or more workers.

Notice that if BMW is producing efficiently and is on the production possibilities frontier, the only way to produce more of one vehicle is to produce less of the other vehicle. Recall from Chapter 1 that the **opportunity cost** of any activity is the highest valued alternative that must be given up to engage in that activity. For BMW, the opportunity cost of producing one SUV is the number of roadsters the company will not be able to produce because it has already devoted those resources to producing SUVs. For example, in moving from point *B* to point *C*, the opportunity cost of producing 200 more SUVs per day is the 200 fewer roadsters that can be produced.

What point on the production possibilities frontier is best? We can't tell without further information. If consumer demand for SUVs is greater than demand for roadsters, the company is likely to choose a point closer to *E*. If demand for roadsters is greater than demand for SUVs, the company is likely to choose a point closer to *A*.

Opportunity cost The highest-valued alternative that must be given up to engage in an activity.

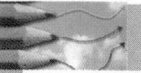

SOLVED PROBLEM 2-1

① **LEARNING OBJECTIVE**
Use a production possibilities frontier to analyze opportunity costs and trade-offs.

Drawing a Production Possibilities Frontier for Rosie's Boston Bakery

Rosie's Boston Bakery specializes in cakes and pies. Rosie has 5 hours per day to devote to baking. In 1 hour, Rosie can prepare 2 pies or 1 cake.

a. Use the information given to complete the following table:

	HOURS SPENT MAKING		QUANTITY MADE	
CHOICE	CAKES	PIES	CAKES	PIES
A	5	0		
B	4	1		
C	3	2		
D	2	3		
E	1	4		
F	0	5		

b. Use the data in the table to draw a production possibilities frontier graph illustrating Rosie's trade-offs between making cakes and making pies. Label the vertical axis "Quantity of cakes made." Label the horizontal axis "Quantity of pies made." Make sure to label the values where Rosie's production possibilities frontier intersects the vertical and horizontal axes.

c. Label the points representing choice *D* and choice *E*. If Rosie is at choice *D*, what is her opportunity cost of making more pies?

Solving the Problem:

Step 1: Review the chapter material. This problem is about using production possibilities frontiers to analyze trade-offs, so you may want to review the section "Graphing the Production Possibilities Frontier," which begins on page 34.

Step 2: Answer question (a) by filling in the table. If Rosie can produce 1 cake in 1 hour, then with choice *A* she will make 5 cakes and 0 pies. Because she can produce 2 pies in 1 hour, with choice *B* she will make 4 cakes and 2 pies. By similar reasoning, you can fill in the remaining cells in the following table:

	HOURS SPENT MAKING		QUANTITY MADE	
CHOICE	CAKES	PIES	CAKES	PIES
A	5	0	5	0
B	4	1	4	2
C	3	2	3	4
D	2	3	2	6
E	1	4	1	8
F	0	5	0	10

Step 3: Answer question (b) by drawing the production possibilities frontier graph. Using the data in the table in question (a), you should draw a graph that looks like this:

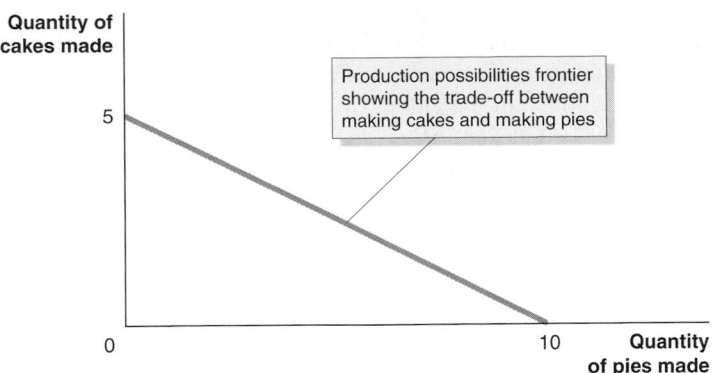

If Rosie devotes all 5 hours to making cakes, she will make 5 cakes. Therefore, her production possibilities frontier will intersect the vertical axis at 5 cakes made. If Rosie devotes all 5 hours to making pies, she will make 10 pies. Therefore, her production possibilities frontier will intersect the horizontal axis at 10 pies made.

Step 4: Answer question (c) by showing choices *D* and *E* on your graph. The points for choices *D* and *E* can be plotted using the information from the table:

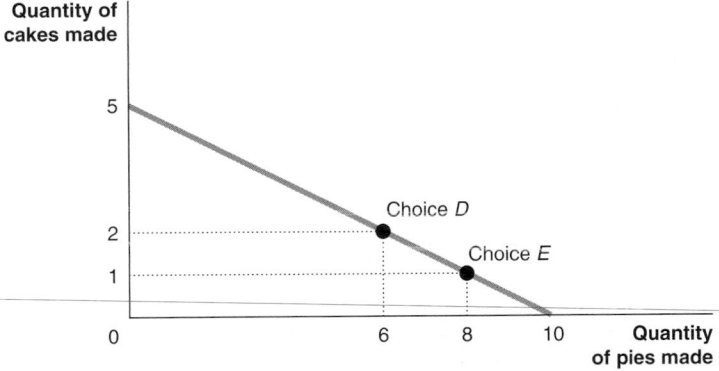

Moving from choice *D* to choice *E* increases Rosie's production of pies by 2 but lowers her production of cakes by 1. Therefore, her opportunity cost of making 2 more pies is making 1 less cake.

YOUR TURN: For more practice do related problem 6 on page 58 at the end of this chapter. Visit www.prenhall.com/hubbard for an interactive exercise related to this Solved Problem.

2-1 *Making the Connection*

Trade-offs and Tsunami Relief

In December 2004, an earthquake caused a tidal wave—or tsunami—to flood coastal areas of Indonesia, Thailand, Sri Lanka, and other countries bordering the Indian Ocean. Over 280,000 people died, and billions of dollars worth of property was destroyed. Governments and individuals around the world moved quickly to donate to relief efforts. The U.S. government donated $950 million, and individual U.S. citizens donated more than an additional $500 million. Both governments and individuals face limited budgets, however, and funds used for one purpose are unavailable to be used for another purpose. Although governments and individuals did increase their total charitable giving following the tsunami disaster, much of the funds spent on tsunami relief appear to have been diverted from other uses. A difficult trade-off resulted: Giving funds to victims of the tsunami meant fewer funds were available to aid other good causes.

For example, some of the funds provided by the U.S. government for reconstruction in the tsunami-devastated areas came from existing aid programs. As a result, spending on other aid projects in the region declined. Similarly, nonprofit organizations in New York City reported sharp declines in donations to the homeless and the poor, as donors gave funds for tsunami relief instead. According to a report in the newspaper *Crain's New York Business,* "Some groups such as Bailey House, which helps homeless people who have AIDS, have even started receiving letters from longtime donors warning that this year's gifts are being redirected to the tsunami relief effort." As one commentator observed, "The milk of human kindness is probably flowing at the usual rate in the United States. It's just getting channeled in different directions."

More funds for tsunami relief meant less funds for other charities.

Governments in the area also faced a trade-off in considering whether to spend funds to install tsunami warning systems, similar to existing systems in the Pacific Ocean. Tsunamis are fairly common in the Pacific Ocean but quite rare in the Indian Ocean. Records dating back to the early 1500s indicate that the tsunami of 2004 was by far the worst in the last 500 years. Funds that governments in poor countries, such as Indonesia, would spend on tsunami warning systems would have to be diverted from spending on health, education, or other programs.

Source: Daniel Gross, "Zero-Sum Charity," *Slate,* January 20, 2005.

Increasing Marginal Opportunity Costs

We can also use the production possibilities frontier to explore issues related to the economy as a whole. For example, suppose we divide all the many goods and services produced in the economy into just two types: military goods and civilian goods. In Figure 2-2, we let tanks represent military goods and automobiles represent civilian goods. If all the country's resources are devoted to producing military goods, 400 tanks can be produced in one year. If all resources are devoted to producing civilian goods, 500 automobiles can be produced in one year. Devoting resources to producing both goods results in the economy being at other points along the production possibilities frontier.

Notice that this production possibilities frontier is bowed outward, rather than being a straight line. Because the curve is bowed out, the opportunity cost of automobiles in terms of tanks depends upon where the economy currently is on the production

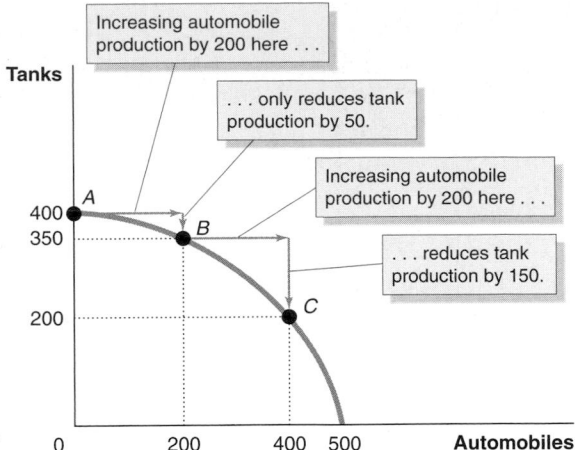

FIGURE 2-2

Increasing Marginal Opportunity Cost

As the economy moves down the production possibilities frontier, it experiences *increasing marginal opportunity costs* because increasing automobile production by a given quantity requires larger and larger decreases in tank production. For example, to increase automobile production from 0 to 200—moving from point *A* to point *B*—the economy only has to give up 50 tanks. But to increase automobile production by another 200 vehicles—moving from point *B* to point *C*—the economy has to give up 150 tanks.

possibilities frontier. For example, to increase automobile production from zero to 200—moving from point *A* to point *B*—the economy only has to give up 50 tanks. But to increase automobile production by another 200 vehicles—moving from point *B* to point *C*—the economy has to give up 150 tanks.

As the economy moves down the production possibilities frontier, it experiences *increasing marginal opportunity costs* because increasing automobile production by a given quantity requires larger and larger decreases in tank production. Increasing marginal opportunity costs occur because some workers, machines, and other resources are better suited to one use than to another. At point *A* some resources that are well suited to producing automobiles are being forced to produce tanks. Shifting these resources into producing automobiles by moving from point *A* to point *B* allows a substantial increase in automobile production, without much loss of tank production. But as the economy moves down the production possibilities frontier, more and more resources that are better suited to tank production are switched into automobile production. As a result, the increases in automobile production become increasingly smaller while the decreases in tank production become increasingly larger. We would expect in most situations that production possibilities frontiers will be bowed outward, rather than linear as in the BMW example we discussed earlier.

The idea of increasing marginal opportunity costs illustrates an important economic concept: *The more resources already devoted to any activity, the smaller the payoff to devoting additional resources to that activity.* The more hours you have already spent studying economics, the smaller the increase in your test grade from each additional hour you spend—and the greater the opportunity cost of using the hour in that way. The more funds a firm has devoted to research and development during a given year, the smaller the amount of useful knowledge it receives from each additional dollar—and the greater the opportunity cost of using the funds in that way. The more funds the federal government spends cleaning up the environment during a given year, the smaller the reduction in pollution from each additional dollar—and, once again, the greater the opportunity cost of using the funds in that way.

Economic Growth

At any given time, the total resources available to any economy are fixed. Therefore, if the United States produces more automobiles, it must produce less of something else—tanks in our example. Over time, though, the resources available to an economy may increase. For example, both the labor force and the capital stock—the amount of physical capital available in the country—may increase. The increase in the available labor force and the capital stock shifts the production possibilities frontier outward for the U.S. economy and makes it possible to produce both more automobiles and more tanks.

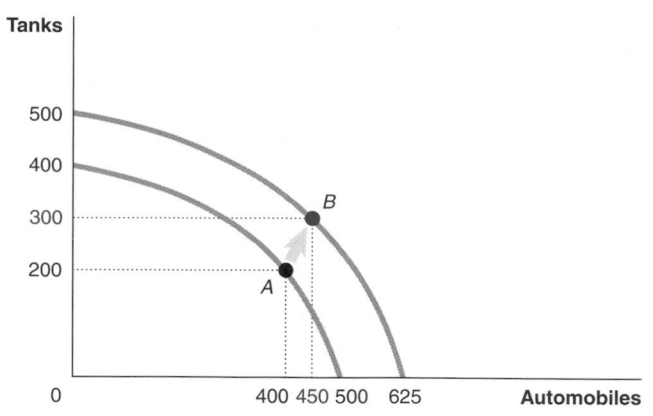

(a) Shifting out the production possibilities frontier

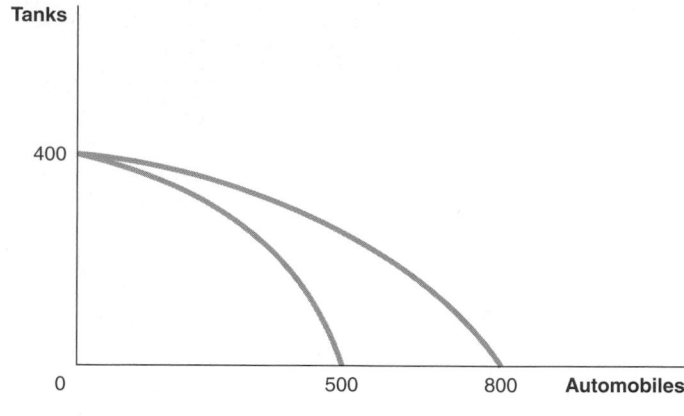

(b) Technological change in the automobile undustry

FIGURE 2-3   **Economic Growth**

Panel (a) shows that as more economic resources become available and technological change occurs, the economy can move from point *A* to point *B*, producing more tanks and more automobiles.

Panel (b) shows the results of technological advance in the automobile industry that increases the quantity of vehicles workers can produce per year, while leaving the maximum quantity of tanks that can be produced unchanged. Shifts in the production possibilities frontier represent *economic growth*.

Economic growth The ability of the economy to produce increasing quantities of goods and services.

Panel (a) of Figure 2-3 shows that the economy can move from point *A* to point *B*, producing more tanks and more automobiles.

Similarly, technological advance makes it possible to produce more goods with the same amount of workers and machinery, which also shifts the production possibilities frontier outward. Technological advance need not affect all sectors equally. Panel (b) of Figure 2-3 shows the results of technological advance in the automobile industry that increases the quantity of vehicles workers can produce per year, while leaving unchanged the quantity of tanks that can be produced.

Shifts in the production possibilities frontier represent **economic growth** because they allow the economy to increase the production of goods and services, which ultimately raises the standard of living. In the United States and other high-income countries, the market system has aided the process of economic growth, which over the past two hundred years has greatly increased the health and well-being of the average person.

② LEARNING OBJECTIVE

Understand comparative advantage and explain how it is the basis for trade.

Trade The act of buying or selling.

Trade

Having discussed the important ideas of production possibilities frontiers and opportunity costs, we can use them to understand the basic economic activity of *trade*. Markets are fundamentally about **trade**, which is the act of buying and selling. Many of the trades in which we engage take place indirectly: We sell our labor services as, say, an accountant, salesperson, or nurse for money, and then use the money to buy goods and services. Ultimately an accountant, salesperson, or nurse is trading his or her services for food, clothing, and other goods and services. One of the great benefits to trade is that it makes it possible for people to become better off by increasing both their production and their consumption.

Specialization and Gains from Trade

Consider the following situation: You and your neighbor both have fruit trees on your property. Initially, suppose that you have only apple trees and your neighbor has only cherry trees. In this situation, if you both like apples and cherries there is an obvious opportunity for both of you to gain from trade: You trade some of your apples for some of your neighbor's cherries, making you both better off. But what if there are apple and

	You		Your Neighbor	
	Apples	Cherries	Apples	Cherries
All time devoted to picking apples	20 pounds	0 pounds	30 pounds	0 pounds
All time devoted to picking cherries	0 pounds	20 pounds	0 pounds	60 pounds

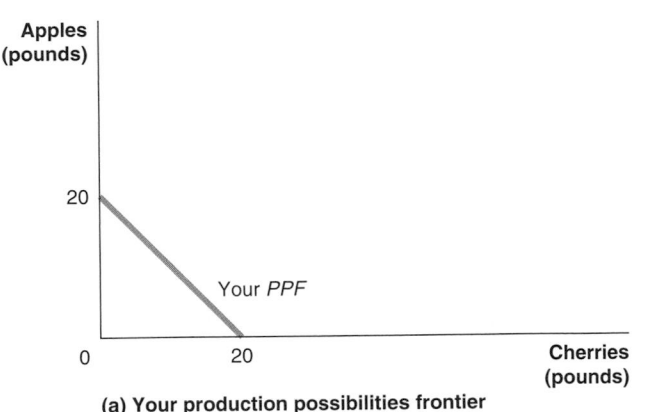

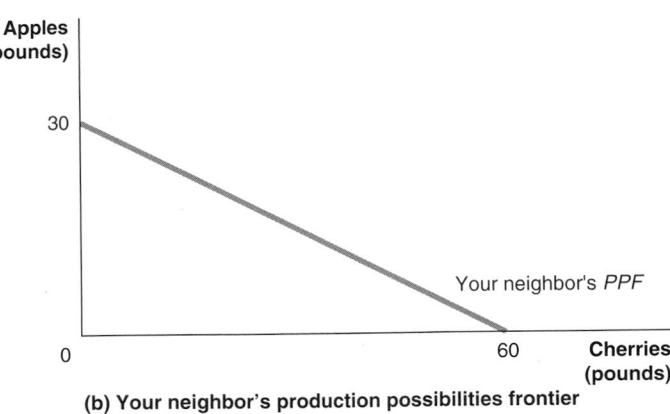

(a) Your production possibilities frontier

(b) Your neighbor's production possibilities frontier

FIGURE 2-4   Production Possibilities for You and Your Neighbor, without Trade

The table in Figure 2-4 shows how many pounds of apples and how many pounds of cherries you and your neighbor can each pick in one month. The graphs in the figure use the data from the table to construct production possibilities frontiers (*PPF*s) for you and your neighbor. Panel (a) shows your *PPF*. If you devote all of your time to picking apples and none of your time to

picking cherries, you can pick 20 pounds. If you devote all of your time to picking cherries, you can pick 20 pounds. Panel (b) shows that if your neighbor devotes all of her time to picking apples, she can pick 30 pounds. If she devotes all of her time to picking cherries, she can pick 60 pounds.

cherry trees growing on both of your properties? In that case there can still be gains from trade. For example, your neighbor might be very good at picking apples and you might be very good at picking cherries. In that case, it makes sense that both can benefit if your neighbor concentrates on picking apples and you concentrate on picking cherries. You can then trade some of your cherries for some of your neighbor's apples. But what if your neighbor is actually better at picking both apples and cherries than you are? It might not seem that in this case your neighbor has anything to gain from trading with you, but in fact she does.

We can use production possibilities frontiers (*PPF*s) to show how your neighbor can benefit from trading with you even though she is better than you are at picking both apples and cherries. (For simplicity, and because it will not have any effect on the conclusions we draw, we will assume that the *PPF*s in this example are straight lines.) The table in Figure 2-4 shows how many apples and how many cherries you and your neighbor can pick in one month. The graph in the figure uses the data from the table to construct *PPF*s for you and your neighbor. Panel (a) shows your *PPF*. If you devote all your time to picking apples and none of your time to picking cherries, you can pick 20 pounds of apples per month. If you devote all your time to picking cherries, you can pick 20 pounds per month. Panel (b) shows that if your neighbor devotes all her time to picking apples, she can pick 30 pounds. If she devotes all her time to picking cherries, she can pick 60 pounds.

The production possibilities frontiers in Figure 2-4 show the opportunities you and your neighbor have to consume apples and cherries, *without trade*. Suppose that when you don't trade with your neighbor, you pick and consume 8 pounds of apples and 12 pounds of cherries per month. This combination of apples and cherries is represented by point *A* in panel (a) of Figure 2-5. When she doesn't trade with you, your neighbor picks and consumes 9 pounds of apples and 42 pounds of cherries per

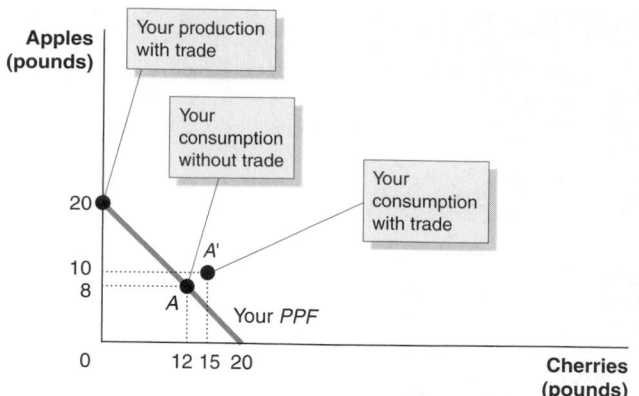

(a) Your production and consumption after trade

(b) Your neighbor's production and consumption with trade

FIGURE 2-5   Gains from Trade

When you don't trade with your neighbor, you pick and consume 8 pounds of apples and 12 pounds of cherries per month—point A in panel (a). When your neighbor doesn't trade with you, she picks and consumes 9 pounds of apples and 42 pounds of cherries per month—point B in panel (b). If you specialize in picking apples, you can pick 20 pounds. If your neighbor specializes in picking cherries, she can pick 60 pounds. If you trade 10 pounds of your apples for 15 pounds of your neighbor's cherries, you will be able to consume 10 pounds of apples and 15 pounds of cherries—point A' in panel (a). Your neighbor can now consume 10 pounds of apples and 45 pounds of cherries—point B' in panel (b). You and your neighbor are both better off as a result of trade.

month. This combination of apples and cherries is represented by point B in panel (b) of Figure 2-5.

After years of picking and consuming your own apples and cherries, suppose your neighbor comes to you one day with the following proposition: She offers next month to trade you 15 pounds of her cherries for 10 pounds of your apples. Should you accept this offer? You will have more apples and more cherries to consume if you do. To take advantage of her offer, first, rather than splitting your time between picking apples and picking cherries, you should specialize in picking only apples. We know this will allow you to pick 20 pounds of apples. You can trade 10 of those 20 pounds of apples to your neighbor for 15 pounds of her cherries. The result is you will be able to consume 10 pounds of apples and 15 pounds of cherries (point A' in panel (a) of Figure 2-5). You are clearly better off as a result of trading with your neighbor: You now can consume 2 more pounds of apples and 3 more pounds of cherries than you were consuming without trading. You have moved beyond your *PPF!*

Your neighbor has also benefited. By specializing in picking only cherries, she can pick 60 pounds. She trades 15 pounds of cherries to you for 10 pounds of apples. The result is she can consume 10 pounds of apples and 45 pounds of cherries (point B' in panel (b) of Figure 2-5). This is 1 more pound of apples and 3 more pounds of cherries than she was consuming before trading with you. She also has moved beyond her *PPF.* Table 2-1 summarizes the changes in production and consumption that result from your trade with your neighbor.

Absolute Advantage versus Comparative Advantage

Absolute advantage The ability of an individual, firm, or country to produce more of a good or service than competitors using the same amount of resources.

Perhaps the most remarkable aspect of the preceding example is that your neighbor benefits from trading with you even though she is better at picking both apples and cherries than you are. **Absolute advantage** is the ability to produce more of a good or service than competitors using the same amount of resources. Your neighbor has an absolute advantage over you in producing both apples and cherries because she can pick more of each fruit than you can in the same amount of time. This observation seems to suggest that your neighbor should pick her own apples *and* her own cherries. We have just seen, however, that she is better off if she specializes in cherry picking and leaves the apple picking to you.

TABLE 2-1

A Summary of the Gains from Trade

	YOU		YOUR NEIGHBOR	
	APPLES (IN POUNDS)	CHERRIES (IN POUNDS)	APPLES (IN POUNDS)	CHERRIES (IN POUNDS)
Production *and* consumption *without* trade	8	12	9	42
Production *with* trade	20	0	0	60
Consumption *with* trade	10	15	10	45
Gains from trade (increased consumption)	2	3	1	3

We can consider further why both you and your neighbor benefit from specializing in picking only one fruit. First, think about the opportunity cost to each of you of picking the two fruits. We saw from the *PPF* in Figure 2-4 that if you devoted all your time to picking apples, you would be able to pick 20 pounds of apples per month. As you move down your *PPF* and shift time away from picking apples to picking cherries, you have to give up 1 pound of apples for each pound of cherries you pick (the slope of your *PPF* is −1—for a review of calculating slopes, see the appendix to Chapter 1). Therefore, your opportunity cost of picking 1 pound of cherries is 1 pound of apples. By the same reasoning, your opportunity cost of picking 1 pound of apples is 1 pound of cherries. Your neighbor's *PPF* has a different slope, and so she faces a different trade-off. As she shifts time from picking apples to picking cherries, she has to give up 0.5 pound of apples for every 1 pound of cherries she picks (the slope of your neighbor's *PPF* is −0.5). As she shifts time from picking cherries to picking apples, she gives up 2 pounds of cherries for every 1 pound of apples she picks. Therefore, her opportunity cost of picking 1 pound of apples is 2 pounds of cherries, and her opportunity cost of picking 1 pound of cherries is 0.5 pound of apples.

Table 2-2 summarizes the opportunity costs for you and your neighbor of picking apples and cherries. Note that even though your neighbor can pick more apples in a month than you can, the *opportunity cost* of picking apples is higher for her than for you because when she picks apples she gives up more cherries than you do. So, even though she has an absolute advantage over you in picking apples, it is more costly for her to pick apples than it is for you. The table also shows us that her opportunity cost of picking cherries is lower than your opportunity cost of picking cherries. **Comparative advantage** is the ability of an individual, firm, or country to produce a good or service at a lower opportunity cost than other producers. In apple picking, your neighbor has an *absolute advantage* over you, but you have a *comparative advantage* over her. Your neighbor has both an absolute and a comparative advantage over you in picking cherries. As we have seen, you are better off specializing in picking apples, and your neighbor is better off specializing in picking cherries. Another way of thinking about why it would be costly for your neighbor to spend time picking apples is that even though she can pick 1.5 times as many apples in a month as you can—30 pounds per month for her versus 20 pounds per month for you—she can pick 3 times as many cherries—60 pounds per month for her versus 20 pounds for you. So, by specializing in picking apples she is spending her time in the activity where her absolute advantage over you is the greatest.

Comparative advantage The ability of an individual, firm, or country to produce a good or service at a lower opportunity cost than other producers.

	OPPORTUNITY COST OF PICKING 1 POUND OF APPLES	OPPORTUNITY COST OF PICKING 1 POUND OF CHERRIES
You	1 pound of cherries	1 pound of apples
Your neighbor	2 pounds of cherries	0.5 pound of apples

TABLE 2-2

Opportunity Costs of Picking Apples and Cherries

Don't Let This Happen To You!

Don't Confuse Absolute Advantage and Comparative Advantage

First, make sure you know the definitions:

➤ *Absolute advantage:* The ability of an individual, firm, or country to produce more of a good or service than competitors using the same amount of resources. In our example, your neighbor has an absolute advantage over you both in picking apples and in picking cherries.

➤ *Comparative advantage:* The ability of an individual, firm, or country to produce a good or service at a lower opportunity cost than other producers. In our example, your neighbor has a comparative advantage

in picking cherries, but you have a comparative advantage in picking apples.

Keep these two key points in mind:

1. It is possible to have an absolute advantage in producing a good or service without having a comparative advantage. This would be the case with your neighbor picking apples.
2. It is possible to have a comparative advantage in producing a good or service without having an absolute advantage. This would be the case with you picking apples.

YOUR TURN: Test your understanding by doing related problem 14 on page 59 at the end of this chapter.

Comparative Advantage and the Gains from Trade

We have just derived an important economic principle: *The basis for trade is comparative advantage, not absolute advantage.* The fastest apple pickers do not necessarily do much apple picking. If the fastest apple pickers have a comparative advantage in some other activity—picking cherries, playing major league baseball, or being industrial engineers—they are better off specializing in that other activity. Individuals, firms, and countries are better off if they specialize in producing goods and services for which they have a comparative advantage and obtain the other goods and services they need by trading. We will return to the important concept of comparative advantage in Chapter 8, which is devoted to the subject of international trade.

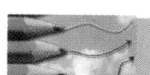

SOLVED PROBLEM 2-2

② **LEARNING OBJECTIVE**

Understand comparative advantage and explain how it is the basis for trade.

Comparative Advantage and the Gains from Trade

We will see in Chapter 8 the important role that comparative advantage plays in analyzing international trade. For now, consider this simple problem. Suppose that Canada and the United States both produce maple syrup and honey. These are the combinations of the two goods that each country can produce in one day:

CANADA		UNITED STATES	
HONEY (IN TONS)	MAPLE SYRUP (IN TONS)	HONEY (IN TONS)	MAPLE SYRUP (IN TONS)
0	60	0	50
10	45	10	40
20	30	20	30
30	15	30	20
40	0	40	10
		50	0

a. Who has a comparative advantage in producing maple syrup? Who has a comparative advantage in producing honey?

b. Suppose that Canada is currently producing 30 tons of honey and 15 tons of maple syrup and the United States is currently producing 10 tons of honey and 40 tons of maple syrup. Demonstrate that Canada and the United States can both be better off if they specialize in producing only one good and then engage in trade.

c. Illustrate your answer to question (b) by drawing a *PPF* for the United States and a *PPF* for Canada. Show on your *PPF*s the combinations of honey and maple syrup produced and consumed in each country before and after trade.

Solving the Problem:

Step 1: Review the chapter material. This problem concerns comparative advantage, so you may want to review the section "Absolute Advantage versus Comparative Advantage," which begins on page 42.

Step 2: Answer question (a) by calculating who has a comparative advantage in each activity. Remember that a country has a comparative advantage in producing a good if it can produce the good at the lowest opportunity cost. When Canada produces 1 more ton of honey, it produces 1.5 fewer tons of maple syrup. On the one hand, when the United States produces 1 more ton of honey, it produces 1 less ton of maple syrup. Therefore, the United States's opportunity cost of producing honey—1 ton of maple syrup—is lower than Canada's—1.5 tons of maple syrup. On the other hand, when Canada produces 1 more ton of maple syrup, it produces ⅔ less of a ton of honey. When the United States produces 1 more ton of maple syrup, it produces 1 less ton of honey. Therefore, Canada's opportunity cost of producing maple syrup—⅔ of a ton of honey—is lower than that of the United States—1 ton of honey. We can conclude that the United States has a comparative advantage in the production of honey and Canada has a comparative advantage in the production of maple syrup.

Step 3: Answer question (b) by showing that specialization makes Canada and the United States better off. We know that Canada should specialize where it has a comparative advantage and the United States should specialize where it has a comparative advantage. If both countries specialize, Canada will produce 60 tons of maple syrup and 0 tons of honey, and the United States will produce 0 tons of maple syrup and 50 tons of honey. After both countries specialize, the United States could then trade 30 tons of honey to Canada in exchange for 40 tons of maple syrup (other mutually beneficial trades are possible as well). We can summarize the results in a table:

	BEFORE TRADE		AFTER TRADE	
	HONEY (IN TONS)	MAPLE SYRUP (IN TONS)	HONEY (IN TONS)	MAPLE SYRUP (IN TONS)
Canada	30	15	30	20
United States	10	40	20	40

The United States is better off after trade because it can consume the same amount of maple syrup and 10 more tons of honey. Canada is better off after trade because it can consume the same amount of honey and 5 more tons of maple syrup.

Step 4: Answer question (c) by drawing the PPFs.

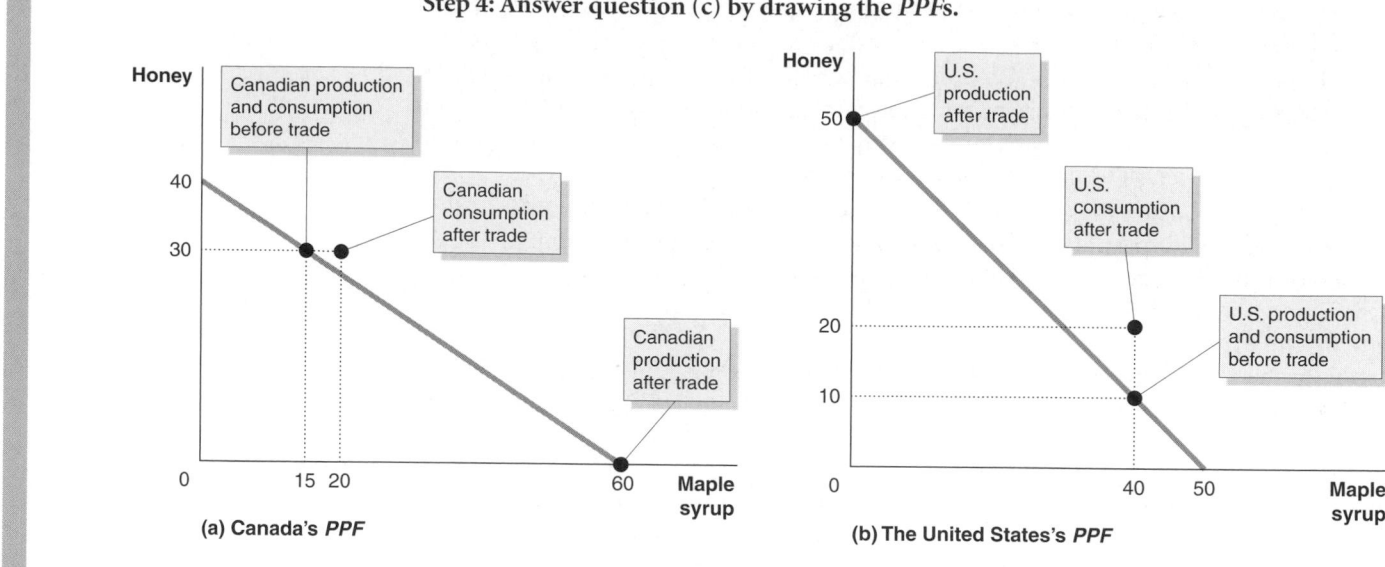

(a) Canada's *PPF*

(b) The United States's *PPF*

YOUR TURN: For more practice, do related problems 12 and 13 on page 59 at the end of this chapter. Visit www.prenhall.com/hubbard for an interactive exercise related to this Solved Problem.

③ **LEARNING OBJECTIVE**

Explain the basic idea of how a market system works.

The Market System

We have seen that households, firms, and the government face trade-offs and incur opportunity costs because of the scarcity of resources. We have also seen that trade allows people to specialize according to their comparative advantage. By engaging in trade, people can raise their standard of living. Of course, trade in the modern world is much more complex than the examples we have considered so far. Trade today involves the decisions of millions of people spread around the world. But how does an economy make trade possible, and how are the decisions of these millions of people coordinated? In the United States and most other countries, trade is carried out in markets. Markets also determine the answers to the three fundamental questions discussed in Chapter 1: *What* goods and services will be produced? *How* will the goods and services be produced? *Who* will receive the goods and services?

Recall that the definition of a **market** is a group of buyers and sellers of a good or service and the institution or arrangement by which they come together to trade. Markets take many forms: They can be physical places, like the local pizza parlor or the New York Stock Exchange, or virtual places, like eBay. In a market, the buyers are demanders of goods or services, and the sellers are suppliers of goods or services. Households and firms interact in two types of markets: *product markets* and *factor markets.* **Product markets** are markets for goods—such as computers—and services—such as medical treatment. In product markets, households are demanders and firms are suppliers. **Factor markets** are markets for the *factors of production,* such as labor, capital, natural resources, and entrepreneurial ability. In factor markets, households are suppliers and firms are demanders. Most people earn most of their income by selling their labor services to firms in the labor market.

Market A group of buyers and sellers of a good or service and the institution or arrangement by which they come together to trade.

Product markets Markets for goods—such as computers—and services—such as medical treatment.

Factor markets Markets for the factors of production, such as labor, capital, natural resources, and entrepreneurial ability.

The Circular Flow of Income

Two key groups participate in markets:

➤ A *household* consists of all the individuals in a home. Households are suppliers of factors of production—particularly labor—used by firms to make goods and services. Households use the income they receive from selling the factors of production to purchase the goods and services supplied by firms.

➤ *Firms* are suppliers of goods and services. Firms use the funds they receive from selling goods and services to buy the factors of production needed to make the goods and services.

We can use a simple economic model called a **circular-flow diagram** to see how participants in markets are linked. Figure 2-6 shows that in factor markets households supply labor and other factors of production in exchange for wages and other payments from firms. In product markets, households use the payments they earn in factor markets to purchase the goods and services supplied by firms. Firms produce these goods and services using the factors of production supplied by households. In the figure, the

Circular-flow diagram A model that illustrates how participants in markets are linked.

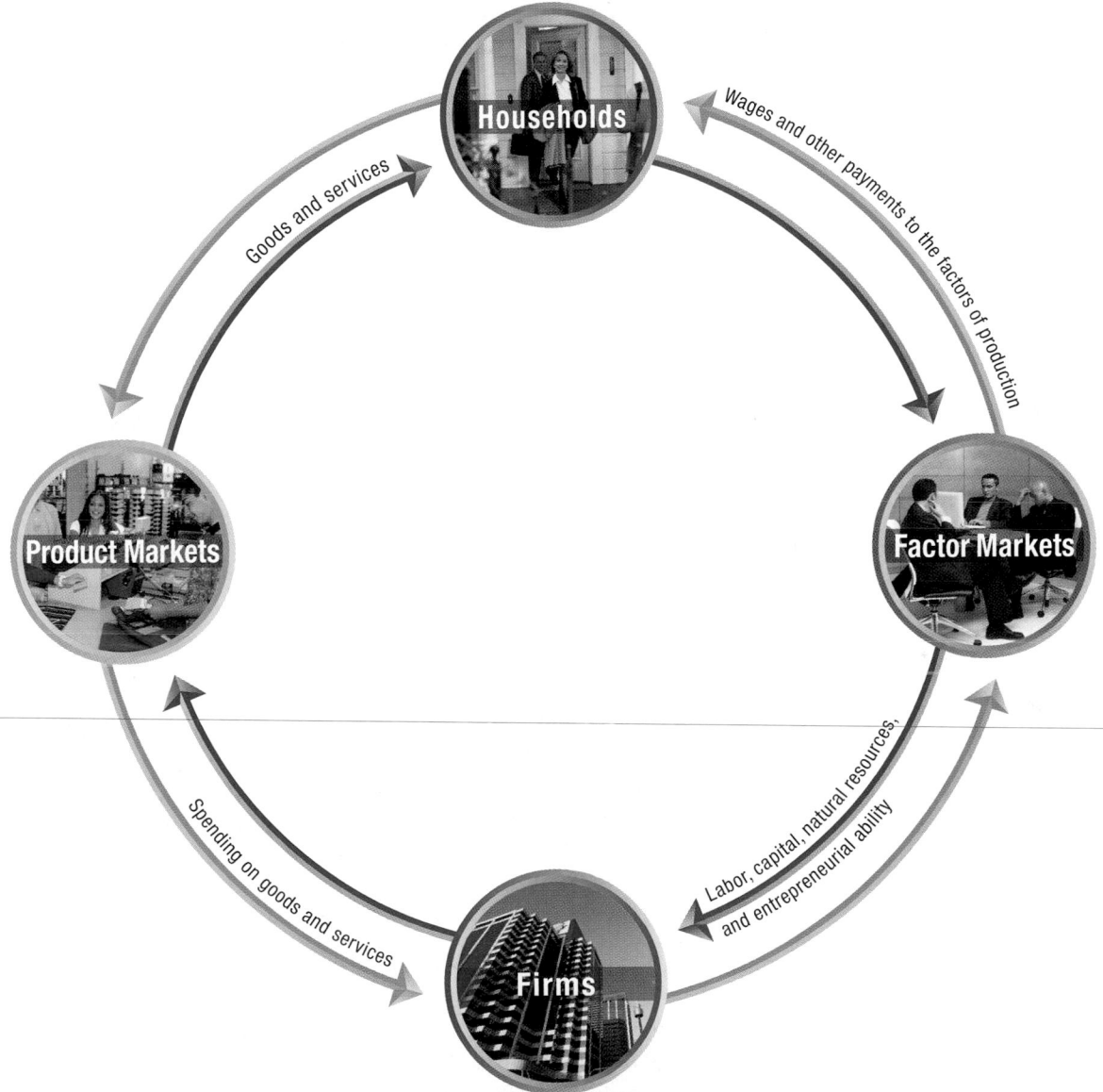

FIGURE 2-6 **The Circular-Flow Diagram**

Households and firms are linked together in a circular flow of production, income, and spending. The blue arrows show the flow of the factors of production. In factor markets, households supply labor, entrepreneurial ability, and other factors of production to firms. Firms use these factors of production to make goods and services that they supply to households in product markets. The red arrows show the flow of goods and services from firms to households. The green arrows show the flow of funds. In factor markets, households receive wages and other payments from firms in exchange for supplying the factors of production. Households use these wages and other payments to purchase goods and services from firms in product markets. Firms sell goods and services to households in product markets, and they use the funds to purchase the factors of production from households in factor markets.

blue arrows show the flow of factors of production from households through factor markets to firms. The red arrow shows the flow of goods and services from firms through product markets to households. The green arrows show the flow of funds from firms through factor markets to households, and the flow of spending from households through product markets to firms.

Like all economic models, the circular-flow diagram is a simplified version of reality. For example, Figure 2-6 leaves out the important role played by government in buying goods from firms and in making payments, such as Social Security or unemployment insurance payments, to households. The figure also leaves out the role played by banks, the stock and bond markets, and other parts of the *financial system* in aiding the flow of funds from lenders to borrowers. Finally, the figure does not show that some goods and services purchased by domestic households are produced in foreign countries, and some goods and services produced by domestic firms are sold to foreign households. The government, the financial system, and the international sector are explored further in later chapters. Despite these simplifications, the circular-flow diagram in Figure 2-6 is useful in seeing how product markets, factor markets, and their participants are linked together. One of the great mysteries of the market system is that it manages successfully to coordinate the independent activities of so many households and firms.

The Gains from Free Markets

Free market A market with few government restrictions on how a good or service can be produced or sold, or on how a factor of production can be employed.

A **free market** exists when the government places few restrictions on how a good or a service can be produced or sold, or on how a factor of production can be employed. Governments in all modern economies intervene more than is consistent with a fully free market. In that sense, we can think of the free market as being a benchmark against which we can judge actual economies. Relatively few government restrictions are placed on economic activity in the United States, Canada, the countries of Western Europe, Hong Kong, Singapore, and Estonia. So these countries come close to the free market benchmark. In countries such as Cuba and North Korea, the free market system has been rejected in favor of centrally planned economies with extensive government control over product and factor markets. Countries that come closest to the free market benchmark have been more successful than countries with centrally planned economies in providing their people with rising living standards.

The Scottish philosopher Adam Smith is considered the father of modern economics because one of his books, *An Inquiry into the Nature and Causes of the Wealth of Nations,* published in 1776, was an early and very influential argument for the free market system. Smith was writing at a time when extensive government restrictions on markets were still very common. In many parts of Europe the *guild system* still prevailed. Under this system, governments would give guilds, or organizations of producers, the authority to control the production of a good. For example, the shoemakers' guild controlled who was allowed to produce shoes, how many shoes they could produce, and what price they could charge. In France, the cloth makers' guild even dictated the number of threads that were allowed in the weave of the cloth.

Smith argued that such restrictions reduced the income or wealth of a country and its people by restricting the quantity of goods produced. Some people at the time supported the restrictions of the guild system because it was in their financial interest to do so. If you were a member of a guild, the restrictions served to reduce the competition you would face. But other people sincerely believed that the alternative to the guild system was economic chaos. Smith argued that these people were wrong and that a country could enjoy a smoothly functioning economic system if firms were freed from guild restrictions.

The Market Mechanism

In Smith's day, defenders of the guild system worried that if, for instance, the shoemakers' guild did not control shoe production, either too many or too few shoes would be produced. Smith argued that prices would do a better job of coordinating the activities of buyers and sellers than the guilds could. A key to understanding Smith's argument is the assumption that *individuals usually act in a rational, self-interested way.* In particular, individuals take those actions most likely to make themselves better off financially. This assumption of rational, self-interested behavior underlies nearly all economic analysis. In fact, economics can be distinguished from other fields that study human behavior—such as sociology and psychology—by its emphasis on the assumption of self-interested behavior. Adam Smith understood—as economists today understand—that people's motives can be complex. But in analyzing people in the act of buying and selling, the motivation of financial reward usually provides the best explanation for the actions people take.

For example, suppose that a significant number of consumers switch from buying cars to buying SUVs, as in fact happened in the United States during the 1990s. Firms will find that they can charge higher prices for SUVs than they can for cars. The self-interest of these firms will lead them to respond to consumers' wishes by producing more SUVs and fewer cars. Or suppose that consumers decide that they want to eat less bread, pasta, and other foods high in carbohydrates, as many did following the increase in popularity of the Atkins and South Beach diets. Then the prices firms can charge for bread and pasta will fall. The self-interest of firms will lead them to produce less bread and pasta, which in fact is what happened.

In the case where consumers want more of a product, and in the case where they want less of a product, the market system responds without a guild or anyone else giving orders about how much to produce or what price to charge. In a famous phrase, Smith said that firms would be led by the "invisible hand" of the market to provide consumers with what they wanted. Firms would respond to changes in prices by making decisions that ended up satisfying the wants of consumers.

Story of the Market System in Action: "I, Pencil"

2-2 Making the Connection

The pencil seems like a very simple product. In fact, its production requires the coordinated activities of many different people, spread around the world. The economist Leonard Read showed how markets achieve this coordination by writing an "autobiography" of a pencil sold by the Eberhard Faber Pencil Company of California. It is one of the most famous accounts of how the market system works. The pencil writes that:

> My family tree begins with a [cedar] tree that grows in Northern California and Oregon. Now contemplate all the saws and trucks and rope and the countless other gear used in harvesting and carting the cedar logs to the railroad siding. . . .
>
> The logs are shipped to a mill in San Leandro, California. . . . The cedar logs are cut into small, pencil-length slats less than one-fourth of an inch in thickness. . . . Once in the pencil factory . . . each slat is given eight grooves by a complex machine, after which another machine lays leads in every other slat. . . .
>
> My "lead" itself—it contains no lead at all—is complex. The graphite is mined in Ceylon . . . [and] is mixed with clay from Mississippi in which ammonium hydroxide is used in the refining process. . . . To increase their strength and smoothness the leads are then treated with a hot mixture which includes candelilla wax from Mexico, paraffin wax, and hydrogenated natural fats.
>
> My cedar receives six coats of lacquer. Do you know all the ingredients of lacquer? Who would think that the growers of castor beans and the refiners of castor oil are a part of it? They are.
>
> My bit of metal–the ferrule–is brass. Think of all the persons who mine zinc and copper and those who have the skills to make shiny sheet brass from these products of nature.
>
> Then there's my crowning glory . . . the part man uses to erase the errors he makes with me. . . . It is a rubber-like product made by reacting rape-seed oil from the Dutch

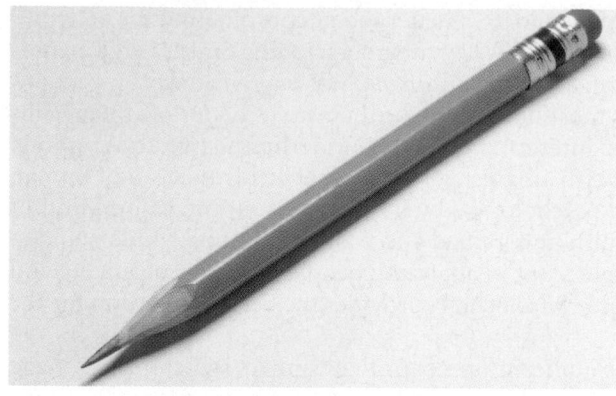

The market coordinates the activities of the many people spread around the world who contribute to the making of a pencil.

East Indies with sulfur chloride. . . . Then, too, there are numerous vulcanizing and accelerating agents. The pumice comes from Italy; and the pigment which gives [the eraser] its color is cadmium sulfide.

[M]illions of human beings have had a hand in my creation, no one of whom even knows more than a very few of the others. . . . There isn't a single person in all these millions, including the president of the pencil company, who contributes more than a tiny, infinitesimal bit of know-how. . . .

There is a fact still more astounding: the absence of a master mind, of anyone dictating or forcibly directing these countless actions which bring me into being. No trace of such a person can be found. Instead, we find the Invisible Hand at work.

Source: Leonard E. Read, *"I, Pencil,"* Irvington-on-Hudson, NY: Foundation for Economic Education, Inc. 1999. Used with permission of Foundation for Economic Education, Inc. Available online at www.econlib.org/library/Essays/rdPncl1.html.

The Role of the Entrepreneur

Entrepreneur Someone who operates a business, bringing together the factors of production—labor, capital, and natural resources—to produce goods and services.

Entrepreneurs are central to the working of the market system. An **entrepreneur** is someone who operates a business. Entrepreneurs must first determine what goods and services they believe consumers want, and then decide how those goods and services might be produced most profitably. Entrepreneurs bring together the factors of production—labor, capital, and natural resources—to produce goods and services. They put their own funds at risk when they start businesses. If they are wrong about what consumers want or about the best way to produce goods and services, they can lose those funds. In fact, it is not unusual for entrepreneurs who eventually achieve great success to fail at first. For instance, early in their careers both Henry Ford and Sakichi Toyoda, whose company eventually became the Toyota Motor Corporation, started companies that quickly failed.

The Legal Basis of a Successful Market System

In a free market, government does not restrict how firms produce and sell goods and services, or how they employ factors of production, but the absence of government intervention is not enough for a market system to work well. Government has to provide secure rights to private property for a market system to work at all. In addition, government can aid the working of the market by enforcing contracts between private individuals through an independent court system. Many economists would also say the government has a role in facilitating the development of an efficient financial system as well as systems of education, transportation, and communication. The protection of private property and the existence of an independent court system to impartially enforce the law provide a *legal environment* that will allow a market system to succeed.

PROTECTION OF PRIVATE PROPERTY For a market system to work well, individuals must be willing to take risks. Someone with $250,000 can be cautious and keep it safely in a bank—or even in cash, if the person doesn't trust the banking system. But the market system won't work unless a significant number of people are willing to risk their funds by investing them in businesses. Investing in businesses is risky in any country. Many businesses fail every year in the United States and other high-income countries. But in the high-income countries, someone who starts a new business or invests in an existing business doesn't have to worry that the government, the military, or criminal gangs might decide to seize the business or demand payments for not destroying the business. Unfortunately, in many poor countries owners of businesses are not well protected from having their businesses seized by the government or from having their profits taken by criminals. Where these problems exist, opening a business can be extremely risky. Cash can be concealed easily, but a business is difficult to conceal and difficult to move.

Property rights refer to the rights individuals or firms have to the exclusive use of their property, including the right to buy or sell it. Property can be tangible, physical property, such as a store or factory. Property can also be intangible, such as the right to an idea.

Two amendments to the U.S. Constitution guarantee property rights: The 5th Amendment states that the federal government shall not deprive any person "of life, liberty, or property, without due process of law." The 14th Amendment extends this guarantee to the actions of state governments: "No state . . . shall deprive any person of life, liberty, or property, without due process of law." Similar guarantees exist in every high-income country. Unfortunately, in many developing countries such guarantees do not exist or are poorly enforced.

In any modern economy, *intellectual property rights* are very important. Intellectual property includes books, films, software, and ideas for new products or new ways of producing products. To protect intellectual property, the federal government will grant a *patent* that gives an inventor—which is often a firm—the exclusive right to produce and sell a new product for a period of 20 years from the date the product was invented. For instance, because Microsoft has a patent on the Windows operating system, other firms cannot sell their own versions of Windows. The government grants patents to encourage firms to spend money on the research and development necessary to create new products. If other companies could freely copy Windows, Microsoft would not have spent the funds necessary to develop it. Just as a new product or a new method of making a product receives patent protection, books, films, and software receive *copyright* protection. Under U.S. law, the creator of a book, film, or piece of music has the exclusive right to use the creation during the creator's lifetime. The creator's heirs retain this exclusive right for 50 years.

> **Property rights** The rights individuals or firms have to the exclusive use of their property, including the right to buy or sell it.

Property Rights in Cyberspace: Napster, Kazaa, and iTunes

2-3 Making the Connection

The development of the Internet has led to new problems in protecting intellectual property rights. Songs, newspaper and magazine articles, and even entire motion pictures can be copied and e-mailed from one computer to another. Controlling unauthorized copying is harder today than it was when "copying" meant making a printed copy. The problem of unauthorized copying of music became particularly severe in 1999 when Napster, a small firm in San Mateo, California, created software that allowed people to download music from the Web without the authorization of the copyright holders. Needless to say, this was not good news for record companies. An article in *Newsweek* quoted a high-school student in Falls Church, Virginia: "I haven't purchased a CD in quite some time." Another student said, "Napster's the best thing ever created. I don't have to spend any money." In fact, a sharp decline in music CD sales occurred in the early 2000s.

The record companies and some artists—including the heavy metal band Metallica—sued Napster for copyright infringement. In spring 2001, a federal court ruled that Napster was violating the copyrights on the songs it allowed to be downloaded and ordered the firm to stop allowing users to swap copyrighted material. Unfortunately for the record companies, a new service called Kazaa quickly replaced Napster. Legal action against Kazaa proved

Metallica sued to stop copyright infringement of their songs on the Internet.

difficult because it was harder to determine the names of people using the service and because the developers of Kazaa live outside the United States and have proved difficult to sue in U.S. courts.

Music companies have attempted to combat free downloads of music by offering inexpensive legal downloads. Some of these legal Web sites, such as Apple's iTunes and Sony's Connect, have been successful. During 2004, legal music downloads increased more than ten times over the previous year. But legal Internet sales still represented only about 1 percent of total music sales worldwide. Not surprisingly, overall music sales were still declining. The failure to give full protection of property rights in music continued to reduce the willingness of music companies to offer as many CDs for sale. The reduction in the quantity of CDs that would be produced if property rights were fully enforced represents a loss of efficiency to the economy.

Sources: Steven Levy, "The Noisy War Over Napster," *Newsweek,* June 5, 2000; "Skype: Catch Us If You Can," *Fortune,* January 26, 2004; Eric Pfanner, "More People Paying for Online Music," *International Herald Tribune,* January 20, 2005.

ENFORCEMENT OF CONTRACTS AND PROPERTY RIGHTS Much business activity involves someone agreeing to carry out some action in the future. For example, you may borrow $20,000 to buy a car and promise the bank—by signing a loan contract—that you will pay back the money over the next five years. Or Microsoft may sign a licensing agreement with a small technology company, agreeing to use that company's technology for a period of several years in return for a fee. Usually these agreements take the form of legal contracts. For a market system to work, businesses and individuals have to rely on these contracts being carried out. If one party to a legal contract does not fulfill its obligations—perhaps the small company had promised Microsoft exclusive use of its technology, but then began licensing it to other companies—the other party can go to court to have the agreement enforced. Similarly, if a property owners in the United States believes that the federal or state government has violated their rights under the 5th or 14th Amendments, they can go to court to have their rights enforced.

But going to court to enforce a contract or private property rights will only be successful if the court system is independent and judges are able to make impartial decisions on the basis of the law. In the United States and other high-income countries, the court systems have enough independence from other parts of the government and enough protection from intimidation by outside forces—such as criminal gangs—that they are able to make their decisions based on the law. In many developing countries, the court systems lack this independence and will not provide a remedy if the government violates private property rights or if a person with powerful political connections decides to violate a business contract.

If property rights are not well enforced, the production of goods and services will be reduced. This reduces economic efficiency, leaving the economy inside its production possibilities frontier.

Conclusion

We have seen that by trading in markets, people are able to specialize and pursue their comparative advantage. Trading on the basis of comparative advantage makes all participants in trade better off. The key role of markets is to facilitate trade. In fact, the market system is a very effective means of coordinating the decisions of millions of consumers, workers, and firms. At the center of the market system is the consumer. To be successful, firms must respond to the desires of consumers. These desires are communicated to firms through prices. To explore how markets work, we must study the behavior of consumers and firms. We continue this exploration of markets in Chapter 3 when we develop the model of demand and supply.

Before moving on to Chapter 3, read *An Inside Look* on the next page to learn how BMW allocates its scarce resources in its Munich plant.

WALL STREET JOURNAL, MAY 6, 2004

BMW's Net Profit Rises 2.5% As New Models Benefit Sales

Bayerische Motoren Werke AG posted a 2.5% increase in first-quarter net profit, as the launches of the 6-Series coupe and X3 sport-utility vehicle boosted sales.

The luxury-car manufacturer, which sells the BMW, Mini and Rolls-Royce brands, benefited from new products that allowed it to outpace rival Mercedes, a unit of Daimler-Chrysler AG, in terms of vehicle sales in the year's first three months.

BMW's net profit rose to €523 million ($632.3 million) from €510 million a year earlier. Revenue climbed 4.9% to €10.8 billion from €10.3 billion. The rise in revenue outpaced the gain in car sales, which climbed 3.2% to 269,973 vehicles from 261,573.

The company, based in Munich, got off to a slow start in 2004 as renovation work at its Munich plant through the end of January slowed production of the 3-Series. The second quarter began well, as the company sold 9% more cars in April compared with a year earlier, Chief Executive Helmut Panke said.

That jump in car sales suggests that a stronger earnings rise is in store for the current quarter. Mr. Panke said he expects earnings growth to roughly track a projected rise in car sales.

The company repeated a forecast for record 2004 earnings, aiming to top 2002's net profit of €2.02 billion. "What's encouraging is that they still expect to achieve record earnings," said Michael Raab, an analyst at Sal. Oppenheim.

BMW's first-quarter performance was enough for the company to overtake Mercedes as the world's leading maker of premium cars—at least for now. BMW's car sales exceeded those of Mercedes, although Mercedes had the upper hand in revenue terms.

"BMW is definitely faring way better than Mercedes, but the two companies are in different stages in their product cycles," said Thomas Ryard, an analyst with forecaster World Markets Research Centre. "I'm not sure it's going to be a long-lasting trend. By 2005, Mercedes should come back."

Last year, BMW launched its flagship 5-Series. This year, it is rolling out the 6-Series, X3, Mini convertible and 1-Series compact. Most of the development expenses for these models have already been booked.

By contrast, Mercedes is at the beginning of the biggest product offensive in its history. It launched a redesigned C-Class in March and is bringing out new versions of its compact A-Class this fall. In 2005, Mercedes expects to introduce two sport-utility vehicles, a redesign of the company's luxury S-Class, and a crossover family, known as the R-Class.

But Mercedes, which produces the Mercedes-Benz, Smart and Maybach brands, won't realize the benefits of these new models until later this year and in 2005.

Mercedes's first-quarter car sales declined 9% to 266,000 vehicles, burdened by the new-model program. But the Mercedes-Benz brand still topped BMW's core brand, selling 246,000 cars during the first quarter, compared with the BMW brand's 222,000.

Key Points in the Article

The article discusses the strong performance of BMW during the first months of 2004. The firm's sales rose sufficiently for it to overtake Mercedes for the lead in production of high-priced, or "premium," cars. The article spotlights the strong sales of the X3 SUV, which along with the Z8 roadster, is assembled at the company's plant in Munich, Germany. Renovations of the Munich plant reduced production of the X3 at the beginning of the year. BMW had been introducing new models and also increasing its capacity to produce existing models.

Analyzing the News

a We can use the economic model of production possibilities frontiers to analyze this news article. First, note that the renovations at the Munich plant meant that initially the company was operating inside its production possibilities frontier at this plant. This is shown in Figure 1, where production in early 2004 is represented by point A. Moving to the frontier makes it possible for BMW to produce more roadsters and more SUVs.

b The strong demand for the X3 SUV has caused BMW to allocate more workers and machines to producing this model. Once BMW is on the production possibilities frontier at the Munich plant, its opportunity cost of producing more X3 SUVs is the reduction in the quantity of Z8 roadsters produced. (Actually, we are simplifying a little here, because at various times BMW has produced other models in the Munich plant as well. We could show this by drawing a production possibilities frontier with the quantity of X3 SUVs on the horizontal axis and the quantity of all other models produced in the plant on the vertical axis. But the point would be the same: Once BMW is on the production possibilities frontier for this plant, it can only produce more X3s by producing less of something else.) In Figure 2 the popularity of the X3 causes BMW to move from point B to point C.

Thinking Critically
ABOUT POLICY

1. Launching the 6-Series coupe and the X3 SUV boosted BMW's sales in early 2004. If launching new products boosts sales, should BMW launch a new line of cars *every* year? Every month? Explain.

2. Some BMW's are made in Germany, some in South Carolina, some in other places. Should the U.S. government encourage the domestic production of BMW's by banning imports of BMWs?

Source: *Wall Street Journal.* Eastern Edition [Staff produced copy only] by Chris Reiter. Copyright 2004 by Dow Jones & Co. Inc. Reproduced with permission of Dow Jones & Co. Inc. in the format Textbook via Copyright Clearance Center.

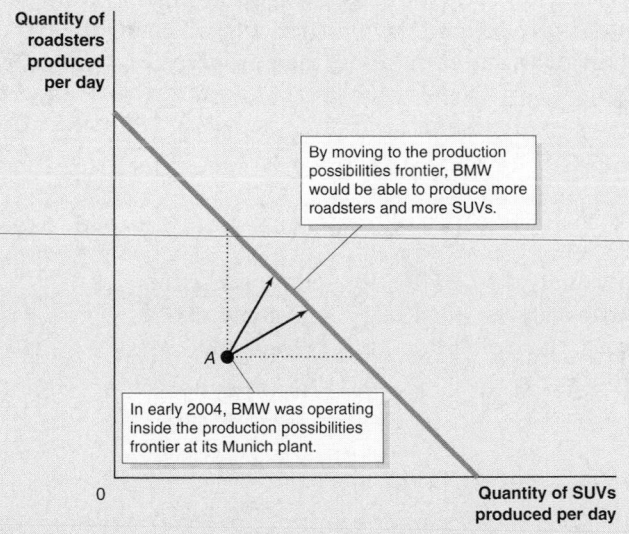

Figure 1: BMW was operating inside the Munich plant's production possibilities frontier in early 2004.

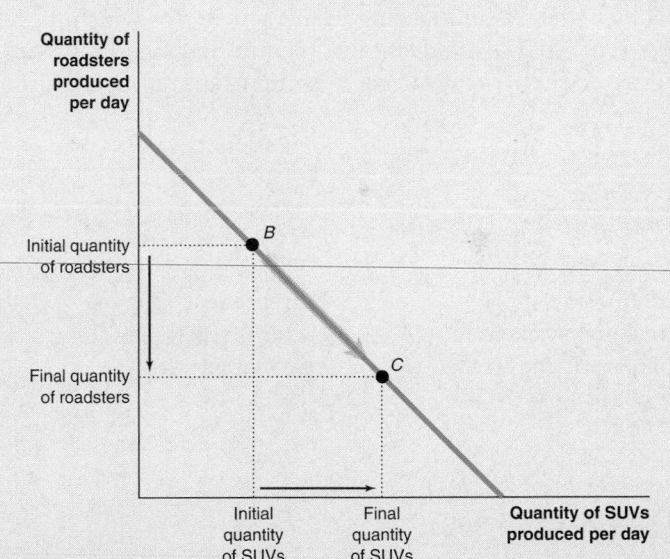

Figure 2: Once BMW is on the production possibilities frontier in its Munich plant, a larger quantity of X3 SUVs produced is only possible if a smaller quantity of Z8 roadsters is produced.

LEARNING OBJECTIVE ① Use a production possibilities frontier to analyze opportunity costs and trade-offs. The production possibilities frontier is a curve showing the maximum attainable combinations of two products that may be produced with available resources. It is used to illustrate the trade-offs that arise from scarcity. Points on the frontier are technically efficient. Points inside the frontier are inefficient and points outside the frontier are unattainable. Because of increasing marginal opportunity costs, production possibilities frontiers are usually bowed-out, or concave, rather than straight lines. This illustrates the important economic concept that the more resources that are already devoted to any activity, the smaller the payoff to devoting additional resources to that activity is likely to be.

LEARNING OBJECTIVE ② Understand comparative advantage and explain how it is the basis for trade. Fundamentally, markets are about *trade,* which is the act of buying or selling. People trade on the basis of *comparative advantage.* An individual, firm, or country has a comparative advantage in producing a good or service if it can produce the good or service at the lowest opportunity cost. People are usually better off specializing in the activity for which they have a comparative advantage and trading for the other goods and services they need. It is important not to confuse comparative advantage with *absolute advantage.* An individual, firm, or country has an *absolute advantage* in producing a good or service if it can produce more of that good or service from the same amount of resources. It is possible to have an absolute advantage in producing a good or service without having a comparative advantage.

LEARNING OBJECTIVE ③ Explain the basic idea of how a market system works. A *market* is a group of buyers and sellers of a good or service and the institution or arrangement by which they come together to trade. *Product markets* are markets for goods and services, such as computers and medical treatment. *Factor markets* are markets for the factors of production, such as labor, capital, natural resources, and entrepreneurial ability. Adam Smith argued in his 1776 book, *The Wealth of Nations,* that in a free market where the government does not control the production of goods and services, changes in prices lead firms to produce the goods and services most desired by consumers. If consumers demand more of a good, its price will rise. Firms respond to rising prices by increasing production. If consumers demand less of a good, its price will fall. Firms respond to falling prices by producing less of a good. A market system will only work well if there is protection for *property rights,* which are the rights of individuals and firms to use their property.

Absolute advantage 42
Circular-flow diagram 47
Comparative advantage 43
Economic growth 40

Entrepreneur 50
Factor markets 46
Free market 48
Market 46

Opportunity cost 35
Product markets 46
Production possibilities
 frontier 34

Property rights 51
Scarcity 34
Trade 40

1. What do economists mean by scarcity? Can you think of anything that is not scarce according to the economic definition?
2. What is a production possibilities frontier? How can we show economic efficiency on a production possibilities frontier? How can we show inefficiency? What causes a production possibilities frontier to shift outward?
3. What does increasing marginal opportunity costs mean? What are the implications of this idea for the shape of the production possibilities frontier?
4. What is absolute advantage? What is comparative advantage? Is it possible for a country to have a comparative advantage in producing a good without also having an absolute advantage? Briefly explain.
5. What is the basis for trade? What advantages are there to specialization?
6. What is the circular-flow diagram, and what does it demonstrate?

7. What are the two main categories of participants in markets? Which participants are of greatest importance in determining what goods and services are produced?

8. What is a free market? In what ways does a free market economy differ from a centrally planned economy?

9. What is an entrepreneur? Why do entrepreneurs play a key role in a market system?

10. Under what circumstances are firms likely to produce more of a good or service? Under what circumstances are firms likely to produce less of a good or service?

11. What are private property rights? What role do they play in the working of a market system? Why are independent courts important for a well-functioning economy?

PROBLEMS AND APPLICATIONS

Please visit **www.prenhall.com/hubbard** *for solutions to the even-numbered problems as well as multiple-choice and true or false self-assessment quizzes.*

1. Draw a production possibilities frontier showing the trade-off between the production of cotton and the production of soybeans.
   a. Show the effect that a prolonged drought would have on the initial production possibilities frontier.
   b. Suppose genetic modification makes soybeans resistant to insects, allowing yields to double. Show the effect of this technological change on the initial production possibilities frontier.

2. **[Related to the *Chapter Opener*]** One of the trade-offs faced by BMW is between safety and gas mileage. For example, adding steel to a car makes it safer but also heavier, which results in lower gas mileage. Draw a hypothetical production possibilities frontier facing BMW engineers that shows this trade-off.

3. Suppose you win free tickets to a movie plus all you can eat at the snack bar for free. Would there be a cost to you to attend this movie? Explain.

4. Suppose we can divide all the goods produced by an economy into two types: consumption goods and capital goods. Capital goods, such as machinery, equipment, and computers, are goods used to produce other goods.
   a. Use a production possibilities frontier graph to illustrate the trade-off to an economy between producing consumption goods and producing capital goods. Is it likely that the production possibilities frontier in this situation would be a straight line (as in Figure 2-1) or concave (as in Figure 2-2)? Briefly explain.
   b. Suppose that technological advance occurs that affects the production of capital goods but not consumption goods. Show the effect on the production possibilities frontier.

c. Suppose that country A and country B currently have identical production possibilities frontiers, but that country A devotes only 5 percent of its resources to producing capital goods over each of the next 10 years, whereas country B devotes 30 percent. Which country is likely to experience more rapid economic growth in the future? Illustrate using a production possibilities frontier graph. Your graph should include production possibilities frontiers for country A today and in 10 years, and for country B today and in 10 years.

5. Use the following production possibilities frontier for a country to answer the questions:

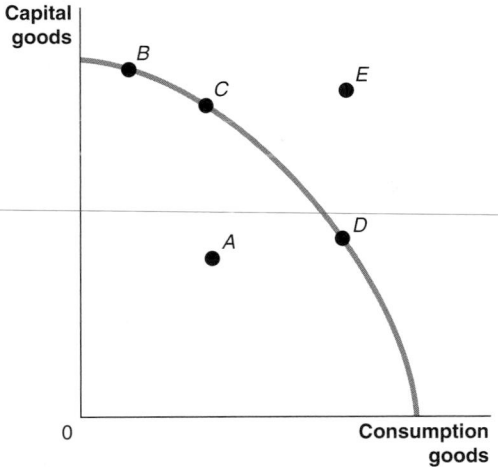

a. Which point(s) are unattainable? Briefly explain why.
b. Which point(s) are efficient? Briefly explain why.
c. Which point(s) are inefficient? Briefly explain why.
d. At which point is the country's future growth rate likely to be the highest? Briefly explain why.

6. **[Related to *Solved Problem 2-1*]** You have exams in economics and chemistry coming up and 5 hours available for studying. The table shows the trade-offs you face in allocating the time you will spend in studying each subject.

	HOURS SPENT STUDYING		MIDTERM SCORE	
CHOICE	ECONOMICS	CHEMISTRY	ECONOMICS	CHEMISTRY
A	5	0	95	70
B	4	1	93	78
C	3	2	90	84
D	2	3	86	88
E	1	4	81	90
F	0	5	75	91

a. Use the data in the table to draw a production possibilities frontier graph. Label your vertical axis "Score on economics exam" and label your horizontal axis "Score on chemistry exam." Make sure to label the values where your production possibilities frontier intersects the vertical and horizontal axes.

b. Label the points representing choice *C* and choice *D*. If you are at choice *C*, what is your opportunity cost of increasing your chemistry score?

c. Under what circumstances would *A* be a sensible choice?

7. Suppose the president is attempting to decide whether the federal government should spend more on research to find a cure for heart disease. He asks you, one of his economic advisors, to prepare a report discussing the relevant factors he should consider. Discuss the main issues you would deal with in your report.

8. Congress has given the Environmental Protection Agency (EPA) the authority to write regulations to implement the provisions of the Clean Air Act, a law aimed at reducing air pollution. According to the Clean Air Act, the EPA is not to consider the cost of complying with the regulations. Why do you suppose Congress would have constrained the EPA in this way? Do you agree that costs should not be taken into account when drafting environmental regulations?

9. Lawrence Summers was a professor of economics at Harvard and served as Secretary of the Treasury in the Clinton administration before becoming president of Harvard. He has been quoted as giving the following moral defense of the economic approach:

> There is nothing morally unattractive about saying: We need to analyze which way of spending money on health care will produce more benefit and which less, and using our money as efficiently as we can. I don't think there is anything immoral about seeking to achieve environmental benefits at the lowest possible costs.

Would it be more moral to reduce pollution without worrying about the cost or by taking the cost into account? Briefly explain.
Source: David Wessel, "Precepts from Professor Summers," *Wall Street Journal*, October 17, 2002.

10. In *The Wonderful Wizard of Oz* and his other books about the Land of Oz, L. Frank Baum observed that if people's wants were modest enough, most goods would not be scarce. According to Baum, this was the case in Oz:

> There were no poor people in the Land of Oz, because there was no such thing as money. . . . Each person was given freely by his neighbors whatever he required for his use, which is as much as anyone may reasonably desire. Some tilled the lands and raised great crops of grain, which was divided equally among the whole population, so that all had enough. There were many tailors and dressmakers and shoemakers and the like, who made things that any who desired them might wear. Likewise there were jewelers who made ornaments for the person, which pleased and beautified the people, and these ornaments also were free to those who asked for them. Each man and woman, no matter what he or she produced for the good of the community, was supplied by the neighbors with food and clothing and a house and furniture and ornaments and games. If by chance the supply ever ran short, more was taken from the great storehouses of the Ruler, which were afterward filled up again when there was more of any article than people needed. . . .

> You will know, by what I have told you here, that the Land of Oz was a remarkable country. I do not suppose such an arrangement would be practical with us.

Do you agree with Baum that the economic system in Oz wouldn't work in the contemporary United States? Briefly explain why or why not.
Source: L. Frank Baum, *The Emerald City of Oz*, pp. 30–31. First edition published in 1910.

11. Using the same amount of resources, the United States and Canada can both produce lumberjack shirts and lumberjack boots as shown in the following production possibilities frontiers:

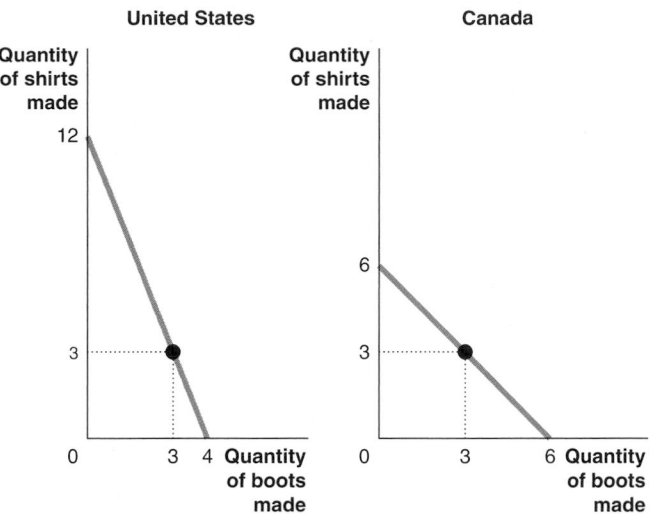

a. Who has a comparative advantage in producing lumberjack boots? Who has a comparative advantage in producing lumberjack shirts? Explain your reasoning.

b. Does either country have an absolute advantage in producing both goods? Explain.

c. Suppose that both countries are currently producing three pairs of boots and three shirts. Show that both can be better off if they specialize in producing one good and then engage in trade.

12. **[Related to *Solved Problem 2-2*]** Suppose Iran and Iraq both produce oil and olive oil. The table shows combinations of both goods that each country can produce in a day, measured in thousands of barrels.

IRAQ		IRAN	
OIL	OLIVE OIL	OIL	OLIVE OIL
0	8	0	4
2	6	1	3
4	4	2	2
6	2	3	1
8	0	4	0

a. Who has the comparative advantage in producing oil? Explain.

b. Can these two countries gain from trading oil and olive oil? Explain.

13. **[Related to *Solved Problem 2-2*]** Suppose that France and Germany both produce schnitzel and wine. The following table shows combinations of the goods that each country can produce in a day:

FRANCE		GERMANY	
WINE (BOTTLES)	SCHNITZEL (POUNDS)	WINE (BOTTLES)	SCHNITZEL (POUNDS)
0	8	0	15
1	6	1	12
2	4	2	9
3	2	3	6
4	0	4	3
		5	0

a. Who has a comparative advantage in producing wine? Who has a comparative advantage in producing schnitzel?

b. Suppose that France is currently producing 1 bottle of wine and 6 pounds of schnitzel and Germany is currently producing 3 bottles of wine and 6 pounds of schnitzel. Demonstrate that France and Germany can both be better off if they specialize in producing only one good and then engage in trade.

14. **[Related to *Don't Let This Happen To You!*]** In the 1950s, the economist Bela Balassa compared 28 manufacturing industries in the United States and Britain. In every one of the 28 industries, Balassa found that the United States had an absolute advantage. In these circumstances, would there have been any gain to the United States from importing any of these products from Britain? Explain.

15. Identify whether each of the following transactions will take place in the factor market or in the product market, and whether households or firms are supplying the good or service, or demanding the good or service:

a. George buys a BMW X5 SUV.

b. BMW increases employment at its Spartanburg plant.

c. George works 20 hours per week at McDonald's.

d. George sells land he owns to McDonald's so it can build a new restaurant.

16. In *The Wealth of Nations*, Adam Smith wrote the following (Book I, Chapter II):

> It is not from the benevolence of the butcher, the brewer, or the baker, that we expect our dinner, but from their regard to their own interest.

Briefly discuss what he meant by this.

17. In a commencement address to economics graduates at the University of Texas, Robert McTeer Jr., who was then the president of the Federal Reserve Bank of Dallas, argued, "For my money, Adam Smith's invisible hand is the most important thing you've learned by studying economics." What's so important about the idea of the invisible hand? Source: Robert D. McTeer Jr., "The Dismal Science? Hardly!" *Wall Street Journal*, June 4, 2003.

18. Evaluate the following argument: "Adam Smith's analysis is based on a fundamental flaw: He assumes that people are motivated by self-interest. But this isn't true. I'm not selfish, and most people I know aren't selfish."

19. Writing in the *New York Times,* Michael Lewis argued that "a market economy is premised on a system of incentives designed to encourage an ignoble human trait: self-interest." Do you agree that self-interest is an "ignoble human trait"? What incentives does a market system provide to encourage self-interest?
Source: Michael Lewis, "In Defense of the Boom," *New York Times,* October 27, 2002.

20. An editorial in *Business Week* magazine offered this opinion:

    Economies should be judged on a simple measure: their ability to generate a rising standard of living for all members of society, including people at the bottom.

    Briefly discuss whether or not you agree.
    Source: "Poverty: The Bigger Picture," *Business Week,* October 7, 2002.

21. An estimated 400 million to 600 million people worldwide are squatters who live on land to which they have no legal title, usually on the outskirts of cities in less-developed countries. Economist Hernando de Soto persuaded Peru's government to undertake a program to make it cheap and easy for these squatters to obtain a title to the land they had been occupying. How would this creation of property rights be likely to affect the economic opportunities available to these squatters?
Source: Alan B. Krueger, "A Study Looks at Squatters and Land Title in Peru," *New York Times,* January 9, 2003.

22. In colonial America, the population was spread thinly over a large area and transportation costs were very high because it was difficult to ship products by road for more than short distances. As a result, most of the free population lived on small farms where they not only grew their own food but also usually made their own clothes and very rarely bought or sold anything for money. Explain why the incomes of these farmers were likely to rise as transportation costs fell. Use the concept of comparative advantage in your answer.

23. During the 1928 presidential election campaign, Herbert Hoover, the Republican candidate, argued that the United States should only import those products that could not be produced here. Do you believe that this would be a good policy? Explain.

chapter

three

Where Prices Come From:
The Interaction of Demand and Supply

How Hewlett-Packard Manages the Demand for Printers

▶ In early 2005 the board of directors at Hewlett-Packard (H-P) ousted chief executive officer Carly Fiorina and replaced her with Mark Hurd, then the chief executive officer of NCR Corporation. What happened?

Carly Fiorina had been a business celebrity for many years. In July 1999 she became H-P's chief executive officer, which made her the first woman to head one of the 100 largest firms in the United States. In 2002, she brought about the largest merger of two technology firms in U.S. history when H-P purchased Compaq Computer Corporation. By 2004, she presided over a firm that employed 150,000 workers and had total sales of $80 billion. Fiorina's ouster in 2005 from H-P reflected the relatively weak performance of the firm during her time as chief executive officer. In particular, the merger with Compaq had failed to improve

H-P's performance in the personal computer market.

Printers, and not personal computers, are H-P's most successful product. Although printers account for only about 30 percent of the firm's sales, they account for 70 percent of its profits. In fact, as *An Inside Look* at the end of this chapter discusses, to increase the demand for printers the firm is willing to sell its personal computers at low prices.

Hewlett-Packard's success, like that of any firm, depends on its ability to analyze changes in demand and supply. Because of the importance of printers to H-P, the firm devotes significant resources to monitoring and forecasting consumer demand. Its forecasts of demand, however, are not always successful. In 2001, for example, Carly Fiorina announced that sales

of H-P printers had declined sharply in the first half of that year compared to the first half of 2000. Two events caused this decline: First, many individuals and small businesses unexpectedly decided not to upgrade their existing computers to faster and more powerful machines. Purchasers of new PCs are a key part of the market for printers. Second, the U.S. economy moved into recession, lowering the incomes of many consumers and reducing the profits of many businesses. Fiorina admitted she had been taken by surprise by this decline in sales: "Stuff happens that you're not able to see even with a ton of information, and the downturn in the economy was a clear case of that. Everybody had loads of information, and everybody missed it."

H-P did a better job anticipating changes in the types of printers con-

After studying this chapter, you should be able to:

① Discuss the variables that influence demand.

② Discuss the variables that influence supply.

③ Use a graph to illustrate market equilibrium.

④ Use demand and supply graphs to predict changes in prices and quantities.

LEARNING OBJECTIVES

sumers would demand. For example, increasing sales of digital cameras have had an important impact on the market for printers. During 2003, 50 million digital cameras were sold, and many people bought both a camera and a new printer designed to print digital photos. Printers aimed at the digital photo market usually include a slot for memory cards from the cameras, and an LCD (liquid crystal display) screen for previews of photos. Many of these printers are multifunction devices (MFD) that combine printing, scanning, copying, and faxing. These MFDs sell for higher prices—and are more profitable—than basic printers. In 2004, H-P had a 58 percent share of the MFD market in the United States. Lexmark was second but far behind with a 21 percent share.

Unfortunately for Carly Fiorina,

matched by success with personal computers. Some members of the firm's board of directors were particularly concerned that H-P had relied too heavily on selling personal computers in retail stores, rather than building up direct sales to consumers through the Internet as Dell Computer had done so successfully. The board gave Mark Hurd, the new chief executive officer, the responsibility of increasing the firm's competitiveness in the personal computer market. *An Inside Look* on page 88 discusses HP's strategy for competing with Dell.

Sources: Olga Kharif, "Printing a Record of Growth," Business Week Online, February 17, 2004; Pui-Wing Tam, "Copy Machine: H-P, Post-Compaq, Looks Like Its Old Self," Wall Street Journal, May 7, 2004; quote from Carly Fiorina: "A Conversation with Carly Fiorina—Forbes 5th Annual CIO Forum," December 2, 2003, Dallas,

➤ In Chapter 1, we learned how economists use models to predict human behavior. In Chapter 2, we used the model of production possibilities frontiers to analyze scarcity and trade-offs. In this chapter and the next, we explore the model of demand and supply, which is the most powerful tool in economics, and use it to explain how prices are determined. We begin by discussing consumers and the demand side of the market, then we turn to firms and the supply side. As you will see, we will apply the model of demand and supply again and again throughout this book to understand business and the economy.

① LEARNING OBJECTIVE

Discuss the variables that influence demand.

The Demand Side of the Market

Chapter 2 explained that in a market system consumers ultimately determine which goods and services will be produced. The most successful businesses are the ones that respond best to consumer demand. But what determines consumer demand for a product? Certainly, many factors influence the willingness of consumers to buy a particular product. For example, consumers who are considering buying a printer will make their decisions based on, among other factors, the income they have available to spend, whether they have recently purchased a personal computer or digital camera, and the effectiveness of the advertising campaigns of the companies that sell printers. The main factor in consumer decisions, though, will be the price of the printers. Thus, it makes sense to begin with price when analyzing the decisions of consumers to buy a product. It is important to note that when we discuss demand, we are considering not what a consumer *wants* to buy, but what the consumer is both willing and *able* to buy.

The Demand of an Individual Buyer

Households, firms, and government agencies all buy printers. Suppose the Prudential Insurance Company intends to purchase printers for a number of its employees. We might determine the relationship between the price of printers and the number of printers the company would be willing to buy during a particular period of time by asking Kate, the company's purchasing manager, "If the price of a printer were $125, how many printers would you be willing to buy over the next month?"

Quantity demanded The amount of a good or service that a consumer is willing and able to purchase at a given price.

Suppose Kate responds that she would be willing to purchase 5 printers over the next month at a price of $125 each. The amount of a good or a service that a consumer is willing and able to purchase at a particular price is referred to as the **quantity demanded**. Figure 3-1 shows Kate's quantity demanded at a price of $125. On the vertical axis, we measure the price of printers, and on the horizontal axis we measure the number of printers demanded during the next month.

Demand Schedules and Demand Curves

Demand schedule A table showing the relationship between the price of a product and the quantity of the product demanded.

Demand curve A curve that shows the relationship between the price of a product and the quantity of the product demanded.

We can repeat our question using different prices. The table in Figure 3-2 shows the number of printers Kate would be willing to buy at five different prices. Tables that show the relationship between the price of a product and the quantity of the product demanded are called **demand schedules**. The graph in Figure 3-2 plots the numbers from the table as a **demand curve**, a curve that shows the relationship between the price of a product and the quantity of a product demanded.

Although we have asked Kate only about her willingness to buy printers at five different prices, we can connect the points in Figure 3-2 to form a continuous downward-sloping demand curve. The demand curve slopes downward because Kate

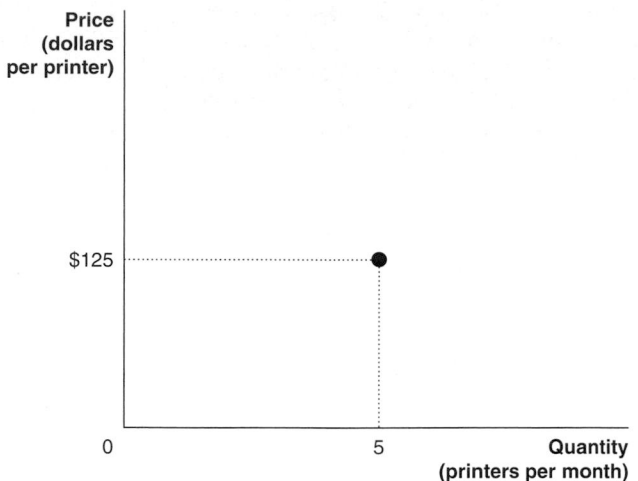

FIGURE 3-1

Plotting a Price–Quantity Combination on a Graph

At a price of $125 per printer, Kate, the purchasing manager for the Prudential Insurance Company, will be willing to buy 5 printers in the next month.

will buy more printers as the price falls. When the price of a printer is $175, Kate buys 3 printers. When the price of a printer falls to $150, Kate buys 4 printers. Buyers demand a larger quantity of a product as the price falls because the product becomes cheaper relative to other products and because they can afford to buy more at a lower price.

Individual Demand and Market Demand

Figure 3-2 shows an individual demand curve. To understand how a market works, however, we need to examine **market demand**, or the demand by all the consumers of a given good or service. We can determine market demand by asking additional consumers how many printers they would purchase at various prices. Ordinarily, the market that we would be interested in would include at least all of the consumers of the product in a city and might include all of the consumers in the world. To keep things simple, let's assume that the market for printers consists of Kate from the Prudential Insurance Company and two individual consumers: Sam and Paul. Figure 3-3 shows that we can find the market demand for printers by adding the number of printers demanded by Kate, Sam, and Paul at each price. The table shows the demand schedules for printers of these three consumers. We plot the numbers from the demand schedule in graphs 3-3(a), 3-3(b), and 3-3(c).

Market demand The demand by all the consumers of a given good or service.

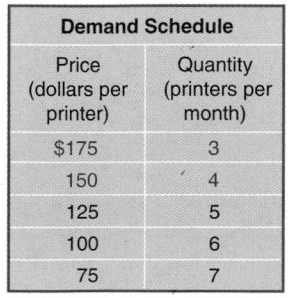

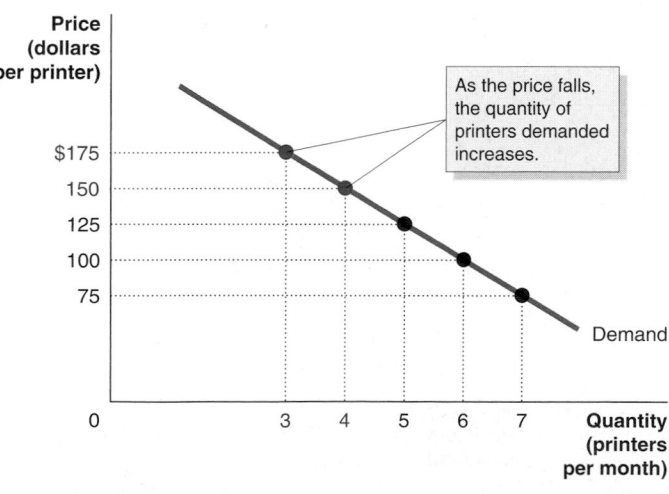

FIGURE 3-2

Kate's Demand Schedule and Demand Curve

As the price changes, Kate changes the quantity of printers she is willing to buy. We can show this as a *demand schedule* in a table, or as a *demand curve* on a graph. The table and graph both show that as the price of printers falls, the quantity demanded rises. When the price of a printer is $175, Kate buys 3 printers. When the price of a printer drops to $150, Kate buys 4 printers. Therefore, Kate's demand curve is downward sloping.

Figure 3-3(d) on page 67 shows the market demand curve for printers. The market demand curve tells us how many units of the product consumers in this market would be willing to buy at each price during a certain period of time. For instance, consumers in this market would be willing to buy a total of 26 printers during the next month at a price of $100 per printer: Kate is willing to buy 6, Sam is willing to buy 11, and Paul is willing to buy 9.

The Law of Demand

Law of demand Holding everything else constant, when the price of a product falls, the quantity demanded of the product will increase, and when the price of a product rises, the quantity demanded of the product will decrease.

The market demand curve for printers shown in Figure 3-3(d) is downward sloping: As the price of printers falls, the quantity of printers demanded increases. The inverse relationship between the price of a product and the quantity of the product demanded is known as the **law of demand**: Holding everything else constant, when the price of a product falls, the quantity demanded of the product will increase, and when the price of a product rises, the quantity demanded of the product will decrease. The law of demand holds for any market demand curve. Economists have never found an exception to it. In fact, Nobel Prize–winning economist Paul Samuelson once remarked that the surest way for an economist to become famous would be to discover a market demand curve that sloped upward rather than downward.

What Explains the Law of Demand?

It makes sense that consumers will buy more of a good when the price falls and less of a good when the price rises, but let's look more closely at why this is true. When the price of printers falls, consumers buy a larger quantity of printers because of the *substitution effect* and the *income effect*.

FIGURE 3-3   **Deriving the Market Demand Curve from Individual Demand Curves**

The table shows that the total quantity demanded in a market is the sum of the quantities demanded by each buyer at each price. We find the market demand curve by adding horizontally the individual demand curves in parts (a), (b), and (c). At a price of $100, Kate demands 6 printers, Sam demands 11 printers, and Paul demands 9 printers. Therefore, part (d) shows that a price of $100 and a quantity demanded of 26 is a point on the market demand curve.

	Quantity (printers per month)			
Price (dollars per printer)	Kate	Sam	Paul	Market
$175	3	5	6	14
150	4	7	7	18
125	5	9	8	22
100	6	11	9	26
75	7	13	10	30

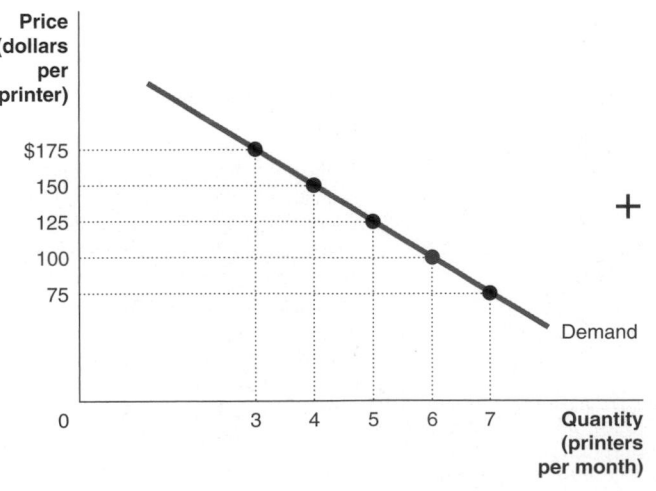

(a) Kate's demand curve

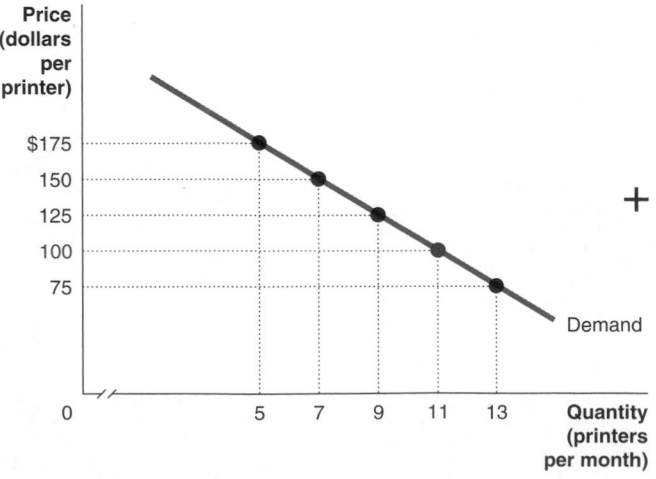

(b) Sam's demand curve

SUBSTITUTION EFFECT The **substitution effect** of a price change refers to the fact that a fall in price makes a good less expensive *relative* to other goods that are *substitutes*. This change leads consumers to buy more of a good when its price falls—or less of a good when its price rises. When the price of printers falls, consumers will substitute buying printers for buying other goods or services. For example, a consumer who has digital camera pictures printed at Wal-Mart might instead buy a printer if the price of printers falls.

Substitution effect The change in the quantity demanded of a good that results from a change in price making the good more or less expensive relative to other goods that are substitutes.

THE INCOME EFFECT The **income effect** of a price change refers to the change in the quantity demanded of a good that results from the effect of a change in the good's price on consumers' purchasing power. Purchasing power refers to the quantity of goods that can be bought with a fixed amount of income. When the price of a good falls, the increased purchasing power of consumers' incomes will usually lead them to purchase a larger quantity of the good. When the price of a good rises, the decreased purchasing power of consumers' incomes will usually lead them to purchase a smaller quantity of the good.

Income effect The change in the quantity demanded of a good that results from the effect of a change in the good's price on consumer purchasing power.

Thus, a fall in the price of printers leads consumers to buy more printers, both because they are now cheaper relative to substitute products and because the purchasing power of the consumers' incomes has increased.

Holding Everything Else Constant: The Ceteris Paribus *Condition*

Notice that the definition of the law of demand contains the phrase "holding everything else constant." In constructing the market demand curve for printers, we focused only on the effect that changes in the price of printers would have on the quantity of printers consumers would be willing and able to buy. We were holding constant other variables that might affect the willingness of consumers to buy printers. Economists refer to the necessity of holding all variables other than price constant in constructing a demand curve as the **ceteris paribus** condition—*ceteris paribus* is Latin for "all else equal."

What would happen if we allowed a variable—other than price—to change that might affect the willingness of consumers to buy printers? Consumers would then change the quantity they demand at each price. We can illustrate this by shifting the market demand curve. A shift of a demand curve is *an increase or decrease in demand*. A movement along a demand curve is *an increase or decrease in the quantity demanded*. As

Ceteris paribus ("all else equal") The requirement that when analyzing the relationship between two variables—such as price and quantity demanded—other variables must be held constant.

FIGURE 3-3   continued

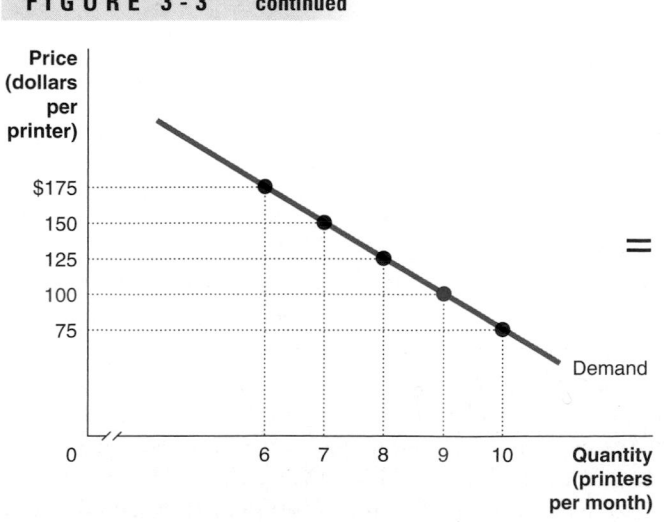

(c) Paul's demand curve

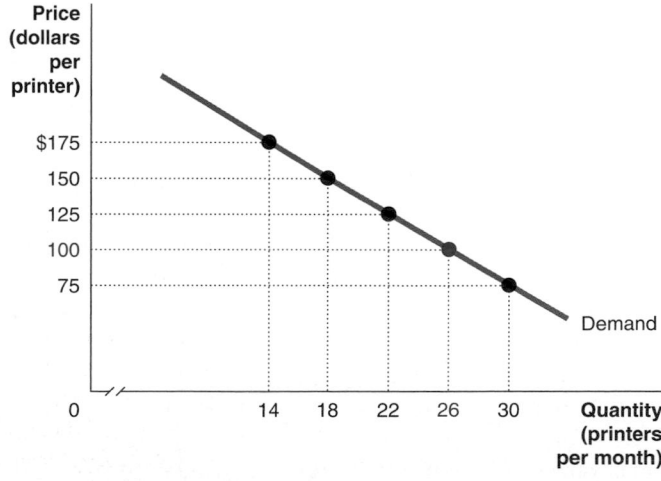

(d) Market demand curve

FIGURE 3-4

Shifting the Demand Curve

When consumers increase the quantity of a product they wish to buy at a given price, the market demand curve shifts to the right from D_1 to D_2. When consumers decrease the quantity of a product they wish to buy at any given price, the demand curve shifts to the left from D_1 to D_3.

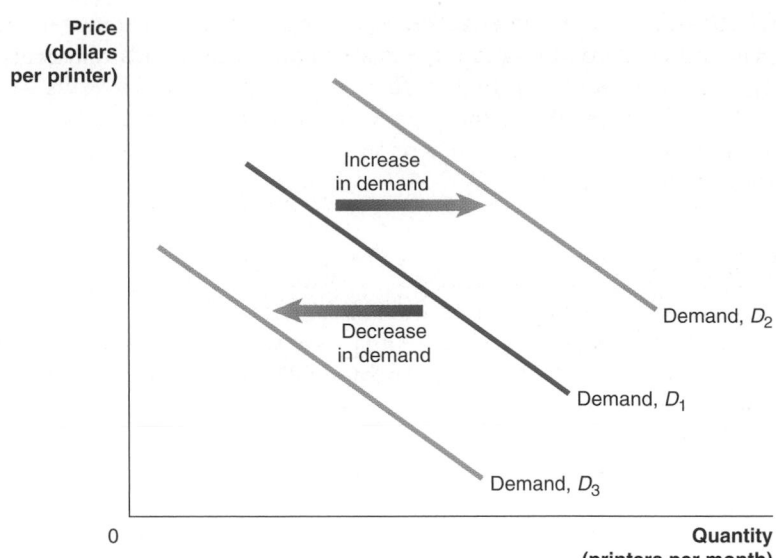

Figure 3-4 shows, we shift the demand curve to the right if consumers decide to buy more of the good at each price, and we shift the demand curve to the left if consumers decide to buy less.

Variables That Shift Market Demand

Many variables other than price can influence market demand. These five are the most important:

➤ Prices of related goods

➤ Income

➤ Tastes

➤ Population and demographics

➤ Expected future prices

We can discuss how changes in each of these variables affects the market demand curve for printers.

PRICES OF RELATED GOODS Consider again the market demand curve for printers. Suppose that the market demand curve in Figure 3-3(d) represents the willingness and ability of consumers to buy printers during a period when Wal-Mart charges $0.50 to print one digital photo. If Wal-Mart lowers the price to $0.25 per photo, how will the market demand for printers change? Fewer printers will be demanded at every price. We show this by shifting the demand curve for printers to the left.

Goods and services that can be used for the same purpose—like printers and having digital photos printed at stores—are **substitutes**. When two goods are substitutes, the more you buy of one, the less you will buy of the other. A decrease in the price of a substitute causes the demand curve for a good to shift to the left. An increase in the price of a substitute causes the demand curve for a good to shift to the right.

Many consumers purchase a new printer when they buy a new computer. Suppose the market demand curve in Figure 3-3(d) represents the willingness of consumers to buy Hewlett-Packard's printers at a time when the average price of a new personal computer is $1,300. If the price of PCs falls to $1,100, consumers will buy more PCs *and* more printers: The demand curve for printers will shift to the right.

Products that are used together—such as personal computers and printers—are **complements.** When two goods are complements, the more you buy of one, the more

Substitutes Goods and services that can be used for the same purpose.

Complements Goods that are used together.

you will buy of the other. A decrease in the price of a complement causes the demand curve for a good to shift to the right. An increase in the price of a complement causes the demand curve for a good to shift to the left.

Why Supermarkets Need to Understand Substitutes and Complements

Supermarkets sell what sometimes seems like a bewildering variety of goods. The first row of the following table shows the varieties of eight products stocked by five Chicago supermarkets.

	COFFEE	FROZEN PIZZA	HOT DOGS	ICE CREAM	POTATO CHIPS	REGULAR CEREAL	SPAGHETTI SAUCE	YOGURT
Varieties in Five Chicago Supermarkets	391	337	128	421	285	242	194	288
Varieties Introduced in a 2-Year Period	113	109	47	129	93	114	70	107
Varieties Removed in a 2-Year Period	135	86	32	118	77	75	36	51

Source: Juin-Kuan Chong, Teck-Hua Ho, and Christopher S. Tang, "A Modeling Framework for Category Assortment Planning," *Manufacturing & Service Operations Management*, 2001, Vol. 3, No. 3, pp. 191–210.

Supermarkets are also constantly adding new varieties of goods to their shelves and removing old varieties. The second row of the table shows that these five Chicago supermarkets added 113 new varieties of coffee over a two-year period, while the third row shows they eliminated 135 existing varieties. How do supermarkets decide which varieties to add and which to remove?

Christopher Tang is a professor at the Anderson Graduate School of Management at the University of California, Los Angeles (UCLA). In an interview with the *Baltimore Sun*, Tang argues that supermarkets should not necessarily remove the slowest-selling goods from their shelves but should consider the relationships among the goods. In particular, they should consider whether the goods being removed are substitutes or complements with the remaining goods. A lobster bisque soup, for example, could be a relatively slow seller but might be a complement to other soups because it can be used with them to make a sauce. In that case, removing the lobster bisque would hurt sales of some of the remaining soups. Tang suggests the supermarket would be better off removing a slow-selling soup that is a substitute for another soup. For example, the supermarket might want to remove one of two brands of cream of chicken soup.

Source: Lobster bisque example from Lorraine Mirabella, "Shelf Science in Supermarkets," *Baltimore Sun*, March 17, 2002, p. 16.

3-1 Making the Connection

A supermarket shouldn't remove a slow-selling soup from its shelves without researching whether shoppers use that soup as a substitute or a complement for another soup.

INCOME In addition to the prices of other goods, the income that consumers have available to spend also affects their willingness and ability to buy a good. Suppose that the market demand curve in Figure 3-3(d) reflects the willingness of consumers to buy printers when average household income is $43,000. If household income rises to $45,000, the demand for printers will increase, which we show by shifting the demand curve to the right. A good is a **normal good** when demand increases following an increase in income and decreases following a decrease in income. Most goods are normal goods, but the demand for some goods falls when income rises, and rises when income falls. For instance, as your income rises you might buy less canned tuna fish or fewer hot dogs, and buy more prime rib or shrimp. A good is an **inferior good** when demand decreases following an increase in income and increases following a decrease in income. So, hot dogs and tuna fish would be examples of inferior goods, not because they are of low quality, but because you buy less of them as your income increases.

Normal good A good for which the demand increases as income rises and decreases as income falls.

Inferior good A good for which the demand increases as income falls, and decreases as income rises.

TASTES Consumers can also be influenced by an advertising campaign for a product. If Hewlett-Packard and other companies begin to heavily advertise their printers on television and in magazines, consumers are more likely to buy them at every price and the demand curve will shift to the right. An economist would say that the advertising campaign has affected consumers' *taste* for printers. Taste is a catchall category that refers to the many subjective elements that can enter into a consumer's decision to buy a product. A consumer's taste for a product can change for many reasons. Sometimes trends play a substantial role. For example, the popularity of low-carbohydrate diets caused a decline in demand for some goods, such as bread and donuts, and an increase in demand for beef. In general, when consumers' taste for a product increases, the demand curve will shift to the right, and when consumers' taste for a product decreases, the demand curve for the product will shift to the left.

POPULATION AND DEMOGRAPHICS Population and demographic factors can affect the demand for a product. As the population of the United States increases, so will the number of consumers, and the demand for most products will increase. The **demographics** of a population refers to its characteristics, with respect to age, race, and gender. As the demographics of a country or region change, the demand for particular goods will increase or decrease because different categories of people tend to have different preferences for those goods. For instance, the demand for baby food will be greatest when the fraction of the population under the age of two is the greatest.

Demographics The characteristics of a population with respect to age, race, and gender.

3-2 *Making the* **Connection**

Firms are responding to the tastes of a growing Hispanic population. Some Home Depot stores, for example, include signs in both English and Spanish.

Companies Respond to a Growing Hispanic Population

In the fall of 2002, Blockbuster Video began stocking more than 1,000 videos and DVDs that had been dubbed in Spanish. Kmart began selling a clothing line named after Thalia, a Mexican singer. The Ford Motor Company hired Mexican actress and singer Salma Hayek to appear in commercials. A used car dealer in Pennsylvania displayed a sign stating "Salga Manejando Hoy Mismo" (or "Drive Out Today" in English). These companies were responding to the rising spending power of Hispanic Americans. The increase in spending by Hispanic households was due partly to increased population growth and partly to rising incomes. By 2020, the Hispanic share of the U.S. consumer market is expected to grow to more than 13 percent—almost twice what it had been in 2000. The Selig Center for Economic Growth at the University of Georgia has forecast that the incomes of Hispanic households will increase more than twice as fast between 2003 and 2007 as the incomes of non-Hispanic households.

As the demand for goods purchased by Hispanic households increases, more can be sold at every price. Not surprisingly, companies have responded by devoting more resources to serving this demographic group.

Source: Eduardo Porter, "Buying Power of Hispanics Is Set to Soar," *Wall Street Journal*, April 18, 2003, p. B1.

EXPECTED FUTURE PRICES Consumers choose not only which products to buy but also when to buy them. On the one hand, if enough consumers become convinced that printers will be selling for lower prices three months from now, the demand for printers will decrease now, as consumers postpone their purchases to wait for the expected price decrease. On the other hand, if enough consumers become convinced that the price of printers will be higher three months from now, the demand for printers will increase now, as consumers try to beat the expected price increase.

Table 3-1 summarizes the most important variables that cause market demand curves to shift. You should note that the table shows the shift in the demand curve that results from an *increase* in each of the variables. A *decrease* in these variables would cause the demand curve to shift in the opposite direction.

TABLE 3-1

Variables That Shift Market Demand Curves

An increase in ...	Shifts the demand curve ...	Because ...
the price of a substitute good		consumers buy less of the substitute good and more of this good.
the price of a complementary good		consumers buy less of the complementary good and less of this good.
income (and the good is normal)		consumers spend more of their higher income on the good.
income (and the good is inferior)		consumers spend less of their higher income on the good.
taste for the good		consumers are willing to buy a larger quantity of the good at every price.
population		additional consumers result in a greater quantity demanded at every price.
the expected price of the good in the future		consumers buy more of the good today to avoid the higher price in the future.

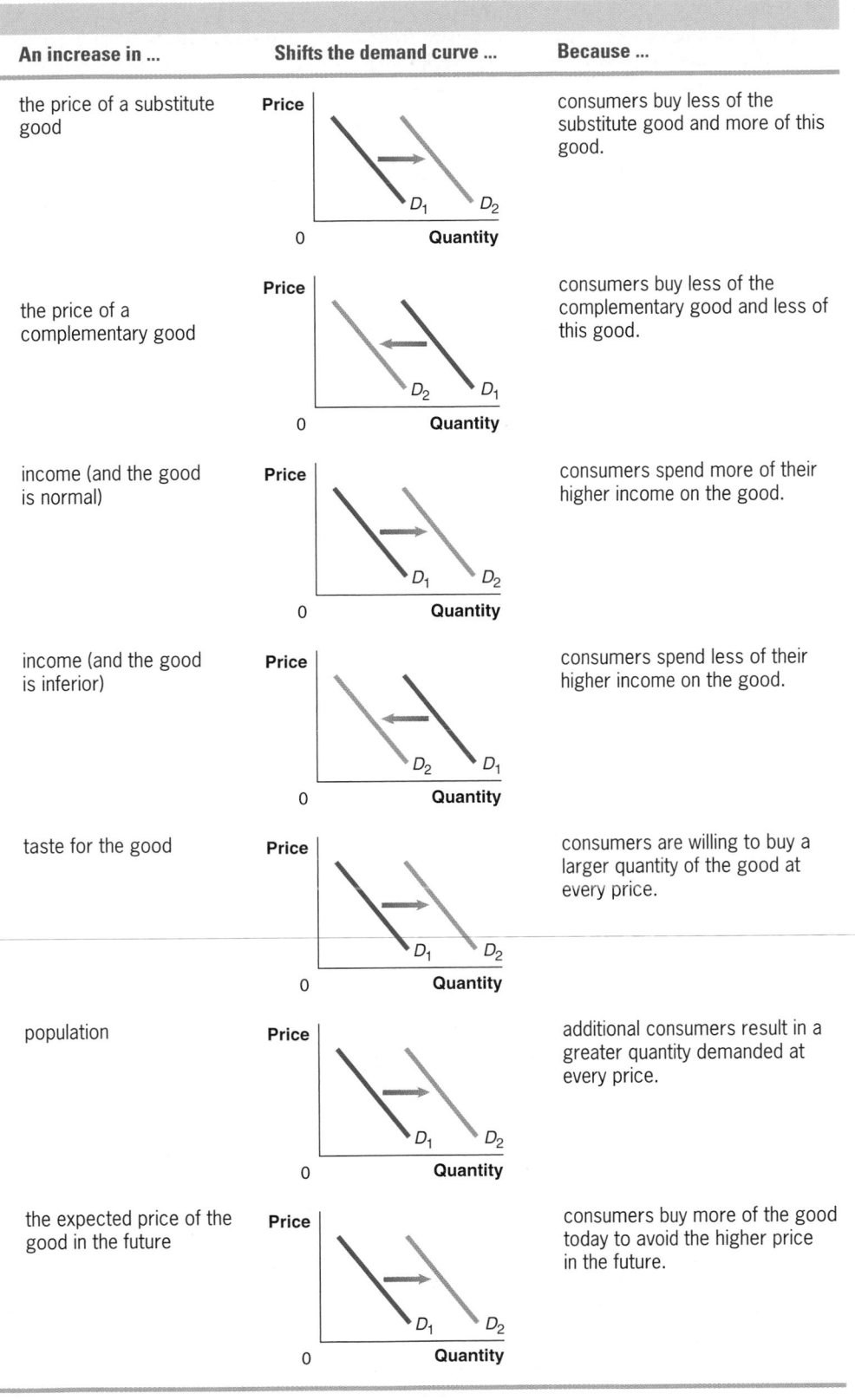

FIGURE 3-5

A Change in Demand versus a Change in the Quantity Demanded

If the price of printers falls from $175 to $150, the result will be a movement along the demand curve from point A to point B—an increase in quantity demanded from 50,000 to 60,000. If consumers' income increases, or another factor changes that makes consumers want more of the product at every price, the demand curve will shift to the right—an increase in demand. In this case, the increase in demand from D_1 to D_2 causes the quantity of printers demanded at a price of $175 to increase from 50,000 at point A to 70,000 at point C.

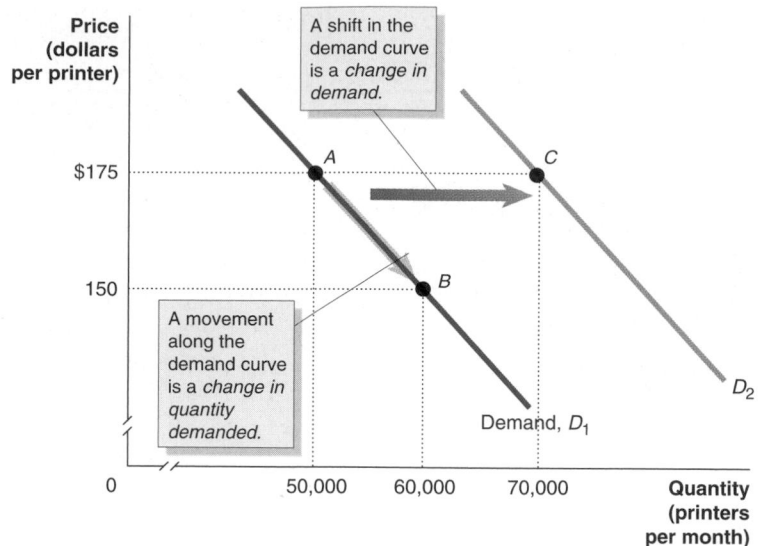

A Change in Demand versus a Change in Quantity Demanded

It is important to understand the difference between a *change in demand* and a *change in quantity demanded*. A change in demand refers to a shift of the demand curve. A shift occurs if there is a change in one of the variables, *other than the price of the product,* that affects the willingness of consumers to buy the product. A change in quantity demanded refers to a movement along the demand curve as a result of a change in the product's price. Figure 3-5 illustrates this important distinction. If the price of printers falls from $175 to $150, the result will be a movement along the demand curve from point A to point B—an increase in quantity demanded from 50,000 to 60,000. If consumers' incomes increase, or another factor changes that makes consumers want more of the product at every price, the demand curve will shift to the right—an increase in demand. In this case, the increase in demand from D_1 to D_2 causes the quantity of printers demanded at a price of $175 to increase from 50,000 at point A to 70,000 at point C.

3-3 *Making the Connection*

Estimating the Demand for Printers at Hewlett-Packard

Conceptually, it is easy to sum up individual demand curves to construct the market demand curve, as we did in Figure 3-3(d). In practice, though, economists usually estimate market demand curves directly, without estimating individual demand curves first. The most detailed information on the relationship between price and quantity demanded can be obtained from statistically estimating demand curves. The use of statistical methods to estimate economic relationships is called *econometrics*.

Forecasters at Hewlett-Packard statistically estimate demand curves using data on the quantity of printers sold, the price of printers, advertising expenditures, and other variables that can affect sales. Because characteristics of printers change very rapidly, the forecasters specifically control for shifts of the demand curve to the right as a result of improvements to the printers being offered for sale. Throughout the 1990s, Hewlett-Packard had great success with its forecasting techniques. During the 1999 Christmas season, many companies selling products on the Internet were taken by surprise by the volume of orders they received and disappointed many customers when they couldn't fill their orders. Hewlett-Packard's forecasting system, however, allowed them to avoid this problem.

Unfortunately for Hewlett-Packard, their forecasters were less successful in 2001. During the first half of that year, the demand for printers was much lower than had been forecast and the company was stuck with large numbers of unsold printers. Two events caused the shift to the left of the demand curve for printers in the first half of 2001. The first was the surprising decline in personal computer sales for use in homes and small offices, resulting from the unexpected decisions by many families and small businesses not to upgrade their existing computers. The drop in PC sales caused a drop in printer sales, because printers are a complementary good. The second event was the U.S. economy moving into recession, lowering the incomes of many consumers and reducing the profits of many businesses. As Hewlett-Packard's experiences in 2001 show, forecasting demand can greatly aid the planning of business managers but can never be perfectly accurate.

Sources: Joel Bryant and Kim Jensen, "Forecasting Inkjet Printers at Hewlett-Packard Company," *Journal of Business Forecasting*, Summer 1994; and Scott Culbertson, Jim Burruss, and Lee Buddress, "Control System Approach to E-Commerce Fulfillment: Hewlett-Packard's Experience," *Journal of Business Forecasting*, Winter 2000–2001.

Inaccurate forecasts in 2001 caused Hewlett-Packard to produce more printers than they could sell.

The Supply Side of the Market

Just as many variables influence the willingness and ability of consumers to buy a particular good or service, many variables also influence the willingness and ability of firms to sell a good or service. The most important of these variables is price. The amount of a good or service that a firm is willing and able to supply at a given price is the **quantity supplied.** Holding other variables constant, when the price of a good rises, producing the good is more profitable and the quantity supplied will increase. When the price of a good falls, the good is less profitable and the quantity supplied will decrease.

② **LEARNING OBJECTIVE**

Discuss the variables that influence supply.

Quantity supplied The amount of a good or service that a firm is willing and able to supply at a given price.

Supply Schedules and Supply Curves

A **supply schedule** is a table that shows the relationship between the price of a product and the quantity of the product supplied. The table in Figure 3-6 is a supply schedule showing the quantity of printers that Hewlett-Packard would be willing to supply per month at different prices. The graph in Figure 3-6 plots the numbers from the supply schedule as a *supply curve.* A **supply curve** shows the relationship between the price of a product and the quantity of the product supplied. The supply schedule and supply curve both show that as the price of printers rises, Hewlett-Packard will increase the quantity it supplies. At a price of $150 per printer, H-P will supply 9.5 million printers. At the higher price of $175, it will supply 10 million.

Supply schedule A table that shows the relationship between the price of a product and the quantity of the product supplied.

Supply curve A curve that shows the relationship between the price of a product and the quantity of the product supplied.

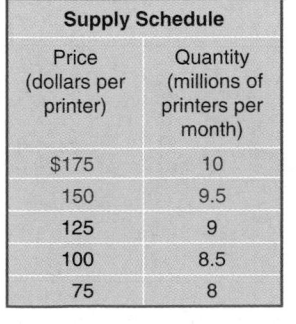

Supply Schedule	
Price (dollars per printer)	Quantity (millions of printers per month)
$175	10
150	9.5
125	9
100	8.5
75	8

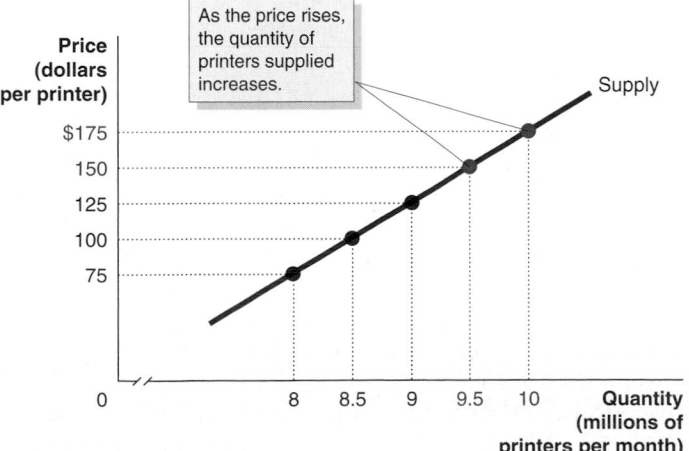

FIGURE 3-6

Hewlett-Packard's Supply Schedule and Supply Curve

As the price changes, Hewlett-Packard changes the quantity of printers it is willing to supply. We can show this as a *supply schedule* in a table, or as a *supply curve* on a graph. The supply schedule and supply curve both show that as the price of printers rises, Hewlett-Packard will increase the quantity it supplies. At a price of $150 per printer, H-P will supply 9.5 million printers. At a price of $175, it will supply 10 million.

Individual Supply and Market Supply

To construct the *market supply curve* for printers, we add the number of printers supplied at each price by each company producing printers. To keep things simple, suppose that Lexmark and Epson are the only other companies producing printers. Figure 3-7 shows that we can find the market supply curve by adding the number of printers supplied by Hewlett-Packard, Lexmark, and Epson at each price. Figure 3-7(d) at the bottom of page 75 shows the market supply curve for printers. For example, at a price of $125, Epson supplies 5 million printers, Lexmark supplies 7.5 million printers, and Hewlett-Packard supplies 9 million printers. Therefore, the quantity supplied in the market at a price of $125 is 21.5 million printers.

The Law of Supply

Law of supply Holding everything else constant, increases in price cause increases in the quantity supplied, and decreases in price cause decreases in the quantity supplied.

The market supply curve in Figure 3-7(d) is upward sloping. This pattern reflects the **law of supply**, which states that, holding everything else constant, increases in price cause increases in the quantity supplied, and decreases in price cause decreases in the quantity supplied. Notice that the definition of the law of supply—like the definition of the law of demand—contains the phrase "holding everything else constant." If only the price of the product changes, there is a movement along the supply curve, which is *an increase or decrease in the quantity supplied*. As Figure 3-8 shows, if any other variable that affects the willingness of firms to supply a good changes, the supply curve will shift, *which is an increase or decrease in supply*. When firms increase the quantity of a product they wish to sell at a given price, the supply curve shifts to the right. The shift from S_1 to S_3 represents an *increase in supply*. When firms decrease the quantity of a product they wish to sell at a given price, the supply curve shifts to the left. The shift from S_1 to S_2 represents a *decrease in supply*.

FIGURE 3-7 **Deriving the Market Supply Curve from the Individual Supply Curves**

The table shows that the total quantity supplied in a market is the sum of the quantities supplied by each seller. We can find the market supply curve by adding horizontally the individual supply curves. For example, at a price of $125, Epson supplies 5 million printers, Lexmark supplies 7.5 million printers, and Hewlett-Packard supplies 9 million printers. Therefore, the quantity supplied in the market at a price of $125 is 21.5 million printers.

	Quantity (millions of printers per month)			
Price (dollars per printer)	Epson	Lexmark	Hewlett-Packard	Market
$175	7	8.5	10	25.5
150	6	8	9.5	23.5
125	5	7.5	9	21.5
100	4	7	8.5	19.5
75	3	6.5	8	17.5

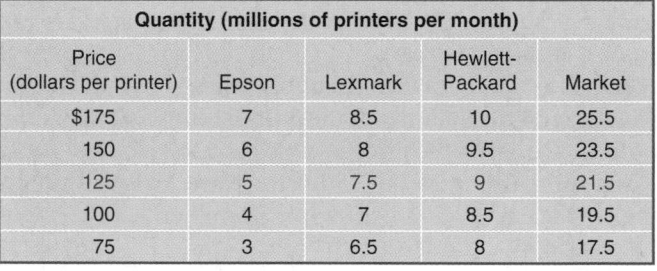

(a) Epson's supply curve

(b) Lexmark's supply curve

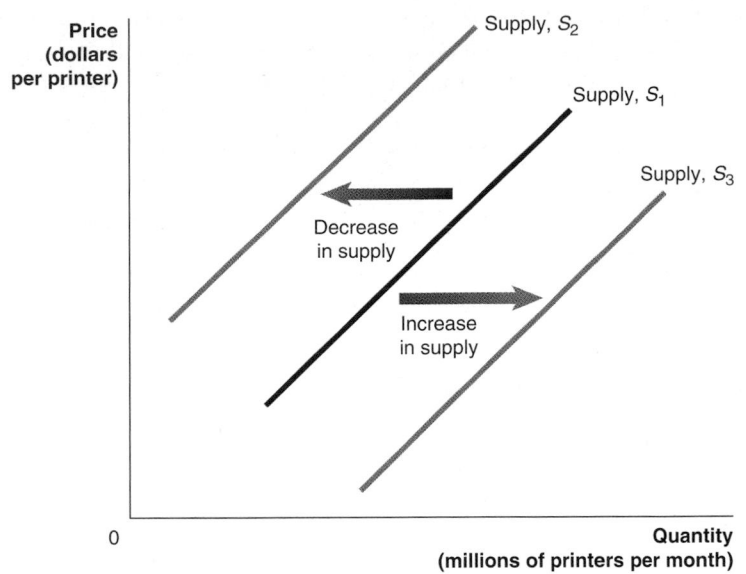

FIGURE 3-8

Shifting the Supply Curve

When firms increase the quantity of a product they wish to sell at a given price, the supply curve shifts to the right. The shift from S_1 to S_3 represents an *increase in supply.* When firms decrease the quantity of a product they wish to sell at a given price, the supply curve shifts to the left. The shift from S_1 to S_2 represents a *decrease in supply.*

Variables That Shift Supply

The following are the most important variables that shift supply:

➤ Prices of inputs
➤ Technological change
➤ Prices of substitutes in production
➤ Expected future prices
➤ Number of firms in the market

We can discuss how each of these variables affects the supply of printers.

PRICES OF INPUTS The factor most likely to cause the supply curve for a product to shift is a change in the price of an *input.* (An *input* is anything used in the production of

FIGURE 3-7   **continued**

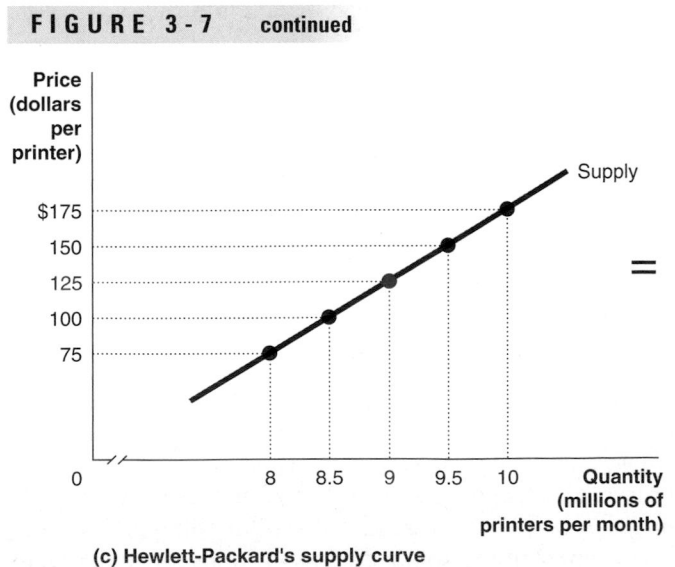

(c) Hewlett-Packard's supply curve

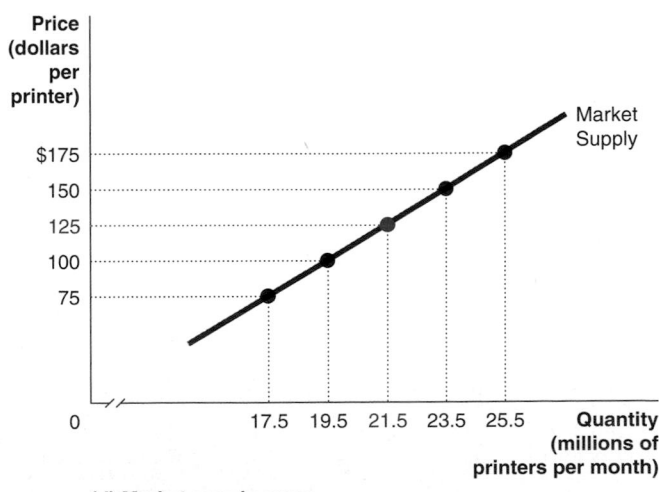

(d) Market supply curve

a good or service.) For instance, if the price of a component of laser printers, such as the laser scanner, rises, the cost of producing printers will increase and printers will be less profitable at every price. The supply of printers will decline, and the market supply curve for printers will shift to the left. Similarly, if the price of an input declines, the supply of printers will increase, and the supply curve will shift to the right.

TECHNOLOGICAL CHANGE   A second factor that causes a change in supply is *technological change*. **Technological change** is a positive or negative change in the ability of a firm to produce a given level of output with a given amount of inputs. Positive technological change occurs whenever a firm is able to produce more output using the same amount of inputs. This shift will happen when the *productivity* of workers or machines increases. If a firm can produce more output with the same amount of inputs, its costs will be lower and the good will be more profitable to produce at any given price. As a result, when positive technological change occurs, the firm will increase the quantity supplied at every price and its supply curve will shift to the right. Normally, we expect technological change to have a positive impact on a firm's willingness to supply a product. Negative technological change is relatively rare, although it could result from a natural disaster or a war that reduces the ability of a firm to supply as much output with a given amount of inputs. Negative technological change will raise a firm's costs, and the good will be less profitable to produce. Therefore, negative technological change causes a firm's supply curve to shift to the left.

PRICES OF SUBSTITUTES IN PRODUCTION   Firms often choose which good or service they will produce. Alternative products that a firm could produce are called *substitutes in production*. For instance, if the price of color printers increases, color printers will become more profitable and Hewlett-Packard, Lexmark, and the other printer companies will shift some of their productive capacity away from black-and-white printers toward color printers. They will offer fewer black-and-white printers for sale at every price, so the supply curve for black-and-white printers will shift to the left.

EXPECTED FUTURE PRICES   If a firm expects that the price of its product will be higher in the future than it is today, it has an incentive to decrease supply now and increase it in the future. For instance, if Hewlett-Packard believes that printer prices are temporarily low—perhaps because of a price war among firms making printers—it may store some of its production today to sell tomorrow when it expects prices will be higher.

NUMBER OF FIRMS IN THE MARKET   Finally, a change in the number of firms in the market will change supply. When new firms *enter* a market, the supply curve shifts to the right, and when existing firms leave, or *exit*, a market, the supply curve shifts to the left. For instance, when Xerox decided that it would no longer produce printers for home use, the market supply curve shifted to the left.

Table 3-2 summarizes the most important variables that cause market supply curves to shift. You should note that the table shows the shift in the supply curve that results from an *increase* in each of the variables. A *decrease* in these variables would cause the supply curve to shift in the opposite direction.

A Change in Supply versus a Change in Quantity Supplied

We noted earlier that it is important to understand the difference between a change in demand and a change in quantity demanded. It is also important to understand the difference between a *change in supply* and a *change in quantity supplied*. A change in supply refers to a shift of the supply curve. The supply curve will shift when there is a change in one of the variables, *other than the price of the product,* that affects the willingness of suppliers to sell the product. A change in quantity supplied refers to a movement along the

Technological change A positive or negative change in the ability of a firm to produce a given level of output with a given amount of inputs.

TABLE 3-2

Variables That Shift Market Supply Curves

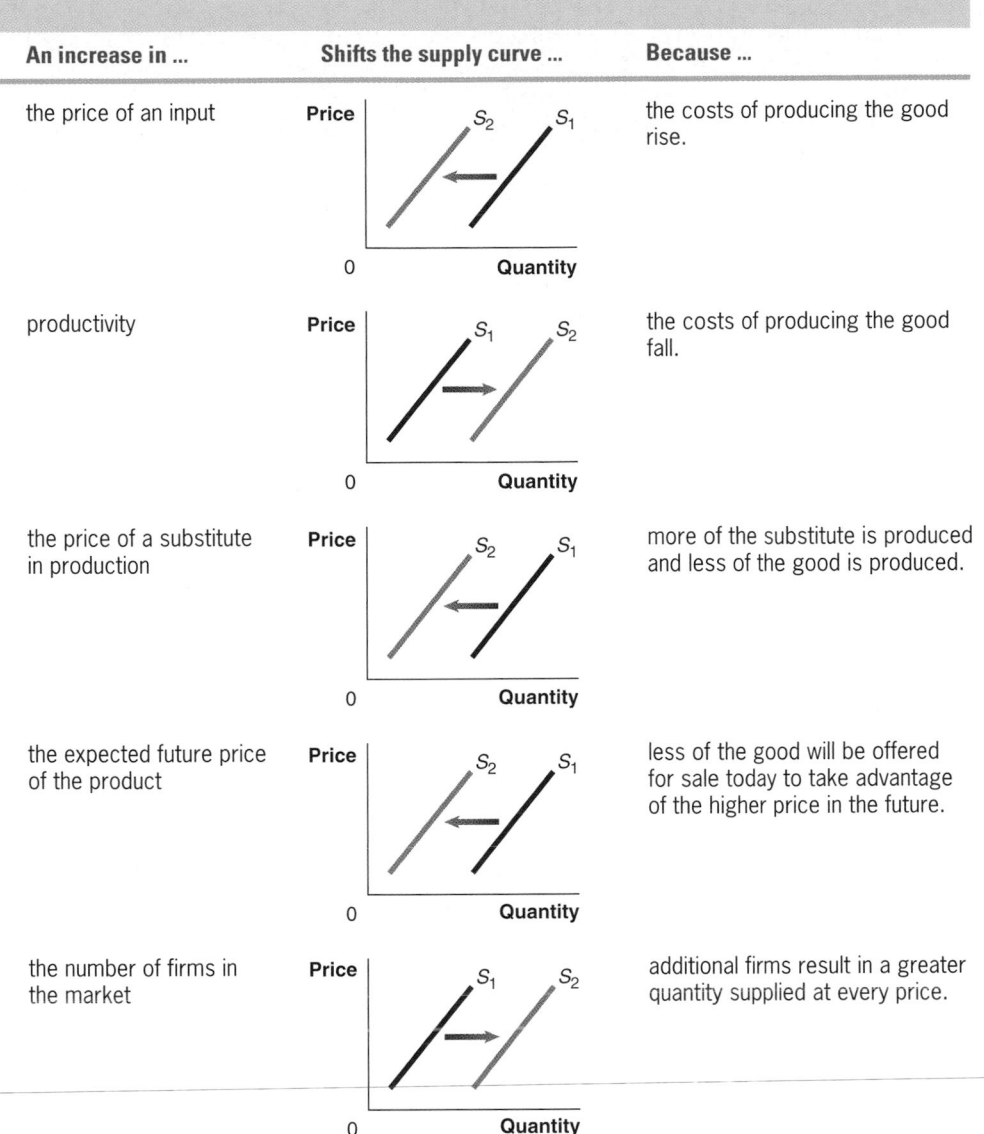

An increase in ...	Shifts the supply curve ...	Because ...
the price of an input		the costs of producing the good rise.
productivity		the costs of producing the good fall.
the price of a substitute in production		more of the substitute is produced and less of the good is produced.
the expected future price of the product		less of the good will be offered for sale today to take advantage of the higher price in the future.
the number of firms in the market		additional firms result in a greater quantity supplied at every price.

supply curve as a result of a change in the product's price. Figure 3-9 illustrates this important distinction. If the price of printers rises from $125 to $150, the result will be a movement up the supply curve from point *A* to point *B*—an increase in quantity supplied from 21.5 million to 23.5 million. If the price of an input decreases or another factor makes sellers supply more of the product at every price change, the supply curve will shift to the right—an increase in supply. In this case, the increase in supply from S_1 to S_2 causes the quantity of printers supplied at a price of $150 to increase from 23.5 million at point *B* to 27.0 million at point *C*.

Market Equilibrium: Putting Demand and Supply Together

The purpose of markets is to bring buyers and sellers together. As we saw in Chapter 2, instead of being chaotic and disorderly, the interaction of buyers and sellers in markets ultimately results in firms being led to produce those goods and services most desired by consumers. To understand how this process happens, we first need to see how markets manage to reconcile the plans of buyers and sellers.

③ LEARNING OBJECTIVE
Use a graph to illustrate market equilibrium.

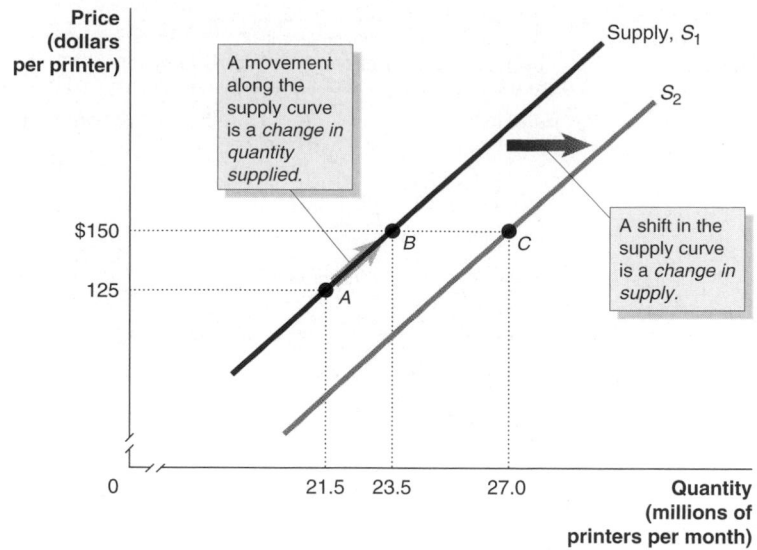

A Change in Supply versus a Change in the Quantity Supplied

If the price of printers rises from $125 to $150, the result will be a movement up the supply curve from point *A* to point *B*—an increase in quantity supplied from 21.5 million to 23.5 million. If the price of an input decreases or another factor changes that makes sellers supply more of the product at every price, the supply curve will shift to the right—an increase in supply. In this case, the increase in supply from S_1 to S_2 causes the quantity of printers supplied at a price of $150 to increase from 23.5 million at point *B* to 27.0 million at point *C*.

Market equilibrium A situation in which quantity demanded equals quantity supplied.

Competitive market equilibrium A market equilibrium with many buyers and many sellers.

In Figure 3-10, we bring together the market demand curve for printers and the market supply curve. Notice that the demand curve crosses the supply curve at only one point. This point represents a price of $100 and a quantity of 19.5 million printers. Only at this point is the quantity of printers consumers are willing to buy equal to the quantity of printers firms are willing to sell. This is the point of **market equilibrium**. Only at market equilibrium will the quantity demanded equal the quantity supplied. In this case, the *equilibrium price* is $100 and the *equilibrium quantity* is 19.5 million. Markets that have many buyers and many sellers are *competitive markets*, and equilibrium in these markets is a **competitive market equilibrium**.

How Markets Eliminate Surpluses and Shortages

A market that is not in equilibrium moves toward equilibrium. Once a market is in equilibrium, it remains in equilibrium. To see why, consider what happens if a market is not

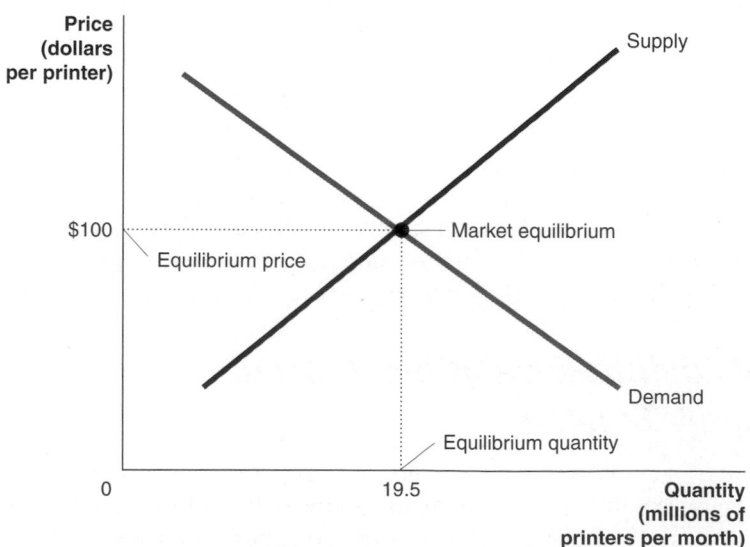

Market Equilibrium

Where the demand curve crosses the supply curve determines market equilibrium. In this case, the demand curve for printers crosses the supply curve at a price of $100 and a quantity of 19.5 million. Only at this point is the quantity of printers consumers are willing to buy equal to the quantity of printers firms are willing to sell: The quantity demanded is equal to the quantity supplied.

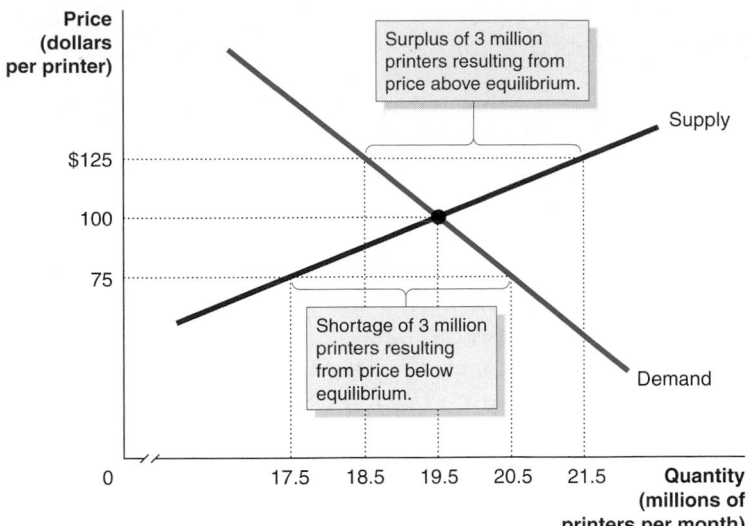

FIGURE 3-11

The Effect of Surpluses and Shortages on the Market Price

When the market price is above equilibrium, there will be a *surplus*. In the figure, a price of $125 for printers results in 21.5 million being supplied, but only 18.5 million being demanded, or a surplus of 3 million. As firms cut the price to dispose of the surplus, the price will fall to the equilibrium of $100. When the market price is below equilibrium, there will be a *shortage*. A price of $75 results in 20.5 million printers being demanded, but only 17.5 million being supplied, or a shortage of 3 million. As consumers who are unable to buy a printer offer to pay higher prices, the price will rise to the equilibrium of $100.

in equilibrium. For instance, suppose that the price in the printer market was $125, rather than the equilibrium price of $100. As Figure 3-11 shows, at a price of $125, the quantity of printers supplied would be 21.5 million and the quantity of printers demanded would be 18.5 million. When the quantity supplied is greater than the quantity demanded, there is a **surplus** in the market. In this case, the surplus is equal to 3 million printers (21.5 million − 18.5 million = 3 million). When there is a surplus, firms have unsold goods piling up, which gives them an incentive to increase their sales by cutting the price. Cutting the price will simultaneously increase the quantity demanded and decrease the quantity supplied. This adjustment will reduce the surplus, but as long as the price is above $100, there will be a surplus and downward pressure on the price will continue. Only when the price has fallen to $100 will the market be in equilibrium.

If, however, the price were $75, the quantity supplied would be 17.5 million and the quantity demanded would be 20.5 million, as shown in Figure 3-11. When the quantity demanded is greater than the quantity supplied, there is a **shortage** in the market. In this case, the shortage is equal to 3 million printers (20.5 million − 17.5 million = 3 million). When a shortage occurs, some consumers will be unable to obtain the product and will have an incentive to offer to buy the product at a higher price. A higher price will simultaneously increase the quantity supplied and decrease the quantity demanded. This adjustment will reduce the shortage, but as long as the price is below $100, there will be a shortage and upward pressure on the price will continue. Only when the price has risen to $100 will the market be in equilibrium.

At a competitive market equilibrium, all consumers willing to pay the market price will be able to buy as much of the product as they want, and all firms willing to accept the market price will be able to sell as much of the product as they want. As a result, there will be no reason for the price to change unless either the demand curve or the supply curve shifts.

Surplus A situation in which the quantity supplied is greater than the quantity demanded.

Shortage A situation in which the quantity demanded is greater than the quantity supplied.

Demand and Supply Both Count

Always keep in mind that it is the interaction of demand and supply that determines the equilibrium price. Neither consumers nor firms can dictate what the equilibrium price will be. No firm can sell anything at any price unless it can find a willing buyer, and no consumer can buy anything at any price without finding a willing seller.

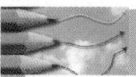

③ **LEARNING OBJECTIVE**

Use a graph to illustrate market equilibrium.

Demand and Supply Both Count: A Tale of Two Letters

Which letter is likely to be worth more: one written by Abraham Lincoln or one written by his assassin, John Wilkes Booth? Lincoln is one of the greatest presidents, and many people collect anything written by him. The demand for letters written by Lincoln surely would seem to be much greater than the demand for letters written by Booth. Yet when R. M. Smythe and Co. auctioned off on the same day a letter written by Lincoln and a letter written by Booth, the Booth letter sold for $31,050 and the Lincoln letter sold for only $21,850. Use a demand and supply graph to explain how the Booth letter has a higher market price than the Lincoln letter, even though the demand for letters written by Lincoln is greater than the demand for letters written by Booth.

Solving the Problem:

Step 1: Review the chapter material. This problem is about prices being determined at market equilibrium, so you may want to review the section "Market Equilibrium: Putting Demand and Supply Together," which begins on page 77.

Step 2: Draw demand curves that illustrate the greater demand for Lincoln's letters. Begin by drawing two demand curves. Label one "Demand for Lincoln's letters" and the other "Demand for Booth's letters." Make sure that the Lincoln demand curve is much farther to the right than the Booth demand curve.

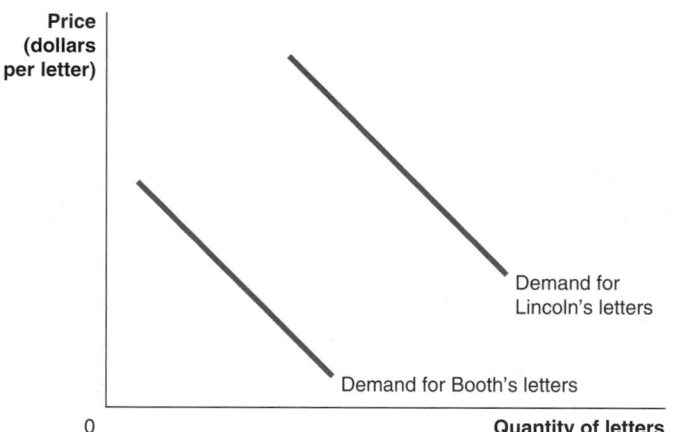

Step 3: Draw supply curves that illustrate the equilibrium price of Booth's letters being higher than the equilibrium price of Lincoln's letters. Based on the demand curves you have just drawn, think about how it might be possible for the market price of Lincoln's letters to be lower than the market price of Booth's letters. The only way this can be true is if the supply of Lincoln's letters is much greater than the supply of Booth's letters. Draw on your graph a supply curve for Lincoln's letters and a supply curve for Booth's letters that will result in an equilibrium price of Booth's letters of $31,050 and an equilibrium price of Lincoln letters of $21,850. You have now solved the problem.

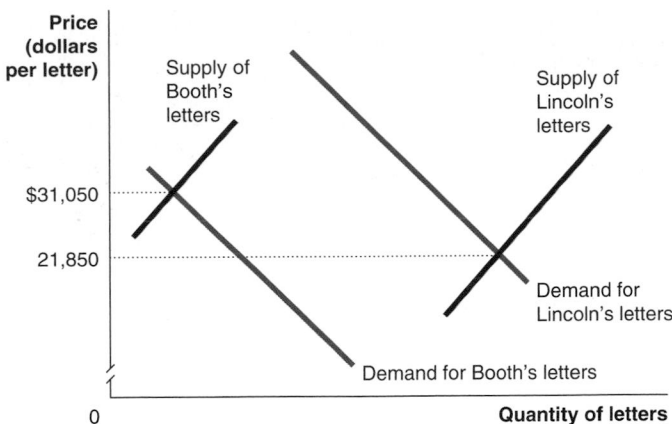

Extra Credit: The explanation for this puzzle is that both demand and supply count when determining market price. The demand for Lincoln's letters is much greater than the demand for Booth's letters, but the supply of Booth's letters is very small. Historians believe that only eight letters written by Booth exist today. (Note that the supply curves for letters written by Booth and by Lincoln slope up even though only a fixed number of each of these types of letters is available and, obviously, no more can be produced. The upward slope of the supply curves occurs because the higher the price, the larger the quantity of letters that will be offered for sale by people who currently own them.)

YOUR TURN: For more practice, do problem 9 on page 92 at the end of this chapter. Visit www.prenhall.com/hubbard for an interactive exercise related to this Solved Problem.

The Effect of Demand and Supply Shifts on Equilibrium

④ LEARNING OBJECTIVE
Use demand and supply graphs to predict changes in prices and quantities.

We have seen that the interaction of demand and supply in markets determines the quantity of a good that is produced and the price at which it sells. We have also seen that several variables cause demand curves to shift, and other variables cause supply curves to shift. As a result, demand and supply curves in most markets are constantly shifting, and the prices and quantities that represent equilibrium are constantly changing. In this section, we see how shifts in demand and supply curves affect equilibrium price and quantity.

The Effect of Shifts in Supply on Equilibrium

When Xerox decided to stop producing printers for the home market, the market supply curve for printers shifted to the left. Figure 3-12 shows the supply curve shifting from S_1 to S_2. This caused a shortage of printers at the original equilibrium price, P_1. The shortage was eliminated as the equilibrium price of printers rose to P_2, and the equilibrium quantity fell from Q_1 to Q_2. If new firms enter the printer market, the supply curve will shift to the right, causing the equilibrium price to fall and the equilibrium quantity to rise.

FIGURE 3-12

The Effect of a Decrease in Supply on Equilibrium

If a firm exits a market, as Xerox did from the market for home printers, the equilibrium price will rise and the equilibrium quantity will fall.

1. As Xerox exits the market for printers, a smaller quantity of printers will be supplied at every price, so the market supply curve shifts to the left from S_1 to S_2, which causes a shortage of printers at the original price, P_1.
2. The equilibrium price rises from P_1 to P_2.
3. The equilibrium quantity falls from Q_1 to Q_2.

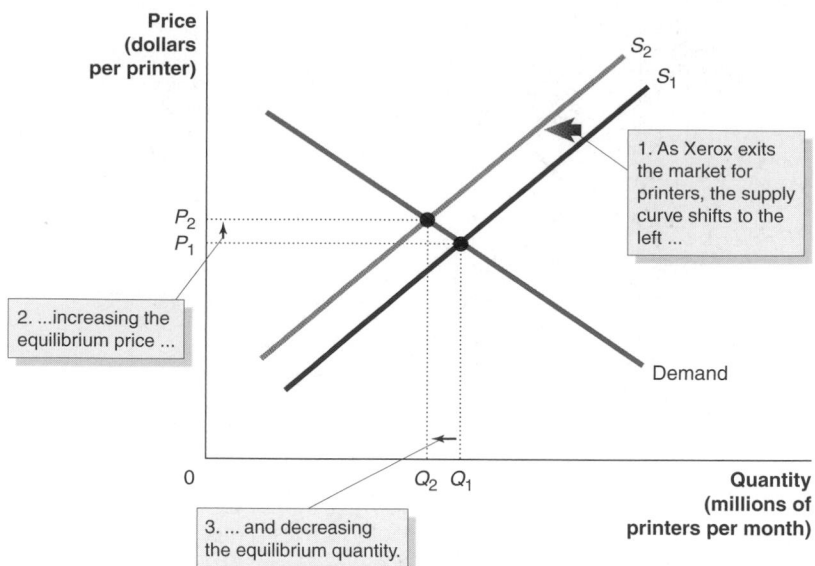

3-4 Making the Connection

The Falling Price of Large Flat-Screen Televisions

Research on flat-screen televisions using liquid crystal displays (LCDs) began in the 1960s. However, it was surprisingly difficult to use this research to produce a television priced low enough for many consumers to purchase. One researcher noted, "In the 1960s, we used to say 'In ten years, we're going to have the TV on the wall.' We said the same thing in the seventies and then in the eighties." A key technical problem in manufacturing LCD televisions was making glass sheets large enough, thin enough, and clean enough to be used as LCD screens. Finally, in 1999, Corning, Inc., developed a process to manufacture glass less than 1 millimeter thick that was very clean because it was produced without being touched by machinery.

Corning's breakthrough led to what the *Wall Street Journal* described as a "race to build new, better factories." The firms producing the flat screens are all located in Taiwan, South Korea, and Japan. The leading firms are Korea's Samsung Electronics and LG Phillips LCD, Taiwan's AU Optronics, and Japan's Sharp Corporation. In 2004, AU Optronics opened a new factory with 2.4 million square feet of clean room in which the LCD screens are manufactured. This factory is nearly five times as large as the largest factory in which Intel makes computer chips. In all, 10 new factories manufacturing LCD screens were scheduled to come into operation between late 2004 and late 2005. The figure shows that this increase in supply was expected to drive the

Corning's breakthrough spurred the manufacture of LCD televisions in Taiwan, South Korea, and Japan, and an eventual decline in price.

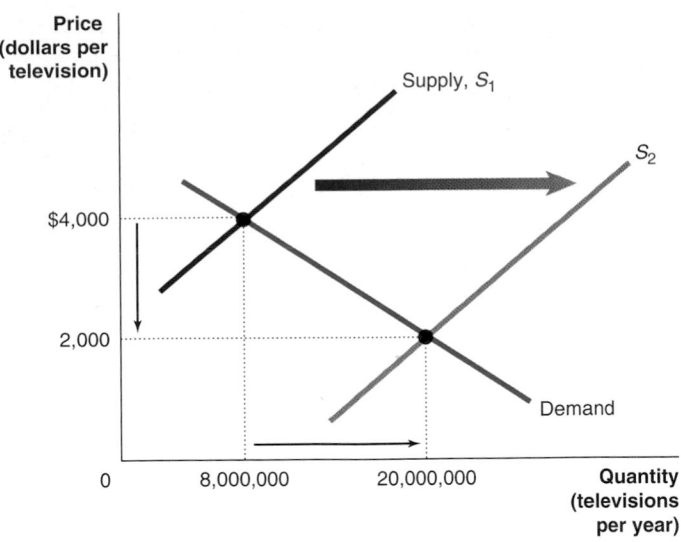

price of a typical large LCD television from $4,000 in the fall of 2004 to $2,000 in 2006, increasing the quantity demanded worldwide from 8,000,000 to 20,000,000.

Sources: Evan Ramstad, "Big Display: Once a Footnote, Flat Screens Grow into Huge Industry," *Wall Street Journal*, August 30, 2004, p. A1; and Michael Schuman, "Flat Chance: Prices on Cool TVs Are Dropping as New Factories Come on Line," *Time*, October 18, 2004, pp. 64–66.

The Effect of Shifts in Demand on Equilibrium

When population growth and income growth occur, the market demand for printers shifts to the right. Figure 3-13 shows the effect of a demand curve shifting to the right from D_1 to D_2. This shift causes a shortage at the original equilibrium price, P_1. To eliminate the shortage, the equilibrium price rises to P_2, and the equilibrium quantity rises from Q_1 to Q_2. However, if the price of a complementary good, such as personal computers, were to rise, the demand for printers would decrease. This change would cause the demand curve for printers to shift to the left, and the equilibrium price and quantity would both decrease.

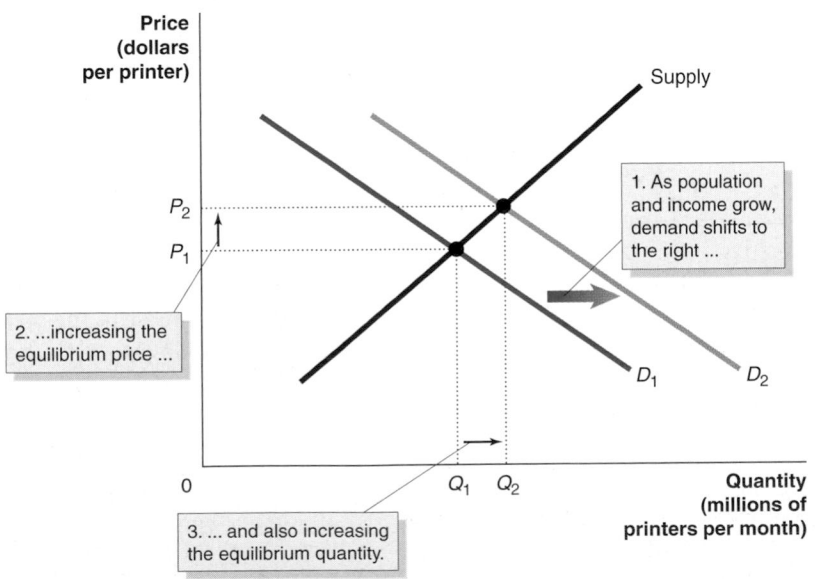

FIGURE 3-13

The Effect of an Increase in Demand on Equilibrium

Increases in income and population will cause the equilibrium price and quantity to rise.

1. As population and income grow, the quantity demanded increases at every price, and the market demand curve shifts to the right from D_1 to D_2, which causes a shortage of printers at the original price, P_1.
2. The equilibrium price rises from P_1 to P_2.
3. The equilibrium quantity rises from Q_1 to Q_2.

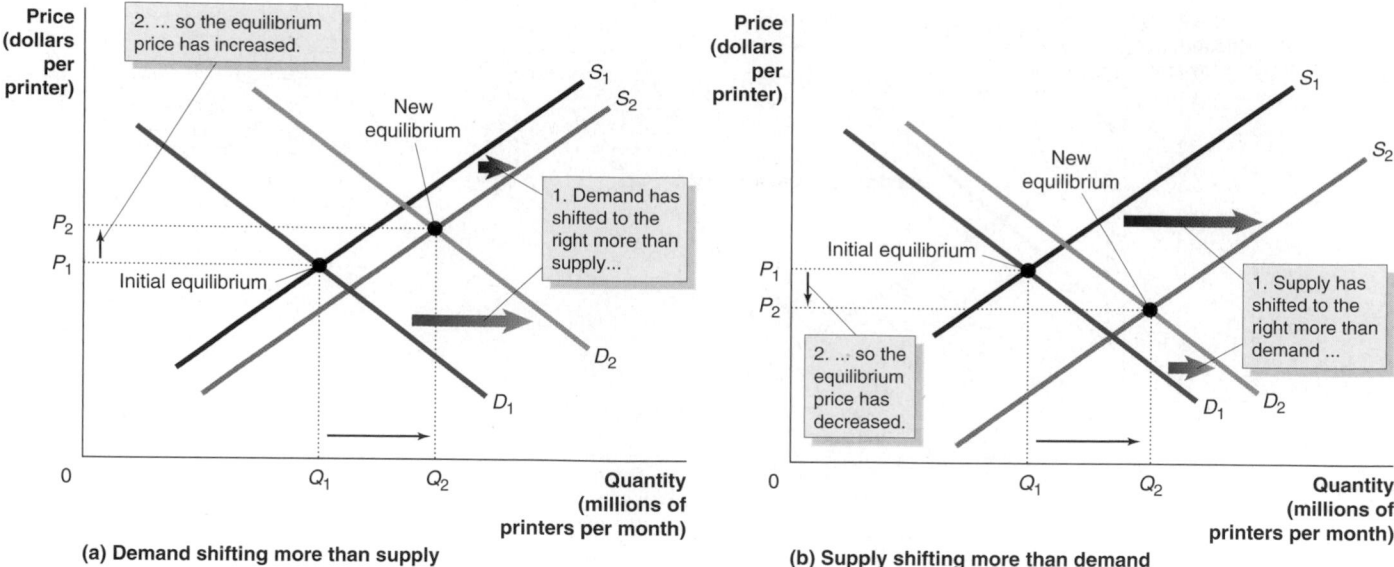

(a) Demand shifting more than supply

(b) Supply shifting more than demand

FIGURE 3-14 **Shifts in Demand and Supply over Time**

Whether the price of a product rises or falls over time depends on whether or not demand shifts to the right more than supply.
In panel (a), demand shifts to the right more than supply and the equilibrium price rises.
1. Demand shifts to the right more than supply.
2. Equilibrium price rises from P_1 to P_2.

In panel (b), supply shifts to the right more than demand and the equilibrium price falls.
1. Supply shifts to the right more than demand.
2. Equilibrium price falls from P_1 to P_2.

The Effect of Shifts in Demand and Supply over Time

Whenever only demand or only supply shifts, we can easily predict the effect on equilibrium price and quantity. But what happens if *both* curves shift? For instance, in many markets, the demand curve shifts to the right over time, as population and income grow. The supply curve also often shifts to the right as new firms enter the market and positive technological change occurs. Whether the equilibrium price in a market rises or falls over time usually depends on whether demand shifts to the right more than does supply. Panel (a) of Figure 3-14 shows that when demand shifts to the right more than supply, the equilibrium price rises. But, as panel (b) shows, when supply shifts to the right more than demand, the equilibrium price falls.

For instance, during the 1990s the demand for chicken increased rapidly, as many consumers attempted to avoid the potential health problems associated with eating too much red meat. At the same time, according to a U.S. Department of Agriculture report, positive technological change occurred in the "feed, hatchery, processing, and breeding stages" of producing chickens. Whether the retail price of chicken would be higher in 2000 than it was in 1991 depended on whether the increase in the demand for chicken was greater or smaller than the increase in the supply. Figure 3-15 shows that, in fact, demand shifted farther to the right than did supply, and the retail price of chicken rose from an average of $0.88 per pound in 1991 to an average of $1.07 per pound in 2000.

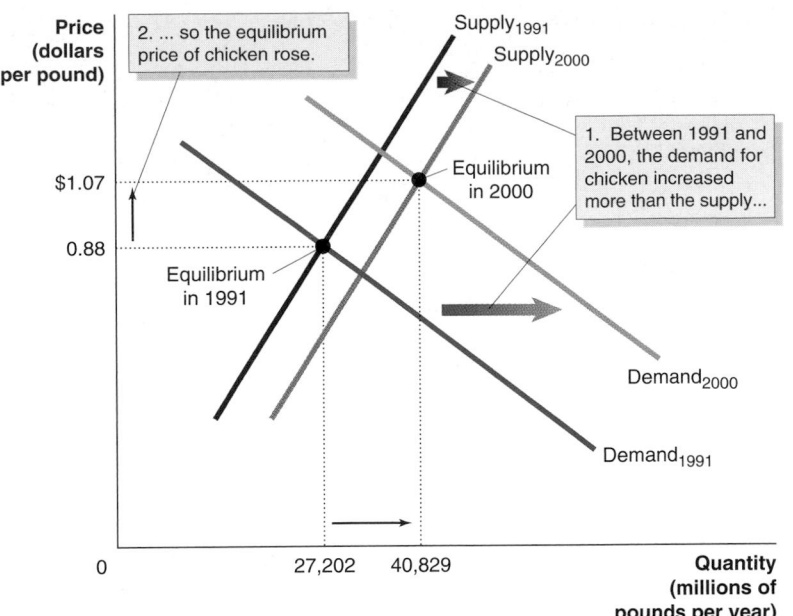

FIGURE 3-15

The Demand for Chicken Has Increased More Than the Supply

The supply of chicken increased rapidly during the 1990s, but the demand increased even faster. The result was that the equilibrium price of chicken rose. (The prices have been adjusted for the effects of inflation.)
1. Between 1991 and 2000, the demand for chicken shifted to the right more than supply.
2. The equilibrium price of chicken rose from $0.88 per pound in 1991 to $1.07 per pound in 2000.

SOLVED PROBLEM   3-2

High Demand and Low Prices in the Lobster Market?

During the spring when demand for lobster is relatively low, Maine lobster fishermen are able to sell their lobster catches for about $4.50 per pound. During the summer when demand for lobster is much higher, Maine lobster fishermen are able to sell their lobster catches for only about $3.00 per pound. It may seem strange that the market price is higher when demand is low than when demand is high. Can you resolve this paradox with the help of a demand and supply graph?

④ LEARNING OBJECTIVE

Use demand and supply graphs to predict changes in prices and quantities.

Solving the Problem:
Step 1: Review the chapter material. This problem is about how shifts in demand and supply curves affect the equilibrium price, so you may want to review the section "The Effects of Shifts in Demand and Supply over Time," which begins on page 84.

Step 2: Draw the demand and supply graph. Draw a demand and supply graph, showing the market equilibrium in the spring. Label the equilibrium price $4.50. Label both the demand and supply curves "spring."

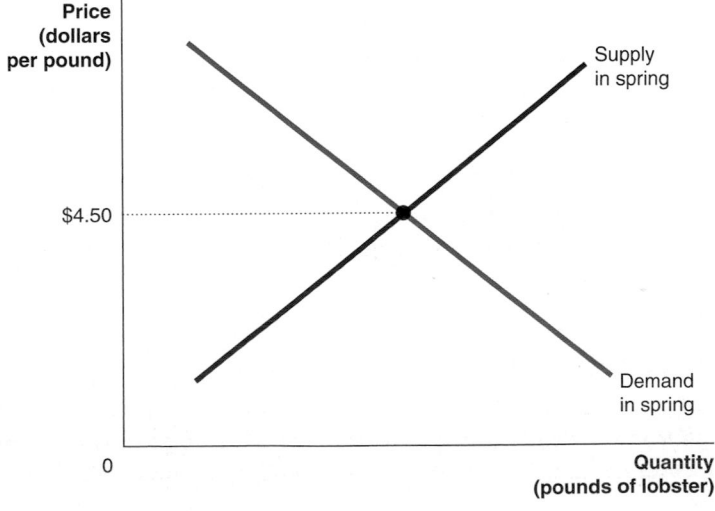

Step 3: Add a demand curve for summer to your graph.

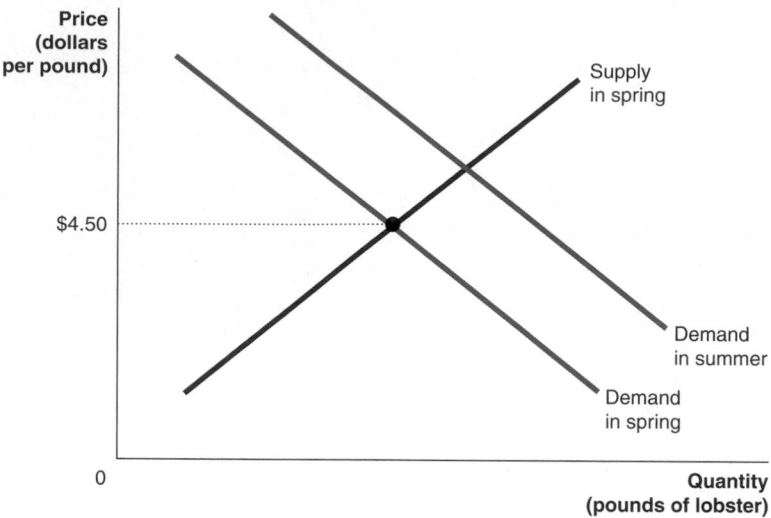

Step 4: Explain the graph. After studying the graph, it is possible to see how the equilibrium price can fall from $4.50 to $3.00 despite the increase in demand: The supply curve must have shifted to the right by enough so that the new equilibrium price is $3.00. Draw in this new supply curve, label it "summer," and label the new equilibrium price $3.00. The demand for lobster does increase in summer compared with the spring. But the increase in the supply of lobster between spring and summer is even greater. So, the equilibrium price falls.

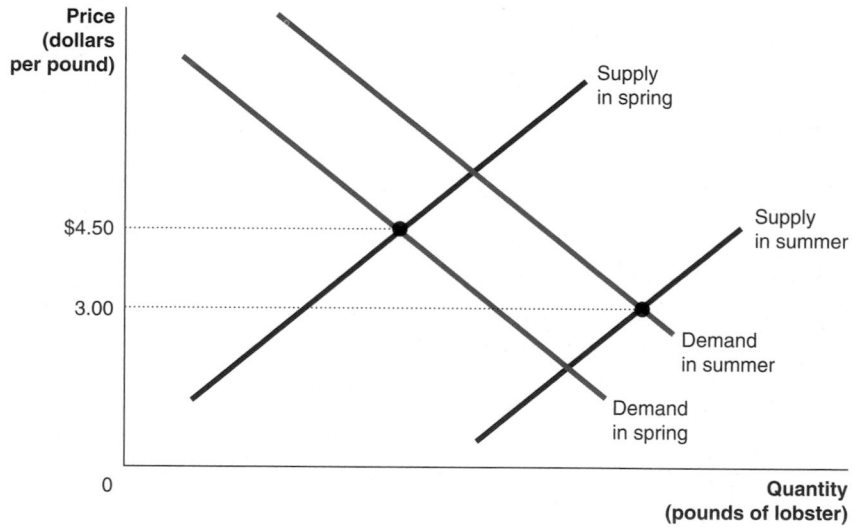

Source: Carey Goldberg, "Down East, the Lobster Hauls Are Up Big," *New York Times*, May 31, 2001.

YOUR TURN: For more practice, do related problem 13 on page 92 at the end of this chapter. Visit www.prenhall.com/hubbard for an interactive exercise related to this Solved Problem.

Shifts in a Curve versus Movements along a Curve

When analyzing markets using demand and supply curves, it is important to remember that *when a shift in a demand or supply curve causes a change in equilibrium price, the change in price does not cause a further shift in demand or supply.* For instance, suppose an

Don't Let This Happen To You!

Remember: A Change in a Good's Price Does *Not* Cause the Demand or Supply Curve to Shift.

Suppose a student is asked to draw a demand and supply graph to illustrate how an increase in the price of oranges would affect the market for apples, other things being constant. He draws the graph below and explains it as follows: "Because apples and oranges are substitutes, an increase in the price of oranges will cause an initial shift to the right in the demand curve for apples from D_1 to D_2. However, because this initial shift in the demand curve for apples results in a higher price for apples, P_2 consumers will find apples less desirable and the demand curve will shift to the

left from D_2 to D_3, resulting in a final equilibrium price of P_3." Do you agree or disagree with the student's analysis?

You should disagree. The student has correctly understood that an increase in the price of oranges will cause the demand curve for apples to shift to the right. But the second demand curve shift the student describes, from D_2 to D_3, will not take place. Changes in the price of a product do not result in shifts in the product's demand curve. Changes in the price of a product result only in movements along a demand curve.

YOUR TURN: Test your understanding by doing related problems 6 and 23 on pages 91 and 94 at the end of this chapter.

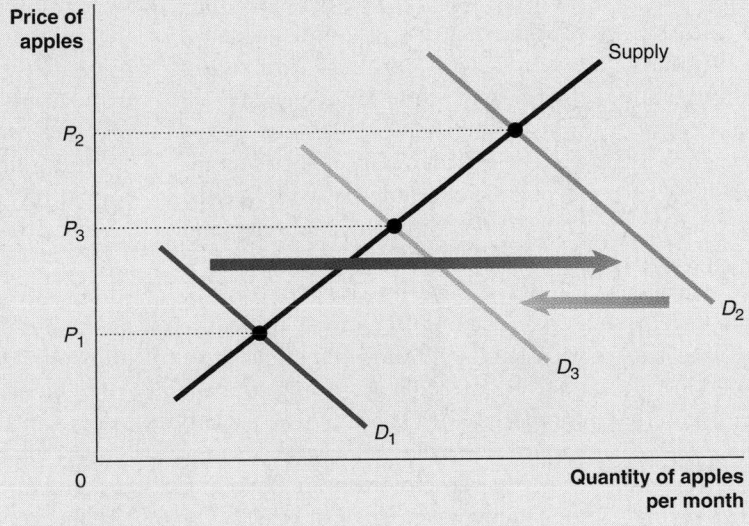

increase in supply causes the price of a good to fall, while everything else that affects the willingness of consumers to buy the good is constant. The result will be an increase in the quantity demanded, but not an increase in demand. For demand to increase, the whole curve must shift. The point is the same for supply: If the price of the good falls, but everything else that affects the willingness of sellers to supply the good is constant, the quantity supplied decreases but not the supply. For supply to decrease, the whole curve must shift.

Conclusion

The interaction of demand and supply determines market equilibrium. When many buyers and many sellers participate in the market, the result is a competitive market equilibrium. In a competitive market equilibrium, all consumers willing to pay the market price will be able to buy as much of the good as they want, and all firms willing to accept the market price will be able to sell as much of the product as they want. The model of demand and supply provides us with a powerful tool for predicting how changes in the actions of consumers and firms will cause changes in equilibrium prices and quantities. We will use the model of demand and supply in the next chapter to evaluate consumer surplus, producer surplus, price floors, and price ceilings. Before moving on, read *An Inside Look* on the next page to learn about H-P's strategy for competing with Dell.

WALL STREET JOURNAL, MAY 12, 2004

Picking a Big Fight with Dell, H-P Cuts PC Profits Razor-Thin

In the past decade, Dell Inc. has surpassed International Business Machines Corp., Gateway Inc., and Compaq Computer Corp., riding direct sales and ruthless efficiency to become the world's largest seller of personal computers.

Two years ago, Hewlett-Packard Co. looked like the next victim. Instead, H-P is fighting back, briefly overtaking Dell in PC sales late last year, and drawing Dell into a bloody war of attrition in which consumers are the big winners.

a H-P's radical strategy for challenging Dell: selling PCs without worrying about profit.

"We think the PC business is strategic," says Chief Executive Carly Fiorina. She says she is willing to allow the company's $22 billion computer division to do little more than break even because PC sales help H-P make money on printers, consulting and consumer electronics. . . .

The result is the biggest threat yet to Dell, the PC industry's most profitable company. Having acquired Compaq in 2002, H-P is using its size to slash prices, in an attempt to undercut Dell's formula for gleaning profits in one of the nation's most competitive markets.

Still, for H-P, the strategy is a serious gamble. By cutting prices, the company earns less on each sale, leaving it with less of a cushion to absorb the inevitable shocks that roil competitive markets. H-P's profit margins in its PC division haven't exceeded 1% since the merger.

Dell continues to post solid profits; its operating profit margins of more than 8% are the widest in the industry. But its executives are complaining that H-P is subsidizing its PC business with earnings from other divisions, which to some suggests Dell is beginning to feel H-P's heat.

b The subsidies impair "the economics of the overall industry," adds Michael S. Dell, the company's founder and chairman. "It's not a healthy process."

It is healthy for customers. Personal-computer prices industry-wide fell by 9% during the first three quarters of 2003, according to Dell, compared with 4.5% a year earlier. Laptop prices fell even faster.

Corporate customers are exploiting the competition. Late last year, Getty Images, the Seattle photo distributor, asked H-P and Dell to compete for a sale of 500 desktop computers and 165 laptops. Kenneth Stringer, Getty's vice president of technical operations, specified how much he expected to pay for each computer.

"They both said, 'OK, we're ready to go there,' " Mr. Stringer says. But then H-P offered free advice for improving Getty's disaster-recovery plan and creating a digital archive of more than 70,000 film clips.

With $73 billion in annual sales, H-P offers a broader line of goods and services than Dell, with $41 billion in sales. And H-P isn't shy about tapping other parts of its empire to help sell PCs. Its credit arm offers generous financing terms. The consulting unit advises customers on how to save money on their technology operations . . .

c Only a few years ago . . . neither H-P nor Compaq could match Dell's mastery of the computer industry's central dynamic: falling prices. Most PCs are assembled from standard parts that all manufacturers buy at similar prices. Technological advances continually shrink the cost of disk drives, display screens and computer chips. . . .

Beginning in the mid-1990s, Dell turned this to its advantage. It flourished by building computers to order and selling them directly to consumers and businesses over the telephone and the Internet. Dell PCs are built only after a sale is made, with components procured at the cheapest prices available . . .

As Dell was thriving, executives from H-P and Compaq mapped out plans to take the company on, even before H-P's $19 billion acquisition of Compaq became final.

The team made plans to stop losing money in the soon-to-be-combined PC units of the two companies, agreeing to cut costs and close weak businesses as soon as the deal closed in May 2002.

Within months, H-P had shaved an average of $26 from the cost of building a PC, compared with Compaq's pre-merger costs, according to an H-P executive.

The result: H-P cut losses in the PC unit by roughly two-thirds in the fiscal year ended October 2002. . . .

In the fourth quarter of last year, H-P sold more computers than Dell . . .

But the victory would soon be reversed, as Dell retook the lead in the first quarter of 2004. . . .

Key Points in the Article

The article discusses the rivalry between Dell and Hewlett-Packard. Hewlett-Packard is willing to sell PCs for a little or no profit, because selling PCs increases demand for complementary products, such as printers. The article also notes that personal computer prices fell during 2003, as they have every year since 1981. These price declines result from positive technological change that reduces the cost of making PCs, and shifts the market supply curve to the right.

Analyzing the News

a Hewlett-Packard management sees PCs playing a strategic role in their plan to maximize profits for Hewlett-Packard as a whole. Printers, consulting provided to firms purchasing PCs, and consumer electronics are all complementary goods to PCs. We can use the economic model of demand and supply developed in this chapter to analyze this strategy.

Because PCs and printers are complementary goods, a decease in the price of PCs will cause an increase in the demand for print-

ers. This pattern is shown in Figure 1, where the demand curve for printers shifts from D_1 to D_2. This causes a shortage of printers at the original price, P_1. To eliminate the shortage, the equilibrium price increases from P_1 to P_2, and the equilibrium quantity increases from Q_1 to Q_2.

b Hewlett-Packard's strategy of increasing printer sales by reducing PC prices has no guarantee of success. Because Dell's own profits are made primarily from selling PCs, rather than related products, it is unlikely to pursue a strategy similar to H-P's. When Michael Dell complains that H-P's strategy is hurting "the economics of the overall industry," he means that the low prices H-P is charging for PCs hurts the profits of all PC makers. In fact, as discussed in the opener to this chapter, one of the reasons that Carly Fiorina was ousted as chief executive officer in 2005 was that H-P's board of directors became dissatisfied with the inability of the firm to earn significant profits from selling personal computers.

c Positive technological change reduces the cost of making PCs. The article notes that: "Technological advances continually shrink the cost of disk drives, display screens and

computer chips." Reductions in cost make PCs more profitable to produce at every price. This causes the supply of PCs to increase, or shift to the right. This pattern is shown in Figure 2, where the supply curve for PCs shifts from S_1 to S_2. This causes a surplus of PCs at the original price, P_1. To eliminate the surplus, the equilibrium price decreases from P_1 to P_2, and the equilibrium quantity increases from Q_1 to Q_2.

Thinking Critically

1. Suppose Dell Inc., IBM, and *Gateway* Inc., simply refused to cut their prices as a result of Hewlett-Packard's strategy. What would happen to the quantity of computers sold by these companies?

2. Further suppose that one manufacturer's computers were not particularly good substitutes for another's. How would that affect your answer to the previous question?

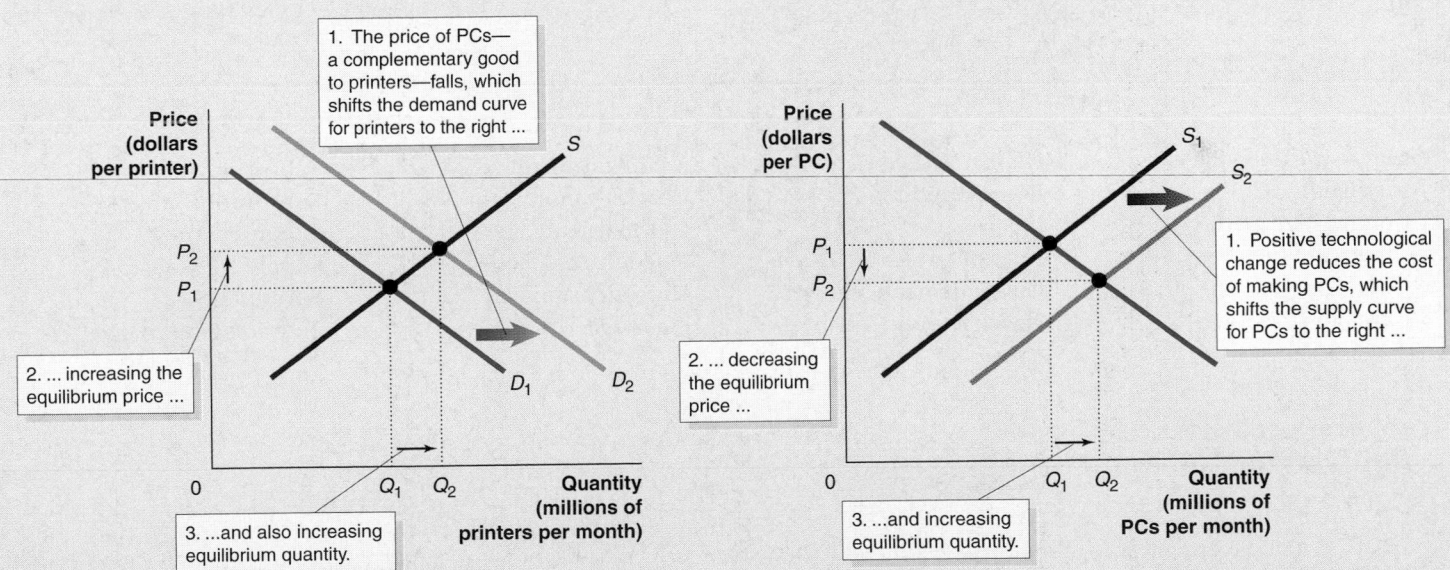

Figure 1: The fall in the price of PCs causes the demand for printers to shift to the right.

Figure 2: A fall in the cost of PCs shifts the supply curve for PCs to the right.

SUMMARY

LEARNING OBJECTIVE ① Discuss the variables that influence demand. The types and quantities of goods and services produced ultimately depend on the desires of consumers. A *demand curve* is a graph showing the relationship between the price of a good and the quantity of the good consumers are willing and able to buy over a period of time. We can find the market demand curve by adding horizontally the individual demand curves of each buyer. The *law of demand* states that *ceteris paribus*—holding everything else constant—the quantity of a product demanded increases when the price falls and decreases when the price rises. Changes in the prices of related goods, income, tastes, population and demographics, and expected future prices all cause the demand curve to shift. Demand curves always slope downward. A *change in demand* refers to a shift of the demand curve. A *change in quantity demanded* refers to a movement along the demand curve as a result of a change in the product's price.

LEARNING OBJECTIVE ② Discuss the variables that influence supply. When the price of a product rises, producing the product is more profitable and a greater amount will be supplied. The *law of supply* states that, holding everything else constant, the quantity of a product supplied increases when the price rises and decreases when the price falls. Changes in the prices of inputs, technology, the prices of substitutes in production, expected future prices, and the number of firms in a market all cause the supply curve to shift. A *change in supply* refers to a shift of the supply curve. A *change in quantity supplied* refers to a movement along the supply curve as a result of a change in the product's price.

LEARNING OBJECTIVE ③ Use a graph to illustrate market equilibrium. *Market equilibrium* occurs where the supply curve intersects the demand curve. Only at this point is the quantity supplied equal to the quantity demanded. Prices above equilibrium result in *surpluses*, which cause the market price to fall. Prices below equilibrium result in *shortages*, which cause the market price to rise.

LEARNING OBJECTIVE ④ Use demand and supply graphs to predict changes in prices and quantities. In most markets, demand and supply curves shift frequently, causing changes in equilibrium prices and quantities. Over time, if demand increases more than supply, equilibrium price will rise. If supply increases more than demand, equilibrium price will fall.

KEY TERMS

Ceteris paribus ("all else equal") 67	Demand schedule 64	Market demand 65	Substitutes 68
Competitive market equilibrium 78	Demographics 70	Market equilibrium 78	Substitution effect 67
Complements 68	Income effect 67	Normal good 69	Supply curve 73
Demand curve 64	Inferior good 69	Quantity demanded 64	Supply schedule 73
	Law of demand 66	Quantity supplied 73	Surplus 79
	Law of supply 74	Shortage 79	Technological change 76

REVIEW QUESTIONS

1. In a market system, who ultimately decides which goods and services will be produced?

2. What do economists mean when they use the Latin expression *ceteris paribus*?

3. What is the difference between a change in demand and a change in quantity demanded?

4. What is the law of demand? What are the main variables that will cause the demand curve to shift? Give an example of each.

5. What is the law of supply? What are the main variables that will cause a supply curve to shift? Give an example of each.

6. What do economists mean by "market equilibrium"? What will happen in a market if the current price is above the equilibrium price? What will happen if the current price is below the equilibrium price?

7. What happens to the equilibrium price in a market if the demand curve shifts to the right? Draw a demand and supply graph to illustrate your answer.

8. What happens to the equilibrium price in a market if the supply curve shifts to the left? Draw a demand and supply graph to illustrate your answer.

9. If, over time, the demand curve for a product shifts to the right more than the supply curve does, what will happen to the equilibrium price? What will happen to the equilibrium price if the supply curve shifts to the right more than the demand curve? For each case, draw a demand and supply graph to illustrate your answer.

PROBLEMS AND APPLICATIONS

Please visit **www.prenhall.com/hubbard** *for solutions to the even-numbered problems as well as multiple-choice and true or false self-assessment quizzes.*

1. Suppose the market for ice cream cones is made up of three consumers: Pedro, Curt, and Tim. Use the information in the following table to construct the market demand curve for ice cream cones. Show the information in a table and in a graph.

	PEDRO	CURT	TIM
PRICE	QUANTITY DEMANDED (CONES PER WEEK)	QUANTITY DEMANDED (CONES PER WEEK)	QUANTITY DEMANDED (CONES PER WEEK)
$1.75	2	1	0
1.50	4	3	2
1.25	6	4	3
1.00	7	6	4
0.75	9	7	5

2. For each of the following pairs of products, state which are complements, which are substitutes, and which are unrelated.
   a. Pepsi and Coke
   b. Oscar Mayer hot dogs and Wonder hot dog buns
   c. Jiffy peanut butter and Smucker's strawberry jam
   d. Hewlett-Packard printers and Texas Instruments hand calculators

3. State whether each of the following events will result in a movement along the demand curve for McDonald's Big Mac hamburgers or whether it will cause the curve to shift. If the demand curve shifts, indicate whether it will shift to the left or to the right and draw a graph to illustrate the shift.
   a. The price of Burger King's Whopper hamburger declines.
   b. McDonald's distributes coupons for $1.00 off on a purchase of a Big Mac.
   c. Because of a shortage of potatoes, the price of French fries increases.
   d. Kentucky Fried Chicken raises the price of a bucket of fried chicken.

4. Is it possible for a good to be an inferior good for one person and a normal good for another person? If it is possible, can you cite some examples?

5. Suppose the data in the following table present the price of a base model Ford Explorer sports utility vehicle and the number of Explorers sold. Do these data indicate that the demand curve for Explorers is upward sloping? Explain.

YEAR	PRICE	QUANTITY
2003	$27,865	325,265
2004	28,325	330,648
2005	28,765	352,666

6. [Related to *Don't Let This Happen To You!*] A student writes the following: "Increased production leads to a lower price, which in turn increases demand." Do you agree with his reasoning? Briefly explain.

7. Following are four graphs and four market scenarios, each of which would cause either a movement along the supply curve for Pepsi or a shift of the supply curve. Match each scenario with the appropriate diagram.
   a. A decrease in the supply of Coke
   b. Average household income in the United States drops from $42,000 to $41,000
   c. An improvement in soft-drink bottling technology
   d. An increase in the price of sugar

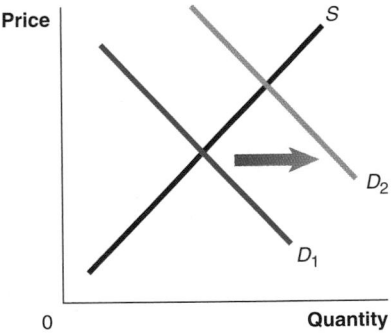

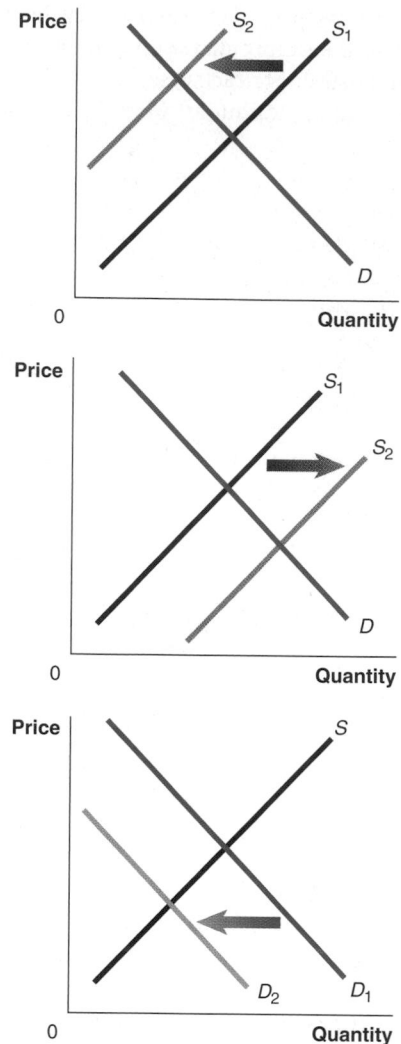

8. Suppose the pizza industry is made up of three firms: The Mark Company, Mike, Inc., and Bill Enterprises. Use the information in the following table to construct the market supply curve for pizzas. Show the information in a table and in a graph.

PRICE	MARK QUANTITY SUPPLIED (PIZZAS PER WEEK)	MIKE QUANTITY SUPPLIED (PIZZAS PER WEEK)	BILL QUANTITY SUPPLIED (PIZZAS PER WEEK)
$5.00	25	30	20
5.50	30	40	25
5.75	35	50	30
6.00	40	60	35
6.25	45	70	40

9. **[Related to *Solved Problem 3–1*]** In *The Wealth of Nations*, Adam Smith discussed what has come to be known as the "diamond and water paradox":

Nothing is more useful than water: but it will purchase scarce anything; scarce anything can be had in exchange for it. A diamond, on the contrary, has scarce any value in use; but a very great quantity of other goods may frequently be had in exchange for it.

Graph the market for diamonds and the market for water. Show how it is possible for the price of water to be much lower than the price of diamonds, even though the demand for water is much greater than the demand for diamonds.

10. Briefly explain under what conditions zero would be the equilibrium quantity.

11. According to an article in the *New York Times*, "Sales of DVD's in the United States have risen dramatically since the discs first went on the market in 1997, thanks in part to a drop in the price of DVD players." Draw a demand and supply graph for the DVD market and use it to show the effect on this market of a decline in the price of DVD players. Now draw a demand and supply graph for the VCR market and use it to show the effect on this market of a decline in the price of DVD players. On both graphs, make sure to indicate the equilibrium price and quantity before and after the decline in the price of DVD players.
Source: Rick Lyman, "Revolt in the Den: DVD Sends the VCR Packing to the Attic," *New York Times*, August 26, 2002.

12. A recent study indicated that "Stricter college alcohol policies, such as raising the price of alcohol, or banning alcohol on campus, decrease the number of students who use marijuana."
   a. On the basis of this information, are alcohol and marijuana substitutes or complements?
   b. Suppose that campus authorities reduce the supply of alcohol on campus. Use demand and supply graphs to illustrate the impact on the campus alcohol and marijuana markets.
Source: Jenny Williams, Rosalie Pacula, Frank Chaloupka, and Henry Wechsler, "Alcohol and Marijuana Use Among College Students: Economic Complements or Substitutes?" *Health Economics*, Volume 13, Issue 9, September 2005, pages 825–843.

13. **[Related to *Solved Problem 3-2*]** The demand for watermelons is highest during summer and lowest during winter. Yet watermelon prices are normally lower in summer than in winter. Use a demand and supply graph to demonstrate how this is possible. Be sure to carefully label the curves in your graph and to clearly indicate the equilibrium summer price and the equilibrium winter price.

14. The following appeared in the *Wall Street Journal:* "U.S. farmers are headed for the lowest corn harvest since 1997, but the soybean crop is expected to reach an all-time high. Prices for both crops are expected to rise." Draw demand and supply graphs illustrating the market for corn and the market for soybeans. Show the impact of a larger soybean crop on the equilibrium price in each market. Holding

everything else constant, what must be happening to the demand for soybeans for the equilibrium price of soybeans to rise?

15. According to an article in the *Wall Street Journal*, the price of flat-screen televisions fell between 2001 and 2004 from more than $8,000 to about $3,000. During that period Sharp, Matsushita Electric Industrial, and Samsung all began producing flat-screen televisions. Use a demand and supply graph to explain what happened to the quantity of flat-screen televisions sold during this period.
Source: Evan Ramstad and Gary McWilliams, "Flat-TV Prices Are Falling," *Wall Street Journal*, November 3, 2004, p. 81.

16. According to an article in the *New York Times*, during the summer of 2001 in San Francisco the quantity supplied of commercial real estate space—such as space in office buildings—was four million square feet more than the quantity of commercial real estate space demanded. Draw a demand and supply graph illustrating the San Francisco commercial real estate market. Predict what was likely to happen to rents for office space in San Francisco.
Source: Matt Richtel, "A City Takes a Breath after the Dot-Com Crash," *New York Times*, July 24, 2001.

17. During the late 1990s many consumers were having their vision problems corrected by laser surgery. An article in the *Wall Street Journal* in early 2001 noted two developments in the market for laser eye surgery. The first was about increasing concerns related to side effects from the surgery, including blurred vision and, occasionally, blindness. The second development was that the companies renting eye-surgery machinery to doctors had reduced their charges. One large company had cut its charge from $250 per patient to $100. Use a demand and supply graph to illustrate the effects of these two developments on the market for laser eye surgery.
Source: Laura Johannes and James Bandler, "Slowing Economy, Safety Concerns Zap Growth in Laser Eye Surgery," *Wall Street Journal*, January 8, 2001, p. B1.

18. Following the September 11, 2001, terrorist attacks, automobile companies became worried that the demand for new cars would decline. To maintain their sales, they reduced the prices of new cars. The following chart shows the effect this had on the prices of some *used* cars:

VEHICLE	PERCENTAGE CHANGE IN PRICE, JULY TO NOVEMBER
2000 Cadillac de Ville	−11.3%
1998 Lexus LS540	−12.2
1999 BMW 3231	−11.3
1999 Chevrolet Tahoe	−14.0
2000 Ford Explorer	−15.9
2000 Ford F-Series	−11.4

Explain why the prices of used cars fell in these circumstances. Use a demand and supply graph of the used car market to illustrate your answer.

19. The market for autographs, including letters or other documents signed by famous people, is subject to frequent large price changes, as are markets for most collectibles. The following table is adapted from one originally appearing in an article in the *Wall Street Journal*. It gives the 1997 price for an autograph, the 2001 price, and a brief comment by the *Wall Street Journal* reporter. Use the information contained in the Comment Column of the table to draw a demand and supply graph for each of the three autographs listed that can account for the change in its market price from 1997 to 2001.

AUTOGRAPH	1997 PRICE	2001 PRICE	COMMENT
The Beatles	$2,500	$7,475	"As boomers get rich, so do prices for pieces . . . signed by the Fab Four."
Princess Diana	14,000	2,000	"Demand rose after her death in 1997, but now the market's full of items like her signed Christmas cards."
Robert E. Lee	200,000	100,000	"The Civil War's out."

Source: Brooks Barnes, "Signature Market: Hard to Read," *Wall Street Journal*, July 13, 2001.

20. Historically, the production of many perishable foods, such as dairy products, was highly seasonal. Thus, as the supply of those products fluctuated, prices tended to fluctuate tremendously—typically by 25 to 50 percent or more—over the course of the year. One impact of mechanical refrigeration, which was commercialized on a large scale in the last decade of the nineteenth century, was that suppliers could store perishables from one season to the next. Economists have estimated that as a result of refrigerated storage, wholesale prices rose by roughly 10 percent during peak supply periods, while they fell by almost the same amount during the off season. Use a demand and supply graph for each season to illustrate how refrigeration affected the market for perishable food.
Source: Lee A. Craig, Barry Goodwin, and Thomas Grennes, "The Effect of Mechanical Refrigeration on Nutrition in the U.S.," *Social Science History*, Vol. 28, No. 2 (Summer 2004), pp. 327–328.

21. Briefly explain whether each of the following statements is true or false.
   a. If the demand and supply for a product both increase, the equilibrium quantity of the product must also increase.
   b. If the demand and supply for a product both increase, the equilibrium price of the product must also increase.

c. If the demand for a product decreases and the supply of the product increases, the equilibrium price of the product may increase or decrease, depending upon whether supply or demand has shifted by more.

22. According to an article in the *Wall Street Journal,* "Online auctioneers like eBay are having a huge impact on the price of fame. After Cal Ripken Jr. announced his retirement from baseball . . . dozens of Ripken-autographed game jerseys, baseball cards and Wheaties boxes flooded the online bazaar." Use a demand and supply graph to illustrate the impact of eBay on the equilibrium price of Cal Ripken memorabilia.

23. **[Related to** *Don't Let This Happen To You!***]** A student was asked to draw a demand and supply graph to illustrate the effect on the personal computer market of a fall in the price of computer hard drives, *ceteris paribus.* She drew the graph below and explained it as follows:

> Hard drives are an input to personal computers, so a fall in the price of hard drives will cause the supply curve for personal computers to shift to the right (from S_1 to S_2). Because this shift in the supply curve results in a lower price (P_2), consumers will want to buy more personal computers and the demand curve will shift to the right (from D_1 to D_2). We know that more personal computers will be sold, but we can't be sure whether the price of personal computers will rise or fall. That depends on whether the supply curve or the demand curve has shifted farther to the right. I assume that the effect on supply is greater than the effect on demand, so I show the final equilibrium price (P_3) as being lower than the initial equilibrium price (P_1).

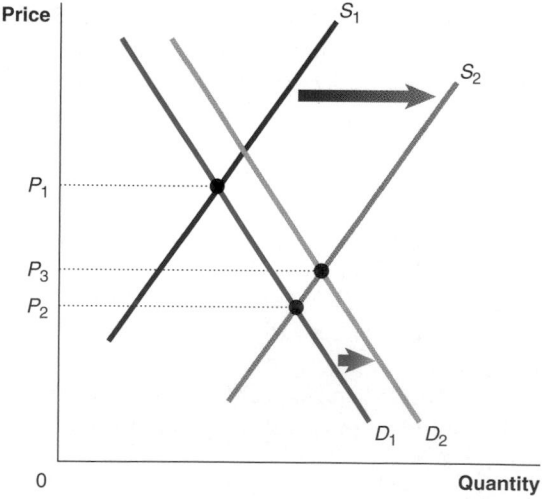

Explain whether you agree or disagree with the student's analysis. Be careful to explain exactly what—if anything— you find wrong with her analysis.

24. David Surdam, an economist at Loyola University of Chicago, makes the following observation of the world cotton market at the beginning of the Civil War:

> [A]s the supply of American-grown raw cotton decreased and the price of raw cotton increased, there would be a *movement along* the supply curve of non-American raw cotton suppliers and the quantity supplied by these producers would increase.

Illustrate this observation with one demand and supply graph for the market for American-grown cotton and another demand and supply graph for the market for non-American cotton. Make sure that your graphs clearly show: (1) the initial equilibrium before the decrease in the supply of American-grown cotton and (2) the final equilibrium. Also clearly show any shifts in the demand and supply curves for each market.

Source: David G. Surdam, "King Cotton: Monarch or Pretender? The State of the Market for Raw Cotton on the Eve of the American Civil War," *The Economic History Review,* Vol. 51, No. 1 (February 1998), p. 116.

25. Proposals have been made to increase government regulation of childcare businesses by, for instance, setting education requirements for childcare workers. Suppose that these regulations increase the quality of childcare and cause the demand for childcare services to increase. At the same time, assume that complying with the new government regulations increases the costs of childcare businesses. Draw a demand and supply graph to illustrate the effects of these changes in the market for childcare services. Briefly explain whether the total quantity of childcare services purchased will increase or decrease as a result of regulation.

26. Below are the supply and demand functions for two markets. One of the markets is for BMW automobiles, and the other is for a cancer-fighting drug, without which lung cancer patients will die. Briefly explain which diagram most likely represents which market.

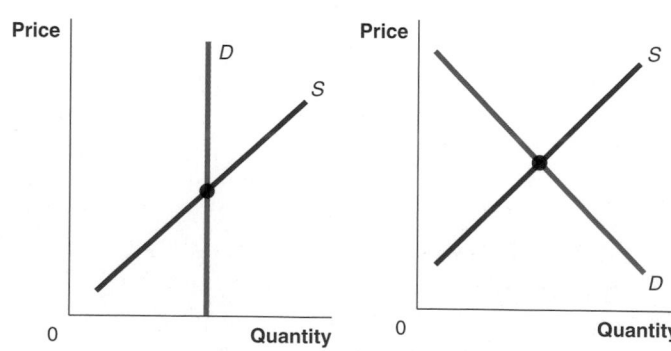

chapter

four

Economic Efficiency, Government Price Setting, and Taxes

Should the Government Control Apartment Rents?

➤ Robert F. Moss owns one apartment building in New York City. He deals with more government red tape than the average businessperson. Unlike most business owners, for example, he is not free to charge the prices he would like for the service he offers. In New York, San Francisco, Los Angeles, and nearly 200 smaller cities, apartments are subject to rent control by the local government. Rent control puts a ceiling on the maximum rent that landlords can charge for an apartment.

About one million of New York City's two million apartments are subject to rent control. The other one million apartments have their rents determined in the market by the demand and supply for apartments.

Mr. Moss's building includes apartments that are rent-controlled and apartments that are not. The market-determined rents are usually far above the controlled rents. The government regulations that determine what rent Mr. Moss can charge for a rent-controlled apartment are very complex. The following is Mr. Moss's description:

[W]hen [an apartment] is vacated state rent laws entitle landlords to raise rents in three primary ways: a vacancy increase of 20 percent for a new tenant's two-year lease (a bit less for a one-year lease); one-fortieth per month of the cost of any improvements, and a "longevity bonus" for longtime residents (calculated at six-tenths

of 1 percent times the tenant's last legal rent multiplied by the number of years of residency beyond eight). . . . (Apartments renting for $2,000 a month are automatically deregulated if they are vacant. Occupied apartments whose rent reaches that figure can be deregulated if the income of the tenants has been $175,000 or more for two years.)

Needless to say, a businessperson who earns a living by renting out apartments in one or two buildings in New York has to deal with much more complex government regulation of prices than a businessperson who owns, say, a McDonald's restaurant.

After studying this chapter, you should be able to:

① Understand the concepts of consumer surplus and producer surplus.

② Understand the concept of economic efficiency, and use a graph to illustrate how economic efficiency is reduced when a market is not in competitive equilibrium.

③ Use demand and supply graphs to analyze the economic impact of price ceilings and price floors.

④ Use demand and supply graphs to analyze the economic impact of taxes.

Larger companies also struggle with the complexity of rent control regulations. This was the case for several companies that built multiple apartment buildings in New York during the 1970s. In exchange for renting apartments to moderate- and low-income tenants at controlled rents, the companies were allowed to charge market rents after 20 years. Unfortunately for the companies, when the 20 years were over, attempts to start charging market rents were often met with lawsuits from unhappy tenants. In 2004, New York Mayor Michael Bloomberg proposed that the law be changed to keep many of these apartment buildings under rent control.

Tenants in rent-controlled apartments in New York are very reluctant to see rent control end because rents for rent-controlled apartments are much lower than rents for apartments that aren't rent-controlled. It turns out, however, that rent control actually drives up the rents of apartments that aren't rent controlled. *An Inside Look* on page 118 shows how a magazine reporter and his family ended up paying a higher rent for an apartment in New York than they would have if there had been no rent control.

Source: Robert F. Moss, "A Landlord's Lot Is Sometimes Not an Easy One," *New York Times*, August 3, 2003, Section 11, p. 1.

Price ceiling A legally determined maximum price that sellers may charge.

Price floor A legally determined minimum price that sellers may receive.

➤ We saw in Chapter 3 that, in a competitive market, the price adjusts to ensure that the quantity demanded equals the quantity supplied. Stated another way, in equilibrium, every consumer willing to pay the market price is able to buy as much of the product as the consumer wants and every firm willing to accept the market price can sell as much as it wants. Despite this, consumers would naturally prefer to pay a lower price, and sellers would prefer to receive a higher price. Normally, consumers and firms have no choice but to accept the equilibrium price if they wish to participate in the market. Occasionally, however, consumers succeed in having the government impose a **price ceiling,** which is a legally determined maximum price that sellers may charge. Rent control is an example of a price ceiling. Firms also sometimes succeed in having the government impose a **price floor,** which is a legally determined minimum price that sellers may receive. In markets for farm products such as milk, the government has been setting price floors that are above the equilibrium market price since the 1930s.

Another way in which the government intervenes in markets is by imposing taxes. The government relies on the revenue raised from taxes to finance its operations. As we will see, though, imposing taxes alters the equilibrium in a market.

Unfortunately, whenever the government imposes a price ceiling, a price floor, or a tax, there are predictable negative economic consequences. It is important for government policymakers and for voters to understand these negative consequences when evaluating the effects of these policies. Economists have developed the concepts of *consumer surplus, producer surplus,* and *economic surplus,* which we discuss in the next section. In the following sections we use them to analyze the economic effects of price ceilings, price floors, and taxes. (As we will see in later chapters, these concepts are also useful in many other contexts.)

① LEARNING OBJECTIVE
Understand the concepts of consumer surplus and producer surplus.

Consumer Surplus and Producer Surplus

We can analyze the effects of government interventions in markets, such as imposing price ceilings and price floors, using the concepts of consumer surplus, producer surplus, and economic surplus. Consumer surplus measures the dollar benefit consumers receive from buying goods or services in a particular market. Producer surplus measures the dollar benefit firms receive from selling goods or services in a particular market. Economic surplus in a market is the sum of consumer surplus plus producer surplus. As we will see, *when the government imposes a price ceiling or a price floor, the amount of economic surplus in a market is reduced*—in other words, price ceilings and price floors reduce the total benefit to consumers and firms from buying and selling in a market. To understand why this is true, we need to understand how consumer surplus and producer surplus are determined.

Consumer Surplus

Demand curves show the willingness of consumers to purchase a product at different prices. For instance, Figure 4-1 shows Joe Irvin's demand curve for chai tea. If the price is $3.00 per cup, Joe will buy 4 cups per week. If the price is $2.00 per cup, Joe will buy 5 cups per week. The fact that Joe is willing to pay $3.00 for the fourth cup means that the *marginal benefit* to him from that cup is $3.00. Similarly, the fact that Joe is willing to pay $2.00 for the fifth cup means that the marginal benefit to him from that cup is $2.00. The **marginal benefit** is the additional benefit to a consumer from consuming one more unit of a good or service. In fact, we can think of Joe's demand curve as representing his marginal benefit curve for chai tea.

> **Marginal benefit** The additional benefit to a consumer from consuming one more unit of a good or service.

Suppose that the market price for chai tea is $2.00 per cup. In this case, for the fifth cup Joe buys in a week, his marginal benefit is equal to the price. For the other 4 cups he buys in a week, however, his marginal benefit is greater than the price he pays. In other words, for the first 4 cups of tea Joe buys in a week, he is paying less than the maximum price he would have been willing to pay, as shown by his marginal benefit. The difference between the highest price a consumer is willing to pay and the price the consumer actually pays is called **consumer surplus.**

> **Consumer surplus** The difference between the highest price a consumer is willing to pay and the price the consumer actually pays.

Figure 4-2 shows the market demand curve for chai tea. In the figure, the quantity demanded at a price of $2.00 is 15,000 cups per week. An important point to understand is that nearly all consumers in this market receive some consumer surplus from their purchases because the marginal benefit they receive is greater than the price they pay. The only consumers who receive no consumer surplus are those who would not have purchased any chai tea if the price had been higher than $2.00. We can calculate total consumer surplus in the market by adding up the consumer surplus received on each unit purchased. Because the demand curve measures the marginal benefit received by consumers, we can draw the following important conclusion: *The total amount of consumer surplus in a market is equal to the area below the demand curve and above the market price.* Consumer surplus is shown as the blue area in Figure 4-2, and represents the benefit to consumers in excess of the price they paid to purchase the product—in this case, chai tea.

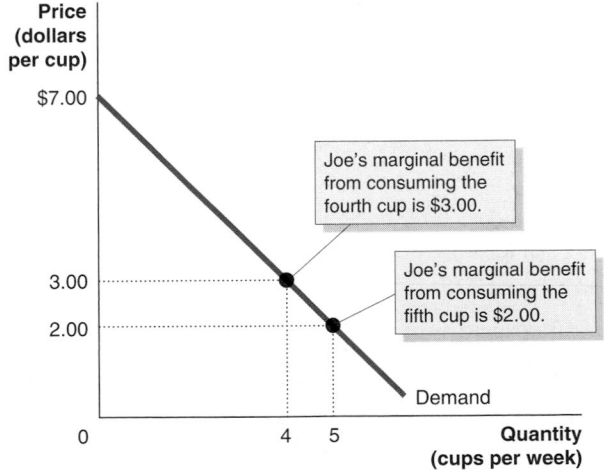

Joe's marginal benefit from consuming the fourth cup is $3.00.

Joe's marginal benefit from consuming the fifth cup is $2.00.

FIGURE 4-1

The Demand Curve Is Also the Marginal Benefit Curve

The demand curve shows a consumer's willingness to purchase a product at various prices. In this case, we know that Joe's willingness to pay $3.00 to purchase 4 cups of chai tea per week means that his *marginal benefit* from consuming the fourth cup is $3.00. Similarly, his willingness to pay $2.00 to purchase 5 cups of tea per week means that his marginal benefit from consuming the fifth cup is $2.00. So, the demand curve is also a marginal benefit curve.

FIGURE 4-2

Total Consumer Surplus in the Market for Chai Tea

The demand curve tells us that most buyers of chai tea would have been willing to pay more than the market price of $2.00. For each buyer, consumer surplus is equal to the difference between the highest price he or she is willing to pay and the market price actually paid. Therefore, the total amount of consumer surplus in the market for chai tea is equal to the area below the demand curve and above the market price. Consumer surplus represents the benefit to consumers in excess of the price they paid to purchase the product.

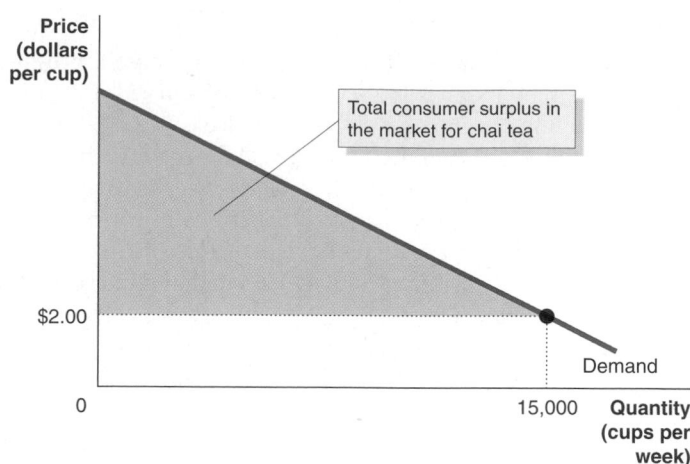

4-1 *Making the Connection*

The Consumer Surplus from Satellite Television

Consumer surplus allows us to measure the benefit consumers receive in excess of the price they paid to purchase the product. Recently, Austan Goolsbee and Amil Petrin, economists at the Graduate School of Business at the University of Chicago, have estimated the consumer surplus that households receive from subscribing to satellite television. To do this, they estimated the demand curve for satellite television and then computed the shaded area shown in the graph.

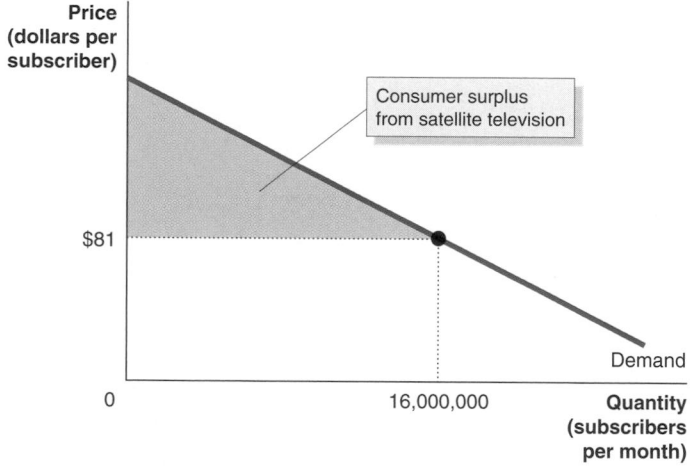

Sixteen million consumers paid an average price of $81 per month to subscribe to DirectTV or DISH Network, the two main providers of satellite television in 2001, the year for which the study was conducted. The demand curve shows that many consumers would have been willing to pay more than $81 rather than do without satellite television. Goolsbee and Petrin calculated that the consumer surplus for households subscribing to satellite television averaged $127 per month, which is the difference between the price they would have paid, and the $81 they did pay. The shaded area on the graph represents the total consumer surplus in the market for satellite television. Goolsbee and Petrin estimate the value of this area is $2 billion. This is one year's benefit to the consumers who subscribe to satellite television.

Source: Austan Goolsbee and Amil Petrin, "The Consumer Gains from Direct Broadcast Satellites and the Competition with Cable TV," *Econometrica*, Vol. 72, No. 2, March 2004, pp. 351–381.

How much consumer surplus will the owner of this satellite dish receive?

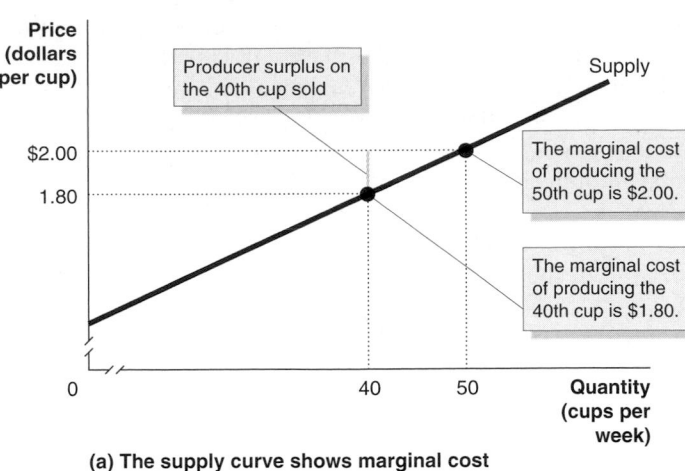

(a) The supply curve shows marginal cost

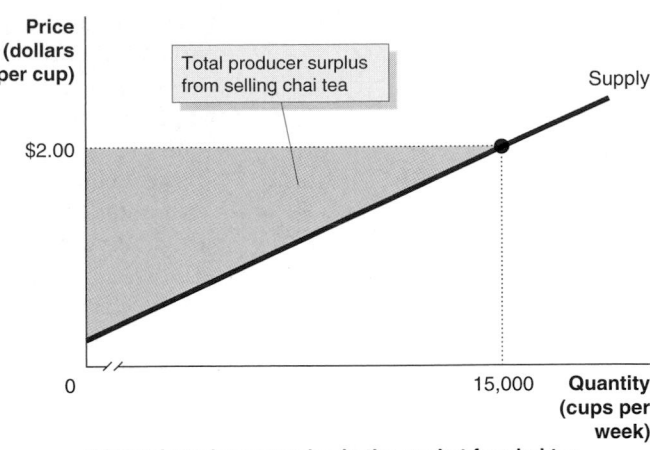

(b) Total producer surplus in the market for chai tea

FIGURE 4-3   **Producer Surplus**

The supply curve shows a firm's willingness to supply a product at various prices. In panel (a), we know that Heavenly Tea's willingness to supply 40 cups of chai tea at a price of $1.80 per cup means that the *marginal cost* of producing the 40th cup is $1.80. Similarly, the firm's willingness to supply 50 cups at a price of $2.00 per cup means its marginal cost of producing the 50th cup is $2.00. Producer surplus on the 40th cup sold is the difference

between the $2.00 market price of the cup and $1.80, which is the lowest price tea sellers would have been willing to accept. In panel (b), the total amount of producer surplus tea sellers receive from selling chai tea can be calculated by adding up for the entire market the producer surplus received on each cup sold. In the figure, this is equal to the area above the supply curve and below the market price, shown in red.

Producer Surplus

Supply curves show the willingness of firms to supply a product at different prices. The willingness to supply a product depends on the cost of producing it. Firms will supply an additional unit of a product only if they receive a price equal to the additional cost of producing that unit. **Marginal cost** is the additional cost to a firm of producing one more unit of a good or service. In Figure 4-3(a), we know that because Heavenly Tea is willing to supply 50 cups of chai tea at a price of $2.00 per cup, the 50th cup must have a marginal cost of $2.00. The supply curve also shows us that Heavenly Tea would be willing to supply 40 cups at a price of $1.80 per cup. So, the marginal cost of the 40th cup is $1.80. The supply curve, then, is also a marginal cost curve.

Notice, though, that if the market price of chai tea is $2.00, Heavenly Tea is able to sell the 40th cup for $0.20 more than the lowest price—$1.80—it would have been willing to accept. This $0.20 is the *producer surplus* on that particular cup of tea. **Producer surplus** is the difference between the lowest price a firm would have been willing to accept and the price it actually receives. The supply curve shows us that Heavenly Tea receives some producer surplus on nearly every cup of chai tea supplied. The marginal cost of the 50th cup is $2.00, and Heavenly Tea receives a price of $2.00, so it receives no producer surplus on that cup. The total amount of producer surplus tea sellers receive from selling chai tea can be calculated by adding up the producer surplus received on each cup sold. Therefore, *the total amount of producer surplus in a market is equal to the area above the market supply curve and below the market price*. The total producer surplus tea sellers receive from selling chai tea is shown as the red area in Figure 4-3(b).

Marginal cost   The additional cost to a firm of producing one more unit of a good or service.

Producer surplus   The difference between the lowest price a firm would have been willing to accept and the price it actually receives.

What Consumer Surplus and Producer Surplus Measure

We have seen that consumer surplus measures the benefit to consumers from participating in a market, and producer surplus measures the benefit to producers from participating in a market. It is important, however, to be clear what we mean by this. In a sense, consumer surplus is measuring the *net* benefit to consumers from participating in a market, rather than the *total* benefit. That is, if the price of a product were zero, then the consumer surplus in a market would be all of the area under the demand curve. When the price is not zero, consumer surplus is the area below the demand curve and above the market price. So, consumer surplus in a market is equal to the total benefit received by consumers minus the total amount they must pay to buy the good.

Similarly, producer surplus measures the net benefit received by producers from participating in a market. If producers could supply a good at zero cost, the producer surplus in a market would be all of the area below the market price. When cost is not zero, producer surplus is the area below the market price and above the supply curve. So, producer surplus in a market is equal to the total amount firms receive from consumers minus the cost of producing the good.

As we apply the concepts of consumer surplus and producer surplus in this chapter, it is important to remember what they measure.

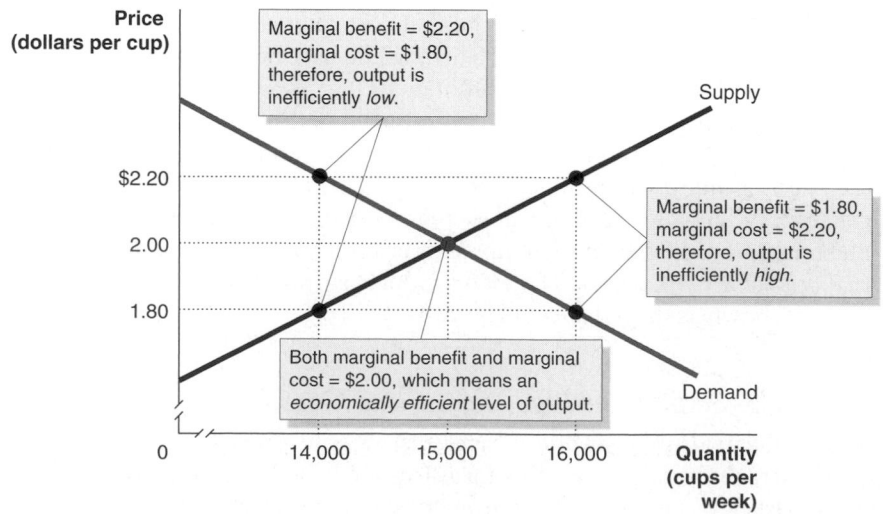
(Circled 2) **LEARNING OBJECTIVE**

Understand the concept of economic efficiency, and use a graph to illustrate how economic efficiency is reduced when a market is not in competitive equilibrium.

The Efficiency of Competitive Markets

In Chapter 3, we defined a *competitive market* as a market with many buyers and many sellers. An important advantage of the market system is that it results in efficient economic outcomes. But what do we mean by economic efficiency? The concepts we have developed so far in this chapter give us two ways to think about the economic efficiency of competitive markets. We can think in terms of marginal benefit and marginal cost. We can also think in terms of consumer surplus and producer surplus. As we will see, these two approaches lead to the same outcome, but using both can increase our understanding of economic efficiency.

Marginal Benefit Equals Marginal Cost in Competitive Equilibrium

Figure 4-4 again shows the market for chai tea. Recall that the demand curve shows the marginal benefit received by consumers, and the supply curve shows the marginal cost of production. To achieve economic efficiency in this market, the marginal benefit from the last unit sold should equal the marginal cost of production. The figure shows that this equality occurs at competitive equilibrium where 15,000 cups per week are produced, and marginal benefit and marginal cost are both equal to $2.00. Why is this outcome economically efficient? Because every cup of chai tea has been produced where the marginal benefit to buyers is greater than or equal to the marginal cost to producers.

FIGURE 4-4

Marginal Benefit Equals Marginal Cost Only at Competitive Equilibrium

In a competitive market, equilibrium occurs at a quantity of 15,000 cups and price of $2.00 per cup, where marginal benefit equals marginal cost. This is the economically efficient level of output because every cup has been produced where the marginal benefit to buyers is greater than or equal to the marginal cost to producers.

Another way to see why the level of output at competitive equilibrium is efficient is to consider what would be true if output were at a different level. For instance, suppose that output of chai tea were 14,000 cups per week. Figure 4-4 shows that at this level of output, the marginal benefit from the last cup sold is $2.20, whereas the marginal cost is only $1.80. This level of output is not efficient because 1,000 more cups could be produced for which the additional benefit to consumers is greater than the additional cost of production. Consumers would willingly purchase those cups, and tea sellers would willingly supply them, making both consumers and sellers better off. Similarly, if the output of chai tea were 16,000 cups per week, the marginal cost of the 16,000th cup is $2.20, whereas the marginal benefit is only $1.80. Tea sellers would only be willing to supply this cup at a price of $2.20, which is $0.40 higher than consumers would be willing to pay. In fact, consumers would not be willing to pay the price tea sellers would need to receive for any cup beyond the 15,000th.

To summarize, we can say this: *Equilibrium in a competitive market results in the economically efficient level of output, where marginal benefit equals marginal cost.*

Economic Surplus

Economic surplus in a market is the sum of consumer surplus and producer surplus. In a competitive market, with many buyers and sellers and no government restrictions, economic surplus is at a maximum when the market is in equilibrium. To see this, let's look one more time at the market for chai tea, which is shown in Figure 4-5. The consumer surplus in this market is the blue area below the demand curve and above the line indicating the equilibrium price of $2.00. The producer surplus is the red area above the supply curve and below the price line.

Economic surplus The sum of consumer surplus and producer surplus.

Deadweight Loss

To show that economic surplus is maximized at equilibrium, consider the situation when the price of chai tea is *above* the equilibrium price, as shown in Figure 4-6. At a price of $2.20 per cup, the number of cups consumers are willing to buy per week drops from 15,000 to 14,000. At competitive equilibrium, consumer surplus is equal to the sum of areas A, B, and C. At a price of $2.20, fewer cups are sold at a higher price, so consumer surplus declines to just the area of A. At competitive equilibrium, producer surplus is equal to the sum of areas D and E. At the higher price of $2.20, producer surplus changes to be equal to the sum of areas B and D. The sum of consumer and producer surplus—economic surplus—has been reduced to the sum of areas A, B, and D. Notice that this is less than the original economic surplus by an amount equal to areas C and E. Economic surplus has declined because at a price of $2.20, all the cups between the 14,000th and the 15,000th, which would have been produced in competitive

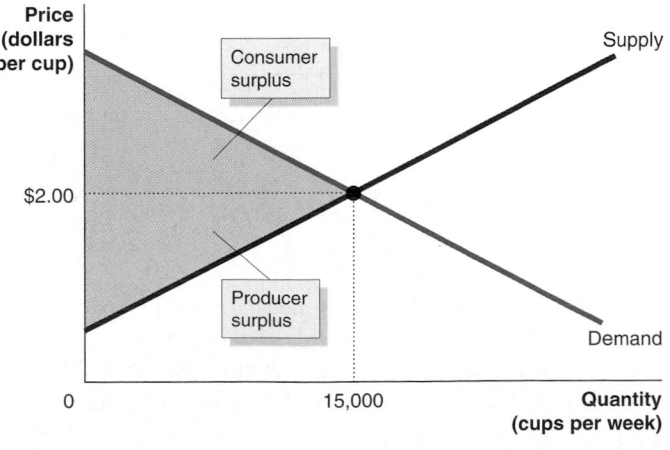

FIGURE 4-5

Economic Surplus Equals the Sum of Consumer Surplus and Producer Surplus

The economic surplus in a market is the sum of the blue area representing consumer surplus and the red area representing producer surplus.

When a Market Is Not in Equilibrium There Is a Deadweight Loss

Economic surplus is maximized when a market is in competitive equilibrium. When a market is not in equilibrium, there is a deadweight loss. When the price of chai tea is $2.20, instead of $2.00, consumer surplus declines from an amount equal to the sum of areas *A*, *B*, and *C*, to just area *A*. Producer surplus increases from the sum of areas *D* and *E*, to the sum of areas *B* and *D*. At competitive equilibrium, there is no deadweight loss. At a price of $2.20, there is a deadweight loss equal to the sum of areas *C* and *E*.

	At Competitive Equilibrium	At a Price of $2.20
Consumer Surplus	A + B + C	A
Producer Surplus	D + E	B + D
Deadweight Loss	None	C + E

equilibrium, are not being produced. These "missing" cups are not providing any consumer or producer surplus, so economic surplus has declined. The reduction in economic surplus resulting from a market not being in competitive equilibrium is called the **deadweight loss**. In the figure, it is equal to the sum of areas *C* and *E*.

Deadweight loss The reduction in economic surplus resulting from a market not being in competitive equilibrium.

Economic Surplus and Economic Efficiency

Consumer surplus measures the benefit to consumers from buying a particular product, such as chia tea. Producer surplus measures the benefit to firms from selling a particular product. Therefore, economic surplus—which is the sum of the benefit to firms plus the benefit to consumers—is the best measure we have of the benefit to society from the production of a particular good or service. This gives us a second way of characterizing the economic efficiency of a competitive market: *Equilibrium in a competitive market results in the greatest amount of economic surplus, or total net benefit to society, from the production of a good or service.* Anything that causes the market for a good or service not to be in competitive equilibrium reduces the total benefit to society from the production of that good or service.

Now we can give a more general definition of *economic efficiency* in terms of our two approaches: **Economic efficiency** is a market outcome in which the marginal benefit to consumers of the last unit produced is equal to its marginal cost of production, and in which the sum of consumer surplus and producer surplus is at a maximum.

Economic efficiency A market outcome in which the marginal benefit to consumers of the last unit produced is equal to its marginal cost of production, and in which the sum of consumer surplus and producer surplus is at a maximum.

③ **LEARNING OBJECTIVE**

Use demand and supply graphs to analyze the economic impact of price ceilings and price floors.

Government Intervention in the Market: Price Floors and Price Ceilings

Notice that we have *not* concluded that every *individual* is better off if a market is at its competitive equilibrium. We have only concluded that economic surplus, or the *total* net benefit to society, is greatest at competitive equilibrium. Any individual producer would rather charge a higher price, and any individual consumer would rather pay a lower

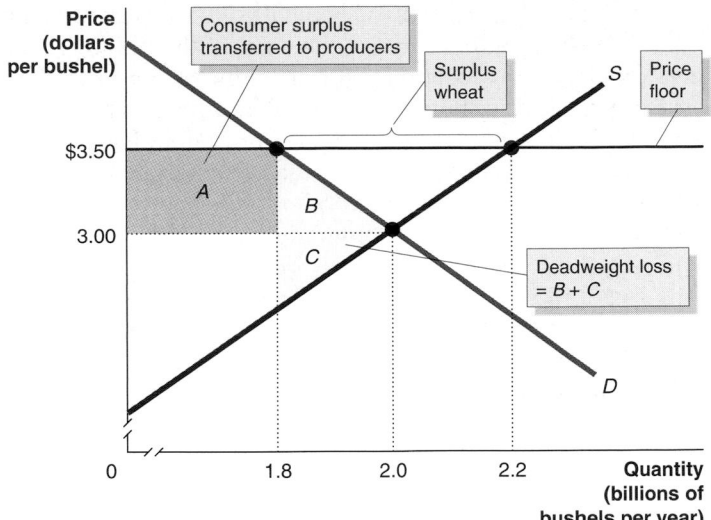

FIGURE 4-7

The Economic Effect of a Price Floor in the Wheat Market

If wheat farmers convince the government to impose a price floor of $3.50 per bushel, the amount of wheat sold will fall from 2.0 billion bushels per year to 1.8 billion. If we assume that farmers produce 1.8 billion bushels, producer surplus then increases by the red rectangle *A*—which is transferred from consumer surplus—and falls by the yellow triangle *C*. Consumer surplus declines by the red rectangle *A* plus the yellow triangle *B*. There is a deadweight loss equal to the yellow triangles *B* and *C*, representing the decline in economic efficiency due to the price floor. In reality, a price floor of $3.50 per bushel will cause farmers to expand their production from 2.0 billion to 2.2 billion bushels, resulting in a surplus of wheat.

price, but usually producers can sell and consumers can buy only at the competitive equilibrium price.

Producers or consumers who are dissatisfied with the competitive equilibrium price can lobby the government to legally require that a different price be charged. The U.S. government only occasionally overrides the market outcome by setting prices. When the government does intervene, it can either attempt to aid sellers by requiring that a price be above equilibrium—a price floor—or to aid buyers by requiring that a price be below equilibrium—a price ceiling. To affect the market outcome, a price floor must be set above the equilibrium price, and a price ceiling must be set below the equilibrium price. Otherwise, the price ceiling or price floor will not be *binding* on buyers and sellers. The preceding section demonstrates that moving away from competitive equilibrium will reduce economic efficiency. We can use the concepts of producer and consumer surplus and deadweight loss to see more clearly the economic inefficiency of binding price floors and price ceilings.

Price Floors: The Example of Agricultural Markets

The Great Depression of the 1930s was the greatest economic disaster in U.S. history, affecting every sector of the U.S. economy. Many farmers were unable to sell their products or could sell them only at very low prices. Farmers were able to convince the federal government to intervene to raise prices by setting price floors for many agricultural products. Government intervention in agriculture—often referred to as the "farm program"—has continued ever since. To see how a price floor in an agricultural market works, suppose that the equilibrium price in the wheat market is $3.00 per bushel but the government decides to set a price floor of $3.50 per bushel. As Figure 4-7 shows, the price of wheat rises from $3.00 to $3.50 and the quantity of wheat sold falls from 2.0 billion bushels per year to 1.8 billion. Suppose, initially, that production of wheat also falls to 1.8 billion bushels.

Just as we saw in the earlier example of the market for chai tea (see Figure 4-6), the producer surplus received by wheat farmers increases by an amount equal to the area of the red rectangle *A* and falls by an amount equal to the area of the yellow triangle *C*. The area of the red rectangle *A* represents a transfer from consumer surplus to producer surplus. The total fall in consumer surplus is equal to the area of the red rectangle *A* plus the area of the yellow triangle *B*. Wheat farmers benefit from this program, but consumers lose. There is also a deadweight loss equal to the areas of the yellow triangles *B* and *C*, which represents the decline in economic efficiency due to the price floor. There is a deadweight loss because the price floor has reduced the amount of economic surplus in the market for wheat. Or, looked at another way, the price floor has caused the marginal benefit of the last bushel of wheat to be greater than the marginal cost of producing it. We can conclude that a price floor reduces economic efficiency.

The actual federal government farm programs have been more complicated than just legally requiring farmers not to sell their output below a minimum price. We assumed initially that farmers reduce their production of wheat to the amount consumers are willing to buy. In fact, as Figure 4-7 shows, a price floor will cause the quantity of wheat that farmers want to supply to increase from 2.0 billion to 2.2 billion bushels. Because the higher price also reduces the amount of wheat consumers wish to buy, the result is a surplus of 0.4 billion bushels of wheat (the 2.2 billion bushels supplied minus the 1.8 billion demanded).

The federal government's farm programs often have resulted in large surpluses of wheat and other agricultural products. The government has usually either bought the surplus food or paid farmers to restrict supply by taking some land out of cultivation. Because both of these options are expensive, Congress passed the Freedom to Farm Act of 1996. The intent of the act was to phase out price floors and government purchases of surpluses and return to a free market in agriculture. To allow farmers time to adjust, the federal government began paying farmers *subsidies*, or cash payments based on the number of acres planted. Although the subsidies were originally scheduled to be phased out, Congress has continued to pay them.

4-2 Making the Connection

Price Floors in Labor Markets: The Minimum Wage

The minimum wage may be the most controversial "price floor." Supporters see the minimum wage as a way of raising the incomes of low-skilled workers. Opponents argue that it results in fewer jobs and imposes large costs on small businesses.

Congress has set a national minimum wage of $5.15 per hour for most occupations. It is illegal for an employer to pay less than this wage in those occupations. For most workers, the minimum wage is irrelevant because it is well below the wage employers are voluntarily willing to pay them. But for low-skilled workers—such as workers in fast-food restaurants—the minimum wage is above the wage they would otherwise receive. The figure shows the effect of the minimum wage on employment in the market for low-skilled labor.

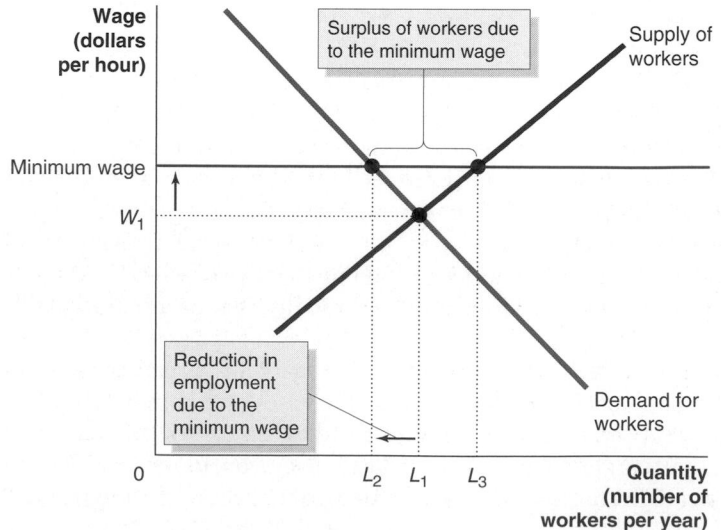

Without a minimum wage, the equilibrium wage would be W_1, and the number of workers hired would be L_1. With a minimum wage set above the equilibrium wage, the quantity of workers demanded by employers declines from L_1 to L_2 and the quantity of labor supplied increases to L_3 leading to a surplus of workers unable to find jobs equal to $L_3 - L_2$. The quantity of labor supplied increases because the higher wage attracts more people to work. For instance, some teenagers may decide that working after school is worthwhile at the minimum wage of $5.15 per hour, but would not have been worthwhile at a lower wage.

This analysis is very similar to our analysis of the wheat market in Figure 4-7. Just as a price floor in the wheat market leads to less wheat consumed, a price floor in the labor market should lead to fewer workers hired. Views differ sharply among economists, however, concerning how large a reduction in employment the minimum wage causes. For instance, David Card of the University of California, Berkeley and Alan Krueger of Princeton University conducted a study of fast-food restaurants in New Jersey and Pennsylvania that indicates the effect of minimum wage increases on employment is very small. Card and Krueger's study has been very controversial, however. Other economists have examined similar data and have come to the different conclusion that the minimum wage does lead to a significant decrease in employment.

Whatever the extent of employment losses from the minimum wage, because it is a price floor, it will cause a deadweight loss, just as a price floor in the wheat market does. Therefore, many economists favor alternative policies for attaining the goal of raising the incomes of low-skilled workers. One policy many economists support is the *earned income tax credit*. The earned income tax credit reduces the amount of tax that low-income wage earners would otherwise pay to the federal government. Workers with very low incomes who do not owe any tax receive a payment from the government. Compared with the minimum wage, the earned income tax credit can increase the incomes of low-skilled workers without reducing employment. The earned income tax credit also places a lesser burden on the small businesses that employ many low-skilled workers, and it might cause a smaller loss of economic efficiency.

Many economists believe there are better policies than the minimum wage for raising the incomes of low-skilled workers.

Sources: David Card and Alan B. Krueger, *Myth and Measurement: The New Economics of the Minimum Wage*, Princeton, NJ: Princeton University Press, 1995; David Neumark and William Wascher, "Minimum Wages and Employment: A Case Study of the Fast-Food Industry in New Jersey and Pennsylvania: Comment," *American Economic Review*, Vol. 90, No. 5, December 2000, pp. 1,362–1,396; and David Card and Alan B. Krueger, "Minimum Wages and Employment: A Case Study of the Fast-Food Industry in New Jersey and Pennsylvania: Reply," *American Economic Review*, Vol. 90, No. 5, December 2000, pp. 1,397–1,420.

Price Ceilings: The Example of Rent Controls

Support for governments setting price floors typically comes from sellers, but support for governments setting price ceilings typically comes from consumers. For example, when there is a sharp increase in gasoline prices, there will often be proposals for the government to impose a price ceiling on the market for gasoline. As we saw in the opening to this chapter, New York is one of the cities that imposes rent controls, which put a ceiling on the maximum rent that landlords can charge for an apartment. Figure 4-8 shows the market for apartments in a city that has rent controls.

Without rent control, the equilibrium rent would be $1,500 per month and 2,000,000 apartments would be rented. With a maximum legal rent of $1,000 per month, landlords reduce the quantity of apartments supplied to 1,900,000. The fall in the quantity of apartments supplied is the result of some apartments being converted to offices or sold off as condominiums, some small apartment buildings being converted to single-family homes, and, over time, some apartment buildings being abandoned. In New York City, rent control has resulted in whole city blocks being abandoned by landlords who were unable to cover their costs with the rents they were allowed to charge. In London, when rent controls were applied to rooms and apartments located in a landlord's own home, the quantity of these apartments supplied dropped by 75 percent.

FIGURE 4-8

The Economic Effect of a Rent Ceiling

Without rent control, the equilibrium rent is $1,500 per month. At that price, 2,000,000 apartments would be rented. If the government imposes a rent ceiling of $1,000, the quantity of apartments supplied falls to 1,900,000, while the quantity of apartments demanded increases to 2,100,000, resulting in a shortage of 200,000 apartments. Producer surplus equal to the area of the blue rectangle *A* is transferred from landlords to renters, and there is a deadweight loss equal to the areas of yellow triangles *B* and *C*.

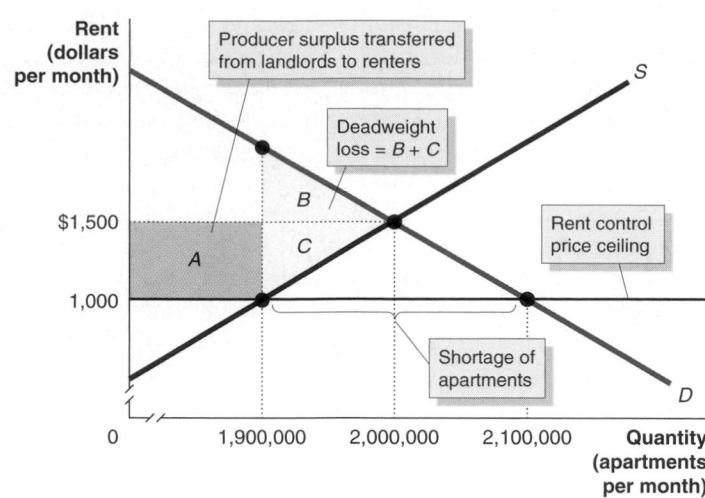

In Figure 4-8, with the rent ceiling of $1,000, the quantity of apartments demanded rises to 2,100,000. There is a shortage of 200,000 apartments. Consumer surplus increases by rectangle *A* and falls by triangle *B*. Rectangle *A* would have been part of producer surplus if rent control were not in place. With rent control, it is part of consumer surplus. Rent control causes the producer surplus received by landlords to fall by rectangle *A* plus triangle *C*. Triangles *B* and *C* represent the deadweight loss. There is a deadweight loss because rent control has reduced the amount of economic surplus in the market for apartments. Rent control has caused the marginal benefit of the last apartment rented to be greater than the marginal cost of supplying it. We can conclude that a price ceiling, such as rent control, reduces economic efficiency. The Appendix to this chapter shows how we can make quantitative estimates of the deadweight loss, and the changes in consumer surplus and producer surplus that result from rent control.

Renters as a group benefit from rent controls—total consumer surplus is larger—but landlords lose. Because of the deadweight loss, the total loss to landlords is greater than the gain to renters. Notice also that although renters as a group benefit, the number of renters is reduced, so some renters are made worse off by rent controls because they are unable to find an apartment at the legal rent.

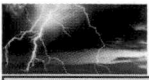

Don't Let This Happen To You!

Don't Confuse "Scarcity" with a "Shortage"

At first glance, the following statement seems correct: "There is a shortage of every good that is scarce." In everyday conversation, we describe a good as "scarce" if we have trouble finding it. For instance, if you are looking for a present for a child, you might call the latest hot toy "scarce" if you are willing to buy it at its listed price but can't find it online or in any store. But recall from Chapter 2 that economists have a broad definition of

scarce. In the economic sense, almost everything—except undesirable things like garbage—is scarce. A shortage of a good occurs only if the quantity demanded is greater than the quantity supplied at the current price. Therefore, the preceding statement—"There is a shortage of every good that is scarce"—is incorrect. In fact, there is no shortage of most scarce goods.

YOUR TURN: Test your understanding by doing related problem 10 on page 123 at the end of this chapter.

Black Markets

To this point, our analysis of rent controls is incomplete. In practice, renters may be worse off and landlords may be better off than Figure 4-8 makes it seem. We have assumed that renters and landlords actually abide by the price ceiling, but sometimes they don't. Because rent control leads to a shortage of apartments, renters who would otherwise not be able to find apartments have an incentive to offer landlords rents above the legal maximum. When governments try to control prices by setting price ceilings or price floors, buyers and sellers often find a way around the controls. The result is a **black market** where buying and selling take place at prices that violate government price regulations.

In a housing market with rent controls, the total amount of consumer surplus received by renters may be reduced and the total amount of producer surplus received by landlords may be increased if apartments are being rented at prices above the legal price ceiling.

Black market Buying and selling at prices that violate government price regulations.

SOLVED PROBLEM   4-1

What's the Economic Effect of a "Black Market" for Apartments?

In many cities with rent controls, the actual rents paid can be much higher than the legal maximum. Because rent controls cause a shortage of apartments, desperate tenants will often be willing to pay landlords rents that are higher than the law allows, perhaps by writing a check for the legally allowed rent and paying an additional amount in cash. Look again at Figure 4-8. Suppose that competition among tenants results in the black market rent rising to $2,000 per month. At this rent, tenants demand 1,900,000 apartments. Use a graph showing the market for apartments to compare this situation with the one shown in Figure 4-8. Be sure to note any differences in consumer surplus, producer surplus, and deadweight loss.

③ **LEARNING OBJECTIVE**
Use demand and supply graphs to analyze the economic impact of price ceilings and price floors.

Solving the Problem:
Step 1: Review the chapter material. This problem is about price controls in the market for apartments, so you may want to review the section "Price Ceilings: The Example of Rent Controls," which begins on page 107.

Step 2: Draw a graph similar to Figure 4-8, with the addition of the black market price.

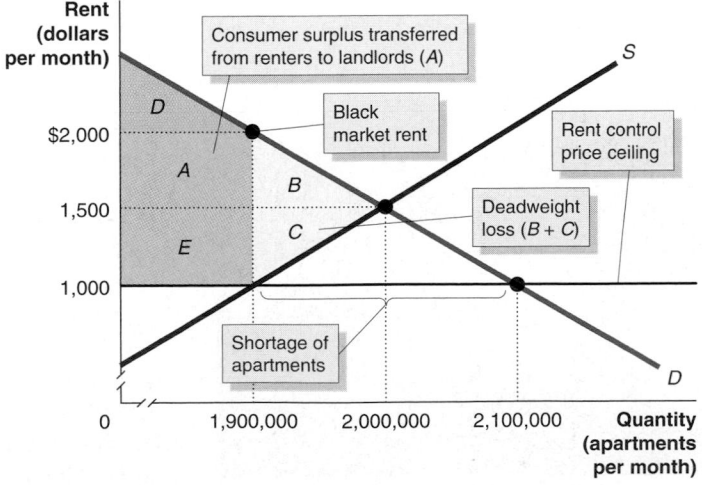

Step 3: Analyze the changes from Figure 4-8. Because the black market rent is now $2,000—even higher than the original competitive equilibrium rent of $1,500—compared with Figure 4-8 consumer surplus declines by an amount equal to the red rectangle *A* plus the red rectangle *E*. The remaining consumer surplus is the blue triangle *D*. Note that the rectangle *A*, which would have been part of consumer surplus without rent control, represents a transfer from renters to landlords. Compared with the situation shown in Figure 4-8, producer surplus has increased by an amount equal to rectangles *A* and *E*, and consumer surplus has declined by the same amount. Deadweight loss is equal to triangles *B* and *C*, the same as in Figure 4-8.

Extra Credit: This analysis leads to a surprising result: With an active black market in apartments, rent control may leave renters as a group worse off—with less consumer surplus—than if there were no rent control. There is one more possibility to consider, however. If enough landlords become convinced that they can get away with charging rents above the legal ceiling, the quantity of apartments supplied will increase. Eventually, the market could even end up at the competitive equilibrium with an equilibrium rent of $1,500 and equilibrium quantity of 2,000,000 apartments. In that case the rent control price ceiling becomes nonbinding, not because it was set below the equilibrium price, but because it was not legally enforced.

YOUR TURN: **For more practice, do related problem 8 on page 122 and problem 16 on page 123 at the end of this chapter. Visit www.prenhall.com/hubbard for an interactive exercise related to this Solved Problem.**

Rent controls can also lead to an increase in racial and other types of discrimination. With rent controls, more renters will be looking for apartments than there are apartments to rent. Landlords can afford to indulge their prejudices by refusing to rent to people they don't like. In cities without rent controls, landlords face more competition, which makes it more difficult to turn down tenants on the basis of irrelevant characteristics, such as race.

4-3 *Making the Connection*

Does Holiday Gift Giving Have a Deadweight Loss?

The deadweight loss that results from rent control occurs, in part, because consumers rent fewer apartments than they would in a competitive equilibrium. Their choices are *constrained* by government. When someone receives a gift, she is also constrained because the person who gave the gift has already chosen the product. In many cases, the recipient would have chosen a different gift for herself. Economist Joel Waldfogel of the University of Pennsylvania points out that gift giving results in a deadweight loss. The amount of the deadweight loss is equal to the difference between the gift's price and the dollar value the recipient places on the gift. Waldfogel surveyed his students, asking them to list every gift they had received for Christmas, to estimate the retail price of each gift, and to state how much they would have been willing to pay for each gift. Waldfogel's students estimated that their families and friends had paid $438 on average on the students' gifts. The students themselves, however, would have

Caution: Gift giving may lead to deadweight loss.

been willing to pay only $313 to buy the presents. If the deadweight losses experienced by Waldfogel's students were extrapolated to the whole population, the deadweight loss of Christmas gift giving could be as much as $13 billion.

If the gifts had been cash, the people receiving the gifts would not have been constrained by the gift givers' choices, and there would have been no deadweight loss. If your sister had given you cash instead of that sweater you didn't like, you could have bought whatever you wanted. Why then do people continue giving presents rather than cash? One answer is that most people receive more satisfaction from giving a present than from giving cash. If we take this satisfaction into account, the deadweight loss from gift giving will be lower than in Waldfogel's calculations.

Source: Joel Waldfogel, "The Deadweight Loss of Christmas," *American Economic Review*, Vol. 83, No. 4, December 1993, pp. 328–336.

The Results of Government Intervention: Winners, Losers, and Inefficiency

When the government imposes price floors or price ceilings, three important results occur:

➤ Some people win.
➤ Some people lose.
➤ There is a loss of economic efficiency.

The winners with rent control are the people who are paying less for rent because they live in rent-controlled apartments. Landlords may also gain if they break the law by charging rents above the legal maximum for their rent-controlled apartments, provided these illegal rents are higher than the competitive equilibrium rents would have been. The losers from rent control are the landlords of rent-controlled apartments who abide by the law, and renters who are unable to find apartments to rent at the controlled price. Rent control reduces economic efficiency because fewer apartments are rented than would be in a competitive market (refer again to Figure 4-8). The resulting deadweight loss measures the decrease in economic efficiency.

Positive and Normative Analysis of Price Ceilings and Price Floors

Are rent controls, government farm programs, and other price ceilings and price floors bad? As we saw in Chapter 1, questions of this type have no right or wrong answers. Economists are generally skeptical of government attempts to interfere with competitive market equilibrium. Economists know the role competitive markets have played in raising the average person's standard of living. They also know that too much government intervention has the potential to reduce the ability of the market system to produce similar increases in living standards in the future.

But recall from Chapter 1 the difference between positive and normative analysis. Positive analysis is concerned with *what is*, and normative analysis is concerned with *what should be*. Our analysis of rent control and of the federal farm programs in this chapter is positive analysis. We discussed what the economic results of these programs are. Whether these programs are desirable or undesirable is a normative question. Whether the gains to the winners more than make up for the losses to the losers and for the decline in economic efficiency is a matter of judgment and not strictly an economic question. Price ceilings and price floors continue to exist partly because they are supported by people who understand their downside but still believe they are good policies. They also persist because many people do not understand their downside, because they are unfamiliar with the economic analysis we have used in this chapter.

④ LEARNING OBJECTIVE

Use demand and supply graphs to analyze the economic impact of taxes.

The Economic Impact of Taxes

Supreme Court Justice Oliver Wendell Holmes once remarked that: "Taxes are what we pay for a civilized society." When the government taxes a good, however, it affects the market equilibrium for that good. Just as with a price ceiling or price floor, one result of a tax is a decline in economic efficiency. Analyzing taxes is an important part of the field of economics known as *public finance*. In this section, we will use the model of demand and supply, and the concepts of consumer surplus, producer surplus, and deadweight loss to analyze the economic impact of taxes.

The Effect of Taxes on Economic Efficiency

Whenever a government taxes a good or service, less of that good or service will be produced. For example, a tax on cigarettes will raise the cost of smoking and reduce the quantity of smoking that takes place. We can use a demand and supply graph to illustrate this point. Figure 4-9 shows the market for cigarettes.

Without the tax, the equilibrium price of cigarettes would be $2.00 per pack and 4 billion packs of cigarettes would be sold per year (point *A*). If the federal government requires sellers of cigarettes to pay a $1.00 per pack tax, then their cost of selling cigarettes will increase by $1.00 per pack. This causes the supply curve for cigarettes to shift up by $1.00 because sellers will now require a price that is $1 greater to supply the same quantity of cigarettes. In Figure 4-9, for example, without the tax, sellers would be willing to supply a quantity of 3.7 billion packs of cigarettes at a price of $1.90 per pack (point *C*). With the tax, they will supply only 3.7 billion packs of cigarettes if the price is $2.90 per pack (point *B*). The shift in the supply curve will result in a new equilibrium price of $2.90 and a new equilibrium quantity of 3.7 billion packs (point *B*).

The federal government will collect tax revenue equal to the tax per pack multiplied by the number of packs sold, or $3.7 billion. The area shaded in green in Figure 4-9 represents the government's tax revenue. Consumers will pay a higher price of $2.90 per pack. Although sellers appear to be receiving a higher price per pack, after they have paid the tax, the price they receive falls from $2.00 per pack to $1.90 per pack. There is a loss of consumer surplus because consumers are paying a higher price. The price producers receive falls, so there is also a loss of producer surplus. Therefore, the tax on cigarettes has reduced *both* consumer surplus and producer surplus. Some of the reduction in consumer and producer surplus becomes tax revenue for the government. The rest of the reduction in consumer and producer surplus is equal to the deadweight loss from the tax, shown by the yellow-shaded triangle in the figure.

We can conclude that the true burden of a tax is not just the amount paid to government by consumers and producers, but also includes the deadweight loss. The deadweight loss from a tax is referred to as the *excess burden* of the tax. *A tax is efficient if it imposes a small excess burden relative to the tax revenue it raises.* One contribution economists make to government tax policy is to provide advice to policymakers on which taxes are most efficient.

Tax Incidence: Who Actually Pays a Tax?

The answer to the question "Who pays a tax?" seems obvious: Whoever is legally required to send a tax payment to the government pays the tax. But there can be an important difference between who is legally required to pay the tax and who actually *bears the burden* of the tax. The actual division of the burden of a tax is referred to as **tax incidence.** The federal government currently levies an excise tax of 18.4 cents per

Tax incidence The actual division of the burden of a tax between buyers and sellers in a market.

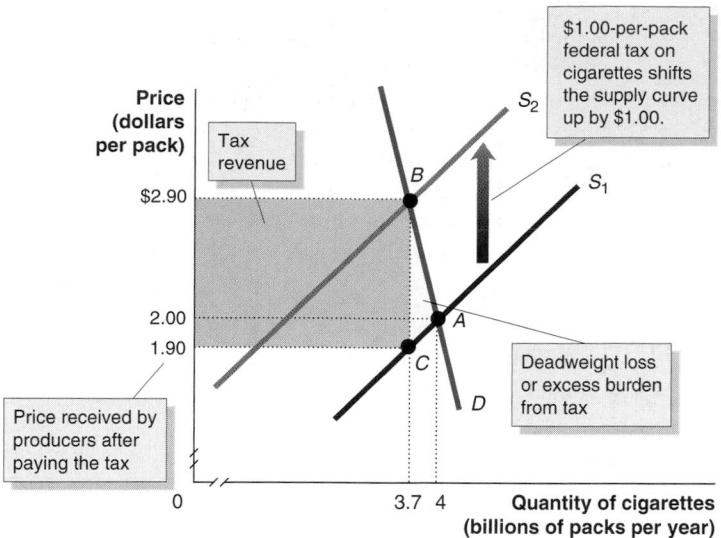

FIGURE 4-9 **The Effect of a Tax on the Market for Cigarettes**

Without the tax, market equilibrium occurs at point *A*. The equilibrium price of cigarettes is $2.00 per pack and 4 billion packs of cigarettes are sold per year. A $1.00-per-pack tax on cigarettes will cause the supply curve for cigarettes to shift up by $1 from S_1 to S_2. The new equilibrium occurs at point *B*. The price of cigarettes will increase by $0.90 to $2.90 per pack, and the quantity sold will fall to 3.7 billion packs. The tax on cigarettes has increased the price paid by consumers from $2.00 to $2.90 per pack. Producers receive a price of $2.90 per pack (point *B*), but after paying the $1.00 tax they are left with $1.90 (point *C*). The government will receive tax revenue equal to the green shaded box. Some consumer surplus and some producer surplus will become tax revenue for the government and some will become deadweight loss, shown by the yellow-shaded area.

gallon of gasoline sold. This tax is collected by gas station owners and forwarded to the federal government, but who actually bears the burden of the tax?

DETERMINING TAX INCIDENCE ON A DEMAND AND SUPPLY GRAPH Suppose that the retail price of gasoline—including the federal excise tax—is $2.08 per gallon, 20 billion gallons of gasoline are sold in the United States per year, and the federal excise tax is 10 cents per gallon. Figure 4-10 allows us to analyze the incidence of the tax.

First, consider the market for gasoline if there were no federal excise tax on gasoline. This equilibrium occurs at the intersection of the demand curve and supply curve S_1. The equilibrium price is $2.00 per gallon and the equilibrium quantity is 24 billion gallons. If the federal government imposes a 10-cents-per-gallon tax, the supply curve for gasoline will shift up by 10 cents per gallon. At the new equilibrium, where the demand curve intersects the supply curve S_2, the price has risen by 8 cents per gallon from $2.00 to $2.08. Notice that only in the extremely unlikely case that demand is a vertical line will the market price rise by the full amount of the tax. Consumers are paying 8 cents more per gallon. Sellers of gasoline receive a new higher price of $2.08 per gallon, but after paying the 10-cents-per-gallon tax, they are left with $1.98 per gallon, or 2 cents less than they had been receiving in the old equilibrium.

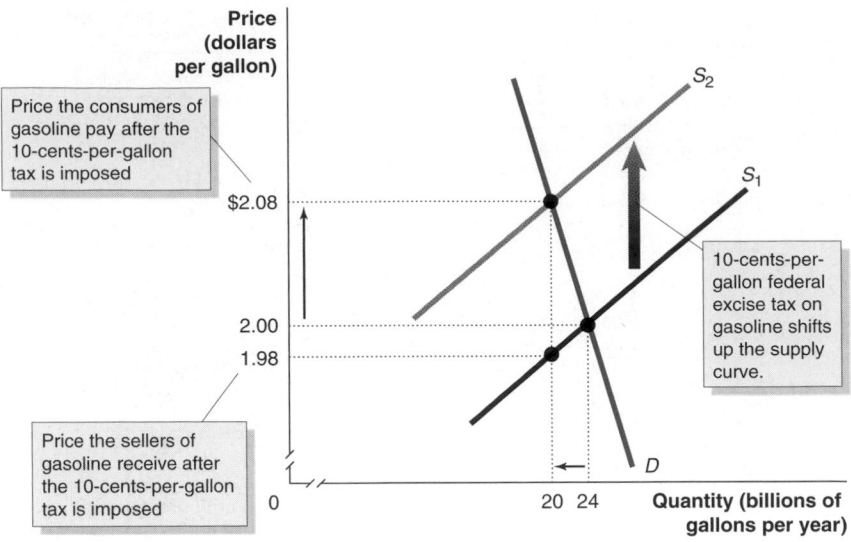

FIGURE 4-10   **The Incidence of a Tax on Gasoline**

With no tax on gasoline, the price would be $2.00 per gallon and 24 billion gallons of gasoline would be sold each year. A 10-cents-per-gallon excise tax shifts up the supply curve from S_1 to S_2, raises the price consumers pay from $2.00 to $2.08, and lowers the price producers receive from $2.00 to $1.98. Therefore, consumers pay 8 cents of the 10-cents-per-gallon tax on gasoline and producers pay 2 cents.

Although the sellers of gasoline are responsible for collecting the tax and sending the tax receipts to the government, they do not bear most of the burden of the tax. In this case, consumers pay 8 cents of the tax, because the market price has risen by 8 cents, and sellers pay 2 cents of the tax, because after sending the tax to the government, they are receiving 2 cents less per gallon of gasoline sold. Expressed in percentage terms, consumers pay 80 percent of the tax and sellers pay 20 percent of the tax.

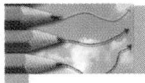

SOLVED PROBLEM   4-2

④ LEARNING OBJECTIVE

Use demand and supply graphs to analyze the economic impact of taxes.

When Do Consumers Pay All of a Sales Tax Increase?

Briefly explain whether you agree with the following statement: "If the federal government raises the sales tax on gasoline by $0.25, then the price of gasoline will rise by $0.25. Consumers can't get by without gasoline, so they have to pay the whole amount of any increase in the sales tax." Illustrate your answer with a graph.

Solving the Problem:

Step 1: Review the chapter material. This problem is about tax incidence, so if you need to you should review the section "Tax Incidence: Who Actually Pays a Tax?", which begins on page 112.

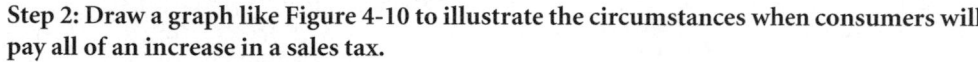

Step 2: Draw a graph like Figure 4-10 to illustrate the circumstances when consumers will pay all of an increase in a sales tax.

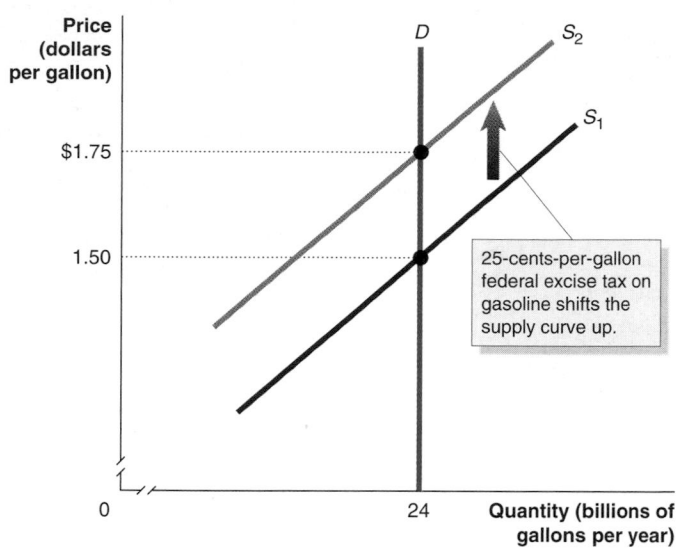

Step 3: Use the graph to evaluate the statement. The graph shows that consumers will pay all of an increase in a sales tax only if the demand curve is a vertical line. It is very unlikely that the demand for gasoline looks like this, because we expect that for every good an increase in price will cause a decrease in the quantity demanded. Because the demand curve for gasoline is not a vertical line, the statement is incorrect.

YOUR TURN: **For more practice do related problem 21 on page 124 at the end of the chapter. Visit www.prenhall.com/hubbard for an interactive exercise related to this Solved Problem.**

DOES IT MATTER WHETHER THE TAX IS ON BUYERS OR SELLERS? We have already seen the important distinction between the true burden of a tax and whether buyers or sellers are required legally to pay a tax. We can reinforce this point by noting explicitly that the incidence of a tax does *not* depend on whether a tax is collected from the buyers of a good or from the sellers. Figure 4-11 illustrates this point by showing the effect on equilibrium in the market for gasoline if a 10-cents-per-gallon tax is imposed on buyers, rather than on sellers. That is, we are now assuming that instead of sellers having to collect the 10-cents-per-gallon tax at the pump, buyers are responsible for keeping track of how many gallons of gasoline they purchase, and sending the tax to the government. (Of course, it would be very difficult for buyers to keep track of their purchases, or for the government to check whether they were paying all of the tax they owed. That is why the government collects the tax on gasoline from sellers.)

Figure 4-11 is similar to Figure 4-10, except that it shows the gasoline tax being imposed on buyers rather than sellers. In Figure 4-11, the supply curve does not shift because nothing has happened to change the willingness of sellers to change the quantity of gasoline they supply. The demand curve, however, has shifted because consumers now have to pay a 10 cent tax on every gallon of gasoline they buy. Therefore, at every quantity they are willing to pay a price 10 cents less than they would have without the tax. We indicate this in the figure by shifting the demand curve down by 10 cents from D_1 to D_2. Once the tax has been imposed and the demand curve has shifted down, the

FIGURE 4-11

The Incidence of a Tax on Gasoline Paid by Buyers

With no tax on gasoline, the demand curve is D_1. If a 10-cents-per-gallon tax is imposed that consumers are responsible for paying, the demand curve shifts down by the amount of the tax from D_1 to D_2. In the new equilibrium, consumers pay a price of $1.50 per gallon, including the tax. Producers receive $1.40 per gallon. This is the same result we saw when producers were responsible for paying the tax.

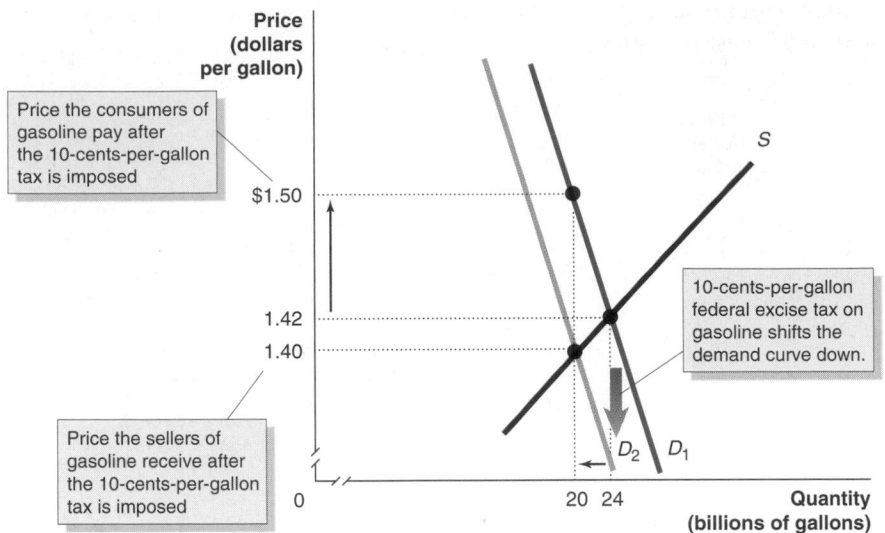

Price the consumers of gasoline pay after the 10-cents-per-gallon tax is imposed

10-cents-per-gallon federal excise tax on gasoline shifts the demand curve down.

Price the sellers of gasoline receive after the 10-cents-per-gallon tax is imposed

new equilibrium quantity of gasoline is 20 billion gallons, which is exactly the same as in Figure 4-10.

The new equilibrium price after the tax is imposed appears to be different in Figure 4-11 than it was in Figure 4-10, but if we include the tax, then buyers will pay and sellers will receive the same price in both figures. To see this, notice that in Figure 4-10 buyers paid sellers a price of $1.50 per gallon. In Figure 4-11 they pay sellers only $1.40, but they must also pay the government a tax of 10 cents per gallon. So, the total price buyers pay remains $1.50 per gallon. In Figure 4-10, sellers receive $1.50 per gallon from buyers, but after they pay the tax of 10 cents per gallon, they are left with $1.40, which is the same amount they receive in Figure 4-11.

4-4 *Making the Connection*

How much FICA do you think this employee pays?

Is the Burden of the Social Security Tax Really Shared Equally between Workers and Firms?

Everyone who receives a paycheck has several different taxes withheld from it by their employers, who forward these taxes directly to the government. In fact, many people are shocked after getting their first job when they discover the gap between their gross pay and their net pay after taxes have been deducted. The largest tax many people of low or moderate income pay is the FICA, which stands for the Federal Insurance Contributions Act. The FICA funds the Social Security and Medicare programs, which provide income and health care to the elderly and disabled. The FICA is sometimes referred to as the payroll tax. When Congress passed the FICA, it wanted the burden of the tax to be shared equally by employers and workers. Currently, the FICA is 15.3 percent of wages, with 7.65 percent paid by workers by being withheld from their paychecks and the other 7.65 percent paid by employers.

But does requiring workers and employers to each pay half the tax mean that the burden of the tax is also shared equally? Our discussion in this chapter shows us that the answer is "No." In the labor market, employers are buyers and workers are sellers. As we saw in the example of federal taxes on gasoline, whether the tax is collected from buyers or from sellers does not affect the incidence of the tax. Most economists believe, in fact, that the burden of FICA falls almost entirely on workers. The figure on the next page, which shows the market for labor, illustrates why.

In the market for labor, the demand curve reflects the quantity of labor demanded by employers at various wages, and the supply curve reflects the quantity of labor supplied by workers at various wages. The intersection of the demand curve and the supply curve determines the equilibrium wage. In both panels the equilibrium wage without a Social Security

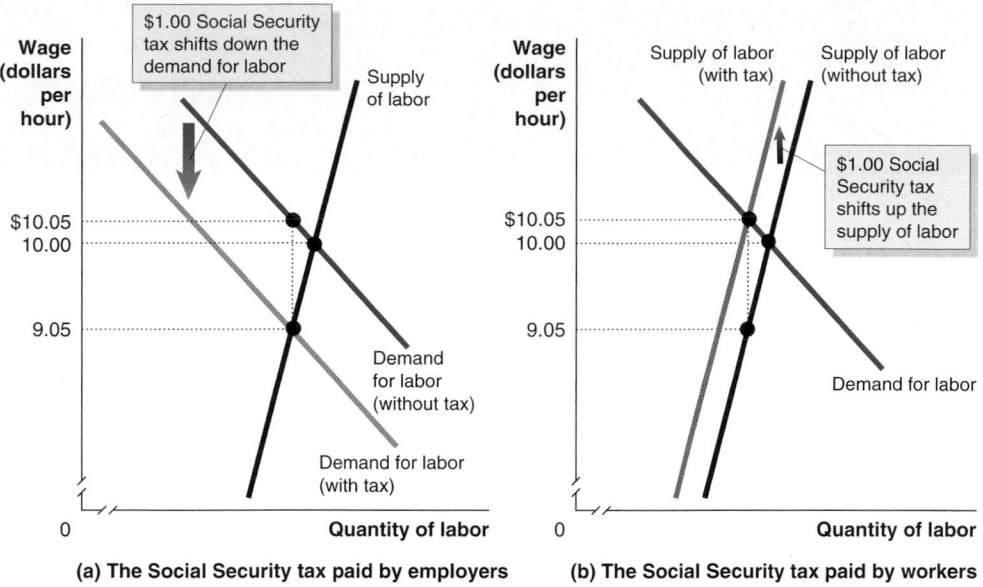

(a) The Social Security tax paid by employers

(b) The Social Security tax paid by workers

payroll tax is $10 per hour. For simplicity, let's assume that the payroll tax equals $1 per hour of work. In panel (a) we assume that the tax must be paid by employers. Imposing the tax causes the demand for labor curve to shift down by $1 at every quantity of labor, because firms now must pay a $1 tax for every hour of labor they hire. We have drawn the supply curve for labor as being very steep to reflect the fact that most economists believe the quantity of labor supplied by workers does not change much as the wage rate changes. In panel (a), after the tax is imposed, the equilibrium wage declines from $10 per hour to $9.05 per hour. Firms are now paying a total of $10.05 for every hour of work they hire: $9.05 in wages to workers and $1 in tax to the government. In other words, workers have paid $0.95 of the $1 tax, and firms have paid only $0.05.

Panel (b) shows that this result is exactly the same if the tax is imposed on workers, rather than on firms. In this case, the tax causes the supply curve for labor to shift up by $1 at every quantity of labor, because workers must now pay a tax of $1 for every hour they work. After the tax is imposed, the equilibrium wage increases to $10.05 per hour. But workers receive only $9.05 after they have paid the $1.00 tax. Once again, workers have paid $0.95 of the $1 tax, and firms have paid only $0.05.

Although the figure presents a simplified analysis, it does reflect the conclusion of most economists who have studied the incidence of FICA: Even though Congress requires half the tax to be paid by employers and the other half to be paid by workers, in fact the burden of the tax falls almost entirely on workers. The forces of demand and supply working in the labor market, and not Congress, determine the incidence of the tax.

Conclusion

The model of demand and supply introduced in Chapter 3 showed that markets free from government intervention eliminate surpluses and shortages, and do a good job of responding to the wants of consumers. We have seen in this chapter that both consumers and firms sometimes try to use the government to change market outcomes in their favor. The concepts of consumer and producer surplus and deadweight loss allow us to measure the benefits consumers and producers receive from competitive market equilibrium. They also allow us to measure the effects of government price floors and price ceilings and the economic impact of taxes.

Read *An Inside Look* on the next page to learn how rent control affects people looking for apartments in New York City.

SLATE, MAY 18, 1997

The Romance of Rent Control

If you want to understand the bitter debate over rent control that now dominates social interaction in New York, you have to begin by ignoring arguments about social justice, market economics, and all appeals to principle. Instead, apply crude Marxist dogma: It's a battle of naked class interest. The catch is that the "classes" glowering at each other across the barricades aren't rich and poor. They're the New Yorkers with scandalously sweet deals vs. all those who get screwed as a result.

Recent experience has done much to reinforce my own class consciousness as a member of the latter group. **a** My wife and I were minding our own business in an unregulated apartment in the rapidly gentrifying East Village when we returned from work one day to a letter informing us that our already (to non-New Yorkers) alarming rent of $1,950 was going up $700. That's for a largish one-bedroom in a marginal neighborhood. . . . Thanks to a connection, we fell into a nice, $2,000 one-bedroom in Chelsea, without paying a finder's fee. Absent the artificial shortage created by rent regulation, we would either have a bigger place or pay much less for the one we've got.

The moral and economic arguments against rent control are pretty much unassailable. Under the present system, government intervenes in the market to protect a class of people defined to some extent by long-term residency, but to an even larger extent by luck. This massive intrusion in the real-estate market, which might be hard to justify even if it had purely beneficial consequences, has a number of obviously disastrous ones. It deters young people and new immigrants from moving to New York City; it encourages landlords to neglect their buildings; it makes them hate their tenants. . . .

b What would happen if rent regulations were really abolished? It's a pretty safe bet that in most parts of Manhattan, market rents would settle in somewhere between the $2,000 a month I pay and the $600 that others pay for nearly identical apartments in the same building. Using the estimates promoted by the Rent Stabilization Association (the newspeak name for the group representing landlords who actually wish to *end* rent stabilization), the typical one-bedroom in the Village or on the Upper West Side might go for $1,300 to $1,400 after the shakeout. A rent like that calls for a pretax income of at least $50,000. Once you figure in New York City and state taxes, a more realistic figure would be $60,000.

c The poor, who are subsidized directly, and are likely to be exempted even in the case of radical decontrol, would stay put. What Manhattan would lose is what remains of its middle class, those earning between $25,000 and, say, $75,000. This would mean a tremendous blow to the city's social variety and cultural vitality. Gone would be the used-bookstore owner, the public-school teacher, the family that's been in the same Upper West Side building for 100 years.

One of the big points made by opponents of rent control is that the present system prevents the construction of new buildings. Because rent regulations say you can't evict people when their leases are up (if they even have leases), one obstinate tenement dweller can block the creation of a 50-story high-rise. But who wants new buildings in Manhattan? What an apartment building looks like—on the outside—affects everybody, not just the landlord and the tenant. New York's old buildings are gracious and charming, even those that are run-down. Its new ones—at least those of the residential variety—are generally horrible. It is rent control that has preserved the aesthetic as well as the social fabric of the kind of variegated, low-rise neighborhoods Jane Jacobs celebrated in *The Death and Life of Great American Cities*. . . .

The goal of a rent-regulation compromise should be to diminish unfairness and mitigate perverse side effects without giving a shock to the city's social system. This argues for a fairly straightforward means test for rent control, say $100,000 a year. . . . There will be people, some of them elderly, who make more than $100,000 but still can't afford the rents their apartments could command on the free market. They will have to move. How big a tragedy is that?

Key Points in the Article

This article provides a look at the market for rental apartments in New York City. Jacob Weisberg, the author of the article, is the managing editor of *Slate*, the online magazine owned by Microsoft. Weisberg's experiences highlight key aspects of life in a city with rent control. Weisberg also presents an argument in favor of rent control, even though he has been made worse off by it financially.

Analyzing the News

We can use the concepts from this chapter to analyze the article:

a Jacob Weisberg and his wife were living in an unregulated apartment, so the rent adjusted according to movements in demand and supply. Because higher-income people were moving into the neighborhood, it was becoming more desirable, and the demand for apartments shifted to the right. This increase in demand caused the equilib-

rium rent to increase from $1,950 to $2,650 per month.

b The author is correct in noting that: "Absent the artificial shortage created by rent regulation, we would either have a bigger place or pay much less for the one we've got." Figure 1 (a) shows the market for apartments currently subject to rent control. For these apartments, eliminating rent control would increase the quantity of apartments rented from Q_1 to Q_2. The rent would rise from $1,000, the rent control ceiling, to $1,500, the competitive equilibrium rent. Figure 1 (b) shows the market for apartments not currently subject to rent control. The elimination of rent control would cause the demand curve for these apartments to shift to the left from D_1 to D_2, which would lower the equilibrium rent from $2,000 to $1,500 per month.

c Although the author is well aware that rent control has resulted in his paying more for his apartment than he would have in a competitive market, he is reluctant to see rent control eliminated. In other words, he under-

stands the positive analysis that shows the economic costs of rent control, but his normative analysis leads him still to support the policy.

Thinking Critically
ABOUT POLICY

1. The author of the article notes that a rent control law "encourages landlords to neglect their buildings. . . ." How does rent control do this?

2. Despite his complaints, the author supports rent control laws. He implicitly balances the cost and benefits of the policy. How might his conclusion change if he were confronted with an estimate of the deadweight loss of the policy? How large would such deadweight loss have to be before you would predict the author would change his mind? Against what measure of benefit would the deadweight loss have to be weighed?

Source: Copyright 1997, Slate.com and Washington post.Newsweek Interactive. All Rights Reserved.

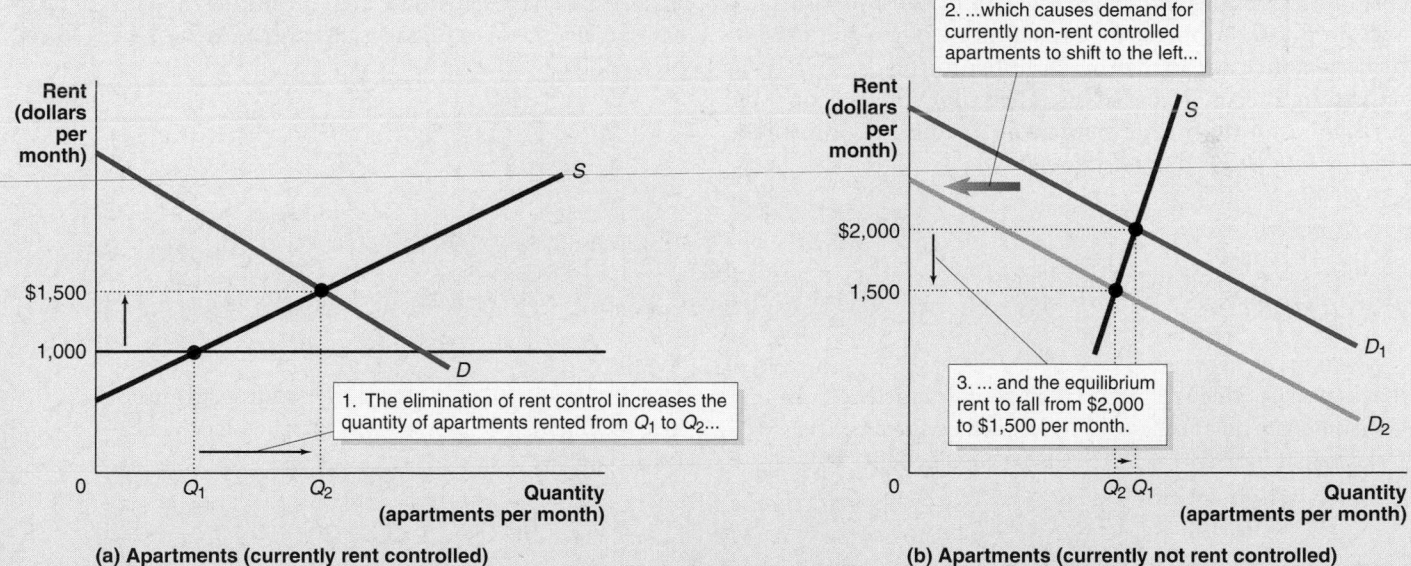

(a) Apartments (currently rent controlled)

(b) Apartments (currently not rent controlled)

Figure 1: In (a), the elimination of rent control causes an increase from Q_1 to Q_2 in the quantity of apartments being rented. In (b) this causes the demand for currently non-rent-controlled apartments to shift to the left from D_1 to D_2. The equilibrium rent declines from $2,000 to $1,500.

LEARNING OBJECTIVE ① Understand the concepts of consumer surplus and producer surplus. *Marginal benefit* is the additional benefit to a consumer from consuming one more unit of a good or service. The demand curve is also a marginal benefit curve. *Consumer surplus* is the difference between the highest price a consumer is willing to pay for a product and the price the consumer actually pays. The total amount of consumer surplus in a market is equal to the area below the demand curve and above the market price. *Marginal cost* is the additional cost to a firm of producing one more unit of a good or service. The supply curve is also a marginal cost curve. *Producer surplus* is the difference between the lowest price a firm is willing to accept and the price it actually receives. The total amount of producer surplus in a market is equal to the area above the supply curve and below the market price.

LEARNING OBJECTIVE ② Understand the concept of economic efficiency, and use a graph to illustrate how economic efficiency is reduced when a market is not in competitive equilibrium. Equilibrium in a competitive market is *economically efficient*. *Economic surplus* is the sum of consumer surplus and producer surplus. Economic efficiency is a market outcome in which the marginal benefit to consumers from the last unit produced is equal to the marginal cost of production, and where the sum of consumer surplus and producer surplus is at a maximum. When the market price is above or below the equilibrium price, there is a reduction in economic surplus. The reduction in economic surplus resulting from a market not being in competitive equilibrium is called the *deadweight loss.*

LEARNING OBJECTIVE ③ Use demand and supply graphs to analyze the economic impact of price ceilings and price floors. Producers or consumers who are dissatisfied with the market outcome can attempt to convince the government to impose *price floors* or *price ceilings*. Price floors usually increase producer surplus, decrease consumer surplus, and cause a deadweight loss. Price ceilings usually increase consumer surplus, reduce producer surplus, and cause a deadweight loss. The results of the government imposing price ceilings and prices floors are that some people win, some people lose, and a loss of economic efficiency occurs. Positive analysis is concerned with what is, and normative analysis is concerned with what should be. Positive analysis shows that price ceilings and price floors cause deadweight losses. Whether these policies are desirable or undesirable, though, is a normative question.

LEARNING OBJECTIVE ④ Use demand and supply graphs to analyze the economic impact of taxes. Most taxes result in a loss of consumer surplus, a loss of producer surplus, and a deadweight loss. The true burden of a tax is not just the amount paid to government by consumers and producers, but also includes the deadweight loss. The deadweight loss from a tax is the excess burden of the tax. *Tax incidence* is the actual division of the burden of a tax. In most cases, consumers and firms share the burden of a tax levied on a good or service.

KEY TERMS

Black market 109	Economic efficiency 104	Marginal cost 101	Producer surplus 101
Consumer surplus 99	Economic surplus 103	Price ceiling 98	Tax incidence 112
Deadweight loss 104	Marginal benefit 99	Price floor 98	

REVIEW QUESTIONS

1. What is marginal benefit? Why is the demand curve referred to as a marginal benefit curve?
2. What is marginal cost? Why is the supply curve referred to as a marginal cost curve?
3. What is consumer surplus? How does consumer surplus change as the equilibrium price of a good rises or falls?
4. What is producer surplus? How does producer surplus change as the equilibrium price of a good rises or falls?
5. What is economic efficiency? Why do economists define efficiency in this way?
6. Why would some consumers tend to favor price controls, while others would be against them?

7. Do producers tend to favor price floors or price ceilings? Why?

8. What is a "black" market? Under what circumstances do black markets arise?

9. Can economic analysis provide a final answer to the question of whether the government should intervene in mar-

kets by imposing price ceilings and price floors? Why or why not?

10. What is meant by tax incidence? Do the people who are legally required to pay a tax always bear the burden of the tax? Briefly explain.

PROBLEMS AND APPLICATIONS

Please visit **www.prenhall.com/hubbard** *for solutions to the even-numbered problems as well as multiple-choice and true or false self-assessment quizzes.*

1. The figure below illustrates the market for apples in which the government has imposed a price floor of $10 per crate.

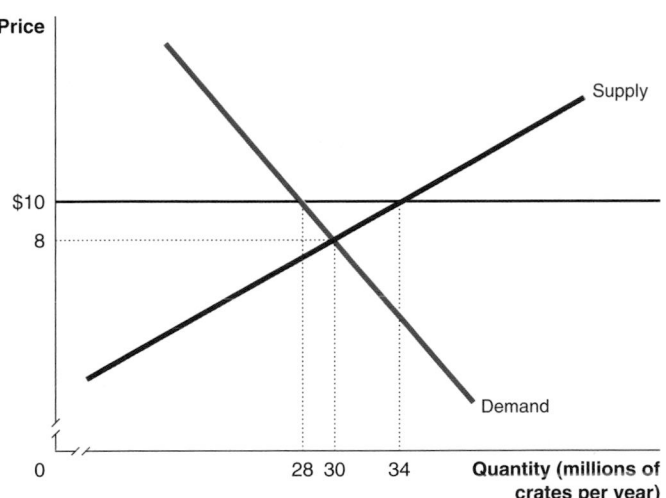

a. How many crates of apples will be sold after the price floor has been imposed?

b. Will there be a shortage or a surplus? If there is a shortage or a surplus, how large will it be?

c. Will apple producers benefit from the price floor? If so, explain how they will benefit.

2. Use the information on the kumquat market in the following table to answer the questions.

PRICE (PER CRATE)	QUANTITY DEMANDED (MILLIONS OF CRATES PER YEAR)	QUANTITY SUPPLIED (MILLIONS OF CRATES PER YEAR)
$10	120	20
15	110	60
20	100	100
25	90	140
30	80	180
35	70	220

a. What are the equilibrium price and quantity? How much revenue do kumquat producers receive when the market is in equilibrium? Draw a graph showing the market equilibrium and the area representing the revenue received by kumquat producers.

b. Suppose the federal government decides to impose a price floor of $30 per crate. Now how many crates of kumquats will consumers purchase? How much revenue will kumquat producers receive? Assume that the government does not purchase any surplus kumquats. On your graph from question (a), show the price floor, the change in the quantity of kumquats purchased, and the revenue received by kumquat producers after the price floor is imposed.

c. Suppose the government imposes a price floor of $30 per crate and purchases any surplus kumquats from producers. Now how much revenue will kumquat producers receive? How much will the government spend purchasing surplus kumquats? On your graph from question (a), show the area representing the amount the government spends to purchase the surplus kumquats.

3. Suppose that the government sets a price floor for milk that is above the competitive equilibrium price.

a. Draw a graph showing this situation. Be sure that your graph shows the competitive equilibrium price, the price floor, the quantity that would be sold in competitive equilibrium, and the quantity that is sold with the price floor.

b. Compare the economic surplus in this market when there is a price floor and when there is no price floor.

4. Suppose that the government restricts the number of dairy farmers, which results in the supply curve for milk shifting to the left. Briefly explain whether each of the following will increase or decrease.

a. Consumer surplus

b. Producer surplus

c. Economic surplus

Using a demand and supply graph, illustrate your answer in each case.

5. To drive a taxicab legally in New York City, you must have a medallion issued by the city government. Only 12,187 medallions have been issued. Let's assume this puts an absolute limit on the number of taxi rides that can be supplied in New York City on any day, because no one breaks the law by driving a taxi without a medallion. Let's also assume that each taxi can provide 6 trips per day. In that case, the supply of taxi rides is fixed at 73,122 (or 6 rides per taxi × 12,187 taxis). We show this in the following graph with a vertical line at this quantity. *Assume that there are no government controls on the prices that drivers can charge for rides.* Use the figure to answer the following questions.

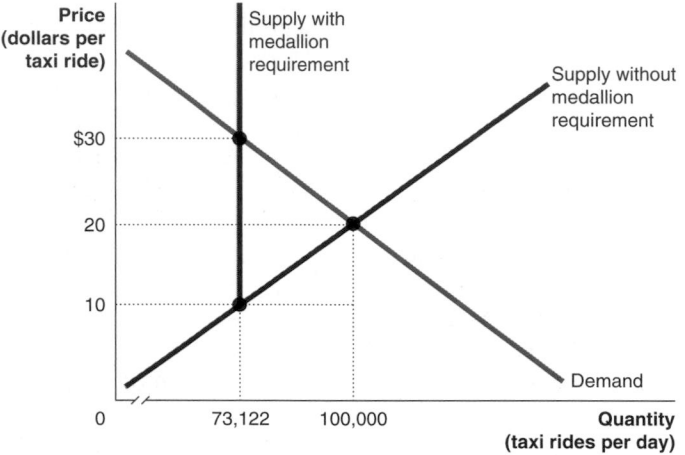

a. What would the equilibrium price and quantity be in this market if there were no medallion requirement?
b. What are the price and quantity with the medallion requirement?
c. Indicate on the graph the areas representing consumer surplus and producer surplus if there were no medallion requirement.
d. Indicate on the graph the areas representing consumer surplus, producer surplus, and deadweight loss with the medallion requirement.

6. If the goal of the federal government's farm program is to raise the incomes of poor family farmers, is the current system of price floors and subsidy payments based on the number of acres farmed a good way to reach the goal? Briefly explain. What other ways might the federal government attempt to reach its goals?

7. Suppose the competitive equilibrium rent for a standard two-bedroom apartment in Lawrence is $600. Now suppose the city council passes a rent control law imposing a price ceiling of $500. Use a demand and supply graph to illustrate the impact of the rent control law. Suppose that shortly after the law is passed, a large employer in the area announces that it will close a plant in Lawrence and lay off 5,000 workers. Show on your graph how this will affect the market for rental property in Lawrence.

8. **[Related to *Solved Problem 4–1*]** Use the information in the following table on the market for apartments in Bay City to answer the following questions.

RENT	QUANTITY DEMANDED	QUANTITY SUPPLIED
$500	375,000	225,000
600	350,000	250,000
700	325,000	275,000
800	300,000	300,000
900	275,000	325,000
1000	250,000	350,000

a. In the absence of rent control, what is the equilibrium rent and what is the equilibrium quantity of apartments rented? Draw a demand and supply graph of the market for apartments to illustrate your answer. In equilibrium, will there be any renters who are unable to find an apartment to rent or any landlords who are unable to find a renter for an apartment?
b. Suppose the government sets a ceiling on rents of $600 per month. What is the quantity of apartments demanded, and what is the quantity of apartments supplied?
c. Assume that all landlords abide by the law. Use a demand and supply graph to illustrate the impact of this price ceiling on the market for apartments. Be sure to indicate on your diagram each of the following: (i) the area representing consumer surplus after the price ceiling has been imposed, (ii) the area representing producer surplus after the price ceiling has been imposed, and (iii) the area representing the deadweight loss after the ceiling has been imposed.
d. Assume that the quantity of apartments supplied is the same as you determined in (b). But now assume that landlords ignore the law and rent this quantity of apartments for the highest rent they can get. Briefly explain what this rent will be.

9. The following is from an article in the *New York Times*:

Imagine finding the perfect apartment, only to learn that the landlord is denying you the place because you are on a blacklist of supposedly high-risk renters. Nothing is wrong with your credit rating, but your name showed up on the list because a private screening service found it in housing court records about a dispute you had with a previous landlord—a dispute that was resolved in your favor.

Is it more likely that a "blacklist" of "high-risk" tenants will exist in a city with rent control, or one without rent control? Briefly explain.
Source: Motoko Rich, "A Blacklist of Renters," *New York Times*, April 8, 2004.

10. [Related to *Don't Let This Happen To You!*] Briefly explain whether you agree or disagree with the following statement: "If there is a shortage of a good it must be scarce, but there is not a shortage of every scarce good."

11. A student makes the following argument:

    > A price floor reduces the amount of a product that consumers buy, because it keeps the price above the competitive market equilibrium. A price ceiling, on the other hand, increases the amount of a product that consumers buy, because it keeps the price below the competitive market equilibrium.

    Do you agree with the student's reasoning? Use a demand and supply graph to illustrate your answer.

12. An advocate of medical care system reform makes the following argument:

    > The 15,000 kidneys that are transplanted in the United States each year are received free from organ donors. Despite this, because of hospital and doctor's fees, the average price of a kidney transplant is $250,000. As a result, only rich people or people with very good health insurance can afford these transplants. The government should put a ceiling of $100,000 on the price of kidney transplants. That way, middle-income people will be able to afford them, the demand for kidney transplants will increase, and more kidney transplants will take place.

    Do you agree with the advocate's reasoning? Use a demand and supply graph to illustrate your answer.

13. [Related to the *Chapter Opener*] The cities of Peabody and Woburn are five miles apart. Woburn enacts a rent control law that puts a ceiling on rents well below their competitive market value. Predict the impact of this law on the competitive equilibrium rent in Peabody, which does not have a rent control law. Illustrate your answer with a demand and supply graph.

14. [Related to the *Chapter Opener*] Rent controls were first imposed in New York City in the early 1940s during a housing shortage brought on by World War II. Why do you think that, once established, rent controls continued in New York City for many decades?

15. [Related to the *Chapter Opener*] The political commentator George Will asked the following question in a column in *Newsweek* magazine:

    > Are rent controls compassionate, or do they create a shortage of rental units and a disincentive for landlords to spend on maintenance?

    How would you answer Will's question?
    Source: George F. Will, "One Judge's Conservatism," *Newsweek*, March 3, 2003.

16. [Related to *Solved Problem 4–1*] Suppose that initially the gasoline market is in equilibrium at a price of $2.00 per gallon and a quantity of 45 million gallons per month. Then a war in the Middle East disrupts imports of oil into the United States, shifting the supply curve for gasoline from S_1 to S_2. The price of gasoline begins to rise and consumers protest. The federal government responds by setting a price ceiling of $2.00 per gallon. Use the graph to answer the following questions.

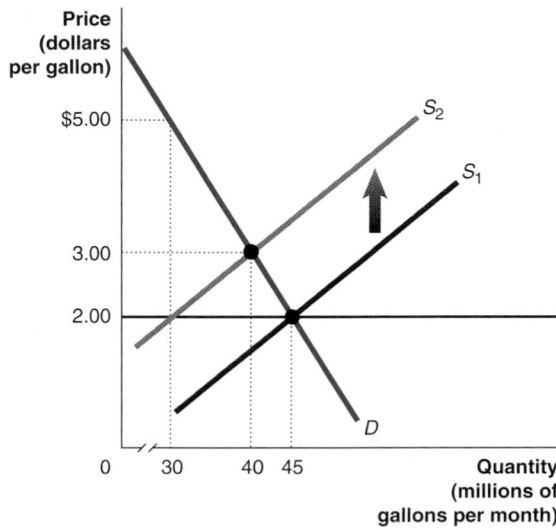

a. If there were no price ceiling, what would be the equilibrium price of gasoline, the quantity of gasoline demanded, and the quantity of gasoline supplied? Now assume that the price ceiling is imposed and that there is no black market in gasoline. What are the price of gasoline, the quantity of gasoline demanded, and the quantity of gasoline supplied? How large is the shortage of gasoline?

b. Assume that the price ceiling is imposed and there is no black market in gasoline. Show on the graph the areas representing consumer surplus, producer surplus, and deadweight loss.

c. Now assume there is a black market and the price of gasoline rises to the maximum that consumers are willing to pay for the amount supplied by producers at $2.00 per gallon. Show on the graph the areas representing producer surplus, consumer surplus, and deadweight loss.

d. Are consumers made better off by the price ceiling? Briefly explain.

17. In the United States, Amazon.com, BarnesandNoble.com, and many other retailers sell books, DVDs, and music CDs for less than the price marked on the package. In Japan, retailers are not allowed to discount prices in this way. Who benefits and who loses from this Japanese law?

18. Most family businesses in the United States receive little direct support from the federal government. However, family farms have been receiving support from the federal government since the 1930s. Why do you suppose family farms have been singled out as meriting special support from the government?

19. The competitive equilibrium rent in the city of Lowell is currently $1,000 per month. The government decides to enact rent control and to establish a price ceiling for apartments of $750 per month. Briefly explain whether rent control is likely to make you personally better or worse off if you are:
    a. someone currently renting an apartment in Lowell.
    b. someone who will be moving to Lowell next year and who intends to rent an apartment.
    c. a landlord who intends to abide by the rent control law.
    d. a landlord who intends to ignore the law and illegally charge the highest rent you can for your apartments.

20. Use this diagram of the market for cigarettes to answer the following questions.

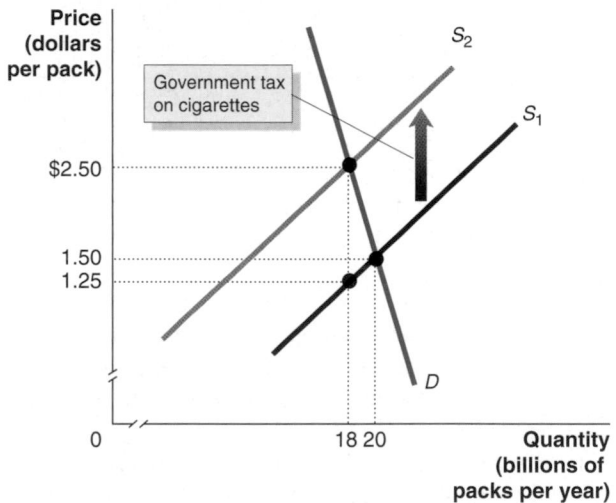

    a. According to the diagram, how much is the government tax on cigarettes?
    b. What price do producers receive after paying the tax?
    c. How much tax revenue does the government collect?

21. [Related to *Solved Problem 4–2*] Suppose the federal government decides to levy a sales tax on pizza of $1.00 per pie. Briefly explain whether you agree with the following statement by a representative of the pizza industry: "The pizza industry is very competitive. As a result, pizza sellers will have to pay the whole tax, because they are unable to pass any of it on to consumers in the form of higher prices.

Therefore, a sales tax of $1.00 per pie will result in pizza sellers receiving $1 less on each pie sold, after paying the tax." Illustrate your answer with a graph.

22. The following figure illustrates the market for a breast-cancer-fighting drug, without which breast cancer patients cannot survive. What is the consumer surplus in this market? How does it differ from the consumer surplus in the markets you have studied up to this point?

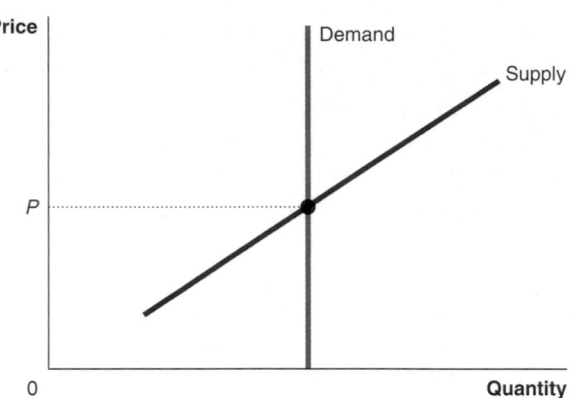

23. The diagram below illustrates the market for seats at a concert, which will be held in a local stadium that seats 15,000 people. What is the producer surplus in this market? How does it differ from the producer surplus in the markets you have studied up to this point?

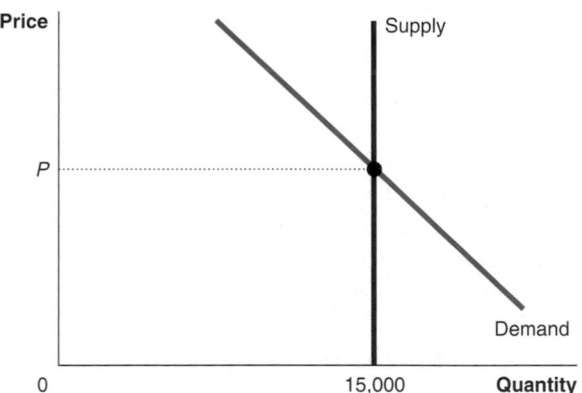

24. Suppose you were assigned the task of developing an economic indicator that measured the "wealth of a nation"— that is, come up with a single number that would allow someone to compare the economic activity in one country to that in another country or to another point in time. How might such a number be related to economic efficiency and consumer and producer surplus?

Quantitative Demand and Supply Analysis

Graphs help us understand economic change *qualitatively*. For instance, a demand and supply graph can tell us that if household incomes rise, the demand curve for a normal good will shift to the right and its price will rise. Often, though, economists, business managers, and policymakers want to know more than the qualitative direction of change, they want a *quantitative estimate* of the size of the change.

In Chapter 4, we carried out a qualitative analysis of rent controls. We saw that imposing rent controls involves a trade-off: Renters as a group gain, but landlords lose and the market for apartments becomes less efficient, as shown by the deadweight loss. To better evaluate rent controls we need to know more than just that these gains and losses exist; we need to know how large they are. A quantitative analysis of rent controls will tell us how large the gains and losses are.

Demand and Supply Equations

The first step in a quantitative analysis is to supplement our use of demand and supply curves with demand and supply *equations*. We noted briefly in Chapter 3 that economists often statistically estimate equations for demand curves. Supply curves can also be statistically estimated. For example, suppose that economists have estimated that the demand for apartments in New York City is

$$Q^D = 3,000,000 - 1,000P,$$

and the supply of apartments is

$$Q^S = -450,000 + 1,300P.$$

We have used Q^D for the quantity of apartments demanded per month, Q^S for the quantity of apartments supplied per month, and P for the apartment rent in dollars per month. In reality, both the quantity of apartments demanded and the quantity of apartments supplied will depend on more than just the rental price of apartments in New York City. For instance, the demand for apartments in New York City will also depend on the average incomes of families in the New York area and on the rents of apartments in surrounding cities. For simplicity, we will ignore these other factors.

With no government intervention, we know that at competitive market equilibrium the quantity demanded must equal the quantity supplied, or

$$Q^D = Q^S.$$

We can use this equation, which is called an *equilibrium condition*, to solve for the equilibrium monthly apartment rent by setting the demand equation equal to the supply equation:

$$3,000,000 - 1,000P = -450,000 + 1,300P$$

$$3,450,000 = 2,300P$$

$$P = \frac{3,450,000}{2,300} = \$1,500$$

FIGURE 4A-1

Graphing Supply and Demand Equations

After statistically estimating supply and demand equations, we can use the equations to draw supply and demand curves. In this case, the equilibrium rent for apartments is $1,500 per month and the equilibrium quantity of apartments rented is 1,500,000. The supply equation tells us that at a rent of $346, the quantity of apartments supplied will be zero. The demand equation tells us that at a rent of $3,000, the quantity of apartments demanded will be zero. The areas representing consumer surplus and producer surplus are also indicated on the graph.

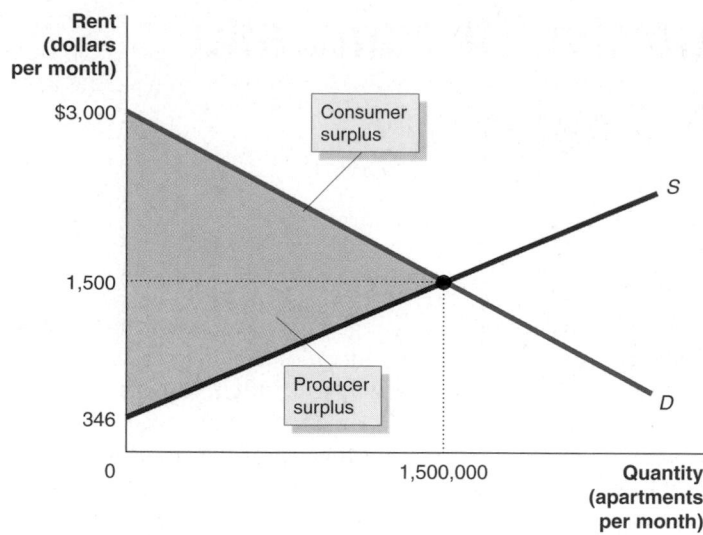

We can then substitute this price back into either the supply equation or the demand equation to find the equilibrium quantity of apartments rented:

$$Q^D = 3,000,000 - 1,000P = 3,000,000 - 1,000(1,500) = 1,500,000$$

$$Q^S = -450,000 + 1,300P = -450,000 + 1,300(1,500) = 1,500,000$$

Figure 4A-1 illustrates the information from these equations in a graph. The figure shows the values for rent when the quantity supplied is zero and when the quantity demanded is zero. These values can be calculated from the demand equation and the supply equation by setting Q^D and Q^S equal to zero and solving for price:

$$Q^D = 0 = 3,000,000 - 1,000P$$

$$P = \frac{3,000,000}{1,000} = \$3,000$$

and

$$Q^S = 0 = -450,000 + 1,300P$$

$$P = \frac{-450,000}{-1,300} = \$346.15.$$

Calculating Consumer Surplus and Producer Surplus

Figure 4A-1 also shows consumer surplus and producer surplus in this market. Recall that the sum of consumer surplus and producer surplus equals the net benefit that renters and landlords receive from participating in the market for apartments. We can use the values from the demand and supply equations to calculate the value of consumer surplus and producer surplus. Remember that consumer surplus is the area below the demand curve and above the line representing market price. Notice that this area forms a right triangle, because the demand curve is a straight line—it is *linear*. As we noted in the Appendix to Chapter 1, the area of a triangle is equal to ½ multiplied by the base of the triangle multiplied by the height of the triangle. In this case, the area is

$$\tfrac{1}{2} \times (1,500,000) \times (3,000 - 1,500) = \$1,125,000,000.$$

So, this calculation tells us that the consumer surplus in the market for rental apartments in New York City would be about $1.125 billion.

We can calculate producer surplus in a similar way. Remember that producer surplus is the area above the supply curve and below the line representing market price. Because our supply curve is also a straight line, producer surplus on the figure is equal to the area of the right triangle:

$$\tfrac{1}{2} \times (1{,}500{,}000) \times (1{,}500 - 346) = \$865{,}500{,}000.$$

This calculation tells us that the producer surplus in the market for rental apartments in New York City is about $865 million.

We can use this same type of analysis to measure the impact of rent control on consumer surplus, producer surplus, and economic efficiency. For instance, suppose the city imposes a rent ceiling of $1000 per month. Figure 4A-2 below can help guide us as we measure the impact. First, we can calculate the quantity of apartments that will actually be rented by substituting the rent ceiling of $1,000 into the supply equation:

$$Q^S = -450{,}000 + (1{,}300 \times 1{,}000) = 850{,}000.$$

We also need to know the price on the demand curve when the quantity of apartments is 850,000. We can do this by substituting in 850,000 for quantity in the demand equation and solving for price:

$$850{,}000 = 3{,}000{,}000 - 1{,}000P$$

$$P = \frac{-2{,}150{,}000}{-1{,}000} = \$2{,}150.$$

Compared with its value in competitive equilibrium, consumer surplus has been reduced by a value equal to the area of the yellow triangle B, but increased by a value equal to the area of the blue rectangle A. The area of the yellow triangle B is

$$\tfrac{1}{2} \times (1{,}500{,}000 - 850{,}000) \times (2{,}150 - 1{,}500) = \$211{,}250{,}000,$$

and the area of the blue rectangle A is base multiplied by height, or

$$(\$1{,}500 - \$1{,}000) \times (850{,}000) = \$425{,}000{,}000.$$

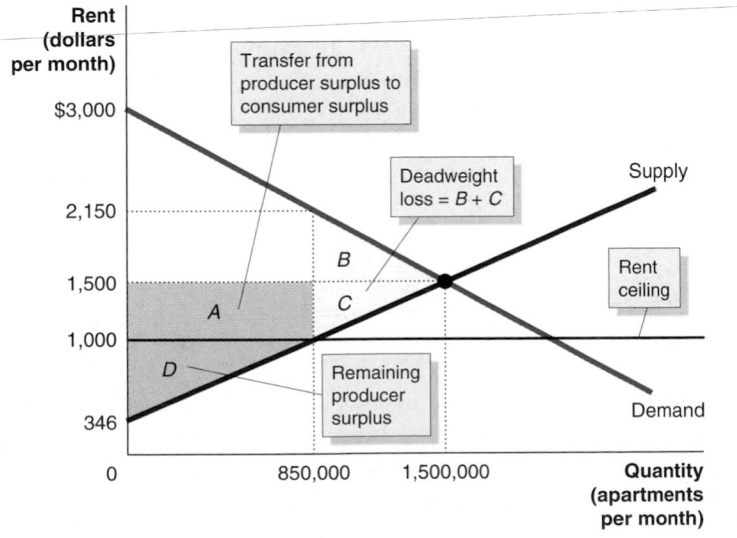

FIGURE 4A-2

Calculating the Economic Effect of Rent Controls

Once we have estimated equations for the demand and supply of rental housing, a diagram can guide our numerical estimates of the economic effects of rent control. Consumer surplus falls by an amount equal to the area of the yellow triangle B and increases by an amount equal to the area of the blue rectangle A. The difference between the values of these two areas is $213,750,000. Producer surplus falls by an amount equal to the area of the blue rectangle A plus the area of the yellow triangle C. The value of these two areas is $587,500,000. The remaining producer surplus is equal to the area of triangle D, or $278,000,000. Deadweight loss is equal to the area of triangle B plus the area of triangle C, or $373,750,000.

The value of consumer surplus in competitive equilibrium was \$1,125,000,000. As a result of the rent ceiling it will be increased to

$$(\$1,125,000,000 + \$425,000,000) - \$211,250,000 = \$1,338,750,000.$$

Compared with its value in competitive equilibrium, producer surplus has been reduced by a value equal to the area of the yellow triangle C plus a value equal to the area of the blue rectangle. The area of the yellow triangle C is

$$\tfrac{1}{2} \times (1,500,000 - 850,000) \times (1,500 - 1,000) = \$162,500,000.$$

We have already calculated the area of the blue rectangle A as \$425,000,000. The value of producer surplus in competitive equilibrium was \$865,500,000. As a result of the rent ceiling it will be reduced to

$$\$865,500,000 - \$162,500,000 - \$425,000,000 = \$278,000,000.$$

The loss of economic efficiency, as measured by the deadweight loss, is equal to the value represented by the areas of the yellow triangles B and C, or

$$\$211,250,000 + \$162,500,000 = \$373,750,000.$$

The following table summarizes the results of the analysis (the values are in millions of dollars):

CONSUMER SURPLUS		PRODUCER SURPLUS		DEADWEIGHT LOSS	
COMPETITIVE EQUILIBRIUM	RENT CONTROL	COMPETITIVE EQUILIBRIUM	RENT CONTROL	COMPETITIVE EQUILIBRIUM	RENT CONTROL
\$1,125	\$1,338.75	\$865.50	\$278	\$0	\$373.75

Qualitatively, we know that imposing rent controls will make consumers better off, landlords worse off, and decrease economic efficiency. The advantage of the analysis that we have just gone through is that it puts dollar values on the qualitative results. We can now see how much consumers have gained, how much landlords have lost, and how great the decline in economic efficiency has been. Sometimes the quantitative results can be surprising. Notice, for instance, that after the imposition of rent control, the deadweight loss is actually greater than the remaining producer surplus.

Economists often study issues where the qualitative results of actions are apparent, even to non-economists. You don't have to be an economist to understand who wins and loses from rent control, or that if a company cuts the price of its product, its sales will increase. Business managers, policymakers, and the general public do, however, need economists to measure quantitatively the effects of different actions—including policies such as rent control—so that they can better assess the results of these actions.

REVIEW QUESTIONS

1. In a linear demand equation, what economic information is conveyed by the intercept on the price axis?

2. Suppose you were assigned the task of choosing a price that maximized economic surplus in a market. What price would you choose? Why?

3. Consumer surplus is used as a measure of a consumer's net benefit from purchasing a good or service. Explain why consumer surplus is a measure of net benefit.

4. Why would economists use a term like "deadweight loss" to describe the impact on consumer and producer surplus from a price control?

PROBLEMS AND APPLICATIONS

Please visit **www.prenhall.com/hubbard** *for solutions to the even-numbered problems as well as multiple-choice and true or false self-assessment quizzes.*

1. Suppose that you have been hired to analyze the impact on employment from the imposition of a minimum wage in the labor market. Further suppose that you estimate the supply and demand functions for labor, where L stands for the quantity of labor (measured in thousands of workers), and W stands for the wage rate (measured in dollars per hour):

   Demand: $L^D = 100 - 4W$
   Supply: $L^S = 6W$

   First, calculate the free-market equilibrium wage and quantity of labor. Now suppose the proposed minimum wage is $12. How large will the surplus of labor in this market?

2. The diagrams below illustrate the markets for two different types of labor. Suppose an identical minimum wage is imposed in both markets. In which market will the minimum wage have the largest impact on employment? Why?

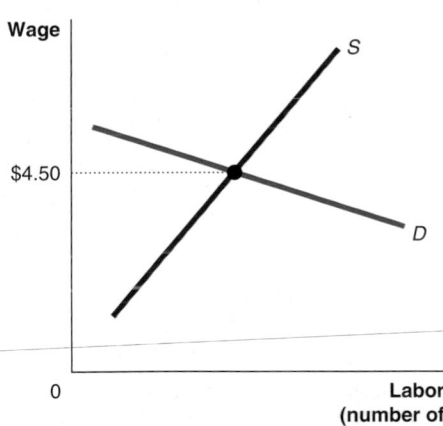

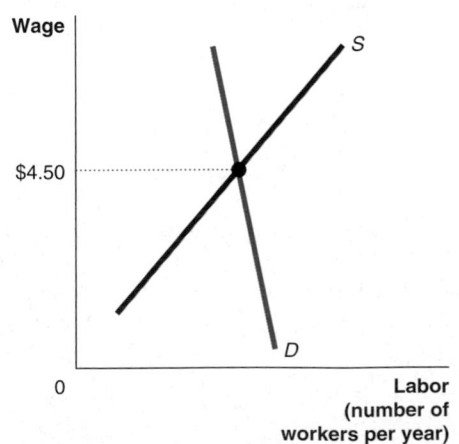

3. Suppose that you are the vice president of operations of a manufacturing firm, which sells an industrial lubricant in a competitive market. Further suppose that your economist gives you the following supply and demand functions:

   Demand: $Q^D = 45 - 2P$
   Supply: $Q^S = -15 + P$

   What is the consumer surplus in this market? What is the producer surplus?

4. The diagram below shows a market in which a price floor has been imposed. Identify the following: (a) the deadweight loss; (b) the transfer of producer surplus to consumers or the transfer of consumer surplus to producers; (c) the remaining producer surplus; (d) the remaining consumer surplus.

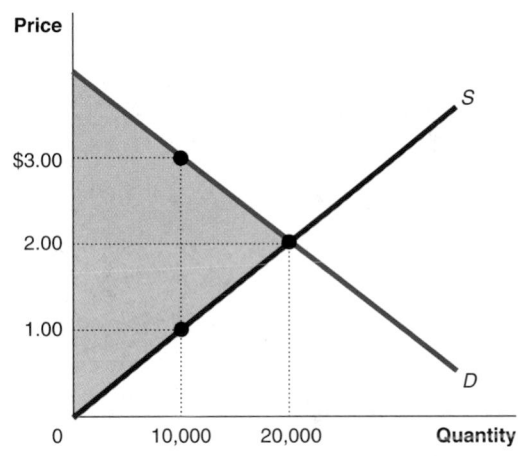

5. Construct a table like the one in this Appendix under the assumption that the rent ceiling is $1,200, rather than $1,000.

chapter

five

Externalities, Environmental Policy, and Public Goods

Economic Incentives Spur Duke Energy Corporation to Reduce Pollution

➤ Pollution is a part of economic life. Consumers create air pollution by burning gasoline to power their cars or natural gas to heat their homes. Firms create air pollution when they produce electricity, pesticides, or plastics, among other products. This air pollution produces acid rain that can damage trees, crops, and buildings and greenhouse gases that can increase global warming. In 1970, the U.S. government passed the Clean Air Act to promote the reduction of air pollution. In 1990, Congress amended the Clean Air Act to deal with the problem of acid rain by reducing the levels of sulfur dioxide emitted by electric utilities. Utilities produce sulfur dioxide when they burn coal to generate electricity. In

the past, Congress mandated the methods firms used to reduce pollution. But many economists were critical of this approach—known as *command and control*—because some companies were able to reduce their emissions much more cheaply if they are allowed to choose the method. To encourage reducing sulfur dioxide emissions in the most efficient way, economists recommended, and Congress adopted, a *market-based approach* called *tradeable emissions allowances*.

Under this system, which went into operation in 1995, the federal government gives utility companies allowances to produce a target amount of sulfur dioxide emissions. Utilities are free to buy and sell

allowances, although they must end up with allowances equal to the amount of sulfur dioxide they wish to emit: one allowance for every ton of sulfur dioxide emitted. Utilities that initially lack sufficient allowances either must reduce the amount of sulfur dioxide they emit or buy allowances from other utilities that are polluting less.

The Duke Power Company, now known as the Duke Energy Corporation, was founded in Charlotte, North Carolina, in 1904. It began generating electricity by using the water power of the Catawba River. By the 1930s, growing demand for electricity was greater than could be met using water power, so the company began building plants that generated electricity by burning coal. Today,

LEARNING OBJECTIVES

After studying this chapter, you should be able to:

① Identify examples of positive and negative externalities and use graphs to show how externalities affect economic efficiency.

② Discuss the Coase theorem and explain how private bargaining can lead to economic efficiency in a market with an externality.

③ Analyze government policies to achieve economic efficiency in a market with an externality.

④ Explain how goods can be categorized on the basis of whether they are rival or excludable.

⑤ Define a public good and a common resource, and use graphs to illustrate the efficient quantities of public goods and common resources.

Duke Energy continues to operate coal-burning plants, which emit sulfur dioxide. Because Duke Energy already burns low-sulfur coal, reducing emissions of sulfur dioxide even further would be expensive. Many electric utilities in the Midwest, however, burn high-sulfur coal and their emissions can be reduced greatly by installing anti-pollution devices known as "scrubbers." As a result, these utilities can drastically reduce their emissions and still have allowances left that they can sell to utilities like Duke Energy. According to the manager in charge of environmental compliance at the company, reducing emissions of sulfur dioxide would cost Duke Energy about $300 per ton. A midwestern utility could reduce emissions for only about $100 per ton. These utilities were willing to sell allowances to Duke Energy for $200 each. As the manager put it, "They would make $100, and Duke would save $100." Not only would the utilities gain, but sulfur dioxide emissions would be reduced at a lower total cost to the economy.

An Inside Look on page 156 discusses how tradeable emissions permits are also being used to reduce emissions of carbon dioxide, one of the gases suspected of contributing to global warming.

Source: Daniel Altman, "Just How Far Can Trading of Emissions Be Extended?", *New York Times*, May 31, 2002.

Externality A benefit or cost that affects someone who is not directly involved in the production or consumption of a good or service.

➤ Air pollution is just one example of an *externality*. An **externality** is a benefit or cost that affects someone who is not directly involved in the production or consumption of a good or service. In the case of air pollution, there is a *negative externality* because, for example, people with asthma may bear a cost even though they were not involved in the buying or selling of the electricity that caused the pollution. *Positive externalities* are also possible. For instance, medical research can provide a positive externality because people who are not directly involved in producing it or paying for it can benefit. A competitive market usually does a good job of producing the economically efficient amount of a good or service. This may not be true, though, if there is an externality in the market. When there is a negative externality, the market may produce a quantity of the good that is greater than the efficient amount. When there is a positive externality, the market may produce a quantity that is less than the efficient amount. In Chapter 4, we saw that government interventions in the economy—such as price floors on agricultural products or price ceilings on rents—can reduce economic efficiency. But when there are externalities, government intervention may actually increase economic efficiency and enhance the well-being of society. The way in which government intervenes is important, however. As the example of the acid rain program shows, economists can help policymakers ensure that government programs are as efficient as possible.

In this chapter, we explore how best to deal with the problem of pollution, as well as other externalities. We also look at *public goods,* which are goods that may not be produced at all unless the government produces them.

① **LEARNING OBJECTIVE**

Identify examples of positive and negative externalities and use graphs to show how externalities affect economic efficiency.

Externalities and Efficiency

When you consume a Big Mac, only you benefit, but when you consume a college education, other people will also benefit. College-educated people are less likely to commit crimes and, by being better informed voters, more likely to contribute to better government policies. So, although you capture most of the benefits of your college education, you do not capture all of them.

When you buy a Big Mac, the price you pay covers all of McDonald's costs of producing the Big Mac. When you buy electricity from a utility that burns coal and generates acid rain, the price you pay for the electricity does not cover the cost of the damage caused by the acid rain.

So, there is a *positive externality* in the production of college educations, because people who do not pay for college educations will nonetheless benefit from them. There is a *negative externality* in the generation of electricity because, for example, people with homes on a lake from which fish and wildlife have disappeared because of acid rain have incurred a cost, even though they might not have bought their electricity from the polluting utility.

The Effect of Externalities

Externalities interfere with the *economic efficiency* of a market equilibrium. We saw in Chapter 4 that a competitive market achieves economic efficiency by maximizing the sum of consumer surplus and producer surplus. *But that result only holds if there are no externalities in production or consumption.* An externality causes a difference between the *private cost* of production and the *social cost,* or the *private benefit* from consumption and the *social benefit*. The **private cost** is the cost borne by the producer of a good or service. The **social cost** is the private cost plus any external cost resulting from production, such as the cost of pollution. Unless there is an externality, the private cost and the social cost will be equal. The **private benefit** is the benefit received by the consumer of a good or service. The **social benefit** is the private benefit plus any external benefit, such as the benefit to others resulting from your college education. Unless there is an externality, the private benefit and the social benefit will be equal.

HOW A NEGATIVE EXTERNALITY IN PRODUCTION REDUCES ECONOMIC EFFICIENCY

Consider first how a negative externality in production affects economic efficiency. In Chapters 3 and 4, we assumed that the producer of a good or service must bear all of the costs of production. We now know that this observation is not always true. In producing electricity, some private costs are borne by the utility, but some external costs of acid rain are borne by farmers, fishermen, and the general public. The social cost of producing electricity is the sum of the private cost plus the external cost. Figure 5-1 shows the effect on the market for electricity of a negative externality in production.

S_1 is the market supply curve and reflects only the private costs that utilities have to bear in generating electricity. If utilities also had to bear the cost of acid rain, the supply curve would be S_2, which reflects the true social cost of generating electricity. The equilibrium with a price P_2 and quantity Q_2 is efficient. The equilibrium with a price P_1 and quantity Q_1 is not efficient. To see why, remember from Chapter 4 that an equilibrium is economically efficient if economic surplus—which is the sum of consumer surplus plus producer surplus—is at a maximum. When economic surplus is at a maximum, the net benefit to society from the production of the good or service is at a maximum. With an equilibrium quantity of Q_2, economic surplus is at a maximum, so this equilibrium is efficient. But with an equilibrium quantity of Q_1, economic surplus is reduced by the deadweight loss, shown in Figure 5-1 by the yellow triangle, and the equilibrium is not efficient. The deadweight loss occurs because the supply curve is above the demand curve for the production of the units of electricity between Q_2 and Q_1. That is, the additional cost—including the external cost—of producing these units is greater than the marginal benefit to consumers. In other words, because of the cost of the acid rain, economic efficiency would be improved if less electricity were produced.

Private cost   The cost borne by the producer of a good or service.

Social cost   The total cost of producing a good, including both the private cost and any external cost.

Private benefit   The benefit received by the consumer of a good or service.

Social benefit   The total benefit from consuming a good, including both the private benefit and any external benefit.

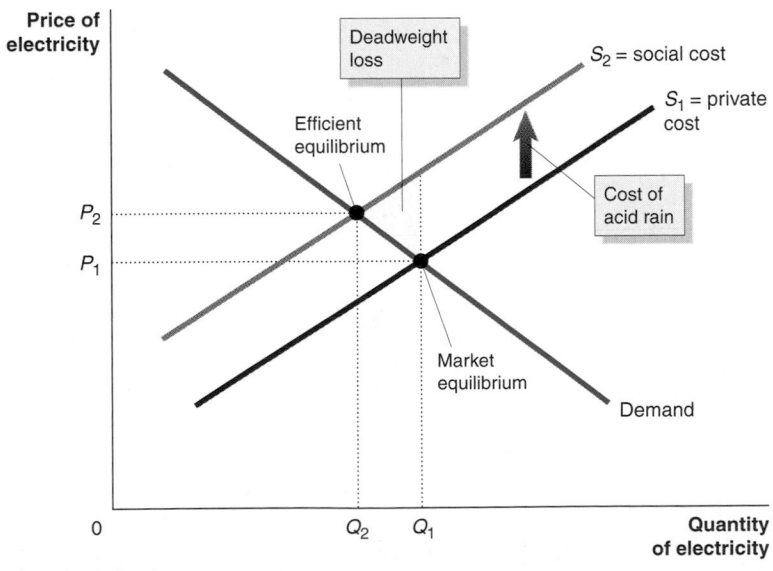

FIGURE 5-1

The Effect of Pollution on Economic Efficiency

Because utilities do not bear the cost of acid rain, they produce electricity beyond the economically efficient level. Supply curve S_1 represents just the private cost that the utility has to pay. Supply curve S_2 represents the social cost, which includes the costs to those affected by acid rain. The figure shows that if the supply curve were S_2, rather than S_1, market equilibrium would occur at a price of P_2 and a quantity of Q_2, the economically efficient level of output. But when the supply curve is S_1, the market equilibrium occurs at a price of P_1 and a quantity of Q_1 where there is a deadweight loss equal to the area of the yellow triangle. Because of the deadweight loss, this equilibrium is not efficient.

We can conclude the following: *When there is a negative externality in producing a good or service, too much of the good or service will be produced at market equilibrium.*

HOW A POSITIVE EXTERNALITY IN CONSUMPTION REDUCES ECONOMIC EFFICIENCY

We have seen that a negative externality interferes with achieving economic efficiency. The same holds true for a positive externality. In Chapters 3 and 4, we assumed that the demand curve reflects all the benefits that come from consuming a good. But we have seen that a college education generates benefits that are not captured by the student receiving the education and so will not be reflected in the market demand curve for college education. Figure 5-2 shows the effect of a positive externality in consumption on the market for a college education.

If students receiving a college education could capture all its benefits, the demand curve would be D_2, which reflects the social benefits. The actual demand curve is D_1, however, reflecting only the private benefits received by students. The efficient equilibrium would come at price P_2 and quantity Q_2. At this equilibrium, economic surplus is maximized. The market equilibrium, at price P_1 and quantity Q_1, will not be efficient because the demand curve is above the supply curve for production of the units between Q_1 and Q_2. That is, the additional benefit—including the external benefit—for producing these units is greater than the marginal cost. As a result, there is a deadweight loss equal to the area of the yellow triangle. Because of the positive externality, economic efficiency would be improved if more college educations were produced. We can conclude the following: *When there is a positive externality in consuming a good or service, too little of the good or service will be produced at market equilibrium.*

Externalities Can Result in Market Failure

We have seen that because of externalities, the efficient level of output may not occur in either the market for electricity or the market for college educations. These are examples of **market failure:** situations in which the market fails to produce the efficient level of output. Later we will discuss possible solutions to problems of externalities. But first we need to consider why externalities occur.

What Causes Externalities?

We saw in Chapter 2 that governments need to guarantee *property rights* for a market system to function well. **Property rights** refer to the rights individuals or businesses have to the exclusive use of their property, including the right to buy or sell it. Property

Market failure Situations in which the market fails to produce the efficient level of output.

Property rights The rights individuals or businesses have to the exclusive use of their property, including the right to buy or sell it.

FIGURE 5-2

The Effect of a Positive Externality on Efficiency

People who do not consume college educations can still benefit from them. As a result, the social benefit from a college education is greater than the private benefit as seen by college students. Because only the private benefit is reflected in the market demand curve D_1, the quantity of college educations produced, Q_1, is too low. If the market demand curve were D_2 instead of D_1, the level of college educations produced would be Q_2, which is the efficient level. At the market equilibrium of Q_1, there is a deadweight loss equal to the area of the yellow triangle.

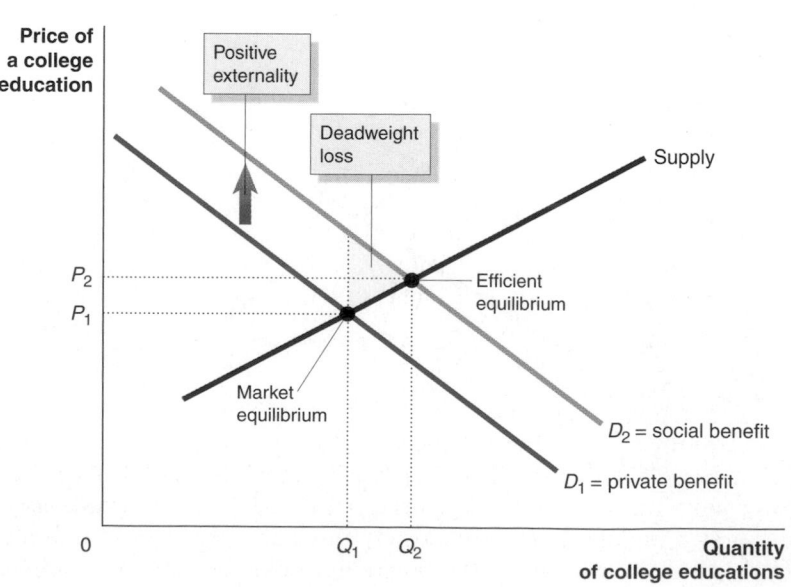

can be tangible, physical property, such as a store or factory. Property can also be intangible, such as the right to an idea. Most of the time, the U.S. government and the governments of other high-income countries do a good job of enforcing property rights, but in certain situations property rights do not exist or cannot be legally enforced.

Consider the following situation: Lee owns land that includes a lake. A paper company wants to lease some of Lee's land to build a pulp and paper mill. The paper mill will discharge pollutants into Lee's lake. Because Lee owns the lake, he can charge the paper company the cost of cleaning up the pollutants. The result is that the cost of the pollution is a private cost to the paper company and is reflected in the price of the paper it sells. There is no externality, the efficient level of paper is produced, and there is no market failure.

Now suppose that the paper company builds its paper mill on privately owned land on the banks of a lake that is owned by the state. In the absence of any government regulations, the company will be free to discharge pollutants into the lake. The cost of the pollution will be external to the company because it doesn't have to pay the cost of cleaning it up. More than the economically efficient level of paper will be produced, and a market failure will occur. Or, suppose that Lee owns the lake, but the pollution is caused by acid rain generated by an electric utility hundreds of miles away. The law does not allow Lee to charge the utility for the damage caused by the acid rain. Even though someone is damaging Lee's property, the law does not allow him to enforce his property rights in this situation. Once again, there is an externality, and the market failure will result in too much electricity being produced.

Similarly, if you buy a house, the government will protect your right to exclusive use of that house. No one else can use the house without your permission. Because of your property rights in the house, your private benefit from the house and the social benefit are the same. When you buy a college education, however, other people are, in effect, able to benefit from your college education. You have no property right that will enable you to prevent them from benefiting or to charge them for the benefits they receive. As a result, there is a positive externality and the market failure will result in too few college educations being supplied.

We can conclude the following: *Externalities and market failures result from incomplete property rights or from the difficulty of enforcing property rights in certain situations.*

Private Solutions to Externalities: The Coase Theorem

② LEARNING OBJECTIVE

Discuss the Coase theorem and explain how private bargaining can lead to economic efficiency in a market with an externality.

As noted at the beginning of this chapter, government intervention may actually increase economic efficiency and enhance the well-being of society when externalities are present. It is also possible, however, that private solutions to the problem of externalities can be found.

Can the market cure market failure? In an important article written in 1960, Ronald Coase of the University of Chicago, winner of the 1991 Nobel Prize in Economics, argued that under some circumstances private solutions to the problem of externalities will occur. To understand Coase's argument it is important to recognize that completely eliminating an externality usually is not economically efficient. Consider pollution, for example. There is, in fact, an *economically efficient level of pollution reduction*. At first, this seems paradoxical. Pollution is bad and the efficient amount of a bad thing should be zero. But it isn't zero.

The Economically Efficient Level of Pollution Reduction

Chapter 1 introduced the important idea that the optimal decision is to continue any activity up to the point where the marginal benefit equals the marginal cost. This applies to reducing pollution just as much as to other activities. As sulfur dioxide emissions—or any other type of pollution—decline, society benefits: Fewer trees die, fewer buildings are damaged, and fewer people suffer breathing problems. But a key point is that the additional benefit—or, *marginal benefit*—received from eliminating another ton of sulfur dioxide declines as sulfur dioxide emissions are reduced. To see why this is true, consider what happens with no reduction in sulfur dioxide emissions. In this situation, many smoggy days will occur in the cities of the Midwest and Northeast. Even healthy people may experience breathing problems. As sulfur dioxide emissions are reduced, the number of smoggy days will fall and healthy people will no longer experience breathing problems. Eventually, if emissions of sulfur dioxide fall to low levels, even people with asthma will no longer be affected. Further reductions in sulfur dioxide will have little additional benefit. The same will be true of the other benefits from reducing sulfur dioxide emissions: As the reductions increase, the additional benefits from fewer buildings and trees being damaged and lakes polluted will decline.

5-1 *Making the Connection*

The Reduction in Infant Mortality Due to the Clean Air Act

The following bar graph shows that tremendous progress has been made in the United States in reducing air pollution since the Clean Air Act was passed by Congress in 1970: Emissions of the six main air pollutants have fallen by almost half. Over the same period, real U.S. gross domestic product—which measures the value, corrected for inflation, of all the final goods and services produced in the country—increased 175 percent, energy consumption increased 42 percent, and the number of miles traveled by all vehicles increased 155 percent.

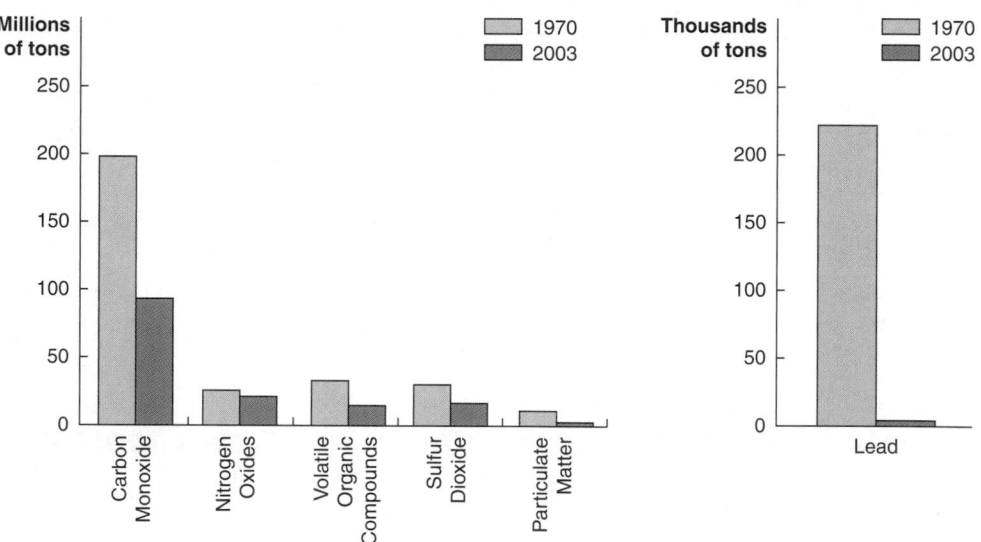

Source: U.S. Environmental Protection Agency, "Air Emissions Trends—Continued Progress Through 2003," September 2004.

As we have seen, when levels of pollution are high, the marginal benefit of reducing pollution also is high. We would expect, then, that the benefit of reducing air pollution in 1970 was much higher than the benefit from a proportional reduction in air pollution would be today, when the level of pollution is much lower. Kenneth Y. Chay of the University of California, Berkeley and Michael Greenstone of MIT have shown that the benefits from the air pollution reductions that occurred in the period immediately after passage of the Clean Air Act were indeed high. Chay and Greenstone argue that the exposure of pregnant women to high levels of air pollution can be damaging to their unborn fetuses, possibly by retarding lung functioning. This damage would increase the chance that the infant would die in the first weeks after being born. In the two years following passage of the Clean Air Act, there was a sharp reduction in air pollution and also a reduction in infant mortality. The decline in infant mortality mainly was due to a reduction in deaths within one month of birth. Of course, other factors also may have been responsible for the decline in infant mortality, but Chay and Greenstone use statistical analysis to isolate the effect of the decline in air pollution. They conclude that "1,300 fewer infants died in 1972 than would have in the absence of the Clean Air Act."

Source: Kenneth Y. Chay and Michael Greenstone, "Air Quality, Infant Mortality, and the Clean Air Act of 1970," NBER Working Paper 10053, October 2003.

Reduction in air pollution has been linked to a decline in infant mortality.

We saw in Chapter 4 that *marginal cost* is the additional cost to a firm of producing one more unit of a good or service. What about the marginal cost to electric utilities of reducing pollution? To reduce sulfur dioxide emissions, utilities have to switch from burning high-sulfur coal to burning more costly fuel, or they have to install pollution control devices, such as scrubbers. As the level of pollution falls, further reductions become increasingly costly. To reduce emissions or other types of pollution to very low levels can require complex and expensive new technologies. For example, Arthur Fraas of the federal Office of Management and Budget and Vincent Munley of Lehigh University have shown that the marginal cost of removing 97 percent of pollutants from municipal wastewater is more than twice as high as the marginal cost of removing 95 percent.

The *net benefit* to society from reducing pollution is equal to the difference between the benefit of reducing pollution and the cost. To maximize the net benefit to society, sulfur dioxide emissions—or any other type of pollution—should be reduced up to the point where the marginal benefit from another ton of reduction is equal to the marginal cost. Figure 5-3 illustrates this point.

In Figure 5-3, we measure *reductions* in sulfur dioxide emissions on the horizontal axis. We measure the marginal benefit and marginal cost in dollars from eliminating another ton of sulfur dioxide emissions on the vertical axis. As reductions in pollution increase, the marginal benefit declines and the marginal cost increases. The economically efficient amount of pollution reduction occurs where the marginal benefit equals the marginal cost. The figure shows that in this case the economically efficient reduction of sulfur dioxide emissions is 8.5 million tons per year, which is the amount of reduction Congress decided should occur by 2010. At that level of emission reduction, the marginal benefit and the marginal cost of the last ton of sulfur dioxide emissions eliminated are both $200 per ton. Suppose instead that the emissions target was only 7 million tons. The figure shows that, at that level of reduction, the last ton of reduction adds $250 to the benefits received by society, but it adds only $175 to the costs of utilities. There was a net benefit to society from this ton of pollution reduction of $75. In fact, the figure shows a net benefit to society from pollution reduction for every ton from 7 million to 8.5 million. Only when sulfur dioxide emissions are reduced by 8.5 million tons per year will marginal benefit fall enough and marginal cost rise enough that the two are equal.

Suppose Congress had set the target for sulfur dioxide emissions reduction at 10 million tons per year. The figure shows the marginal benefit at that level of reduction has fallen to only $150 per ton and the marginal cost has risen to $225 per ton. The last ton of reduction has actually *reduced* the net benefit to society by $75 per ton. In fact, every ton of reduction beyond 8.5 million reduces the net benefit to society.

To summarize: If the marginal benefit of reducing sulfur dioxide emissions is greater than the marginal cost, further reductions will make society better off. But if the marginal cost of reducing sulfur dioxide emissions is greater than the marginal benefit, reducing sulfur dioxide emissions will actually make society worse off.

FIGURE 5-3

The Marginal Benefit from Pollution Reduction Should Equal the Marginal Cost

If the reduction of sulfur dioxide emissions is at 7 million tons per year, the marginal benefit of $250 per ton is greater than the marginal cost of $175 per ton. Further reductions in emissions will increase the net benefit to society. If the reduction of sulfur dioxide emissions is at 10 million tons, the marginal cost of $225 per ton is greater than the marginal benefit of $150 per ton. An increase in sulfur dioxide emissions will increase the net benefit to society. Only when the reduction is at 8.5 million tons is the marginal benefit equal to the marginal cost. This level is the economically efficient level of pollution reduction.

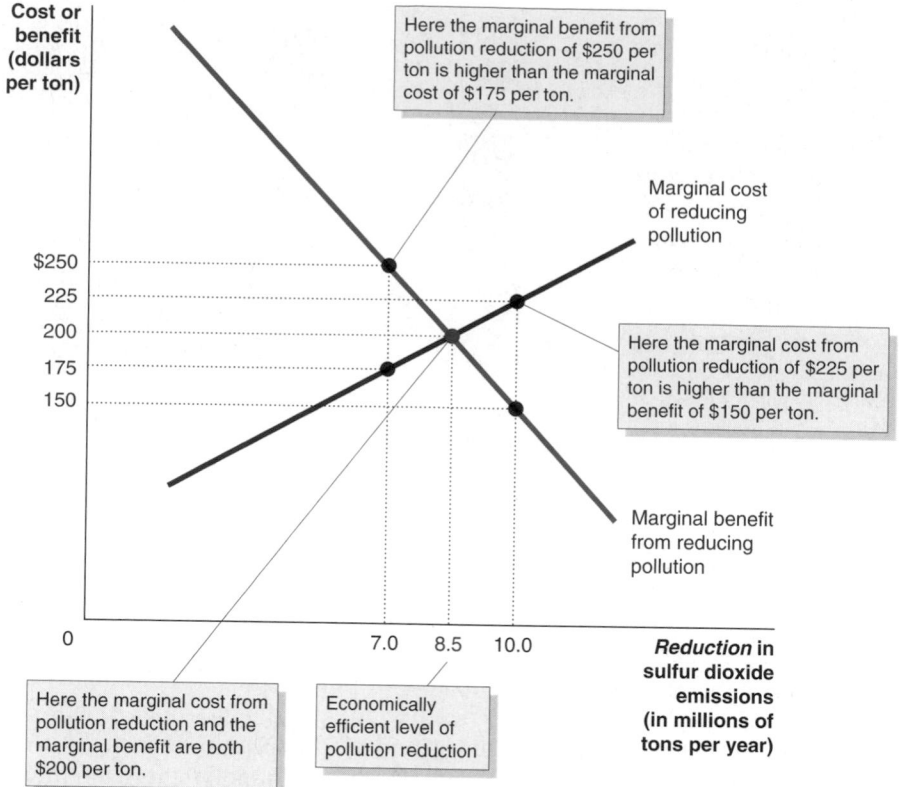

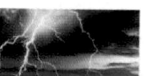

Don't Let This Happen To You!

Remember That It's the *Net* Benefit That Counts

There is always a temptation to want to eliminate completely anything unpleasant. As long as any person suffers any unpleasant consequences from air pollution, the marginal benefit of reducing air pollution will be positive. So, removing every particle of air pollution results in the largest *total* benefit to society. But removing every particle of air pollution is not optimal for the same reason that it is not optimal to remove every particle of dirt or dust from a room when cleaning it. The cost of cleaning your room is not just the price of the cleaning products but also the opportunity cost of your time. The more time you devote to cleaning your room, the less time you have available for other activities. As you devote additional hours to cleaning your room, the alternative activities you have to give up are likely to increase in value, raising the opportunity cost of cleaning—cleaning instead of eating or sleeping is costly! Optimally, you should eliminate dirt in your room up to the point where the marginal benefit of the last dirt removed equals the marginal cost of removing it. Society should take the same approach to air pollution. The result is the largest *net* benefit to society.

YOUR TURN: Test your understanding by doing related problem 10 on page 160 at the end of this chapter.

The Basis for Private Solutions to Externalities

In arguing that private solutions to the problem of externalities were possible, Ronald Coase emphasized that when more than the optimal level of pollution is occurring, the benefits from reducing the pollution to the optimal level are greater than the costs. Figure 5-4 illustrates this point.

The marginal benefit curve shows the additional benefit from each reduction in a ton of sulfur dioxide emissions. The *total* benefit received from reducing emissions

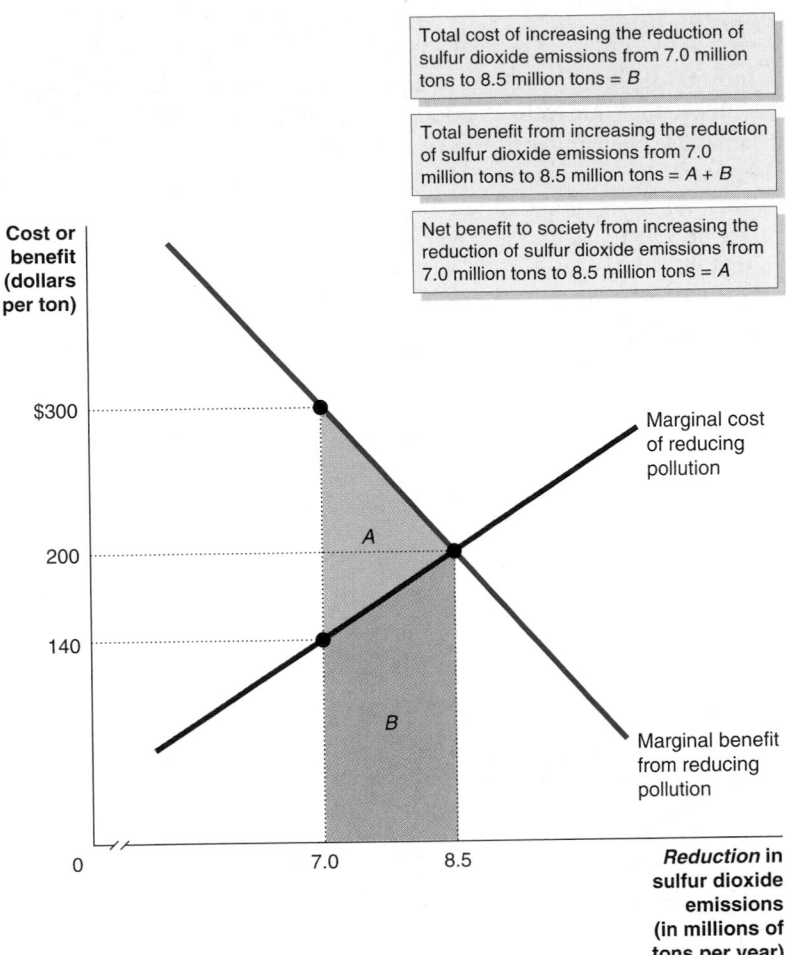

Total cost of increasing the reduction of
sulfur dioxide emissions from 7.0 million
tons to 8.5 million tons = B

Total benefit from increasing the reduction
of sulfur dioxide emissions from 7.0
million tons to 8.5 million tons = A + B

Net benefit to society from increasing the
reduction of sulfur dioxide emissions from
7.0 million tons to 8.5 million tons = A

FIGURE 5-4

The Benefits of Reducing Pollution to the Optimal Level Are Greater Than the Costs

Increasing the reduction in sulfur dioxide emissions from 7.0 million tons to 8.5 millions tons results in total benefits equal to the area under the marginal benefit curve, or the sum of the areas *A* and *B*. The total cost of this decrease in pollution is equal to the area under the marginal cost curve, the area *B*. The total benefits are greater than the total costs by an amount equal to the area of triangle *A*. Because the total benefits from reducing pollution are greater than the total costs, it's possible for those receiving the benefits to arrive at a private agreement with polluters to pay them to reduce pollution.

from one level to another is shown as the area under the marginal benefit curve between the two emission levels. For instance, in Figure 5-4, the total benefit from increasing the reduction in sulfur dioxide emissions from 7.0 million tons to 8.5 million tons is the sum of the areas of *A* and *B*. The marginal cost curve shows the additional cost from each reduction in a ton of emissions. The *total* cost of reducing emissions from one level to another is the area under the marginal cost curve between the two emissions levels. The total cost from increasing the reduction in emissions from 7.0 million tons to 8.5 million tons is the area *B*. The net benefit from reducing emissions is the difference between the total cost and the total benefit, which is equal to the area of triangle *A*.

In Figure 5-4, the benefits from further reductions in sulfur dioxide emissions are much greater than the costs. In the Appendix to Chapter 1, we reviewed the formula for calculating the area of a triangle, which is ½ × base × height, and the formula for the area of a rectangle, which is base × height. Using these formulas, we can calculate the value of the total benefits from the reduction in emissions and the value of the total costs. The value of the benefits (*A* + *B*) is $375 million. The value of the costs (*B*) is $255 million. If the people who would benefit from a reduction in pollution could get together, they could offer to pay the electric utilities $255 million to reduce the pollution to the optimal level. After making the payment, they would still be left with a net benefit of $120 million. In other words, a private agreement to reduce pollution to the optimal level is possible, without any need for government intervention.

5-2 *Making* the *Connection*

The Fable of the Bees

Apple trees must be pollinated by bees to bear fruit. Bees need the nectar from apple trees (or other plants) to produce honey. In a famous article published in the early 1950s, the British economist James Meade, winner of the 1977 Nobel Prize in Economics, argued that there were positive externalities in both apple growing and beekeeping. The more apple trees growers planted, the more honey would be produced in the hives of local beekeepers. And the more hives beekeepers kept, the larger the apple crops in neighboring apple orchards. Meade assumed that beekeepers were not being compensated by apple growers for the pollination services they were providing to apple growers, and that apple growers were not being compensated by beekeepers for the use of their nectar in honey making. Therefore, he concluded that unless the government intervened, the market would not supply enough apple trees and beehives.

Steven Cheung of the University of Washington showed, however, that government intervention was not necessary because beekeepers and apple growers had long since arrived at private agreements. In fact, in Washington State, farmers with fruit orchards had been using beehives to pollinate their trees since at least World War I. According to Cheung, "Pollination contracts usually include stipulations regarding the number and strength of the [bee] colonies, the rental fee per hive, the time of delivery and removal of hives, the protection of bees from pesticide sprays, and the strategic placing of hives."

Today many beekeepers travel from state to state renting out their bees to farmers. The

doubling of the number of acres of almond trees in California between 1983 and 2003 greatly increased the demand for bees in that state. Currently, more than one million beehives are required to pollinate the California almond crop. Beehives are shipped into the state in February and March to pollinate the almond trees, and then they are shipped to Oregon and Washington to pollinate the cherry, pear, and apple orchards in those states during April and May.

Some apple growers and beekeepers make private arrangements to arrive at an economically efficient outcome.

Sources: J. E. Meade, "External Economies and Diseconomies in a Competitive Situation," *Economic Journal,* Vol. 62, March 1952, pp. 54–67; Steven N. S. Cheung, "The Fable of the Bees: An Economic Investigation," *Journal of Law and Economics,* Vol. 16, 1973, pp. 11–33; Anna Oberthur, "Almond Growers Scramble for Pollinating Honey Bees," Associated Press story printed in the *San Jose Mercury-News,* February 24, 2004.

Do Property Rights Matter?

In discussing the bargaining between the electric utilities and the people suffering the effects of the pollution, we assumed that the electric utilities were not legally liable for the damage they were causing. In other words, the victims of pollution could not legally enforce the right of their property not to be damaged. But would it make any difference if the utilities were liable for the damages? Surprisingly, as Coase was the first to point out, it does not matter for the amount of pollution reduction. The only difference would be that now the electric utilities would have to pay the victims of pollution for the right to pollute, rather than the victims having to pay the utilities. Because the marginal benefits and marginal costs of pollution reduction would not change, the bargaining would still result in the efficient level of pollution reduction—in this case 8.5 million tons.

In other words, in the absence of the utilities being legally liable, the victims of pollution have an incentive to pay the utilities to reduce pollution up to the point where the marginal benefit of the last ton of reduction is equal to the marginal cost. If the utilities are legally liable, they have an incentive to pay the victims of pollution to allow them to pollute up to the same point.

The Problem of Transactions Costs

Although the possibility of a private solution to the problem of externalities always exists, practical difficulties often arise when creating one. In cases of pollution, for example, there are often both many polluters and many people suffering from the negative effects of pollution. Bringing together all those suffering from pollution with all those causing the pollution and negotiating an agreement often fails due to *transactions costs*. **Transactions costs** are the costs in time and other resources that parties incur in the process of agreeing to and carrying out an exchange of goods or services. In this case the transactions costs would include the time and other costs of negotiating an agreement, drawing up a binding contract, purchasing insurance, and monitoring the agreement. Unfortunately, when many people are involved, the transactions costs are often higher than the net benefits from reducing the externality. Thus, the cost of transacting ends up exceeding the gain from the transaction. In such cases, a private solution to an externality problem is not feasible.

Transactions costs The costs in time and other resources that parties incur in the process of agreeing to and carrying out an exchange of goods or services.

The Coase Theorem

Coase's argument that private solutions to the problem of externalities are possible is summed up in the **Coase theorem:** If transactions costs are low, private bargaining will result in an efficient solution to the problem of externalities. We have seen the basis for the Coase theorem in the preceding example of pollution by electric utilities: Because the benefits from reducing an externality are often greater than the costs, private bargaining can arrive at an efficient outcome. But we also have seen that this outcome will occur only if transactions costs are low, and in the case of pollution usually are not. In general, private bargaining is most likely to reach an efficient outcome if the number of parties bargaining is small.

In practice, we must add a couple of other qualifications to the Coase theorem. In addition to low transactions costs, private solutions to the problem of externalities will occur only if all parties to the agreement have full information about the costs and benefits associated with the externality, and all parties must be willing to accept a reasonable agreement. For example, if those suffering from the effects of pollution do not have information on the costs of reducing pollution, it is unlikely the parties can reach an agreement. Unreasonable demands can also hinder an agreement. For instance, in the example of pollution by electric utilities, even if transactions costs were very low, if the utilities insist on being paid more than $375 million to reduce sulfur dioxide emissions, no agreement will be reached because the amount paid exceeds the value of the reduction to those suffering from the emissions.

Coase theorem The argument of economist Ronald Coase that if transactions costs are low, private bargaining will result in an efficient solution to the problem of externalities.

Government Solutions to Externalities

When private solutions to externalities are not feasible, how should the government intervene? The first economist to analyze market failure systematically was A. C. Pigou, a British economist at Cambridge University. Pigou argued that to deal with a negative externality in production, the government should impose a tax equal to the cost of the externality. The effect of such a tax is shown in Figure 5-5, which reproduces the negative externality from acid rain shown in Figure 5-1.

By imposing a tax on the production of electricity equal to the cost of acid rain, the government will cause electric utilities to *internalize* the externality. As a consequence, the

③ LEARNING OBJECTIVE
Analyze government policies to achieve economic efficiency in a market with an externality.

FIGURE 5-5

When There Is a Negative Externality, a Tax Can Bring about the Efficient Level of Output

Because utilities do not bear the cost of acid rain, they produce electricity beyond the economically efficient level. If the government imposes a tax equal to the cost of acid rain, the utilities will internalize the externality. As a consequence, the supply curve will shift up from S_1 to S_2. As a result, market equilibrium changes from Q_1, where an inefficiently high level of electricity is produced, to Q_2, the economically efficient equilibrium. The price of electricity will rise from P_1—which does not reflect the cost of acid rain—to P_2—which does reflect the cost.

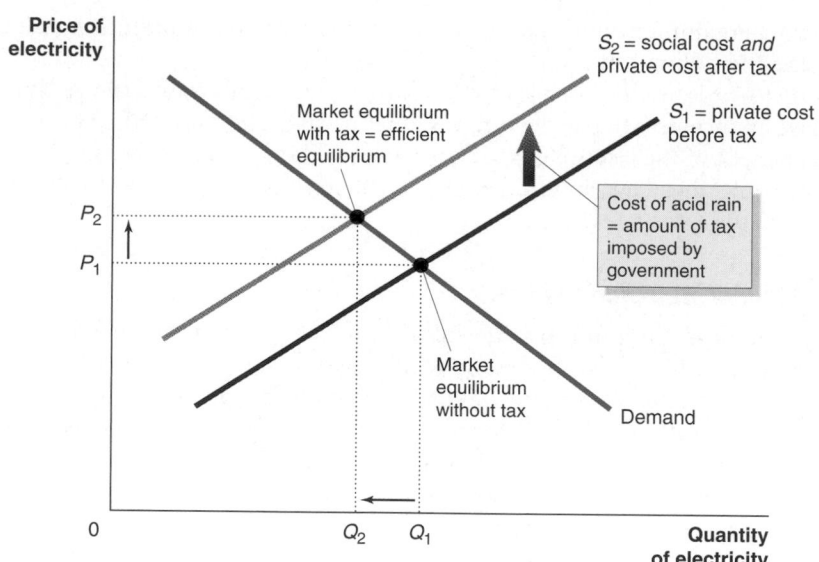

cost of the acid rain will become a private cost borne by the utilities, and the supply curve for electricity will shift from S_1 to S_2. The result will be a decrease in the equilibrium output of electricity from Q_1 to the efficient level Q_2. The price of electricity will rise from P_1—which does not reflect the cost of acid rain—to P_2—which does reflect the cost.

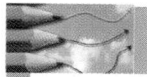

SOLVED PROBLEM   5-1

(3) LEARNING OBJECTIVE

Analyze government policies to achieve economic efficiency in a market with an externality.

Using a Tax to Deal with a Negative Externality

Companies producing toilet paper bleach the paper to make it white. The bleach is discharged into rivers and lakes and causes substantial environmental damage. Suppose the following graph illustrates the situation in the toilet paper market:

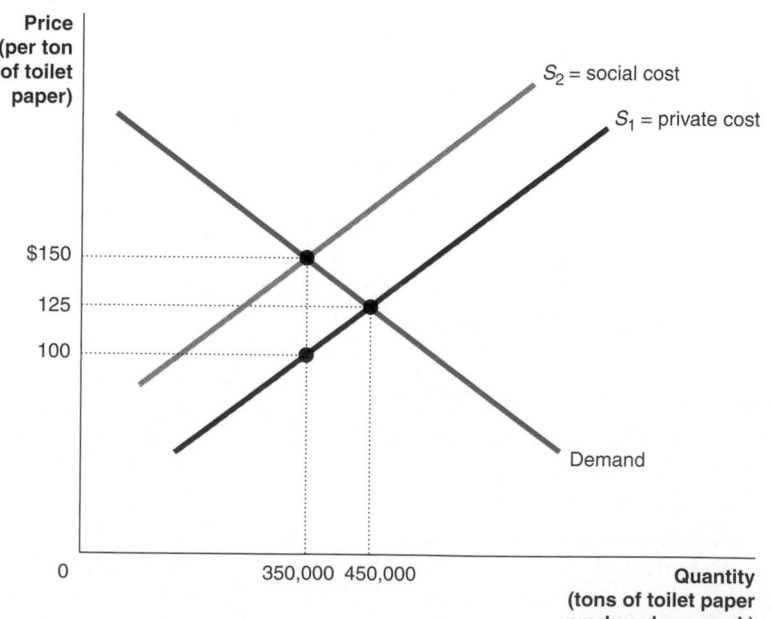

Explain how the federal government can use a tax on toilet paper to bring about the efficient level of production. What should the value of the tax be?

Solving the Problem:

Step 1: Review the chapter material. This problem is about the government using a tax to deal with a negative externality in production, so you may want to review the section "Government Solutions to Externalities," which begins on page 141.

Step 2: Use the information from the graph to determine the necessary tax. The efficient level of toilet paper production will occur where the price of toilet paper is equal to the marginal social cost of production. The graph shows that this will occur at a price of $150 per ton and production of 350,000 tons. In the absence of government intervention, the price will be $125 per ton and production will be 450,000 tons. It is tempting—but incorrect!—to think that the government could bring about the efficient level of production by imposing a per-ton tax equal to the difference between the price when production is at its optimal level and the current market price. But this would be a tax of only $25. The diagram shows that at the optimal level of production, the difference between the marginal private cost and the marginal social cost is $50. Therefore, a tax of $50 per ton is required to shift the supply curve up from S_1 to S_2.

YOUR TURN: For more practice, do related problem 14 on page 160 at the end of this chapter. Visit www.prenhall.com/hubbard for an interactive exercise related to this Solved Problem.

Pigou also argued that the government can deal with a positive externality in consumption by giving consumers a subsidy, or payment, equal to the value of the externality. The effect of the subsidy is shown in Figure 5-6, which reproduces the positive externality from college education shown in Figure 5-2.

By paying college students a subsidy equal to the external benefit from a college education, the government will cause students to *internalize* the externality. That is, the external benefit from a college education will become a private benefit received by college students, and the demand curve for college educations will shift from D_1 to D_2. The equilibrium number of college educations supplied will increase from Q_1 to the efficient level Q_2. In fact, the government does heavily subsidize college educations. All states have government-operated universities that charge tuitions well below the cost of providing the education. The state and federal governments also provide students with

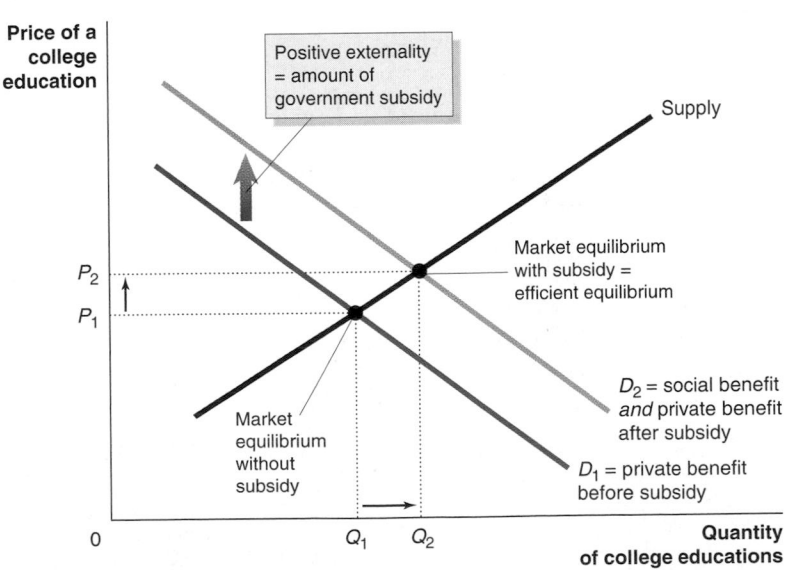

FIGURE 5-6

When There Is a Positive Externality, a Subsidy Can Bring about the Efficient Level of Output

People who do not consume college educations can still benefit from them. As a result, the social benefit from a college education is greater than the private benefit seen by college students. If the government pays a subsidy equal to the external benefit, students will internalize the externality. The subsidy will cause the demand curve to shift up from D_1 to D_2. The result will be that market equilibrium shifts from Q_1, where an inefficiently low level of college educations is supplied, to Q_2, the economically efficient equilibrium.

grants and low-interest loans that subsidize college educations. The economic justification for these programs is that college educations provide an external benefit to society.

Because using government taxes and subsidies to deal with externalities was first proposed by A. C. Pigou, they are sometimes referred to as **Pigovian taxes and subsidies.**

Pigovian taxes and subsidies
Government taxes and subsidies intended to bring about an efficient level of output in the presence of externalities.

Command and control approach
Government-imposed quantitative limits on the amount of pollution firms are allowed to generate, or government-required installation by firms of specific pollution control devices.

Command and Control versus Tradeable Emissions Allowances

Although the federal government has sometimes used taxes and subsidies to deal with externalities, in dealing with pollution it has traditionally used a *command and control approach* with firms that pollute. A **command and control approach** to reducing pollution involves the government imposing quantitative limits on the amount of pollution firms are allowed to generate, or requiring that firms install specific pollution control devices. For example, in 1983, the federal government required the installation of catalytic converters to reduce auto emissions on all new automobiles.

Congress could have used direct pollution controls to deal with the problem of acid rain. To achieve its objective of a reduction of 8.5 million tons per year in sulfur dioxide emissions by 2010, it could have required every utility to reduce sulfur dioxide emissions by the same specified amount. However, this approach would not have been an economically efficient solution to the problem. As we saw at the beginning of this chapter, utilities can have very different costs of reducing sulfur dioxide emissions. Some utilities, like Duke Energy, that already use low-sulfur coal can reduce emissions further only at a high cost. Other utilities, particularly those in the Midwest, are able to reduce emissions at a lower cost.

As a result, Congress decided to use a market-based approach by setting up a system of tradeable emissions allowances to reduce sulfur dioxide emissions. The federal government gave utilities allowances equal to the total amount of allowable emissions. The utilities were then free to buy and sell the allowances. An active market where the allowances can be bought and sold is conducted on the Chicago Mercantile Exchange. Utilities that could reduce emissions at low cost did so and sold their allowances. Utilities that could only reduce emissions at high cost bought allowances. Using tradeable emissions allowances to reduce acid rain has been a great success and has made it possible for utilities to meet Congress's emissions goal at a much lower cost than expected. As Figure 5-7 shows, just before Congress enacted the allowances program in 1990, the Edison Electrical Institute estimated that the cost to utilities of complying with the program would be $7.4 billion by 2010. By 1994, the federal government's

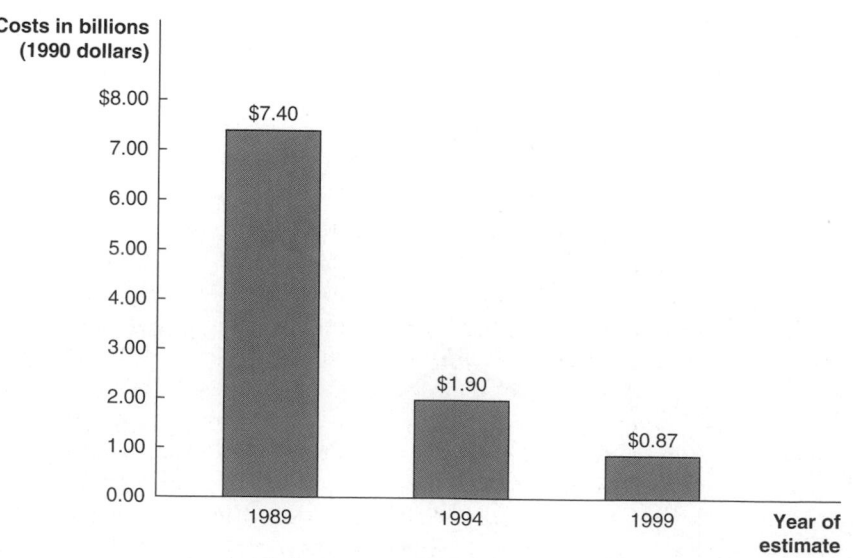

FIGURE 5-7

Estimated Cost of the Acid Rain Program in 2010

The Edison Electric Institute estimated in 1989 that the program to reduce acid rain pollution would cost utilities a total of $7.4 billion by 2010. The system of tradeable emissions allowances used in the program resulted in the bulk of the reduction in pollution being carried out by the utilities that could do it at the lowest cost. As a result, the program is likely to cost $870 million, which is almost 90 percent less than the original estimate.

Note: To correct for the effect of inflation, the costs are measured in dollars of 1990 purchasing power.

Source: Environmental Protection Agency, *Progress Report on the EPA Acid Rain Program,* November 1999, Figure 2.

General Accounting Office estimated the cost would be less than $2 billion. In practice, the cost appears likely to be almost 90 percent less than the initial estimate, or only about $870 *million.*

Licenses to Pollute?

Some environmentalists have criticized tradeable emissions allowances, labeling them "licenses to pollute." They argue that just as the government does not issue licenses to rob banks or to drive drunk, it should not issue licenses to pollute. But this criticism ignores one of the central lessons of economics: Resources are scarce and trade-offs exist. Resources that are spent reducing one type of pollution are not available to reduce other types of pollution or for any other use. Because reducing acid rain using tradeable emissions allowances cost utilities $870 million, rather than $7.4 billion as originally estimated, society saved more than $6.5 billion.

Can Tradeable Permits Reduce Global Warming?

5-3 Making
the **Connection**

In the past 25 years, the global surface temperature has increased about three-quarters of 1 degree Fahrenheit (or four-tenths of 1 degree Centigrade) compared with the average for the previous 30 years. The following graph shows changes in temperature over the years since 1880.

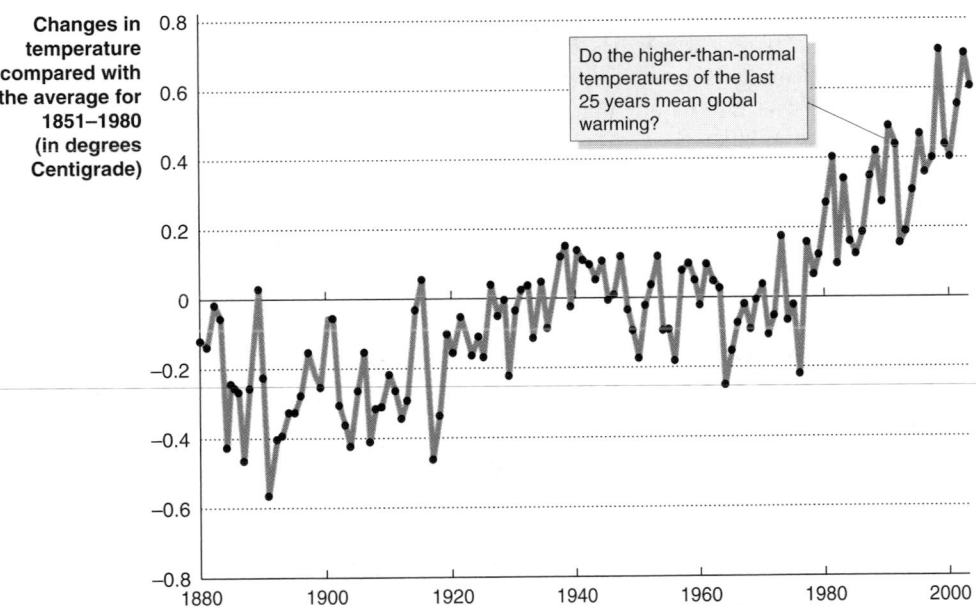

Do the higher-than-normal temperatures of the last 25 years mean global warming?

Changes in temperature compared with the average for 1851–1980 (in degrees Centigrade)

Global temperatures have gone through many periods of warming and cooling. In fact, the below-normal temperatures that prevailed before 1970 led some scientists to predict the eventual arrival of a new ice age. Nevertheless, many scientists are convinced that the recent warming is not part of the natural fluctuations in temperature but is instead due to the burning of fossil fuels, such as coal, natural gas, and petroleum. Burning these fuels releases CO_2 (carbon dioxide), which accumulates in the atmosphere as a "greenhouse gas." Greenhouse gases cause some of the heat released from the earth to be reflected back, increasing temperatures.

If greenhouse gases continue to accumulate in the atmosphere, according to some estimates, global temperatures could increase by 3 degrees Fahrenheit or more during the next 100 years. Such increases in temperature could lead to significant changes in climate, which might result in more storms and flooding as well as other problems. By 1995, a number of nations had concluded that the threat of global warming was significant enough to take steps toward reducing emissions of CO_2 and other greenhouse gases. The result was the 1997 Kyoto Treaty, which, if accepted, would have required the high-income countries to reduce

Rapid growth in India has led to rapid increases in CO_2 emissions.

their CO_2 emissions by more than 5 percent compared with their 1990 levels. However, President George W. Bush was not willing to commit the United States to the treaty. He argued that the costs to the United States of complying with the treaty were too high, particularly because some scientists were still skeptical that CO_2 emissions actually were causing the increase in temperature. Even scientists who believed that CO_2 emissions contribute to rising temperatures were skeptical that the Kyoto Treaty would have much effect on global warming. President Bush also argued that developing countries should be included in any agreement. Some developing countries, such as China and India, are experiencing rapid economic growth, which in turn has led to rapid increases in CO_2 emissions.

The mechanism by which reductions in CO_2 emissions would occur has also been in dispute. The United States has favored a global system of tradeable emission permits for CO_2 that would be similar to the system for sulfur dioxide we discussed earlier in this chapter. As we have seen, this type of system has the potential to reduce CO_2 emissions at the lowest cost. Most European countries, however, have been reluctant to give full acceptance to such a system, preferring instead to require that each country reduce emissions by a specified amount. It seems unlikely that the debate over the costs and benefits of reducing CO_2 emissions will be resolved any time soon.

Source for data in graph: NASA, Goddard Institute for Space Studies, www.giss.nasa.gov/data/update/gistemp/graphs.

---

(4) **LEARNING OBJECTIVE**

Explain how goods can be categorized on the basis of whether they are rival or excludable.

Rivalry The situation that occurs when one person's consuming a unit of a good means no one else can consume it.

Excludability The situation in which anyone who does not pay for a good cannot consume it.

Private good A good that is both rival and excludable.

Four Categories of Goods

We can explore further the question of when the market is likely to succeed in supplying the efficient quantity of a good by noting that goods differ on the basis of whether their consumption is *rival* and *excludable*. **Rivalry** occurs when one person's consuming a unit of a good means no one else can consume it. If you consume a Big Mac, no one else can consume it. **Excludability** means that anyone who does not pay for a good cannot consume it. If you don't pay for a Big Mac, MacDonald's can exclude you from consuming it. The consumption of a Big Mac is rival and excludable. The consumption of some goods, however, can be either *nonrival or nonexcludable*. Nonrival means that one person's consumption does not interfere with another person's consumption. Nonexcludable means that it is impossible to exclude others from consuming the good, whether they have paid for it or not. Figure 5-8 shows four possible categories into which goods can fall.

We can consider each of the four categories:

1. **Private Goods.**   A good that is both rival and excludable is a **private good.** Food, clothing, haircuts, and many other goods and services fall into this category. One person's consuming these goods precludes other people from consuming them, and anyone who does not buy these goods can't consume them. Although we didn't state it explicitly, when we analyzed the demand and supply for goods and services in Chapter 3, we assumed the goods and services were all private goods.

2. **Natural Monopolies.**   Some goods are excludable but not rival. An example is cable television. People who do not pay for cable television do not receive it, but one person's watching it doesn't affect other people's watching it. The same is true of a

	Excludable	Nonexcludable
Rival	**Private Goods** *Examples:* *Big Macs* *Running shoes*	**Common Resources** *Examples:* *Tuna in the ocean* *Public pasture land*
Nonrival	**Natural Monopolies** *Examples:* *Cable TV* *Toll road*	**Public Goods** *Examples:* *National defense* *Court system*

FIGURE 5-8

Four Categories of Goods

Goods and services can be divided into four categories on the basis of whether consumption of them is rival or excludable.

toll road. Anyone who doesn't pay the toll doesn't get on the road, but one person using the road doesn't interfere with someone else using the road (unless so many people are using the road that it becomes congested). Goods that fall into this category are called *natural monopolies.*

3. **Common Resources.**   If a good is rival but not excludable, it is a **common resource.** Forest land in many poor countries is a common resource. If one person cuts down a tree, no one else can use the tree. But if no one has a property right to the forest, no one can be excluded from using it. As we will discuss in more detail later, common resources will often be overused.

Common resource   A good that is rival but not excludable.

4. **Public Goods.**   A **public good** is both nonrivalrous and nonexcludable. Public goods are often, although not always, supplied by a government rather than by private firms. The classic example of a public good is national defense. Your consuming national defense does not interfere with your neighbor's consuming it, so consumption is nonrivalrous. You also cannot be excluded from consuming it, whether you pay for it or not. No private firm would be willing to supply national defense, because everyone can consume national defense without paying for it. The behavior of consumers in this situation is referred to as **free riding.** Free riding involves individuals benefiting from a good—in this case, the provision of national defense—without paying for it.

Public good   A good that is both nonrivalrous and nonexcludable.

Free riding   Benefiting from a good without paying for it.

Should the Government or the Airlines Screen Luggage at Airports?

5-4 Making the Connection

Governments often directly supply public goods, but not always. Governments can also use subsidies to provide incentives for a public good to be supplied by private firms, or it can use regulations to require that private firms supply the good. Without government intervention, airlines are unlikely to provide the efficient level of aviation security. The figure shows that there is a positive externality to aviation security because people who are not airline passengers benefit from aviation security. Demand curve D_1 reflects just the private benefits to airline passengers. Demand curve D_2 reflects the social benefits, which include the external benefits not received by airline passengers. The tragic events of September 11, 2001 show that a lapse in aviation security could result in the deaths of thousands of people who were not airline passengers. In the figure, the efficient quantity of aviation security is Q_2, but the airlines will only supply Q_1.

Should the government be responsible for supplying aviation security?

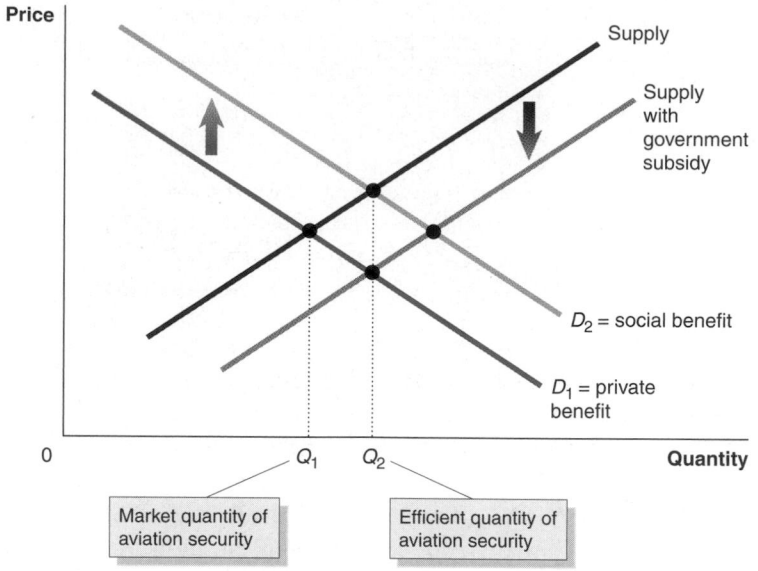

The federal government first began tackling aviation security in a significant way in the early 1970s following a series of airline hijackings. At that time, the federal government decided not to directly provide aviation security itself. Instead, the Federal Aviation Administration issued regulations that required the airlines to meet standards for the screening of passengers and luggage. Over the next 30 years, additional regulations were issued to tighten security, and the federal government began paying subsidies to the airlines to reduce their costs of providing security. The preceding figure shows that subsidizing the airlines' provision of aviation security can shift the supply curve down and cause the efficient quantity to be supplied.

Following the events of September 11, 2001, Congress and the administration of President George W. Bush reexamined the issue of aviation security. The discussion involved whether the federal government should continue to rely on the airlines to provide security or should begin providing security directly through a new government agency. As discussed in earlier chapters, goods and services are usually provided more efficiently by private firms than by governments. Some members of Congress and some economists opposed the establishment of a government aviation security agency on these grounds. Others raised the additional objection that government agencies respond less flexibly to changes in conditions and in technology than do private firms. Finally, a concern arose that a government agency might be less sensitive to costs of increasing security—including the opportunity cost of passengers' time as they wait to be screened—leading it to supply more than the efficient level of security. Proponents of the new agency, however, argued that in the past, passenger and baggage screeners had often been low paid and poorly trained. They believed that a government agency would be more successful in raising pay and increasing training.

In the end, Congress decided the issue in favor of the government directly supplying this service when it passed the Aviation and Transportation Security Act, which established the Transportation Security Administration. The Transportation Security Administration was given responsibility for hiring screeners to monitor all security checkpoints in airports.

Source: Cletus C. Coughlin, Jeffrey P. Cohen, and Sarosh R. Khan, "Aviation Security and Terrorism: A Review of the Economic Issues," Federal Reserve Bank of St. Louis, *Review*, September/October 2002.

⑤ **LEARNING OBJECTIVE**

Define a public good and a common resource, and use graphs to illustrate the efficient quantities of public goods and common resources.

Public Goods and Common Resources

The demand and supply for private goods was discussed in Chapter 3, and private goods are discussed further in later chapters. Natural monopolies are analyzed in Chapter 14. For the remainder of this chapter, we focus on the other two categories of goods: public goods and common resources. To determine the optimal quantity of a public good, we have to modify the demand and supply analysis of Chapter 3 to take into account that a public good is both nonrivalrous and nonexcludable.

The Demand for a Public Good

We saw in Chapter 3 that the market demand curve for a good or service is determined by adding up the quantity of the good demanded by each consumer at each price. To keep things simple, let's review the concept for the case of a market with only two consumers. Figure 5-9 shows that the market demand curve for hamburgers depends on the individual demand curves of Jill and Joe.

At a price of $4.00, Jill demands 2 hamburgers per week and Joe demands 4. Adding horizontally, the combination of a price of $4.00 per hamburger and a quantity demanded of 6 hamburgers will be a point on the market demand curve for hamburgers. Similarly, adding horizontally at a price of $1.50, we have a price of $1.50 and a quantity demanded of 11 as another point on the market demand curve.

How can we find the demand curve for a public good? Once again, for simplicity assume that Jill and Joe are the only consumers. Unlike a private good, where Jill and Joe can end up consuming different quantities, with a public good they will consume *the same quantity*. Suppose that Jill owns a service station on an isolated rural road and next door Joe owns a car dealership. These are the only two businesses around for miles. Both Jill and Joe are afraid that unless they hire a security guard at night, their businesses may be burgled. Like national defense, the services of a security guard are in this case a public good: Once hired, the guard will be able to protect both businesses, so the good is nonrival. It also will not be possible to exclude either business from being protected, so the good is nonexcludable.

To arrive at a demand curve for a public good, we don't add quantities at each price, as with a private good. Instead, we add the price each consumer is willing to pay for each quantity of the public good. This value represents the total dollar amount consumers as a group would be willing to pay for that quantity of the public good. Put another way, for private goods we add individual demand curves horizontally to find market demand, whereas for public goods we add individual demand curves vertically. Figure 5-10 shows how the demand curve for security guard services depends on the individual demand curves of Jill and Joe.

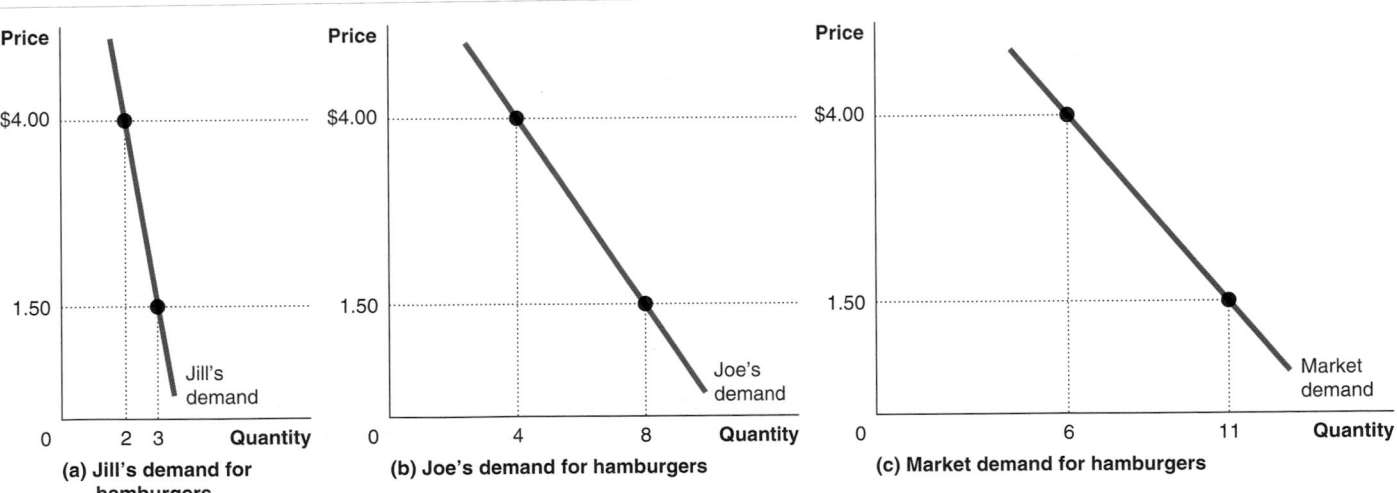

FIGURE 5-9 Constructing the Market Demand Curve for a Private Good

The market demand curve for private goods is determined by adding horizontally the quantity of the good demanded at each price by each consumer. For instance, in panel (a), Jill demands 2 hamburgers when the price is $4.00 and in panel (b), Joe demands 4 hamburgers when the price is $4.00. So, a quantity of 6 hamburgers and a price of $4.00 is a point on the market demand curve in panel (c).

FIGURE 5-10

Constructing the Market Demand Curve for a Public Good

To find the demand curve for a public good, we add up the price at which each consumer is willing to purchase each quantity of the good. In panel (a), Jill is willing to pay $8 per hour for a security guard to provide 10 hours of protection. In panel (b), Joe is willing to pay $10 for that level of protection. Therefore, in panel (c), the price of $18 per hour and the quantity of 10 hours will be a point on the market demand curve for security guard services.

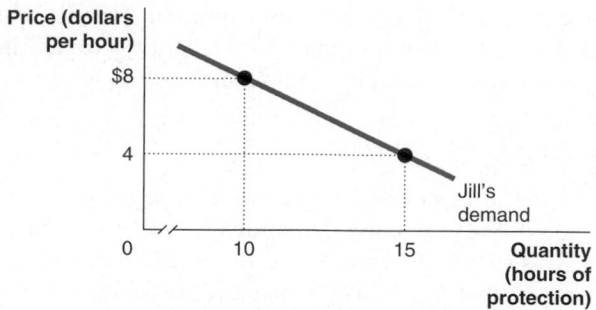

(a) Jill's demand for security guard services

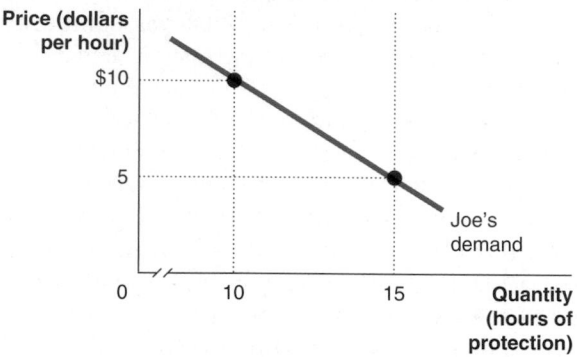

(b) Joe's demand for security guard services

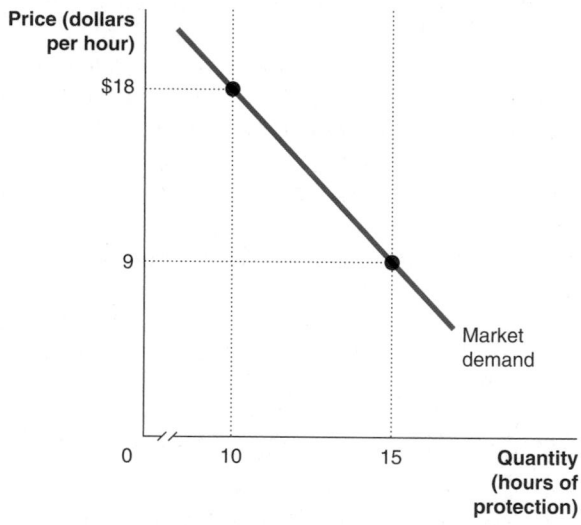

(c) Market demand for security guard services

The figure shows that Jill is willing to pay $8 per hour for the guard to provide 10 hours of protection per night. Joe would suffer a greater loss from a burglary, so he is willing to pay $10 per hour for the same amount of protection. Adding the dollar amount that each is willing to pay gives us a price of $18 per hour and a quantity of 10 hours as a point on the demand curve for security guard services. Because Jill is willing to spend $4 per hour for the protection provided by 15 hours of guard services and Joe is willing to pay $5, a price of $9 per hour and a quantity of 15 hours is also a point on the demand curve for security guard services.

The Optimal Quantity of a Public Good

We know that to achieve economic efficiency, a good or service should be produced up to the point where the sum of consumer surplus and producer surplus is maximized.

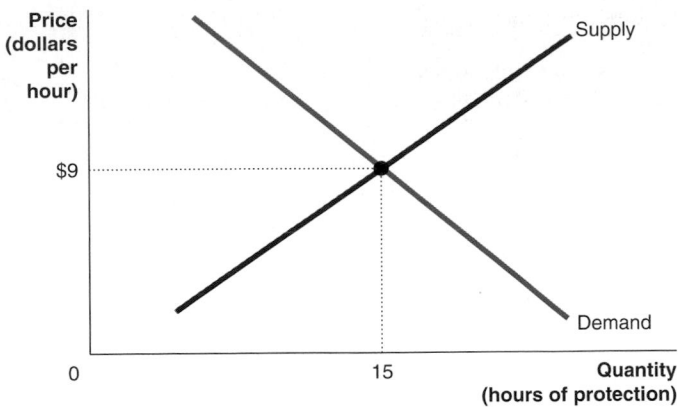

FIGURE 5-11

The Optimal Quantity of a Public Good

The optimal quantity of a public good is produced where the sum of consumer surplus and producer surplus is maximized, which occurs where the demand curve intersects the supply curve. In this case, the optimal quantity of security guard services is 15 hours at a price of $9 per hour.

The optimal quantity of security guard services—or any other public good—will occur where the demand curve intersects the supply curve, just as with the market for private goods. As with private goods, the supply curve represents the costs to producers of supplying the good. Figure 5-11 shows that the optimal quantity of security guard services supplied is 15 hours, at a price of $9 per hour.

Will the economically efficient quantity of security guard services actually be achieved? One difficulty is that the individual preferences of consumers, as shown by their demand curves, are not revealed in this market. This difficulty does not arise with private goods because consumers must reveal their preferences in order to purchase private goods. If the market price of Big Macs is $4.00, Joe either reveals he is willing to pay that much by buying it, or he does without it. In our example, neither Jill nor Joe can be excluded from consuming the services provided by a security guard once one is hired, and, therefore, neither has an incentive to reveal her or his preferences. In this case, though, with only two consumers it is likely that private bargaining will result in an efficient quantity of the public good. This outcome is not likely for a public good—such as national defense—that is supplied by the government to millions of consumers.

Governments sometimes use *cost-benefit analysis* to determine what quantity of a public good should be supplied. For example, before building a dam on a river, the federal government will attempt to weigh the costs against the benefits. The costs include the opportunity cost of other projects that will not be carried out if this dam is built. The benefits include improved flood control or new recreational opportunities on the lake formed by the dam. However, for many public goods, including national defense, the government does not use a formal cost-benefit analysis. Instead, the quantity of national defense supplied is determined by a political process involving Congress and the president. Even here, of course, Congress and the president realize that trade-offs are involved: The more resources used for national defense, the fewer resources available for other public goods or for private goods.

SOLVED PROBLEM   5-2

Determining the Optimal Level of Public Goods

Suppose, once again, that Jill and Joe run isolated businesses that are next door to each other and in need of the services of a security guard. Their demand schedules for security guard services are as follows:

⑤ **LEARNING OBJECTIVE**

Define a public good and a common resource, and use graphs to illustrate the efficient quantities of public goods and common resources.

JOE		JILL	
PRICE (DOLLARS PER HOUR)	QUANTITY (HOURS OF PROTECTION)	PRICE (DOLLARS PER HOUR)	QUANTITY (HOURS OF PROTECTION)
$20	0	$20	1
18	1	18	2
16	2	16	3
14	3	14	4
12	4	12	5
10	5	10	6
8	6	8	7
6	7	6	8
4	8	4	9
2	9	2	10

The supply schedule for security guard services is as follows:

PRICE (DOLLARS PER HOUR)	QUANTITY (HOURS OF PROTECTION)
$8	1
10	2
12	3
14	4
16	5
18	6
20	7
22	8
24	9

a. Draw a graph showing the optimal level of security guard services. Be sure to label the curves on your graph.

b. Briefly explain why 8 hours of security guard protection is not an optimal quantity.

Solving the Problem:
Step 1: Review the chapter material. This problem is about the determination of the optimal level of public goods, so you may want to review the section "The Optimal Quantity of a Public Good," which begins on page 150.

Step 2: Begin by deriving the demand curve for security guard services. To calculate demand, we must add the prices that Jill and Joe are willing to pay at each quantity:

DEMAND	
PRICE (DOLLARS PER HOUR)	QUANTITY (HOURS OF PROTECTION)
$38	1
34	2
30	3
26	4
22	5
18	6
14	7
10	8
6	9

Step 3: Answer question (a) by plotting the demand and supply curves. The graph shows that the optimal level of security guard services is 6 hours.

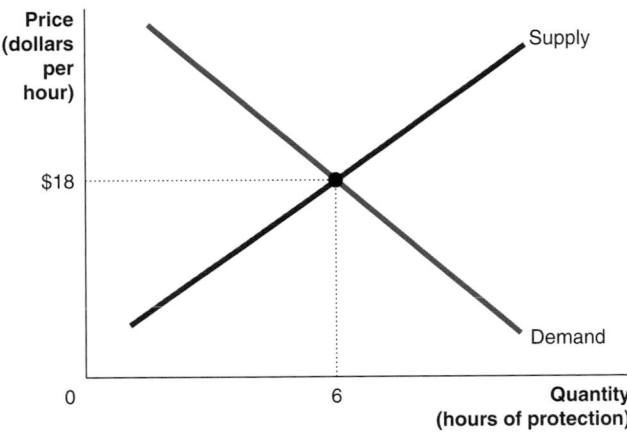

Step 4: Answer question (b) by explaining why 8 hours of security guard protection is not an optimal quantity. For each hour beyond 6, the supply curve is above the demand curve. Therefore, the additional benefits received will be less than the additional cost of supplying these hours. This results in a deadweight loss and a reduction in economic surplus.

YOUR TURN: For more practice, do related problem 16 on page 161 at the end of this chapter. Visit www.prenhall.com/hubbard for an interactive exercise related to this Solved Problem.

Common Resources

In England during the Middle Ages, each village had an area of pasture, known as a *commons,* on which any family in the village was allowed to graze its cows or sheep without charge. The grass eaten by one family's cow, of course, was not available for another family's cow, so consumption was rival. But every family in the village had the right to use the commons, so it was nonexcludable. Without some type of restraint on usage, the commons would end up overgrazed. To see why, consider the economic incentives facing a family that was thinking of buying another cow and grazing it on the commons. The family would gain the benefits from increased milk production, but adding another cow to the commons would create a negative externality by reducing the amount of grass available for the cows of other families. Because this family—and the other families in the village—did not take this negative externality into account when deciding whether to add another cow to the commons, too many cows would be added. The grass on the commons would eventually be depleted and no family's cow would get enough to eat.

Tragedy of the commons The tendency for a common resource to be overused.

THE TRAGEDY OF THE COMMONS The tendency for a common resource to be overused is called the **tragedy of the commons.** A modern example is the forests in many poor countries. When a family chops down a tree in a public forest, it takes into account the benefits of gaining firewood or wood for building, but it does not take into account the costs of deforestation. Haiti, for example, was once heavily forested. Today, 80 percent of the country's forests have been cut down, primarily to be burned to create charcoal, which is used for heating and cooking. Because the mountains no longer have tree roots to hold the soil, heavy rains lead to devastating floods. The following is from a newspaper account of tree cutting in Haiti:

> "No Tree Cutting" signs hang over the park entrance, but without money and manpower, there is no way to enforce that. Loggers make nightly journeys, hacking away at trees until they fall. The next day, they're on a truck out. Days later, they've been chopped up, burned and packaged in white bags offered for sale by soot-covered women. "This is the only way I can feed my four kids," said Vena Verone, one of the vendors. "I've heard about the floods and deforestation that caused them, but there's nothing I can do about that."

Figure 5-12 shows that with a common resource such as wood from a forest, the efficient level of use, Q_2, is determined by the intersection of the demand curve—which represents the marginal benefit received by consumers—and S_2, which reflects the social cost of cutting the wood. As in our discussion of negative externalities, the social cost is equal to the private cost of cutting the wood plus the external cost. In this case, the external cost reflects the fact that the more wood each person cuts, the less wood there is available for others, and the greater the deforestation, which increases the chances of floods. Because each individual tree cutter ignores the external cost, the equilibrium quantity of wood cut is Q_1, which is greater than the efficient quantity. At the equilibrium level of output there is a deadweight loss, as shown in Figure 5-12 by the yellow triangle.

FIGURE 5-12

Overuse of a Common Resource

For a common resource such as wood from a forest, the efficient level of use, Q_2, is determined by the intersection of the demand curve—which represents the marginal benefit received by consumers—and S_2, which reflects the marginal social cost of cutting the wood. Because each individual tree cutter ignores the external cost, the equilibrium quantity of wood cut is Q_1, which is greater than the efficient quantity. At the equilibrium level of output there is a deadweight loss, as shown by the yellow triangle.

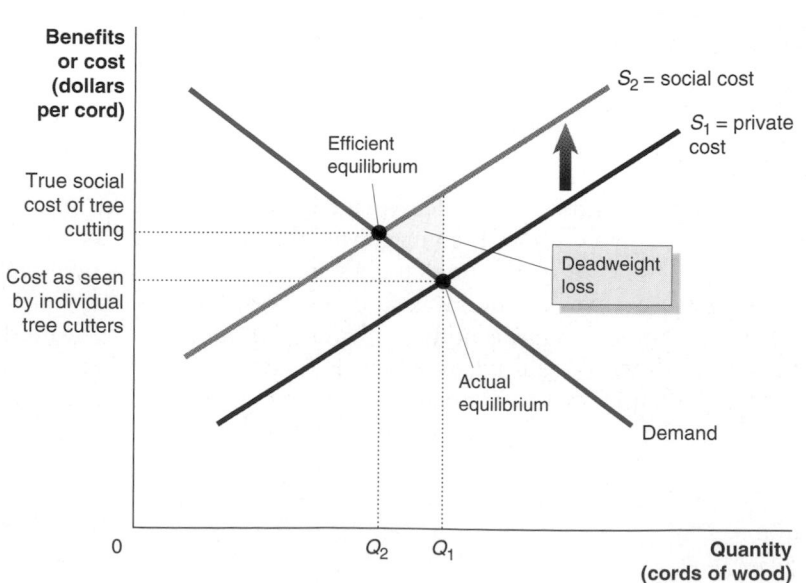

IS THERE A WAY OUT OF THE TRAGEDY OF THE COMMONS? Notice that our discussion of the tragedy of the commons was very similar to our earlier discussion of negative externalities. The source of the tragedy of the commons is the same as the source of negative externalities: lack of clearly defined and enforced property rights. For instance, if instead of being held as a collective resource, a single person owns a piece of pastureland, that person would take into account the effect of adding another cow on the food available to cows already using the pasture. As result, the optimal number of cows will be placed on the pasture. Over the years, most of the commons lands in England were converted to private property. Most of the forest land in Haiti and other developing countries is actually the property of the government. The failure of the government to protect the forests against trespassers is the key to their overuse.

In some situations, though, enforcing property rights is not feasible. An example is the oceans. Because no country owns the oceans beyond its own coastal waters, the fish and other resources of the ocean will remain a common resource. In situations in which enforcing property rights is not feasible, two types of solutions to the tragedy of the commons are possible. If the geographic area involved is limited and the number of people involved is small, access to the commons can be restricted through community norms and laws. If the geographic area or the number of people involved is large, legal restrictions on access to the commons are required. As an example of the first type of solution, the tragedy of the commons was avoided in the Middle Ages by traditional limits on the number of animals each family was allowed to put on the common pasture. Although these traditions were not formal laws, they usually were enforced adequately through social pressure.

With the second type of solution, the government imposes restrictions on access to the common resources. These restrictions can take several different forms, of which taxes, quotas, and tradeable permits, are the most common. By setting a tax equal to the external cost, governments can ensure that the efficient quantity of a resource is used. Quotas, or legal limits, on the quantity of the resource that can be taken during a given time period have been used in the United States to limit access to pools of oil when the pool is beneath property owned by many different persons. The governments of Canada, New Zealand, and Iceland have used a system of tradeable permits to restrict access to ocean fisheries. Under this system, a total quota is set on the number of fish that can be caught during a season. Fishermen are then assigned permits that are equal to the quota. This system operates like the tradeable emissions allowances described earlier in this chapter. The fishermen are free to use the permits or to sell them, which ensures that the permits are used by the fishermen with the lowest costs.

Conclusion

In Chapter 4, we saw that government intervention in the economy can reduce economic efficiency. In this chapter, however, we have seen that the government has an indispensable role to play in the economy when the absence of well-defined and enforceable property rights keeps the market from operating efficiently. Because no one has a property right for clean air, in the absence of government intervention, firms will produce too great a quantity of products that generate air pollution. We also saw that public goods are nonrivalrous and nonexcludable and are, therefore, often supplied directly by the government.

Read *An Inside Look,* which begins on the following page, to learn about two approaches to fighting global warming.

NEW YORK TIMES, JUNE 13, 2004

A Hamstrung Market Fights Global Warming

In "The Day After Tomorrow," the disaster movie, millions die while politicians and scientists squabble about global warming.

Real life, of course, is a bit more complicated. For more than a decade, there has been a fierce international debate over how to curb the buildup of heat-trapping greenhouse gases like carbon dioxide. While the environmental results of the dispute may not be clear for years, some economic consequences are already apparent.

On one side of the argument is the United States government, which opposes mandatory caps on emissions of carbon dioxide and other greenhouse gases. On the other are more than 100 nations, including most of the developed world, that have signed the treaty known as the Kyoto Protocol.

The Kyoto signatories have agreed that developed nations will cut greenhouse gas emissions by 2012 to a level 5.2 percent below the total in 1990. To reach that goal, each nation is expected to establish caps on its various polluters, caps that add up to the requisite cuts.

Some trading in emissions allowances for greenhouse gases has begun. . . . While the Kyoto Protocol isn't binding on its signers—it won't become so unless Russia makes good on President Vladimir V. Putin's pledge that his nation will join—the European Union has already adopted an emissions program that complies with the treaty's terms. In Europe, trading has started in the emissions allowances issued by European Union members, and in credits given for projects that cut emissions.

. . . [A] group called the Chicago Climate Exchange has been formed to pursue a private approach to trading in emissions allowances, and the Bush administration has endorsed its efforts. Led by members like American Electric Power, DuPont, International Paper and Ford Motor, the exchange created a framework defining how to measure, report and audit emissions and credits for cutting them.

Each participating company agreed to cut emissions 1 percent annually for four years, starting last year, either through its own projects or by buying credits for cuts made by others. They began trading in December. The exchange calls itself a pilot program and says its goal is to explore trading in greenhouse gases, not to set itself up as the arbiter of which cuts are needed to combat global warming.

So far, the results suggest that businesses and investors do not see the makings of a serious market in this voluntary approach. How can one tell? Even though trading is thin everywhere, prices are far higher in Europe, where government-mandated emissions caps begin taking effect next year. At the Chicago prices, the signal from the market is that only the most minimal investments make economic sense.

Some environmental advocates say opposition from the Bush administration to emissions caps has heartened companies that are trying to roll back the emissions limits in Europe. In this view, prices have declined in Europe this year because of market fears that European policy makers will retreat, reducing the incentive for companies to invest in emissions cuts.

This may not be a disaster, but it is hardly a recipe for reducing the risk of global warming.

Key Points in the Article

The article discusses the use of tradeable emissions permits to reduce carbon dioxide, which may be contributing to global warming (for a brief discussion of global warming, see Making the Connection 5-3: Can Tradeable Permits Reduce Global Warming?). The United States has not endorsed the Kyoto Treaty, which would put mandatory caps on carbon dioxide emissions. The Bush administration instead has urged the development of new technologies and the use of voluntary reductions by firms that currently emit carbon dioxide. The countries of the European Union and Russia already have adopted the caps in the Kyoto Treaty. In both the United States and Europe, trading in emissions allowances has begun. The allowances are similar to the tradeable emissions permits for sulfur dioxide that were discussed in this chapter.

Analyzing the News

a We can use the economic analysis of externalities to analyze this news article. One source of carbon dioxide emissions is cars and trucks burning gasoline. If carbon dioxide contributes to global warming, an externality in using gasoline is not included in the private costs incurred by oil companies. Figure 1 shows that market equilibrium will occur at quantity Q_1, which is larger than the efficient quantity Q_2. Note that this figure is very similar to Figure 5-1.

b Using tradeable emissions permits is an attempt to reverse the gradual upward trend in carbon dioxide emissions in the United States, which is shown in Figure 2. The Kyoto Protocol calls for a reduction in carbon dioxide emissions to 5 percent below 1990 levels. The figure shows that for the United States to meet this target, carbon dioxide emissions would have to be reduced by about 20 percent from current levels.

c The article raises doubts about the effectiveness of reducing carbon dioxide emissions through a voluntary system of emissions allowances. Emissions allowances are trading at high prices in Europe, where government-imposed limits on carbon dioxide emissions will begin in 2005, but at low prices in the United States, where there are no government-imposed limits. The prices for the allowances are low in the United States, apparently, because a relatively limited number of firms have developed plans to reduce emissions.

Thinking Critically
ABOUT POLICY

1. Michael Crichton's thriller *State of Fear* argues that worries over global warming are vastly overblown because carbon dioxide emissions don't do much to harm the environment. Suppose that a Pigovian tax was put in place on carbon dioxide emissions but that carbon dioxide emissions *don't* harm the environment. Would the tax bring the economy toward efficiency?

2. Some critics of the Kyoto Accords argue that carbon dioxide emissions generate *benefits* to the environment and the economy: Plants grow faster and stronger when more carbon dioxide is in the environment and when the growing season is longer, for example. If the external benefits from carbon dioxide emissions equal the external costs, what should the government do in terms of taxing or subsidizing carbon dioxide emissions? If the external benefits are larger, what should the government do? If the external benefits exist but are smaller than the external costs, what should the government do?

Source: A Hamstrung Market Fights Global Warming by Barnaby J. Feder, New York Times, June 13, 2004. Copyright © 2004 by *New York Times*. Reprinted with permission.

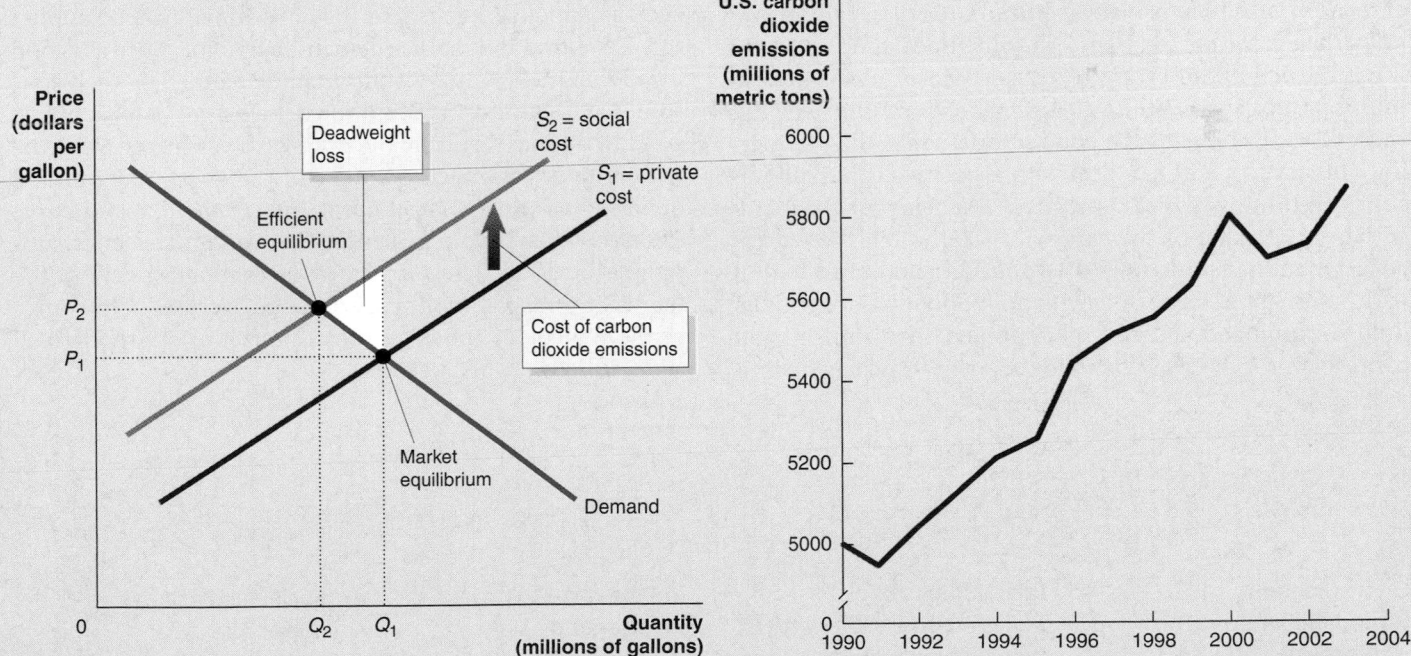

Figure 1: If carbon dioxide contributes to global warming, a negative externality results from burning gasoline in automobiles.

Figure 2: Carbon dioxide emissions have slowly increased in the United States.

Source: U.S. Department of Energy, Energy Information Administration, "Emission of Greenhouse Gases in the United States, 2003," December 13, 2004.

LEARNING OBJECTIVE ① Identify examples of positive and negative externalities and use graphs to show how externalities affect economic efficiency. An *externality* is a benefit or cost to parties who are not involved in a transaction. Pollution and other externalities in production cause a difference between the *private cost* borne by the producer of a good or services and the *social cost,* which includes any external cost, such as the cost of pollution. An externality in consumption causes a difference between the *private benefit* received by the consumer and the *social benefit,* which includes any external benefit. If externalities exist in production or consumption, the market will not produce the optimal level of a good or service. This outcome is referred to as *market failure.*

LEARNING OBJECTIVE ② Discuss the Coase theorem and explain how private bargaining can lead to economic efficiency in a market with an externality. Externalities and market failures result from incomplete property rights or from the difficulty of enforcing property rights in certain situations. According to the *Coase theorem,* if *transactions costs* are low, private bargaining will result in an efficient solution to the problem of externalities.

LEARNING OBJECTIVE ③ Analyze government policies to achieve economic efficiency in a market with an externality. When private solutions to externalities are unworkable, the government will sometimes intervene. One way to deal with a negative externality in production is to impose a tax equal to the cost of the externality. The tax causes the producer of the good to internalize the externality. The government can deal with a positive externality in consumption by giving consumers a subsidy, or payment, equal to the value of the externality. Although the federal government has sometimes used subsidies and taxes to deal with externalities, in dealing with pollution it has more often used a "command and control approach." A command and control approach involves the government imposing quanti-

tative limits on the amount of pollution allowed or requiring that specific pollution control devices be installed. Direct pollution controls are not economically efficient, however. As a result, Congress decided to use a system of tradeable emissions allowances to reduce sulfur dioxide emissions.

LEARNING OBJECTIVE ④ Explain how goods can be categorized on the basis of whether they are rival or excludable. *Rivalry* means that when one person consumes a unit of a good, no one else can consume that unit. *Excludability* means that anyone who does not pay for a good cannot consume it. *Private goods* are both rival and excludable. Natural monopolies are excludable but not rival. *Common resources* are rival, but not excludable. *Public goods* are both nonrivalrous and nonexcludable.

LEARNING OBJECTIVE ⑤ Define a public good and a common resource, and use graphs to illustrate the efficient quantities of public goods and common resources. A *public good* has two characteristics. First, consumption of a public good is nonrivalrous, which means that one person's consumption does not interfere with another person's consumption. Second, the public good is nonexcludable, which means that it is impossible to exclude anyone from consuming the good. Firms cannot profitably supply public goods, such as national defense, so the government often supplies them. We find the market demand curve for a private good by adding the quantity of the good demanded by each consumer at each price. We find the demand curve for a public good by adding vertically the price each consumer would be willing to pay for each quantity of the good. The optimal quantity of a public good occurs where the demand curve intersects the curve representing the marginal cost of supplying the good. The *tragedy of the commons* refers to the tendency for a common resource to be overused. The source of the tragedy of the commons is a lack of clearly defined and enforced property rights.

Coase theorem 141
Command and control
  approach 144
Common resource 147
Excludability 146
Externality 132

Free riding 147
Market failure 134
Pigovian taxes and
  subsidies 144
Private benefit 133

Private cost 133
Private good 146
Property rights 134
Public good 147
Rivalry 146

Social benefit 133
Social cost 133
Tragedy of the
  commons 154
Transactions costs 141

REVIEW QUESTIONS

1. What is an externality? Give an example of a positive externality and of a negative externality.

2. When will the private cost of producing a good differ from the social cost? Give an example. When will the private benefit from consuming a good differ from the social benefit? Give an example.

3. What is economic efficiency? How do externalities affect the economic efficiency of a market equilibrium?

4. What is market failure? When is market failure likely to arise?

5. Briefly discuss the relationship between property rights and the existence of externalities.

6. What do economists mean by "an economically efficient level of pollution"?

7. What is the Coase theorem? What are transactions costs? When are we likely to see private solutions to the problem of externalities?

8. What is a Pigovian tax? At what level must a Pigovian tax be set to achieve efficiency?

9. Why do most economists favor tradeable emissions allowances to the command and control approach to pollution?

10. Define rivalry and excludability and use these terms to discuss the four categories of goods.

11. What is a public good? What is free riding? How is free riding related to the tendency of a public good to create market failure?

12. What is the tragedy of the commons? How can it be avoided?

PROBLEMS AND APPLICATIONS

Please visit **www.prenhall.com/hubbard** for solutions to the even-numbered problems as well as multiple-choice and true or false self-assessment quizzes.

1. The chapter states that your consuming a Big Mac does not create an externality. But suppose you arrive at your favorite McDonald's at lunchtime and get in a long line to be served. By the time you reach the counter, there are 10 people in line behind you. Because you decided to have a Big Mac for lunch—instead of, say, a pizza—each of those 10 people must wait in line an additional 2 minutes. Or suppose that after a lifetime of consuming Big Macs you develop heart disease. Because you are now over age 65, the government must pay most of your medical bills through the Medicare system. Is it still correct to say that your consuming a Big Mac created no externalities? Might there be a justification here for the government to intervene in the market for Big Macs? Explain.

2. The chapter discusses the cases of consumption generating a positive externality and production generating a negative externality. Is it possible for consumption to generate a negative externality? If so, give an example. Is it possible for production to generate a positive externality? If so, give an example.

3. Why does the government subsidize the purchase of college educations but not the purchase of hamburgers?

4. For several years, *The Sopranos* television series was available only on the HBO cable network. The series was a hit and attracted more viewers than many programs available on the broadcast networks NBC, CBS, ABC, and Fox. But Chris Albrecht, the chairman of HBO, found that he was unable to use the popularity of *The Sopranos* to increase the number of subscribers to HBO. To receive HBO, cable viewers usually had to pay for a "premium package" that included not just HBO but other services, like Showtime, that were owned by other companies. As Albrecht put it, "That means we're just part of everything else. First the consumer is asked to pay $60 for the basic cable service and then it's another $40 for the platinum package, and they're selling Showtime and Starz in with us." Is there an externality involved here? If so, is it an externality in production or consumption, and is it positive or negative? If there is an externality, discuss possible solutions.

Source: Excerpt from Bill Carter, "Cable Conquered, What's Next for 'The Sopranos'?" *New York Times*, October 7, 2002. Copyright © 2002 by The New York Times Co. Reprinted with permission.

5. Is it ever possible for an *increase* in pollution to make society better off? Briefly explain using a graph like Figure 5-3.

6. If the marginal cost of reducing a certain type of pollution is zero, should all of that pollution be eliminated? Briefly explain.

7. Discuss the factors that determine the marginal cost of reducing crime. Discuss the factors that determine the marginal benefit of reducing crime. Would it be economically efficient to reduce the amount of crime to zero? Briefly explain.

8. A columnist for the *Wall Street Journal* observes:

    > No one collects money from those who benefit from the flood control a wetland provides, or the nutrient recycling a forest does. . . . In a nutshell, market failures help drive habitat loss.

    What does she mean by market failures? What does she mean by habitat loss? Explain why she believes one is causing the other. Illustrate your argument with a graph showing the market for land to be used for development.
    Source: Sharon Begley, "Furry Math? Market Has Failed to Capture True Value of Nature," *Wall Street Journal*, August 9, 2002, p. B1.

9. Writing in the *New York Times*, Michael Lewis argues:

    > Good new technologies are a bit like good new roads: Their social benefits far exceed what any one person or company can get paid for creating them.

    Does this observation justify the government subsidizing the production of new technologies? If so, how might the government do this?
    Source: Michael Lewis, "In Defense of the Boom," *New York Times*, October 27, 2002.

10. **[Related to *Don't Let This Happen To You!*]** Briefly explain whether you agree or disagree with the following statement: "Sulfur dioxide emissions cause acid rain and breathing difficulties for people with respiratory problems. The total benefit to society is greatest if we completely eliminate sulfur dioxide emissions. Therefore, the economically efficient level of emissions is zero."

11. In discussing cleaning up oil spills, Gary Shigenka of the National Oceanographic and Atmospheric Agency observed that "The first 90% of any cleanup comes easy. But the tradeoffs for the remaining bits are brutal." He estimates that the last 1 percent of oil removed can cost seven times as much as the first 99 percent. Why should it be any more costly to clean up the last 1 percent of an oil spill than to clean up the first 1 percent? What trade-offs do you think Shigenka was referring to?
    Source: Keith Johnson and Gautam Naik, "For Spain, Exxon Valdez Offers Some Surprising Lessons," *Wall Street Journal*, November 22, 2002.

12. We saw in this chapter that market failure occurs when firms ignore the costs generated by pollution in deciding how much to produce. Government intervention usually is necessary to bring about a more efficient level of production. Before 1989, the Communist governments of Eastern Europe directly controlled the production of most goods and were free to choose how much of each good would be produced and what production process would be used. When these Communist governments collapsed, it was revealed that the countries of Eastern Europe suffered from very high levels of pollution, much higher than had existed in the United States and other high-income countries even before there was government anti-pollution legislation. Discuss reasons why the non-market Communist system generated more pollution than market economies.

13. Bjorn Lomborg, director of the Environmental Assessment Institute in Denmark, argued in a column in the *New York Times*:

    > Traditionally, the developed nations of the West have shown a greater concern for environmental sustainability, while the third world countries have a stronger desire for economic development.

    Recall the definition of a normal good given in Chapter 3. Is environmental protection a normal good? If so, is there any connection between this fact and Lomborg's observation? Briefly explain. How do the marginal cost and marginal benefit of environmental protection change with economic development?
    Source: Bjorn Lomborg, "The Environmentalists Are Wrong," *New York Times*, August 26, 2002.

14. **[Related to *Solved Problem 5-1*]** The fumes from dry cleaners can contribute to air pollution. Suppose the following diagram illustrates the situation in the dry cleaning market:

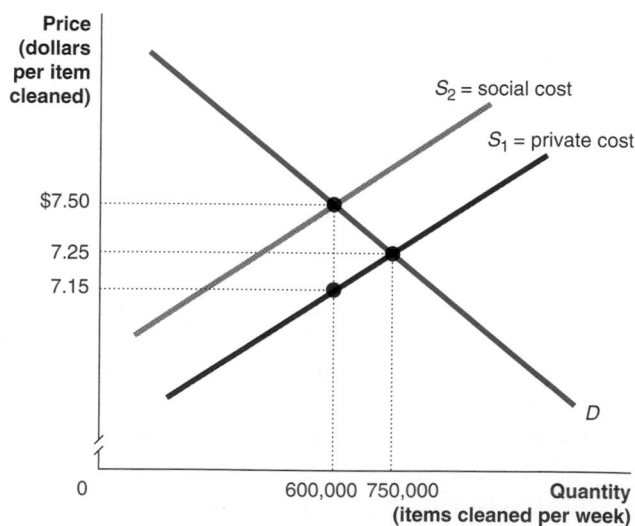

a. Explain how a government can use a tax on dry cleaning to bring about the efficient level of production. What should the value of the tax be?

b. How large is the deadweight loss (in dollars) from excessive dry cleaning, according to the figure?

15. The following diagram illustrates the situation in the dry cleaning market. In contrast to problem 14, the marginal social cost of the pollution rises as the quantity of items cleaned per week rises. In addition, there are two demand curves, one for a smaller city D_S, the other for a larger city D_L.

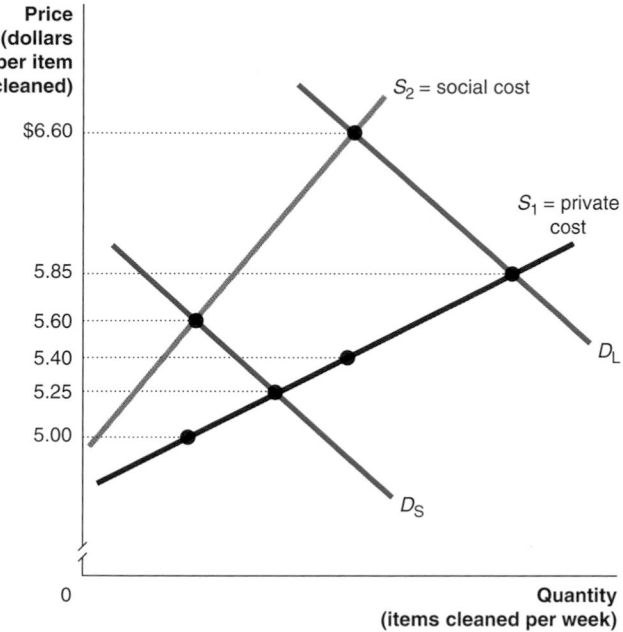

a. Explain why the social cost curve has a different slope than the private cost curve.
b. What tax rate per item cleaned will achieve economic efficiency in the smaller city? In the larger city? Explain why the tax rate differs from one city to the next.

16. **[Related to *Solved Problem 5-2*]** Suppose that Jill and Joe are the only two people in the small town of Andover. Andover has land available to build a park of no more than nine acres. Jill and Joe's demand schedules for the park are as follows:

JOE	
PRICE PER ACRE	NUMBER OF ACRES
$10	0
9	1
8	2
7	3
6	4
5	5
4	6
3	7
2	8
1	9

JILL	
PRICE PER ACRE	NUMBER OF ACRES
$15	0
14	1
13	2
12	3
11	4
10	5
9	6
8	7
7	8
6	9

The supply curve is as follows:

PRICE	NUMBER OF ACRES
$11	1
13	2
15	3
17	4
19	5
21	6
23	7
25	8
27	9

a. Draw a graph showing the optimal size park. Be sure to label the curves on your graph.
b. Briefly explain why a park of two acres is not optimal.

17. Commercial whaling has been described as a modern example of the tragedy of the commons. Briefly explain whether you agree or disagree.

18. According to an article in the *Wall Street Journal*, economist Paul Romer of Stanford University has argued:

> The market mechanism and property rights are excellent at conserving scarce resources and putting them to the most profitable use. . . . They aren't so good at encouraging the production and distribution of new ideas, which are critical to progress.

What characteristics of the production and distribution of new ideas might make it difficult for the market to produce the optimal amount?
Source: David Wessel, "Precepts from Professor Summers," *Wall Street Journal*, October 17, 2002.

19. The more frequently bacteria are exposed to antibiotics, the more quickly the bacteria will develop resistance to the antibiotics. A columnist for the *Wall Street Journal* observes:

> Each parent will press a pediatrician for a drug if there's any chance it will cure a child. Yet if every parent and pediatrician does the same, they will speed the evolution of drug-resistant microbes. And what drug company will enlist its marketers to prod doctors to prescribe its antibiotics less?

Briefly discuss in what sense antibiotics can be considered a common resource.
Source: David Wessel, "Losing the Race with Bugs: Bacteria Beats New Drugs," *Wall Street Journal*, April 25, 2002.

20. **[Related to the *Chapter Opener*]** Anyone can purchase sulfur dioxide emissions allowances on the Chicago Mercantile Exchange. Several environmental groups have raised money to buy allowances. As part of their fund-raising, these groups have urged contributors to buy the allowances as gifts. As one newspaper story put it, "For the environmentalist in your life, here's a gift that is sold by the ton, fits in an envelope and will last forever." What would be the impact of environmental groups buying emission allowances on the total amount of sulfur dioxide pollution in the United States? What would be the impact on the price of the emission allowances?
Source for quote: Randall Edwards, "Dear Santa: Please Bring Me Sulfur Dioxide for Christmas," *Columbus Dispatch*, December 19, 1999.

21. Review Making the Connection 5-3 on global warming. Briefly discuss why you agree or disagree with the following statement: "The position of the United States is that CO_2 emissions should be reduced by a system of tradeable permits. This is more economically efficient than the European position of requiring each country to reduce its emissions by a specific amount. But I think the European position is fairer, because no country should be allowed to buy its way out of having to reduce CO_2 emissions. Therefore, I support that European position."

22. A recent study of a large state university where students were randomly assigned roommates found that, on aver-age, males assigned to roommates who reported drinking alcohol in the year prior to entering college had one quarter-point lower GPAs than those assigned to non-drinking roommates. For males who themselves drank frequently prior to college, assignment to a roommate who drank frequently prior to college reduced GPAs by two-thirds of a point. Draw a graph showing the price of alcohol and the quantity of alcohol consumption on college campuses. Include in the graph the private and social cost of drinking. Label any deadweight loss that arises in this market.
Source: Michael Kremer and Dan M. Levy, "Peer Effects and Alcohol Use Among College Students," National Bureau of Economic Research Working Paper, 9876, July 2003.

23. Tom and Jacob are college students. Both of them will probably get married later and have two or three children. Each knows that if he studies more in college he'll get a better job and earn more. Earning more means the ability to spend more on things for future kids—things like cool computer games, braces, nice clothes, admission to a more expensive college, and travel. Tom thinks about the potential benefits to his potential children when he decides how much studying to do. Jacob doesn't.
   a. What type of externality arises from studying?
   b. Draw a graph showing this externality, contrasting the responses of Tom and Jacob. Who studies more? Who acts more efficiently? Why?

24. Put each of these goods or services into one of the boxes in Figure 5-8. That is, categorize them as private goods, common resources, natural monopolies, or public goods.
   a. A television broadcast of the World Series
   b. Mail delivery
   c. Education in a public school
   d. Education in a private school
   e. Hiking in a park surrounded by a fence
   f. Hiking in a park not surrounded by a fence
   g. An apple

chapter

six

Elasticity: The Responsiveness of Demand and Supply

Do People Care about the Prices of Books?

➤ Some observers have been predicting for years that the printed book will be replaced with an electronic version. The printed book is still holding its own, however. In 2004, U.S. consumers spent almost $38 billion to buy the 2.5 billion copies of books that were published that year. By contrast, although thousands of books were available in electronic format, total sales amounted to only a few million dollars.

While the printed book lives on, the book publishing industry has undergone substantial change. Until recently, most book publishers were relatively small firms, usually located in New York or Boston, and often run by the families that founded them. Today, many U.S. publishers have become part of multinational corporations. For example, Doubleday was

founded by Frank Nelson Doubleday in 1897, and Knopf was founded by Alfred and Blanche Knopf in 1915. For decades, both companies were among the leading publishers in the United States. Today, both are owned by Bertelsmann, AG, a German firm that also owns other publishers, as well as radio and television stations and music companies.

Whether independent or part of larger companies, book publishers face a common problem unique to the industry: When retail stores buy most products from manufacturers, they have no legal right to return unsold items. For example, when a local supermarket orders shampoo, apple juice, or dog food, it knows that if it has overestimated consumer demand, it will be stuck with the unsold items. Bookstores were in

the same situation until the Great Depression of the 1930s. During that period of extreme economic hardship, many bookstores went bankrupt and most others were reluctant to order books from publishers unless they were certain of being able to sell them. To give bookstores an incentive to order more books, publishers began to give them the right to return unsold copies. This practice continues today. On average, bookstores return 35 percent of books to publishers.

The high return rate of books means that publishers have to be very careful when deciding how many copies of a book to print and ship to bookstores. In 2004, Knopf published *My Life*, the memoirs of former President Bill Clinton. Knopf could not simply print all the books ordered by bookstores because it feared that the

bookstores might overestimate the quantity of books actually demanded by consumers. As one bookseller put it, "No retailer ever wants to lose a sale. Of course, it's Knopf that is taking the big risks. If the books don't sell, we say 'Sorry, here are your books back.'" Executives at Knopf knew that the number of copies of the book demanded by consumers would depend in part on the price of the book. Publishers debate how responsive consumers are to changes in the prices of books.

For example, Stephen Rubin, publisher of Doubleday, has made the following argument about book prices: "I am just convinced that there is no difference between $22 and $23. Let's face it. If you want a book in translation from a Czech writer, you are going to buy the book—price is not a factor if it is a book that you really want." Is Rubin correct that book buyers don't care about the prices of books? If so, why charge $23 for a book, rather than $100 or $200? Does it matter whether the book is a "translation from a Czech writer" or a horror novel by Stephen King? In this chapter we will see how to measure the responsiveness of the quantity demanded of a product to changes in its price. *An Inside Look* on page 190 discusses the effectiveness of price cutting at Amazon.com, the online bookseller.

Sources: Quote about Knopf from Jeffrey Trachtenberg, "Clinton Will Be Star Salesman of His Memoir," *Wall Street Journal*, June 9, 2004; Rubin quote from Virginia Postrel, "Often, Basic Concepts in Economics Are Taken for Granted," *New York Times*, January 3, 2002.

LEARNING OBJECTIVES

After studying this chapter, you should be able to:

① Define the price elasticity of demand and understand how to calculate it.

② Understand the determinants of the price elasticity of demand.

③ Understand the relationship between the price elasticity of demand and total revenue.

④ Define the cross-price elasticity of demand and the income elasticity of demand, and understand their determinants and how they are calculated.

⑤ Use price elasticity and income elasticity to analyze economic issues.

⑥ Define the price elasticity of supply, and understand its main determinants and how it is calculated.

Elasticity A measure of how much one economic variable responds to changes in another economic variable.

➤ Whether you are managing a publishing company, bookstore, or coffee shop, you need to know how an increase or decrease in the price of your products will affect the quantity consumers are willing to buy. We saw in Chapter 3 that cutting the price of a good increases the quantity demanded, and that raising the price reduces the quantity demanded. But the critical question is this: *How much* will the quantity demanded change as a result of a price increase or decrease? Economists use the concept of **elasticity** to measure how one economic variable—such as the quantity demanded—responds to changes in another economic variable—such as the price. For example, the responsiveness of the quantity demanded of a good to changes in its price is called the *price elasticity of demand.* Knowing the price elasticity of demand allows you to compute the effect of a price change on the quantity demanded.

We also saw in Chapter 3 that the quantity of a good that consumers demand depends not just on the price of the good but also on consumer income and on the prices of related goods. As a manager, you would also be interested in measuring the responsiveness of demand to these other factors. As we will see, we can use the concept of elasticity here as well. We also are interested in the responsiveness of the quantity supplied of a good to changes in its price, which is called the *price elasticity of supply.*

Elasticity is an important concept not just for business managers but for policymakers as well. If the government wants to discourage teenage smoking, it can raise the price of cigarettes by increasing the tax on them. If we know the price elasticity of demand for cigarettes, we can calculate how many fewer cigarettes will be demanded at a higher price. In this chapter, we will also see how policymakers use the concept of elasticity.

① **LEARNING OBJECTIVE**

Define the price elasticity of demand and understand how to calculate it.

Price elasticity of demand The responsiveness of the quantity demanded to a change in price, measured by dividing the percentage change in the quantity demanded of a product by the percentage change in the product's price.

The Price Elasticity of Demand and Its Measurement

We know from the law of demand that when the price of a product falls, the quantity demanded of the product increases. But the law of demand tells firms only that the demand curves for their products slope downward. More useful is a measure of the responsiveness of the quantity demanded to a change in price. This measure is called the **price elasticity of demand.**

Measuring the Price Elasticity of Demand

We might measure the price elasticity of demand using the slope of the demand curve, because the slope of the demand curve tells us how much quantity changes as price changes. Using the slope of the demand curve to measure price elasticity has a drawback, however: The measurement of slope is sensitive to the units chosen for quantity and price. For example, suppose a $1 decrease in the price of wheat leads to an increase in the quantity of wheat demanded from 1.1 billion bushels to 1.2 billion bushels. The change in quantity is 0.1 billion bushels and the change in price is −$1, so the slope is $0.1/-1 = -0.1$. But if we measure price in cents, rather than dollars, the slope is $0.1/-100 = -0.001$. If we measure price in dollars, and wheat in millions of bushels, the slope is: $100/-1 = -100$. Clearly the value we compute for the slope can change dramatically depending on the units we use for quantity and price.

To avoid this confusion over units, economists use *percentage changes* when measuring the price elasticity of demand. Percentage changes are not dependent on units. (For a review of calculating percentage changes, see the Appendix to Chapter 1.) No matter what units we use to measure the quantity of wheat, 10 percent more wheat is 10 percent more wheat. Therefore, the price elasticity of demand is measured by dividing the percentage change in the quantity demanded by the percentage change in the price. Or,

$$\text{Price elasticity of demand} = \frac{\text{Percentage change in quantity demanded}}{\text{Percentage change in price}}.$$

It's important to remember that *the price elasticity of demand is not the same as the slope of the demand curve.*

If we calculate the price elasticity of demand for a price cut, the percentage change in price will be negative and the percentage change in quantity demanded will be positive. Similarly, if we calculate the price elasticity of demand for a price increase, the percentage change in price will be positive and the percentage change in quantity will be negative. Therefore, the price elasticity of demand is always negative. In comparing elasticities, though, we are usually interested in their relative size. So, we often drop the minus sign and compare their absolute values. In other words, although -3 is actually a smaller number than -2, a price elasticity of -3 is larger than a price elasticity of -2.

Elastic Demand and Inelastic Demand

If the quantity demanded is responsive to changes in price, the percentage change in quantity demanded will be *greater* than the percentage change in price, and the price elasticity of demand will be greater than 1 in absolute value. In this case, demand is **elastic.** For example, if a 10 percent fall in the price of bagels results in a 20 percent increase in the quantity of bagels demanded, then

$$\text{Price elasticity of demand} = \frac{20\%}{-10\%} = -2,$$

and we can conclude that the price of bagels is *elastic.*

When the quantity demanded is not very responsive to price, however, the percentage change in quantity demanded will be *less* than the percentage change in price, and the price elasticity of demand will be less than 1 in absolute value. In this case demand is **inelastic.** For example, if a 10 percent fall in the price of wheat results in a 5 percent increase in the quantity of wheat demanded, then

$$\text{Price elasticity of demand} = \frac{5\%}{-10\%} = -0.5,$$

and we can conclude that the demand for wheat is *inelastic.*

In the special case in which the percentage change in the quantity demanded is equal to the percentage change in price, the price elasticity of demand equals -1 (or 1 in absolute value). In this case, demand is **unit-elastic.**

An Example of Computing Price Elasticities

Suppose you own a small bookstore and you are trying to decide whether to cut the price you are charging for the new John Grisham mystery novel. You are currently at point A in Figure 6-1: selling 16 copies of the novel per day at a price of $30 per copy. How many more copies you will sell by cutting the price to $20 depends on the price elasticity of demand for this novel. Let's consider two possibilities: If D_1 is the demand curve for this novel in your store, your sales will increase to 28 copies per day, point B.

Elastic demand Demand is elastic when the percentage change in quantity demanded is *greater* than the percentage change in price, so the price elasticity is *greater* than 1 in absolute value.

Inelastic demand Demand is inelastic when the percentage change in quantity demanded is *less* than the percentage change in price, so the price elasticity is *less* than 1 in absolute value.

Unit-elastic demand Demand is unit-elastic when the percentage change in quantity demanded is *equal to* the percentage change in price, so the price elasticity is equal to 1 in absolute value.

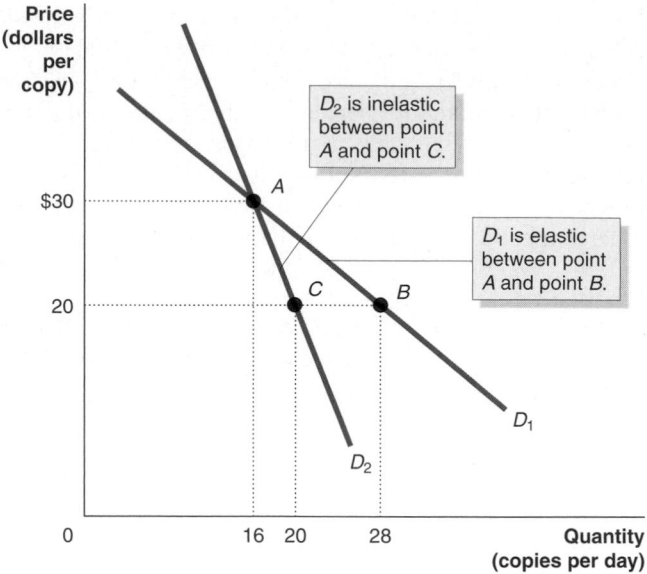

FIGURE 6-1

Elastic and Inelastic Demand Curves

Along D_1, demand is elastic between point A and point B, so cutting price from $30 to $20 increases the number of copies sold from 16 per day to 28 per day. Along D_2, demand is inelastic between point A and point C, so cutting price from $30 to $20 increases the number of copies sold from 16 per day to only 20 per day.

But if D_2 is your demand curve, your sales will increase only to 20 copies per day, point C. We might expect—correctly, as we will see—that between these points demand curve D_1 is *elastic* and demand curve D_2 is *inelastic*.

To confirm that D_1 is elastic between these points and that D_2 is inelastic, we need to calculate the price elasticity of demand for each curve. In calculating price elasticity between two points on a demand curve, though, we run into a problem because we get a different value for price increases than for price decreases. For example, suppose we calculate the price elasticity for D_1 as the price is cut from $30 to $20. This reduction is a 33 percent price cut that increases the quantity demanded from 16 books to 20 books, or by 25 percent. Therefore, the price elasticity of demand between points A and C is $25/-33 = -0.8$. Now let's calculate the price elasticity for D_1 as the price is *increased* from $20 to $30. This is a 50 percent price increase that decreases the quantity demanded from 20 books to 16 books, or by 20 percent. So, now our measure of the price elasticity of demand between points A and C is $-20/50 = -0.4$. It is not very satisfactory to have different values for the price elasticity of demand between the same two points on the same demand curve.

The Midpoint Formula

We can use the *midpoint formula* to ensure that we have only one value of the price elasticity of demand between the same two points on the same demand curve. The midpoint formula uses the *average* of the initial and final quantity and the initial and final price. If Q_1 and P_1 are the initial quantity and price and Q_2 and P_2 are the final quantity and price, the midpoint formula is:

$$\text{Price elasticity of demand} = \frac{(Q_2 - Q_1)}{\left(\frac{Q_1 + Q_2}{2}\right)} \div \frac{(P_2 - P_1)}{\left(\frac{P_1 + P_2}{2}\right)}.$$

The midpoint formula may seem challenging at first, but the numerator is just the change in quantity divided by the average of the initial and final quantities, and the denominator is just the change in price divided by the average of the initial and final prices.

Let's apply the formula to calculating the price elasticity of D_2 in Figure 6-1. Between point A and point C on D_2, the change in quantity is 4, and the average of the two quantities is 18. Therefore, there is a 22.2 percent change in quantity. The change in price is $-\$10$, and the average of the two prices is \$25. Therefore, there is a -40 percent change in price. So, the price elasticity of demand is $22.2/-40.0 = -0.6$. Notice these three results from calculating the price elasticity of demand using the midpoint formula: First, as we suspected from examining Figure 6-1, demand curve D_2 is inelastic between points A and C. Second, our value for the price elasticity calculated using the midpoint formula is between the two values we calculated earlier. Third, the midpoint formula will give us the same value whether we are moving from the higher price to the lower price, or from the lower price to the higher price.

We can also use the midpoint formula to calculate the elasticity of demand between point A and point B on D_1. In this case, there is a 54.5 percent change in quantity and a -40 percent change in price. So, the elasticity of demand is $54.5/-40.0 = -1.4$. Once again, as we suspected, demand curve D_1 is price elastic between points A and B.

SOLVED PROBLEM 6-1

Calculating the Price Elasticity of Demand for Wheat Using the Midpoint Formula

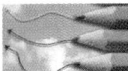 **① LEARNING OBJECTIVE**
Define the price elasticity of demand and understand how to calculate it.

Suppose the following table gives data on the price of wheat and the number of bushels of wheat sold in 2010 and 2011. Assuming that the demand curve for wheat did not shift between 2010 and 2011, use the information in the table and the midpoint formula to calculate the price elasticity of demand for wheat.

YEAR	PRICE (PER BUSHEL)	QUANTITY (BILLIONS OF BUSHELS)
2010	\$3.00	3.0
2011	3.60	2.8

Solving the Problem:
Step 1: Review the chapter material. This problem requires calculating the price elasticity of demand, so you may want to review the material in the section "The Midpoint Formula," which begins on page 168.

Step 2: As the first step in using the midpoint formula, calculate the average quantity and the average price.

$$\text{Average quantity} = \frac{3.0 + 2.8}{2} = 2.9$$

$$\text{Average price} = \frac{\$3.00 + \$3.60}{2} = \$3.30$$

Step 3: Now calculate the percentage change in the quantity demanded and the percentage change in price.

$$\text{Percentage change in quantity demanded} = \frac{2.8 - 3.0}{2.9} \times 100 = -6.9\%$$

$$\text{Percentage change in price} = \frac{\$3.60 - \$3.00}{\$3.30} \times 100 = 18.2\%$$

Step 4: Finally, divide the percentage change in the quantity demanded by the percentage change in price to arrive at the correct answer.

$$\text{Price elasticity of demand for wheat} = \frac{-6.9\%}{18.2\%} = -0.4$$

Notice that because this calculation was for a price increase, the percentage change in the quantity demanded was negative and the percentage change in the price was positive.

YOUR TURN: **For more practice, do related problem 1 on page 193 at the end of this chapter. Visit www.prenhall.com/hubbard for an interactive exercise related to this Solved Problem.**

When Demand Curves Intersect, the Flatter Curve Is More Elastic

Remember that elasticity is not the same thing as slope. Slope is calculated using changes in quantity and price, whereas elasticity is calculated using percentage changes. But it *is* true that when two demand curves intersect, the one with the smaller slope (in absolute value)—the flatter demand curve—is more elastic, and the one with the larger slope (in absolute value)—the steeper demand curve—is less elastic. In Figure 6-1, demand curve D_1 is more elastic than demand curve D_2.

Polar Cases of Perfectly Elastic and Perfectly Inelastic Demand

Perfectly inelastic demand Demand is perfectly inelastic when a change in price results in no change in quantity demanded.

Although they do not occur frequently, you should be aware of the extreme, or polar, cases of price elasticity. If a demand curve is a vertical line, it is **perfectly inelastic.** In this case, the quantity demanded is completely unresponsive to price, and the price elasticity of demand equals zero. However much price may increase or decrease, the quantity remains the same. For only a very few products will the quantity demanded be completely unresponsive to the price, making the demand curve a vertical line. The drug insulin is an example. Diabetics must take a certain amount of insulin each day. If the price of insulin declines, it will not affect the required dose and thus will not increase the quantity demanded. Similarly, a price increase will not affect the required dose or decrease the quantity demanded. (Of course, some diabetics will not be able to afford insulin at a higher price. If so, even in this case the demand curve may not be completely vertical and, therefore, not perfectly inelastic.)

Perfectly elastic demand Demand is perfectly elastic when a change in price results in an infinite change in quantity demanded.

If a demand curve is a horizontal line, it is **perfectly elastic.** In this case, the quantity demanded would be infinitely responsive to price, and the price elasticity of demand equals infinity. If a demand curve is perfectly elastic, an increase in price causes the quantity demanded to fall to zero. Once again, perfectly elastic demand curves are rare and it is important not to confuse elastic with perfectly elastic. Table 6-1 summarizes the different price elasticities of demand.

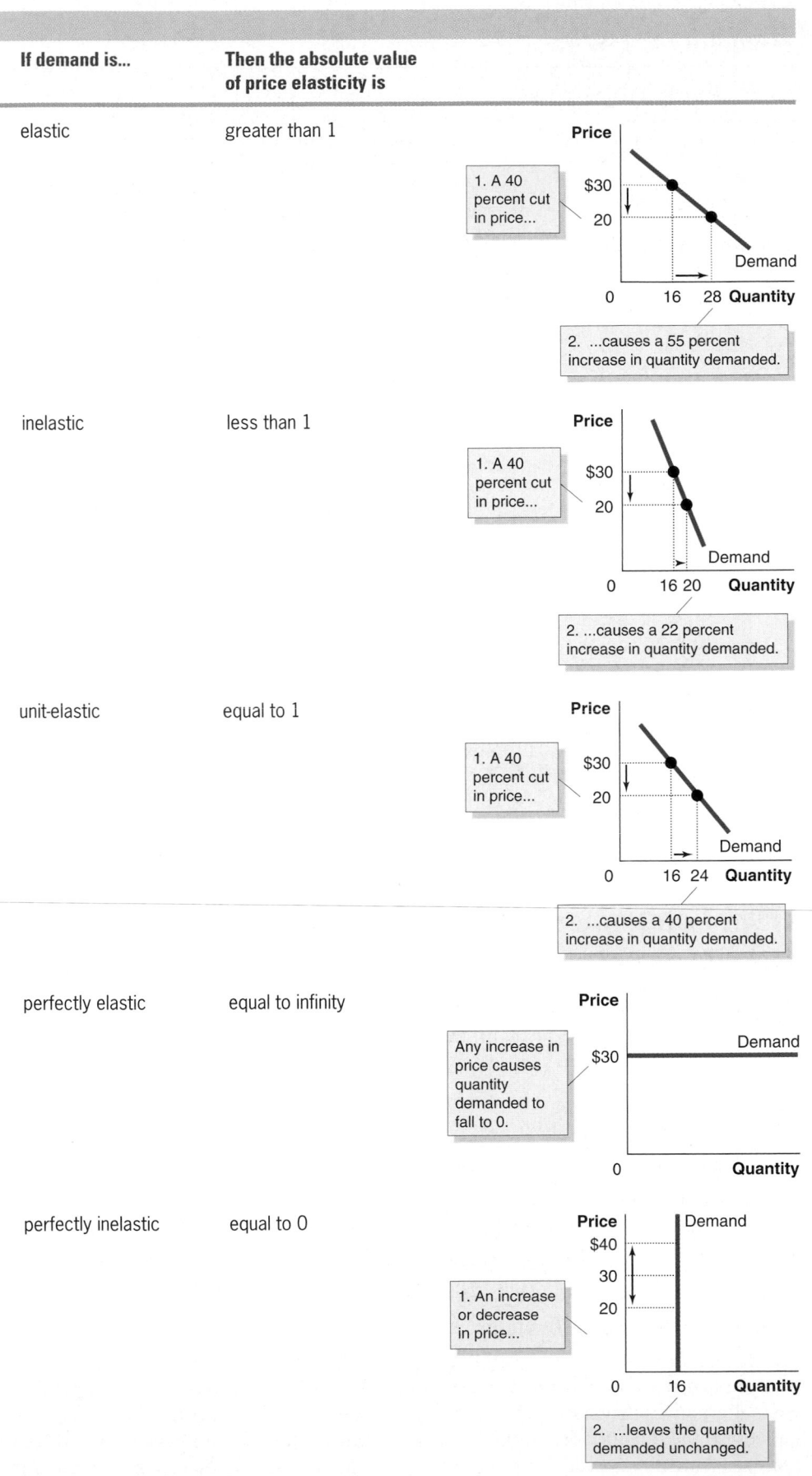

TABLE 6-1

Summary of the Price Elasticities of Demand

If demand is...	Then the absolute value of price elasticity is
elastic	greater than 1
inelastic	less than 1
unit-elastic	equal to 1
perfectly elastic	equal to infinity
perfectly inelastic	equal to 0

elastic

1. A 40 percent cut in price...

Price

$30

20

Demand

0   16   28   **Quantity**

2. ...causes a 55 percent increase in quantity demanded.

inelastic

1. A 40 percent cut in price...

Price

$30

20

Demand

0   16 20   **Quantity**

2. ...causes a 22 percent increase in quantity demanded.

unit-elastic

1. A 40 percent cut in price...

Price

$30

20

Demand

0   16 24   **Quantity**

2. ...causes a 40 percent increase in quantity demanded.

perfectly elastic

Any increase in price causes quantity demanded to fall to 0.

Price

$30   Demand

0   **Quantity**

perfectly inelastic

1. An increase or decrease in price...

Price   Demand

$40

30

20

0   16   **Quantity**

2. ...leaves the quantity demanded unchanged.

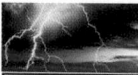

Don't Let This Happen To You!

Don't Confuse Inelastic with *Perfectly* Inelastic

You may be tempted to simplify the concept of elasticity by assuming that any demand curve described as being inelastic is *perfectly* inelastic. You should never assume this because perfectly inelastic demand curves are rare. For example, consider the following problem: "Use a demand and supply graph to show how a decrease in supply affects the equilibrium quantity of gasoline. Assume that the demand for gasoline is inelastic."

The following graph would be an *incorrect* answer to this problem:

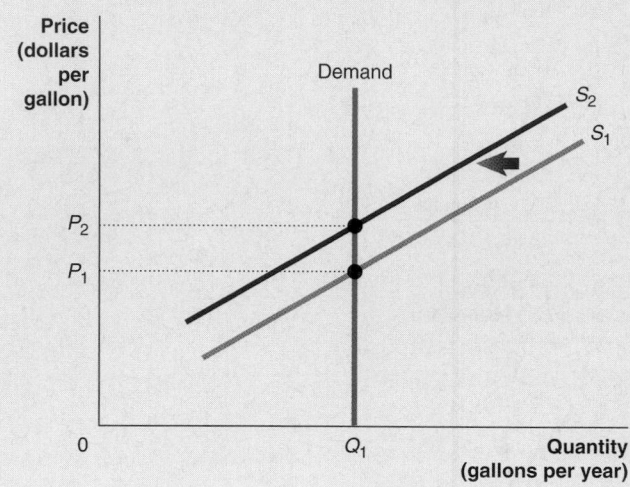

The demand for gasoline is inelastic, but it is not *perfectly* inelastic. When the price of gasoline rises, the quantity demanded falls. So, the graph that would be the correct answer to this problem would show a normal downward-sloping demand curve, rather than a vertical demand curve:

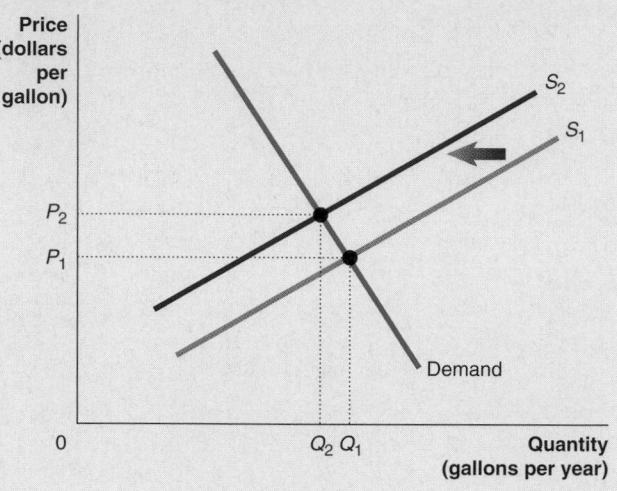

YOUR TURN: Test your understanding by doing related problem 16 on page 195 at the end of this chapter.

---

(2) **LEARNING OBJECTIVE**

Understand the determinants of the price elasticity of demand.

What Determines the Price Elasticity of Demand for a Product?

We have seen that the demand for some products may be elastic, while the demand for other products may be inelastic. In this section, we examine why price elasticities differ among products. The key determinants of the price elasticity of demand are as follows:

➤ Availability of close substitutes
➤ Passage of time
➤ Necessities versus luxuries
➤ Definition of the market
➤ Share of the good in the consumer's budget

Availability of Close Substitutes

The availability of substitutes is the most important determinant of price elasticity of demand because how consumers react to a change in the price of a product depends on what alternatives they have. When the price of gasoline rises, consumers have few alternatives, so the quantity demanded falls only a little. But if Domino's raises the price of pizza, consumers have many alternatives, so the quantity demanded is likely to fall quite a lot. In fact, a key constraint on a firm's pricing policies is how many close substitutes exist for its product. In general, *if a product has more substitutes available, it will have more elastic demand. If a product has fewer substitutes available, it will have less elastic demand.*

Passage of Time

It usually takes consumers some time to adjust their buying habits when prices change. If the price of chicken falls, it will take a while before consumers decide to change from eating chicken for dinner once per week to eating it twice per week. If the price of gasoline increases, it will also take a while for consumers to decide to shift toward buying more fuel-efficient cars, reducing the quantity of gasoline they buy. *The more time that passes, the more elastic the demand for a product becomes.*

Luxuries versus Necessities

Goods that are luxuries will usually have more elastic demand curves than goods that are necessities. For example, the demand for milk is inelastic because milk is a necessity and the quantity that people buy is not very dependent on its price. Tickets to a concert are a luxury, so the demand for concert tickets is much more elastic than the demand for milk. *The demand curve for a luxury is more elastic than the demand curve for a necessity.*

Definition of the Market

In a narrowly defined market consumers will have more substitutes available. If the price of Kellogg's Raisin Bran rises, many consumers will start buying another brand of raisin bran. If the prices of all brands of raisin bran rise, the responsiveness of consumers will be lower. If the prices of all breakfast cereals rise, the responsiveness of consumers will be even lower. *The more narrowly we define a market, the more elastic demand will be.*

The Price Elasticity of Demand for Breakfast Cereal

6-1 Making the Connection

MIT economist Jerry Hausman has estimated the price elasticity of demand for breakfast cereal. He divided breakfast cereals into three categories: children's cereals, such as Trix or Froot Loops; adult cereals, such as Special K or Grape-Nuts; and family cereals, such as Corn Flakes and Raisin Bran. Some of the results of his estimates are given in the following table.

CEREAL	PRICE ELASTICITY OF DEMAND
Post Raisin Bran	−2.5
All family breakfast cereals	−1.8
All types of breakfast cereals	−0.9

Source: Jerry A. Hausman, "The Price Elasticity of Demand for Breakfast Cereal" in *The Economics of New Goods*, TF Bresnahan & RJ Gordon, eds. Used with permission of The University of Chicago Press.

Just as we would expect, the price elasticity for a particular brand of raisin bran was larger in absolute value than the elasticity for all family cereals, and the elasticity for all family cereals was larger than the elasticity for all types of breakfast

What happens when the price of cereal rises?

cereals. If Post increases the price of its Raisin Bran by 10 percent, sales will decline by 25 percent, as many consumers switch to another brand of raisin bran. If the prices of all family breakfast cereals rise by 10 percent, sales will drop by 18 percent, as consumers switch to child or adult cereals. In both of these cases, demand is elastic. But if the prices of all types of breakfast cereals rise by 10 percent, sales will only decline by 9 percent. Demand for all breakfast cereals is inelastic.

Source: Jerry A. Hausman, "Valuation of New Goods under Perfect and Imperfect Competition," in Timothy F. Bresnahan and Robert J. Gordon, eds., *The Economics of New Goods*, Chicago and London: University of Chicago Press, 1997.

Share of the Good in the Consumer's Budget

Goods that take only a small fraction of a consumer's budget tend to have less elastic demand. For example, most people buy salt infrequently and in relatively small quantities. The share of the average consumer's budget that is spent on salt is very low. As a result, even a doubling of the price of salt is likely to result in only a small decline in the quantity of salt demanded. "Big-ticket items," such as houses, cars, and furniture, take up a larger share in the average consumer's budget. Increases in the prices of these goods are likely to result in significant declines in quantity demanded. In general, *the demand for a good will be less elastic the smaller the share of the good in the average consumer's budget.*

Is the Demand for Books Perfectly Inelastic?

At the beginning of the chapter we quoted Stephen Rubin, publisher of Doubleday Books, as saying, "I am just convinced that there is no difference between $22 and $23. . . . [P]rice is not a factor if it is a book that you really want." Taken literally, Rubin seems to be arguing that the demand for books is perfectly inelastic, because only when demand is perfectly inelastic is price "not a factor." It's unlikely that this is what he means, because if demand were really perfectly inelastic, he could charge $200 or $2,000 instead of charging $23 and still sell the same number of books. It is more likely he is arguing that demand is inelastic, so that even though he will sell fewer books at a price of $23 than at a price of $22, the decline in sales will be small.

Notice also that the book he mentions is a "translation from a Czech writer." Specialized books of this type will have relatively few substitutes. A cut in price is unlikely to attract many new customers, and an increase in price is unlikely to lose many existing customers. This lack of substitutes is the main factor that makes demand inelastic. The situation may be different for light fiction written by popular novelists, like John Grisham, Stephen King, or Dean Koontz. Many consumers see books written by these authors as close substitutes. Someone looking for a "good read" on an airplane trip or at the beach may switch from Stephen King to Dean Koontz if the price of the Stephen King book is significantly higher.

③ **LEARNING OBJECTIVE**

Understand the relationship between the price elasticity of demand and total revenue.

Total revenue The total amount of funds received by a seller of a good or service, calculated by multiplying price per unit by the number of units sold.

The Relationship between Price Elasticity and Total Revenue

A firm is interested in price elasticity because it allows the firm to calculate how changes in price will affect its **total revenue,** which is the total amount of funds it receives from selling a good or service. Total revenue is calculated by multiplying price per unit by the number of units sold. When demand is inelastic, price and total revenue move in the same direction: An increase in price raises total revenue, and a decrease in price reduces total revenue. When demand is elastic, price and total revenue move inversely: An increase in price reduces total revenue, and a decrease in price raises total revenue.

To understand the relationship between price elasticity and total revenue, consider Figure 6-2. Panel (a) shows a demand curve for a John Grisham novel (as in Figure 6-1).

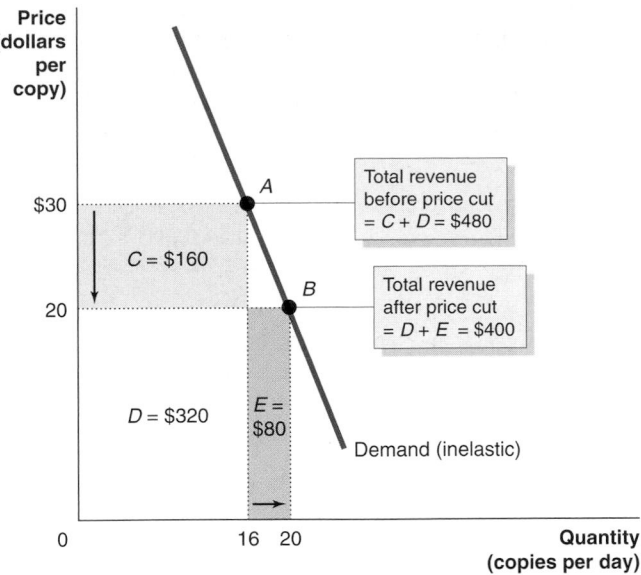

(a) Cutting price when demand is inelastic reduces total revenue.

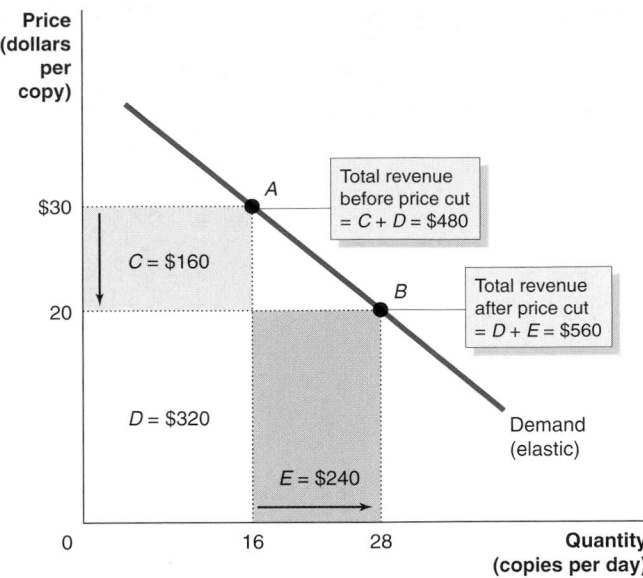

(b) Cutting price when demand is elastic increases total revenue.

FIGURE 6-2   The Relationship between Price Elasticity and Total Revenue

When demand is inelastic, a cut in price will decrease total revenue. In panel (a), at point A the price is $30, 16 copies are sold, and total revenue received by the bookseller equals $30 × 16 copies, or $480. At point B, cutting price to $20 increases the quantity demanded to 20 copies, but the fall in price more than offsets the increase in quantity. As a result, revenue falls to $20 × 20 copies, or $400. When demand is elastic, a cut in price will increase total revenue. In panel (b), at point A the area of rectangles C and D is still equal to $480. But at point B the area of rectangles D and E is equal to $20 × 28 copies, or $560. In this case, the increase in the quantity demanded is large enough to offset the fall in price, so total revenue increases.

This demand curve is inelastic between point A and point B. The total revenue received by a bookseller at point A equals the price of $30 multiplied by the 16 copies sold, or $480. This amount equals the areas of the rectangles C and D in the figure, because together the rectangles have a height of $30 and a base of 16 copies. Because this demand curve is inelastic between point A and point B (it was demand curve D_2 in Figure 6-1), cutting the price to $20 (point B) reduces total revenue. The new total revenue is shown by the areas of rectangles D and E, and it is equal to $20 multiplied by 20 copies, or $400. Total revenue falls because the increase in the quantity demanded is not large enough to make up for the decrease in price. As a result, the $80 increase in revenue gained as a result of the price cut—dark-green rectangle E—is less than the $160 in revenue lost—light-green rectangle C.

Panel (b) of Figure 6-2 shows a demand curve that is elastic between point A and point B (it was demand curve D_1 in Figure 6-1). In this case, cutting the price increases total revenue. At point A, the areas of rectangles C and D are still equal to $480, but at point B, the areas of rectangles D and E are equal to $20 multiplied by 28 copies, or $560. Here total revenue rises because the increase in the quantity demanded is large enough to offset the lower price. As a result, the $240 increase in revenue gained as a result of the price cut—dark-green rectangle E—is greater than the $160 in revenue lost—light-green rectangle C.

The third, less common possibility is that demand is unit-elastic. In that case, a change in price is exactly offset by a proportional change in quantity demanded, leaving revenue unaffected. Therefore, when demand is unit-elastic, neither a decrease in price nor an increase in price affects revenue. Table 6-2 summarizes the relationship between price elasticity and revenue.

Elasticity and Revenue with a Linear Demand Curve

Along most demand curves, elasticity is not constant at every point. For example, a straight-line, or linear, demand curve for DVDs is shown in panel (a) of Figure 6-3. The

TABLE 6-2	IF DEMAND IS...	THEN...	BECAUSE...
The Relationship between Price Elasticity and Revenue	elastic	an increase in price reduces revenue	the decrease in quantity demanded is proportionally *greater* than the increase in price.
	elastic	a decrease in price increases revenue	the increase in quantity demanded is proportionally *greater* than the decrease in price.
	inelastic	an increase in price increases revenue	the decrease in quantity demanded is proportionally *smaller* than the increase in price.
	inelastic	a decrease in price reduces revenue	the increase in quantity demanded is proportionally *smaller* than the decrease in price.
	unit-elastic	an increase in price does not affect revenue	the decrease in quantity demanded is proportionally *the same as* the increase in price.
	unit-elastic	a decrease in price does not affect revenue	the increase in quantity demanded is proportionally *the same as* the decrease in price.

demand curve shows that when the price falls by $1, consumers always respond by buy-ing 2 more DVDs per month. When the price is high and the quantity demanded is low, demand is elastic. This is true because a $1 fall in price is a smaller percentage change when the price is high, and an increase of 2 DVDs is a larger percentage change when the quantity of DVDs is small. By similar reasoning, we can see why Jill's demand is inelastic when the price is low and the quantity demanded is high.

As panel (b) in Figure 6-3 shows, because over the price range from $8 to $4 demand is elastic, total revenue will increase as price falls. For example, as price falls from $7 to $6, total revenue increases from $14 to $24. Over the price range from $4 to zero, demand is inelastic, so total revenue will decrease as price falls. For example, as price falls from $3 to $2, total revenue decreases from $30 to $24.

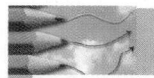

SOLVED PROBLEM   6-2

③ LEARNING OBJECTIVE

Understand the relationship between the price elasticity of demand and total revenue.

Price and Revenue Don't Always Move in the Same Direction

Briefly explain whether you agree or disagree with the following statement: "The only way to increase the revenue from selling a product is to increase the product's price."

Solving the Problem:

Step 1: Review the chapter material. This problem deals with the effect of a price change on a firm's revenue, so you may want to review the section "The Relationship between Price Elasticity and Total Revenue," which begins on page 174.

Step 2: Analyze the statement. We have seen that a price increase will increase revenue only if demand is inelastic. In Figure 6-3, for example, increasing the rental price of DVDs from $1 to $2 *increases* revenue from $14 to $24 because demand is inelastic along this portion of the demand curve. But increasing the price from $5 to $6 *decreases* revenue from $30 to $24 because demand is elastic along this portion of the demand curve. If the price is currently $5, increasing revenue would require a price *cut*, not a price increase. As this example shows, the statement is incorrect and you should disagree with it.

YOUR TURN: **For more practice, do related problem 11 on page 195 at the end of this chapter. Visit www.prenhall.com/hubbard for an interactive exercise related to this Solved Problem.**

Price	Quantity Demanded	Total Revenue
$8	0	$0
7	2	14
6	4	24
5	6	30
4	8	32
3	10	30
2	12	24
1	14	14
0	16	0

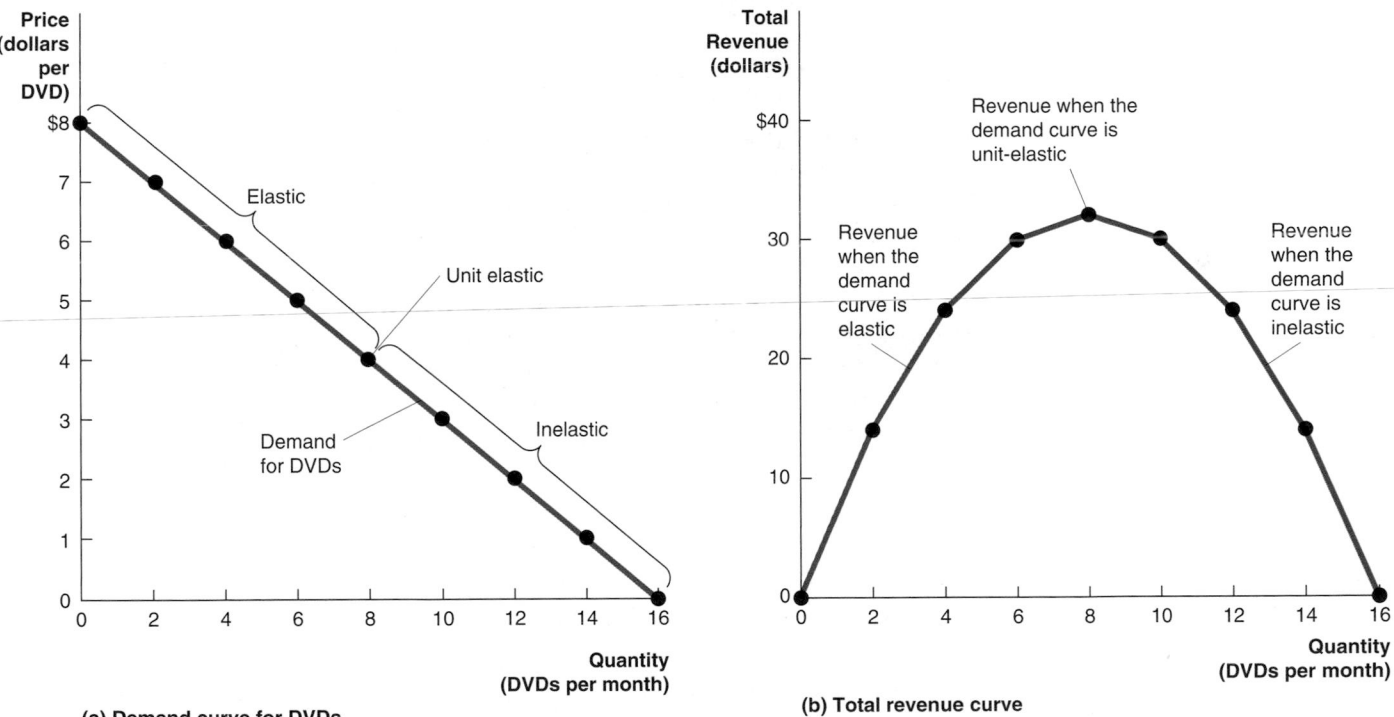

(a) Demand curve for DVDs

(b) Total revenue curve

FIGURE 6-3   **Elasticity Is Not Constant Along a Linear Demand Curve**

The data from the table are plotted in the graphs. Panel (a) shows that as we move down the demand curve for DVDs, the price elasticity of demand declines. In other words, at higher prices demand is elastic and at lower prices demand is inelastic. Panel (b) shows that as the quantity of DVDs sold increases from zero, revenue will increase until it reaches a maximum of $32 when 8 DVDs are sold. As sales increase beyond 8 DVDs, revenue falls because demand is inelastic on this portion of the demand curve.

Estimating Price Elasticity of Demand

To estimate the price elasticity of demand, economists need to know the demand curve for a product. In Chapter 3, we briefly discussed the fact that economists often use statistical methods to estimate the demand curve for a product. Economists generally use the same methods to estimate the price elasticity of demand. When trying to calculate the price elasticity of demand for new products, however, firms often rely on market experiments. With market experiments, firms will try different prices and observe the change in quantity demanded that results.

6-2 *Making* the *Connection*

Determining the Price Elasticity of Demand for DVDs by Market Experiment

DVDs were a relatively new product in 2001. The movie studios producing them were unsure of the price elasticity of the demand curves they were facing, so they experimented with different prices to help determine the price elasticity. Following are four films and the prices for DVDs and VHS tapes that the studios suggested stores such as Blockbuster Video charge for them:

FILM	DVD PRICE	VHS PRICE
Rugrats in Paris	$22.46	$22.99
The Mummy Returns	26.98	22.98
Miss Congeniality	16.69	22.98
The Perfect Storm	24.98	22.99

When DVDs were first introduced, the movie studios were uncertain of their price elasticity of demand.

VHS tapes had been on the market for many years, and the studios had determined their pricing strategies, given their estimates of the price elasticity of demand. As a result, the prices of VHS tapes were usually very similar—for these four films the prices were almost identical. The prices of DVDs were much less standardized because the studios were unsure of their price elasticities. Tom Adams, the head of Adams Market Research, a company that does research on the home video market, summed up the situation: "The studios have different views of the market, so they are setting different suggested retail prices, and the stores are discounting those prices to different degrees."

Sources: Geraldine Fabrikant, "Sale of DVDs Are Challenging Movie Rental Business," *The New York Times,* April 16, 2001; prices from Amazon.com Web site.

④ LEARNING OBJECTIVE

Define the cross-price elasticity of demand and the income elasticity of demand, and understand their determinants and how they are calculated.

Other Demand Elasticities

Elasticity is an important concept in economics because it allows us to quantify the responsiveness of one economic variable to changes in another economic variable. In addition to price elasticity, two other demand elasticities are important: *cross-price elasticity of demand* and *income elasticity of demand*.

Cross-Price Elasticity of Demand

Suppose you work at Hewlett-Packard and you need to predict the effect of an increase in the price of Canon printers on the quantity of Hewlett-Packard printers demanded holding other factors constant. You can do this by calculating the **cross-price elasticity of demand,** which is the percentage change in the quantity of Hewlett-Packard printers demanded divided by the percentage change in the price of Canon printers—or, in general:

$$\text{Cross-price elasticity of demand} = \frac{\text{Percentage change in quantity demanded of one good}}{\text{Percentage change in price of another good}}.$$

Cross-price elasticity of demand
The percentage change in quantity demanded of one good divided by the percentage change in the price of another good.

The cross-price elasticity of demand will be positive or negative depending on whether the two products are substitutes or complements. Recall that substitutes are products that can be used for the same purpose, such as two brands of printers. Complements are products that are used together, such as printers and printer toner cartridges. An increase in the price of a substitute will lead to an increase in quantity demanded, so the cross-price elasticity of demand will be positive. An increase in the price of a complement will lead to a decrease in the quantity demanded, so the cross-price elasticity of demand will be negative. Of course, if the two products are unrelated, the cross-price elasticity of demand will be zero. Table 6-3 summarizes the key points concerning the cross-price elasticity of demand.

Cross-price elasticity of demand is important to firm managers because it allows them to measure whether products sold by other firms are close substitutes for their products. For example, Amazon.com and Barnesandnoble.com are the leading online booksellers. We might predict that if Amazon raises the price of a new John Grisham novel, many consumers will buy it from Barnesandnoble.com instead. But Jeff Bezos, Amazon's chief executive officer, has argued that because of Amazon's reputation for good customer service and because more customers are familiar with the site, ordering a book from Barnesandnoble.com is not a good substitute for ordering a book from Amazon. In effect, Bezos is arguing that the cross-price elasticity between Amazon's books and Barnesandnoble.com's books is low. Economists Judith Chevalier of Yale University and Austan Goolsbee of the University of Chicago have used data on prices and quantities of books sold on these Web sites to estimate the cross-price elasticity. They found that the cross-price elasticity of demand between books at Amazon and books at Barnesandnoble.com was 3.5. This estimate means that if Amazon raises its prices by 10 percent, the quantity of books demanded on Barnesandnoble.com will increase by 35 percent. This result indicates that, contrary to Jeff Bezos's argument, consumers do consider books sold on the two Web sites to be close substitutes.

IF THE PRODUCTS ARE...	THEN THE CROSS-PRICE ELASTICITY OF DEMAND WILL BE...	EXAMPLE
Substitutes	Positive	Two brands of printers
Complements	Negative	Printers and toner cartridges
Unrelated	Zero	Printers and peanut butter

TABLE 6-3

Summary of Cross-Price Elasticity of Demand

Income elasticity of demand A measure of the responsiveness of quantity demanded to changes in income, measured by the percentage change in quantity demanded divided by the percentage change in income.

Income Elasticity of Demand

The **income elasticity of demand** measures the responsiveness of quantity demanded to changes in income. It is calculated as follows:

$$\text{Income elasticity of demand} = \frac{\text{Percentage change in quantity demanded}}{\text{Percentage change in income}}.$$

As we saw in Chapter 3, if the quantity demanded of a good increases as income increases, then the good is a *normal good*. Normal goods are often further subdivided into *luxury goods* and *necessity goods*. A good is a luxury if the quantity demanded is very responsive to changes in income, so that a 10 percent increase in income results in more than a 10 percent increase in quantity demanded. Expensive jewelry or vacation homes are examples of luxuries. A good is a necessity if the quantity demanded is not very responsive to changes in income, so that a 10 percent increase in income results in less than a 10 percent increase in quantity demanded. Food and clothing are examples of necessities. A good is *inferior* if the quantity demanded falls when income increases. Ground beef with a high fat content is an example of an inferior good.

Because most goods are normal goods, during periods of economic expansion when consumer income is rising most firms can expect—holding other factors constant—that the quantity demanded of their products will increase. Sellers of luxuries can expect particularly large increases. During the late 1990s, rapid increases in income resulted in large increases in demand for luxuries, such as meals in expensive restaurants, luxury apartments, and high-performance automobiles. During recessions, falling consumer income can cause firms to experience increases in demand for inferior goods. Supermarkets will find the demand for hamburger increasing relative to the demand for steak. The demand for bus trips will also increase as consumers cut back on air travel. Table 6-4 summarizes the key points about income elasticity.

6-3 Making the Connection

An "inferior good"?

Price Elasticity, Cross-Price Elasticity, and Income Elasticity in the Market for Alcoholic Beverages

Many public policy issues are related to the consumption of alcoholic beverages. These issues include underage drinking, drunk driving, and the possible beneficial effects of red wine in lowering the risk of heart disease. X. M. Gao, an economist who works at American Express, and two colleagues have estimated statistically the following elasticities (*spirits* refer to all beverages that contain alcohol, other than beer and wine).

Price elasticity of demand for beer	−0.23
Cross-price elasticity of demand between beer and wine	0.31
Cross-price elasticity of demand between beer and spirits	0.15
Income elasticity of demand for beer	−0.09
Income elasticity of demand for wine	5.03
Income elasticity of demand for spirits	1.21

The demand for beer is inelastic. A 10 percent increase in the price of beer will result in a 2.3 percent decline in the quantity of beer demanded. Not surprisingly, both wine and spirits are substitutes for beer. A 10 percent increase in the price of wine will result in a 3.1 percent *increase* in the quantity of beer demanded. A 10 percent increase in income will result in a little less than a 1 percent *decline* in the quantity of beer demanded. So, beer is an inferior good. Both wine and spirits are categorized as luxuries because their income elasticities are greater than 1.

Source: X. M. Gao, Eric J. Wailes, and Gail L. Cramer, "A Microeconometric Model Analysis of U.S. Consumer Demand for Alcoholic Beverages," *Applied Economics*, January 1995.

IF THE INCOME ELASTICITY OF DEMAND IS . . .	THEN THE GOOD IS . . .	EXAMPLE
Positive, but less than 1	Normal and a necessity	Milk
Positive and greater than 1	Normal and a luxury	Caviar
Negative	Inferior	High-fat meat

TABLE 6-4

Summary of Income Elasticity of Demand

Using Elasticity to Analyze the Disappearing Family Farm

⑤ **LEARNING OBJECTIVE**

Use price elasticity and income elasticity to analyze economic issues.

The concepts of price elasticity and income elasticity can help us understand many economic issues. For example, some people are concerned that the family farm is becoming an endangered species in the United States. Although food production continues to grow rapidly, the number of farms and the number of farmers continues to dwindle. In 1950, more than 5 million farms could be found in the United States and more than 23 million people lived on farms. By 2004, fewer than 2 million farms remained and fewer than 3 million people lived on them. In Chapter 4, we discussed several federal government programs designed to slow the movement of people out of farming. Many of these programs have been aimed at helping small, family-operated farms, but rapid growth in farm production has combined with low price and income elasticities for most food products to make family farming difficult in the United States.

Productivity measures the ability of firms to produce goods and services with a given amount of economic inputs, such as workers, machines, and land. Productivity has grown very rapidly in U.S. agriculture. In 1950, the average U.S. wheat farmer harvested about 17 bushels from each acre of wheat planted. By 2004, because of the development of superior strains of wheat and improvements in farming techniques, the average American wheat farmer harvested 43 bushels per acre. So, even though the total number of acres devoted to growing wheat declined from about 62 million to about 50 million, total wheat production rose from about 1 billion bushels to about 2.2 billion.

Unfortunately for U.S. farmers, this increase in wheat production resulted in a substantial decline in wheat prices. Two key factors explain this decline in wheat prices: (1) The demand for wheat is inelastic and (2) the income elasticity of demand for wheat is low. Even though the U.S. population has increased greatly since 1950 and the income of the average American is much higher than it was in 1950, the demand for wheat has increased only moderately. For all of the additional wheat to be sold, the price has had to decline. Because the demand for wheat is inelastic, the price decline has been substantial. Figure 6-4 illustrates these points.

A large shift in supply, a small shift in demand, and an inelastic demand curve combined to drive down the price of wheat from $13.13 per bushel in 1950 to $3.40 per bushel in 2004 (the 1950 price is measured in terms of prices in 2004, to adjust for the general increase in prices since 1950). With low prices, only the most efficiently run farms have been able to remain profitable. Smaller, family-run farms have found it difficult to survive, and many of these farms have disappeared. The markets for most food products are similar to the market for wheat. They also are characterized by rapid output growth, and low income and price elasticities. The result is the paradox of American farming: ever more abundant and cheaper food, supplied by fewer and fewer farms. American consumers have benefited, but most family farmers have not.

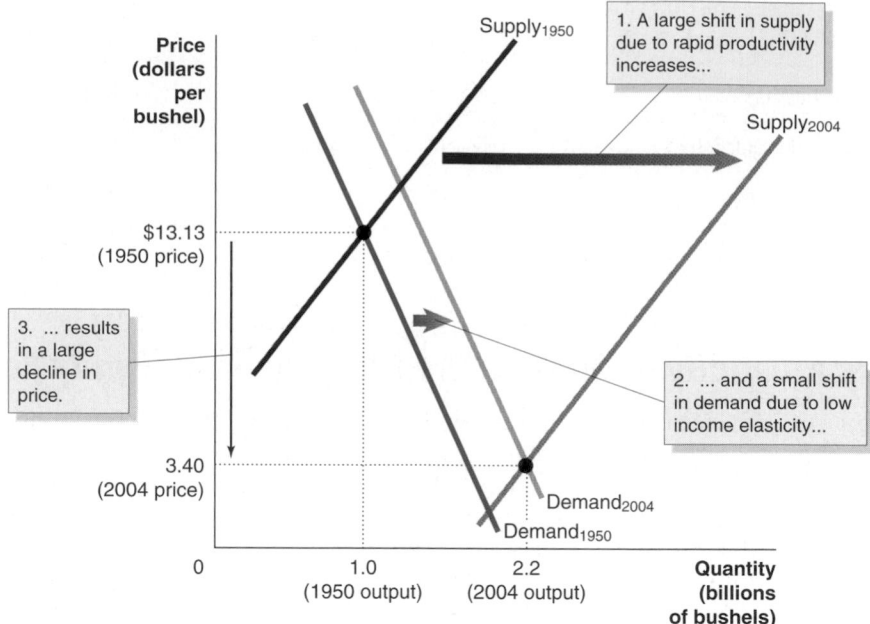

FIGURE 6-4

Elasticity and the Disappearing Farm

In 1950, U.S. farmers produced 1.0 billion bushels of wheat at a price of $13.13 per bushel. Over the next 50 years, rapid increases in farm productivity caused a large shift to the right in the supply curve for wheat. The income elasticity of demand for wheat is low, so the demand for wheat increased relatively little over this period. Because the demand for wheat is also inelastic, the large shift in the supply curve and the small shift in the demand curve resulted in a sharp decline in the price of wheat from $13.13 per bushel in 1950 to $3.40 per bushel in 2004.

SOLVED PROBLEM   6-3

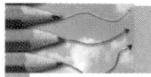 **⑤ LEARNING OBJECTIVE**

Use price elasticity and income elasticity to analyze economic issues.

Using Price Elasticity to Analyze the Drug Problem

An ongoing policy debate concerns whether to legalize the use of drugs such as marijuana and cocaine. Some researchers estimate that legalizing cocaine would cause its price to fall by as much as 95 percent. Proponents of legalization argue that legalizing drug use would lower crime rates by eliminating the main reason for the murderous gang wars that plague many big cities and by reducing the incentive for drug addicts to commit robberies and burglaries. Opponents of legalization argue that lower drug prices would lead more people to use drugs.

a. Suppose the price elasticity of demand for cocaine is −2. If legalization causes the price of cocaine to fall by 95 percent, what will be the percentage increase in the quantity of cocaine demanded?

b. If the price elasticity is −0.02, what will be the percentage increase in the quantity demanded?

c. Discuss how the size of the price elasticity of demand for cocaine is relevant to the debate over its legalization.

Solving the Problem:

Step 1: Review the chapter material. This problem deals with applications of the price elasticity of demand formula, so you may want to review the section "Measuring the Price Elasticity of Demand," which begins on page 166.

Step 2: Answer question (a) using the formula for the price elasticity of demand.

$$\text{Price elasticity of demand} = \frac{\text{Percentage change in quantity demanded}}{\text{Percentage change in price}}.$$

We can plug into this formula the values we are given for the price elasticity and the percentage change in price:

$$-2 = \frac{\text{Percentage change in quantity demanded}}{-95\%}.$$

Or, rearranging:

Percentage change in quantity demanded $= -2 \times -95\% = 190\%$

Step 3: Use the same method to answer question (b). We only need to substitute -0.02 for -2 as the price elasticity of demand:

Percentage change in quantity demanded $= -0.02 \times -95\% = 1.9\%$

Step 4: Answer question (c) by discussing how the size of the price elasticity of demand for cocaine helps us to understand the effects of legalization. Clearly, the higher the absolute value of the price elasticity of demand for cocaine, the greater the increase in cocaine use that would result from legalization. If the price elasticity is as high as in question (a), legalization will lead to a large increase in use. If, however, the price elasticity is as low as in question (b), legalization will lead to only a small increase in use.

Extra Credit: One estimate puts this price elasticity at -0.28, which suggests that even a large fall in the price of cocaine might lead to only a moderate increase in cocaine use. However, even a moderate increase in cocaine use would have its costs. Some studies have shown that cocaine users are more likely to commit crimes, to abuse their children, to have higher medical expenses, and to be less productive workers. Moreover, many people object to the use of cocaine and other narcotics on moral grounds and would oppose legalization even if it led to no increase in use. Ultimately, whether the use of cocaine and other drugs should be legalized is a normative issue. Economics can contribute to the discussion but cannot decide the issue.

Source for estimate of price elasticity of cocaine: Henry Saffer and Frank Chaloupka, "The Demand for Illicit Drugs," *Economic Inquiry*, Vol. 37, No. 3, July 1999, pp. 401–411.

YOUR TURN: For more practice, do related problems 3 and 4 on pages 193–194 at the end of this chapter. Visit www.prenhall.com/hubbard for an interactive exercise related to this Solved Problem.

The Price Elasticity of Supply

6 LEARNING OBJECTIVE
Define the price elasticity of supply, and understand its main determinants and how it is calculated.

We can use the concept of elasticity to measure the responsiveness of firms to a change in price just as we used it to measure the responsiveness of consumers. We know from the law of supply that when the price of a product increases, the quantity supplied increases. To measure how much quantity supplied increases when price increases, we use the *price elasticity of supply*.

Measuring the Price Elasticity of Supply

Just as with the price elasticity of demand, we calculate the **price elasticity of supply** using percentage changes:

$$\text{Price elasticity of supply} = \frac{\text{Percentage change in quantity supplied}}{\text{Percentage change in price}}.$$

Notice that because supply curves are upward sloping, the price elasticity of supply will be a positive number. We categorize the price elasticity of supply the same way we categorized the price elasticity of demand. If the price elasticity of supply is less than one, then supply is *inelastic*. For example, the price elasticity of supply of gasoline from U.S. oil refineries is about 0.20, and so it is inelastic. A 10 percent increase in the price of gasoline will result in only a 2 percent increase in the quantity supplied. If the price elasticity of supply is greater than 1, then supply is *elastic*. If the price elasticity of supply is equal to 1, then supply is *unit-elastic*. As with other elasticity calculations, when we calculate the price elasticity of supply, we hold the values of other factors constant.

Price elasticity of supply The responsiveness of the quantity supplied to a change in price, measured by dividing the percentage change in the quantity supplied of a product by the percentage change in the product's price.

Determinants of the Price Elasticity of Supply

Whether supply is elastic or inelastic depends on the ability and willingness of firms to alter the quantity they produce as price increases. Often firms have difficulty increasing the quantity of the product they supply during any short period of time. For example, a pizza parlor cannot produce more pizzas on any one night than is possible using the ingredients on hand. Within a day or two it can buy more ingredients, and within a few months it can hire more cooks and install additional ovens. As a result, the supply curve for pizza and most other products will be inelastic if we measure it over a short period of time, but increasingly elastic the longer the period of time over which we measure it. Products that require resources that are themselves in fixed supply are an exception to this rule. For example, a French winery may rely on a particular variety of grape. If all the land on which that grape can be grown is already planted in vineyards, then the supply of that wine will be inelastic even over a long period.

6-4 *Making* the *Connection*

Why Are Oil Prices So Unstable?

Bringing oil to market is a long process. Oil companies hire geologists to search for oil. Once a likely field has been found, the company will drill an exploratory well. If the exploratory well indicates that significant amounts of oil are present, then full-scale development of the field can begin. The whole process from exploration to pumping significant amounts of oil can take years. Because it takes so long to bring additional quantities of oil to market, the price elasticity of supply for oil is very low. Substitutes are limited for oil-based products—such as gasoline—so the price elasticity of demand for oil is also low.

As the following graph shows, the combination of inelastic supply and inelastic demand results in shifts in supply causing large changes in price. In the graph, a reduction in supply that shifts the market supply curve from S_1 to S_2 causes the equilibrium quantity of oil to fall only from 80 million barrels per day to 76 million, but the equilibrium price rises by 25 percent, from $40 per barrel to $50 per barrel.

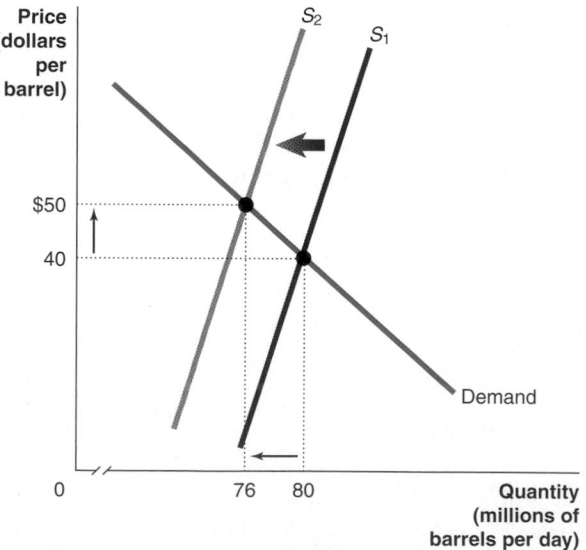

The world oil market is heavily influenced by the Organization of Petroleum Exporting Countries (OPEC). OPEC has 11 members, including Saudi Arabia, Kuwait, and other Arab countries, as well as Iran, Venezuela, Nigeria, and Indonesia. Together these countries own

75 percent of the world's proven oil reserves. Periodically, OPEC has attempted to force up the price of oil by reducing the quantity of oil its members supply. As we will discuss further in Chapter 13, since the 1970s, the attempts by OPEC to reduce the quantity of oil on world markets have been successful only sporadically: Periods during which OPEC members cooperate and reduce supply alternate with periods in which the members fail to cooperate and supply increases. As a result, the supply curve for oil shifts fairly frequently. Combined with the low price elasticities of oil supply and demand, these shifts in supply have caused the price of oil to fluctuate significantly over the past 30 years, from as low as $11 dollars per barrel to as high as $55 per barrel.

Over longer periods of time, higher oil prices also lead to greater increases in the quantity supplied—in other words, the price elasticity of supply for oil increases. This increase happens because higher prices increase the economic incentive to explore for oil and to recover oil from more costly sources, such as under the oceans or at greater depths in the earth. When supply is more elastic, a given shift in supply results in a smaller increase in price. This effect is illustrated in the following graph. Compared with the preceding graph, a decrease in supply increases the equilibrium price to $45 per barrel, rather than $50 per barrel.

Why do oil prices fluctuate so much?

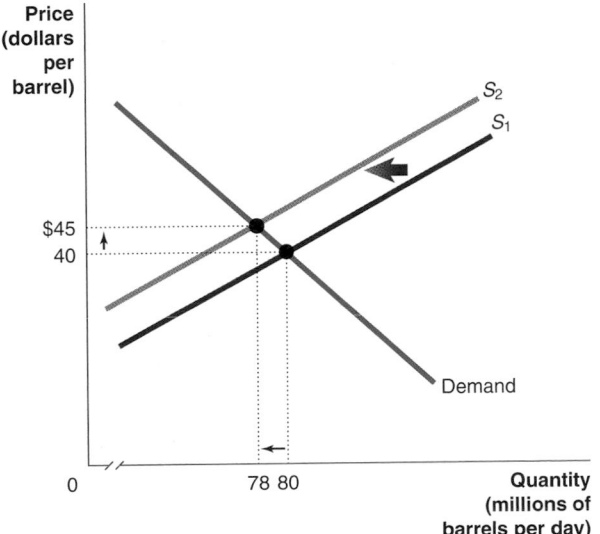

Polar Cases of Perfectly Elastic and Perfectly Inelastic Supply

Although it occurs infrequently, it is possible for supply to fall into one of the polar cases of price elasticity. If a supply curve is a vertical line, it is *perfectly inelastic*. In this case, the quantity supplied is completely unresponsive to price, and the price elasticity of supply equals zero. However much price may increase or decrease, the quantity remains the same. Over a brief period of time, the supply of some goods and services may be perfectly inelastic. For example, a parking lot may have only a fixed number of parking spaces. If demand increases, the price to park in the lot may rise, but no more spaces will become available. Of course, if demand increases permanently, over a longer period of time the owner of the lot may decide to buy more land to add additional spaces.

If a supply curve is a horizontal line, it is *perfectly elastic*. In this case, the quantity supplied is infinitely responsive to price, and the price elasticity of supply equals infinity. If a supply curve is perfectly elastic, a very small increase in price causes a very large increase in quantity supplied. Just as with demand curves, it is important not to confuse

TABLE 6-5

Summary of the Price Elasticities of Supply

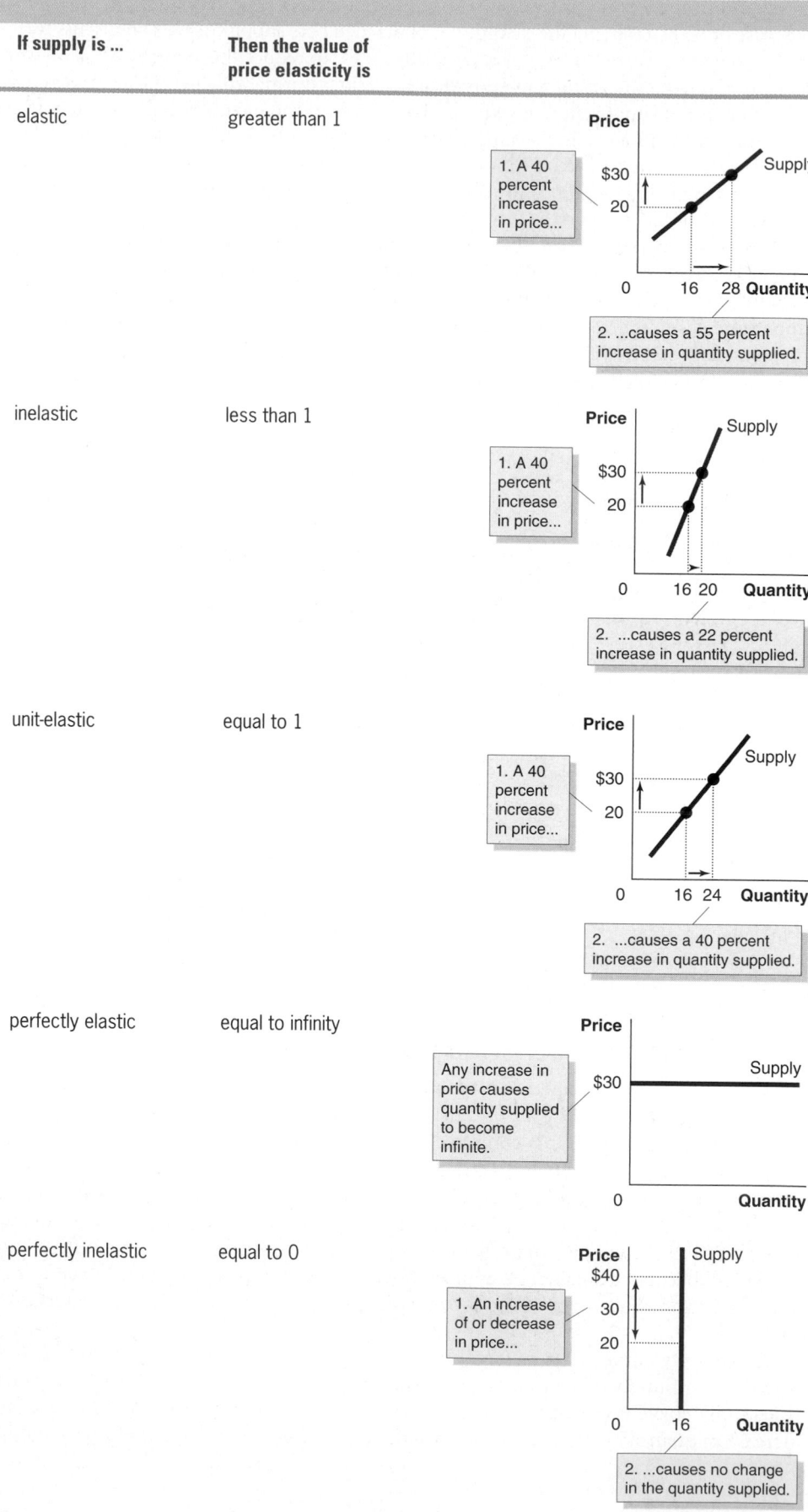

If supply is ...	Then the value of price elasticity is
elastic	greater than 1
inelastic	less than 1
unit-elastic	equal to 1
perfectly elastic	equal to infinity
perfectly inelastic	equal to 0

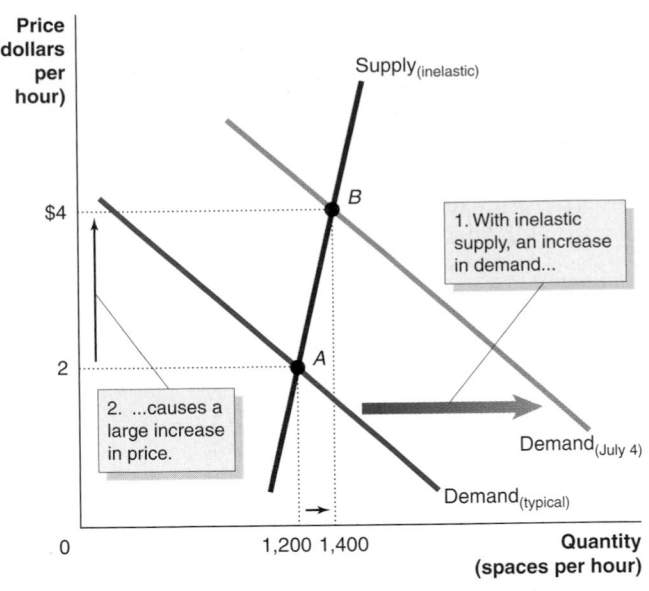

(a) Price increases more when supply is inelastic.

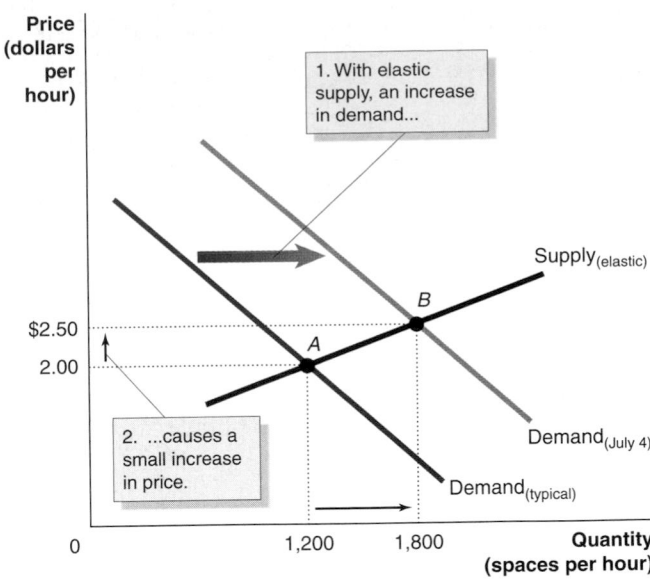

(b) Price increases less when supply is elastic.

FIGURE 6-5   **Changes in Price Depend on the Price Elasticity of Supply**

In panel (a), Demand (typical) represents the typical demand for parking spaces on a summer weekend at a beach resort. Demand (July 4) represents demand on the Fourth of July. Because supply is inelastic, the shift in equilibrium from point A to point B results in a large increase in price—from $2.00 per hour to $4.00—but only a small increase in the quantity of spaces supplied—from 1,200 to 1,400. In panel (b), supply is elastic. As a result, the shift in equilibrium from point A to point B results in a smaller increase in price and a larger increase in the quantity supplied. An increase in price from $2.00 per hour to $2.50 is sufficient to increase the quantity of parking supplied from 1,200 to 2,100.

Using Price Elasticity of Supply to Predict Changes in Price

Figure 6-5 illustrates the important point that, when demand increases, the amount that price increases depends on the price elasticity of supply. The figure shows the demand and supply for parking spaces at a beach resort. In panel (a), on a typical summer weekend, equilibrium occurs at point A, where Demand (typical) intersects a supply curve that is inelastic. The increase in demand for parking spaces on the Fourth of July shifts the demand curve to the right, moving the equilibrium to point B. Because the supply curve is inelastic, the increase in demand results in a large increase in price—from $2.00 per hour to $4.00—but only a small increase in the quantity of spaces supplied—from 1,200 to 1,400.

In panel (b), supply is elastic, perhaps because the resort has vacant land that can be used for parking during periods of high demand. As a result, the shift in equilibrium from point A to point B results in a smaller increase in price and a larger increase in the quantity supplied. An increase in price from $2.00 per hour to $2.50 is sufficient to increase the quantity of parking supplied from 1,200 to 2,100. Knowing the price elasticity of supply makes it possible to predict more accurately how much price will change following an increase or decrease in demand.

Conclusion

In this chapter, we have explored the important concept of elasticity. Table 6-6 summarizes the various elasticities we discussed in this chapter. Computing elasticities is of importance in economics because it allows us to measure how one variable changes in response to changes in another variable. For example, by calculating the price elasticity of demand for its product, a firm can make a numerical estimate of the effect of a price change on the revenue it receives. Similarly, by calculating the price elasticity of demand for cigarettes, the government can better estimate the effect of an increase in cigarette taxes on smoking.

Before going further in analyzing how firms decide on the prices to charge and the quantities to produce, we need to look at how firms are organized. We do this in the next chapter. Read *An Inside Look* on the next page to use the concept of elasticity to analyze revenue at Amazon.com.

PRICE ELASTICITY OF DEMAND

$$\text{Formula}: \frac{\text{Percentage change in quantity demanded}}{\text{Percentage change in price}}$$

$$\text{Midpoint Formula}: \frac{(Q_2 - Q_1)}{\left(\dfrac{Q_1 + Q_2}{2}\right)} \div \frac{(P_2 - P_1)}{\left(\dfrac{P_1 + P_2}{2}\right)}$$

	ABSOLUTE VALUE OF PRICE ELASTICITY	EFFECT ON TOTAL REVENUE OF AN INCREASE IN PRICE
Elastic	Greater than 1	Total revenue falls
Inelastic	Less than 1	Total revenue rises
Unit-elastic	Equal to 1	Total revenue unchanged

CROSS-PRICE ELASTICITY OF DEMAND

$$\text{Formula}: \frac{\text{Percentage change in quantity demanded of one good}}{\text{Percentage change in price of another good}}$$

TYPES OF PRODUCTS	VALUE OF CROSS-PRICE ELASTICITY
Substitutes	Positive
Complements	Negative
Unrelated	Zero

INCOME ELASTICITY OF DEMAND

$$\text{Formula}: \frac{\text{Percentage change in quantity demanded}}{\text{Percentage change in income}}$$

TYPES OF PRODUCTS	VALUE OF INCOME ELASTICITY
Normal and a necessity	Positive, but less than 1
Normal and a luxury	Positive and greater than 1
Inferior	Negative

PRICE ELASTICITY OF SUPPLY

$$\text{Formula}: \frac{\text{Percentage change in quantity supplied}}{\text{Percentage change in price}}$$

	VALUE OF PRICE ELASTICITY
Elastic	Greater than 1
Inelastic	Less than 1
Unit-elastic	Equal to 1

TABLE 6-6

Summary of Elasticities

USA TODAY, APRIL 23, 2004

Amazon, Microsoft Earnings Better than Expected

Seattle-area tech giants Microsoft and Amazon both reported better-than-expected earnings Thursday—another sign of a slow-but-steady economic recovery. A pickup in corporate technology spending propelled revenue at the world's largest software maker to $9.2 billion, a 17% jump from $7.8 billion a year ago. "Business PC demand in the (fiscal) third quarter was more than we expected," CFO [Chief Financial Officer] John Connors said. "We are in the midst of a corporate recovery." . . .

(a) Amazon.com posted its biggest non-holiday profit Thursday because of aggressive pricing, free-shipping offers and more products. The largest online retailer, which has evolved from an online bookseller to the equivalent of a virtual shopping mall, reported first-quarter earnings of $111 million, or 26 cents a share, compared with a loss of $10 million, or 3 cents a share, last year. The average earnings estimate of analysts surveyed by Thomson First Call was 19 cents a share.

Revenue soared 41% to $1.5 billion, compared with $1.1 billion a year ago, when Amazon was struggling to make its first profit outside a holiday season. Products delivered outside the USA accounted for half of Amazon's net sales, the company said.

Amazon CFO Tom Szkutak credited the strong sales to lowered prices, expanded selection and the company's continued offer of free shipping on orders of more than $25 in the USA. The Seattle-based company also offers free shipping on some orders in Japan, Germany, France, the United Kingdom and Canada.

"The lower-pricing strategy drives volume and sales, but the question is whether they are giving away so much it affects the bottom line," says analyst Dan Geiman of McAdams Wright Ragen.

(b) Amazon also launched an online jewelry store Thursday. Shares of Amazon dipped 2.8% to $47.50 in after-hours trading on the news, released after market close. Microsoft shares rose 4.8% to $27.20 during that time.

Key Points in the Article

The article discusses the financial performance of Amazon.com during the first quarter of 2004. Revenue and profit both increased for the firm compared with the same period during 2003. (Remember that revenue equals price multiplied by the number of units sold. Profit equals revenue minus costs.) Tom Szkutak—Amazon's chief financial officer (CFO)—identified three reasons why the firm's revenue and profit increased:

1. Lower prices
2. More types of products offered for sale
3. Free shipping on some orders

But Dan Geiman, an industry analyst, raises the possibility that lowering prices might have hurt Amazon's profits.

Analyzing the News

a In this chapter, we have seen that whether lowering price increases or decreases a firm's *revenue* depends on the price elasticity of demand. The Amazon executive quoted believes that demand for the firm's product is elastic. So, Amazon is in the situation we illustrated in Figure 6-1 (which we reproduce here slightly altered as Figure 1): If demand is elastic in the relevant range, Amazon's demand curve is D_1, lowering the price per book from \$30.00 to \$20.00 increases sales from 16,000 copies per day to 28,000, and that increases revenue.

b Dan Geiman, the analyst quoted in the article, refers to Amazon's profit, rather than its revenue. But because Amazon's cost per book—or other item—sold doesn't change much with changes in the quantity of books sold, increases (or decreases) in revenue from cutting the price should result in increases (or decreases) in profits. If the analyst is correct, Amazon faces an inelastic demand curve like D_2, and cutting the price per book from \$30.00 to \$20.00 increases sales only from 16,000 copies per day to 20,000, and it decreases revenue.

Can we tell whether the Amazon executive or the industry analyst is correct? Because Amazon sells many products, it is difficult to determine what the price elasticity of demand is for every product it sells. Economists Judith Chevalier and Austan Goolsbee have estimated Amazon's price elasticity of demand for books is −0.45. If this estimate is correct, cutting the price will actually reduce the revenue Amazon receives from selling books, and the analyst is correct to question the firm's policy.

Source: Austan Goolsbee and Judith Chevalier, "Price Competition Online: Amazon Versus Barnes and Noble," *Quantitative Marketing and Economics*, 1(2), June 2003, 203–222.

Thinking Critically

1. If the price elasticity of demand for one of Amazon.com's books is inelastic (−0.45), then as its price rises, the firm's total revenue from sales of the book will rise. However, price elasticity of demand generally changes with a movement along a demand curve. What implication does this have for Amazon's pricing strategy and for the total revenue Amazon receives from sales of the book as the book's price gets higher and higher?

2. Over time, more and more of Amazon's competitors have gone online. What implication does this have for the price elasticity of demand for Amazon's products? Explain.

Source: Michelle Kessler and Jon Swartz, "Amazon, Microsoft Earnings Better than Expected," *USA Today*, April 23, 2004. Reprinted with permission.

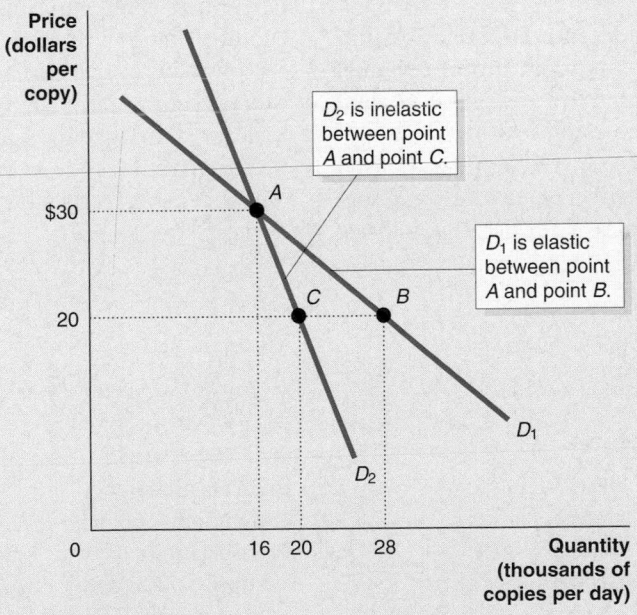

Figure 1: Potential demand curves facing Amazon.com.

SUMMARY

LEARNING OBJECTIVE ① Define the price elasticity of demand and understand how to calculate it. The *price elasticity of demand* measures how responsive quantity demanded is to changes in price. The price elasticity of demand is equal to the percentage change in quantity demanded divided by the percentage change in price. If the quantity demanded changes more than proportionally when price changes, the price elasticity of demand is greater than 1 in absolute value and demand is *elastic*. If the quantity demanded changes less than proportionally when price changes, the price elasticity of demand is less than 1 in absolute value and demand is *inelastic*. If the quantity demanded changes proportionally when price changes, the price elasticity of demand is equal to 1 in absolute value and demand is *unit-elastic*. Perfectly inelastic demand curves are vertical lines and perfectly elastic demand curves are horizontal lines. Relatively few products have perfectly elastic or perfectly inelastic demand curves.

LEARNING OBJECTIVE ② Understand the determinants of the price elasticity of demand. The main determinants of the price elasticity of demand for a product are the availability of close substitutes, the passage of time, whether the good is a necessity or a luxury, how narrowly the market for the good is defined, and the share of the good in the consumer's budget.

LEARNING OBJECTIVE ③ Understand the relationship between the price elasticity of demand and total revenue. When demand is inelastic, a decrease in price reduces total revenue and an increase in price increases total revenue. When demand is elastic, a decrease in price increases total revenue and an increase in price decreases total revenue. When demand is unit-elastic, an increase or decrease in price leaves total revenue unchanged.

LEARNING OBJECTIVE ④ Define the cross-price elasticity of demand and the income elasticity of demand, and understand their determinants and how they are calculated. Other important demand elasticities are the *cross-price elasticity of demand*, which is equal to the percentage change in quantity demanded divided by the percentage change in the price of another good and the *income elasticity of demand*, which is equal to the percentage change in the quantity demanded divided by the percentage change in income.

LEARNING OBJECTIVE ⑤ Use price elasticity and income elasticity to analyze economic issues. Price elasticity and income elasticity can be used to analyze many economic issues. One example is the disappearance of the family farm in the United States. Because the income elasticity of demand for food is low, the demand for food has not increased proportionally as incomes in the United States have grown. As farmers have become more productive, they have increased the supply of most foods. Because the price elasticity of demand for food is low, increasing supply has resulted in continually falling food prices.

LEARNING OBJECTIVE ⑥ Define the price elasticity of supply, and understand its main determinants and how it is calculated. The price elasticity of supply is equal to the percentage change in quantity supplied divided by the percentage change in price. The supply curves for most goods are inelastic over a short period of time, but they become increasingly elastic over longer periods of time. Perfectly inelastic demand curves are vertical lines, and perfectly elastic supply curves are horizontal lines. Relatively few products have perfectly elastic or perfectly inelastic supply curves.

KEY TERMS

Cross-price elasticity of demand 179
Elastic demand 167
Elasticity 166
Income elasticity of demand 180

Inelastic demand 167
Perfectly elastic demand 170
Perfectly inelastic demand 170

Price elasticity of demand 166
Price elasticity of supply 183

Total revenue 174
Unit-elastic demand 167

REVIEW QUESTIONS

1. Write the formula for the price elasticity of demand. Why isn't elasticity just measured by the slope of the demand curve?

2. If a 10 percent increase in the price of Cap'n Crunch cereal causes a 25 percent reduction in the number of boxes of cereal demanded, what is the price elasticity of demand for Cap'n Crunch cereal? Is demand for Cap'n Crunch elastic or inelastic?

3. What is the midpoint method for calculating price elasticity of demand? How else can the price elasticity of demand be calculated? What advantage does the midpoint method have?

4. If the demand for orange juice is inelastic, will an increase in the price of orange juice increase or decrease the revenue received by orange juice sellers?

5. Is the demand for most agricultural products elastic or inelastic? Why?

6. What are the key determinants of the price elasticity of demand for a product? Which determinant is the most important?

7. Draw a graph of a perfectly inelastic demand curve. Think of a product that would have a perfectly inelastic demand curve. Explain why demand for this product would be perfectly inelastic.

8. Define the cross-price elasticity of demand. What does it mean if the cross-price elasticity of demand is negative? What does it mean if the cross-price elasticity of demand is positive?

9. Define the income elasticity of demand. Use income elasticity to distinguish a normal good from an inferior good. Is it possible to tell from the income elasticity of demand whether a product is a luxury good or a necessity good?

10. Write the formula for the price elasticity of supply. If an increase of 10 percent in the price of frozen pizzas results in a 9 percent increase in the quantity of frozen pizzas supplied, what is the price elasticity of supply for frozen pizzas? Is the supply of pizzas elastic or inelastic?

PROBLEMS AND APPLICATIONS

Please visit **www.prenhall.com/hubbard** *for solutions to the even-numbered problems as well as multiple-choice and true or false self-assessment quizzes.*

1. **[Related to *Solved Problem 6-1*]** Suppose the following table gives data on the price of rye and the number of bushels of rye sold in 2007 and 2008.

YEAR	PRICE (DOLLARS PER BUSHEL)	QUANTITY (BUSHELS)
2007	$3.00	8 million
2008	2.00	12 million

   a. Calculate the change in the quantity of rye demanded divided by the change in the price of rye. Measure the quantity of rye in bushels.

   b. Calculate the change in the quantity of rye demanded divided by the change in the price of rye, but this time measure the quantity of rye in millions of bushels. Compare your answer to the one you computed in a.

   c. Finally, assuming that the demand curve for rye did not shift between 2007 and 2008, use the information in the table to calculate the price elasticity of demand for

rye. Use the midpoint formula in your calculation. Compare the value for the price elasticity of demand to the values you calculated in a and b.

2. A newspaper story on the effect of higher milk prices on the market for ice cream contained the following:

   > As a result [of the increase in milk prices], retail prices for ice cream are up 4 percent from last year. . . . And ice cream consumption is down 3 percent.

   Given this information, compute the price elasticity of demand for ice cream. Will the revenue received by ice cream suppliers have increased or decreased following the price increase? Briefly explain.

   Source: John Curran, "Ice Cream, They Scream: Milk Fat Costs Drive Up Ice Cream Prices," Associated Press, July 23, 2001.

3. **[Related to *Solved Problem 6-3*]** According to a study by the federal Centers for Disease Control and Prevention, the price elasticity of demand for cigarettes is −0.25. Americans purchase about 480 billion cigarettes each year.

   a. If the federal tax on cigarettes were increased enough to raise the price of cigarettes by 50 percent, what would be the effect on the quantity of cigarettes demanded?

b. Is raising the tax on cigarettes a more effective way to reduce smoking if the demand for cigarettes is elastic or if it is inelastic? Briefly explain.
Source: "Response to Increases in Cigarette Prices by Race/Ethnicity, Income, and Age Groups—United States, 1976–1993," *Morbidity and Mortality Weekly Report,* July 31, 1998.

4. [Related to *Solved Problem 6-3*] The price elasticity of demand for cocaine has been estimated as equal to −0.28. Suppose that a successful war on illegal drugs reduces the supply of cocaine in the United States enough to result in a 20 percent increase in its price. What will be the percentage reduction in the quantity of cocaine demanded?
Source: Henry Saffer and Frank Chaloupka, "The Demand for Illicit Drugs," *Economic Inquiry,* Vol. 37, No. 3, July 1999, pp. 401–411.

5. A study of the price elasticities of products sold in supermarkets contained the following data:

PRODUCT	PRICE ELASTICITY OF DEMAND
Soft Drinks	−3.18
Canned Soup	−1.62
Cheese	−0.72
Toothpaste	−0.45

a. The demand for which products is inelastic? Discuss reasons why the demand for each product is either elastic or inelastic.

b. Use the information in the table to predict the change in the quantity demanded for each product following a 10 percent price increase.
Source: Stephen J. Hoch, Byung-do Kim, Alan L. Montgomery, and Peter E. Rossi, "Determinants of Store-Level Price Elasticity," *Journal of Marketing Research,* Vol. 32, February 1995, pp. 17–29.

6. On most days the price of a rose is $1 and 8,000 roses are purchased. On Valentine's Day, the price of a rose jumps to $2 and 30,000 roses are purchased.

a. Draw a supply and demand diagram showing why the price jumps.

b. Based on this information, what do we know about the price elasticity of demand for roses? What do we know about the price elasticity of supply for roses? Calculate values for the price elasticity of demand and the price elasticity of supply, or explain why you can't calculate values.

7. According to an article in the *Wall Street Journal:*

Unlike airlines, even elite hotels don't have sophisticated systems that can react quickly to changes in demand. Even if they could, many hoteliers say people don't respond that much to lower rates. "We've tested this, cutting our rates by $50 [per night], and we didn't see an appreciable response in occupancy," says Jim Schultenover, a vice president for Ritz-Carlton.

On the basis of this information, would you conclude that the demand for hotel rooms is elastic or inelastic? Briefly explain.
Source: Jesse Drucker, "In Times of Belt-Tightening, We Seek Reasonable Rates," *Wall Street Journal,* April 6, 2001.

8. Use the following graph for Yolanda's Frozen Yogurt Stand to answer the questions that follow:

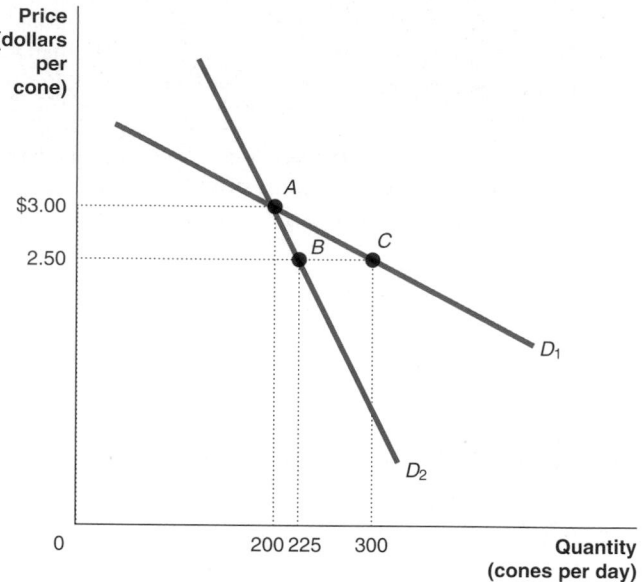

a. Use the midpoint formula to calculate the price elasticity of demand for D_1 between point A and point C, and the price elasticity of demand for D_2 between point A and point B. Which demand curve is more elastic, D_1 or D_2? Briefly explain.

b. Suppose Yolanda is initially selling 200 cones per day at a price of $3.00 per cone. If she cuts her price to $2.50 per cone and her demand curve is D_1, what will be the change in her revenue? What will be the change in her revenue if her demand curve is D_2?

9. An article in the *Wall Street Journal* noted the following:

Instead of relying on a full-coach, round-trip unrestricted fare of about $2,000 between Cleveland and Los Angeles . . . Continental [Airlines] since June has offered a $716 unrestricted fare in that market. . . . Through October, the test resulted in about the same revenue that Continental thinks it would have collected with its higher fare.

What is the value of the price elasticity of demand on this airline route? Is Continental likely to be better off charging the low fare or the high fare? Briefly explain.
Source: Scott McCartney, "Airlines Try Cutting Business Fares, Find They Don't Lose Revenue," *Wall Street Journal,* November 22, 2002.

10. In 1916, the Ford Motor Company sold 500,000 Model T Fords at a price of $440. Henry Ford believed that he could increase sales of the Model T by 1,000 cars for every dollar he cut the price. Use this information to calculate the price elasticity of demand for Model T Fords. Use the midpoint formula in your calculation.

11. [Related to *Solved Problem 6-2*] Briefly explain whether you agree or disagree with Manager 2's reasoning:
    Manager 1: "The only way we can increase the revenue we receive from selling our frozen pizzas is by cutting the price."
    Manager 2: "Cutting the price of a product never increases the amount of revenue you receive. If we want to increase revenue, we have to increase price."

12. [Related to the *Chapter Opener*] Consider the following description of a pricing decision by academic book publishers:

    A publisher may have issued a monograph several years ago, when both costs and book prices were lower, and priced it at $14.95. The book is still selling reasonably well and would continue to do so at $19.95. Why not, then, raise the price? The only danger is miscalculation: By raising the price you may reduce sales to the point where you make less money overall, even while making more per copy.

    Assume that the situation described in the last sentence happens. What does this tell us about the price elasticity of demand for that book? Briefly explain.
    Source: Beth Luey, *Handbook for Academic Authors,* 4th ed., Cambridge University Press, 2002, p. 250.

13. Each summer the city of Bethlehem, Pennsylvania holds Musikfest, an outdoor music festival. The city had been charging $7 per day to park in city parking lots. One year it raised the fee to $10 per day. According to an article in a local newspaper: "Fewer parkers used city lots, but this year's parking rate increase [from $7 to $10] gave the [parking] authority record [parking] lot revenues for the annual festival." Use the information in the following table to calculate the price elasticity of demand for parking spaces in Bethlehem city parking lots during Musikfest (use the midpoint price elasticity of demand formula). Assume that nothing happened to shift the demand curve for parking places. Be sure to state whether demand is elastic or inelastic.

MUSIKFEST PARKING RATE REVENUE

YEAR	RATE	REVENUE
1999	$10	$83,760
1998	7	77,792

Source: Matt Assad, "Grinch Alive and Well in Bethlehem Parking Authority," Allentown *Morning Call,* September 29, 1999, page B4.

14. Briefly explain whether the demand for each of the following products is likely to be elastic or inelastic:
    a. Milk
    b. Frozen cheese pizza
    c. Cola
    d. Prescription medicine

15. The price elasticity of demand for most agricultural products is quite low. What impact is this likely to have on how much the prices of these products change from year to year? Illustrate your answer with a supply and demand diagram.

16. [Related to *Don't Let This Happen To You!*] The publisher of a magazine gives his staff the following information:

Current price	$2.00 per issue
Current sales	150,000 copies per month
Current total costs	$450,000 per month

He tells them, "Our costs are currently $150,000 more than our revenues each month. I propose to eliminate this problem by raising the price of the magazine to $3.00 per issue. This will result in our revenue being exactly equal to our cost." Do you agree with the publisher's analysis? Explain.

17. An article about the newspaper industry that appeared in the *Wall Street Journal* noted the following:

    Declining circulation hasn't stopped Knight Ridder papers from raising subscription prices. Such increases, while boosting revenue per copy, almost always trigger a readership decline.

    a. What is a newspaper's "circulation"?
    b. To what is "revenue per copy" equal?
    c. Why would a newspaper's management increase its subscription price if the result was a decline in the quantity of newspapers sold?
    Source: Patricia Callahan and Kevin Helliker, "Subscriptions Fall, But Knight Ridder Lifts Advertising Rates," *Wall Street Journal,* June 18, 2001.

18. During their last year in power in Afghanistan, the Taliban outlawed growing poppies, the flower from which opium is made. As a result, opium production declined by 95 percent and the price of opium rose from 2,000 rupees per kilogram to 40,000 rupees per kilogram. What is the price elasticity of demand for opium in Afghanistan?
    Source: Craig S. Smith, "Poppy Ban Pleases Dealers in Opium," *New York Times,* January 19, 2002.

19. [Related to the *Chapter Opener*] Look again at the quote from Stephen Rubin of Doubleday Books that began this chapter. Doubleday Books is selling John Grisham's novel, *The Broker,* at a price of $27.95.
    a. If the demand for this book is perfectly inelastic, draw a demand curve showing the effect on the quantity demanded of raising the price from $27.95 to $39.95.

Assume sales are 500,000 at a price of $27.95. What is the change in revenue as a result of the price change?

b. Now assume that the price elasticity of demand is −2. Draw another demand curve showing the effect of raising the price from $27.95 to $39.95. Be sure to show the quantity demanded at each price. Now what is the change in revenue as a result of the price change?

20. The head of the United Kumquat Growers Association makes the following statement: "The federal government is considering implementing a price floor in the market for kumquats. The government will not be able to buy any surplus kumquats produced at the price floor or to pay us any other subsidy. Because the demand for kumquats is elastic, I believe this program will make us worse off, and I say we should oppose it." Explain whether you agree or disagree with this reasoning.

21. Review the concept of economic efficiency from Chapter 4 before answering the following question: Will there be a greater loss of economic efficiency from a price ceiling when demand is elastic or inelastic? Illustrate your answer with a demand and supply graph.

22. In the spring of 2002, lettuce prices doubled from about $1.50 per head to about $3.00. The reaction of one consumer was quoted in a newspaper article:

"I will not buy [lettuce] when it's $3 a head," she said, adding that other green vegetables can fill in for lettuce. "If bread were $5 a loaf we'd still have to buy it. But lettuce is not that important in our family."

a. For this consumer's household, which product has the higher price elasticity of demand: bread or lettuce? Briefly explain.

b. Is the cross-price elasticity of demand between lettuce and other green vegetables positive or negative for this consumer? Briefly explain.

Source: Justin Bachman, "Sorry, Romaine Only," Associate Press, March 29, 2002.

23. In the following graph, the demand for hot dog buns has shifted outward because the price of hot dogs has fallen from $2.20 to $1.80 per package.

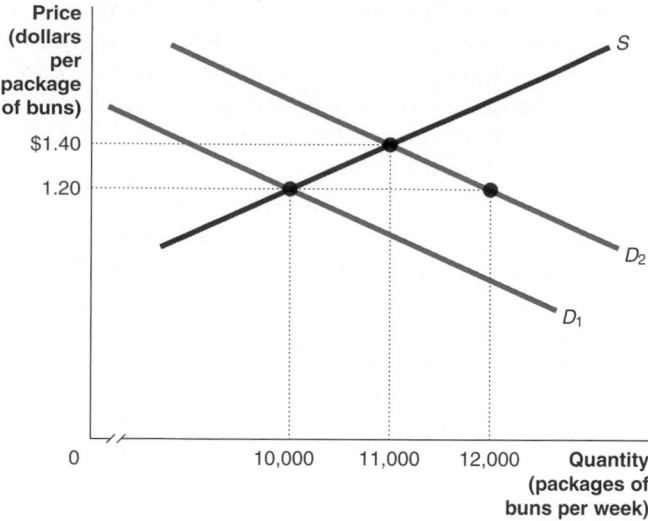

a. Calculate the cross-price elasticity of demand between hot dogs and hot dog buns.

b. Calculate the price elasticity of supply for hot dog buns.

24. Are the cross-price elasticities of demand between the following pairs of products likely to be positive or negative? Briefly explain.

a. Pepsi and Coke

b. French fries and ketchup

c. Steak and chicken

d. DVD players and DVDs

25. After World War II, the Japanese government intervened in the economy to provide aid to certain industries that it believed would be most important in the recovery from war. One of the requirements for receiving government aid was that an industry had to be producing a good with a high income elasticity of demand. Why do you think the Japanese government made this a requirement?

26. Rank the following four goods from lowest income elasticity of demand to highest income elasticity of demand. Briefly explain your ranking.

a. Bread

b. Pepsi

c. Mercedes-Benz automobiles

d. Personal computers

27. For the 2003 baseball season, the Chicago White Sox cut the prices of tickets by 50 percent for tickets to games on Monday nights. The number of Monday night game tickets sold increased by 80 percent. Is this enough information to allow us to calculate the price elasticity of demand for tickets to White Sox games? Briefly explain.

28. The Delaware River Joint Toll Bridge Commission increased the toll on the bridges on Route 22 and Interstate 78 from New Jersey to Pennsylvania from $0.50 to $1.00. Use the information in the table to answer the questions (assume nothing other than the toll change occurred during the months that would affect consumer demand).

| | | NUMBER OF VEHICLES CROSSING THE BRIDGE | |
MONTH	TOLL	ROUTE 22 BRIDGE	INTERSTATE 78 BRIDGE
November	$0.50	519,337	728,022
December	1.00	433,691	656,257

a. Calculate the price elasticity of demand for each bridge using the midpoint formula.

b. How much total revenue did the Commission collect from these bridges in November? How much did they collect in December? Relate your answer to your answer in part a.

Source: Garrett Therolf, "Frugal Drivers Flood Free Bridge," Allentown *Morning Call*, January 20, 2003.

29. Use the midpoint formula for calculating elasticity to calculate the price elasticity of supply between point *A* and point *B* for each panel of Figure 6-5.

chapter

seven

Firms, the Stock Market, and Corporate Governance

Google: From Dorm Room to Wall Street

> There could be no question that Google was cool. The world's most widely used Internet search engine, Google had become the essence of cool as a way to research information stored on Web sites. Founded in 1998 by Larry Page and Sergey Brin, Google grew quickly. In 2005, Google employed 3,000 people and earned $3.2 billion in revenue. Google's founders had transformed the Internet search engine and brought value to users through a combination of intellect, technology, and the talents of many employees. Google's key advantage over competitors such as A9 and Ask Jeeves was its search algorithms that allowed users to find easily Web sites

most relevant to a subject. Google had other advantages as well, such as its automatic foreign-language translation. Google had become so dominant that other major Web sites, such as AOL and Yahoo, were using it as their search engine. And "Google" had even become a verb: "I couldn't remember the name of the founder of Microsoft, so I googled it." Google's huge popularity allowed it to do what most other Internet sites could not: make money selling advertising.

And Google was hot. In 2004, Google sold part of the firm to outside investors by offering stock— and partial ownership—to the public. This stock offering vaulted Larry

Page and Sergey Brin to the ranks of the super-rich. Google's stock offering also gained significant press attention, as the firm bypassed conventional financial practice and used an automated online auction to help set the share price and determine who should receive stock. The offering's size grabbed attention, too: It was the most anticipated stock sale since the 1995 launch of Netscape, a deal that sparked the late-1990s Internet gold rush on Wall Street. *An Inside Look* on page 214 discusses movements in Google's stock price in the months following the firm's first sale of stock in August 2004.

LEARNING OBJECTIVES

After studying this chapter, you should be able to:

① Categorize the major types of business in the United States.

② Describe the typical management structure of corporations and understand the concepts of separation of ownership from control and the principal-agent problem.

③ Explain how firms obtain the funds they need to operate and expand.

④ Understand the information provided in firms' financial statements.

⑤ Understand the business accounting scandals of 2002, as well as the role of government in corporate governance.

A business like Google is more than a black box, transforming inputs into outputs. As the firm grew larger, it was less the informal organization put together by the founders and more a complex organization with greater need for management and funds to grow. Indeed, Google's offering of stock to outside investors provided the firm with a major inflow of funds for growth.

Once a firm grows very large, its owners often do not continue to manage it. The large modern corporation is owned by millions of individual investors who have purchased the firm's stock. With ownership so dispersed, the top managers who actually run the firm have the opportunity to make decisions that are in the managers' best interests, but that may not be in the best interests of the stockholders who own the firm.

Against this backdrop, Google faced significant costs associated with selling stock to the public. High-profile corporate accounting scandals in 2001 and 2002 at major U.S. firms, such as Enron, WorldCom, and Tyco, led to the passage of stronger—and more costly—securities regulation under the Sarbanes-Oxley Act, enacted by Congress in 2002. Google's growth prospects and the health of the financial system were intertwined.

➤ In this chapter, we look at the firm: how it is organized, how it raises funds, and the information it provides to investors. As we have already discussed, in a market system, firms are responsible for organizing the factors of production to produce goods and services. Firms are the vehicles entrepreneurs use to earn profits by responding to consumer wants as expressed in the market. To succeed, entrepreneurs must meet consumer wants by producing new or better goods and services, or by finding ways of producing existing goods and services at a lower cost so they can be sold at a lower price. Entrepreneurs also need access to sufficient funds, and they must be able to efficiently organize production. As the typical firm in many industries has become larger during the past hundred years, the task of efficiently organizing production has become more difficult. The problem of successfully coordinating the activities of large firms is one of the causes of the recent business scandals in the United States. Toward the end of this chapter, we look at why these scandals occurred and at the steps businesses and the government have taken to avoid similar problems in the future.

Types of Firms

① **LEARNING OBJECTIVE**

Categorize the major types of business in the United States.

Sole proprietorship A firm owned by a single individual and not organized as a corporation.

Partnership A firm owned jointly by two or more persons and not organized as a corporation.

Corporation A legal form of business that provides the owners with limited liability.

Asset Anything of value owned by a person or a firm.

In studying a market economy, it is important to understand the basics of how firms operate. In the United States, there are three legal categories of firms: *sole proprietorships, partnerships,* and *corporations.* A **sole proprietorship** is a firm owned by a single individual. Although most sole proprietorships are small, some are quite large in terms of sales, number of persons employed, and profits earned. **Partnerships** are firms owned jointly by two or more—sometimes many—persons. Most law and accounting firms are partnerships. The famous Lloyd's of London insurance company is a partnership. Although some partnerships, such as Lloyd's, can be quite large, most large firms are organized as *corporations.* A **corporation** is a legal form of business that provides the owners with limited liability.

Who Is Liable? Limited and Unlimited Liability

A key distinction among these three types of firms is that the owners of sole proprietorships and partnerships have unlimited liability. Unlimited liability means there is no legal distinction between the personal assets of the owners of the firm and the assets of the firm. An **asset** is anything of value owned by a person or a firm. If a sole proprietorship or a partnership owes a lot of money to the firm's suppliers or employees, the suppliers and employees have a legal right to sue the firm for payment, even if this requires the firm's owners to sell some of their personal assets, such as stocks or bonds. In other words, with sole proprietorships and partnerships, the owners are not legally distinct from the firms they own.

It may seem only fair that the owners of a firm be responsible for a firm's debts. But early in the nineteenth century it became clear to many state legislatures in the United States that unlimited liability was a significant problem for any firm that was attempting to raise funds from large numbers of investors. An investor might be interested in making a relatively small investment in a firm but be unwilling to become a partner in the firm for fear of placing at risk all of his or her personal assets if the firm were to fail. To get around this problem, state legislatures began to pass *general incorporation laws,* which allowed firms to be organized as corporations. Under the corporate form of business, the owners of a firm have **limited liability,** which means that if the firm fails, the owners can never lose more than the amount they had invested in the firm. The personal assets of the owners of the firm are not affected by the failure of the firm. In fact, in the eyes of the law, a corporation is a legal "person" separate from its owners. Limited liabil-

Limited liability The legal provision that shields owners of a corporation from losing more than they have invested in the firm.

	SOLE PROPRIETORSHIP	**PARTNERSHIP**	**CORPORATION**
Advantages	• Control by owner	• Ability to share work	• Limited personal liability
	• No layers of management	• Ability to share risks	• Greater ability to raise funds
Disadvantages	• Unlimited personal liability	• Unlimited personal liability	• Costly to organize
	• Limited ability to raise funds	• Limited ability to raise funds	• Possible double taxation of income

TABLE 7-1

Differences among Business Organizations

ity has made it possible for corporations to raise funds by issuing shares of stock to large numbers of investors. For example, if you buy a share of Google stock, you are part owner of the firm, but even if Google were to go bankrupt, you would not be personally responsible for any of Google's debts. Therefore, you could not lose more than the amount you had paid for the stock.

Corporate organizations also have some disadvantages. In the United States, corporate profits are taxed twice—once at the corporate level and again when investors receive a share of corporate profits. Corporations, because they generally are larger than sole proprietorships and partnerships, also are more difficult to organize and harder to run. Table 7-1 reviews the advantages and disadvantages of different forms of business organization.

What's in a "Name"? Lloyd's of London Learns about Unlimited Liability the Hard Way

7-1 Making the Connection

The world-famous insurance company Lloyd's of London got its start in Edward Lloyd's coffeehouse in London in the late 1600s. Ship owners would come to the coffeehouse looking for someone to insure (or "underwrite") their ships and cargos in exchange for a flat fee (or "premium"). The customers of the coffeehouse, themselves merchants or ship owners, who agreed to insure ships or cargos would have to make payment from their personal funds if an insured ship were lost at sea. By the late 1700s the system had become more formal: Each underwriter would recruit investors, known as "Names," and use the funds raised to back insurance policies sold to a wide variety of clients. In the twentieth century Lloyd's became famous for some of its unusual insurance policies. It issued an insurance policy on the legs of Betty Grable, a 1940s movie star. One man bought an insurance policy against seeing a ghost.

By the late 1980s, 34,000 persons around the world had invested in Lloyd's as Names. A series of disasters in the late 1980s and early 1990s—including the *Exxon Valdez* oil spill in Alaska, Hurricane Hugo in South Carolina, and an earthquake in San Francisco—resulted in huge payments on insurance policies written by Lloyd's. In 1989, Lloyd's lost $3.85 billion. In 1990 it lost an additional $4.4 billion. It then became clear to many of the Names that Lloyd's was not a corporation and that the Names did not have the limited liability enjoyed by corporate shareholders. On the contrary, the Names were personally responsible for paying the losses on the insurance policies. Many Names lost far more than they had invested. Some investors, such as Charles Schwab, the discount stockbroker, were wealthy enough that their losses were sustainable, but others were less fortunate. One California investor ended up living in poverty after having to sell his $1 million house to pay his share of the losses. Another Name, Sir Richard Fitch, a British admiral, committed suicide after most of his wealth was wiped out. As many as 30 Names may have committed suicide as a result of their losses.

By 2004, only 2,500 Names—undoubtedly sadder but wiser—remained as investors in Lloyd's. New rules have allowed insurance companies to underwrite Lloyd's policies for the first time. Today, Names provide only about 20 percent of Lloyd's funds.

Investors in Lloyd's of London lost billions of dollars during the 1980s and 1990s.

Sources: Charles Fleming, "The Master of Disaster Is Trying to Avoid One," *Wall Street Journal*, November 17, 2003 and "Lloyd's of London: Insuring for the Future," *Economist*, September 16, 2004.

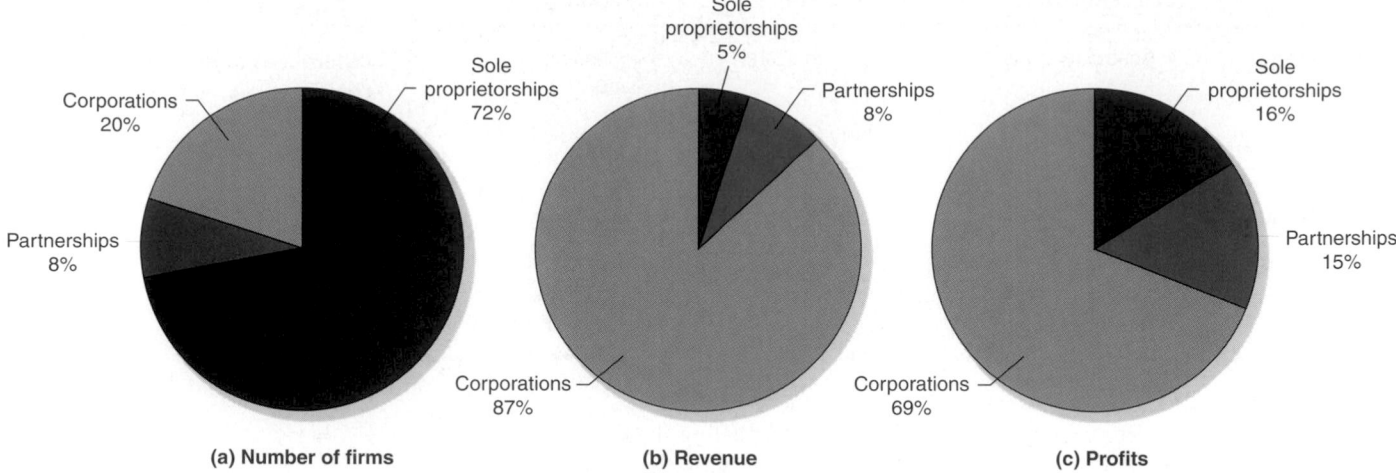

FIGURE 7-1   Business Organizations: Sole Proprietorships, Partnerships, and Corporations

The three types of firms in the United States are sole proprietorships, partnerships, and corporations. Panel (a) shows that only 20 percent of all firms are corporations. Yet, as panels (b) and (c) show, corporations account for a majority of the total revenue and profits earned by all firms.

Source: *Statistical Abstract of the United States, 2004–2005.*

Corporations Earn the Majority of Revenue and Profits

Figure 7-1 gives basic statistics on the three types of business organizations. Panel (a) shows that almost three-quarters of all firms are sole proprietorships. Panels (b) and (c) show that although only 20 percent of all firms are corporations, corporations account for the majority of revenue and profits earned by all firms. *Profit* is the difference between revenue and the total cost to the firm of producing the goods and services it offers for sale.

There are nearly 5 million corporations in the United States, but only 22,000 have annual revenues of more than $50 million. We can think of these 22,000 firms—including Microsoft, General Electric, and Exxon Mobil—as representing "big business." These large firms account for more than four-fifths of all U.S. corporate profits.

② LEARNING OBJECTIVE

Describe the typical management structure of corporations and understand the concepts of separation of ownership from control and the principal-agent problem.

Corporate governance The way in which a corporation is structured and the impact a corporation's structure has on the firm's behavior.

The Structure of Corporations and the Principal-Agent Problem

Because large corporations account for most sales and profits in the economy, it is important to know how they are managed. Most large corporations have a similar management structure. This structure can lead to problems on the scale of the 2002 business scandals, which we will discuss later. The way in which a corporation is structured and the impact a corporation's structure has on the firm's behavior is referred to as **corporate governance.**

Corporate Structure and Corporate Governance

Corporations are legally owned by their *shareholders,* the owners of the corporation's stock. Unlike founder-dominated businesses, such as family businesses, a corporation's shareholders, although they are the firm's owners, do not manage the firm directly. Instead, they elect a *board of directors* to represent their interests. The board of directors appoints a *chief executive officer* (CEO) to run the day-to-day operations of the corporation. Sometimes the board of directors will also appoint other members of *top management,* such as the *chief financial officer* (CFO). At other times the CEO appoints other members of top management. Members of top management, including the CEO and CFO, will often serve on the board of directors. Members of management serving on the board of directors are referred to as *inside directors*. Members of the board of directors who do not have a direct management role in the firm are referred to as *outside directors*. The outside directors are intended to act as checks on the decisions of top managers, but the distinction between an outside director and an inside director is not always clear. For example, the CEO of a firm that sells a good or service to a large corporation may sit on the board of directors of that corporation. Although an outside director, this person may be reluctant to displease the top managers because the top managers have the power to stop purchasing from his firm. In some instances, top managers have effectively controlled their firms' boards of directors.

Unlike founder-dominated businesses, the top management of large corporations does not generally own a large share of the firm's stock, so large corporations have a **separation of ownership from control.** Although the shareholders actually own the firm, top management controls the day-to-day operations of the firm. Because top managers do not own the entire firm, they may have an incentive to decrease the firm's profits by spending money to purchase private jets or schedule management meetings at luxurious resorts. Economists refer to the conflict between the interests of shareholders and the interests of top management as a **principal-agent problem.** This problem occurs when agents—in this case, a firm's top management—pursue their own interests rather than the interests of the principal who hired them—in this case, the shareholders of the corporation. To reduce the impact of the principal-agent problem, in the 1990s, many boards of directors began to tie the salaries of top managers to the profits of the firm or to the price of the firm's stock. They hoped this would give top managers an incentive to make the firm as profitable as possible, thereby benefiting its shareholders.

Separation of ownership from control In many large corporations the top management, rather than the shareholders, control day-to-day operations.

Principal-agent problem A problem caused by an agent pursuing his own interests rather than the interests of the principal who hired him.

SOLVED PROBLEM   7-1

Does the Principal-Agent Problem Also Apply to the Relationship between Managers and Workers?

Briefly explain whether you agree or disagree with the following argument: "The principal-agent problem applies not just to the relationship between shareholders and top managers. It also applies to the relationship between managers and workers. Just as shareholders have trouble monitoring whether top managers are earning as much profit as possible, managers have trouble monitoring whether workers are working as hard as possible."

② **LEARNING OBJECTIVE**

Describe the typical management structure of corporations and understand the concepts of separation of ownership from control and the principal-agent problem.

Solving the Problem:
Step 1: Review the chapter material. This problem concerns the principal-agent problem, so you may want to review the section "Corporate Structure and Corporate Governance," which begins on page 202.

Step 2: Evaluate the argument. You should agree with the argument. A corporation's shareholders have difficulty monitoring the activities of top managers. In practice, they attempt to do so indirectly through the corporation's board of directors. But a board of directors may be influenced heavily by—or even controlled by—the firm's top managers. Even if a board of directors is not controlled by top management, it may be difficult for the board to know whether actions taken by top managers—say, opening a branch office in Paris—will increase the profitability of the firm or just increase the enjoyment of the top managers.

To answer the problem, we must extend this analysis to the relationship between managers and workers: Managers would like workers to work as hard as possible. Workers would often rather not work hard, particularly if they do not see a direct financial reward for doing so. Managers can have trouble monitoring whether workers are working hard or goofing off. Is that worker in his cubicle diligently staring at a computer screen because he is hard at

work on a report or because he is surfing the Web for sports scores or writing a long e-mail to his girlfriend? Thus, the principal-agent problem does apply to the relationship between managers and workers.

Extra Credit: Boards of directors try to reduce the principal-agent problem by designing compensation policies for top managers that give them financial incentives to increase profits. (Although, as we will see later in this chapter, these plans can sometimes backfire.) Similarly, managers try to reduce the principal-agent problem by designing compensation policies that give workers an incentive to work harder. For example, some manufacturers pay factory workers on the basis of how much they produce, rather than on the basis of how many hours they work.

YOUR TURN: For more practice, do related problems 6 and 7 on page 217 at the end of this chapter. Visit www.prenhall.com/hubbard for an interactive exercise related to this Solved Problem.

---

③ **LEARNING OBJECTIVE**

Explain how firms obtain the funds they need to operate and expand.

How Firms Raise Funds

Owners and managers of firms try to earn a profit. To earn a profit, a firm must raise funds to pay for its operations, including paying its employees and buying machines. Indeed, a central challenge for anyone running a firm, whether that person is a sole proprietor or a top manager of a large corporation, is raising the funds needed to operate and expand the business. Suppose you decide to open an online trading service using $100,000 you have saved in a bank. You use the $100,000 to rent a building for your firm, to buy computers, and to pay other start-up expenses. Your firm is a great success and you decide to expand by moving to a larger building and buying more computers. You can obtain the funds for this expansion in three ways:

1. If you are making a profit, you could reinvest the profits back into your firm. Profits that are reinvested in a firm, rather than taken out of a firm and paid to the firm's owners, are *retained earnings*.

2. You could also obtain funds by taking on one or more partners who would invest in the firm. This arrangement would increase the firm's *financial capital*.

3. Finally, you could borrow the funds from relatives, friends, or a bank.

Sources of External Funds

Indirect finance A flow of funds from savers to borrowers through financial intermediaries such as banks. Intermediaries raise funds from savers to lend to firms (and other borrowers).

Unless firms rely on retained earnings, they have to obtain the *external funds* they need from others who have funds available to invest. It is the role of an economy's *financial system* to transfer funds from savers to borrowers—directly through financial markets or indirectly through financial intermediaries such as banks.

Firms can raise external funds in two distinct ways. The first relies on financial intermediaries such as banks and is called **indirect finance.** If you put $1,000 in a checking account or a savings account, or if you buy a $1,000 certificate of deposit (CD), the bank will loan most of those funds to borrowers. The bank will combine your funds with those of other depositors and, for example, make a $100,000 loan to a local business.

Direct finance A flow of funds from savers to firms through financial markets.

The second way for firms to acquire external funds is through *financial markets.* Raising funds in these markets, such as the New York Stock Exchange on Wall Street in New York, is called **direct finance.** Direct finance usually takes the form of the borrower selling the lender a *financial security.* A financial security is a document—sometimes in electronic form—that states the terms under which the funds have passed from the buyer of the security—who is lending funds—to the borrower. *Bonds* and *stocks* are the two main types of financial securities.

BONDS   **Bonds** are financial securities that represent promises to repay a fixed amount of funds. When General Electric (GE) sells a bond to raise funds, it promises to pay the purchaser of the bond an interest payment each year for the term of the bond, as well as a final payment of the amount of the loan, or the *principal*, at the end of the term. GE may need to raise many millions of dollars to build a factory, but each individual bond has a principal or *face value*, of $1,000, which is the amount each bond purchaser is lending GE. So, GE must sell many bonds to raise all the funds it needs. Suppose GE promises it will pay interest of $60 per year to anyone who will buy one of its bonds. The interest payments on a bond are referred to as **coupon payments.** The **interest rate** is the cost of borrowing funds, usually expressed as a percentage of the amount borrowed. If we express the coupon as a percentage of the face value of the bond, we have the interest rate on the bond, called the *coupon rate*. In this case the interest rate is

$$\frac{\$60}{\$1,000} = 0.06, \text{ or } 6\%.$$

Bond   A financial security that represents a promise to repay a fixed amount of funds.

Coupon payment   Interest payment on a bond.

Interest rate   The cost of borrowing funds, usually expressed as a percentage of the amount borrowed.

Many bonds issued by corporations have terms, or *maturities*, of 30 years. If you bought a bond from GE, GE would pay you $60 per year for 30 years, and at the end of the thirtieth year GE would pay you back the $1,000 principal.

STOCKS   When you buy a newly issued bond from a firm, you are lending funds to that firm. When you buy **stock** issued by a firm, you are actually buying part ownership of the firm. When a corporation sells stock, it is doing the same thing the owner of a small business does when she takes on a partner: The firm is increasing its financial capital by bringing additional owners into the firm. Any individual shareholder usually owns only a small fraction of the total shares of stock issued by a corporation. As we discussed earlier, corporations are run by their top managers who answer to the corporation's board of directors, which is elected by the shareholders. Although some individuals may own enough of a firm's stock to influence the actions of the firm, the average shareholder does not.

Stock   A financial security that represents partial ownership of a firm.

A shareholder is entitled to a share of the corporation's profits, if there are any. Corporations generally keep some of their profits—known as retained earnings—to finance future expansion. The remaining profits are paid to shareholders as **dividends.** If investors expect the firm to earn economic profits on its retained earnings, the firm's share price will rise, providing a *capital gain* for investors. If a corporation is unable to make a profit, it usually will not pay a dividend. Under the law, corporations must make payments on any debt they have before making payments to their owners. That is, the corporation must make promised payments to bondholders before it may make any dividend payments to shareholders. In addition, when firms sell stock, they acquire from investors an open-ended commitment of funds to the firm. Therefore, unlike bonds, stocks do not have a maturity date, so the firm is not obliged to return the investor's funds at any particular date.

Dividends   Payments by a corporation to its shareholders.

Stock and Bond Markets Provide Capital—and Information

The original purchasers of stocks and bonds may resell them to other investors. In fact, most of the buying and selling of stocks and bonds that takes place each day is investors reselling existing stocks and bonds to each other, rather than corporations selling new stocks and bonds to investors. The buyers and sellers of stocks and bonds together make up the *stock and bond markets*. There is no single place where stocks and bonds are bought and sold. Some trading of stocks and bonds takes place in buildings known as *exchanges*, such as the New York Stock Exchange or Tokyo Stock Exchange. In the United States, the stocks and bonds of the largest corporations are traded on the New York Stock Exchange. The development of computer technology has spread the trading of stocks and bonds outside of exchanges to *securities dealers* linked by computers. These

Don't Let This Happen To You!

When Google Shares Change Hands, Google Doesn't Get the Money

If Google becomes a popular investment, with shares changing hands often as views about the firm's valuation shift, that's great for Google, right? Think of all that money flowing into Google's coffers as shares change hands and the stock price goes up. *Wrong.* Google raises funds in a primary market, but shares change hands in a secondary market. Those trades don't put money into Google's hands, but they do give important information to the firm's managers. Let's see why.

Primary markets are those in which newly issued claims are sold to initial buyers by the issuer. Businesses can raise funds in a primary financial market in two ways—by borrowing or by selling shares—which result in different types of claims on the borrower's future income. Although you hear about the stock market fluctuations each night on the evening news, debt instruments actually account for more of the funds raised by borrowers. In mid-2005, the value of debt instruments in the United States was about $25 trillion compared to $12 trillion for equities.

In *secondary markets,* claims that have already been issued are sold by one investor to another. If Google sells shares to the public, it is turning to a primary market for new funds. Once Google shares are issued, investors trade the shares in the secondary market. The founders of Google do not receive any new funds when Google shares are traded on secondary markets. The initial seller of a financial instrument raises funds from a lender only in the primary market. Secondary markets convey information to firms' managers and to investors by determining the price of financial instruments. For example, a major increase in Google's stock price conveys the market's good feelings about the firm, and the firm may decide to raise funds to expand. Hence, secondary markets are valuable sources of information for corporations that are considering raising funds.

Primary and secondary markets are both important, but they play different roles. As an investor, you principally will trade financial instruments in a secondary market. As a corporate manager, you may help decide how to raise new funds to expand the firm where you work.

YOUR TURN: Test your understanding by doing related problem 14 on page 218 at the end of this chapter.

dealers comprise the *over-the-counter market.* The stocks of many computer and other high-technology firms—including Microsoft and Intel—are traded in the most important of the over-the-counter markets, the *National Association of Securities Dealers' Automated Quotation System,* which is referred to by its acronym, NASDAQ.

Shares of stock represent claims on the profits of the firms that issue them. Therefore, as the fortunes of the firms change and they earn more or less profit, the prices of the stock the firms have issued should also change. Similarly, bonds represent claims to receive coupon payments and one final payment of principal. Therefore, a particular bond that was issued in the past may have its price go up or down depending upon whether the coupon payments being offered on newly issued bonds are higher or lower than on existing bonds. If you hold a bond with a coupon of $80 per year and newly issued bonds have coupons of $100 per year, the price of your bond will fall because it is less attractive to investors. The price of a bond will be affected by changes in investors' perceptions of the issuing firm's ability to make the coupon payments. For example, if investors begin to believe that a firm may soon go out of business and stop making coupon payments to its bondholders, the price of the firm's bonds will fall to very low levels.

Changes in the value of a firm's stocks and bonds offer important information for a firm's managers, as well as for investors. An increase in the stock price means that investors are more optimistic about the firm's profit prospects, and the firm's managers may wish to expand the firm's operations as a result. By contrast, a decrease in the firm's stock price indicates that investors are less optimistic about the firms' profit prospects, so that management may want to shrink the firm's operations. Likewise, changes in the value of the firm's bonds imply changes in the cost of external funds to finance the firm's investment in research and development or in new factories. A higher bond price indicates a lower cost of new external funds, while a lower bond price indicates a higher cost of new external funds.

Following General Electric's Stock and Bond Prices in the Financial Pages

If you read the stock and bond listings in your local paper or the *Wall Street Journal*, you will notice that newspapers manage to pack into a small space a lot of information about what happened to stocks and bonds during the previous day's trading. The following figure reproduces a section from one page of the stock quotations from the *Wall Street Journal*. Let's focus on the highlighted listing for General Electric, and examine the information in each column.

➤ The first column (YLD %CHG) gives the percentage change in the price of the stock from the beginning of the year to date. In this case, the price of GE's stock had fallen 1.1 percent since the beginning of 2005.

➤ The second column (52-WEEK HI) and the third column (52-WEEK LO) give the highest price GE stock has traded for and the lowest price GE has traded for during the previous year. These numbers tell you how *volatile* the stock price is—that is, how much it fluctuates over the course of the year.

➤ The fourth column (STOCK (SYM)) gives a compact version of the firm's name followed by the firm's "ticker" symbol, which you may have seen scrolling along the bottom of the screen on cable financial news channels.

➤ The fifth column (DIV) gives the dividend expressed in dollars. In this case, .88 means that GE paid a dividend of $0.88 per share.

➤ The sixth column (YLD %) gives the *dividend yield*, which is calculated by dividing the dividend by the *closing price* of the stock—that is, the price at which GE stock last sold before the close of trading on the previous day.

➤ The seventh column (PE) gives the *P-E ratio* (or price-earnings ratio), which is calculated by dividing the price of the firm's stock by its earnings per share (remember that because firms retain some earnings, earnings per share is not necessarily the same as dividends per share). GE's P-E ratio was 22, meaning that its price per share was 22 times its earnings per share. You would have to pay $22 to buy $1 of GE earnings.

➤ The eighth column (VOL 100s) gives the number of shares of stock traded on the previous day (in hundreds of shares). So, 26,135,600 shares of GE stock were traded the previous day on the New York Stock Exchange.

➤ The ninth column (CLOSE) is the price the stock sold for the last time it was traded before the close of trading on the previous day, which in this case was $36.10.

➤ The tenth and final column (NET CHG) gives the amount by which the closing price changed from the closing price the day before. In this case, the price of GE's stock had fallen by $0.15 per share from its closing price the day before. Changes in GE's stock price give the firm's managers a signal that they may want to expand or contract the firm's operations.

Stock and bond tables in local newspapers help investors track a firm's prospects.

YTD % CHG	52-WEEK HI	LO	STOCK (SYM)	DIV	YLD %	PE	VOL 100s	CLOSE	NET CHG
−14.9	14.10	6.79	GenlCbl BGC	...		51	2066	11.79	−0.26
0.9	109.98	90.61	GenDynam GD	1.60F	1.5	16	7304	105.57	0.06
−1.1	37.75	29.55	GenElec GE	.88	2.4	22	261356	36.10	−0.15
3.8	39.30	24.31	GenGrthProp GGP	1.44	3.8	31	21099	37.53	−0.86
11.7	53.98	17.75	GenMaritime GMR	1.77p	...	6	5522	44.64	−0.46

Now we can look at the listings for corporate bonds. As with stocks, to understand the information printed on bonds, you must understand the conventions used. Look at the highlighted Ford bond, and once again we examine the information in each column of the listing.

➤ The first column (COMPANY (TICKER)) gives the firm name and ticker symbol.

➤ The second column (COUPON) gives the coupon rate. It is always expressed as a percentage of $1,000. So, this corporate bond pays a coupon of $50.00 per year and has a coupon rate of 5.00%.

➤ The third column (MATURITY) gives the date on which the bond matures, when the investor will receive a payment of the face value, or principle, of $1,000.

➤ The fourth column (LAST PRICE) gives the price that the bond sold for the last time it was traded before the close of trading the previous day. (Because this listing is from the paper of May 4, the listed price is for May 3.) The price is expressed as a percentage of $1,000. So, the price was 101.666 percent of $1,000, or $1,016.66.

➤ The fifth column (LAST YIELD) shows the interest rate on the bond if an investor purchased the bond at its current price. The yield of 4.739% is lower than the coupon rate of 5.00% because the bond is currently selling for a price greater than $1,000.

➤ The sixth column (EST SPREAD) and seventh column (UST) allow an investor to compare the interest rate on this bond to the interest rate on a corresponding bond issued by the United States Treasury. The spread is quoted in *basis points,* with 100 basis points equal to one percentage point. The 10 under UST indicates that the spread is calculated relative to the interest rate on a 10-year Treasury note. Therefore, we know that the interest rate on the Treasury note must have been 4.739% − 0.54% = 4.199%.

➤ Finally, the eighth column (EST $ VOL) gives the dollar value of the bonds traded the previous day in thousands of dollars. In this case, $53,979,000 worth of these GE bonds were traded.

	COUPON	MATURITY	LAST PRICE	LAST YIELD	*EST SPREAD	UST†	EST $ VOL (000's)
Morgan Stanley	5.300	May 01, 2013	102.064	4.977	78	10	57,739
Clear Channel Communications Inc. (CCU)	4.900	May 15, 2015	89.270	6.364	220	10	55,270
General Electric (GE)	5.000	Feb 01, 2013	101.666	4.739	54	10	53,979
Clear Channel Communications Inc. (CCU)	5.500	Sep 15, 2014	94.359	6.306	214	10	53,535
May Department Stores (MAY)	5.750	Jul 15, 2014	103.837	5.218	105	10	53,200

Source: Wall Street Journal Eastern Edition [Staff produced copy only] by *Wall Street Journal.* Copyright 2005 by Dow Jones & Co Inc. Reproduced with permission of Dow Jones & Co. Inc. in the format Textbook via Copyright Clearance Center.

④ **LEARNING OBJECTIVE**

Understand the information provided in firms' financial statements.

Using Financial Statements to Evaluate a Corporation

To raise funds, a firm's managers must persuade financial intermediaries or buyers of its bonds or stock that it will be profitable. Before a firm can sell new issues of stock or bonds, it must first provide investors and financial regulators with information about its finances. To borrow from a bank or other financial intermediary, the firm must disclose financial information to the lender as well.

In most high-income countries, government agencies set requirements for information disclosure for firms that desire to sell securities in financial markets. In the United States, the Securities and Exchange Commission requires publicly owned firms to report their performance in financial statements prepared using standard accounting methods, often referred to as *generally accepted accounting principles.* Such disclosure reduces information costs, but it doesn't eliminate them, for two reasons. First, some firms may be too young to have much information for potential investors to evaluate. Second, managers may try to present the required information in the best possible light so that investors will overvalue their securities.

Private firms also collect information on business borrowers and sell the information to lenders and investors. As long as the information-gathering firm does a good job, lenders and investors purchasing the information will be better able to judge the quality of borrowing firms. Firms specializing in information—including Moody's Investor Service, Standard & Poor's Corporation, Value Line, and Dun and Bradstreet—collect information from businesses and sell it to subscribers. Buyers include individual investors, libraries, and financial intermediaries. You can find some of these publications in your college library or through online information services.

A Bull in China's Financial Shop

Prospects for Sichuan Changhong Electric Co., manufacturer of plasma televisions and liquid crystal displays, looked excellent in 2004, with rapidly growing output, employment, and profits earned from trade in the world economy. And Changhong was not alone. In the early 2000s the Chinese economy was sizzling. China's output grew by 9.5 percent during 2004, dominated by an astonishing 26 percent growth in investment in plant and equipment. The Chinese economic juggernaut caught the attention of the global business community—and charged onto the U.S. political stage, as China's growth fueled concerns about job losses in the United States.

Yet at the same time many economists and financial commentators worried that the Chinese expansion—which was fueling rising living standards in a rapidly developing economy with 1.3 billion people—would come to an end. Indeed, the debate seemed to be over whether China's boom would have a "soft landing" (with gradually declining growth) or a "hard landing" (possibly leading to an economic financial crisis).

Why? Although China's saving rate was estimated to be a very high 40 percent of GDP, the financial system was doing a poor job of allocating capital. Excessive expansion in office construction and factories was fueled less by careful financial analysis than by the directions of national and local government officials trying to encourage growth. With nonperforming loans—where the borrower cannot make promised payments to lenders—at unheard-of levels, China's banks were in financial trouble. Worse still, they continued to lend to weak, politically connected borrowers.

China's prospects for long-term economic growth depend importantly on a better developed financial system to generate information for borrowers and lenders. Many economists have urged Chinese officials to improve accounting transparency and information disclosure so that stock and bond markets can flourish. In the absence of well-functioning financial markets, banks are crucial allocators of capital. There, too, information disclosure and less government direction of lending will help oil the Chinese growth machine in the long run.

Chinese firms, like Changhong, may well play a major role on the world's economic stage. For Chinese firms to add enough value to raise the standard of living for Chinese workers over the long run, though, China's creaky financial system needs repair.

Will China's weak financial system derail economic growth?

What kind of information do investors and firm managers need? A firm must answer three basic questions: what to produce, how to produce it, and what price to charge. To answer these questions, a firm's managers need two pieces of information: The first is the firm's revenues and costs, and the second is the value of the property and other assets the firm owns and the firm's debts, or other **liabilities,** that it owes to other persons and firms. Potential investors in the firm also need this information to decide whether to buy the firm's stocks or bonds. Managers and investors find this information in the firm's *financial statements,* principally its

Liability Anything owed by a person or a firm.

income statement and balance sheet. We discuss each of these statements and then use them to understand the business scandals of 2002 we mentioned at the beginning of this chapter.

The Income Statement

Income statement A financial statement that sums up a firm's revenues, costs, and profit over a period of time.

A firm's **income statement** sums up its revenues, costs, and profit over a period of time. Corporations issue annual income statements, although the 12-month *fiscal year* covered may be different from the calendar year to reflect the seasonal pattern of the business better. We explore an income statement in greater detail in the appendix to this chapter.

GETTING TO ACCOUNTING PROFIT The income statement shows a firm's revenue, costs, and profit for the firm's fiscal year. To determine profitability, the income statement starts with the firm's revenue and subtracts its operating expenses and taxes paid. The remainder, *net income*, is the **accounting profit** of the firm.

Accounting profit A firm's net income measured by revenue less operating expenses and taxes paid.

Opportunity cost The highest-valued alternative that must be given up to engage in an activity.

Explicit cost A cost that involves spending money.

Implicit cost A nonmonetary opportunity cost.

. . . AND ECONOMIC PROFIT Accounting profit is not the ideal measure of a firm's profits because it neglects some of the firm's costs. Remember that economists always measure cost as *opportunity cost*. The **opportunity cost** of any activity is the highest-valued alternative that must be given up to engage in that activity. Costs are either *explicit* or *implicit*. When the firm spends money, an **explicit cost** results. If the firm incurs an opportunity cost but does not spend money, an **implicit cost** results. For example, firms pay explicit labor costs to employees. They have many other explicit costs as well, such as the cost of the electricity used to light their office buildings.

Some costs are implicit, however. The most important of these is the opportunity cost to investors of the funds they have invested in the firm. Economists refer to the minimum amount that investors must earn on the funds they invest in a firm, expressed as a percentage of the amount invested, as a *normal rate of return*. If a firm fails to provide investors with at least a normal rate of return, it will not be able to remain in business over the long run because investors will not continue to invest their funds in the firm. For example, Bethlehem Steel was once the second-leading producer of steel in the United States and a very profitable firm with stock that sold for more than $50 per share. By 2002, investors became convinced that the firm's uncompetitive labor costs in world markets meant that the firm would never be able to provide investors with a normal rate of return. Many investors expected the firm would eventually have to declare bankruptcy, and as a result, the price of Bethlehem Steel's stock plummeted to $1 per share. Shortly thereafter the firm declared bankruptcy, and its remaining assets were sold off to a competing steel firm. The return (in dollars) that investors require to continue investing in the firm is a true cost to the firm and should be subtracted from the firm's revenues to calculate its profits.

The necessary rate of return that investors must receive to continue investing in a firm varies from firm to firm. If the investment is risky—as would be the case with a biotechnology start-up—investors will require a high rate of return to compensate them for the risk. Investors in firms in more established industries, such as electric utilities, may require lower rates of return. With respect to any particular firm, the exact rate of return required by investors is difficult to calculate, which also makes it difficult to include in an income statement. Firms have other implicit costs besides the return required by investors that can also be difficult to calculate. As a result, the rules of accounting generally require that only explicit costs be recognized for purposes of keeping the firm's financial records and for paying taxes. *Economic costs* include both explicit costs *and* implicit costs. **Economic profit** is equal to the firm's revenues minus all of its costs, implicit and explicit. Because accounting profit excludes some implicit costs, it will be larger than economic profit.

Economic profit A firm's revenues minus all of its costs, implicit and explicit.

The Balance Sheet

A firm's **balance sheet** sums up its financial position on a particular day, usually the end of a quarter or a year. We analyze a balance sheet in detail in the appendix to this chapter. Recall that an asset is anything of value that the firm owns, and a liability is a debt or obligation owed by the firm. Subtracting the value of a firm's liabilities from the value of its assets leaves its *net worth*. We can think of the net worth as what the firm's owners would be left with if the firm were closed, its assets were sold, and its liabilities were paid off. Investors can determine a firm's net worth by inspecting its balance sheet.

Balance sheet A financial statement that sums up a firm's financial position on a particular day, usually the end of a quarter or a year.

Understanding the Business Scandals of 2002

(5) LEARNING OBJECTIVE

Understand the business accounting scandals of 2002, as well as the role of government in corporate governance.

A firm's financial statements provide important information on the firm's ability to add value for investors and the economy. Accurate and easy-to-understand financial statements are inputs for decisions by the firm's managers and investors. Indeed, the information in accounting statements helps guide resource allocation in the economy.

Firms disclose financial statements in periodic filings to the federal government and in *annual reports* to shareholders. An investor is more likely to buy a firm's stock if the firm's income statement shows a large after-tax profit and if its balance sheet shows a large net worth. The top management of a firm has at least two reasons to attract investors and keep the firm's stock price high. First, a higher stock price increases the funds the firm can raise when it sells a given amount of stock. Second, to reduce the principal-agent problem, boards of directors will often tie the salaries of top managers to the firm's stock price or to the profitability of the firm.

Top managers clearly have an incentive to maximize the profits reported on the income statement and the net worth reported on the balance sheet. If top managers make good decisions, the firm's profits will be high, and the firm's assets will be large relative to its liabilities. The business scandals that came to light in 2002 revealed, however, that some top managers inflated profits and hid liabilities that should have been listed on their balance sheets.

At Enron, an energy trading firm, chief financial officer Andrew Fastow was accused of creating partnerships that were supposedly independent of Enron, but in fact were owned by the firm. He was accused of transferring large amounts of Enron's debts to these partnerships, which reduced the liabilities on Enron's balance sheet, thereby increasing the firm's net worth. Falstow's deception made Enron more attractive to investors, increasing its stock price—and Fastow's compensation. In 2001, however, Enron was forced into bankruptcy. The firm's shareholders lost billions of dollars, and many employees lost their jobs. In 2004, Fastow pleaded guilty to conspiracy and was sentenced to 10 years in federal prison.

At WorldCom, a telecommunications firm, David Myers, the firm's controller, pleaded guilty to falsifying "WorldCom's books, to reduce WorldCom's reported actual costs and therefore increase WorldCom's reported earnings." Myers's actions caused WorldCom's income statement to overstate the firm's profits by more than $10 billion. The scandals at Enron and WorldCom were the largest cases of corporate fraud in U.S. history.

How was it possible for corporations such as Enron and WorldCom to falsify their financial statements? The federal government does regulate how financial statements are prepared, but this regulation cannot by itself guarantee the accuracy of the statements. All firms that issue stock to the public have their statements *audited* by a certified public accountant. The accountant is an employee of an accounting firm, *not* of the firm being audited. The audit is intended to provide investors with an independent opinion as to whether the firm's financial statements fairly reflect the true financial condition of the firm. Unfortunately, as the Enron and WorldCom scandals revealed, top managers who are determined to deceive investors about the true financial condition of their firms also can deceive outside auditors.

The private sector's response to the corporate scandals was almost immediate. In addition to the reexamination of corporate governance practices at many corporations, the New York Stock Exchange and the NASDAQ put forth initiatives to ensure the accuracy and accessibility of information.

To guard against future scandals, new federal legislation was enacted in 2002. The landmark *Sarbanes-Oxley Act* of 2002 requires that corporate directors have a certain level of expertise with financial information and mandates that chief executive officers personally certify the accuracy of financial statements. The Sarbanes-Oxley Act also requires that financial analysts and auditors disclose whether any conflicts of interest might exist that would limit their independence in evaluating a firm's financial condition. The purpose of this provision is to ensure that analysts and auditors are acting in the best interests of shareholders. The Act promotes management accountability by specifying the responsibilities of corporate officers and by increasing penalties (including long jail sentences) for managers who do not meet their responsibilities.

Perhaps the most noticeable corporate governance reform under the Sarbanes-Oxley Act is the creation of the Public Company Accounting Oversight Board, a special national board to oversee the auditing of public companies' financial reports. The board's mission is to promote the independence of auditors to ensure they disclose accurate information. On balance, most observers acknowledge that the Sarbanes-Oxley Act brought back confidence in the U.S. corporate governance system, though questions remain for the future about whether the Act may chill legitimate business risk-taking by diverting management attention from the core business toward regulatory compliance. And the high accounting costs of implementing Sarbanes-Oxley are borne by all shareholders.

Outside the United States, the European Commission released plans in 2003 to tighten corporate governance rules, and Japan has debated such reforms as well. The challenge of ensuring the accurate reporting of firms' economic profits is a global one.

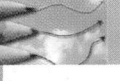

SOLVED PROBLEM　　7-2

⑤ LEARNING OBJECTIVE

Understand the business accounting scandals of 2002, as well as the role of government in corporate governance.

What Makes a Good Board of Directors?

Business Week magazine has listed 3M Company as having one of the best boards of directors of any U.S. corporation:

> With just one insider on its nine-member board, the company gets high marks for independence. Outside directors include the CEOs of Lockheed-Martin, Allstate, and Amgen. . . . No directors have business ties to the company.

a. What is an "insider" on a board of directors?

b. Why might having too many insiders be a problem?

c. Why would having outside directors who are CEOs of large firms be a good thing?

d. Why would directors not having business ties to the firm be a good thing?

Source: "The Best Boards and the Worst Boards," *Business Week*, October 7, 2002, p. 107.

Solving the Problem:

Step 1: Review the chapter material. The context of this problem is the business scandals of 2002 and the underlying principal-agent problem that arises because of the separation of ownership from control in large corporations, so you may want to review the section "Understanding the Business Scandals of 2002," which begins on page 211.

Step 2: Answer question (a) by defining "insiders." "Insiders" are members of top management who also serve on the board of directors.

Step 3: Answer question (b) by explaining why having too many insiders on a board may be a problem. Having members of top management on the board of directors provides the board with information about the firm that only top managers possess. Having too many insiders on a board, however, means that top managers may end up controlling the board rather than the other way around. A corporation's board of directors is supposed to provide the monitoring and control of top managers that shareholders cannot provide directly.

Step 4: Answer question (c) by explaining why having directors who are CEOs of large firms may be a good thing. Members of boards of directors are sometimes retired politicians, academics, or philanthropists. Although these people may be well intentioned and hard working, some of them may lack the knowledge and experience to successfully monitor top managers. CEOs of other large corporations, on the other hand, do have the experience to judge better whether top managers are making decisions in the best interests of the firm.

Step 5: Answer question (d) by stating why directors should not have business ties to the firm. If a CEO of Firm 1 sits on the board of directors of Firm 2, she is an outside director, but if her company does a significant amount of business with Firm 2, she may be reluctant to do anything to displease the top managers because the top managers have the power to stop doing business with her firm.

YOUR TURN: For more practice, do related problems 16 and 17 on page 218 at the end of this chapter. Visit www.prenhall.com/hubbard for an interactive exercise related to this Solved Problem.

Conclusion

In a market system, firms make independent decisions about which goods and services to produce, how to produce them, and what prices to charge. In modern high-income countries, such as the United States, large corporations account for a majority of the sales and profits earned by firms. Generally, the managers of these corporations do a good job of representing the interests of stockholders, while providing the goods and services demanded by consumers. As the business scandals of 2002 showed, however, some top managers enriched themselves at the expense of stockholders and consumers by manipulating financial statements. Legislative strengthening of financial regulation in the Sarbanes-Oxley Act of 2002 and greater financial market scrutiny of financial statements have helped restore investor and management confidence in firms' financial statements.

Read *An Inside Look* on the next page about Google's initial pubic offering (IPO) for a discussion of the role expectations of future profits play in determining stock prices.

An Inside Look   Google's Initial Public Offering

WALL STREET JOURNAL, JANUARY 3, 2005

Technology Shares Slip, But Google Passes $200

Google shares soared past $200 Monday, with an upbeat note from Goldman Sachs buoying Web search stocks as the broader technology market fell. Goldman Sachs raised its earnings and revenue estimates for Google and Yahoo, sending Google shares up $9.92, or 5.1%, to $202.71 on the Nasdaq Stock Market. It was the company's highest close since its initial public offering, and marked the first time the search giant's shares finished above the $200 mark.

Search companies fared well last year, helped by Google's high-profile IPO in August. Since then, the company's shares have more than doubled. Goldman raised its fourth-quarter revenue estimate for Google to $592 million from $579 million. The firm also increased its earnings-per-share forecast to 76 cents from 74 cents.

The Goldman note helped push other search stocks higher. Yahoo climbed 50 cents to $38.18 on Nasdaq as Goldman increased its fourth-quarter sales estimate for the company to $773 million from $747 million.

The note also lifted search rival Ask Jeeves $1.07, or 4%, to $27.82 on Nasdaq.

But the broader tech market didn't fare as well, with lackluster manufacturing numbers for December and the onset of jitters ahead of this month's slew of earnings news. The Nasdaq Composite Index shed 23.29, or 1.1%, to close at 2152.15 in the first session of the new year. The tech heavy index gained 8.6% last year.

Morgan Stanley's high-tech index declined 5.17 to 502.50, and the Nasdaq 100 Index of nonfinancial stocks fell 17.61 to 1603.51.

Among some individual stocks, Sun Microsystems lost 28 cents, or 5.2%, to $5.11 on Nasdaq after Sanford Bernstein cut the network giant's shares to "underperform" from "market perform." The firm says the company's calendar fourth quarter didn't experience a material acceleration, and that it doesn't see upside to its revenue expectations for the fiscal second-quarter of 2005.

Shares of Corning eased 6 cents to $11.71 on the Big Board after the technology giant announced that the Chinese Ministry of Commerce found Saturday that the company had not dumped standard single-mode optical fiber into the Chinese market.

Nortel Networks rose 6 cents to $3.55 on the New York Stock Exchange. The telecommunications-equipment supplier said the Big Board has granted it an additional three months to file its 2003 annual report with the Securities and Exchange Commission. The exchange will allow Nortel to continue listing while the company continues to sort through accounting irregularities in 2003.

Shares of Tellabs gained 59 cents, or 6.9%, to $9.18 on Nasdaq after Robert W. Baird upgraded the maker of telecom equipment to "outperform" from "neutral." Analysts expect solid bookings due to improved international and fiber-to-the-premises business.

Key Points in the Article

The Money and Investing section (or C section) of the *Wall Street Journal* is devoted to analyzing the stock and bond markets. Because technology stocks, such as Google, have been an important part of the stock market, the *Wall Street Journal* prints an article each day called "Tech Stocks." This particular article discusses price changes in the stocks of Google, Ask Jeeves, Nortel, and several other companies. In each case, the author attempts to explain why the prices of the stocks changed as they did.

Analyzing the News

a Buying a share of stock in Google, or any other firm, means buying part ownership of the firm. As a part owner, you have a claim to your share of the firm's profits. Therefore, firms that earn large profits have high stock prices. Investors are always searching for new information on the future profitability of firms. In the instance discussed here, an analyst for Goldman Sachs, an investment firm, issued a "research note" that forecast higher profits for Google than most investors had been expecting. Apparently, enough investors believed the Goldman Sachs analyst was correct, because demand for Google's shares increased, raising the price per share by almost $10 during the day.

Google sold stock to the public for the first time on August 19, 2004. This *initial public offering,* or IPO, was unusual because the firm used an Internet auction to determine the price and who would receive the shares. Most firms use investment bankers to handle their IPOs, with the result that small investors sometimes have difficulty buying shares on the day they are first issued. Figure 1 shows movements in the price of Google's stock from the time of the IPO through mid-January 2005.

b As discussed earlier in this chapter, the stocks of many computer and other high-technology firms, including Google, are traded on NASDAQ. The NASDAQ Composite Index declined during the day discussed in the article. The NASDAQ Composite Index converts the stock prices of all the stocks that are traded on Nasdaq into a single index number. This index makes it possible for investors to gauge the overall performance of these stocks. Although the stocks of some firms, such as Google and Ask Jeeves, rose during the day, investors at that time were worried about the profitability of high-technology firms, so on average, the prices of NASDAQ stocks declined.

c In the chapter, we discussed some of the accounting problems that had plagued many firms. For a firm's stock to be traded on the New York Stock Exchange—the "Big Board"—the firm needs to meet certain requirements, including the filing of accurate financial statements with the Securities and Exchange Commission. Failure to meet these requirements can cause a firm to be "delisted," which means its stock can no longer be traded on the Big Board. Being delisted makes it extremely difficult for a firm to continue selling stock. Nortel, which is based in Ontario, Canada, and manufactures telecommunications equipment, had failed to file its 2003 annual report with the Securities and Exchange Commission because the firm had discovered accounting irregularities that resulted in its reported profits being higher than its actual profits. The firm had fired ten executives and finance officials. Several of the executives gave back $8.6 million in salary bonuses they had received on the basis of the firm's profits being overstated.

Thinking Critically
ABOUT POLICY

1. According to Figure 1, on October 22, 2004, Google's stock was selling for about $150 per share, then Google reported its net profit at $52 million and the stock's price jumped to over $175 per share.
   a. Did investors as a group expect the stock to jump by over $25 per share before the company announced its net profit?
   b. Do stocks' prices always jump upward when companies announce that they've earned a profit? Explain.
2. Someone who knew that Google was about to announce a big profit—for example, someone in Google's top management—could have earned a bundle quickly by buying Google stock at $150 per share and then selling it at $175 per share a day or so later. Such "insider trading" is illegal, however. Do you think that "insider trading" should be illegal? What are the benefits associated with it? What are the problems associated with it?

Source: *Wall Street Journal,* Eastern Edition [Staff produced copy only] by Vauhina Vara. Copyright 2005 by Dow Jones & Co., Inc. Reproduced with permission of Dow Jones & Co., Inc. in the format Textbook via Copyright Clearance Center.

Figure 1: Movements in Google's stock price, August 2004–January 2005.

SUMMARY

LEARNING OBJECTIVE ① **Categorize the major types of business in the United States.** There are three types of firms: *sole proprietorships, partnerships,* and *corporations.* The owners of sole proprietorships and partners have *unlimited liability,* which means there is no legal distinction between the personal assets of the owners of the business and the assets of the business. The owners of corporations have *limited liability,* which means they can never lose more than their investment in the firm. Although only 20 percent of firms are corporations, they account for the majority of revenue and profit earned by all firms.

LEARNING OBJECTIVE ② **Describe the typical management structure of corporations and understand the concepts of separation of ownership from control and the principal-agent problem.** Most corporations have a similar management structure: The shareholders elect a board of directors that appoints the corporation's top managers, such as the chief executive officer. Because the top management often does not own a large fraction of the stock in the corporation, large corporations have a *separation of ownership from control.* Because top managers have less incentive to increase the corporation's profits than to increase their own salaries and their own enjoyment, corporations can suffer from a *principal-agent problem.* A principal-agent problem exists when the principals—in this case, the shareholders of the corporation—have difficulty in getting the agent—the corporation's top management—to carry out their wishes.

LEARNING OBJECTIVE ③ **Explain how firms obtain the funds they need to operate and expand.** Firms rely on *retained earnings*—which are profits retained by the firm and not paid out to the firm's owners—or on using the savings of households for the funds they need to operate and expand. The savings of households flow directly to businesses when investors buy stocks and bonds in financial markets. Savings flow indirectly to businesses when households deposit money in saving and checking accounts in banks and the banks lend these funds to businesses. Federal, state, and local governments also sell bonds in financial markets and households also borrow funds from banks. When a firm sells a bond, it is borrowing money from the buyer of the bond. When a firm sells stock, it is selling part ownership of the firm to the buyer of the stock. The original purchasers of stocks and bonds may resell them in stock and bond markets, such as the New York Stock Exchange.

LEARNING OBJECTIVE ④ **Understand the information provided in firms' financial statements.** A firm's *income statement* sums up its revenues, costs, and profit over a period of time. A firm's *balance sheet* sums up its financial position on a particular day, usually the end of a quarter or year. Firms report their *accounting profit* on their income statements. Because accounting profit excludes some implicit costs, it is larger than *economic profit.*

LEARNING OBJECTIVE ⑤ **Understand the business accounting scandals of 2002, as well as the role of government in corporate governance.** Because their compensation often rises with the profitability of the corporation, top managers have an incentive to overstate the profits reported on their firm's income statements. During 2002, it became clear that the top managers of several large corporations had done this, even though intentionally falsifying financial statements is illegal. The *Sarbanes-Oxley Act* of 2002 and greater scrutiny of financial statements have helped to restore investor and management confidence in firm's financial statements.

KEY TERMS

Accounting profit 210
Asset 200
Balance sheet 211
Bond 205
Corporate governance 202
Corporation 200
Coupon payment 205

Direct finance 204
Dividends 205
Economic profit 210
Explicit cost 210
Implicit cost 210
Income statement 210

Indirect finance 204
Interest rate 205
Liability 209
Limited liability 200
Opportunity cost 210
Partnership 200

Principal-agent
  problem 203
Separation of ownership
  from control 203
Sole proprietorship 200
Stock 205

REVIEW QUESTIONS

1. What are the three major types of business in the United States? Briefly discuss the most important characteristics of each type.

2. What is limited liability? Why are owners of corporations granted limited liability by the government?

3. What do we mean by the separation of ownership from control in large corporations? How is this related to the principal-agent problem?

4. What is the difference between direct finance and indirect finance? If you borrow money from a bank to buy a new car, are you using direct finance or indirect finance?

5. Why is a bond considered to be a loan but a share of stock is not? Why do corporations issue both bonds and shares of stock?

6. How do the stock and bond markets provide information to businesses? Why do stock and bond prices change over time?

7. What is the Sarbanes-Oxley Act? Why was it passed?

PROBLEMS AND APPLICATIONS

Please visit **www.prenhall.com/hubbard** *for solutions to the even-numbered problems as well as multiple-choice and true or false self-assessment quizzes.*

1. Suppose that shortly after graduating from college you decide to start your own business. Will you organize the business as a sole proprietorship, a partnership, or a corporation? Explain your reasoning.

2. In a May 10, 2003, opinion piece in the *New York Times,* sociologist Dalton Conley proposed the *elimination* of limited liability to corporate shareholders. Do you think that corporations should be granted limited liability? What are the benefits of limited liability? What is its downside? Would you be more willing to buy bonds from a company with limited liability? Would you be more willing to buy the stock of a company with limited liability?

3. Suppose that a firm in which you have invested is losing money. Would you rather own the firm's stock or the firm's bonds? Explain.

4. Suppose you originally invested in a firm when it was small and unprofitable. Now the firm has grown considerably and is large and profitable. Would you be better off if you had bought the firm's stock or the firm's bonds? Explain.

5. The principal-agent problem arises almost everywhere in the business world—but it also crops up even closer to home. Discuss the principal-agent problem that exists in the college classroom. Who is the principal? Who is the agent? What is the problem between this principal and this agent?

6. [Related to *Solved Problem 7-1*] Briefly explain whether you agree or disagree with the following argument: "The separation of ownership from control in large corporations and the principal-agent problem means that top managers can work short days, take long vacations, and otherwise slack off."

7. [Related to *Solved Problem 7-1*] An economic consultant gives the board of directors of a firm the following advice: "You can increase the profitability of the firm if you change your method of compensating top management. Instead of paying your top management a straight salary, you should pay them a salary plus give them the right to buy the firm's stock in the future at a price above the stock's current market price." Explain the consultant's reasoning. To what difficulties might this compensation scheme lead?

8. The following is from an article in the *New York Times:*

   > In theory, boards [of directors] design pay packages to attract and inspire good chief executives and to align their interests with those of shareholders. . . . But what kind of pay packages are appropriate at companies still run by the founding family?

   The article quotes one expert as arguing: "There is little or no justification for treating an owner-manager in exactly the same way as a standard CEO."

   What does the article mean by saying that pay packages should "align [chief executives'] interests with those of shareholders"? What kind of pay packages would achieve this objective? Do you agree that an "owner-manager" should have a pay package different from that of a CEO who is not a member of the family that started the firm? Briefly explain.

   Source: Diana B. Henriques, "What's Fair Pay for Running the Family Store?," *New York Times,* January 12, 2003.

9. If you deposit $20,000 in a savings account at a bank, you might earn 3 percent interest per year. Someone who borrows $20,000 from a bank to buy a new car might have to pay an interest rate of 8 percent per year on the loan. Knowing this, why don't you just lend your money directly to the car buyer, cutting out the bank?

10. [Related to the *Chapter Opener*] When Google's owners wanted to raise funds for expansion in 2004, they decided to sell stock in their company rather than to borrow the money. Why do some companies fund their expansion by borrowing, while others fund expansion by issuing new stock?

11. The following listing for a corporate bond issued by Sara Lee Corporation appeared in the *Wall Street Journal* on May 4, 2005:

COUPON	MATURITY	LAST PRICE	LAST YIELD	EST SPREAD	UST	EST $ VOL (000s)
3.875	June 15, 2013	91.047	5.244	108	10	84,860

   a. If you bought this bond, what is the total coupon payment you would receive during the next year (in dollars)?

   b. For what price did this bond sell at the close of trading on May 3?

   c. What was the yield on a 30-year U.S. Treasury bond on May 3?

12. Consider again the information for the Sara Lee bond in problem 11. Why weren't investors willing to pay $1,000 for this bond, which has a face value of $1,000?

13. In 2005, the French government began issuing bonds with 50-year maturities. Would this bond be purchased only by very young investors who expect to still be alive when the bond matures? Briefly explain.

14. [Related to *Don't Let This Happen To You!*] Briefly explain whether you agree or disagree with the following statement: "The total value of the shares of Microsoft stock traded on the NASDAQ last week was $250 million, so the firm actually received more revenue from stock sales than from selling software."

15. Loans from banks are the most important external source of funds to businesses because most businesses are too small to borrow in financial markets by issuing stocks or bonds. Most investors are reluctant to buy the stocks or bonds of small businesses because of the difficulty of gathering accurate information on the financial strength and profitability of the businesses. Nevertheless, news about the stock market is included in nearly every network news program and is often the lead story in the business section of most newspapers. Is there a contradiction here? Why is the average viewer of TV news or the average reader of a newspaper interested in the fluctuations in prices in the stock market?

16. [Related to *Solved Problem 7-2*] In the fall of 2002, Buford Yates, director of accounting at WorldCom, pleaded guilty to fraud. In federal court he said that top managers at WorldCom ordered him to make certain adjustments to the firm's financial statements.

> I came to believe that the adjustments I was being directed to make in WorldCom's financial statements had no justification and contravened generally accepted accounting principles. I concluded that the purpose of these adjustments was to incorrectly inflate WorldCom's reported earnings.

What are "generally accepted accounting principles"? How would the "adjustments" Yates was ordered to make benefit top managers at WorldCom? Would these adjustments also benefit WorldCom's stockholders? Briefly explain.
Source: Devlin Barrett, "Ex-WorldCom Exec Pleads Guilty," Associated Press, October 8, 2002.

17. [Related to *Solved Problem 7-2*] In 2002, *Business Week* listed Apple Computer as having one of the worst boards of directors:

> Founder Steve Jobs owns just two shares in the company. . . . The CEO of Micro Warehouse, which accounted for nearly 2.9% of Apple's net sales in 2001, sits on the compensation committee. . . . There is an interlocking directorship—with Gap CEO Mickey Drexler and Jobs sitting on each other's boards.

Why might investors be concerned that a top manager like Steve Jobs owns only two shares in the firm? Why might investors be concerned if a member of the board of directors also has a business relationship with the firm? What is an "interlocking directorship"? Why is it a bad thing?
Source: "The Best Boards and the Worst Boards," *Business Week*, October 7, 2002, p. 107.

18. The following is from a *Business Week* editorial:

> Welcome to the revolution. After years of paying lip service to reform, Enron Corp. and the ensuing wave of business scandal has finally produced a dramatic change in corporate governance. . . . [I]nvestors are rewarding companies with good governance and punishing those without it.

How are investors able to reward or punish firms? What impact will these rewards and punishments have on boards of directors and top managers?
Source: "Boardrooms Are Starting to Wake Up," *Business Week*, October 7, 2002, p. 107.

19. Dane decides to give up a job earning $100,000 per year as a corporate lawyer and converts the duplex that he owns into a UFO museum. (He had been renting out the duplex for $20,000 a year.) His direct expenses include $50,000 per year paid to his assistants and $10,000 per year for utilities. Fans flock to the museum to see his collection of extraterrestrial paraphernalia, which he easily could sell on eBay for $1,000,000. Over the course of the year, the museum brings in revenues of $100,000.
  a. How much is Dane's accounting profit for the year?
  b. Is he earning an economic profit? Explain.

20. **[Related to the *Chapter Opener*]** What impact would these events be likely to have on the price of Google's stock?
  a. A competitor launches a search engine that's just as good as Google's.
  b. The corporate income tax is abolished.
  c. Google's board of directors becomes dominated by close friends and relatives of its top management.
  d. The price of wireless Internet connections unexpectedly drops, so more and more people use the Internet.
  e. Google announces a huge profit of $1 billion, but everybody anticipated that Google would earn a huge profit of $1 billion.

Tools to Analyze Firms' Financial Information

As we saw in the chapter, modern business organizations are not just "black boxes" transforming inputs into output. Most business revenues and profits are earned by large corporations. Unlike founder-dominated firms, the typical large corporation is run by managers who generally do not own a controlling interest in the firm. Large firms raise funds from outside investors, and outside investors seek information on firms and the assurance that the managers of firms will act in the interests of the investors.

This chapter showed how corporations raise funds by issuing stocks and bonds. This appendix provides more detail to support that discussion. We begin by analyzing *present value* as a key concept in determining the prices of financial securities. We then provide greater information on *financial statements* issued by corporations, using Google as an example.

Using Present Value to Make Investment Decisions

Firms raise funds equity (stock) and debt (bonds and loans) to investors and lenders. If you own shares of stock or a bond, you will receive payments in the form of dividends or coupons over a number of years. Most people value funds they already have more highly than funds they will not receive until some time in the future. For example, you would probably not trade $1,000 you already have for $1,000 you will not receive for one year. The longer you will have to wait to receive a payment, the less value it will have for you. One thousand dollars you will not receive for two years is worth less to you than $1,000 you will receive after one year. The value you give today to money you will receive in the future is called the future payment's **present value.** The present value of $1,000 you will receive in one year will be less than $1,000.

Why is this true? Why is the $1,000 you will not receive for one year less valuable to you than the $1,000 you already have? The most important reason is that if you have $1,000 today, you can use that $1,000 today. You can buy goods and services with the money and receive enjoyment from them. The $1,000 you receive in one year does not have direct use to you now.

Also, prices likely will rise during the year you are waiting to receive your $1,000. So, when you finally do receive the $1,000 in one year you will not be able to buy as much with it as you could with $1,000 today. Finally, there is some risk that you will not receive the $1,000 in one year. The risk may be very great if an unreliable friend borrows $1,000 from you and vaguely promises to pay you back in one year. The risk may be very small when you lend money to the federal government by buying a United States Treasury bond. In either case, there is at least some risk that you will not receive the funds promised.

When someone lends money, the lender expects to be paid back both the amount of the loan and some additional interest. If you decide that to be willing to lend your $1,000 today and you must be paid back $1,100 one year from now, you are charging $100/$1,000 = 0.10 or 10 percent interest on the funds you have loaned. Economists would say that you value $1,000 today as equivalent to the $1,100 to be received one year in the future.

Notice that $1,100 can be written as $1,000 (1 + 0.10). That is, the value of money received in the future is equal to the value of money in the present multiplied by 1 plus the interest rate, with the interest rate expressed as a decimal. Or,

$$\$1,100 = 1,000 (1 + 0.10).$$

Notice, also, that if we divide both sides by (1 + 0.10), we can rewrite this formula as:

$$\$1,000 = \frac{\$1,100}{(1+0.10)}.$$

Present value The value in today's dollars of funds to be paid or received in the future.

The rewritten formula states that the present value is equal to the future value to be received in one year divided by one plus the interest rate. This formula is an important one because it can be used to convert any amount to be received in one year into its present value. Writing the formula generally, we have:

$$\text{Present Value} = \frac{\text{Future Value}_1}{(1+i)}.$$

The present value of funds to be received in one year—Future Value$_1$—can be calculated by dividing the amount of those funds to be received by 1 plus the interest rate. With an interest rate of 10 percent, the present value of $1,000,000 to be received one year from now is:

$$\frac{\$1,000,000}{(1+0.10)} = \$909,090.91.$$

This method is a very useful way of calculating the value today of funds that won't be received for one year. But financial securities such as stocks and bonds involve promises to pay funds over many years. Therefore, it would be even more useful if we could expand this formula to calculate the present value of funds to be received more than one year in the future.

This expansion is easy to do. Go back to the original example where we assumed you were willing to loan out your $1,000 for one year, provided you received 10 percent interest. Suppose you are asked to lend the funds for two years and that you are promised 10 percent interest per year for each year of the loan. That is, you are lending $1,000, which at 10 percent interest will grow to $1,100 after one year, and you are agreeing to loan that $1,100 out for a second year at 10 percent interest. So, after two years you will be paid back $1,100 (1 + 0.10) or $1,210. Or,

$$\$1,210 = \$1,000 (1 + 0.10)(1 + 0.10)$$

or,

$$\$1,210 = \$1,000 (1 + 0.10)^2.$$

This formula can also be rewritten as:

$$\$1,000 = \frac{\$1,210}{(1+0.10)^2}.$$

To put the formula in words, the $1,210 you receive two years from now has a present value equal to $1,210 divided by the quantity 1 plus the interest rate squared. If you were to agree to lend out your $1,000 for three years at 10 percent interest, you would receive:

$$\$1,331 = \$1,000 (1 + 0.10)^3.$$

Notice, again, that:

$$\$1,000 = \frac{\$1,331}{(1+0.10)^3}.$$

You can probably see a pattern here. We can generalize the concept to say that the present value of funds to be received n years in the future—whether n is 1, 20, or 85 does not matter—equals the amount of the funds to be received divided by the quantity 1 plus the interest rate raised to the nth power. For instance, with an interest rate of 10 percent, the value of $1,000,000 to be received 25 years in the future is:

$$\text{Present Value} = \frac{\$1,000,000}{(1+0.10)^{25}} = \$92,296.$$

Or, more generally:

$$\text{Present Value} = \frac{\text{Future Value}_n}{(1+i)^n},$$

where Future Value$_n$ represents funds that will be received in n years.

SOLVED PROBLEM 7A-1

How to Receive Your Contest Winnings

Suppose you win a contest and are given the choice of the following prizes:

Prize 1: $50,000 to be received right away, with four additional payments of $50,000 to be received each year for the next four years
Prize 2: $175,000 to be received right away

Explain which prize you would choose and the basis for your decision.

Solving the Problem:
Step 1: Review the material. This problem involves applying the concept of present value, so you may want to review the section "Using Present Value to Make Investment Decisions," which begins on page 220.

Step 2: Explain the basis for choosing the prize. Unless you need immediate cash, you should choose the prize with the highest present value.

Step 3: Calculate the present value of each prize. Prize 2 consists of one payment of $175,000 received right away, so its present value is $175,000. Prize 1 consists of five payments spread out over time. To find the present value of the prize, we must find the present value of each of these payments and add them together. To calculate present value we must use an interest rate. Let's assume an interest rate of 10 percent. In that case the present value of Prize 1 is:

$$\$50,000 + \frac{\$50,000}{(1+0.10)} + \frac{\$50,000}{(1+0.10)^2} + \frac{\$50,000}{(1+0.10)^3} + \frac{\$50,000}{(1+0.10)^4} =$$

$$\$50,000 + \$45,454.55 + \$41,322.31 + \$37,565.74 + \$34,150.67 = \$208,493.$$

Step 4: State your conclusion. Prize 1 has the greater present value, so you should choose it rather than Prize 2.

YOUR TURN: For more practice, do related problems 1, 3, 4, and 5 on page 228 at the end of this appendix. Visit www.prenhall.com/hubbard for an interactive exercise related to this Solved Problem.

Using Present Value to Calculate Bond Prices

Anyone who buys a financial asset, such as shares of stock or a bond, is really buying a promise to receive certain payments—dividends in the case of shares of stock or coupons in the case of a bond. The price investors are willing to pay for a financial asset should be equal to the value of the payments they will receive as a result of owning the asset. Because most of the coupon or dividend payments will be received in the future, it is their present value that matters. Put another way, we have the following important idea: *The price of a financial asset should be equal to the present value of the payments to be received from owning that asset.*

Let's consider an example. Suppose that in 1980 General Electric issued a bond with an $80 coupon that will mature in 2010. It is now 2008 and that bond has been bought and sold by investors many times. You are considering buying it. If you buy the bond, you will receive two years of coupon payments plus a final payment of the bond's principal or face value of $1,000. Suppose, once again, that you need an interest rate of 10 percent to invest your funds. If the bond has a coupon of $80, the present value of the payments you receive from owning the bond—and, therefore, the present value of the bond—will be:

$$\text{Present Value} = \frac{\$80}{(1+0.10)} + \frac{\$80}{(1+0.10)^2} + \frac{\$1,000}{(1+0.10)^2} = \$965.29.$$

That is, the present value of the bond will equal the present value of the three payments you will receive during the two years you own the bond. You should, therefore, be willing to pay $965.29 to own this bond and have the right to receive these payments from GE. This process of calculating present values of future payments is used to determine bond prices, with one qualification. The relevant interest rate used by investors in the bond market to calculate the present value and, therefore, the price of an existing bond is usually the coupon rate on comparable newly issued bonds. Therefore, the general formula for the price of a bond is:

$$\text{Bond Price} = \frac{\text{Coupon}_1}{(1+i)} + \frac{\text{Coupon}_2}{(1+i)^2} + \dots + \frac{\text{Coupon}_n}{(1+i)^n} + \frac{\text{Face Value}}{(1+i)^n},$$

where Coupon_1 is the coupon payment to be received after one year, Coupon_2 is the coupon payment to be received after two years, up to Coupon_n, which is the coupon payment received in the year the bond matures. The ellipsis takes the place of the coupon payments—if any—received between the second year and the year the bond matures. Face Value is the face value of the bond, to be received when the bond matures. The interest rate on comparable newly issued bonds is i.

Using Present Value to Calculate Stock Prices

When you own a firm's stock, you are legally entitled to your share of the firm's profits. Remember that the profits a firm pays out to its shareholders are referred to as dividends. The price of a share of stock should be equal to the present value of the dividends investors expect to receive as a result of owning that stock. Therefore, the general formula for the price of a stock is:

$$\text{Stock Price} = \frac{\text{Dividend}_1}{(1+i)} + \frac{\text{Dividend}_2}{(1+i)^2} + \dots$$

Notice that this formula looks very similar to the one we used to calculate the price of a bond, with a couple of important differences. First, unlike a bond, stock has no maturity date, so we have to calculate the present value of an infinite number of dividend payments. At first, it may seem that the stock's price must be infinite as well, but remember that dollars you don't receive for many years are worth very little today. For instance, a dividend payment of $10 that will be received 40 years in the future is worth only a little more than $0.20 today at a 10 percent interest rate. The second difference between the stock price formula and the bond price formula is that whereas the coupon payments you receive from owning the bond are known with certainty—they are written on the bond and cannot be changed—you don't know for sure what the dividend payments from owning a stock will be. How large a dividend payment you will receive depends upon how profitable the company will be in the future.

Although it is possible to forecast the future profitability of a company, this cannot be done with perfect accuracy. To emphasize this point, some economists rewrite the basic stock price formula by adding a superscript *e* to each Dividend term to emphasize that these are *expected* dividend payments. Because the future profitability of companies is often very difficult to forecast, it is not surprising that differences of opinion exist over what the price of a particular stock should be. Some investors will be very optimistic about the future profitability of a company and will, therefore, believe that the company's stock should have a high price. Other investors might be very pessimistic and believe that the company's stock should have a low price.

A Simple Formula for Calculating Stock Prices

It is possible to simplify the formula for determining the price of a stock, if we assume that dividends will grow at a constant rate:

$$\text{Stock Price} = \frac{\text{Dividend}}{(i - \text{Growth Rate})},$$

where Dividend is the dividend being received currently and Growth Rate is the rate at which those dividends are expected to grow. If a company currently is paying a dividend of $1 per share and Growth Rate is 10 percent, the company is expected to pay a dividend of $1.10 next year, $1.21 the year after that, and so on.

Now suppose that IBM currently is paying a dividend of $5 per share, the consensus of investors is that these dividends will increase at a rate of 5 percent per year for the indefinite future, and the interest rate is 10 percent. Then the price of IBM's stock should be:

$$\text{Stock Price} = \frac{\$5.00}{(0.10 - 0.05)} = \$100.00.$$

Particularly during the years 1999 and 2000, there was much discussion of whether the high prices of many Internet stocks—such as the stock of Amazon.com—were justified given that many of these companies had not made any profit yet and so had not paid any dividends. Is there any way that a rational investor would pay a high price for the stock of a company currently not earning profits? The formula for determining stock prices shows that it is possible, provided the investor's assumptions are optimistic enough! For example, during 1999, one stock analyst predicted that Amazon.com would soon be earning $10 per share of stock. That is, Amazon.com's total earnings divided by the number of shares of its stock outstanding would be $10. Suppose Amazon.com pays out that $10 in dividends and that the $10 will grow rapidly over the years, by, say, 7 percent per year. Then our formula indicates that the price of Amazon.com stock should be:

$$\text{Stock Price} = \frac{\$10.00}{(0.10 - 0.07)} = \$333.33.$$

If you are sufficiently optimistic about the future prospects of a company, a high stock price can be justified even if the company currently is not earning a profit. But investors in growth stocks must be careful. Suppose that investors believe that growth prospects for Amazon are only 4 percent per year instead of 7 percent because the firm turns out not to be as profitable as initially believed. Then our formula indicates that the price of Amazon.com stock should be:

$$\text{Stock Price} = \frac{\$10.00}{(0.10 - 0.04)} = \$166.67,$$

or only half the value assuming a more optimistic growth rage. Hence investors use information about firms' profitability and growth prospects to determine what the firm is worth.

Going Deeper into Financial Statements

Corporations disclose substantial information about their business operations and financial position to actual and potential investors. Some of this information meets the demands of participants in financial markets and of information-collection agencies, such as Moody's Investors Service, which develops credit ratings that help investors judge the riskiness of corporate bonds. Other information meets the requirements of the U.S. Securities and Exchange Commission.

Key sources of information about a corporation's profitability and financial position are its principal financial statements—the *income statement* and the *balance sheet*. These important information sources were first introduced in the chapter. Here we go into more detail, using recent data for Google as an example.

Analyzing Income Statements

As discussed in the chapter, a firm's income statement summarizes its revenues, costs, and profit over a period of time. Figure 7A-1 shows Google's income statement for 2004.

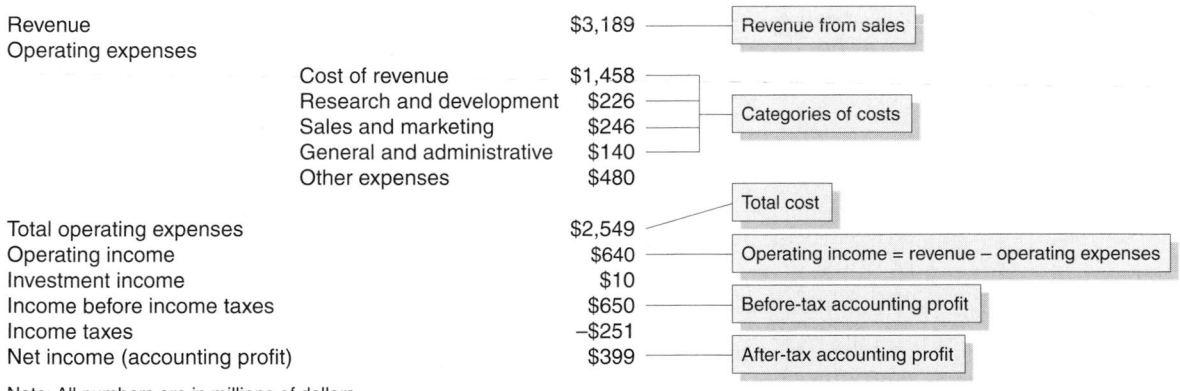

Revenue	$3,189	Revenue from sales
Operating expenses		
Cost of revenue	$1,458	
Research and development	$226	Categories of costs
Sales and marketing	$246	
General and administrative	$140	
Other expenses	$480	
		Total cost
Total operating expenses	$2,549	
Operating income	$640	Operating income = revenue − operating expenses
Investment income	$10	
Income before income taxes	$650	Before-tax accounting profit
Income taxes	−$251	
Net income (accounting profit)	$399	After-tax accounting profit

Note: All numbers are in millions of dollars.

FIGURE 7A-1

Google's Income Statement for 2004

Google's income statement shows the company's revenue, costs, and profit for 2004. The difference between its revenue ($3,189 million) and its operating expenses ($2,549 million) is its operating income ($640 million). Most corporations also have investments, such as government or corporate bonds, that generate some income for them. In this case, Google earned $10 million, giving the firm an income before taxes of $650 million. After paying taxes of $251 million, Google was left with a net income, or accounting profit, of $399 million for the year.

Source: Google's Income Statement for 2004. Google Inc. "Consolidated Statements of Income," February 1, 2005. Used with permission of Google, Inc.

Google's income statement presents the results of the company's operations during the year. Listed first are the revenues it earned, largely from selling advertising on its Web site, from January 1, 2004 to December 31, 2004: $3,189 million. Listed next are Google's operating expenses, the most important of which is its *cost of revenue*—which is commonly known as *cost of sales* or *cost of goods sold*: $1,458 million. Cost of revenue is the direct cost of producing the products sold, including in this case the salaries of the computer programmers Google hires to write the software for its Web site. Google also has substantial costs for researching and developing its products ($226 million) and for advertising and marketing them ($246 million). General and administrative expenses ($140 million) includes costs such as the salaries of top managers.

The difference between a firm's revenue and its costs is its profit. "Profit" shows up in several forms on an income statement. A firm's *operating income* is the difference between its revenue and its operating expenses. Most corporations, including Google, also have investments, such as government and corporate bonds, that normally generate some income for them. In this case, Google earned $10 million on its investments, which increased its *income before taxes* to $650 million. The federal government taxes the profits of corporations. During 2004, Google paid $251 million—or about 39 percent of its profits—in taxes. *Net income* after taxes was $399 million. The net income that firms report on their income statements is referred to as their after-tax *accounting profit*.

Analyzing Balance Sheets

As discussed in the chapter, whereas a firm's income statement reports a firm's activities for a period of time, a firm's balance sheet summarizes its financial position on a particular day, usually the end of a quarter or a year. To understand how a balance sheet is organized, first recall that an asset is anything of value that the firm owns and a liability is a debt or obligation owed by the firm. Subtracting the value of a firm's liabilities from the value of its assets leaves its *net worth*. Because a corporation's stockholders are its owners, net worth is often listed as **stockholders' equity** on a balance sheet. Using these definitions, we can state the balance sheet equation (also called the basic accounting equation) as follows:

Stockholders' equity The difference between the value of a corporation's assets and the value of its liabilities; also known as net worth.

$$\text{Assets} - \text{Liabilities} = \text{Stockholders' Equity}$$

or,

$$\text{Assets} = \text{Liabilities} + \text{Stockholders' Equity.}$$

This formula tells us that the value of a firm's assets must equal the value of its liabilities plus the value of stockholders' equity. An important accounting rule dating back to the beginning of modern bookkeeping in fifteenth-century Italy holds that balance sheets should list assets on the left side and liabilities and net worth or stockholders' equity on the right side. Notice that this means that *the value of the left side of the balance sheet must always equal the value of the right side.* Figure 7A-2 shows Google's balance sheet as of December 31, 2004.

A couple of the entries on the asset side of the balance sheet may be unfamiliar: *Current assets* are assets that the firm could convert into cash quickly, such as the balance in its checking account or its accounts receivable, which is money currently owed to the firm for products that have been delivered but not yet paid for. *Goodwill* represents the difference between the purchase price of a company and the market value of its assets. It represents the ability of a business to earn an economic profit from its assets. For example, if you buy a restaurant that is located on a busy intersec-

ASSETS		LIABILITIES AND STOCKHOLDERS' EQUITY	
Current assets	$2,693	Current liabilities	$340
Property and equipment	379	Long-term liabilities	44
Investments	71	Total liabilities	384
Goodwill	123	Stockholders' equity	2,929
Other long-term assets	47		
Total assets	3,313	Total liabilities and stockholders' equity	3,313

FIGURE 7A-2

Google's Balance Sheet as of December 31, 2004

Corporations list their assets on the left of their balance sheets and their liabilities on the right. The difference between the value of the firm's assets and the value of its liabilities equals the net worth of the firm, or stockholders' equity. Stockholders' equity is listed on the right side of the balance sheet. Therefore, the value of the left side of the balance sheet must always equal the value of the right side.

Note: All numbers are in millions of dollars.

Source: Google's Balance Sheet as of December 31, 2004, source: Google, Inc., "Consolidated Balance Sheets," February 1, 2004. Used with permission of Google, Inc.

tion and you employ a chef with a reputation for preparing delicious food, you may pay more than the market value of the tables, chairs, ovens, and other assets. This additional amount you pay will be entered on the asset side of your balance sheet as goodwill.

Current liabilities are short-term debts such as accounts payable, which is money owed to suppliers for goods received but not yet paid for, or bank loans that will be paid back in less than one year. Long-term bank loans and the value of outstanding corporate bonds are *long-term liabilities*.

KEY TERMS

Present value   221   Stockholders' equity   226

REVIEW QUESTIONS

1. Why is money you receive at some future date worth less than money you receive today? If the interest rate rises, what effect does this have on the present value of payments you receive in the future?

2. Give the formula for calculating the present value of a bond that will pay a coupon of $100 per year for 10 years and that has a face value of $1,000.

3. Compare the formula for calculating the present value of the payments you will receive from owning a bond to the

formula for calculating the present value of the payments you will receive from owning a stock. What are the key similarities? What are the key differences?

4. How is operating income calculated? How does operating income differ from net income? How does net income differ from accounting profit?

5. What's the key difference between a firm's income statement and its balance sheet? What is listed on the left side of a balance sheet? What is listed on the right side?

PROBLEMS AND APPLICATIONS

Please visit **www.prenhall.com/hubbard** *for solutions to the even-numbered problems as well as multiple-choice and true or false self-assessment quizzes.*

1. **[Related to *Solved Problem 7A-1*]** If the interest rate is 10 percent, what is the present value of a bond that matures in two years, pays $85 one year from now, and pays $1,085 two years from now?

2. The following is from an Associated Press story on the contract of baseball star Carlos Beltran:

   > Beltran's contract calls for his $11 million signing bonus to be paid in four installments: $5 million upon approval and $2 million each this June 15, 2005, and on Jan. 15, 2006, and Jan. 15, 2007. He gets a $10 million salary this year, $12 million in each of the following two seasons and $18.5 million in each of the final four seasons, with $8.5 million deferred annually from 2008–11. The players' association calculated the present day value of the contract at $115,726,946, using a 6 percent discount rate (the prime rate [which is the interest rate banks charge on loans to their best customers] plus 1 percent, rounded to the nearest whole number). For purposes of baseball's luxury tax, which currently uses a 3.62 percent discount rate, the contract is valued at $116,695,898.

   Briefly explain why the present value of Beltran's contract is lower if a higher interest is used to make the calculation than if a lower interest rate is used.

   Source: "Like Pedro, Beltran Gets Suite on Road," Associated Press, January 18, 2005.

3. **[Related to *Solved Problem 7A-1*]** Before the 2005 season pitcher Armando Benitez signed a contract with the San Francisco Giants baseball team that would pay him the following amounts: $4.1 million in 2005, $6.6 million in 2006, $7.6 million in 2007, $1.6 million in 2008, and $1.6 million in 2009. Assume that he receives each payment as a lump sum at the end of the season and that he received his 2005 payment one year after he signed the contract.

   a. Some newspaper reports described Benitez as having signed a "$21.5 million contract" with the Giants. Do you agree that $21.5 million was the value of this contract? Briefly explain.

   b. What was the present value of Benitez's contract at the time he signed it (assume an interest rate of 10 percent)?

   c. If you use an interest rate of 5 percent, what was the present value of his contract?

4. **[Related to *Solved Problem 7A-1*]** A winner of the Pennsylvania Lottery was given the choice of receiving $18 million at once or $1,440,000 per year for 25 years.

   a. If the winner had opted for the 25 annual payments, how much in total would she have received?

   b. At an interest rate of 10 percent, what would be the present value of the 25 payments?

   c. At an interest rate of 5 percent, what would be the present value of the 25 payments?

   d. What interest rate would make the present value of the 25 payments equal to the one payment of $18 million? (This question is difficult and requires the use of a financial calculator or a spreadsheet. *Hint:* If you are familiar with the Excel spreadsheet program, use the RATE function. Questions b and c can be answered by using the Excel NPV—Net Present Value—function.)

5. **[Related to *Solved Problem 7A-1*]** Before the start of the 2000 baseball season, the New York Mets decided they didn't want Bobby Bonilla playing for them any longer. But Bonilla had a contract with the Mets for the 2000 season that would have obliged the Mets to pay him $5.9 million. When the Mets released Bonilla, he agreed to take the following payments in lieu of the $5.9 million the Mets would have paid him in the year 2000: He will receive 25 equal payments of $1,193,248.20 each July 1 from 2011 to 2035. If you were Bobby Bonilla, which would you rather have had, the lump sum $5.9 million or the 25 payments beginning in 2011? Explain the basis for your decision.

6. Suppose that eLake, an online auction site, is paying a dividend of $2.00 per share. You expect this dividend to grow 2 percent per year, and the interest rate is 10 percent. What is the most you would be willing to pay for a share of stock in eLake? If the interest rate is 5 percent, what is the most you would be willing to pay? When interest rates in the economy decline, would you expect stock prices in general to rise or fall? Explain.

7. Suppose you buy the bond of a large corporation at a time when the inflation rate is very low. If the inflation rate increases during the time you hold the bond, what is likely to happen to the price of the bond?

8. Use the information in the following table for calendar year 2004 to prepare the McDonald's Corporation's income statement. Be sure to include entries for operating income and net income.

Revenue from company restaurants	$14,224 million
Revenue from franchised restaurants	4,841 million
Cost of operating company-owned restaurants	12,100 million
Income taxes	924 million
Interest expense	338 million
General and administrative cost	1,980 million
Cost of restaurant leases	1,003 million
Other operating costs	441 million

Source: McDonald's Corporation, *Consolidated Statement of Income, 2004,* January 28, 2005.

9. Use the information in the following table on the financial situation of Starbucks Corporation as of October 3, 2004, to prepare the firm's balance sheet. Be sure to include an entry for stockholders' equity.

Current assets	$1,359 million
Current liabilities	774 million
Property and equipment	1,471 million
Long-term liabilities	58 million
Goodwill	69 million
Other assets	419 million

Source: Starbucks Corporation, *Annual Report, 2004.*

10. The *current ratio* is equal to a firm's current assets divided by its current liabilities. Use the information in Figure 7A-2 to calculate Google's current ratio on December 31, 2004. Investors generally prefer that a firm's current ratio is greater than 1.5. What problems might a firm encounter if the value of its current assets is low relative to the value of its current liabilities?

chapter

eight

Comparative Advantage and the Gains from International Trade

Sugar Quota Drives U.S. Candy Manufacturers Overseas

➤ Trade is, simply, the act of buying or selling. Is there a difference when trade takes place within a country or when the trade is international? Within the United States, domestic trade makes it possible for consumers in Ohio to eat salmon caught in Alaska or for consumers in Montana to drive cars built in Michigan. Similarly, international trade makes it possible for consumers in the United States to drink wine from France or use DVD players from Japan. But one significant difference between domestic trade and international trade is that international trade is more controversial. At one time, nearly all the televisions, shoes, clothing, and toys consumed in the United States were also produced in the United States. Today, these goods are produced mainly by firms in

other countries. This shift has benefited U.S. consumers because foreign-made goods have lower prices than the U.S.-made goods they have replaced. But at the same time, many U.S. firms that produced these goods have gone out of business and their workers have lost their jobs. Not surprisingly, opinion polls show that many Americans favor reducing international trade because they believe this would preserve jobs in the United States.

But would it? Congress enacted a sugar quota to preserve jobs in the U.S. sugar industry by reducing the quantity of sugar allowed into the United States. Several countries around the world can produce sugar at lower costs than can U.S. sugar producers. As a result the *world price* of sugar, which is the price at

which sugar can be bought on the world market, is too low for U.S. sugar companies to cover their costs. The sugar quota allows U.S. companies to sell sugar domestically for a price that is about three times as high as the world price. Without the sugar quota, competition from foreign sugar producers would drive many U.S. producers out of business. But the United States also has a large candy industry, which uses many tons of sugar. So how have U.S. candy firms and their employees been affected by high sugar prices in the United States?

Life Savers used to be called the "All-American Candy." Life Savers were invented in 1912 by Clarence Crane, who wanted to develop a candy that would not melt in the heat of the summer. Because the sinking

LEARNING OBJECTIVES

After studying this chapter, you should be able to:

① Discuss the increasing importance of international trade to the United States.

② Understand the difference between comparative advantage and absolute advantage.

③ Explain how countries gain from international trade.

④ Discuss the sources of comparative advantage.

⑤ Analyze the economic effects of government policies that restrict international trade.

⑥ Evaluate the arguments for and against government policies that restrict international trade.

of the cruise liner *Titanic* had been the most publicized event of the year, Crane hit on the idea of selling a hard candy in the shape of a life preserver. Today, Life Savers is no longer advertised as the all-American candy because in 2003 it moved production from Holland, Michigan, to Montreal, Canada. The six hundred workers employed at the Michigan Life Savers plant lost their jobs. The price of sugar is about 21 cents per pound in the United States, but the world price is only about 8 cents per pound. In Canada, Life Savers can be made using sugar purchased at the world price, which saves almost $9 million per year in lower sugar costs.

Life Savers is only one of several candies no longer produced in the United States. Brach's Confections, maker of Star Brites mints, closed its

factory in Illinois and moved production to Argentina. Bob's Candies, the largest manufacturer of candy canes, and the Spangler Candy Company, maker of Cherry Balls, have both moved to Mexico.

Should the United States have a sugar quota? The sugar quota creates winners—U.S. sugar companies and their employees—and losers—U.S. companies that use sugar, their employees, and U.S. consumers who must pay higher prices for goods that contain sugar. In this chapter, we will explore who wins and who loses from international trade and review the political debate over whether international trade should be restricted. *An Inside Look* on page 256 discusses a recent trade agreement between the United States and Australia.

➤ Markets for internationally traded goods and services can be analyzed using the tools of demand and supply that we developed in Chapter 3. We saw in Chapter 2 that trade in general—whether within a country or between countries—is based on the principle of comparative advantage. In this chapter, we look more closely at how this principle is applied to international trade. We can also use the concepts of consumer surplus, producer surplus, and deadweight loss that were developed in Chapter 4 to analyze government policies, such as the sugar quota, that interfere with trade. With this background we can return to the political debate over the desirability of international trade. We begin by looking at how large a role international trade plays in the U.S. economy.

① **LEARNING OBJECTIVE**
Discuss the increasing importance of international trade to the United States.

Tariff A tax imposed by a government on imports.

Imports Goods and services bought domestically but produced in other countries.

Exports Goods and services produced domestically but sold to other countries.

An Overview of International Trade

International trade has grown tremendously over the past 50 years. The increase in trade is the result of the falling costs of shipping products around the world, the spread of cheap and reliable communications, and changes in government policies. Businesspeople today can travel to Europe or Asia using fast, cheap, and reliable air transportation. The Internet allows managers to communicate instantaneously and at a very low cost with customers and suppliers around the world. Firms can use large container ships to send their products across the oceans at low cost. These and other improvements in transportation and communication have created a global marketplace only dreamed about by earlier generations of businesspeople.

In addition, over the past 50 years many governments have changed policies to facilitate international trade. For example, tariff rates have fallen. A **tariff** is a tax imposed by a government on *imports* of a good into a country. **Imports** are goods and services bought domestically but produced in other countries. In the 1930s, the United States charged an average tariff rate above 50 percent. Today, the rate is less than 2 percent. In North America, most tariffs between Canada, Mexico, and the United States were eliminated in 1994 with passage of the North American Free Trade Agreement (NAFTA). Twenty-five countries in Europe have formed the European Union, which has eliminated all tariffs among member countries, greatly increasing both imports and **exports,** which are goods and services produced domestically, but sold to other countries.

The Importance of Trade to the U.S. Economy

U.S. consumers buy increasing quantities of goods and services produced in other countries. At the same time, U.S. businesses sell increasing quantities of goods and services to consumers in other countries. Figure 8-1 shows that since 1950, both exports and imports have been steadily increasing as a fraction of U.S. gross domestic product (GDP). Recall that GDP is the value of all the goods and services produced in a country during a year. In 1950, exports and imports were both about 4 percent of GDP. In 2004, exports were about 10 percent of GDP, and imports were about 15 percent.

Not all sectors of the U.S. economy are affected equally by international trade. On the one hand, it's difficult to import or export some services, such as haircuts or appendectomies. On the other hand, a large percentage of U.S. agricultural production is exported. Each year the United States exports about 50 percent of the wheat crop, 40 percent of the rice crop, and 20 percent of the corn crop.

Many U.S. manufacturing industries also depend on trade. About 20 percent of U.S. manufacturing jobs depend directly or indirectly on exports. In some industries, such as computers, the products these workers make are directly exported. In other industries, such as steel, the products are used to make other products, such as bulldoz-

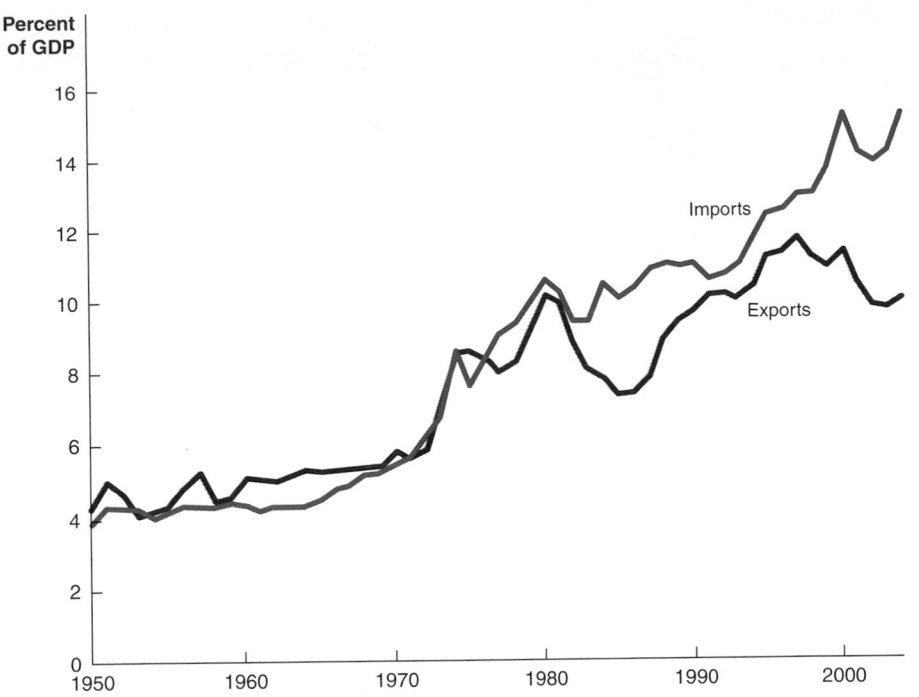

FIGURE 8-1

International Trade Is of Increasing Importance to the United States

Exports and imports of goods and services as a percentage of total production—measured by GDP—show the importance of international trade to an economy. Since 1950, both imports and exports have been steadily rising as a fraction of U.S. GDP.

Source: U.S. Department of Commerce, Bureau of Economic Analysis.

ers or machine tools, that are then exported. In all, about two-thirds of U.S. manufacturing industries depend on exports for at least 10 percent of jobs.

U.S. International Trade in a World Context

The United States is the largest exporter in the world, as Figure 8-2 illustrates. Six of the other seven leading exporting countries are also large, high-income countries. The rapid growth of the Chinese economy over the past 20 years has resulted in its becoming the fifth largest exporter.

International trade remains less important to the United States than it is to most other countries. Figure 8-3 on the next page shows that imports and exports remain smaller fractions of GDP in the United States than in other countries. In some smaller countries, like Belgium, imports and exports make up more than half of GDP. Japan is the only high-income country that is less dependent on international trade than is the United States.

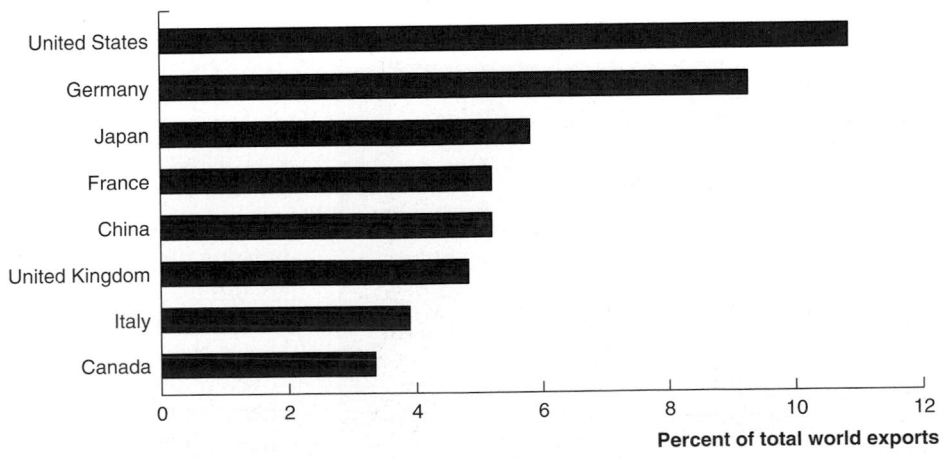

FIGURE 8-2

The Eight Leading Exporting Countries

The United States is the leading exporting country, accounting for about 11 percent of total world exports. The values are the shares of total world exports of merchandise and commercial services.

Source: World Trade Organization, *International Trade Statistics*, 2004.

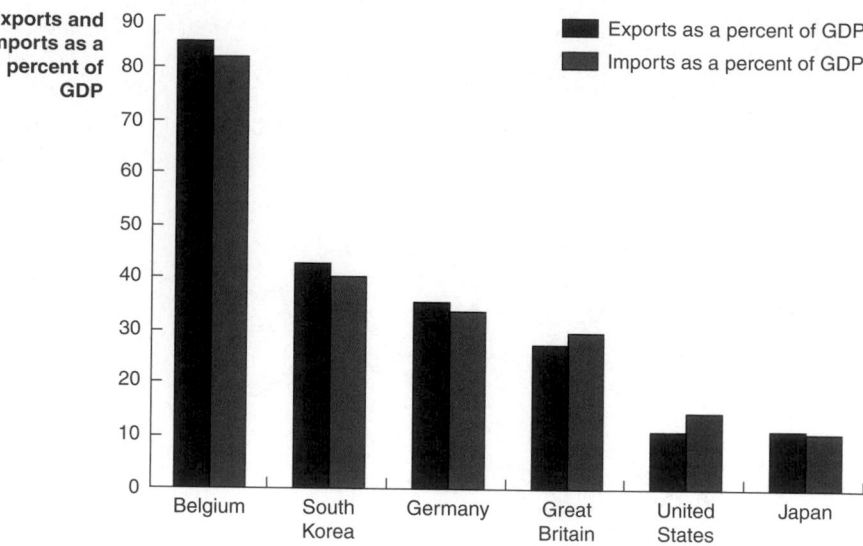

8-1 *Making the Connection*

Has Outsourcing Hurt the U.S. Economy?

One aspect of the increase in international trade that has been particularly controversial in recent years is *outsourcing*. Outsourcing—sometimes called "offshoring"—occurs when a domestic firm uses workers in a foreign country to produce a good or service that is then sold to domestic consumers. An example is Dell Computer using workers in Bangalore, India, to provide telephone technical support to U.S. buyers of Dell's computers. From the viewpoint of the Indian economy, this would be *insourcing*. The increase in outsourcing and insourcing reflects advances in communications and information technology that make it easier for firms to coordinate the activities of their employees in foreign countries. Outsourcing became a source of political controversy during the early 2000s as employment in the United States grew slowly following the 2001 recession. Some political commentators believed that outsourcing played a significant role in this slow employment growth.

Exact statistics are not available, but the number of jobs outsourced by U.S. companies appears to be small relative to the size of the economy. For example, a study by the U.S. Bureau of Labor Statistics indicates that during the first three months of 2003, outsourcing accounted for only 4,633 of 239,361 jobs lost at a large group of firms. The study covered only firms that employed at least 50 employees and that had eliminated at least 50 jobs, so it was not complete. It seems unlikely, however, that including smaller firms in the study would have significantly changed the results. In a market economy, new jobs are constantly being created as old jobs are destroyed. For example, during 2003, more than 30 million jobs were created and about the same number were destroyed. Some of the job creation was due to insourcing—as foreign firms increased production in the United States—and some of the job destruction was due to outsourcing—as U.S. firms moved jobs overseas. But outsourcing and insourcing are not major factors in the employment situation in the United States.

How does outsourcing affect the economy? We know that firms outsource to reduce their costs. Com-

Some companies outsource technical support services to India.

petition among firms ensures that lower costs are passed on to consumers in the form of lower prices. In this sense, outsourcing has an effect similar to a technological change that lowers cost. The lower prices that outsourcing makes possible are spread widely among consumers, but the costs of outsourcing are concentrated among workers who lose their jobs. Although jobs that are outsourced are lost to U.S. workers, other jobs are created in the United States to take their place. The same is true of jobs lost to technological change. Over the last 20 years, the U.S. economy has created 30 million more jobs than have been destroyed due to outsourcing, technological change, and all other causes. Nevertheless, individual workers whose jobs are lost to outsourcing may have difficulty finding jobs as desirable as the ones they have lost.

Source: U.S. Bureau of Labor Statistics, "Extended Mass Layoffs Associated with Domestic and Overseas Relocations, First Quarter 2004," June 10, 2004.

Comparative Advantage: The Basis of All Trade

② **LEARNING OBJECTIVE**
Understand the difference between comparative advantage and absolute advantage.

Why have businesses around the world increasingly looked for markets in other countries? Why have consumers increasingly purchased goods and services made in other countries? People trade for one reason: Trade makes them better off. Whenever a buyer and seller agree to a sale, they must both believe they are better off—otherwise there would be no sale. This outcome must hold whether the buyer and seller live in the same city or in different countries. As we will see, governments are more likely to interfere with international trade than they are with domestic trade, but the reasons for the interference are more political than they are economic.

A Brief Review of Comparative Advantage

In Chapter 2, we discussed the key economic concept of *comparative advantage*. **Comparative advantage** is the ability of an individual, firm, or country to produce a good or service at a lower opportunity cost than other producers. Recall that **opportunity cost** is the highest-valued alternative that must be given up to engage in an activity. People specialize in those economic activities in which they have a comparative advantage. In trading, we benefit from the comparative advantage of other people (or firms or countries), and other people benefit from our comparative advantage.

Comparative advantage The ability of an individual, firm, or country to produce a good or service at a lower opportunity cost than other producers.

Opportunity cost The highest-valued alternative that must be given up to engage in an activity.

A good way to think of comparative advantage is to recall the example in Chapter 2 of you and your neighbor picking fruit. Your neighbor is better at picking both apples and cherries than you are. Why, then, doesn't your neighbor pick both types of fruit? Because the opportunity cost of picking her own apples is very high: She is a particularly skilled cherry picker, and every hour spent picking apples is an hour taken away from picking cherries. You can pick apples at a much lower opportunity cost than your neighbor, so you have a comparative advantage in picking apples. Your neighbor can pick cherries at a much lower opportunity cost than you can, so your neighbor has a comparative advantage in picking cherries. Your neighbor is better off specializing in picking cherries, and you are better off specializing in picking apples. You can then trade some of your apples for some of your neighbor's cherries and both of you will end up with more of each fruit.

Comparative Advantage in International Trade

The principle of comparative advantage can explain why people pursue different occupations. It can also explain why countries produce different goods and services. International trade involves many countries importing and exporting many different goods and services. Countries are better off if they specialize in producing the goods for which they have a comparative advantage. They can then trade for the goods for which other countries have a comparative advantage.

We can illustrate why specializing on the basis of comparative advantage makes countries better off with a simple example involving just two countries and two

TABLE 8-1

An Example of Japanese Workers
Being More Productive Than
American Workers

	OUTPUT PER HOUR OF WORK	
	CELL PHONES	MP3 PLAYERS
Japan	12	6
United States	2	4

Absolute advantage The ability to
produce more of a good or service
than competitors when using the
same amount of resources.

products. Suppose the United States and Japan produce only cell phones and MP3 players, like Apple's iPod. Assume that each country uses only labor to produce each good, and that Japanese and U.S. cell phones and MP3 players are exactly the same. Table 8-1 shows how much each country can produce of each good with one hour of labor.

Notice that Japanese workers are more productive than U.S. workers in making both goods. In 1 hour of work, Japanese workers can make six times as many cell phones and one and one-half times as many MP3 players as U.S. workers. Japan has an *absolute advantage* over the United States in producing both goods. **Absolute advantage** is the ability to produce more of a good or service than competitors when using the same amount of resources. In this case, Japan can produce more of both goods using the same amount of labor as the United States.

It might seem at first that Japan has nothing to gain from trading with the United States because it has an absolute advantage in producing both goods. However, Japan should specialize and produce only cell phones and obtain the MP3 players it needs by exporting cell phones to the United States in exchange for MP3 players. The reason that Japan benefits from trade is that although it has an *absolute advantage* in the production of both goods, it has a *comparative advantage* only in the production of cell phones. The United States has a comparative advantage in the production of MP3 players.

If this seems contrary to common sense, think about the opportunity cost to each country of producing each good. If Japan wants to produce more MP3 players, it has to switch labor away from cell phone production. Every hour of labor switched from producing cell phones to producing MP3 players increases MP3 player production by 6 and reduces cell phone production by 12. Japan has to give up 12 cell phones for every 6 MP3 players it produces. Therefore, the opportunity cost to Japan of producing one more MP3 player is 12/6, or 2 cell phones.

If the United States switches 1 hour of labor from cell phones to MP3 players, production of cell phones falls by 2 and production of MP3 players rises by 4. Therefore, the opportunity cost to the United States of producing one more MP3 player is 2/4, or 0.5 cell phone. The United States has a lower opportunity cost of producing MP3 players and, therefore, has a comparative advantage in making this product. By similar reasoning, we can see that Japan has a comparative advantage in producing cell phones. Table 8-2 summarizes this result.

③ **LEARNING OBJECTIVE**

Explain how countries gain from
international trade.

The Gains from Trade

Can Japan really gain from producing only cell phones and trading with the United States for MP3 players? To see that it can, assume at first that Japan and the United States

TABLE 8-2

The Opportunity Costs of
Producing Cell Phones and MP3
Players

	OPPORTUNITY COSTS	
	CELL PHONES	MP3 PLAYERS
Japan	0.5 MP3 player	2 cell phones
United States	2 MP3 players	0.5 cell phone

WITHOUT TRADE			TABLE 8-3
PRODUCTION AND CONSUMPTION			Production without Trade
	CELL PHONES	MP3 PLAYERS	
Japan	9,000	1,500	
United States	1,500	1,000	

do not trade with each other. A situation in which a country does not trade with other countries is called **autarky.** Assume that in autarky each country has 1,000 hours of labor available to produce the two goods, and each country produces the quantities of the two goods shown in Table 8-3. Because there is no trade, these quantities also represent consumption of the two goods in each country.

Autarky   A situation in which a country does not trade with other countries.

Increasing Consumption through Trade

Suppose now that Japan and the United States begin to trade with each other. The **terms of trade** is the ratio at which a country can trade its exports for imports from other countries. As Table 8-1 on the previous page shows, it takes twice as much labor in Japan to produce one MP3 player as to produce one cell phone. In the United States, the situation is reversed: It takes twice as much labor to produce a cell phone as it does to produce an MP3 player. For simplicity, let's assume that the terms of trade end up with Japan and the United States being willing to trade one cell phone for one MP3 player.

Terms of trade   The ratio at which a country can trade its exports for imports from other countries.

Once trade has begun, the United States and Japan can exchange MP3 players for cell phones or cell phones for MP3 players. For example, if Japan specializes by using all 1,000 available hours of labor to produce cell phones, it will be able to produce 12,000. It then could export 1,500 cell phones to the United States in exchange for 1,500 MP3 players (remember we are assuming the terms of trade are one cell phone for one MP3 player). Japan ends up with 10,500 cell phones and 1,500 MP3 players. Compared with the situation before trade, Japan has the same number of MP3 players, but 1,500 more cell phones. If the United States specializes in producing MP3 players, it will be able to produce 4,000. It then could export 1,500 MP3 players to Japan in exchange for 1,500 cell phones. The United States ends up with 2,500 MP3 players and 1,500 cell phones. Compared with the situation before trade, the United States has the same number of cell phones, but 1,500 more MP3 players. Trade has allowed both countries to increase the quantities of goods consumed. Table 8-4 summarizes the gains from trade for the United States and Japan.

By trading, Japan and the United States are able to consume more than they could without trade. This outcome is possible because world production of both goods increases after trade (remember, in this example, our "world" consists of just the United States and Japan):

WORLD PRODUCTION		
	BEFORE TRADE	AFTER TRADE
Cell Phones	10,500	12,000
MP3 Players	2,500	4,000

Why does total production of cell phones and MP3 players increase when the United States specializes in producing MP3 players and Japan specializes in producing cell phones? A domestic analogy helps to answer this question: If a company shifts production from an old factory to a more efficient modern factory, its output will increase. In effect, the same thing happens in our example. Producing MP3 players in Japan and cell phones in the United States is inefficient. Shifting production to the more efficient

TABLE 8-4

The Gains from Trade for Japan
and the United States

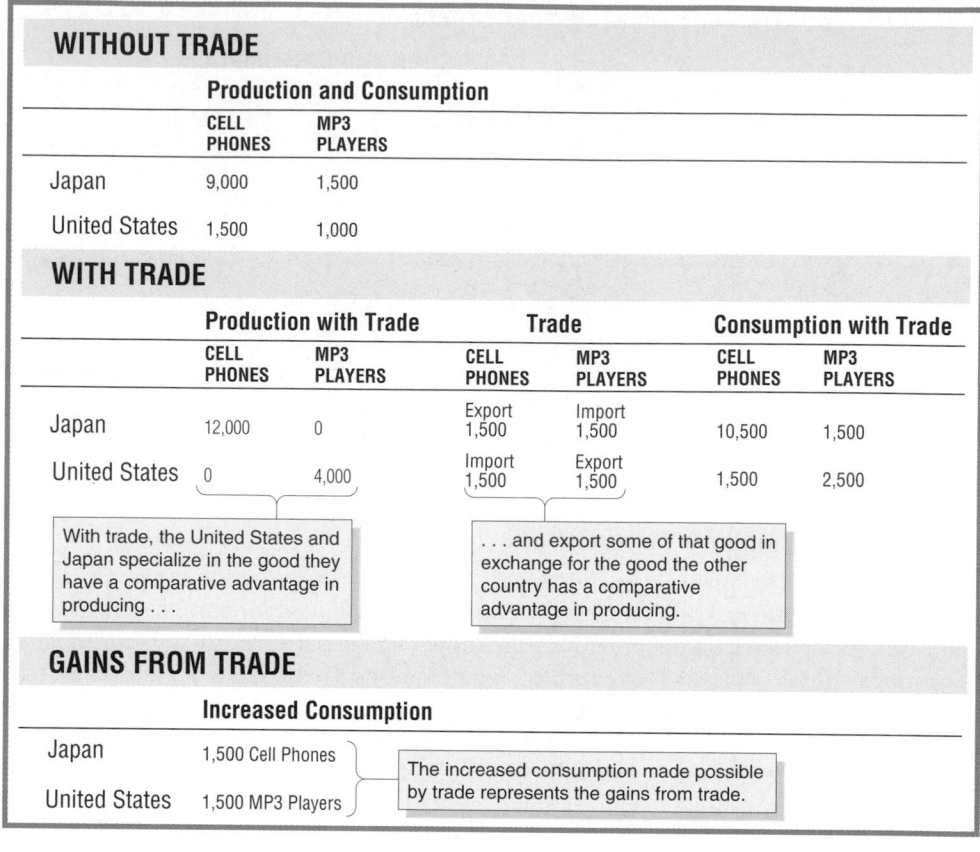

TABLE 8-4

The Gains from Trade for Japan
and the United States

WITHOUT TRADE

Production and Consumption

	CELL PHONES	MP3 PLAYERS
Japan	9,000	1,500
United States	1,500	1,000

WITH TRADE

	Production with Trade		Trade		Consumption with Trade	
	CELL PHONES	MP3 PLAYERS	CELL PHONES	MP3 PLAYERS	CELL PHONES	MP3 PLAYERS
Japan	12,000	0	Export 1,500	Import 1,500	10,500	1,500
United States	0	4,000	Import 1,500	Export 1,500	1,500	2,500

With trade, the United States and Japan specialize in the good they have a comparative advantage in producing . . .

. . . and export some of that good in exchange for the good the other country has a comparative advantage in producing.

GAINS FROM TRADE

Increased Consumption

Japan	1,500 Cell Phones
United States	1,500 MP3 Players

The increased consumption made possible by trade represents the gains from trade.

country—the one with the comparative advantage—increases total production. The key point is this: *Countries gain from specializing in producing goods in which they have a comparative advantage and trading for goods in which other countries have a comparative advantage.*

SOLVED PROBLEM **8-1**

③ LEARNING OBJECTIVE

Explain how countries gain from international trade.

The Gains from Trade

The first discussion of comparative advantage appears in *On the Principles of Political Economy and Taxation*, a book written by David Ricardo in 1817. Ricardo provided a famous example of the gains from trade using wine and cloth production in Portugal and England. The following table is adapted from Ricardo's example, with cloth measured in sheets and wine measured in kegs:

	OUTPUT PER YEAR OF LABOR	
	CLOTH	WINE
Portugal	100	150
England	90	60

  a. Explain which country has an absolute advantage in the production of each good.
  b. Explain which country has a comparative advantage in the production of each good.

c. Suppose that Portugal and England currently do not trade with each other. Each has 1,000 years of labor to use producing cloth and wine, and the countries are currently producing the amounts of each good shown in the table:

	CLOTH	WINE
Portugal	18,000	123,000
England	63,000	18,000

Show that Portugal and England can both gain from trade. Assume that the terms of trade are that one sheet of cloth can be traded for one keg of wine.

Solving the Problem:

Step 1: Review the chapter material. This problem is about absolute and comparative advantage and the gains from trade, so you may want to review the section "Comparative Advantage: The Basis of All Trade," which begins on page 235, and the section "The Gains from Trade," which begins on page 236.

Step 2: Answer question (a) by determining which country has an absolute advantage. Remember that a country has an absolute advantage over another country when it can produce more of a good using the same resources. The table shows that Portugal can produce more cloth *and* more wine with 1 year's worth of labor than can England. Thus, Portugal has an absolute advantage in the production of both goods and, therefore, England does not have an absolute advantage in the production of either good.

Step 3: Answer question (b) by determining which country has a comparative advantage. A country has a comparative advantage when it can produce a good at a lower opportunity cost. To produce 100 sheets of cloth, Portugal must give up 150 kegs of wine. Therefore, the opportunity cost to Portugal of producing one sheet of cloth is 150/100 or 1.5 kegs of wine. England has to give up 60 kegs of wine to produce 90 sheets of cloth, so its opportunity cost of producing one sheet of cloth is 60/90 or 0.67 keg of wine. The opportunity costs of producing wine can be calculated in the same way. The following table shows the opportunity cost to Portugal and England of producing each good.

OPPORTUNITY COSTS		
	CLOTH	WINE
Portugal	1.5 kegs of wine	0.67 sheets of cloth
England	0.67 keg of wine	1.5 sheets of cloth

Portugal has a comparative advantage in wine because its opportunity cost is lower. England has a comparative advantage in cloth because its opportunity cost is lower.

Step 4: Answer question (c) by showing that both countries can benefit from trade. By now it should be clear that both countries would be better off if they specialize where they have a comparative advantage and trade for the other product. The following table is very similar to Table 8-4 and shows one example of trade making both countries better off (to test your understanding, construct another example):

WITHOUT TRADE		
	PRODUCTION AND CONSUMPTION	
	CLOTH	WINE
Portugal	18,000	123,000
England	63,000	18,000

WITH TRADE						
	PRODUCTION WITH TRADE		TRADE		CONSUMPTION WITH TRADE	
	CLOTH	WINE	CLOTH	WINE	CLOTH	WINE
Portugal	0	150,000	Import 18,000	Export 18,000	18,000	132,000
England	90,000	0	Export 18,000	Import 18,000	72,000	18,000

GAINS FROM TRADE	
	INCREASED CONSUMPTION
Portugal	9,000 wine
England	9,000 cloth

YOUR TURN: For more practice, do related problems 3 and 10 on pages 259 and 260 at the end of this chapter. Visit www.prenhall.com/hubbard for an interactive exercise related to this Solved Problem.

Why Don't We See Complete Specialization?

In our example of two countries producing only two products, each country specializes in producing one of the goods. In the real world, many goods and services are produced in more than one country. For example, the United States and Japan both produce automobiles. We do not see complete specialization in the real world for three main reasons:

➤ *Not all goods and services are traded internationally.* Even if, for example, Japan had a comparative advantage in the production of medical services, it would be difficult for Japan to specialize in their production and export them. There is no easy way for U.S. patients in need of appendectomies to receive them from Japanese surgeons.

➤ *Production of most goods involves increasing opportunity costs.* Recall from Chapter 2 that production of most goods involves increasing opportunity costs. As a result, when the United States devotes more workers to producing MP3 players, the opportunity cost of producing more MP3 players will increase. At some point, the opportunity cost of producing MP3 players in the United States will rise to the level of the opportunity cost of producing MP3 players in Japan. Once that happens, international trade will no longer push the United States further toward complete specialization. The same will be true of Japan: Increasing opportunity cost will cause Japan to stop short of complete specialization in producing cell phones.

➤ *Tastes for products differ.* Most products are *differentiated.* Cell phones, MP3 players, cars, and televisions—to name just a few products—come with a wide variety of features. When buying automobiles, some people are looking for reliability and good gasoline mileage, others are looking for room to carry seven passengers, and still others want styling and high performance. So, some car buyers prefer Toyota Corollas, some prefer Ford minivans, and others prefer BMWs. As a result, Japan, the United States, and Germany may each have a comparative advantage in producing different types of automobiles.

Does Anyone Lose as a Result of International Trade?

In our cell phone and MP3 player example, consumption increases in both the United States and Japan as a result of trade. Everyone gains and no one loses. Or do they? In our example, we referred repeatedly to "Japan" or the "United States" producing cell phones or MP3 players. But countries do not produce goods—firms do. In a world without trade, there would be cell phone and MP3 player firms in both Japan and the

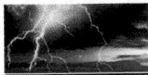

Don't Let This Happen To You!

Remember That Trade Creates Both Winners and Losers

The following statement is from a Federal Reserve publication: "Trade is a win–win situation for all countries that participate." Statements like this are sometimes taken to mean that there are no losers from international trade. But notice that the statement refers to *countries,* not individuals. When countries participate in trade, they make their consumers better off by increasing the quantity of goods and services available to them. As we have seen, however, expanding trade eliminates the jobs of workers employed at companies that are less efficient than foreign companies. Trade also creates new jobs at companies that export to foreign markets. It may be difficult, though, for workers who

lose their jobs because of trade to easily find others. That is why in the United States the federal government uses the Trade Adjustment Assistance program to provide funds for workers who have lost their jobs due to international trade. These funds can be used for retraining, for searching for new jobs, or for relocating to areas where new jobs are available. This program—and similar programs in other countries—recognizes that there are losers from international trade as well as winners.

Source: Quote from Federal Reserve Bank of Dallas Web site, "International Trade and the Economy," www.dallasfed.org/educate/everyday/ev7.html.

YOUR TURN: Test your understanding by doing related problem 24 on page 262 at the end of this chapter.

United States. In a world with trade, there would only be Japanese cell phone firms and U.S. MP3 player firms. Japanese MP3 player firms and U.S. cell phone firms would disappear. The owners of Japanese MP3 player firms, the owners of U.S. cell phone firms, and the people who work for them are likely to do their best to convince the Japanese and U.S. governments to interfere with trade by barring imports of the competing products from the other country or by imposing high tariffs on them. Later in this chapter we will discuss government policies that restrict trade.

Where Does Comparative Advantage Come From?

Among the main sources of comparative advantage are the following:

➤ *Climate and natural resources.*   This source of comparative advantage is the most obvious. Because of geology, Saudi Arabia has a comparative advantage in the production of oil. Because of climate and soil conditions, Costa Rica has a comparative advantage in the production of bananas, and the United States has a comparative advantage in the production of wheat.

➤ *Relative abundance of labor and capital.*   Some countries, such as the United States, have many highly skilled workers and a great deal of machinery. Other countries, such as China, have many unskilled workers and relatively little machinery. As a result, the United States has a comparative advantage in the production of goods that require highly skilled workers or sophisticated machinery to manufacture, such as aircraft, semiconductors, and computer software. China has a comparative advantage in the production of goods that require unskilled workers and small amounts of simple machinery, such as children's toys.

➤ *Technology.*   Broadly defined, *technology* is the process firms use to turn inputs into goods and services. At any given time, firms in different countries do not all have access to the same technologies. In part, this difference reflects past investments countries have made in supporting higher education or in providing support for research and development. Some countries are strong in *product technologies,* which involve the ability to develop new products. For example, firms in the United States have pioneered the development of such products as televisions, digital computers, airliners, and many prescription drugs. Other countries are strong in *process technologies,* which involve the ability to improve the processes used to make existing products. For example, firms in Japan, such as Toyota and Nissan, succeeded by greatly improving the processes for making automobiles.

④   **LEARNING OBJECTIVE**

Discuss the sources of comparative advantage.

> *External economies.* It is difficult to explain the location of some industries on the basis of climate, natural resources, the relative abundance of labor and capital, or technology. For example, why does southern California have a comparative advantage in making movies or Switzerland in making watches or New York in providing financial services? The answer is that once an industry becomes established in an area, firms that locate in that area gain advantages over firms located elsewhere. The advantages include the availability of skilled workers, the opportunity to interact with other firms in the same industry, and being close to suppliers. These advantages result in lower costs to firms located in the area. Because these lower costs result from increases in the size of the industry in an area, economists refer to them as **external economies.**

External economies Reductions in a firm's costs that result from an expansion in the size of an industry.

8-2 Making the Connection

Why Is Dalton, Georgia, the Carpet-Making Capital of the World?

Factories within a 65-mile radius of Dalton, Georgia, account for 80 percent of U.S. carpet production and more than half of world carpet production. Carpet production is highly automated and relies primarily on synthetic fibers. Dalton, a small city located in rural northwest Georgia, would not seem to have any advantages in carpet production. In fact, the location of the carpet industry in Dalton was an historical accident.

In the early 1900s, Catherine Evans Whitener started making bedspreads using a method called "tufting," in which she sewed cotton yarn through the fabric and then cut the ends of the yarn so it would fluff up. These bedspreads became very popular. By the 1930s, the process was mechanized and was then applied to carpets. In the early years, the industry used cotton grown in Georgia, but today synthetic fibers, such as nylon and olefin, have largely replaced cotton and wool in carpet manufacturing.

More than 170 carpet factories are now located in the Dalton area. Supporting the carpet industry are local yarn manufacturers, machinery suppliers, and maintenance firms. Dye plants have opened solely to supply the carpet industry. Printing shops have opened whose whole business is printing tags and labels for carpets. Box factories have opened to produce cartons designed specifically for shipping carpets. The local workforce has developed highly specialized skills for running and maintaining the carpet-making machinery.

A company establishing a carpet factory outside the Dalton area is unable to use the suppliers or the skilled workers available to factories in Dalton. As a result, carpet factories located outside of Dalton may have higher costs than factories located in Dalton. Although there is no particular reason why the carpet industry should have originally located in Dalton, external economies gave the area a comparative advantage in carpet making once it began to grow there.

Because Catherine Evans Whitener started making bedspreads by hand in Dalton, Georgia, a hundred years ago, a multibillion-dollar carpet industry is now located there.

Comparative Advantage Over Time: The Rise and Fall—and Rise—of the U.S. Consumer Electronics Industry

A country may develop a comparative advantage in the production of a good, then as time passes and circumstances change, the country may lose its comparative advantage in producing that good and develop a comparative advantage in producing other goods. For several decades, the United States had a comparative advantage in the production of consumer electronic goods, such as televisions, radios, and stereos. The comparative advantage of the United States in these products was based on having developed most of the underlying technology, having the most modern factories, and having a skilled and experienced workforce. Gradually, however, other countries, particularly Japan, gained access to the technology, built modern factories, and developed skilled workforces. As mentioned earlier, Japanese firms have excelled in process technologies, which involve the ability to improve the processes used to make existing products. By the 1970s and 1980s, Japanese firms were able to produce many consumer electronic goods more cheaply and with higher quality than could U.S. firms. Sony, Panasonic, and Pioneer replaced Magnavox, Zenith, and RCA as world leaders in consumer electronics.

By 2005, however, as the technology underlying consumer electronics evolved, comparative advantage began to shift again, and several U.S. firms surged ahead of their Japanese competitors. For example, Apple Computer developed the iPod; palmOne developed the Treo smartphone that has the capacity for e-mail, Web surfing, and picture taking; and Kodak developed digital cameras with EasyShare software that made it easy to organize, enhance, and share digital pictures. As pictures and music converted to digital data, process technologies became less important than the ability to design and develop new products. These new consumer electronics products required skills similar to those in computer design and software writing where the United States had long maintained a comparative advantage.

Once a country has lost its comparative advantage in producing a good, its income will be higher and its economy will be more efficient if it switches from producing the good to importing it, as the United States did when it switched from producing televisions to importing them. As we will see in the next section, however, there is often political pressure on governments to attempt to preserve industries that have lost their comparative advantage.

Government Policies That Restrict Trade

Free trade, or trade between countries that is without government restrictions, makes consumers better off. We can expand on this idea using the concepts of consumer surplus and producer surplus developed in Chapter 4. Figure 8-4 shows the market for lumber in the United States assuming autarky, where the United States does not trade with other countries. The equilibrium price of lumber is $3 per board foot and the equilibrium quantity is 1,000,000 board feet. (A board foot is a piece of lumber one inch thick and one foot wide by one foot long.) The blue area represents consumer surplus and the red area represents producer surplus.

Now suppose that the United States begins importing lumber from Canada and other countries, and that lumber is selling in these countries for $2 per board foot. Because the world market for lumber is large, we will assume that the United States can buy as much lumber as it wants to without causing the *world price* of $2 to rise. Therefore, once imports of lumber are permitted into the United States, U.S. lumber companies will not be able to sell lumber at prices higher than the world price of $2, and the U.S. price will become equal to the world price.

Figure 8-5 shows the result of allowing imports of lumber into the United States. With the price lowered from $3 to $2, U.S. consumers increase their purchases from 1,000,000 board feet to 1,200,000 board feet. Equilibrium moves from point E to point F. In the new equilibrium, U.S. producers have reduced the quantity of lumber they supply from 1,000,000 board feet to 700,000 board feet. Imports will equal 500,000 board feet, which is the difference between U.S. consumption and U.S. production.

⑤ LEARNING OBJECTIVE
Analyze the economic effects of government policies that restrict international trade.

Free trade Trade between countries that is without government restrictions.

FIGURE 8-4

The U.S. Lumber Industry under Autarky

This figure shows the market for lumber in the United States assuming autarky, where the United States does not trade with other countries. The equilibrium price of lumber is $3 per board foot and the equilibrium quantity is 1,000,000 board feet. The blue area represents consumer surplus, and the red area represents producer surplus.

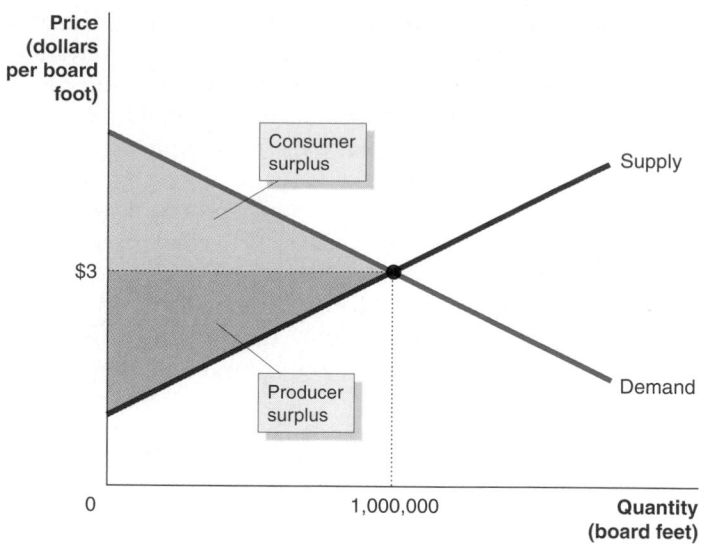

Under autarky, consumer surplus would be area *A* in Figure 8-5. With imports, the reduction in price increases consumer surplus, so it is now equal to the sum of areas *A*, *B*, *C*, and *D*. Although the lower price increases consumer surplus, it reduces producer surplus. Under autarky, producer surplus was equal to the sum of the areas *B* and *E*. With imports, producer surplus is equal to only area *E*. Recall that economic surplus equals the sum of consumer surplus and producer surplus. Moving from autarky to allowing imports increases economic surplus in the United States by an amount equal to the sum of areas *C* and *D*.

We can conclude that international trade helps consumers, but hurts firms that are less efficient than foreign competitors. As a result, these firms and their workers are

FIGURE 8-5

The Effect of Imports on the U.S. Lumber Market

When imports are allowed into the United States, the price of lumber falls from $3 to $2. U.S. consumers increase their purchases from 1,000,000 board feet to 1,200,000 board feet. Equilibrium moves from point *F* to point *G*. U.S. producers reduce the quantity of lumber they supply from 1,000,000 board feet to 700,000 board feet. Imports equal 500,000 board feet, which is the difference between U.S. consumption and U.S. production. Consumer surplus equals the areas *A*, *B*, *C*, and *D*. Producer surplus equals the area of *E*.

	Under Autarky	With Imports
Consumer Surplus	A	A + B + C + D
Producer Surplus	B + E	E
Economic Surplus	A + B + E	A + B + C + D + E

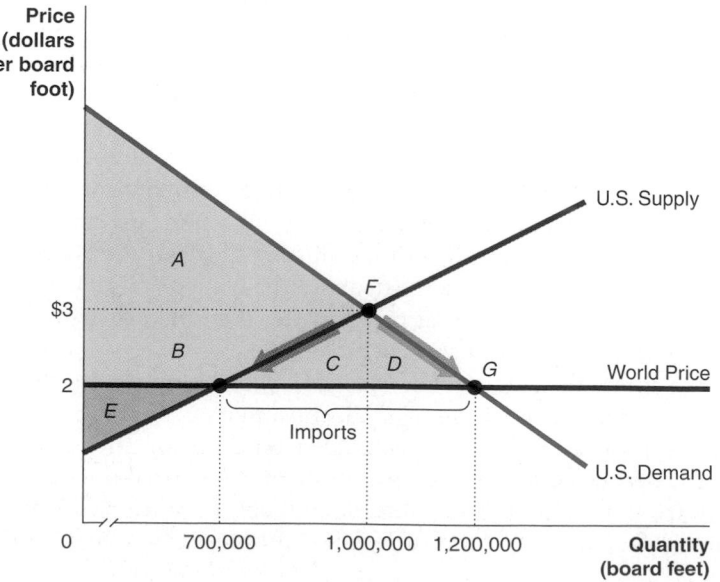

often strong supporters of government policies that restrict trade. These policies usually take one of two forms:

➤ Tariffs

➤ Quotas and voluntary export restraints

Tariffs

The most common interferences with trade are *tariffs,* which are taxes imposed by a government on goods imported into a country. Like any other tax, a tariff will increase the cost of selling a good. Figure 8-6 shows the impact of a tariff of $0.50 per board foot on lumber imports into the United States. The $0.50 tariff raises the price of lumber in the United States from the world price of $2.00 per board foot to $2.50 per board foot. At this higher price, U.S. lumber producers increase the quantity they supply from 700,000 board feet to 900,000 board feet. U.S. consumers, though, cut back their purchases of lumber from 1,200,000 board feet to 1,100,000 board feet. Imports decline from 500,000 board feet (1,200,000 − 700,000) to 200,000 board feet (1,100,000 − 900,000). Equilibrium moves from point E to point F.

By raising the price of lumber from $2.00 to $2.50, the tariff reduces consumer surplus by the sum of areas A, B, C, and D. Area A is the increase in producer surplus from the higher price. The government collects tariff revenue equal to the tariff of $0.50 per board feet multiplied by the 200,000 board feet imported. Area C represents the government's tariff revenue. Areas B and D represent losses to U.S. consumers that are not captured by anyone. They are deadweight loss and represent the decline in economic efficiency resulting from the lumber tariff. Area B shows the effect on U.S. consumers of being forced to buy from U.S. producers who are less efficient than foreign producers, and area D shows the effect of U.S. consumers buying less lumber than they would have at the world price. As a result of the tariff, economic surplus has been reduced by the

Loss of Consumer Surplus	=	Increase in Producer Surplus	+	Government Tariff Revenue	+	Deadweight Loss
A + B + C + D		A		C		B + D

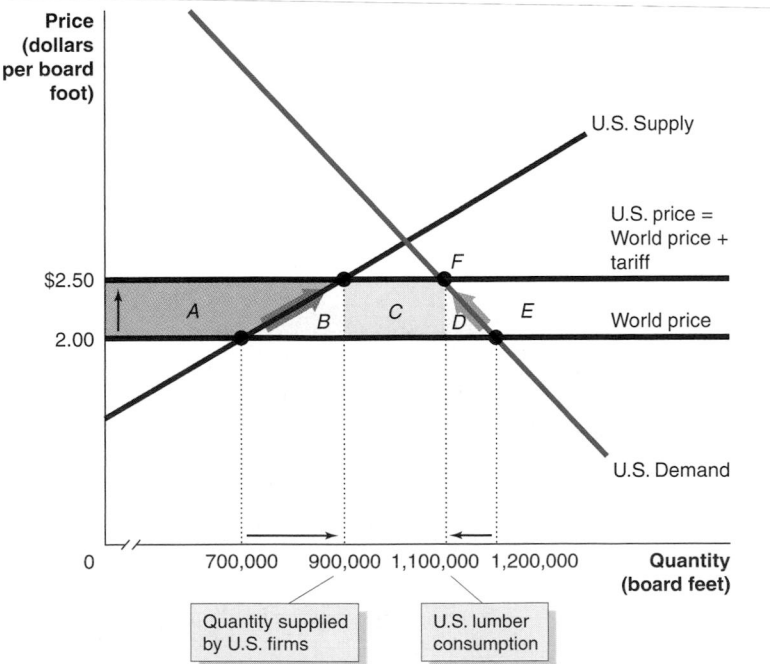

FIGURE 8-6

The Effects of a Tariff on Lumber

Without a tariff on lumber, U.S. lumber producers will sell 700,000 board feet of lumber, U.S. consumers will purchase 1,200,000 board feet, and imports will be 500,000 board feet. The U.S. price will equal the world price of $2.00 per board foot. The $0.50 per board foot lumber tariff raises the price of lumber in the United States to $2.50 per board foot and U.S. producers increase the quantity they supply to 900,000 board feet. U.S. consumers reduce their purchases to 1,100,000 board feet. Equilibrium moves from point E to point F. The lumber tariff causes a loss of consumer surplus equal to the area A + B + C + D. The area A is the increase in producer surplus due to the higher price. The area C is the government's tariff revenue. The areas B and D represent deadweight loss.

sum of areas *B* and *D*. Recall from Chapter 4 that deadweight loss represents a loss of economic efficiency.

We can conclude that the tariff succeeds in helping U.S. lumber producers, but hurts U.S. consumers and the efficiency of the U.S. economy.

Quotas

Quota A numerical limit imposed by the government on the quantity of a good that can be imported into a country.

Voluntary export restraint An agreement negotiated between two countries that places a numerical limit on the quantity of a good that can be imported by one country from the other country.

A **quota** is a numerical limit on the quantity of a good that can be imported, and it has an effect similar to a tariff. A quota is imposed by the government of the importing country. A **voluntary export restraint** is an agreement negotiated between two countries that places a numerical limit on the quantity of a good that can be imported by one country from the other country. In the early 1980s, the United States and Japan negotiated a voluntary export restraint that limited the quantity of automobiles the United States would import from Japan. Quotas and voluntary export restraints have similar economic effects.

The main purpose of most tariffs and quotas is to reduce the foreign competition faced by domestic firms. We saw an example of this at the beginning of this chapter when we discussed the sugar quota, which Congress imposed to protect U.S. sugar producers. Figure 8-7 shows the actual statistics for the U.S. sugar market in 2003. The effect of a quota is very similar to the effect of a tariff. By limiting imports, a quota forces the domestic price of a good above the world price. In this case, the sugar quota limits sugar imports to 3.5 billion pounds (shown by the bracket in Figure 8-7), forcing the U.S. price of sugar up to $0.21 per pound, or

FIGURE 8-7

The Effect of the U.S. Sugar Quota

Without a sugar quota, U.S. sugar producers would have sold 1.0 billion pounds of sugar, U.S. consumers would have purchased 24.3 billion pounds of sugar, and imports would have been 23.3 billion pounds. The U.S. price would have equaled the world price of $0.08 per pound. Because the sugar quota limits imports to 3.5 billion pounds (the bracket in the graph), the price of sugar in the United States rises to $0.21 per pound and U.S. producers increase the quantity of sugar they supply to 16.8 billion pounds. U.S. consumers reduce their sugar purchases to 20.3 billion pounds. Equilibrium moves from point *E* to point *F*. The price of sugar in the United States is now $0.13 per pound higher than the world price. The sugar quota causes a loss of consumer surplus equal to the area *A* + *B* + *C* + *D*. The area *A* is the gain to U.S. sugar producers. The area *C* is the gain to foreign sugar producers. The areas *B* and *D* represent deadweight loss. The total loss to U.S. consumers in 2003 was $2.91 billion.

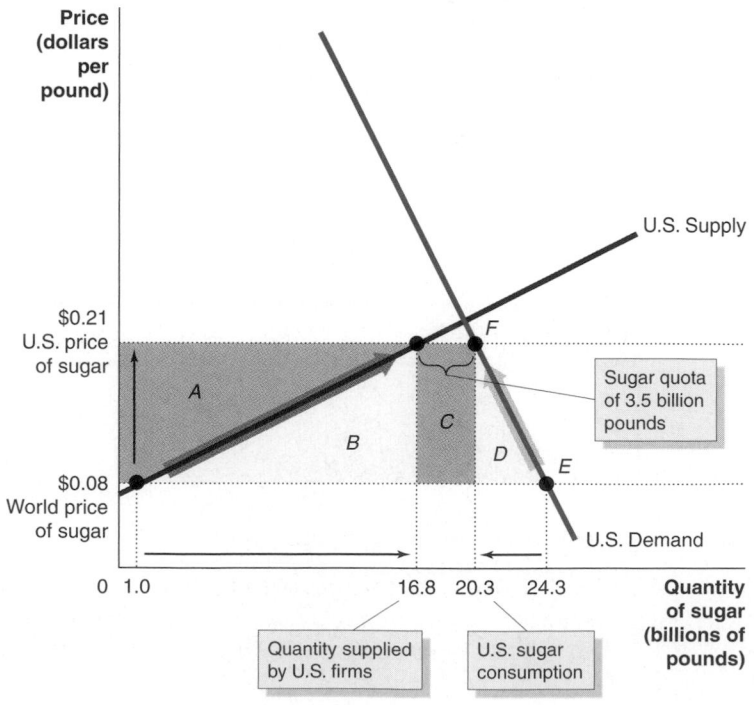

Loss of Consumer Surplus	=	Gain by U.S. Sugar Producers	+	Gain to Foreign Sugar Producers	+	Deadweight Loss
A + *B* + *C* + *D*		*A*		*C*		*B* + *D*
$2.91 billion	=	$1.16 billion	+	$.46 billion	+	$1.29 billion

$0.13 higher than the world price. The U.S. price is above the world price because the quota keeps foreign sugar producers from selling the additional sugar in the United States that would drive the price down to the world price. At a price of $0.21 cents per pound, U.S. producers increased the quantity of sugar they supply from 1.0 billion pounds to 16.8 billion pounds, and U.S. consumers cut back their purchases of sugar from 24.3 billion pounds to 20.3 billion pounds. Equilibrium moves from point E to point F.

Measuring the Economic Impact of the Sugar Quota

Once again, we can use the concepts of consumer surplus, producer surplus, and deadweight loss to measure the economic impact of the sugar quota. Without a sugar quota, the world price of $0.08 per pound would also be the U.S. price. In Figure 8-7, consumer surplus equals the area above the $0.08 price line and below the demand curve. The sugar quota causes the U.S. price to rise to $0.21 cents and reduces consumer surplus by the area $A + B + C + D$. Without a sugar quota, producer surplus received by U.S. sugar producers would be equal to the area below the $0.08 price line and above the supply curve. The higher U.S. price resulting from the sugar quota increases the producer surplus of U.S. sugar producers by an amount equal to area A.

A license from the U.S. government is required to import sugar under the quota system. These import licenses are distributed to foreign producers. Therefore, foreign sugar producers who are lucky enough to have an import license also benefit from the quota because they are able to sell sugar on the U.S. market at $0.21 per pound instead of $0.08 per pound. The gain to foreign sugar producers is area C. Areas A and C represent transfers from U.S. consumers of sugar to U.S. and foreign producers of sugar. Areas B and D represent losses to U.S. consumers that are not captured by anyone. They are deadweight losses and represent the decline in economic efficiency resulting from the sugar quota. Area B shows the effect of U.S. consumers being forced to buy from U.S. producers who are less efficient than foreign producers, and area D shows the effect of U.S. consumers buying less sugar than they would have at the world price.

Enough information is available in the figure to calculate the dollar value of each of the four areas. The results of these calculations are shown in the table in Figure 8-7. The total loss to consumers from the sugar quota was $2.91 billion in 2003. About 40 percent of this loss, or $1.16 billion, was gained by U.S. sugar producers as increased producer surplus. About 16 percent, or $0.46 billion, was gained by foreign sugar producers as increased producer surplus, and about 44 percent, or $1.29 billion, was a deadweight loss to the U.S. economy. The U.S. International Trade Commission estimates that eliminating the sugar quota would result in the loss of about 3,000 jobs in the U.S. sugar industry. The cost to U.S. consumers of saving these jobs is equal to $2.91 billion/3,000 or about $970,000 per job. In fact, this cost is an underestimate because eliminating the sugar quota would result in new jobs being created, particularly in the candy industry. As we saw at the beginning of this chapter, U.S. candy companies have been moving factories to other countries to escape the impact of the sugar quota.

SOLVED PROBLEM 8-2

Measuring the Economic Effect of a Quota

⑤ LEARNING OBJECTIVE
Analyze the economic effects of government policies that restrict international trade.

Suppose that the United States currently both produces apples and imports them. The U.S. government then decides to restrict international trade in apples by imposing a quota that allows imports of only four million boxes of apples into the United States each year. The figure shows the results of imposing the quota:

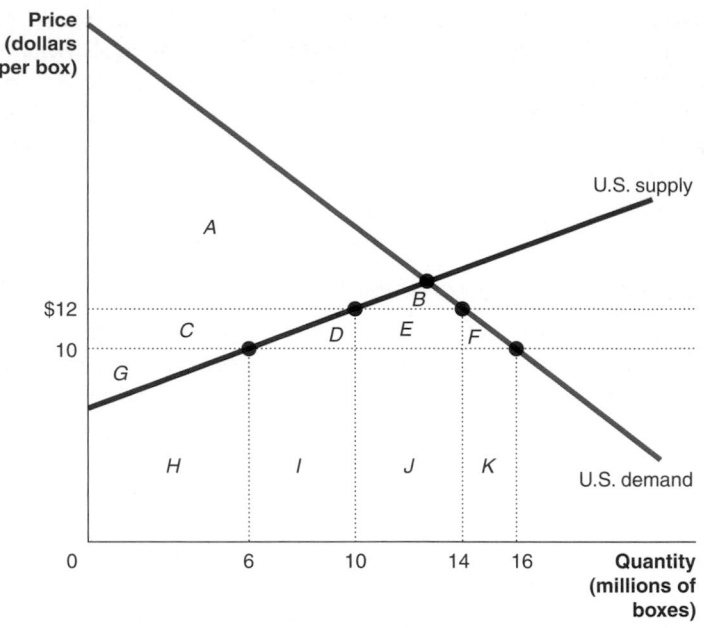

Fill in the following table using the prices, quantities, and letters in the figure:

	WITHOUT QUOTA	WITH QUOTA
World price of apples	_____	_____
U.S. price of apples	_____	_____
Quantity supplied by U.S. firms	_____	_____
Quantity demanded by U.S. consumers	_____	_____
Quantity imported	_____	_____
Area of consumer surplus	_____	_____
Area of producer surplus	_____	_____
Area of deadweight loss	_____	_____

Solving the Problem:

Step 1: Review the chapter material. This problem is about measuring the economic effects of a quota, so you may want to review the section "Quotas," which begins on page 246, and "Measuring the Economic Impact of the Sugar Quota," which begin on page 247.

Step 2: Fill in the table. After studying Figure 8-7, you should be able to fill in the table. Remember that consumer surplus is the area below the demand curve and above the market price.

	WITHOUT QUOTA	WITH QUOTA
World price of apples	$10	$10
U.S. price of apples	$10	$12
Quantity supplied by U.S. firms	6 million boxes	10 million boxes
Quantity demanded by U.S. consumers	16 million boxes	14 million boxes
Quantity imported	10 millions boxes	4 million boxes
Area of consumer surplus	A + B + C + D + E + F	A + B
Area of domestic producer surplus	G	G + C
Area of deadweight loss	No deadweight loss	D + F

YOUR TURN: For more practice, do related problem 25 on page 262 at the end of this chapter. Visit www.prenhall.com/hubbard for an interactive exercise related to this Solved Problem.

PRODUCT	NUMBER OF JOBS SAVED	COST TO CONSUMERS PER YEAR FOR EACH JOB SAVED
Benzenoid chemicals	216	$1,376,435
Luggage	226	1,285,078
Softwood lumber	605	1,044,271
Dairy products	2,378	685,323
Frozen orange juice	609	635,103
Ball bearings	146	603,368
Machine tools	1,556	479,452
Women's handbags	773	263,535
Canned tuna	390	257,640

TABLE 8-5

Preserving U.S. Jobs with Tariffs and Quotas Is Expensive

Source: Federal Reserve Bank of Dallas, *2002 Annual Report,* Exhibit 11.

The High Cost of Preserving Jobs with Tariffs and Quotas

The sugar quota is not alone in imposing a high cost on U.S. consumers to save jobs at U.S. firms. Table 8-5 shows the cost tariffs and quotas impose on U.S. consumers per year for each job saved for several other industries.

Many other countries also use tariffs and quotas to try to protect jobs. Table 8-6 shows the cost to Japanese consumers per year for each job saved as a result of tariffs and quotas in the listed industries. Note the staggering cost imposed on Japanese consumers by the Japanese government's restrictions on imports of rice.

Just as the sugar quota costs jobs in the candy industry, other tariffs and quotas cost jobs outside the industries immediately affected. For example, in 1991, the United States imposed tariffs on flat-panel displays used in laptop computers. This was good news for U.S. producers of these displays but bad news for companies producing laptop computers. Toshiba, Sharp, and Apple all closed their U.S. laptop production facilities and moved production overseas. In fact, whenever one industry receives tariff or quota protection, jobs will be lost in other domestic industries.

Gains from Unilateral Elimination of Tariffs and Quotas

Some politicians argue that eliminating U.S. tariffs and quotas will help the U.S. economy only if other countries eliminate their tariffs and quotas in exchange. It is easier to gain

PRODUCT	COST TO CONSUMERS PER YEAR FOR EACH JOB SAVED
Rice	$51,233,000
Natural gas	27,987,000
Gasoline	6,329,000
Paper	3,813,000
Beef, pork, and poultry	1,933,000
Cosmetics	1,778,000
Radio and television sets	915,000

TABLE 8-6

Preserving Japanese Jobs with Tariffs and Quotas Is Also Expensive

Source: Yoko Sazabami, Shujiro Urata, and Hiroki Kawai, "Measuring the Cost of Protection in Japan," Washington, DC: Institute for International Economics, 1995. Used with permission.

political support for reducing or eliminating a tariff or quota if it is done as part of an agreement with other countries that involves their eliminating some of their tariffs or quotas. But as the example of the sugar quota shows, *the U.S. economy would gain from the elimination of tariffs and quotas, even if other countries do not reduce their tariffs and quotas.*

Other Barriers to Trade

In addition to tariffs and quotas, governments sometimes erect other barriers to trade. For example, all governments require that imports meet certain health and safety requirements. Sometimes, however, health and safety requirements are used to shield domestic firms from foreign competition. This can be true when a government imposes stricter health and safety requirements on imported goods than on goods produced by domestic firms.

Many governments also restrict imports of certain products on national security grounds. The argument is that in time of war, a country should not be dependent on imports of critical war materials. Once again, these restrictions are sometimes used more to protect domestic companies from competition than to protect national security. For example, for years, the United States government would only buy military uniforms from U.S. manufacturers, even though uniforms are not a critical war material.

⑥ **LEARNING OBJECTIVE**

Evaluate the arguments for and against government policies that restrict international trade.

The Argument over Trade Policies and Globalization

The argument over whether the U.S. government should regulate international trade dates back to the beginning of the country. One particularly controversial attempt to restrict trade took place during the Great Depression of the 1930s. At that time the United States and other countries attempted to help domestic firms by raising tariffs on foreign imports. The United States started the process by passing the Smoot-Hawley Tariff in 1930, which raised average tariff rates to more than 50 percent. As other countries retaliated by raising their tariffs, international trade collapsed.

By the end of World War II in 1945, government officials in the United States and Europe were looking for a way to reduce tariffs and revive international trade. To help achieve this goal, they set up the General Agreement on Tariffs and Trade (GATT) in 1948. Countries that joined the GATT agreed not to impose new tariffs or import quotas. In addition, a series of *multilateral negotiations,* called *trade rounds,* took place, in which countries agreed to reduce tariffs from the very high levels of the 1930s.

In the 1940s, most international trade was in goods, and the GATT agreement covered only goods. In the following decades, trade in services and in products incorporating *intellectual property,* such as software programs and movies, grew in importance. Many GATT members pressed for a new agreement that would cover services and intellectual property, as well as goods. A new agreement was negotiated, and in January 1995 the GATT was replaced by the **World Trade Organization (WTO),** headquartered in Geneva, Switzerland. More than 130 countries are currently members of the WTO.

World Trade Organization (WTO) An international organization that enforces international trade agreements.

Why Do Some People Oppose the World Trade Organization?

During the years immediately after World War II, many low-income, or developing, countries erected high tariffs and restricted investment by foreign companies. When these policies failed to produce much economic growth, many of these countries decided during the 1980s to become more open to foreign trade and investment. This process became known as **globalization.** Most developing countries joined the WTO and began to follow its policies.

Globalization The process of countries becoming more open to foreign trade and investment.

During the 1990s, opposition to globalization began to increase. In 1999, this opposition took a violent turn at a meeting of the WTO in Seattle, Washington. The purpose of the meeting was to plan a new round of negotiations aimed at further reductions in trade barriers. A large number of protestors assembled in Seattle to meet the WTO delegates. Protests started peacefully but quickly became violent. Protesters looted stores and burned cars, and many delegates were unable to leave their hotel rooms.

Why would attempts to reduce trade barriers with the objective of increasing income around the world cause such a furious reaction? The opposition to the WTO comes from three sources. First, some opponents are specifically against the globalization process that began in the 1980s and became widespread in the 1990s. Second, other opponents have the same motivation as the supporters of tariffs in the 1930s—to erect trade barriers to protect domestic firms from foreign competition. Third, some critics of the WTO support globalization in principle but believe that the WTO favors the interests of the high-income countries at the expense of the low-income countries. Because of the importance of this issue, we will look more closely at the sources of opposition to the WTO.

ANTI-GLOBALIZATION Many of the protestors in Seattle distrust globalization. Some believe that free trade and foreign investment destroy the distinctive cultures of many countries. As developing countries began to open their economies to imports from the United States and other high-income countries, these imports of food, clothing, movies, and other goods began to replace the equivalent local products. So, a teenager in Thailand might be sitting in a McDonald's restaurant, wearing Levi's jeans and a Ralph Lauren shirt, listening to a recording by U2 on his iPod, before going to the local movie theater to watch *Spider-Man 2*. Globalization has increased the variety of products available to consumers in developing countries, but some people argue this is too high a price to pay for what they see as the damage to local cultures.

Globalization has also allowed multinational corporations to relocate factories from high-income countries to low-income countries. These new factories in Indonesia, Malaysia, Pakistan, and other countries pay much lower wages than are paid in the United States, Europe, and Japan and often do not meet the environmental or safety regulations that are imposed in high-income countries. Some factories use child labor, which is illegal in high-income countries. Some people have argued that firms with factories in developing countries should pay workers wages as high as those paid in the high-income countries. They also believe these firms should follow the health, safety, and environmental regulations that exist in the high-income countries.

The governments of most developing countries have resisted these proposals. They argue that when the currently rich countries were poor, they also lacked environmental or safety standards, and their workers were paid low wages. They argue that it is easier for rich countries to afford high wages and environmental and safety regulations than it is for poor countries. They also point out that many jobs that seem very poorly paid by high-income country standards are often better than the alternatives available to workers in low-income countries.

The Unintended Consequences of Banning Goods Made with Child Labor

8-3 Making the Connection

In many developing countries, such as Indonesia, Thailand, and Peru, children as young as seven or eight work 10 or more hours a day. Reports of very young workers laboring long hours producing goods for export have upset many people in the high-income countries. In the United States, boycotts have been organized against stores that stock goods made in developing countries with child labor. Many people assume that if child workers in developing countries weren't working in factories making clothing, toys, and other products, they would be in school, as are children in the high-income countries.

In fact, there are usually few good alternatives to work for children in developing countries. Schooling is frequently available for only a few months each year, and even children who attend school rarely do so for more than a few years. Poor families are often unable to afford even the small costs of sending their children to school. Families may even rely on the earnings of very young children to survive, as once did poor families in the the United States,

Would eliminating child labor in developing countries be a good thing?

Europe, and Japan. The United States did not outlaw child labor until 1938. In developing countries, jobs producing export goods are usually better paying and less hazardous than the alternatives.

As preparations began in France for the 1998 World Cup, there were protests that Baden Sports—the main supplier of soccer balls— was purchasing the balls from suppliers in Pakistan who used child workers. France decided to ban all use of soccer balls made by child workers. Bowing to this pressure, Baden Sports moved production from Pakistan, where the balls were hand-stitched by child workers, to China, where the balls were machine-stitched by adult workers in factories. There was some criticism of the boycott of hand-stitched soccer balls at the time. In a broad study of child labor, three economists argued:

> [O]f the array of possible employment in which impoverished children might engage, soccer ball stitching is probably one of the most benign. . . . [In Pakistan] children generally work alongside other family members in the home or in small workshops. . . . Nor are the children exposed to toxic chemicals, hazardous tools or brutal working conditions. Rather, the only serious criticism concerns the length of the typical child stitcher's work-day and the impact on formal education.

In fact, the alternatives to soccer ball stitching for child workers in Pakistan turned out to be extremely grim. According to Keith Maskus, an economist at the University of Colorado and the World Bank, a "large proportion" of the children who lost their jobs stitching soccer balls ended up begging or in prostitution.

Sources: Drusilla K. Brown, Alan V. Deardorff, and Robert M. Stern, "U.S. Trade and Other Policy Options to Deter Foreign Exploitation of Child Labor," in Magnus Blomstrom and Linda S. Goldberg, eds., *Topics in Empirical International Economics: A Festschrift in Honor of Bob Lipsey,* Chicago: University of Chicago Press, 2001; and Tomas Larsson, *The Race to the Top: The Real Story of Globalization,* 2001,p. 48.

"OLD-FASHIONED" PROTECTIONISM The anti-globalization argument against free trade and the WTO is relatively new. Another argument against free trade is called *protectionism* and has been around for centuries. **Protectionism** is the use of trade barriers to shield domestic firms from foreign competition. For as long as international trade has existed, governments have attempted to restrict it to protect domestic firms. As we saw with the analysis of the sugar quota, protectionism causes losses to consumers and eliminates jobs in the domestic industries that use the protected product. In addition, by reducing the ability of countries to produce according to comparative advantage, protectionism reduces incomes.

Why, then, does protectionism attract support? Protectionism is usually justified on the basis of one of the following arguments:

Protectionism The use of trade barriers to shield domestic firms from foreign competition.

➤ *Saving jobs.* Supporters of protectionism argue that free trade reduces employment by driving domestic firms out of business. It is true that when more-efficient foreign firms drive less-efficient domestic firms out of business, jobs are lost, but jobs are also lost when more-efficient domestic firms drive less-efficient domestic firms out of business. These job losses are rarely permanent. In the U.S. economy, jobs are being lost and new jobs are being created continually. No economic study has ever found a connection in the long run between the total number of jobs available and the level of tariff protection for domestic industries. In addition, trade restrictions destroy jobs in some industries at the same time that they preserve jobs in others. The U.S. sugar quota may have saved jobs in the U.S. sugar industry, but, as we saw at the beginning of this chapter, it also has destroyed jobs in the U.S. candy industry.

➤ *Protecting high wages.*   Some people worry that firms in the high-income countries will have to start paying much lower wages to compete with firms in the developing countries. This fear is misplaced, however, because free trade actually raises living standards by increasing economic efficiency. When a country practices protectionism and produces goods and services it could obtain more cheaply from other countries, it reduces its standard of living. The United States could ban imports of coffee and begin growing it domestically. But this would entail a very high opportunity cost because coffee could only be grown in the U.S. in greenhouses and would require large amounts of labor and equipment. The coffee would have to sell for a very high price to cover these costs. Suppose the United States did ban coffee imports: Eliminating the ban at some future time would eliminate the jobs of U.S. coffee workers, but the standard of living in the United States would rise as coffee prices declined and labor, machinery, and other resources moved out of coffee production and into production of goods and services for which the U.S. has a comparative advantage.

➤ *Protecting infant industries.*   It is possible that firms in a country may have a comparative advantage in producing a good, but because the country begins production of the good later than other countries, its firms initially have higher costs. In producing some goods and services, substantial "learning by doing" occurs. As workers and firms produce more of the good or service, they gain experience and become more productive. Over time, costs and prices will fall. As the firms in the "infant industry" gain experience, their costs will fall and they will be able to compete successfully with foreign producers. Under free trade, however, they may not get the chance. The established foreign producers can sell the product at a lower price and drive domestic producers out of business before they gain enough experience to compete. To economists, this is the most persuasive of the protectionist arguments. It does have a significant drawback, however. Tariffs used to protect an infant industry eliminate the need for the firms in the industry to become productive enough to compete with foreign firms. After World War II, the governments of many developing countries used the "infant industry" argument to justify high tariff rates. Unfortunately, most of their infant industries never grew up and they continued for years as inefficient drains on their economies.

➤ *Protecting national security.*   As already discussed, a country should not rely on other countries for goods that are critical to its military defense. For example, the United States would probably not want to import all of its jet fighter engines from China. The definition of which goods are critical to military defense is a slippery one, however. In fact, it is rare for an industry to ask for protection without raising the issue of national security even if its products have mainly nonmilitary uses.

Has NAFTA Helped or Hurt the U.S. Economy?

8-4 Making the Connection

The North American Free Trade Agreement (NAFTA) was very controversial when it was being negotiated in the early 1990s. During the 1992 presidential campaign, independent candidate Ross Perot claimed to hear a "giant sucking sound" as jobs were pulled out of the United States and into Mexico. NAFTA went into effect in 1994 and eliminated most tariffs on products shipped between the United States, Canada, and Mexico. This policy change made it possible for each country to better pursue its comparative advantage. For example, before NAFTA the Mexican government had used tariffs to protect its domestic automobile industry, but the industry was much less efficient than the U.S. automobile industry. Once tariffs were removed, Mexican consumers could take advantage of the efficiency of the U.S. industry, and U.S. exports of motor vehicles to Mexico soared. Similarly, Canadian consumers could take advantage of lower-priced U.S. beef, and U.S. consumers could take advantage of lower-priced Canadian lumber. As we would expect, expanding trade increased consumption in all three countries. In the United States, consumption increased about $400 per year for a family of four as a result of NAFTA.

Contrary to Ross Perot's prediction, NAFTA did not lead to a loss of jobs in the United States. Between 1994, when NAFTA went into effect, and 2004, the number of jobs in the United States increased by more than 17 million. Some commentators argued that jobs in the United States could be preserved with NAFTA, but only if wages for U.S. workers declined to the much lower levels being paid Mexican workers. In fact, a study by Gordon Hanson of the University of California, San Diego, showed that the opposite occurred: wages for both U.S. and Mexican workers increased following NAFTA. In addition, the gap between U.S. wages and Mexican wages did not close.

There were, of course, people in all three countries who were made worse off by NAFTA. Some firms in each country were no longer competitive once tariffs had been lowered. In the United States, government assistance helped workers who lost their jobs to retrain or relocate. Overall, most economists have concluded that NAFTA helped the U.S. economy become more efficient, thereby expanding the consumption of U.S. households.

Despite resistance to NAFTA, time proved that the U.S. economy gained jobs.

Sources: Gordon H. Hanson, "What Has Happened to Wages in Mexico Since NAFTA? Implications for Hemispheric Free Trade" in Toni Estevadeordal, Dani Rodrick, Alan Taylor Andres Velasco, eds., *FTAA and Beyond: Prospects for Integration in the Americas*, Cambridge: Harvard University Press, 2004.

Dumping

Dumping Selling a product for a price below its cost of production.

In recent years, the United States has extended protection to some domestic industries by using a provision in the WTO agreement that allows governments to impose tariffs in the case of *dumping*. **Dumping** is selling a product for a price below its cost of production. Although allowable under the WTO agreement, using tariffs to offset the effects of dumping is very controversial.

In practice, it is difficult to determine if foreign companies are dumping goods because the true production costs of a good are not easy for foreign governments to calculate. As a result, the WTO allows countries to determine that dumping has occurred if a product is exported for a lower price than it sells for on the home market. There is a problem with this approach, however. Often there are good business reasons for a firm to sell a product for different prices to different consumers. For example, the airlines charge business travelers higher ticket prices than leisure travelers. Firms also use "loss leaders"—products that are sold below cost, or even given away free—when introducing a new product or, in the case of retailing, to attract customers who also will buy full-price products. For example, when Sun Microsystems attempted to establish StarOffice as a competitor to Microsoft's Office, it gave it away free on its Web site. During the Christmas season, Wal-Mart sometimes offers toys at prices below what they pay to buy them from manufacturers. It's unclear why these normal business practices should be unacceptable when used in international trade.

Positive versus Normative Analysis (Once Again)

Economists emphasize the burden on the economy imposed by tariffs, quotas, and other government restrictions on free trade. Does it follow that these interferences are bad? Remember from Chapter 1 the distinction between *positive analysis* and *normative analysis*. Positive analysis concerns what *is*. Normative analysis concerns what *ought to be*. Measuring the impact of the sugar quota on the U.S. economy is an example of positive analysis. Asserting that the sugar quota is bad public policy and should be eliminated is normative analysis. The sugar quota—like all other interferences with trade—makes some people better off, some people worse off, and reduces total income and consumption. Whether increasing the profits of U.S. sugar companies and the number of workers they employ justifies the costs imposed on consumers and the reduction in economic efficiency is a normative question.

Most economists do not support interferences with trade, such as the sugar quota. Few people become economists if they don't believe that markets should usually be as free as possible. But the opposite view is certainly intellectually respectable. It is possible for someone to understand the costs of tariffs and quotas but still believe that tariffs and quotas are a good idea, perhaps because they believe unrestricted free trade would cause too much disruption to the economy.

The success of industries in getting the government to erect barriers to foreign competition depends partly on some members of the public knowing full well the costs of trade barriers but supporting them anyway. Two other factors are also at work:

1. The costs tariffs and quotas impose on consumers are large in total but relatively small per person. For example, the sugar quota imposes a total burden of about $3 billion per year on consumers. Spread across 295 million Americans, the burden is only about $10 per person: too little for most people to worry about, even if they know the burden exists.

2. The jobs lost to foreign competition are easy to identify, but the jobs created by foreign trade are less easy to identify.

In other words, the industries that benefit from tariffs and quotas benefit a lot—the sugar quota increases the profits of U.S. sugar producers by more than $1 billion—whereas each consumer loses relatively little. This concentration of benefits and widely spread burdens makes it easy to understand why members of Congress receive strong pressure from some industries to enact tariffs and quotas and relatively little pressure from the general public to reduce them.

Conclusion

There are few issues economists agree upon more than the economic benefits of free trade. However, there are few political issues as controversial as government policy toward trade. Many people who would be reluctant to see the government interfere with domestic trade are quite willing to see it interfere with international trade. The damage high tariffs inflicted on the world economy during the 1930s shows what can happen when governments around the world abandon free trade. Whether future episodes of that type can be avoided is by no means certain.

Read *An Inside Look* on the next page to learn how eliminating tariffs on wine benefits the United States and Australia.

SAN FRANCISCO CHRONICLE, MAY 15, 2004

U.S., Australia Commerce to Leap Forward

An already close commercial and cultural relationship will grow even closer Tuesday, when the United States and Australia sign a bilateral free trade agreement that will slash tariffs, streamline investment rules and open up access to a broad spectrum of each country's markets. The free trade agreement, this country's first with a developed nation since Washington struck a free trade deal with Canada in 1988, won't take effect for months to come.

The legislatures of both nations will have to approve it before it becomes law. Australia's Parliament is expected to approve the agreement without too much fuss, while a spokesperson for the U.S. Trade Representative's office said Friday that the Bush administration plans to submit the pact to Congress "sometime this summer. We are seeing good bipartisan support for it."

Two-way trade between Washington and Canberra is already robust, with annual two-way trade of $28 billion. Australia, with a population of just 20 million, is the 13th-largest export market for the United States, while this country is Australia's top export market. Unusually, the United States, which ran a record $46 billion trade deficit with the rest of the world last month, racks up a trade surplus with Australia; the annual surplus crested at $9 billion in 2002.

California, in particular, finds an eager Aussie market for its computers, electronic gizmos, farm produce, Hollywood movies and Silicon Valley software in Australian shops and homes. The Golden State shipped out $1.9 billion worth of goods to Australia in 2002, and ranks just behind Washington State as this country's largest exporting state to Australia.

"It's hugely positive, it's a winner for both countries," said Robert Hunt, senior investment commissioner for North America at Invest Australia, an Australian federal agency. The agreement, said Hunt, who is based in Invest Australia's San Francisco office, means "the virtual elimination of tariffs, except on beef, dairy and sugar. But they are very far from being the main game. It's probably the most comprehensive agreement anywhere by any two countries."

Even in this ambitious agreement, some sectors of the economy are off-limits to the Aussies. Notwithstanding its free-trade rhetoric, Washington shelters beef, dairy and sugar industries from foreign competition. In line with that, the proposed agreement would allow no increase in quotas for inexpensive Australian sugar and only modest increases in Aussie beef and dairy products in the huge U.S. market.

But while the free trade agreement won't change everything, it will, if enacted, be far-reaching. The rules of the game for investors, for example, will be radically revised, according to Hunt, whose agency is charged with attracting foreign direct investment. Aussie rules barring foreigners from buying more than a $37 million stake in Australian businesses would be raised to $600 million, for example, enabling Americans to buy into Australian companies and giving Aussie firms much greater access to U.S. capital.

Companies that do businesses with Australia are broadly supportive of the trade agreement. "We have a big interest in Australia, and in general, we support free trade agreements," said Johnny Ng, a spokesman for San Ramon's Chevron Texaco. The energy company is exploring for natural gas on Australia's northwest coast, where it owns 57.1 percent of a natural gas project on the northwest shelf and has a one-sixth stake in a project in the Indian Ocean called Gorgon.

Key Points in the Article

The article discusses a new trade agreement between the United States and Australia that will reduce most restrictions on trade between the two countries. Agreements, such as this one, to expand trade between two countries are known as *bilateral agreements*. The trade agreements worked out by the World Trade Organization are *multilateral agreements*. As the article predicted, both the Australian parliament and the U.S. Congress approved the agreement later in 2004. The U.S. market is the largest in the world. As the article points out, Australia exports more to the United States than to any other country, despite the great distance that separates the two countries.

Analyzing the News

a In this chapter, we have seen that expanding trade raises living standards by increasing consumption and economic efficiency. Reducing tariffs on trade between Australia and the United States will aid consumers in both countries. Figure 1 shows the U.S. market for wine following the elimination of the tariff on Australian wine (just for simplicity, we assume that there are no remaining U.S. tariffs on wine). The price of wine in the United States falls from P_1 to P_2, and equilibrium in the U.S.

wine market moves from point E to point F. U.S. consumption of wine increases from Q_3 to Q_4, the quantity of wine supplied by U.S. winemakers declines from Q_2 to Q_1, and imports increase from $Q_3 - Q_2$ to $Q_4 - Q_1$. Consumer surplus increases by the sum of areas A, B, C, and D. Area A represents a transfer from producer surplus under the tariff to consumer surplus. Areas B and D represent the conversion of deadwight loss to consumer surplus. Area C represents a conversion of government tariff revenue to consumer surplus. Eliminating the tariff reduces the cost to California wine producers of selling their product in Australia. We show this lower cost in the diagram by shifting the supply curve from Supply (including tariff) to Supply (without tariff). The equilibrium shifts from price P_1 and quantity Q_1 to price P_2 and quantity Q_2. Australian consumers purchase a larger quantity of California wine at a lower price.

b Figure 1 shows that eliminating the tariff on wine also eliminates the revenue the U.S. government had been collecting from this tariff. In high-income countries, such as Australia and the United States, governments receive most of their revenue from taxes on personal and corporate income. For example, tariff revenue in the United States for 2004 amounted to only about 1 percent of all revenue received by the federal government, but

governments in low-income countries often have difficulty collecting income taxes, so they rely heavily on tariffs for revenue. In these countries, the government's need for revenue can pose a serious barrier to expanding international trade by reducing tariffs, because governments have difficulty replacing the revenues lost from tariff reductions. This was also true in the United States early in its history. In 1800, tariffs brought in 90 percent of all federal government revenue. As late as the 1950s, tariffs accounted for 14 percent of federal revenues.

c Political factors enter into most trade negotiations. In this case, for political reasons the United States was unwilling to reduce its quotas on beef, dairy products, and sugar. In this chapter, we analyzed the sugar quota's economic effect on the United States.

Thinking Critically
ABOUT POLICY

1. Import quotas on sugar, beef, and dairy products save jobs for Americans working in those industries. Do you support these quotas? Why or why not?
2. In which goods mentioned in the article does the United States have a comparative advantage? In which does Australia have a comparative advantage? Explain your reasoning.

Source: San Francisco Chronicle (1865–) [Staff produced copy only] by Staff. Copyright 2004 by San Francisco Chronicle. Reproduced with permission of San Francisco Chronicle in the format Textbook via Copyright Clearance Center.

Increase in Consumer Surplus	=	Decrease in Producer Surplus	+	Decrease in Government Tariff Revenue	+	Decrease in Deadweight Loss
$A + B + C + D$		A		C		$B + D$

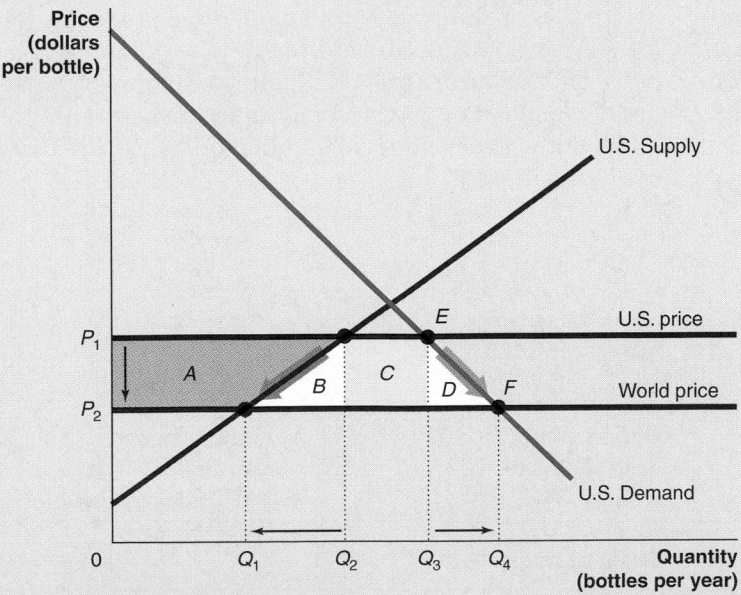

Figure 1: The market for wine in the United States after the tariff on Australian wine is eliminated.

LEARNING OBJECTIVE ① **Discuss the increasing importance of international trade to the United States.** The quantity of goods and services the United States imports and exports has been continually increasing. Today, the United States is the leading exporting country in the world, and about 20 percent of U.S. manufacturing jobs depend upon exports.

LEARNING OBJECTIVE ② **Understand the difference between comparative advantage and absolute advantage.** *Comparative advantage* is the ability of an individual, business, or country to produce a good or service at the lowest opportunity cost. *Absolute advantage* is the ability to produce more of a good or service than competitors when using the same amount of resources. Countries trade on the basis of comparative advantage, not on the basis of absolute advantage.

LEARNING OBJECTIVE ③ **Explain how countries gain from international trade.** When a country specializes in producing goods where it has a comparative advantage and trades for the other goods it needs, the country will have a higher level of income and consumption. We do not see complete specialization in production for three reasons: Not all goods and services are traded internationally; production of most goods involves increasing opportunity costs; and tastes for products differ across countries. Although the population of a country as a whole benefits from trade, companies—and their workers—that are unable to compete with lower-cost foreign producers lose.

LEARNING OBJECTIVE ④ **Discuss the sources of comparative advantage.** Among the main sources of comparative advantage are these: climate and natural resources, relative abundance of labor and capital, technology, and *external economies*. A country may develop a comparative advantage in the production of a good, then as time passes and circumstances change, the country may lose its comparative advantage in producing that good and develop a comparative advantage in producing other goods.

LEARNING OBJECTIVE ⑤ **Analyze the economic effects of government policies that restrict international trade.** Government policies that interfere with trade usually take the form of: *tariffs, quotas,* or *voluntary export restraints.* A tariff is a tax imposed by a government on imports. A quota is a numerical limit imposed by the government on the quantity of a good that can be imported into a country. A voluntary export restraint is an agreement negotiated between two countries that places a numerical limit on the quantity of a good that can be imported by one country from the other country. The federal government's sugar quota costs U.S. consumers $2.91 billion per year, or about $970,000 per year for each job saved in the sugar industry. Saving jobs by using tariffs and quotas is often very expensive.

LEARNING OBJECTIVE ⑥ **Evaluate the arguments for and against government policies that restrict international trade.** The *World Trade Organization (WTO)* is an international organization that enforces international trade agreements. The WTO has promoted *globalization,* the process of countries becoming more open to foreign trade and investment. Some critics of the WTO argue that globalization has damaged local cultures around the world. Other critics oppose the WTO because they believe governments should be free to use tariffs and quotas to protect domestic industries. The WTO allows countries to use tariffs in cases of *dumping,* when an imported product is sold for a price below its cost of production. Economists can point out the burden imposed on the economy by tariffs, quotas, and other government interferences with free trade. But whether these policies should be used is a normative decision.

KEY TERMS

Absolute advantage 236	Exports 232	Opportunity cost 235	Voluntary export
Autarky 237	External economies 242	Protectionism 252	restraint 246
Comparative	Free trade 243	Quota 246	World Trade Organization
advantage 235	Globalization 250	Tariff 232	(WTO) 250
Dumping 254	Imports 232	Terms of trade 237	

REVIEW QUESTIONS

1. Briefly explain whether you agree or disagree with the following statement: "International trade is more important to the U.S. economy than to most other economies."

2. A World Trade Organization publication calls comparative advantage "arguably the single most powerful insight in economics." What is comparative advantage? What makes it such a powerful insight?
Source: World Trade Organization, *Trading into the Future*, April 1999.

3. What is the difference between absolute advantage and comparative advantage? Will a country always be an exporter of a good where it has an absolute advantage in production?

4. Briefly explain how international trade increases a country's consumption.

5. What is meant by a country specializing in the production of a good? Is it typical for countries to be completely specialized? Briefly explain.

6. What are the main sources of comparative advantage?

7. What is a tariff? What is a quota? Give an example of a non-tariff barrier to trade.

8. Who gains and who loses when a country imposes a tariff or a quota on imports of a good?

9. What events led to the General Agreement on Tariffs and Trade? Why did the World Trade Organization eventually replace the GATT?

10. What is globalization? Why are some people opposed to globalization?

11. What is protectionism? Who benefits and who loses from protectionist policies? What are the main arguments people use to justify protectionism?

12. What is dumping? Who benefits and who loses from dumping? What problems arise when implementing antidumping laws?

PROBLEMS AND APPLICATIONS

Please visit **www.prenhall.com/hubbard** *for solutions to the even-numbered problems as well as multiple-choice and true or false self-assessment quizzes.*

1. Why do the goods that countries import and export change over time? Use the concept of comparative advantage in your answer.

2. In 1987, an economic study showed that, on average, workers in the Japanese consumer electronics industry produced less output per hour than did U.S. workers producing the same goods. Despite this fact, Japan exported large quantities of consumer electronics to the United States. Briefly explain how this is possible.
Source: Study cited in Douglas A. Irwin, *Free Trade under Fire*, Princeton: Princeton University Press, 2002, p. 27.

3. [Related to *Solved Problem 8-1*] The following table shows the hourly output per worker in two industries in Chile and Argentina:

	OUTPUT PER HOUR OF WORK	
	HATS	BEER
Chile	8	6
Argentina	1	2

a. Explain which country has an absolute advantage in the production of hats and which country has an absolute advantage in the production of beer.

b. Explain which country has a comparative advantage in the production of hats and which country has a comparative advantage in the production of beer.

c. Suppose that Chile and Argentina currently do not trade with each other. Each has 1,000 hours of labor to use producing hats and beer, and the countries are currently producing the amounts of each good shown in the following table:

	HATS	BEER
Chile	7,200	600
Argentina	600	800

Using this information, give a numerical example of how Chile and Argentina can both gain from trade. Assume that after trading begins, one hat can be exchanged for one barrel of beer.

4. Demonstrate how the opportunity costs of producing cell phones and MP3 players in Japan and the United States in Table 8-2 were calculated.

5. Briefly explain whether you agree or disagree with the following statement: "Most countries exhaust their comparative advantage in producing a good or service before they reach complete specialization."

6. Patrick J. Buchanan, a former presidential candidate, argues in his book on the global economy that there is a flaw in David Ricardo's theory of comparative advantage:

> [C]lassical free trade theory fails the test of common sense. According to Ricardo's law of comparative advantage . . . if America makes better computers and textiles than China does, but our advantage in computers is greater than our advantage in textiles, we should (1) focus on computers, (2) let China make textiles, and (3) trade U.S. computers for Chinese textiles. . . .
>
> The doctrine begs a question. If Americans are more efficient than Chinese in making clothes . . . why surrender the more efficient American industry? Why shift to a reliance on a Chinese textile industry that will take years to catch up to where American factories are today?

Do you agree with Buchanan's argument? Briefly explain.
Source: Patrick J. Buchanan, *The Great Betrayal: How American Sovereignty and Social Justice Are Being Sacrificed to the Gods of the Global Economy*, Boston: Little, Brown, 1998, p. 66.

7. Is free trade likely to benefit a large populous country more than a small country with fewer people? Briefly explain.

8. An editorial in *Business Week* argued the following:

> [President] Bush needs to send a pure and clear signal that the U.S. supports free trade on its merits. . . . That means resisting any further protectionist demands by lawmakers. It could even mean unilaterally reducing tariffs or taking down trade barriers rather than erecting new ones. Such moves would benefit U.S. consumers while giving a needed boost to struggling economies overseas.

What does the editorial mean by "protectionist demands"? How would the unilateral elimination of U.S. trade barriers benefit both U.S. consumers and economies overseas?
Source: "The Threat of Protectionism," *Business Week*, June 3, 2002.

9. Political commentator B. Bruce-Biggs once wrote the following in the *Wall Street Journal*:

> This is not to say that the case for international free trade is invalid; it is just irrelevant. It is an "if only everybody . . . " argument. . . . In the real world almost everybody sees benefits in economic nationalism.

What do you think he means by "economic nationalism"? Do you agree that a country only benefits from free trade if every other country also practices free trade? Briefly explain.
Source: B. Bruce-Biggs, "The Coming Overthrow of Free Trade," *Wall Street Journal*, February 24, 1983, p. 28.

10. **[Related to *Solved Problem 8-1*]** A political commentator makes the following statement:

> The idea that international trade should be based on the comparative advantage of each country is fine for rich countries like the United States and Japan. Rich countries have educated workers and large quantities of machinery and equipment. These advantages allow them to produce every product more efficiently than poor countries can. Poor countries like Kenya and Bolivia have nothing to gain from international trade based on comparative advantage.

Do you agree with this argument? Briefly explain.

11. Explain why there are advantages to a movie studio operating in Southern California, rather than in, say, Florida.

12. The United States produces beef and also imports beef from other countries.
    a. Draw a graph showing the supply and demand for beef in the United States. Assume that the United States can import as much as it wants at the world price of beef without causing the world price of beef to increase. Be sure to indicate on your diagram the quantity of beef imported.
    b. Now show on your graph the effect of the United States imposing a tariff on beef. Be sure to indicate on your diagram the quantity of beef sold by U.S. producers before and after the tariff is imposed, the quantity of beef imported before and after the tariff, and the price of beef in the United States before and after the tariff.
    c. Discuss who benefits and who loses when the U.S. imposes a tariff on beef.

13. The following excerpt is from a newspaper story on President Bill Clinton's proposals for changes in the World Trade Organization. The story was published just before the 1999 World Trade Organization meeting in Seattle that ended in rioting:

> [President Clinton] suggested that a working group on labor be created within the WTO to develop core labor standards that would become "part of every trade agreement. And ultimately I would favor a system in which sanctions would come for violating any provision of a trade agreement. . . . " But the new U.S. stand is sure to meet massive resistance

from developing countries, which make up more than 100 of the 135 countries in the WTO. They are not interested in adopting tougher U.S. labor standards.

What did President Clinton mean by "core labor standards"? Why would developing countries resist adopting these standards?

14. **[Related to the *Chapter Opener*]** Which industries are affected unfavorably by the sugar quota? Are any industries (other than the sugar industry) affected favorably by the sugar quota? (*Hint:* Think about what sugar is used for and whether substitutes exist for these uses.)

15. When Congress was considering a bill to impose quotas on imports of textiles, shoes, and other products, Milton Friedman, a Nobel Prize–winning economist, made the following comment:

   The consumer will be forced to spend several extra dollars to subsidize the producers [of these goods] by one dollar. A straight handout would be far cheaper.

Why would a quota result in consumers paying much more than domestic producers receive? Where do the other dollars go? What does Friedman mean by a "straight handout"? Why would this be cheaper than a quota?
Source: Milton Friedman, "Free Trade," *Newsweek*, August 27, 1970.

16. The European Union is an organization of more than 20 European countries. Half of the spending by the European Union consists of subsidies to farmers. These payments result in European farmers producing much more food than they otherwise would. A substantial amount of this food is exported. According to an article in the *Wall Street Journal*, Monica Shandu, a farmer in South Africa, works full-time raising sugar cane on her four-acre farm:

   Ms. Shandu was named South Africa's small-scale Cane Grower of the Year for a top-quality harvest in 2001. Yet . . . she earned only $200 after costs on that harvest. Sugar prices depressed by [European] subsidies cut her annual income by about a third.

Why would subsidies paid by European governments to European sugar farmers reduce the income of a sugar farmer in South Africa?
Source: Roger Thurow and Geoff Winestock, "Addiction to Sugar Subsidies Chokes Poor Nations' Exports," *Wall Street Journal*, September 16, 2002.

17. An economic analysis of a proposal to impose a quota on steel imports into the United States indicated that the quota would save 3,700 jobs in the steel industry but cost about 35,000 jobs in other U.S. industries. Why would a quota on steel imports cause employment to fall in other industries? Which other industries are likely to be most affected?
Source: Study cited in Douglas A. Irwin, *Free Trade Under Fire*, Princeton: Princeton University Press, 2002, p. 82.

18. A student makes the following argument: "Tariffs on imports of foreign goods into the United States will cause the foreign companies to add the amount of the tariff to the prices they charge in the United States for those goods. Instead of putting a tariff on imported goods, we should ban importing them. Banning imported goods is better than putting tariffs on them because U.S. producers benefit from the reduced competition and U.S. consumers don't have to pay the higher prices caused by tariffs." Briefly explain whether you agree with the student's reasoning.

19. Steven Landsburg, an economist at the University of Rochester, wrote the following in an article in the *New York Times*:

   Free trade is not only about the right of American consumers to buy at the cheapest possible price; it's also about the right of foreign producers to earn a living. Steelworkers in West Virginia struggle hard to make ends meet. So do steelworkers in South Korea. To protect one at the expense of the other, solely because of where they happened to be born, is a moral outrage.

How does the U.S. government protect steelworkers in West Virginia at the expense of steelworkers in South Korea? Is Landsburg making a positive or a normative statement? A few days later, Tom Redburn published an article disagreeing with Landsburg:

   It is not some evil character flaw to care more about the welfare of people nearby than about that of those far away—it's human nature. And it is morally—and economically—defensible. . . . A society that ignores the consequences of economic disruption on those among its citizens who come out at the short end of the stick is not only heartless, it also undermines its own cohesion and adaptability.

Which of the two arguments do you find most convincing?
Source: Steven E. Landsburg, "Who Cares If the Playing Field Is Level?" *New York Times*, June 13, 2001; and Tom Redburn, "Economic View: Of Politics, Free Markets, and Tending to Society," *New York Times*, June 17, 2001.

20. Suppose China decides to pay large subsidies to any Chinese company that exports goods or services to the United States. As a result, these companies are able to sell products in the United States at far below their cost of production. In addition, China decides to bar all imports from the United States. The dollars that the United States pays to import Chinese goods are left in banks in China. Will this strategy raise or lower the standard of living in China? Will it raise or lower the standard of living in the United States? Briefly explain. Be sure to indicate your definition of "standard of living" in your answer.

21. A Federal Reserve publication offers the following observation: "Too many U.S. citizens associate free trade with job
losses rather than opportunities and a higher standard of
living." Do you agree? Briefly explain.
Source: Surya Sen and Dan Wassmann, "The Great Trade Debate: From
Rhetoric to Reality," Federal Reserve Bank of Chicago, January 1999.

22. Hal Varian, an economist at the University of California,
Berkeley, has made two observations about international
trade:

1. Trade allows a country "to produce more with less."

2. There is little doubt who wins [from trade] in the long
   run: consumers.

Briefly explain whether or not you agree with either or
both of these observations.
Source: Hal R. Varian, "The Mixed Bag of Productivity," New York Times,
October 23, 2003.

23. [Related to the *Chapter Opener*] According to an editorial
in the *New York Times,* because of the sugar quota, "Sugar
growers in this country, long protected from global competition, have had a great run at the expense of just about
everyone else—refineries, candy manufacturers, other food
companies, individual consumers and farmers in the developing world." Briefly explain how each group mentioned in
this editorial is affected by the sugar quota.
Source: "America's Sugar Daddies," New York Times, November 29, 2003.

24. [Related to *Don't Let This Happen To You!*] Briefly explain
whether you agree or disagree with the following statement: "I can't believe that anyone opposes expanding international trade. After all, when international trade expands,
everyone wins."

25. [Related to *Solved Problem 8-2*] Suppose that the United
States currently both produces kumquats and imports
them. The U.S. government then decides to restrict international trade in kumquats by imposing a quota that
allows imports of only six million pounds of kumquats

into the United States each year. The figure shows the
results of imposing the quota:

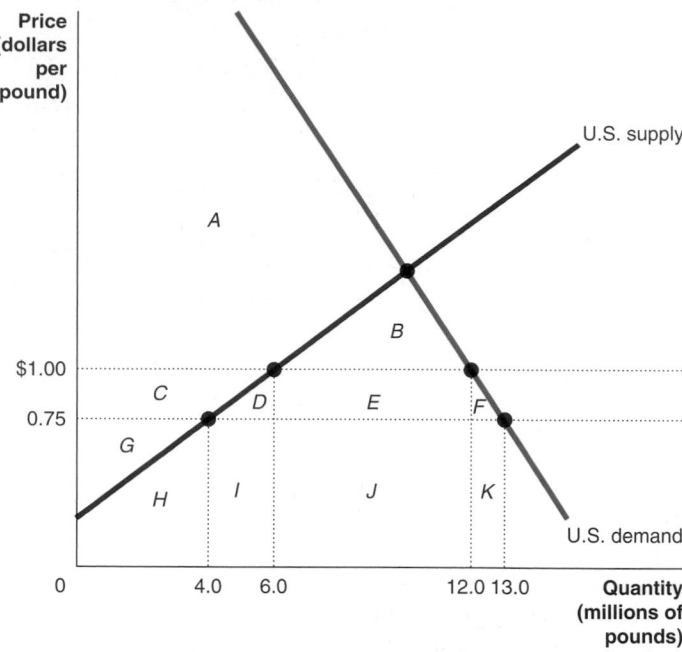

Fill in the following table using the letters in the figure:

	WITHOUT QUOTA	WITH QUOTA
World price of kumquats	_____	_____
U.S. price of kumquats	_____	_____
Quantity supplied by U.S. firms	_____	_____
Quantity demanded	_____	_____
Quantity imported	_____	_____
Area of consumer surplus	_____	_____
Area of domestic producer surplus	_____	_____
Area of deadweight loss	_____	_____

Multinational Firms

Multinational Firms

Most large corporations are multinational. **Multinational enterprises** are firms that conduct operations in more than one country—as opposed to simply trading with other countries. For example, the U.S. firm General Electric employs nearly 300,000 people in more than one hundred countries. Toyota Motor Corporation of Japan has invested more than $10 billion in factories and other facilities in the United States and assembles more than a million cars and trucks in North American factories (almost two-thirds of the cars and trucks Toyota sells in the United States are assembled in North American factories). The Nestlé Company is headquartered in the small city of Vevey, Switzerland, but it produces and sells food products in practically every country in the world. It has more than 500 factories worldwide, employing more than 240,000 people.

Table 8A-1 shows the top 25 multinational corporations ranked by the value of their revenues in 2004. Large corporations based in the United States generally established multinational operations earlier than did firms based in other countries. Today, 5 of the top 10 multinational corporations in the world are based in the United States. The table shows that large corporations in the motor vehicle, electronics, insurance, and petroleum refining industries are most likely to have extensive multinational operations.

A Brief History of Multinational Enterprises

From at least 2500 B.C., companies have traded over long distances. Well-developed systems of long-distance trade existed in the eastern Mediterranean by 1500 B.C. By the Middle Ages, a number of multinational firms had been established in Europe. For example, the Medici bank was based in Florence, Italy, but had branches in France, Switzerland, and England. Some multinational companies founded during these years still exist. The Austrian freight forwarding firm Gerbrueder Weiss, which had offices in several countries in the fourteenth century, continues to operate today. Before the twentieth century, multinational firms were still relatively rare, however.

In the late nineteenth and early twentieth centuries, a few large U.S. corporations began to expand their operations beyond the domestic market. Two key technological innovations made it possible for these firms to coordinate operations on several continents. The first innovation was the successful completion of the transatlantic cable in 1866, which made possible instant communication by telegraph between the United States and Europe. The second innovation was the development of more efficient steam engines, which reduced the cost and increased the speed of long ocean voyages. U.S. firms such as Standard Oil, the Singer Sewing Machine Company, and the American Tobacco Company took advantage of these innovations to establish factories and distribution networks around the world. When firms build or buy facilities in foreign countries they are engaging in **foreign direct investment.** When an individual or firm buys stocks or bonds issued in another country, they are engaging in **foreign portfolio investment.** In the early twentieth century, most U.S. firms expanded abroad through foreign direct investment because the stock and bond markets in other countries were often too poorly developed to make foreign portfolio investment practical.

Appendix

	RANK	CORPORATION	HOME COUNTRY	INDUSTRY
TABLE 8A-1 **The Top 25 Multinational Corporations, 2004**	1	Wal-Mart Stores	United States	Retailing
	2	BP	Great Britain	Petroleum Refining
	3	Exxon Mobil	United States	Petroleum Refining
	4	Royal Dutch/Shell Group	Netherlands/United Kingdom	Petroleum Refining
	5	General Motors	United States	Motor Vehicles
	6	Ford Motor	United States	Motor Vehicles
	7	DaimlerChrysler	Germany	Motor Vehicles
	8	Toyota Motor	Japan	Motor Vehicles
	9	General Electric	United States	Diversified Financials
	10	Total	France	Petroleum Refining
	11	Allianz	Germany	Insurance
	12	ChevronTexaco	United States	Petroleum Refining
	13	Axa	France	Insurance
	14	ConocoPhillips	United States	Petroleum
	15	Volkswagen	Germany	Motor Vehicles
	16	Nippon Telephone and Telegraph	Japan	Telecommunications
	17	ING Group	Netherlands	Insurance
	18	Citigroup	United States	Banking
	19	International Business Machines	United States	Computers
	20	American International Group	United States	Insurance
	21	Siemens AG	Germany	Electronics
	22	Carrefour	France	Food and Drug Stores
	23	Hitachi	Japan	Electronics
	24	Hewlett-Packard	United States	Computers
	25	Honda Motor	Japan	Motor Vehicles

Source: "Fortune Global 500," *Fortune*, July 26, 2004 ©2004 Time Inc. All rights reserved.
Note: Corporations are ranked by their revenue in 2004.

Multinational enterprise A firm that conducts operations in more than one country.

Foreign direct investment The purchase or building by a domestic firm of a facility in a foreign country.

Foreign portfolio investment The purchase by an individual or firm of stocks or bonds issued in another country.

Strategic Factors in Moving from Domestic to Foreign Markets

Today, most large U.S. corporations have established factories and other facilities overseas. Corporations expand their operations outside the United States when they expect to increase their profitability by doing so. Firms might expect to increase their profits through overseas operations for five main reasons:

➤ *To avoid tariffs or the threat of tariffs.* As we saw in this chapter, tariffs are taxes imposed by countries on imports from other countries. Sometimes firms will establish factories in other countries to avoid the need to pay tariffs. At other times, firms will establish a factory in a country to which they are exporting because they fear the other country's government will impose a tariff or some other restriction on their product. Governments often are less concerned about domestic production by foreign-owned companies than they are about imports. As we also saw in this chapter, government restrictions on imports frequently result from a fear that imports will cause job losses in domestic industries. For example, in the 1970s and 1980s many Americans feared that imports of Japanese automobiles would reduce employment in the U.S. automobile industry. Members of Congress threatened to increase tariffs or impose quotas on imports of Japanese automobiles. In fact, beginning in 1981, a voluntary export restraint did reduce imports of Japanese automobiles. In response to this political pressure, the Japanese automobile companies established assembly plants in the United States. Now that a majority of Japanese automobiles sold in the United States are also assembled in the United States by U.S. workers, the Japanese share of the U.S. automobile market is a less heated political issue than it was during the 1970s and 1980s.

➤ *To gain access to raw materials.*   Some U.S. firms have expanded abroad to secure supplies of raw materials. U.S. oil firms—beginning with Standard Oil in the late nineteenth century—have had extensive overseas operations aimed at discovering, recovering, and refining crude oil. In early 2001, one of Standard Oil's successor firms, ChevronTexaco, headquartered in San Francisco, opened its largest oil field in Kazakstan, in the former Soviet Union. ChevronTexaco also constructed a 990-mile pipeline to bring the oil from this field on the Caspian Sea across Russia to a port on the Black Sea.

➤ *To gain access to low-cost labor.*   In the past 20 years, some U.S. firms have located factories or other facilities in countries such as China, India, Malaysia, and El Salvador to take advantage of the lower wages paid to workers in those countries. As we saw in "Making the Connection 8-1," most economists believe that this *outsourcing* ultimately improves the efficiency of the economy and raises the consumption of U.S. households, but it also can disrupt the lives of U.S. workers who lose their jobs. For this reason outsourcing has caused political controversy.

➤ *To minimize exchange-rate risk.*   The exchange rate tells us how many units of foreign currency are received in exchange for a unit of domestic currency. Fluctuations in exchange rates can reduce the profits of a firm that exports goods to other countries. The J. M. Smucker Company is headquartered in Orrville, Ohio, and ships jams, ice cream toppings, peanut butter, and other products to more than 70 countries. Suppose Smucker's has contracted to sell 200,000 cases of jam to a British importer. The British importer will be paying for the shipment in British currency, the pound (the symbol for the pound is £). The importer will pay Smucker's £21 million in 60 days. It is currently possible to exchange 1 dollar for 0.7 British pounds, so Smucker's expects to receive $30 million (£21 million/£0.70 per dollar) in 60 days. But if the value of the pound falls against the dollar during the next 60 days, the amount Smucker's receives in dollars could be significantly reduced. For example, if the value of the pound falls to 0.80 pounds per dollar, then Smucker's will only receive $26.25 million (£21 million/£0.80 per dollar).

Firms, like Smucker's, that have extensive international operations are exposed to significant risk to their profits from fluctuations in the values of international currencies. This risk is known as *exchange-rate risk*. If Smucker's began producing jam in Britain, it would reduce its exposure to exchange-rate risk.

➤ *To respond to industry competition.*   In some instances, companies expand overseas as a competitive response to an industry rival. The worldwide competition for markets between Pepsi and Coke is an example of this kind of expansion. Coke began expanding overseas before World War II and by the 1970s was earning more from its foreign sales than from its sales in the United States. It became clear to

Pepsi's management that the firm needed to compete with Coke in foreign as well as domestic markets. In 1972, Pepsi had a major success when it signed an agreement with the Soviet Union to become the first foreign product sold in that country. Coke and Pepsi continue to compete vigorously in many countries, with their shares of the market often fluctuating significantly.

8A-1 *Making the Connection*

Many U.S. jobs require technical training.

Have Multinational Corporations Reduced Employment and Lowered Wages in the United States?

During the 1990s, some U.S. corporations responded to the greater economic openness of many poorer countries by relocating manufacturing operations to these countries. For example, most U.S. toy firms, such as Mattel, now produce nearly all their toys in factories in China. Most U.S. clothing manufacturers now produce the bulk of their goods in factories in Central America or Asia. These firms have reduced their production costs by paying much lower wages in their overseas factories than they were paying in the United States. The workers who lost their jobs in U.S. factories have often experienced periods of unemployment and have sometimes had to accept lower wages when they find new jobs. Towns and cities where factories closed also have been hurt by losses of tax revenues to support schools and other local services.

Most economists, however, do not believe that relocating jobs abroad has reduced either total employment in the United States or the average wage paid to U.S. workers. The overall level of employment in the United States in the long run is not affected by job losses in particular industries, however painful the losses may be to those experiencing them. The U.S. economy creates more than 2 million additional new jobs during a typical year. Nearly all workers who lose jobs at one firm eventually find new ones at another firm.

Competition from low-wage foreign workers has not reduced the average wages of U.S. workers. Wages are determined by the ability of workers to produce goods and services. This ability depends in part on the workers' education and training and in part on the machinery and equipment available to them. American workers have high wages because, on average, they are well trained and because of the quantity and quality of the machinery and equipment they work with. Low-wage foreign workers are generally less well trained and work with smaller amounts of machinery and equipment than do American workers.

During the 1990s and early 2000s, the gap in the United States between the wages of skilled workers and the wages of unskilled workers increased. It has been suggested that competition from low-wage foreign workers forced unskilled U.S. workers to accept lower wages to keep their jobs. To a small extent, the increase in the wage gap in the United States may have been due to this cause. But careful economic studies have shown that most of the increase in the wage gap is due to developments within the U.S. economy—such as the increasing number of jobs that require technical training—that have resulted in higher pay to skilled workers, rather than to competition from low-wage foreign workers.

Most U.S. firms have followed similar steps in expanding their operations overseas: Newly established firms usually begin by selling only within the United States. If successful in the domestic market, they will begin to export. They initially use foreign firms to market and distribute their products. If sales are good in these foreign markets, U.S. firms will establish their own overseas marketing and distribution networks. Finally, firms will establish their own production facilities in these foreign countries. Since World War II, many U.S. firms have switched from building their own production facilities to a strategy of acquiring local firms that were already producing the good. Some firms have first licensed production to local firms, only later acquiring the firms. U.S.-based Colgate-Palmolive, for example, typically has entered a foreign market first by licensing a foreign soap manufacturer to produce its brands, while keeping control over marketing and distribution. Typically, Colgate-Palmolive eventually has acquired ownership of the foreign firm.

Challenges to U.S. Firms in Foreign Markets

It seems obvious that any successful firm will want to expand into foreign markets. After all, it is always better to have more customers than fewer customers. In fact, however, expanding into foreign markets can often be quite difficult and the additional costs incurred may end up being greater than the additional revenue gained. One problem encountered by U.S. firms is differences in tastes between U.S. and foreign consumers. Although products like Coke seem to appeal to consumers everywhere in the world, other products run into problems because of cultural differences among countries. For example, Singapore banned Janet Jackson's album *All for You* because, according to a government spokesman, its "sexually explicit lyrics" were "not acceptable to our society." In 2002, eBay closed its online auction site in Japan. Although eBay is successful selling collectibles in the United States, many Japanese consumers do not like to buy used goods.

Some U.S. companies have had difficulty adapting their employment practices to deal with the differences between U.S. and foreign labor markets. Many countries have much stronger labor unions than does the United States, and many foreign governments regulate labor markets much more than does the U.S. government. For example, government regulations in most European countries make it much more difficult than it is in the United States to lay off workers.

Competitive Advantages of U.S. Firms

Some U.S. firms have successful foreign operations because of the strength of their brand names. Many producers of soft drinks and many fast food restaurants can be found in nearly every foreign country, but Coca-Cola and McDonald's have such strong name recognition that their appeal extends around the world. Other firms have developed a significant technological edge over foreign rivals. Microsoft, the software giant, and Hewlett-Packard, the computer and printer firm, are examples. Some U.S. firms, such as Dell Computer and Boeing, have advantages over foreign manufacturers based on having developed the most efficient and low-cost way of producing a good.

A U.S. firm's global competitive advantage changes over time. This change is illustrated dramatically by the experience of U.S. semiconductor firms. The semiconductor industry originated in the United States with the invention of the transistor at Bell Telephone Laboratories in 1947. United States predominance in the industry was enhanced further in 1959 with the invention of the integrated circuit, which contains multiple transistors on a single silicon chip. Through 1980, U.S. firms held between 60 and 80 percent of the global market for semiconductors. Beginning in the 1970s, the Japanese government moved to establish a strong domestic semiconductor industry by subsidizing domestic firms and by limiting imports of semiconductors from the United States. The Japanese policy was very successful with respect to DRAM—dynamic random access memory—the most basic chip. By the mid-1980s, Japanese firms dominated the global market and nearly all U.S. chipmakers had abandoned DRAM manufacture. Many observers predicted the collapse of the U.S. semiconductor industry. Even Intel Corporation, the most successful U.S. semiconductor firm, appeared close to bankruptcy.

From this low point, U.S. semiconductor firms rebounded to regain global predominance by the 1990s. The key to the rebound of U.S. firms was the decreasing demand for simple memory chips and the increasing demand for two products: microprocessors—such as Intel's Pentium 4 chip used in personal computers—and ASICs—application-specific integrated circuits—which are used in many electronic products. In manufacturing microprocessors and ASICs, a firm's ability to rapidly design and develop new products is more important than using low-cost production processes. U.S. firms, such as Intel, have proven to be much better at designing and rapidly bringing to market advanced microprocessors and ASICs than have competing firms in Japan, South Korea, and elsewhere.

KEY TERMS

Foreign direct
   investment 264

Foreign portfolio
   investment 264

Multinational
   enterprise 264

REVIEW QUESTIONS

1. When did large U.S. corporations first begin to operate internationally? What key technological changes made it easier for U.S. corporations to operate overseas?
2. What is the difference between foreign direct investment and foreign portfolio investment? Is the Camry assembly plant that Toyota operates in Kentucky an example of foreign direct investment or foreign portfolio investment?
3. What are the five main reasons why firms expand their operations overseas? Which of these reasons explains why U.S.-based oil companies have extensive overseas operations?
4. What are the main reasons U.S. firms succeed overseas?

PROBLEMS AND APPLICATIONS

Please visit **www.prenhall.com/hubbard** *for solutions to the even-numbered problems as well as multiple-choice and true or false self-assessment quizzes.*

1. Suppose that in 1850 you are operating a large factory manufacturing cotton cloth. You are considering expanding your operations overseas. What technical problems are you likely to encounter in coordinating your overseas and domestic operations?
2. The Ford Motor Company and the International Harvester Company were two of the first U.S. firms to establish extensive manufacturing operations overseas. Why might a producer of automobiles and a producer of farm machinery find it particularly advantageous to manufacture their products in countries in which they had substantial sales?
3. Why might many U.S. firms that were expanding their operations overseas after World War II have been more likely to acquire an existing firm in the market they were entering rather than building new facilities there?
4. Would a firm based in the United States ever produce a good in another country if it cost less to produce it in the United States and ship it to the other country? Explain.
5. Is expanding a firm's operations internationally really any different than expanding within a nation? For example, if a firm is based in Texas, what's the difference between it expanding operations to Mexico, Canada, Singapore, or Germany rather than to North Carolina or Pennsylvania?
6. Is expanding a firm's operations internationally really any different than expanding into a new product market? For example, is Whirlpool's expansion into Europe different than Whirlpool expanding by making a new line of appliances, such as dehumidifiers?
7. If you ran a successful U.S. firm like Wal-Mart, IBM, or Hershey's, into which countries would you first expand? Why?

chapter

nine

Consumer Choice and Behavioral Economics

Can LeBron James Get You to Drink Powerade?

➤ When Coca-Cola hired LeBron James to endorse its Powerade drink, it announced that he would create his own flavor—Flava23—and that DC Comics had been hired by the company to create a LeBron James comic book. Celebrity endorsements of this type are very common, of course. Over the years, Coca-Cola has used other celebrities, including Lance Armstrong, Paula Abdul, and Ray Charles, to advertise its products. Nor is Coca-Cola alone in using celebrity endorsements. From Britney Spears and Sean "P. Diddy" Combs endorsing Pepsi to Michael Jordan endorsing Nike basketball shoes to Oprah Winfrey endorsing Pontiac cars, celebrities appear constantly in radio, television, and magazine advertising. What do firms hope

to gain from celebrity endorsements? The obvious answer is that firms expect celebrity advertising will increase sales of their products. But why should consumers buy more of a product just because it is endorsed by a celebrity?

In this chapter, we will examine how consumers make decisions about which products to buy. Firms must understand consumer behavior to determine whether strategies such as using celebrities in their advertising are likely to be effective. Coca-Cola has been a leader in innovative advertising, including the use of celebrity endorsements.

Firms have been advertising for centuries. Josiah Wedgwood, who manufactured dishes and other dinnerware in England in the late 1700s, was probably the first to use

celebrity endorsements. He sold fine china to prominent people of the time, including Catherine the Great of Russia, at reduced prices, hoping that the publicity from these sales would increase his sales to the general public. However, true modern advertising campaigns with firms spending large amounts year in and year out only began in the late nineteenth and early twentieth centuries. Coca-Cola was founded in Atlanta, Georgia, in 1886 by John Styth Pemberton. After Asa G. Candler bought the company in 1891, Coke began to be sold nationally, first primarily in drugstore soda fountains. The firm's advertising in magazines, newspapers, billboards, and calendars featured pictures of attractive young women drinking Coke—instead of emphasizing the taste or other quali-

After completing this chapter, you should be able to:

① Define utility and explain how consumers choose goods and services to maximize their utility.

② Use the concept of utility to explain how the law of demand results from consumers adjusting their consumption choices to changes in prices.

③ Explain how social influences can affect consumption choices.

④ Describe how people can improve their decision making by taking into account nonmonetary opportunity costs, ignoring sunk costs, and being more realistic about their future behavior.

ties of the cola. According to one business historian these young women

presented an ideal of femininity. Young women aspired to be like the girls in the advertisements; young men aspired to date them. And these girls drank Coca-Cola.

By the 1910s, Coca-Cola had moved from using unnamed women in its advertising to using movie stars. The attempt to associate Coke with celebrities in the minds of consumers continued through the following decades. Even Santa Claus was pressed into service. The modern image of Santa Claus as cheerful, chubby, and with a full white beard was actually created in 1931 by artist Haddon Sundblom for a

Coke advertisement. From the 1950s on, Coke's television commercials often featured popular singers or sports figures of the time, including the Supremes, the Moody Blues, Ray Charles, and football star "Mean" Joe Greene.

Firms' attempts to distinguish their products in the minds of consumers from the products of rival firms will be an important theme in several of the following chapters. Advertising is one way in which firms try to distinguish their products. *An Inside Look* on page 292 shows that celebrity endorsements can sometimes be a risky form of advertising.

Source: Richard S. Tedlow, *New and Improved: The Story of Mass Marketing in America*, New York: Basic Books, 1990, p. 48.

➤ We begin this chapter by exploring how consumers make decisions. In Chapter 2, we saw that economists usually assume that people act in a rational, self-interested way. In explaining consumer behavior, this means economists believe consumers make choices that will leave them as satisfied as possible, given their *tastes,* their *incomes,* and the *prices* of the goods and services available to them. We will see how the downward-sloping demand curves we encountered in Chapters 3 through 5 result from the economic model of consumer behavior. We will also see that in certain situations, knowing the best decision to make can be difficult. In these cases, economic reasoning provides a powerful tool for consumers to improve their decision making. Finally, we will see that *experimental economics* has shown that factors such as social pressure and notions of fairness can affect consumer behavior. We will look at how businesses take these factors into account when setting prices. In the appendix to this chapter, we extend the analysis by using indifference curves and budget lines to understand consumer behavior.

Utility and Consumer Decision Making

① LEARNING OBJECTIVE

Define utility and explain how consumers choose goods and services to maximize their utility.

We saw in Chapter 3 that the model of demand and supply is a powerful tool for analyzing how prices and quantities are determined. We also saw in Chapter 3 that, according to the *law of demand,* whenever the price of a good falls, the quantity demanded increases. Now we will show how the economic model of consumer behavior leads to the law of demand.

The Economic Model of Consumer Behavior in a Nutshell

Imagine walking through a shopping mall trying to decide how to spend your clothing budget. If you had an unlimited budget, your decision would be easy: Just buy as much of everything as you want. Given that you have a limited budget, what do you do? Economists assume that consumers act so as to make themselves as well off as possible. Therefore, you should choose among those combinations of clothes that you can afford, the one combination that makes you as well off as possible. Stated more generally, the economic model of consumer behavior predicts that consumers will choose to buy the combination of goods and services that makes them as well off as possible from among all the combinations that their budgets allow them to buy.

This prediction may seem obvious and not particularly useful. But as we explore the implication of this prediction, we will see that it leads to conclusions that are both useful and not obvious.

Utility

Utility The enjoyment or satisfaction people receive from consuming goods and services.

Ultimately, how well off you are from consuming a particular combination of goods and services depends upon your tastes, or preferences. There is an old saying—"There's no accounting for tastes"—and economists don't try to. If you buy Powerade instead of Gatorade, even though Gatorade has a lower price, you must receive more enjoyment or satisfaction from drinking Powerade. Economists refer to the enjoyment or satisfaction people receive from consuming goods and services as **utility.** So we can say that the goal of a consumer is to spend available income so as to maximize utility. But utility is a difficult concept to measure, because there is no way of knowing exactly how much enjoyment or satisfaction a consumer receives from consuming a product. Similarly, it is not possible to compare utility across consumers. There is no way of knowing for sure whether Jill receives more or less satisfaction than Jack from drinking a bottle of Powerade.

Two hundred years ago, economists had hoped it would be possible to measure utility in units called "utils." The util would be an objective measure in the same way that temperature is. If it is 70 degrees in New York and 70 degrees in Los Angeles, it is just as warm in both cities. These economists hoped it would be possible to say that if Jack's utility from eating a hamburger is 10 utils and Jill's utility is 5 utils, then Jack receives exactly twice the satisfaction from eating a hamburger that Jill does. In fact, it is not possible to measure utility across people. It turns out that none of the important conclusions of the economic model of consumer behavior depend on utility being directly measurable (this point is demonstrated in the appendix). Nevertheless, the economic model of consumer behavior is easier to understand if we assume that utility is something directly measurable, like temperature.

The Principle of Diminishing Marginal Utility

To make the model of consumer behavior more concrete, let's see how a consumer makes decisions in a case involving just two products: pepperoni pizza and Coke. To begin, consider how the utility you receive from consuming a good changes with the amount of the good you consume. For example, suppose that you have just arrived at a Super Bowl party where the hosts are serving pepperoni pizza, and you are very hungry. In this situation, you are likely to receive quite a lot of enjoyment, or utility, from consuming the first slice of pizza. Suppose this satisfaction is measurable and is equal to 20. After eating the first slice, you decide to have a second slice. Because you are no longer as hungry, the satisfaction you receive from eating the second slice of pizza will be less than the satisfaction you received from eating the first slice. Consuming the second slice would increase your utility by only an *additional* 16, which would raise your *total* utility from eating the two slices to 36. If you continue eating slices, each additional slice will give you less and less additional satisfaction.

The table in Figure 9-1 shows the relationship between the number of slices of pizza you consume while watching the Super Bowl and the amount of utility you receive. The second column in the table shows the total utility you receive from eating a particular number of slices. The third column shows the additional utility or **marginal utility** (*MU*) you receive from consuming one additional slice. (Remember that in economics "marginal" means additional.) For example, as you increase your consumption from 2 slices to 3 slices, your total utility increases from 36 to 46, so your marginal utility from consuming the third slice is 10. As the table shows, by the time you eat the fifth slice of pizza that evening, your marginal utility will be very low: only 2. If you were to eat a sixth slice, we will assume that you would become slightly nauseous and your marginal utility would actually be a *negative* 3.

Figure 9-1 also plots the numbers from the table as graphs. Panel (a) shows how your total utility rises as you eat the first five slices of pizza, and then falls as you eat the sixth slice. Panel (b) shows how your marginal utility declines with each additional slice you eat and finally becomes negative when you eat the sixth slice. The height of the marginal utility line at any quantity of pizza in panel (b) represents the change in utility as a result of consuming that additional slice. For example, the change in utility as a result of consuming 4 slices instead of 3 is 6, so the height of the marginal utility line in panel (b) is 6.

The relationship illustrated in Figure 9-1 between consuming additional units of a product during a period of time and the marginal utility received from consuming each additional unit is referred to as the **law of diminishing marginal utility.** For nearly every good or service, the more you consume during a period of time, the less you increase your total satisfaction from each additional unit you consume.

Marginal utility (*MU*) The change in total utility a person receives from consuming one additional unit of a good or service.

Law of diminishing marginal utility Consumers experience diminishing additional satisfaction as they consume more of a good or service during a given period of time.

The Rule of Equal Marginal Utility per Dollar Spent

The key challenge for consumers is to decide how to allocate their limited incomes among all the products they wish to buy. Every consumer has to make trade-offs: If you have $100 to spend on entertainment for the month, then the more DVDs you buy, the

FIGURE 9-1

Total and Marginal Utility from Eating Pizza on Super Bowl Sunday

The table shows that for the first 5 slices of pizza, the more you eat, the more your total satisfaction or utility will increase. If you eat the sixth slice, you will start to feel ill from eating too much pizza, and your total utility will fall. Each additional slice increases your utility by less than the previous slice, so your marginal utility from each slice is less than the one before. Panel (a) shows your total utility rising as you eat the first 5 slices, and falling with the sixth slice. Panel (b) shows your marginal utility falling with each additional slice you eat, and becoming negative with the sixth slice. The height of the marginal utility line at any quantity of pizza in panel (b) represents the change in utility as a result of consuming that additional slice. For example, the change in utility as a result of consuming 4 slices instead of 3 is 6, so the height of the marginal utility line in panel (b) for the fourth slice is 6.

Number of Slices	Total Utility from Eating Pizza	Marginal Utility from the Last Slice Eaten
0	0	—
1	20	20
2	36	16
3	46	10
4	52	6
5	54	2
6	51	−3

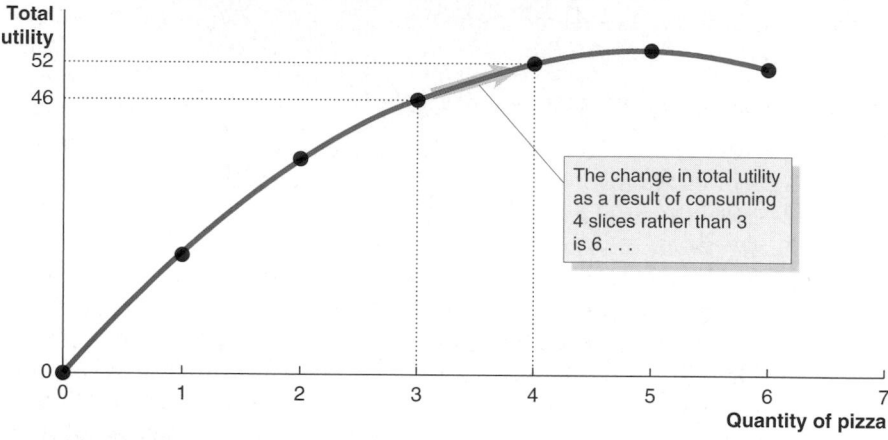

The change in total utility as a result of consuming 4 slices rather than 3 is 6 . . .

(a) Total utility

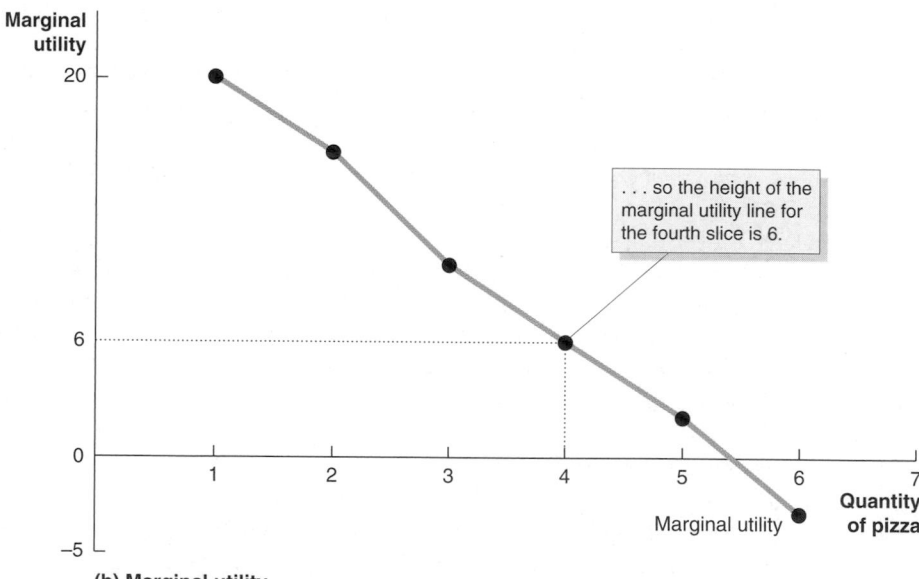

. . . so the height of the marginal utility line for the fourth slice is 6.

Marginal utility

(b) Marginal utility

fewer movies you can see in the theater. Economists refer to the limited amount of income you have available to spend on goods and services as your **budget constraint.** The principle of diminishing marginal utility helps us understand how consumers can best spend their limited incomes on the products available to them.

Suppose you attend a Super Bowl party at a restaurant and you have $10 to spend on refreshments. Pizza is selling for $2 per slice and Coke is selling for $1 per cup. Table 9-1 shows the relationship between the amount of pizza you eat, the amount of Coke you drink, and the amount of satisfaction or utility you receive. The values for pizza are repeated from the table in Figure 9-1. The values for Coke also follow the principle of diminishing marginal utility.

How many slices of pizza and how many cups of Coke do you buy if you want to maximize your utility? If you did not have a budget constraint, you would buy 5 slices of pizza and 5 cups of Coke, because that would give you total utility of 107 (54 + 53), which is the maximum utility you can achieve. Eating another slice of pizza or drinking another cup of Coke during the evening would lower your utility. Unfortunately, you do have a budget constraint: You have only $10 to spend. To buy 5 slices of pizza (at $2 per slice) and 5 cups of Coke (at $1 per cup), you would need $15.

To select the best way to spend your $10, remember this key economic principle: *Optimal decisions are made at the margin.* That is, most of the time economic decision makers—consumers, firms, and the government—are faced with decisions about whether to do a little more of one thing or a little more of an alternative. In this case, you are choosing between a little more pizza or a little more Coke. BMW chooses between manufacturing more roadsters or more SUVs in its South Carolina factory. Congress and the president choose between spending more dollars for research on heart disease or more dollars for research on breast cancer. Every economic decision maker faces a budget constraint, and every economic decision maker faces trade-offs.

The key to making the best consumption decision is to maximize utility by following the *rule of equal marginal utility per dollar:* As you decide how to spend your income, you should buy pizza and Coke up to the point where the last slice of pizza purchased and the last cup of Coke purchased give you equal increases in utility *per dollar.* By doing this, you will have maximized your total utility.

It is important to remember that to follow this rule you must equalize your marginal utility per dollar spent, *not* your marginal utility from each good. Buying season tickets for your favorite NFL team or for the opera, or buying a BMW may give you a lot

Budget constraint   The limited amount of income available to consumers to spend on goods and services.

TABLE 9-1   Total Utility and Marginal Utility from Eating Pizza and Drinking Coke

NUMBER OF SLICES OF PIZZA	TOTAL UTILITY FROM EATING PIZZA	MARGINAL UTILITY FROM THE LAST SLICE	NUMBER OF CUPS OF COKE	TOTAL UTILITY FROM DRINKING COKE	MARGINAL UTILITY FROM THE LAST CUP
0	0		0	0	
1	20	20	1	20	20
2	36	16	2	35	15
3	46	10	3	45	10
4	52	6	4	50	5
5	54	2	5	53	3
6	51	−3	6	52	−1

TABLE 9-2   Converting Marginal Utility to Marginal Utility per Dollar

(1) SLICES OF PIZZA	(2) MARGINAL UTILITY (MU_{Pizza})	(3) MARGINAL UTILITY PER DOLLAR $\left(\dfrac{MU_{Pizza}}{P_{Pizza}}\right)$	(4) CUPS OF COKE	(5) MARGINAL UTILITY (MU_{Coke})	(6) MARGINAL UTILITY PER DOLLAR $\left(\dfrac{MU_{Coke}}{P_{Coke}}\right)$
1	20	10	1	20	20
2	16	8	2	15	15
3	10	5	3	10	10
4	6	3	4	5	5
5	2	1	5	3	3
6	−3	−	6	−1	−

more satisfaction than drinking a cup of Coke, but the NFL tickets may well give you less satisfaction *per dollar* spent. To decide how many slices of pizza and how many cups of Coke to buy you must take the values for marginal utility in Table 9-1 and convert them to marginal utility per dollar. You can do this by dividing marginal utility by the price of each good, as shown in Table 9-2.

In column (3), we calculate marginal utility per dollar spent on pizza. Because the price of pizza is $2 per slice, the marginal utility per dollar from eating one slice of pizza equals 20 divided by $2, or 10 units of utility per dollar. Similarly, we show in column (6) that because the price of Coke is $1 per cup, the marginal utility per dollar from drinking 1 cup of Coke equals 20 divided by $1, or 20 units of utility per dollar. To maximize the total utility you receive, you must make sure that the utility per dollar of pizza for the last slice of pizza is equal to the utility per dollar of Coke for the last cup of Coke. Table 9-2 shows that there are three combinations of slices of pizza and cups of Coke where marginal utility per dollar is equalized. Table 9-3 lists these combinations, along with the total amount of money needed to buy each combination, and the total utility received from consuming each combination.

If you buy 4 slices of pizza, the last slice gives you 3 units of utility per dollar. If you buy 5 cups of Coke, the last cup also gives you 3 units of utility per dollar, so you have equalized your marginal utility per dollar. Unfortunately, as the third column in the table shows, to buy 4 slices and 5 cups, you would need $13 and you have only $10. You could also equalize your marginal utility per dollar by buying 1 slice and 3 cups, but that would cost just $5, leaving you with $5 to spend. Only when you buy 3 three slices and

TABLE 9-3   Equalizing Marginal Utility per Dollar Spent

COMBINATIONS OF PIZZA AND COKE WITH EQUAL MARGINAL UTILITIES PER DOLLAR	MARGINAL UTILITY PER DOLLAR (MARGINAL UTILITY/PRICE)	TOTAL SPENDING	TOTAL UTILITY
1 Slice of Pizza and 3 Cups of Coke	10	$2 + $3 = $5	20 + 45 = 65
3 Slices of Pizza and 4 Cups of Coke	5	$6 + $4 = $10	46 + 50 = 96
4 Slices of Pizza and 5 Cups of Coke	3	$8 + $5 = $13	52 + 53 = 105

4 cups have you equalized your marginal utility per dollar and spent neither more nor less than the $10 available.

We can compactly summarize the two conditions for maximizing utility as follows:

1. $\dfrac{MU_{Pizza}}{P_{Pizza}} = \dfrac{MU_{Coke}}{P_{Coke}}$

2. Spending on pizza + Spending on Coke = Amount available to be spent

The first condition shows that the marginal utility per dollar spent must be the same for both goods. The second condition is the budget constraint, which states that total spending on both goods must equal the amount available to be spent. Of course, these conditions for maximizing utility apply not just to pizza and Coke, but to any two pairs of goods.

SOLVED PROBLEM   9-1

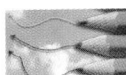

Finding the Optimal Level of Consumption

The following table shows Lee's utility from consuming ice cream cones and cans of Lime Fizz Soda:

① LEARNING OBJECTIVE
Define utility and explain how consumers choose goods and services to maximize their utility.

NUMBER OF ICE CREAM CONES	TOTAL UTILITY FROM ICE CREAM CONES	MARGINAL UTILITY FROM LAST CONE	NUMBER OF CANS OF LIME FIZZ	TOTAL UTILITY FROM CANS OF LIME FIZZ	MARGINAL UTILITY FROM LAST CAN
0	0	–	0	0	–
1	30	30	1	40	40
2	55	25	2	75	35
3	75	20	3	101	26
4	90	15	4	119	18
5	100	10	5	134	15
6	105	5	6	141	7

a. Ed inspects this table and says to Travis, "Lee's optimal choice would be to consume 4 ice cream cones and 5 cans of Lime Fizz, because with that combination his marginal utility from ice cream cones is equal to his marginal utility from Lime Fizz." Do you agree with Ed's reasoning? Briefly explain.

b. Suppose that Lee has an unlimited budget to spend on ice cream cones and cans of Lime Fizz. Under these circumstances, how many ice cream cones and how many cans of Lime Fizz will he consume?

c. Suppose Lee has $7 per week to spend on ice cream cones and Lime Fizz. The price of an ice cream cone is $2 and the price of a can of Lime Fizz is $1. If Lee wants to maximize his utility, how many ice cream cones and how many cans of Lime Fizz should he buy?

Solving the Problem:
Step 1: Review the chapter material. This problem involves finding the optimal consumption of two goods, so you may want to review the section "The Rule of Equal Marginal Utility per Dollar Spent," which begins on page 273.

Step 2: Answer question (a) by analyzing Ed's reasoning. Ed's reasoning is incorrect. To maximize utility, Lee needs to equalize marginal utility per dollar for the two goods.

Step 3: Answer question (b) by determining how Lee would maximize utility with an unlimited budget. With an unlimited budget, consumers maximize utility by continuing to buy each good as long as their utility is increasing. In this case, Lee will maximize utility by buying 6 ice cream cones and 6 cans of Lime Fizz.

Step 4: Answer question (c) by determining Lee's optimal combination of ice cream cones and cans of Lime Fizz. Lee will maximize his utility if he spends his $7 per week so that the marginal utility of ice creams cones divided by the price of ice cream cones is equal to the marginal utility of Lime Fizz divided by the price of Lime Fizz. We can use the following table to solve this part of the problem:

	ICE CREAM CONES		CANS OF LIME FIZZ	
QUANTITY	MU	$\dfrac{MU}{P}$	MU	$\dfrac{MU}{P}$
1	30	15	40	40
2	25	12.5	35	35
3	20	10	26	26
4	15	7.5	18	18
5	10	5	15	15
6	5	2.5	7	7

Lee will maximize utility by buying 1 ice cream cone and 5 cans of Lime Fizz. At this combination, the marginal utility of each good divided by its price equals 15. He has also spent all of his $7.

YOUR TURN: For more practice, do related problems 4 and 5 on pages 295–296 at the end of this chapter. Visit www.prenhall.com/hubbard for an interactive exercise related to this Solved Problem.

What If the Rule of Equal Marginal Utility per Dollar Does Not Hold?

The idea of getting the maximum utility by equalizing the ratio of marginal utility to price for the goods you are buying can be difficult to grasp, so it is worth thinking about in another way. Suppose that instead of buying 3 slices of pizza and 4 cups of Coke, you buy 4 slices and 2 cups. Four slices and 2 cups cost $10, so you would meet your budget constraint by spending all the money available to you, but would you have gotten the maximum amount of utility? No, you wouldn't have. From the information in Table 9-1, we can list the additional utility per dollar you are getting from the last slice and the last cup and the total utility from consuming 4 slices and 2 cups:

> Marginal utility per dollar for the fourth slice of pizza = 3 units of utility per dollar
>
> Marginal utility per dollar for the second cup of Coke = 15 units of utility per dollar
>
> Total utility from 4 slices of pizza and 2 cups of Coke = 87

Obviously, the marginal utilities per dollar are not equal. The last cup of Coke gave you considerably more satisfaction per dollar than did the last slice of pizza. You could raise your total utility by buying less pizza and more Coke. Buying 1 less slice of pizza frees up $2 that will allow you to buy 2 more cups of Coke. Eating 1 less slice of pizza reduces your utility by 6, but drinking 2 additional cups of Coke raises your utility by 15 (make sure you see this), for a net increase of 9. You end up equalizing your marginal utility per dollar (5 units of utility per dollar for both the last slice and the last cup) and raising your total utility from 87 to 96.

Don't Let This Happen To You!

Equalize Marginal Utilities *per Dollar*

Consider the information in the following table, which gives Harry's utility from buying CDs and DVDs:

HARRY'S UTILITY FROM BUYING CDs AND DVDs

QUANTITY OF CDs	TOTAL UTILITY FROM CDs	MARGINAL UTILITY FROM LAST CD	QUANTITY OF DVDs	TOTAL UTILITY FROM DVDs	MARGINAL UTILITY FROM LAST DVD
0	0		0	0	
1	50	50	1	60	60
2	85	35	2	105	45
3	110	25	3	145	40
4	130	20	4	175	30
5	140	10	5	195	20
6	145	5	6	210	15

Can you determine from this information what the optimal combination of CDs and DVDs is for Harry? It is very tempting to say that Harry should buy 4 CDs and 5 DVDs because his marginal utility from CDs is equal to his marginal utility from DVDs with that combination. In fact, we can't be sure this is the best combination because we are lacking some critical information: Harry's budget constraint—how much he has available to spend on CDs and DVDs—and the prices of CDs and DVDs.

Let's say that Harry has $100 to spend this month, the price of CDs is $10, and the price of DVDs is $20. Using the information from the first table, we can now calculate Harry's marginal utility per dollar for both goods, as is shown in the following table:

HARRY'S MARGINAL UTILITY AND MARGINAL UTILITY PER DOLLAR FROM BUYING CDs AND DVDs

QUANTITY OF CDs	MARGINAL UTILITY FROM LAST CD (MU_{CD})	MARGINAL UTILITY PER DOLLAR $\left(\dfrac{MU_{CD}}{P_{CD}}\right)$	QUANTITY OF DVDs	MARGINAL UTILITY FROM LAST DVD (MU_{DVD})	MARGINAL UTILITY PER DOLLAR $\left(\dfrac{MU_{DVD}}{P_{DVD}}\right)$
1	50	5	1	60	3
2	35	3.5	2	45	2.25
3	25	2.5	3	40	2
4	20	2	4	30	1.5
5	10	1	5	20	1
6	5	0.5	6	15	0.75

Harry's marginal utility per dollar is the same for two combinations of CDs and DVDs:

COMBINATIONS OF CDs AND DVDs WITH EQUAL MARGINAL UTILITIES PER DOLLAR	MARGINAL UTILITY PER DOLLAR (MARGINAL UTILITY/PRICE)	TOTAL SPENDING	TOTAL UTILITY
5 CDs and 5 DVDs	1	$50 + $100 = $150	140 + 195 = 335
4 CDs and 3 DVDs	2	$40 + $60 = $100	130 + 145 = 275

Unfortunately, 5 CDs and 5 DVDs would cost Harry $150, and he has only $100. The best Harry can do is to buy 4 CDs and 3 DVDs. This combination provides him with the maximum amount of utility attainable, given his budget constraint.

The key point, which we also saw in "Solved Problem 9-1," is that consumers maximize their utility when they equalize marginal utility *per dollar* for every good they buy, not when they equalize marginal utility.

YOUR TURN: Test your understanding by doing related problem 7 on page 296 at the end of this chapter.

The Income Effect and Substitution Effect of a Price Change

We can use the rule of equal marginal utility per dollar to analyze how consumers adjust their buying decisions when a price changes. Suppose you are back at the restaurant for the Super Bowl party, but this time the price of pizza is $1.50 per slice, rather than $2. You still have $10 to spend on pizza and Coke.

When the price of pizza was $2 per slice and the price of Coke was $1 per cup, your optimal choice was to consume 3 slices of pizza and 4 cups of Coke. The fall in the price of pizza to $1.50 per slice has two effects on the quantity of pizza you consume: the *income effect* and the *substitution effect*. First, consider the income effect. When the price of a good falls, you now have more purchasing power. In our example, 3 slices of pizza and 4 cups of Coke now cost a total of only $8.50, instead of $10.00. An increase in purchasing power is essentially the same thing as an increase in income. The change in the quantity of pizza you will demand because of this increase in purchasing power—holding all other factors constant—is the **income effect** of the price change. Recall from Chapter 3 that if a product is a *normal good*, a consumer increases the quantity demanded as the consumer's income rises, but if a product is an *inferior good*, a consumer decreases the quantity demanded as the consumer's income rises. So, if we assume that for you pizza is a normal good, the income effect of a fall in price causes you to consume more pizza. If pizza had been an inferior good for you, the income effect of a fall in the price would have caused you to consume less pizza.

The second effect of the price change is the substitution effect. When the price of pizza falls, pizza becomes cheaper *relative* to Coke, and the marginal utility per dollar for each slice of pizza eaten increases. If we hold constant the effect of the price change on your purchasing power, and just focus on the effect of the price being lower relative to the price of the other good, we have isolated the **substitution effect** of the price change. The lower price of pizza relative to the price of Coke has lowered the *opportunity cost* to you of consuming pizza because now you have to give up less Coke to consume the same quantity of pizza. Therefore, the substitution effect from the fall in the price of pizza relative to the price of Coke will cause you to eat more pizza and drink less Coke. In this case, both the income effect and the substitution effect of the fall in price cause you to eat more pizza. If the price of pizza had risen, both the income effect and the substitution effect would have caused you to eat less pizza. Table 9-4 summarizes the effect of a price change on the quantity demanded.

We can determine the effect of the fall in the price of pizza on your optimal consumption with the aid of Table 9-5. Table 9-5 has the same information as Table 9-2 with one change: The marginal utility per dollar from eating pizza has been adjusted to reflect the new lower price of $1.50 per slice. Examining the table, we can see that the fall in the

Income effect The change in the quantity demanded of a good that results from the effect of a change in price on consumer purchasing power, holding all other factors constant.

Substitution effect The change in the quantity demanded of a good that results from a change in price making the good more or less expensive relative to other goods, holding constant the effect of the price change on consumer purchasing power.

TABLE 9-4			INCOME EFFECT		SUBSTITUTION EFFECT
Income Effect and Substitution Effect of a Price Change			**NORMAL GOOD**	**INFERIOR GOOD**	
	Price Decrease	Increases the consumer's purchasing power, which . . .	. . . causes the quantity demanded to increase.	. . . causes the quantity demanded to decrease.	Lowers the opportunity cost of consuming the good, which causes the quantity of the good demanded to increase.
	Price Increase	Decreases the consumer's purchasing power, which . . .	. . . causes the quantity demanded to decrease.	. . . causes the quantity demanded to increase.	Raises the opportunity cost of consuming the good, which causes the quantity of the good demanded to decrease.

TABLE 9-5 Adjusting Optimal Consumption to a Lower Price of Pizza

NUMBER OF SLICES OF PIZZA	MARGINAL UTILITY FROM LAST SLICE (MU_{Pizza})	MARGINAL UTILITY PER DOLLAR $\left(\dfrac{MU_{Pizza}}{P_{Pizza}}\right)$	NUMBER OF CUPS OF COKE	MARGINAL UTILITY FROM LAST CUP (MU_{COKE})	MARGINAL UTILITY PER DOLLAR $\left(\dfrac{MU_{Coke}}{P_{Coke}}\right)$
1	20	13.33	1	20	20
2	16	10.67	2	15	15
3	10	6.67	3	10	10
4	6	4	4	5	5
5	2	1.33	5	3	3
6	−3	–	6	−1	–

price of pizza will result in your eating 1 more slice of pizza, so your optimal consumption now becomes 4 slices of pizza and 4 cups of Coke. You will be spending all of your $10, and the last dollar you spend on pizza will provide you with about the same marginal utility per dollar as the last dollar you spend on Coke. You will not be receiving exactly the same marginal utility per dollar spent on the two products. As Table 9-5 shows, the last slice of pizza gives you 4 units of utility per dollar, and the last cup of Coke gives you 5 units of utility per dollar. But this is as close as you can come to equalizing marginal utility per dollar for the two products, unless you can buy a fraction of a slice of pizza or a fraction of a cup of Coke.

Where Demand Curves Come From

We saw in Chapter 3 that, according to the *law of demand*, whenever the price of a product falls, the quantity demanded increases. Now that we have covered the concepts of total utility, marginal utility, and the budget constraint, we can look more closely at why the law of demand holds.

In our example of optimal consumption of pizza and Coke at the Super Bowl party, we found the following:

Price of pizza = $2 per slice ⇒ Quantity of pizza demanded = 3 slices

Price of pizza = $1.50 per slice ⇒ Quantity of pizza demanded = 4 slices

In panel (a) of Figure 9-2, we plot the two points showing the optimal number of pizza slices you choose to consume at each price. In panel (b) of Figure 9-2, we draw a line connecting the two points. This downward-sloping line represents your demand curve for pizza. We could find more points on the line by changing the price of pizza and using the information in Table 9-2 to find the new optimal number of slices of pizza you would demand at each price.

Remember that according to the law of demand, demand curves always slope downward. We now know that this is true because the income and substitution effects of a fall in price cause consumers to increase the quantity of the good they demand. There is a complicating factor, however. As we discussed earlier, only for normal goods will the income effect result in consumers increasing the quantity of the good they demand when the price falls. If the good is an inferior good, then the income effect leads consumers to *decrease* the quantity of the good they demand. The substitution effect, on the other

② **LEARNING OBJECTIVE**
Use the concept of utility to explain how the law of demand results from consumers adjusting their consumption choices to changes in prices.

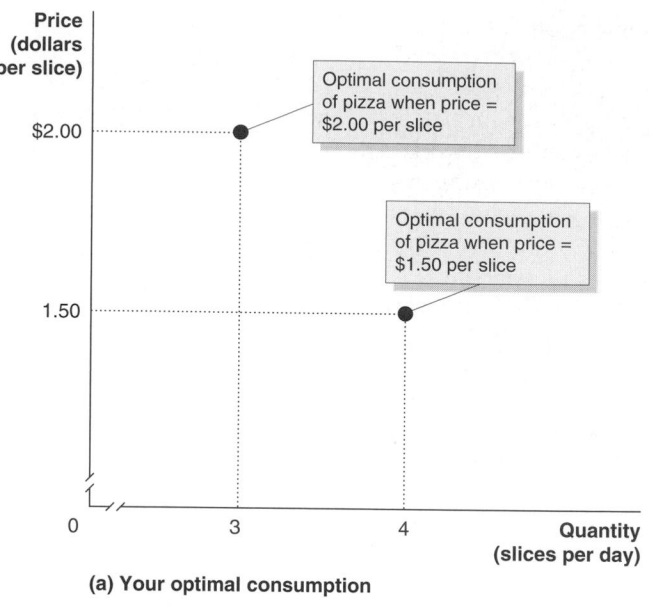

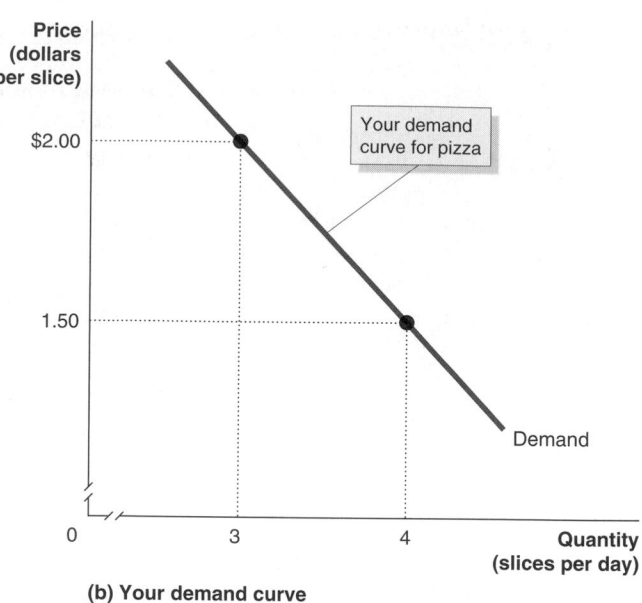

FIGURE 9-2   **Deriving the Demand Curve for Pizza**

A consumer responds optimally to the fall in the price of a product by consuming more of that product. In panel (a), the price of pizza falls from $2 per slice to $1.50, and optimal quantity of slices consumed rises from 3 to 4. When we graph this result in panel (b), we have the consumer's demand curve.

hand, results in consumers increasing the quantity they demand of both normal and inferior goods when the price falls. So, when the price of an inferior good falls, the income and substitution effects work in opposite directions: The income effect causes consumers to decrease the quantity of the good they demand, whereas the substitution effect causes consumers to increase the quantity of the good they demand. Is it possible, then, that consumers might actually buy less of a good when the price falls? If this happened, the demand curve would be upward-sloping. (Be sure you see why this would be true.)

For a demand curve to be upward-sloping, the good would have to be an inferior good, and the income effect would have to be larger than the substitution effect. Goods that have both these characteristics are called *Giffen goods*. Although we can conceive of there being Giffen goods, none has ever been discovered because for all actual goods the substitution effect is larger than the income effect. Therefore, even for an inferior good, a fall in price leads to an increase in quantity demanded and a rise in price leads to a decrease in the quantity demanded.

(3) **LEARNING OBJECTIVE**

Explain how social influences can affect consumption choices.

Social Influences on Decision Making

Sociologists and anthropologists have argued that social factors such as culture, customs, and religion are very important in explaining the choices consumers make. Economists have traditionally seen such factors as being relatively unimportant, if they take them into consideration at all. Recently, however, some economists have begun to study how social factors influence consumer choice.

For example, people seem to receive more utility from consuming goods they believe are popular. As the economists Gary Becker and Kevin Murphy put it:

The utility from drugs, crime, going bowling, owning a Rolex watch, voting Democratic, dressing informally at work, or keeping a neat lawn depends on whether friends and neighbors take drugs, commit crimes, go bowling, own Rolex watches, vote Democratic, dress informally, or keep their lawns neat.

This reasoning can help to explain why one restaurant is packed, while another restaurant that serves essentially the same food and has a similar décor has many fewer customers. Consumers decide which restaurant to go to partly on the basis of food and décor, but also on the basis of the restaurant's popularity. People receive utility from being seen eating at a popular restaurant because they believe it makes them appear knowledgeable and fashionable. Whenever consumption takes place publicly, many consumers will base their purchasing decisions on what other consumers buy. Examples include eating in restaurants, attending sporting events, wearing clothes or jewelry, or driving cars. In all these cases, the decision to buy a product will depend partly on the characteristics of the product and partly on how many other people are buying the product.

The Effects of Celebrity Endorsements

In many cases, it is not just the number of people who use a product that makes it desirable, but the types of people who use it. If consumers believe that movie stars or professional athletes use a product, demand for the product will often increase. This may be partly because consumers believe public figures are particularly knowledgeable about products: "Tiger Woods knows more about cars than I do, so I'll buy the same car he drives." But many consumers also feel more fashionable and closer to famous people if they use the same products these people do. All these considerations help to explain why companies are willing to pay millions of dollars to have celebrities endorse their products. As we saw at the beginning of this chapter, Coke has been using celebrities in its advertising for decades.

Why Do Firms Pay Tiger Woods to Endorse Their Products?

Tiger Woods may be the best golfer who ever lived. In his first five years as a professional, he won 27 tournaments on the Professional Golfers Association (PGA) Tour. When he won the Masters Tournament in 2001, he became the first golfer ever to hold all four major professional golf championships at the same time. Even though Tiger Woods is a great golfer, should consumers care what products he uses? A number of major companies apparently believe consumers do care. The Nike, Titleist, American Express, Buick, and Rolex companies collectively pay him more than $50 million per year to endorse their products.

There seems little doubt that consumers do care what products Tiger uses, but *why* do they care? It might be that they believe Tiger has better information than they do about the products he endorses. The average weekend golfer might believe that if Tiger endorses Titleist golf clubs, maybe Titleist clubs are better than other golf clubs. But it seems more likely that people buy products associated with Tiger Woods or other celebrities because using these products makes them feel closer to the celebrity endorser or because it makes them appear to be fashionable.

Network Externalities

Technology can also play a role in explaining why consumers buy products that many other consumers are already buying. There are **network externalities** in the consumption of a product if the usefulness of the product increases with the number of consumers who use it. For example, if you owned the only telephone in the world, it would not be very useful. The usefulness of telephones increases with the number of people who own them and use them. Similarly, your willingness to buy a DVD player will depend in part on the number of other people who have DVD players. The more people who have DVD players, the more movies that will be available in DVD format and the more useful a DVD player is to you.

Some economists have raised the possibility that network externalities may have a significant downside because they might result in consumers buying products that contain inferior technologies. This outcome could occur because network externalities can create significant *switching costs* to changing products. Therefore, once a product becomes established, consumers may find it too costly to switch to a new product that

9-1 Making
the Connection

When consumers buy the same products as celebrities, they feel fashionable and closer to the celebrities.

Network externalities Network externalities exist when the usefulness of a product increases with the number of consumers who use it.

contains a better technology. The selection of products may be *path dependent*. That means that because of switching costs, the technology that was first available may have advantages over better technologies that were developed later—in other words, the path along which the economy has developed in the past is important.

One possible example of path dependency and the use of an inferior technology is computers with QWERTY keyboards. QWERTY refers to the order of the letters along the top row of most keyboards. This order first became widespread when manual typewriters were developed in the late nineteenth century. The metal keys on these typewriters would stick together if a user typed too fast. Some economists have argued that the QWERTY keyboard was designed actually to slow down typists. With computers, the problem that QWERTY was developed to solve no longer exists, so keyboards could be changed easily to have letters in a more efficient layout. But because the overwhelming majority of people have learned to use keyboards with the QWERTY layout, there might be significant costs to them from switching even if a new layout ultimately made them faster typists.

Other products that supposedly embodied inferior technologies are VHS video recorders—supposedly inferior to Sony Betamax recorders—and the Windows computer operating system—supposedly inferior to the Macintosh operating system. Some economists have argued that because of path dependence and switching costs, network externalities can result in *market failures*. As we saw in Chapter 5, a market failure is a situation in which the market fails to produce the efficient level of output. If network externalities result in market failure, government intervention in these markets might improve economic efficiency. Many economists are skeptical, however, that network externalities really do lead to consumers being locked into products with inferior technologies. In particular, economists Stan Leibowitz of the University of Texas, Dallas, and Stephen Margolis of North Carolina State University have argued that in practice the gains from using a superior technology are larger than the losses due to switching costs. After carefully studying the cases of the QWERTY keyboard, VHS video recorders, and the Windows computer operating system, they have concluded that there is no good evidence that the alternative technologies were actually superior. The implications of network externalities for economic efficiency remain controversial among economists.

Does Fairness Matter?

If people were only interested in making themselves as well off as possible in a material sense, they would not be concerned with fairness. There is a great deal of evidence, however, that people like to be treated fairly and that they usually attempt to treat others fairly, even if doing so makes them worse off financially. Tipping servers in restaurants is an example. Diners in restaurants typically add 15 percent to their food bills as tips to their servers. Tips are not *required*, but most people see it as very unfair not to tip, unless the service has been exceptionally bad. You could argue that people leave tips not to be fair but because they are afraid that if they don't leave a tip, the next time they visit the restaurant they will receive poor service. Studies have shown, however, that most people leave tips at restaurants even while on vacation or in other circumstances where they are unlikely to visit the restaurant again.

There are many other examples where people willingly part with money when they are not required to do so and when they receive nothing material in return. The most obvious example is making donations to charity. Apparently donating money to charity or leaving tips in restaurants that they will never visit again gives people more utility than they would receive from keeping the money and spending it on themselves.

A TEST OF FAIRNESS IN THE ECONOMIC LABORATORY: THE ULTIMATUM GAME EXPERIMENT Economists have used experiments to increase their understanding of the role that fairness plays in consumer decision making. Experimental economics has been widely used during the last two decades, and a number of experimental economics laboratories exist in the United States and Europe. Economists Maurice Allais, Reinhard Selten, and Vernon Smith were awarded the Nobel Prize in Economics in part because of their contributions to experimental economics. Experiments make it possible to focus on a single aspect of consumer behavior. The *ultimatum game* is an experiment that tests whether fairness is important in consumer decision making. Various economists have conducted the ultimatum game experiment under slightly different conditions, but with generally the same result. In this game, a group of volunteers—often college students—are divided into pairs. One member of each pair is the "allocator" and the other member of the pair is the "recipient."

Each pair is given an amount of money, say $20. The allocator decides how much of the $20 each member of the pair will get. There are no restrictions on how the allocator divides up the money. He or she could keep it all, give it all to the recipient, or anything in between. The recipient must then decide whether to accept the allocation or reject it. If the recipient decides to accept the allocation, each member of the pair gets to keep his or her share. If the recipient decides to reject the allocation, both members of the pair receive nothing.

If neither the allocator nor the recipient cared about fairness, optimal play in the ultimatum game is straightforward: The allocator should propose a division of the money in which the allocator receives $19.99 and the recipient receives $0.01. The allocator has maximized his or her gain. The recipient should accept the division, because the alternative is to reject the division and receive nothing at all: Even a penny is better than nothing.

In fact, when the ultimatum game experiment is carried out, both allocators and recipients act as if fairness is important. Allocators usually offer recipients at least a 40 percent share of the money, and recipients almost always reject offers of less than a 10 percent share. Why do allocators offer recipients more than a negligible amount? It might be that allocators do not care about fairness but fear that recipients do care and will reject offers they consider unfair. This possibility was tested in an experiment known as the *dictator game* carried out by Daniel Kahneman (a psychologist who shared the Nobel Prize in Economics in 2002), Jack Knetsch, and Richard Thaler using students at Cornell University. In this experiment, the allocators were given only two possible divisions of $20: either $18 for themselves and $2 for the recipient, or an even division of $10 for themselves and $10 for the recipient. One important difference from the ultimatum game was that *the recipient was not allowed to reject the division*. Of the 161 allocators, 122 chose the even division of the $20. Because there was no possibility of the $18/$2 split being rejected, the allocators must have chosen the even split because they valued acting fairly.

Why would recipients in the ultimatum game ever reject any division of the money in which they receive even a very small amount, given that even a small amount of money is better than nothing? Apparently, most people value fairness enough that they will refuse to participate in transactions they consider unfair, even if they are worse off financially as a result.

BUSINESS IMPLICATIONS OF FAIRNESS If consumers value fairness, how does that affect firms? One consequence is that firms will sometimes not raise prices of goods and services, even when there is a large increase in demand, because they are afraid their customers will consider the price increases unfair and may buy elsewhere.

For example, the Broadway play *The Producers* was extremely popular during its first year in production. Even though ticket prices were an average of $75, on most nights many more people wanted to buy tickets at that price than could be accommodated in the St. James Theater, where the play was running. Figure 9-3 illustrates this situation.

Notice that the supply curve in Figure 9-3 is a vertical line, which indicates that the capacity of the St. James Theater is fixed at 1,644 seats. At a price of $75 per ticket, there was a shortage of more than 400 tickets. Why didn't the theater raise

FIGURE 9-3

The Market for Tickets to the *Producers*

The St. James Theater could have raised prices for the Broadway musical *The Producers* to $125 per ticket and still sold all of the 1,644 tickets available. Instead, the theater kept the price of tickets at $75, even though the result was a shortage of more than 400 seats. Is it possible that this strategy maximized profits?

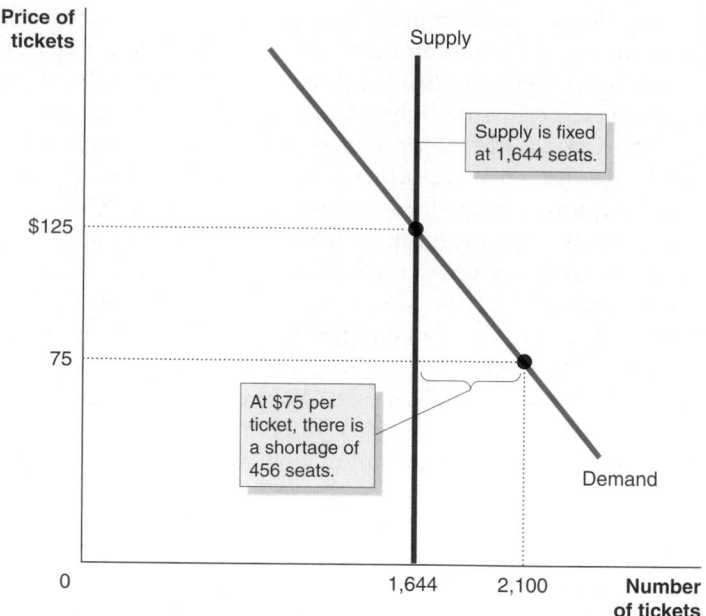

ticket prices to $125, where the quantity supplied would equal the quantity demanded?

The following are two other examples in which it seems that businesses could increase their profits by raising prices: Each year many more people would like to buy tickets to see the Super Bowl than there are tickets for them to buy at the price the National Football League charges. Why doesn't the National Football League raise prices? At popular restaurants, there are often long lines of people waiting to be served. Some of the people will wait hours to be served, and some won't be served at all before the restaurant closes. Why doesn't the restaurant raise prices high enough to eliminate the lines?

In each of these cases, it appears that a firm could increase its profits by raising prices. The seller would be selling the same quantity—of seats in a theater or a football stadium or meals in a restaurant—at a higher price, so profits should increase. Economists have provided two explanations why firms will sometimes not raise prices in these situations. Gary Becker, winner of the Nobel Prize in Economics, has suggested that the products involved—theatrical plays, football games, rock concerts, or restaurant meals—are all products that buyers consume together with other buyers. In those situations, the amount consumers wish to buy may be related to how much of the product other people are consuming. People like to consume, and be seen consuming, a popular product. In this case, a popular restaurant that increased its prices enough to eliminate lines might find that it had also eliminated its popularity.

Daniel Kahneman, Jack Knetsch, and Richard Thaler have offered another explanation for why firms don't always raise prices when doing so would seem to increase their profits. In surveys of consumers, these researchers found that most people considered it fair for firms to raise their prices following an increase in costs but unfair to raise prices following an increase in demand. For example, Kahneman, Knetsch, and Thaler conducted a survey in which people were asked their opinion of the following situation: "A hardware store has been selling snow shovels for $15. The morning after a large snowstorm, the store raises the price to $20." Eighty-two percent of those surveyed responded that they considered the hardware store's actions to be unfair. Kahneman, Knetsch, and Thaler have concluded that firms may sometimes not raise their prices even when the quantity demanded of their product is greater than the quantity supplied out of fear that in the long run they will lose customers who believe the price increases were unfair.

These explanations share the same basic idea: Sometimes firms will give up some profits in the short run to keep their customers happy and increase their profits in the long run.

Professor Krueger Goes to the Super Bowl

Economist Alan Krueger of Princeton University has studied the question of why the National Football League does not charge a price for Super Bowl tickets that is high enough to make the quantity of tickets demanded equal to the quantity of tickets available. The prices may seem high—$400 for the best seats, $325 for the rest—but the quantity demanded still greatly exceeds the quantity supplied. Most Super Bowl tickets are allocated to the two teams playing in the game or to the league's corporate sponsors. To give ordinary fans a chance to attend the game, in 2001 the NFL set aside 500 pairs of tickets. They held a lottery for the opportunity to buy these tickets, and more than 36,000 people applied. Some fans were willing to pay as much as $5,000 to buy a ticket from ticket scalpers. (Scalpers buy tickets at their face value and then resell them at much higher prices, even though in Florida, where the 2001 Super Bowl was held, ticket scalping is illegal.)

Why didn't the NFL simply raise the price of tickets to clear the market? Krueger decided to survey football fans attending the game to see if their views could help explain this puzzle. Krueger's survey provides support for the Kahneman, Knetsch, and Thaler explanation of why companies do not always raise prices when the quantity demanded is greater than the quantity supplied. When asked whether it would "be fair for the NFL to raise the [price of tickets] to $1,500 if that is still less than the amount most people are willing to pay for tickets," 92 percent of the fans surveyed answered "no." Even 83 percent of the fans who had paid more than $1,500 for their tickets answered "no." Krueger concluded that whatever the NFL might gain in the short run from raising ticket prices, it would more than lose in the long run from alienating football fans.

Source: Alan B. Krueger, "Supply and Demand: An Economist Goes to the Super Bowl," *The Milken Institute Review,* Second Quarter 2001.

9-2 *Making the Connection*

Should the NFL raise the price of Super Bowl tickets?

Behavioral Economics: Do People Make Their Choices Rationally?

When economists say that consumers and firms are behaving "rationally," they mean that consumers and firms are taking actions that are appropriate to reach their goals, given the information available to them. In recent years, some economists have begun studying situations in which people do not appear to be making choices that are economically rational. This new area of economics is called **behavioral economics.** Why might consumers or businesses not act rationally? The most obvious reason would be that they do not realize that their actions are inconsistent with their goals. As we discussed in Chapter 1, one of the goals of economics is to suggest ways to make better decisions. In this section, we discuss ways in which consumers can improve their decisions by avoiding some common pitfalls.

Consumers commonly commit the following three mistakes when making decisions:

➤ They take into account monetary costs but ignore nonmonetary opportunity costs.

➤ They fail to ignore sunk costs.

➤ They are overly optimistic about their future behavior.

Ignoring Nonmonetary Opportunity Costs

Remember from Chapter 2 that the **opportunity cost** of any activity is the highest-valued alternative that must be given up to engage in that activity. For example, if you own something you could sell, using it yourself involves an opportunity cost. It is often difficult for people to think of opportunity costs in these terms.

Consider the following example: Some of the fans at the 2001 Super Bowl had participated in a lottery run by the National Football League that allowed the winners to purchase tickets at their face value, which was either $325 or $400, depending on where

④ LEARNING OBJECTIVE

Describe how people can improve their decision making by taking into account nonmonetary opportunity costs, ignoring sunk costs, and being more realistic about their future behavior.

Behavioral economics The study of situations in which people act in ways that are not economically rational.

Opportunity cost The highest-valued alternative that must be given up to engage in an activity.

in the stadium the seats were. Alan Krueger surveyed the lottery winners, asking them two questions:

Question 1: If you had not won the lottery, would you have been willing to pay $3,000 for your ticket?

Question 2: If after winning your ticket (and before arriving in Florida for the Super Bowl) someone had offered you $3,000 for your ticket, would you have sold it?

In answer to the first question, 94 percent said that if they had not won the lottery they would not have paid $3,000 for a ticket. In answer to the second question, 92 percent said they would not have sold their ticket for $3,000. But these answers are contradictory! If someone offers you $3,000 for your ticket, then by using the ticket rather than selling it you incur an opportunity cost of $3,000. There really is a $3,000 cost involved in using that ticket, even though you do not pay $3,000 in cash. The alternatives of either paying $3,000 or not receiving $3,000 amount to exactly the same thing.

If the ticket is really not worth $3,000 to you, you should sell it. If it is worth $3,000 to you, you should be willing to pay $3,000 in cash to buy it. Not being willing to sell a ticket you already own for $3,000, while at the same time not being willing to buy a ticket for $3,000 if you didn't already own one, is inconsistent behavior. The inconsistency comes from a failure to take into account nonmonetary opportunity costs. Behavioral economists believe this inconsistency is caused by the **endowment effect,** which is the tendency of people to be unwilling to sell a good they already own even if they are offered a price that is greater than the price they would be willing to pay to buy the good if they didn't already own it.

> **Endowment effect** The tendency of people to be unwilling to sell something they already own even if they are offered a price that is greater than the price they would be willing to pay to buy the good if they didn't already own it.

The failure to take into account opportunity costs is a very common error in decision making. Suppose, for example, that a friend is in a hurry to have his room cleaned—it's the Friday before Parents Weekend—and he offers you $50 to do it for him. You turn him down and spend the time cleaning your own room, even though you know somebody down the hall who would be willing to clean your room for $20. Leave aside complicating details—the guy who asked you to clean his room is a real slob, or you don't want the person who offered to clean your room for $20 to go through your stuff—and you should see the point being made here. The opportunity cost of cleaning your own room is $50—the amount your friend offered to pay you to clean his room. It is inconsistent to turn down an offer from someone else to clean your room for $20 when you are doing it for yourself at a cost of $50. The key point here is this: *Nonmonetary opportunity costs are just as real as monetary costs and should be taken into account when making decisions.*

Business Implications of Consumers Ignoring Nonmonetary Opportunity Costs

Behavioral economist Richard Thaler has studied several examples of how businesses make use of consumers' failure to take into account opportunity costs. Whenever you buy something with a credit card, the credit card company charges the merchant a fee to process the bill. Credit card companies generally do not allow stores to charge higher prices to customers who use credit cards. A bill was introduced in Congress that would have made it illegal for credit card companies to enforce this rule. The credit card industry was afraid that if this law passed, credit card usage would drop because stores might begin charging a fee to credit card users. They attempted to have the law amended so that stores would be allowed to give a cash discount to people not using credit cards but would not be allowed to charge a fee to people using credit cards. There really is no difference in opportunity-cost terms between being charged a fee and not receiving a discount. The credit card industry was relying on the fact that *not* receiving a discount is a nonmonetary opportunity cost—and, therefore, likely to be ignored by consumers—but a fee is a monetary cost that people do take into account.

Film processing companies provide another example. Many of these companies have a policy of printing every picture on a roll of film, even if the picture is very fuzzy. Customers are allowed to ask for refunds on pictures they don't like. Once again, the companies are relying on the fact that passing up a refund once you have already paid for a picture is a nonmonetary opportunity cost, rather than a direct monetary cost. In fact, customers rarely ask for refunds.

Failing to Ignore Sunk Costs

A **sunk cost** is a cost that has already been paid and cannot be recovered. Once you have paid money and can't get it back, you should ignore that money in any later decisions you make. Consider the following two situations:

Sunk cost A cost that has already been paid and cannot be recovered.

Situation 1: You have paid $75 to buy a ticket to a play. The ticket is nonrefundable and must be used on Tuesday night, which is the only night the play will be performed. On Monday a friend calls and invites you to a local comedy club to see a comedian you both like who is appearing only on Tuesday night. Your friend offers to pay the cost of going to the club.

Situation 2: It's Monday night and you are about to buy a ticket for the Tuesday night performance of the same play as in situation 1. As you are leaving to buy the ticket, your friend calls and invites you to the comedy club.

Would your decision to go to the play or to the comedy club be different in situation 1 than in situation 2? Most people would say that in situation 1 they would go to the play, because otherwise they would lose the $75 they had paid for the ticket. In fact, though, the $75 is "lost" no matter what you do, because the ticket is not refundable. The only real issue for you to decide is whether you would prefer to see the play or prefer to go with your friend to the comedy club. If you would prefer to go to the club, the fact that you have already paid $75 for the ticket to the play is irrelevant. Your decision should be the same in situation 1 and situation 2.

Psychologists Daniel Kahneman and Amos Tversky explored the tendency of consumers not to ignore sunk costs by asking a sample of people the following questions:

Question 1: "Imagine that you have decided to see a play and have paid the admission price of $10 per ticket. As you enter the theater, you discover that you have lost the ticket. The seat was not marked and the ticket cannot be recovered. Would you pay $10 for another ticket?" Of those asked, 46 percent answered "yes" and 54 percent answered "no."

Question 2: A different sample of people was asked the following question: "Imagine that you have decided to see a play where admission is $10 per ticket. As you enter the theater, you discover that you have lost a $10 bill. Would you still pay $10 for a ticket to the play?" Of those asked, 88 percent answered "yes" and 12 percent answered "no."

The situations presented in the two questions are actually the same and should have received the same fraction of yes and no responses. Many people, though, have trouble seeing that in question 1 when deciding whether to see the play they should ignore the $10 already paid for a ticket because it is a sunk cost.

Being Unrealistic about Future Behavior

Studies have shown that a majority of adults in the United States are overweight. Why do many people choose to eat too much? One possibility is that they receive more utility from eating too much than they would from being thin. A more likely explanation, however, is that many people eat a lot today because they expect to eat less tomorrow. But they never do eat less, and so they end up overweight. (Of course, some people also suffer from medical problems that lead to weight gain.) Similarly, some people continue smoking today because they expect to be able to give it up sometime in the future. Unfortunately, for many people that time never comes and they suffer the health consequences of prolonged smoking. In both these cases, people are overvaluing the utility from current choices—eating chocolate cake or smoking—and undervaluing the utility to be received in the future from being thin or not getting lung cancer.

Economists who have studied this question argue that many people have preferences that are not consistent over time. In the long run, you would like to be thin or give up smoking or achieve some other goal, but each day you make decisions to eat too much or to smoke that are not consistent with this long-run goal. Because you are unrealistic about your future behavior, you underestimate the costs of choices—like overeating or smoking—that you make today. A key way of avoiding this problem is to be realistic about your future behavior.

9-3 *Making the Connection*

Why Don't Students Study More?

Government statistics show that students who do well in college earn at least $10,000 more per year than students who fail to graduate or who graduate with low grades. So, over the course of a career of 40 years or more, students who do well in college will have earned upwards of $400,000 more than students who failed to graduate or who received low grades. Most colleges advise that students study at least two hours outside of class for every hour they spend in class. Surveys show that students often ignore this advice.

If the opportunity cost of not studying is so high, why do many students choose to study relatively little? Some students have work or family commitments that limit the amount of time they can study. But many other students study less than they would if they were more realistic about their future behavior. On any given night, a student has to choose between studying and other activities—like watching television, going to the movies, or going to a party—that may seem to provide higher utility in the short run. Many students choose one of these activities over studying because they expect to study tomorrow or the next day, but tomorrow they face the same choices and make similar decisions. As a result they do not study enough to meet their long-run goal of graduating with high grades. If they were more realistic about their future behavior, they would not make the mistake of overvaluing the utility from activities like watching television or partying because they would realize that those activities can endanger their long-run goal of graduating with honors.

If the payoff to studying is so high, why don't students study more?

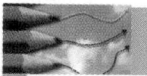

SOLVED PROBLEM 9-2

④ **LEARNING OBJECTIVE**

Describe how people can improve their decision making by taking into account nonmonetary opportunity costs, ignoring sunk costs, and being more realistic about their future behavior.

How Do You Get People to Save More of Their Income?

An article in the *New York Times* states the following:

> When it comes to saving for retirement, Americans . . . know they do not put away enough. . . . But ask them to save more in their [retirement] plans and they balk. A buck in the hand is irresistibly spent. Try a different approach. Ask them to commit now to increasing their savings in the future, make the increase coincide with the next raise, and they cheerfully sign up.

Why would people refuse to increase their savings now, but agree to increase their savings in the future?

Source: Louis Uchitelle, "Why It Takes Psychology to Make People Save," *New York Times*, January 13, 2002.

Solving the Problem:

Step 1: Review the chapter material. This problem is about how people are not always realistic about their future behavior, so you may want to review the section "Being Unrealistic about Future Behavior," which begins on page 289.

Step 2: Use your understanding of consumer decision making to show that this plan may work. We have seen that many people are unrealistic about their future behavior. They spend money today that they should be saving for retirement, partly because they expect to increase their saving in the future. A savings plan that gets people to commit today to saving in the future takes advantage of people's optimism about their future behavior. They agree to save more in the future because they expect to be doing that anyway. In fact, without being part of a plan that automatically saves their next raise, they probably would not have increased their savings.

YOUR TURN: For more practice, do related problems 21, 22, and 23 on page 297 at the end of this chapter. Visit www.prenhall.com/hubbard for an interactive exercise related to this Solved Problem.

Taking into account nonmonetary opportunity costs, ignoring sunk costs, and being more realistic about future behavior are three ways in which consumers are able to improve the decisions they make.

Conclusion

In a market system, consumers are in the driver's seat. Goods are produced only if consumers want them to be. Therefore, how consumers make their decisions is an important area for economists to study, a fact that was highlighted when Daniel Kahneman—whose research was mentioned several times in this chapter—shared the 2002 Nobel Prize in Economics. Economists expect that consumers will spend their incomes so that the last dollar spent on each good provides them with equal additional amounts of satisfaction, or utility. In practice, there are significant social influences on consumer decision making, particularly when a good or service is consumed in public. Fairness also seems to be an important consideration for most consumers. Finally, many consumers could improve the decisions they make if they would take into account non-monetary opportunity costs and ignore sunk costs.

In this chapter, we studied consumers' choices. In the next several chapters, we will study firms' choices. Before moving on to the next chapter, read *An Inside Look* on the next page to learn how firms respond when celebrities they hired to endorse their products offend rather than attract consumers.

BOSTON GLOBE, JULY 20, 2004

A Celebrity Endorser Who Doesn't Offend? Slim Chance

Somewhere out there, a celebrity is doing or saying something unfortunate, and Madison Avenue is getting very nervous.

A famous face is getting pulled over for erratic driving, checking into rehab, or making a statement either too impolitic or too political. In a few days, perhaps even a few hours, some ad executive, trembling in his $500 loafers, will learn a very old lesson about the perils of connecting a product with a well-known personality.

Last week, Whoopi Goldberg became the latest celebrity dumped for behavior deemed detrimental to the image of the product she was endorsing. Slim-Fast execs kicked Goldberg to the curb after her appearance at a recent star-studded fund-raiser for Democratic presidential candidate John Kerry, where she made several off-color remarks about President George W. Bush.

In severing ties with Goldberg, Terry Olson, Slim-Fast's vice president of marketing, said in a statement, "We are disappointed by the manner in which Ms. Goldberg chose to express herself, and sincerely regret that her recent remarks offended some of our consumers. Ads featuring Ms. Goldberg will no longer air. . . ."

Also taking a hit recently were sisters Mary-Kate and Ashley Olsen, who were dropped from the "Got Milk?" campaign after Mary-Kate sought help for what reportedly is an eating disorder. Officials from the Milk Processor Education Program said they yanked the magazine ads "out of sensitivity for her situation." And while that may be true, it's more likely that the company didn't want their product, promoted as a cornerstone of a nutritious diet, associated with someone struggling with eating issues.

It costs millions of dollars to launch advertising campaigns, so it's a safe bet that companies don't shut these things down without a lot of hand-wringing and teeth-gnashing. Of course, it also raises questions as to why corporations are so eager to swoon for celebrity endorsers in the first place.

Presumably, companies hire some rappers, athletes, and actors for their edgy personas, in hopes that an accessible version of that attitude will magically transfer to their products. . . .

Personally, I've never understood the point—either consumers want a product or they don't. I'm hard pressed to believe that simply because Catherine Zeta-Jones smiles pretty and bats her big brown eyes I'm going to switch my cellphone service. There's always been something absurd in the idea that consumers will buy something simply because a famous face tells them to do so.

292

Key Points in the Article

This article discusses the problems firms may encounter when they use celebrity endorsements in their advertising. Whoopi Goldberg was dropped as an endorser by Slim-Fast after she made critical and vulgar comments about President George W. Bush. Mary-Kate and Ashley Olson were dropped from the "Got Milk?" campaign after Mary-Kate was reportedly hospitalized with an eating disorder. The author of the article argues that firms run the risk of negative publicity whenever they use celebrity endorsers. The author is also skeptical that celebrity endorsements really do have a significant effect on consumer choice.

Analyzing the News

a We saw in Chapter 3 that when consumers' taste for a product increases, the demand curve will shift to the right, and when consumers' taste for a product decreases, the demand curve for the product will shift to the left. When a firm hires a celebrity to endorse its products, it is hoping to increase consumers' taste for its product. If the endorsement is successful in increasing consumers' taste for the product, the result is shown in Figure 1. The figure shows the demand curve for Slim-Fast shifting from D_1 to D_2. The increase in demand allows the firm to sell more cans at every price. For example, at a price of P_1 it could sell Q_1 cans without the endorsement but Q_2 cans with the endorsement.

b As the author points out, if a celebrity generates negative publicity, consumers' taste for the product may decrease. Presumably, this is what Slim-Fast was afraid was happening with Whoopi Goldberg. The result is shown in Figure 2, where the demand curve shifts to the left and fewer cans of Slim-Fast are sold at every price.

c Advertising increases a firm's costs and—if it is successful—the demand for the firm's product, and, therefore, its revenues. If, because of some of the problems mentioned in this article, an advertising campaign reduces the demand for a product, the firm's profits will decline. But does a "successful" advertising campaign always increase a firm's profits? In fact, a firm's profits will increase only if the additional revenue the firm receives from selling a larger quantity of the product is greater than the additional cost resulting from the advertising campaign.

Thinking Critically
ABOUT POLICY

1. The article's author says, "It costs millions of dollars to launch advertising campaigns, so it's a safe bet that companies don't shut these things down without a lot of hand-wringing and teeth-gnashing." Should a company whose celebrity endorser was just arrested base its decision about whether or not to cancel its ad campaign based on the amount it has already poured into making the ads? Should they do more "hand-wringing and teeth-gnashing" if creating the ad campaign costs an extra million dollars? Explain.

2. Some critics argue that advertising using celebrity endorsements serves no useful social purpose and should be banned or discouraged by the government. Do you agree? Explain.

Source: Boston Globe [Staff Produced Copy Only] by Renee Graham. Copyright 2004 by Globe Newspaper Co (MA). Reproduced with permission of Globe Newspaper Co (MA) in the format Textbook via Copyright Clearance Center.

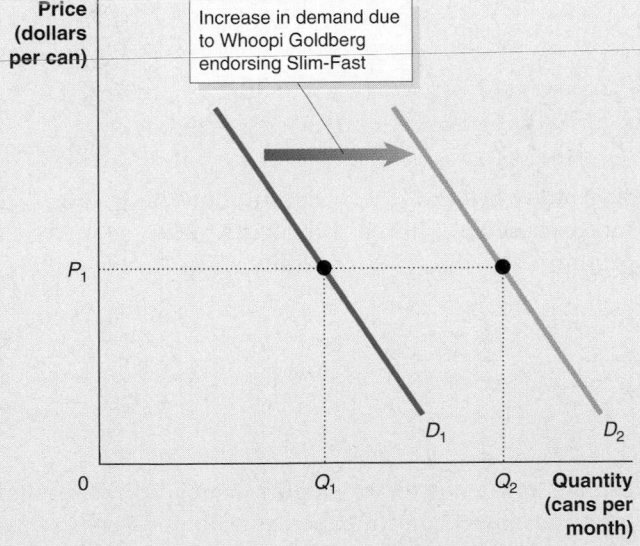

Figure 1: When successful, a celebrity endorsement can shift the demand curve for a product to the right, from D_1 to D_2.

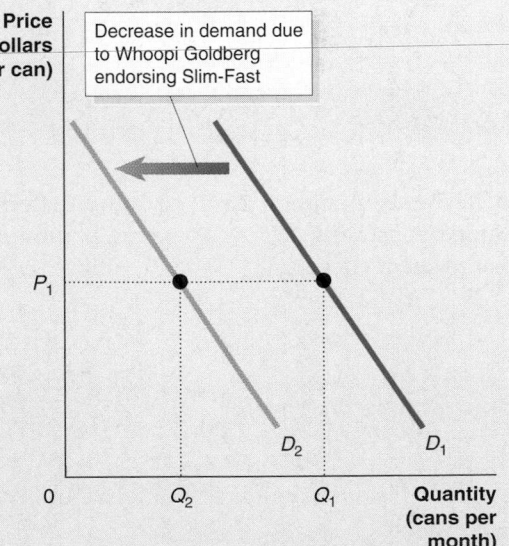

Figure 2: If a celebrity endorsing a product generates bad publicity, the demand curve for the product may shift to the left, from D_1 to D_2.

293

LEARNING OBJECTIVE ① **Define utility and explain how consumers choose goods and services to maximize their utility.** *Utility* is the enjoyment or satisfaction that people receive from consuming goods and services. The goal of a consumer is to spend available income so as to maximize utility. The *law of diminishing marginal utility* states that consumers receive diminishing additional satisfaction as they consume more of a good or service during a given period of time. The *budget constraint* is the amount of income consumers have available to spend on goods and services. To maximize utility, consumers should make sure they spend their income so that the last dollar spent on each product gives them the same marginal utility. The *income effect* is the change in the quantity demanded of a good that results from the effect of a change in the price on consumer purchasing power. The *substitution effect* is the change in the quantity demanded of a good that results from a change in price making the good more or less expensive relative to other goods, holding constant the effect of the price change on consumer purchasing power.

LEARNING OBJECTIVE ② **Use the concept of utility to explain how the law of demand results from consumers adjusting their consumption choices to changes in prices.** When the price of a good declines, the ratio of the marginal utility to price rises. This leads consumers to buy more of that good. As a result, whenever the price of a product falls, the quantity demanded increases. We saw in Chapter 3 that this is known as the *law of demand*.

LEARNING OBJECTIVE ③ **Explain how social influences can affect consumption choices.** Social factors can have an influence on consumption. For example, the amount of utility people receive from consuming a good often depends upon how many other people they know who also consume the good. There are *network externalities* in the consumption of a product if the usefulness of the product increases with the number of consumers who use it. There is also evidence that people like to be treated fairly and that they usually attempt to treat others fairly, even if doing so makes them worse off financially. This result has been demonstrated in laboratory experiments, such as the ultimatum game. When firms set prices, they take into account consumers' preference for fairness. For example, hardware stores often will not increase the price of snow shovels to take advantage of a temporary increase in demand following a snowstorm.

LEARNING OBJECTIVE ④ **Describe how people can improve their decision making by taking into account nonmonetary opportunity costs, ignoring sunk costs, and being more realistic about their future behavior.** *Behavioral economics* is the study of situations in which people act in ways that are not economically rational. People would improve their decision making if they took into account nonmonetary opportunity costs, ignored sunk costs, and were more realistic about their future behavior.

Behavioral economics 287	Income effect 280	Marginal utility (*MU*) 273	Substitution effect 280
Budget constraint 275	Law of diminishing marginal	Network externalities 283	Sunk cost 289
Endowment effect 288	utility 273	Opportunity cost 287	Utility 272

1. What is the economic definition of utility? Is utility measurable?

2. What is the definition of marginal utility? What is the law of diminishing marginal utility? Why is marginal utility more useful than total utility in consumer decision making?

3. What is meant by a consumer's budget constraint? What is the rule of equal marginal utility per dollar?

4. Explain how a downward-sloping demand curve results from consumers adjusting their consumption choices to changes in price. What is the income effect? What is the substitution effect?

5. In which of the following situations are social influences on consumer decision making likely to be greater: choosing a restaurant for dinner or choosing a brand of toothpaste to buy? Briefly explain.

6. Why do consumers pay attention to celebrity endorsements of products?

7. What are network externalities? For what types of products are network externalities likely to be important? What is path dependence?

8. What is the ultimatum game? What insight does it give us into consumer decision making?

9. How does the fact that consumers apparently value fairness affect the decisions that businesses make?

10. What does it mean to be economically rational? Define behavioral economics, and give an example of three common mistakes that consumers often make.

PROBLEMS AND APPLICATIONS

Please visit www.prenhall.com/hubbard *for solutions to the even-numbered problems as well as multiple-choice and true or false self-assessment quizzes.*

1. Does the law of diminishing marginal utility hold true in every situation? Is it possible to think of goods for which consuming additional units will result in increasing marginal utility?

2. If consumers should allocate their income so that the last dollar spent on every product gives them the same amount of additional utility, how should they decide the amount of their income to save?

3. You have 6 hours to study for 2 exams tomorrow. The relationship between hours of study and test scores is as follows:

ECONOMICS		PSYCHOLOGY	
HOURS	SCORE	HOURS	SCORE
0	54	0	54
1	62	1	60
2	69	2	65
3	75	3	69
4	80	4	72
5	84	5	74
6	87	6	75

a. Use the rule for determining optimal purchases to decide how many hours you should study each subject. Treat each point on an exam like 1 unit of utility and assume you are equally interested in doing well in economics and psychology.

b. Suppose now that you are a psychology major and that you value each point you earn on a psychology exam as being worth three times as much as each point you earn on an economics exam. Now how many hours will you study each subject?

4. **[Related to *Solved Problem 9-1*]** Joe has $16 to spend on Twinkies and Ho-Hos. Twinkies have a price of $1 per pack and Ho-Hos have a price of $2 per pack. Use the information in the following graphs to determine the number of Twinkies packs and the number of Ho-Hos packs Joe should buy to maximize his utility. Briefly explain your reasoning.

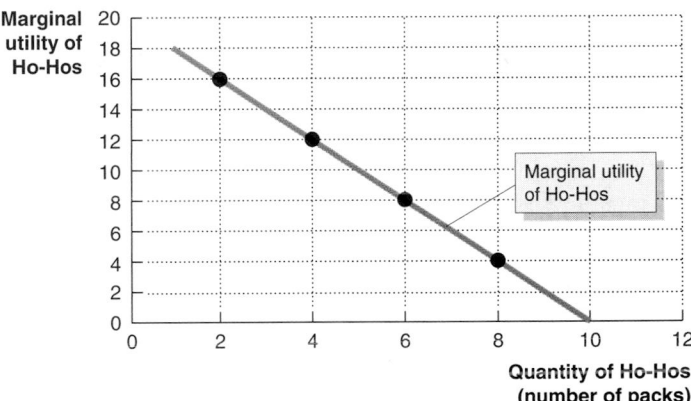

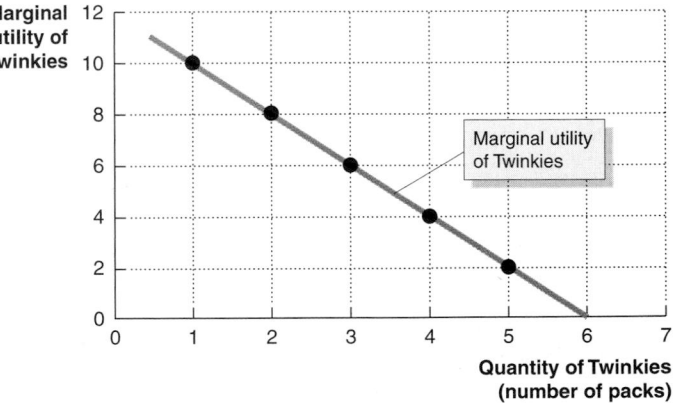

5. [Related to *Solved Problem 9-1*] Joe has $55 to spend on apples and oranges. Given the information in the following table, is Joe maximizing utility? Briefly explain.

PRODUCT	PRICE	QUANTITY	TOTAL UTILITY	MARGINAL UTILITY OF LAST UNIT
Apples	$0.50	50	1,000	20
Oranges	$0.75	40	500	30

6. Suppose the price of a bag of Frito's Corn Chips declines from $0.69 to $0.59. Which is likely to be larger: the income effect or the substitution effect? Briefly explain.

7. [Related to *Don't Let This Happen To You!*] Mary is buying corn chips and soda. She has 4 bags of corn chips and 5 bottles of soda in her shopping cart. The marginal utility of the fourth bag of corn chips is 10, and the marginal utility of the sixth bottle of soda is also 10. Is Mary maximizing utility? Briefly explain.

8. When the price of pizza falls in the Super Bowl example on pages 280, both the income and the substitution effect cause you to want to consume more pizza. If pizza were an inferior good, how would the analysis be changed? In this case, is it possible that a lower price of pizza might lead you to buy less pizza? Briefly explain.

9. Suppose the wage you are being paid increases. Is there an income and substitution effect involved? If so, what is being substituted for what?

10. Which of the following products are most likely to have significant network externalities? Explain.
   a. Fax machines
   b. Dog food
   c. Board games
   d. Conventional (CRT) television sets
   e. Plasma television sets

11. Linux is a computer operating system that is an alternative to Microsoft's Windows system. According to a newspaper article:

   The dominance of the Windows operating system, which runs 95 per cent of the world's PCs, is coming under greater attack in Asia than in any other part of the world, analysts say. Linux for PCs sold three times as many copies in Asia as in the US last year. . . . "In emerging markets such as India and China, where PC growth rates are the highest, Linux's momentum seems to be accelerating," said Robert Stimson, a Bank of America analyst in San Francisco.

   If network externalities are important in choosing a computer operating system, why might Linux be more successful in Asia than in the United States?

Source: "Gates Blitzes Asia to Stem Linux Threat," *New Zealand Herald*, June 29, 2004.

12. Suppose your little brother tells you on Tuesday that one of his friends offered him $20 for his Barry Bonds rookie baseball card, but your brother decided not to sell the card. On Wednesday your brother loses the card. Your parents feel sorry for him and give him $20 to make up the loss. Instead of buying another Barry Bonds card with the money (which we will assume he could have done), your brother uses the money to go to the movies. Explain your brother's actions by using the concepts in this chapter.

13. Economist Richard Thaler has argued that the behavior of professional football teams during the college draft is an example of the endowment effect. Professional football teams take turns drafting eligible college players. Suppose that it's the New England Patriots' turn to pick, and the best college player not yet drafted is a quarterback. Suppose also that the Patriots already have a great quarterback and don't need another one. What should they do? Their optimal choice would appear to be to draft the quarterback and then trade him to another team that needs a quarterback. The Patriots could then receive in return a player from the other team who plays a position for which the Patriots need help. In fact, teams very rarely draft a college player and immediately trade him. Explain how the endowment effect could be involved here. (*Hint:* Consider the potential reaction of a team's fans to the team drafting a star college player and immediately trading him.)

Source: Richard Thaler, *Quasi Rational Economics*, New York: Russell Sage Foundation, 1991, p. 10.

14. An article in the *New York Times* published during the 2002 Winter Olympics held in Utah indicated that many businesses raised prices during the two-week event. The article described one incident as follows:

   Susanne and Heather McDonald, sisters from the northwest Wyoming town of Moose, said a friend was having sushi at a restaurant in Park City, where skiing events are held, and the waiter was adding $3 for every side dish until the man identified himself as a local resident. "Then he got them for free," Susanne McDonald said.

   When setting the price for a meal, why would it matter to the restaurant whether the customer was a local resident or not?

Source: Michael Janofsky, "Olympic Boom Leaves Visitors Feeling Busted," *New York Times*, February 19, 2002.

15. Suppose U2 can sell out a concert at Madison Square Garden with tickets priced at $45. U2's manager estimates that they could still sell out the Garden at $85 per ticket. Why might U2 and their manager want to keep ticket prices at $45?

16. Suppose that *Spider-Man 3* comes out and hundreds of people arrive at the Cineplex only to discover that the movie is already sold out. Meanwhile, the Cineplex is also showing a boring movie in its third week of release in a mostly empty theater. Why would this firm charge the same $7.50 for a ticket to either movie, when the quantity of tickets demanded is much greater than the quantity supplied for one movie, and the quantity of tickets demanded is much less than the quantity supplied for the other?

17. Oldies 93 has a promotion in which it announces that a local gas station will sell gasoline at 93 cents per gallon beginning in 30 minutes. Jack hops in his car and drives to the station to fill up his half-empty tank. He pays only $9.30 for 10 gallons, instead of the going price of $19.30. Did Jack save $10.00? Is the radio station doing its listeners a favor by offering this promotion? Briefly explain.

18. You have tickets to see Bruce Springsteen in concert at a stadium 50 miles away. A severe thunderstorm on the night of the concert makes driving hazardous. Will your decision to attend the concert be different if you paid $70 for the tickets than if you received the tickets for free? Explain your answer.

19. Rob Neyer is a baseball writer for ESPN.com. He described attending a Red Sox game at Fenway Park in Boston and having a seat in the sun on a hot, humid day:

> Granted, I could have moved under the overhang and enjoyed today's contest from a nice, cool, shady seat. But when you paid forty-five dollars for a ticket in the fourth row, it's tough to move back to the twenty-fourth [row].

Evaluate Neyer's reasoning.
Source: Rob Neyer, *Feeding the Green Monster*, New York: iPublish.com, 2001, p. 50.

20. After owning a used car for two years, you start having problems with it. You take it into the shop and are told that it will cost $4,000 to repair it. What factors will you take into account in deciding whether to have the repairs done or to junk the car and buy another one? Will the price you paid for the car be one of those factors? Briefly explain.

21. **[Related to *Solved Problem 9-2*]** In an article in the *Quarterly Journal of Economics*, Ted O'Donoghue and Matthew Rabin make the following observation: "[P]eople have self-control problems caused by a tendency to pursue immediate gratification in a way that their 'long-run selves' do not appreciate." What do they mean by a person's "long-run self"? Give two examples of people pursuing immediate gratification that their long-run selves would not appreciate.
Source: Ted O'Donoghue and Matthew Rabin, "Choice and Procrastination," *Quarterly Journal of Economics*, February 2001, pp. 125–26.

22. **[Related to *Solved Problem 9-2*]** Briefly explain whether you agree or disagree with the following statement: "If people were more realistic about their future behavior, the demand curve for potato chips would shift to the left."

23. **[Related to *Solved Problem 9-2*]** Data from health clubs show that members who choose a contract with a flat monthly fee over $70 attend, on average, 4.8 times per month. They pay a price per expected visit of more than $14, even though a $10-per-visit fee is also available. Why would these consumers choose a monthly contract when they lose money on it?

24. The following excerpt is from a letter sent to a financial advice columnist:

> My wife and I are trying to decide how to invest a $250,000 windfall. She wants to pay off our $114,000 mortgage, but I'm not eager to do that because we refinanced only nine months ago, paying $3,000 in fees and costs.

Briefly discuss what effect the $3,000 refinancing cost should have on this couple's investment decision.
Source: Liz Pulliam, *Los Angeles Times* advice column, March 24, 2004.

25. **[Related to the *Chapter Opener*]** Think of some businesses that don't use celebrities to endorse their products. Why do some firms, like Coca-Cola, use celebrity endorsers, while these other firms don't?

Using Indifference Curves and Budget Lines to Understand Consumer Behavior

Consumer Preferences

In this chapter, we analyzed consumer behavior using the assumption that satisfaction, or *utility*, is measurable in utils. Although this assumption made our analysis easier to understand, it is unrealistic. Instead, we can use the more realistic assumption that consumers are able to *rank* different combinations of goods and services in terms of how much utility they provide. In other words, a consumer is able to determine whether he or she prefers 2 slices of pizza and 1 can of Coke or 1 slice of pizza and 2 cans of Coke, even if the consumer is unsure exactly how much utility he or she would receive from consuming these goods. This approach has the advantage that it allows us to actually draw a map of a consumer's preferences.

To begin with, suppose a consumer is presented with the following alternatives, or *consumption bundles:*

CONSUMPTION BUNDLE A	CONSUMPTION BUNDLE B
2 slices of pizza and 1 can of Coke	1 slice of pizza and 2 cans of Coke

We assume that the consumer will always be able to decide which of the following is true:

➤ The consumer prefers bundle A to bundle B.

➤ The consumer prefers bundle B to bundle A.

➤ The consumer is indifferent between bundle A and bundle B; that is, the consumer receives equal utility from either bundle.

For consistency, we also assume that the consumer's preferences are *transitive.* For example, if a consumer prefers pepperoni pizza to mushroom pizza and prefers mushroom pizza to anchovy pizza, the consumer must prefer pepperoni pizza to anchovy pizza.

Indifference Curves

Given these assumptions, we can draw a map of a consumer's preferences using indifference curves. An **indifference curve** shows combinations of consumption bundles that give the consumer the same utility. In reality, consumers choose among consumption bundles containing many goods and services, but to make the discussion easier to follow, we will assume that only two goods are involved. Nothing important would change if we expanded the discussion to include many goods, instead of just two.

The table in Figure 9A-1 gives Dave's preferences for pizza and Coke. The graph plots the information from the table. Every possible combination of pizza and Coke will have an indifference curve passing through it, although in the figure we have shown only four of Dave's indifference curves. Dave is indifferent among all the consumption bundles that are on the same indifference curve. So, he is indifferent among bundles *E, B,*

Consumption Bundle	Slices of Pizza	Cans of Coke
A	1	2
B	3	4
C	4	5
D	1	6
E	2	8
F	5	2

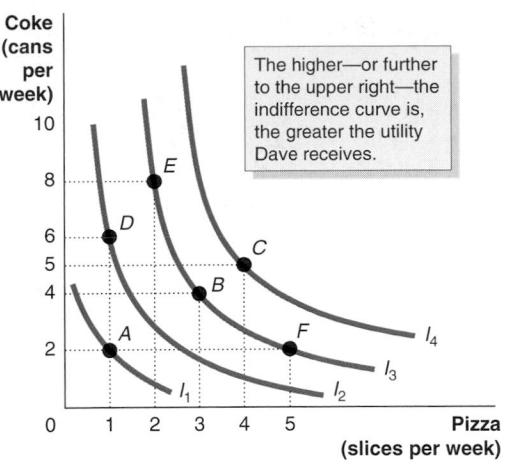

The higher—or further to the upper right—the indifference curve is, the greater the utility Dave receives.

FIGURE 9A-1

Plotting Dave's Preferences for Pizza and Coke

Every possible combination of pizza and Coke will have an indifference curve passing through it, although in the figure we show just four of Dave's indifference curves. Dave is indifferent among all the consumption bundles that are on the same indifference curve. So, he is indifferent among bundles *E, B,* and *F* because they all lie on indifference curve I_3. Moving to the upper right in the graph increases the quantities of both goods available for Dave to consume. Therefore, the further to the upper right the indifference curve is, the greater the utility Dave receives.

and *F* because they all lie on indifference curve I_3. Even though Dave has 4 fewer cans of Coke with bundle *B* than with bundle *E*, the additional slice of pizza he has in bundle *B* leaves him with the same amount of utility.

Even without looking at Dave's indifference curves, we know he will prefer consumption bundle *D* to consumption bundle *A* because in *D* he receives the same quantity of pizza as in *A* but 4 additional cans of Coke. But we need to know Dave's preferences, as shown by his indifference curves, to know how he will rank bundle *B* and bundle *D*. Bundle *D* contains more Coke but less pizza than bundle *B*, so Dave's ranking will depend on how much pizza he would be willing to give up to receive more Coke. The higher the indifference curve is—that is, the further to the upper right on the graph—the greater the amounts of both goods that are available for Dave to consume, and the greater his utility. In other words, Dave receives more utility from the consumption bundles on indifference curve I_2 than from the consumption bundles on indifference curve I_1, more utility from the bundles on I_3 than from the bundles on I_2, and so on.

Indifference curve A curve that shows the combinations of consumption bundles that give the consumer the same utility

The Slope of an Indifference Curve

Remember that the slope of a curve is the ratio of the change in the variable on the vertical axis to the change in the variable on the horizontal axis. Along an indifference curve, the slope tells us the rate at which the consumer is willing to trade off one product for another, while keeping the consumer's utility constant. The slope of an indifference curve is referred to as the **marginal rate of substitution (MRS).**

We expect that the *MRS* will change as we move down an indifference curve. In Figure 9A-1, at a point like *E* on indifference curve I_3, Dave's indifference curve is relatively steep. As we move down the curve, it becomes less steep until it becomes relatively flat at a point like *F*. This is the usual shape of indifference curves: They are bowed in or convex. A consumption bundle like *E* contains a lot of Coke and not much pizza. We would expect that Dave could give up a significant quantity of Coke for a smaller quantity of additional pizza and still have the same level of utility. Thus, the *MRS* will be high. As we move down the indifference curve, Dave moves to bundles, like *B* and *F*, which have more pizza and less Coke. As a result, Dave is willing to trade less Coke for pizza, and the *MRS* declines.

Marginal rate of substitution (MRS) The slope of an indifference curve; represents the rate at which a consumer would be willing to trade off one good for another.

Can Indifference Curves Ever Cross?

Remember that we assume that consumers have transitive preferences. That is, if Dave prefers consumption bundle *X* to consumption bundle *Y* and he prefers consumption bundle *Y* to consumption bundle *Z*, he must prefer bundle *X* to bundle *Z*. If indifference

Indifference Curves Cannot Cross

Because bundle *X* and bundle *Z* are both on indifference curve I_1, Dave must be indifferent between them. Similarly, because bundle *X* and bundle *Y* are on indifference curve I_2, Dave must be indifferent between them. The assumption of transitivity means that Dave should also be indifferent between bundle *Z* and bundle *Y*. We know that this is not true, however, because bundle *Y* contains more pizza and more Coke than bundle *Z*. So Dave will definitely prefer bundle *Y* to bundle *Z*, which violates the assumption of transitivity. *Therefore, none of Dave's indifference curves can cross.*

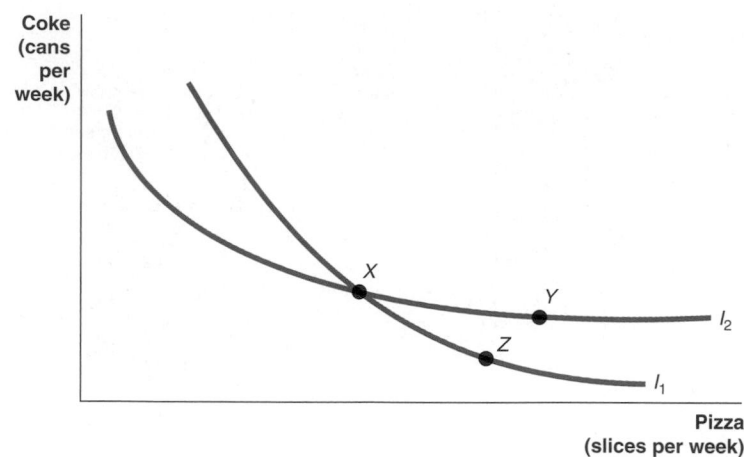

curves cross, this assumption is violated. To understand why, look at Figure 9A-2, which shows two of Dave's indifference curves crossing.

Because bundle *X* and bundle *Z* are both on indifference curve I_1, Dave must be indifferent between them. Similarly, because bundle *X* and bundle *Y* are on indifference curve I_2, Dave must be indifferent between them. The assumption of transitivity means that Dave should also be indifferent between bundle *Z* and bundle *Y*. We know that this is not true, however, because bundle *Y* contains more pizza and more Coke than bundle *Z*. So, Dave will definitely prefer bundle *Y* to bundle *Z*, which violates the assumption of transitivity. Therefore, none of Dave's indifference curves can cross.

The Budget Constraint

Remember that a consumer's *budget constraint* is the amount of income he or she has available to spend on goods and services. Suppose that Dave has $10 per week to spend on pizza and Coke. The table in Figure 9A-3 shows the combinations that he can afford to buy if the price of pizza is $2 per slice and the price of Coke is $1 per can. As you can see, all the points lie on a straight line. This line represents Dave's budget constraint. The line intersects the vertical axis at the maximum number of cans of Coke Dave can afford to buy with $10, which is consumption bundle *G*. The line intersects the horizontal axis at the maximum number of slices of pizza Dave can afford to buy with $10, which is consumption bundle *L*. As he moves down his budget constraint from bundle *G*, he gives up 2 cans of Coke for every slice of pizza he buys.

Any consumption bundle along the line or inside the line is *affordable* for Dave because he has the income to buy those combinations of pizza and Coke. Any bundle that lies outside the line is *unaffordable*, because these bundles cost more than the income he has available to spend.

The slope of the budget constraint is constant because the budget constraint is a straight line. The slope of the line equals the change in the number of cans of Coke divided by the change in the number of slices of pizza—or the "rise" over the "run." In this case, moving down the budget constraint from one point to another point, the change in the number of cans of Coke equals −2 and the change in the number of slices of pizza equals 1, so the slope equals −2/1, or −2. Notice that with the price of pizza equal to $2 per slice and the price of Coke equal to $1 per can, the slope of the budget constraint is equal to the ratio of the price of pizza to the price of Coke (multiplied by negative 1). In fact, this result will always hold: *The slope of the budget constraint is equal to the ratio of the*

Combinations of Pizza and Coke Dave Can Buy with $10			
Consumption Bundle	Slices of Pizza	Cans of Coke	Total Spending
G	0	10	$10.00
H	1	8	10.00
I	2	6	10.00
J	3	4	10.00
K	4	2	10.00
L	5	0	10.00

Dave's Budget Constraint

Dave's budget constraint shows the combinations of slices of pizza and cans of Coke he can buy with $10. The price of Coke is $1 per can, so if he spends all of his $10 on Coke he can buy 10 cans (bundle *G*). The price of pizza is $2 per slice, so if he spends all of his $10 on pizza he can buy 5 slices (bundle *L*). As he moves down his budget constraint from bundle *G*, he gives up 2 cans of Coke for every slice of pizza he buys. Any consumption bundles along the line or inside the line are affordable. Any bundles that lie outside the line are unaffordable.

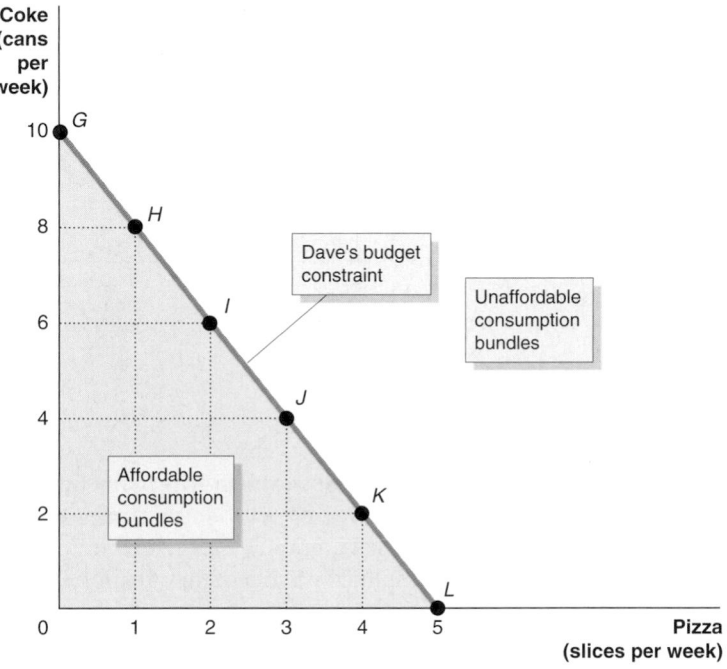

price of the good on the horizontal axis divided by the price of the good on the vertical axis, multiplied by negative 1.

Choosing the Optimal Consumption of Pizza and Coke

Dave would like to be on the highest possible indifference curve, because higher indifference curves represent more pizza and more Coke. But Dave can only buy those bundles that lie on or inside his budget constraint. In other words, *to maximize utility, a consumer needs to be on the highest indifference curve, given his budget constraint.*

Figure 9A-4 plots the consumption bundles from Figure 9A-1 along with the budget constraint from Figure 9A-3. The figure also shows the indifference curves that pass through each consumption bundle. In Figure 9A-4 the highest indifference curve shown is I_4. Unfortunately, Dave lacks the income to purchase consumption bundles—like *C*—that lie on I_4. He has the income to purchase bundles like *A* and *D*, but he can do better. If he consumes bundle *B*, he will be on the highest indifference curve he can reach, given his budget constraint of $10. The resulting combination of 3 slices of pizza and 4 cans of Coke represents optimal consumption of pizza and Coke, given Dave's preferences and given his budget constraint. Notice that at point *B*, Dave's budget constraint just touches—or, is *tangent* to—I_3. In fact, bundle *B* is the only bundle on I_3 that Dave is able to purchase for $10.

Finding Optimal Consumption

Dave would like to be on the highest possible indifference curve, but he cannot reach indifference curves like I_4 that are outside his budget constraint. Dave's optimal combination of slices of pizza and cans of Coke comes at point *B,* where his budget constraint just touches—or is *tangent* to—the highest indifference curve he can reach. At point *B,* he buys 3 slices of pizza and 4 cans of Coke.

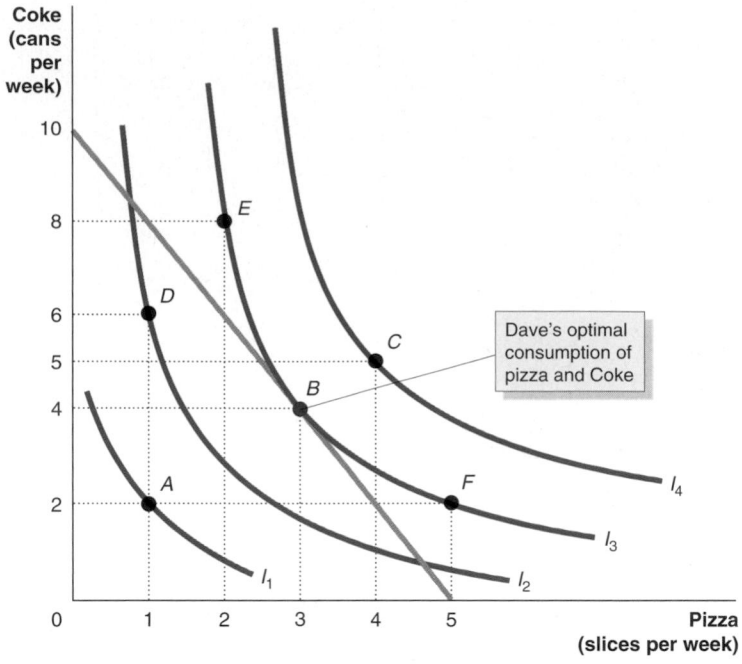

9A-1 *Making*
the Connection

Dell Determines the Optimal Mix of Products

Consumers have different preferences, which helps explain why many firms offer products with a variety of characteristics. For example, Dell sells laptop computers with different screen sizes, processor speeds, hard drive sizes, graphic cards, and so on. We can use the model of consumer choice to analyze a simplified version of the situation Dell faces in deciding which features to offer consumers.

Assume that consumers have $2,000 each to spend on laptops and that they are concerned with only two laptop characteristics: screen size and processor speed. Because larger screens and faster processors increase Dell's cost of producing laptops, consumers will face a trade-off: the larger the screen, the slower the processor speed. Consumers in panel (a) of the figure prefer screen size to processor speed. For this group, the point of tangency between a typical consumer's indifference curve and the budget constraint shows an optimal choice of a 17-inch screen and a 1.5-gigahertz processor. Consumers in panel (b) prefer processor speed to screen size. For this group, the point of tangency between a typical consumer's indifference curve and the budget constraint shows an optimal choice of a 12-inch screen and 3.0-gigahertz processor.

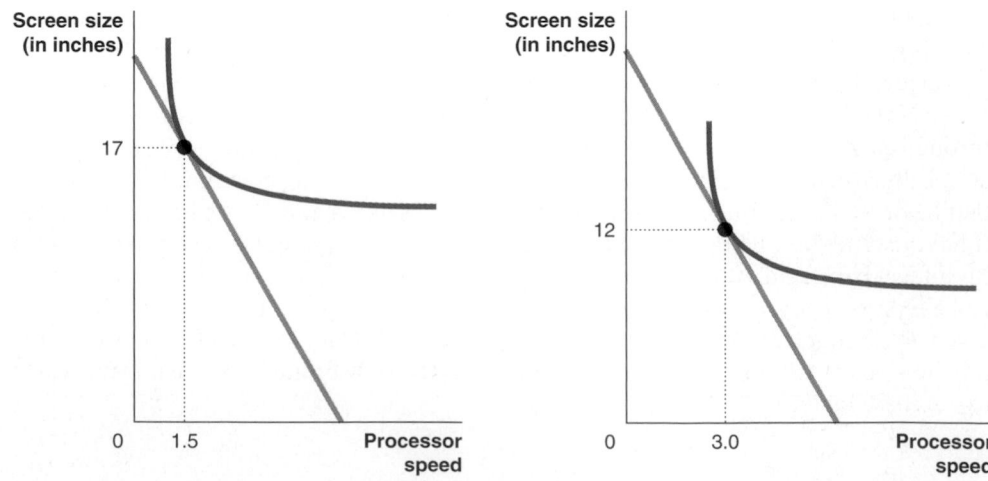

Companies like Dell use surveys and other means to gather information about consumer preferences. With knowledge of consumers' preferences and data on the costs of producing different laptop components, Dell can determine the mix of components to offer consumers.

Dell has to determine which mix of computer components matches consumers' preferences.

How a Price Change Affects Optimal Consumption

Suppose the price of pizza falls from $2 per slice to $1 per slice. How will this affect Dave's decision about which combination of pizza and Coke is optimal? First, notice what happens to Dave's budget constraint when the price of pizza falls. As Figure 9A-5 shows, when the price of pizza is $2 per slice, the maximum number of slices Dave can buy is 5. After the price of pizza falls to $1 per slice, Dave can buy a maximum of 10 slices. His budget constraint rotates outward from point *A* to point *B* to reflect this. (Notice that the fall in the price of pizza does not affect the maximum number of cans of Coke Dave can buy with his $10.)

When his budget constraint rotates outward, Dave is able to purchase consumption bundles that were previously unaffordable. Figure 9A-6 shows that the combination of 3 slices of pizza and 4 cans of Coke was optimal when the price of pizza was $2 per slice, but the combination of 7 slices of pizza and 3 cans of Coke is optimal when the price of pizza falls to $1. The lower price of pizza causes Dave to consume more pizza and less Coke and to end up on a higher indifference curve.

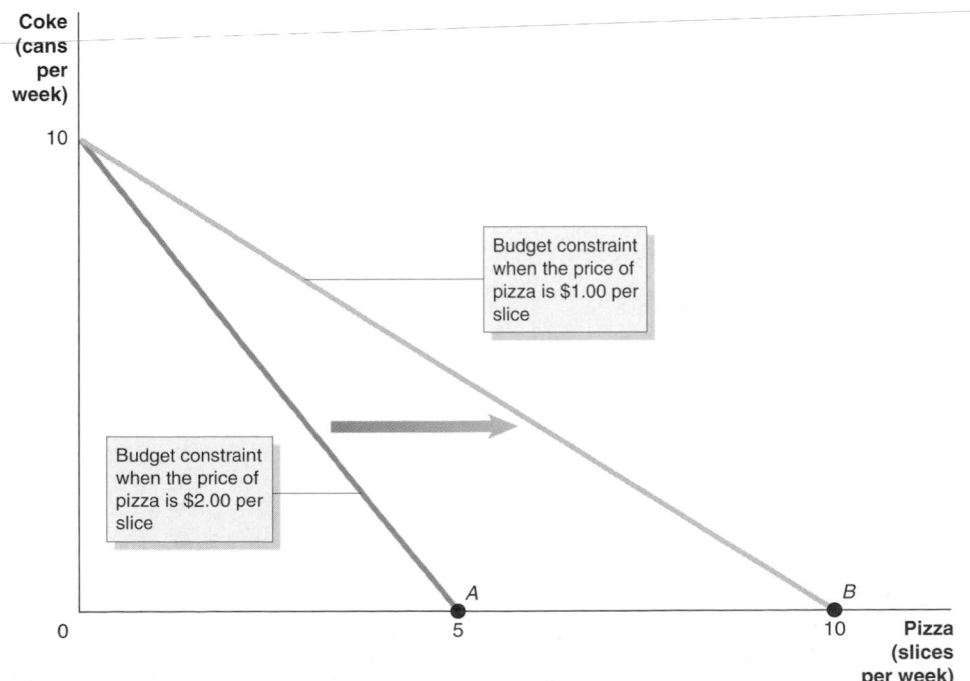

FIGURE 9A-5

How a Price Decrease Affects the Budget Constraint

A fall in the price of pizza from $2 per slice to $1 per slice increases the maximum number of slices Dave can buy with $10 from 5 to 10. The budget constraint rotates outward from point *A* to point *B* to show this.

How a Price Change Affects Optimal Consumption

A fall in the price of pizza results in Dave consuming less Coke and more pizza.

1. A fall in the price of pizza rotates the budget constraint outward, because Dave can now buy more pizza with his $10.
2. In the new optimum on indifference curve I_2, Dave changes the quantities he consumes of both goods. His consumption of Coke falls from 4 cans to 3 cans.
3. In the new optimum, Dave's consumption of pizza increases from 3 slices to 7 slices.

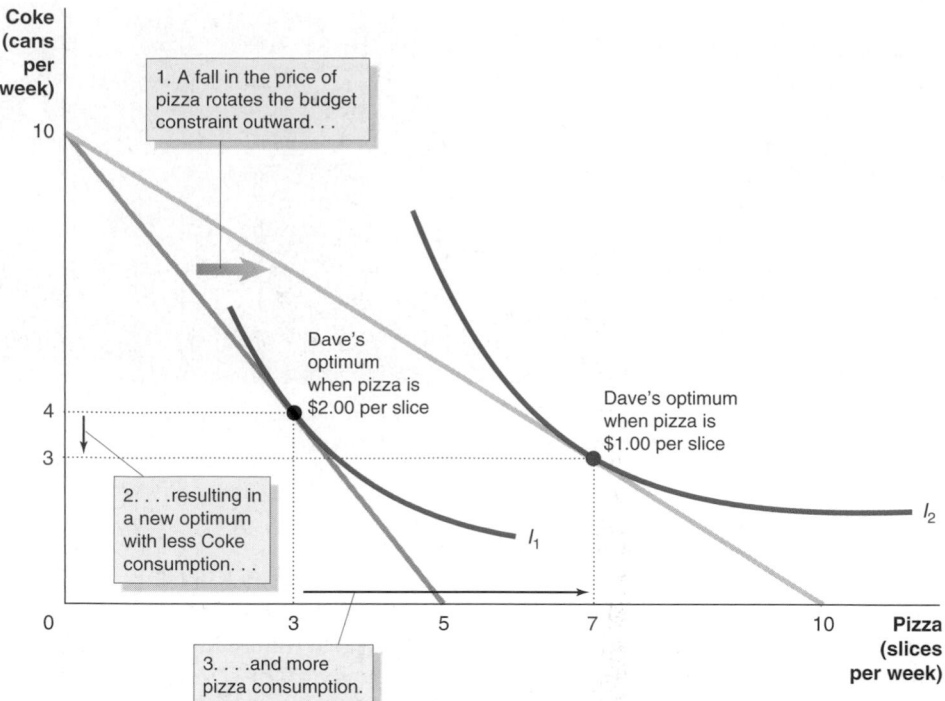

1. A fall in the price of pizza rotates the budget constraint outward. . .

Dave's optimum when pizza is $2.00 per slice

Dave's optimum when pizza is $1.00 per slice

2. . . .resulting in a new optimum with less Coke consumption. . .

3. . . .and more pizza consumption.

SOLVED PROBLEM 9A-1

When Does a Price Change Make a Consumer Better Off?

Dave has $300 to spend each month on DVDs and CDs. DVDs and CDs both currently have a price of $10, and Dave is maximizing his utility by buying 20 DVDs and 10 CDs. Suppose Dave still has $300 to spend, but the price of CDs rises to $20, while the price of DVDs drops to $5. Is Dave better or worse off than he was before the price change? Use a budget constraint–indifference curve graph to illustrate your answer.

Solving the Problem:

Step 1: Review the chapter material. This problem concerns the effect of price changes on optimal consumption, so you may want to review the section "How a Price Change Affects Optimal Consumption," which begins on page 303.

Step 2: Answer the problem by drawing the appropriate graph. We can begin by drawing the budget constraint, indifference curve, and point of optimal consumption for the original prices:

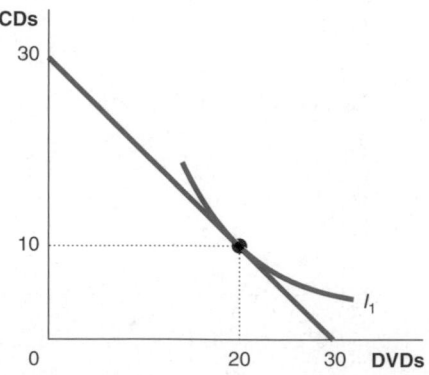

Now we can draw a graph that shows the results of the price changes. Notice that in this problem, the prices of *both* goods change. However, we can determine the position of the new budget constraint by calculating the maximum quantity of DVDs and CDs Dave can buy after the price changes. You should also note that after the price changes, Dave can still buy his original optimal consumption bundle—20 DVDs and 10 CDs—by spending all of his $300, so his new budget constraint must pass through this point.

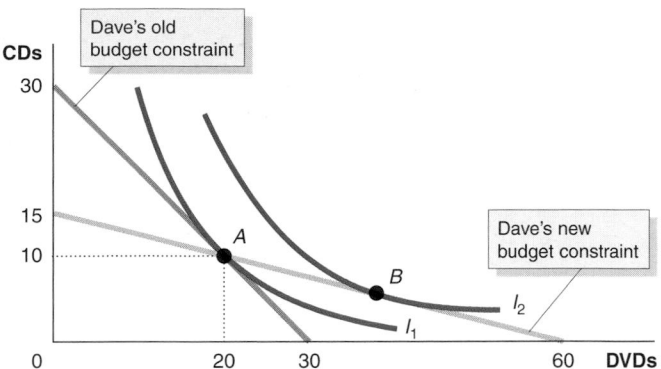

At the new prices, Dave can buy a maximum of 60 DVDs or 15 CDs. Both his old and his new budget constraints pass through the consumption bundle at point A. This consumption bundle is no longer optimal, however, because with the new prices it is possible for him to reach an indifference curve that is higher than I_1. We can draw in the new highest indifference curve he can reach—I_2—and show the new optimal consumption bundle—point B.

Because Dave can now reach a higher indifference curve, we can conclude that he is better off as a result of the price change.

YOUR TURN: For more practice, do related problem 7 on page 311 at the end of this appendix. Visit www.prenhall.com/hubbard for an interactive exercise related to this Solved Problem.

Deriving the Demand Curve

The change in Dave's optimal consumption of pizza as the price changes explains why demand curves slope downward. Dave adjusted his consumption of pizza as follows:

Price of pizza = $2 per slice ⇒ Quantity of pizza demanded = 3 slices

Price of pizza = $1 per slice ⇒ Quantity of pizza demanded = 7 slices

In panel (a) of Figure 9A-7, we plot the two points of optimal consumption. In panel (b) of Figure 9A-7, we draw a line connecting the points. This downward-sloping line is Dave's demand curve for pizza. We could find more points on the demand curve by changing the price of pizza and finding the new optimal number of slices of pizza Dave would demand.

Remember that according to the law of demand, demand curves always slope downward. We have just shown that the law of demand results from the optimal adjustment by consumers to changes in prices. A fall in the price of a good will rotate *outward* the budget constraint and make it possible for a consumer to reach higher indifference curves. As a result, the consumer will increase the quantity of the good demanded. An increase in price will rotate *inward* the budget constraint and force the consumer to a lower indifference curve. As a result, the consumer will decrease the quantity of the good demanded.

The Income Effect and the Substitution Effect of a Price Change

We saw in this chapter that a price change has two effects on the quantity of a good consumed: the *income effect* and the *substitution effect*. The income effect is the change

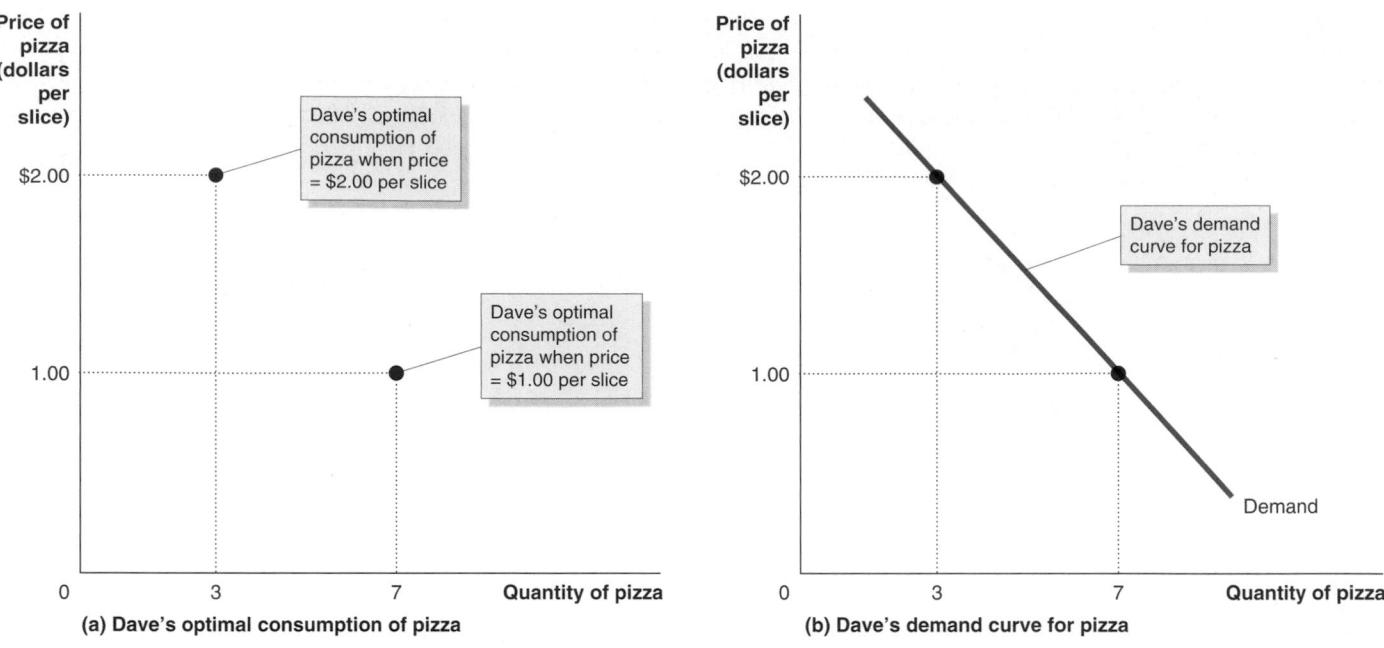

Dave responds optimally to the fall in the price of a product by consuming more of that product. In panel (a) the price of pizza falls from $2 per slice to $1, and the optimal quantity of slices consumed rises from 3 to 7. When we graph this result in panel (b), we have Dave's demand curve for pizza.

in the quantity demanded of a good that results from the effect of a change in price on consumer purchasing power, holding all other factors constant. The substitution effect is the change in the quantity demanded of a good that results from a change in price making the good more or less expensive relative to other goods, holding constant the effect of the price change on consumer purchasing power. We can use indifference curves and budget constraints to analyze these two effects more exactly.

Figure 9A-8 illustrates the same situation as Figure 9A-7: The price of pizza has fallen from $2 per slice to $1 per slice, and Dave's budget constraint has rotated outward. As before, Dave's optimal consumption of pizza increases from 3 slices (point A in Figure 9A-8) per week to 7 slices per week (point C). We can think of this movement from point A to point C as taking place in two steps: The movement from point A to point B represents the substitution effect, and the movement from point B to point C represents the income effect. To isolate the substitution effect, we have to hold constant the effect of the price change on Dave's income. We do this by changing the price of pizza relative to the price of Coke, *but at the same time holding his utility constant by keeping Dave on the same indifference curve.* In Figure 9A-8, in moving from point A to point B, Dave remains on indifference curve I_1. Point A is a point of tangency between I_1 and Dave's original budget constraint. Point B is a point of tangency between I_1 and a new, *hypothetical* budget constraint that has a slope equal to the new ratio of the price of pizza to the price of Coke. At point B, Dave has increased his consumption of pizza from 3 slices to 5 slices. Because we are still on indifference curve I_1, we know that this increase is Dave's response only to the change in the relative price of pizza and, therefore, that the increase represents the substitution effect of the fall in the price of pizza.

At point B, Dave has not spent all his income. Remember that the fall in the price of pizza has increased Dave's purchasing power. In Figure 9A-8, we illustrate the additional pizza Dave consumes because of the income effect of increased purchasing power by the movement from point B to point C. Notice that in moving from point B to point C, the price of pizza relative to the price of Coke is constant because the slope of the new

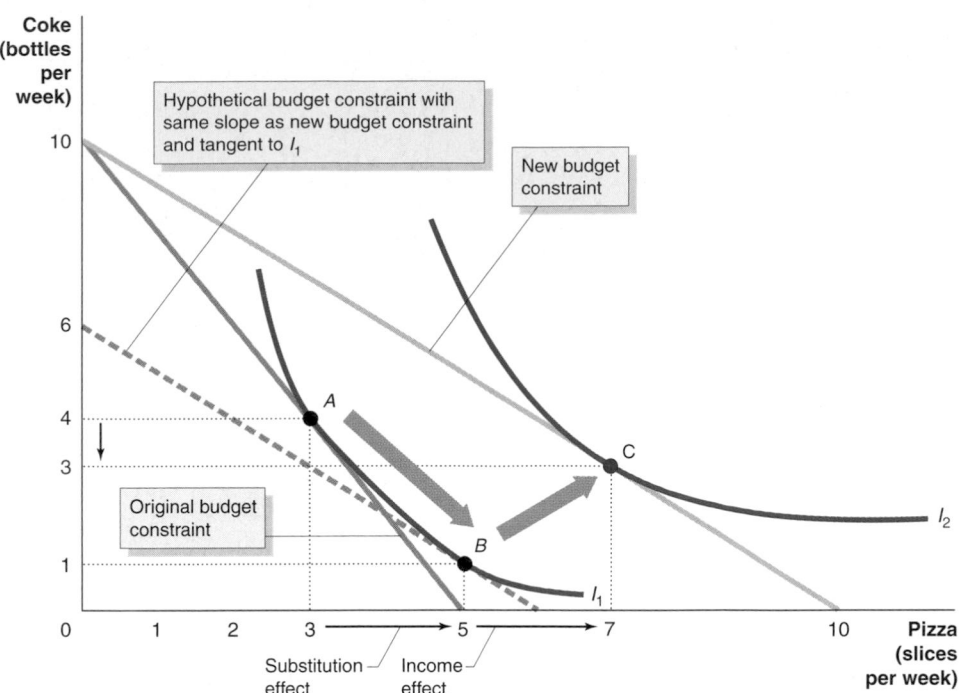

Income and Substitution Effects of a Price Change

Following a decline in the price of pizza, Dave's optimal consumption of pizza increases from 3 slices (point *A*) per week to 7 slices per week (point *C*). We can think of this movement from point *A* to point *C* as taking place in two steps: The movement from point *A* to point *B* along indifference curve I_1 represents the substitution effect, and the movement from point *B* to point *C* represents the income effect. Dave increases his consumption of pizza from 3 slices per week to 5 slices per week because of the substitution effect of a fall in the price of pizza, and from 5 slices per week to 7 slices per week because of the income effect.

budget constraint is the same as the slope of the hypothetical budget constraint that is tangent to I_1 at point *B*.

We can conclude that Dave increases his consumption of pizza from 3 slices per week to 5 slices per week because of the substitution effect of a fall in the price of pizza, and from 5 slices per week to 7 slices per week because of the income effect. Recall from our discussion of income and substitution effects in this chapter that the income effect of a price decline causes consumers to buy more of a normal good and less of an inferior good. Because the income effect causes Dave to increase his consumption of pizza, pizza must be a normal good for him.

How a Change in Income Affects Optimal Consumption

Suppose that the price of pizza remains at $2 per slice, but the income Dave has to spend on pizza and Coke increases from $10 to $20. Figure 9A-9 shows how this affects his budget constraint. With an income of $10, Dave could buy a maximum of 5 slices of pizza or 10 cans of Coke. With an income of $20 he can buy 10 slices of pizza or 20 cans of Coke. The additional income allows Dave to increase his consumption of both pizza and Coke and to move to a higher indifference curve. Figure 9A-10 shows Dave's new optimum. Dave is able to increase his consumption of pizza from 3 slices per week to 7 and his consumption of Coke from 4 cans per week to 6.

The Slope of the Indifference Curve, the Slope of the Budget Line, and the Rule of Equal Marginal Utility per Dollar

In this chapter, we saw that consumers maximize utility when they consume each good up to the point where the marginal utility per dollar spent is the same for every good. This condition seems different from the one we stated earlier in this appendix that to maximize utility a consumer needs to be on the highest indifference curve, given his budget constraint. In fact, though, the two conditions are equivalent. To see this, begin

FIGURE 9A-9

How a Change in Income Affects the Budget Constraint

When the income Dave has to spend on pizza and Coke increases from $10 to $20, his budget constraint shifts outward. With $10, Dave could buy a maximum of 5 slices of pizza or 10 cans of Coke. With $20, he can buy a maximum of 10 slices of pizza or 20 cans of Coke.

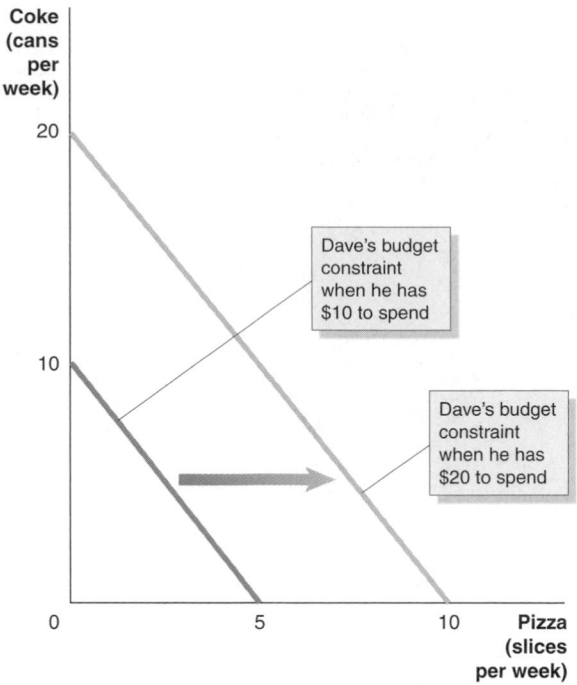

FIGURE 9A-10

How a Change in Income Affects Optimal Consumption

An increase in income leads Dave to consume more Coke and more pizza.

1. An increase in income shifts Dave's budget constraint outward because he can now buy more of both goods.
2. In the new optimum on indifference curve I_2, Dave changes the quantities he consumes of both goods. His consumption of Coke increases from 4 cans to 6 cans.
3. In the new optimum, Dave's consumption of pizza increases from 3 slices to 7 slices.

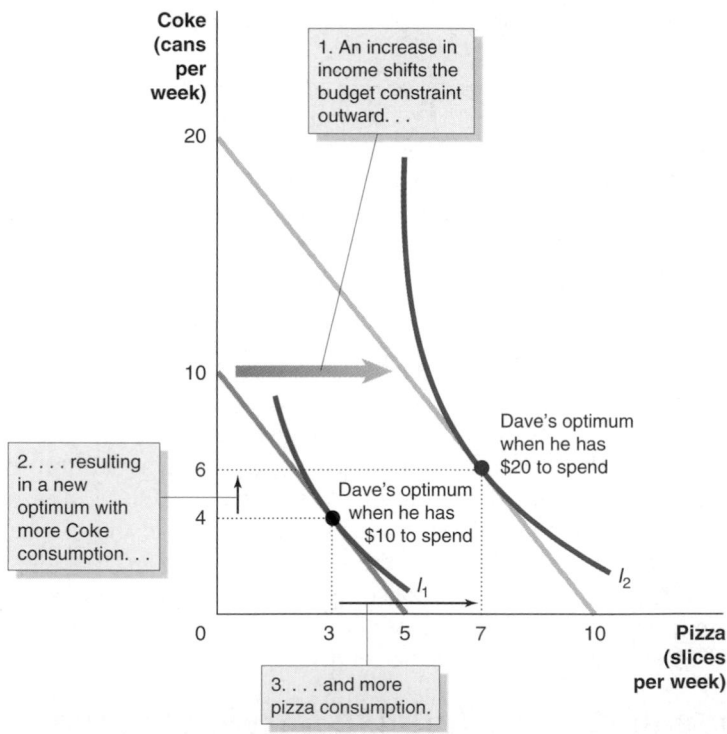

by looking at Figure 9A-11, which again combines Dave's indifference curve and budget constraint. Remember that at the point of optimal consumption the indifference curve and the budget constraint are tangent, so they have the same slope. Therefore: *At the point of optimal consumption, the marginal rate of substitution (MRS) is equal to the ratio of the price of the product on the horizontal axis to the price of the product on the vertical axis.*

The slope of the indifference curve tells us the rate at which a consumer is *willing* to trade off one good for the other. The slope of the budget constraint tells us the rate at

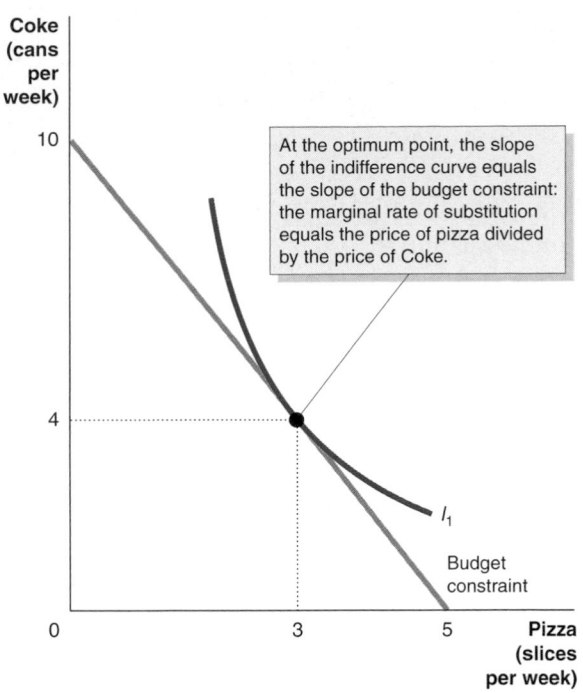

At the optimum point, the slope of the indifference curve equals the slope of the budget constraint: the marginal rate of substitution equals the price of pizza divided by the price of Coke.

FIGURE 9A-11

At the Optimum Point, the Slopes of the Indifference Curve and Budget Constraint Are the Same

At the point of optimal consumption, the marginal rate of substitution is equal to the ratio of the price of the product on the horizontal axis to the price of the product on the vertical axis.

which a consumer is *able* to trade off one good for the other. Only at the point of optimal consumption is the rate at which a consumer is willing to trade off one good for the other equal to the rate at which he can trade off one good for the other.

The Rule of Equal Marginal Utility per Dollar Revisited

Recall from this chapter the *rule of equal marginal utility per dollar,* which states that to maximize utility, consumers should spend their income so that the last dollar spent on each product gives them the same marginal utility. We can use our indifference curve and budget constraint analysis to see why this rule holds. When we move from one point on an indifference curve to another we end up with more of one product and less of the other product but the same amount of utility. For example, as Dave moves down an indifference curve, he consumes less Coke and more pizza, but he has the same amount of utility.

Remember that marginal utility (MU) tells us how much additional utility a consumer gains (or loses) from consuming more (or less) of a good. So when Dave consumes less Coke by moving down an indifference curve, he loses utility equal to:

$$-\text{Change in the quantity of Coke} \times MU_{Coke},$$

but he consumes more pizza, so he gains utility equal to:

$$\text{Change in the quantity of pizza} \times MU_{Pizza}.$$

We know that the gain in utility from the additional pizza is equal to the loss from the smaller quantity of Coke because Dave's total utility remains the same along an indifference curve. Therefore we can write:

$$-(\text{Change in the quantity of Coke} \times MU_{Coke}) = (\text{Change in the quantity of pizza} \times MU_{Pizza}).$$

Loss in utility from consuming less Coke

Gain in utility from consuming more pizza

If we rearrange terms, we have:

$$\frac{- \text{Change in the quantity of Coke}}{\text{Change in the quantity of pizza}} = \frac{MU_{Pizza}}{MU_{Coke}}$$

because the

$$\frac{- \text{Change in the quantity of Coke}}{\text{Change in the quantity of pizza}}$$

is the slope of the indifference curve, or the marginal rate of substitution, we can write:

$$\frac{- \text{Change in the quantity of Coke}}{\text{Change in the quantity of pizza}} = MRS = \frac{MU_{Pizza}}{MU_{Coke}}.$$

The slope of Dave's budget constraint equals the price of pizza divided by the price of Coke. At the point of optimal consumption, the slope of the indifference curve is equal to the slope of the budget line. Therefore,

$$\frac{MU_{Pizza}}{MU_{Coke}} = \frac{P_{Pizza}}{P_{Coke}}.$$

We can rewrite this to show that at the point of optimal consumption:

$$\frac{MU_{Pizza}}{P_{Pizza}} = \frac{MU_{Coke}}{P_{Coke}}.$$

This last expression is the rule of equal marginal utility per dollar that we first developed in this chapter. So we have shown how this rule follows from the indifference curve and budget constraint approach to analyzing consumer choice.

KEY TERMS

Indifference curve   299

Marginal rate of substitution (*MRS*)   299

PROBLEMS AND APPLICATIONS

Please visit **www.prenhall.com/hubbard** *for solutions to the even-numbered problems as well as multiple-choice and true or false self-assessment quizzes.*

1. Jacob receives an allowance of $5 per week. He spends all his allowance on ice cream cones and cans of Lemon Fizz soda.
   a. If the price of ice cream cones is $0.50 per cone and the price of Lemon Fizz is $1 per can, draw a diagram showing Jacob's budget constraint. Be sure to indicate on your diagram the maximum number of ice cream cones and the maximum number of cans of Lemon Fizz that Jacob can buy.
   b. Jacob buys 8 cones and 1 can of Lemon Fizz. Draw an indifference curve representing Jacob's choice, assuming he has chosen the optimal combination.

   c. Suppose the price of ice cream cones rises to $1 per cone. Draw in Jacob's new budget constraint and his new optimal consumption of ice cream cones and Lemon Fizz.

2. Suppose that Jacob's allowance in problem 1 climbs from $5 per week to $10 per week.
   a. Show how this alters his budget constraint.
   b. Draw a set of indifference curves showing how Jacob's choice of cones and Lemon Fizz will change when his allowance increases. Assume that both goods are normal.
   c. Draw a set of indifference curves showing how Jacob's choice of cones and Lemon Fizz will change when his allowance increases. Assume that Lemon Fizz is normal but cones are inferior.

3. Suppose that Calvin considers Pepsi and Coke to be perfect substitutes. They taste the same to him, and he gets exactly the same amount of enjoyment from drinking a can of Pepsi or a can of Coke.
   a. Will Calvin's indifference curves showing his trade-off between Pepsi and Coke have the same curvature as the indifference curves drawn in the figures in this appendix? Briefly explain.
   b. How will Calvin decide whether to buy Pepsi or to buy Coke?
4. In the following budget constraint–indifference curve graph, Nikki has $200 to spend on blouses and skirts.
   a. What is the price of blouses? What is the price of skirts?
   b. Is Nikki making the optimum choice if she buys 4 blouses and 2 skirts? Explain how you know this.

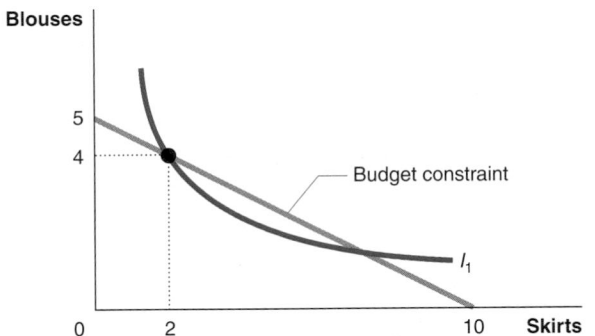

5. Marilou and Hunter both purchase milk and doughnuts at the same Quik Mart. They have different tastes for milk and doughnuts and different incomes. They both buy some milk and some doughnuts, but they buy considerably different quantities of the two goods. Can we conclude that their marginal rate of substitution between milk and doughnuts is the same? Draw a graph showing their budget constraints and indifference curves and explain.
6. Sunsweet decides that prune juice has a bad image problem, so it launches a slick advertising campaign to convince young people that prune juice is very hip. They hire Eminem, Ludacris, and Trick Daddy to tout their product. The campaign works! Prune juice sales soar, even though Sunsweet hasn't cut the price. Draw a budget constraint and indifference curve diagram with Sunsweet Prune Juice on one axis and other drinks on the other axis and show how the celebrity endorsements have changed things.
7. [Related to *Solved Problem 9A-1*] Dave has $300 to spend each month on DVDs and CDs. DVDs and CDs both currently have a price of $10, and Dave is maximizing his utility by buying 20 DVDs and 10 CDs. Suppose Dave still has $300 to spend, but the price of DVDs rises to $12, while the price of CDs drops to $6. Is Dave better or worse off than he was before the price change? Use a budget constraint–indifference curve graph to illustrate your answer.

chapter

ten

10

Technology, Production, and Costs

Sony Uses a Cost Curve to Determine the Price of Radios

> In early 2005, a high-profile management shake-up at Sony Corporation resulted in Howard Stringer being named the firm's first non-Japanese chairman and chief executive officer. The Tokyo-based firm remains a giant of the international economy, manufacturing televisions, computers, satellite systems, semiconductors, telephones, and LCDs, among other products. It is the third-largest manufacturing firm in Japan, after Toyota and Hitachi, and the thirtieth-largest firm in the world. In a survey of top business managers and financial analysts, Sony was the third most admired non-U.S. company in the world behind only Nokia, the Finnish cell phone manufacturer, and Toyota. In 2005, Sony employed more than 160,000 workers and had revenue of more than $72 billion. Like most firms, Sony started small. Its early

success resulted from the vision and energy of two young entrepreneurs, Akio Morita and Masaru Ibuka. Sony was founded in 1945, and its first product was a rice cooker. Soon Morita and Ibuka decided to concentrate on manufacturing electronic goods. Their first successful product was a tape recorder.

In 1953, Sony purchased a license that allowed it to use transistor technology developed in the United States at Western Electric's Bell Laboratories. Sony used the technology to develop a transistor radio that was small enough to fit in a shirt pocket and far smaller than any other radio then available. At that time, hearing aids were the only consumer products that used transistors. In 1955, Morita, Sony's chairman, arrived in New York hoping to convince one of the U.S.

department store chains to carry the Sony radios.

Morita offered to sell one department store chain 5,000 radios at a price of $29.95 each. If the chain wanted more than 5,000 radios, the price would change. As Morita described it later:

I sat down and drew a curve that looked something like a lopsided letter U. The price for five thousand would be our regular price. That would be the beginning of the curve. For ten thousand there would be a discount, and that was at the bottom of the curve. For thirty thousand the price would begin to climb. For fifty thousand the price per unit would be higher than for five thousand, and for one hundred thousand units the price per unit would

LEARNING OBJECTIVES

After studying this chapter, you should be able to:

① Define technology and give examples of technological change.

② Distinguish between the economic short run and the economic long run.

③ Understand the relationship between the marginal product of labor and the average product of labor.

④ Explain and illustrate the relationship between marginal cost and average total cost.

⑤ Graph average total cost, average variable cost, average fixed cost, and marginal cost.

⑥ Understand how firms use the long-run average cost curve to plan.

have to be much higher than for the first five thousand.

Why would the prices Morita offered the department store follow a U-shape? Because Sony's cost per unit, or *average cost*, of manufacturing the radios would have the same shape. Curves that show the relationship between the level of output and per unit cost are called *average total cost curves*. Average total cost curves typically have the U-shape of Morita's curve. As we explore the relationship between production and costs in this chapter, we will see why average total cost curves have this shape.

Today, Sony is one of the largest electronics firms in the world, but more than 50 years ago, when it was a small, struggling company, Akio Morita used a simple economic

tool—the average cost curve—to help make an important business decision. Every day, in companies large and small, managers use economic tools to make decisions. *An Inside Look* on page 334 discusses the cost analysis underlying Sony's joint venture with Samsung to build a large factory to manufacture LCD panels for televisions and computers. In this chapter, we will focus on the relationship between a firm's technology and its production costs. In Chapter 11, we will see how firms use information about costs of production and about demand to determine how much to produce and what price to charge.

Source: Akio Morita, with Edwin M. Reingold and Mitsuko Shimomura, *Made in Japan: Akio Morita and Sony*, New York: Signet Books, 1986, p. 94.

➤ In Chapter 9, we looked behind the demand curve to understand consumer decision making better. In this chapter, we look behind the supply curve to understand firm decision making better. Earlier chapters showed that supply curves are upward-sloping because marginal cost increases as firms increase the quantity they supply of a good. In this chapter, we look more closely at why this is true. In the appendix to this chapter, we extend the analysis by using isoquants and isocost lines to understand the relationship between production and costs. Once we have a good understanding of production and cost, we can proceed in the following chapters to understand how firms decide what level of output to produce and what price to charge.

Technology: An Economic Definition

The basic activity of a firm is to use *inputs*, such as workers, machines, and natural resources, to produce *outputs* of goods and services. A pizza parlor, for example, uses inputs such as pizza dough, pizza sauce, cooks, and ovens to produce pizza. A firm's **technology** is the processes it uses to turn inputs into outputs of goods and services. Notice that this economic definition of technology is broader than the everyday definition. In everyday language, "technology" is often used to mean only the development of new products. In the economic sense, a firm's technology depends on many factors, such as the skill of its managers, the training of its workers, and the speed and efficiency of its machinery and equipment. The technology of pizza production, for example, includes not only the capacity of the pizza ovens and how quickly they bake the pizza, but also how quickly the cooks can prepare the pizza for baking, how well the manager motivates the workers to work hard, and how well the manager has arranged the facilities to allow the cooks to quickly prepare the pizzas and get them in the ovens.

Whenever a firm experiences positive **technological change,** it is able to produce more output using the same inputs, or the same output using fewer inputs. Positive technological change can come from many sources. The firm's managers may rearrange the factory floor or the layout of a retail store, thereby increasing production and sales. The firm's workers may go through a training program. The firm may install faster or more reliable machinery or equipment. It is also possible for a firm to experience negative technological change. If a firm hires less-skilled workers or if its facilities are damaged during a hurricane or other natural disaster, the quantity of output it can produce from a given quantity of inputs may decline.

① **LEARNING OBJECTIVE**

Define technology and give examples of technological change.

Technology The processes a firm uses to turn inputs into outputs of goods and services.

Technological change A change in the ability of a firm to produce a given level of output with a given quantity of inputs.

10-1 *Making the Connection*

Improving Inventory Control at Wal-Mart

Inventories are goods that have been produced but not yet sold. For a retailer such as Wal-Mart, inventories at any point in time include the goods on the store shelves, as well as goods in warehouses. Inventories are an input into Wal-Mart's output of goods sold to consumers. Holding inventories is costly, so firms have an incentive to hold as few inventories as possible and to *turn over* their inventories as rapidly as possible by ensuring that goods do not remain on the shelves long. Holding too few inventories, however, results in *stockouts*, where sales are lost because the goods were not on the shelf for customers to buy.

Improvements in inventory control meet the economic definition of positive technological change because they allow firms to produce the same output with fewer inputs. In recent years, many firms have adopted *just-in-time* inventory systems in which firms accept shipments from suppliers as close as possible to the time they will be needed. The just-in-time system was pioneered by Toyota, which used it to reduce the inventories of parts in its automobile assembly plants. Wal-Mart has been a pioneer in using similar inventory control systems in its stores.

Wal-Mart actively manages its *supply chain* stretching from the manufacturers of the goods it sells to its retail stores. Entrepreneur Sam Walton, the company founder, built a series of distribution centers spread across the country to supply goods to the retail stores. As goods are sold in the stores, this *point-of-sale* information is sent electronically to the firm's distribution centers. The information on sales is used to determine what products will be shipped to each store. Depending on a store's location relative to a distribution center, goods may be shipped overnight, using Wal-Mart's own trucks. This distribution system allows Wal-Mart to minimize its inventory holdings without running the risk of many stockouts. Because Wal-Mart sells 15 percent to 25 percent of all the toothpaste, disposable diapers, dog food, and many other products sold in the United States, it has been able to involve many manufacturers closely in its supply chain. For example, a company such as Procter & Gamble, which is one of the world's largest manufacturers of toothpaste, laundry detergent, toilet paper, and other products, receives Wal-Mart's point-of-sale and inventory information electronically. Procter & Gamble uses this information to help determine its production schedules and the quantities it should ship to Wal-Mart's distribution centers.

Technological change has been a key to Wal-Mart's becoming the largest firm in the United States, with 1.7 million employees and revenue of more than $285 billion in 2004.

Better inventory controls have helped reduce firms' costs.

The Short Run and the Long Run

When firms analyze the relationship between their level of production and their costs, they separate the time period involved into the short run and the long run. In the **short run,** at least one of the firm's inputs is fixed. In particular, in the short run the firm's technology and the size of its physical plant–its factory, store, or office—are both fixed, while the number of workers the firm hires is variable. In the **long run,** the firm is able to vary all of its inputs, and can adopt new technology and increase or decrease the size of its physical plant. Of course, the actual length of calendar time in the short run will be different from firm to firm. A pizza parlor may be able to increase its physical plant by adding another pizza oven and some tables and chairs in just a few weeks. BMW, in contrast, may take more than a year to increase the capacity of one of its automobile assembly plants by installing new equipment.

The Difference between Fixed Costs and Variable Costs

Total cost is the cost of all the inputs a firm uses in production. We have just seen that in the short run some inputs are fixed and others are variable. The costs of the fixed inputs are *fixed costs,* and the costs of the variable inputs are *variable costs.* We can also think of **variable costs** as the costs that change as output changes. Similarly, **fixed costs** are costs that remain constant as output changes. A typical firm's variable costs include its labor costs, its raw material costs, and its costs of electricity and other utilities. Typical fixed costs include lease payments for factory or retail space, payments for fire insurance, and payments for newspaper and television advertising. All of a firm's costs are either fixed or variable, so we can state the following:

Total Cost = Fixed Cost + Variable Cost

or, using symbols:

$$TC = FC + VC$$

② **LEARNING OBJECTIVE**
Distinguish between the economic short run and the economic long run.

Short run The period of time during which at least one of the firm's inputs is fixed.

Long run A period of time long enough to allow a firm to vary all of its inputs, to adopt new technology, and to increase or decrease the size of its physical plant.

Total cost The cost of all the inputs a firm uses in production.

Variable costs Costs that change as output changes.

Fixed costs Costs that remain constant as output changes.

10-2 *Making the Connection*

The salaries of editors are considered a fixed cost by publishers.

Fixed Costs in the Publishing Industry

An editor at Cambridge University Press gives the following estimates of the annual fixed cost for a medium-size academic book publisher:

COST	AMOUNT
Salaries and Benefits	$437,500
Rent	$75,000
Utilities	$20,000
Supplies	$6,000
Postage	$4,000
Travel	$8,000
Subscriptions, etc.	$4,000
Miscellaneous	$5,000
Total	$559,500

Academic book publishers hire editors, designers, and production and marketing managers who help prepare books for publication. Because these employees work on several books simultaneously, the number of people the company hires will not go up and down with the quantity of books the company publishes during any particular year. Publishing companies therefore consider the salaries and benefits of people in these job categories as fixed costs.

In contrast, for a company that *prints* books, the quantity of workers will vary with the quantity of books printed. The wages and benefits of the workers operating the printing presses, for example, would be a variable cost.

The other costs listed in the preceding table are typical of fixed costs at many firms.

Source: Beth Luey, *Handbook for Academic Authors*, 4th ed., Cambridge: Cambridge University Press, 2002, p. 244.

Implicit Costs versus Explicit Costs

Opportunity cost The highest-valued alternative that must be given up to engage in an activity.

Explicit cost A cost that involves spending money.

Implicit cost A nonmonetary opportunity cost.

It is important to remember that economists always measure costs as *opportunity costs.* The **opportunity cost** of any activity is the highest-valued alternative that must be given up to engage in that activity. As we saw in Chapter 7, costs are either *explicit* or *implicit.* When a firm spends money, it incurs an **explicit cost**. When a firm experiences a nonmonetary opportunity cost, it incurs an **implicit cost.**

For example, suppose that Jill Johnson owns a copy store. In operating her store, Jill has explicit costs, such as the wages she pays her workers and the payments she makes for electricity and paper. But some of Jill's most important costs are implicit. Before opening her own store, Jill earned a salary of $30,000 per year managing a store for someone else. To start her store, Jill quit her job, withdrew $50,000 from her bank account—where it earned her interest of $3,000 per year—and used the funds to equip her store with tables, shelves, a cash register, and other equipment. To open her store, Jill had to give up the $30,000 salary and the $3,000 in interest. This $33,000 is a cost to Jill of running her store. It is an implicit cost because it does not represent payments that Jill has to make. All the same, giving up that $33,000 per year is a real cost to Jill. In addition, during the course of the year, the $50,000 worth of equipment in Jill's store will lose some of its value due partly to wear and tear and partly to better equipment becoming available. *Economic depreciation* is the difference between what Jill paid for the equipment at the beginning of the year, and what she could sell the equipment for at the end of the year. If Jill's equipment could be sold for $40,000 at the end of the year, then the $10,000 in economic depreciation represents another implicit cost. (Note that the whole $50,000 she spent on the equipment is not a cost, because she still has the equipment at the end of the year, although it is now worth only $40,000.)

Table 10-1 lists Jill's costs. The entries in red are explicit costs and the entries in blue are implicit costs. As we saw in Chapter 7, the rules of accounting generally require that

Paper	$20,000
Wages	48,000
Lease payment for copy machines	10,000
Electricity	6,000
Lease payment for store	24,000
Foregone salary	30,000
Foregone interest	3,000
Economic depreciation	10,000
Total	151,000

TABLE 10-1

Jill Johnson's Costs per Year

only explicit costs be recognized for purposes of keeping the company's financial records and for paying taxes. Therefore, explicit costs are sometimes called *accounting costs*. *Economic costs* include both accounting costs and implicit costs.

The Production Function

Let's look at the relationship between the level of production and costs in the short run for Jill Johnson's copy store. To keep things simple, let's assume that Jill uses only labor—workers—and capital—machines—to produce a single good: photocopies. Many firms use more than two inputs and produce more than one good, but we can understand the relationship between output and cost more easily by focusing on the case of a firm using only two inputs and producing only one good. In the short run, Jill doesn't have time to build a larger store, bring in additional copy machines, or redesign the layout of her store. So, in the short run, she can increase or decrease the quantity of photocopies she produces only by increasing or decreasing the quantity of workers she employs.

The first three columns of Table 10-2 show the relationship between the quantity of workers and machines Jill uses each day and the quantity of copies she can produce. The relationship between the inputs employed by a firm and the maximum output it can produce with those inputs is called the firm's **production function.** Because a firm's technology is the processes it uses to turn inputs into output, the production function represents the firm's technology. In this case, Table 10-2 shows Jill's *short-run*

Production function The relationship between the inputs employed by the firm and the maximum output it can produce with those inputs.

TABLE 10-2 Short-Run Production and Cost at Jill Johnson's Copy Store

QUANTITY OF WORKERS	QUANTITY OF COPY MACHINES	QUANTITY OF COPIES	COST OF COPY MACHINES (FIXED COST)	COST OF WORKERS (VARIABLE COST)	TOTAL COST OF COPIES	COST PER COPY (AVERAGE TOTAL COST)
0	2	0	$30	$0	$30	—
1	2	625	30	50	80	$0.13
2	2	1325	30	100	130	0.10
3	2	2200	30	150	180	0.08
4	2	2600	30	200	230	0.09
5	2	2900	30	250	280	0.10
6	2	3100	30	300	330	0.11

production function because we are assuming the time period is too short for Jill to increase or decrease the quantity of copy machines she is using.

A First Look at the Relationship between Production and Cost

Table 10-2 also gives us information on Jill's costs. We can determine the total cost of producing a given quantity of copies if we know how many workers and machines are required to produce that quantity of copies and what Jill has to pay for those workers and machines. Suppose Jill leases 2 copy machines for $15 each per day. Therefore, her fixed costs will be $30 per day. If Jill pays $50 per day to each worker she hires, her variable costs will depend on how many workers she hires. In the short run, Jill can increase the quantity of copies she produces only by hiring more workers. The table shows that if she hires 1 worker she produces 625 copies during the day; if she hires 2 workers she produces 1,325 copies; and so on. On a particular day, Jill's total cost of producing copies is equal to the $30 she pays to lease the copy machines plus the amount she pays to hire workers. If Jill decides to hire 4 workers and produce 2,600 copies, her total cost will be $230: $30 to lease the copy machines and $200 to hire the workers. Her cost per copy is equal to her total cost of producing copies divided by the quantity of copies produced. If she produces 2,600 copies at a total cost of $230, her cost per copy, or **average total cost**, is $230/2,600 = $0.09.

Average total cost Total cost divided by the quantity of output produced.

Panel (a) of Figure 10-1 uses the numbers in the next-to-last column of Table 10-2 to graph Jill's total cost. Panel (b) uses the numbers in the last column to graph her average total cost. Notice in panel (b) that Jill's average cost roughly has the same U-shape as

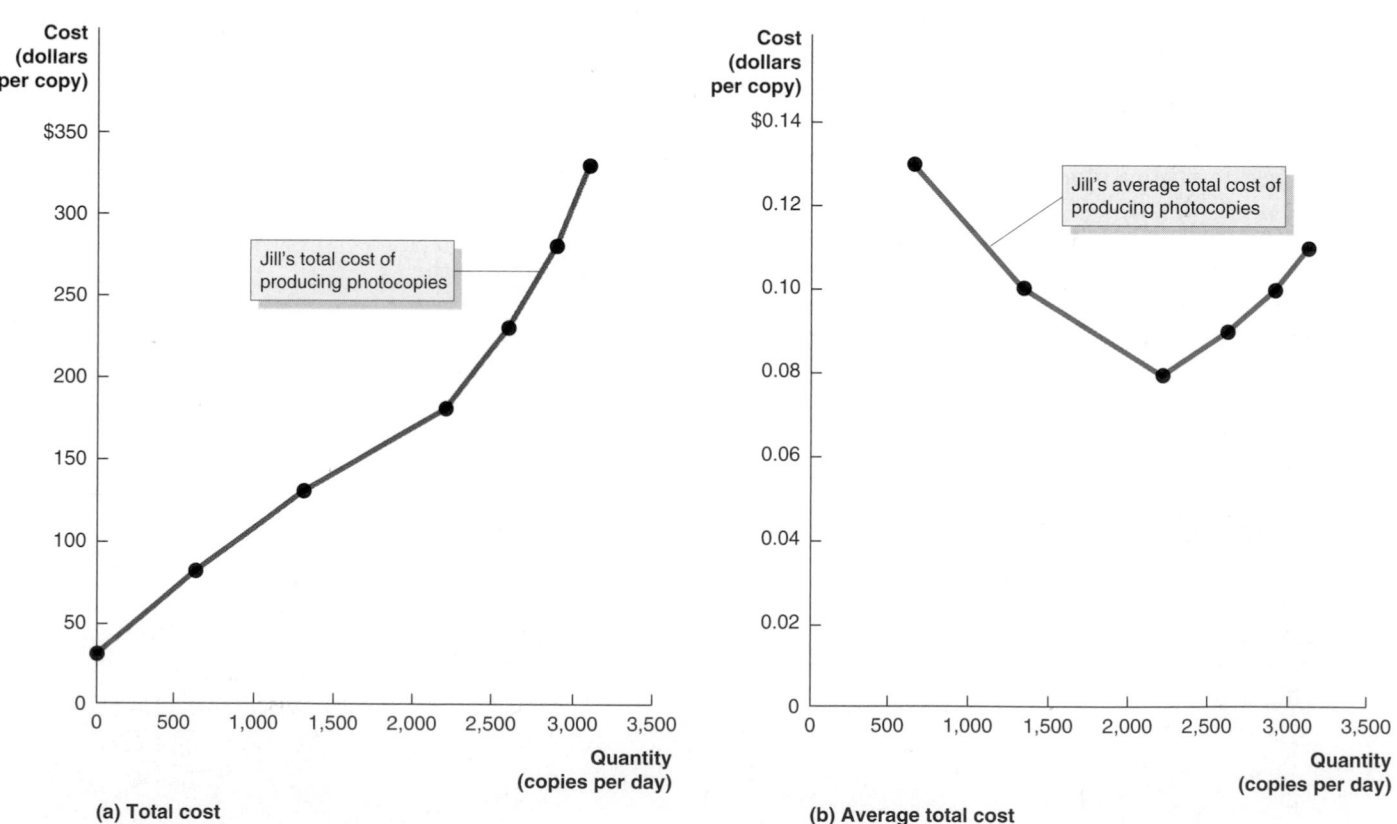

(a) Total cost

(b) Average total cost

FIGURE 10-1 Graphing Total Cost and Average Total Cost at Jill Johnson's Copy Store

We can use the information from Table 10-2 to graph the relationship between the quantity of photocopies Jill produces and her total cost and average total cost. Panel (a) shows that total cost increases as the level of production increases. In panel (b), we see that average total cost is roughly U-shaped:

As production increases from low levels, average cost falls before rising at higher levels of production. To understand why average cost has this shape, we must look more closely at the technology of producing photocopies, as shown by the production function.

the average cost curve we saw Akio Morita calculate for Sony transistor radios at the beginning of this chapter. As production increases from low levels, average cost falls. Average cost then becomes fairly flat before rising at higher levels of production. To understand why average cost has this U-shape, we first need to look more closely at the technology of producing photocopies, as shown by the production function for Jill's store. Then we need to look at how this technology determines the relationship between production and cost.

The Marginal Product of Labor and the Average Product of Labor

To have a better understand of the choices Jill faces given the technology available to her, think first about the situation in her store if she hires only one worker. That one worker will have to perform several different activities, including receiving orders from customers, answering customers' questions, running the copying jobs on the two copy machines, and ringing up sales on the cash registrar. If Jill hires two workers, some of these activities can be divided up: One worker could be assigned to the copy machines, and one worker could be assigned to take orders and work the cash register. With this division of tasks, Jill will find that hiring two workers actually allows her to produce more than twice as many copies as she could produce with just one worker.

The additional output produced by a firm as a result of hiring one more worker is called the **marginal product of labor.** We can calculate the marginal product of labor by determining how much total output increases as each additional worker is hired. We do this for Jill's copy store in Table 10-3.

When Jill hires only one worker, she produces 625 copies per day. When she hires two workers, she produces 1,325 copies per day. Hiring the second worker increases her production by 700 copies per day. So, the marginal product of labor for one worker is 625 copies. For two workers, the marginal product of labor rises to 700 copies. If Jill hires a third worker, total output rises to 2,200, an increase of 875 copies. So, the marginal product of labor for three workers rises to 875. These increases in marginal product result from the *division of labor* and from *specialization.* By dividing the tasks to be performed—the division of labor—Jill reduces the time workers lose moving from one activity to the next. She also allows them to become more specialized at their tasks. For example, a worker who concentrates on operating a copy machine will become skilled at using it quickly and efficiently.

The Law of Diminishing Returns

In the short run, the quantity of copy machines Jill leases is fixed, so as she hires more workers the marginal product of labor eventually begins to decline. This happens

Understand the relationship between the marginal product of labor and the average product of labor.

Marginal product of labor   The additional output a firm produces as a result of hiring one more worker.

QUANTITY OF WORKERS	QUANTITY OF COPY MACHINES	QUANTITY OF COPIES	MARGINAL PRODUCT OF LABOR
0	2	0	—
1	2	625	625
2	2	1,325	700
3	2	2,200	875
4	2	2,600	400
5	2	2,900	300
6	2	3,100	200

TABLE 10-3

The Marginal Product of Labor at Jill Johnson's Copy Store

Law of diminishing returns The principle that, at some point, adding more of a variable input, such as labor, to the same amount of a fixed input, such as capital, will cause the marginal product of the variable input to decline.

because at some point Jill uses up all the gains from the division of labor and from specialization and starts to experience the effects of the **law of diminishing returns.** This law states that adding more of a variable input, such as labor, to the same amount of a fixed input, such as capital, will eventually cause the marginal product of the variable input to decline. For Jill, this happens when she hires the fourth worker. Hiring four workers raises the quantity of copies she produces from 2,200 per day to 2,600. But the increase in the quantity of copies—400—is less than the increase when she hired the third worker—875.

If Jill kept adding more and more workers to the same quantity of machines, eventually workers would begin to get in each other's way and the marginal product of labor would actually become negative. When the marginal product is negative, the level of total output declines. No firm actually would hire so many workers as to experience a negative marginal product of labor and falling total output.

Graphing Production

Panel (a) in Figure 10-2 shows the relationship between the quantity of workers Jill hires and her total output of photocopies, using the numbers from Table 10-3. Panel (b) shows the marginal product of labor. In panel (a), output increases as more workers are hired, but the increase in output does not occur at a constant rate. Because of specialization and the division of labor, output will at first increase at an increasing rate, with each additional worker hired causing production to increase by a *greater* amount than did the hiring of the previous worker. But after the third worker has been hired, hiring more workers while keeping the amount of machinery constant results in diminishing returns. Once the point of diminishing returns has been reached, production increases at a decreasing rate. Each additional worker hired after the third worker causes production to increase by a *smaller* amount than did the hiring of the previous worker. In panel (b), the marginal product of labor curve rises initially because of the effects of specialization and division of labor, and then falls due to the effects of diminishing returns.

Average product of labor The total output produced by a firm divided by the quantity of workers.

10-3 Making the Connection

The gains from division of labor and specialization are as important to firms today as they were in the eighteenth century when Adam Smith first discussed them.

Adam Smith's Famous Account of the Division of Labor in a Pin Factory

In *The Wealth of Nations,* Adam Smith uses production in a pin factory as an example of the gains in output resulting from the division of labor. The following is an excerpt from his account of how pin making was divided into a series of tasks:

> One man draws out the wire, another straightens it, a third cuts it, a fourth points it, a fifth grinds it at the top for receiving the head; to make the head requires two or three distinct operations; to put it on is a [distinct operation], to whiten the pins is another; it is even a trade by itself to put them into the paper; and the important business of making a pin is, in this manner, divided into eighteen distinct operations.

Because the labor of pin making was divided up in this way, the average worker was able to produce about 4,800 pins per day. Smith speculated that a single worker using the pin-making machinery alone would make only about 20 pins per day. This lesson from more than 225 years ago showing the tremendous gains from division of labor and specialization remains relevant to most business situations today.

Source: Adam Smith, *An Inquiry into the Nature and Causes of the Wealth of Nations,* Vol. I, Oxford University Press edition, 1976, pp. 14–15.

The Relationship between Marginal and Average Product

The marginal product of labor tells us how much total output changes as the quantity of workers hired changes. We can also calculate how many copies workers produce on average. The **average product of labor** is the total output produced divided by the quantity of workers. For example, using the numbers in Table 10-3, if Jill hires four workers to produce 2,600 copies, the average product of labor is 2,600/4 = 650.

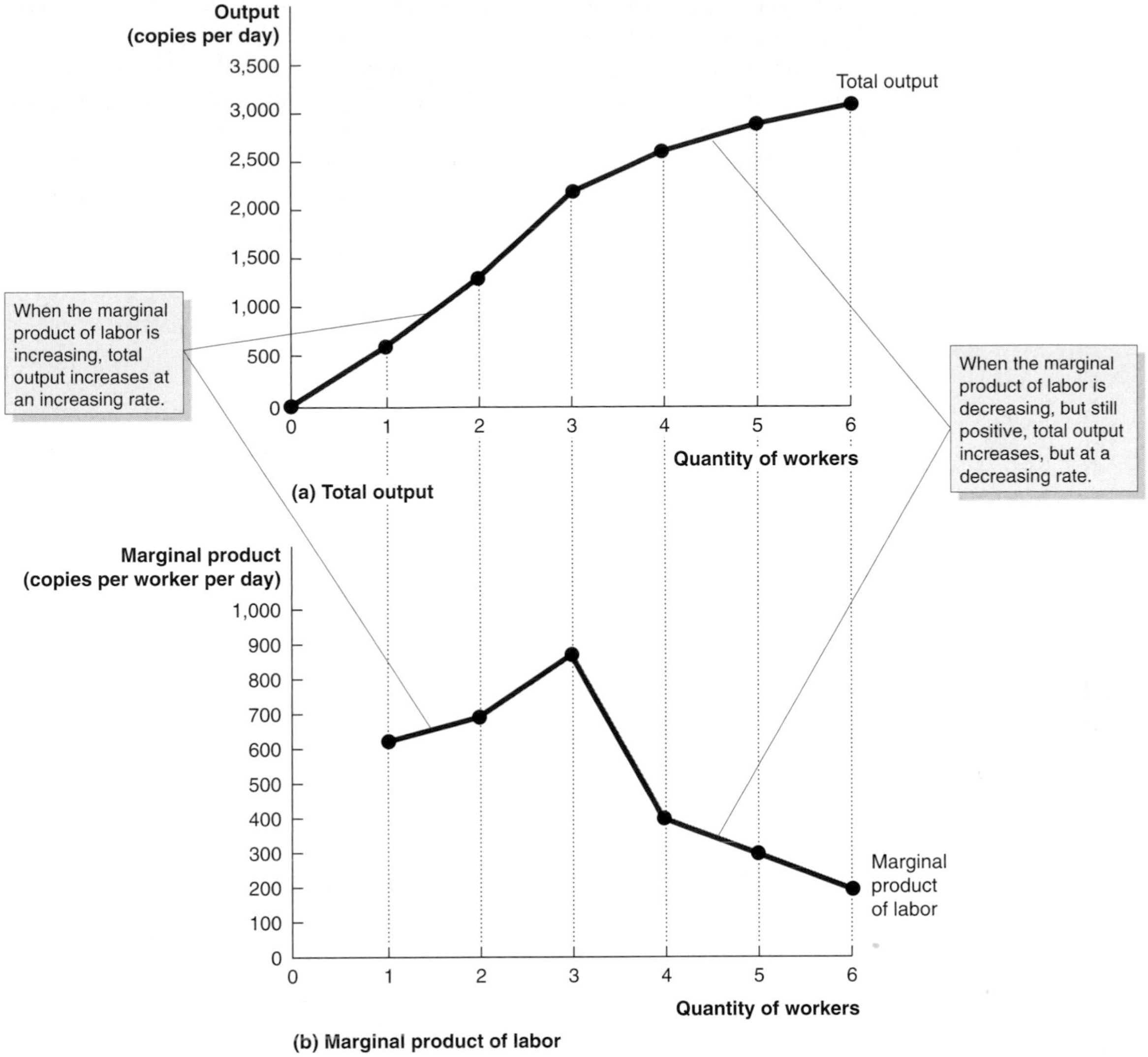

**Output
(copies per day)**

When the marginal product of labor is increasing, total output increases at an increasing rate.

Total output

When the marginal product of labor is decreasing, but still positive, total output increases, but at a decreasing rate.

(a) Total output

**Marginal product
(copies per worker per day)**

Marginal product of labor

Quantity of workers

(b) Marginal product of labor

FIGURE 10-2   Total Output and the Marginal Product of Labor

In panel (a), output increases as more workers are hired, but the increase in output does not occur at a constant rate. Because of specialization and the division of labor, output will at first increase at an increasing rate, with each additional worker hired causing production to increase by a *greater* amount than did the hiring of the previous worker. After the third worker has been hired, hiring more workers while keeping the amount of machinery constant results in diminishing returns. Once the point of diminishing returns has been reached, production increases at a decreasing rate. Each additional worker hired after the third worker causes production to increase by a *smaller* amount than did the hiring of the previous worker. In panel (b), the *marginal product of labor* is the additional output produced as a result of hiring one more worker. The marginal product of labor rises initially because of the effects of specialization and division of labor, and then falls due to the effects of diminishing returns.

We can state the relationship between the marginal and average products of labor this way: *The average product of labor is the average of the marginal products of labor.* For example, the numbers from Table 10-3 show that the marginal product of the first worker Jill hires is 625, the marginal product of the second worker is 700, and the marginal product of the third worker is 875. Therefore, the average product of labor for three workers is 733.3:

$$733.3 = (625 + 700 + 875) / 3$$

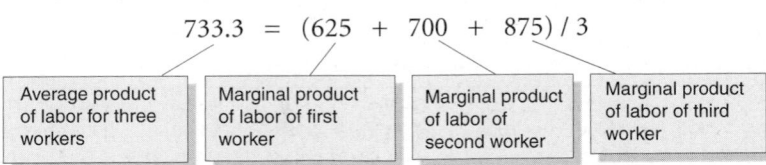

Average product of labor for three workers

Marginal product of labor of first worker

Marginal product of labor of second worker

Marginal product of labor of third worker

By taking the average of the marginal products of the first three workers, we have the average product of the three workers.

Whenever the marginal product of labor is greater than the average product of labor, the average product of labor must be increasing. This statement is true for the same reason that a person 6 feet, 2 inches tall entering a room where the average height is 5 feet, 10 inches raises the average height of people in the room. Whenever the marginal product of labor is less than the average product of labor, the average product of labor must be decreasing. The marginal product of labor equals the average product of labor for the quantity of workers where the average product of labor is at its maximum.

An Example of Marginal and Average Values: College Grades

The relationship between the marginal product of labor and the average product of labor is the same as the relationship between the marginal and average values of any variable. To see this more clearly, think about the familiar relationship between a student's grade point average (GPA) in one semester and his overall, or cumulative, grade point average. The table in Figure 10-3 shows Paul's college grades for each semester,

FIGURE 10-3

Marginal and Average GPAs

The relationship between marginal and average values for a variable can be illustrated using grade point averages (GPAs). We can calculate the GPA Paul earns in a particular semester (his "marginal GPA"), and we can calculate his cumulative GPA for all the semesters he has completed so far (his "average GPA"). Paul's GPA is only 1.50 in the fall semester of his freshman year. In each following semester through fall of his junior year, his GPA for the semester increases—raising his cumulative GPA. In Paul's junior year, even though his semester GPA declines from fall to spring, his cumulative GPA rises. Only in the fall of his senior year, when his semester GPA drops below his cumulative GPA, does his cumulative GPA decline.

	Semester GPA (Marginal) GPA	Cumulative GPA (Average) GPA
Freshman Year		
Fall	1.50	1.50
Spring	2.00	1.75
Sophomore Year		
Fall	2.20	1.90
Spring	3.00	2.18
Junior Year		
Fall	3.20	2.38
Spring	3.00	2.48
Senior Year		
Fall	2.40	2.47
Spring	2.00	2.41

> Average GPA continues to rise, although marginal GPA falls.

> With the marginal GPA below the average, the average GPA falls.

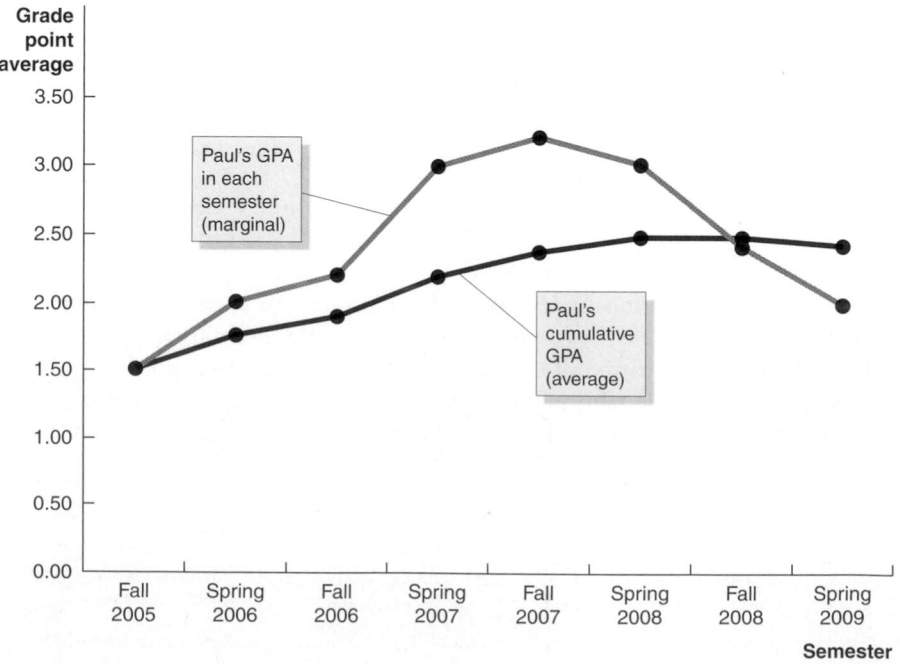

beginning with fall 2005. The graph in Figure 10-3 plots the grades from the table. Just as each additional worker hired adds to a firm's total production, each additional semester adds to Paul's total grade points. We can calculate what each individual worker hired adds to total production (marginal product), and we can calculate the average production of the workers hired so far (average product).

Similarly, we can calculate the GPA Paul earns in a particular semester (his "marginal GPA"), and we can calculate his cumulative GPA for all the semesters he has completed so far (his "average GPA"). As the table shows, Paul gets off to a weak start in college with only a 1.50 GPA in the fall semester of his freshman year. In each subsequent semester through the fall of his junior year, his GPA for the semester increases from the previous semester—raising his cumulative GPA. As the graph shows, however, his cumulative GPA does not increase as rapidly as his semester-by-semester GPA, because his cumulative GPA is held back by the low GPAs of his first few semesters. Notice that in Paul's junior year, even though his semester GPA declines from fall to spring, his cumulative GPA rises. Only in the fall of his senior year, when his semester GPA drops below his cumulative GPA, does his cumulative GPA decline.

The Relationship between Short-Run Production and Short-Run Cost

④ **LEARNING OBJECTIVE**
Explain and illustrate the relationship between marginal cost and average total cost.

We have seen that technology determines the values of the marginal product of labor and the average product of labor. In turn, the marginal and average products of labor will affect the firm's costs. Keep in mind that the relationships we are discussing are *short-run* relationships: We are assuming the time period is too short for the firm to change its technology or the size of its plant.

At the beginning of this chapter, we saw how Akio Morita used an average total cost curve to determine the price of radios. The average total cost curve Morita used and the average total cost curve in Figure 10-1 for Jill Johnson's copy store both have a U-shape. As we will soon see, the U-shape of the average total cost curve is determined by the shape of the curve that shows the relationship between *marginal cost* and the level of production.

Marginal Cost

As we saw in Chapter 1, one of the key ideas in economics is that optimal decisions are made at the margin. Consumers, firms, and government officials usually make decisions about doing a little more or a little less. As Jill Johnson considers whether to hire additional workers to produce additional photocopies, she needs to consider how much she will add to her total cost by producing the additional copies. **Marginal cost** is the change in a firm's total cost from producing one more unit of a good or service. We can calculate marginal cost for a particular increase in output by dividing the change in cost by the change in output. Expressing this idea mathematically (remembering that the Greek letter delta, Δ, means "change in") we can write:

Marginal cost The change in a firm's total cost from producing one more unit of a good or service.

$$MC = \frac{\Delta TC}{\Delta Q}.$$

In the table in Figure 10-4, we use this equation to calculate Jill's marginal cost of producing copies.

Why Are the Marginal and Average Cost Curves U-Shaped?

Notice in the graph in Figure 10-4 that Jill's marginal cost of producing copies declines at first and then increases, giving the marginal cost curve a U-shape. The table in Figure 10-4 also shows the marginal product of labor. This table allows us to see the important

FIGURE 10-4

Jill Johnson's Marginal Cost and Average Total Cost of Producing Copies

We can use the information in the table to calculate Jill's marginal cost and average total cost of producing copies. For the first three workers hired, the marginal product of labor is increasing. This increase causes the marginal cost of production to fall. For the last three workers hired, the marginal product of labor is falling. This causes the marginal cost of production to increase. Therefore, the marginal cost curve falls and then rises—has a U-shape—because the marginal product of labor rises and then falls. As long as marginal cost is below average total cost, average total cost will be falling. When marginal cost is above average total cost, average total cost will be rising. The relationship between marginal cost and average total cost explains why the average total cost curve also has a U-shape.

Quantity of Workers	Quantity of Copies	Marginal Product of Labor	Total Cost of Copies	Marginal Cost of Copies	Average Total Cost of Copies
0	0	—	$30	—	—
1	625	625	80	$0.08	$0.13
2	1,325	700	130	0.07	0.10
3	2,200	875	180	0.06	0.08
4	2,600	400	230	0.13	0.09
5	2,900	300	280	0.17	0.10
6	3,100	200	330	0.25	0.11

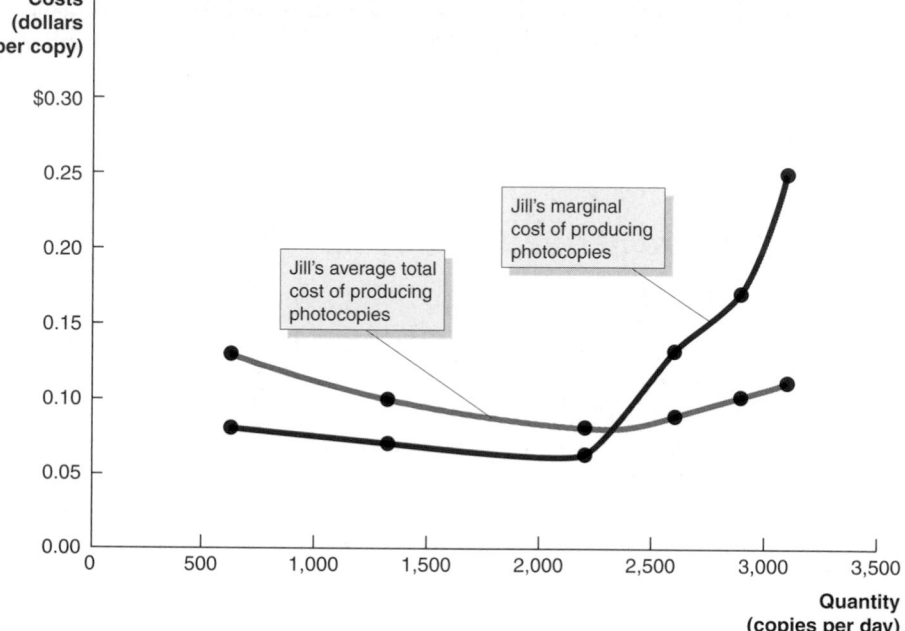

relationship between the marginal product of labor and the marginal cost of production: The marginal product of labor is *rising* for the first three workers, but the marginal cost of the copies produced by these workers is *falling*. The marginal product of labor is *falling* for the last three workers, but the marginal cost of copies produced by these workers is *rising*. To summarize this point: *When the marginal product of labor is rising, the marginal cost of output will be falling. When the marginal product of labor is falling, the marginal cost of production will be rising.*

One way to understand why this point is true is first to notice that the only additional cost to Jill from producing more copies is the additional wages she pays to hire more workers. She pays each new worker the same $50 per day. So the marginal cost of the additional copies each worker makes depends upon that worker's additional output, or marginal product. As long as the additional output from each new worker is rising, the marginal cost of that output will be falling. Once the additional output from each new worker is falling, the marginal cost of that output will be rising. *We can conclude that the marginal cost of production falls and then rises—a U-shape—because the marginal product of labor rises and then falls.*

The relationship between marginal cost and average total cost follows the usual relationship between marginal and average values. As long as marginal cost is below average total cost, average total cost will fall. When marginal cost is above average total cost, average total cost will rise. Marginal cost will equal average total cost when average total cost is at its lowest point. Therefore, the average total cost curve has a U-shape because the marginal cost curve has a U-shape.

SOLVED PROBLEM 10-1

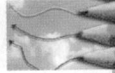

The Relationship between Marginal Cost and Average Cost

Is Jill Johnson right or wrong when she says the following? "I am currently producing 10,000 copies per day at a total cost of $500.00. If I produce 10,001 copies my total cost will rise to $500.11. Therefore, my marginal cost of producing copies must be increasing." Draw a graph to illustrate your answer.

④ **LEARNING OBJECTIVE**
Explain and illustrate the relationship between marginal cost and average total cost.

Solving the Problem:

Step 1: Review the chapter material. This problem requires understanding the relationship between marginal and average cost, so you may want to review the section "Why Are the Marginal and Average Cost Curves U-Shaped?" which begins on page 323.

Step 2: Calculate average total cost and marginal cost. Average total cost is total cost divided by total output. In this case, average total cost is $500.11/10,000 = $0.05. Marginal cost is the change in total cost divided by the change in output. In this case, marginal cost is $0.11/1 = $0.11.

Step 3: Use the relationship between marginal cost and average total cost to answer the question. When marginal cost is greater than average total cost, marginal cost must be increasing. You have shown in step 2 that marginal cost is greater than average total cost. Therefore, Jill is right: Her marginal cost of producing copies must be increasing.

Step 4: Draw the graph.

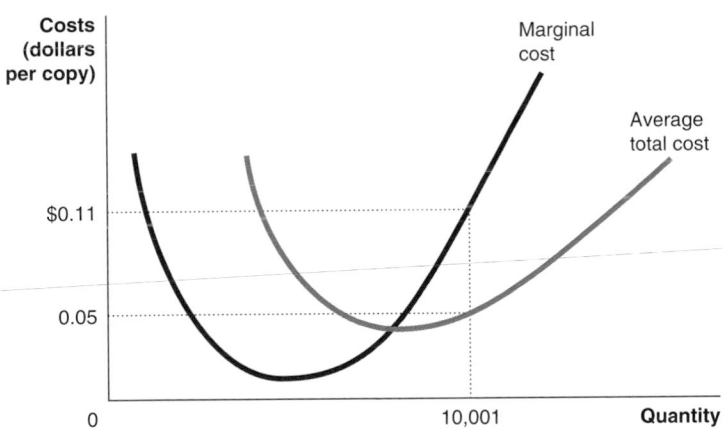

YOUR TURN: For more practice, do related problems 11, 15, 17, and 29 on pages 338, 339, and page 341 at the end of this chapter. Visit www.prenhall.com/hubbard for an interactive exercise related to this Solved Problem.

Graphing Cost Curves

We have seen that we calculate average total cost by dividing total cost by the quantity of output produced. Similarly, we can calculate **average fixed cost** by dividing fixed cost by the quantity of output produced. And we can calculate **average variable cost** by dividing variable cost by the quantity of output produced. Or, mathematically, with Q being the level of output, we have:

⑤ **LEARNING OBJECTIVE**
Graph average total cost, average variable cost, average fixed cost, and marginal cost.

$$\text{Average total cost} = ATC = \frac{TC}{Q}$$

Average fixed cost Fixed cost divided by the quantity of output produced.

$$\text{Average fixed cost} = AFC = \frac{FC}{Q}$$

Average variable cost Variable cost divided by the quantity of units produced.

$$\text{Average variable cost} = AVC = \frac{VC}{Q}.$$

Finally, notice that average total cost is just the sum of average fixed cost plus average variable cost:

$$ATC = AFC + AVC.$$

The only fixed cost Jill incurs in operating her copy store is the $30 per day she pays to lease two copy machines. Her variable costs are the wages she pays her workers. The table and graph in Figure 10-5 show Jill's costs.

We will use graphs like the one in Figure 10-5 in the next several chapters to analyze how firms decide the level of output to produce and the price to charge. Before going further, be sure you understand the following three key facts about Figure 10-5:

FIGURE 10-5

Costs at Jill Johnson's Copy Store

Jill's costs of making copies are shown in the table and plotted in the graph. Notice three important facts about the graph: (1) The marginal cost (*MC*), average total cost (*ATC*), and average variable cost (*AVC*) curves are all U-shaped, and the marginal cost curve intersects both the average variable cost curve and average total cost curve at their minimum points. (2) As output increases, average fixed cost (*AFC*) gets smaller and smaller. (3) As output increases, the difference between average total cost and average variable cost decreases. Make sure you can explain why each of these three facts is true. You should spend time becoming familiar with this graph, because it is one of the most important graphs in microeconomics.

Quantity of Workers	Quantity of Copy Machines	Quantity of Copies	Cost of Copy Machines (Fixed Cost)	Cost of Workers (Variable Cost)	Total Cost of Copies	ATC	AFC	AVC	MC
0	2	0	$30	0	$30	—	—	—	—
1	2	625	30	$50	80	$0.13	$0.05	$0.08	$0.08
2	2	1,325	30	100	130	0.10	0.02	0.08	0.07
3	2	2,200	30	150	180	0.08	0.01	0.07	0.06
4	2	2,600	30	200	230	0.09	0.01	0.08	0.13
5	2	2,900	30	250	280	0.10	0.01	0.09	0.17
6	2	3,100	30	300	330	0.11	0.01	0.10	0.25

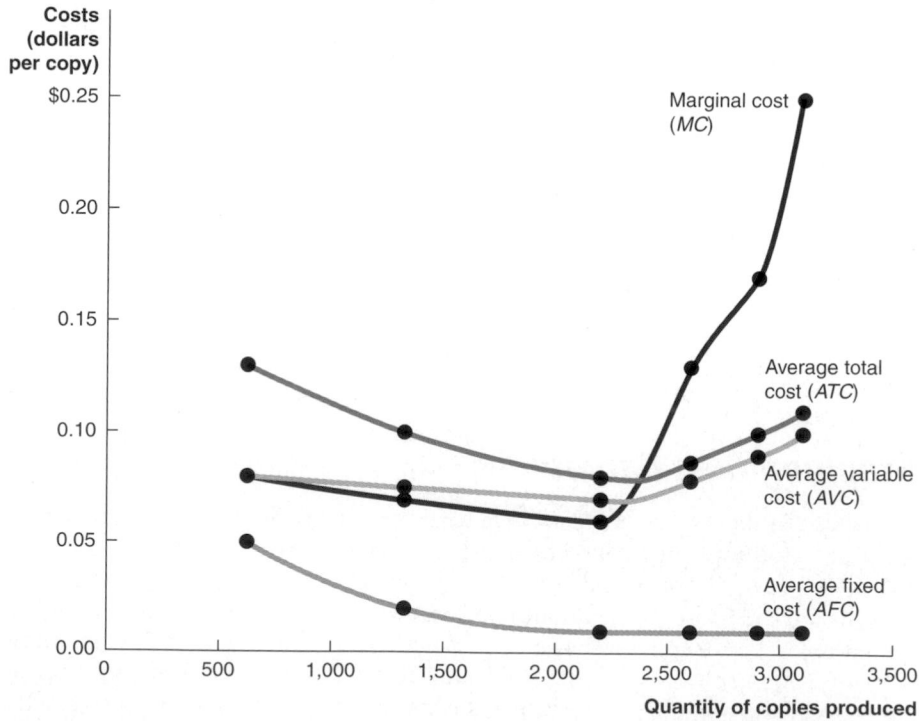

1. The marginal cost (*MC*), average total cost (*ATC*), and average variable cost (*AVC*) curves are all U-shaped, and the marginal cost curve intersects the average variable cost and average total cost curves at their minimum points. When marginal cost is less than either average variable cost or average total cost, it causes them to decrease. When marginal cost is above average variable cost or average total cost, it causes them to increase. Therefore, when marginal cost equals average variable cost or average total cost, they must be at their minimum points.

2. As output increases, average fixed cost gets smaller and smaller. This happens because in calculating average fixed cost we are dividing something that gets larger and larger—output—into something that remains constant—fixed cost. Firms often refer to this process of lowering average fixed cost by selling more output as "spreading the overhead." By "overhead" they mean fixed costs.

3. As output increases, the difference between average total cost and average variable cost decreases. This happens because the difference between average total cost and average variable cost is average fixed cost, which gets smaller as output increases.

Costs in the Long Run

(6) **LEARNING OBJECTIVE**
Understand how firms use the long-run average cost curve to plan.

The distinction between fixed cost and variable cost that we just discussed applies to the short run but *not* to the long run. For example, in the short run, Jill Johnson has fixed costs of $30 a day because she has signed an agreement to lease two copy machines for six months. When the six months are over, that cost becomes variable because Jill can choose whether or not to sign another agreement. The same would be true of any other fixed costs a company like Jill's might have. Once a company has purchased a fire insurance policy, the cost of the policy is fixed. But when the policy expires, the company must decide whether or not to renew it and the cost becomes variable. The important point here is that: *In the long run all costs are variable. There are no fixed costs in the long run.* In other words, in the long run, total cost equals variable cost and average total cost equals average variable cost.

Managers of successful companies simultaneously consider how they can most profitably run their current store, factory, or office and also whether in the long run they would be more profitable if they became larger or, possibly, smaller. Jill must consider how to run her current store, which has only two copy machines, but she also must plan what to do when her current lease agreements end. Should she lease more copy machines? Should she lease a larger store?

Economies of Scale

Short-run average cost curves represent the costs a firm faces when some input, such as the quantity of machines it uses, is fixed. The **long-run average cost curve** shows the lowest cost at which the firm is able to produce a given level of output in the long run, when no inputs are fixed. Many firms experience **economies of scale,** which means the firm's long-run average costs fall as it increases the quantity of output it produces. We can illustrate the effects of economies of scale in Figure 10-6, which shows the relationship between short-run and long-run average cost curves. Managers can use long-run average cost curves for planning because they show the effect on cost of expanding output by, for example, building a larger factory or store.

Long-run average cost curve A curve showing the lowest cost at which the firm is able to produce a given quantity of output in the long run, when no inputs are fixed.

Economies of scale Exist when a firm's long-run average costs fall as it increases output.

Long-Run Average Total Cost Curves for Bookstores

Figure 10-6 shows long-run average cost in the retail bookstore industry. If a bookstore expects to be able to sell only 1,000 books per month, the small store represented by the *ATC* curve on the left of the figure will allow it to sell this quantity of books at the lowest average cost. A much larger bookstore, such as one run by a national chain like Barnes &

The Relationship between Short-Run Average Cost and Long-Run Average Cost

If a bookstore expects to sell only 1,000 books per month, the small store represented by the *ATC* curve on the left of the figure will allow it to sell this quantity of books at the lowest average cost, which would be $22 per book. A larger bookstore will be able to sell 20,000 books per month at a lower cost of $18 per book. A bookstore selling 20,000 books per month and a bookstore selling 40,000 books per month will experience constant returns to scale and have the same average cost. A bookstore selling 20,000 books per month will have reached minimum efficient scale. Very large bookstores will experience diseconomies of scale, and their average costs will rise as sales increase beyond 40,000 books per month.

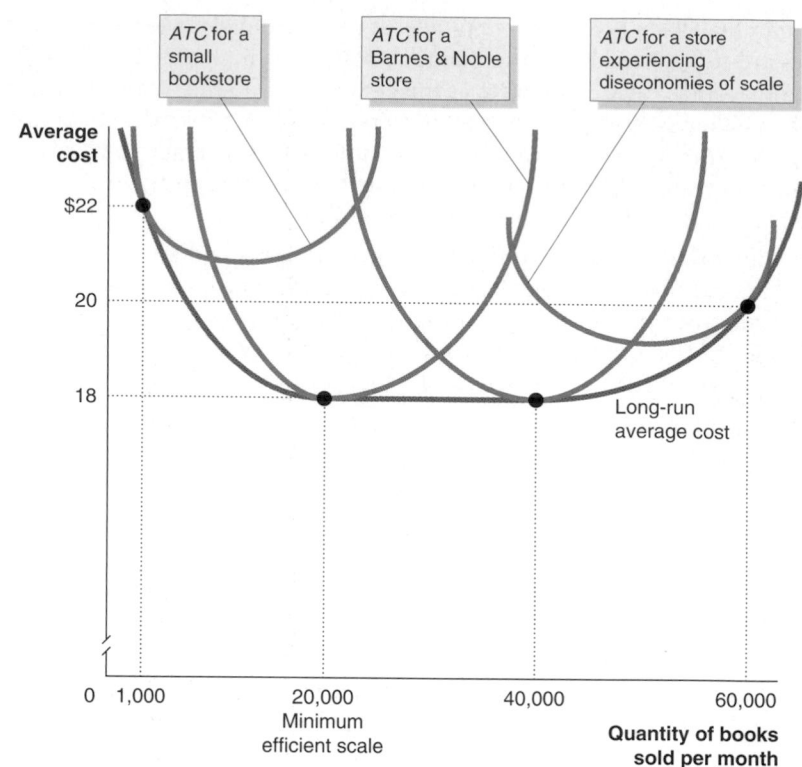

Constant returns to scale Exist when a firm's long-run average costs remain unchanged as it increases output.

Minimum efficient scale The level of output at which all economies of scale have been exhausted.

Noble, will be able to sell 20,000 books per month at a much lower average cost. For the small bookstore, the average total cost of selling 1,000 books per month would be $22 per book. For a Barnes & Noble store, the average total cost of selling 20,000 books would be only $18 per book. This decline in average cost represents the economies of scale that exist in bookselling. Why would the larger bookstore have lower average costs? One important reason is that the Barnes & Noble store is selling 20 times as many books per month as the small store but might need only six times as many workers. This saving in labor cost would reduce Barnes & Noble's average cost of selling books.

Firms may encounter economies of scale for several reasons. First, as with the case of Barnes & Noble, the firm's technology may make it possible to increase production with a smaller proportional increase in at least one input. Second, both workers and managers can become more specialized, enabling them to become more productive, as output expands. Third, large firms, like Barnes & Noble, Wal-Mart, and General Motors, may be able to purchase inputs at lower costs than smaller competitors. In fact, as Wal-Mart expanded, its bargaining power with respect to its suppliers increased and its average costs fell. Finally, as a firm expands it may be able to borrow money more cheaply, thereby lowering its costs.

Economies of scale do not continue forever. The long-run average cost curve in most industries has a flat segment that often stretches over a substantial range of output. As Figure 10-6 shows, a bookstore selling 20,000 books per month and a bookstore selling 40,000 books per month will have the same average cost. Over this range of output, firms in the industry will experience **constant returns to scale.** As these firms increase their output, they will have to increase their inputs, such as the size of the store and the quantity of workers, proportionally. The level of output at which all economies of scale have been exhausted is known as **minimum efficient scale.** A bookstore selling 20,000 books per month has reached minimum efficient scale.

Very large bookstores will experience increasing average costs as managers begin to have difficulty coordinating the operation of the store. Figure 10-6 shows that for sales above 40,000 books per month, firms in the industry will experience **diseconomies of scale.** Toyota ran into diseconomies of scale in 2004. The firm found that as it expanded production at its Georgetown, Kentucky, plant and its plants in China, its managers had difficulty keeping costs from rising. The president of Toyota's Georgetown plant was quoted as saying, "Demand for . . . high volumes saps your energy. Over a period of time, it eroded our focus . . . [and] thinned out the expertise and knowledge we painstakingly built up over the years." One analysis of the problems Toyota faced in expanding production concluded: "It is the kind of paradox many highly successful companies face: Getting bigger doesn't always mean getting better."

Diseconomies of scale Exist when a firm's long-run average costs rise as it increases output.

SOLVED PROBLEM 10-2

Using Long-Run Average Cost Curves to Understand Business Strategy

⑥ **LEARNING OBJECTIVE**
Understand how firms use the long-run average cost curve to plan.

In the fall of 2002, Motorola and Siemens were each manufacturing both mobile phone handsets and wireless infrastruture—the base stations needed to operate a wireless communications network. The firms discussed the following arrangement: Motorola would give Siemens its wireless infrastructure business in exchange for Siemens giving Motorola its mobile phone handsets business. The main factor motivating the trade was the hope of taking advantage of economies of scale in each business. Use long-run average total cost curves to explain why this trade might make sense for Motorola and Siemens.

Solving the Problem:
Step 1: Review the chapter material. This problem is about the long-run average cost curve, so you may want to review the material in the section "Costs in the Long Run," which begins on page 327.

Step 2: Draw long-run average cost graphs for Motorola and Siemens. The question does not provide us with the details of the quantity of each product each company is producing before the trade or their average costs of production. If economies of scale were an important reason for the trade, we can assume that Motorola and Siemens were not yet at minimum efficient scale in the wireless infrastructure and phone handset businesses. Therefore, we can draw the following graphs:

Handsets

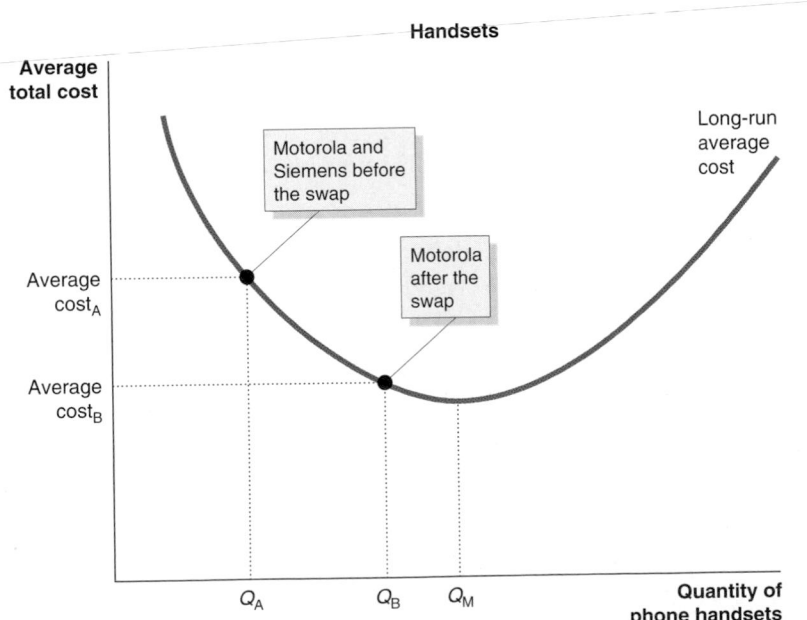

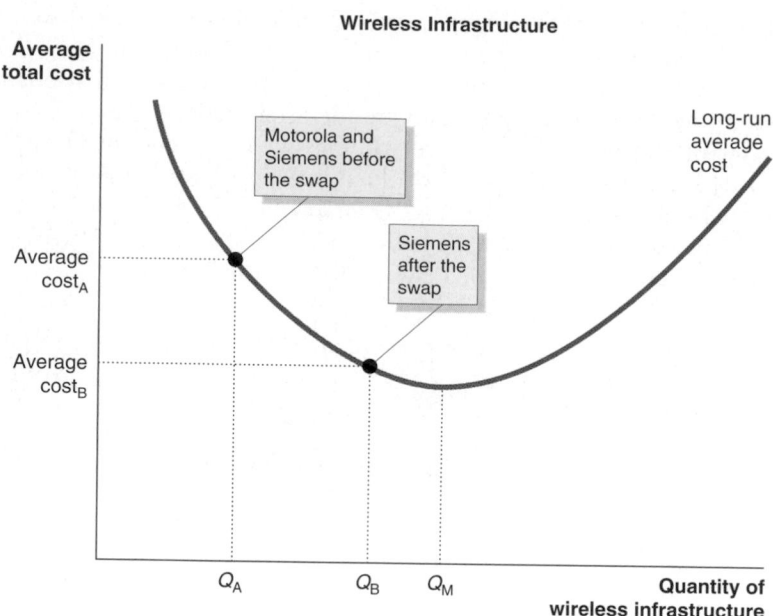

Step 3: Explain the curves in the graphs. Before the proposed trade, Motorola and Siemens are producing both products at less than the minimum efficient scale, which is Q_M in both graphs. After the trade, Motorola's production of handsets will increase, moving it from Q_A to Q_B in the first graph. This increase in production allows it to take advantage of economies of scale and reduce its average cost from Average Cost$_A$ to Average Cost$_B$. Similarly, production of wireless infrastructure by Siemens will increase from Q_A to Q_B, lowering its average cost from Average Cost$_A$ to Average Cost$_B$. As drawn, the graphs show that both firms will still be short of minimum efficient scale after the trade, although their average costs have fallen.

Extra Credit: These were new technologies at the time the trade was being discussed. As a result, companies making these products were only beginning to understand how large minimum efficient scale was. To survive in the industry, the managements of both companies wanted to lower their costs by taking advantage of economies of scale. As one industry analyst put it:

> Motorola and Siemens may be driven by the conviction that they have little choice. Most observers believe consolidation in both the [wireless] networking and handset areas is inevitable.

Source for quote: Ray Hegarty, "Rumored Motorola–Siemens Business Unit Swap? A Compelling M&A Story," www.thefeature.com.

YOUR TURN: **For more practice, do related problems 14, 18, 19, 24, and 25 on pages 338, 339, and 340 at the end of this chapter. Visit www.prenhall.com/hubbard for an interactive exercise related to this Solved Problem.**

Over time, most firms in an industry will build factories or stores that are at least as large as the minimum efficient scale but not so large that diseconomies of scale occur. In the bookstore industry, stores will sell between 20,000 and 40,000 books per month. However, firms often do not know the exact shape of their long-run average cost curves. As a result, they may mistakenly build factories or stores that are either too large or too small.

The Colossal River Rouge: Diseconomies of Scale at the Ford Motor Company

10-4 Making the Connection

When Henry Ford started the Ford Motor Company in 1903, automobile companies produced cars in small workshops using highly skilled workers. Ford introduced two new ideas that allowed him to take advantage of economies of scale. First, Ford used identical—or, interchangeable—parts so that unskilled workers could be used to assemble the cars. Second, instead of having groups of workers

Is it possible for a factory to be too big?

moving from one stationary automobile to the next, he had the workers remain stationary while the automobiles moved along an assembly line. Ford built a large factory at Highland Park, outside of Detroit, where he used these ideas to produce the famous Model T at an average cost well below what his competitors could match using older production methods in smaller factories.

Ford believed that he could produce automobiles at an even lower average cost by building a still larger plant along the River Rouge. Unfortunately, Ford's River Rouge plant was too large and suffered from diseconomies of scale. Ford's managers had great difficulty coordinating the production of automobiles in such a large plant. The following description of the River Rouge comes from the biography of Ford by Allan Nevins and Frank Ernest Hill:

> A total of 93 separate structures stood on the [River Rouge] site. . . . Railroad trackage covered 93 miles, conveyors 27 [miles]. About 75,000 men worked in the great plant. A force of 5000 did nothing but keep it clean, wearing out 5000 mops and 3000 brooms a month, and using 86 tons of soap on the floors, walls, and 330 acres of windows. The Rouge was an industrial city, immense, concentrated, packed with power. . . . By its very massiveness and complexity, it denied men at the top contact with and understanding of those beneath, and gave those beneath a sense of being lost in inexorable immensity and power.

Beginning in 1927, Ford produced the Model A—its only car model at that time—at the River Rouge plant. Ford failed to achieve economies of scale, and actually *lost money* on each of the four Model A body styles.

Ford could not raise the price of the Model A to make it profitable, because at a higher price the car could not compete with similar models produced by competitors such as General Motors and Chrysler. He eventually reduced the cost of making the Model A by constructing smaller factories spread out across the country. These smaller factories produced the Model A at a lower average cost than was possible at the River Rouge plant.

Sources: Quote from Allan Nevins and Frank Ernest Hill, *Ford: Expansion and Challenge, 1915–1933*, New York: Charles Scribner's Sons, 1957, pp. 293, 295.

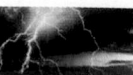

Don't Let This Happen To You!

Don't Confuse Diminishing Returns with Diseconomies of Scale

The concepts of diminishing returns and diseconomies of scale may seem similar, but, in fact, they are unrelated. Diminishing returns applies only to the short run, when at least one of the firm's inputs, such as the quantity of machinery it uses, is fixed. The law of diminishing returns

tells us that in the short run hiring more workers will, at some point, result in less additional output. Diminishing returns explains why marginal cost curves eventually slope upward. Diseconomies of scale apply only in the long run, when the firm is free to vary all its inputs, can adopt new technology, and can vary the amount of machinery it uses and the size of its facility. Diseconomies of scale explain why long-run average cost curves eventually slope upward.

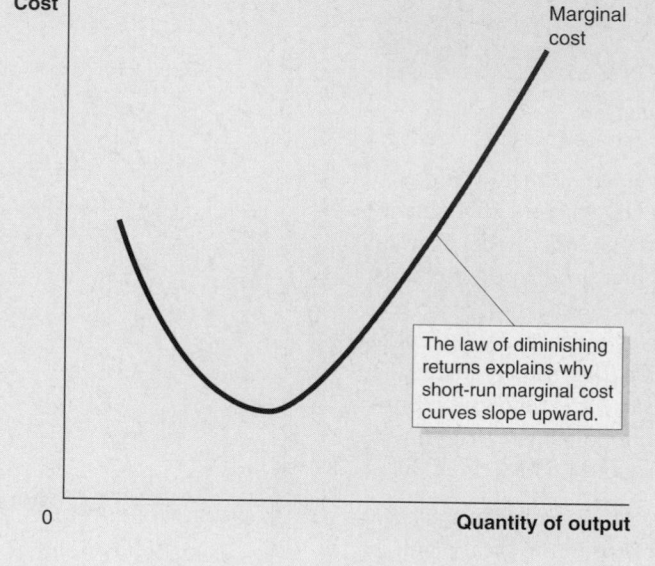

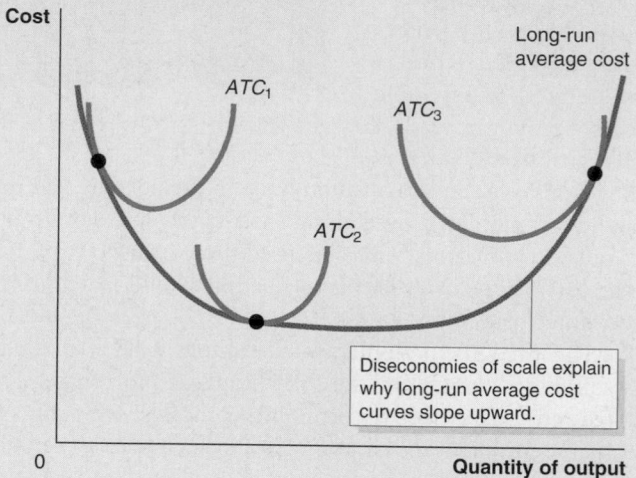

YOUR TURN: Test your understanding by doing related problem 21 on page 340 at the end of this chapter.

Conclusion

In this chapter, we discussed the relationship between a firm's technology, its production, and its costs. During the discussion, we encountered a number of definitions of costs. Because we will use these definitions in later chapters, it is useful to bring them together in Table 10-4 for you to review.

We have seen the important relationship between a firm's level of production and its costs. Just as this information was vital to Akio Morita in deciding which price to charge for his transistor radios, so it remains vital today to all firms as they attempt to decide the optimal level of production and the optimal prices to charge for their products. We will explore this point further in Chapter 11. Before moving on to that chapter, read *An Inside Look* on pages 334–335 to see how we can use long-run average cost curves to understand the motives behind the joint venture between Sony and Samsung.

TERM	DEFINITION	SYMBOLS AND EQUATIONS
Total cost	Value of all the inputs used by a firm	TC
Fixed cost	Costs that remain constant when a firm's level of output changes	FC
Variable cost	Costs that change when the firm's level of output changes	VC
Marginal cost	Increase in total cost resulting from producing another unit of output	$MC = \dfrac{\Delta TC}{\Delta Q}$
Average total cost	Total cost divided by the quantity of units produced	$ATC = \dfrac{TC}{Q}$
Average fixed cost	Fixed cost divided by the quantity of units produced	$AFC = \dfrac{FC}{Q}$
Average variable cost	Variable cost divided by the quantity of units produced	$AVC = \dfrac{VC}{Q}$
Implicit cost	A nonmonetary opportunity cost	—
Explicit cost	A cost that involves spending money	—

TABLE 10-4

A Summary of Definitions of Cost

FINANCIAL TIMES, JULY 16, 2004

It's 'Win-Win' as Samsung, Sony Join on Flat Screens

It was a handshake that brought together the world's largest television-maker with the biggest producer of liquid crystal displays to create what they hope will be a new force in the flat-screen market. Nobuyuki Idei, chairman of Sony, and Yun Jong-yong, chief executive of Samsung Electronics, were marking the launch of S-LCD, the two companies' display-making joint-venture, at a sprawling new technology park in Asan, South Korea, yesterday. . . .

a By joining forces, Sony and Samsung have pitted themselves against LG Electronics of South Korea and Philips of the Netherlands. . . . Together with Sharp and a handful of Taiwanese manufacturers, S-LCD and LG Philips are investing billions of dollars in plants to make flat panel displays. The companies are anticipating years of rapid growth in the sector as households and offices replace bulky cathode ray tube TVs and computer monitors with slimmer LCD models. . . .

In addition to producing flat panel displays, Samsung, Sony, Sharp, LG and Philips are also among the world's biggest makers of TVs and monitors. That means they must seek a balance between keeping LCD prices high enough to make profits but low enough to attract consumers. Samsung and Sony are each investing [1,050 billion Korean won or $902 million] in S-LCD to build a so-called seventh-generation plant that will churn out 60,000 panels a month, starting in the first half of next year.

b The facility will produce bigger glass panels than the sixth-generation plants recently opened by Sharp and planned by LG Philips. This will allow S-LCD to make larger-sized TVs and cut more screens from each panel, reducing costs. By focusing on large-sized TVs, up to 46-inches in width, Samsung and Sony are aiming for potentially the most profitable part of the LCD market, in contrast to lower-margin small TVs and monitors.

Each company will be entitled to half the plant's output to feed their rival TV businesses and Samsung is building a second seventh-generation plant by itself. Keiji Nakazawa, the Sony-appointed chief finance officer of S-LCD, said the two companies would decide in the future whether to build more facilities together. . . .

The joint-venture with Samsung marks a first foray into LCD manufacturing for Sony. The Japanese company has fallen behind Sharp in the flat screen TV market and needed a reliable source of LCDs to catch up. In the first quarter of this year, Sharp made 26.5 per cent of global LCD TV sales, while Samsung and Sony each commanded 11.9 per cent, followed by Philips, LG and Toshiba.

Key Points in the Article

This article discusses the joint venture between Sony and Samsung to build a new plant to manufacture liquid crystal displays (LCDs) for flat-screen television sets. The joint venture will be known as "S-LCD." Sony, which manufacturers both television sets and computers that use LCDs, had previously purchased the LCDs it needed from other firms. Sony and Samsung expect output will expand as consumers and firms switch from televisions and computer monitors that use bulky cathode-ray tubes to thinner models that use LCDs. The plant will be a "seventh-generation" facility that will produce larger glass panels. Because it will be possible to cut more screens from each panel, costs will be lower than in existing plants.

Analyzing the News

a We can use the idea of long-run average cost from this chapter to analyze this article. We have seen that firms can use the concepts that underlie the long-run average cost curve to plan for future expansion. In this case, Sony and Samsung expect that they will be able to sell a larger output of flat-screen, LCD televisions and computer monitors as consumers and businesses switch away from bulky cathode-ray tube technology. In the new "seventh-generation" facility, the firms will be able to produce larger glass panels from which more television and computer screens can be cut. This change will reduce their average cost of production.

b Figure 1 shows the effects of the new technology used in the seventh-generation LCD plant. $LRAC_1$ is the long-run average cost curve for plants that use sixth-generation technology. ATC_1 is the optimal size plant using this technology. $LRAC_2$ is the long-run average cost curve for plants that use seventh-generation technology. ATC_2 is the optimal size plant using this technology. Notice that the average cost of producing LCDs is lower when the firm produces Q_3 in a seventh-generation plant (ATC_2) than when it produces Q_1 in a sixth-generation plant (ATC_1). Also notice, though, that if the demand for LCD panels results in output of less than Q_2 screens per month, a sixth-generation plant will actually allow production at lower average cost. Sony and Samsung expect that output will exceed Q_2, so they can lower their average cost of production by building a seventh-generation plant.

Thinking Critically

1. The figure below shows the $LRAC$ curves for sixth- and seventh-generation factories. What is an eighth-generation factory's $LRAC$ likely to look like? Explain.
2. The educational systems of South Korea and Japan are geared toward training in math, science, and engineering. For example, 5 percent of bachelor's degrees in the United States are in engineering, while this figure is 27 percent in South Korea and 19 percent in Japan. How are increases in these countries' engineering skills likely to affect the $LRAC$ of producing LCD screens?

Source: Andrew Ward, "It's 'Win-Win' as Samsung, Sony Join on Flat Screens," *Financial Times*, July 16, 2004. Used with permission of Financial Times.

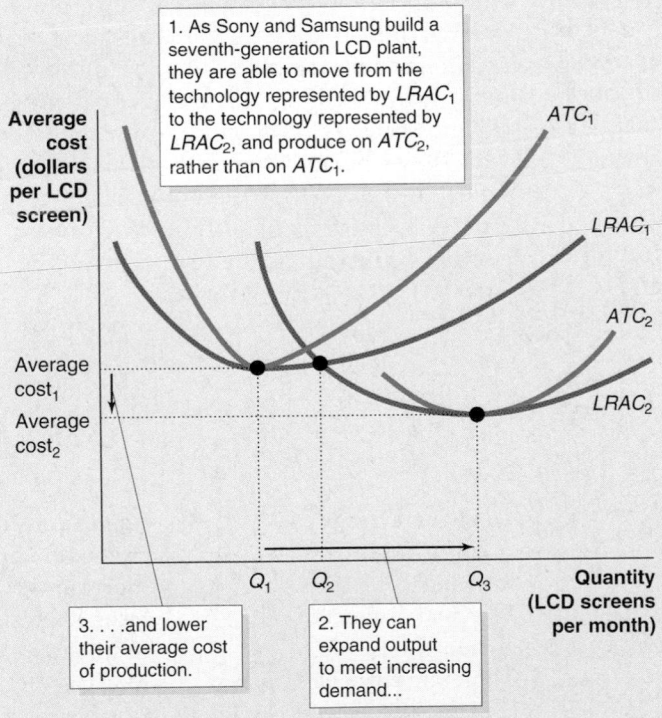

Figure 1: Seventh-generation LCD factories have lower average costs than sixth-generation factories.

LEARNING OBJECTIVE ① Define technology and give examples of technological change. The basic activity of a firm is to use inputs, such as workers, machines, and natural resources, to produce goods and services. The firm's *technology* is the processes it uses to turn inputs into goods and services.

LEARNING OBJECTIVE ② Distinguish between the economic short run and the economic long run. In the *short run,* the firm's technology and the size of its factory, store, or office are fixed. In the *long run,* the firm is able to adopt new technology and to increase or decrease the size of its physical plant. The relationship between the inputs employed by the firm and the maximum output it can produce with those inputs is called the firm's *production function.*

LEARNING OBJECTIVE ③ Understand the relationship between the marginal product of labor and the average product of labor. The *marginal product of labor* is the additional output produced by a firm as a result of hiring one more worker. Specialization and division of labor cause the marginal product of labor to rise for the first few workers hired. Eventually, the *law of diminishing returns* causes the marginal product of labor to decline. The *average product of labor* is the total amount of output produced by a firm divided by the quantity of workers hired. When the marginal product of labor is greater than the average product of labor, the average product of labor increases. When the marginal product of labor is less than the average product of labor, the average product of labor decreases.

LEARNING OBJECTIVE ④ Explain and illustrate the relationship between marginal cost and average total cost.

The *marginal cost* of production is the increase in total cost resulting from producing another unit of output. The marginal cost curve has a U-shape, because when the marginal product of labor is rising, the marginal cost of output will be falling. When the marginal product of labor is falling, the marginal cost of output will be rising. When marginal cost is less than average total cost, average total cost falls. When marginal cost is greater than average total cost, average total cost rises.

LEARNING OBJECTIVE ⑤ Graph average total cost, average variable cost, average fixed cost, and marginal cost. *Variable costs* are costs that change when the firm's level of output changes. *Fixed costs* are costs that remain constant when the firm's level of output changes. *Average total cost* is equal to total cost divided by the level of output. Average fixed cost is equal to fixed cost divided by the level of output. Average variable cost is equal to variable cost divided by the level of output. Figure 10-5 shows the relationship among marginal cost, average total cost, average variable cost, and average fixed cost. It is one of the most important graphs in microeconomics.

LEARNING OBJECTIVE ⑥ Understand how firms use the long-run average cost curve to plan. The *long-run average cost curve* shows the lowest cost at which a firm is able to produce a given level of output in the long run. For many firms, the long-run average cost curve falls as output expands because of *economies of scale.* After economies of scale have been exhausted, firms experience *constant returns to scale,* where their long-run average cost curve is flat. At high levels of output, the long-run average cost curve will turn up as the firm experiences *diseconomies of scale.*

Average fixed cost 326
Average product of
  labor 320
Average total cost 318
Average variable cost 326
Constant returns to
  scale 328
Diseconomies of scale 329

Economies of scale 327
Explicit cost 316
Fixed costs 315
Implicit cost 316
Law of diminishing
  returns 320
Long run 315

Long-run average cost
  curve 327
Marginal cost 323
Marginal product of
  labor 319
Minimum efficient
  scale 328

Opportunity cost 316
Production function 317
Short run 315
Technological change 314
Technology 314
Total cost 315
Variable costs 315

REVIEW QUESTIONS

1. What is the difference between technology and technological change? Is it possible for technological change to be negative? If so, give an example.

2. What is the difference between the short run and the long run? Is the amount of time that separates the short run from the long run the same for every firm?

3. What are implicit costs? How are they different from explicit costs?

4. Draw a graph showing the usual relationship between the marginal product of labor and the average product of labor. Why do the marginal product of labor and the average product of labor have the shapes you drew?

5. What is the law of diminishing returns? Does it apply in the long run?

6. Is a firm likely to stop hiring if the marginal product of the last worker hired is greater than the marginal product of the next-to-last worker hired? Explain.

7. Explain why the marginal cost curve intersects the average variable cost curve at the level of output where average variable cost is at a minimum.

8. What is the difference between total cost and variable cost in the long run?

9. What is minimum efficient scale? What is likely to happen in the long run to firms that do not reach minimum efficient scale?

10. What are economies of scale? What are diseconomies of scale? What is the main reason that firms eventually encounter diseconomies of scale as they keep increasing the size of their store or factory?

PROBLEMS AND APPLICATIONS

Please visit **www.prenhall.com/hubbard** *for solutions to the even-numbered problems as well as multiple-choice and true or false self-assessment quizzes.*

1. Which of the following are examples of a firm experiencing positive technological change?
   a. The firm is able to cut each worker's wage rate by 10 percent and still produce the same level of output.
   b. A training program makes the firm's workers more productive.
   c. An exercise program makes the firm's workers more healthy and productive.
   d. The firm cuts its workforce and is able to maintain its initial level of output.
   e. The firm rearranges the layout of its factory and finds that by using its initial set of inputs it can produce exactly as much as before.

2. Fill in the missing values in the following table:

QUANTITY OF WORKERS	TOTAL OUTPUT	MARGINAL PRODUCT OF LABOR	AVERAGE PRODUCT OF LABOR
0	0		
1	400		
2	900		
3	1,500		
4	1,900		
5	2,200		
6	2,400		
7	2,300		

3. Use the numbers from problem 2 to draw one graph showing how total output increases with the quantity of workers hired and a second graph showing the marginal product of labor and the average product of labor.

4. Suppose the total cost of producing 10,000 tennis balls is $30,000 and the fixed cost is $10,000.
   a. What is the variable cost?
   b. When output is 10,000, what are the average variable cost and the average fixed cost?
   c. Assuming that the cost curves have the usual shape, is the dollar difference between the average total cost and the average variable cost greater when the output is 10,000 tennis balls or when the output is 30,000 tennis balls? Explain.

5. A student looks at the data in Table 10-3 and draws this conclusion: "The marginal product of labor is increasing for the first 3 workers hired, then it declines for the next 3 workers. I guess each of the first 3 workers must have been hard workers. Then Jill must have had to settle for increasingly poor workers." Do you agree with the student's analysis? Briefly explain.

6. Sally looks at her college transcript and says to Sam, "How is this possible? My grade point average for this semester's courses is higher than my grade point average for last semester's courses, but my cumulative grade point average still went down from last semester to this semester." Explain to Sally how this is possible.

7. Is it possible for a firm to experience a technological change that would increase the marginal product of labor while leaving the average product of labor unchanged? Explain.

8. Jill Johnson operates her copy business in a building she owns in the center of the city. Similar buildings in the neighborhood rent for $4,000 per month. Jill is considering selling her building and renting space in the suburbs for $3,000 per month. Jill decides not to make the move. She reasons, "I would like to have a store in the suburbs, but I pay no rent for my store now and I don't want to see my costs rise by $3,000 per month." What do you think of Jill's reasoning?

9. When the DuPont chemical company first attempted to enter the paint business, it was not successful. According to a company report, in one year it "lost nearly $500,000 in actual cash in addition to an expected return on investment of nearly $500,000, which made a total loss of income to the company of nearly a million." Why did this report include as part of the company's loss the amount it had expected to earn—but didn't—on its investment in manufacturing paint?

   Source: Alfred D. Chandler Jr., Thomas K. McCraw, and Richard Tedlow, *Management Past and Present*, Cincinnati: South-Western, 2000, pp. 3–92.

10. An account of Benjamin Franklin's life notes that he started his career as a printer and publisher of the newspaper the *Pennsylvania Gazette*. He also opened a store where he sold stationery, books, and food. According to this account, "He could without expense apprise the public of items on hand by advertisements in his *Gazette*." Is the author correct that Franklin did not incur a cost when he used space in his newspaper to run advertisements for his store? Briefly explain.

    Source: Richard Tedlow, "Benjamin Franklin and the Definition of American Values," in Alfred D. Chandler Jr., Thomas K. McCaw, and Richard S. Tedlow, *Management Past and Present: A Casebook on the History of American Business*, Cincinnati: South-Western College Publishing, 2000.

11. **[Related to *Solved Problem 10-1*]** Is Jill Johnson right or wrong when she says the following: "Currently, I am producing 20,000 copies per day at a total cost of $750.00. If I produce 20,001 copies my total cost will rise to $750.02, therefore my marginal cost of producing copies must be increasing." Illustrate your answer with a graph.

12. One description of the costs of operating a railroad makes the following observation: "The fixed . . . expenses which attach to the operation of railroads . . . are in the nature of a tax upon the business of the road; the smaller the [amount of] business, the larger the tax." Briefly explain why fixed costs are like a tax. In what sense is this tax smaller when the amount of business is larger?

    Source: Quoted in Alfred D. Chandler, Jr., Thomas K. McCraw, and Richard Tedlow, *Management Past and Present*, Cincinnati: South-Western, 2000, pp. 2–27.

13. In the ancient world, a book could be produced either on a scroll or as a codex, which was made of folded sheets glued together, something like a modern book. One scholar has estimated the following variable costs (in Greek drachmas) of the two methods:

	SCROLL	CODEX
Cost of writing (wage of a scribe)	11.33 drachmas	11.33 drachmas
Cost of paper	16.50 drachmas	9.25 drachmas

    Another scholar points out that a significant fixed cost was involved in producing a codex:

    > In order to copy a codex . . . the amount of text and the layout of each page had to be carefully calculated in advance to determine the exact number of sheets . . . needed. No doubt, this is more time-consuming and calls for more experimentation than the production of a scroll would. But for the next copy these calculations would be used again.

    a. Suppose that the fixed cost of preparing a codex was 58 drachmas and that there was no similar fixed cost for a scroll. Would an ancient book publisher who intended to sell 5 copies of a book be likely to publish it as a scroll or as a codex? What if he intended to sell 10 copies? Briefly explain.

    b. Although most books were published as scrolls in the first century A.D., by the third century most were published as codices. Considering only the factors mentioned in this problem, explain why this changeover may have taken place.

    Sources: T. C. Skeat, "The Length of the Standard Papyrus Roll and the Cost-Advantage of the Codex," *Zeitschrift fur Papyrologie and Epigraphik*, 1982, p. 175; and David Trobisch, *The First Edition of the New Testament*, New York: Oxford University Press, 2000, p. 73.

14. **[Related to *Solved Problem 10-2*]** Suppose that Jill Johnson has to choose between building a smaller store or a larger store. In the following graph, the relationship between costs and output for the smaller store is represented by the curve ATC_1 and the relationship between costs and output for the larger store is represented by the curve ATC_2.

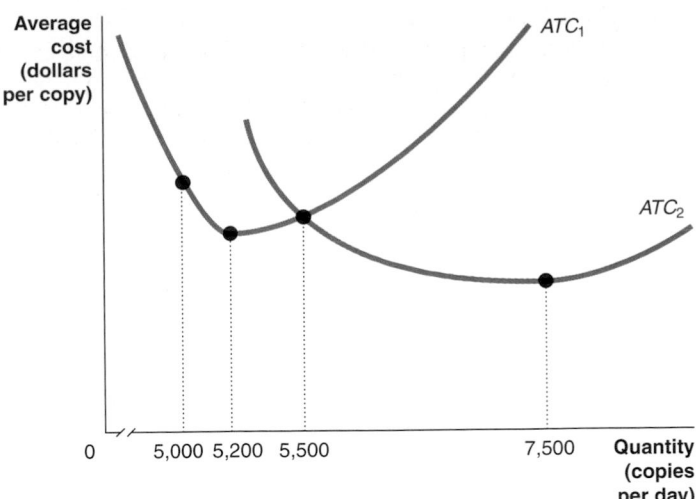

a. If Jill expects to produce 5,100 copies per day, should she build a smaller store or a larger store? Briefly explain.

b. If Jill expects to produce 6,000 copies per day, should she build a smaller store or a larger store? Briefly explain.

c. A student asks, "If the average cost of producing copies is lower in the larger store when Jill produces 7,500 copies per day, why isn't it also lower when Jill produces 5,200 copies per day?" Give a brief answer to the student's question.

15. [Related to **Solved Problem 10-1**] Use the information in the following graph to find the values for the following at an output level of 1,000:
   a. Marginal cost
   b. Total cost
   c. Variable cost
   d. Fixed cost

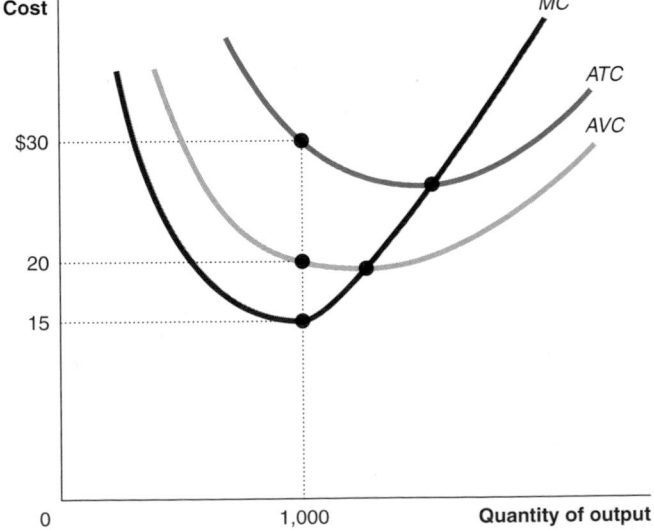

16. List the errors in the following graph. Carefully explain why the curves drawn this way are wrong. In other words, why can't these curves be as they are shown in the graph?

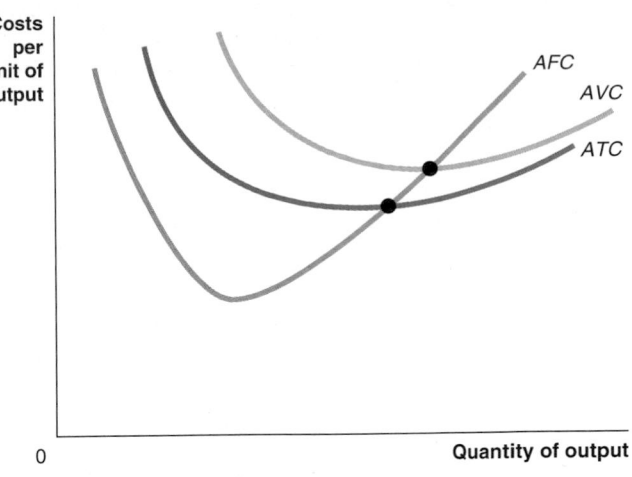

17. [Related to **Solved Problem 10-1**] Explain how the listed events (a–d) would affect the following at the Ford Motor Company:
   i. marginal cost
   ii. average variable cost
   iii. average fixed cost
   iv. average total cost
   a. Ford signs a new contract with the United Automobile Workers Union that requires the company to pay higher wages.
   b. The federal government starts to levy a $1,500 per vehicle tax on sport utility vehicles.
   c. The company decides to give its senior executives a one-time $100,000 bonus.
   d. Ford decides to increase the amount it spends on designing new car models.

18. [Related to **Solved Problem 10-2**] Suppose that Henry Ford had continued to experience increasing returns to scale no matter how large an automobile factory he built. Discuss what the implications of this would have been for the automobile industry.

19. [Related to **Solved Problem 10-2**] Read the following description of U.S. manufacturing in the late nineteenth century:

> [W]hen . . . Standard Oil . . . reorganized its refinery capacity in 1883 and concentrated almost two-fifths of the nation's refinery production in three huge refineries, the unit cost dropped from 1.5 cents a gallon to 0.5 cents. A comparable concentration of two-fifths of the nation's output of textiles or shoes in three plants would have been impossible, and in any

case would have brought huge diseconomies of scale and consequently higher prices.

   a. Use this information to draw a long-run average cost curve for an oil-refining firm and a long-run average cost curve for a firm manufacturing shoes.

   b. Is it likely that there were more oil refineries in the United States in the late nineteenth century or more shoe factories? Briefly explain.

   c. Why would concentrating two-fifths of total shoe output in three factories have led to higher shoe prices?

Source: Alfred D. Chandler Jr., Thomas K. McCraw, and Richard Tedlow, *Management Past and Present*, Cincinnati: South-Western, 2000, pp. 4–53.

20. One scholar has made the following comment on the publishing industry:

   If publishers were able to determine exactly what sells a book, they all would feature fewer titles and produce them in larger numbers.

What must be true about the costs of publishing books for this statement to be correct? Briefly explain.

Source: David Trobisch, *The First Edition of the New Testament*, New York: Oxford University Press, 2000, p. 75.

21. **[Related to *Don't Let This Happen To You!*]** Explain whether you agree or disagree with the following statement: "Henry Ford expected to be able to produce cars at a lower average cost at his River Rouge plant. Unfortunately, because of diminishing returns, his costs were actually higher."

22. **[Related to the *Chapter Opener*]** Review the discussion at the beginning of the chapter of Akio Morita selling transistor radios in the United States. Suppose that Morita became convinced that Sony would be able to sell more than 75,000 transistor radios each year in the United States. What steps would he have taken?

23. TIAA-CREF is a retirement system for people who work at colleges and universities. For some years, TIAA-CREF also sold long-term care insurance before deciding to sell that business to MetLife, a large insurance company. TIAA-CREF's chairman and chief executive officer explained the decision this way (a "premium" is the price a buyer has to pay for an insurance policy):

   In recent years, the long-term care insurance market has experienced significant consolidation. A few large insurance companies now own most of the business. MetLife has 428,000 policies, for example—nearly 10 times the number we have—and can achieve economies of scale that we can't. Over time, we would have had difficulty holding down premium rates.

Briefly explain what economies of scale have to do with the premiums that insurance companies can charge for their policies.

Source: "Long-Term Care Sale in Best Interest of Policyholders," *Advance*, Spring 2004, p. 6.

24. **[Related to *Solved Problem 10-2*]** The company eToys sold toys on the Internet. In 1999, the total value of the company was about $7.7 billion, but by early 2001 the company was in deep financial trouble and it eventually closed. One of the company's key mistakes was the decision in 2000 to build a large distribution center from which it would ship toys throughout the United States. The following description of this decision appeared in an article in the *Wall Street Journal*:

   [eToys built] a giant automated distribution center in Virginia. . . . Although many analysts agreed that the costly move was a sound decision for the long run . . . [the] decision meant eToys needed to generate much higher sales to justify its costs. . . . Despite a spiffy TV ad campaign and an expanded line of goods, there weren't enough customers.

What does the author mean that eToys "needed to generate much higher sales to justify its costs"? Use a graph like Figure 10-6 to illustrate your answer.

Source: Lisa Bannon, "The eToys Saga: Costs Kept Rising but Sales Slowed," *Wall Street Journal*, January 22, 2001.

25. **[Related to *Solved Problem 10-2*]** In 2003, Time Warner and the Walt Disney Company discussed merging their news operations. Time Warner owns the Cable News Network (CNN) and Disney owns ABC News. After analyzing the situation, the companies decided that a combined news operation would have higher average costs than either CNN or ABC News had separately. Use a long-run average cost curve graph to illustrate why the companies did not merge their news operations.

Source: Martin Peers and Joe Flint, "AOL Calls Off CNN–ABC Deal, Seeing Operating Difficulties," *Wall Street Journal*, February 14, 2003.

26. According to one account of the problems DuPont had in entering the paint business, "the du Ponts had assumed that large volume would bring profits through lowering unit costs." In fact, according to one company report, "The more paint and varnish we sold, the more money we lost." Draw an average cost curve graph showing the relationship between paint output and average cost as DuPont expected it to be. Draw another graph that would explain the result that the more paint the company sold, the more money it lost.

Source: Alfred D. Chandler Jr., Thomas K. McCraw, and Richard Tedlow, *Management Past and Present*, Cincinnati: South-Western, 2000, pp. 3–88.

27. According to a study of chicken processing plants by the U.S. Department of Agriculture, the largest plants have average costs that are 20 percent lower than the smallest plants. The report concludes, "These cost differentials are

consistent with the near-disappearance of small plants." Briefly explain the reasoning behind this conclusion.

Source: Michael Ollinger, James MacDonald, and Milton Madison, "Structural Change in U.S. Chicken and Turkey Slaughter," Economic Research Service, U.S. Department of Agriculture, Agricultural Economic Report No. 787.

28. Michael Korda was for many years editor-in-chief at the Simon & Schuster book publishing company. He has described how during the 1980s many publishing companies merged together to form larger firms. He claims that publishers hoped to take advantage of economies of scale. But, he concludes, "sheer size did not make publishing necessarily more profitable, and most of these big publishing monoliths would continue to disappoint their corporate owners in terms of earnings." On the basis of this information, draw a long-run average cost curve for a publishing firm reflecting the economies of scale that were expected to result from the mergers. Draw another long-run average cost curve reflecting the actual results experienced by the new larger publishing firms.

Source: Michael Korda, *Making the List: A Cultural History of the American Bestseller, 1900–1999*, New York: Barnes & Noble Books, 2001, p. 166.

29. **[Related to *Solved Problem 10-1*]** The following problem is somewhat more advanced. Using symbols, we can write that the marginal product of labor is equal to $\Delta Q/\Delta L$. Marginal cost is equal to $\Delta TC/\Delta Q$. Because fixed costs by definition don't change, marginal cost is also equal to $\Delta VC/\Delta Q$. If Jill Johnson's only variable cost is labor cost, then her variable cost is just the wage times the quantity of workers hired, or wL.

a. If the wage Jill pays is constant, then what is ΔVC in terms of w and L?

b. Use your answer to question a. and the expressions given above for the marginal product of labor and the marginal cost of output to find an expression for marginal cost, $\Delta TC/\Delta Q$, in terms of the wage, w, and the marginal product of labor, $\Delta Q/\Delta L$.

c. Use your answer to question b to determine Jill's marginal cost of producing copies if the wage is $75 per day and the marginal product of labor is 15. If the wage falls to $60 per day, while the marginal product of labor is unchanged, what happens to Jill's marginal cost? If the wage is unchanged at $75 per day and the marginal product rises to 25, what happens to Jill's marginal cost?

Using Isoquants and Isocosts to Understand Production and Cost

Isoquants

In this chapter, we studied the important relationship between a firm's level of production and its costs. In this appendix, we will look more closely at how firms choose the combination of inputs to produce a given level of output. Firms usually have a choice of how they will produce their output. For example, Jill Johnson is able to produce 5,000 photocopies per day using 10 workers and 2 machines, or using 6 workers and 3 machines. We will see that firms search for the *cost-minimizing* combination of inputs that will allow them to produce a given level of output. The cost-minimizing combination of inputs will depend on two factors: technology—which determines how much output a firm receives from employing a given quantity of inputs—and input prices—which determine the total cost of each combination of inputs.

An Isoquant Graph

We begin by graphing the levels of output that Jill can produce using different combinations of two inputs: labor—the quantity of workers she hires per day—and capital—the quantity of machines she rents per day. In reality, of course, Jill uses more than just these two inputs to produce photocopies, but nothing important would change if we expanded the discussion to include many inputs, instead of just two. Figure 10A-1 measures capital along the vertical axis and labor along the horizontal axis. The curves in the graph are **isoquants,** which show all the combinations of two inputs, in this case capital and labor, that will produce the same level of output.

The isoquant labeled $Q = 5,000$ shows all the combinations of workers and machines that enable Jill to produce that quantity of photocopies per day. For example, at point *A*, she produces 5,000 copies using 6 workers and 3 machines, and at point *B* she produces the same output using 10 workers and 2 machines. With more workers and machines, she can move to a higher isoquant. For example, with 12 workers and 4 machines she can produce at point *C* on the isoquant $Q = 10,000$. With even more workers and machines, she could move to the isoquant $Q = 13,000$. The higher the isoquant is—that is, the further to the upper right on the graph—the more output the firm produces. Although we have shown only three isoquants in this graph, in fact, there are an infinite number of isoquants—one for every level of output.

The Slope of an Isoquant

Remember that the slope of a curve is the ratio of the change in the variable on the vertical axis to the change in the variable on the horizontal axis. Along an isoquant the slope tells us the rate at which a firm is able to substitute one input for another, while keeping the level of output constant. The slope of an isoquant is called the **marginal rate of technical substitution (***MRTS***).**

We expect that the *MRTS* will change as we move down an isoquant. In Figure 10A-1, at a point like *A* on isoquant $Q = 5,000$, the isoquant is relatively steep. As we move down the curve, it becomes less steep at a point like *B*. This shape is the usual one for

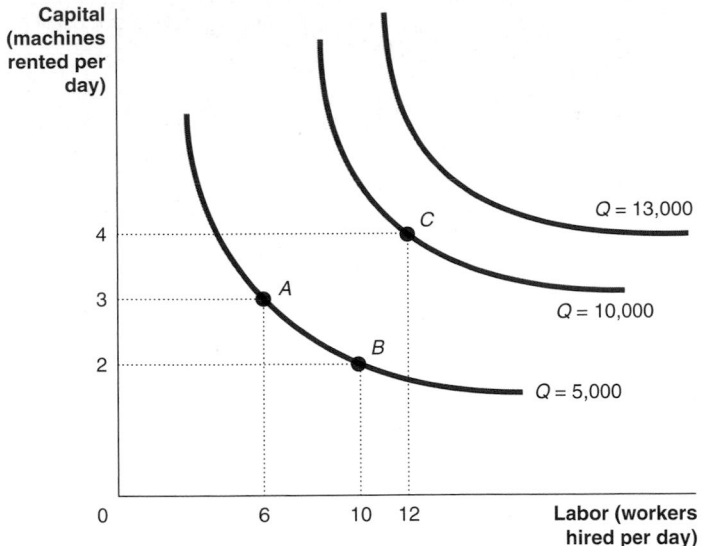

FIGURE 10A-1

Isoquants

Isoquants show all the combinations of two inputs, in this case capital and labor, that will produce the same level of output. For example, the isoquant labeled $Q = 5,000$ shows all the combinations of machines and workers that enable Jill to produce that quantity of photocopies per day. At point A, she produces 5,000 copies using 3 machines and 6 workers, and at point B she produces the same output using 2 machines and 10 workers. With more machines and workers, she can move to a higher isoquant. For example, with 4 machines and 12 workers she can produce at point C on the isoquant $Q = 10,000$. With even more machines and workers, she could move to the isoquant $Q = 13,000$.

isoquants: They are bowed in or convex. The reason isoquants have this shape is that as we move down the curve we continue to substitute labor for capital. As the firm produces the same quantity of output using less capital, the additional labor it needs increases because of diminishing returns. Remember from the chapter that, as a consequence of diminishing returns, for a given decline in capital, increasing amounts of labor are necessary to produce the same level of output. Because the *MRTS* is equal to the change in capital divided by the change in labor, it will become smaller (in absolute value) as we move down an isoquant.

Isoquant A curve showing all the combinations of two inputs, such as capital and labor, that will produce the same level of output.

Marginal rate of technical substitution (*MRTS*) The slope of an isoquant; represents the rate at which a firm is able to substitute one input for another, while keeping the level of output constant.

Isocost Lines

Any firm wants to produce a given quantity of output at the lowest possible cost. We can show the relationship between the quantity of inputs used and the firm's total cost using an *isocost* line. An **isocost line** shows all the combinations of two inputs, such as capital and labor, that have the same total cost.

Isocost line All the combinations of two inputs, such as capital and labor, that have the same total cost.

Graphing the Isocost Line

Suppose Jill has $600 per day to spend on capital and labor. The table in Figure 10A-2 shows the combinations of capital and labor available to her if the rental price of machines is $100 per day and the wage rate is $50 per day. The graph uses the data in the table to construct an isocost line. The isocost line intersects the vertical axis at the maximum number of machines Jill can rent per day, which is shown by point *A*. The line intersects the horizontal axis at the maximum number of workers Jill can hire per day, which is point *G*. As Jill moves down the isocost line from point *A*, she gives up renting 1 machine for every 2 workers she hires. Any combination of inputs along the line or inside the line can be purchased with $600. Any combination that lies outside the line cannot be purchased, because it would have a total cost to Jill of more than $600.

The Slope and Position of the Isocost Line

The slope of the isocost line is constant, and equals the change in the quantity of machines divided by the change in the quantity of workers. In this case, in moving from any point on the isocost line to any other point, the change in the quantity of machines

FIGURE 10A-2

An Isocost Line

The isocost line shows the combinations of inputs with a total cost of $600. The rental price of machines is $100 per day, so if Jill spends the whole $600 on machines she can rent 6 machines (point A). The wage rate is $50 per day, so if Jill spends the whole $600 on workers, she can hire 12 workers. As she moves down the isocost line, she gives up renting 1 machine for every 2 workers she hires. Any combinations of inputs along the line or inside the line can be purchased with $600. Any combinations that lie outside the line cannot be purchased with $600.

Point	Machines	Workers	Total Cost	
A	6	0	(6 x $100) + (0 x $50)	= $600
B	5	2	(5 x $100) + (2 x $50)	= 600
C	4	4	(4 x $100) + (4 x $50)	= 600
D	3	6	(3 x $100) + (6 x $50)	= 600
E	2	8	(2 x $100) + (8 x $50)	= 600
F	1	10	(1 x $100) + (10 x $50)	= 600
G	0	12	(0 x $100) + (12 x $50)	= 600

Combinations of Workers and Machines with a Total Cost of $600

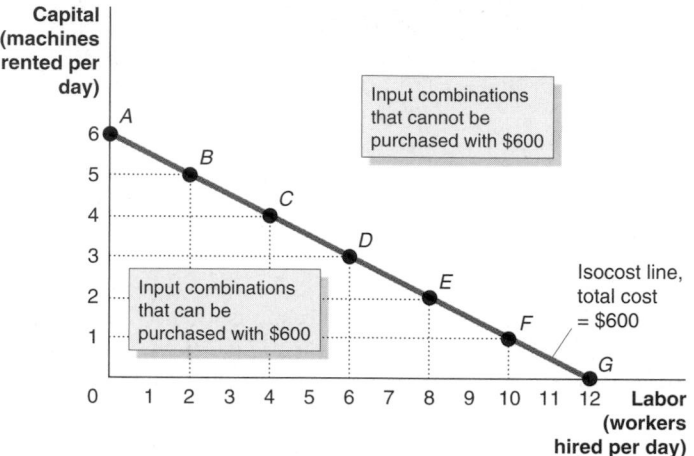

equals −1 and the change in the quantity of workers equals 2, so the slope equals −1/2. Notice that with a rental price of machines of $100 per day and a wage rate for labor of $50 per day, the slope of the isocost line is equal to the ratio of the wage rate divided by the rental price of capital, multiplied by negative 1: −$50/$100 = −1/2. In fact, this result will always hold, whatever inputs are involved and whatever their prices may be: *The slope of the isocost line is equal to the ratio of the price of the input on the horizontal axis divided by the price of the input on the vertical axis, multiplied by negative 1.*

The position of the isocost line depends on the level of total cost. Higher levels of total cost shift the isocost line outward, and lower levels of total cost shift the isocost line inward. This can be seen in Figure 10A-3, which shows isocost lines for total costs of $300, $600, and $900. We have shown only three isocost lines in the graph, but there are in fact an infinite number of isocost lines—one for every level of total cost.

Choosing the Cost-Minimizing Combination of Capital and Labor

Suppose Jill wants to produce 5,000 photocopies per day. Figure 10A-1 showed that there are many combinations of machines and workers that will allow her to produce this level of output. There is only one combination of machines and workers, however, that will allow her to produce 5,000 photocopies *at the lowest total cost.* Figure 10A-4 shows the isoquant Q = 5,000 along with three isocost lines. Point B is the lowest-cost combination of inputs shown in the graph, but this combination of 1 machine and 4 workers will produce less than the 5,000 photocopies needed. Points C and D are combinations of machines and workers that will produce 5,000 copies, but their total cost is $900. The combination of 3 machines and 6 workers at point A produces 5,000 photocopies at the lowest total cost of $600.

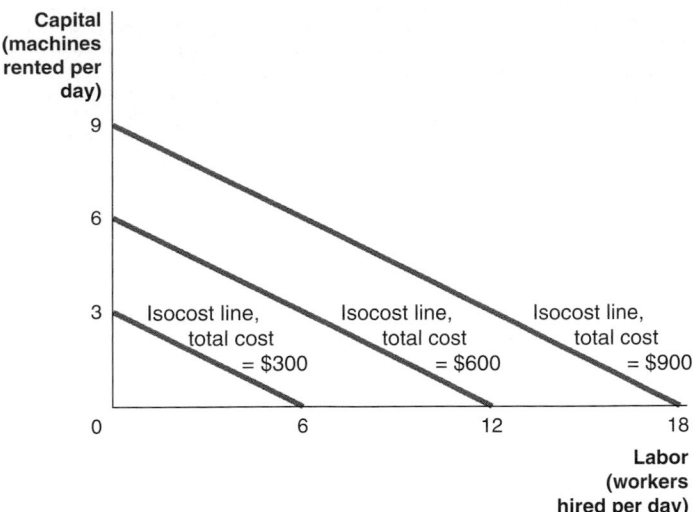

FIGURE 10A-3

The Position of the Isocost Line

The position of the isocost line depends on the level of total cost. As total cost increases from $300 to $600 to $900 per day, the isocost line shifts outward. For each isocost line shown, the rental price of machines is $100 per day, and the wage rate is $50 per day.

The graph shows that moving to an isocost line with a total cost of less than $600 would mean producing less than 5,000 photocopies. Being at any point along the isoquant $Q = 5{,}000$ other than point A would increase total cost above $600. In fact, the combination of inputs at point A is the only one on isoquant $Q = 5{,}000$ that has a total cost of $600. All other input combinations on this isoquant have higher total costs. Notice also that at point A the isoquant and the isocost lines are tangent, so the slope of the isoquant is equal to the slope of the isocost line at that point.

Different Input Price Ratios Lead to Different Input Choices

Jill's cost-minimizing choice of 3 machines and 6 workers is determined jointly by the technology available to her—as represented by her firm's isoquants—and by input prices—as represented by her firm's isocost lines. If the technology of making photocopies changes, perhaps because new photocopy machines are developed, her isoquants will be affected and her choice of inputs may change. If her isoquants remain unchanged but input prices change, then her choice of inputs may also change. This fact can explain why firms in different countries that face different input prices may produce

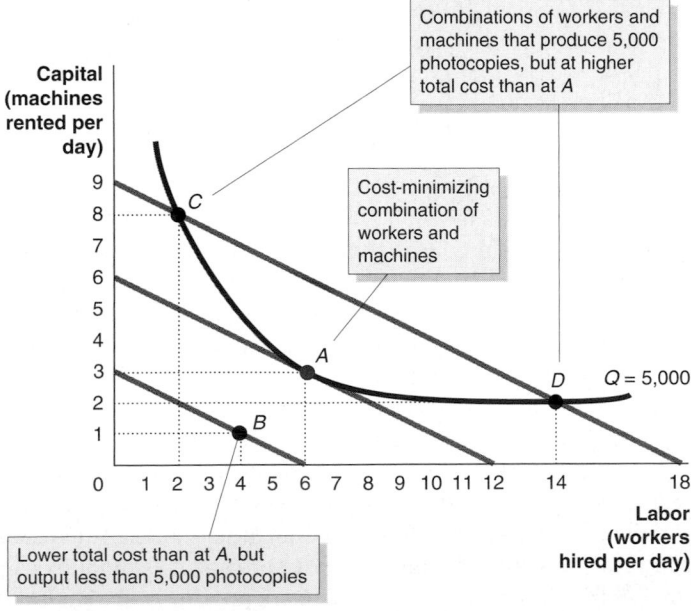

FIGURE 10A-4

Choosing Capital and Labor to Minimize Total Cost

Jill wants to produce 5,000 photocopies per day at the lowest total cost. Point B is the lowest-cost combination of inputs shown in the graph, but this combination of 1 machine and 4 workers will produce less than the 5,000 photocopies needed. Points C and D are combinations of machines and workers that will produce 5,000 copies, but their total cost is $900. The combination of 3 machines and 6 workers at point A produces 5,000 photocopies at the lowest total cost of $600.

FIGURE 10A-5

Changing Input Prices Affects the Cost-Minimizing Input Choice

As the graph shows, the input combination at point *A*, which was optimal for Jill, is not optimal for a businessperson in China. Using the input combination at point *A* would cost businesspeople in China more than $600. Instead, the Chinese isocost line is tangent to the isoquant at point *B*, where the input combination is 2 machines and 10 workers. Because machinery costs more in China, but workers cost less, a Chinese firm will use fewer machines and more workers than a U.S. firm, even if it has the same technology as the U.S. firm.

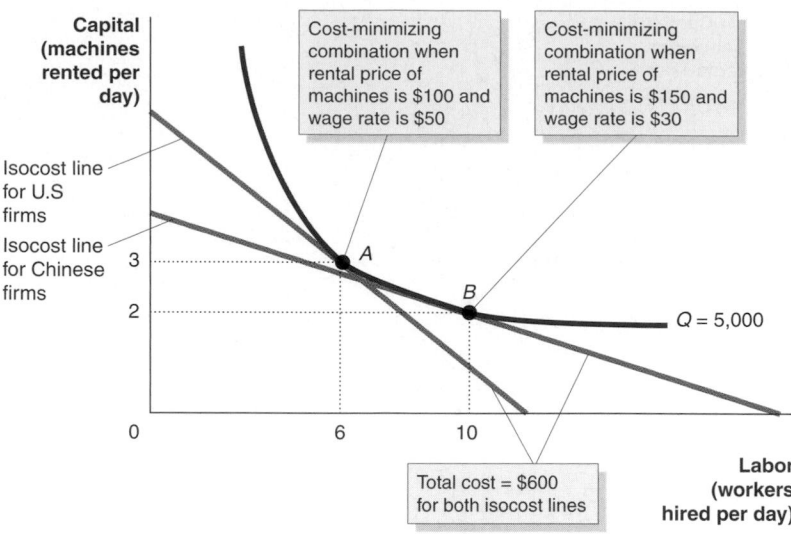

the same good using different combinations of capital and labor, even though they have the same technology available.

For example, suppose that in China machines are higher-priced and labor is lower-priced than in the United States. In our example, Jill Johnson pays $100 per day to rent photocopy machines, and $50 per day to hire workers. Suppose a businessperson in China must pay a price of $150 per day to rent the identical photocopy machines, but, can hire Chinese workers, who are as productive as U.S. workers, at a wage of $30 per day. Figure 10A-5 shows how the cost-minimizing input combination for the businessperson in China differs from Jill's.

Remember that the slope of the isocost line equals the wage rate divided by the rental price of capital, multiplied by negative one. The slope of the isocost line faced by Jill and other U.S. firms is −$50/$100, or −1/2. Firms in China, however, face an isocost line with a slope of −$30/$150, or −1/5. As the graph shows, the input combination at point *A*, which was optimal for Jill, is not optimal for a firm in China. Using the input combination at point *A* would cost a firm in China more than $600. Instead, the Chinese isocost line is tangent to the isoquant at point *B*, where the input combination is 2 machines and 10 workers. This result makes sense: Because machinery costs more in China, but workers cost less, a Chinese firm will use fewer machines and more workers than a U.S. firm, even if it has the same technology as the U.S. firm.

10A-1 *Making the Connection*

The Changing Input Mix in Walt Disney Film Animation

The inputs used to make feature-length animated films have changed dramatically in the past 15 years. Prior to the early 1990s, the Walt Disney Company dominated the market for animated films. Disney's films were produced using hundreds of animators drawing most of the film by hand. Each film would contain as many as 170,000 individual drawings. Then, two developments dramatically affected how animated films are produced. First, in 1994 Disney had a huge hit with *The Lion King*, which cost only $50 million, but earned the company more than $1 billion in profit. As a result of this success, Disney and other film studios began to produce more animated films, increasing the demand for animators, and more than doubling their salaries. The second development came in 1995 when Pixar Animation Studios released the film *Toy Story*. This was the first successful feature-length film produced using computers, with no hand-drawn animation. In the following years, technological advance continued to reduce the cost of the computers and software necessary to produce an animated film.

As a result of these two developments, the price of capital—computers and software—fell relative to the price of labor—animators. As the figure shows, the change in the price of computers relative to animators changed the slope of the isocost line and resulted in film studios now producing animated films using many more computers and many fewer animators than in the early 1990s.

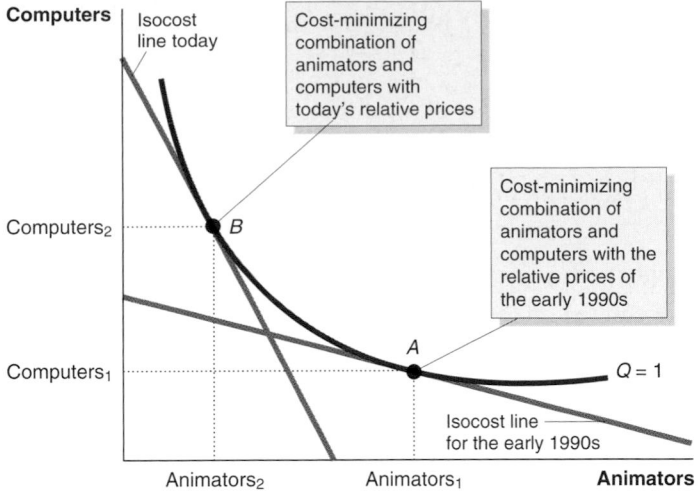

Film studios produce animated films like Toy Story *by using many more computers and many fewer animators than they did in the early 1990s.*

Source: Bruce Orwall, "Disney Delivers 'Lilo and Stitch' on Competition-Driven Budget," *Wall Street Journal,* June 18, 2002, p. A1.

Another Look at Cost Minimization

In Chapter 9, we saw that consumers maximize utility when they consume each good up to the point where the marginal utility per dollar spent is the same for every good. We can derive a very similar cost-minimization rule for firms. Remember that at the point of cost minimization the isoquant and the isocost line are tangent, so they have the same slope. Therefore, *at the point of cost minimization, the marginal rate of technical substitution* (MRTS) *is equal to the wage rate divided by the rental price of capital.*

The slope of the isoquant tells us the rate at which a firm is able to substitute labor for capital, *given existing technology.* The slope of the isocost line tells us the rate at which a firm is able to substitute labor for capital, *given current input prices.* Only at the point of cost minimization are these two rates the same.

When we move from one point on an isoquant to another, we end up using more of one input and less of the other input, but the level of output remains the same. For example, as Jill moves down an isoquant, she uses fewer machines and more workers, but produces the same quantity of photocopies. In this chapter we defined the *marginal product of labor* (MP_L) as the additional output produced by a firm as a result of hiring one more worker. Similarly, we can define the *marginal product of capital* (MP_K) as the additional output produced by a firm as a result of using one more machine. So, when Jill uses fewer machines by moving down an isoquant, she loses output equal to:

   −Change in the quantity of machines x MP_K.

But she uses more workers, so she gains output equal to:

   Change in the quantity of workers x MP_L.

We know that the gain in output from the additional workers is equal to the loss from the smaller quantity of machines because total output remains the same along an isoquant. Therefore we can write:

   − Change in the quantity of machines x MP_K = Change in the quantity of workers x MP_L.

Loss in output from using fewer machines

Gain in output from using more workers

If we rearrange terms, we have the following:

$$\frac{-\text{Change in the quantity of machines}}{\text{Change in the quantity of workers}} = \frac{MP_L}{MP_K}.$$

Because the

$$\frac{-\text{Change in the quantity of machines}}{\text{Change in the quantity of workers}}$$

is the slope of the isoquant, or the marginal rate of technical substitution (*MRTS*), we can write:

$$\frac{-\text{Change in the quantity of machines}}{\text{Change in the quantity of workers}} = MRTS = \frac{MP_L}{MP_K}.$$

The slope of the isocost line equals the wage rate (w) divided by the rental price of capital (r). At the point of cost minimization, the slope of the isoquant is equal to the slope of the isocost line. Therefore,

$$\frac{MP_L}{MP_K} = \frac{w}{r}.$$

We can rewrite this to show that at the point of cost minimization:

$$\frac{MP_L}{w} = \frac{MP_K}{r}.$$

This last expression tells us that to minimize cost, a firm should hire inputs up to the point where the last dollar spent on each input results in the same increase in output. If this equality did not hold, a firm could lower its costs by using more of one input and less of the other. For example, if the left-hand side of the equation were greater than the right-hand side, a firm could rent fewer machines, hire more workers, and produce the same output at lower cost.

SOLVED PROBLEM   **10A-1**

Determining the Optimal Combination of Inputs

Consider the information in the following table for Jill Johnson's copy store:

Marginal product of capital	3,000 copies
Marginal product of labor	100 copies
Wage rate	$50 per day
Rental price of machines	$600 per day

Briefly explain whether Jill is minimizing costs. If she is not minimizing costs, explain whether she should rent more machines and hire fewer workers, or rent fewer machines and hire more workers.

Solving the Problem:
Step 1: Review the chapter material. This problem is about determining the optimal choice of inputs by comparing the ratios of the marginal products of inputs to their prices, so you may want to review the section "Another Look at Cost Minimization," which begins on page 347.

Step 2: Compute the ratios of marginal product to input price to determine whether Jill is minimizing costs. If Jill is minimizing costs, then the following relationship should hold:

$$\frac{MP_L}{w} = \frac{MP_K}{r}.$$

In this case, we have:

$$MP_L = 100$$
$$MP_K = 3,000$$
$$w = \$50$$
$$r = \$600.$$

So,

$$\frac{MP_L}{w} = \frac{100}{\$50} = 2 \text{ copies per dollar, and } \frac{MP_K}{r} = \frac{3,000}{\$600} = 5 \text{ copies per dollar.}$$

Because the two ratios are not equal, Jill is not minimizing cost.

Step 3: Determine how Jill should change the mix of inputs she uses. Jill produces more copies per dollar from the last machine than from the last worker. This indicates that she has too many workers and too few machines. Therefore, to minimize cost, Jill should rent more machines and hire fewer workers.

YOUR TURN: For more practice, do problem 3 on page 351 at the end of this appendix. Visit www.prenhall.com/hubbard for an interactive exercise related to this Solved Problem.

The Expansion Path

We can use isoquants and isocost lines to examine what happens as a firm expands its level of output. Figure 10A-6 shows three isoquants for a firm producing bookcases. The isocost lines are drawn assuming that the rental price of machines is $100 per day and the wage rate is $25 per day. The point where each isoquant is tangent to an isocost line determines the cost-minimizing combination of capital and labor for producing that level of output. For example, 10 machines and 40 workers is the cost-minimizing combination of inputs for producing 50 bookcases per day. The cost-minimizing points *A, B,* and *C* lie along the firm's **expansion path,** which is a curve showing the cost-minimizing combination of inputs for every level of output.

> **Expansion path** A curve showing a firm's cost-minimizing combination of inputs for every level of output.

An important point to note is that the expansion path represents the least-cost combination of inputs to produce a given level of output *in the long run,* when the firm is able to vary the levels of all of its inputs. We know, though, that in the short run, at least one input is fixed. We can use Figure 10A-6 to show that as the firm expands in the short run, its costs will be higher than in the long run. For example, suppose that the firm is currently at point *B,* using 15 machines and 60 workers to produce 75 bookcases per day. The firm wants to expand its output to 100 bookcases per day, but in the short run it is unable to increase the quantity of machines it uses. Therefore, to expand output, it must hire more workers. The figure shows that in the short run, to produce 100 bookcases per day using 15 machines, the lowest costs it can attain are at point *D,* where it employs 110 workers. With a rental price of machines of $100 per day and a wage rate of $25 per day, in the short run the firm will have total costs of $4,250 to produce 100 bookcases per day. In the long run, though, the firm can increase the number of machines it uses from 15 to 20, and reduce the number of workers from 110 to 80. This change allows it

FIGURE 10A-6

The Expansion Path

The tangency points *A, B,* and *C* lie along the firm's expansion path, which is a curve showing the cost-minimizing combination of inputs for every level of output. In the short run, when the quantity of machines is fixed, the firm can expand output from 75 bookcases per day to 100 bookcases per day at the lowest cost only by moving from point *B* to point *D,* and increasing the number of workers from 80 to 110. In the long run, when it can increase the quantity of machines it uses, the firm can move from point *D* to point *C,* thereby reducing its total costs of producing 100 bookcases per day from $4,250 to $4,000.

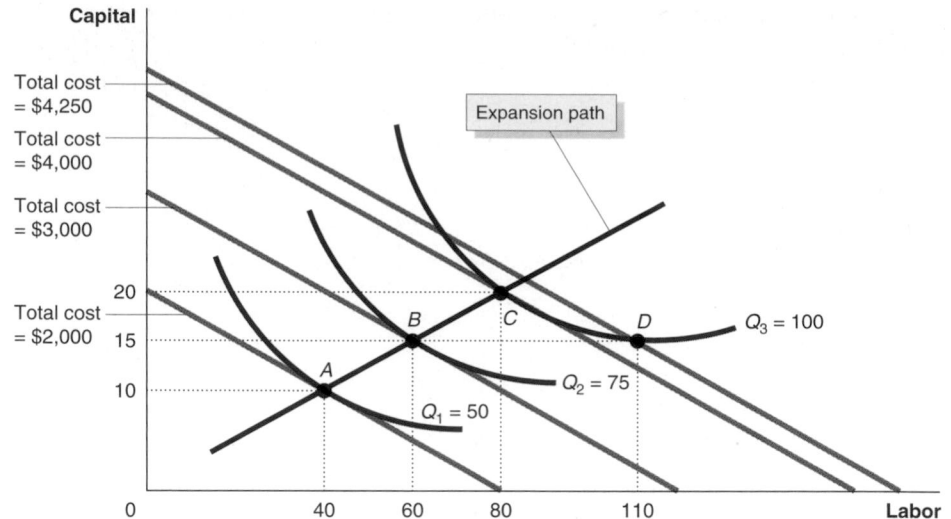

to move from point *D* to point *C* on its expansion path, and to lower its total costs of producing 100 bookcases per day from $4,250 to $4,000. The firm's minimum total costs of production are lower in the long run than in the short run.

KEY TERMS

Expansion path   349   Isoquant   343   Marginal rate of technical
Isocost line   343   substitution (*MRTS*)   343

PROBLEMS AND APPLICATIONS

Please visit **www.prenhall.com/hubbard** *for solutions to the even-numbered problems as well as multiple-choice and true or false self-assessment quizzes.*

1. Draw an isoquant–isocost line graph to illustrate the following situation: Jill Johnson can rent photocopy machines for $200 per day and hire workers for $100 per day. She is currently using 5 machines and 10 workers to produce 20,000 copies per day and has total costs of $2,000. Make sure to label your graph showing the cost-minimizing input combination and the maximum quantity of labor and capital she can use with total costs of $2,000.

2. Use the following graph to answer the questions:
   a. If the wage rate and the rental price of machines are both $100 and total cost is $2,000, then is the cost-minimizing point *A, B,* or *C?* Briefly explain.
   b. If the wage rate is $25 and the rental price of machines is $100, then is the cost-minimizing point *A, B,* or *C?* Briefly explain.
   c. If the wage rate and the rental price of machines are both $100 and total cost is $4,000, then is the cost-minimizing point *A, B,* or *C?* Briefly explain.

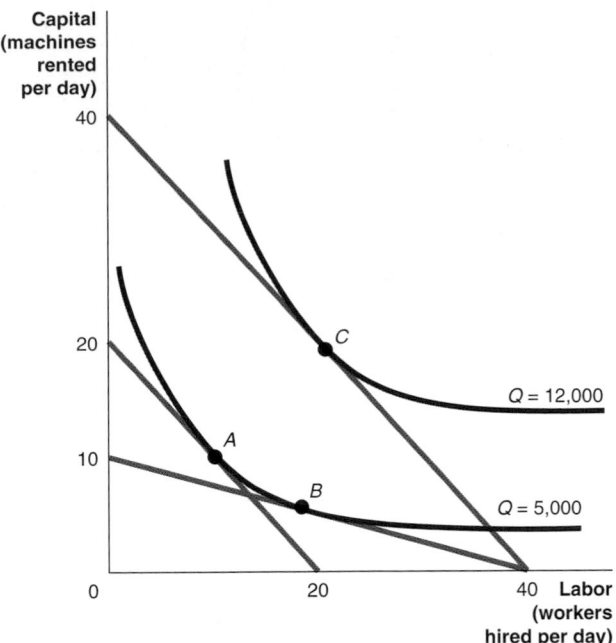

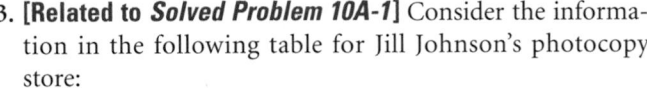

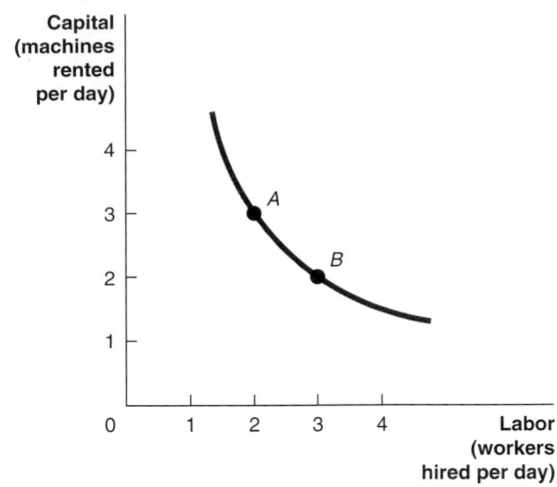

3. **[Related to Solved Problem 10A-1]** Consider the information in the following table for Jill Johnson's photocopy store:

Marginal product of capital	4,000
Marginal product of labor	100
Wage rate	$10
Rental price of machines	$500

Briefly explain whether Jill is minimizing costs. If she is not minimizing costs, explain whether she should rent more machines and hire fewer workers, or rent fewer machines and hire more workers.

4. Draw an isoquant–isocost line graph to illustrate the following situation and the change that occurs: Jill Johnson can rent photocopy machines for $200 per day and hire workers for $100 per day. Currently, she is using 5 machines and 10 workers to produce 20,000 copies per day and has total costs of $2,000. Then Jill reorganizes the way things are done in her business and achieves positive technological change.

5. Use the following graph to answer these questions about Jill Johnson's isoquant curve:
   a. Which combination of inputs yields more output: combination A (3 machines and 2 workers) or combination B (2 machines and 3 workers)?
   b. What will determine whether Jill selects A, B, or some other point along this isoquant curve?
   c. Is the marginal rate of technical substitution (MRTS) greater at point A or point B?

6. Draw an isoquant–isocost line graph to illustrate the following situation: Jill Johnson can rent photocopy machines for $200 per day and hire workers for $100 per day. She can minimize the cost of producing 20,000 copies per day by using 5 machines and 10 workers at a total cost of $2,000. She can minimize the cost of producing 45,000 copies per day by using 10 machines and 20 workers at a total cost of $4,000. And, she can minimize the cost of producing 60,000 copies per day by using 15 machines and 30 workers at a total cost of $6,000. Now draw Jill's long-run average cost curve and discuss the economies and diseconomies of scale that it possesses.

7. Draw an isoquant–isocost line graph to illustrate the following situation: Jill Johnson can rent photocopy machines for $200 per day and hire workers for $100 per day. Currently, she is using 5 machines and 10 workers to produce 20,000 copies per day and has total costs of $2,000. Jill's marginal rate of technical substitution (MRTS) equals −1. Explain why this means that she's not minimizing costs and what she could do to minimize costs.

8. In Brazil, a grove of oranges is picked using 20 workers, ladders, and baskets. In Florida a grove of oranges is picked using 1 worker and a machine that shakes the oranges off the trees and scoops up the fallen oranges. Using an isoquant–isocost line graph, illustrate why these two different methods are used to pick the same number of oranges per day in these two locations.

9. Jill Johnson is minimizing the costs of producing copies. The cost of one of her machines is $20 per day and the wage rate is $60 per day. The marginal product of capital in her business is 2,000 copies. What must be the marginal product of her workers?

chapter

eleven

Firms in Perfectly Competitive Markets

Perfect Competition in the Market for Organic Apples

➤ The market for organically grown food has expanded rapidly in the United States. As recently as 15 years ago, organic food was sold primarily in small health food stores. Today, organic food makes up an increasing fraction of all the food sold in supermarkets. By 2001, more than two-thirds of U.S. consumers were buying at least some organic food, and 12 percent of consumers were buying organic food almost exclusively. In 2002, the U.S. Department of Agriculture (USDA) established standards for organic food labeling. The standards were intended to protect consumers from false and misleading claims and to make it easier for U.S. farmers to export to foreign countries whose governments also require organic

food labeling. According to the USDA, a firm can label and advertise food as "organic" only if that food is "produced without using most conventional pesticides; fertilizers made with synthetic ingredients or sewage sludge; bioengineering; or ionizing radiation." The USDA inspects the farm where the food is grown and all firms that handle the food before it arrives at the supermarket or restaurant.

More organic fresh fruits and vegetables are sold than any other food category. Organically grown apples became popular with consumers during the late 1990s. Farmers growing apples organically use only organic fertilizers and control insects with sprays made from soil compounds. These growing

methods add about 15 percent to the cost of growing apples. The Yakima Valley of Washington State is particularly suited to growing apples organically because of the absence of certain insects. In 2004, Washington State accounted for more than half of U.S. organic apple production. In 1997, Yakima Valley apple farmers were able to sell organically grown apples for a price 50 percent higher than the price of regular apples, more than offsetting the higher costs of organic growing methods. This price difference made organically grown apples considerably more profitable than apples grown using traditional methods.

Between 1997 and 2001, many apple farmers switched from tradi-

tional to organic growing methods, increasing production of organically grown apples from 1.2 million boxes per year to more than 3 million boxes. The additional supply of organically grown apples forced down prices and made them no more profitable than apples grown using traditional methods. As one farmer in the Yakima Valley put it, "It's like anything else in agriculture. If people see an economic opportunity, usually it only lasts for a few years."

What the organic apple farmer experienced is not unique to agriculture. Throughout the economy, entrepreneurs are continually introducing new products, which—when successful—enable them to earn economic profits in the short run. But in the long run, competition

among firms forces prices to the level where they just cover the costs of production. This process of competition is at the heart of the market system and is the focus of this chapter. *An Inside Look* on page 378 discusses how the increasing demand for organic food has affected the sales of organic snacks.

Sources: USDA Web site: www.ams.usda. gov/nop/Consumers/brochure.html, "Organic Food Industry Taps Growing American Market," *Agricultural Outlook*, October 2002; Emily Green, "Study Gives Nod to Organic Apples, but It's Crunch Time for All State Growers," *Seattle Times*, April 19, 2001; quote from farmer from the NPR Web site: www.npr.org, National Public Radio, *All Things Considered*, April 18, 2001.

LEARNING OBJECTIVES

After studying this chapter, you should be able to:

① Define a perfectly competitive market, and explain why a perfect competitor faces a horizontal demand curve.

② Explain how a perfect competitor decides how much to produce.

③ Use graphs to show a firm's profit or loss.

④ Explain why firms may shut down temporarily.

⑤ Explain how entry and exit ensure that perfectly competitive firms earn zero economic profit in the long run.

⑥ Explain how perfect competition leads to economic efficiency.

➤ Organic apple growing is an example of a *perfectly competitive* industry. Firms in perfectly competitive industries are unable to control the prices of the products they sell and are unable to earn an economic profit in the long run. There are two main reasons for this result: (1) Firms in these industries sell identical products; and (2) It is easy for new firms to enter these industries. Studying how perfectly competitive industries operate is the best way to understand how markets answer the fundamental economic questions we discussed in Chapter 1:

➤ What goods and services will be produced?

➤ How will the goods and services be produced?

➤ Who will receive the goods and services produced?

In fact, though, most industries are not perfectly competitive. In most industries, firms do *not* produce identical products, and in some industries it may be difficult for new firms to enter. There are thousands of industries in the United States. Although in some ways each industry is unique, industries share enough similarities that economists group them into four market structures. In particular, any industry has three key characteristics:

➤ The number of firms in the industry

➤ The similarity of the good or service produced by the firms in the industry

➤ The ease with which new firms can enter the industry

Economists use these characteristics to classify industries into the four market structures listed in Table 11-1.

Many industries, including restaurants, hardware stores, and other retailers, have many firms selling products that are differentiated, rather than identical, and fall into the category of *monopolistic competition*. Some industries, such as computers and automobiles, have only a few firms and are *oligopolies*. Finally, a few industries, such as the delivery of first-class mail by the U.S. Postal Service, have only one firm and are *monopolies*. After discussing perfect competition in this chapter, we will devote a chapter to each of these other market structures.

T A B L E 1 1 - 1   **The Four Market Structures**

CHARACTERISTIC	MARKET STRUCTURE			
	PERFECT COMPETITION	MONOPOLISTIC COMPETITION	OLIGOPOLY	MONOPOLY
Number of firms	Many	Many	Few	One
Type of product	Identical	Differentiated	Identical or differentiated	Unique
Ease of entry	High	High	Low	Entry blocked
Examples of industries	• Wheat • Apples	• Selling DVDs • Restaurants	• Manufacturing computers • Manufacturing automobiles	• First-class mail delivery • Tap water

Perfectly Competitive Markets

Why are firms in a **perfectly competitive market** unable to control the prices of the goods they sell, and why are the owners of these firms unable to earn economic profits in the long run? We can begin our analysis by listing the three conditions that make a market perfectly competitive:

1. There must be many buyers and many firms, all of whom are small relative to the market.
2. The products sold by all firms in the market must be identical.
3. There must be no barriers to new firms entering the market.

All three of these conditions hold in the market for organic apples. No single consumer or producer of organic apples buys or sells more than a tiny fraction of the total apple crop. The apples sold by each apple grower are identical, and there are no barriers to a new firm entering the organic apple market by purchasing land and planting apple trees. As we will see, it is the existence of many firms, all selling the same good, that keeps any single organic apple farmer from affecting the price of organic apples.

Although the market for organic apples meets the conditions for perfect competition, the markets for most goods and services do not. In particular, the second and third conditions are very restrictive. In most markets that have many buyers and sellers, firms do not sell identical products. For example, not all restaurant meals are the same, nor is all women's clothing the same. In Chapter 12, we will explore the common situation of monopolistic competition where many firms are selling similar but not identical products. In Chapters 13 and 14, we will analyze industries that are oligopolies or monopolies, where it is difficult for new firms to enter. In this chapter, we concentrate on perfectly competitive markets so we can use as a benchmark the situation in which firms are facing the maximum possible competition.

A Perfectly Competitive Firm Cannot Affect the Market Price

Prices in perfectly competitive markets are determined by the interaction of demand and supply. The actions of any single consumer or any single firm have no effect on the market price. Consumers and firms have to accept the market price if they want to buy and sell in a perfectly competitive market.

Because a firm in a perfectly competitive market is very small relative to the market and because it is selling exactly the same product as every other firm, it can sell as much as it wants without having to lower its price. But if a perfectly competitive firm tries to raise its price, it won't sell anything at all, because consumers will switch to buying from the firm's competitors. Therefore, the firm will be a **price taker,** and will have to charge the same price as every other firm in the market. Although we don't usually think of firms as being too small to affect the market price, consumers are often in the position of being price takers. For instance, suppose your local supermarket is selling bread for $1.50 per loaf. You can load up your shopping cart with 10 loaves of bread and the supermarket will gladly sell them all to you for $1.50 per loaf. But if you go to the cashier and offer to buy the bread for $1.49 per loaf, he or she will not sell it to you. As a buyer, you are too small relative to the bread market to have any effect on the equilibrium price. Whether you leave the supermarket and buy no bread or you buy 10 loaves, you are unable to change the market price of bread by even one cent.

The situation you face as a bread buyer is the same one a wheat farmer faces as a wheat seller. More than 225,000 farmers grow wheat in the United States. The market price of wheat is determined not by any individual wheat farmer but by the interaction in the wheat market of all the buyers and all the sellers. If any one wheat farmer has the best crop the farmer has ever had, or if any one wheat farmer stops growing wheat altogether, the market price of wheat will not be affected *because the market supply curve for wheat will not shift by enough to change the equilibrium price by even one cent.*

① **LEARNING OBJECTIVE**
Define a perfectly competitive market, and explain why a perfect competitor faces a horizontal demand curve.

Perfectly competitive market A market that meets the conditions of (1) many buyers and sellers, (2) all firms selling identical products, and (3) no barriers to new firms entering the market.

Price taker A buyer or seller that is unable to affect the market price.

FIGURE 11-1

A Perfectly Competitive Firm Faces a Horizontal Demand Curve

A firm in a perfectly competitive market is selling exactly the same product as many other firms. Therefore, it can sell as much as it wants at the current market price, but it cannot sell anything at all if it raises the price by even one cent. As a result, the demand curve for a perfectly competitive firm's output is a horizontal line. In the figure, whether the wheat farmer sells 3,000 bushels per year or 7,500 bushels has no effect on the market price of $4.

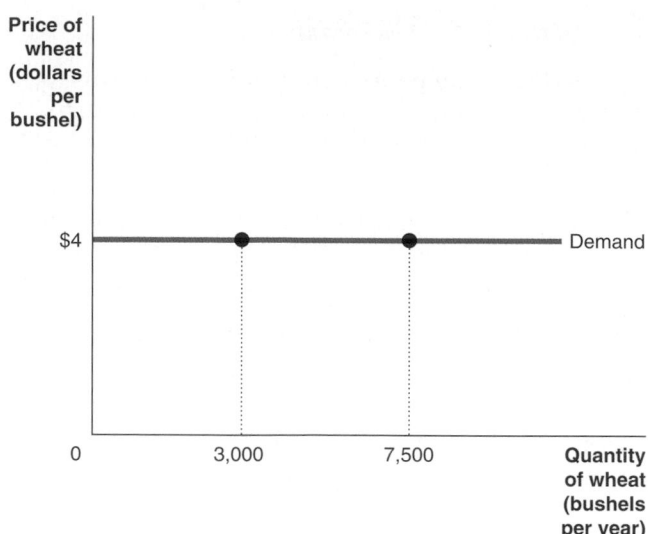

The Demand Curve for the Output of a Perfectly Competitive Firm

Suppose Robert Whaples grows wheat on a 250-acre farm in Washington State. Farmer Whaples is selling wheat in a perfectly competitive market, so he is a price taker. Because he can sell as much wheat as he chooses at the market price—but can't sell any wheat at all at a higher price—the demand curve for his wheat has an unusual shape: It is horizontal, as shown in Figure 11-1. With a horizontal demand curve, Farmer Whaples must accept the market price, which in this case is $4. Whether Farmer Whaples sells 3,000 bushels per year or 7,500 has no effect on the market price.

The demand curve for Farmer Whaples's wheat is very different from the market demand curve for wheat. Panel (a) of Figure 11-2 shows the market for wheat. The demand curve in panel (a) is the *market demand curve for wheat* and has the normal downward slope we are familiar with from the market demand curves in Chapter 3. Panel (b) of Figure 11-2 shows the demand curve for Farmer Whaples's wheat, which is a horizontal line. By viewing these graphs side by side, you can see that the price Farmer Whaples receives for his wheat in panel (b) is determined by the interaction of all sellers and all buyers of wheat in the wheat market in panel (a). Keep in mind, however, that the scales on the horizontal axes in the two panels are very different. In panel (a), the equilibrium quantity of wheat is 2 *billion* bushels. In panel (b), Farmer Whaples is producing only 7,500 bushels, or less than 0.0004 percent of market output. We need to use different scales in the two panels so we can display both of them on one page. Keep in mind the key point: Farmer Whaples's output of wheat is very small relative to the total market output.

② **LEARNING OBJECTIVE**

Explain how a perfect competitor decides how much to produce.

How a Firm Maximizes Profit in a Perfectly Competitive Market

Profit Total revenue minus total cost.

We have seen that Farmer Whaples cannot control the price of his wheat. In this situation, how does he decide how much wheat to produce? We assume that Farmer Whaples's objective is to maximize profits. This is a reasonable assumption for most firms, most of the time. Remember that **profit** is the difference between total revenue (*TR*) and total cost (*TC*):

$$\text{Profit} = TR - TC.$$

To maximize his profit, Farmer Whaples should produce the quantity of wheat where the difference between the total revenue he receives and his total cost is as large as possible.

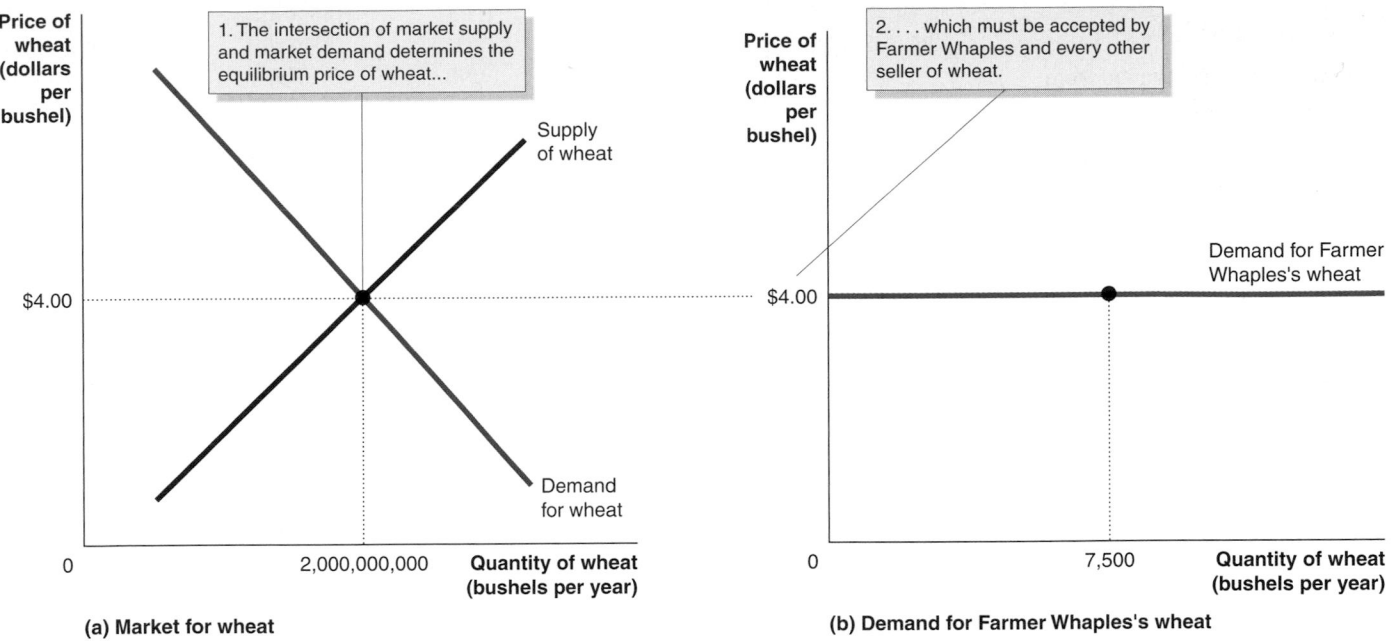

(a) Market for wheat   **(b) Demand for Farmer Whaples's wheat**

FIGURE 11-2   **The Market Demand for Wheat versus the Demand for One Farmer's Wheat**

In a perfectly competitive market, price is determined by the intersection of market demand and market supply. In panel (a), the demand and supply curves for wheat intersect at a price of $4 per bushel. An individual wheat farmer like Farmer Whaples has no ability to affect the market price for wheat. Therefore, as panel (b) shows, the demand curve for Farmer Whaples's wheat is a horizontal line. To understand this figure, it is important to notice that the scales on the horizontal axes in the two panels are very different. In panel (a), the equilibrium quantity of wheat is 2 *billion* bushels and in panel (b) Farmer Whaples is producing only 7,500 bushels of wheat.

Revenue for a Firm in a Perfectly Competitive Market

To understand how Farmer Whaples maximizes profits, let's first consider his revenue. To keep the numbers simple, we will assume that he owns a very small farm and produces at most 10 bushels of wheat per year. Table 11-2 shows the revenue Farmer Whaples will earn from selling various quantities of wheat if the market price for wheat is $4.

 *Don't Let This Happen To You!*

Don't Confuse the Demand Curve for Farmer Whaples's Wheat with the Market Demand Curve for Wheat

The demand curve for wheat has the normal downward-sloping shape. If the price of wheat goes up, the quantity of wheat demanded goes down, and if the price of wheat goes down, the quantity of wheat demanded goes up. But the demand curve for the output of a single wheat farmer is *not* downward-sloping: It is a horizontal line. If an individual wheat farmer tries to increase the price he charges for his wheat, the quantity demanded falls to zero because buyers will purchase from one of the other 225,000 wheat farmers. But any one farmer can sell as much wheat as the farmer can produce without needing to cut the price. Both of these things are true because each wheat farmer is very small relative to the overall market for wheat.

When we draw graphs of the wheat market, we usually show the market equilibrium quantity in millions or billions of bushels. When we draw graphs of the demand for wheat produced by one farmer, we usually show the quantity produced in thousands of bushels. It is important to remember this difference in scale when interpreting these graphs.

Finally, it is not just wheat farmers who have horizontal demand curves for their products; any firm in a perfectly competitive market faces a horizontal demand curve.

YOUR TURN: **Test your understanding by doing related problem 2 on page 381 at the end of this chapter.**

TABLE 11-2	NUMBER OF BUSHELS (Q)	MARKET PRICE (PER BUSHEL) (P)	TOTAL REVENUE (TR)	AVERAGE REVENUE (AR)	MARGINAL REVENUE (MR)
Farmer Whaples's Revenue from Wheat Farming	0	$4	$0	—	—
	1	4	4	$4	$4
	2	4	8	4	4
	3	4	12	4	4
	4	4	16	4	4
	5	4	20	4	4
	6	4	24	4	4
	7	4	28	4	4
	8	4	32	4	4
	9	4	36	4	4
	10	4	40	4	4

The third column in Table 11-2 shows that Farmer Whaples's *total revenue* rises by $4 for every additional bushel he sells because he can sell as many bushels as he wants at the market price of $4 per bushel. The fourth and fifth columns in the table show Farmer Whaples's *average revenue* and *marginal revenue* from selling wheat. His **average revenue (AR)** is his total revenue divided by the number of bushels he sells. For example, if he sells 5 bushels for a total of $20, his average revenue is $20/5 = $4. Notice that his average revenue is also equal to the market price of $4. In fact, for any level of output, a firm's average revenue is always equal to the market price. One way to see this is to note that total revenue equals price times quantity ($TR = P \times Q$), and average revenue equals total revenue divided by quantity ($AR = TR/Q$). So, $AR = TR/Q = (P \times Q)/Q = P$.

Average revenue (AR) Total revenue divided by the number of units sold.

Farmer Whaples's **marginal revenue (MR)** is the change in his total revenue from selling one more bushel:

Marginal revenue (MR) Change in total revenue from selling one more unit.

$$\text{Marginal Revenue} = \frac{\text{Change in total revenue}}{\text{Change in quantity}}, \text{ or } MR = \frac{\Delta TR}{\Delta Q}.$$

Because for each additional bushel sold he always adds $4 to his total revenue, his marginal revenue is $4. This outcome occurs because Farmer Whaples is selling wheat in a perfectly competitive market and can sell as much as he wants at the market price. In fact, Farmer Whaples's marginal revenue and average revenue are both equal to the market price. This is an important point: *For a firm in a perfectly competitive market, price is equal to both average revenue and marginal revenue.*

Determining the Profit-Maximizing Level of Output

To determine how Farmer Whaples can maximize profit, we have to consider his costs as well as his revenue. A wheat farmer will have many costs, including seed, fertilizer, and the wages of farm workers. In Table 11-3, we bring together the revenue data from Table 11-1 with cost data for Farmer Whaples's farm. Recall from Chapter 10 that a firm's *marginal cost* is the increase in total cost resulting from producing another unit of output.

Profit is shown in the fourth column and is calculated by subtracting total cost in the third column from total revenue in the second column. The fourth column shows that as long as Farmer Whaples produces between 2 and 9 bushels of wheat, he will earn a profit. His maximum profit is $9.00, which he will earn by producing 6 bushels of wheat. Producing more than 6 bushels reduces his profit. For example, if he produces

QUANTITY (BUSHELS) (Q)	TOTAL REVENUE (TR)	TOTAL COST (TC)	PROFIT (TR − TC)	MARGINAL REVENUE (MR)	MARGINAL COST (MC)
0	$0.00	$1.00	−$1.00	—	—
1	4.00	4.00	0.00	$4.00	$3.00
2	8.00	6.00	2.00	4.00	2.00
3	12.00	7.50	4.50	4.00	1.50
4	16.00	9.50	6.50	4.00	2.00
5	20.00	12.00	8.00	4.00	2.50
6	24.00	15.00	9.00	4.00	3.00
7	28.00	19.50	8.50	4.00	4.50
8	32.00	25.50	6.50	4.00	6.00
9	36.00	32.50	3.50	4.00	7.00
10	40.00	40.50	−0.50	4.00	8.00

TABLE 11-3

Farmer Whaples's Profits from Wheat Farming

7 bushels of wheat, his profit will decline from $9.00 to $8.50. The values for marginal cost given in the last column of the table help us understand why Farmer Whaples's profits will decline if he produces more than 6 bushels of wheat. After the sixth bushel of wheat, rising marginal cost causes Farmer Whaples's profits to fall.

In fact, we can use the values for marginal cost and marginal revenue given in the table to calculate Farmer Whaples's profits using a different method than comparing total cost and total revenue. To help compare the two methods of calculating profits, we illustrate one in panel (a) and one in panel (b) of Figure 11-3. Panel (a) shows Farmer Whaples's total revenue, total cost, and profit. Total revenue is a straight line on the graph because it increases at a constant rate of $4 for each additional bushel sold. Farmer Whaples's profits are maximized when the vertical distance between the line representing total revenue and the total cost curve is as large as possible. Just as we saw in Table 11-3, this occurs at an output of 6 bushels.

The last two columns of Table 11-3 provide information on the marginal revenue (MR) Farmer Whaples receives from selling another bushel of wheat and his marginal cost (MC) of producing another bushel of wheat. Panel (b) is a graph of Farmer Whaples's marginal revenue and marginal cost. Because marginal revenue is always equal to $4, it is a horizontal line at the market price. We have already seen that the demand curve for a perfectly competitive firm is also a horizontal line at the market price. *Therefore, the marginal revenue curve for a perfectly competitive firm is the same as its demand curve.* Farmer Whaples's marginal cost of producing wheat first falls and then rises, following the usual pattern we discussed in Chapter 10.

We know from panel (a) that profit is at a maximum at 6 bushels of wheat. In panel (b), profit is also at a maximum at 6 bushels of wheat. To understand why this result is true, remember a key economic principle that we discussed in Chapter 1: *Optimal decisions are made at the margin.* Firms use this principle to decide the quantity to produce. In deciding how much to produce, Farmer Whaples needs to compare the marginal revenue he earns from selling another bushel of wheat to the marginal cost of producing that bushel. The difference between the marginal revenue and the marginal cost is the additional profit (or loss) from producing one more bushel. As long as marginal revenue is greater than marginal cost, Farmer Whaples's profits are increasing and he will want to expand production. For example, he will not stop producing at 5 bushels of wheat because producing and selling the sixth bushel adds $4 to his revenue, but only $3 to his cost, so his profit increases by $1. He wants to continue producing until the marginal revenue he receives from selling another bushel is equal to the marginal cost of producing it. At that

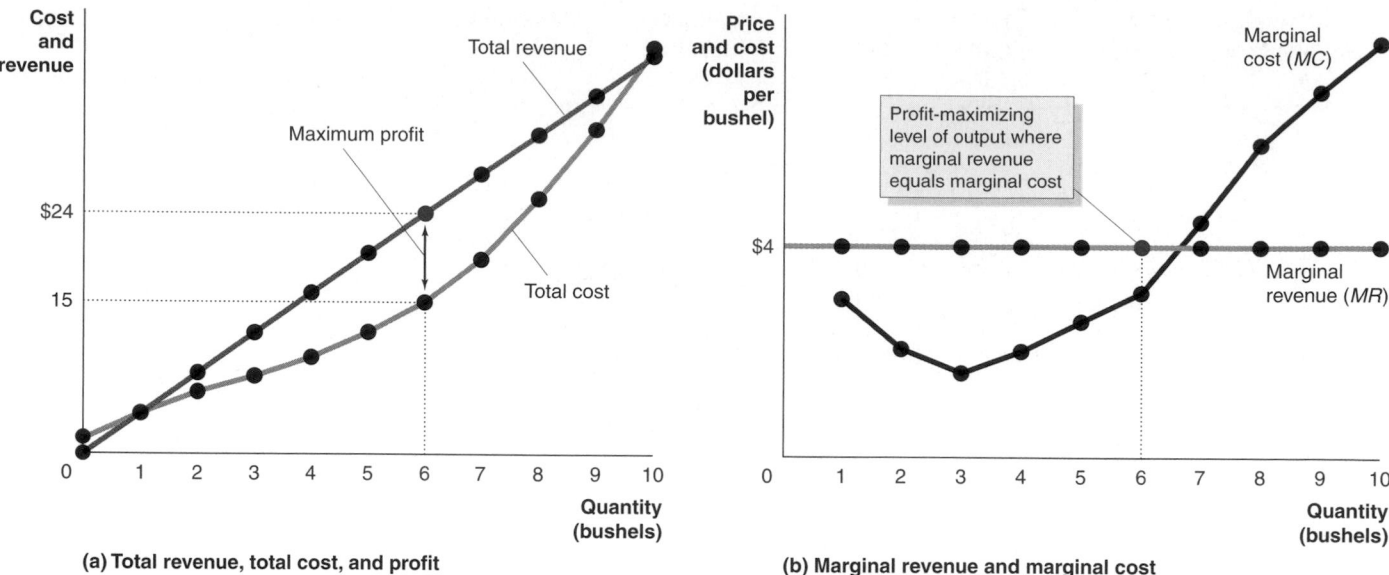

FIGURE 11-3   **The Profit-Maximizing Level of Output**

In panel (a), Farmer Whaples maximizes his profit where the vertical distance between total revenue and total cost is the largest. This happens at an output of 6 bushels. Panel (b) shows that Farmer Whaples's marginal revenue (*MR*) is equal to a constant $4 per bushel. Farmer Whaples maximizes profits by producing wheat up to the point where the marginal revenue of the last bushel produced is equal to its marginal cost, or *MR = MC*. In this case, at no level of output does marginal revenue exactly equal marginal cost. The closest Farmer Whaples can come is to produce 6 bushels of wheat. He will not want to continue to produce once marginal cost is greater than marginal revenue because this will reduce his profits. Panels (a) and (b) show alternative ways of thinking about how Farmer Whaples can determine the profit-maximizing quantity of wheat to produce.

level of output, he will make no *additional* profit by selling another bushel, so he will have maximized his profits.

Inspecting the table, we can see that at no level of output does marginal revenue exactly equal marginal cost. The closest Farmer Whaples can come is to produce 6 bushels of wheat. He will not want to continue to produce once marginal cost is greater than marginal revenue because this will reduce his profits. For example, the seventh bushel of wheat adds $4.50 to his cost, but only $4.00 to his revenue, so producing the seventh bushel *reduces* his profit by $0.50.

From the information in Table 11-3 and Figure 11-3, we can draw the following conclusions:

1. The profit-maximizing level of output is where the difference between total revenue and total cost is the greatest.

2. The profit-maximizing level of output is also where marginal revenue equals marginal cost, or *MR = MC*.

Both these conclusions are true for any firm, whether or not it is in a perfectly competitive industry. We can draw one other conclusion about profit maximization that is true only of firms in perfectly competitive industries: For a firm in a perfectly competitive industry, price is equal to marginal revenue, or *P = MR*. So, we can restate the *MR = MC* condition as *P = MC*.

③ **LEARNING OBJECTIVE**

Use graphs to show a firm's profit or loss.

Illustrating Profit or Loss on the Cost Curve Graph

We have seen that profit is the difference between total revenue and total cost. We can also express profit in terms of *average total cost (ATC)*. This allows us to show profit on the cost curve graph we developed in Chapter 10.

To begin, we need to work through the several steps necessary to determine the relationship between profit and average total cost. Because profit is equal to total rev-

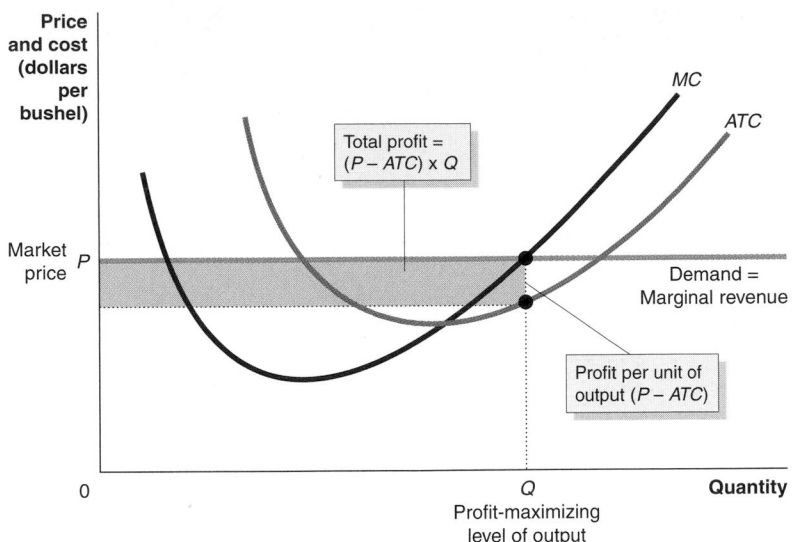

FIGURE 11-4

The Area of Maximum Profit

A firm maximizes profit at the level of output at which marginal revenue equals marginal cost. The difference between price and average total cost equals profit per unit of output. Total profit equals profit per unit multiplied by the number of units produced. Total profit is represented by the area of the green-shaded rectangle, which has a height equal to ($P - ATC$) and a width equal to Q.

enue minus total cost (TC) and total revenue is price times quantity, we can write the following:

$$\text{Profit} = (P \times Q) - TC.$$

If we divide both sides of this equation by Q we have:

$$\frac{\text{Profit}}{Q} = \frac{(P \times Q)}{Q} - \frac{TC}{Q},$$

or

$$\frac{\text{Profit}}{Q} = P - ATC,$$

because TC/Q equals ATC. This equation tells us that profit per unit (or average profit) equals price minus average total cost. Finally, we obtain the expression for the relationship between total profit and average total cost by multiplying through again by Q:

$$\text{Profit} = (P - ATC) \times Q.$$

This expression tells us that a firm's total profit is equal to the quantity produced multiplied by the difference between price and average total cost.

Showing a Profit on the Graph

Figure 11-4 shows the relationship between a firm's average cost and its marginal cost that we discussed in Chapter 10. In this figure, we also show the firm's marginal revenue curve (which is the same as its demand curve) and the area representing total profit. Using the relationship between profit and average total cost that we just determined, we can say that the area representing total profit has a height equal to ($P - ATC$) and a base equal to Q. This area is shown by the green-shaded rectangle.

SOLVED PROBLEM   11-1

Determining Profit-Maximizing Price and Quantity

Suppose that Andy sells basketballs in the perfectly competitive basketball market. His output per day and his costs are as follows:

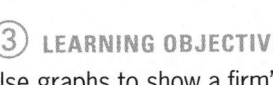
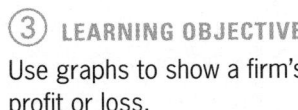

③ LEARNING OBJECTIVE

Use graphs to show a firm's profit or loss.

OUTPUT PER DAY	TOTAL COST
0	$10.00
1	15.00
2	17.50
3	22.50
4	30.00
5	40.00
6	52.50
7	67.50
8	85.00
9	105.00

a. If the current equilibrium price in the basketball market is $12.50, to maximize profits how many basketballs will Andy produce, what price will he charge, and how much profit (or loss) will he make? Draw a graph to illustrate your answer. Your graph should be labeled clearly and should include Andy's demand, *ATC*, *AVC*, *MC*, and *MR* curves, the price he is charging, the quantity he is producing, and the area representing his profit (or loss).

b. Suppose the equilibrium price of basketballs falls to $5.00. Now how many basketballs will Andy produce, what price will he charge, and how much profit (or loss) will he make? Draw a graph to illustrate this situation, using the instructions in question (a).

Solving the Problem:

Step 1: Review the chapter material. This problem is about using cost curve graphs to analyze perfectly competitive firms, so you may want to review the section "Illustrating Profit or Loss on the Cost Curve Graph," which begins on page 360.

Step 2: Calculate Andy's marginal cost, average total cost, and average variable cost. To maximize profits, Andy will produce the level of output where marginal revenue is equal to marginal cost. We can calculate marginal cost from the information given in the table. We can also calculate average total cost and average variable cost, in order to draw the required graph. Average total cost (*ATC*) equals total cost (*TC*) divided by the level of output (*Q*). Average variable cost (*AVC*) equals variable cost (*VC*) divided by output (*Q*). To calculate variable cost, recall that total cost equals variable cost plus fixed cost. When output equals zero, total cost equals fixed cost. In this case fixed cost equals $10.00.

OUTPUT PER DAY (Q)	TOTAL COST (TC)	FIXED COST (FC)	VARIABLE COST (VC)	AVERAGE TOTAL COST (ATC)	AVERAGE VARIABLE COST (AVC)	MARGINAL COST (MC)
0	$ 10.00	$10.00	$ 0.00	—	—	—
1	15.00	10.00	5.00	$15.00	$ 5.00	$ 5.00
2	17.50	10.00	7.50	8.75	3.75	2.50
3	22.50	10.00	12.50	7.50	4.17	5.00
4	30.00	10.00	20.00	7.50	5.00	7.50
5	40.00	10.00	30.00	8.00	6.00	10.00
6	52.50	10.00	42.50	8.75	7.08	12.50
7	67.50	10.00	57.50	9.64	8.21	15.00
8	85.00	10.00	75.00	10.63	9.38	17.50
9	105.00	10.00	95.00	11.67	10.56	20.00

Step 3: Use the information from the table in Step 2 to calculate how many basketballs Andy will produce, what price he will charge, and how much profit he will earn if the market price of basketballs is $12.50. Andy's marginal revenue is equal to the market price of

$12.50. Marginal revenue equals marginal cost when Andy produces 6 basketballs per day. So, Andy will produce 6 basketballs per day and charge a price of $12.50 per basketball. Andy's profits are equal to his total revenue minus his total costs. His total revenue equals the 6 basketballs he sells multiplied by the $12.50 price, or $75.00. So, his profits equal $75.00 − $52.50 = $22.50.

Step 4: Use the information from the table in Step 2 to illustrate your answer to question (a) with a graph.

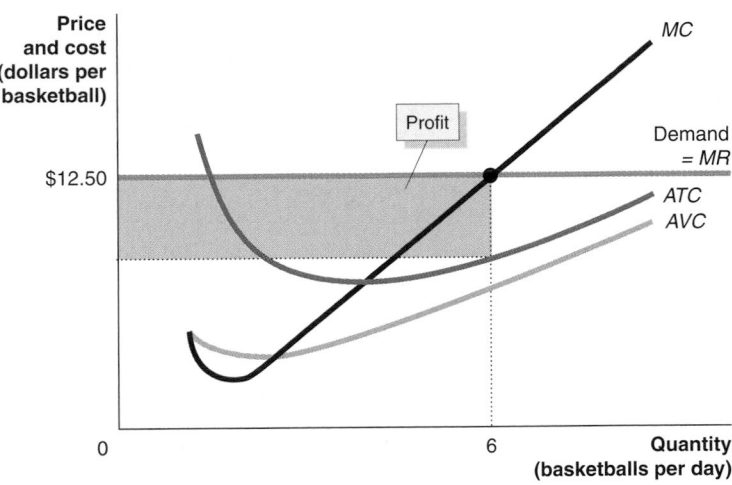

Step 5: Calculate how many basketballs Andy will produce, what price he will charge, and how much profit he will earn when the market price of basketballs is $5.00. Referring to the table in Step 2, we can see that marginal revenue equals marginal cost when Andy produces 3 basketballs per day. He charges the market price of $5.00 per basketball. His total revenue is only $15.00, while his total costs are $22.50, so he will have a loss of $7.50. (Can we be sure that Andy will continue to produce even though he is operating at a loss? We answer this question in the next section.)

Step 6: Illustrate your answer to question (b) with a graph.

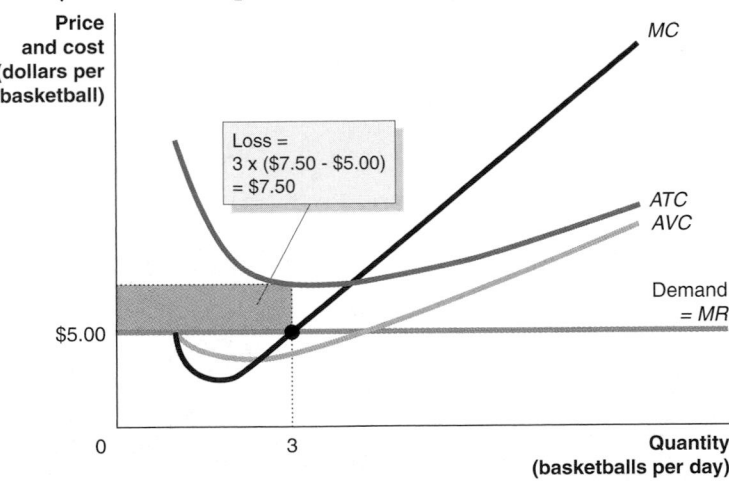

YOUR TURN: For more practice, do related problems 5 and 9 on pages 381 and 382 at the end of this chapter. Visit www.prenhall.com/hubbard for an interactive exercise related to this Solved Problem.

Illustrating When a Firm Is Breaking Even or Operating at a Loss

We have already seen that to maximize profits a firm produces the level of output where marginal revenue equals marginal cost. But will the firm actually make a profit at that

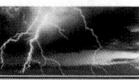

Don't Let This Happen To You!

Remember That Firms Maximize Total Profit, Not Profit per Unit

A student examines the following graph and argues, "I believe that a firm will want to produce at Q_1, not Q_2. At Q_1 the distance between price and average total cost is the greatest. Therefore, at Q_1 the firm will be maximizing its profits per unit." Briefly explain whether you agree with the student's argument.

The student's argument is incorrect because firms are interested in maximizing their *total* profits and not their profits per unit. We know that profits are not maximized at Q_1 because at that level of output marginal revenue is greater than marginal cost. A firm can always increase its profits by producing any unit that adds more to its revenue than it does to its costs. Only when the firm has expanded production to Q_2 will it have produced every unit for which marginal revenue is greater than marginal cost. At that point, it will have maximized profit.

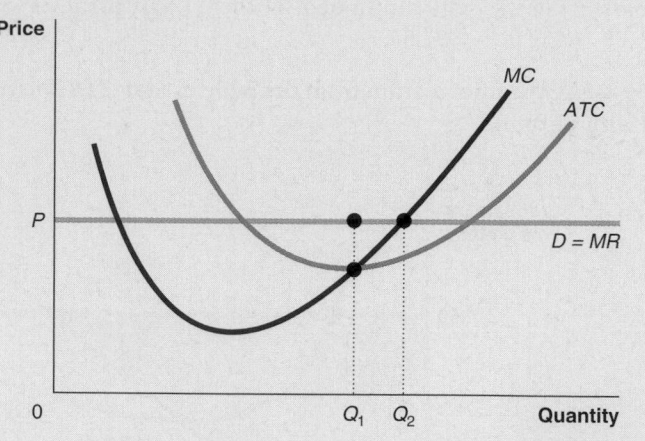

YOUR TURN: Test your understanding by doing related problem 12 on page 382 at the end of this chapter.

level of output? It depends on the relationship of price to average total cost. There are three possibilities:

1. $P > ATC$, which means the firm makes a profit.
2. $P = ATC$, which means the firm *breaks even* (its total cost equals its total revenue).
3. $P < ATC$, which means the firm experiences losses.

Figure 11-4 illustrated the first possibility, where the firm makes a profit. Panels (a) and (b) of Figure 11-5 show the situations where a firm experiences losses or breaks even.

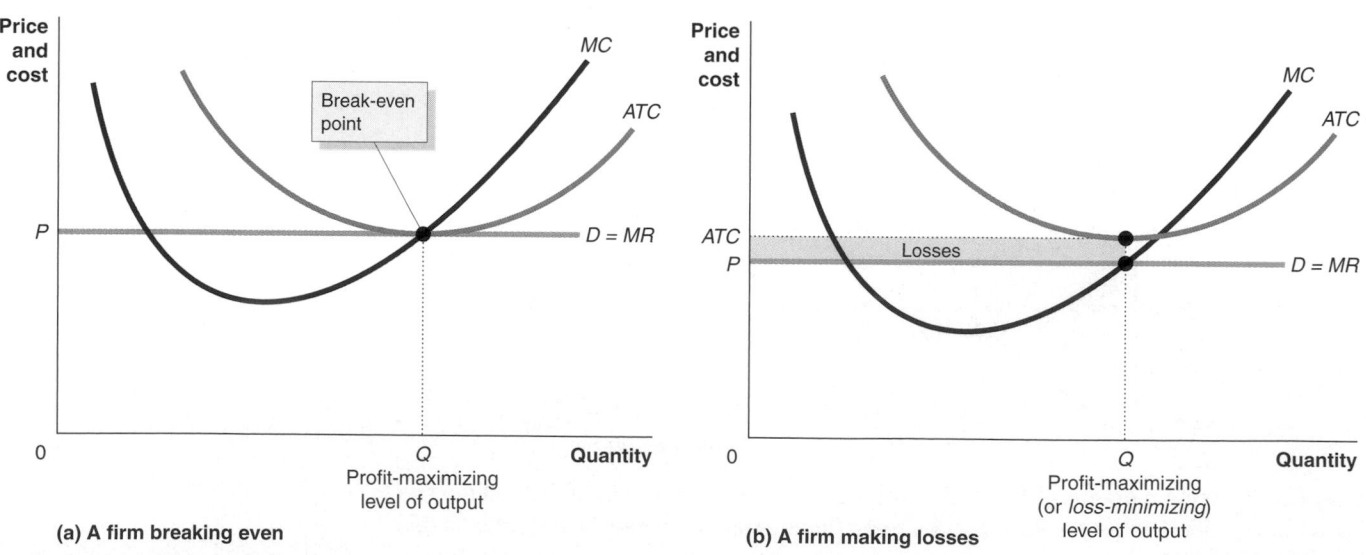

(a) A firm breaking even

(b) A firm making losses

FIGURE 11-5   **A Firm Breaking Even and a Firm Experiencing Losses**

In panel (a), price equals average total cost and the firm breaks even because its total revenue will be equal to its total cost. In this situation, the firm makes zero economic profit. In panel (b), price is below average total cost and the firm experiences a loss. The loss is represented by the area of the red-shaded rectangle, which has a height equal to ($ATC - P$) and a width equal to Q.

In panel (a) of Figure 11-5, at the level of output at which $MR = MC$, price is equal to average total cost. Therefore, total revenue is equal to total cost and the firm will break even, making zero economic profit. In panel (b), at the level of output at which $MR = MC$, price is less than average total cost. Therefore, total revenue is less than total cost and the firm has losses. In this case, maximizing profits amounts to *minimizing* losses.

Losing Money in the Medical Screening Industry

Some ideas for new products work out; others don't. In a market system, a good or service becomes available to consumers only if an entrepreneur brings the product to market. Thousands of new businesses open every week in the United States. Each new business represents an entrepreneur risking his or her funds trying to earn a profit by offering a good or service to consumers. Of course, there are no guarantees of success, and many new businesses experience losses rather than earn the profits their owners hoped for.

In the early 2000s, technological advance reduced the price of computed tomography (CT) scanning equipment. For years, doctors and hospitals have prescribed CT scans to diagnose patients showing symptoms of heart disease, cancer, and other disorders. The declining price of CT scanning equipment convinced many entrepreneurs that it would be profitable to offer preventive body scans to apparently healthy people. The idea was that the scans would provide early detection of diseases before the customers had begun experiencing symptoms. Unfortunately, the new firms offering this service ran into several difficulties: First, because the CT scan was a voluntary procedure, it was not covered under most medical insurance plans. Second, very few consumers used the service more than once, so there was almost no repeat business. Finally, as with any medical test, some "false positives" occurred where the scan appeared to detect a problem that did not actually exist. Negative publicity from people who had to have expensive additional—and unnecessary—medical procedures as a result of false positive CT scans also hurt these new businesses.

As a result of these difficulties, the demand for CT scans was less than most of these entrepreneurs had expected, and the new businesses operated at a loss. For example, the owner of California HeartScan would have broken even if the market price had been $495 per heart scan, but suffered losses because the actual market price was only $250. The following figure shows the owner's situation.

11-1 *Making*
the **Connection**

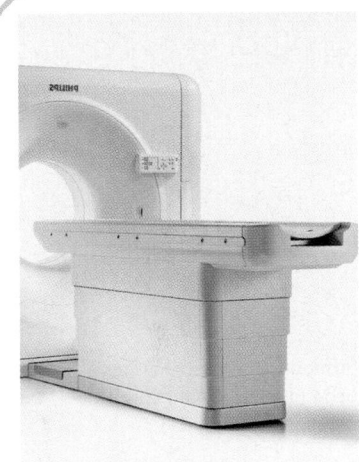

Providing preventive medical scans turned out not to be a profitable business.

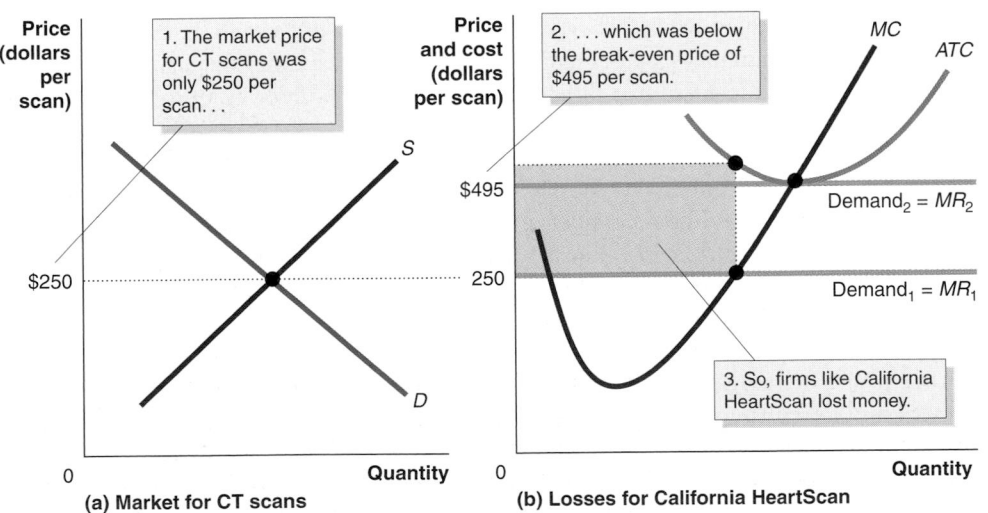

(a) Market for CT scans

(b) Losses for California HeartScan

Why didn't California HeartScan and other medical clinics just raise the price to the level they needed to break even? We have already seen that any firm that tries to raise the price it charges above the market price loses customers to competing firms. By fall 2003, many scanning businesses began to close. Most of the entrepreneurs who had started these businesses lost their investments.

Source: Patricia Callahan, "Scanning for Trouble," *Wall Street Journal,* September 11, 2003, p. B1.

④ **LEARNING OBJECTIVE**
Explain why firms may shut down
temporarily.

Deciding Whether to Produce or to Shut Down in the Short Run

In panel (b) of Figure 11-5, we assumed the firm would continue to produce, even though it was operating at a loss. In fact, in the short run a firm suffering losses has two choices:

1. Continue to produce
2. Stop production by shutting down temporarily

In many cases, a firm experiencing losses will consider stopping production temporarily. Even during a temporary shutdown a firm must still pay its fixed costs. For example, if the firm has signed a lease for its building, the landlord will expect to receive a monthly rent payment, even if the firm is not producing anything that month. Therefore, if a firm does not produce, it will suffer a loss equal to its fixed costs. This loss is the maximum the firm will accept. If, by producing, the firm would lose an amount greater than its fixed costs, it will shut down.

A firm may be able to reduce its loss below the amount of its total fixed cost by continuing to produce. This outcome will occur if the total revenue it receives is greater than its variable cost. The revenue over and above variable cost can be used to cover part of the firm's fixed cost. As a result, in this case the firm will have a smaller loss by continuing to produce than if it shut down.

Sunk cost A cost that has already been paid and that cannot be recovered.

In analyzing the firm's decision to shut down, we are assuming that its fixed costs are *sunk costs*. Remember from Chapter 9 that a **sunk cost** is a cost that has already been paid and cannot be recovered. We assume, as is usually the case, that the firm cannot recover its fixed costs by shutting down. Those funds have been spent and cannot be recovered, so the firm should treat its sunk costs as irrelevant to its decision making. Whether the firm's total revenue is greater or less than its variable costs is the key to deciding whether to shut down.

11-2 Making the Connection

When to Close a Laundry

An article in the *Wall Street Journal* describes what happened to Robert Kjelgaard when he quit his job writing software code at Microsoft and bought a laundry by paying the previous owner $80,000. For this payment, he received 76 washers and dryers and the existing lease on the building. The lease had six years remaining and required a monthly payment of $3,300. Unfortunately, Mr. Kjelgaard had difficulty operating the laundry at a profit. His explicit costs were $4,000 per month more than his revenue.

Keeping a business open even when suffering losses can sometimes be the best decision in the short run.

He tried to sell the laundry but was unable to do so. As he told a reporter, "It's hard to sell a business that's losing money." He considered closing the laundry, but as a sole proprietor he would be responsible for the remainder of the lease. At $3,300 per month for six years, he would be responsible for paying almost $200,000 out of his personal savings. Closing the laundry would still seem to be the better choice, because his $3,300 per month in sunk costs were less than the $4,000 per month plus the opportunity cost of his time, which he was losing from operating the laundry.

In the end he reorganized his business and hired a professional manager. This change allowed him to return to Microsoft and still reduce his losses to $2,000 per month. Because this amount was less than the $3,300 per month he would lose by shutting down, it made sense for him to continue to operate the laundry. But he was still suffering losses and, according to the article, his wife was "counting the days until the lease runs out."

Source: G. Pascal Zachary, "How a Success at Microsoft Washed Out at a Laundry," *Wall Street Journal*, May 30, 1995.

One option not available to a firm with losses in a perfectly competitive market is to raise its price. If the firm did raise its price, it would lose all its customers and its sales would drop to zero. For example, in a recent year the price of wheat in the United States was $3.16 per bushel. At that price, the typical U.S. wheat farmer lost $9,500. At a price of about $4.25 per bushel, the typical wheat farmer would have broken even. But any wheat farmer who tried to raise his price to $4.25 per bushel would have seen his sales quickly disappear because consumers could buy all the wheat they wanted at $3.16 per bushel from the thousands of other wheat farmers.

The Supply Curve of the Firm in the Short Run

Remember that the supply curve for a firm tells us how many units of a product the firm is willing to sell at any given price. Notice that the marginal cost curve for a firm in a perfectly competitive market tells us the same thing. The firm will produce at the level of output where $MR = MC$. Because price equals marginal revenue for a firm in a perfectly competitive market, the firm will produce where $P = MC$. For any given price, we can determine from the marginal cost curve the quantity of output the firm will supply. *Therefore, the perfectly competitive firm's marginal cost curve also is its supply curve.* There is, however, an important qualification to this. We have seen that if a firm is experiencing losses, it will shut down if its total revenue is less than its variable cost:

Total Revenue < Variable Cost,

or, in symbols:

$P \times Q < VC.$

If we divide both sides by Q, we have the result that the firm will shut down if:

$P < AVC.$

If the price drops below average variable cost, the firm will have a smaller loss if it shuts down and produces no output. *So, the firm's marginal cost curve is its supply curve only for prices at or above average variable cost.* The red line in Figure 11-6 shows the supply curve for the firm in the short run.

Recall that the marginal cost curve intersects the average variable cost where the average variable cost curve is at its minimum point. Therefore, the firm's supply curve is its marginal cost curve above the minimum point of the average variable cost curve. For prices below minimum average variable cost (P_{MIN}), the firm will shut down and its

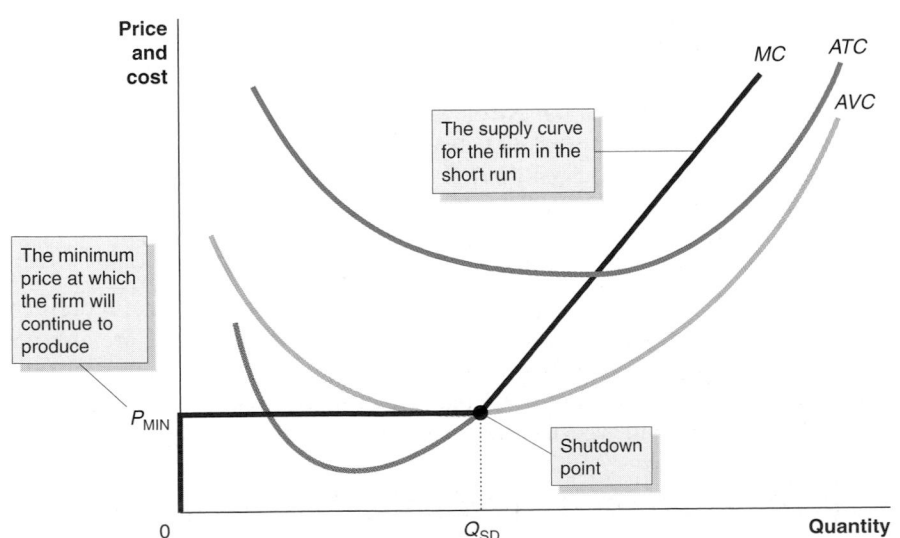

FIGURE 11-6

The Firm's Short-Run Supply Curve

The firm will produce at the level of output at which $MR = MC$. Because price equals marginal revenue for a firm in a perfectly competitive market, the firm will produce where $P = MC$. For any given price, we can determine the quantity of output the firm will supply from the marginal cost curve. In other words, the marginal cost curve is the firm's supply curve. But remember that the firm will shut down if the price falls below average variable cost. The marginal cost curve crosses the average variable cost at the firm's shutdown point. This point occurs at output level Q_{SD}. For prices below P_{MIN}, the supply curve is a vertical line along the price axis, which shows that the firm will supply zero output at those prices. The red line in the figure is the firm's short-run supply curve.

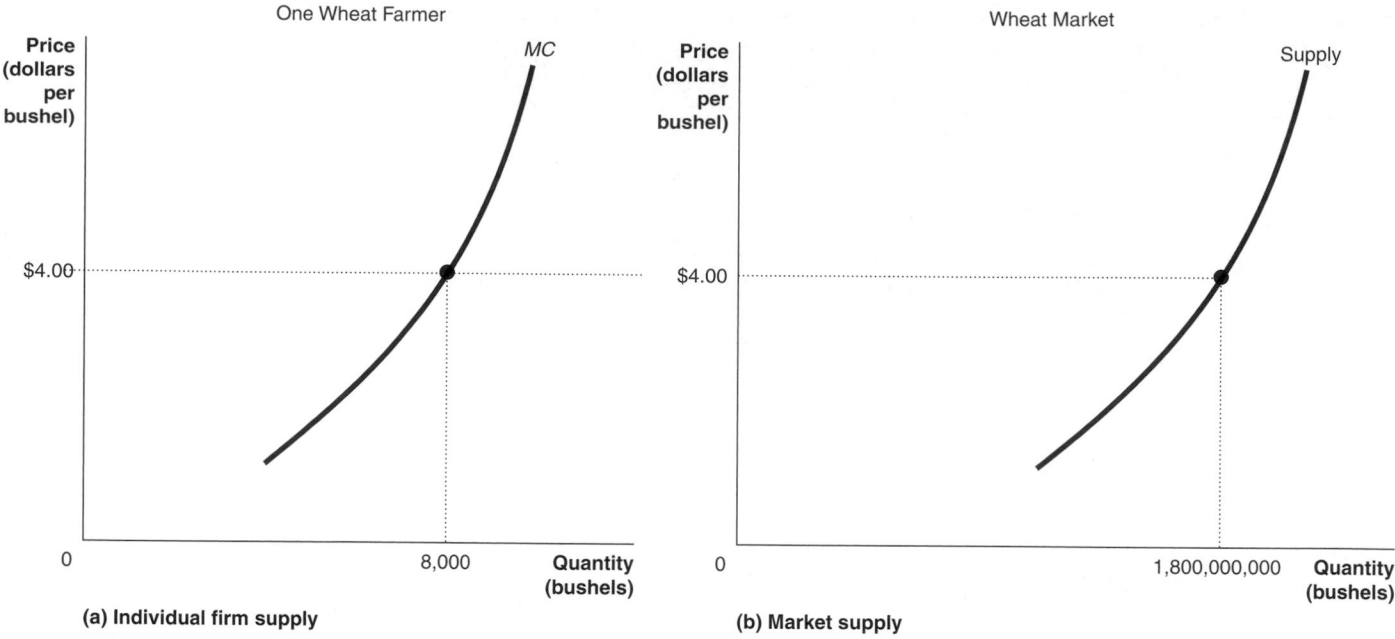

FIGURE 11-7 **Firm Supply and Market Supply**

We can derive the market supply curve by adding up the quantity that each firm in the market is willing to supply at each price. In panel (a), one wheat farmer is willing to supply 8,000 bushels of wheat at a price of $4 per bushel. If every wheat farmer supplies the same amount of wheat at this price and if there are 225,000 wheat farmers, the total amount of wheat supplied at a price of $4 will equal 8,000 bushels per farmer × 225,000 farmers = 1.8 billion bushels of wheat. This is one point on the market supply curve for wheat shown in panel (b). We can find the other points on the market supply curve by seeing how much wheat each farmer is willing to supply at each price.

Shutdown point The minimum point on a firm's average variable cost curve; if the price falls below this point, the firm shuts down production in the short run.

output will fall to zero. The minimum point on the average variable cost curve is called the **shutdown point** and occurs in Figure 11-6 at output level Q_{SD}.

The Market Supply Curve in a Perfectly Competitive Industry

We saw in Chapter 3 that the market supply curve is determined by adding up the quantity supplied by each firm in the industry at each price. Each firm's marginal cost curve tells us how much that firm will supply at each price. So, the market supply curve can be derived directly from the marginal cost curves of the firms in the industry. Panel (a) of Figure 11-7 shows the marginal cost curve for one wheat farmer. At a price of $4, this wheat farmer supplies 8,000 bushels of wheat. If every wheat farmer supplies the same amount of wheat at this price and if there are 225,000 wheat farmers, the total amount of wheat supplied at a price of $4 will be:

8,000 bushels per farmer × 225,000 farmers = 1.8 billion bushels of wheat.

Panel (b) shows a price of $4 and a quantity of 1.8 billion bushels as a point on the market supply curve for wheat. In reality, of course, not all wheat farms are alike. Some wheat farms will supply more at the market price than the typical farm; other wheat farms will supply less. The key point is that we can derive the market supply curve by adding up the quantity that each firm in the market is willing to supply at each price.

(5) **LEARNING OBJECTIVE**

Explain how entry and exit ensure that perfectly competitive firms earn zero economic profit in the long run.

"If Everyone Can Do It, You Can't Make Money at It" — The Entry and Exit of Firms in the Long Run

In the long run, unless a firm can cover all its costs, it will shut down and exit the industry. In a market system, firms continually enter and exit industries. In this section, we will see how profits and losses provide signals to firms that lead to entry and exit.

Economic Profit and the Entry or Exit Decision

To begin, let's look more closely at how economists characterize the profits earned by the owners of a firm. Suppose Anne Moreno decides to start her own business. After considering her interests and preparing a business plan, she decides to start an organic apple farm rather than open a restaurant or gift shop. After 10 years of effort, Anne has saved $100,000 and borrowed another $900,000 from a bank. With these funds, she has bought the land, apple trees, and farm equipment necessary to start her organic apple business. As we saw in Chapter 10, when someone invests her own funds in her firm, the opportunity cost to the firm is the return the funds would have earned in their best alternative use. If Farmer Moreno could have earned a 10 percent return on her $100,000 in savings in their best alternative use—which might have been, for example, to buy a small restaurant—then her apple business incurs a $10,000 opportunity cost. We can also think of this $10,000 as being the minimum amount that Farmer Moreno needs to earn on her $100,000 investment in her farm to remain in the industry in the long run.

Table 11-4 lists Farmer Moreno's costs. In addition to her explicit costs, we assume that she has two implicit costs: the $10,000, which represents the opportunity cost of the funds she invested in her farm, and the $30,000 salary she could have earned managing someone else's farm instead of her own. Her total costs are $125,000. If the market price of organic apples is $15 per box and Farmer Moreno sells 10,000 boxes, her total revenue will be $150,000 and her economic profit will be $25,000 (total revenue of $150,000 minus total costs of $125,000). Recall from Chapter 7 that **economic profit** equals a firm's revenues minus all of its costs, implicit and explicit. So, Farmer Moreno is covering the $10,000 opportunity cost of the funds invested in her firm, and she also is earning an additional $25,000 in economic profit.

Economic profit A firm's revenues minus all its costs, implicit and explicit.

ECONOMIC PROFIT LEADS TO ENTRY OF NEW FIRMS Unfortunately, Farmer Moreno is unlikely to earn an economic profit for very long. Suppose other apple farmers are just breaking even by growing apples using conventional methods. In that case, they will have an incentive to convert to organic growing methods so they can begin earning an economic profit. Remember that the more firms there are in an industry, the further to the right the market supply curve is. Panel (a) of Figure 11-8 shows that more farmers entering the market for organically grown apples will cause the market supply curve to shift to the right. Farmers will continue entering the market until the market supply curve has shifted from S_1 to S_2.

At that point, the market price will have fallen to $10 per box. Panel (b) shows the effect on Farmer Moreno, who we assume has the same costs as other organic apple

EXPLICIT COSTS		**TABLE 11-4**
Water	$10,000	**Farmer Moreno's Costs per Year**
Wages	$15,000	
Organic fertilizer	$10,000	
Electricity	$5,000	
Payment on bank loan	$45,000	
IMPLICIT COSTS		
Foregone salary	$30,000	
Opportunity cost of the $100,000 she has invested in her farm	$10,000	
Total Cost	$125,000	

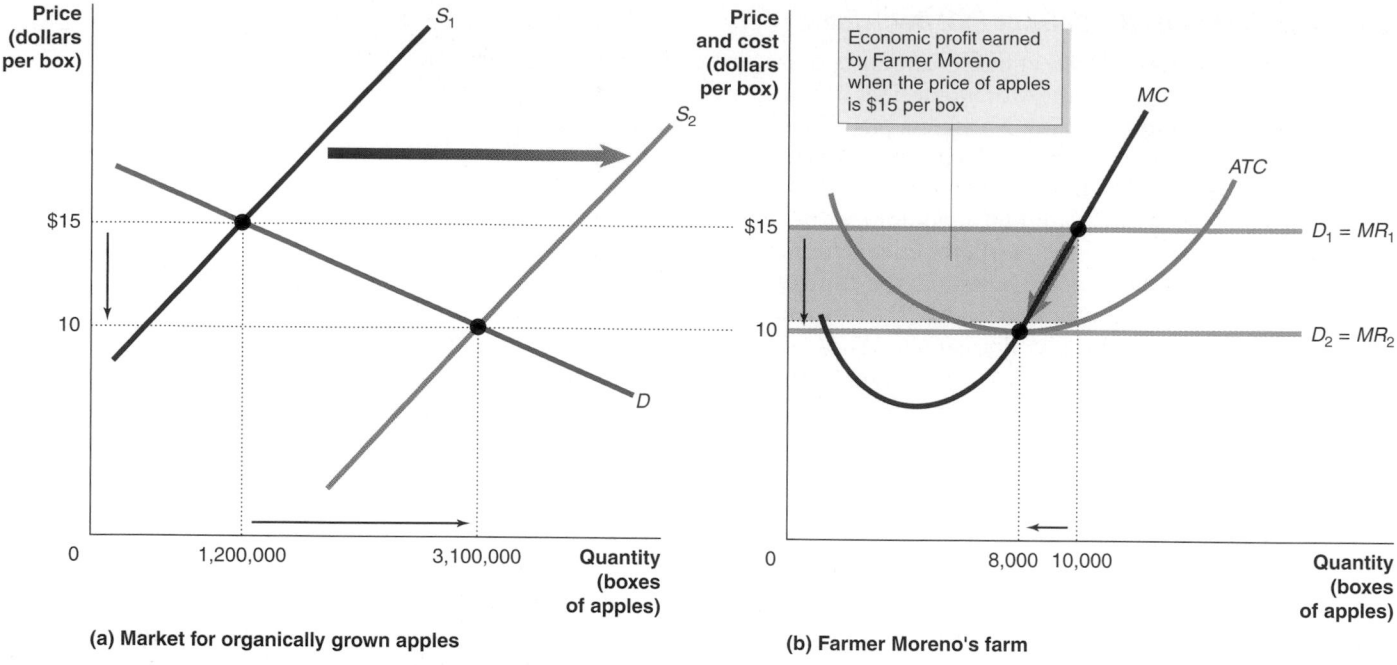

(a) Market for organically grown apples

(b) Farmer Moreno's farm

FIGURE 11-8   The Effect of Entry on Economic Profits

We assume that Farmer Moreno's costs are the same as the costs of other organic apple growers. Initially, she and other producers of organically grown apples are able to charge $15 per box and earn an economic profit. Farmer Moreno's economic profit is represented by the area of the green box. Panel (a) shows that as other farmers begin to grow apples using organic methods, the market supply curve shifts to the right from S_1 to S_2 and the market price drops

to $10 per box. Panel (b) shows that the falling price causes Farmer Moreno's demand curve to shift down from D_1 to D_2, and she reduces her output from 10,000 boxes to 8,000. At the new market price of $10 per box, organic apple growers are just breaking even: Their total revenue is equal to their total cost, and they are earning zero economic profit. Notice the difference in scale between the graph in panel (a) and the graph in panel (b).

farmers. As the market price falls from $15 to $10 per box, Farmer Moreno's demand curve shifts down from D_1 to D_2. In the new equilibrium, Farmer Moreno is selling 8,000 boxes at a price of $10 per box. She and the other organic apple growers are no longer earning any economic profit. They are just breaking even, and the return on their investment is just covering the opportunity cost of these funds. New farmers will stop entering the market for organic apples because the rate of return is no better than they can earn elsewhere.

Will Farmer Moreno continue to grow organic apples even though she is just break-ing even? She will because growing organic apples earns her as high a return on her invest-ment as she could earn elsewhere. It may seem strange that new firms will continue to enter a market until all economic profits are eliminated and that established firms remain in a market despite not earning any economic profit. It only seems strange because we are used to thinking in terms of accounting profits, rather than *economic* profits. Remember that accounting rules generally require that only explicit costs be included on a firm's financial statements. The opportunity cost of the funds Farmer Moreno invested in her firm—$10,000—and her foregone salary—$30,000—are economic costs, but neither is an accounting cost. So, although an accountant would see Farmer Moreno as earning a profit of $40,000, an economist would see her as just breaking even. Farmer Moreno must pay attention to her accounting profit when preparing her financial statements and when paying her income tax. But because economic profit takes into account all her costs, it gives a truer indication of the financial health of her farm.

ECONOMIC LOSSES LEAD TO EXIT OF FIRMS Suppose some consumers decide there are no important benefits from eating organically grown apples and they switch back to buying conventionally grown apples. Panel (a) of Figure 11-9 shows that the demand

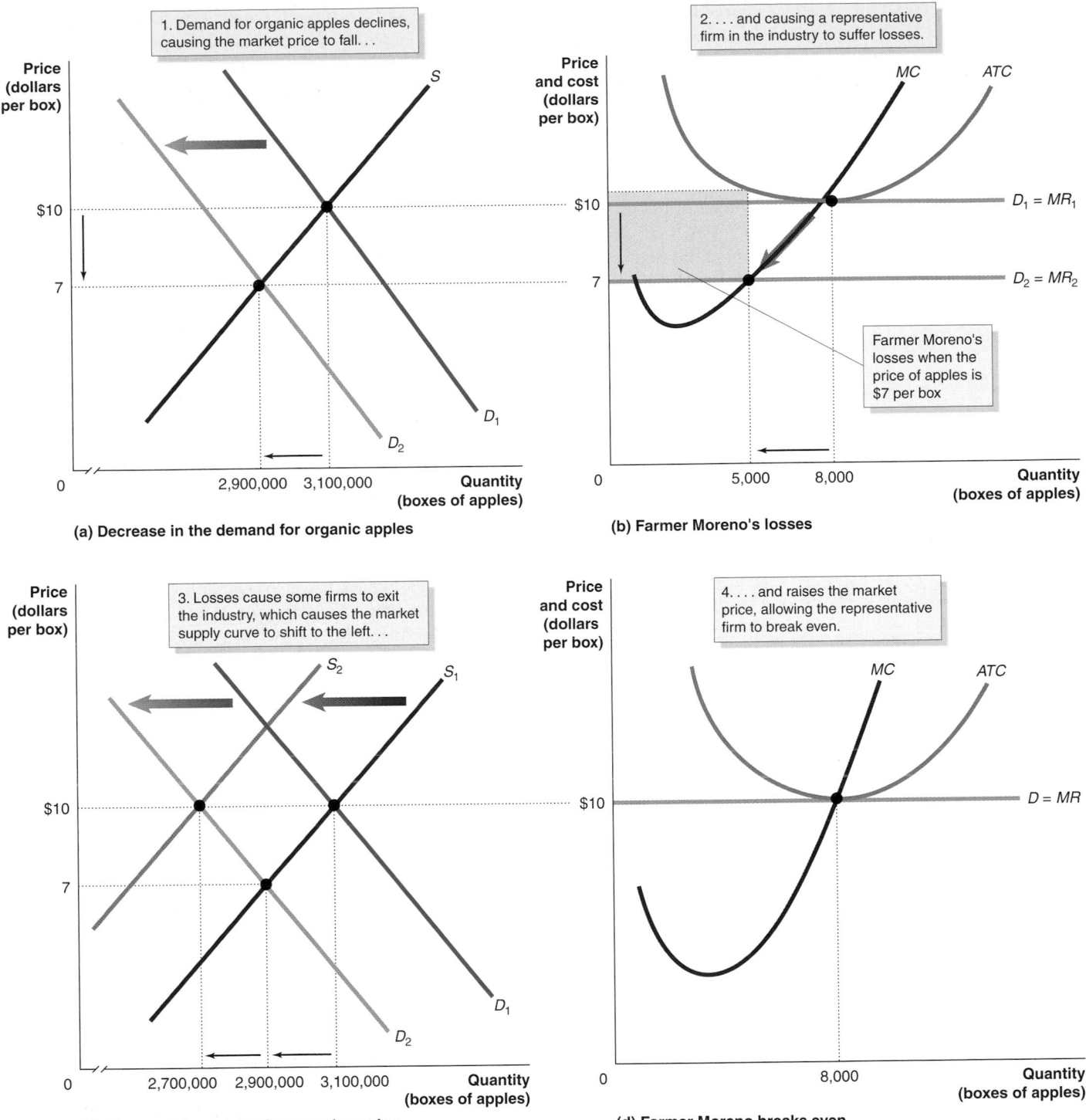

(a) Decrease in the demand for organic apples

1. Demand for organic apples declines, causing the market price to fall. . .

(b) Farmer Moreno's losses

2. . . . and causing a representative firm in the industry to suffer losses.

Farmer Moreno's losses when the price of apples is $7 per box

(c) Firms exit the market for organic apples

3. Losses cause some firms to exit the industry, which causes the market supply curve to shift to the left. . .

(d) Farmer Moreno breaks even

4. . . . and raises the market price, allowing the representative firm to break even.

FIGURE 11-9   The Effect of Exit on Economic Losses

When the price of apples is $10 per box, Farmer Moreno and other producers of organically grown apples are breaking even. A total quantity of 3,100,000 boxes is sold in the market. She sells 8,000 boxes. Panel (a) shows a decline in the demand for organically grown apples from D_1 to D_2 that reduces the market price to $7 per box. Panel (b) shows that the falling price causes Farmer Moreno's demand curve to shift down from D_1 to D_2 and her output to fall from 8,000 to 5,000 boxes. At a market price of $7 per box, farmers have economic

losses, represented by the area of the red box. As a result, some farmers will exit the market, which shifts the market supply curve to the left. Panel (c) shows that exit continues until the supply curve has shifted from S_1 to S_2 and the market price has risen from $7 back to $10. Panel (d) shows that with the price back at $10, Farmer Moreno will break even. In the new market equilibrium, total production of organic apples has fallen from 3,100,000 to 2,700,000 boxes.

Economic loss The situation in which a firm's total revenue is less than its total cost, including all implicit costs.

curve for organically grown apples will shift to the left from D_1 to D_2, and the market price will fall from $10 per box to $7. Panel (b) shows that as the price falls, a typical organic apple farmer, like Anne Moreno, will move down her marginal cost curve to a lower level of output. At the lower level of output and lower price, she will be suffering an **economic loss** because she will not cover all her costs. As long as price is above average variable cost, she will continue to produce in the short run, even when suffering losses. But in the long run, firms will exit an industry if they are unable to cover all their costs. In this case, some organic apple growers will switch back to growing apples using conventional methods.

Panel (c) of Figure 11-9 shows that firms exiting the organic apple industry will cause the market supply curve to shift to the left. Firms will continue to exit and the supply curve will continue shifting to the left until the price has risen back to $10 and the market supply curve is at S_2. Panel (d) shows that when the price is back to $10, the remaining firms in the industry will be breaking even.

Long-Run Equilibrium in a Perfectly Competitive Market

We have seen that economic profits attract firms to enter an industry. The entry of firms forces down the market price until the typical firm is breaking even. Economic losses cause firms to exit an industry. The exit of firms forces up the equilibrium market price until the typical firm is breaking even. This process of entry and exit results in *long-run competitive equilibrium.* In **long-run competitive equilibrium,** entry and exit have resulted in the typical firm breaking even. The *long-run equilibrium market price* is at a level equal to the minimum point on the typical firm's average total cost curve.

Long-run competitive equilibrium The situation in which the entry and exit of firms has resulted in the typical firm breaking even.

The long run in the organic apple market is three to four years, which is the amount of time it takes farmers to convert from conventional growing methods to organic growing methods. As discussed at the beginning of this chapter, only during the years from 1997 to 2001 was it possible for organic apple farmers to earn economic profits. By 2002 the entry of new firms had eliminated economic profits in the industry.

Firms in perfectly competitive markets are in a constant struggle to stay one step ahead of their competitors. They are always looking for new ways to provide a product, such as growing apples organically. It is possible for firms to find ways to earn an economic profit for a while, but to repeat the quote from a Yakima Valley organic apple farmer at the beginning of this chapter, "It's like anything else in agriculture. If people see an economic opportunity, usually it only lasts for a few years." There is no need to restrict this observation to agriculture. In any perfectly competitive market, an opportunity to make economic profits never lasts for long. As Sharon Oster, an economist at Yale University has put it, "If everyone can do it, you can't make money at it."

The Long-Run Supply Curve in a Perfectly Competitive Market

If the typical organic apple grower breaks even at a price of $10 per box, in the long run the market price will always return to this level. If an increase in demand causes the market price to rise above $10, farmers will be earning economic profits. This profit will attract additional farmers into the market, and the market supply curve will shift to the right until the price is back to $10. Panel (a) in Figure 11-10 illustrates the long-run effect of an increase in demand. An increase in demand from D_1 to D_2 causes the market price to temporarily rise from $10 per box to $15. At this price, farmers are making economic profits growing organic apples, but these profits attract entry of new farmers organic apples. The result is an increase in supply from S_1 to S_2, which forces the price back down to $10 per box and eliminates the economic profits.

Similarly, if a decrease in demand causes the market price to fall below $10, farmers will experience economic losses. These losses will cause some farmers to exit the market, the supply curve will shift to the left, and the price will return to $10. Panel (b)

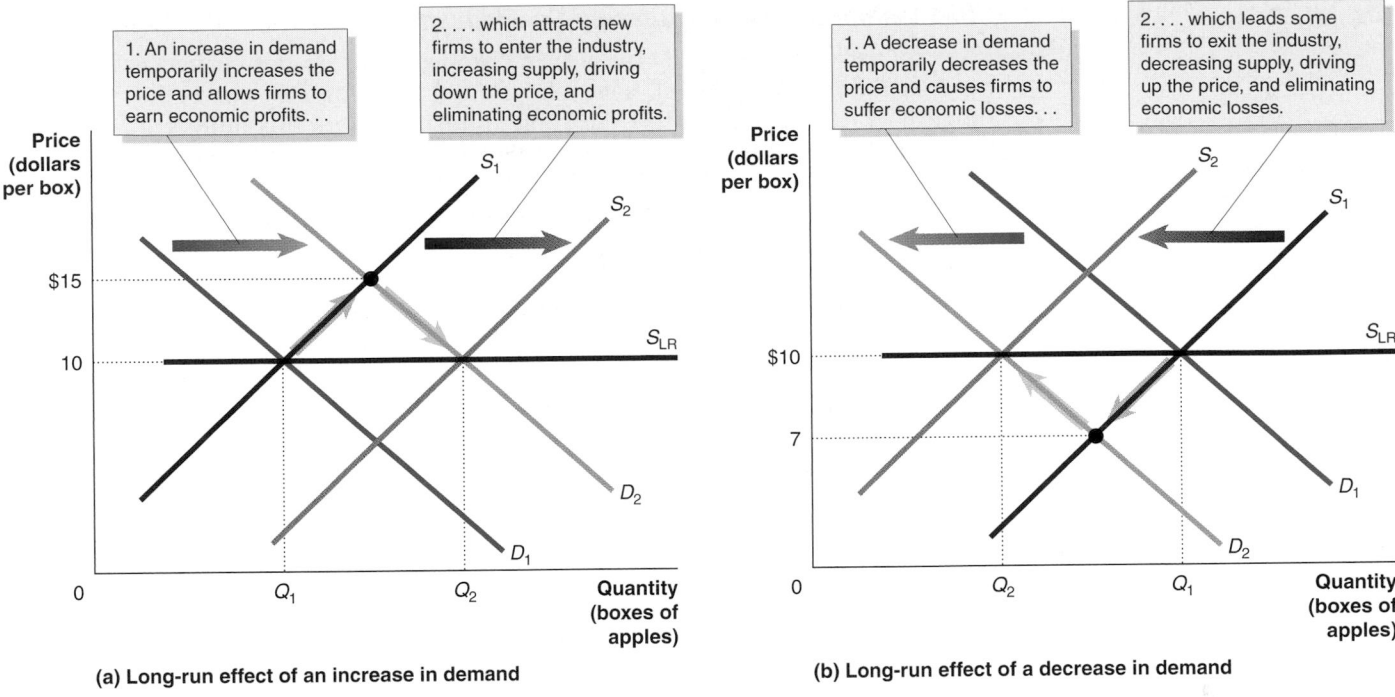

FIGURE 11-10 The Long-Run Supply Curve in a Perfectly Competitive Industry

Panel (a) shows that an increase in demand for organic apples will lead to a temporary increase in price from $10 to $15 per box, as the market demand curve shifts to the right from D_1 to D_2. The entry of new firms shifts the market supply curve to the right from S_1 to S_2, which will cause the price to fall back to its long-run level of $10. Panel (b) shows that a decrease in demand will lead to a temporary decrease in price from $10 to $7 per box, as the market demand

curve shifts to the left from D_1 to D_2. The exit of firms shifts the market supply curve to the left from S_1 to S_2, which causes the price to rise back to its long-run level of $10. The long-run supply curve (S_{LR}) shows the relationship between market price and the quantity supplied in the long run. In this case, the long-run supply curve is a horizontal line.

in Figure 11-10 illustrates the long-run effect of a decrease in demand. A decrease in demand from D_1 to D_2 causes the market price to fall temporarily from $10 per box to $7. At this price, farmers are suffering economic losses growing organic apples, but these losses cause some farmers to exit the market for organic apples. The result is a decrease in supply from S_1 to S_2, which forces the price back up to $10 per box and eliminates the losses.

The **long-run supply curve** shows the relationship in the long run between market price and the quantity supplied. In the long run, the price in the organic apple market will be $10 per box, no matter how many boxes of apples are produced. So, as Figure 11-10 shows, the long-run supply curve (S_{LR}) for organic apples is a horizontal line at a price of $10. Remember that the reason the price returns to $10 in the long run is that this is the price at which the typical firm in the industry just breaks even. The typical firm breaks even at this price because it is at the minimum point on the firm's average total cost curve. We can draw the important conclusion that *in the long run, a perfectly competitive market will supply whatever amount of a good consumers demand at a price determined by the minimum point on the typical firm's average total cost curve.*

Because the position of the long-run supply curve is determined by the minimum point on the typical firm's average total cost curve, anything that raises or lowers the costs of the typical firm in the long run will cause the long-run supply curve to shift. For example, if a disease infects apple trees and the costs of treating the disease adds $2 per box to the cost of producing apples, the long-run supply curve will shift up by $2.

Long-run supply curve A curve showing the relationship in the long run between market price and the quantity supplied.

Increasing-Cost and Decreasing-Cost Industries

Any industry in which the typical firm's average costs do not change as the industry expands production will have a horizontal long-run cost curve, like the one in Figure 11-10. Industries, like the apple industry, where this holds true are called *constant-cost industries*. It's possible, however, for the typical firm's average costs to change as an industry expands.

For example, if an input used in producing a good is available in only limited quantities, the cost of the input will rise as the industry expands. If only a limited amount of land is available on which to grow the grapes to make a certain variety of wine, an increase in demand for wine made from these grapes will result in competition for the land and will drive up its price. As a result, more of the wine will be produced in the long run only if the price rises to cover the higher average costs of the typical firm. In this case, the long-run supply curve will slope upward. Industries with upward-sloping long-run supply curves are called *increasing-cost industries*.

Finally, in some cases the typical firm's costs may fall as the industry expands. Suppose that a new electronic product uses as an input a specialized memory chip that is currently produced only in small quantities. If demand for the electronic product increases, firms will increase their orders for the memory chip. We saw in Chapter 10 that if there are economies of scale in producing a good, its average cost will decline as output increases. If there are economies of scale in producing this memory chip, the average cost of producing it will fall, and competition will result in its price falling as well. This price decline, in turn, will lower the average cost of producing the new electronic product. In the long run, competition will force the price of the electronic product to fall to the level of the new lower average cost of the typical firm. In this case, the long-run supply curve will slope downward. Industries with downward-sloping long-run supply curves are called *decreasing-cost industries*.

⑥ **LEARNING OBJECTIVE**
Explain how perfect competition leads to economic efficiency.

Perfect Competition and Efficiency

Notice how powerful consumers are in a market system. If consumers want more organic apples, the market will supply them. This happens not because orders are given by a bureaucrat in a government office in Washington, DC, or by an official in an apple growers association. The additional apples are produced because an increase in demand results in higher prices and a higher rate of return on investments in organic growing techniques. Apple growers, trying to get the highest possible return on their investment, begin to switch from using conventional growing methods to using organic growing methods. If consumers lose their taste for organic apples and demand falls, the process works in reverse.

11-3 *Making the Connection*

The Decline of Apple Production in New York State

Although New York State is second only to Washington State in production of apples, production has been declining during the past 20 years. The decline has been particularly steep in counties close to New York City. In 1985, there were more than 11 thousand acres of apple orchards in Ulster County, which is 75 miles north of New York City. Today, fewer than five thousand acres remain. As it became difficult for apple growers in the county to compete with lower-cost producers elsewhere, the resources these entrepreneurs were using to produce apples—particularly land—became more valuable in other uses. Many farmers sold their land to housing developers. As one apple farmer put it, "Over the last ten years or so, [apple] prices have been stagnant or going down. I didn't see a return on the money, and I didn't want to continue."

In a market system, entrepreneurs will not continue to employ economic resources to produce a good or service unless consumers are willing to pay a price at least high enough for them to break even. Consumers were not willing to pay a high-enough price for apples for many New York State apple growers to break even on their investments. As a result, resources left apple production in that state.

When apple growers in New York State stopped breaking even, many sold their land to housing developers.

Sources: Lisa W. Foderaro, "Where Apples Don't Pay, Developers Will," *New York Times*, June 23, 2001; USDA, *2002 Census of Agriculture, Volume 1, Chapter 2,* New York County Level Data, Table 31.

Productive Efficiency

In the market system, consumers get as many apples as they want, produced at the lowest average cost possible. The forces of competition will drive the market price to the minimum average cost of the typical firm. **Productive efficiency** refers to the situation in which a good or service is produced at the lowest possible cost. As we have seen, perfect competition results in productive efficiency.

The managers of every firm strive to earn an economic profit by reducing costs. But in a perfectly competitive market, other firms quickly copy ways of reducing costs, so that in the long run, only the consumer benefits from cost reductions.

Productive efficiency The situation in which a good or service is produced at the lowest possible cost.

SOLVED PROBLEM 11-2

How Productive Efficiency Benefits Consumers

Writing in the *New York Times* on the technology boom of the late 1990s, Michael Lewis argues:

> The sad truth, for investors, seems to be that most of the benefits of new technologies are passed right through to consumers free of charge.

a. What do you think Lewis means by the benefits of new technology being "passed right through to consumers free of charge"? Use a graph like Figure 11-8 to illustrate your answer.

b. Explain why this result is a "sad truth" for investors.

(6) LEARNING OBJECTIVE
Explain how perfect competition leads to economic efficiency.

Solving the Problem:

Step 1: Review the chapter material. This problem is about perfect competition and efficiency, so you may want to review the section "Perfect Competition and Efficiency," which begins on page 374.

Step 2: Explain what Lewis means using the concepts from this chapter. By "new technologies," Lewis means new products—like cell phones or DVD players—or lower-cost ways of producing existing products. In either case, new technologies will allow firms to earn economic profits for a while, but these profits will lead new firms to enter the market in the long run.

Step 3: Use a graph like Figure 11-8 to illustrate why the benefits of new technologies are "passed right through to consumers free of charge." Figure 11-8 shows the situation in which a firm is making economic profits in the short run but has these profits eliminated by entry in the long run. We can draw a similar graph to analyze what happens in the long run in the market for DVD players:

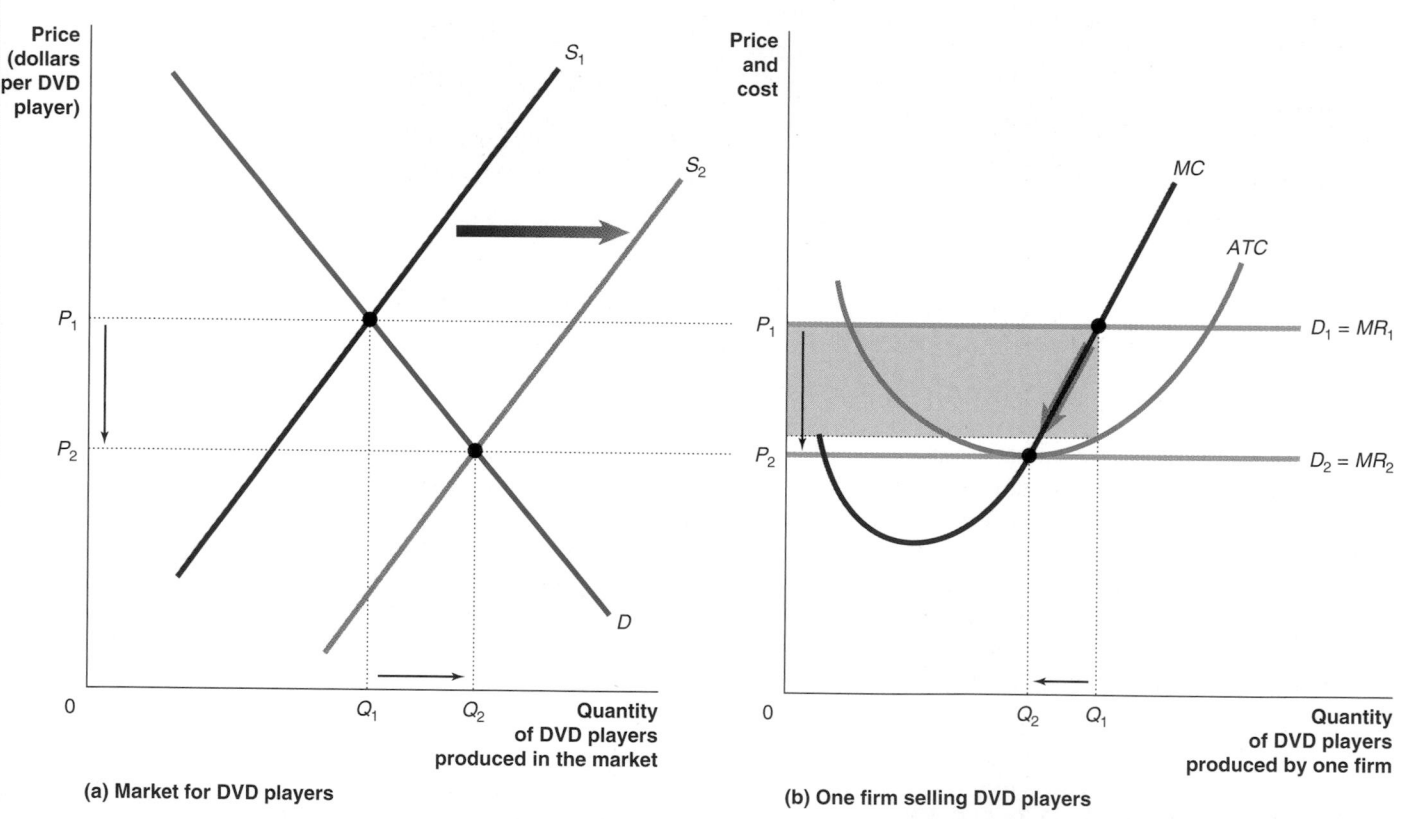

(a) Market for DVD players

(b) One firm selling DVD players

When DVD players were first introduced, prices were high and only a few firms were in the market. Panel (a) shows that the initial equilibrium price in the market for DVD players is P_1. Panel (b) shows that at this price the typical firm in the industry is earning an economic profit, which is shown by the green-shaded box. The economic profit attracts new firms into the industry. This entry shifts the market supply curve from S_1 to S_2 in panel (a) and lowers the equilibrium price from P_1 to P_2. Panel (b) shows that at the new market price P_2, the typical firm is breaking even. Therefore, DVD players are being produced at the lowest possible cost and productive efficiency is achieved. Consumers receive the new technology "free of charge" in the sense that they only have to pay a price equal to the lowest possible cost of production.

Step 4: Answer question (b) by explaining why the result in question (a) is a "sad truth" for investors. We have seen in answering question (a) that in the long run, firms only break even on their investment in producing high-technology goods. That result implies that investors in these firms are also unlikely to earn an economic profit in the long run.

Extra Credit: Lewis is using a key result from this chapter: In the long run, entry of new firms competes away economic profits. We should notice that, strictly speaking, the high-technology industries Lewis is discussing are not perfectly competitive. Cell phones or DVD players, for instance, are not identical and each cell phone company produces a quantity large enough to affect the market price. However, as we will see in Chapter 12, these deviations from perfect competition do not change the important conclusion that the entry of new firms benefits consumers by forcing prices down to the level of average cost. In fact, the price of DVD players dropped by more than 95 percent within five years of their first becoming available.

Source: Michael Lewis, "In Defense of the Boom," *New York Times*, October 27, 2002.

YOUR TURN: For more practice, do related problems 18 and 19 on page 383 at the end of this chapter. Visit www.prenhall.com/hubbard for an interactive exercise related to this Solved Problem.

Allocative Efficiency

Not only do perfectly competitive firms produce goods and services at the lowest possible cost, they also produce the goods and services that consumers value most. Firms will produce a good up to the point where the marginal cost of producing another unit is equal to the marginal benefit consumers receive from consuming that unit. In other words, firms will supply all those goods that provide consumers with a marginal benefit at least as great as the marginal cost of producing them. We know this is true because:

1. The price of a good represents the marginal benefit consumers receive from consuming the last unit of the good sold.
2. Perfectly competitive firms produce up to the point where the price of the good equals the marginal cost of producing the last unit.
3. Therefore, firms produce up to the point where the last unit provides a marginal benefit to consumers equal to the marginal cost of producing it.

These statements are another way of saying that entrepreneurs in a market system efficiently *allocate* labor, machinery, and other inputs to produce the goods and services that best satisfy consumer wants. In this sense, perfect competition achieves **allocative efficiency.** As we will explore in the next few chapters, many goods and services sold in the U.S. economy are not produced in perfectly competitive markets. Nevertheless, productive efficiency and allocative efficiency are useful benchmarks against which to compare the actual performance of the economy.

Allocative efficiency A state of the economy in which production reflects consumer preferences; in particular, every good or service is produced up to the point where the last unit provides a marginal benefit to consumers equal to the marginal cost of producing it.

Conclusion

The competitive forces of the market impose relentless pressure on firms to produce new and better goods and services at the lowest possible cost. Firms that fail to adequately anticipate changes in consumer tastes or that fail to adopt the latest and most efficient technology do not survive in the long run. In the nineteenth century, the biologist Charles Darwin developed a theory of evolution based on the idea of the "survival of the fittest." Only those plants and animals that were best able to adapt to the demands of their environment were able to survive. Darwin wrote that he first realized the important role that the struggle for existence plays in the natural world after reading early nineteenth-century economists discuss the role it plays in the economic world. Just as "survival of the fittest" is the rule in nature, so it is in the economic world.

At the start of this chapter, we saw that there are four market structures: perfect competition, monopolistic competition, oligopoly, and monopoly. Now that we have studied perfect competition, in the following chapters we move on to the other three market structures. Before turning to those chapters, read *An Inside Look* on the next page to learn how firms are rushing to enter the market for organic snacks.

USA TODAY, JUNE 17, 2004

Organic Food Trend Chips Out a Niche in Snack Food Aisle

Organic food is breaking out of the produce section to a spot few anticipated: the snack aisle. Forget stereotypes of pristine strawberries or zucchinis untouched by preservatives, pesticides, hormones or antibiotics. It's sales of organic snacks, also produced in accordance with government rules to be labeled "organic," that are on fire.

a Sales of organic chips, nuts, nutrition bars and candy jumped 29.6% last year. That was outpaced only by organic meats (including poultry and fish), reports the Organic Trade Association.

All the good things about the $23 billion organic food industry are being processed by foodmakers at a near-frenetic pace into convenient snack foods. Organics are Frito-Lay's fastest-growing line. In a year, Frito-

Lay has emerged as the No. 1 seller of organic snacks. It recently introduced organic Tostitos chips. Now, it's working on an organic Doritos line; perhaps, someday, potato chips.

"There's a perception that the organic consumer is living in a commune somewhere," says Stephen Quinn, marketing chief at Frito-Lay. "She's not. She's my wife."

Adding to the trend: more snacking of all kinds. For many time-pressed, two-worker families, a stream of snacks has replaced family meal time. That's one reason a record 120 organic snacks are scheduled to be introduced this year, up 40% from last year, estimates Lynn Dornblaser, director of consulting services at Mintel, a research firm. For some consumers, there's a who'd-a-thunk-it factor to organics' growth in snacks. "It seems to be a disconnect," says Dornblaser.

Nor are nutritionists overjoyed. "These are all dead, processed foods," laments Cynthia Lair, author of *Feed-*

ing the Whole Family. "Organic or not, they won't make you healthier or give you more vitality. It's better to eat an apple." Organic snacks are late to the party, says Peter Meehan, CEO of Newman's Own Organics. "Things like organic produce and dairy have all grown years ahead of them."

Perhaps that's why sales of Garden of Eden's organic tortilla chips grew 41% in the past year. The company's organic snack business has grown more than 20% in the past year, says Ellen Deutsch, chief growth officer at parent company Hain Celestial Group.

b Such numbers have even some organic specialty companies that don't make processed snacks trying to squeeze into the snacking arena. Take Earthbound Farm, the biggest producer of organic produce, including those familiar bags of baby carrots. "My snack as a kid was a Twinkie," says Larry Hamwey, head of marketing. "But my three kids all know they have to have healthy snacks."

Key Points in the Article

At the beginning of this chapter, we discussed the increase in production of organically grown apples. This article discusses how the increasing demand for organic food has led to sales of organic snacks being "on fire." Large firms, such as Frito-Lay, are entering the market, with organic versions of Tostitos and Doritos. Medium-sized firms, such as Garden of Eden and Newman's Own Organics, are also entering the market. Even firms, such as Earthbound Farm, that don't currently produce snacks are planning to "squeeze into the snacking arena."

Analyzing the News

a One of the key points of this chapter is that, ultimately, it is *consumers* who decide which goods should be produced. If consumers increase their demand for organic snacks, then firms will redirect workers, machines, and natural resources toward producing those goods. In early 2003, an industry

analyst (not quoted in the article) observed, "Organic is a niche, but a very profitable niche. Give consumers what they truly want/need and they will dig deeply into their pockets."

In fact, it is those profits that signal to entrepreneurs that demand for organic foods has increased. We know from the analysis in this chapter, though, that these profits will not persist in the long run. Figure 1 shows the short-run result of an increase in demand for organic snacks. The increased consumer demand for organic snacks raises the price of organic snacks from P_1 to P_2, which results in the typical firm earning economic profits.

b Figure 2 shows the long-run result. The economic profit earned by producing organic snacks will attract additional firms— such as Earthbound Farm, mentioned in the article—to enter the industry. This causes the market price to fall back to P_1. At a price of P_1, the typical firm is once again breaking even. The increase in consumer demand for organic snacks results in the quantity supplied rising in

the long run, as new firms enter the industry, but the typical firm does not make an economic profit.

Thinking Critically
ABOUT POLICY

1. Show, using a demand and supply graph and a cost-curve graph, what would happen if the government tightened its regulations, making it more difficult for the snacks mentioned in the article to be labeled as organic.
2. Show, using a demand and supply graph and a cost-curve graph, why organic snacks are likely to be more expensive than non-organic snacks.

Source: "Organic Food Trend Chips Out a Niche in Snack Food Aisle," by Bruce Horovitz, *USA Today*, June 17, 2004. Reprinted with permission.

Source for quote: Jerry Dryer, "Market Trends: Organic Lessons," *Prepared Foods*, January 2003.

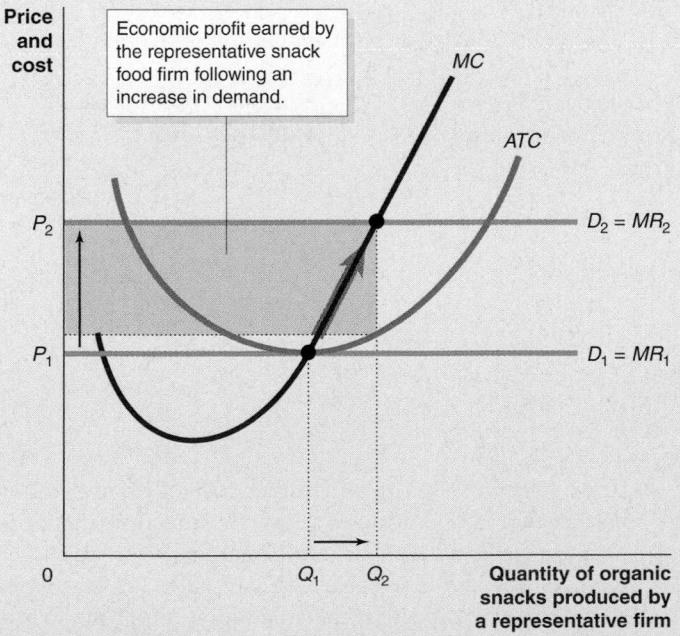

Figure 1: The short-run effects of an increase in demand for organic snack foods.

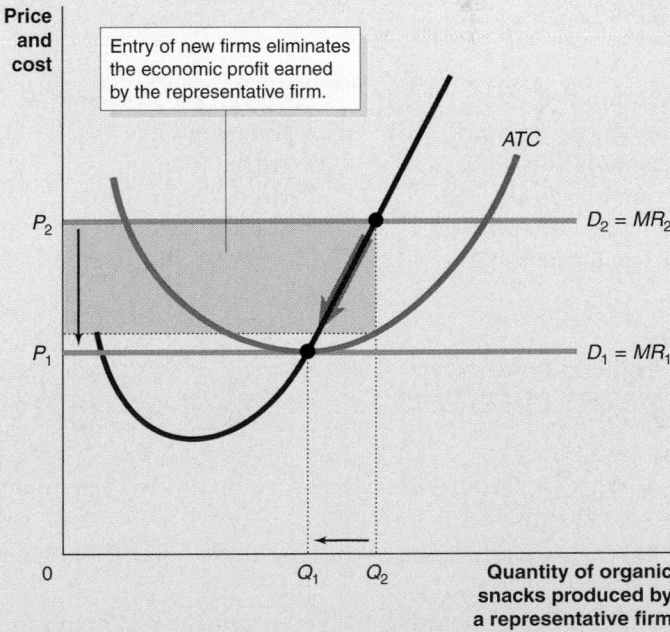

Figure 2: The long-run effects of an increase in demand for organic snack foods.

SUMMARY

LEARNING OBJECTIVE ① Define a perfectly competitive market, and explain why a perfect competitor faces a horizontal demand curve. A *perfectly competitive market* must have many buyers and sellers, firms must be producing identical products, and there must be no barriers to entry of new firms. The demand for a good or service produced in a perfectly competitive market will be downward-sloping, but the demand curve for the output of one firm in a perfectly competitive market will be a horizontal line at the market price. Firms in perfectly competitive markets are *price takers* and will see their sales drop to zero if they attempt to charge more than the market price.

LEARNING OBJECTIVE ② Explain how a perfect competitor decides how much to produce. A firm maximizes profit by producing the level of output where the difference between revenue and cost is the greatest. This is the same level of output where marginal revenue is equal to marginal cost.

LEARNING OBJECTIVE ③ Use graphs to show a firm's profit or loss. On a cost-curve graph, the area of profit or loss is a box with a height equal to price minus average total cost (for profit) or average total cost minus price (for loss) and a base equal to the level of output.

LEARNING OBJECTIVE ④ Explain why firms may shut down temporarily. In the short run, a firm will continue to produce as long as its price is at least equal to its average variable cost. If price falls below average variable cost, the firm will shut down. In the long run, a firm will shut down if price falls below average total cost.

LEARNING OBJECTIVE ⑤ Explain how entry and exit ensure that perfectly competitive firms earn zero economic profit in the long run. If firms make economic profits in the short run, new firms will enter the industry until the market price has fallen enough to wipe out the profits. If firms make economic losses, firms will exit the industry until the market price has risen enough to wipe out the losses. In the long run, firms in perfectly competitive markets break even.

LEARNING OBJECTIVE ⑥ Explain how perfect competition leads to economic efficiency. Perfect competition results in *productive efficiency*, which means that goods and services are produced at the lowest possible cost. Perfect competition also results in *allocative efficiency*, which means that the goods and services are produced up to the point where the last unit provides a marginal benefit to consumers equal to the marginal cost of producing it.

KEY TERMS

Allocative efficiency 377	Long-run supply curve 373	Price taker 355	Shutdown point 368
Average revenue (*AR*) 358	Marginal revenue	Productive efficiency 375	Sunk cost 366
Economic loss 372	(*MR*) 358	Profit 356	
Economic profit 369	Perfectly competitive		
Long-run competitive	market 355		
equilibrium 372			

REVIEW QUESTIONS

1. What are the three conditions for a market to be perfectly competitive?

2. What is a price taker? When are firms likely to be price takers?

3. Draw a graph showing the market demand and supply for corn and the demand for the corn produced by one corn farmer. Be sure to indicate the market price and the price received by the corn farmer.

4. Draw a graph showing a firm in a perfectly competitive market that is operating at a loss. Be sure your diagram includes the firm's demand curve, marginal revenue curve, marginal cost curve, average total cost curve, average variable cost curve, and that the area representing the firm's losses is indicated.

5. Discuss why it is true that for a firm in a perfectly competitive market, the profit-maximizing condition $MR = MC$ is equivalent to the condition $P = MC$.

6. What is the difference between the firm's shutdown point in the short run and in the long run? Why are firms willing to accept losses in the short run but not in the long run?

7. When are firms likely to enter an industry? When are they likely to exit an industry?

8. Would a firm earning zero economic profit continue to produce, even in the long run?

9. Discuss the shape of the long-run supply curve in a perfectly competitive market. Suppose that a perfectly com-

petitive market is initially at long-run equilibrium and then there is a permanent decrease in the demand for the product. Draw a graph showing how the market adjusts in the long run.

10. What is meant by allocative efficiency? What is meant by productive efficiency? Briefly discuss the difference between these two concepts.

PROBLEMS AND APPLICATIONS

Please visit **www.prenhall.com/hubbard** *for solutions to the even-numbered problems as well as multiple-choice and true or false self-assessment quizzes.*

1. Explain whether each of the following is a perfectly competitive market. For each market that is not perfectly competitive explain why it is not.
   a. Corn farming
   b. Retail bookselling
   c. Manufacturing automobiles
   d. Constructing new homes

2. **[Related to *Don't Let This Happen To You!*]** Explain whether you agree or disagree with the following remark: "According to the model of perfectly competitive markets, the demand for wheat should be a horizontal line. But this can't be true: When the price of wheat rises, the quantity of wheat demanded falls, and when the price of wheat falls, the quantity of wheat demanded rises. Therefore, the demand for wheat is not a horizontal line."

3. Suppose an assistant professor of economics is earning a salary of $65,000 per year. One day she quits her job, sells $100,000 worth of bonds that had been earning 5 percent per year, and uses the funds to open a bookstore. At the end of the year she shows an accounting profit of $80,000 on her income tax return. What is her economic profit?

4. Suppose that you and your sister both decide to open copy stores. Your parents always liked your sister better than you, so they purchase and give to her free of charge the three copiers she needs to operate her store. You, however, have to rent your copiers for $1,500 per month each. Does your sister have lower costs in operating her copier store than you have in operating your copier store because of this? Explain.

5. **[Related to *Solved Problem 11-1*]** Frances sells earrings in the perfectly competitive earring market. Her output per day and costs are as follows:

OUTPUT PER DAY	TOTAL COST
0	$1.00
1	2.50
2	3.50
3	4.20
4	4.50
5	5.20
6	6.80
7	8.70
8	10.70
9	13.00

   a. If the current equilibrium price in the earring market is $1.80, how many earrings will Frances produce, what price will she charge, and how much profit (or loss) will she make? Draw a graph to illustrate your answer. Your graph should be clearly labeled and should include Frances's demand, *ATC*, *AVC*, *MC*, and *MR* curves, the price she is charging, the quantity she is producing, and the area representing her profit (or loss).
   b. Suppose the equilibrium price of earrings falls to $1.00. Now how many earrings will Frances produce, what price will she charge, and how much profit (or loss) will she make? Show your work. Draw a graph to illustrate this situation, using the instructions in question a.
   c. Suppose the equilibrium price of earrings falls to $0.25. Now how many earrings will Frances produce, what price will she charge, and how much profit (or loss) will she make?

6. The financial writer Andrew Tobias has described an incident when he was a student at the Harvard Business School: Each student in the class was given large amounts of information about a particular firm and asked to determine a pricing strategy for the firm. Most of the students spent hours preparing their answers and came to class carrying many sheets of paper with their calculations. Tobias came up with the correct answer after just a few minutes and without having made any calculations. When his professor called on him in class for an answer, Tobias stated, "The case said the XYZ Company was in a very competitive industry . . . and the case said that the company had all the business it could handle." Given this information, what price do you think Tobias argued the company should charge? Briefly explain. (Tobias says the class greeted his answer with "thunderous applause.")

Source: Andrew Tobias, *The Only Investment Guide You'll Ever Need,* San Diego: Harcourt, 2002, pp. 6–8.

7. Harry Ellis produces table lamps in the perfectly competitive desk lamp market.
   a. Fill in the missing values in the table.

OUTPUT PER WEEK	TOTAL COSTS	AFC	AVC	ATC	MC
0	$100				
1	150				
2	175				
3	190				
4	210				
5	240				
6	280				
7	330				
8	390				
9	460				
10	540				

   b. Suppose the equilibrium price in the desk lamp market is $50. How many table lamps should Harry produce, and how much profit will he make?
   c. If next week the equilibrium price of desk lamps drops to $30, should Harry shut down? Explain.

8. The following graph represents the situation of a perfectly competitive firm. Indicate on the graph the areas that represent:
   a. Total cost
   b. Total revenue
   c. Variable cost
   d. Profit or loss

   Briefly explain whether the firm will continue to produce in the short run.

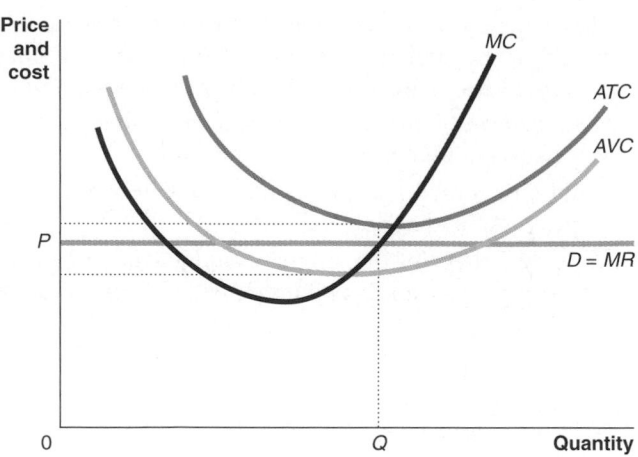

9. [Related to *Solved Problem 11-1*] Review Solved Problem 11-1, and then answer the following: Suppose the equilibrium price of basketballs falls to $2.50. Now how many basketballs will Andy produce? What price will he charge? How much profit (or loss) will he make?

10. Do you agree or disagree with the following statement? "The products for which demand is the greatest will also be the products that are most profitable to produce." Explain.

11. In panel (b) of Figure 11-9, Anne Moreno reduces her output from 8,000 to 5,000 boxes of apples when the price falls to $7. At this price and this output level she is operating at a loss. Why doesn't she just continue charging the original $10 and continue producing 8,000 boxes of apples?

12. [Related to *Don't Let This Happen To You!*] A student examines the following graph and argues, "I believe that a firm will want to produce at Q_1, not Q_2. At Q_1, the distance between price and marginal cost is the greatest. Therefore, at Q_1, the firm will be maximizing its profits." Briefly explain whether you agree with the student's argument.

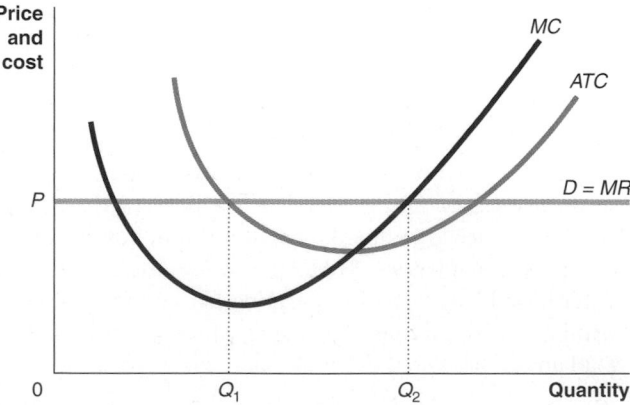

13. According to a report in the *Wall Street Journal,* during the fourth quarter of 2003 the profits of British Airways rose to 83 million pounds from 13 million pounds one year earlier. At the same time "the average amount the airline makes on each paying passenger fell 0.8%." If profit per passenger fell, how could total profits rise? Illustrate your answer with a graph. Be sure to indicate profit per passenger and total profit on the graph.
    Source: Emma Blake, "British Airways Reports Sharp Jump in Net Profits," *Wall Street Journal,* February 9, 2004.

14. The following is from an article in the *Los Angeles Times:*

    > Gerald Lasseigne, a 53-year-old information systems technician in Donaldsonville, La., lost his job last month when steep natural gas prices forced Triad Nitrogen to shut down its fertilizer plant on the banks of the Mississippi River.

    Draw a graph showing the Triad Nitrogen company earning a profit from its fertilizer plant before the increase in the price of natural gas. Draw a second graph showing why Triad Nitrogen shuts down the plant following the increase in the price of natural gas.
    Source: Warren Vieth and Aparna Kumar, "Higher Oil Prices Ooze into Economy," *Los Angeles Times,* March 25, 2003, p. C1.

15. Suppose you decide to open a copy store. You rent store space (signing a one-year lease), and you take out a loan at a local bank and use the money to purchase 10 copiers. Six months later a large chain opens a copy store two blocks away from yours. As a result, the revenue you receive from your copy store, while sufficient to cover the wages of your employees, and the costs of paper and utilities, doesn't cover all of your rent and the interest and repayment costs on the loan you took out to purchase the copiers. Should you continue operating your business?

16. The following statement appeared in a Congressional analysis of the airline industry: "In lean times, airlines can operate for extended periods of time [while making losses] . . . because revenues will cover a large part of their costs (Pan Am lost money for about a decade before finally closing down)." Why would Pan Am—or any airline—continue losing money for 10 years, rather than shut down immediately? In the statement "revenues will cover a large part of their costs," does it matter if the costs being referred to are fixed costs or variable costs? Briefly explain.
    Source: Joint Economic Committee, Democratic Staff, *Assessing Losses for the Airline Industry and Its Workers in the Aftermath of the Terrorist Attacks,* October 3, 2001.

17. Club Mediterranee operates 120 Club Med resorts around the world. Following the September 11, 2001, terrorist attacks on the United States, many American tourists were reluctant to travel to foreign resorts. As a result, the prices Club Med could charge visitors to its resorts declined. In November 2001, Club Med decided to temporarily shut down 15 of its resorts. Analyze possible reasons for Club Med's decision. Be sure to discuss the likely relationship between the revenue Club Med received from operating these resorts and the resorts' fixed and variable costs.
    Source: Rafer Guzmán, "Club Med Plans to Temporarily Close 15 Resorts," *Wall Street Journal,* November 9, 2001, p. B1.

18. **[Related to *Solved Problem 11-2*]** Discuss the following statement: "In a perfectly competitive market, in the long run consumers benefit from reductions in costs, but firms don't." Don't firms also benefit from cost reductions because they are able to earn greater profits?

19. **[Related to *Solved Problem 11-2*]** Suppose you read the following item in a newspaper article under the headline, "Price Gouging Alleged in Pencil Market:"

    > Consumer advocacy groups charged at a press conference yesterday that there is widespread price gouging in the sale of pencils. They released a study showing that whereas the average retail price of pencils was $1.00, the average cost of producing pencils was only $0.50. "Pencils can be produced without complicated machinery or highly skilled workers, so there is no justification for companies charging a price that is twice what it costs them to produce the product. Pencils are too important in the life of every American for us to tolerate this sort of price gouging any longer," said George Grommet, chief spokesperson for the consumer groups. The consumer groups advocate passage of a law that would allow companies selling pencils to charge a price no more than 20 percent greater than their average cost of production.

    Do you believe such a law would be advisable in a situation like this? Explain.

20. A student in a principles of economics course makes the following remark: "The economic model of perfectly competitive markets is fine in theory but not very realistic. It predicts that in the long run a firm in a perfectly competitive market will earn no profits. No firm in the real world would stay in business if it earned zero profits." Do you agree with this remark?

21. The following is an excerpt from a newspaper story on the state of the lettuce market in the spring of 2002:

    > The shortage [of lettuce] began with freezing weather that cut per-acre yields by more than half in parts of California, where more than half of the nation's supply is grown. At the same time, many farmers grew less lettuce, fearing a drop in demand after Sept. 11 [2001] because many people dined out less. The result has been high prices. In some parts of the country, iceberg lettuce has topped $3 per head at grocery stores, up from the regular $1 to $2.

Prices are expected to drop to their usual levels in the next two to three weeks as new supplies catch up to demand, said Ashraf Zaki, a market price reporter for the Agriculture Department in Forest Park, Ga.

Use a demand-and-supply graph to illustrate the changes in the lettuce market described in this story. Briefly explain any shifts of the demand and supply curves in your graph. Why was the market price reporter for the Agriculture Department confident that prices would drop "to their usual levels"?

Source: Justin Bachman, "Light on Lettuce at the Salad Bar," Associated Press, March 29, 2002.

22. Suppose that the laptop computer industry is perfectly competitive and that the firms that assemble laptops do not also make the displays for them. Suppose that the laptop display industry is perfectly competitive. Suppose that because the demand for laptop displays is currently relatively small, firms in the laptop display industry have not been able to take advantage of all the economies of scale in laptop display production. Use a graph of the laptop computer market to illustrate the long-run effects on equilibrium price and quantity in the laptop computer market of a substantial and sustained increase in the demand for laptop computers. Use another graph to show the impact on the cost curves of a typical firm in the laptop computer industry. Briefly explain your graphs. Do your graphs indicate that the laptop computer industry is a constant-cost industry, an increasing-cost industry, or a decreasing-cost industry?

23. **[Related to the *Chapter Opener*]** If in the long run apple growers who use organic methods of cultivation make no greater rate of return on their investment than apple growers who use conventional methods, why did a significant number of apple growers switch from conventional to organic methods in the first place?

chapter twelve

12

Monopolistic Competition:
The Competitive Model in a More Realistic Setting

Starbucks: Growth through Product Differentiation

➤ Starbucks coffee shops seem to be everywhere—in malls, downtown shopping districts, airports, Barnes & Noble bookstores, and practically everywhere else you can imagine. By 2005, Starbucks operated 8,300 stores worldwide, with the company planning to eventually open 25,000. More than 25 million people visit a Starbucks each day.

Like many firms that are currently large, Starbucks started small. The first Starbucks was opened in Seattle in 1971 by entrepreneurs Gordon Bowker, Gerald Baldwin, and Zev Siegl. There were only five Starbucks stores in 1982 when Howard Schultz was hired to manage the firm's retail sales and marketing. Schultz, who would become chairman of the board

and chief executive officer, was determined to make the company first a national chain, and then a worldwide chain. By 1993, Starbucks was opening stores on the East Coast, and in 1996 it opened its first store outside North America, in Tokyo, Japan.

Of course, fresh-brewed coffee has always been widely available in restaurants, diners, and donut shops. What Howard Schultz and the other Starbucks executives realized, however, was that a significant consumer demand existed for coffeehouses where customers could sit, relax, read the newspaper, and drink higher-quality coffee than was typically served in diners or donut shops. The espresso-based coffees

served at Starbucks were relatively difficult to find elsewhere during the 1990s, as Starbucks expanded nationally.

Still Starbucks is not unique: You probably know of three or more coffeehouses in your neighborhood. The coffeehouse market is competitive because it is inexpensive to open a new store by leasing store space and buying espresso machines. Hundreds of firms in the United States operate coffeehouses. Some firms are large nationwide chains, such as Diedrich Coffee, which has more than 2,400 stores in the United States and 10 foreign countries. Others are regional chains, such as Caribou Coffee, which operates

LEARNING OBJECTIVES

After studying this chapter, you should be able to:

① Explain why a monopolistically competitive firm has a downward-sloping demand curve.

② Explain how a monopolistically competitive firm decides the quantity to produce and the price to charge.

③ Analyze the situation of a monopolistically competitive firm in the long run.

④ Compare the efficiency of monopolistic competition and perfect competition.

⑤ Define marketing and explain how firms use it to differentiate their products.

⑥ Identify the key factors that determine a firm's profitability.

250 stores in nine states. Still others are small firms that operate only one store.

In Chapter 11, we discussed the situation of firms in perfectly competitive markets. These markets share three key characteristics:

1. There are many firms.
2. The products sold by all firms are identical.
3. There are no barriers to new firms entering the industry.

The market Starbucks competes in shares two of these characteristics: There are many other coffeehouses—with the number increasing all the time—and the barriers to entering the market are very low.

But unlike the products offered by perfectly competitive firms, such as wheat farms, consumers do not view coffeehouses as identical. The coffee at Starbucks, as well as the muffins and other snacks, are not identical to what is offered by competing coffeehouses. Selling coffee in coffeehouses is not like selling wheat: The products sold by Starbucks and its competitors are *differentiated,* rather than identical. So, the coffeehouse market is *monopolistically competitive,* rather than perfectly competitive. *An Inside Look* on page 404 explores one of the ways that businesses like Starbucks attempt to differentiate themselves from the competition.

> Many markets in the U.S. economy are similar to the coffeehouse market in that these markets have many buyers and sellers and the barriers to entry are low, but the goods and services offered for sale are differentiated, rather than identical. Examples of these markets include video stores, restaurants, movie theaters, supermarkets, and manufacturers of men's and women's clothing. In fact, the majority of the businesses you patronize are competing in **monopolistically competitive** markets.

Monopolistic competition A market structure in which barriers to entry are low, and many firms compete by selling similar, but not identical, products

In Chapter 11, we saw how perfect competition benefits consumers and results in economic efficiency. Will these same desirable outcomes also hold for monopolistically competitive markets? This question is important because monopolistically competitive markets are so common, and it is a key issue we will explore in this chapter.

(1) **LEARNING OBJECTIVE**

Explain why a monopolistically competitive firm has a downward-sloping demand curve.

Demand and Marginal Revenue for a Firm in a Monopolistically Competitive Market

If the Starbucks coffeehouse located one mile from your house raises the price for a caffè latte from $3.00 to $3.25, it will lose some, but not all, of its customers. Some customers will switch to buying their coffee at another store, but other customers will be willing to pay the higher price for a variety of reasons: This store may be closer to them, or they may prefer Starbucks caffè lattes to similar coffees at competing stores. Because changing the price affects the quantity of caffè lattes sold, a Starbucks store will face a downward-sloping demand curve, rather than the horizontal demand curve faced by a wheat farmer.

The Demand Curve for a Monopolistically Competitive Firm

Figure 12-1 shows how a change in price affects the quantity of caffè lattes Starbucks sells. The increase in the price from $3.00 to $3.25 decreases the quantity of caffè lattes sold from 3,000 per week to 2,400 per week.

FIGURE 12-1

The Downward-Sloping Demand for Caffè Lattes at a Starbucks

If a Starbucks increases the price of caffè lattes, it will lose some, but not all, of its customers. In this case, raising the price from $3.00 to $3.25 reduces the quantity of caffè lattes sold from 3,000 to 2,400. Therefore, unlike a perfect competitor, a Starbucks store faces a downward-sloping demand curve.

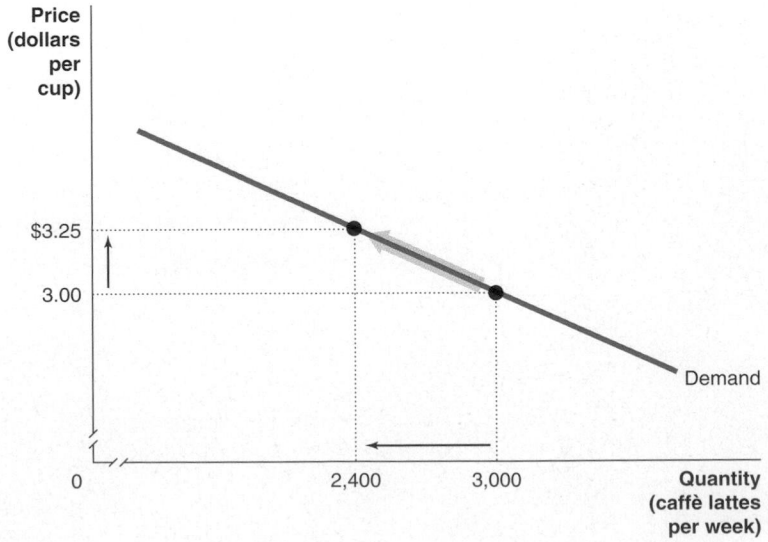

Marginal Revenue for a Firm with a Downward-Sloping Demand Curve

Recall from Chapter 11 that for a firm in a perfectly competitive market, the demand curve and the marginal revenue curve are the same. A perfectly competitive firm faces a horizontal demand curve and does not have to cut the price to sell a larger quantity. A monopolistically competitive firm, however, must cut the price to sell more, so its marginal revenue curve will slope downward and will be below its demand curve.

The data in Table 12-1 illustrate this point. To keep the numbers simple, let's assume that your local Starbucks coffeehouse is very small and only sells at most 10 caffè lattes per week. If Starbucks charges a price of $6.00 or more, all of its potential customers will buy their coffee somewhere else. If it charges $5.50, it will sell one caffè latte per week. For each additional $0.50 Starbucks reduces the price, it increases the number of caffè lattes it sells by one. The third column in the table shows how the firm's *total revenue* changes as it sells more caffè lattes. The fourth column shows the firm's revenue per unit, or its *average revenue*. Average revenue is equal to total revenue divided by quantity. Because total revenue equals price multiplied by quantity, dividing by quantity leaves just price. Therefore, *average revenue is always equal to price*. This result will be true for firms selling in any of the four market structures we discussed in Chapter 11.

The last column shows the firm's marginal revenue, or the amount that total revenue changes as the firm sells one more caffè latte. For a perfectly competitive firm, the additional revenue received from selling one more unit is just equal to the price. That will not be true for Starbucks because to sell another caffè latte it has to reduce the price. When the firm cuts the price by $0.50, one good thing and one bad thing happens:

➤ *The good thing:*   It sells one more caffè latte; we can call this the *output effect.*

➤ *The bad thing:*   It receives $0.50 less for each caffè latte that it could have sold at the higher price; we can call this the *price effect.*

Figure 12-2 illustrates what happens when the firm cuts the price from $3.50 to $3.00. Selling the sixth caffè latte adds the $3.00 price to the firm's revenue; this is the output effect. But Starbucks now receives a price of $3.00, rather than $3.50, on the first 5 caffè lattes sold; this is the price effect. As a result of the price effect, the firm's revenue on

CAFFÈ LATTES SOLD PER WEEK (Q)	PRICE (P)	TOTAL REVENUE ($TR = P \times Q$)	AVERAGE REVENUE $\left(AR = \dfrac{TR}{Q} \right)$	MARGINAL REVENUE $\left(MR = \dfrac{\Delta TR}{\Delta Q} \right)$
0	$6.00	$0.00	—	—
1	5.50	5.50	$5.50	$5.50
2	5.00	10.00	5.00	4.50
3	4.50	13.50	4.50	3.50
4	4.00	16.00	4.00	2.50
5	3.50	17.50	3.50	1.50
6	3.00	18.00	3.00	0.50
7	2.50	17.50	2.50	−0.50
8	2.00	16.00	2.00	−1.50
9	1.50	13.50	1.50	−2.50
10	1.00	10.00	1.00	−3.50

TABLE 12-1

Demand and Marginal Revenue at a Starbucks

FIGURE 12-2

How a Price Cut Affects a Firm's Revenue

If the local Starbucks reduces the price of a caffè latte from $3.50 to $3.00, the number of caffè lattes it sells per week will increase from 5 to 6. Its marginal revenue from selling the sixth caffè latte will be $0.50, which is equal to the $3.00 additional revenue from selling one more caffè latte (the area of the green box) minus the $2.50 loss in revenue from selling the first 5 caffè lattes for $0.50 less each (the area of the red box).

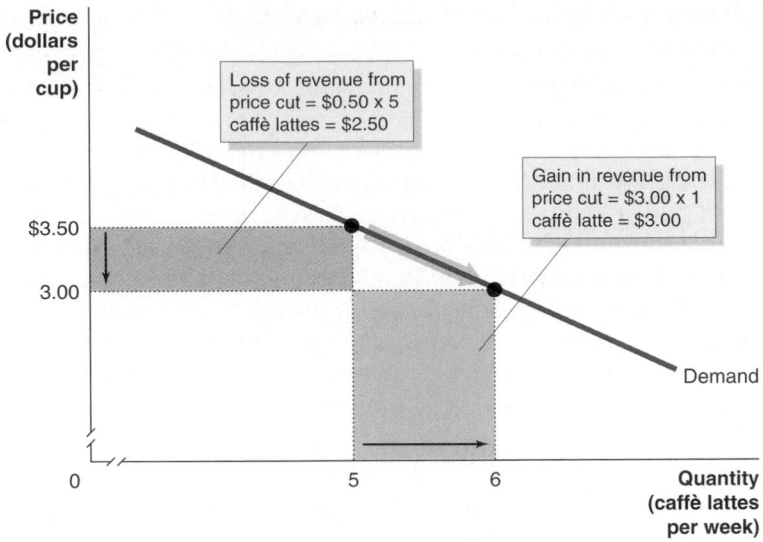

these 5 caffè lattes is $2.50 less than it would have been if the price had remained at $3.50. So, the firm has gained $3.00 in revenue on the sixth caffè latte and lost $2.50 in revenue on the first 5 caffè lattes, for a net change in revenue of $0.50. Marginal revenue is the change in total revenue from selling one more unit. Therefore, the marginal revenue of the sixth caffè latte is $0.50. Notice that the marginal revenue of the sixth unit is far below its price of $3.00. In fact, for each additional caffè latte Starbucks sells, marginal revenue will be less than price. There is an important general point: *Every firm that has the ability to affect the price of the good or service it sells will have a marginal revenue curve that is below its demand curve.* Only firms in perfectly competitive markets, which can sell as many units as they want at the market price, have marginal revenue curves that are the same as their demand curves.

Figure 12-3 shows the relationship between the demand curve and the marginal revenue curve for the local Starbucks. Notice that after the sixth caffè latte, marginal rev-

FIGURE 12-3

The Demand and Marginal Revenue Curves for a Monopolistically Competitive Firm

Any firm that has the ability to affect the price of the product it sells will have a marginal revenue curve that is below its demand curve. The demand and marginal revenue curves in the figure graph the data from Table 12-1. After the sixth caffè latte, marginal revenue becomes negative because the additional revenue received from selling one more caffè latte is smaller than the revenue lost from receiving a lower price on the caffè lattes that could have been sold at the original price.

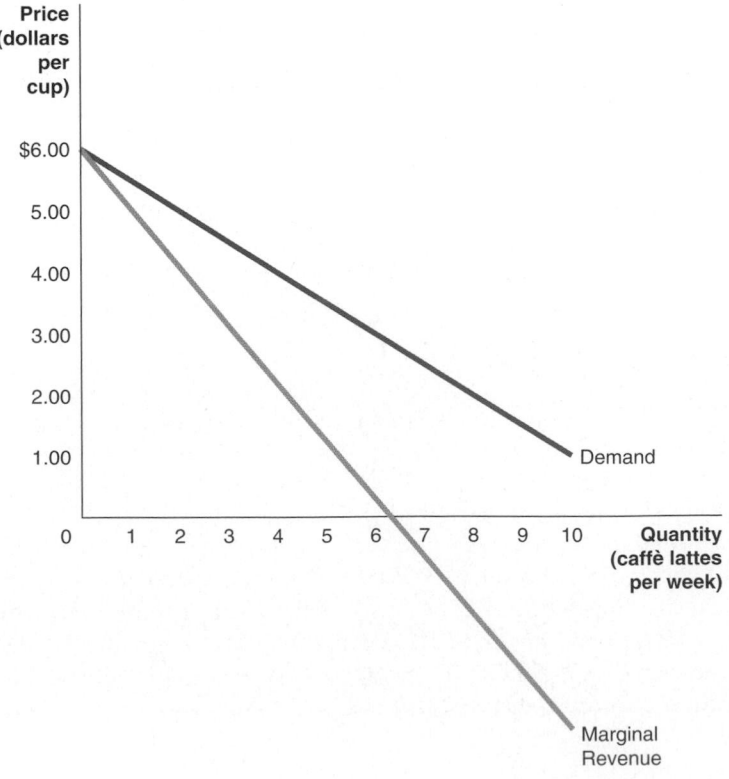

enue becomes negative. This outcome occurs because the additional revenue received from selling one more caffè latte is smaller than the revenue lost from receiving a lower price on the caffè lattes that could have been sold at the original price.

How a Monopolistically Competitive Firm Maximizes Profits in the Short Run

② **LEARNING OBJECTIVE**

Explain how a monopolistically competitive firm decides the quantity to produce and the price to charge.

All firms use the same approach to maximize profits: They produce where marginal revenue is equal to marginal cost. For the local Starbucks, this means selling the quantity of caffè lattes for which the last caffè latte sold adds the same amount to the firm's revenue as to its costs. To begin our discussion of how monopolistically competitive firms maximize profits, let's consider the situation the local Starbucks faces in the short run. Recall from Chapter 10 that in the short run at least one factor of production is fixed and there is not enough time for new firms to enter the market. A Starbucks will have many costs, including the cost of purchasing the ingredients for its caffè lattes and other coffees, the electricity it uses, and the wages of its employees. Recall that a firm's *marginal cost* is the increase in total cost resulting from producing another unit of output. We have seen that for many firms, marginal cost has a U-shape. We will assume that Starbucks's marginal cost has this usual shape.

In the table in Figure 12-4, we bring together the revenue data from Table 12-1 with the cost data for Starbucks. The graphs in Figure 12-4 plot the data from the table. In panel (a), we see how Starbucks can determine its profit-maximizing quantity and price. As long as the marginal cost of selling one more caffè latte is less than the marginal revenue, the firm should sell additional caffè lattes. For example, increasing the quantity of caffè lattes sold from 3 per week to 4 per week increases marginal cost by $1.00 but increases marginal revenue by $2.50. So, the firm's profits are increased by $1.50 as a result of selling the fourth caffè latte.

As Starbucks sells more caffè lattes, rising marginal cost will eventually equal marginal revenue and the firm will be selling the profit-maximizing quantity of caffè lattes. This outcome happens with the fifth caffè latte, which adds $1.50 to the firm's costs and $1.50 to its revenues—point *A* in Figure 12-4 (a). The demand curve tells us the price at which the firm is able to sell 5 caffè lattes per week. In Figure 12-4, if we draw a vertical line from 5 caffè lattes up to the demand curve, we can see that the price at which the firm can sell 5 caffè lattes per week is $3.50 (point *B*). We can conclude that Starbucks's profit-maximizing quantity is 5 caffè lattes and its profit-maximizing price is $3.50. If the firm sells more than 5 caffè lattes per week, its profits fall. For example, if it sells a sixth caffè latte, it will add $2.00 to its costs and only $0.50 to its revenues. So, its profit will fall from $5.00 to $3.50.

Panel (b) adds Starbucks's average total cost curve. The panel shows that the average total cost of selling 5 caffè lattes is $2.50. Recall from Chapter 11 that:

$$\text{Profit} = (P - ATC) \times Q.$$

In this case, profit = ($3.50 − $2.50) × 5 = $5.00. The green box in panel (b) shows the amount of profit. The box has a base equal to Q and a height equal to $(P - ATC)$, so its area equals profit.

Notice that, unlike a perfectly competitive firm, which produces where $P = MC$, a monopolistically competitive firm produces where $P > MC$. In this case, Starbucks is charging a price of $3.50, although marginal cost is $1.50. For the perfectly competitive firm, price equals marginal revenue, $P = MR$. Therefore, to fulfill the $MR = MC$ condition for profit maximization, a perfectly competitive firm will produce where $P = MC$. Because $P > MR$ for a monopolistically competitive firm—which results from the marginal revenue curve being below the demand curve—a monopolistically competitive firm will maximize profits where $P > MC$.

ITALIC)

CROSS - OUT

Caffè Lattes Sold per Week (Q)	Price (P)	Total Revenue (TR)	Marginal Revenue (MR)	Total Cost (TC)	Marginal Cost (MC)	Average Total Cost (ATC)	Profit
0	$6.00	$0.00		$5.00			—$5.00
1	5.50	5.50	$5.50	8.00	$3.00	$8.00	—2.50
2	5.00	10.00	4.50	9.50	1.50	4.75	0.50
3	4.50	13.50	3.50	10.00	0.50	3.33	3.50
4	4.00	16.00	2.50	11.00	1.00	2.75	5.00
5	3.50	17.50	1.50	12.50	1.50	2.50	5.00
6	3.00	18.00	0.50	14.50	2.00	2.42	3.50
7	2.50	17.50	—0.50	17.00	2.50	2.43	0.50
8	2.00	16.00	—1.50	20.00	3.00	2.50	—4.00
9	1.50	13.50	—2.50	23.50	3.50	2.61	—10.00
10	1.00	10.00	—3.50	27.50	4.00	2.75	—17.50

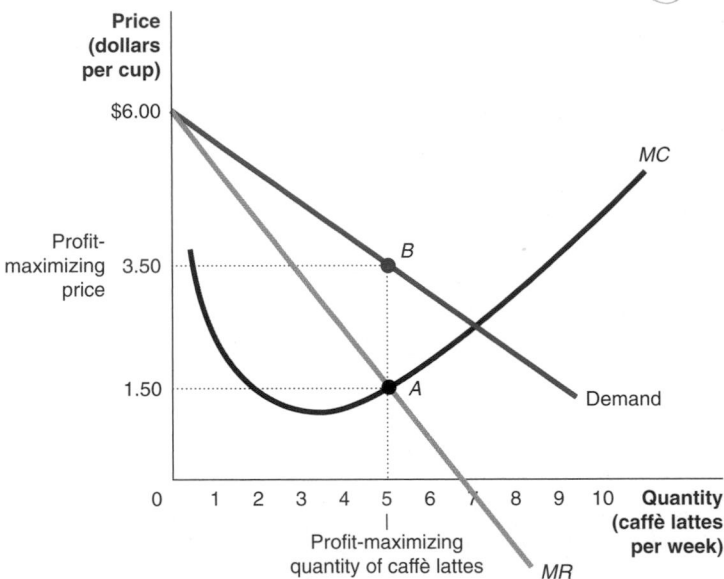

(a) Profit-maximizing quantity and price for a monopolistic competitor

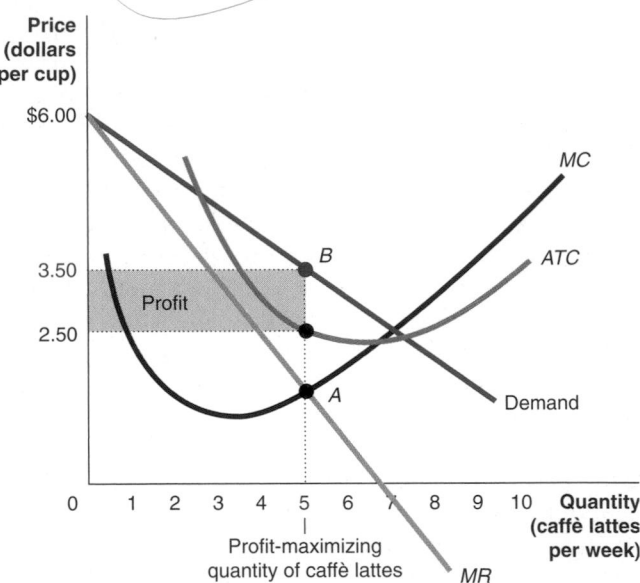

(b) Short-run profits for a monopolistic competitor

FIGURE 12-4   **Maximizing Profit in a Monopolistically Competitive Market**

To maximize profit, Starbucks coffeehouse wants to sell caffè lattes up to the point where the marginal revenue from selling the last caffè latte is just equal to the marginal cost. As the information in the table shows, this happens with the fifth caffè latte—point *A* in panel (a)—which adds $1.50 to the firm's costs and $1.50 to its revenues. The firm then uses the demand curve to find the price

that will lead consumers to buy this quantity of caffè lattes (point *B*). In panel (b), the green box represents the firm's profits. The box has a height equal to $1.00, which is the price of $3.50 minus the average total cost of $2.50, and a base equal to the quantity of 5 caffè lattes. So, this Starbucks profit equals $1 × 5 = $5.00.

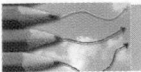

SOLVED PROBLEM 12-1

② **LEARNING OBJECTIVE**

Explain how a monopolistically competitive firm decides the quantity to produce and the price to charge.

How Not to Maximize Profits

In an article in the *New York Times*, Virginia Postrel states that when deciding the "question of whether printing another copy of a given, already published book, is a profitable thing to do" managers at publishing firms begin by calculating the cost of printing an additional copy of the book. But these managers "often fall prey to the mistake of adding up every expense associated with a book, including the overhead like rent and editors' salaries, and then dividing by the number of copies." Will the process described in the previous sentence give an accurate estimate of marginal cost? If you were a manager at a publishing firm, how would you determine whether producing one more copy of a book will increase your profits?

Source: Virginia Postrel, "Often, Basic Concepts in Economics Are Taken for Granted," *New York Times*, January 3, 2002.

Solving the Problem:

Step 1: Review the chapter material. This problem is about how monopolistically competitive firms maximize profits, so you may want to review the section "How a Monopolistically Competitive Firm Maximizes Profits in the Short Run," which begins on page 391.

Step 2: Analyze the costs described in the problem. We have seen that to maximize profits, firms should produce up to the point where marginal revenue equals marginal cost. Marginal cost is the increase in total cost resulting from producing another unit of output. Rent and editors' salaries are part of a publishing company's fixed costs because they do not change as the company increases its output of books. Therefore, managers at publishing companies should not include them in calculating marginal cost.

Step 3: Explain how a manager at a publishing firm should decide whether to publish one more copy of a book. To determine whether producing one more copy of a book will increase your profits, you need to compare the marginal revenue received from selling the book with the marginal cost of producing it. If the marginal revenue is greater than the marginal cost, producing the book will increase your profits.

YOUR TURN: For more practice, do related problem 8 on page 408 at the end of this chapter. Visit www.prenhall.com/hubbard for an interactive exercise related to this Solved Problem.

What Happens to Profits in the Long Run?

Remember that a firm makes an economic profit when its total revenue is greater than all of its opportunity costs, including the opportunity cost of the funds invested in the firm by its owners. Because cost curves include the owners' opportunity costs, the Starbucks coffeehouse represented in Figure 12-4 is making an economic profit. This economic profit gives entrepreneurs an incentive to enter this market and establish new firms. If a Starbucks is earning economic profit selling caffè lattes, new coffeehouses are likely to open in the same area.

How Does Entry of New Firms Affect the Profits of Existing Firms?

As new coffeehouses open near the local Starbucks, the firm's demand curve will shift to the left. The demand curve will shift because Starbucks will sell fewer caffè lattes at each price now that there are additional coffeehouses in the area selling similar drinks. The demand curve will also become more elastic because consumers now have additional coffeehouses from which to buy coffee, so Starbucks will lose more sales if it raises its prices. Figure 12-5 shows how the demand curve for the local Starbucks shifts as new firms enter its market.

In panel (a) of Figure 12-5, the short-run demand curve shows the relationship between the price of caffè lattes and the quantity of caffè lattes Starbucks sells per week before the entry of new firms. With this demand curve, Starbucks can charge a price above average total cost—shown as point A in panel (a)—and make a profit. But this profit attracts additional coffeehouses to the area and shifts the demand curve for the Starbucks's caffè lattes to the left. As long as Starbucks is making an economic profit, there is an incentive for additional coffeehouses to open in the area and the demand curve will continue shifting to the left. As panel (b) shows, eventually the

3 **LEARNING OBJECTIVE**

Analyze the situation of a monopolistically competitive firm in the long run.

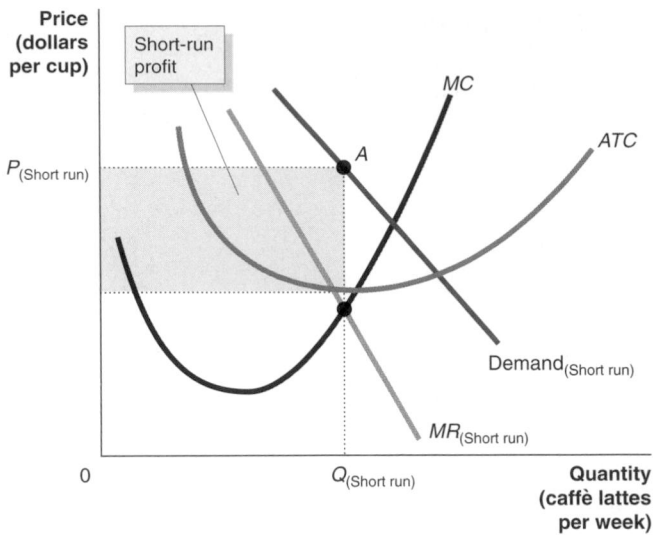

(a) A monopolistic competitor may earn a short-run profit

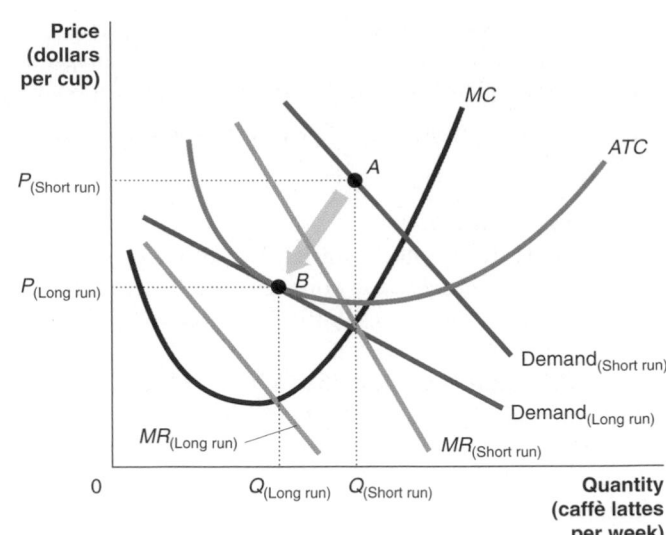

(b) A monopolistic competitor's profits are eliminated in the long run

FIGURE 12-5   **How Entry of New Firms Eliminates Profits**

In the short run—panel (a)—the local Starbucks faces the demand and marginal revenue curves labeled "Short run." With this demand curve, Starbucks coffeehouse can charge a price above average total cost (point A) and make a profit, shown by the green rectangle. But this profit attracts new firms to enter the market, which shifts the demand and marginal revenue curves to the ones labeled "Long run" in panel (b). Because price is now equal to average total cost (point B), Starbucks breaks even and no longer earns an economic profit.

demand curve will have shifted to the point where it is just touching—or tangent to—the average cost curve.

In the long run, at the point at which the demand curve is tangent to the average cost curve, price is equal to average total cost (point B), the firm is breaking even, and it no longer earns an economic profit. In the long run, the demand curve is also more elastic because the more coffeehouses there are in the area, the more sales Starbucks will lose to other coffeehouses if it raises its price.

Of course, it is possible that a monopolistically competitive firm will suffer economic losses in the short run. As a consequence, the owners of the firm will not be covering the opportunity cost of their investment. In the long run, we would expect firms will exit an industry if they are suffering economic losses. If firms exit, the demand curve for the output of a remaining firm will shift to the right. This process will continue until the representative firm in the industry is able to charge a price

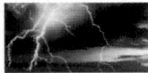

Don't Let This Happen To You!

Don't Confuse Zero Economic Profit with Zero Accounting Profit

Remember that economists count the opportunity cost of the owner's investment in a firm as a cost. For example, suppose you invest $200,000 opening a video store and the return you could earn on those funds each year in a similar investment—such as opening a pizza parlor—is 10 percent. Therefore, the annual opportunity cost of investing the funds in your own business is 10 percent of $200,000 or $20,000. This $20,000 is part of your profit in the account-

ing sense, and you would have to pay taxes on it. But in an economic sense, the $20,000 is a cost. In long-run equilibrium, we would expect that entry of new firms would keep you from earning more than 10 percent on your investment. So, you would end up breaking even and earning zero economic profit, even though you were earning an accounting profit of $20,000.

YOUR TURN: Test your understanding by doing related problem 9 on page 408 at the end of this chapter.

TABLE 12-2 The Short Run and the Long Run for a Monopolistically Competitive Firm

Relationship between Price and Marginal Cost	Relationship between Price and Average Total Cost	Profits and Losses	Elasticity of Demand Curve
Short Run $P > MC$	**Short Run** $P > ATC$	**Short Run** Economic profit	**Short Run** Less elastic demand curve

[Graphs for each column — Short Run row]

| | or $P < ATC$ | or Economic loss | |

[Graphs — middle row for Price and ATC, and Profits and Losses columns]

| **Long Run**
$P > MC$ | **Long Run**
$P = ATC$ | **Long Run**
Zero economic profit | **Long Run**
More elastic demand curve |

[Graphs for each column — Long Run row]

equal to its average cost and break even. Therefore, in the long run, monopolistically competitive firms will experience neither economic profits nor economic losses. Table 12-2 summarizes the short run and the long run for a monopolistically competitive firm.

The Rise and Fall of Apple's Macintosh Computer

12-1 Making the Connection

In 1983, there were more than 15 firms selling personal computers nationally, as well as many smaller firms in local markets that sold computers assembled from purchased components. None of these personal computers operated using the current system of clicking on icons with a mouse. Instead, users had to type in commands to call up word processing, spreadsheet, and other software programs. This awkward system required

Macintosh lost its differentiation, but still has a loyal—if small—following.

users to memorize many commands or constantly consult computer manuals. In January 1984, Apple Computer introduced the Macintosh, which used a mouse and could be operated by clicking on icons. The average cost of producing Macintoshes was about $500. Apple sold them for prices between $2,500 and $3,000. This price was more than twice that of comparable personal computers sold by IBM and other companies, but the Macintosh was so easy to use that it was able to achieve a 15 percent share of the market. Apple had successfully introduced a personal computer that was strongly differentiated from its competitors. One journalist covering the computer industry has gone so far as to call the Macintosh "the most important consumer product of the last half of the twentieth century."

Microsoft produced the operating system known as MS-DOS (Microsoft Disk Operating System), which was used by almost all non-Apple computers. The financial success of the Macintosh led Microsoft to develop an operating system that would also use a mouse and icons. In 1992, Microsoft introduced the operating system Windows 3.1, which succeeded in reproducing many of the key features of the Macintosh. By August 1995, when Microsoft introduced Windows 95, non-Apple computers had become as easy to use as Macintosh computers. By that time, most personal computers operated in a way very similar to the Macintosh, and Apple was no longer able to charge prices that were significantly above those charged by its competitors. The Macintosh had lost its differentiation. Although the Macintosh continues to have a loyal following, particularly among graphic designers, today it has only a 3 percent share of the personal computer market.

Source: The quote in the first paragraph is from Steven Levy, *Insanely Great: The Life and Times of Macintosh, the Computer that Changed Everything*, New York: Viking, 1994, p. 7.

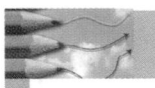

SOLVED PROBLEM 12-2

③ **LEARNING OBJECTIVE**

Analyze the situation of a monopolistically competitive firm in the long run.

The Short Run and the Long Run for the Macintosh

Use the information in Making the Connection 12-1 to draw a graph showing changes in the market for Macintosh computers between 1984 and 1995.

Solving the Problem:

Step 1: Review the chapter material. This problem is about how the entry of new firms affected the market for the Macintosh, so you may want to review the section "How Does the Entry of New Firms Affect the Profits of Existing Firms?" which begins on page 393.

Step 2: Draw the graph. Making the Connection 12-1 indicates that in 1984, when the Macintosh was first introduced, its differentiation from other computers allowed Apple to make a substantial economic profit. In 1995, the release of Windows 95 meant that non-Macintosh computers were as easy to use as Macintosh computers. Apple's product differentiation was eliminated, as was its ability to earn economic profits. The change over time in Apple's situation is shown in the following graph, which combines panels (a) and (b) from Figure 12-5 in one graph.

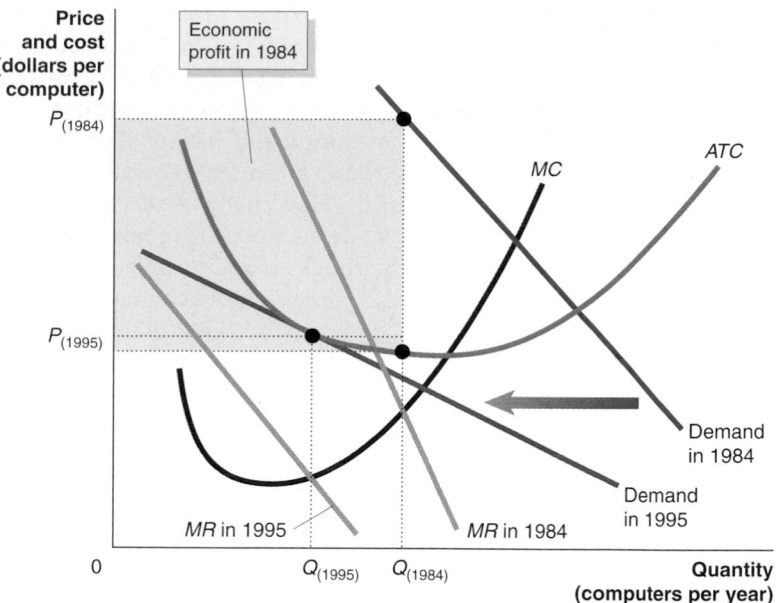

Between 1984 and 1995, Microsoft's development of the Windows operating system eliminated Macintosh's product differentiation. The demand curve for Macintoshes shifted to the left and became more elastic throughout the relevant range of prices.

Extra Credit: Note that this analysis is simplified. The Macintosh of 1995 was a different—and better—computer than the Macintosh of 1984. Apple has made changes to the Macintosh, such as the introduction of the colorful iMac computer in 1999, that have sometimes led to increases in sales. But the Macintosh has never been able to regain the high demand and premium prices it enjoyed from the mid-1980s to the early 1990s.

YOUR TURN: For more practice, do related problem 14 on page 409 at the end of this chapter. Visit www.prenhall.com/hubbard for an interactive exercise related to this Solved Problem.

Is Zero Economic Profit Inevitable in the Long Run?

The economic analysis of the long run shows the effects of market forces over time. In the case of Starbucks, the effect of market forces is to eliminate the economic profit earned by a monopolistically competitive firm. Owners of monopolistically competitive firms, of course, do not have to passively accept this long-run result. The key to earning economic profits is either to sell a differentiated product or to find a way of producing an existing product at a lower cost. If a monopolistically competitive firm selling a differentiated product is earning profits, these profits will attract the entry of additional firms and the entry of these firms eventually will eliminate the firm's profits. If a firm introduces new technology that allows it to sell a good or service at a lower cost, competing firms eventually will be able to duplicate this technology and eliminate the firm's profits. *But this result holds only if the firm stands still and fails to find new ways of differentiating its product or fails to find new ways of lowering the cost of producing its product.* Firms continually struggle to find new ways of differentiating their products as they try to stay one step ahead of other firms that are attempting to copy their success. As new coffeehouses enter the area served by the Starbucks coffeehouse, the owners can expect to see their economic profits competed away, unless they can find ways to differentiate their product.

In 2004, Howard Schultz, the chairman of Starbucks, was well aware of this fact. Although the firm had already opened 7,500 coffeehouses worldwide, he declared, "We are in the second inning of a nine-inning game. We are just beginning to tap into all sorts of new markets, new customers, and new products." In fact, Starbucks has used various strategies to differentiate itself from competing coffeehouses. Competitors have found it difficult to duplicate Starbucks's European espresso bar atmosphere, with its large, comfortable chairs, music playing, and groups of friends dropping in and out during the day. Most importantly, Starbucks has continued to be very responsive to its customers' preferences. As one observer put it, "How many retailers could put up with 'I'll have a grande low-fat triple-shot half-caf white-chocolate mocha, extra hot, easy on the whipped cream. And I'm in a rush'?" Starbucks has been able to maintain greater control over the operations of its coffeehouses, because unlike many of its competitors, all of its coffeehouses are company-owned; none are *franchises*. A franchise is a business with the legal right to sell a good or service in a particular area. When a firm uses franchises, local businesspeople are able to buy and run the stores in their area. This makes it easier for a firm to finance its expansion, but forces the firm to give up some control over its stores.

Starbucks experienced great success during the 1990s and the early 2000s, but history shows that in the long run competitors will be able to duplicate most of what it does. In the face of that competition, it will be very difficult for Starbucks to continue earning economic profits.

The owner of a competitive firm is in a position similar to that of Ebenezer Scrooge in Charles Dickens's *A Christmas Carol* when Scrooge is confronted by the Ghost of Christmas Yet to Come. When Scrooge is shown visions of his own death, he asks the Ghost, "Are these the shadows of the things that Will be, or are they shadows of things that May be, only?" The shadow of the end of their profits haunts owners of every firm. Firms try to avoid losing profits by reducing costs, by improving their products, or by convincing consumers their products are indeed different from what competitors offer. To stay one step ahead of its competitors, a firm has to offer consumers goods or services that they perceive to have greater *value* than those offered by competing firms. Value can take the form of product differentiation that makes the good or service more suited to consumers' preferences, or it can take the form of a lower price.

12-2 Making the Connection

Staying One Step Ahead of the Competition: Eugène Schueller and L'Oréal

Today, L'Oréal, with headquarters in the Paris suburb of Clichy, is the largest seller of perfumes, cosmetics, and hair care products in the world. In addition to L'Oréal, its brands include Lancôme, Maybelline, Soft Sheen/Carson, Garnier, Redken, Ralph Lauren, and Matrix. Like most large firms, L'Oréal was started by an entrepreneur with an idea. Eugène Schueller was a French chemist who experimented in the evenings trying to find a safe and reliable hair coloring for women. In 1907, he founded the firm that became L'Oréal and began selling his hair coloring preparations to Paris hair salons. Schueller was able to take advantage of changes in fashion. In the early twentieth century, women began to cut their hair much shorter than had been typical in the nineteenth century, and it had become socially acceptable to spend time and money styling it. The number of hair salons in Europe and the United States increased rapidly. By the 1920s and 1930s, the international popularity of Hollywood films, many starring "platinum blonde bombshells" such as Jean Harlow, made it fashionable for women to color their hair. By the late 1920s, L'Oréal was selling its products throughout Europe, the United States, and Japan.

Perfumes, cosmetics, and hair coloring are all products that should be easy for rival firms to duplicate. We would expect, then, that the economic profits L'Oréal earned in its early years would have been competed away in the long run through the entry of new firms. In fact, though, the firm has remained profitable through the decades, following a strategy of developing new products, improving existing products, and expanding into new markets. For example, when French workers first received paid holidays during the 1930s, L'Oréal moved quickly to dominate the new market for suntan lotion. Today, the firm's SoftSheen brand is experiencing rapid sales increases in Africa. In early 2005, L'Oréal launched a new line of men's skin-care products, including shaving cream. As one observer put it, at L'Oréal "brands don't stay at home serving the same old clientele. They get spruced up, put in a new set of traveling clothes, and sent abroad to meet new customers." L'Oréal has maintained its ability to innovate by spending more on research and development than do competing firms. The firm has a research staff of more than 1,000.

One reason L'Oréal has been able to follow a focused strategy is that the firm has had only three chairmen in its nearly century of existence: founder Eugène Schueller, François Dalle, and Lindsay Owen-Jones, who became chairman in 1988. Owen-Jones has described the firm's strategy: "Each brand is positioned on a very precise [market] segment, which overlaps as little as possible with the others." The story of L'Oréal shows that it is possible for a firm to stay one step ahead of the competition, but it takes a top management committed to an entrepreneurial spirit of continually developing new products.

Source for quotes: Richard Tomlinson, "L'Oréal's Global Makeover," *Fortune*, September 30, 2002.

Unlike many monopolistically competitive firms, L'Oréal has earned economic profits for a very long time.

Comparing Perfect Competition and Monopolistic Competition

We have seen that monopolistic competition and perfect competition share the characteristic that in long-run equilibrium firms earn zero economic profits. As Figure 12-6 shows, however, there are two important differences between long-run equilibrium in the two markets.

➤ Monopolistically competitive firms charge a price greater than marginal cost.

➤ Monopolistically competitive firms do not produce at minimum average total cost.

④ **LEARNING OBJECTIVE**
Compare the efficiency of monopolistic competition and perfect competition.

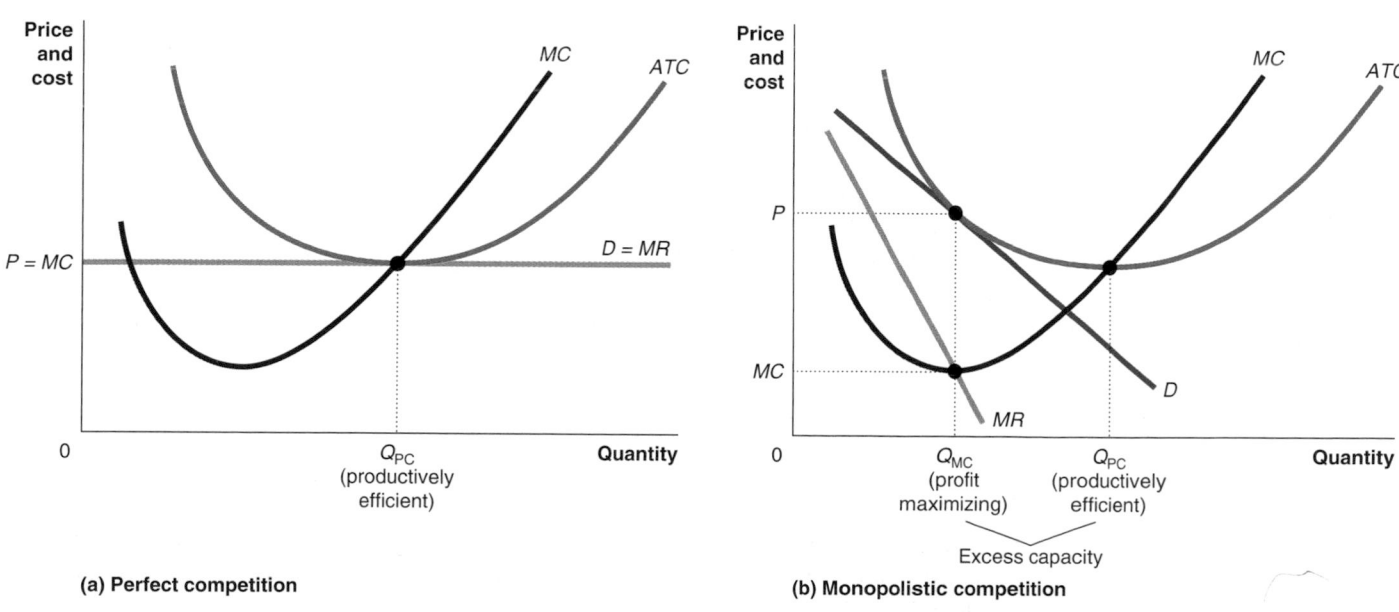

(a) Perfect competition

(b) Monopolistic competition

FIGURE 12-6 Comparing Long-Run Equilibrium under Perfect Competition and Monopolistic Competition

In panel (a), the perfectly competitive firm in long-run equilibrium produces at Q_{PC}, where price equals marginal cost and average total cost is at a minimum. The perfectly competitive firm is both allocatively efficient and productively efficient. In panel (b), the monopolistically competitive firm produces at Q_{MC}, where price is greater than marginal cost and average total cost is not at a minimum. As a result, the monopolistically competitive firm is neither allocatively efficient nor productively efficient. The monopolistically competitive firm has excess capacity equal to the difference between its profit-maximizing level of output and the productively efficient level of output.

Excess Capacity under Monopolistic Competition

Recall that a firm in a perfectly competitive market faces a perfectly elastic demand curve that is also its marginal revenue curve. Therefore, the firm maximizes profit by producing where price equals marginal cost. As panel (a) of Figure 12-6 shows, in long-run equilibrium, a perfectly competitive firm produces at the minimum point of its average total cost curve.

Panel (b) of Figure 12-6 shows that the profit-maximizing level of output for a monopolistically competitive firm comes at a level of output where price is greater than marginal cost and the firm is not at the minimum point of its average total cost curve. A monopolistically competitive firm has *excess capacity*: If it increased its output, it could produce at a lower average cost.

Is Monopolistic Competition Inefficient?

In Chapter 11, we discussed *productive efficiency* and *allocative efficiency*. Productive efficiency refers to the situation where a good is produced at the lowest possible cost. Allocative efficiency refers to the situation where every good or service is produced up to the point where the last unit provides a marginal benefit to consumers equal to the marginal cost of producing it. For productive efficiency to hold, firms must produce at the minimum point of average total cost. For allocative efficiency to hold, firms must charge a price equal to marginal cost. In a perfectly competitive market, both productive efficiency and allocative efficiency are achieved, but in a monopolistically competitive market, neither is achieved. Economists have debated whether the fact that monopolistically competitive markets are not productively or allocatively efficient means that there is a significant loss of well-being to society in these markets when compared with perfectly competitive markets.

How Consumers Benefit from Monopolistic Competition

Looking again at Figure 12-6, you can see that the only difference between the monopolistically competitive firm and the perfectly competitive firm is that the demand curve for the monopolistically competitive firm slopes downward, whereas the demand curve for the perfectly competitive firm is a horizontal line. The demand curve for the monopolistically competitive firm slopes downward because the good or service the firm is selling is differentiated from the goods or services being sold by competing firms. The perfectly competitive firm is selling a good or service identical to those being sold by its competitors. A key point to remember is that *firms differentiate their products to appeal to consumers*. When Starbucks coffeehouses begin offering new flavors of coffee, when Blockbuster stores begin carrying more DVDs and fewer VHS tapes, when General Mills introduces Apple-Cinnamon Cheerios, or when PepsiCo introduces caffeine-free Diet Pepsi, they are all attempting to attract and retain consumers through product differentiation. The success of these product differentiation strategies indicates that some consumers find these products preferable to the alternatives. Consumers, therefore, are better off than they would have been had these companies not differentiated their products.

We can conclude that consumers face a trade-off when buying the product of a monopolistically competitive firm: They are paying a price that is greater than marginal cost and the product is not being produced at minimum average cost, but they benefit from being able to purchase a product that is differentiated and more closely suited to their tastes.

12-3 *Making* the *Connection*

Abercrombie and Fitch: Can the Product Be Too Differentiated?

Business managers often refer to differentiating their products as finding a "market niche." The larger the niche, the greater the potential profit but the more likely that other firms will be able to compete against you. Too small a niche, however, may reduce competition but also reduce profits. In 2004, some analysts believed that the market niche chosen by the managers of the Abercrombie and Fitch clothing stores was too small. Chief Executive Mike Jeffries was quoted as saying that his store's target customer was an "18-to-22 [year old] college guy who has a good body and is aspirational." He admitted that his was a narrow niche: "If I exclude people—absolutely. Delighted to do so."

But was A&F excluding too many people? One analyst argued "they've . . .

Did Abercrombie and Fitch narrow its target market too much?

pushed a lot of people out of the brand." A&F's sales results seemed to indicate that this analyst was correct. Managers of retail stores closely monitor "same-store sales," which measures how much sales have increased on average in the same stores from one year to the next. To offset the effects of inflation—or general increases in prices in the economy—same-store sales need to increase at least 2 percent to 3 percent each year. A firm whose strategy of product differentiation succeeds will experience increases in same-store sales of at least 5 percent to 6 percent each year. By 2004, A&F's 350 stores had experienced four consecutive years of *negative* same-store results. The company apparently had gone too far in narrowing its market niche.

Source: Shelly Branch, "Maybe Sex Doesn't Sell, A&F Is Discovering," *Wall Street Journal*, December 12, 2003.

How Marketing Differentiates Products

Firms can differentiate their products through marketing. **Marketing** refers to all the activities necessary for a firm to sell a product to a consumer. Marketing includes activities such as determining which product to produce, designing the product, advertising the product, deciding how to distribute the product—for example, in retail stores or through a Web site—and monitoring how changes in consumer tastes are affecting the market for the product. Peter F. Drucker, a leading business strategist, describes marketing as follows: "It is the whole business seen from the point of view of its final result, that is, from the consumer's point of view. . . . True marketing . . . does not ask, 'What do we want to sell?' It asks, 'What does the consumer want to buy?'"

As we have seen, for monopolistically competitive firms to earn economic profits and to defend those profits from competitors, they must differentiate their products. Firms use two marketing tools to differentiate their products: brand management and advertising.

Brand Management

Once a firm has succeeded in differentiating its product, it must try to maintain that differentiation over time through **brand management.** As we have seen, whenever a firm successfully introduces a new product or a significantly different version of an old product, it earns economic profits in the short run. But the success of the firm inspires competitors to copy the new or improved product and, in the long run, the firm's economic profits will be competed away. Firms use brand management to postpone the time when they will no longer be able to earn economic profits.

Advertising

An innovative advertising campaign can make even long-established and familiar products, such as Coke or McDonald's Big Mac hamburgers, seem more desirable than

⑤ **LEARNING OBJECTIVE**

Define marketing and explain how firms use it to differentiate their products.

Marketing   All the activities necessary for a firm to sell a product to a consumer.

Brand management   The actions of a firm intended to maintain the differentiation of a product over time.

competing products. When a firm advertises a product, it is trying to shift the demand curve for the product to the right and to make it more inelastic. If the firm is successful, it will sell more of the product at every price and it will be able to increase the price it charges without losing as many customers. Of course, advertising also increases a firm's costs. If the increase in revenue that results from the advertising is greater than the increase in costs, the firm's profits will rise.

Needless to say, advertising campaigns are not always successful. In 1957, the Ford Motor Company introduced a new car, the Edsel, designed to compete with the Buick from General Motors. Ford set up a new division of the company to produce the Edsel in five different models and hired the advertising firm of Foote, Cone & Belding to direct a massive advertising campaign. Among other things, Ford purchased an hour of prime television time on the CBS network to broadcast *The Edsel Show*, hosted by Frank Sinatra, Bing Crosby, and Louis Armstrong. Ford set a sales goal of 200,000 cars during the first year of production. Unfortunately, most of the car-buying public found the styling of the Edsel, with its oversized headlights and elaborate front grill, to be unappealing. First-year sales were only about 63,000 cars. During the same period, General Motors sold more than 230,000 Buicks. Ford decided to shift its advertising account for the Edsel from Foote, Cone & Belding to Kenyon & Eckhardt. Despite a revised advertising campaign, sales of the Edsel remained very low. Fewer than 45,000 Edsels were sold during its second year of production. In November 1959, after only two years in production, Ford stopped making the Edsel. Even one of the largest advertising campaigns in history had failed to make the Edsel successful.

Defending a Brand Name

Once a firm has established a successful brand name, it has a strong incentive to defend it. A firm can apply for a *trademark,* which grants legal protection against other firms using its product's name.

One threat to a trademarked name is the possibility that it will become so widely used for a type of product that it will no longer be associated with the product of a specific company. Courts in the United States have ruled that when this happens, a firm is no longer entitled to legal protection of the brand name. For example, "aspirin," "escalator," and "thermos" originally were all brand names of the products of particular firms, but each became so widely used to refer to a type of product that none remains a legally protected brand name. Firms will spend substantial amounts of money trying to make sure that this does not happen to them. Coca-Cola, for example, employs workers to travel around the country stopping at restaurants and asking to be served a "Coke" with their meal. If the restaurant serves Pepsi or some other cola, rather than Coke, the restaurant will receive a letter from Coca-Cola's legal department reminding it that "Coke" is a trademarked name and not a generic name for any cola. Similarly, Xerox Corporation spends money on advertising to remind the public that "Xerox" is not a generic term for making photocopies.

Legally enforcing trademarks can be difficult. Estimates are that each year U.S. firms lose hundreds of billions of dollars in sales worldwide as a result of unauthorized use of their trademarked brand names. U.S. firms often find it difficult to enforce their trademarks in the courts of some foreign countries. Recent international agreements have increased the legal protections for trademarks.

Firms that sell their products through franchises rather than through company-owned stores encounter the problem that if a franchisee does not run his or her business well, the firm's brand may be damaged. Automobile firms send "roadmen" to visit their dealers to make sure that the dealerships are clean and well maintained and that the service departments employ competent mechanics and are well equipped with spare parts. Similarly, McDonald's sends employees from corporate headquarters to visit McDonald's franchises to make sure that the bathrooms are clean and the French fries are hot.

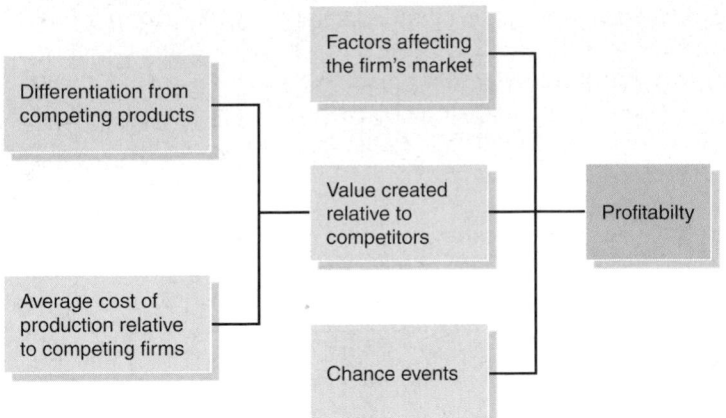

FIGURE 12-7

What Makes a Firm Successful?

The factors under a firm's control—the ability to differentiate its product and the ability to produce it at lower cost—combine with the factors beyond its control to determine the firm's profitability.

Source: Adapted from Figure 11.3 in David Besanko, David Dranove, Mark Shanley, and Scott Schaefer, *The Economics of Strategy,* 3rd ed., New York: John Wiley & Sons, 2004.

What Makes a Firm Successful?

A firm's owners and managers control some of the factors that make a firm successful and allow it to earn economic profits. The most important of these are the firm's ability to differentiate its product and to produce its product at a lower average cost than competing firms. A firm that successfully does these things creates *value* for its customers. Consumers will buy a product if they believe it meets a need not met by competing products or if its price is below that of competitors.

Some factors that affect a firm's profitability are not directly under the firm's control. Certain factors will affect all the firms in a market. For example, rising prices for jet fuel will reduce the profitability of all airlines. If consumers decide that they would rather watch pay-for-view movies delivered to their homes by cable or satellite than buy DVDs, the profitability of all stores selling DVDs will be reduced.

Sheer chance also plays a role in business, as it does in all other aspects of life. A struggling McDonald's franchise may see profits increase dramatically after the county unexpectedly decides to build a new road nearby. Many businesses in New York City, including restaurants, hotels, and theaters, experienced a marked drop in customers and profits following the September 11, 2001 terrorist attacks. Figure 12-7 illustrates the important point that factors within the firm's control and factors outside the firm's control interact to determine the firm's profitability.

(6) LEARNING OBJECTIVE

Identify the key factors that determine a firm's profitability.

Conclusion

In this chapter, we have applied many of the ideas about competition we developed in Chapter 11 to the more common market structure of monopolistic competition. We have seen that these ideas apply to monopolistically competitive markets, just as they did to perfectly competitive markets. At the end of Chapter 11, we concluded that "The competitive forces of the market produce relentless pressure on firms to produce new and better goods and services, and to produce them at lower cost. Firms that fail to adequately anticipate changes in consumer tastes or that fail to adopt the latest and most efficient production techniques usually do not survive in the long run." These conclusions are as true for coffeehouses and firms in other monopolistically competitive markets as they are for wheat farmers or apple growers.

In Chapter 13 and Chapter 14, we discuss the remaining market structures: oligopoly and monopoly. Before moving on to those chapters, read *An Inside Look* on the next page to learn how some Starbucks and McDonald's locations differentiate themselves from competitors by extending their hours of operation.

WALL STREET JOURNAL, JULY 15, 2004

Midnight Snack

SCHILLER PARK, III.— At about 3 a.m. recently, Michael Johnson sat at a table at a suburban Chicago McDonald's here eating lunch: Big Mac, with fries. This time of night, the 57-year-old truck driver says, few restaurants along his route from northern Indiana to western Illinois are open, and those that are tend to be far from the main highway.

Mr. Johnson eats in the middle of his 11 p.m. to 8 a.m. shift because, he says, "if you eat early, you come in sluggish, you're not as alert as you should be." So he's stopped at this highway rest stop regularly since it opened three weeks ago.

Having thoroughly squeezed the lunchtime market dry, the fast-food industry is chasing late-night customers like Mr. Johnson. Desperate for growth in a highly competitive business, chains from McDonald's Corp. to Wendy's International Inc. to Starbucks Corp. are keeping their doors open longer. . . .

To cater to insomniacs, Starbucks has opened 41 all-night units in places such as Miami, Wheaton, Colo., Kenosha, Wis., and Atlanta, a striking departure for a company that generally closed at 6 p.m. just a few years ago.

Restaurants' impetus for rushing into the late-night market is clear: With more Americans working the overnight shift, society is increasingly operating around-the-clock. Wendy's, for instance, found that 25% of its late-night customers stop in on their way home from work, while 22% ducked out of the house for a snack or meal, and 19% were returning home from nightclubs, bars and other social venues.

"Americans are working later hours. Mom's working days. Dad's working nights, and the night shift people are looking for good meals," says Mike Roberts, president of McDonald's USA. "It's such an integral part of how many Americans are living today. It's going to be very important to our business."

A decade ago, Taco Bell, subsidiary of Yum! Brands Inc., led the fast-food charge into the late-night market once dominated by White Castle Management Co., Denny's Corp. and IHOP Corp. The company has invested millions of dollars in promoting its "Open 'Til Midnight or Later" slogan in television, print and radio ads, and many of its commercials end with a late-night shot. Still, only recently has competition followed. . . .

The six-hour traditional breakfast time, which is 5 a.m. to 11 a.m., accounted for 12% of all quick-service meals, compared with lunch, which was nearly half of all fast-food sales, and the dinner rush, which accounted for just over one-third. Several years ago, when franchisee Dennis Stabile started opening one of his suburban Chicago McDonald's restaurants ear-

lier, at 5 a.m., sales between 7 a.m. and 8 a.m. grew by 50%. He saw similar results 9 p.m. to 11 p.m. after extending his hours past midnight. "Now that customers know you're open later, there's no question, 'Will McDonald's be open?,' because we always are," he says.

Restaurant owners and executives say extending hours doesn't require developing a new menu. Overnight workers can transition the restaurant from the dinner to breakfast periods. And extended hours simply maximize use of space. "You're not paying any more taxes to be open 24 hours than you are by staying open 18 hours. The more profit you make, the more money you have to remodel," Mr. Stabile says.

Restaurants say security during late-night periods is of little concern, especially since many have invested heavily in such items as closed-circuit cameras within view of customers at cash registers. Others offer free meals to law-enforcement officials, hoping their presence will be a crime deterrent. Fast-food outlets with drive-thrus can close the unit and leave the drive-thru open, which provides safety for patrons and workers, says Dennis Lombardi, executive vice president at Technomic Inc., a food-consulting firm. The majority of McDonald's restaurants open for extended hours do so only with drive-thrus. Half of Starbucks's new 24-hour units are drive-thrus. . . .

Key Points in the Article

This article discusses a new trend of restaurants staying open 24 hours per day. At one time, the market for late-night (or early-morning) meals was dominated by "family-style" restaurants, such as Denny's and the International House of Pancakes (IHOP). Recently, many other restaurants have begun to stay open 24 hours, including McDonald's, Wendy's, and Starbucks. Demand for late-night meals has increased as more U.S. workers are scheduled for night shifts, rather than the traditional 9-to-5 day shift.

Analyzing the News

a We saw in this chapter how important it is for firms to differentiate their products from those of their competitors. As a McDonald's owner asserted in this article, opening at 5:00 A.M. helped his normal 7:00 A.M. to 8:00 A.M. breakfast sales and being open after midnight helped his evening sales because "Now that customers know you're open later, there's no question, 'Will McDonald's be open?,' because we always are." In other words, by differentiating his product from that of other restaurants—that are not open early—the McDonald's owner is able to shift his firm's demand curve to the right. We show this in Figure 1, where the demand curve $D_{open\ 24\ hours}$ is to the right of $D_{open\ 16\ hours}$. Because price, $P_{open\ 24\ hours}$, is above ATC, this strategy allows the McDonald's owner to earn economic profits, at least in the short run.

b As we saw in Chapter 10, business managers sometimes attempt to reduce their average fixed costs by "spreading the overhead." The article explains that for a restaurant "extended hours simply maximize use of space." Figure 2 shows that if staying open longer allows a restaurant to increase the quantity it sells from Q_1 to Q_2, its average fixed costs will decline from AFC_1 to AFC_2.

Thinking Critically

1. Suppose that a law was passed banning restaurants from staying open past 10:00 P.M. Who would be harmed by this law? Would the law reduce profits in the fast-food market in the short run? In the long run? Use a graph like Figure 1 in your answer.

2. Suppose that a law was passed requiring fast-food firms to pay their night-shift employees twice as much as their daytime employees. What impact would this have on fast-food profits in the short run? In the long run? Use a graph like Figure 2 in your answer.

Source: *Wall Street Journal*, Eastern Edition [Staff Produced Copy Only] by Steven Gray. Copyright 2004 by Dow Jones & Co Inc. Reproduced with permission of Dow Jones and Co Inc. in the format Textbook via Copyright Clearance Center.

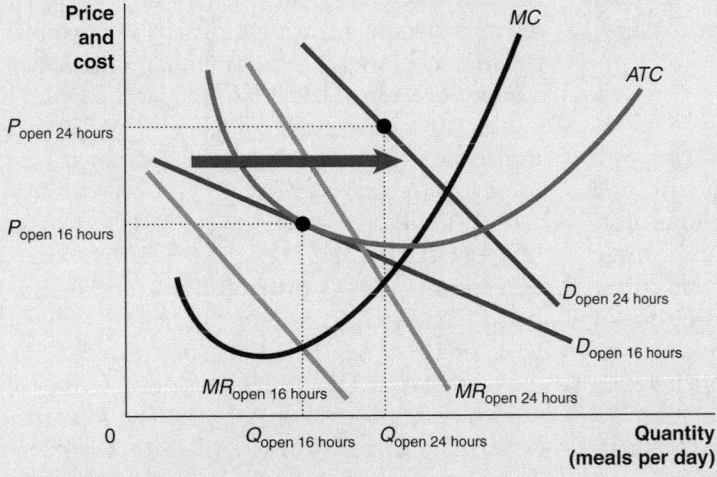

Figure 1: Product differentiation shifting the demand curve for a monopolistic competitor.

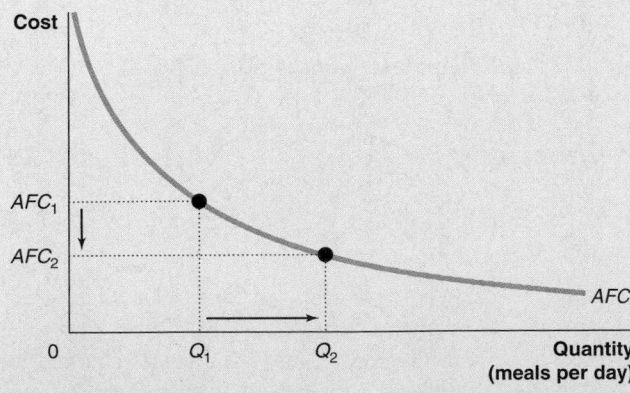

Figure 2: Spreading the overhead

SUMMARY

LEARNING OBJECTIVE ① Explain why a monopolistically competitive firm has a downward-sloping demand curve. A *monopolistically competitive* firm sells a differentiated product. Therefore, unlike a perfectly competitive firm, it faces a downward-sloping demand curve. When a monopolistically competitive firm cuts the price of its product, it sells more units, but must accept a lower price on the units it could have sold at the higher price. As a result, its marginal revenue curve is downward-sloping.

LEARNING OBJECTIVE ② Explain how a monopolistically competitive firm decides the quantity to produce and the price to charge. A monopolistically competitive firm maximizes profits at the level of output where marginal revenue equals marginal cost. Price equals marginal revenue for a perfectly competitive firm, but price is greater than marginal revenue for a monopolistically competitive firm. Therefore, unlike a perfectly competitive firm, which produces where $P = MC$, a monopolistically competitive firm produces where $P > MC$.

LEARNING OBJECTIVE ③ Analyze the situation of a monopolistically competitive firm in the long run. If a monopolistically competitive firm is earning economic profits in the short run, entry of new firms will eliminate those profits in the long run. If a monopolistically competitive firm is suffering economic losses in the short run, exit of existing firms will eliminate those losses in the long run. Monopolistically competitive firms continually struggle to find new ways of differentiating their products as they try to stay one step ahead of other firms that are attempting to copy their success.

LEARNING OBJECTIVE ④ Compare the efficiency of monopolistic competition and perfect competition. Perfectly competitive firms produce where price equals marginal cost and at minimum average total cost. Perfectly competitive firms achieve both allocative and productive efficiency. Monopolistically competitive firms produce where price is greater than marginal cost and above minimum average total cost. Monopolistically competitive firms do not achieve either allocative or productive efficiency. Consumers face a trade-off when buying the product of a monopolistically competitive firm: They are paying a price that is greater than marginal cost and the product is not being produced at minimum average cost, but they benefit from being able to purchase a product that is differentiated and more closely suited to their tastes.

LEARNING OBJECTIVE ⑤ Define marketing and explain how firms use it to differentiate their products. *Marketing* refers to all the activities necessary for a firm to sell a product to a consumer. Firms use two marketing tools to differential their products: *brand management* and *advertising*. Once a firm has established a successful brand name, it has a strong incentive to defend it. A firm can apply for a *trademark*, which grants legal protection against other firms using its product's name.

LEARNING OBJECTIVE ⑥ Identify key factors that determine a firm's profitability. The firm's owners and managers control some of the factors that determine the profitability of the firm. Other factors affect all the firms in the market or are the result of chance, so they are not under the control of the firm's owners. The interactions between factors the firm controls and factors it does not control determine its profitability.

KEY TERMS

Brand management 401   Marketing 401   Monopolistic competition 388

REVIEW QUESTIONS

1. What are the most important differences between perfectly competitive markets and monopolistically competitive markets? Give two examples of products sold in perfectly competitive markets and two examples of products sold in monopolistically competitive markets.

2. Why does the local McDonald's face a downward-sloping demand curve for Big Macs? If it raises the price it charges for Big Macs above the prices charged by other McDonald's, won't it lose all its customers?

3. Explain the differences between total revenue, average revenue, and marginal revenue.

4. Sally runs a McDonald's franchise. She is selling 350 Big Macs per week at a price of $3.25. If she lowers the price to $3.20, she will sell 351 Big Macs. What is the marginal revenue of the 351st Big Mac?

5. Sam runs a Hollywood Video store. Sam is currently renting 3,525 DVDs per week. If instead of renting 3,525 DVDs, he rents 3,526 DVDs, he will add $2.95 to his costs and $2.75 to his revenues. What will be the effect on his profits of renting 3,526 DVDs instead of 3,525 DVDs?

6. The text states, "Every firm that has the ability to affect the price of the good or service it sells will have a marginal revenue curve that is below its demand curve." Why is this true?

7. What are the differences between the long-run equilibrium of a perfectly competitive firm and the long-run equilibrium of a monopolistically competitive firm?

8. Does the fact that monopolistically competitive markets are not allocatively or productively efficient mean that there is a significant loss in economic well-being to society in these markets? In your answer, be sure to define what you mean by "economic well-being."

9. Define marketing. Why are many companies so concerned about brand management?

10. What are the key factors that determine the profitability of a firm in a monopolistically competitive market? How could a monopolistically competitive firm continually earn economic profit greater than zero?

PROBLEMS AND APPLICATIONS

Please visit **www.prenhall.com/hubbard** *for solutions to the even-numbered problems as well as multiple-choice and true or false self-assessment quizzes.*

1. Complete the following table:

DVDs RENTED PER WEEK (Q)	PRICE (P)	TOTAL REVENUE (TR = P × Q)	AVERAGE REVENUE (AR = TR/Q)	MARGINAL REVENUE (MR = ΔTR/ΔQ)
0	$8.00			
1	7.50			
2	7.00			
3	6.50			
4	6.00			
5	5.50			
6	5.00			
7	4.50			
8	4.00			

2. If Daniel sells 350 Big Macs at a price of $3.25 and his average cost of producing 350 Big Macs is $3.00, what is his profit?

3. Alicia manages a Hollywood Video store and has the following information on demand and costs:

DVDs RENTED PER WEEK (Q)	PRICE (P)	TOTAL COST (TC)
0	$6.00	$3.00
1	5.50	7.00
2	5.00	10.00
3	4.50	12.50
4	4.00	14.50
5	3.50	16.00
6	3.00	17.00
7	2.50	18.50
8	2.00	21.00

a. To maximize profit, how many DVDs should Jill rent, what price should she charge, and how much profit will she make?

b. What is the marginal revenue received by renting the profit-maximizing DVD? What is the marginal cost of renting the profit-maximizing DVD?

4. A trucking company investigates the relationship between the gas mileage of its trucks and the average speed at which the trucks are driven on the highway. The company finds the relationship shown in the following graph:

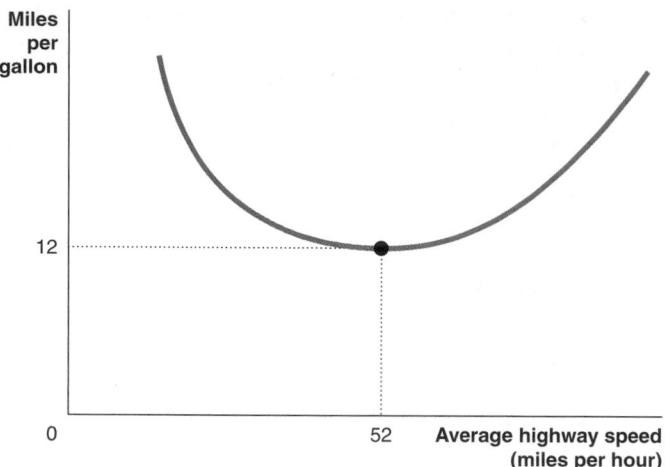

Will the firm maximize profits if it instructs its drivers to maintain an average speed of 52 miles per hour? Briefly explain.

5. Use the following graph to answer the questions.

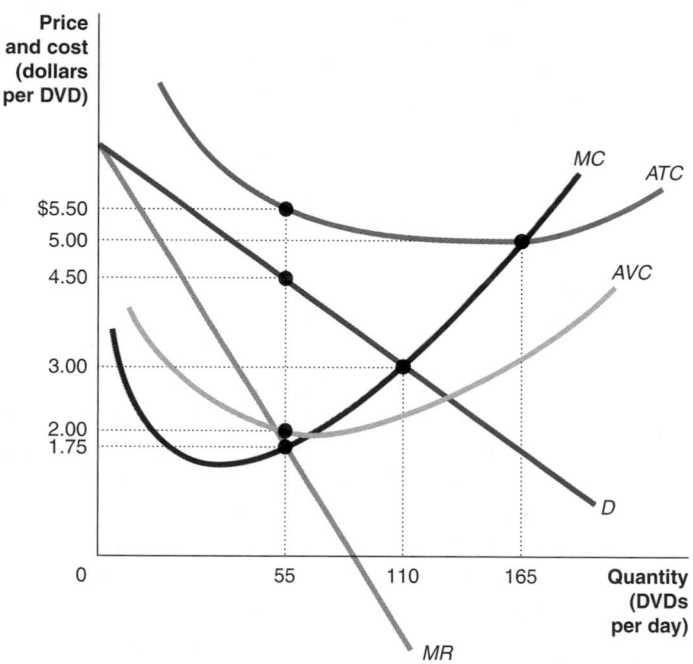

a. If the owner of this video store wants to maximize profits, how many DVDs should she rent per day and what rental price should she charge? Briefly explain your answer.

b. How much economic profit (or loss) is she making? Briefly explain.

c. Is the owner likely to continue renting this number of DVDs in the long run? Briefly explain.

6. The following is from an article in the *Wall Street Journal:* "Krispy Kreme Doughnuts Inc. reported its profit fell 56% in its second quarter despite an 11% increase in revenue." Briefly explain how it is possible for a firm's revenue to increase at the same time its profits decrease.
Source: "Krispy Kreme's Net Falls 56%; Company Cuts Sales Forecast," *Wall Street Journal,* August 26, 2004.

7. During 2003, General Motors cut the prices of most of its car models. As a result, GM earned a profit of only $184 per car, compared to the profit of $555 per car it had earned in 2002. Does the decline in GM's profits per car indicate that cutting prices was not a profit-maximizing strategy? Briefly explain.
Source: Karen Lundergaard and Sholnn Freeman, "Detroit's Challenge: Weaning Buyers from Years of Deals," *Wall Street Journal,* January 6, 2004.

8. **[Related to *Solved Problem 12-1*]** William Germano is vice president and publishing director at the Routledge publishing company. He has given the following description of how a publisher might deal with an unexpected increase in the cost of publishing a book:

> It's often asked why the publisher can't simply raise the price [if costs increase]. . . . It's likely that the editor [is already] . . . charging as much as the market will bear. . . . In other words, you might be willing to pay $50.00 for a . . . book on the Brooklyn Bridge, but if . . . production costs [increase] by 25 percent, you might think $62.50 is too much to pay, though that would be what the publisher needs to charge. And indeed the publisher may determine that $50.00 is this book's ceiling—the most you would pay before deciding to rent a movie instead.

According to what you have learned in this chapter, how do firms adjust the price of a good when there is an increase in cost? Use a graph to illustrate your answer. Why does this model not seem to fit Germano's description? If a publisher does not raise the price of a book following an increase in its production cost, what will be the result?
Source: William Germano, *Getting It Published: A Guide to Scholars and Anyone Else Serious about Serious Books,* Chicago: University of Chicago Press, 2001, pp. 110–111.

9. **[Related to *Don't Let This Happen To You!*]** A student remarks, "If firms in a monopolistically competitive industry are earning economic profits, new firms will enter the industry. Eventually, the representative firm will find its demand curve has shifted to the left until it is just tangent to its average cost curve and it is earning zero profit. Because firms are earning zero profit at that point, some firms will leave the industry and the representative firm will find its demand curve will shift to the right. In long-run equilibrium, price will be above average total cost by just enough so that each firm is just breaking even." Briefly explain whether you agree with this analysis.

10. Ernest Claremont, who served as chairman of the Rolls-Royce automobile company, once remarked that a factory "of excessive capacity is apt to induce excessive production, with the inevitable result of spoiling one's own market, since one in such a case is anxious to employ his [factory] at . . . full capacity, which can only be done by reducing prices and making goods in large quantity, which is often not to one's advantage." Why might "making goods in large quantity" not be to a firm's advantage? Rolls-Royce is a very expensive automobile that is produced in small quantities and sold to wealthy consumers. Are Claremont's remarks only relevant to this type of product? Why or why not?

    Source: Quoted in Peter Botticelli, "Rolls-Royce and the Rise of High-Technology Industry," in Thomas K. McCraw, *Creating Modern Capitalism*, Cambridge: Harvard University Press, 1997, p. 101.

11. The following excerpt is from an article in the *Wall Street Journal*:

    [Amazon.com], whose sales stagnated last year, increased revenue [this quarter] by 21 percent, to $806 million. . . . It attributed the increase to its price-cutting strategy: discounting books that cost more than $15 each and offering free shipping on orders of at least $49.

    a. If Amazon.com's revenue increased after it cut the price of books, what must be true about the price elasticity of demand for ordering books online?

    b. Suppose that before the price cut, Amazon.com was not selling the profit-maximizing quantity of books, but after the price cut it was. Draw a graph showing Amazon.com's situation before and after the price cut. (For simplicity, assume that Amazon charges the same price for all books.) Be sure your graph includes the price Amazon was charging and the quantity of books it was selling before the price cut; the price and quantity after the price cut; Amazon's demand, marginal revenue, average total cost, and marginal cost curves; and the areas representing its profits before and after the price cut.

    Source: Saul Hansell, "Citing Its Price Strategy, Amazon Pares Loss," *Wall Street Journal*, July 24, 2002.

12. Writing in the *Economist* magazine, Clive Crook argues:

    A fashionable strand of skepticism argues that governments have surrendered their power to capitalism—that the world's biggest companies are nowadays more powerful than many of the world's governments. Democracy is a sham. Profits rule, not people. These claims are patent nonsense. On the other hand, there is no question that companies would run the world for profit if they could. What stops them is not governments, powerful as they may be, but markets.

How do markets stop companies from "running the world for profit"?

Source: Clive Crook, "Globalisation and Its Critics," *Economist*, September 27, 2001.

13. Before the fall of Communism, most basic consumer products in Eastern Europe and the Soviet Union were standardized. For example, government-run stores would offer for sale only one type of bar soap or one type of toothpaste. Soviet economists often argued that this system of standardizing basic consumer products avoided the waste associated with the differentiated goods and services produced in Western Europe and the United States. Do you agree with this argument?

14. **[Related to *Solved Problem 12-2*]** Michael Porter, an economist at the Harvard Business School, argues that firms in the U.S. commercial-printing industry have been "Investing heavily in the same new equipment, running their presses faster, and reducing crew sizes. But the resulting major productivity gains are being captured by customers and equipment suppliers, not retained in superior profitability." How would consumers gain from these productivity increases? Why haven't the productivity increases made the printing firms more profitable?

    Source: Michael E. Porter, "What Is Strategy?" *Harvard Business Review*, November–December 1996, p. 63.

15. According to an article in the *New York Times*, by 2003, "J. Crew, once a stylish powerhouse of preppy catalog retailing, had been floundering. . . ." Millard S. Drexler took over as chief executive officer and tried to restore the company's fortunes by offering new styles of clothes, "made of much more expensive materials: tight, military-style suede jackets, Shetland sweaters and sleek coats, designed in a range of colors—from pimento red to green the shade of a new-mown lawn." Drexler also raised the prices of most products the company sells. Use the model of monopolistic competition to analyze this situation.

    a. Draw a graph showing the impact Drexler hoped to have on J. Crew's profitability. For simplicity, your graph will be for a single J. Crew product and should include the demand curve, marginal cost, average total cost, the profit-maximizing price, and J. Crew's profits before and after Drexler changed the firm's strategy.

    b. Would Drexler's strategy likely be successful in increasing J. Crew's profits in the short run? Briefly explain. How about in the long run?

    Source: Tracie Rozhon, "Chief Seeks to Revive J. Crew's Preppy Heyday," *New York Times*, May 6, 2003.

16. 7-Eleven, Inc., operates more than 20,000 convenience stores worldwide. Edward Moneypenny, 7-Eleven's chief financial officer, was asked to name the biggest risk the

company faced. He replied, "I would say that the biggest risk that 7-Eleven faces, like all retailers, is competition . . . because that is something that you've got to be aware of in this business." In what sense is competition a "risk" to a business? Why would a company in the retail business need to be particularly aware of competition?
Source: Company Report, CEO Interview: Edward Moneypenny—7-Eleven, Inc., The Wall Street Transcript Corporation.

17. In 1916, the Ford Motor Company produced 500,000 Model T Fords at a price of $440. The company made a profit of $60,000,000 that year. Henry Ford told a newspaper reporter that he intended to reduce the price of the Model T to $360 and he expected to be able to sell 800,000 cars at that price. Ford said, "[L]ess profit on each car, but more cars, more employment of labor, and in the end we get all the total profit we ought to make."
   a. Did Ford expect the total revenue he received from selling Model Ts to rise or fall following the price cut?
   b. Use the information given above to calculate the price elasticity of demand for Model Ts. Use the midpoint formula (see Chapter 6) to make your calculation.
   c. What would the average total cost of producing 800,000 Model Ts have to be for Ford to make as much profit selling 800,000 Model Ts as it made selling 500,000 Model Ts? Is this smaller or larger than the average total cost of producing 500,000 Model Ts?
   d. Assume that Ford would make the same total profit when selling 800,000 cars as when selling 500,000 cars. Was Henry Ford correct in saying he would make less profit per car when selling 800,000 cars than when selling 500,000 cars?

18. Michael Korda for many years was editor-in-chief at the Simon & Schuster book publishing company. He has described the many books that become bestsellers by promising to give readers financial advice that will make them wealthy, by, for example, buying and selling real estate. Korda is very skeptical about how useful the advice in these books is: "I have yet to meet anybody who got rich by buying a book, though quite a few people got rich by writing one." On the basis of the analysis in this chapter, discuss why it may be very difficult to become rich by following the advice found in a book.
Source: Michael Korda, *Making the List: A Cultural History of the American Bestseller, 1900–1999*, New York: Barnes & Noble Books, 2001, p. 168.

19. Draw a graph showing the impact on a firm's profits when it increases spending on advertising and the increased advertising has *no* effect on the demand for the firm's product.

20. A skeptic says, "Marketing research and brand management are redundant. If a company wants to find out what customers want, it should simply look at what they're already buying." Do you agree with the comment? Explain.

21. Some companies have done a lousy job at protecting their products' images. For example, Hormel's Spam brand name is widely ridiculed and has escaped from the company's control in cyberspace. Think of other cases where companies have failed to protect their brand names. What can they do about it now? Should they re-brand their products?

22. **[Related to the *Chapter Opener*]** According to an article in *Fortune* magazine in early 2004, "The big question for [Starbucks's chairman Howard] Schultz is whether Starbucks can keep it up. There are those on Wall Street who say that Starbucks's game is almost over." What do you think the article means by "Starbucks's game is almost over"? Why would some people on Wall Street be making this prediction about a firm that in 2004 was making substantial economic profits?
Source: Andy Serwer, "Hot Starbucks to Go," *Fortune*, January 12, 2004.

chapter thirteen

Oligopoly: Firms in Less Competitive Markets

Competing with Wal-Mart

> Many of the largest corporations in the United States began as small businesses. Henry Ford founded the Ford Motor Company in 1903 with only $28,000 and a small factory that had been used to make horse-drawn wagons. In 1975, Bill Gates and Paul Allen founded the Microsoft Corporation in Albuquerque, New Mexico, with themselves as the only employees. Michael Dell started the Dell computer company in 1984 from his dorm room at the University of Texas. Sam Walton, founder of Wal-Mart, bought his first store in 1945 with $20,000 borrowed from his father-in-law. Eventually, Wal-Mart would become the largest company in the world. Today, Wal-Mart employs more than 1.4 million people—three times more than the next largest private employer in the United States.

When each of these firms was founded, their industries included many more firms than they do now. Today, in the automobile, software, and computer industries, fewer than 10 firms account for the great majority of sales. Wal-Mart accounts for a large share of several segments of retail sales. In 2004, it was the leading seller of groceries in the United States, with a 19 percent share of the market. It sells more than 25 percent of all the disposable diapers, toothpaste, dog food, and photographic film sold in the United States. It is also the leading seller of CDs, videos, and DVDs, with market shares of 15 to 20 percent in each of those markets.

An industry with only a few firms is an *oligopoly*. In an oligopoly, a firm's profitability depends crucially on its interactions with other firms. In

these industries, firms must develop *business strategies*, which involve not just deciding what price to charge and how many units to produce, but also how much to advertise, which new technologies to adopt, how to manage relations with suppliers, and which new markets to enter, among other things.

A key part of Sam Walton's business strategy for Wal-Mart involved placing stores in small towns, where the main competition was from small, locally owned stores. By buying in bulk directly from manufacturers, Walton was able to lower costs, which enabled him to charge lower prices than his competitors. As early as the 1970s, Wal-Mart also made large investments in information technology (IT). Unlike most of its competitors, who had to count unsold goods by

LEARNING OBJECTIVES

After studying this chapter, you should be able to:

① Show how barriers to entry explain the existence of oligopolies.

② Use game theory to analyze the actions of oligopolistic firms.

③ Use sequential games to analyze business strategies.

④ Use the five competitive forces model to analyze competition in an industry.

hand to find out how many were left in inventory, Wal-Mart had a computerized system for tracking goods. To aid this system, Wal-Mart insisted in the early 1980s that its suppliers use UPC barcodes on products. This helped spread the use of barcodes to nearly every product sold in the United States. Today, Wal-Mart is pioneering the use of radio frequency identification tracking tags that may ultimately replace barcodes. With this system, employees will no longer have to manually scan barcodes. Instead, a radio signal will automatically record the arrival of a product in the warehouse, its shipment to a Wal-Mart store, and its purchase by the consumer. Soon it will be possible for the contents of a customer's shopping cart to be automatically scanned and the customer's debit card

charged, without the customer having to go through a checkout stand.

In recent years, Wal-Mart has been criticized for several practices, including selling goods produced in foreign factories by low-paid workers, paying low wages to its own workers, and driving smaller competitors into bankruptcy. As a result, Wal-Mart has run into some difficulty getting local government approvals to open new stores. Wal-Mart's competitors, however, continue to search for ways to successfully compete. In 2004, Kmart purchased Sears, Roebuck and Company to compete better with Wal-Mart. As *An Inside Look* on page 434 discusses, one approach firms take in competing with Wal-Mart is to offer products or services that Wal-Mart has difficulty offering.

Oligopoly A market structure in which a small number of interdependent firms compete.

➤ In Chapters 11 and 12, we studied perfectly competitive and monopolistically competitive industries. Our analysis focused on the determination of a firm's profit-maximizing price and quantity. We concluded that firms maximize profit by producing where marginal revenue equals marginal cost. To determine marginal revenue and marginal cost, we used graphs that included the firm's demand, marginal revenue, and marginal cost curves. In this chapter, we will study **oligopoly**—a market structure in which a small number of interdependent firms compete—and for two reasons we need to take a different approach.

First, we need to use economic models that allow us to analyze the more complex business strategies of large oligopoly firms. Second, even in determining the profit-maximizing price and output of an oligopoly firm, demand curves and cost curves are not as useful as in the cases of perfect competition and monopolistic competition. We are able to draw the demand curves for competitive firms by assuming that the prices charged by these firms have no impact on the prices charged by other firms in their industries. This assumption is realistic when each firm is small relative to the market. It is not a realistic assumption, however, for firms that are as large relative to their markets as Ford, Dell, or Wal-Mart.

When large firms cut their prices, their rivals in the industry often—but not always—respond by also cutting their prices. Because we don't know for sure how other firms will respond to a price change, we don't know the quantity an oligopolist will sell at a particular price. In other words, it is difficult to know what an oligopolist's demand curve will look like. As we have seen, a firm's marginal revenue curve depends on its demand curve. If we don't know what an oligopolist's demand curve looks like, we also don't know what its marginal revenue curve looks like. Not knowing marginal revenue, we can't calculate the profit-maximizing level of output and the profit-maximizing price the way we did for competitive firms.

The approach we use to analyze competition among oligopolists is called *game theory*. Game theory can be used to analyze any situation in which groups or individuals interact. In the context of economic analysis, game theory is the study of the decisions of firms in industries where the profits of each firm depend on its interactions with other firms. It has been applied to strategies for nuclear war, for international trade negotiations, and for political campaigns, among many other examples. In this chapter, we focus on how game theory can be used to analyze the business strategies of large firms.

① **LEARNING OBJECTIVE**
Show how barriers to entry explain the existence of oligopolies.

Oligopoly and Barriers to Entry

Oligopolies are industries with only a few firms. This market structure lies between the competitive industries we studied in Chapters 11 and 12, which have many firms, and the monopolies we will study in Chapter 14, which have only a single firm. One measure of the extent of competition in an industry is the *concentration ratio*. Every five years, the U.S. Bureau of the Census publishes four-firm concentration ratios that state the fraction of each industry's sales accounted for by its four largest firms. Most economists believe that a four-firm concentration ratio of greater than 40 percent indicates that an industry is an oligopoly.

The concentration ratio has some flaws as a measure of the extent of competition in an industry. For example, concentration ratios do not include sales in the United States by foreign firms. Concentration ratios are also calculated for the national market, even though the competition in some industries, such as restaurants or college bookstores, is mainly local. Finally, competition sometimes exists between firms in different industries. For example, Wal-Mart is included in the discount department stores industry, but also competes with firms in the supermarket industry and the retail toy store industry. As we will see in Chapter 14, some economists prefer another measure of competition, known as the *Herfindahl-Hirschman Index*. Despite these shortcomings, concentration ratios can be useful in providing a general idea of the extent of competition in an industry.

Table 13-1 lists examples of oligopolies in manufacturing and retail trade. Notice that the "Discount Department Stores" industry that includes Wal-Mart is highly concentrated. Wal-Mart also operates Sam's Club stores, which are in the also heavily concentrated "Warehouse Clubs and Superstores" industry.

Barriers to Entry

Why do oligopolies exist? Why aren't there many more firms in the discount department store industry, the beer industry, or the automobile industry? We saw in Chapters 11 and 12 that new firms will enter industries where existing firms are earning economic profits. But new firms often have difficulty entering an oligopoly. Anything that keeps new firms from entering an industry in which firms are earning economic profits is called a **barrier to entry.** Three barriers to entry are: economies of scale, ownership of a key input, and government-imposed barriers.

Barrier to entry Anything that keeps new firms from entering an industry in which firms are earning economic profits.

Economies of Scale

The most important barrier to entry is economies of scale. Chapter 10 stated that **economies of scale** exist when a firm's long-run average costs fall as it increases output. The greater the economies of scale, the fewer the number of firms that will be in the industry. Figure 13-1 illustrates this point.

Economies of scale Economies of scale exist when a firm's long-run average costs fall as it increases output.

RETAIL TRADE		MANUFACTURING		**TABLE 13-1**
INDUSTRY	FOUR-FIRM CONCENTRATION RATIO	INDUSTRY	FOUR-FIRM CONCENTRATION RATIO	**Examples of Oligopolies in Retail Trade and Manufacturing**
Discount Department Stores	95%	Cigarettes	99%	
Warehouse Clubs and Supercenters	92%	Beer	90%	
College Bookstores	71%	Aircraft	85%	
Athletic Footwear Stores	70%	Automobiles	80%	
Radio, Television, and Other Electronic Stores	69%	Breakfast Cereal	83%	
Hobby, Toy, and Game Stores	64%	Dog and Cat Food	58%	
Pharmacies and Drugstores	52%	Computers	45%	

Source: For retail trade: U.S. Census Bureau, 2002 Census; for manufacturing: U.S. Census Bureau, 1997 Census.

Economies of Scale Help Determine the Extent of Competition in an Industry

The industry will be competitive if the minimum point on the typical firm's long-run average cost curve *(LRAC₁)* occurs at a level of output that is a small fraction of total industry sales, like Q_1. The industry will be an oligopoly if the minimum point comes at a level of output that is a large fraction of industry sales, like Q_2.

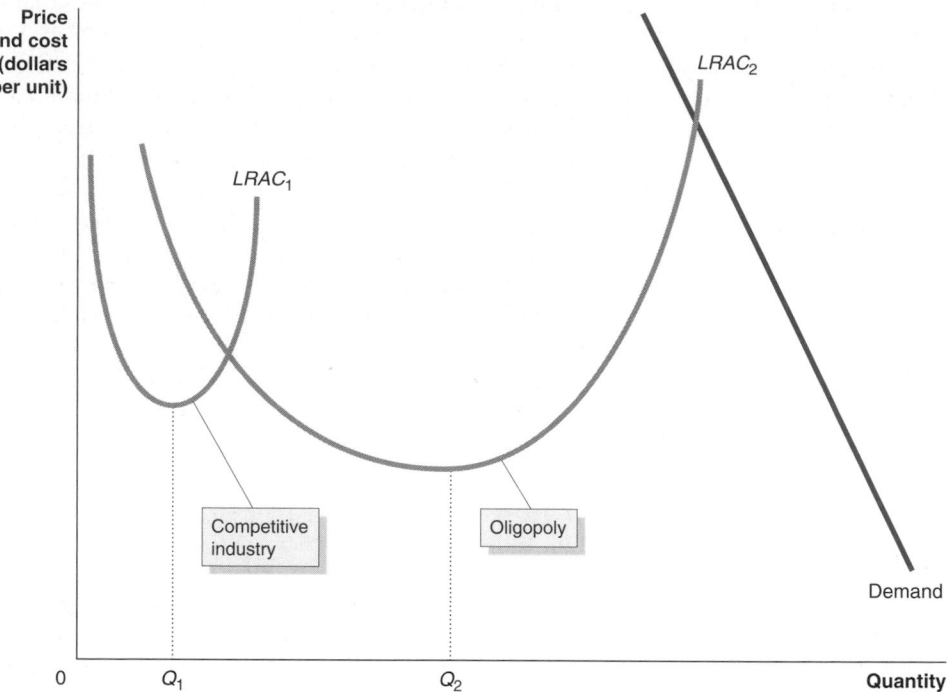

If economies of scale are relatively unimportant in the industry, the typical firm's long-run average cost curve *(LRAC)* will reach a minimum at a level of output that is a small fraction of total industry sales—Q_1 in Figure 13-1. The industry will have room for a large number of firms and will be competitive. If economies of scale are significant, the typical firm will not reach the minimum point on its long-run average cost curve until it has produced a large fraction of industry sales—Q_2 in Figure 13-1. Then the industry will have room for only a few firms and will be an oligopoly.

Economies of scale can explain why there is much more competition in the restaurant industry than in the discount department store industry. Because very large restaurants do not have lower average costs than smaller restaurants, the restaurant industry has room for many firms. In contrast, large discount department stores, such as Wal-Mart, have much lower average costs than small discount department stores, for reasons discussed in the opening to this chapter. As a result, just four firms—Wal-Mart, Target, Kmart, and Costco—account for about 95 percent of all sales in this industry.

Ownership of a Key Input

If production of a good requires a particular input, then control of that input can be a barrier to entry. For many years, the Aluminum Company of America (Alcoa) controlled most of the world's supply of high quality bauxite, the mineral needed to produce aluminum. The only way other companies could enter the industry to compete with Alcoa was to recycle aluminum. The De Beers Company of South Africa was able to block competition in the diamond market by controlling the output of most of the world's diamond mines. Until the 1990s, Ocean Spray had very little competition in the market for fresh and frozen cranberries because it controlled almost the entire supply of cranberries. Even today it controls about 80 percent of the cranberry crop.

Government-Imposed Barriers

Firms sometimes try to have the government impose barriers to entry. Many large firms employ *lobbyists* to try to convice state legislators and members of Congress to pass laws favorable to the economic interests of the firms. There are tens of thousands of lobbyists in Washington, DC alone. Top lobbyists command annual salaries of $300,000 or more, which indicates the value firms place on their activities. Examples of government-imposed barriers to entry are patents, licensing requirements, and barriers to international trade. Governments use patents to encourage firms to carry out research and development of new and better products and better ways of producing existing products. Output and living standards increase faster when firms devote resources to research and development, but a firm that spends money to develop a new product may not earn much profit if other firms can copy the product. For example, the pharmaceutical company Merck spends more than $3 billion per year to develop new prescription drugs. If rival companies could freely produce these new drugs as soon as Merck developed them, most of the firm's investment would be wasted. To avoid this problem, the federal government grants a **patent** that gives the firm the exclusive right to a new product for a period of 20 years from the date the product was invented. During the years the patent is in force, the firm can charge higher prices and make an economic profit on its successful innovation.

The government also restricts competition through occupational licensing. The United States currently has about 500 occupational licensing laws. For example, doctors and dentists in every state need licenses to practice. The justification for the laws is to protect the public from incompetent practitioners, but by restricting the number of people who can enter the licensed professions, the laws also raise prices. Studies have shown that states that make it harder to earn a dentist's license have prices for dental services that are about 15 percent higher than in other states. Similarly, states that require a license for out-of-state firms to sell contact lenses have higher prices for contact lenses. When state licenses are required for occupations like hair braiding, which was done several years ago in California, restricting competition is the main result.

Government also imposes barriers to entering some industries by imposing tariffs and quotas on foreign competition. As we saw in Chapter 8, a quota on foreign sugar imports severely limits competition in the U.S. sugar market. As a result, U.S. sugar companies can charge prices that are more than twice as high as those charged by companies outside the United States.

In summary, to earn economic profits, all firms would like to charge a price well above average cost, but earning economic profits attracts new firms to enter the industry. Eventually the increased competition forces price down to average cost, and firms just break even. In an oligopoly, barriers to entry prevent—or at least slow down—entry, which allows firms to earn economic profits over a longer period.

Using Game Theory to Analyze Oligopoly

As we noted at the beginning of the chapter, economists analyze oligopolies using *game theory*, which was developed during the 1940s by the mathematician John von Neumann and the economist Oskar Morgenstern. **Game theory** is the study of how people make decisions in situations where attaining their goals depends on their interactions with others. In oligopolies, the interactions among firms are crucial in determining profitability because the firms are large relative to the market.

In all games—whether poker, chess, or Monopoly—the interactions among the players are crucial in determining the outcome. In addition, games share three key characteristics:

1. *Rules* that determine what actions are allowable.
2. *Strategies* that players employ to attain their objectives in the game.
3. *Payoffs* that are the results of the interaction among the players' strategies.

In business situations, the rules of the "game" include not just laws that a firm must obey, but also other matters beyond a firm's control—at least in the short run—such as its production function. A **business strategy** is a set of actions taken by a firm to achieve a goal, such as maximizing profits. The *payoffs* are the profits earned as a result of a

Patent The exclusive right to a product for a period of 20 years from the date the product was invented.

② **LEARNING OBJECTIVE**
Use game theory to analyze the actions of oligopolistic firms.

Game theory The study of how people make decisions in situations where attaining their goals depends on their interactions with others; in economics, the study of the decisions of firms in industries where the profits of each firm depend on its interactions with other firms.

Business strategy Actions taken by a firm to achieve a goal, such as maximizing profits.

firm's strategies interacting with the strategies of the other firms. The best way to understand the game theory approach is to look at an example.

A Duopoly Game: Price Competition between Two Firms

In the following simple example, we use game theory to analyze price competition in a *duopoly*—an oligopoly with two firms. Suppose that an isolated town in Alaska has only two stores: Wal-Mart and Target. Both stores sell the new Sony PlayStation 3. For simplicity, let's assume that no other stores stock PlayStation 3 and that consumers in the town can't buy it on the Internet or through mail-order catalogs. The manager of each store decides whether to charge $150 or $200 for the PlayStation. Which price will be more profitable depends on the price being charged by the other store. The decision regarding what price to charge is an example of a business strategy. In Figure 13-2 we organize the possible outcomes that result from the actions of the two firms into a *payoff matrix*. A **payoff matrix** is a table that shows the payoffs that each firm earns from every combination of strategies by the firms.

Payoff matrix A table that shows the payoffs that each firm earns from every combination of strategies by the firms.

Wal-Mart's profits are shown in blue and Target's profits are shown in red. If Wal-Mart and Target both charge $200 for the PlayStation, each store will make a profit of $10,000 per month from sales of the game console. If Wal-Mart charges the lower price of $150, while Target charges $200, Wal-Mart will gain many of Target's customers. Wal-Mart's profits will be $15,000 and Target's will be only $5,000. Similarly, if Wal-Mart charges $200, while Target is charging $150, Wal-Mart's profits will be only $5,000, while Target's profits will be $15,000. If both stores charge $150, each will earn profits of $7,500 per month.

Clearly, the stores will be better off if they both charge $200 for the PlayStation. But will they both charge this price? One possibility is that the manager of the Wal-Mart and the manager of the Target will get together and *collude* by agreeing to charge the higher price. **Collusion** is an agreement among firms to charge the same price, or otherwise not to compete. Unfortunately, for Wal-Mart and Target—but fortunately for their customers—collusion is against the law in the United States. Companies that agree not to compete on price can be fined and the managers involved can be sent to jail.

Collusion An agreement among firms to charge the same price, or otherwise not to compete.

The manager of the Wal-Mart store legally can't discuss his pricing decision with the manager of the Target store, so he has to predict what he thinks the other manager will do. Suppose the Wal-Mart manager is convinced that the Target manager will charge $200 for the PlayStation. In this case, the Wal-Mart manager will definitely charge $150, because that will increase his profit from $10,000 to $15,000. But suppose instead the Wal-Mart manager is convinced that the Target manager will charge $150. Then the Wal-Mart manager also definitely will charge $150, because that will increase his profit from $5,000 to $7,500. In fact, whichever price the Target manager decides to charge, the Wal-Mart manager is better off charging $150. So, we know that the Wal-Mart manager will choose a price of $150 for the PlayStation.

FIGURE 13-2

A Duopoly Game

Wal-Mart's profits are in blue, and Target's profits are in red. Wal-Mart and Target would each make profits of $10,000 per month on sales of PlayStation 3 if they both charged $200. However, each store manager has an incentive to undercut the other by charging a lower price. If both charge $150, they would each make profits of only $7,500 per month.

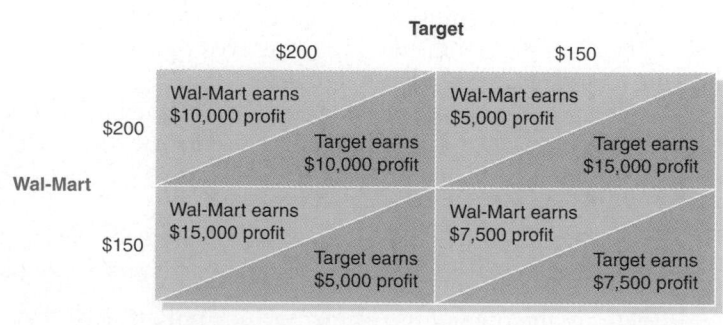

Now consider the situation of the Target manager. The Target manager is in the identical position to the Wal-Mart manager, so we can expect her to make the same decision to charge $150 for the PlayStation. In this situation each manager has a *dominant strategy*. A **dominant strategy** is the best strategy for a firm, no matter what strategies other firms use. The result is an equilibrium where both managers charge $150 for the PlayStation. This situation is an equilibrium because each manager is maximizing profits, *given the price chosen by the other manager*. In other words, neither firm can increase its profits by changing its price, given the price chosen by the other firm. An equilibrium where each firm chooses the best strategy, given the strategies chosen by other firms, is called a **Nash equilibrium,** named after Nobel Prize winner John Nash of Princeton University, a pioneer in the development of game theory.

Dominant strategy A strategy that is the best for a firm, no matter what strategies other firms use.

Nash equilibrium A situation where each firm chooses the best strategy, given the strategies chosen by other firms.

A Beautiful Mind: Game Theory Goes to the Movies

John Nash is the most celebrated game theorist in the world, partly because of his achievements and partly because of his dramatic life. In 1948, at the age of 20, Nash received bachelor's and master's degrees in mathematics from the Carnegie Institute of Technology (now known as Carnegie Mellon University). Two years later he received a Ph.D. from Princeton for his 27-page dissertation on game theory. It was in this dissertation that he first discussed the concept that became known as the *Nash equilibrium*. Nash appeared to be on his way to a brilliant academic career until he developed schizophrenia in the 1950s. He spent decades in and out of mental hospitals. During these years he roamed the Princeton campus, covering blackboards in unused classrooms with indecipherable writings. He became known as the "Phantom of Fine Hall." In the 1970s, Nash gradually began to recover. In 1994, he shared the Nobel Prize in Economics with John Harsanyi of the University of California, Berkeley, and Reinhard Selten of Rheinische Friedrich–Wilhelms Universität, Germany, for his work on game theory.

In 1998, Sylvia Nasar of the *New York Times* wrote a biography of Nash, titled *A Beautiful Mind*. Three years later, the book was adapted into an award-winning film starring Russell Crowe. Unfortunately, the (fictitious) scene in the film that shows Nash discovering the idea of Nash equilibrium misstates the concept. In the scene, Nash is in a bar with several friends when four women with brown hair and one with blonde hair walk in. Nash and all of his friends prefer the blonde to the brunettes. One of Nash's friends points out that if they all compete for the blonde, they are unlikely to get her. In competing for the blonde, they will also insult the brunettes, with the result that none of them will end up with a date. Nash then gets a sudden insight. He suggests that they ignore the blonde and each approach one of the brunettes. That is the only way, he argues, that each of them will end up with a date.

Nash immediately claims that this is also an economic insight. He points out that Adam Smith had argued that the best result comes from everyone in the group doing what's best for himself. Nash argues, however, "The best result comes from everyone in the group doing what's best for himself *and* the group." But this is not an accurate description of the Nash equilibrium. As we have seen, in a Nash equilibrium each player uses a strategy that will make him as well off as possible, *given the strategies of the other players*. The bar situation would not be a Nash equilibrium. Once the other men have chosen a brunette, each man will have an incentive to switch from the brunette he initially chose to the blonde.

In the film, A Beautiful Mind, *Russell Crowe played John Nash, winner of the Nobel Prize in Economics.*

Firm Behavior and the Prisoners' Dilemma

Notice that the equilibrium in Figure 13-2 is not very satisfactory for either firm. The firms earn $7,500 profit each month by charging $150, but they could have earned $10,000 profit if they had both charged $200. By "cooperating" and charging the higher price they would have achieved a *cooperative equilibrium*. In a **cooperative equilibrium** players cooperate to increase their mutual payoff. We have seen, though, that the out-

Cooperative equilibrium An equilibrium in a game in which players cooperate to increase their mutual payoff.

Don't Let This Happen To You!

Don't Misunderstand Why Each Manager Ends Up Charging a Price of $150

It is tempting to think that the Wal-Mart manager and the Target manager would each charge $150 rather than $200 for the PlayStation because each is afraid that the other manager will charge $150. In fact, fear of being undercut by the other firm's charging a lower price is not the key to understanding each manager's pricing strategy. Notice that charging $150 is the most profitable strategy for each man-

ager, no matter which price the other manager decides to charge. For example, even if the Wal-Mart manager somehow knew for sure that the Target manager intended to charge $200, he would still charge $150, because his profits would be $15,000 instead of $10,000. The Target manager is in the same situation. That is why charging $150 is a dominant strategy for both managers.

YOUR TURN: Test your understanding by doing related problem 5 on page 437 at the end of the chapter.

Noncooperative equilibrium An equilibrium in a game in which players do not cooperate but pursue their own self-interest.

Prisoners' dilemma A game where pursuing dominant strategies results in noncooperation that leaves everyone worse off.

come of this game is likely to be a **noncooperative equilibrium,** in which each firm pursues its own self-interest.

A situation like this, in which pursuing dominant strategies results in noncooperation that leaves everyone worse off, is called a **prisoners' dilemma.** The game gets its name from its similarity to the situation of two suspects arrested for a crime by the police. If the police lack other evidence, they may separate the suspects and offer each a reduced prison sentence in exchange for confessing to the crime and testifying against the other criminal. Because each suspect has a dominant strategy to confess to the crime, they will both confess and serve a jail term, even though they would have gone free if they had both remained silent.

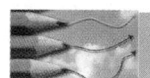

SOLVED PROBLEM 13-1

② **LEARNING OBJECTIVE**

Use game theory to analyze the actions of oligopolistic firms.

Is Advertising a Prisoners' Dilemma for Coca-Cola and Pepsi?

Coca-Cola and Pepsi both advertise aggressively, but would they be better off if they didn't? Their commercials are not designed to convey new information about the products. Instead, they are designed to capture each other's customers. Construct a payoff matrix using the following hypothetical information:

➤ *If neither firm advertises:* Coca-Cola and Pepsi both earn profits of $750 million per year.

➤ *If both firms advertise:* Coca-Cola and Pepsi both earn profits of $500 million per year.

➤ *If Coca-Cola advertises and Pepsi doesn't:* Coca-Cola earns profits of $900 million and Pepsi earns profits of $400 million.

➤ *If Pepsi advertises and Coca-Cola doesn't:* Pepsi earns profits of $900 million and Coca-Cola earns profits of $400 million.

    a. If Coca-Cola wants to maximize profit, will it advertise? Briefly explain.

    b. If Pepsi wants to maximize profit, will it advertise? Briefly explain.

    c. Is there a Nash equilibrium to this advertising game? If so, what is it?

Solving the Problem:

Step 1: Review the chapter material. This problem uses payoff matrixes to analyze a business situation, so you may want to review the section "A Duopoly Game: Price Competition between Two Firms," which begins on page 418.

Step 2: Construct the payoff matrix.

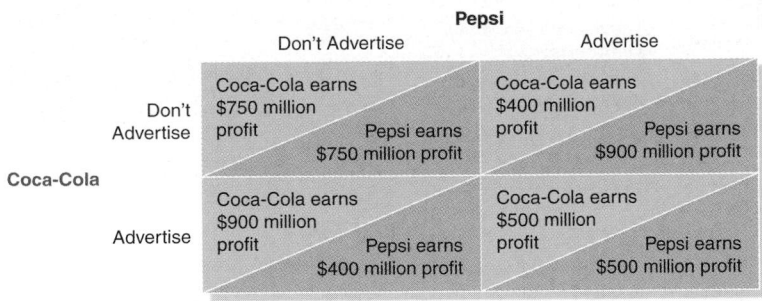

Step 3: Answer question (a) by showing that Coca-Cola has a dominant strategy of advertising. If Pepsi doesn't advertise, then Coca-Cola will make $900 million if it advertises, but only $750 million if it doesn't. If Pepsi advertises, then Coca-Cola will make $500 million if it advertises, but only $400 million if it doesn't. Therefore, advertising is a dominant strategy for Coca-Cola.

Step 4: Answer question (b) by showing that Pepsi has a dominant strategy of advertising. Pepsi is in the same position as Coca-Cola, so it also has a dominant strategy of advertising.

Step 5: Answer question (c) by showing that there is a Nash equilibrium for this game. Both firms advertising is a Nash equilibrium. Given that Pepsi is advertising, Coca-Cola's best strategy is to advertise. Given that Coca-Cola is advertising, Pepsi's best strategy is to advertise. Therefore, advertising is the optimal decision for both firms, *given the decision by the other firm*.

Extra Credit: This is another example of the prisoners' dilemma game. Coca-Cola and Pepsi would be more profitable if they both refrained from advertising, thereby saving the enormous expense of television and radio commercials and newspaper and magazine ads. Each firm's dominant strategy is to advertise, however, so they end up in an equilibrium where both advertise and their profits are reduced.

YOUR TURN: For more practice, do related problems 8, 9, and 10 on page 438 at the end of this chapter. Visit www.prenhall.com/hubbard for an interactive exercise related to this Solved Problem.

Is There a Dominant Strategy for Bidding on eBay?

An auction is a game in which bidders compete to buy a product. The payoff in winning an auction is equal to the difference between the subjective value you place on the product being auctioned and the amount of the winning bid. On eBay, the online auction site, more than 200 million items valued at more than $10 billion are auctioned each year.

EBay is run as a *second-price auction*, where the winning bidder pays the price of the second-highest bidder. If the high bidder on a DVD of *Spiderman 2* bids $15 and the second bidder bids $10, the high bidder wins the auction and pays $10. It may seem that your best strategy when bidding on eBay is to place a bid well below the subjective value you place on the item in the hope of winning it at a low price. In fact, bidders on eBay have a dominant strategy of entering a bid equal to the maximum value they place on the item. For instance, suppose you are looking for a present for your parents' anniversary. They are Rolling Stones fans, and someone is auctioning a pair of Stones concert tickets. If the maximum value you

13-2 Making
the Connection

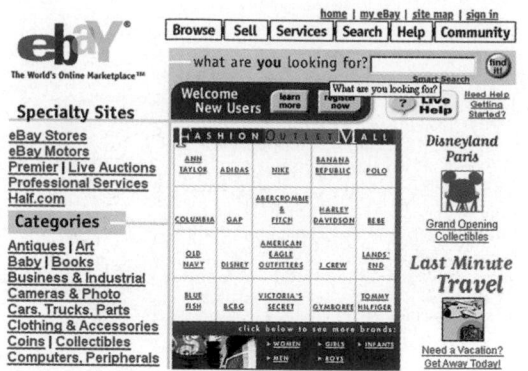

On eBay, bidding the maximum value you place on an item is a dominant strategy.

place on the tickets is $200, that should be your bid. To see why, consider the results of strategies of bidding more or less than $200.

There are two possible outcomes of the auction: Either someone else bids more than you do, or you are the high bidder. First, suppose you bid $200 but someone else bids more than you do. If you had bid less than $200, you would still have lost. If you had bid more than $200, you might have been the high bidder, but because your bid would be for more than the value you place on the tickets, you would have a negative payoff. Second, suppose you bid $200 and you are the high bidder. If you had bid less than $200, you would have run the risk of losing the tickets to someone whose bid you would have beaten by bidding $200. You would be worse off than if you had bid $200 and won. If you had bid more than $200, you would not have affected the price you ended up paying—which, remember, is equal to the amount bid by the second-highest bidder. Therefore, a strategy of bidding $200—the maximum value you place on the tickets—dominates bidding more or less than $200.

Even though making your first bid your highest bid is a dominant strategy on eBay, many bidders don't use it. After an auction is over, a link leads to a Web page showing all the bids. In many auctions, the same bidder bids several times, showing that the bidder had not understood his or her dominant strategy.

Can Firms Escape the Prisoners' Dilemma?

Although the prisoners' dilemma game seems to show that cooperative behavior always breaks down, we know that it doesn't. People often cooperate to achieve their goals, and firms find ways to cooperate by not competing on price. The reason the basic prisoners' dilemma story is not always applicable is that it assumes the game will be played only once. Most business situations, however, are repeated over and over. Each month the Target and Wal-Mart managers will decide again what price they will charge for PlayStation 3. In the language of game theory, the managers are playing a *repeated game.* In a repeated game, the losses from not cooperating are greater, and players can also employ *retaliation strategies* against those who don't cooperate. As a result, we are more likely to see cooperative behavior.

Figure 13-2 on page 420 shows that Wal-Mart and Target are earning $2,500 less per month by both charging $150 instead of $200 for the PlayStation. Every month that passes with both stores charging $150 increases the total amount lost: Two years of charging $150 will cause each store to lose $60,000 in profit. This lost profit increases the incentive for the store managers to cooperate by *implicitly* colluding. Remember that *explicit* collusion—such as the managers meeting and agreeing to charge $200—is illegal. But if the managers can find a way to signal each other that they will charge $200, they may be within the law.

Suppose, for example, that Wal-Mart and Target both advertise that they will match the lowest price offered by any competitor—in our simple example, they are each other's only competitor. These advertisements are signals to each other that they intend to charge $200 for the PlayStation. The signal is clear because each store knows that if it charges $150, the other store will automatically retaliate by also lowering its price to $150. The offer to match prices is a good *enforcement mechanism* because it guarantees that if either store fails to cooperate and charges the lower price it is automatically

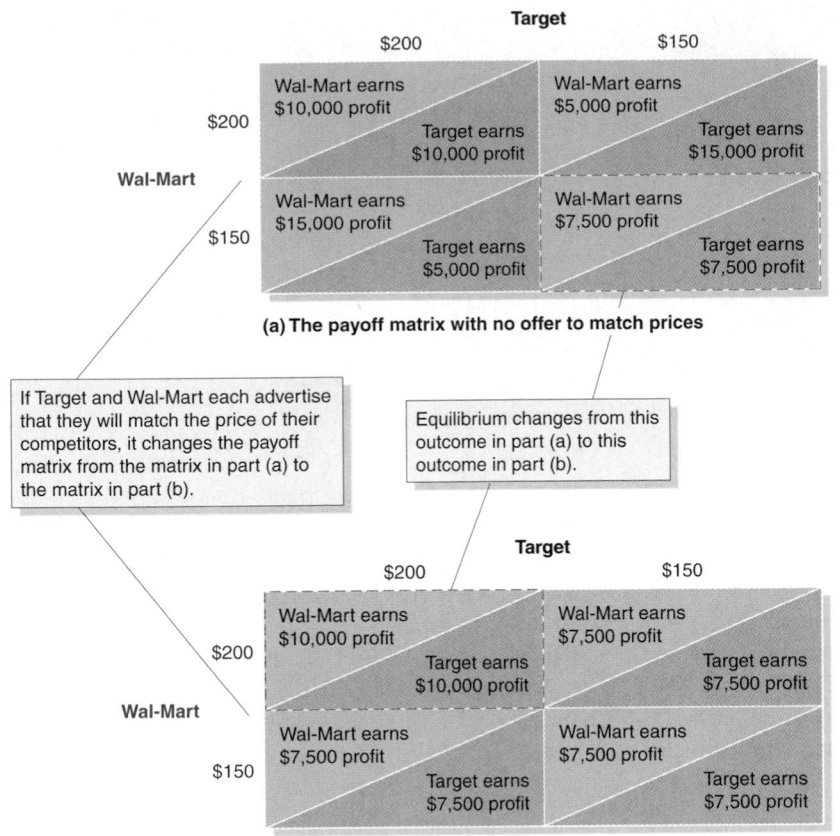

(a) The payoff matrix with no offer to match prices

If Target and Wal-Mart each advertise that they will match the price of their competitors, it changes the payoff matrix from the matrix in part (a) to the matrix in part (b).

Equilibrium changes from this outcome in part (a) to this outcome in part (b).

(b) The payoff matrix with an offer to match prices

FIGURE 13-3

Changing the Payoff Matrix in a Repeated Game

Wal-Mart and Target can change the payoff matrix by advertising that they will match their competitor's price. This retaliation strategy provides a signal that one store charging a lower price will be met automatically by the other store charging a lower price. In payoff matrix (a), there is no matching offer and each store benefits if it charges $150 when the other charges $200. In payoff matrix (b), with the matching offer, the companies have only two choices: They can charge $200 and receive a profit of $10,000 per month, or they can charge $150 and receive a profit of $7,500 per month. The equilibrium shifts from the prisoners' dilemma result of both stores charging the low price and receiving low profits to both stores charging the high price and receiving high profits.

punished by having its competitor also charge the lower price. As Figure 13-3 shows, the stores have changed the payoff matrix they face.

With the original payoff matrix (a), there is no matching offer, and each store makes more profit if it charges $150 when the other charges $200. The matching offer changes the payoff matrix to (b). Now the stores can charge $200 and receive a profit of $10,000 per month, or they can charge $150 and receive a profit of $7,500 per month. The equilibrium shifts from the prisoners' dilemma result of both stores charging the low price and receiving low profits to a result where both stores charge the high price and receive high profits. An offer to match competitors' prices might seem to benefit consumers, but game theory shows that it actually may hurt consumers by helping to keep prices high.

American Airlines and Northwest Airlines Fail to Cooperate on a Price Increase

13-3 Making the Connection

Coordinating prices is easier in some industries than in others. Fixed costs in the airline industry are very large and marginal costs are very small. The marginal cost of flying one more passenger from New York to Chicago is no more than a few dollars: the cost of another snack served and a small amount of additional jet fuel. As a result, airlines often engage in last-minute price cutting to fill the remaining empty seats on a flight. Even a low-price ticket will increase marginal revenue more than marginal cost. As with other oligopolies, if all airlines cut prices, industry profits will decline. Airlines therefore continually adjust their prices, while at the same time monitoring their rivals' prices and retaliating against them either for cutting prices or failing to go along with price increases.

The airlines have trouble raising the price this business traveler pays for a ticket.

Consider the following fairly typical events from the spring of 2002. American Airlines decided to raise some of its ticket prices in a roundabout way. Business travelers are usually willing to pay higher prices for airline tickets than are leisure travelers. Business travelers also often must make their flight plans only a few days before they leave. Airlines take advantage of this fact by requiring 10- to 14-day advance reservations to get a fully discounted ticket. A smaller discount is available with a 3-day advance reservation. This smaller discount is aimed at business travelers. American decided to increase to 7 days the advance purchase requirement for the business travel discount. Because many business travelers cannot make their reservations that far in advance, they would have to buy full-fare tickets.

Continental Airlines matched American's change, but the other airlines refused to go along. They hoped that by not matching American's price increase, they would gain some of its customers. American then retaliated by offering very low $99 one-way tickets in 10 markets where Northwest Airlines, United Airlines, Delta Air Lines, and US Airways offered nonstop service. American did not offer the $99 fares in the markets where Continental offered nonstop service. An airline industry consultant observed that "American is trying to slap the hands of people who wouldn't go along with its increase."

Northwest immediately responded by offering $99 fares in 20 markets where American offers nonstop service. American retaliated by offering the low fare in 10 additional markets served by Northwest. Northwest then further retaliated by offering the low fare in a total of 160 markets served by American. After several days of very low fares and lost profits, American and Northwest restored their normal fares and American went back to a 3-day advance reservation requirement for discounted business-travel tickets.

Did American's aggressive retaliation make it easier for airlines to agree on ticket price increases in the future? Apparently not. A few weeks later, Continental raised its prices for round-trip discounted tickets by $20. Every airline but Northwest matched the price increase. Rather than lose customers to Northwest, Continental and the other airlines rolled back the price increase.

Sources: Scott McCartney, "Airfare Wars Show Why Deals Arrive and Depart," *Wall Street Journal*, March 19, 2002; and Scott McCartney, "Airlines Drop $20 Fare Increase after Northwest Fails to Join In," *Wall Street Journal*, April 16, 2002.

Cartels: The Case of OPEC

In the United States, firms cannot legally meet to agree on what prices to charge and how much to produce. But suppose they could. Would this be enough to guarantee that their collusion would be successful? The example of the Organization of Petroleum Exporting Countries (OPEC) indicates that the answer to this question is "no." OPEC has 11 members, including Saudi Arabia, Kuwait, and other Arab countries, as well as Iran, Venezuela, Nigeria, and Indonesia. Together these countries own 75 percent of the world's proven oil reserves, although they pump a smaller share of the total oil sold each year. OPEC operates as a **cartel**, which is a group of firms that colludes to restrict output to increase prices and profits. The members of OPEC meet periodically and agree on *quotas*, quantities of oil that each country agrees to produce. The quotas are intended to

Cartel A group of firms that colludes by agreeing to restrict output to increase prices and profits.

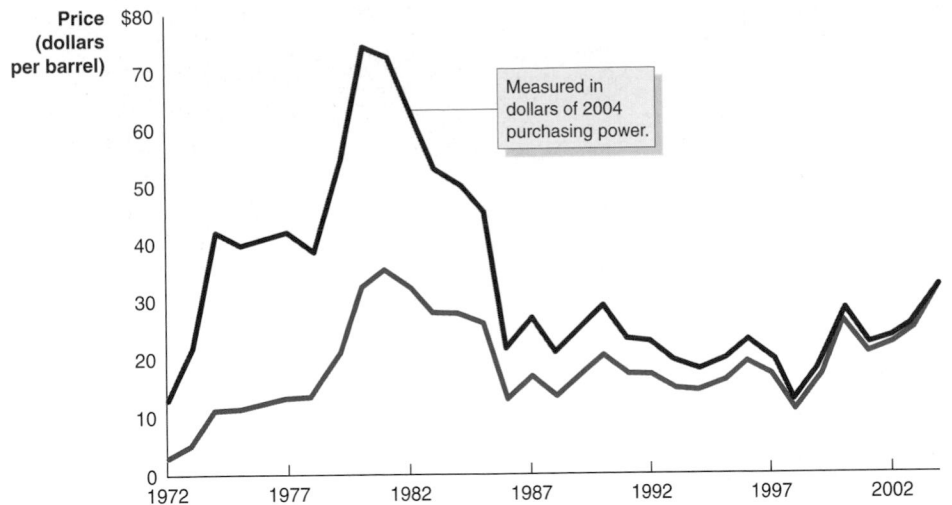

FIGURE 13-4

World Oil Prices, 1972–2004

The blue line shows the price of a barrel of oil in each year. The red line measures the price of a barrel of oil in terms of the purchasing power of the dollar in 2004. By reducing oil production, the Organization of Petroleum Exporting Countries (OPEC) was able to raise the world price of oil in the mid-1970s and early 1980s. Sustaining high prices has been difficult, however, because members often exceed their output quotas.

Source: U.S. Energy Information Agency, *Monthly Energy Review,* May 2005.

reduce oil production well below the competitive level, to force up the price of oil, and to increase the profits of member countries.

Figure 13-4 shows world oil prices from 1972 to 2004. The blue line shows the price of a barrel of oil in each year. Prices in general have risen since 1972, which has reduced the amount of goods and services that can be purchased with a dollar. The red line corrects for this by measuring oil prices in terms of the dollar's purchasing power in 2004. Although political unrest in the Middle East and other factors also affect the price of oil, the figure shows that OPEC had considerable success in raising the price of oil during the mid-1970s and early 1980s. Oil prices, which had been below $3 per barrel in 1972, rose to more than $35 per barrel in 1981, which was more than $70 measured in dollars of 2004 purchasing power. The figure also shows that OPEC has had difficulty sustaining the high prices of 1981 in later years, although in 2004 and 2005 oil prices rose in part due to increasing demand from China and India. Game theory helps us to understand why oil prices have fluctuated. If every member of OPEC cooperates and produces the low output level dictated by its quota, prices will be high and the cartel will earn large profits. Once the price has been driven up, however, each member has an incentive to stop cooperating and to earn even higher profits by increasing output beyond its quota. But if no country sticks to its quota, total oil output will increase and profits will decline. In other words, OPEC is caught in a prisoners' dilemma.

If the members of OPEC always exceeded their production quotas, the cartel would have no effect on world oil prices. In fact, periodically the members of OPEC meet and assign new quotas that, at least for a while, enable them to restrict output enough to raise prices. OPEC's occasional success at behaving as a cartel can be explained by two factors. First, the members of OPEC are participating in a repeated game. As we have seen, this increases the likelihood of a cooperative outcome. Second, Saudi Arabia has far larger oil reserves than any other member of OPEC. Therefore, it has the most to gain from high oil prices, and a greater incentive to cooperate. To see this, consider the payoff matrix shown in Figure 13-5. To keep things simple, let's assume that OPEC has only two members: Saudi Arabia and Nigeria. In Figure 13-5, "low output" corresponds to cooperating with the OPEC assigned output quota, and "high output" corresponds to producing at maximum capacity. The payoff matrix shows the profits received per day by each country.

We can see that Saudi Arabia has a strong incentive to cooperate and maintain its low output quota. By keeping output low, Saudi Arabia can by itself significantly raise the world price of oil, increasing its own profits, as well as those of other members of OPEC. Therefore, Saudi Arabia has a dominant strategy of cooperating with the quota and producing a low output. Nigeria, however, cannot by itself have much impact on the price

The OPEC Cartel with Unequal Members

Because Saudi Arabia can produce so much more oil than Nigeria, its output decisions have a much larger impact on the price of oil. In the figure, "low output" corresponds to cooperating with the OPEC-assigned output quota, and "high output" corresponds to producing at maximum capacity. Saudi Arabia has a dominant strategy to cooperate and produce a low output. Nigeria, on the other hand, has a dominant strategy not to cooperate and produce a high output. Therefore, the equilibrium of this game will occur with Saudi Arabia producing a low output and Nigeria producing a high output.

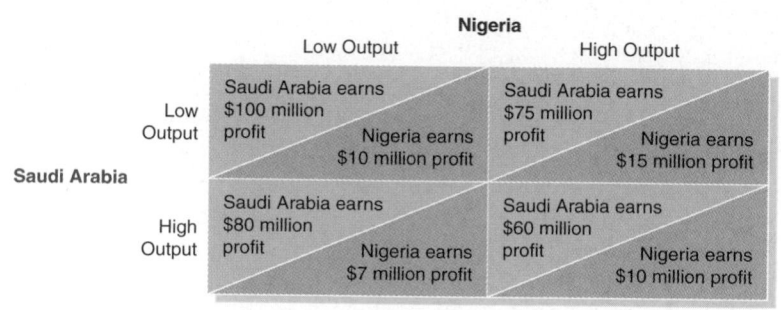

of oil. Therefore, Nigeria has a dominant strategy of not cooperating and producing a high output. The equilibrium of this game will occur with Saudi Arabia producing a low output and Nigeria producing a high output. In fact, OPEC often operates in just this way. Saudi Arabia will cooperate with the quota, while the other 10 members produce at capacity. Because this is a repeated game, however, Saudi Arabia will occasionally produce more oil than its quota to intentionally drive down the price and retaliate against the other members for not cooperating.

Sequential Games

We have been analyzing games where both players move simultaneously. In many business situations, however, one firm will act first, and then other firms will respond. These situations can be analyzed using *sequential games*. We will use sequential games to analyze two business strategies: (1) deterring entry and (2) bargaining between firms. To keep things simple, we consider situations that involve only two firms.

3 LEARNING OBJECTIVE

Use sequential games to analyze business strategies.

Deterring Entry

We saw earlier that barriers to entry are a key to firms continuing to earn economic profits. Can firms create barriers to deter new firms from entering an industry? Some recent research in game theory has focused on this question. To take a simple example, suppose a town in South Dakota currently has no discount department stores. Executives at Wal-Mart decide to enter the market and are considering what size store to build. To cover the opportunity cost of the funds involved, the store must provide a minimum rate of return of 15 percent on the firm's investment. If Wal-Mart builds a small store in the town, it will earn economic profits by receiving a return of 30 percent. If it builds a large store, its costs will be somewhat higher and it will receive a return of only 22 percent.

It seems clear that Wal-Mart should build the small store, but the executives are worried that Target may also build a store in this market. If Wal-Mart builds a small store and Target enters the market, both firms will earn an 18 percent return on their investment in this market. If Wal-Mart builds a large store and Target enters, the stores will have to cut prices, and the firms will each earn only 10 percent return on their investments, which is below the 15 percent return necessary for either firm to break even.

We can analyze a sequential game using a *decision tree*, like the one shown in Figure 13-6. The boxes in the figure represent *decision nodes*, which are points when the firms must make the decision contained in the box. At the left, Wal-Mart makes the initial decision of what size store to build and then Target responds by either entering the market or not. The decisions made are shown beside the arrows. The *terminal nodes* at the right side of the figure show the resulting rates of return.

Let's start with Wal-Mart's initial decision. If Wal-Mart builds a large store, then the arrow directs us to the upper red decision node for Target. If Target decides to enter, it will earn only a 10 percent rate of return on its investment, which represents an economic loss because it is below the opportunity cost of the funds involved. If Target doesn't enter, Wal-Mart will earn 22 percent and Target will not earn anything in this

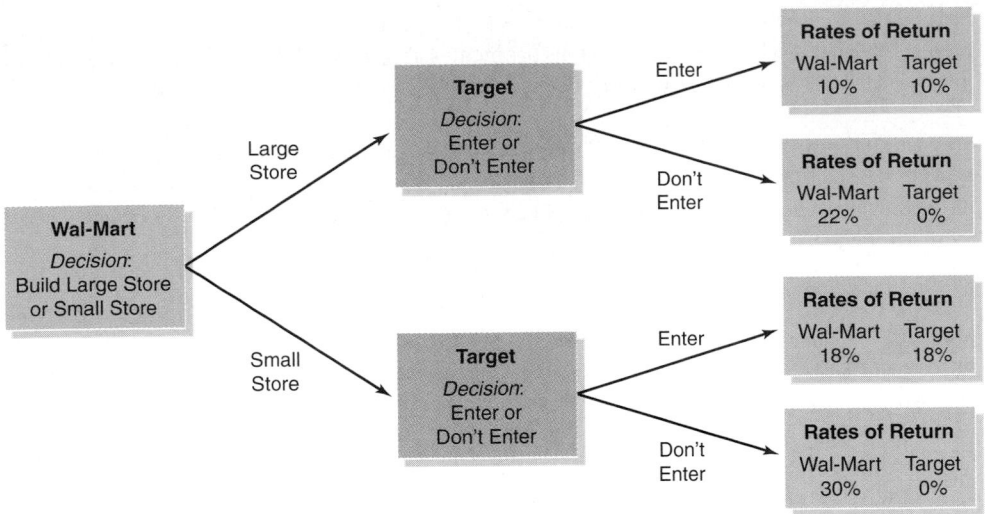

FIGURE 13-6

The Decision Tree for an Entry Game

Wal-Mart earns its highest return if it builds a small store and Target doesn't enter the market. If Wal-Mart builds a small store, Target will enter because it will earn economic profit by receiving an 18 percent return on its investment. Therefore, the best decision for Wal-Mart is to build a large store to deter Target's entry. Once Wal-Mart has built a large store, Target knows that if it enters this market, it will earn only 10 percent on its investment, which represents an economic loss, so it won't enter the market.

market. Wal-Mart executives can conclude that if they build a large store, Target will not enter and Wal-Mart will earn 22 percent on its investment.

If Wal-Mart decides to build a small store, then the arrow directs us to the lower red decision node for Target. If Target decides to enter, it will earn an 18 percent rate of return. If it doesn't enter, Wal-Mart will earn 30 percent and Target will not earn anything in this market. Wal-Mart executives can conclude that if they build a small store, Target will enter and Wal-Mart will earn 18 percent on its investment.

This analysis should lead Wal-Mart executives to conclude that they can build a small store and earn 18 percent—because Target will enter—or they can build a large store and earn 22 percent by deterring Target's entry.

SOLVED PROBLEM 13-2

Is Deterring Entry Always a Good Idea?

Whether deterring entry makes sense depends on how costly it is to the firm doing the deterring. Use the following decision tree to decide whether or not Wal-Mart should deter Target from entering this market. Assume that each firm must earn a 15 percent return on its investment to break even.

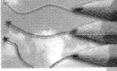

(3) **LEARNING OBJECTIVE**

Use sequential games to analyze business strategies.

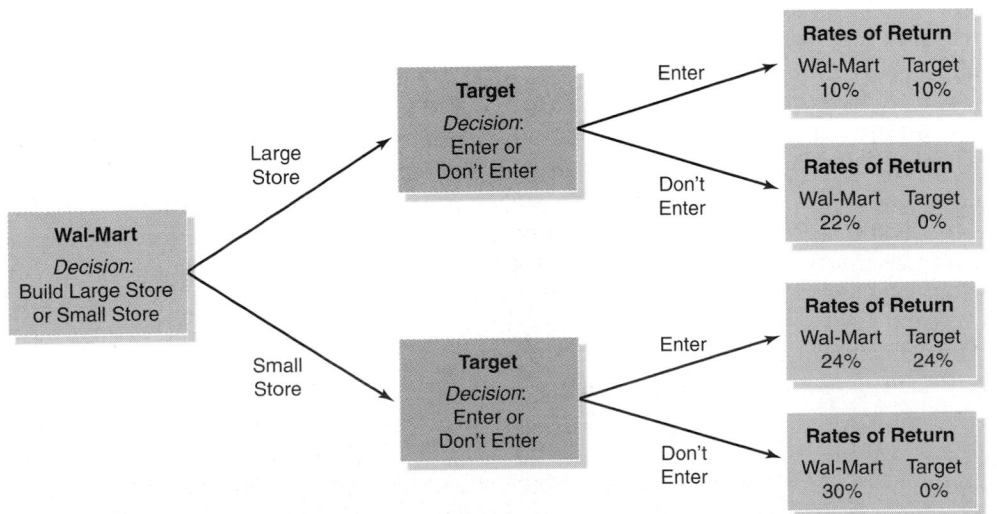

Solving the Problem:

Step 1: Review the chapter material. This problem is about sequential games, so you may want to review the section "Deterring Entry," which begins on page 426.

Step 2: Determine how Target will respond to Wal-Mart's decision. If Wal-Mart builds a large store, Target will not enter this market because the return on its investment represents an economic loss. If Wal-Mart builds a small store, Target will enter because it will earn a return that represents an economic profit.

Step 3: Given how Target will react, determine which strategy maximizes profits for Wal-Mart. If Wal-Mart builds the large store, it will have deterred Target's entry and the rate of return on its investment will be 22 percent. If it builds the small store, Target will enter, but Wal-Mart will actually earn a higher return of 24 percent.

Step 4: State your conclusion. Like any other business strategy, deterrence is worth pursuing only if its costs are not too high. In this case, the high cost of building a large store lowers Wal-Mart's economic profits below what it earns by building a small store, even given that Target will enter the market.

YOUR TURN: For more practice, do related problem 18 on page 439 at the end of this chapter. Visit www.prenhall.com/hubbard for an interactive exercise related to this Solved Problem.

Bargaining

The success of many firms depends on how well they bargain with other firms. For example, firms often must bargain with their suppliers over the prices they pay for inputs. Suppose that TruImage is a small firm that has developed software that improves how pictures from a digital camera are displayed on computer screens. TruImage currently sells its software only on its Web site and earns profits of $2 million per year. Dell Computer informs TruImage that it is considering installing the software on every new computer Dell sells. Dell expects to sell more computers at a higher price if it can install TruImage's software on its computers. The two firms begin bargaining over what price Dell will pay TruImage for its software.

The decision tree in Figure 13-7 illustrates this bargaining game. At the left, Dell makes the initial decision on what price to offer TruImage for its software, and then TruImage responds by either accepting or rejecting the contract offer. First, suppose that Dell offers TruImage a contract price of $30 per copy for its software. If TruImage accepts this contract, its profits will be $5 million per year, and Dell will earn $10 million in additional profits. If TruImage rejects the contract, its profits will be the $2 million per year it earns selling its software on its Web site and Dell will earn zero additional profits.

Now, suppose Dell offers TruImage a contract price of $20 per copy. If TruImage accepts this contract, its profits will be $3 million per year, and Dell will earn $15 million in additional profits. If TruImage rejects this contract, its profits will be the $2 million it earns selling its software on its Web site, and Dell will earn zero additional profits. Clearly, for Dell a contract of $20 per copy is more profitable, while for TruImage a contract of $30 per copy is more profitable.

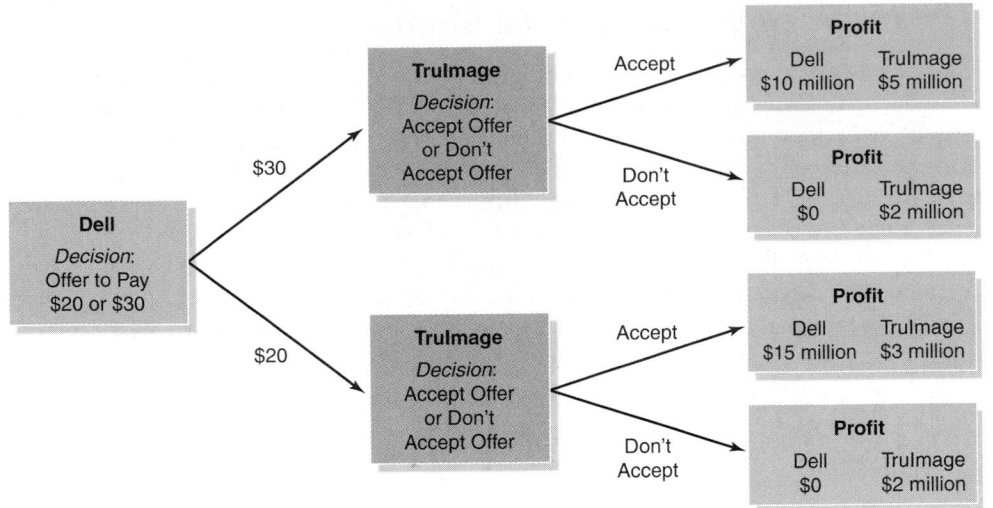

FIGURE 13-7

The Decision Tree for a Bargaining Game

Dell earns the highest profit if it offers a contract price of $20 per copy, and TruImage accepts the contract. TruImage earns the highest profit if Dell offers it a contract of $30 per copy, and it accepts the contract. TruImage may attempt to bargain by threatening to reject a $20 per copy contract. But Dell knows this threat is not credible because once Dell has offered a $20 per copy contract, TruImage's profits are higher if it accepts the contract than if it rejects it.

Suppose TruImage attempts to obtain a favorable outcome from the bargaining by telling Dell that it will reject a $20 per copy contract. If Dell believes this threat, then it will offer TruImage a $30 per copy contract because Dell is better off with the $10 million profit that will result from TruImage's accepting the contract, than with the zero profits Dell will earn if TruImage rejects the $20 per copy contract. This result is a Nash equilibrium because neither firm can increase its profits by changing its choice—*provided Dell believes TruImage's threat.* But is TruImage's threat credible? Once Dell has offered TruImage the $20 contract, then TruImage's choices are to accept the contract and earn $3 million, or reject the contract and earn only $2 million. Because rejecting the contract reduces TruImage's profits, TruImage's threat to reject the contract is not credible and Dell should ignore it.

As a result, we would expect Dell to use the strategy of offering TruImage a $20 per copy contract, and TruImage to use the strategy of accepting the contract. Dell will earn additional profits of $15 million per year, and TruImage will earn profits of $3 million per year. This outcome is called a *subgame-perfect equilibrium.* A subgame-perfect equilibrium is a Nash equilibrium in which no player can make himself better off by changing his decision at any decision node. In our simple bargaining game, each player has only one decision to make. As we have seen, Dell's profits are highest if it offers the $20 per copy contract, and TruImage's profits are highest if it accepts the contract. Typically, in sequential games of this type there is only one subgame-perfect equilibrium.

Decision trees like those in Figures 13-6 and 13-7 are widely used in business planning because they provide managers a systematic way of thinking through the implications of a strategy and of predicting the reactions of rivals. We can see the benefits of decision trees in the simple examples we considered here. In the first example, Wal-Mart managers can conclude that building a large store is more profitable than building a smaller store. In the second example, Dell managers can conclude that TruImage's threat to reject a $20 per copy contract is not credible.

④ LEARNING OBJECTIVE

Use the five competitive forces model to analyze competition in an industry.

The Five Competitive Forces Model

We have seen that the number of competitors in an industry affects a firm's ability to charge a price above average cost and earn an economic profit. The number of firms is not the only determinant of the level of competition in an industry, however. Michael Porter of the Harvard Business School has drawn on the research of a number of economists to develop a model showing how five competitive forces determine the overall level of competition in an industry. Figure 13-8 illustrates Porter's model.

We can look at each of the five competitive forces: (1) competition from existing firms, (2) the threat from potential entrants, (3) competition from substitute goods or services, (4) the bargaining power of buyers, and (5) the bargaining power of suppliers.

Competition from Existing Firms

We have already seen that price competition among firms in an industry can lower profits. Competition in the form of advertising, better customer service, or longer warranties can also reduce profits by raising costs. For example, online booksellers Amazon.com, BarnesandNoble.com, and Buy.com have competed by offering low-cost—or free—shipping, by increasing their customer service staffs, and by building more warehouses to provide faster deliveries. These activities have raised the booksellers' costs and reduced their profits.

The Threat from New Entrants

Firms also face competition from companies that currently are not in the market but might enter. We have already seen how actions taken to deter entry can reduce profits. In our hypothetical example in the previous section, Wal-Mart built a larger store and earned less profit to deter Target's entry. Business managers often take actions aimed at deterring entry. Some of these actions include advertising to create product loyalty, introducing new products—such as slightly different cereals or toothpastes—to fill market

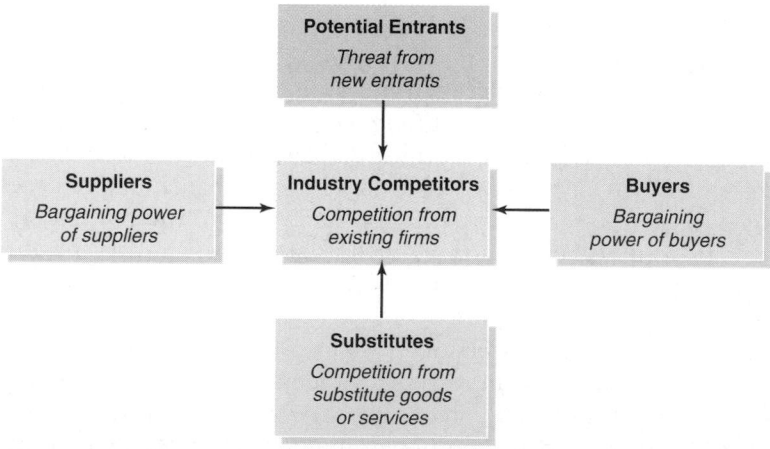

FIGURE 13-8 **The Five Competitive Forces Model**

Michael Porter's model identifies five forces that determine the level of competition in an industry: (1) competition from existing firms, (2) the threat from new entrants, (3) competition from substitute goods or services, (4) the bargaining power of buyers, and (5) the bargaining power of suppliers.

Source: Reprinted with the permission of The Free Press, a Division of Simon & Schuster Adult Publishing Group, from *Competitive Strategy: Techniques for Analyzing Industries and Competitors* by Michael E. Porter. Copyright © 1980, 1998 by The Free Press. All rights reserved.

niches, and setting lower prices to keep profits at a level that would make entry less attractive.

Competition from Substitute Goods or Services

Firms are always vulnerable to the introduction of a new product that fills a consumer need better than their current product does. Consider the encyclopedia business. For decades many parents bought expensive and bulky encyclopedias for their children attending high school or college. By the 1990s, computer software companies were offering electronic encyclopedias that sold for a small fraction of the price of the printed encyclopedias. Encyclopedia Britannica and the other encyclopedia publishers responded by cutting prices and launching advertising campaigns aimed at showing the superiority of printed encyclopedias. Still, profits continued to decline, and by the end of the 1990s, most printed encyclopedias had disappeared.

Bargaining Power of Buyers

If buyers have enough bargaining power, they can insist on lower prices, higher-quality products, or additional services. Automobile companies, for example, have significant bargaining power in the tire market, which tends to lower tire prices and limit the profitability of tire manufacturers. Some retailers have significant buying power over their suppliers. For instance, Wal-Mart has required many of its suppliers to alter their distribution systems to accommodate Wal-Mart's need to control the stocks of goods in its stores.

Bargaining Power of Suppliers

If many firms can supply an input and the input is not specialized, the suppliers are unlikely to have the bargaining power to limit a firm's profits. For instance, suppliers of paper napkins to McDonald's restaurants have very little bargaining power. With only a single or a few suppliers of an input, the purchasing firm may face a high price. During the 1930s and 1940s, for example, the Technicolor Company was the only producer of the cameras and film that studios needed to produce color movies. Technicolor charged the studios high prices to use their cameras, and it had the power to insist that only its technicians could operate the cameras. The only alternative for the movie studios was to make black-and-white movies.

As with other competitive forces, the bargaining power of suppliers can change over time. For instance, when IBM chose Microsoft to supply the operating system for its personal computers, Microsoft was a small company with very limited bargaining power. As Microsoft's Windows operating system became standard in more than 90 percent of personal computers, this large market share increased Microsoft's bargaining power.

Is Southwest's Business Strategy More Important Than the Structure of the Airline Industry?

13-4 Making the Connection

For years, economists and business strategists believed that market structure was the most important factor in explaining the ability of some firms to continue earning economic profits. For example, most economists argued that during the first few decades after World War II steel companies in the United States earned economic profits because barriers to entry were high, there were few firms in the industry, and competition among firms was low. In contrast, restaurants were seen as less profitable because barriers to entry were low and the industry was intensely competitive. One problem with this approach to analyzing the profitability of firms is that it does not explain how firms in the same industry can have very different levels of profit.

Today, economists and business strategists put greater emphasis on the characteristics of individual firms and the strategies their managements use to continue to earn economic profits. This approach helps explain why Nucor continues to be a profitable steel company while Bethlehem Steel, at one time the second-largest steel producer in the United States, was forced into bankruptcy. It also explains why Dell, which began as a small company run by Michael Dell from his dorm room at the University of Texas, went on to become extremely profitable and an industry leader, while other computer companies have disappeared.

Many economists argue that the best strategy for a company is to identify a segment of the market and then shape the company to fit that segment. Doing this makes it very difficult for rivals in the industry to copy it. For example, Southwest Airlines concentrates on customers who fly relatively short distances and who want a low-price, no-frills airline flight. Every aspect of the company is focused on this goal. Southwest's planes have no first class or business sections—only coach seats are available. By flying primarily between midsize cities, it can avoid the delays at the crowded airports near big cities and can keep its planes at the airport gate for only 15 minutes—much less than other airlines. This lowers its costs by allowing it to keep its planes in the air longer and to offer more flights with fewer planes. Southwest also lowers costs by not serving meals, by flying only Boeing 737s to standardize maintenance, and by not checking luggage through to connecting flights.

It is very difficult for the other full-service airlines, such as Delta, American, and United, to compete with Southwest. Because they fly out of larger, more congested airports, they have no hope of turning around their planes at the gate as quickly as Southwest does. Because many of their passengers are flying longer distances—often using connecting flights—they have to serve meals and check luggage through. Many of the other airlines' customers want upgraded seats and service, so these airlines must offer first-class and business-class seats. Even when Delta, American, and United have tried to offer stripped-down service on certain routes in direct competition with Southwest, they have not been successful. Southwest's complete focus on providing low-cost, low-price service has proven very difficult for the other

Southwest's business strategy allowed it to remain profitable when many other airlines faced heavy losses.

airlines to copy. While other airlines suffered heavy losses in 2003–2004 as fuel prices rose and demand declined as a result of the war in Iraq and the spread of the disease SARS (severe acute respiratory syndrome), Southwest continued to earn profits.

Southwest's corporate strategy, rather than the structure of the airline industry, explains why Southwest earns economic profits.

Conclusion

Firms are locked in a never-ending struggle to earn economic profits. As noted in the three preceding chapters, competition erodes economic profits. Even in the oligopolies discussed in this chapter, firms have difficulty earning economic profits in the long run. We have seen that firms attempt to avoid the effects of competition in various ways. For example, they can stake out a secure niche in the market, they can engage in implicit collusion with competing firms, or they can attempt to have the government impose barriers to entry. Read *An Inside Look* on the next page to learn about the business strategies an electronics store and a clothing store use to compete with Wal-Mart. The next chapter focuses on firms that are insulated from competition by being monopolies.

WALL STREET JOURNAL,
MAY 20, 2004

Electronics Retailers Are Starting to Make House Calls

In an effort to win the loyalty of consumers frustrated at trying to make their high-tech gear work like it's supposed to, companies including Best Buy Co. and CompUSA Inc. are quickly adding or expanding their in-home installation and repair services. It's the latest battleground in consumer electronics, where retailers are facing tough new competition from discount-store giant Wal-Mart Stores Inc....

a Retailers are fighting back by trying to refashion themselves as on-call handymen, partly in an effort to stand out from discounters competing mainly on price. Last month, Best Buy launched a national expansion of the Geek Squad, a staff of techies who wear black clip-on ties and offer in-home computer repair and installation. By this summer, the company plans to have Geek Squads in all 614 stores, up from the current 120.

The high-tech house calls cover a wide range of services, from installing wireless networks to rescuing lost computer files. The visits can cost anywhere from $300 to set up a flat-panel TV to about $100 to debug a computer.

Consumer-electronics retailers are so eager to get inside consumers' living rooms that some of them are now teaming up with home builders to wire new houses with high-speed cables and networking equipment. Last month, Best Buy signed a deal to wire 3,000 or so homes being built by Hillwood Development Corp., a Dallas-based developer....

Companies realize that by getting a foot in the door of shoppers' homes, they can see what's there—and suggest more gear to buy....

WALL STREET JOURNAL,
APRIL 27, 2004

Clothing Store Appeals to Plus-Sized Women

a At 5 feet 2 and more than 160 pounds, Alicia Derrick had a tough time finding clothes that fit. She usually left stores empty-handed.

But on a recent trip to a Torrid store in Northridge, Calif., the 26-year-old singer picked up a black lace tank top, silver studded belt and black cargo pants. "It's got everything," she says. In most stores, "you go to the teen section and it's all for stick girls."

Torrid, a national chain with 52 stores, is at the leading edge of a quest to solve an important retailing riddle: What do the growing ranks of overweight young American women want to wear? It is prospering with an unconventional answer: the same clothes other young women want.

With an assortment of tulle prom dresses, fishnet tights, camisole-and-thong lingerie sets and T-shirts with slogans such as, "All this and brains too," Torrid looks like a lot of other retailers catering to teenage girls. The look is Britney Spears wannabe, full of curvy silhouettes with hip-hugging jeans and revealing tops....

"These girls want to feel good and they want as many options as anyone else," says Betsy McLaughlin, the 43-year-old chief executive of teen retailer Hot Topic Inc., which launched Torrid three years ago. Analysts say Torrid became profitable last year and is one reason Hot Topic's profit rose 39% in its most recent fiscal year while its stock price doubled.

The nation's biggest retailers, including Wal-Mart Stores Inc. and Target Corp., have struggled to understand this market....

b Wal-Mart's plus-size "tween" line, for ages 8 to 12, called "Faded Glory," lasted only one year after its 2001 introduction. In January 2003 Wal-Mart started offering the clothing line of teen stars Mary-Kate and Ashley Olsen in extended sizes. But sales have been lackluster, in part because the items were "lost on a rack of regular sizes," says Judy Swartz, executive designer at the Olsen twins' company Dualstar Entertainment Group Inc....

Wal-Mart says since January it has been displaying the Olsens' plus-size clothes on separate racks. Melissa Berryhill, a Wal-Mart spokeswoman, says in an e-mail that the retailer is also "fine tuning" designs in a bid to make the clothes a better fit....

Key Points in the Article

These articles discuss how companies attempt to compete with Wal-Mart. Wal-Mart has been very successful at selling standard products that it purchases in large quantities directly from manufacturers. Because it has lower costs than its competitors, it can charge lower prices. This has led its competitors to look for products and services they can offer that Wal-Mart does not. The first article discusses how Best Buy has formed Geek Squads that offer customers in-home repair and installation services that Wal-Mart does not offer. The second article discusses how Torrid has been successful selling plus-sized women's clothes. So far, Wal-Mart has not been successful in selling these clothes.

Analyzing the News

a We can use the game theory model from this chapter to analyze the business strategies discussed in these articles. In both articles, the firms discussed are not attempting to compete directly with Wal-Mart by offering the same products and services. Instead, they are attempting to find "niches" that Wal-Mart does not currently occupy. Whether or not this strategy is successful depends partly on Wal-Mart's reaction. For instance, whether or not

Best Buy is successful in offering in-home service by Geek Squads depends on whether Wal-Mart decides to offer the same service.

b We can use decision trees to analyze the impact of Wal-Mart deciding to compete with firms offering new services. In Figure 1 we focus on the competition between Wal-Mart and Best Buy, although we could undertake a similar analysis of the competition between Wal-Mart and Torrid. In both panels of the figure, Best Buy chooses first whether to offer in-home service for electronic products, then Wal-Mart decides whether or not to also offer the service. We assume that each company needs a 15 percent return on its investment for the new service to break even. In panel (a), if Best Buy decides not to offer the service, neither firm will offer it. If Best Buy decides to offer the service, Wal-Mart must decide whether or not to respond by also offering the service. If Wal-Mart decides not to offer the service, then Best Buy receives a 20 percent return on its investment. If Wal-Mart does offer the service, it receives a 20 percent return, and Best Buy receives a 10 percent return. We can conclude that Wal-Mart will choose to offer the service. This would be a bad outcome for Best Buy because its return is below 15 percent, so it will incur an economic loss.

In panel (b), the outcome is better for Best Buy. In this case, if Wal-Mart responds by also

offering the service, Wal-Mart's return would be only 10 percent. We can conclude that Wal-Mart will not offer the service, and that Best Buy will end up with a 20 percent return. Before the initial decision to offer the in-home service, Best Buy would have to decide whether it believed that panel (a) or panel (b) more accurately reflected the returns Wal-Mart could expect to make. If panel (a) is accurate, Best Buy should not begin to offer this service. If panel (b) is accurate, then Best Buy should begin to offer this service.

Thinking Critically

1. Do you believe that Wal-Mart will eventually offer plus-sized women's clothing and home installation and repair services for electronic goods? In what ways do these products differ from the typical goods sold at Wal-Mart? Do these differences pose a barrier to Wal-Mart becoming the low-cost supplier of these products? Briefly explain.

2. We have seen that economies of scale are the most important explanation for an industry being an oligopoly. Does Wal-Mart benefit from significant economies of scale? If so, briefly describe what they are.

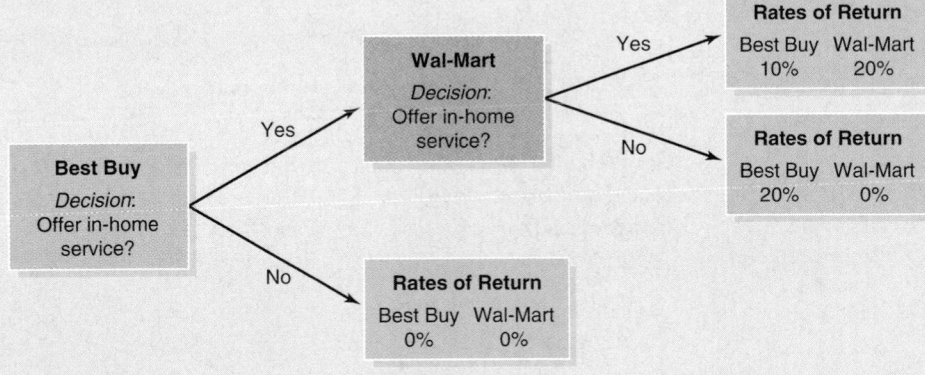

(a) Wal-mart begins offering in-home service

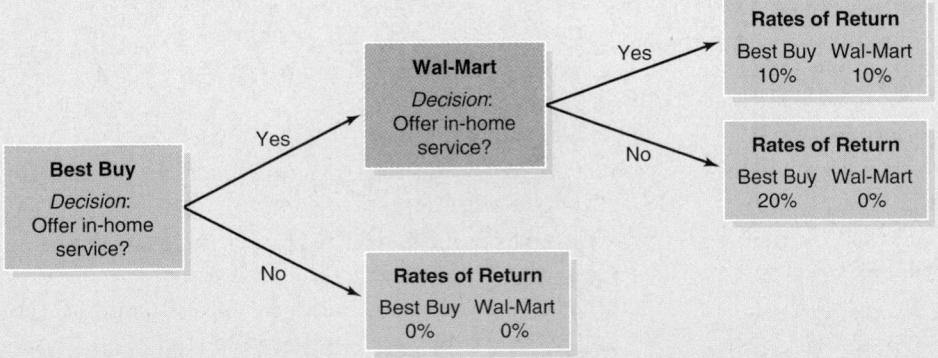

(b) Wal-mart does not begin offering in-home service

Figure 1: Best Buy analyzes whether to offer in-home service for electronic products.

435

SUMMARY

LEARNING OBJECTIVE ① Show how barriers to entry explain the existence of oligopolies. An *oligopoly* is a market structure in which a small number of interdependent firms compete. *Barriers to entry* keep new firms from entering an industry. The three most important barriers to entry are economies of scale, ownership of a key input or raw material, and government barriers. Government barriers include patents, licensing, and barriers to international trade. Economies of scale are the most important barrier to entry.

LEARNING OBJECTIVE ② Use game theory to analyze the actions of oligopolistic firms. Because an oligopoly has only a few firms, interactions among those firms are particularly important. *Game theory* is the study of how people make decisions in situations where attaining their goals depends on their interactions with others; in economics, it is the study of the decisions of firms in industries where the profits of each firm depends on its interactions with other firms. In a *cooperative equilibrium,* firms cooperate to increase their mutual payoff. In a *noncooperative equilibrium,* firms do not cooperate but pursue their own self-interest. A *dominant strategy* is a strategy that is the best for a firm, no matter what

strategies other firms use. A situation where pursuing dominant strategies results in noncooperation that leaves everyone worse off is called a *prisoners' dilemma.* Because many business situations are repeated games, firms may end up implicitly colluding to keep prices high.

LEARNING OBJECTIVE ③ Use sequential games to analyze business strategies. Recent work in game theory has focused on actions firms can take to deter the entry of new firms into an industry. Deterring entry can be analyzed using a sequential game, where first one firm makes a decision and then the other firm reacts to that decision. Sequential games can be illustrated using decision trees.

LEARNING OBJECTIVE ④ Use the five competitive forces model to analyze competition in an industry. Michael Porter of the Harvard Business School argues that the state of competition in an industry is determined by five competitive forces: the degree of competition among existing firms, the threat from new entrants, competition from substitute goods or services, the bargaining power of buyers, and the bargaining power of suppliers.

KEY TERMS

Barrier to entry 415
Business strategy 417
Cartel 424
Collusion 418

Cooperative
 equilibrium 419
Dominant strategy 419
Economies of scale 415

Game theory 417
Nash equilibrium 419
Noncooperative
 equilibrium 420

Oligopoly 414
Patent 417
Payoff matrix 418
Prisoners' dilemma 420

REVIEW QUESTIONS

1. What is an oligopoly? Give three examples of oligopolistic industries in the United States.
2. What do barriers to entry have to do with the extent of competition, or lack thereof, in an industry? What are the most important barriers to entry?
3. Give an example of a government-imposed barrier to entry. Why would the government be willing to erect barriers to entering an industry?
4. Give brief definitions of the following concepts:
   a. game theory
   b. cooperative equilibrium

   c. noncooperative equilibrium
   d. dominant strategy
   e. Nash equilibrium
5. Why do economists refer to the methodology for analyzing oligopolies as game theory?
6. Why do economists refer to the pricing strategies of oligopoly firms as a prisoners' dilemma game?
7. What is the difference between explicit collusion and implicit collusion? Give an example of each.

8. How is the prisoners' dilemma result changed in a repeated game?

9. What is a sequential game? How are decision trees used to analyze sequential games?

10. List the competitive forces in the five competitive forces model. Does the strength of each of these forces remain constant over time? Briefly explain.

PROBLEMS AND APPLICATIONS

Please visit **www.prenhall.com/hubbard** *for solutions to the even-numbered problems as well as multiple-choice and true or false self-assessment quizzes.*

1. Consider two oligopolistic industries. In the first industry, firms always match price changes by any other firm in the industry. In the second industry, firms always ignore price changes by any other firm. In which industry are firms likely to charge higher prices? Briefly explain.

2. Consider the following two excerpts from articles in the *Wall Street Journal:*

   [From February 2003] An attempt by major airlines to raise fares $20 per round-trip ticket fell apart over the weekend as Northwest Airlines, the fourth-largest carrier, refused to go along. . . . By yesterday morning, all airlines had rolled back prices.

   [From August 2003] Northwest Airlines triggered a major round of discounting last week when it launched a fare sale for late summer and early fall travel—setting off a chain reaction in the industry. During the course of one day, airlines cut fares on nearly 35,881 routes.

   Briefly explain why airlines might be more likely to match price cuts than price increases.
   Sources: Scott McCartney and Susan Carey, "Airlines' Move to Raise Fares Falls Apart as Northwest Balks," *Wall Street Journal*, February 18, 2003; and Eleena De Lisser, "Fall Travel Deals Arrive Early," *Wall Street Journal*, August 14, 2003.

3. The city is considering auctioning licenses that would allow one or two vendors to sell ice cream on the local beach.
   a. If the city sells licenses to two vendors, will it receive more in total license fees than if it sells a license to only one vendor?
   b. Will people who use the beach be better off if the city licenses two vendors or one vendor?
   c. Suppose the city licenses two vendors but announces that every year it will sell licenses to two new vendors. The same vendor may not hold a license more than once every five years. Would this make any difference to the prices the vendors charge?

4. Bob and Tom are two criminals who have been arrested for burglary. The police put Tom and Bob in separate cells. They offer to let Bob go free if he confesses to the crime and testifies against Tom. Bob also is told that he will serve a 15-year sentence if he remains silent while Tom confesses. If he confesses and Tom also confesses, they will each serve a 10-year sentence. Separately, the police make the same offer to Tom. Assume that if Bob and Tom both remain silent, the police only have enough evidence to convict them of a lesser crime and they will serve 3-year sentences.
   a. Use this information to write a payoff matrix for Bob and Tom.
   b. Does Bob have a dominant strategy? If so, what is it?
   c. Does Tom have a dominant strategy? If so, what is it?
   d. What sentences do Bob and Tom serve? How might they have avoided this outcome?

5. [Related to *Don't Let This Happen To You!*] A student argues, "The prisoners' dilemma game is unrealistic. Each player's strategy is based on the assumption that the other player won't cooperate. But if each player assumes that the other player *will* cooperate, then the 'dilemma' disappears." Briefly explain whether or not you agree with this argument.

6. Under "early decision" college admission plans, students apply to a college in the fall and, if they are accepted, they must enroll in that college. According to an article in *Business Week*, Yale president Richard Levin argues that early decision plans put too much pressure on students to decide early in their senior years which college they wish to attend. Levin has proposed abolishing early decision plans. But the author of the article is doubtful this will succeed because "as long as some big-name schools offer early admissions, the others feel they must, too, or lose out on the best talent." Do you agree with this conclusion? How can game theory help us analyze this situation?

7. Baseball players who hit the most home runs *relative to other players* usually receive the highest pay. Beginning in the mid-1990s, the typical baseball player became significantly stronger and more muscular. As one baseball

announcer put it, "The players of 20 years ago look like stick figures compared with the players of today." As a result, the average number of home runs hit each year increased dramatically. Some of the increased strength gained by baseball players came from more weight training and better conditioning and diet. As some players admitted, though, some of the increased strength came from taking steroids and other illegal drugs. Taking steroids can significantly increase the risk of developing cancer and other medical problems.

 a. In these circumstances, are baseball players in a prisoners' dilemma? Carefully explain.

 b. Suppose that Major League Baseball begins testing players for steroids and firing players who are caught using them (or other illegal muscle-building drugs). Will this testing make baseball players as a group better off or worse off? Briefly explain.

8. [Related to *Solved Problem 13–1*] Would a ban on advertising beer on television be likely to increase or decrease the profits of beer companies? Briefly explain.

9. [Related to *Solved Problem 13–1*] In 2003, following the coalition declaration of victory in the war in Iraq, the U.S. government spent billions of dollars rebuilding the damaged Iraqi infrastructure. Much of the work was carried out by construction and engineering firms that had to bid for the business. Suppose, hypothetically, that only two companies—Bechtel and Halliburton—enter the bidding and that each firm is deciding whether to bid either $4 billion or $5 billion. (Remember that in this type of bidding, the winning bid is the *low* bid because the bid represents the amount the government will have to pay to have the work done.) Each firm will have costs of $2.5 billion to do the work. If they both make the same bid, they will both be hired and will split the work and the profits. If one makes a low bid and one makes a high bid, only the low bidder will be hired and it will receive all the profits. The result is the following payoff matrix:

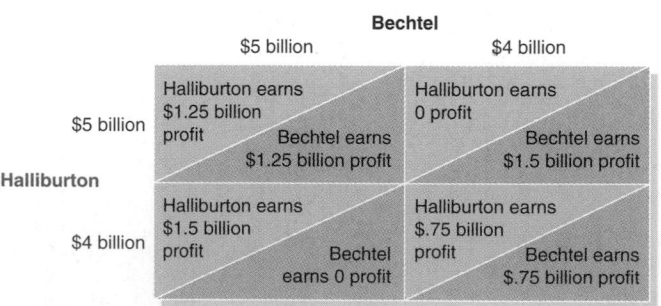

 a. Is there a Nash equilibrium in this game? Briefly explain.

 b. How might the situation be changed if the two companies expect to be bidding on many similar projects in future years?

10. [Related to *Solved Problem 13–1* and the Chapter Opener] Suppose that Wal-Mart and Target are competing on whether to stick with barcodes or switch to radio frequency identification (RFID) tags to monitor the flow of products. Because many suppliers sell to both Wal-Mart and Target, it is much less costly for suppliers to use one system or the other, rather than to use both. The following payoff matrix shows the profits per year for each company resulting from the interaction of their strategies:

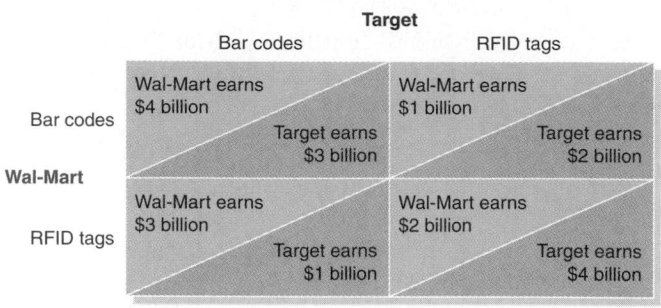

 a. Briefly explain whether Wal-Mart has a dominant strategy.

 b. Briefly explain whether Target has a dominant strategy.

 c. Briefly explain whether there is a Nash equilibrium in this game.

11. An historical account of the development of the cotton textile industry in England argues the following:

 > [T]he cotton textile industry was shaped by ruthless competition. Rapid growth in demand, low barriers to entry, frequent technological innovations, and a high rate of firm bankruptcy all combined to form an environment in which . . . oligopolistic competition became almost impossible.

 Explain how each of the factors described above would contribute to making the cotton textile industry competitive, rather than oligopolistic.
 Source: Thomas K. McCraw, ed., *Creating Modern Capitalism*, Cambridge: Harvard University Press, pp. 61–62.

12. Michael Porter has argued, "The intensity of competition in an industry is neither a matter of coincidence nor bad luck. Rather, competition in an industry is rooted in its underlying economic structure." What does Porter mean by "economic structure"? What factors, other than economic structure, might be expected to determine the intensity of competition in an industry?
 Source: Michael Porter, *Competitive Strategy: Techniques for Analyzing Industries and Competitors*, New York: Free Press, 1980, p. 3.

13. "Less-than-truckload" trucking companies include goods from several shippers in their highway trailers. According to an article in the *Wall Street Journal*:

 > Unlike truckload [companies], a fiercely competitive business it is relatively easy to enter,

less-than-truckload companies face a higher entry barrier due to the cost of an extensive network of terminals to consolidate shipments.

Would you expect truckload companies or less-than-truckload companies to charge higher prices to ship freight? Which companies are likely to earn economic profits? Briefly explain.

Source: Daniel Machalaba, "Yellow Freight to Raise Rates 4.9% on Bet about Lower Inventory Costs," *Wall Street Journal*, July 5, 2001.

14. According to an article in *Fortune* magazine:

> In business terms, "commodity" is typically used to describe a product or service with no differentiation from the competition's, leaving price as the sole factor in the customer's decision.

In 2001, Dell Computer aggressively began cutting the prices of its personal computers. Lou Gerstner, the CEO of IBM, was quoted as saying: "Price wars in a commodity business are really dumb." Is Gerstner correct that personal computers are a "commodity business"? Why would a price war be a worse strategy in a commodity business than in a noncommodity business?

Source: J. William Gurley, "Above the Crowd: Why Dell's War Isn't Dumb," *Fortune*, July 9, 2001.

15. Explain how collusion makes firms better off. Given the incentives to collude, briefly explain why every industry doesn't become a cartel.

16. Thomas McCraw, a professor at the Harvard Business School, has written the following:

> Throughout American history, entrepreneurs have tried, sometimes desperately, to create big businesses out of naturally small-scale operations. It has not worked.

What advantage would entrepreneurs expect to gain from creating "big businesses"? Why would they be unsuccessful in doing so with "naturally small-scale operations"? Illustrate your answer with a graph showing long-run average costs.

Source: Thomas K. McCraw, ed., *Creating Modern Capitalism*, Cambridge, MA: Harvard University Press, 1997, p. 323.

17. Until the late 1990s, airlines would post proposed changes in ticket prices on computer reservations systems several days before the new ticket prices went into effect. Then the federal government took action to end the practice. Now airlines can only post prices on their reservations systems for tickets that are immediately available for sale. Why would the federal government object to the old system of posting prices before they went into effect?

Source: Scott McCartney, "Airfare Wars Show Why Deals Arrive and Depart," *Wall Street Journal*, March 19, 2002.

18. **[Related to *Solved Problem 13–2*]** Bradford is a small town that currently has no fast-food restaurants. McDonald's and Burger King both are considering entering this market. Burger King will wait until McDonald's has made its decision before deciding whether to enter. Use the following decision tree to decide the optimal strategy for each company. Does your answer depend on the rate of return that owners of fast-food restaurants must earn on their investments in order to break even? Briefly explain.

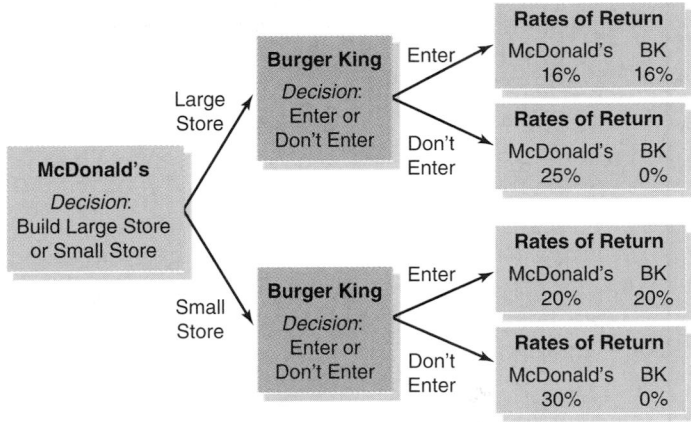

19. Michael Porter has argued that in many industries "strategies converge and competition becomes a series of races down identical paths that no one can win." Briefly explain whether firms in these industries likely will earn economic profits.

Source: Michael E. Porter, "What Is Strategy?" *Harvard Business Review*, November–December 1996, p. 64.

20. An article in the *Wall Street Journal* argues, "Finally, American [Airlines] has figured out what Southwest Airlines and others have known for some time: There is a cost to complexity." What does the author mean by a "cost to complexity"? How does Southwest Airlines avoid this cost? (*Hint:* Review Making the Connection 13-4: Is Business Strategy More Important Than Market Structure?)

Source: Scott McCartney, "Large Carriers Are Beginning to Discover the Benefits of Simplicity," *Wall Street Journal*, August 15, 2002, p. D4.

21. Soldiers in battle may face a prisoners' dilemma. If all soldiers stand and fight, the chance that the soldiers as a unit will survive is maximized. If there is a significant chance that the soldiers will lose the battle, an individual soldier may maximize his chance of survival by running away while the other soldiers hold off the enemy by fighting. If all soldiers run away, however, many of them are likely to be killed or captured by the enemy because no one is left to hold off the enemy. In ancient times, the Roman army practiced "decimation." If a unit of soldiers was guilty of running away during a battle or committing other cowardly acts, all would be lined up and every tenth soldier would be killed by being run through with a sword. No attempt was made to distinguish between soldiers in the unit who had

fought well and those who had been cowardly. Briefly explain under what condition the Roman system of decimation was likely to have solved the prisoners' dilemma of soldiers running away in battle.

22. In early 2004, Yahoo was set to challenge Google as the leading online search engine. According to an article in the *Wall Street Journal*, Yahoo's strategy was "not simply to match what Google does now but to add features its rival can't easily match." The article quoted a senior vice president at Yahoo as stating, "We're not going to beat the competition by being the competition." Briefly explain what the Yahoo executive means by "being the competition." Briefly discuss whether the strategy of "being the competition" ever makes sense.
Source: Mylene Mangalindan, "Yahoo Gets Set to Give Google a Run for Its Money," *Wall Street Journal*, January 6, 2004.

23. The following is from an article in the *Wall Street Journal*:

    As U.S. car makers continue to offer generous cash discounts and cut-rate financing to woo buyers, top Japanese manufacturers are taking a different pricing approach that seems to be working: Hold sticker prices steady but pack cars with alluring new features.

    What happens to the profit a car company makes on each car sold if it cuts the price while holding the car's features constant? What happens to profit per car if the company adds new features while holding the price constant? Briefly discuss how a car company might decide which of these strategies to use.
Source: Todd Zaun, "Japanese Battle U.S. Discounts with Extras," *Wall Street Journal*, January 6, 2004.

24. Alfred Chandler, a professor at the Harvard Business School, has observed, "Imagine the diseconomies of scale—the great increase in unit costs—that would result from placing close to one-fourth of the world's production of shoes, or textiles, or lumber into three factories or mills!" The shoe, textiles, and lumber industries are very competitive with many firms producing each of these products. Briefly explain whether Chandler's observation helps us explain why.
Source: Alfred D. Chandler, Jr., "The Emergence of Managerial Capitalism," in Alfred D. Chandler, Jr. and Richard S. Tedlow, *The Coming of Managerial Capitalism*, New York: Irwin, 1985, p. 406.

25. Alfred Chandler also has written: "The entrepreneurs who invested in plants big enough to exploit the economies of scale . . . in production . . . , and in the managerial organization essential for coordination of those activities brought into being the modern industrial enterprise. The first to do so acquired powerful competitive advantages, or (to use the economists' term) 'first-mover' advantages." What were these advantages in terms of the long-run average cost of production? Illustrate.
Source: Alfred D. Chandler, Jr., *Scale and Scope: The Dynamics of Industrial Capitalism*, Cambridge, MA: Harvard University Press, 1990, p. 34.

26. The figure below illustrates the average total cost curves for two automobile manufacturing firms: LittleAuto and BigAuto. Under which conditions would you expect to see the market composed of firms like LittleAuto and under which conditions would you expect to see the market dominated by firms like BigAuto?
    a. When the market demand curve intersects the quantity axis at less than 1000 units
    b. When the market demand curve intersects the quantity axis at more than 1000 units but less than 10,000 units
    c. When the market demand curve intersects the quantity axis at more than 10,000 units

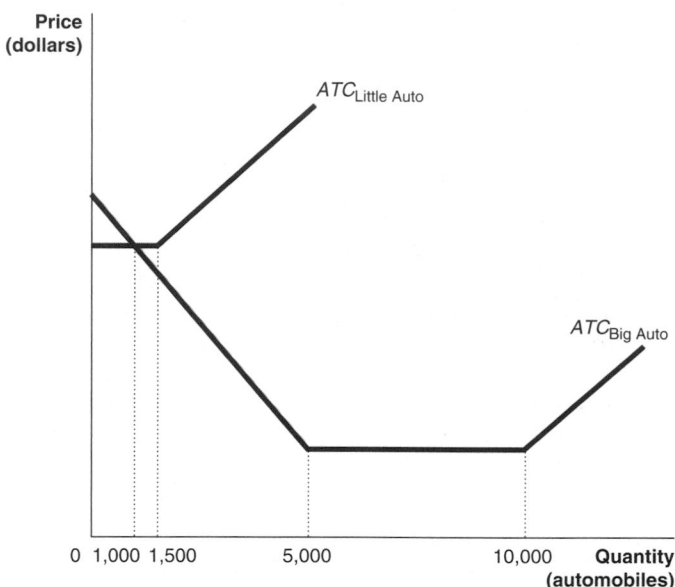

27. The figure below contains two long-run average cost curves. Briefly explain which cost curve would most likely be associated with an oligopoly and which would most likely be associated with a perfectly competitive industry.

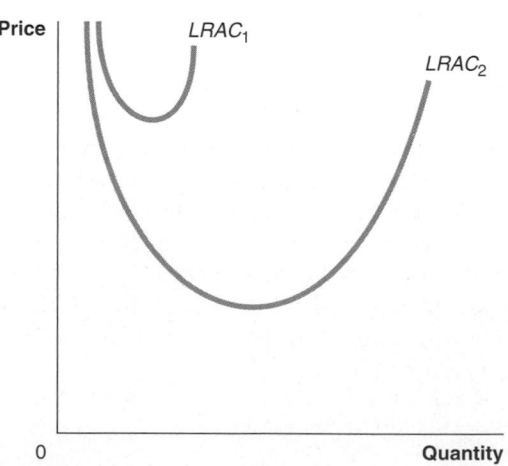

chapter fourteen

Monopoly and Antitrust Policy

Time Warner Rules Manhattan

➤ Today most people can hardly imagine life without cable television. In fact, almost 80 percent of U.S. homes have cable television: a larger fraction than have clothes dryers, dishwashers, air conditioning, or personal computers, and almost as many as have washing machines. The first cable systems were established in the 1940s in cities that were too small to support broadcast stations. Those systems consisted of large antennas set up on hills to receive broadcasts from television stations within range. The signals were then transmitted by cable to individual houses.

The cable industry grew slowly because the technology did not exist to rebroadcast the signals of distant

stations, so cable systems offered few stations. By 1970 only about 7 percent of households had cable television. In addition, the Federal Communications Commission (FCC)—the federal government agency that regulates the television industry—placed restrictions on both rebroadcasting the signals of distant stations and on the fees that could be charged for "premium channels" that would show movies or sporting events. In the late 1970s two key developments occurred: First, satellite relay technology made it feasible for local cable systems to receive signals relayed via satellite from distant broadcast stations. Second, Congress loosened regulations on rebroadcasting distant stations

and premium channels. The result of these developments was the growth of both "superstations," which are local broadcast stations in large cities—such as New York, Chicago, and Atlanta—whose programming is sent by satellite to cable systems around the country, and premium channels, such as Home Box Office (HBO).

One of the most successful of the superstations was WTBS, started by Atlanta entrepreneur Robert Edward "Ted" Turner III. Turner went on to found the Turner Broadcasting System (TBS), which included the Cable News Network (CNN), the first 24-hour news network. In 2001, Turner was involved in the largest merger of entertainment companies in history

LEARNING OBJECTIVES

After studying this chapter, you should be able to:

① Define monopoly.

② Explain the four main reasons monopolies arise.

③ Explain how a monopoly chooses price and output.

④ Use a graph to illustrate how a monopoly affects economic surplus.

⑤ Discuss government policies toward monopoly.

when AOL Time Warner was formed. The company—now known as Time Warner—was made up of leading firms from four segments of the entertainment industry: Warner Brothers (movie making), *Time* (magazine publishing), TBS (cable television), and AOL (Internet). Today, Time Warner operates cable systems in 22 states through Time Warner Cable.

A firm needs a license from the city government to enter a local cable television market. If you live in Manhattan and you want cable television, you have to purchase it from Time Warner Cable. Other cable companies could ask the New York City government for a license to compete against Time Warner Cable in Manhattan, but none has. This is not an unusual situation for a cable television system: Of the 10,000 markets for cable television in the United States, fewer than 400 have competing cable systems.

As the only provider of cable TV in Manhattan, Time Warner has a *monopoly*. Few firms in the United States are monopolies because in a market system whenever a firm earns economic profits, other firms will enter its market. Therefore, it is very difficult for a firm to remain the only provider of a good or service. In this chapter, we will develop an economic model of monopoly that can help us analyze how such firms affect the economy. *An Inside Look* on page 466 explores a cable executive's view of the industry.

➤ Although few firms are monopolies, the economic model of monopoly can still be quite useful. As we saw in Chapter 11, even though perfectly competitive markets are rare, this market model provides a benchmark for how a firm acts in the most competitive situation possible: when it is in an industry with many firms that all supply the same product. Monopoly provides a benchmark for the other extreme, where a firm is the only one in its market and, therefore, faces no competition from other firms supplying its product. The monopoly model is also useful in analyzing situations where firms agree to *collude*, or not compete, and act together as if they were a monopoly. As we will discuss in this chapter, collusion is illegal in the United States, but it occasionally happens.

Monopolies also pose a dilemma for the government. Should the government allow monopolies to exist? Are there circumstances in which the government should actually promote the existence of monopolies? Should the government regulate the prices monopolies charge? If so, will such price regulation increase economic efficiency? In this chapter, we will also explore these public policy issues.

① **LEARNING OBJECTIVE**
Define monopoly.

Monopoly The only seller of a good or service that does not have a close substitute.

Is Any Firm Ever Really a Monopoly?

A **monopoly** is a firm that is the only seller of a good or service that does not have a close substitute. Because substitutes of some kind exist for just about every product, can any firm really be a monopoly? The answer is "yes," provided the substitutes are not "close" substitutes. But how do we decide whether a substitute is a close substitute? A narrow definition of monopoly used by some economists is that a firm has a monopoly if it can ignore the actions of all other firms. In other words, other firms must not be producing close substitutes if the monopolist can ignore other firms' prices. For example, candles are a substitute for electric lights, but your local electric company can ignore candle prices because however low the price of candles falls, almost no customers will give up using electric lights and switch to candles. Therefore, your local electric company is clearly a monopoly.

Many economists, however, use a broader definition of monopoly. For example, suppose Joe Santos owns the only pizza parlor in a small town (we will consider later the question of *why* a market may have only a single firm). Does Joe have a monopoly? Substitutes for pizzas certainly exist. If the price of pizza is too high, people will switch to hamburgers or fried chicken or some other food instead. People do not have to eat at Joe's or starve. Joe is in competition with the local McDonald's and Kentucky Fried Chicken, among other firms. So, Joe does not meet the narrow definition of a monopoly. But many economists would still argue that it is useful to think of Joe as having a monopoly.

Although hamburgers and fried chicken are substitutes for pizza, competition from firms selling them is not enough to keep Joe from earning economic profits. We saw in Chapter 11 that when firms earn economic profits, we can expect new firms to enter the industry, and in the long run the economic profits are competed away. This outcome will not happen to Joe as long as he is the *only* seller of pizza. Using the broader definition, Joe has a monopoly because there are no other firms selling a substitute close enough that his economic profits are competed away in the long run.

*14-1 Making
the Connection*

Is Xbox a Close Substitute for PlayStation 2?

When Microsoft decided to develop a video-game console, it wanted to produce something very different from Nintendo's GameCube and Sony's PlayStation 2 (PS2). Unlike the competing systems, Microsoft's Xbox contains a hard disk and a version of the Windows computer operating system. As a result, the cost of producing it is much higher than the cost to Nintendo of producing the GameCube or the cost to Sony of producing the PS2. This change did not concern Microsoft because it believed it would be able to charge a higher price than Nintendo or Sony charged for their systems. After all, as Bruno Bonnell, the chairman of the French game maker Infogames Entertainment SA, put it, "The Xbox is a full-feature BMW, the PS2 is a Toyota."

To many gamers, PlayStation 2 is a close substitute for Xbox.

Because consumers do not consider Toyotas to be close substitutes for BMWs, BMW can safely ignore competition from Toyota when setting the prices for its cars. Microsoft expected to be in a similar position. Unfortunately for Microsoft, consumers considered the Sony PS2 a close substitute for the Xbox. Microsoft was forced to charge the same price for the Xbox that Sony charged for the PS2. Although Sony was able to make a substantial profit at that price, Microsoft initially lost money on the Xbox because of its higher costs.

Source: *Wall Street Journal.* Eastern Edition [Staff Produced Copy Only] by Rebecca Buckman, Khanh T. L. tran, Robert. Copyright 2002 by Dow Jones & Co Inc. Reproduced with permission of Dow Jones & Co Inc in the format Textbook via Copyright Clearance Center.

Where Do Monopolies Come From?

② LEARNING OBJECTIVE
Explain the four main reasons monopolies arise.

Because monopolies do not face competition, every firm would like to have a monopoly. But to have a monopoly, barriers to entering the market must be so high that no other firms can enter. *Barriers to entry* may be high enough to keep out competing firms for four main reasons:

1. Government blocks the entry of more than one firm into a market.
2. One firm has control of a key raw material necessary to produce a good.
3. There are important *network externalities* in supplying the good or service.
4. Economies of scale are so large that one firm has a *natural monopoly*.

Entry Blocked by Government Action

As we will discuss later in this chapter, governments ordinarily try to promote competition in markets, but sometimes governments take action to block entry into a market. In the United States, government blocks entry in two main ways:

1. By granting a *patent* or *copyright* to an individual or firm, which gives it the exclusive right to produce a product.
2. By granting a firm a *public franchise,* which makes it the exclusive legal provider of a good or service.

PATENTS AND COPYRIGHTS The U.S. government grants patents to firms that develop new products or new ways of making existing products. A **patent** gives a firm

Patent The exclusive right to a product for a period of 20 years from the date the product was invented.

the exclusive right to a new product for a period of 20 years from the date the product was invented. Because Microsoft has a patent on the Windows operating system, other firms cannot sell their own versions of Windows. The government grants patents to encourage firms to spend money on the research and development necessary to create new products. If other firms could have freely copied Windows, Microsoft is unlikely to have spent the money necessary to develop it. Sometimes firms are able to maintain a monopoly without patent protection, provided they can keep secret how the product is made.

Patent protection is of vital importance to pharmaceutical firms as they develop new prescription drugs. Pharmaceutical firms start research and development work on a new prescription drug an average of 12 years before the drug is available for sale. A firm applies for a patent about 10 years before it begins to sell the product. The average 10-year delay between the government granting a patent and the firm actually selling the drug is due to the federal Food and Drug Administration's requirements that the firm demonstrate that the drug is both safe and effective. Therefore, during the period before the drug can be sold, the firm will have substantial costs to develop and test the drug. If the drug does not make it successfully to market, the firm will have a substantial loss.

The profits the firm earns from the drug will increase throughout the period of patent protection—which is usually about 10 years—as the drug becomes more widely known to doctors and patients. After the patent has expired, other firms are free to legally produce chemically identical drugs called *generic drugs*. Gradually, competition from generic drugs will eliminate the profits the original firm had been earning. For example, when patent protection expired for Glucophage, a diabetes drug manufactured by Bristol-Myers Squibb, sales of the drug declined by more than $1.5 billion in the first year due to competition from 12 generic versions of the drug produced by other firms. When the patent expired on Prozac, an antidepressant drug manufactured by Eli Lilly, sales dropped by more than 80 percent. Most economic profits from selling a prescription drug have been eliminated 20 years after the drug was first offered for sale.

14-2 Making the Connection

The End of the Christmas Plant Monopoly

In December, the poinsettia plant seems to be almost everywhere, decorating stores, restaurants, and houses. Although it may seem strange that anyone can have a monopoly on the production of a plant, for many years the Paul Ecke Ranch in Encinitas, California, had a monopoly on poinsettias.

The poinsettia is a wildflower native to Mexico. It was almost unknown in the United States before Albert Ecke, a German immigrant, began selling it in the early twentieth century at his flower stand in Hollywood, California. Unlike almost every other flowering plant, the poinsettia blossoms in the winter. This timing, along with the plant's striking red and green colors, makes the Poinsettia ideal for Christmas decorating.

Albert Ecke's son, Paul, discovered that by grafting together two varieties of poinsettias it was possible to have multiple branches grow from one stem. The result was a plant that had more leaves and was much more colorful than conventional poinsettias. Paul Ecke did not attempt to patent his new technique for growing poinsettias. But because the Ecke family kept the technique secret for decades, it was able to maintain a monopoly on the commercial production of the plants. Unfortunately, for the Ecke family—but fortunately for consumers—a university researcher discovered the technique and published it in an academic journal.

New firms quickly entered the industry, and the price of poinsettias plummeted. Soon consumers could purchase them for as little as three for $10. At those prices, the firm was unable to earn economic profits. In late 2003, Paul Ecke III, the current owner of the company, decided to sell off more than half the firm's land to fund new state-of-the-art greenhouses and research into new varieties of plants that he hoped would earn the firm economic profits once again.

Sources: Cynthia Crossen, "Holiday's Ubiquitous Houseplant," *Wall Street Journal*, December 19, 2000; and Mike Freeman and David E. Graham, "Ecke Ranch Plans to Sell Most of Its Remaining Land," *San Diego Union-Tribune*, December 11, 2003.

At one time, the Ecke family had a monopoly on growing poinsettias, but many new firms entered the industry.

Just as a new product or a new method of making a product receives patent protection, books, films, and software receive **copyright** protection. U.S. law grants the creator of a book, film, or piece of music the exclusive right to use the creation during the creator's lifetime. The creator's heirs retain this exclusive right for 50 years after the creator's death. In effect, copyrights create monopolies for the copyrighted items. Without copyrights, however, individuals and firms would be less likely to invest in creating new books, films, and software.

Copyright A government-granted exclusive right to produce and sell a creation.

PUBLIC FRANCHISES The government will sometimes grant a firm a **public franchise** that allows it to be the only legal provider of a good or service. For example, state and local governments will often designate one company as the sole provider of electricity, natural gas, or water.

Occasionally, the government will decide to provide certain services directly to consumers through a *public enterprise*. This is much more common in Europe than in the United States. For example, the governments in most European countries own the railroad systems. In the United States, many city governments provide water and sewage service themselves, rather than relying on private firms.

Public franchise A designation by the government that a firm is the only legal provider of a good or service.

Control of a Key Resource

Another way for a firm to become a monopoly is by controlling a key resource. This happens infrequently because most resources, including raw materials such as oil or iron ore, are widely available from a variety of suppliers. There are, however, a few prominent examples of monopolies based on control of a key resource, such as the Aluminum Company of America (Alcoa) and the International Nickel Company of Canada.

For many years until the 1940s, Alcoa either owned or had long-term contracts to buy nearly all of the available bauxite, the mineral needed to produce aluminum. Without access to bauxite, competing firms had to use recycled aluminum, which limited the amount of aluminum they could produce. Similarly, the International Nickel Company of Canada controlled more than 90 percent of available nickel supplies. Competition in the nickel market increased when the Petsamo nickel fields in northern Russia were developed after World War II.

In the United States, a key resource for a professional sports team is a large stadium. The teams that make up the major professional sports leagues—Major League Baseball, the National Football League, and the National Basketball Association—usually have long-term leases with the stadiums in major cities. Control of these stadiums is a major barrier to new professional baseball, football, or basketball leagues forming.

Are Diamond (Profits) Forever? The De Beers Diamond Monopoly

The most famous monopoly based on control of a raw material is the De Beers diamond mining and marketing company of South Africa. Before the 1860s, diamonds were extremely rare. Only a few pounds of diamonds were produced each year, primarily from Brazil and India. Then in 1870, enormous deposits of diamonds were discovered along the Orange River in South Africa. It became possible to produce thousands of pounds of diamonds per year,

14-3 Making the Connection

De Beers promoted the sentimental value of diamonds as a way to maintain its position in the diamond market.

and the owners of the new mines feared that the price of diamonds would plummet. To avoid financial disaster, the mine owners decided in 1888 to merge and form De Beers Consolidated Mines, Ltd.

De Beers became one of the most profitable and longest-lived monopolies in history. The company has carefully controlled the supply of diamonds to keep prices high. As new diamond deposits were discovered in Russia and Zaire, De Beers was able to maintain prices by buying most of the new supplies.

Because diamonds are rarely destroyed, De Beers has always worried about competition from the resale of stones. Heavily promoting diamond engagement and wedding rings with the slogan "A Diamond Is Forever" was a way around this problem. Because engagement and wedding rings have great sentimental value, they are seldom resold, even by the heirs of the original recipients. De Beers advertising has been successful even in some countries, such as Japan, that have had no custom of giving diamond engagement rings. As the populations in De Beers's key markets age, its advertising in recent years has focused on middle-aged men presenting diamond rings to their wives as symbols of financial success and continuing love, and on professional women buying "right-hand rings" for themselves.

In the past few years, competition has finally come to the diamond business. By 2000, De Beers directly controlled only about 40 percent of world diamond production. The company became concerned about the amount it was spending to buy diamonds from other sources to keep them off the market. It decided to adopt a strategy of differentiating its diamonds by relying on its name recognition. Each De Beers diamond is now marked with a microscopic brand to reassure consumers of its high quality. Other firms, such as BHP Billiton, which owns mines in northern Canada, have followed suit by branding their diamonds. Sellers of Canadian diamonds stress that they are "mined under ethical, environmentally friendly conditions," as opposed to "blood diamonds," which are supposedly "mined under armed force in war-torn African countries and exported to finance military campaigns." Whether consumers will pay attention to brands on diamonds remains to be seen.

Sources: Edward Jay Epstein, "Have You Ever Tried to Sell a Diamond?" *Atlantic Monthly,* February 1982; Donna J. Bergenstock, Mary E. Deily, and Larry W. Taylor, "A Cartel's Response to Cheating: An Empirical Investigation of the De Beers Diamond Empire," Lehigh University Working Paper, January 2002; Bernard Simon, "Adding Brand Names to Nameless Stones," *New York Times,* June 27, 2002; Blythe Yee, "Ads Remind Women They Have Two Hands," *Wall Street Journal,* August 14, 2003; quote in last paragraph from Joel Baglole, "Political Correctness by the Carat," *Wall Street Journal,* April 17, 2003.

Network Externalities

Network externalities Exist when the usefulness of a product increases with the number of consumers who use it.

There are **network externalities** in the consumption of a product if the usefulness of the product increases with the number of people who use it. If you owned the only cell phone in the world, it would not be very valuable. The more cell phones in use, the more valuable they become to consumers.

Some economists argue that network externalities can serve as a barrier to entry. For example, in the early 1980s Microsoft gained an advantage over other software companies by developing MS-DOS, the operating system for the first IBM personal computers. Because IBM sold more computers than any other company, software developers wrote many application programs for MS-DOS. The more people who used MS-DOS-based programs, the greater the usefulness to a consumer from using an MS-DOS-based program. Today, Windows, the program Microsoft developed to succeed MS-DOS, has a 95 percent share in the market for personal computer operating systems (although Windows has a much lower share in the market for operating systems for servers). If another firm introduced a competing operating system, some economists argue that relatively few people would use it initially and few applications would run on it, which would limit the operating system's value to other consumers.

EBay was the first Internet site to attract a significant number of people to its online auctions. Once a large number of people began to use eBay to buy and sell collectibles, antiques, and many other products, it became a more valuable place to buy and sell. Yahoo.com, Amazon.com, and other Internet sites eventually started online auctions, but they found it difficult to attract buyers and sellers. On eBay, a buyer expects to find more sellers, and a seller expects to find more potential buyers than on Amazon or other auction sites.

As these examples show, network externalities can set off a *virtuous cycle:* If a firm can attract enough customers initially, it can attract additional customers because its product's value has been increased by more people using it, which attracts even more customers, and so on. With products like computer operating systems and online auctions, it might be difficult for new firms to enter the market and compete away the profits being earned by the first firm in the market.

Economists engage in considerable debate, however, about the extent to which network externalities are important barriers to entry in the business world. Some economists argue that the dominant positions of Microsoft and eBay reflect the efficiency of those firms in offering products that satisfy consumer preferences more than the effects of network externalities. In this view, the advantages existing firms gain from network externalities would not be enough to protect them from competing firms offering better products. In other words, a firm entering the operating system market with a program better than Windows, or a firm offering an Internet auction site better than eBay, would be successful despite the effects of network externalities. (We discussed this point in more detail in Chapter 9.)

Natural Monopoly

We saw in Chapter 10 that economies of scale exist when the firm's long-run average costs fall as it increases the quantity of output it produces. A **natural monopoly** occurs when economies of scale are so large that one firm can supply the entire market at a lower average total cost than two or more firms. In that case, there is really only "room" in the market for one firm.

Natural monopoly A situation in which economies of scale are so large that one firm can supply the entire market at a lower average total cost than can two or more firms.

Figure 14-1 shows the average total cost curve for a firm producing electricity and the total demand for electricity in the firm's market. Notice that the average total cost curve is still falling when it crosses the demand curve at point *A*. If the firm is a monopoly and produces 30 billion kilowatt-hours of electricity per year, its average total cost of production will be $0.04 per kilowatt-hour. Suppose instead that two firms are in the market, each producing half of the market output, or 15 billion kilowatt-hours per year. Assume that each firm has the same average total cost curve. The figure shows that producing 15 billion kilowatt-hours would move each firm back up its average cost curve, so that the average cost of producing electricity would rise to $0.06 per kilowatt-hour (point *B*). In this case, if one of the firms expands production, it will move down the average total cost curve. With lower average costs, it will be able to offer electricity at a lower price than the other firm can. Eventually, the other firm will be driven out of business and the remaining firm will have a monopoly. Because a monopoly would develop automatically—or *naturally*—in this market, it is a natural monopoly.

Natural monopolies are most likely to occur in markets where fixed costs are very large relative to variable costs. For example, a firm that produces electricity must make a

FIGURE 14-1

Average Total Cost Curve for a Natural Monopoly

With a natural monopoly, the average total cost curve is still falling when it crosses the demand curve (point *A*). If only one firm is producing electric power in the market and it produces where average cost intersects the demand curve, average total cost will equal $0.04 per kilowatt-hour of electricity produced. If the market is divided between two firms, each producing 15 billion kilowatt-hours, the average cost of producing electricity rises to $0.06 per kilowatt-hour (point *B*). In this case, if one firm expands production, it can move down the average total cost curve, lower its price, and drive the other firm out of business.

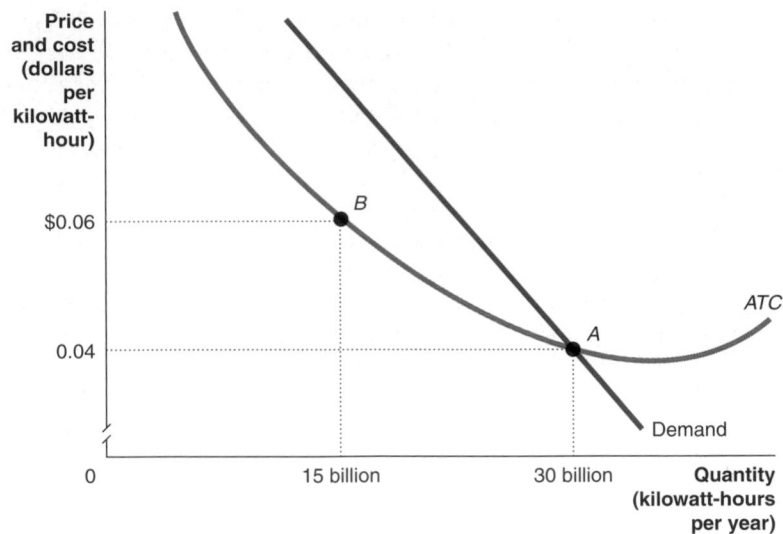

substantial investment in machinery and equipment necessary to generate the electricity and in wires and cables necessary to distribute it. Once the initial investment has been made, however, the marginal cost of producing another kilowatt-hour of electricity is relatively small.

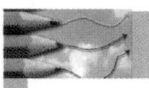

SOLVED PROBLEM   14-1

② **LEARNING OBJECTIVE**

Explain the four main reasons monopolies arise.

Is the "Proxy Business" a Natural Monopoly?

A corporation is owned by its shareholders, who elect members of the corporation's board of directors and who also vote on particularly important issues of corporate policy. The shareholders of large corporations are spread around the country and relatively few of them are present at the annual meetings at which elections take place. Before each meeting, corporations must provide shareholders with annual reports and forms that allow them to vote by mail. Voting by mail is referred to as "proxy voting." Providing annual reports and ballots to shareholders is referred to on Wall Street as the "proxy business." Currently, one company, Automatic Data Processing, Inc. (ADP), controls almost all the proxy business.

According to the *Wall Street Journal*, Don Kittell of the Securities Industry Association has explained ADP's virtual monopoly by arguing that, "The economies of scale and the efficiencies achieved by ADP handling all the brokerage business—rather than multiple companies—resulted in savings to [corporations]."

a. Assuming Kittell is correct, draw a graph showing the market for handling proxy materials. Be sure that the graph contains the demand for proxy materials and ADP's average total cost curve. Explain why cost savings result from having the proxy business handled by a single firm.

b. According to a spokesman for ADP, the proxy business produces a profit rate of about 7 percent, which is lower than the profit rate the company receives from any of its other businesses. Does this information support or undermine Kittell's analysis? Explain.

Solving the Problem:
Step 1: Review the chapter material. This problem is about natural monopoly, so you may want to review the section "Natural Monopoly," which begins on page 449.

Step 2: Answer question (a) by drawing a natural monopoly graph and discussing the potential cost savings in this industry. Kittell is describing a situation of natural monopoly. Otherwise, the entry of another firm into the market would not raise average cost. Draw a natural monopoly graph, like the one in Figure 14-1:

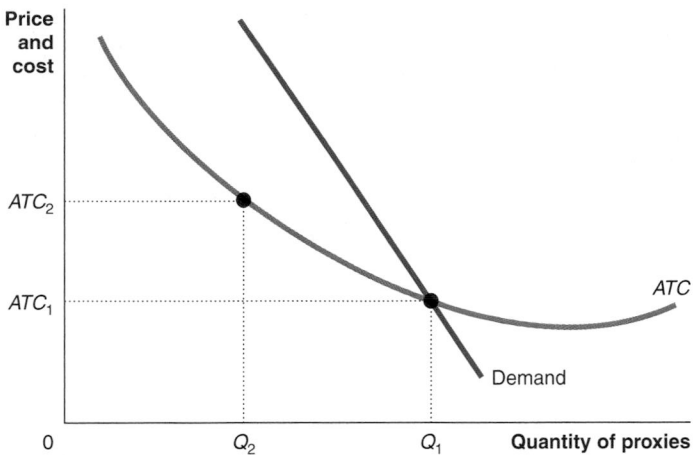

Make sure that your average total cost curve is still declining when it crosses the demand curve. If one firm can supply Q_1 proxies at an average total cost of ATC_1, then dividing the business equally between two firms each supplying Q_2 proxies would raise average total cost to ATC_2.

Step 3: Answer question (b) by discussing the implications of ADP's low profit rate in the proxy business. If ADP earns a low profit rate on its investment in this business even though it has a monopoly, Kittell probably is correct that the proxy business is a natural monopoly.

Extra Credit: Keep in mind that competition is not good for its own sake. It is good because it can lead to lower costs, lower prices, and better products. In certain markets, however, cost conditions are such that competition is likely to lead to higher costs and higher prices. These markets are natural monopolies that are best served by one firm.

Source: Phyllis Plitch, "Competition Remains Issue in Proxy-Mailing Costs," *Wall Street Journal,* January 16, 2002.

YOUR TURN: For more practice, do related problem 12 on page 470 at the end of this chapter. Visit www.prenhall.com/hubbard for an interactive exercise related to this Solved Problem.

How Does a Monopoly Choose Price and Output?

③ LEARNING OBJECTIVE
Explain how a monopoly chooses price and output.

Like every other firm, a monopoly maximizes profit by producing where marginal revenue equals marginal cost. A monopoly differs from other firms in that *a monopoly's demand curve is the same as the demand curve for the product.* We emphasized in Chapter 11 that the market demand curve for wheat was very different from the demand curve for the wheat produced by any one farmer. If, however, that farmer had a monopoly on wheat production, the two demand curves would be exactly the same.

Marginal Revenue Once Again

Recall from Chapter 11 that firms in perfectly competitive markets—such as a farmer in the wheat market—face horizontal demand curves. They are *price takers*. All other firms, including monopolies, are *price makers*. If price makers raise their prices, they will lose some, but not all, of their customers. Therefore, they face a downward-sloping demand curve and a downward-sloping marginal revenue curve as well. Let's review why a firm's marginal revenue curve slopes downward if its demand curve slopes downward.

Remember that when a firm cuts the price of a product, one good thing and one bad thing happens:

➤ *The good thing:*   It sells more units of the product.
➤ *The bad thing:*   It receives less revenue from each unit than it would have received at the higher price.

For example, consider the table in Figure 14-2, which shows the demand curve for Time Warner Cable's basic cable package. For simplicity, we assume the market has only 10 potential subscribers, instead of the millions it actually has. If Time Warner charges a price of $60 per month, it won't have any subscribers. If it charges a price of $57, it sells 1 subscription. At $54, it sells 2, and so on. Time Warner's total revenue is equal to the number of subscriptions sold per month multiplied by the price. The firm's average revenue—or revenue per subscription sold—is equal to its total revenue divided by the quantity of subscriptions sold. Time Warner is particularly interested in marginal revenue because marginal revenue tells the firm how much revenue will increase if it cuts the price to sell one more subscription.

Notice that Time Warner's marginal revenue is less than the price for every subscription sold after the first subscription. To see why, think about what happens if Time Warner cuts the price of its basic cable package from $42 to $39, which increases its sub-

FIGURE 14-2

Calculating a Monopoly's Revenue

Time Warner Cable faces a downward-sloping demand curve for subscriptions to basic cable. To sell more subscriptions, it must cut the price. When this happens, it gains the revenue from selling more subscriptions but loses revenue from selling at a lower price the subscriptions that it could have sold at a higher price. The firm's marginal revenue is the change in revenue from selling another subscription. We can calculate marginal revenue by subtracting the revenue lost as a result of a price cut from the revenue gained. The table shows that Time Warner's marginal revenue is less than the price for every subscription sold after the first subscription. Therefore, Time Warner's marginal revenue curve will be below its demand curve.

Subscribers per Month (Q)	Price (P)	Total Revenue (TR = P x Q)	Average Revenue (AR = TR/Q)	Marginal Revenue (MR = ΔTR/ΔQ)
0	$60	$0	—	—
1	57	57	$57	$57
2	54	108	54	51
3	51	153	51	45
4	48	192	48	39
5	45	225	45	33
6	42	252	42	27
7	39	273	39	21
8	36	288	36	15
9	33	297	33	9
10	30	300	30	3

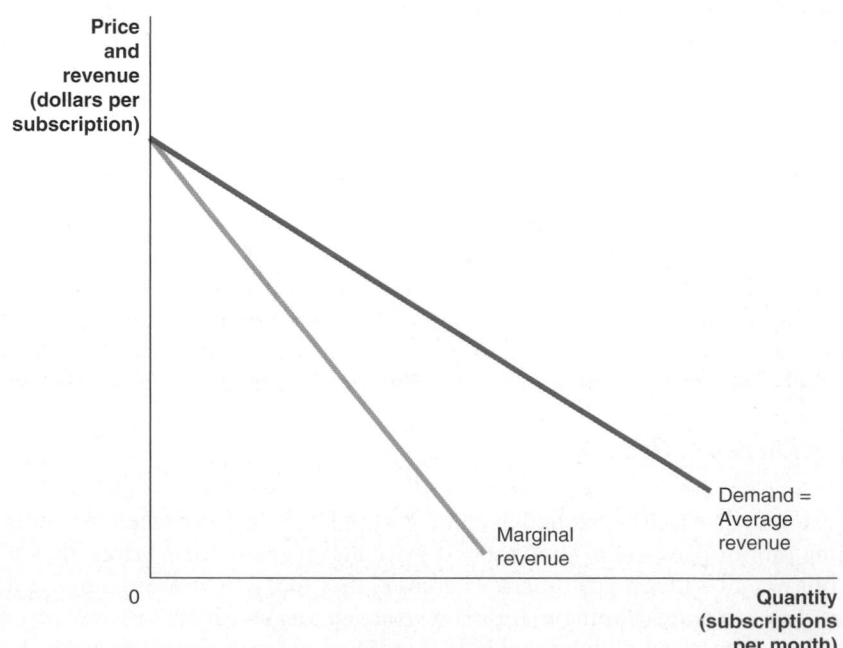

scriptions sold from 6 to 7. Time Warner increases its revenue by the $39 it receives for the seventh subscription. But it also loses revenue of $3 per subscription on the first 6 subscriptions because it could have sold them at the old price of $42. So, its marginal revenue on the seventh subscription is $39 − $18 = $21, which is the value shown in the table. The graph in Figure 14-2 plots Time Warner's demand and marginal revenue curves, based on the information given in the table.

Profit Maximization for a Monopolist

Figure 14-3 shows how Time Warner combines the information on demand and marginal revenue with information on average and marginal costs to decide how many subscriptions to sell and which price to charge. We assume that the firm's marginal cost and average total cost curves have the usual U-shapes we encountered in Chapters 10 and 11. In panel (a), we see how Time Warner can calculate its profit-maximizing quantity and price. As long as the marginal cost of selling one more subscription is less than the marginal revenue, the firm should sell additional subscriptions because it is adding to its profits. As Time Warner sells more cable subscriptions, rising marginal cost will eventually equal marginal revenue and the firm will be selling the profit-maximizing quantity of subscriptions. This happens with the sixth subscription, which adds $27 to the firm's costs and $27 to its revenues (point A in Figure 14-3 [a]). The demand curve tells us that Time Warner can sell 6 subscriptions for a price of $42 per month. We can conclude that Time Warner's profit-maximizing quantity of subscriptions is 6, and its profit-maximizing price is $42.

Panel (b) shows that the average total cost of 6 subscriptions is $30 and that Time Warner can sell 6 subscriptions at a price of $42 per month (point B on the demand curve). Time Warner is making a profit of $12 per subscription—the price of $42 minus the average cost of $30. Its total profit is $72 (6 subscriptions × $12 profit per subscription), which is shown by the area of the green-shaded rectangle in the figure.

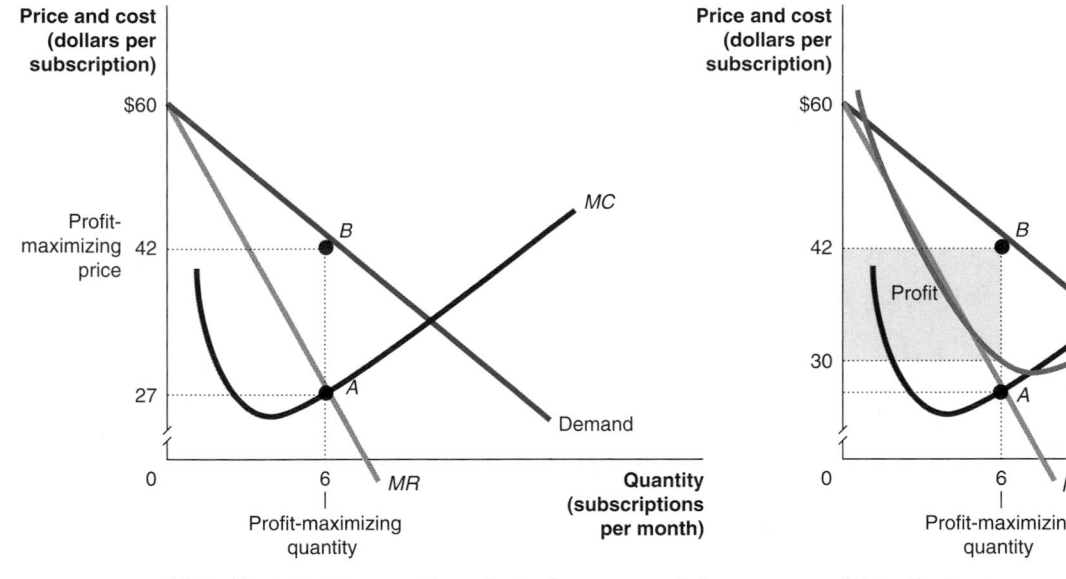

(a) Profit-maximizing quantity and price for a monopolist

(b) Profits for a monopolist

FIGURE 14-3   **Profit-Maximizing Price and Output for a Monopoly**

Panel (a) shows that to maximize profit, Time Warner should sell subscriptions up to the point that the marginal revenue from selling the last subscription equals its marginal cost (point A). In this case, the marginal revenue from selling the sixth subscription and the marginal cost are both $27. Time Warner maximizes profit by selling 6 subscriptions per month and charging a price of

$42 (point B). In panel (b), the green box represents Time Warner's profits. The box has a height equal to $12, which is the price of $42 minus the average total cost of $30, and a base equal to the quantity of 6 cable subscriptions. Time Warner's profit equals $12 × 6 = $72.

We could also have calculated Time Warner's total profit as the difference between its total revenue and its total cost. Its total revenue from selling 6 subscriptions is $252. Its total cost equals its average cost multiplied by the number of subscriptions sold or $30 × 6 = $180. So, its profit is $252 − $180 = $72.

It's important to note that even though Time Warner is earning economic profits, new firms will *not* enter the market. Because Time Warner has a monopoly, it will not face competition from other cable operators. Therefore, if other factors remain unchanged, Time Warner will be able to continue to earn economic profits, even in the long run.

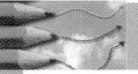

SOLVED PROBLEM 14-2

③ **LEARNING OBJECTIVE**

Explain how a monopoly chooses price and output.

Finding Profit-Maximizing Price and Output for a Monopolist

Suppose that Comcast has a cable monopoly in Philadelphia. The following table gives Comcast's demand and costs per month for subscriptions to basic cable (for simplicity, we once again keep the number of subscribers artificially small):

PRICE	QUANTITY	TOTAL REVENUE	MARGINAL REVENUE ($MR = \Delta TR/\Delta Q$)	TOTAL COST	MARGINAL COST ($MC = \Delta TC/\Delta Q$)
$17	3			$56	
16	4			63	
15	5			71	
14	6			80	
13	7			90	
12	8			101	

a. Fill in the missing values in the table.

b. If Comcast wants to maximize profits, what price should it charge and how many cable subscriptions per month should it sell? How much profit will it make? Briefly explain.

c. Suppose the local government imposes a $2.50 per month tax on cable companies. Now what price should Comcast charge, how many subscriptions should it sell, and what will its profits be?

Solving the Problem:
Step 1: Review the chapter material. This problem is about finding the profit-maximizing quantity and price for a monopolist, so you may want to review the section "Profit Maximization for a Monopolist," which begins on page 453.

Step 2: Answer question (a) by filling in the missing values in the table. Remember that to calculate marginal revenue and marginal cost, you must divide the change in total revenue or total cost by the change in quantity.

PRICE	QUANTITY	TOTAL REVENUE	MARGINAL REVENUE ($MR = \Delta TR/\Delta Q$)	TOTAL COST	MARGINAL COST ($MC = \Delta TC/\Delta Q$)
$17	3	$51	–	$56	–
16	4	64	$13	63	$7
15	5	75	11	71	8
14	6	84	9	80	9
13	7	91	7	90	10
12	8	96	5	101	11

We don't have enough information from the table to fill in the values for marginal revenue or marginal cost in the first row.

Step 3: Answer question (b) by determining the profit-maximizing quantity and price. We know that Comcast will maximize profits by selling subscriptions up to the point where marginal cost equals marginal revenue. In this case, that means selling 6 subscriptions per month. From the information in the first two columns, we know Comcast can sell 6 subscriptions at a price of $14 each. Comcast's profits are equal to the difference between its total revenue and its total cost: Profit = $84 − $80 = $4 per month.

Step 4: Answer question (c) by analyzing the impact of the tax. This tax is a fixed cost to Comcast because it is a flat $2.50, no matter how many subscriptions it sells. Because the tax has no impact on Comcast's marginal revenue or marginal cost, the profit-maximizing level of output has not changed. So, Comcast will still sell 6 subscriptions per month at a price of $14, but its profits will fall by the amount of the tax from $4.00 per month to $1.50.

YOUR TURN: For more practice, do related problems 13 and 14 on page 470 at the end of this chapter. Visit www.prenhall.com/hubbard for an interactive exercise related to this Solved Problem.

Don't Let This Happen To You!

Don't Assume That Charging a Higher Price Is Always More Profitable for a Monopolist

In answering question (c) of Solved Problem 14-2, it's tempting to argue that Comcast should increase its price to make up for the tax. After all, Comcast is a monopolist, so why can't it just pass along the tax to its customers? The reason it can't is that Comcast, like any other monopolist, must pay attention to demand. Comcast is not interested in charging high prices for the sake of charging high prices; it is interested in maximizing profits. Charging a price of $1,000 for a basic cable subscription sounds nice, but if no one will buy at that price, Comcast would hardly be maximizing profits.

To look at it another way, before the tax is imposed Comcast has already determined $14 is the price that will maximize its profits. After the tax is imposed, it must determine if $14 is still the profit-maximizing price. Because the tax has not affected Comcast's marginal revenue or marginal cost (or had any effect on consumer demand), $14 is still the profit-maximizing price, and Comcast should continue to charge it. The tax cuts into Comcast's profits but doesn't cause it to increase the price of cable subscriptions.

YOUR TURN: Test your understanding by doing related problems 15 and 16 on page 471 at the end of this chapter.

Does Monopoly Reduce Economic Efficiency?

 LEARNING OBJECTIVE
Use a graph to illustrate how a monopoly affects economic surplus.

We saw in Chapter 11 that a perfectly competitive market is economically efficient. How would economic efficiency be affected if instead of being perfectly competitive, a market were a monopoly? In Chapter 4, we developed the idea of *economic surplus*. Economic surplus provides a way of characterizing the economic efficiency of a perfectly competitive market: *Equilibrium in a perfectly competitive market results in the greatest amount of economic surplus, or total benefit to society, from the production of a good or service.* What happens to economic surplus under monopoly? We can begin the analysis by considering the hypothetical case of what would happen if the television industry begins as perfectly competitive and then becomes a monopoly. (In reality the television industry is not perfectly competitive, but assuming that it is simplifies our analysis.)

Comparing Monopoly and Perfect Competition

Panel (a) in Figure 14-4 illustrates the situation if the market for televisions is perfectly competitive. Price and quantity are determined by the intersection of the demand and supply curves. Remember that none of the individual firms in a perfectly competitive

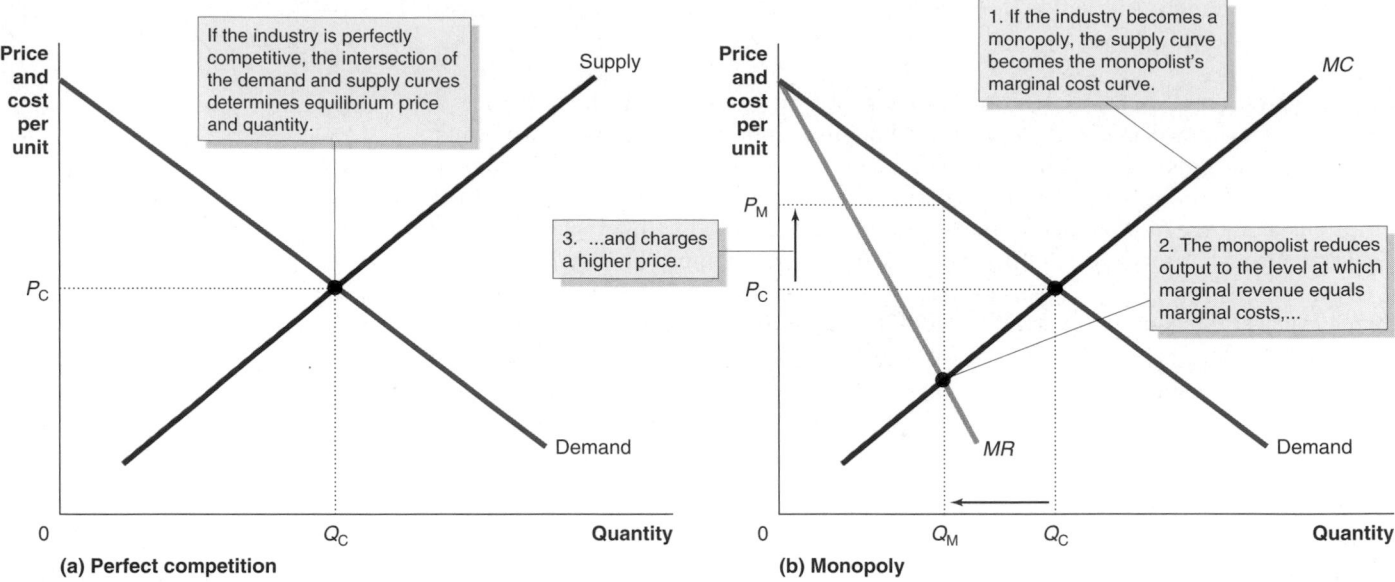

FIGURE 14-4   **What Happens If a Perfectly Competitive Industry Becomes a Monopoly?**

In panel (a), the television industry is perfectly competitive and price and quantity are determined by the intersection of the demand and supply curves. In panel (b), the perfectly competitive television industry became a monopoly. As a result, the equilibrium quantity falls, and the equilibrium price rises.

1. The industry supply curve becomes the monopolist's marginal cost curve.
2. The monopolist reduces output to where marginal revenue equals marginal cost, Q_M.
3. The monopolist raises the price from P_C to P_M.

industry has any control over price. Each firm must accept the price determined by the market. Panel (b) shows the consequences of the television industry becoming a monopoly. We know that the monopoly will maximize profits by producing where marginal revenue equals marginal cost. To do this, the monopoly reduces the quantity of televisions that would have been produced if the industry were perfectly competitive and increases the price. Panel (b) illustrates an important conclusion: *A monopoly will produce less and charge a higher price than would a perfectly competitive industry producing the same good.*

Measuring the Efficiency Losses from Monopoly

Figure 14-5 uses panel (b) from Figure 14-4 to illustrate how monopoly affects consumers, producers, and the efficiency of the economy. Recall from Chapter 4 that *consumer surplus* measures the net benefit received by consumers from purchasing a good or service. We measure consumer surplus as the area below the demand curve and above the market price. The higher the price, the smaller the consumer surplus. Because a monopoly raises the market price, it reduces consumer surplus. In Figure 14-5, the loss of consumer surplus is equal to rectangle *A* plus triangle *B*. Remember that *producer surplus* measures the net benefit to producers from selling a good or service. We measure producer surplus as the area above the supply curve and below the market price. The increase in price due to monopoly increases producer surplus by an amount equal to rectangle *A* and reduces it by an amount equal to triangle *C*. Because rectangle *A* is larger than triangle *C*, we know that a monopoly increases producer surplus compared with perfect competition.

Economic surplus is equal to the sum of consumer surplus plus producer surplus. By increasing price and reducing the quantity produced, the monopolist has reduced economic surplus by an amount equal to the areas of triangles *B* and *C*. This reduction in economic surplus is called *deadweight loss* and represents the loss of economic efficiency due to monopoly.

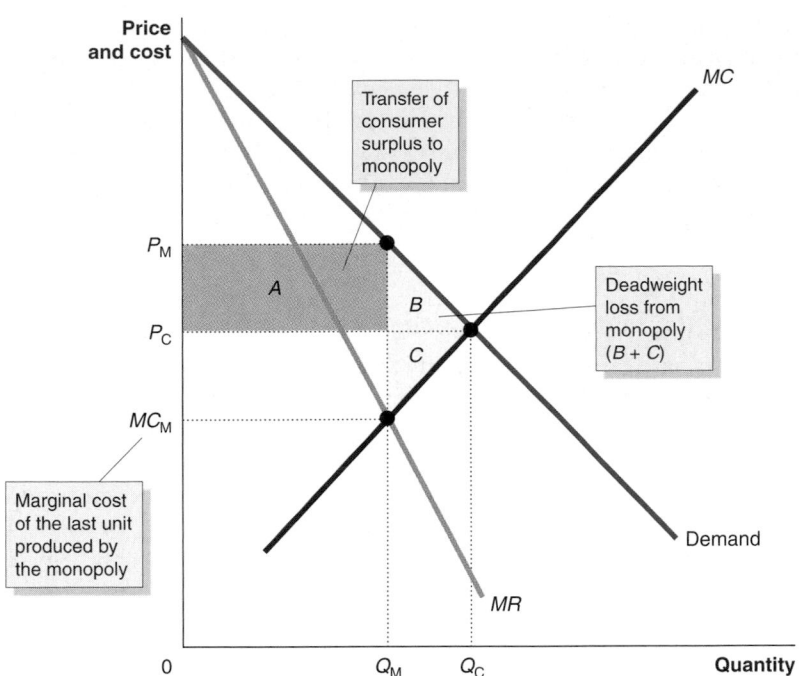

FIGURE 14-5

The Inefficiency of Monopoly

A monopoly charges a higher price, P_M, and produces a smaller quantity, Q_M, than a perfectly competitive industry, which charges a price of P_C and produces at Q_C. The higher price reduces consumer surplus by the area equal to the rectangle A and the triangle B. Some of the reduction in consumer surplus is captured by the monopoly as producer surplus and some becomes deadweight loss, which is the area equal to triangles B and C.

The best way to understand how a monopoly causes a loss of economic efficiency is to recall that price is equal to marginal cost in a perfectly competitive market. As a result, a consumer in a perfectly competitive market is always able to buy a good if she is willing to pay a price equal to the marginal cost of producing it. As Figure 14-5 shows, the monopolist stops producing at a point where the price is well above marginal cost. Consumers are unable to buy some units of the good for which they would be willing to pay a price greater than the marginal cost of producing them. Why doesn't the monopolist produce this additional output? Because the monopolist's profits are greater if it restricts output and forces up the price. A monopoly produces the profit-maximizing level of output, but fails to produce the efficient level of output from the point of view of society.

We can summarize the effects of monopoly as follows:

1. Monopoly causes a reduction in consumer surplus.
2. Monopoly causes an increase in producer surplus.
3. Monopoly causes a deadweight loss, which represents a reduction in economic efficiency.

How Large Are the Efficiency Losses Due to Monopoly?

We know that there are relatively few monopolies, so the loss of economic efficiency due to monopoly must be small. Many firms, though, have **market power,** which is the ability of a firm to charge a price greater than marginal cost. The analysis we just completed shows that some loss of economic efficiency will occur whenever a firm has market power and can charge a price greater than marginal cost, even if the firm is not a monopoly. The only firms that do *not* have market power are firms in perfectly competitive markets, who must charge a price equal to marginal cost. Because few markets are perfectly competitive, *some loss of economic efficiency occurs in the market for nearly every good or service.*

Is the total loss of economic efficiency due to market power large or small? It is possible to put a dollar value on the loss of economic efficiency by estimating for every industry the size of the deadweight loss triangle, as in Figure 14-5. The first economist to do this was Arnold Harberger of the University of Chicago. His estimates—largely confirmed by later researchers—indicated that the total loss of economic efficiency in the

Market power   The ability of a firm to charge a price greater than marginal cost.

U.S. economy due to market power is small. According to his estimates, if every industry in the economy were perfectly competitive, so that price were equal to marginal cost in every market, the gain in economic efficiency would equal less than 1 percent of the value of total production in the United States, or about $300 per person.

The loss of economic efficiency is this small primarily because true monopolies are very rare. In most industries, competition will keep price much closer to marginal cost than would be the case in a monopoly. The closer price is to marginal cost, the smaller the size of the deadweight loss.

Market Power and Technological Change

Some economists have raised the possibility that the economy may actually benefit from firms having market power. This argument is most closely identified with Joseph Schumpeter, an Austrian economist who spent many years as a professor of economics at Harvard. Schumpeter argued that economic progress depended on technological change in the form of new products. For example, the replacement of horse-drawn carriages by automobiles, the replacement of ice boxes by refrigerators, or the replacement of mechanical calculators with electronic computers all represent technological changes that significantly raised living standards. In Schumpeter's view, new products unleash a "gale of creative destruction" in which older products—and, often, the firms that produced them—are driven out of the market. Schumpeter was unconcerned that firms with market power would charge higher prices than perfectly competitive firms:

> It is not that kind of [price] competition which counts but the competition from the new commodity, the new technology, the new source of supply, the new type of organization . . . competition which commands a decisive cost or quality advantage and which strikes not at the margins of the profits and outputs of the existing firms but at their foundations and their very lives.

Economists who support Schumpeter's view argue that the introduction of new products requires firms to spend funds on research and development. It is possible for firms to raise this money by borrowing from investors or from banks. But investors and banks are usually skeptical of ideas for new products that have not yet passed the test of consumer acceptance in the market. As a result, firms are often forced to rely on their profits to finance the research and development needed for new products. Because firms with market power are more likely to earn economic profits than are perfectly competitive firms, they are also more likely to carry out research and development and to introduce new products. In this view, the higher prices charged by firms with market power are unimportant compared with the benefits from the new products these firms introduce to the market.

Some economists disagree with Schumpeter's views. These economists point to the number of new products developed by smaller firms, including, for example, Steve Jobs and Steve Wozniak inventing the first Apple computer in Wozniak's garage, and Larry Page and Sergey Brin inventing the Google search engine as graduate students at Stanford. As we will see in the next section, government policymakers continue to struggle with the issue of whether, on balance, large firms with market power are good or bad for the economy.

⑤ LEARNING OBJECTIVE

Discuss government policies toward monopoly.

Collusion An agreement among firms to charge the same price, or otherwise not to compete.

Government Policy toward Monopoly

Because monopolies reduce consumer surplus and economic efficiency, most governments have policies that regulate their behavior. Recall from Chapter 13 that **collusion** refers to an agreement among firms to charge the same price, or otherwise not to compete. In the United States, *antitrust laws* are government policies that deal with monopolies and collusion. These laws make illegal any attempts to form a monopoly or to collude. Governments also regulate firms that are natural monopolies, often by controlling the prices they charge.

Antitrust Laws and Antitrust Enforcement

The first important law regulating monopolies in the United States was the Sherman Act, which Congress passed in 1890 to promote competition and prevent the formation of monopolies. Section 1 of the Sherman Act outlaws "every contract, combination in the form of trust or otherwise, or conspiracy in restraint of trade." Section 2 states that "every person who shall monopolize, or attempt to monopolize, or combine or conspire with any other person or persons, to monopolize any part of the trade or commerce . . . shall be deemed guilty of a felony."

The Sherman Act targeted firms in several industries that had combined together during the 1870s and 1880s to form "trusts." In a trust, the firms would be operated independently but would give voting control to a board of trustees. The board would enforce collusive agreements for the firms to charge the same price and not to compete for each other's customers. The most notorious of the trusts was the Standard Oil Trust, organized by John D. Rockefeller. After the Sherman Act was passed, trusts disappeared, but the term **antitrust laws** has lived on to refer to the laws aimed at eliminating collusion and promoting competition among firms.

> **Antitrust laws** Laws aimed at eliminating collusion and promoting competition among firms.

The Sherman Act prohibited trusts and collusive agreements, but it left several loopholes. For example, it was not clear whether it would be legal for two or more firms to merge to form a new larger firm that would have substantial market power. A series of Supreme Court decisions interpreted the Sherman Act narrowly, and the result was a wave of mergers at the turn of the twentieth century. Included in these mergers was the United States Steel Corporation, which was formed from dozens of smaller companies. U.S. Steel, organized by J. P. Morgan, was the first billion-dollar corporation and controlled two-thirds of steel production in the United States. The Sherman Act also left unclear whether any business practices short of outright collusion were illegal.

To address the loopholes in the Sherman Act, in 1914 Congress passed the Clayton Act and the Federal Trade Commission Act. Under the Clayton Act, a merger was illegal if its effect was "substantially to lessen competition, or to tend to create a monopoly." The Federal Trade Commission Act set up the Federal Trade Commission (FTC), which was given the power to police unfair business practices. The FTC has brought lawsuits against firms employing a variety of business practices, including deceptive advertising. In setting up the FTC, however, Congress divided the authority to police mergers. Currently, both the Antitrust Division of the U.S. Department of Justice and the FTC are responsible for merger policy. Table 14-1 lists the most important U.S. antitrust laws and the purpose of each.

LAW	DATE	PURPOSE
Sherman Act	1890	Prohibited "restraint of trade," including price fixing and collusion. Also outlawed monopolization.
Clayton Act	1914	Prohibited firms from buying stock in competitors and from having directors serve on the boards of competing firms.
Federal Trade Commission Act	1914	Established the Federal Trade Commission (FTC) to help administer antitrust laws.
Robinson–Patman Act	1936	Prohibited charging buyers different prices if the result would reduce competition.
Cellar–Kefauver Act	1950	Toughened restrictions on mergers by prohibiting any mergers that would reduce competition.

TABLE 14-1

Important U.S. Antitrust Laws

Horizontal merger A merger between firms in the same industry.

Vertical merger A merger between firms at different stages of production of a good.

Mergers: The Trade-off between Market Power and Efficiency

The federal government regulates business mergers because it knows that if firms gain market power by merging, they may use that market power to raise prices and reduce output. As a result, the government is most concerned with **horizontal mergers,** or mergers between firms in the same industry. Horizontal mergers are more likely to increase market power than **vertical mergers,** which are mergers between firms at different stages of the production of a good. An example of a vertical merger would be a merger between a company making personal computers and a company making computer hard drives.

Regulating horizontal mergers can be complicated by two factors. First, the "market" that firms are in is not always clear. For example, if Hershey Foods wants to merge with Mars, Inc., makers of M&Ms, Snickers, and other candies, what is the relevant market? If the government looks just at the candy market, the newly merged company would have more than 70 percent of the market, a level at which the government would likely oppose the merger. What if the government looks at the broader market for "snacks"? In this market, Hershey and Mars compete with makers of potato chips, pretzels, peanuts, and, perhaps, even producers of fresh fruit. Of course, if the government looked at the very broad market for "food," then both Hershey and Mars have very small market shares and there would be no reason to oppose their merger. In practice, the government defines the relevant market on the basis of whether there are close substitutes for the products being made by the merging firms. In this case, potato chips and the other snack foods mentioned are not close substitutes for candy. So, the government would consider the candy market to be the relevant market and would oppose the merger on the grounds that the new firm would have too much market power.

The second factor that complicates merger policy is the possibility that the newly merged firm might be more efficient than the merging firms were individually. For example, one firm might have an excellent product but a poor distribution system for getting the product into the hands of consumers. A competing firm might have built a great distribution system but have an inferior product. Allowing these firms to merge might be good for both the firms and consumers. Or, two competing firms might each have an extensive system of warehouses that are only half full, but if the firms merged, they could consolidate their warehouses and significantly reduce their costs.

An example of the government dealing with the issue of greater efficiency versus reduced competition occurred in early 2000 when Time Warner, which as we have seen owns cable systems with more than 20 million subscribers, and America Online (AOL), which was the country's largest Internet Service Provider (ISP) with more than 26 million subscribers, announced plans to merge. The firms argued that the merger would speed the development of high-speed (or "broadband") Internet access and would lead to the more rapid growth of services such as interactive television. Some competing firms complained that the new firm created by the merger would have excessive market power. In particular, other ISPs were worried that they would be denied access to the cable systems owned by Time Warner. After more than a year of study, the FTC finally approved the merger, subject to certain conditions. One key condition was that Time Warner was required to allow AOL's competitors to offer their services over Time Warner's high-speed cable lines before AOL would be permitted to offer its services over those lines.

Most of the mergers that come under scrutiny by the Department of Justice and the FTC are between large firms. For simplicity, let's consider a case where all the firms in a perfectly competitive industry want to merge to form a monopoly. As we saw in Figure 14-5, as a result of this merger prices will rise and output will fall, leading to a decline in consumer surplus and economic efficiency. But what if the larger, newly merged firm actually is more efficient than the smaller firms had been? Figure 14-6 shows a possible result.

If costs are unaffected by the merger, we get the same result as in Figure 14-5: Price rises from P_C to P_M, quantity falls from Q_C to Q_M, consumer surplus is lower, and a loss

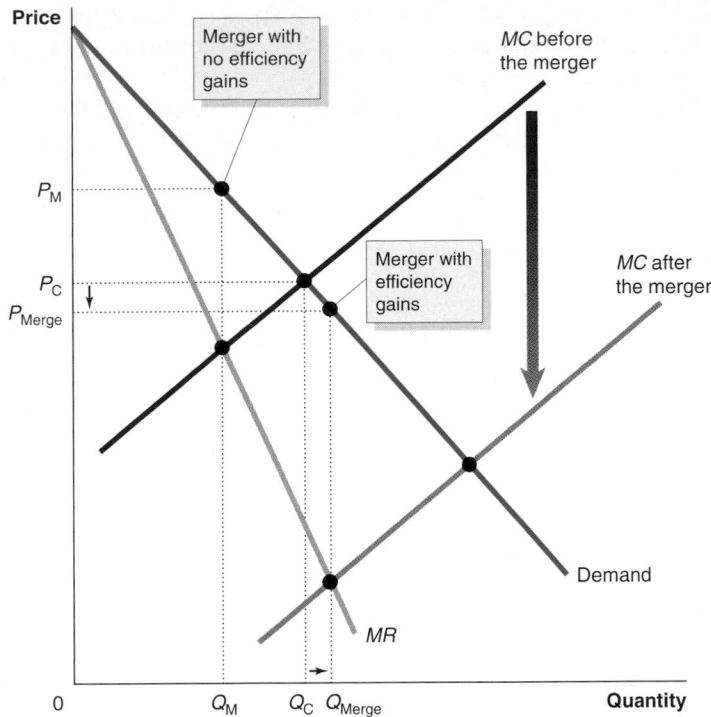

FIGURE 14-6   **A Merger That Makes Consumers Better Off**

This figure shows the result of all the firms in a perfectly competitive industry merging to form a monopoly. If costs are unaffected by the merger, the result is the same as in Figure 14-5: Price rises from P_C to P_M, quantity falls from Q_C to Q_M, consumer surplus declines, and a loss of economic efficiency results. If, however, the monopoly has lower costs than the perfectly competitive firms, it is possible the price will actually decline from P_C to P_{Merge} and output will increase from Q_C to Q_{Merge} following the merger.

of economic efficiency results. If the monopoly has lower costs than the competitive firms, it is possible for price to decline and quantity to increase. In Figure 14-6, price declines after the merger from P_C to P_{Merge} and quantity increases from Q_C to Q_{Merge}. This leads to the following seemingly paradoxical result: *Although the newly merged firm has a great deal of market power, because it is more efficient, consumers are better off and economic efficiency is improved.* Of course, sometimes a merged firm will be more efficient and have lower costs, and other times it won't. Even if a merged firm is more efficient and has lower costs, this may not offset the increased market power of the firm enough to increase consumer surplus and economic efficiency.

As you might expect, whenever large firms propose a merger they claim that the newly merged firm will be more efficient and have lower costs. They realize that without these claims it is unlikely their merger will be approved. It is up to the Department of Justice and the FTC, along with the court system, to evaluate the merits of these claims.

The Department of Justice and the Federal Trade Commission Merger Guidelines

For many years after the passage of the Sherman Antitrust Act in 1890, lawyers from the Department of Justice enforced the antitrust laws. They rarely considered economic arguments, such as the possibility that consumers might be made better off by a merger if economic efficiency were significantly improved. This began to change in 1965 when Donald Turner became the first Ph.D. economist to head the Antitrust Division of the Department of Justice. Under Turner and his successors, antitrust policy was reshaped by economic analysis. In 1973, the Economics Section of the Antitrust Division was established and staffed with economists who evaluate the economic consquences of proposed mergers.

One of the fruits of this economic expertise was the joint development by the Department of Justice and the FTC of merger guidelines in 1982. The guidelines made it possible for economists and attorneys employed by firms considering a merger to understand whether the government was likely to allow the merger or to oppose it. The guidelines have three main parts:

1. Market definition
2. Measure of concentration
3. Merger standards

MARKET DEFINITION A market consists of all firms making products that consumers view as close substitutes. We can identify close substitutes by looking at the effect of a price increase. If our definition of a market is too narrow, a price increase will cause firms to experience a significant decline in sales—and profits—as consumers switch to buying close substitutes.

Identifying the relevant market involved in a proposed merger begins with a narrow definition of the industry. For the hypothetical merger of Hershey Foods and Mars, Inc. discussed previously in this chapter, we might start with the candy industry. If all firms in the candy industry increased price by 5 percent, would their profits increase or decrease? If profits would increase, the market is defined as being just these firms. If profits would decrease, we would try a broader definition—say, by adding in potato chips and other snacks. Would a price increase of 5 percent by all firms in the broader market raise profits? If profits increase, the relevant market has been identified. If profits decrease, we would consider a broader definition. We would continue this procedure until a market has been identified.

MEASURE OF CONCENTRATION A market is *concentrated* if a relatively small number of firms have a large share of total sales in the market. A merger between firms in a market that is already highly concentrated is very likely to increase market power. A merger between firms in an industry that has a very low concentration is unlikely to increase market power and can be ignored. The guidelines use the *Herfindahl-Hirschman Index (HHI)* of concentration, which adds together the squares of the market shares of each firm in the industry. The following are some examples of calculating a Herfindahl-Hirschman Index:

➤ 1 firm, with 100% market share (a monopoly):
  $HHI = 100^2 = 10,000$

➤ 2 firms, each with a 50% market share:
  $HHI = 50^2 + 50^2 = 5,000$

➤ 4 firms, with market shares of 30%, 30%, 20%, and 20%:
  $HHI = 30^2 + 30^2 + 20^2 + 20^2 = 2,600$

➤ 10 firms, each with market shares of 10%:
  $HHI = 10 (10^2) = 1,000$

MERGER STANDARDS The HHI calculation for a market is then used to evaluate proposed horizontal mergers according to these standards:

➤ *Post-Merger HHI below 1,000.*
  These markets are not concentrated, so mergers in them are not challenged.

➤ *Post-Merger HHI between 1,000 and 1,800.*
  These markets are moderately concentrated. Mergers that raise the HHI by less than 100 probably will not be challenged. Mergers that raise the HHI by more than 100 may be challenged.

➤ *Post-Merger HHI above 1,800.*
These markets are highly concentrated. Mergers that increase the HHI by less than 50 points will not be challenged. Mergers that increase the HHI by 50 to 100 points may be challenged. Mergers that increase the HHI by more than 100 points will be challenged.

Increases in economic efficiency will be taken into account and can lead to approval of a merger that otherwise would be opposed, but the burden of showing that the efficiencies exist lies with the merging firms: "The merging firms must substantiate efficiency claims so that the [Department of Justice and the FTC] can verify by reasonable means the likelihood and magnitude of each asserted efficiency. . . . Efficiency claims will not be considered if they are vague or speculative or otherwise cannot be verified by reasonable means."

The Antitrust Case against Microsoft

Microsoft was still a small company in 1981 when IBM chose it to provide the operating system for its personal computers. As other companies "cloned" the IBM PC, Microsoft's business increased. By 1992, it controlled more than 90 percent of the market for PC operating systems. Microsoft required computer manufacturers who installed Windows on any of their computers to pay Microsoft a royalty on every computer sold, whether or not the computer actually had Windows installed on it. The Department of Justice saw this as a potential violation of the antitrust laws because it made it more difficult for new firms to enter the market for operating systems. Any manufacturer of PCs who wanted to use Windows on any of its PCs would likely use it on all of its PCs, because if the manufacturer installed a non-Windows operating system on its PCs it would have to pay twice: once to Microsoft and once to the firm whose operating system it was actually using. To head off the investigation by the Justice Department, Microsoft agreed in 1994 to stop this practice. Thereafter, manufacturers of PCs would have to pay Microsoft only when a computer they sold actually had Windows installed on it.

Still, Microsoft's antitrust problems weren't over. In 1997, Microsoft tried to increase its share of the market for Internet browsers. At the time, the Netscape browser had the largest market share. When Microsoft released a new version of its Internet browser, Internet Explorer 4.0, it required PC firms to install it on all computers sold with Windows. The Justice Department decided that requiring PC firms using Windows to also install Internet Explorer violated Microsoft's 1994 agreement. In May 1998, the Justice Department filed a lawsuit charging that Microsoft had violated the Sherman Act. After a 78-day trial, Judge Thomas Penfield Jackson found that Microsoft had illegally monopolized the PC operating-system market and had illegally attempted to use this monopoly also to monopolize the browser market. Jackson ordered Microsoft to be broken into two companies: One company would produce the Windows operating system, and the other company would produce Microsoft's other software, including Internet Explorer.

Microsoft appealed the case, and the federal Court of Appeals ruled that Microsoft had taken actions to maintain a monopoly on PC operating systems, but it threw out Judge Jackson's order that the company be split up. The appeals court sent the case back to the district court for final resolution. In spring 2002, the Justice Department and Microsoft agreed on a settlement. As part of the settlement, Microsoft agreed to allow removal of the Internet Explorer icon from the Windows "desktop," and to allow computer manufacturers to include other companies' software icons on the desktop. Microsoft also agreed to make it easier for other operating systems to run on computers that had Windows installed on them. Nine states declined to go along with the settlement of the federal antitrust suit and pressed ahead with their own lawsuit.

The Microsoft case illustrates one of the key problems in enforcing the antitrust laws: the trade-off between efficiency and market power. Microsoft argues that embedding software such as Internet Explorer and a media player in Windows benefits consumers by improving

14-4 *Making* *the* **Connection**

Software pioneer, monopolist, or both?

the ease of using the software. At the same time, it may make it more difficult for makers of competing software to break into the market. The government has had little difficulty proving that Microsoft has market power, but as one observer puts it, "Proving that Microsoft's monopoly power harms consumers has always been a difficulty in the government's case against the company."

Sources: Last quote from Amy Harmon, "Why Gates Won't Apologize," *New York Times,* April 29, 2002; other material from Department of Justice Web site: www.usdoj.gov.

Regulating Natural Monopolies

If a firm is a natural monopoly, competition from other firms will not play its usual role of forcing price down to the level where the company earns zero economic profit. As a result, local or state *regulatory commissions* usually set the prices for natural monopolies, such as firms selling natural gas or electricity. What price should these commissions set? Recall from Chapter 11 that economic efficiency requires the last unit of a good or service produced to provide an additional benefit to consumers equal to the additional cost of producing it. We can measure the additional benefit consumers receive by the price and the additional cost by marginal cost. Therefore, to achieve economic efficiency, regulators should require that the monopoly charge a price equal to its marginal cost. There is, however, an important drawback to doing so, which is illustrated in Figure 14-7. This figure shows the situation of a typical regulated natural monopoly.

Remember that with a natural monopoly the average total cost curve is still falling when it crosses the demand curve. If unregulated, the monopoly will charge a price equal to P_M and produce Q_M. To achieve economic efficiency, regulators should require the monopoly to charge a price equal to P_E. The monopoly will then produce Q_E. But here is the drawback: P_E is less than average total cost, so the monopoly will be suffering a loss, shown by the area of the red-shaded rectangle. In the long run, the owners of the monopoly will not continue in business if they are experiencing losses. Realizing this, most regulators will set the regulated price, P_R, equal to the level of average total cost at which the demand curve intersects the *ATC* curve. At that price, the owners of the monopoly are able to break even on their investment by producing the quantity Q_R.

FIGURE 14-7

Regulating a Natural Monopoly

A natural monopoly that is not subject to government regulation will charge a price equal to P_M and produce Q_M. If government regulators want to achieve economic efficiency, they will set the regulated price equal to P_E and the monopoly will produce Q_E. Unfortunately, P_E is below average cost and the monopoly will suffer a loss shown by the shaded rectangle. Because the monopoly will not continue to produce in the long run if it suffers a loss, government regulators set a price equal to average cost, which is P_R in the figure.

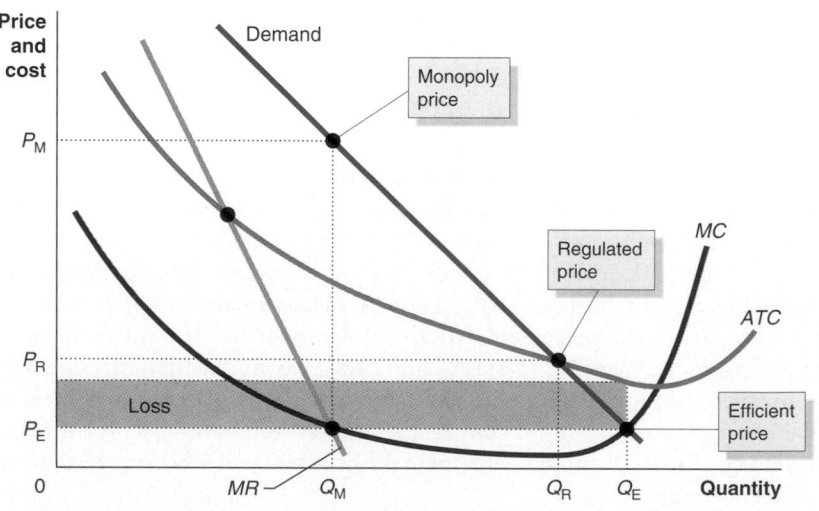

Conclusion

The more intense the level of competition among firms, the better a market works. In this chapter we have seen that with monopoly—where competition is entirely absent—price is higher, output is lower, and consumer surplus and economic efficiency decline compared with perfect competition. Fortunately, true monopolies are rare. Even though most firms resemble monopolies in being able to charge a price above marginal cost, most markets have enough competition to keep the efficiency losses from market power quite low.

We've seen that barriers to entry are an important source of market power. Read *An Inside Look* on the next page to learn how cable companies use barriers to entry.

An Inside Look

A "Monopoly Mindset" in the Cable Industry?

WALL STREET JOURNAL, MAY 21, 2004

Why I'm Filing Chapter 11

Sometime in the next week or so, I anticipate that one of my companies, the cable, phone and video provider RCN, will file for what is known in the business as a consensual, pre-arranged Chapter 11 bankruptcy. That hardly makes me unique. Since 2000, nearly 70 major telecom companies have filed for bankruptcy. Hundreds, if not thousands, never even made it to Chapter 11 . . .

Having built, bought, or started 10 telecom companies in the last 25 years, I think both Wall Street and Washington overlook the most persistent problem: The cable industry remains in the grip of a monopoly mindset. . . . [C]able rates have soared 40% and the industry giants continue to think in terms of how to dominate markets rather than of how to drive innovation. The bankruptcies that sidelined so many upstart cable providers have effectively spared the cable incumbents from facing competitive pressures—at least for the moment.

RCN was one of the "overbuilders" that started constructing a fiber pipeline in densely populated neighborhoods where competition was unknown. I believed—and still do—that a new infrastructure to the home was the critical step to creating a system that can bundle and deliver every type of service that consumers would want. Not just phone, cable and Internet, but home security, energy monitoring and even appliance diagnostics. . . .

That idea of building a network that could attract multiple streams of revenue was drawn on the economics I learned as a freshman in college. Those economic principles dictated that if you have a network, you want to make it as expansive as possible and if you own content you want to deliver it over as big a network and to as many people as possible. Until 1996, the entire telecom industry operated on exactly the opposite principle. The incumbents depended on closed, proprietary systems guarded by regulations and old technology. The strategy was like building a road system that only goes to your store, or a railroad that only goes to your town.

[T]he major cable companies still divide-and-rule territory. When one company buys close to another, the rivals simply exchange geographic service areas, so that each side can expand their local fiefdoms—the same business model championed by Tony Soprano.

The cable companies have also relied on closed, proprietary technology to inhibit open competition. Rather than let customers go to Radio Shack and buy a standardized set-top box, they force you to rent their proprietary converter boxes. Over the last five years, RCN has had to spend nearly half a billion dollars replacing proprietary equipment each time a customer switched to our service. . . .

Comcast's recent bid to acquire Disney would have taken this anticompetitive approach one step further. Had the merger plan taken off—and if not this one, other, similar mergers will—then Disney's content would have been harder to get, more expensive, or less convenient to find for any consumer not part of the Comcast family.

Fortunately, the telecom story is not over. For many telecom companies—including my own—bankruptcy is not the end, but a new lease on life. I believe that the wave of bankruptcy filings will help launch a new era in telecom. Over the next year or two, I suspect we will see many companies re-emerging from bankruptcy, now in a much better position to compete without the dead weight of debt on their back. These may well be the companies that bring Voice-over-IP technology to the cable world, creating "Video-over-IP" competitors who change the way customers bring television into their homes. That possibility should worry today's cable giants who have been ignoring the logic of economics, the possibilities of technology and the interests of consumers for far too long.

Key Points in the Article

This article by David McCourt, the founder of cable television company RCN, discusses problems in the cable industry. He argues that many cable companies have a "monopoly mindset" that causes them to erect barriers to the entry of competing firms in order to make economic profits through high prices. McCourt argues that both the cable firms and the public would be better off if the firms concentrated on making profits through technological change and on being more responsive to consumers.

Analyzing the News

a McCourt argues that most cable companies are relying on barriers to entry to give them monopolies in local markets. Figure 1 shows the now-familiar graph of a monopoly firm making economic profits. The monopolist sells the quantity of subscriptions Q_M, where marginal revenue equals marginal cost, and charges the price P_M. The profits are shown by the area of the light-green rectangle.

b McCourt also argues that cable companies would be better off if they relied on expanding their markets—"if you have a network, you want to make it as expansive as possible"—and technological innovations—"a new infrastructure to the home was the critical step to creating a system that can bundle and deliver every type of service that consumers would want." Figure 2 shows that if McCourt's argument is correct, the new and better services and expanded market will shift out the demand curve the firm faces and increase its profits. Price rises from P_M^{Old} to P_M^{New}, quantity rises from Q_M^{Old} to Q_M^{New}, and profits increase from the area of the light-green rectangle to the area of the dark-green rectangle (which includes the smaller, light-green rectangle).

Thinking Critically
ABOUT POLICY

1. If monopoly generally brings a loss of economic efficiency and consumer surplus, why would a local government give only *one* cable television company a license to enter its market? Should local governments continue this practice?
2. If you were one of the cable giants discussed by David McCourt, would you be willing to open up your network? Explain your answer.

Source: Wall Street Journal, Eastern Edition [Staff Produced Copy Only] by David McCourt. Copyright 2004 by Dow Jones & Co Inc. Reproduced with permission of Dow Jones & Co Inc in the format Textbook via Copyright Clearance Center.

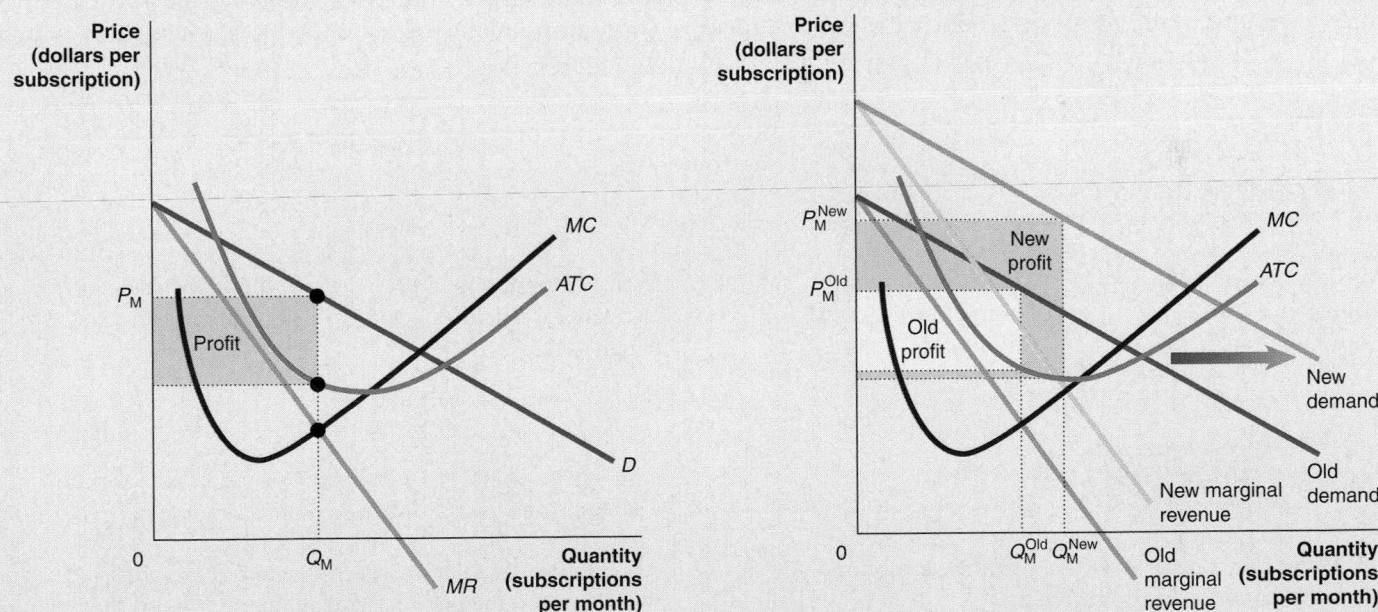

Figure 1: A profitable cable company with a monopoly in a local market.

Figure 2: Better services and an expanded market increase firm profits.

SUMMARY

SUMMARY

LEARNING OBJECTIVE ① Define monopoly. A *monopoly* exists only in the rare situation in which a firm is producing a good or service for which there are no close substitutes. A narrow definition of monopoly used by some economists is that a firm has a monopoly if it can ignore the actions of all other firms. Many economists favor a broader definition of monopoly. Under the broader definition, a firm has a monopoly if no other firms are selling a substitute close enough that the firm's economic profits are competed away in the long run.

LEARNING OBJECTIVE ② Explain the four main reasons monopolies arise. To have a monopoly, barriers to entering the market must be so high that no other firms can enter. *Barriers to entry* may be high enough to keep out competing firms for four main reasons: (1) government blocks the entry of more than one firm into a market by issuing a *patent* or giving a firm a *public franchise*, (2) one firm has control of a key raw material necessary to produce a good, (3) there are important *network externalities* in supplying the good or service, or (4) economies of scale are so large that one firm has a *natural monopoly*.

LEARNING OBJECTIVE ③ Explain how a monopoly chooses price and output. Monopolists face downward-sloping demand and marginal revenue curves and, like all other firms, maximize profit by producing where marginal revenue equals marginal cost. Unlike a perfect competitor, a

monopolist that earns economic profits does not face the entry of new firms into the market. Therefore, a monopolist can earn economic profits, even in the long run.

LEARNING OBJECTIVE ④ Use a graph to illustrate how a monopoly affects economic surplus. Compared with a perfectly competitive industry, a monopoly charges a higher price and produces less, which reduces consumer surplus and economic efficiency. Some loss of economic efficiency will occur whenever firms have *market power* and can charge a price greater than marginal cost. The total loss of economic efficiency in the U.S. economy due to market power is small, however, because true monopolies are very rare. In most industries, competition will keep price much closer to marginal cost than would be the case in a monopoly.

LEARNING OBJECTIVE ⑤ Discuss government policies toward monopoly. Because monopolies reduce consumer surplus and economic efficiency, most governments regulate monopolies. Firms that are not monopolies have an incentive to avoid competition by colluding on output and price. In the United States, *antitrust laws* are aimed at deterring monopoly, eliminating collusion, and promoting competition among firms. The Antitrust Division of the U.S. Department of Justice and the Federal Trade Commission share responsibility for enforcing the antitrust laws. Local governments regulate the prices charged by natural monopolies.

KEY TERMS

Antitrust laws 459	Horizontal merger 460	Natural monopoly 449	Public franchise 447
Collusion 458	Market power 457	Network externalities 448	Vertical merger 460
Copyright 447	Monopoly 444	Patent 445	

REVIEW QUESTIONS

1. What is a monopoly? Can a firm be a monopoly if close substitutes for its product exist?

2. What are the four most important ways a firm becomes a monopoly?

3. What is "natural" about a natural monopoly?

4. If patents reduce competition, why does the federal government grant them?

5. What is a public franchise? Are all public franchises natural monopolies?

6. What is the relationship between a monopolist's demand curve and the market demand curve? What is the relationship between a monopolist's demand curve and its marginal revenue curve?

7. Draw a graph showing a monopolist that is earning a profit. Be sure your diagram includes the monopolist's demand, marginal revenue, average total cost, and marginal cost curves. Be sure to indicate the profit-maximizing level of output and price.

8. Suppose that a perfectly competitive industry becomes a monopoly. Describe the effects of this change on consumer surplus, producer surplus, and deadweight loss.

9. Explain why market power leads to a deadweight loss. Is the total deadweight loss from market power for the economy large or small?

10. What is the purpose of the antitrust laws? Who is in charge of enforcing them?

11. What is the difference between a horizontal merger and a vertical merger? Which type of merger is more likely to increase the market power of the newly merged firm?

12. Why would it be economically efficient to require a natural monopoly to charge a price equal to marginal cost? Why do most regulatory agencies require natural monopolies to charge a price equal to average cost instead?

PROBLEMS AND APPLICATIONS

Please visit **www.prenhall.com/hubbard** *for solutions to the even-numbered problems as well as multiple-choice and true or false self-assessment quizzes.*

1. Is "monopoly" a good name for the game *Monopoly?* What aspects of the game involve monopoly? Explain briefly using the definition of monopoly.

2. The U.S. Postal Service (USPS) is a monopoly because the federal government has blocked entry into the market for delivering first-class mail. Is it also a natural monopoly? How can we tell? What would happen if the law preventing competition in this market were removed?

3. **[Related to the *Chapter Opener*]** Some observers say that changes in the past few years have eroded the monopoly power of local cable TV companies, even though no other cable firms have entered their markets. What are these changes? Do these "monopoly" firms still have monopoly power?

4. Patents are granted for 20 years, but pharmaceutical companies can't use their patent-guaranteed monopoly powers for anywhere near this long because it takes several years to acquire FDA approval of drugs. Should the life of drug patents be extended to 20 year *after* FDA approval? What would be the costs and benefits of this extension?

5. Just as a new product or a new method of making a product receives patent protection from the government, books, articles, and essays receive copyright protection. Under U.S. law, authors have the exclusive right to their writings during their lifetimes—unless they sell this right, as most authors do to their publishers—and their heirs retain this exclusive right for 50 years after their death. The historian Thomas Macaulay once described the copyright law as "a tax on readers to give a bounty to authors." In what sense does the existence of the copyright law impose a tax on readers? What "bounty" do copyright laws give authors? Discuss whether the government would be doing readers a favor by abolishing the copyright law.
Source of quotation from Macaulay: Thomas Mallon, *Stolen Words: The Classic Book on Plagiarism,* San Diego: Harcourt, 2001 (original ed. 1989), p. 59.

6. Before inexpensive pocket calculators were developed, many science and engineering students used slide rules to make numerical calculations. Slide rules are no longer produced, which means nothing prevents you from establishing a monopoly in the slide rule market. Draw a graph showing the situation your slide rule firm would be in. Be sure to include on your graph your demand, marginal revenue, average total cost, and marginal cost curves. Indicate the price you would charge and the quantity you would produce. Are you likely to make a profit or a loss? Show this area on your diagram.

7. Are there any products for which there are no substitutes? Are these the only products for which it would be possible to have a monopoly? Briefly explain.

8. The German company Konig and Bauer has 90 percent of the world market for presses that print currency. Discuss the factors that would make it difficult for new companies to enter this market.

9. Does a monopolist have a supply curve? Briefly explain. (*Hint:* Look again at the definition of a supply curve in Chapter 3 and consider whether this applies to a monopolist.)

10. Use this diagram for a monopoly to answer the questions:

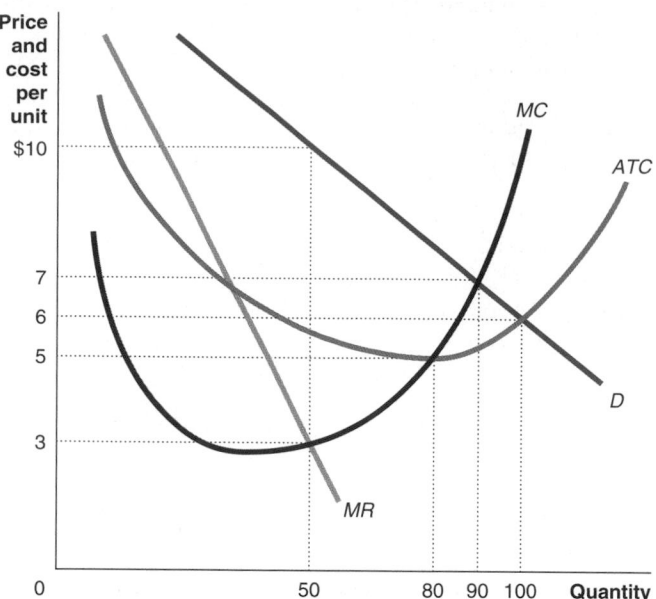

a. What quantity will the monopoly produce, and what price will the monopoly charge?

b. Suppose the monopoly is regulated. If the regulatory agency wants to achieve economic efficiency, what price should it require the monopoly to charge? How much output will the monopoly produce at this price? Will the monopoly make a profit if it charges this price? Briefly explain.

11. Use the following diagram for a monopoly to answer the questions:

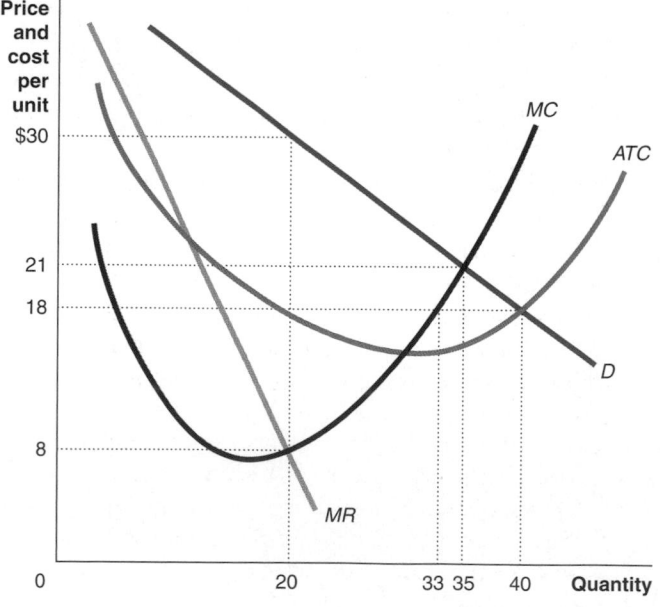

a. What quantity will the monopoly produce, and what price will the monopoly charge?

b. Suppose the government decides to regulate this monopoly and imposes a price ceiling of $18 (in other words, the monopoly can charge less than $18 but can't charge more). Now what quantity will the monopoly produce and what price will the monopoly charge? Will every consumer who is willing to pay this price be able to buy the product? Briefly explain.

12. **[Related to *Solved Problem 14-1*]** Suppose that the quantity demanded per day for a product is 90 when the price is $35. The following table shows costs for a firm with a monopoly in this market:

QUANTITY (PER DAY)	TOTAL COST
30	$1,200
40	1,400
50	2,250
60	3,000

Briefly explain whether this firm has a natural monopoly in this market.

13. **[Related to *Solved Problem 14-2*]** Ed Scahill has acquired a monopoly on the production of baseballs (don't ask how) and faces the demand and cost situation given in the following table:

PRICE	QUANTITY (PER WEEK)	TOTAL REVENUE	MARGINAL REVENUE	TOTAL COST	MARGINAL COST
$20	15,000			$330,000	
19	20,000			365,000	
18	25,000			405,000	
17	30,000			450,000	
16	35,000			500,000	
15	40,000			555,000	

a. Fill in the remaining values in the table.

b. If Joe wants to maximize profits, what price should he charge and how many baseballs should he sell? How much profit will he make?

c. Suppose the government imposes a tax of $50,000 per week on baseball production. Now what price should Joe charge, how many baseballs should he sell, and what will his profits be?

14. **[Related to *Solved Problem 14-2*]** Use the information in Solved Problem 14-2 on pages 454–455 to answer the following questions:

a. What will Comcast do if the tax is $6.00 per month, instead of $2.50? (*Hint:* Will its decision be different in the long run than in the short run?)

b. Suppose that the flat per-month tax is replaced with a tax on the firm of $0.50 per cable subscriber. Now how many subscriptions should Comcast sell if it wants to maximize profit? What price does it charge? What are its profits? (Assume that Comcast will sell only the quantities listed in the table.)

15. **[Related to *Don't Let This Happen To You!*]** A student argues, "If a monopolist finds a way of producing a good at lower cost, he will not lower his price. Because he is a monopolist, he will keep the price and the quantity the same and just increase his profit." Do you agree? Use a graph to illustrate your answer.

16. **[Related to *Don't Let This Happen To You!*]** Discuss whether you agree or disagree with the following statement: "A monopolist maximizes profit by charging the highest price at which it can sell any of the good at all."

17. When home builders construct a new housing development, they will usually sell the rights to lay cable to a single cable television company. As a result, anyone buying a home in that development is not able to choose between competing cable companies. Some cities have begun to ban such exclusive agreements. Williams Township, Pennsylvania, decided to allow any cable company to lay cable in the utility trenches of new housing developments. The head of the township board of supervisors argued, "What I would like to see and do is give the consumers a choice. If there's no choice, then the price [of cable] is at the whim of the provider." In a situation in which the consumers in a housing development have only one cable company available, is the price really at the whim of the company? Would a company in this situation be likely to charge, say, $500 per month for basic cable services? Briefly explain why or why not.
Source: Sam Kennedy, "Williams Township May Ban Exclusive Cable Provider Pacts," Allentown *Morning Call*, November 5, 2004, p. D1.

18. Will a monopoly that maximizes profit also be maximizing revenue? Will it be maximizing production? Briefly explain.

19. Economist Harvey Leibenstein argued that the loss of economic efficiency in industries that are not perfectly competitive has been understated. He argued that when competition is weak, firms are under less pressure to adopt the best techniques or to hold down their costs. He referred to this effect as "x-inefficiency." If x-inefficiency causes a firm's marginal costs to rise, show that the deadweight loss in Figure 14-5 understates the true deadweight loss caused by a monopoly.

20. The following is from an article in the *New York Times*:

> United Airlines and US Airways announced today that they had called off their proposed merger after the Justice Department threatened to file a lawsuit to block the $4.2 billion deal, calling it anticompetitive.

Why would the Justice Department care if two airlines merge? What is "anticompetitive" about two airlines merging?
Source: Kenneth N. Gilpin and Jack Lynch, "United and US Airways Call Off Merger After U.S. Opposes It," *New York Times*, July 27, 2001.

21. A marketing textbook observes, "Pricing actions that violate laws can land executives in jail." Why would executives be thrown in jail because of the prices they charge? Which laws are they likely to have violated?
Source: David W. Cravens, *Strategic Marketing*, 5th ed., Boston: Irwin McGraw-Hill, 1997, p. 343.

22. Draw a graph like Figure 14-6. On your graph, show producer surplus and consumer surplus before a merger and consumer surplus and producer surplus after a merger.

23. The following phone call took place in February 1982 between Robert Crandall, the chief executive officer of American Airlines, and Howard Putnam, the chief executive officer of Braniff Airways. Although Crandall didn't know it, Putnam was recording the call:

Crandall: I think it's dumb . . . to sit here and pound the (obscenity) out of each other and neither one of us making a (obscenity) dime . . .
Putnam: Do you have a suggestion for me?
Crandall: Yes, I have a suggestion for you. Raise your . . . fares 20 percent. I'll raise mine the next morning.
Putnam: Robert, we . . .
Crandall: You'll make more money and I will, too.
Putnam: We can't talk about pricing.
Crandall: Oh (obscenity), Howard. We can talk about any . . . thing we want to talk about.

Who had a better understanding of antitrust law, Crandall or Putnam? Briefly explain.
Source: Mark Potts, "American Airlines Charged with Seeking a Monopoly," *Washington Post*, February 24, 1983; "Blunt Talk on the Phone," *New York Times*, February 24, 1983; and Thomas Petzinger Jr., *Hard Landing: The Epic Contest for Power and Profits that Plunged the Airline Industry into Chaos*, New York: Random House, 1995, pp. 149–50.

24. Look again at the section "The Department of Justice and the Federal Trade Commission Merger Guidelines" that begins on page 461. Evaluate the following situations:
   a. A market initially has 20 firms, each with a 5 percent market share. Of the firms, 4 propose to merge, leaving a total of 16 firms in the industry. Are the Department of Justice and the Federal Trade Commission likely to oppose the merger? Briefly explain.
   b. A market initially has 5 firms, each with a 20 percent market share. Of the firms, 2 propose to merge, leaving a total of 4 firms in the industry. Are the Department of Justice and the Federal Trade Commission likely to oppose the merger? Briefly explain.

25. Industrial gases are used in the electronics industry. For example, nitrogen trifluoride is used for cleaning

semiconductor wafers. The following table shows the market shares for the companies in this industry:

COMPANY	MARKET SHARE
Air Products	29%
Air Liquide	22
BOC Gases	21
Nippon Sanso	17
Praxzir	8
Other	3

In 2000, Air Products discussed a merger with BOC Gases. Use the information in the section "The Department of Justice and the Federal Trade Commission Merger Guidelines" that begins on page 461 to predict whether the Department of Justice and the Federal Trade Commission opposed this merger. Assume that "Other" in the table consists of three firms, each of which has a 1 percent share of the market.

Source for market share data: Graph in Dan Shope, "Air Products Turns a Corner," Allentown *Morning Call,* July 29, 2001.

26. The following table gives the market shares of the companies in the U.S. carbonated soft drink industry:

COMPANY	MARKET SHARE
Coca-Cola	37%
PepsiCo	35
Cadbury Schweppes	17
Other	11

Use the information in the section "The Department of Justice and the Federal Trade Commission Merger Guidelines" that begins on page 461 to predict whether the Department of Justice and the Federal Trade Commission would be likely to approve a merger between any two of the first three companies listed. Does your answer depend on how many companies are included in the "Other" category? Briefly explain.

Source: Pepsico *Annual Report, 2003.*

27. Most cities own the water system that provides water to homes and businesses. Some cities charge a flat monthly fee, while other cities charge by the gallon. Which method of pricing is more likely to result in economic efficiency in the water market? Be sure to refer to the definition of economic efficiency in your answer. Why do you think the same method of pricing isn't used by all cities?

28. Review the concept of externalities on page 130 in Chapter 5. If a market is a monopoly, will a negative externality in production always lead to production beyond the level of economic efficiency? Use a graph to illustrate your answer.

chapter

fifteen

Pricing Strategy

15

Getting into Walt Disney World: One Price Does Not Fit All

➤ When you visit Walt Disney World in Florida, your age, home address, and occupation can determine how much you pay for admission. In the summer of 2005, the price of an annual admission pass for an adult was $421. The same pass for a child, aged three to nine, was $358. Children under three were free. Florida residents paid $318. Florida residents who were also members of Auto Club South paid $307. Active members of the military paid $385. Why does Disney charge so many different prices for the same product?

In previous chapters, we assumed that firms charge all consumers the same price for a given product. In reality, many firms will charge customers different prices, based on differences in their willingness to pay for the product. Firms often face compli-

cated pricing problems. For example, the Walt Disney Company faces the problem of determining the profit-maximizing prices to charge for admission to its Disneyland and Walt Disney World theme parks.

The Walt Disney Company was founded in 1923 by Walt Disney and his brother Roy O. Disney. The Disney brothers risked financial ruin by investing in innovative entertainment ideas. In 1927, they released *Steamboat Willie* starring Mickey Mouse, the first cartoon to feature synchronized sound. The profits from *Steamboat Willie* and other short cartoons helped finance production of *Snow White and the Seven Dwarfs*. Released in 1937, this was the first full-length Technicolor cartoon.

In the early 1950s, Walt Disney began to believe there was a mar-

ket for theme parks. At that time, amusement parks—like Coney Island in New York—were usually collections of unrelated rides, such as roller coasters and Ferris wheels. The parks often had rowdy reputations and appealed more to teenagers and young adults than to families with younger children. Disney believed that a theme park, with attractions that emphasized storytelling over thrills, would be more attractive to families than amusement parks were. Disney had trouble raising the funds necessary to build his new park, however, because it was so strikingly different from existing parks. An economist hired by Disney to evaluate the feasibility of the park interviewed managers of existing parks, and was told, "Tell your boss to save his

LEARNING OBJECTIVES

After studying this chapter, you should be able to:

① Define the law of one price and explain the role of arbitrage.

② Explain how a firm can increase its profits through price discrimination.

③ Explain how some firms increase their profits through the use of odd pricing, cost-plus pricing, and two-part tariffs.

money. Tell him to stick to what he knows and leave the amusement business to people who know it." Eventually, Disney convinced the ABC television network to provide funding in exchange for his providing them with a weekly television program.

When Disneyland opened in Anaheim, California, in July 1955, the Disney company had to set ticket prices. Should the company charge for entry into the park—which most amusements parks did not—and also charge for each ride within the park? Disney decided to charge a low price—$1 for adults and $0.50 for children—for admission into the park and also to charge for tickets to the rides. This system of separate charges for admission and for the rides continued until the early 1980s, when a very different system was implemented. Today there is a high price for admission to Disneyland and Walt Disney World, but once in the parks the rides are free. Why did Disney change its pricing strategy? In this chapter, we will study some common pricing strategies, and we will see how Disney and other firms use these strategies to increase their profits. *An Inside Look* on page 492 discusses the importance of theme park profits to the Disney Company.

Source for quote: Harrison Price, *Walt's Revolution! By the Numbers,* n.p.: Ripley Entertainment, Inc., 2004, p. 31; original Disneyland pricing from Bruce Gordon and David Mumford, *Disneyland: The Nickel Tour,* Santa Clarita, California: Camphor Tree Publishers, 2000, pp. 174–175.

➤ We have seen in previous chapters that entrepreneurs continually seek out economic profit. Pricing strategies are one way firms can attempt to increase their economic profit. One of these strategies is called *price discrimination*. It involves firms setting different prices for the same good or service, as Disney does when setting admission prices at Disney World. In Chapter 14, we analyzed the situation of a monopolist who sets a single price for its product. In this chapter, we will see how a firm can increase its profits by charging a higher price to consumers who value the good more, and a lower price to consumers who value the good less.

We will also analyze the widely used strategies of *odd pricing* and *cost-plus pricing*. Finally, we will analyze situations where firms are able to charge consumers one price for the right to buy a good and a second price for each unit of the good purchased. The ability of Disney to charge for admission to Disney World and also to charge for each ride is an example of this situation, which economists call a *two-part tariff*.

<table>
<tr><td>① LEARNING OBJECTIVE

Define the law of one price and explain the role of arbitrage.</td></tr>
</table>

Pricing Strategy and the Law of One Price

We have seen in the opening to this chapter that sometimes firms can increase their profits by charging different prices for the same good. In fact, many firms rely on economic analysis to practice *price discrimination* by charging higher prices to some customers and lower prices to others. The development of information technology during the past 20 years has made it possible for firms to gather information on consumers' preferences and the responsiveness of consumers to changes in prices, and to use this information to rapidly adjust prices. This practice, called *yield management*, has been particularly important to airlines and hotels. There are limits, though, to the ability of firms to charge different prices for the same product. The key limit is the possibility in some circumstances that consumers who can buy a good at a low price will resell it to consumers who would otherwise have to buy at a high price.

Arbitrage

According to the *law of one price*, identical products should sell for the same price everywhere. Let's explore why the law of one price usually holds true. Suppose that a Sony PlayStation Portable (PSP) hand-held video-game player sells for $249 in stores in Atlanta and for $199 in stores in San Francisco. Anyone who lives in San Francisco could buy PSPs for $199 and resell them for $249 in Atlanta. They could sell them on eBay or ship them to someone they know in Atlanta who could sell them in local flea markets. Buying a product in one market at a low price and reselling it in another market at a high price is referred to as *arbitrage*. The profits received from engaging in arbitrage are referred to as *arbitrage profits*.

As the supply of PSPs in Atlanta increases, the price of PSPs in Atlanta will decline, and as the supply of PSPs in San Francisco decreases, the price of PSPs in San Francisco will rise. Eventually the arbitrage process will eliminate most, but not all, of the price difference. Some price difference will remain because sellers must pay to list PSPs on eBay and to ship them to Atlanta. The costs of carrying out a transaction—by, for example, listing items on eBay and shipping them across the country—are called **transactions costs**. The law of one price holds exactly *only if transactions costs are zero*. As we will soon see, in cases where it is impossible to resell a product, the law of one price will not hold and firms will be able to price discriminate. Apart from this important qualification, we expect that arbitrage will result in a product selling for the same price everywhere.

Transactions costs The costs in time and other resources that parties incur in the process of agreeing to and carrying out an exchange of goods or services.

SOLVED PROBLEM 15-1

Is Arbitrage Just a Rip-off?

People are often suspicious of arbitrage. Buying something at a low price and reselling it a high price exploits the person buying at the high price. Or does it? Is this view correct? If so, do the auctions on eBay serve any useful economic purpose?

① **LEARNING OBJECTIVE**
Define the law of one price and explain the role of arbitrage.

Solving the Problem:
Step 1: Review the chapter material. This problem is about arbitrage, so you may want to review the section "Arbitrage," which begins on page 476. If necessary, also review the discussion of the benefits from trade in Chapters 2 and 8.

Step 2: Use the discussion of arbitrage and the discussion in earlier chapters of the benefits from trade to answer the questions. Many of the goods on eBay have been bought at a low price and are being resold at a higher price. In fact, some people supplement their incomes by buying collectibles and other goods at garage sales and reselling them on eBay. Does eBay serve a useful economic purpose? Economists would say that it does. Consider the case of Lou who buys collectible movie posters and resells them on eBay. Suppose Lou buys a poster for *Spider-Man 2* at a garage sale for $30 and resells it on eBay for $60. Both the person who sold to Lou at the garage sale and the person who bought from him on eBay must have been made better off by the deals, *or they would not have made them.* Lou has performed the useful service of locating the poster and making it available for sale on eBay. In carrying out this service, Lou has incurred costs, including the opportunity cost of his time spent searching garage sales, the opportunity cost of the funds he has tied up in posters he has purchased but not yet sold, and the cost of the fees eBay charges him. It is easy to sell goods on eBay, so over time competition among Lou and other movie poster dealers should cause the difference between the prices of posters sold at garage sales and the prices on eBay to shrink until they are equal to the dealers' costs of reselling the posters.

YOUR TURN: **For more practice, do related problems 1 and 2 on page 495 at the end of this chapter. Visit www.prenhall.com/hubbard for an interactive exercise related to this Solved Problem.**

Why Don't All Firms Charge the Same Price?

The law of one price may appear to be violated even where transactions costs are zero and a product can be resold. For example, different Internet Web sites may sell what seem to be identical products for different prices. We can resolve this apparent contradiction if we look more closely at what "product" an Internet Web site—or other business—actually offers for sale.

Suppose you want to buy a copy of the book *Harry Potter and the Half-Blood Prince.* You use MySimon.com or some other search engine to compare the book's price at various Web sites. You get the results shown in Table 15-1.

Would you automatically buy the book from one of the last two sites listed, rather than from Amazon.com or BarnesandNoble.com? We can think about why you might not. Consider what product is being offered for sale. Amazon.com is not just offering *Harry Potter and the Half-Blood Prince*—it is offering *Harry Potter and the Half-Blood Prince* delivered quickly to your home, well packaged so it's not damaged in the mail, and charged to your credit card using a secure method that keeps your credit card number safe from computer hackers. As we discussed in Chapter 12, firms differentiate the products they sell in many ways. One way is by providing faster and more reliable delivery than competitors.

Amazon.com and BarnesandNoble.com have built reputations for fast and reliable service. New Internet booksellers who lack that reputation will have to differentiate their

TABLE 15-1	PRODUCT: *HARRY POTTER AND THE HALF-BLOOD PRINCE*	
Which Company Would You Buy From?	COMPANY	PRICE
	Amazon.com	$20.95
	BarnesandNoble.com	20.95
	WaitForeverForYourOrder.com	18.50
	JustStartedinBusinessLastWednesday.com	17.75

products on the basis of price, as the two fictitious firms listed in the table have done. So, the difference in the prices of products offered on Web sites does *not* violate the law of one price. A book offered for sale by Amazon.com is not the same product as a book offered for sale by JustStartedinBusinessLastWednesday.com.

② **LEARNING OBJECTIVE**

Explain how a firm can increase its profits through price discrimination.

Price discrimination Charging different prices to different customers for the same product when the price differences are not due to differences in cost.

Price Discrimination: Charging Different Prices for the Same Product

We saw at the beginning of this chapter that the Walt Disney Company charges different prices for the same product: admission to Disney World. Charging different prices to different customers for the same good or service when the price differences are not due to differences in cost is called **price discrimination.** But doesn't price discrimination contradict the law of one price? Why doesn't the possibility of arbitrage profits lead people to buy at the low price and resell at the high price?

The Requirements for Successful Price Discrimination

A successful strategy of price discrimination has three requirements:

1. A firm must possess market power.
2. Some consumers must have a greater willingness to pay for the product than other consumers, and the firm must be able to know what prices customers are willing to pay.
3. The firm must be able to divide up—or *segment*—the market for the product so that consumers who buy the product at a low price are not able to resell it at a high price. In other words, price discrimination will not work if arbitrage is possible.

Note that a firm selling in a perfectly competitive market cannot practice price discrimination because it can only charge the market price. But because most firms do not sell in perfectly competitive markets, they have market power and can set the price of the good they sell. Many firms may also be able to determine that some customers have a greater willingness to pay for the product than others. However, the third requirement—that markets be segmented so that customers buying at a low price will not be able to resell the product—can be difficult to fulfill. For example, some people really love Big Macs and would be willing to pay $10 rather than do without one. Other people would not be willing to pay a penny more than $1 for one. Even if McDonald's could identify differences in the willingness of its customers to pay for Big Macs, it would not be able to charge them different prices. Suppose McDonald's knows that Joe is willing to pay $10, whereas Jill will pay only $1. If McDonald's tries to charge Joe $10, he will just have Jill buy his Big Mac for him.

Only firms that can keep consumers from reselling a product are able to practice price discrimination. Because the product cannot be resold, the law of one price is not contradicted. For example, movie theaters know that many people are willing to pay more to see a movie at night than during the afternoon. As a result, theaters usually charge higher prices for tickets to night showings than for tickets to afternoon showings. They keep these markets separate by making the tickets to afternoon showings a different color or by having the time printed on them, and by having a ticket taker examine the tickets. That makes it difficult for someone to buy a lower-priced ticket in the afternoon and use the ticket to gain admission to an evening showing.

Figure 15-1 illustrates how the owners of movie theaters use price discrimination to increase their profits. The marginal cost to the movie theater owner from another person attending a showing is very small: a little more wear on a theater seat and a few more kernels of popcorn to be swept from the floor. In previous chapters, we have assumed that marginal cost has a U-shape. For our purposes here, we can simplify things by assuming that marginal cost is a constant $0.50, shown as a horizontal line in Figure 15-1. Panel (a) shows the demand for afternoon showings. In this segment of its market, the theater should maximize profit by selling the number of tickets for which marginal revenue equals marginal cost, or 350 tickets. We know from the demand curve that 450 tickets can be sold at a price of $4.50 per ticket. Panel (b) shows the demand for night showings. Notice that charging $4.50 per ticket would *not* be profit-maximizing in this market. At a price of $4.50, the theater sells 850 tickets, which is 225 more tickets than the profit-maximizing number of 625. By charging $4.50 for tickets to afternoon showings and $6.75 for tickets to night showings, the theater has maximized profits.

Figure 15-1 also illustrates another important point about price discrimination: When firms can price discriminate, they will charge customers who are less sensitive to price—those whose demand for the product is *less elastic*—a higher price and charge customers who are more sensitive to price—those whose demand is *more elastic*—a

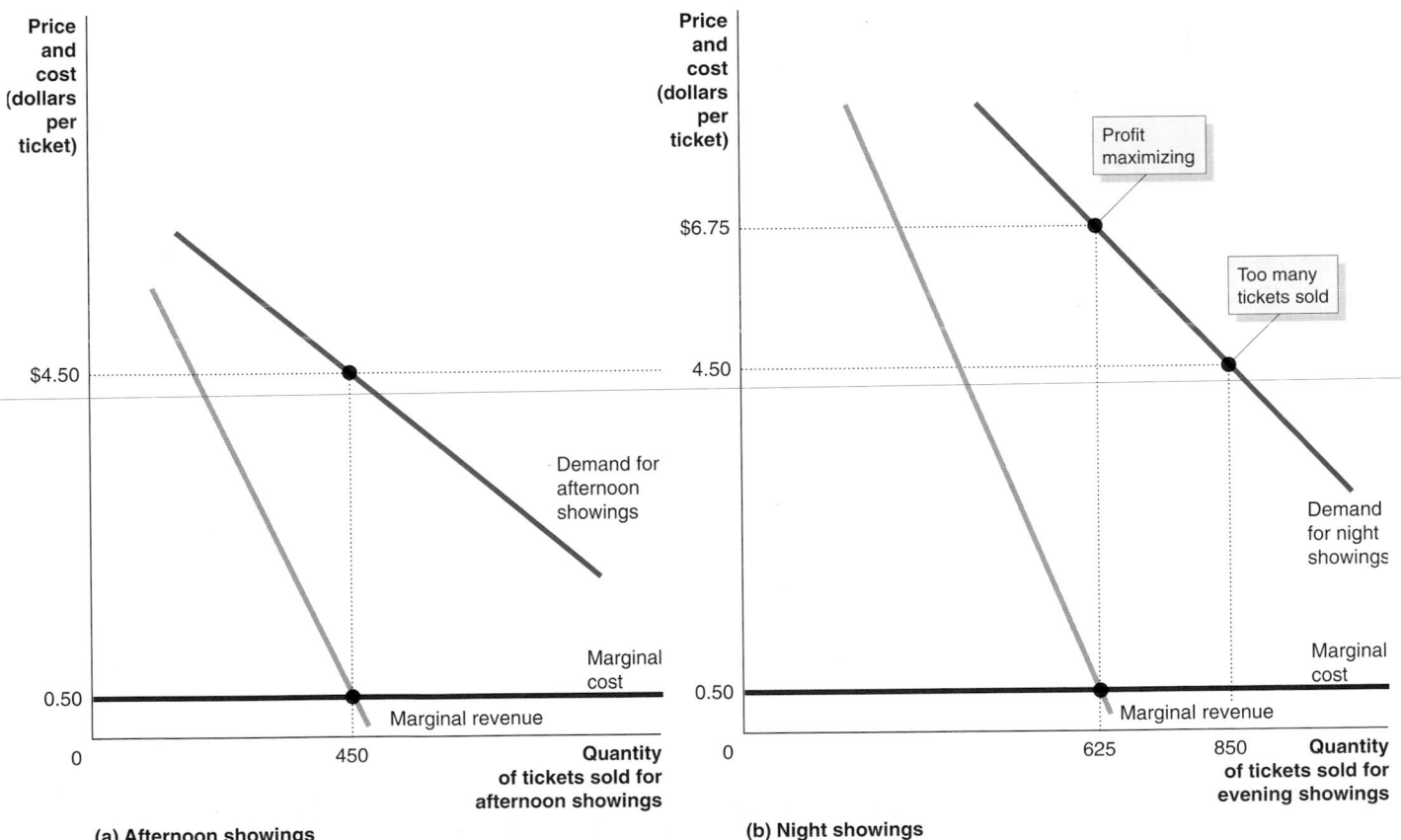

(a) Afternoon showings

(b) Night showings

FIGURE 15-1   **Price Discrimination by a Movie Theater**

Fewer people want to go to the movies in the afternoon than in the evening. In panel (a), the profit-maximizing price for a ticket to an afternoon showing is $4.50. Charging this same price for night showings would not be profit-maximizing, as panel (b) shows. At a price of $4.50, 850 tickets would be sold to night showings, which is more than the profit-maximizing number of 625 tickets. To maximize profits, the theater should charge $6.75 for tickets to night showings.

lower price. In this case, the demand for tickets to night showings is less elastic, so the price charged is higher, and the demand for tickets to afternoon showings is more elastic, so the price charged is lower.

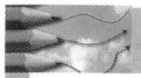

SOLVED PROBLEM 15-2

How Dell Computer Uses Price Discrimination to Increase Profits

According to an article in the *Wall Street Journal,* "On Dell's Web site recently, the same Optiplex business desktop PC priced at $1,498 for education customers was offered at $1,426 on a page devoted to health-care customers." Why would Dell charge different prices for the same computer depending on whether the buyer is an education customer or a health-care customer? Draw a graph to illustrate your answer.

Source: David Bank and Gary McWilliams, "Picking a Big Fight with Dell, H-P Cuts PC Profits Razor-Thin," *Wall Street Journal,* May 12, 2004.

Solving the Problem:

Step 1: Review the chapter material. This problem is about using price discrimination to increase profits, so you may want to review the section "Price Discrimination: Charging Different Prices for the Same Product," which begins on page 478.

Step 2: Explain why charging different prices to education customers and health-care customers will increase Dell's profits. It makes sense for Dell to charge different prices if education customers have a different price elasticity of demand than do health-care customers. In that case, Dell will charge the market segment with the less elastic demand a higher price, and the market segment with the more elastic demand a lower price. Because education customers are being charged the higher price, they must have a less elastic demand than health-care customers.

Step 3: Draw a graph to illustrate your answer. Your diagram should look like the following graph, where we have chosen hypothetical quantities to illustrate the ideas. As in the case of movie theaters, you can assume for simplicity that the marginal cost is constant—in the graph we assume marginal cost is $400.

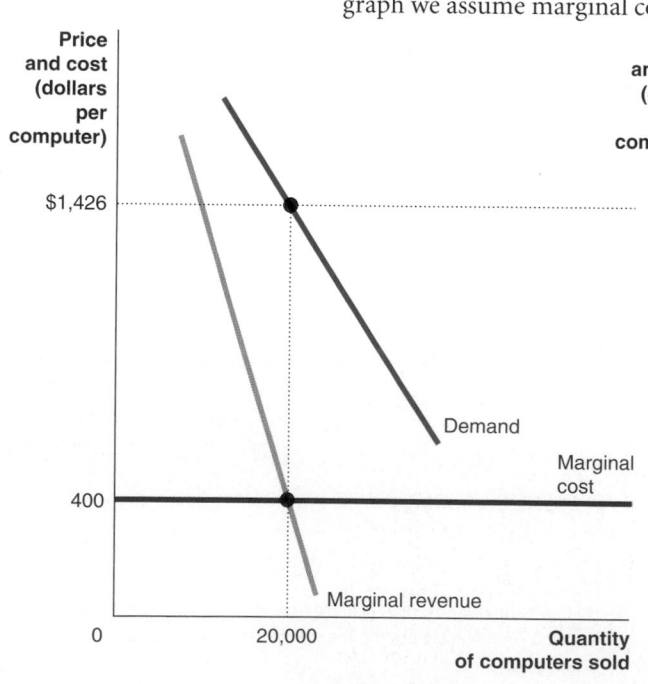

(a) Health-care customers

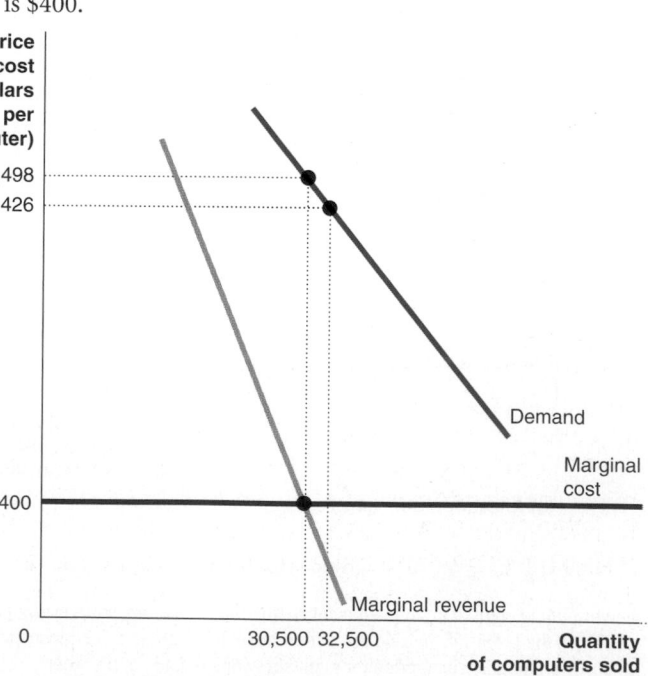

(b) Education customers

The graph shows that in the health-care customers segment of the market, marginal revenue equals marginal cost at 20,000 computers sold. Therefore, Dell should charge a price of $1,426 to maximize profits. But if Dell also charged $1,426 in the education customers segment of the market, it would sell 32,500 computers, which is more than the profit-maximizing quantity. By charging $1,498 to education customers, Dell will sell 30,500 computers, the profit-maximizing quantity. We have shown that Dell maximizes its profits by charging education customers a higher price than health-care customers.

YOUR TURN: For more practice, do problem 12 on page 495 at the end of this chapter. Visit www.prenhall.com/hubbard for an interactive exercise related to this Solved Problem.

Airlines: The Kings of Price Discrimination

Airline seats are a very perishable product. Once a plane has taken off from Chicago for Los Angeles, any seat that has not been sold on that particular flight will never be sold. In addition, the marginal cost of flying one additional passenger is low. This situation gives airlines a strong incentive to manage prices so that as many seats as possible are filled on each flight.

Airlines divide their customers into two main categories: business travelers and leisure travelers. Business travelers often have inflexible schedules, can't commit until the last minute to traveling on a particular day, and, most importantly, are not very sensitive to changes in price. The opposite is true for leisure travelers: They are flexible about when they travel, they are willing to buy their tickets well in advance, and they are sensitive to changes in price. Based on what we discussed earlier in this chapter, you can see that airlines will maximize profits by charging business travelers higher ticket prices than leisure travelers, but they need to determine who is a business traveler and who is a leisure traveler. Some airlines do this by requiring people who want to buy a ticket at the leisure price to buy 14 days in advance and to stay at their destination over a Saturday night. Anyone unable to meet these requirements must pay a much higher price. Because business travelers often cannot make their plans 14 days in advance of their flight and don't want to stay over a weekend, they end up paying the higher ticket price. The gap between leisure fares and business fares is often very substantial. For example, in April 2005, the price of a leisure-fare ticket between New York and San Francisco on United Airlines was $363. The price of a business-fare ticket was $1,143.

The airlines go well beyond a single leisure fare and a single business fare in their pricing strategies. Although they ordinarily charge high prices for tickets sold only a few days in advance, they are willing to reduce prices for seats that they expect will not be sold at existing prices. Since the late 1980s, airlines have employed economists and mathematicians to construct computer models of the market for airline tickets. To calculate a suggested price each day for each seat, these models take into account factors that affect the demand for tickets, such as the season of the year, the length of the route, the day of the week, and whether the flight typically attracts primarily business or leisure travelers. This practice of continually adjusting prices to take into account fluctuations in demand is called *yield management.*

Since the late 1990s, Internet sites such as Priceline.com have helped the airlines to implement yield management. On Priceline.com, buyers commit to paying a price of their choosing for a ticket on a particular day and agree that they will fly at any time on that day. This gives airlines the opportunity to fill seats that otherwise would have gone empty, particularly on late night or early morning flights, even though the price may be well below the normal leisure fare. In 2001, several airlines combined to form the Internet site Orbitz, which became another means of filling seats at discount prices. In fact, in the last few years the chances that you paid the same price for your airline ticket as the person sitting next to you has become quite small. Figure 15-2 shows an actual United

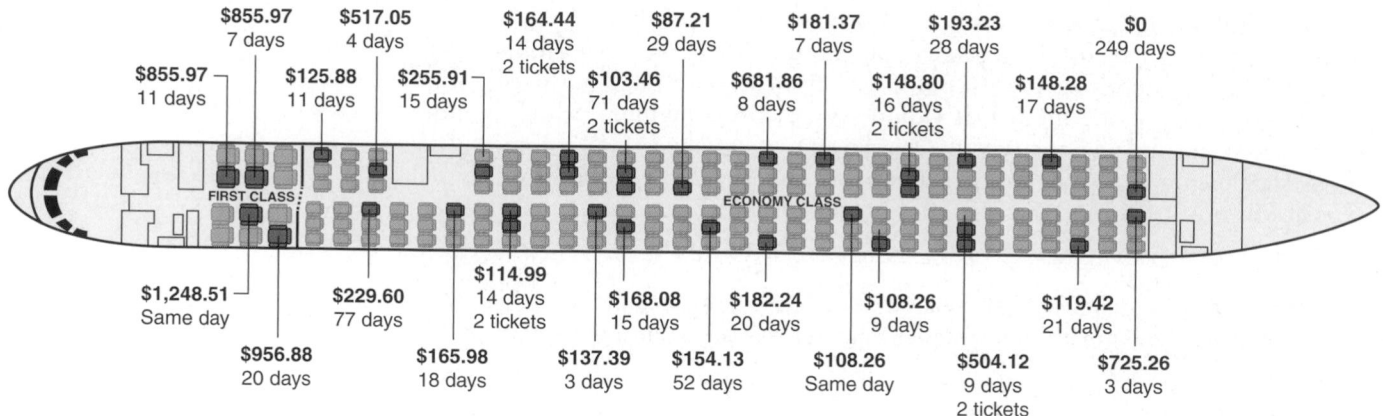

FIGURE 15-2   **33 Customers and 27 Different Prices**

To fill as many seats on a flight as possible, airlines charge many different ticket prices. The 33 passengers on this United Airlines flight from Chicago to Los Angeles paid 27 different prices for their tickets, including one passenger who used frequent flyer miles to obtain a free ticket. The first number in the figure is the price paid for the ticket; the second number is the number of days in advance that the ticket was purchased.

Source: Matthew L. Wald, "So, How Much Did You Pay for Your Ticket?" *New York Times*, April 12, 1998. Used with permission of New York Times Agency.

Airlines flight from Chicago to Los Angeles. The 33 passengers on the flight paid 27 different prices for their tickets, including one passenger who used frequent flyer miles to obtain a free ticket.

15-1 *Making the Connection*

Do colleges practice price discrimination?

How Colleges Use Yield Management

Traditionally, colleges have based financial aid decisions only on the incomes of prospective students. In recent years, however, many colleges have started using yield management techniques, first developed for the airlines, to determine the amount of financial aid they offer different students. Colleges typically use a name like "financial aid engineering" or "student enrollment management" rather than "yield management" to describe what they are doing. However, there is an important difference between the airlines and colleges: Colleges are interested not just in maximizing the revenue they receive from student tuition, but also in improving the academic quality of the students who enroll.

The "price" of a college education equals the tuition charged minus any financial aid received. When colleges use yield management techniques, they increase financial aid offers to students likely to be more price sensitive and they reduce financial aid offers to students likely to be less price sensitive. As Harvard economist Caroline Hoxby puts it, "Universities are trying to find the people whose decisions will be changed by these [financial aid] grants." Some of the factors used to judge how sensitive to price students are likely to be include whether they applied for early admission, whether they came for an on-campus interview, their intended major, their home state, and the level of their family's income. Focusing on one of these factors, William F. Elliot, vice president for enrollment management at Carnegie Mellon University, advises, "If finances are a concern, you shouldn't be applying any place [for] early decision" because you are less likely to receive a large financial aid offer.

Many students (and their parents) are critical of colleges that use yield management techniques in allocating financial aid. Some colleges, such as those in the Ivy League, have large enough endowments to meet all of their students' financial aid needs, so they don't practice yield management. Less well-endowed colleges defend the practice on the grounds that it allows them to recruit the best students at a lower cost in financial aid.

Sources: Steve Stecklow, "Expensive Lesson: Colleges Manipulate Financial-Aid Offers, *Wall Street Journal*, April 1, 1996; and Albert B. Crenshaw, "Price Wars on Campus: Colleges Use Discounts to Draw Best Mix of Top Students, Paying Customers," *Washington Post*, October 15, 2002.

Perfect Price Discrimination

If a firm knew every consumer's willingness to pay—and could keep consumers who bought a product at a low price from reselling it—the firm could charge every consumer a different price. In this case of *perfect price discrimination*—also known as *first-degree price discrimination*—each consumer would have to pay a price equal to the consumer's willingness to pay and, therefore, would receive no consumer surplus. To see that this outcome is true, remember that consumer surplus is the difference between the highest price a consumer is willing to pay for a product and the price the consumer actually pays. But if the price the consumer pays is the maximum the consumer would be willing to pay, there is no consumer surplus.

Figure 15-3 shows the effects of perfect price discrimination. To simplify the discussion, we assume the firm is a monopoly and that it has constant marginal and average costs. Panel (a) should be familiar from Chapter 14. It shows the case of a monopolist who cannot price discriminate and, therefore, can charge only a single price for its product. The monopolist maximizes profits by producing the level of output where marginal revenue equals marginal cost. Recall that the economically efficient level of output occurs where price is equal to marginal cost, which is the level of output in a perfectly competitive market. Because the monopolist produces where price is greater than marginal cost, it causes a loss of economic efficiency, equal to the area of the deadweight loss triangle in the figure.

Panel (b) shows the situation of a monopolist practicing perfect price discrimination. Because the firm can now charge each consumer the maximum the consumer is willing to pay, its marginal revenue from selling one more unit is equal to the price of that unit. Therefore, the monopolist's marginal revenue curve becomes equal to its demand curve, and the firm will continue to produce up to the point where price is equal to marginal cost. It may seem like a paradox, but the ability to perfectly price discriminate causes the monopolist to produce the efficient level of output. By doing so, it converts into profits what in panel (a) had been consumer surplus *and* what had

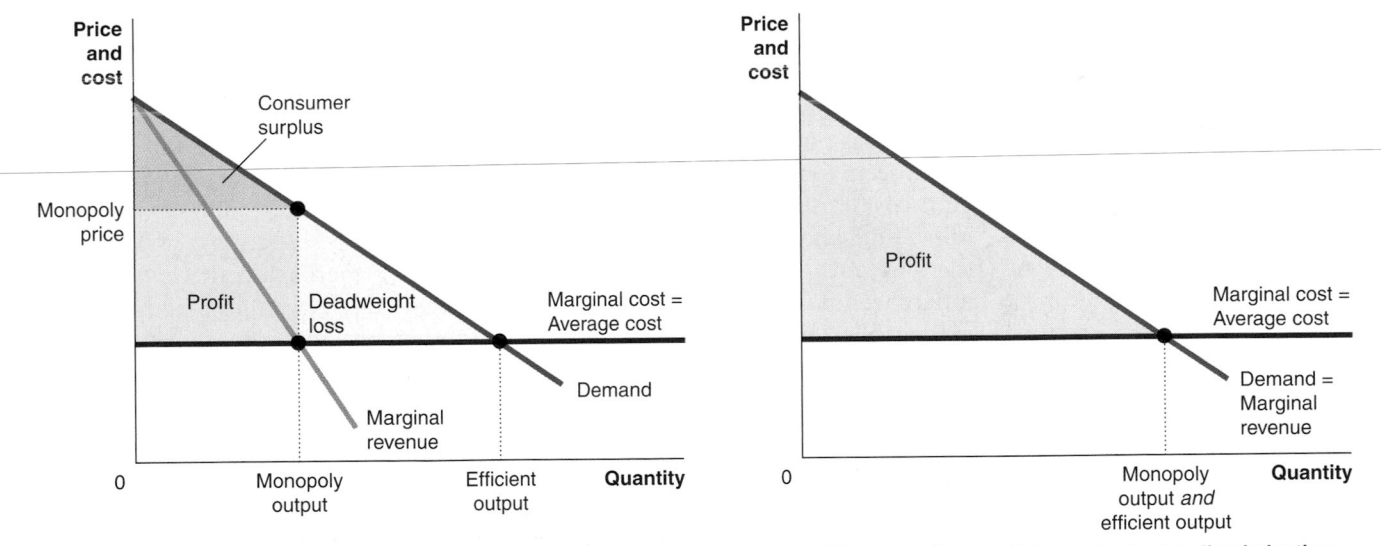

(a) A monopolist who cannot practice price discrimination

(b) A monopolist practicing perfect price discrimination

FIGURE 15-3   **Perfect Price Discrimination**

Panel (a) shows the case of a monopolist who cannot price discriminate and, therefore, can only charge a single price for its product. The graph, like those in Chapter 14, shows that to maximize profits the monopolist will produce the level of output where marginal revenue equals marginal cost. The resulting profit is shown by the area of the green rectangle. Given the monopoly price, the amount of consumer surplus in this market is shown by the area of the blue triangle. The

economically efficient level of output occurs where price equals marginal cost. Because the monopolist stops production at a level of output where price is above marginal cost, there is a deadweight loss equal to the area of the yellow triangle. In panel (b), the monopolist is able to perfectly price discriminate by charging a different price to each consumer. The result is to convert both the consumer surplus *and* the deadweight loss from panel (a) into profit.

been deadweight loss. In both panel (a) and panel (b), the profit shown is also producer surplus.

Even though the result in panel (b) is more economically efficient than the result in panel (a), consumers clearly are worse off because the amount of consumer surplus has been reduced to zero. We probably will never see a case of perfect price discrimination in the real world because firms typically do not know how much each consumer is willing to pay and therefore cannot charge each consumer a different price. Still, this extreme case helps us to see the two key results of price discrimination:

1. Profits increase.
2. Consumer surplus decreases.

With perfect price discrimination, economic efficiency is improved. Can we also say that this will be the case if price discrimination is less than perfect? Often, less than perfect price discrimination will improve economic efficiency. But under certain circumstances, it may actually reduce economic efficiency, so we can't draw a general conclusion.

Price Discrimination across Time

Firms are sometimes able to engage in price discrimination over time. With this strategy, firms charge a higher price for a product when it is first introduced, and a lower price later. Some consumers are *early adopters* who will pay a high price to be among the first to own certain new products. This pattern helps explain why DVD players, digital cameras, and flat-screen plasma televisions all sold for very high prices when first introduced. After the demand of the early adopters was satisfied, the companies reduced prices to attract more price-sensitive customers. For example, the price of DVD players dropped by 95 percent within five years of their introduction. Some of the price reductions over time for these products also reflected falling costs, as companies took advantage of economies of scale, but some represented price discrimination across time.

Book publishers routinely use price discrimination across time to increase profits. Hardcover editions of novels have much higher prices and are published months before paperback editions. For example, the hardcover edition of John Grisham's novel *The Broker* was published in January 2005 at a price of $27.95. The paperback edition was published in November 2005 for $7.99. Although this difference in price might seem to reflect the higher costs of hardcover books, in fact, it does not. The marginal cost of printing another copy of the hardcover is about $1.50. The marginal cost of printing another copy of the paperback edition is only slightly less, about $1.25. So, the difference in price between the hardcover and paperback is driven primarily by differences in demand. John Grisham's most devoted fans want to read his next book at the earliest possible moment and are not too sensitive to price. Many casual readers are also interested in Grisham's books but will read something else if the price is too high. Figure 15-4 shows the result.

As Figure 15-4 shows, a publisher will maximize profits by segmenting the market—in this case across time—and by charging a higher price to the less elastic market segment and a lower price to the more elastic segment. (This example is similar to our earlier analysis of movie tickets.) If the publisher had skipped the hardcover and just issued the paperback version in January at a price of $7.99, its revenue would have dropped by the number of readers who bought the hardcover multiplied by the difference between the price of the hardcover and the price of the paperback, or 500,000 × ($27.95 − 7.99) = $9,980,000.

Can Price Discrimination Be Illegal?

In Chapter 14, we saw that Congress has passed *antitrust laws* to promote competition. Price discrimination may be illegal if its effect is to reduce competition in an industry. In 1936, Congress passed the Robinson-Patman Act, which outlawed price

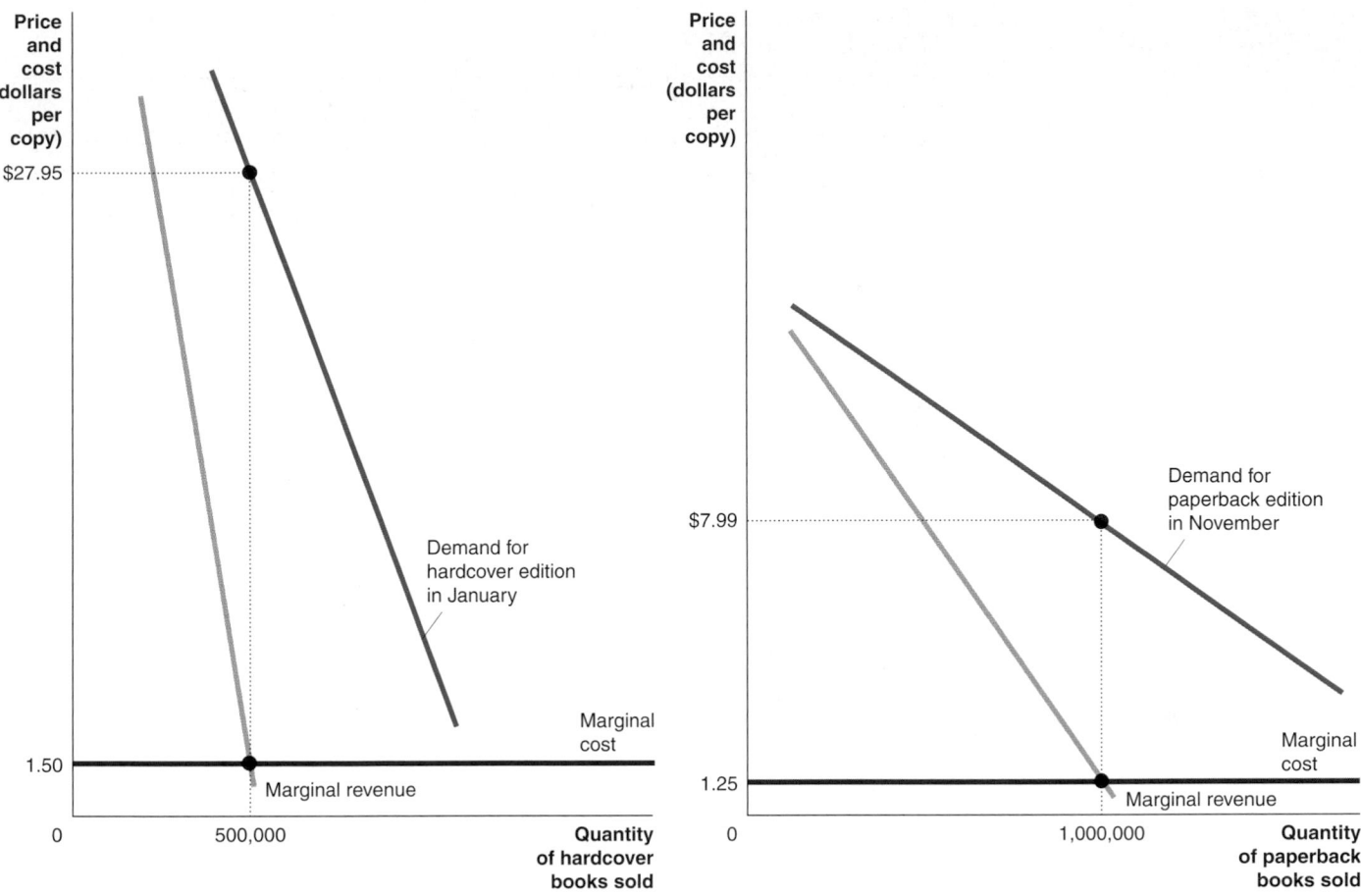

FIGURE 15-4   **Price Discrimination across Time**

Publishers issue most novels in hardcover at high prices to satisfy the demand of the novelists' most devoted fans. Later, they publish paperback editions at much lower prices to capture sales from casual readers. In panel (a), with a marginal cost of $1.50 per copy for a hardcover, the profit-maximizing level of

output is 500,000 copies, which can be sold at a price of $27.95. In panel (b), the more elastic demand of casual readers and the slightly lower marginal cost result in a profit-maximizing output of 1,000,000 for the paperback edition, which can be sold at a price of $7.99.

discrimination that reduced competition, but which also contained language that could be interpreted as making illegal *all* price discrimination not based on differences in cost. In the 1960s, the Federal Trade Commission sued the Borden company under this act because Borden was selling the same evaporated milk for two different prices. Cans with the Borden label were sold for a high price and cans sold to supermarkets to be repackaged with the supermarkets' private labels were sold for a much lower price. The courts ultimately ruled that Borden had not violated the law because the price differences increased, rather than reduced, competition in the market for evaporated milk. In recent years, the courts have interpreted Robinson-Patman narrowly, allowing firms to use the types of price discrimination described in this chapter.

Other Pricing Strategies

In addition to price discrimination, firms use many different pricing strategies, depending on the nature of their products, the level of competition in their markets, and the characteristics of their customers. In this section, we consider three important strategies: odd pricing, cost-plus pricing, and two-part tariffs.

(3) LEARNING OBJECTIVE

Explain how some firms increase their profits through the use of odd pricing, cost-plus pricing, and two-part tariffs.

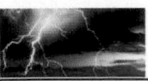
Don't Let This Happen To You!

Don't Confuse Price Discrimination with Other Types of Discrimination

Don't confuse price discrimination with discrimination based on race or gender. Discriminating on the basis of arbitrary characteristics, like race or gender, is illegal under the civil rights laws. Price discrimination is legal because it involves charging people different prices on the basis of their willingness to pay rather than on the basis of arbitrary characteristics. There is a gray area, however, when companies charge different prices on the basis of race or gender. For example, insurance companies usually charge women lower prices than men for automobile insurance. The courts have ruled that this is not illegal discrimination under the civil rights laws because women on average have better driving records than men. Because the costs of insuring men are higher than insuring women, insurance companies are allowed to charge them higher prices. Notice that this is not actually price discrimination as we have defined it here. Price discrimination involves charging different prices for the same product, *where the price differences are not due to differences in cost.*

Insurance companies have been less successful in defending the practice of charging blacks higher life insurance prices than whites. The insurance companies had claimed that this practice, which continued into the 1960s, was based on the shorter average life span of blacks. Even though most insurance companies stopped the practice in the 1960s for new policies, most companies continued to collect the higher prices on policies that were already in effect. When this became widely known, several state insurance commissions launched investigations. Eventually, most companies reimbursed policyholders for the higher prices and paid substantial fines to the government. MetLife, the largest publicly held life insurance company in the United States, paid $250 million to settle a lawsuit by policyholders and to pay fines imposed by the New York State Insurance Department.

YOUR TURN: Test your understanding by doing related problem 13 on page 496 at the end of this chapter.

Odd Pricing: Why Is the Price $2.99 Instead of $3.00?

Many firms use what is called *odd pricing*—that is, charging $4.95 instead of $5.00, or $199 instead of $200. Surveys show that 80 percent to 90 percent of the products sold in supermarkets have prices ending in "9" or "5" rather than "0." Odd pricing has a long history. In the early nineteenth century, most goods in the United States were sold in general stores, and prices were often determined by haggling, much as prices of new cars are often determined today by haggling on dealers' lots. Later in the nineteenth century, when most products began to sell for a fixed price, odd pricing became popular.

Different explanations have been given for the origin of odd pricing. One explanation is that it began because goods imported from Great Britain had a reputation for high quality. When the prices of British goods in British currency—the pound—were translated into U.S. dollars, the result was an odd price. Because customers connected odd prices with high-quality goods, even sellers of domestic goods charged odd prices. Another explanation is that odd pricing began as an attempt to guard against employee theft. An odd price forced an employee to give the customer change, which reduced the likelihood that the employee would simply pocket the customer's money without recording the sale.

Whatever the origins of odd pricing, why do firms still use it today? The most obvious answer is that an odd price, say $9.99, seems somehow significantly—more than a penny—cheaper than $10.00. But do consumers really have this illusion? To find out, three market researchers conducted a study. We saw in Chapter 3 that demand curves can be estimated statistically. If consumers have the illusion that $9.99 is significantly cheaper than $10.00, they will demand a greater quantity of goods at $9.99—and other odd prices—than the estimated demand curve predicts. The researchers surveyed consumers about their willingness to purchase six different products—ranging from a block of cheese to an electric blender—at a series of prices. Ten of the prices were either odd cent prices—99 cents or 95 cents—or odd dollar prices—$95 or $99. Nine of these 10 odd prices resulted in an odd-price effect, with the quantity demanded being greater than predicted using the estimated demand curve. The study was not conclusive because it relied on surveys rather than on observing actual purchasing behavior and because it used only a small group of products, but it does provide some evidence that using odd prices makes economic sense.

Why Do Firms Use Cost-Plus Pricing?

Many firms use *cost-plus pricing,* which involves adding a percentage *markup* to average cost. With this pricing strategy, the firm first calculates average cost at a particular level of production, usually equal to the firm's expected sales. It then increases average cost by a percentage amount, say 30 percent, to arrive at the price. For example, if average cost is $100 and the percentage markup is 30 percent, the price will be $130. In a firm selling multiple products, the markup is intended to cover all costs, including those that the firm cannot assign to any particular product. Most firms have costs that are difficult to assign to one particular product. For example, the work performed by the employees in McDonald's accounting and finance departments applies to all of McDonald's products and can't be assigned directly to Big Macs or Happy Meals.

Cost-Plus Pricing in the Publishing Industry

Book publishing companies incur substantial costs for editing, designing, marketing, and warehousing books. These costs are difficult to assign directly to any particular book. Most publishers arrive at a price for a book by applying a markup to their production costs, which are usually divided into plant costs and manufacturing costs. Plant costs include typesetting the manuscript and preparing graphics or artwork for printing. Manufacturing costs include the cost of printing, paper, and binding the book.

Consider the following example for the hypothetical new book by Adam Smith, *How to Succeed at Economics without Really Trying.* We will assume that the book is 250 pages long, the publisher expects to sell 5,000 copies, and plant and manufacturing costs are as given in the following table:

15-2 *Making*
the **Connection**

How do publishers determine the price of books?

PLANT COST

Typesetting	$3,500
Other plant costs	2,000

MANUFACTURING COST

Printing	$5,750
Paper	6,250
Binding	5,000

TOTAL PRODUCTION COST

	$22,500

With total production cost of $22,500 and production of 5,000 books, per unit production cost is $22,500/5,000 = $4.50. Many publishers multiply the unit production cost number by 7 or 8 to arrive at the retail price they will charge customers in bookstores. In this case, multiplying by 7 results in a price of $31.50 for the book. The markup seems quite high, but publishers typically sell books to bookstores at a 40 percent discount. Although a customer in a bookstore will pay $31.50 for the book—or less, of course, if it is purchased from a bookseller that discounts the retail price—the publisher receives only $18.90. The difference between the $18.90 received from the bookstore and the $4.50 production cost equals the cost of editing, marketing, warehousing, and all other costs, including the opportunity cost of the investment in the firm by its owners, plus any economic profit received by the owners.

Source: Beth Luey, *Handbook for Academic Authors,* 4th ed., New York: Cambridge University Press, 2002, Ch. 11.

A difficulty that firms face when using cost-plus pricing should be obvious to you. In this chapter, as in the previous four chapters, we have emphasized that firms maximize profit by producing the quantity where marginal revenue equals marginal cost and charging a price that will cause consumers to buy this quantity. The cost-plus approach doesn't appear to maximize profits, unless the cost-plus price turns out to be the same as the price that will cause the quantity sold to be where marginal revenue is equal to marginal cost. Economists have two views of cost-plus pricing. One is that cost-plus pricing is simply a mistake that firms should avoid. The other view is that cost-plus pricing is a good way to come close to the profit-maximizing price when either marginal revenue or marginal cost is difficult to calculate.

Small firms often like cost-plus pricing because it is easy to use. Unfortunately, these firms can fall into the trap of mechanically applying a cost-plus pricing rule, which can result in charging prices that do not maximize profits. The most obvious problems with cost-plus pricing are that it ignores demand and focuses on average cost, rather than marginal cost. If the firm's marginal cost is significantly different from its average cost at its current level of production, cost-plus pricing is unlikely to maximize profits.

Despite these problems, cost-plus pricing is used by some large firms, such as General Motors, that clearly have the knowledge and resources to devise a better method of pricing if cost-plus pricing fails to maximize profits. Economists conclude that cost-plus pricing may be the best way to determine the optimal price when:

1. Marginal cost and average cost are roughly equal.
2. The firm has difficulty estimating its demand curve.

In fact, most large firms that use cost-plus pricing do not just mechanically apply a markup to their estimate of average cost. Instead, they adjust the markup to reflect their best estimate of current demand. At General Motors, for example, a pricing policy committee adjusts prices to reflect its views of the current state of competition in the industry and the current state of the economy. If competition is strong in a weak economy, the pricing committee may decide to set price significantly below the cost-plus price—perhaps by offering buyers a rebate.

In general, firms that take demand into account will charge lower markups on products that are more price elastic and higher markups on products that are less elastic. Supermarkets, where cost-plus pricing is widely used, have markups in the 5 percent to 10 percent range for products with more elastic demand, such as soft drinks and breakfast cereals, and markups in the 50 percent range for products with less elastic demand, such as fresh fruits and vegetables.

Pricing with Two-Part Tariffs

Some firms can require consumers to pay an initial fee for the right to buy their product and an additional fee for each unit of the product purchased. For example, many golf and tennis clubs require members to buy an annual membership in addition to paying a fee each time they use the tennis court or golf course. Sam's Club requires consumers to pay a membership fee before shopping at its stores. Cellular phone companies charge a monthly fee and then have a per-minute charge after a certain number of minutes have been used. Economists refer to this situation as a **two-part tariff.**

Two-part tariff A situation in which consumers pay one price (or tariff) for the right to buy as much of a related good as they want at a second price.

The Walt Disney Company is in a position to use a two-part tariff by charging consumers for admission to Disney World or Disneyland and also charging them to use the rides in the parks. As mentioned at the beginning of this chapter, at one time the admission price to Disneyland was low, but people had to purchase tickets to go on the rides. Today, you must pay a high price for admission to Disneyland or Disney World, but the rides are free. Figure 15-5 helps us understand which of these pricing strategies is more profitable for Disney. The numbers in the figure are simplified to make the calculations easier.

Once visitors are inside the park, Disney is in the position of a monopolist—no other firm is operating rides in Disney World. So, we can draw panel (a) in Figure 15-5

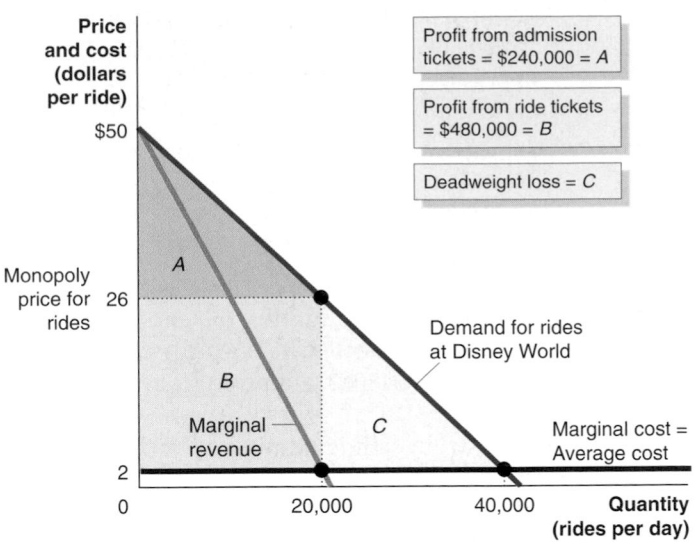

Price
and cost
(dollars
per ride)

$50

Monopoly
price for   26
rides

2
0   20,000   40,000   **Quantity**
                                                            (rides per day)

A

B

C

Marginal
revenue

Demand for rides
at Disney World

Marginal cost =
Average cost

Profit from admission
tickets = $240,000 = A

Profit from ride tickets
= $480,000 = B

Deadweight loss = C

(a) Disney s profit when charging the monopoly price

Price
and cost
(dollars
per ride)

$50

2
0   20,000   40,000   **Quantity**
                                                            (rides per day)

Profit from
admission tickets
= $960,000

Marginal
revenue

Demand for rides
at Disney World

Marginal cost =
Average cost

**(b) Disney s profit when charging the perfectly
competitive price**

FIGURE 15-5   A Two-Part Tariff at Disney World

In panel (a), Disney charges the monopoly price of $26 per ride ticket, and sells 20,000 ride tickets. Its profit from *ride tickets* is shown by the area of the light-green rectangle *B*, $480,000. If Disney is in the position of knowing every consumer's willingness to pay, it can also charge a price for *admission tickets* that would result in the total amount paid for admission tickets being equal to total consumer surplus from the rides. Total consumer surplus from the rides equals the area of the dark-green triangle *A*, or $240,000. So, when charging the monopoly price, Disney's total profit equals $480,000 + $240,000, or $720,000. In panel (b), Disney charges the perfectly competitive price of $2, where marginal revenue equals marginal cost, and sells 40,000 ride tickets. At the lower ride ticket price, Disney can charge a higher price for admission tickets, which will increase its total profits from operating the park to the area of the light-green triangle, or $960,000.

to represent the market for rides at Disney World. This graph looks like the standard monopoly graph from Chapter 14. (Note that the marginal cost of another rider is quite low. We can assume that it is a constant $2 and equal to the average cost.) It seems obvious—but it will turn out to be wrong!—that Disney should determine the profit-maximizing quantity of ride tickets by setting marginal revenue equal to marginal cost. In this case, that would lead to 20,000 ride tickets sold per day at a price of $26 per ride. Disney's profit from selling *ride tickets* is shown by the area of the light-green rectangle *B*. It equals the difference between the $26 price and the average cost of $2, multiplied by the 20,000 tickets sold, or ($26 − $2) × 20,000 = $480,000. Disney also has a second source of profit from selling *admission tickets* to the park. Given the $26 price for ride tickets, what price would Disney be able to charge for admission tickets?

Let's assume the following for simplicity: The only reason people want admission to Disney World is to go on the rides, all consumers have the same individual demand curve for rides, and Disney knows what this demand curve is. This last assumption puts Disney in the position of being able to practice perfect price discrimination. More realistic assumptions would make the outcome of the analysis somewhat different, but would not affect the main point of how Disney uses a two-part tariff to increase its profits. With these assumptions, we can use the concept of consumer surplus to calculate the maximum total amount consumers would be willing to pay for admission. Remember that consumer surplus is equal to the area below the demand curve and above the price line, shown by the dark-green triangle *A* in panel (a). It represents the benefit to buyers from consuming the product. In this case, consumers would not be willing to pay more for admission to the park than the consumer surplus they receive from the rides. In panel (a) of Figure 15-5 the total consumer surplus when Disney charges a price of $26 per ride is $240,000. (This number is easy to calculate if you remember that the formula for the area of a triangle is ½ × base × height, or ½ × 20,000 × $24.) Disney can set the price of admission tickets so that the *total* amount spent by buyers would be $240,000.

TABLE 15-2		MONOPOLY PRICE FOR RIDES	COMPETITIVE PRICE FOR RIDES
Profits per Day from Different Pricing Strategies at Disney World	Profits from admission tickets	$240,000	$960,000
	Profits from ride tickets	480,000	0
	Total profit	720,000	960,000

In other words, Disney can set the price of admission to capture the entire consumer surplus from the rides. So, Disney's total profit from Disney World would be the $240,000 it receives from admission tickets plus the $480,000 in profit from the rides, or $720,000 per day.

Is this the most profit Disney can earn from selling admission tickets and ride tickets? The answer is "no." The key to seeing why is to notice that *the lower the price Disney charges for ride tickets, the higher the price it can charge for admission tickets.* This result is true because lower-priced ride tickets increase consumer surplus from the rides and, therefore, increase the willingness of buyers to pay a higher price for admission tickets. In panel (b) of Figure 15-5, we assume that Disney acts as it would in a perfectly competitive market and charges a price for ride tickets that is equal to marginal cost, or $2. Charging this price increases consumer surplus—*and* the maximum total amount that Disney can charge for admission tickets—from $240,000 to $960,000. (Once again we use the formula for the area of a triangle to calculate the light-green area in panel (b): ½ × 40,000 × $48 = $960,000.) Disney's profits from the rides will decline to zero because it is now charging a price equal to average cost, *but its total profit from Disney World will rise from $720,000 per day to $960,000.* Table 15-2 summarizes this result.

What is the source of Disney's increased profit from charging a price equal to marginal cost? The answer is that Disney has converted what was deadweight loss when the monopoly price was charged—the area of triangle *C* in panel (a)—into consumer surplus. It then turns this consumer surplus into profit by increasing the price of admission tickets.

It is important to note the following about the outcome of a firm using an optimal two-part tariff:

1. Because price equals marginal cost at the level of output supplied, the outcome is economically efficient.

2. All of consumer surplus is transformed into profit.

Disney actually does follow the profit-maximizing strategy of charging a high price for admission to the park and a very low price—zero—for the rides. It seems that Disney could increase its profits by raising the price for the rides from zero to the marginal cost of the rides. But the marginal cost is so low that it would not be worth the expense of printing ride tickets and hiring additional workers to sell the tickets and collect them at each ride. Finally, note that because the demand curves of Disney's customers are not all the same, and because Disney does not actually know precisely what these demand curves are, Disney is not able to convert all of consumer surplus into profit.

Conclusion

Firms in perfectly competitive industries must sell their products at the market price. For firms in other industries—which means, of course, the vast majority of firms—pricing is an important part of the strategy used to maximize profits. We have seen in this chapter, for example, that if firms can successfully segment their customers into different groups on the basis of willingness to pay, they can increase their profits by charging different segments different prices.

Read *An Inside Look* on the next page to learn how increased attendance at Disneyland and Walt Disney World affected the revenue and profits of the Walt Disney Company in 2004.

WALL STREET JOURNAL, FEBRUARY 1, 2005

Disney's Profit Rises 5%, Lifted by TV and Parks

a Keeping its earnings comeback on track, Walt Disney Co. posted a 5% increase in net income for its fiscal first quarter, as strong gains in its cable-television networks and theme parks offset tough comparisons for its movie studio.

For the quarter ended Dec. 31, Disney posted net income of $723 million, or 35 cents a share, on revenue of $8.67 billion, driven by star performers such as its ESPN channel. That compares with a year-earlier profit of $688 million, or 33 cents a share, on revenue of $8.55 billion.

The quarter was helped by a one-cent-a-share benefit from a tax settlement and a one-cent-a-share benefit from a change in the reporting calendar. Still, the results beat the 29 cents a share forecast by a Thomson First Call consensus of analysts.

"As this quarter's earnings helped demonstrate, the broad-based improvement in our businesses continues as does our confidence in delivering ongoing growth this year and over the longer run," said Disney Chief Financial Officer Tom Staggs in a presentation on the results at the company's analyst conference in Orlando, Fla. Mr. Staggs stuck by the company's forecast for double-digit earnings growth through at least 2007.

Disney is coming off a boom year when it posted a 72% leap in per-share earnings on the back of a rebound in its television networks, beating a promised 50% gain for the period. Now the company must prove that its recovery is durable in the face of tougher comparisons this year.

The movie studio, for one, had a tough time in the just-completed quarter matching impressive 2004 first-quarter results. The studio's performance then was boosted by DVDs for blockbusters such as "Finding Nemo" and "Pirates of the Caribbean," as well as a special edition of "The Lion King." In this year's fiscal first quarter, revenue at the movie studio dropped 20% to $2.4 billion and operating earnings fell 27% to $333 million.

The television networks and parks showed solid gains, however. An advertising rebound helped the media networks to post the biggest profit, with operating earnings up 36% to $467 million and revenue increasing 11% to $3.5 billion.

ESPN profited from higher ad prices and fees, but broadcasting income actually fell $8 million, largely because of a decline at the ABC network. Despite ABC's much-trumpeted ratings recovery, Disney didn't see a big benefit from hits "Desperate Housewives" and "Lost" in the quarter because it sold ad time for lower prices last year when the network's ratings were weaker. Ad revenue for

those shows is expected to increase later in the year and help the network become profitable in 2005.

b After hurricanes in Florida hurt the parks and resorts unit in the fourth quarter of 2004, it delivered an 11% increase in operating earnings to $258 million, on revenue 30% higher at $2.1 billion. The improvement was credited in large part to an increase in visitors at Walt Disney World Resort, where visitors were up by mid-single-digit percentages.

On the West Coast, rainy weather kept attendance flat. Per-capita spending at the Disneyland Resort increased 12%, though. The Disneyland 50th anniversary celebrations are expected to give the parks a boost this year.

The sale of Disney Stores affected the consumer-products division, with revenue falling 14% to $725 million and operating earnings down 3% to $231 million. Mr. Staggs said Disney would ramp up investment in videogames over the next few quarters.

The results kicked off Disney's two-day analyst meeting, which last year was marked by an unsolicited takeover bid by cable operator Comcast Corp. hours before the start of the presentations. Since then, Disney has gone through the grinder, with Michael Eisner giving up his chairmanship and then announcing his retirement as chief executive after a shareholder revolt.

Key Points in the Article

This article discusses the effect of increased attendance at Disneyland and Walt Disney World on the revenue and profits of the Walt Disney Company. During the last quarter of 2004, profits—measured here as "operating earnings"—from Walt Disney World increased 11 percent from the same period in 2003. Attendance at the theme parks had declined following the terrorist attacks of September 11, 2001, and had been slow to recover during the following few years. By 2004, attendance was increasing as visitors were attracted by new rides introduced at the parks. International visitors had also been attracted by the relatively low value of the dollar, particularly in exchange for the euro and the British pound, which made theme park attendance less expensive in their domestic currencies.

Analyzing the News

a We saw in this chapter that in the early 1980s, Disney changed the pricing strategy it was using for admission to its theme parks. Previously, it had charged a low fee for admission to the parks and then also charged for each ride. It switched to charging a large fee for admission to the parks and eliminated the charge for the rides. As we discussed in the chapter, Disney had switched from charging the monopoly price for rides to charging the competitive price (which was effectively zero).

In Figure 1, Disney is charging the competitive price for rides. The increase in demand for rides is shown by the shift in the demand curve from Old Demand to New Demand. Price is unchanged, but the equilibrium quantity of rides increases from Q_1 to Q_2. The light green-shaded area shows the increase in economic profit that results from the increase in demand. Remember that Disney is able to charge a price for admission tickets that is high enough to allow the firm to convert the *entire* consumer surplus from the rides into economic profit. As a result, an increase in demand, such as occurred in 2004, can cause a large increase in Disney's profit from its theme parks. The other side of the coin is that a fall in demand, such as occurred following September 11, 2001, will cause a large decrease in profit. Not surprisingly, most newspaper articles like this one that report on the profits of the Disney Company discuss the effect of changes in profits from its theme parks.

b Figure 2 shows that if Disney were still charging the monopoly price for rides, the increase in profits following an increase in demand would be limited. In this case, the increase in demand raises the equilibrium price from P_1 to P_2, and the equilibrium quantity from Q_1 to Q_2. In the figure, the increase in profit is shown by the light-green-shaded area. The dark-green area represents potential profit that Disney would fail to gain if it charges the monopoly price instead of the competitive price.

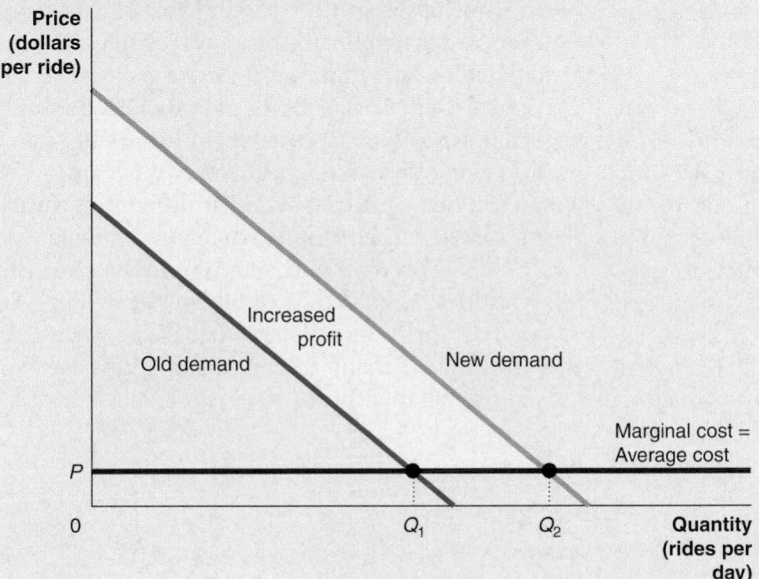

Figure 1: Disney's increase in profits when charging the competitive price.

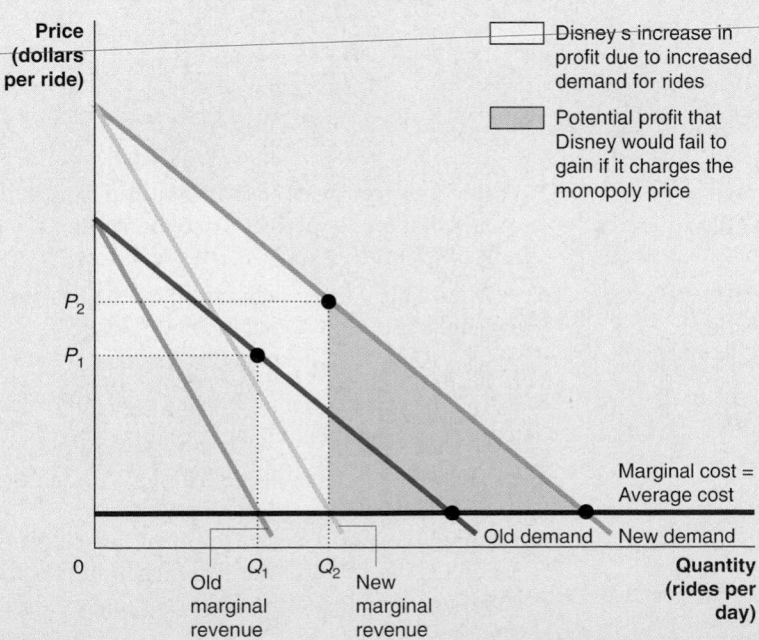

Figure 2: Disney's increase in profits when charging the monopoly price.

Thinking Critically
ABOUT POLICY

1. Suppose that courts began interpreting the Robinson-Patman Act broadly and banned all forms of price discrimination. How would this affect Disney's theme park business? Would this be good for Disney's customers and potential customers?
2. Suppose that on a visit to Orlando, a competitor of Disney's offers you a ticket that allows you to return to its park for free on the following day. Is this price discrimination? Why would the Disney competitor make such an offer?

Source: Wall Street Journal. Eastern Edition [Staff Produced Copy Only] by Merissa Marr. Copyright 2004 by Dow Jones & Co Inc. Reproduced with permission of Dow Jones & Co Inc in the format Textbook via Copyright Clearance Center.

SUMMARY

LEARNING OBJECTIVE ① Define the law of one price and explain the role of arbitrage. According to the *law of one price*, identical products should sell for the same price everywhere. If a product sells for different prices, it will be possible to make a profit through *arbitrage*: buying a product at a low price and reselling it at a high price. The law of one price will hold so long as arbitrage is possible. Arbitrage is sometimes blocked by high *transactions costs* or because the product cannot be resold. Another apparent exception to the law of one price occurs when companies offset the higher price they charge for a product by providing superior or more reliable service to customers.

LEARNING OBJECTIVE ② Explain how a firm can increase its profits through price discrimination. *Price discrimination* occurs if a firm charges different prices for the same product when the price differences are not due to differences in cost. Three requirements must be met for a firm to successfully price discriminate: (1) A firm must possess market power. (2) Some consumers must have a greater willingness to pay for the product than other consumers, and firms must be able to know what customers are willing to pay. (3) Firms must be able to divide up—or, segment—

the market for the product so that consumers who buy the product at a low price cannot resell it a high price. In the case of *perfect price discrimination*, each consumer pays a price equal to the consumer's willingness to pay.

LEARNING OBJECTIVE ③ Explain how some firms increase their profits through the use of odd pricing, cost-plus pricing, and two-part tariffs. In addition to price discrimination, firms also use odd pricing, cost-plus pricing, and two-part tariffs as pricing strategies. Firms use *odd pricing*—charging $1.99, rather than $2.00—because consumers tend to buy more at odd prices than would be predicted from estimated demand curves. With *cost-plus pricing*, firms set the price for a product by adding a percentage markup to average cost. Cost-plus pricing may be a good way to come close to the profit-maximizing price when marginal revenue or marginal cost is difficult to measure. Some firms can require consumers to pay an initial fee for the right to buy their product and an additional fee for each unit of the product purchased. Economists refer to this situation as a *two-part tariff*. Sam's Club, Walt Disney World, cell phone companies, and many golf and tennis clubs use two-part tariffs in pricing their products.

KEY TERMS

Price discrimination   478   Transactions costs   476   Two-part tariff   488

REVIEW QUESTIONS

1. What is the law of one price? What is arbitrage? Does a product always have to sell for the same price everywhere? Briefly explain.

2. What is price discrimination? Under what circumstances can a firm successfully practice price discrimination?

3. During a particular week, America West charged $218 for a round-trip ticket on a flight from New York to San Francisco, provided the ticket was purchased at least 10 days in advance and the ticket buyer was willing to stay over a Saturday night. If the buyer did not meet these conditions, the price for the ticket was $1,361. Why does America West use this pricing strategy?

4. What is yield management? Give an example of a firm using yield management to increase profits.

5. What is perfect price discrimination? Is it likely to ever occur? Explain. Is perfect price discrimination economically efficient? Explain.

6. Is it possible to price discriminate across time? Briefly explain.

7. What is odd pricing?

8. What is cost-plus pricing? Is using cost-plus pricing consistent with a firm maximizing profits?

9. Give an example of a firm using a two-part tariff as part of its pricing strategy.

10. Why did the Walt Disney Company switch from charging for admission to Disneyland and charging for the rides, to charging for admission and *not* charging for the rides?

PROBLEMS AND APPLICATIONS

Please visit **www.prenhall.com/hubbard** *for solutions to the even-numbered problems as well as multiple-choice and true or false self-assessment quizzes.*

1. **[Related to *Solved Problem 15-1*]** Suppose California has many apple trees and the price of apples is low. Nevada has few apple trees and the price of apples is high. Abner buys low-priced California apples and ships them to Nevada, where he resells them at a high price. Is Abner exploiting Nevada consumers by doing this? Is he likely to earn economic profits in the long run? Briefly explain.

2. **[Related to *Solved Problem 15-1*]** Suspicions of arbitrage have a long history. For example, Valerian of Cimiez, a Catholic bishop who lived during the fifth century, wrote, "[W]hen something is bought cheaply only so it can be retailed dearly, doing business always means cheating." What might Valerian think of eBay? Do you agree with his conclusion? Explain.
   Source for quote: Michael McCormick, *The Origins of the European Economy: Communications and Commerce, A.D. 300–900*, New York: Cambridge University Press, 2001, p. 85.

3. Can a firm in a perfectly competitive industry practice price discrimination? Briefly explain.

4. According to an article in the *Wall Street Journal*, the average price of Ford Explorers sold in Dallas, Texas, was $30,142. During the same period, the average price of identically equipped Explorers in Oklahoma was only $27,939. Briefly explain whether or not this is an example of price discrimination.
   Source: Karen Lundegaard, "How to Buy Your Next Car: First, Get a Plane Ticket," *Wall Street Journal*, April 30, 2002.

5. In a column in the *Wall Street Journal*, Walter Mossberg offered the following opinion:

   > There's a sucker in the software business today, and if you're in an average family with a couple of PCs, that sucker is you. . . . Families constitute the only significant customer group not getting a discount on [Microsoft] Office when upgrading multiple PCs. Big corporations, organizations and government agencies get a discount, called a "site license." College students get a discount. Small and medium-size businesses get a discount. But not families.

   Why might Microsoft charge families a higher price for Office than the other groups Mossberg mentions?
   Source: Walter Mossberg, "Microsoft Should Offer Families a Deal with Its Office Program," *Wall Street Journal*, July 18, 2002.

6. Sony will often sell electronic products at lower prices in the United States than in Japan. Does Sony consider the demand of U.S. consumers for these products to be more elastic or less elastic than the demand of Japanese consumers? Briefly explain.

7. An article in the *New York Times* observes that "On US Airways . . . a round-trip ticket between Washington and New Orleans could have been bought yesterday for as little as $198, while the cheapest unrestricted one-way fare was $638." Briefly discuss why this pricing strategy might be profit maximizing for US Airways.
   Source: Ian Ayers and Barry Nalebuff, "The Wrong Ticket to Ride," *New York Times*, March 24, 2004.

8. Political columnist Michael Kinsley writes, "The infuriating [airline] rules about Saturday night stayovers and so on are a crude alternative to administering truth serum and asking, 'So how much are you really willing to pay?'" Would a truth serum—or some other way of knowing how much people would be willing to pay for an airline ticket—really be all the airlines need to price discriminate? Briefly explain.
   Source: Michael Kinsley, "Consuming Gets More Complicated," *Slate*, November 21, 2001.

9. When a firm offers a rebate on a product, the buyer normally has to fill out a form and mail it in to receive a rebate check in the mail. A financial columnist argues:

   > When a manufacturer offers a rebate, you needn't be too suspicious. The manufacturer wants to lower the price temporarily (to move an old product or combat a competitor's new low price), but doesn't have faith that the retailer will pass on the savings.

   But suppose that a manufacturer wants to engage in price discrimination. Would offering rebates be a way of doing this? Briefly explain.
   Source: Carol Vinzant, "The Great Rebate Scam," *Slate*, June 10, 2003.

10. **[Related to the *Chapter Opener*]** Why does Walt Disney World charge a lower admission price for children aged three to nine than for adults? Why does it categorize a 10-year-old as an adult for this purpose? Why does it admit children under three for free? Why does it charge residents of Florida a lower price than residents of other states?

11. Are supermarket coupons a form of price discrimination? Briefly explain why or why not.

12. **[Related to *Solved Problem 15-2*]** Use the graphs on the next page to answer the following questions.
    a. If the firm wants to maximize profits, what price will it charge in Market 1, and what quantity will it sell?
    b. If the firm wants to maximize profits, what price will it charge in Market 2, and what quantity will it sell?

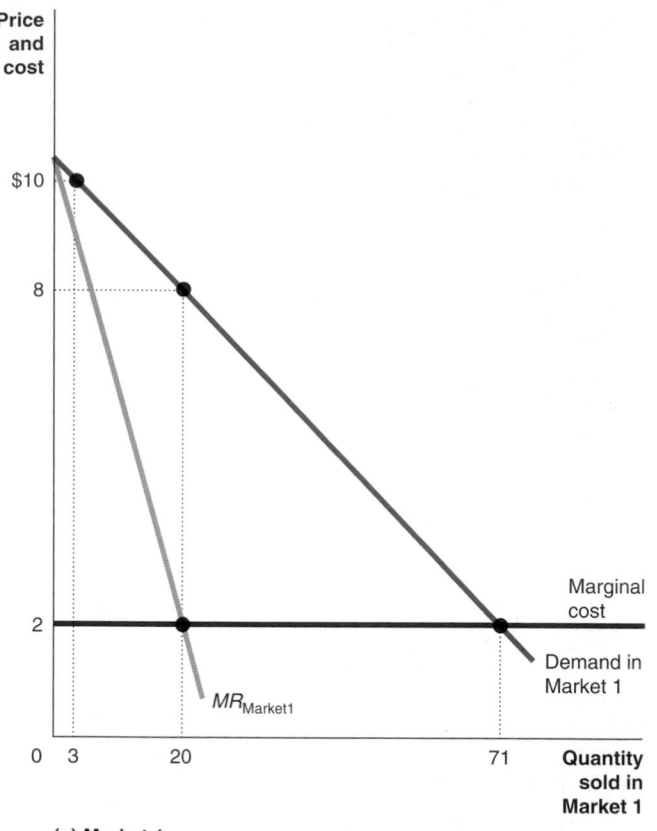

(a) Market 1

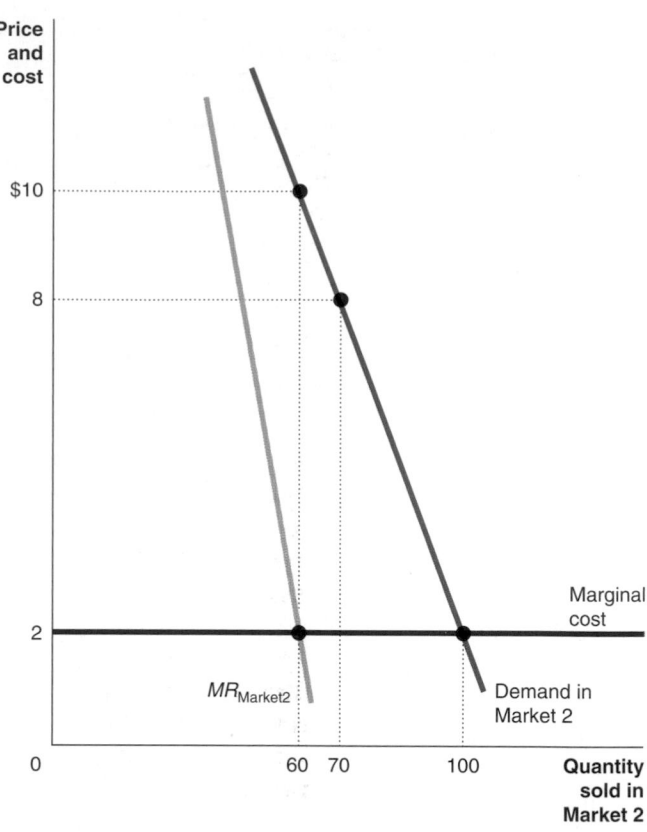

(b) Market 2

13. **[Related to *Don't Let This Happen To You!*]** Beginning in 2002, a state law in California made it illegal for businesses to charge men and women different prices for dry cleaning, laundry, tailoring, or hair grooming. The state legislator who proposed the law did so after a dry cleaner charged her more to have her shirts dry-cleaned than to have her husband's shirts dry-cleaned: "They charged me $1.50 for each of his, and he wears an extra large. They charged $3.50 for each of mine, and I wear a small." According to a newspaper article, "the dry cleaning proprietor told her that the price difference stemmed from the need for hand ironing her shirts because automatic presses are not made to handle small-sized women's garments."

   a. Was the dry cleaner practicing price discrimination, as defined in this chapter? Briefly explain.

   b. Do you support laws like this one? Briefly explain.

Source: Harry Brooks, "Law Mandates Equality in Dry Cleaning, Hair Styling," *North County* [California] *Times*, October 7, 2001.

14. Eric Orkin, the president of Opus 2 Revenue Technologies, Inc., which sells yield management systems to hotels, argues that, "The price-sensitive person gets what he wants as long as he's willing to have some flexibility." Why would a yield management system for hotels result in lower prices for "price-sensitive" customers than the alternative of charging

one price for all customers? Why would a price-sensitive person need to be "flexible" to receive a lower price?

Source: Neal Templin, "Property Report: Your Room Costs $250 . . . No! $200 . . . No . . . , " *Wall Street Journal*, May 5, 1999.

15. Draw a graph showing producer surplus, consumer surplus, and deadweight loss (if any) in a market where the seller practices perfect price discrimination. Profit-maximizing firms select an output at which marginal cost equals marginal revenue. Where is the marginal revenue curve in this graph?

16. One leading explanation for odd pricing is that it allows firms to trick buyers into the illusion that they're paying less than they really are. If this is true, in what types of markets and among what groups of consumers would you be mostly likely to find odd pricing? Should the government ban this practice and force companies to round up their prices to the nearest dollar?

17. Emerson Electric Company of St. Louis makes industrial equipment. Jerry Bernstein, the director of its price improvement team, describes how the company previously determined the prices of its products: "You developed a product, worked at the costs, and said, 'I need to make X [profit],' and you marked it up accordingly." Using this approach, Emerson arrived at a cost of $2,650 for a com-

pact sensor used in pharmaceutical factories. In recent years, Emerson has moved away from a policy of cost-plus pricing, so it ended up charging $3,150, rather than $2,650, for the sensor. Discuss the factors that would lead Emerson to charge a price higher than the cost-plus price.
Source: Timothy Aeppel, "Amid Weak Inflation, Firms Turn Creative to Boost Prices," *Wall Street Journal*, September 18, 2002.

18. Some professional sports teams charge fans a one-time, lump sum "personal seat license." The personal seat license allows fans the right to buy season tickets each year. No one without a personal seat license can buy season tickets. After the original purchase from the team, the personal seat licenses usually can be bought and sold by fans—whoever owns the seat license in a given year can buy season tickets—but the team does not earn any additional revenue from this buying and selling. Suppose a new sports stadium has been built and the team is trying to decide on the price to charge for season tickets.
   a. Will the team make more profit from the combination of selling personal seat licenses and season tickets if it keeps the prices of the season tickets low or if it charges the monopoly price? Briefly explain.
   b. After the first year, is the team's strategy for pricing season tickets likely to change?
   c. Will it matter for the team's pricing strategy for season tickets if all the personal seat licenses were sold in the first year?

19. Most teams in the National Football League sell all of the good seats in their stadiums to season ticket holders—people who agree to buy a ticket to every home game. Most teams require that to buy a season ticket, a buyer also must agree to buy tickets to the team's preseason games. The tickets for the preseason games usually have the same price as the tickets to the regular season games, even though most football fans have much more interest in regular season games than in preseason games. Why don't NFL teams adopt a strategy of charging lower prices for preseason games and higher prices for regular season games, rather than requiring season ticket holders to also purchase tickets—at the same price—to preseason games?

20. During the nineteenth century, the U.S. Congress encouraged railroad companies to build transcontinental railways across the Great Plains by giving them land grants. At that time, the federal government owned most of the land on the Great Plains. The land grants consisted of the land on which the railway was built and alternating sections of 1 square mile each on either side of the railway to a distance of 6 to 40 miles, depending on the location. The railroad companies were free to sell this land to farmers or anyone else who wanted to buy it. The process of selling the land took decades. Some economic historians have argued that the railroad companies charged lower prices to ship freight because they owned so much land along the tracks. Briefly explain the reasoning of these economic historians.

chapter sixteen

The Markets for Labor and Other Factors of Production

16

Why Are the New York Mets Paying Carlos Beltran a $17 Million Salary?

➤ Few businesses arouse in their customers the level of passion that sports teams do. Unlike most industries, the sports industry has an entire section devoted to it in most newspapers. Fred Wilpon made a fortune as a real estate developer with his firm Sterling Equities, and Jerry Jones made a fortune in the oil and gas exploration business in Oklahoma. But neither man was well-known to the general public until Wilpon bought the New York Mets baseball team and Jones bought the Dallas Cowboys football team. Of course, the best-known people in sports are not the owners of teams but some of their employees—the players.

Sports fans admire the skills of star athletes, but many are also fascinated by their high salaries. How is it, fans often wonder, that some athletes are paid salaries in the millions of dollars "just for playing a game"? Many baseball fans also wonder why a few teams, such as the New York Yankees, Boston Red Sox, and New York Mets, are able to pay higher salaries than other teams. For example, before the 2004 baseball season, the Kansas City Royals signed centerfielder Carlos Beltran to a contract that paid him a salary of $9 million for the season (in the middle of the 2004 season, he was traded to the Houston Astros). In 2005, Beltran signed a new contract to play

with the Mets for a salary of $17 million. Why are the New York Mets willing to pay Beltran almost twice as much as the Kansas City Royals? Fordham University in New York City pays professors on its faculty an average salary of $80,000. Why are the Mets willing to pay so much more to hire a baseball player than Fordham University is willing to pay to hire a professor?

The key to answering these questions is to understand that wages are determined in the labor market by the demand and supply of labor, just as the price of apples is determined by the demand and supply of apples and the price of DVDs is determined by the demand and supply of DVDs.

After studying this chapter, you should be able to:

① Explain how firms choose the profit-maximizing quantity of workers to employ.

② Explain how people choose the quantity of labor to supply.

③ Explain how equilibrium wages are determined in labor markets.

④ Use demand and supply analysis to explain how compensating differentials, discrimination, and labor unions cause wages to differ.

⑤ Discuss the role personnel economics can play in helping firms deal with human resources issues.

⑥ Show how equilibrium prices are determined in the markets for capital and natural resources.

In Chapter 3, we developed a model for analyzing the demand and supply of goods and services. We will use some of the same concepts in this chapter to analyze the demand and supply of labor and other factors of production. But there are important ways in which the markets for factors of production are not like markets for goods. The most obvious difference is that in factor markets, firms are demanders and households are suppliers. As we will see, this fact changes how we look at demand curves and supply curves in factor markets.

Another difference between the labor market and the markets for goods and services is that most

people accept the prices determined in the markets for apples or DVDs as "fair," but this is less often true of the labor market. When an athlete like Carlos Beltran signs a contract for millions of dollars, people often make comments like "Why should someone be paid so much for playing a game, when teachers, nurses, and other people doing more important jobs are paid so much less?" Because people typically earn most of their income from wages and salaries, they often view the labor market as being the most important market they participate in. *An Inside Look* on page 526 discusses the salaries of college football coaches.

Factors of production Labor, capital, natural resources, and other inputs used to produce goods and services.

➤ Firms use **factors of production**—such as labor, capital, and natural resources—to produce goods and services. For example, the New York Mets use labor (baseball players), capital (Shea Stadium), and natural resources (the land on which Shea Stadium sits) to produce baseball games. In this chapter, we will explore how firms choose the profit-maximizing quantity of labor and other factors of production. A firm's demand for factors of production is a *derived demand* because it is based on the underlying consumer demand for the good or service the factor is being used to produce. For example, the New York Mets' demand for baseball players is based on the underlying consumer demand for baseball games. The interaction between firm demand for labor and household supply of labor determines the equilibrium wage rate.

Because there are many different types of labor, there are many different labor markets. The equilibrium wage in the market for baseball players is much higher than the equilibrium wage in the market for college professors. We will explore why this is true. We will also explore how factors such as discrimination, unions, and compensation for dangerous or unpleasant jobs help explain differences among wages. We then look at *personnel economics,* which is concerned with how firms can use economic analysis to design their employee compensation plans. Finally, we also analyze the markets for other factors of production.

(1) **LEARNING OBJECTIVE**

Explain how firms choose the profit-maximizing quantity of workers to employ.

Derived demand The demand for a factor of production that is derived from the demand for the good the factor produces.

The Demand for Labor

Up until now we have concentrated on consumer demand for final goods and services. The demand for labor is different from the demand for final goods and services because it is a *derived demand*. A **derived demand** is the demand for a factor of production that is based on the demand for the good the factor produces. You demand a Sony television because of the utility you receive from watching television. Sony's demand for the labor to make televisions is derived from the underlying consumer demand for televisions. As a result, we can say that Sony's demand for labor depends primarily on two factors:

1. The additional televisions Sony will be able to produce if it hires one more worker.
2. The additional revenue Sony receives from selling the additional televisions.

The Marginal Revenue Product of Labor

Consider the following example. To keep the main point clear, let's assume that because we are in the short run, Sony can increase production of televisions only by increasing the quantity of labor it employs. The table in Figure 16-1 shows the relationship between the quantity of workers Sony hires, the quantity of televisions it produces, the additional revenue from selling the additional televisions, and the additional profit from hiring each additional worker.

For simplicity, we are keeping the scale of Sony's factory very small. We will also assume that Sony is a perfect competitor both in the market for selling televisions and in the market for hiring labor. This means that Sony is a *price taker* in both markets. Although this is not realistic, the basic analysis would not change if we assumed that Sony can affect the price of televisions and the wage paid to workers. Given these assumptions, suppose that Sony can sell as many televisions as it wants at a price of $200

Number of Workers	Output of Televisions per Week	Marginal Product of Labor (television sets per week)	Product Price	Marginal Revenue Product of Labor (dollars per week)	Wage (dollars per week)	Additional Profit from Hiring One More Worker (dollars per week)
L	Q	MP	P	MRP = P x MP	W	MRP – W
0	0	—	$200	—	$600	—
1	6	6	200	$1,200	600	$600
2	11	5	200	1,000	600	400
3	15	4	200	800	600	200
4	18	3	200	600	600	0
5	20	2	200	400	600	–200
6	21	1	200	200	600	–400

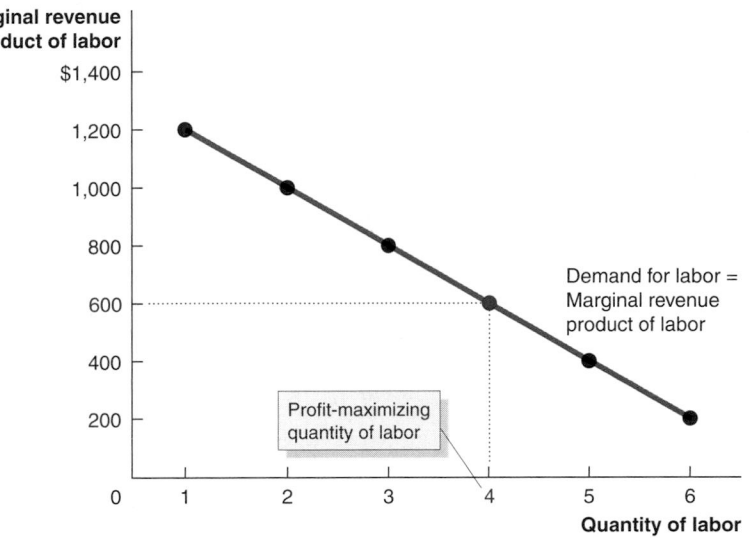

FIGURE 16-1

The Marginal Revenue Product of Labor and the Demand for Labor

The marginal revenue product of labor equals the marginal product of labor multiplied by the price of the good. The marginal revenue product curve slopes downward because diminishing returns causes the marginal product of labor to decline as more workers are hired. A firm maximizes profits by hiring workers up to the point where the wage equals the marginal revenue product of labor. The marginal revenue product of labor curve is the firm's demand curve for labor because it tells the firm the profit maximizing quantity of workers to hire at each wage. For example, using the demand curve shown in this figure, if the wage was $600, the firm will hire 4 workers.

and can hire as many workers as it wants at a wage of $600 per week. Remember from Chapter 10 that the additional output produced by a firm as a result of hiring another worker is called the **marginal product of labor.** In the table, we calculate the marginal product of labor as the change in total output as each additional worker is hired. As we saw in Chapter 10, because of *the law of diminishing returns,* the marginal product of labor declines as a firm hires more workers.

When deciding how many workers to hire, a firm is not interested in how much *output* will increase as it hires another worker but in how much *revenue* will increase as it hires another worker. In other words, what matters is how much the firm's revenue will rise when it sells the additional output it can produce by hiring one more worker. We can calculate this amount by multiplying the additional output produced by the product price. This amount is called the **marginal revenue product of labor (MRP).** For example, consider what happens if Sony increases the number of workers hired from 2 to 3. The table in Figure 16-1 shows that hiring the third worker allows Sony to increase its weekly output of televisions from 11 to 15, so the marginal product of labor is 4 televisions. The price of the televisions is $200, so the marginal revenue product of the third worker is 4 × $200, or $800. In other words, Sony adds $800 to its revenue as a result of hiring the third worker. In the graph, we plot the values of the marginal revenue product of labor at each quantity of labor.

To decide how many workers to hire, Sony must compare the additional revenue it earns from hiring another worker to the increase in its costs from paying that worker. The difference between the additional revenue and the additional cost is the additional profit (or loss) from hiring one more worker. This additional profit is shown in the last

Marginal product of labor   The additional output a firm produces as a result of hiring one more worker.

Marginal revenue product of labor (MRP)   The change in the firm's revenue as a result of hiring one more worker.

TABLE 16-1	WHEN...	THEN THE FIRM...
The Relationship between the Marginal Revenue Product of Labor and the Wage	MRP > W,	should hire more workers to increase profits.
	MRP < W,	should hire fewer workers to increase profits.
	MRP = W,	is hiring the optimal number of workers and is maximizing profits.

column of the table in Figure 16-1 and is calculated by subtracting the wage from the marginal revenue product of labor. As long as the marginal revenue product of labor is greater than the wage, Sony's profits are increasing and it should continue to hire more workers. When the marginal revenue product of labor is less than the wage, Sony's profits are falling and it should hire fewer workers. When the marginal revenue product of labor is equal to the wage, Sony has maximized its profits by hiring the optimal number of workers. The values in the table show that Sony should hire 4 workers. If it hires a fifth worker, the marginal revenue product of $400 will be less than the wage of $600, and its profits will fall by $200. Table 16-1 summarizes the relationship between the marginal revenue product of labor and the wage.

We can see from Figure 16-1 that if Sony has to pay a wage of $600 per week, it should hire 4 workers. If the wage were to rise to $1,000, then applying the rule that profits are maximized where the marginal revenue product of labor equals the wage, Sony should hire only 2 workers. Similarly, if the wage is only $400 per week, Sony should hire 5 workers. In fact, the marginal revenue product curve tells the firm how many workers it should hire at any wage rate. In other words, *the marginal revenue product of labor curve is the demand curve for labor.*

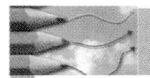

SOLVED PROBLEM   16-1

Hiring Decisions by a Firm That Is a Price Maker

We have assumed that Sony can sell as many televisions as it wants without having to cut the price. Recall from Chapter 11 that this is the case for firms in perfectly competitive markets. These firms are *price takers.* Suppose instead that a firm has market power and is a *price maker,* so that to increase sales it must reduce the price.

Suppose Sony faces the situation shown in the following table. Fill in the blanks and then determine the profit-maximizing number of workers for Sony to hire. Briefly explain why hiring this number of workers is profit-maximizing.

(1) QUANTITY OF LABOR	(2) OUTPUT OF TELEVISIONS PER WEEK	(3) MARGINAL PRODUCT OF LABOR	(4) PRODUCT PRICE	(5) TOTAL REVENUE	(6) MARGINAL REVENUE PRODUCT OF LABOR	(7) WAGE	(8) ADDITIONAL PROFIT FROM HIRING ONE ADDITIONAL WORKER
0	0	—	$200		—	$500	—
1	6	6	180			500	
2	11	5	160			500	
3	15	4	140			500	
4	18	3	120			500	
5	20	2	100			500	
6	21	1	80			500	

Solving the Problem:

Step 1: Review the chapter material. This problem is about determining the profit-maximizing quantity of labor for a firm to hire, so you may want to review the section "The Demand for Labor," which begins on page 500.

Step 2: Fill in the blanks in the table. As Sony hires more workers, it sells more televisions and earns more revenue. We can calculate how revenue increases by multiplying the number of televisions produced—shown in column 2—by the price—shown in column 4. Then we can calculate the marginal revenue product of labor as the change in revenue as each additional worker is hired. Finally, we can calculate the additional profit from hiring one more worker by subtracting the wage—shown in column 7—from each worker's marginal revenue product.

(1) QUANTITY OF LABOR	(2) OUTPUT OF TELEVISIONS PER WEEK	(3) MARGINAL PRODUCT OF LABOR	(4) PRODUCT PRICE	(5) TOTAL REVENUE	(6) MARGINAL REVENUE PRODUCT OF LABOR	(7) WAGE	(8) ADDITIONAL PROFIT FROM HIRING ONE ADDITIONAL WORKER
0	0	—	$200	$0	—	$500	—
1	6	6	180	1,080	$1,080	500	$580
2	11	5	160	1,760	680	500	180
3	15	4	140	2,100	340	500	−160
4	18	3	120	2,160	60	500	−440
5	20	2	100	2,000	−160	500	−660
6	21	1	80	1,680	−320	500	−820

Step 3: Use the information in the table to determine the profit-maximizing quantity of workers to hire. To determine the profit-maximizing quantity of workers to hire, we need to compare the marginal revenue product of labor with the wage. Column 8 does this by subtracting the wage from the marginal revenue product. As long as the values in column 8 are positive, the firm should continue to hire workers. The marginal revenue product of the second worker is $680 and the wage is $500, so column 8 shows that hiring the second worker will add $180 to Sony's profits. The marginal revenue product of the third worker is $340 and the wage is $500, so hiring the third worker would reduce Sony's profits by $160. Therefore, Sony will maximize profits by hiring 2 workers.

YOUR TURN: For more practice, do problem 22 on page 531 at the end of this chapter. Visit www.prenhall.com/hubbard for an interactive exercise related to this Solved Problem.

We can determine the market demand curve for labor in the same way we determine a market demand curve for a good. We saw in Chapter 3 that the market demand curve for a good is determined by adding up the quantity of the good demanded by each consumer at each price. Similarly, the market demand curve for labor is determined by adding up the quantity of labor demanded by each firm at each wage, holding constant all other variables that might affect the willingness of firms to hire workers.

Factors That Shift the Labor Demand Curve

In constructing the demand curve for labor, we held constant all variables that would affect the willingness of firms to demand labor—except for the wage. An increase or decrease in the wage causes *an increase or decrease in the quantity of labor demanded,* which we show by a movement along the demand curve. If any variable other than the wage changes, the result is *an increase or decrease in the demand for labor,* which we show by a shift of the demand curve. The five most important variables that cause the labor demand curve to shift are the following:

➤ *Increases in human capital.* **Human capital** represents the accumulated training and skills that workers possess. For example, workers with a college education generally have more skills and are more productive than workers who have only a high school diploma. If workers become more educated and are therefore able to produce more output per day, the demand for their services will increase, shifting the labor demand curve to the right.

➤ *Changes in technology.* As new and better machinery and equipment are developed, workers become more productive. This effect causes the labor demand curve to shift to the right over time.

➤ *Changes in the price of the product.* The marginal revenue product of labor depends on the price the firm receives for its output. A higher price increases the marginal revenue product and shifts the labor demand curve to the right. A lower price shifts the labor demand curve to the left.

➤ *Changes in the quantity of other inputs.* Workers are able to produce more if they have more machinery and other inputs available to them. The marginal product of labor in the United States is higher than the marginal product of labor in other countries in large part because U.S. firms provide workers with more machinery and equipment. Over time, workers in the United States have had increasing amounts of other inputs available to them, and that has increased their productivity and caused the demand for labor to shift to the right.

➤ *Changes in the number of firms in the market.* If new firms enter the market, the demand for labor will shift to the right. If firms exit the market, the demand for labor will shift to the left. This is similar to the effect that increasing or decreasing the number of consumers in a market has on the demand for a good.

The Supply of Labor

Having discussed the demand for labor, we can now consider the supply of labor. Of the many trade-offs each of us faces in life, one of the most important is how to divide up the 24 hours in the day between labor and leisure. Every hour spent watching television, walking on the beach, or in other forms of leisure is one less hour spent working. Because in devoting an hour to leisure we give up an hour's earnings from working, the *opportunity cost* of leisure is the wage. The higher the wage we could earn working, the higher the opportunity cost of leisure. Therefore, as the wage increases we will take less leisure and work more. This relationship explains why the labor supply curve for most people is upward-sloping, as Figure 16-2 shows.

Although we normally expect the labor supply curves for most individuals to be upward-sloping, it is possible that at very high wage levels the supply curve for an individual might be *backward-bending*, so that higher wages actually result in a *smaller* quantity of labor supplied, as shown in Figure 16-3. To understand why, recall the definitions of the *substitution effect* and the *income effect*, which we introduced in Chapter 3 and discussed more fully in Chapter 9. The substitution effect of a price change refers to the fact that an increase in price makes a good more expensive *relative* to other goods. In the case of a wage change, the substitution effect refers to the fact that an increase in the wage raises the opportunity cost of leisure and causes a worker to devote *more* time to working and less time to leisure.

The income effect of a price change refers to the change in the quantity demanded of a good that results from changes in consumer purchasing power as a result of a price change. For a normal good, the income effect leads to a larger quantity demanded. Because leisure is a normal good, the income effect of a wage change will cause a worker

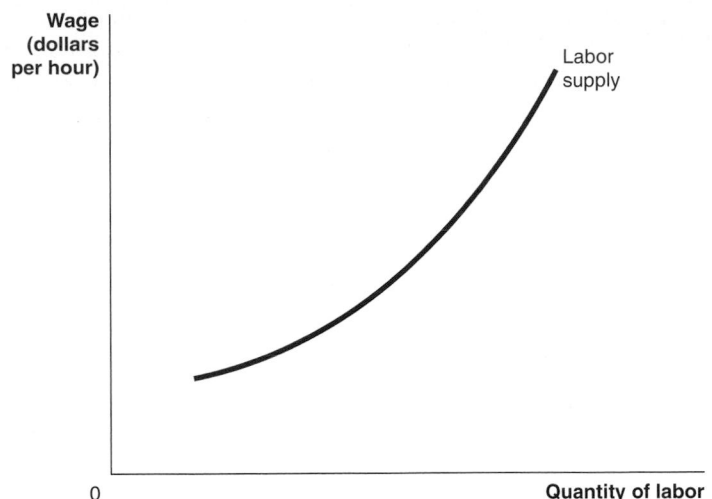

FIGURE 16-2

The Labor Supply Curve

As the wage increases, the opportunity cost of leisure increases, causing individuals to supply a greater quantity of labor. Therefore, the labor supply curve is upward-sloping.

to devote *less* time to working and more time to leisure. So, the substitution effect of a wage increase causes a worker to supply a larger quantity of labor, but the income effect causes a worker to supply a smaller quantity of labor. Whether a worker supplies more or less labor following a wage increase depends on whether the substitution effect is larger than the income effect. Figure 16-3 shows the typical case of the substitution effect being larger than the income effect at low levels of wages—so the worker supplies a larger quantity of labor as the wage rises—and the income effect being larger than the substitution effect at high levels of wages—so the worker supplies a smaller quantity of labor as the wage rises. For example, suppose an attorney has become quite successful and can charge clients very high fees. Or suppose a rock band has become very popular and receives a large payment for every concert it performs. In these cases, there is a high opportunity cost for the lawyer to turn down another client to take a longer vacation or for the band to turn down another concert. But because their incomes are already very high, they may decide to give up additional income for more leisure. For the lawyer or the rock band, the income effect is larger than the substitution effect, and a higher wage causes them to supply *less* labor.

We can determine the market labor supply curve in the same way we determine a market supply curve for a good. We saw in Chapter 3 that the market supply curve for a good is determined by adding up the quantity of the good supplied by each firm at

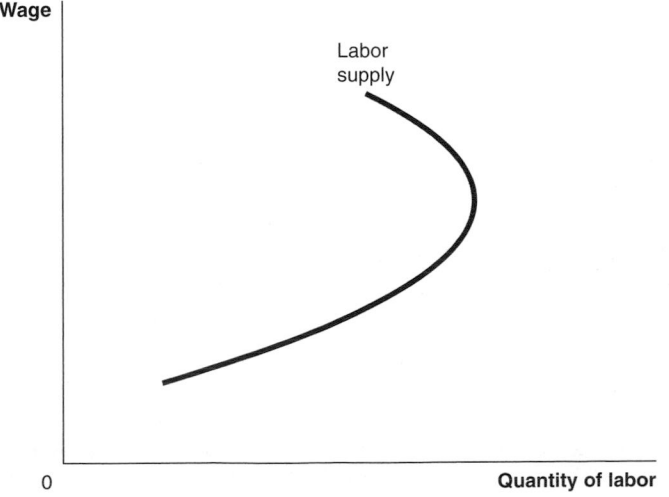

FIGURE 16-3

A Backward-Bending Labor Supply Curve

As the wage rises, a greater quantity of labor is usually supplied. As the wage climbs above a certain level, the individual is able to afford more leisure even though the opportunity cost of leisure is high. The result may be a smaller quantity of labor supplied.

each price. Similarly, the market labor supply curve is determined by adding up the quantity of labor supplied by each worker at each wage, holding constant all other variables that might affect the willingness of workers to supply labor.

Factors That Shift the Labor Supply Curve

In constructing the labor supply curve, we hold constant all other variables that would affect the willingness of workers to supply labor, except the wage. If any of these other variables change, the supply curve will shift. The three most important variables that cause the labor supply curve to shift are the following:

➤ *Increases in population.* As the population grows because of natural increase and immigration, the supply curve of labor will shift to the right. The effects of immigration on labor supply are largest in the markets for unskilled workers. In some large cities in the United States, for example, the majority of taxi drivers and workers in hotels and restaurants are immigrants. Some supporters of reducing immigration argue that wages in these jobs have been depressed by the increased supply of labor from immigrants.

➤ *Changing demographics.* *Demographics* refers to the composition of the population. The more people who are between the ages of 16 and 65, the greater the quantity of labor supplied. During the 1970s and 1980s, the U.S. labor force grew particularly rapidly as members of the baby boom generation—born between 1946 and 1964—first began working. In contrast, a low birth rate in Japan has resulted in an aging population. The number of working-age people in Japan actually began to decline during the 1990s, causing the labor supply curve to shift to the left.

A related demographic issue is the changing role of women in the labor force. In 1900, only 21 percent of women in the United States were in the labor force. By 1950, this had risen to 30 percent, and today it is 60 percent. This increase in the *labor force participation* of women has significantly increased the supply of labor in the United States.

➤ *Changing alternatives.* The labor supply in any particular labor market depends, in part, on the opportunities available in other labor markets. For example, the telecommunications industry bust in 2001 reduced the opportunities for optical engineers. Many workers left this market—causing the labor supply curve to shift to the left—and entered other markets, causing the labor supply curves to shift to the right in those markets. People who have lost jobs or who have low incomes are eligible for unemployment insurance and other payments from the government. The more generous these payments are, the less pressure unemployed workers have to quickly find another job. In many European countries, it is much easier than in the United States for unemployed workers to receive a greater replacement of their wage income from government payments. In one case that received widespread publicity, an unemployed German banker received payments of $2,400 per month from the German government to help pay for his apartment in Miami Beach in a gated community with a swimming pool and sauna. The banker's psychiatrist reportedly argued that the banker needed to remain in sunny Florida because the overcast weather in his hometown in Germany might worsen his depression. Although cases like this are extreme, many economists believe generous unemployment benefits help explain the higher unemployment rates experienced in Europe. For example, in the 10 years from 1995 to 2004, the average of the unemployment rates in the United Kingdom, France, Germany, Italy, and Spain was just under 10 percent, whereas in the United States the unemployment rate averaged just over 5 percent. There have been proposals in some European countries to reduce the size of these government payments with the hope of increasing the labor supply.

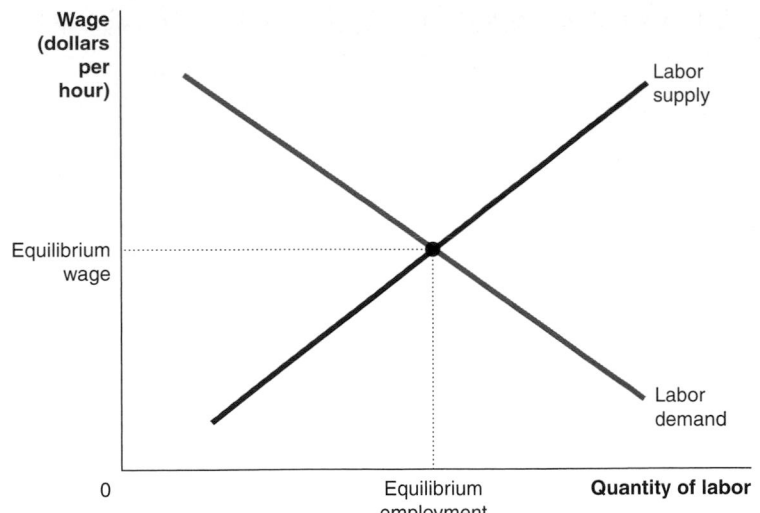

FIGURE 16-4

Equilibrium in the Labor Market

As in other markets, equilibrium in the labor market occurs where the demand curve for labor and the supply curve of labor intersect.

Equilibrium in the Labor Market

In Figure 16-4, we bring labor demand and labor supply together to determine equilibrium in the labor market. We can use demand and supply to analyze changes in the equilibrium wage and the level of employment for the entire labor market, or we can use it to analyze markets for different types of labor, such as baseball players or college professors.

(3) **LEARNING OBJECTIVE**

Explain how equilibrium wages are determined in labor markets.

The Effect on Equilibrium Wages of a Shift in Labor Demand

In many labor markets, increases over time in labor productivity will cause the demand for labor to increase. As Figure 16-5 shows, if labor supply is unchanged, an increase in labor demand will increase both the equilibrium wage and the number of workers employed.

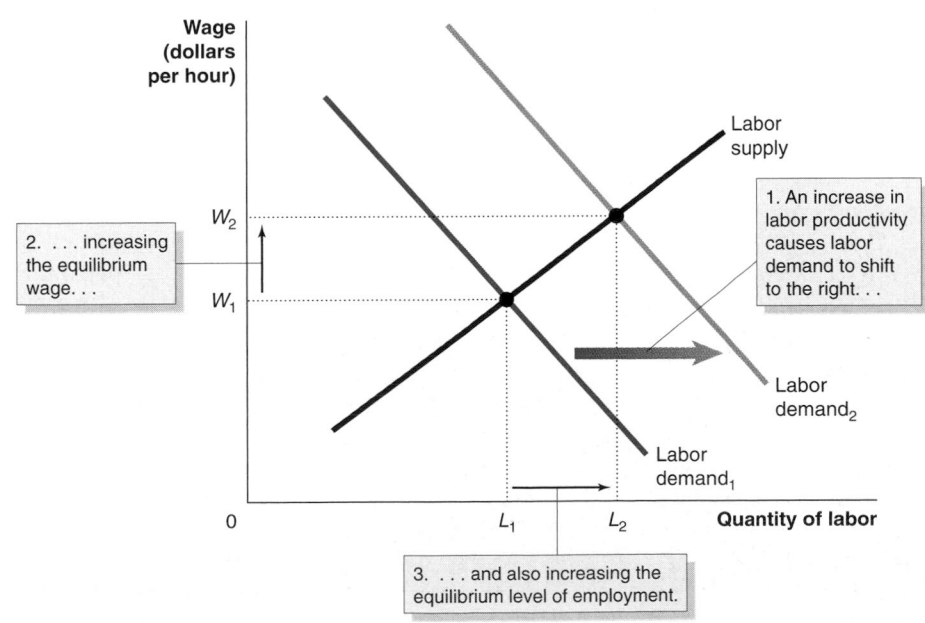

FIGURE 16-5

The Effect of an Increase in Labor Demand

Increases in labor demand will cause the equilibrium wage and the equilibrium level of employment to rise.
1. If the productivity of workers rises, the marginal revenue product increases, causing the labor demand curve to shift to the right.
2. The equilibrium wage rises from W_1 to W_2.
3. The equilibrium level of employment rises from L_1 to L_2.

16-1 *Making the Connection*

Will Your Future Income Depend on Which Courses You Take in College?

Most people realize the value of a college education. As the chart below shows, in 2005, full-time workers age 25 and over with a college degree earned more per week than other workers, including two and one-half times as much as high school dropouts.

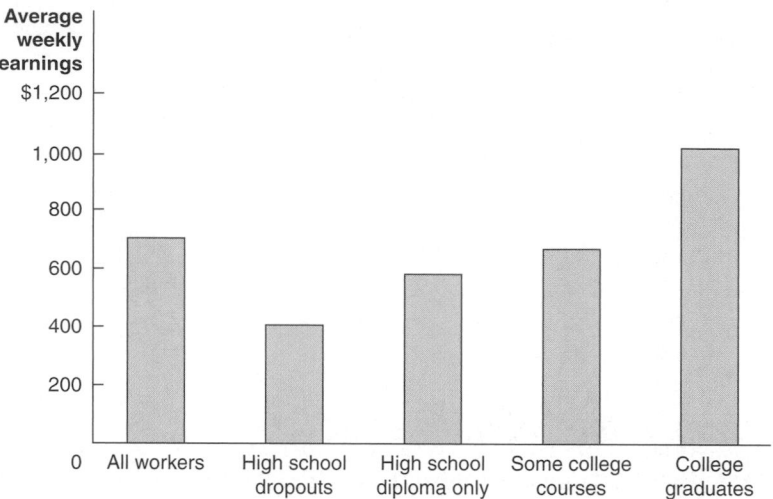

Source: U.S. Bureau of Labor Statistics, "Usual Weekly Earnings of Wage and Salary Workers," April 21, 2005.

Why do college graduates earn more? The obvious answer would seem to be that a college education provides skills that increase productivity. Some economists, though, advocate an alternative explanation known as the *signaling hypothesis,* first proposed by A. Michael Spence of Stanford University, winner of the Nobel Prize in Economics in 2001. This hypothesis is based on the idea that job applicants will always have more information than will potential employers about how productive the applicants are likely to be. Although employers attempt through job interviews and background checks to distinguish "good workers" from "bad workers," they are always looking for more information.

According to the signaling hypothesis, employers see a college education as a signal that workers possess certain desirable characteristics: self-discipline, the ability to meet deadlines, and the ability to make a sustained effort. Even if these characteristics are not related to the specifics of a particular job, employers value them because they usually lead to success in any activity. People generally believe that college graduates possess these characteristics, so employers often require a college degree for their best-paying jobs. In this view, the signal that a college education sends about a person's inherent characteristics—which the person presumably already possessed *before* entering college—is much more important than any skills the person may have learned in college. Or, as a college math professor of one of the authors put it (only half-jokingly), "The purpose of college is to show employers that you can do well something that's boring and hard."

Some recent economic studies have provided evidence that the higher

How does a college degree affect your future earnings?

incomes of college graduates reflect their greater productivity, not just the signal that a college degree sends to employers. Orley Ashenfelter and Cecilia Rouse of Princeton University have studied the relationship between schooling and income among 700 pairs of identical twins. Identical twins have identical genes, so differences in their inherent abilities should be relatively small. Therefore, if they have different numbers of years in school, the impact on their earnings should mainly reflect how their schooling has increased their productivity. Ashenfelter and Rouse found that identical twins had returns of about 9 percent per additional year of schooling, enough to account for most of the gap in income between high school graduates and college graduates.

Daniel Hamermesh and Stephen G. Donald of the University of Texas have studied the determinants of the earnings of college graduates 5 to 25 years after graduation. They collected extensive information on each person in their study, including the person's SAT scores, rank in high school class, grades in every college course taken, and college major. They discovered that, holding constant all other factors, business and engineering majors earned more than graduates with other majors. They also discovered a large impact on future earning of taking science and math courses: "A student who takes 15 credits of upper-division science and math courses and obtains a B average in them will earn about 10 percent more than an otherwise identical student in the same major . . . who takes no upper-division classes in these areas." This result held even after adjusting for a student's SAT score. The study by Hamermesh and Donald contradicts the signaling hypothesis, because if the signaling hypothesis is correct, the choice of courses taken in college should be of minor importance compared with the signal workers send to employers just by having completed college.

Sources: Orley Ashenfelter and Cecilia Rouse, "Income, Schooling, and Ability: Evidence from a New Sample of Identical Twins," *Quarterly Journal of Economics*, Vol. 113, No. 1 (February 1998), pp. 253–284; Daniel S. Hamermesh and Stephen G. Donald, "The Effect of College Curriculum on Earnings: Accounting for Non-Ignorable Non-Response Bias," National Bureau of Economic Research Working Paper 10809, September 2004.

The Effect on Equilibrium Wages of a Shift in Labor Supply

What is the effect on the equilibrium wage of an increase in labor supply due to population growth? As Figure 16-6 shows, if labor demand is unchanged, an increase in labor supply will decrease the equilibrium wage but increase the number of workers employed.

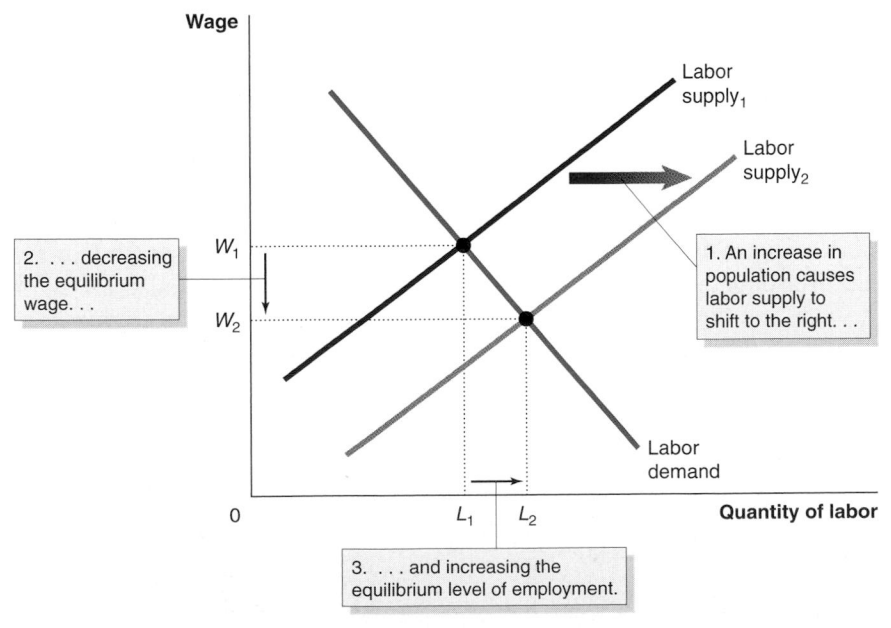

FIGURE 16-6

The Effect of an Increase in Labor Supply

Increases in labor supply will cause the equilibrium wage to fall, but the equilibrium level of employment to rise.

1. As population increases, the labor supply curve shifts to the right.
2. The equilibrium wage falls from W_1 to W_2.
3. The equilibrium level of employment increases from L_1 to L_2.

Whether the wage rises in a market depends on whether demand increases faster than supply. For example, after the success of Walt Disney's animated film *The Lion King* in 1994, most movie studios increased production of animated films, increasing the demand for animators much faster than the supply of animators was increasing. The annual salary for a top animator rose from about $125,000 in 1994 to $550,000 in 1999. These high salaries led more people with artistic ability to choose to get training as film animators, causing the supply of animators to increase after 1999. Several of the animated films released between 1999 and 2001 failed to earn a profit, which caused some companies to stop making these films, thereby decreasing the demand for animators. The decrease in demand for animators and the increase in supply caused the salaries of top animators to fall from $550,000 in 1999 to $225,000 in 2002.

16-2 *Making* the *Connection*

Why Didn't the Great Immigration Waves of the Early Twentieth Century Cause Wages to Fall?

In the early twentieth century, wages rose as technological change increased the demand for labor enough to offset the increase in labor supply resulting from immigration.

Between 1900 and the outbreak of World War I in 1914, about 13.4 million immigrants arrived in the United States. Relative to the U.S. population—which was about 76 million in 1900—this was the largest wave of immigration in the history of the world. Many commentators at the time predicted that this great increase in the U.S. labor supply would cause a sharp fall in wages. Figure 16-6 shows that this is a reasonable prediction of the effect of an increase in labor supply on the equilibrium wage, *but only if the demand for labor remains unchanged.* In fact, the demand for labor increased rapidly during these years as technological progress, such as electrification and the development of mass production techniques, increased the productivity of labor.

As a result, the demand for labor shifted to the right faster than the supply of labor, and wages rose. The following figure shows the situation in manufacturing. Both demand and supply increased, but because the shift in demand was greater than the shift in supply, average hourly earnings rose from less than $0.18 in 1900 to $0.22 in 1914, or by almost 25 percent (the data for both years use 1914 prices to correct for the effects of inflation). During the same years, employment in manufacturing rose from about 5.5 million workers to almost 9 million.

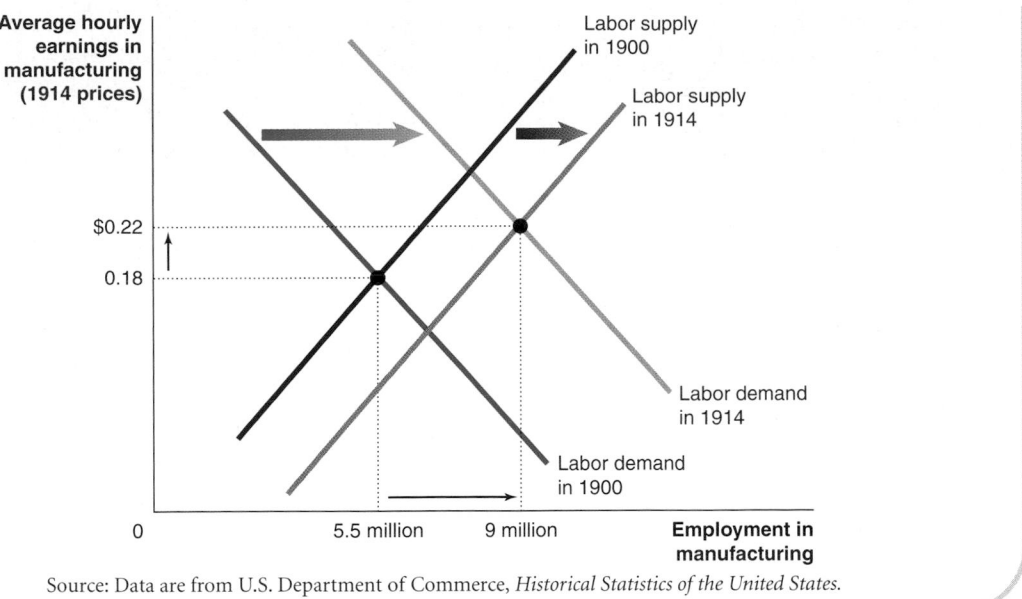

Source: Data are from U.S. Department of Commerce, *Historical Statistics of the United States.*

Explaining Differences in Wages

A key conclusion of our discussion of the labor market is that the equilibrium wage equals the marginal revenue product of labor. The more productive workers are and the higher the price workers' output can be sold for, the higher the wages workers will receive. At the beginning of the chapter, we raised the question of why major league baseball players are paid so much more than college professors. We are now in a position to use demand and supply analysis to answer this question. Figure 16-7 shows the demand and supply curves for major league baseball players and the demand and supply curves for college professors.

④ **LEARNING OBJECTIVE**
Use demand and supply analysis to explain how compensating differentials, discrimination, and labor unions cause wages to differ.

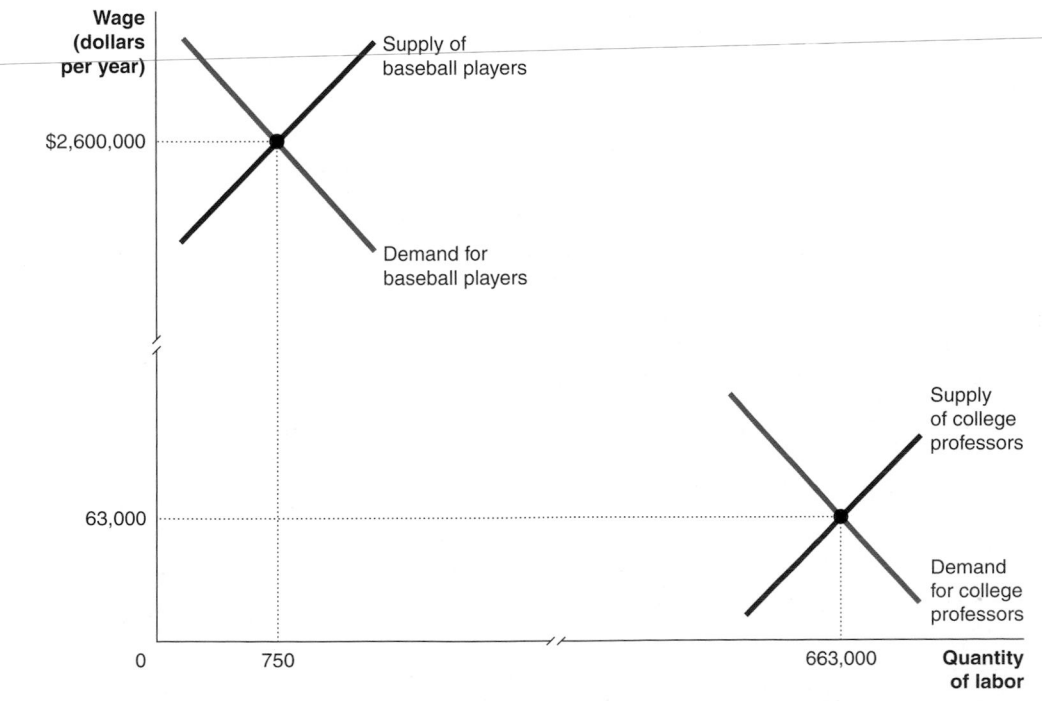

FIGURE 16-7

Baseball Players Are Paid More Than College Professors

The marginal revenue product of baseball players is very high and the supply of people with the ability to play major league baseball is low. The result is that the 750 major league baseball players receive an average wage of $2,600,000. The marginal revenue product of college professors is much lower, and the supply of people with the ability to be college professors is much higher. The result is that the 663,000 college professors in the United States receive an average wage of $63,000, far below that of baseball players.

Consider first the marginal revenue product of baseball players, which is the additional revenue a team owner will receive from hiring one more player. Baseball players are hired to produce baseball games that are then sold to fans who pay admission to baseball stadiums and to radio and television stations that broadcast the games. Because a major league baseball team can sell each baseball game for a large amount, the marginal revenue product of baseball players is high. The supply of people with the ability to play major league baseball is also very limited. As a result, the average annual salary of the 750 major league baseball players is about $2,600,000.

The marginal revenue product of college professors is much lower than for baseball players. College professors are hired to produce college educations that are then sold to students and their parents. Although one year's college tuition is quite high at many colleges, hiring one more professor allows a college to admit at most a few more students. So, the marginal revenue product of a college professor is much lower than the marginal revenue product of a baseball player. There are also many more people who possess the skills to be a college professor than possess the skills to be a major league baseball player. As a result, the country's 663,000 college professors are paid an average salary of about $63,000.

This still leaves unanswered the question raised at the beginning of this chapter: Why are the New York Mets willing to pay Carlos Beltran more than the Kansas City Royals were? Beltran's marginal product—which we can think of as the extra games a team will win by employing him—should be about the same in New York as it was in Kansas City. But his *marginal revenue product* will be much higher in New York. Because the population of the New York metropolitan area is much greater than the population of the Kansas City metropolitan area, winning more games will result in a greater increase in attendance at New York Mets games than it would at Kansas City Royals games. It will also result in a greater increase in viewers for Mets games on television. Therefore, the Mets are able to sell the extra wins that Beltran produces for much more than the Kansas City Royals can. This difference explains why the Mets were willing to pay Beltran $17 million per year, when he had made "only" $9 million with the Royals.

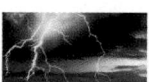

Don't Let This Happen To You!

Remember That Prices and Wages Are Determined at the Margin

You have probably heard some variation of the following remark: "We could live without baseball, but we can't live without the garbage being hauled away. In a more rational world, garbage collectors would be paid more than baseball players." This remark seems logical: The total value to society of having the garbage hauled away certainly is greater than the total value of baseball games. But wages—like prices—do not depend on total value, but on *marginal* value. The *additional* baseball games the Mets expect to win by signing Carlos Beltran will result in millions of dollars in increased revenue. The supply of people with the ability to play major league baseball is very limited. The supply of people with the ability to be trash haulers is much greater. If a trash-hauling firm hires another worker, the *additional* trash-hauling services it can now offer will

bring in a much smaller amount of revenue. The *total* value of baseball games and the *total* value of trash hauling are not relevant in determining the relative salaries of baseball players and garbage collectors.

This point is related to the diamond and water paradox first noted by Adam Smith. On the one hand, water is very valuable—we literally couldn't live without it—but its price is very low. On the other hand, apart from a few industrial uses, diamonds are used only for jewelry, yet their prices are quite high. We resolve the paradox by noting that the price of water is low because the supply is very large and the additional benefit consumers receive from the last gallon purchased is low. The price of diamonds is high because the supply is very small, and the additional benefit consumers receive from the last diamond purchased is high.

YOUR TURN: Test your understanding by doing related problem 10 on page 530 at the end of this chapter.

Technology and the Earnings of "Superstars"

The gap between Carlos Beltran's salary and the salary of the lowest-paid baseball players is much greater than the gap between the salaries paid during the 1950s and 1960s to top players such as Mickey Mantle and Willie Mays and the salaries of the lowest-paid players. Similarly, the gap between the $20 million Julia Roberts is paid to star in a movie and the salary paid to an actor in a minor role is much greater than the gap between the salaries paid during the 1930s and 1940s to stars such as Clark Gable and Cary Grant and the salaries paid to bit players. In fact, in most areas of sports and entertainment the highest-paid performers—the "superstars"—now have much higher incomes relative to other members of their professions than was true a few decades ago.

The increase in the relative incomes of superstars is mainly due to technological advances. The spread of cable television has increased the number of potential viewers of Mets games, but many of those viewers will watch only if the Mets are winning. This increases the value to the Mets of winning games and, therefore, increases Beltran's marginal revenue product and the salary he can earn.

With DVDs, Internet streaming video, and pay-for-view cable, the value to movie studios of producing a hit movie has risen greatly. Not surprisingly, the movie studios have also increased their willingness to pay large salaries to stars like Julia Roberts or Tom Cruise who they think will significantly raise the chances of a film being successful.

This process has been going on for a long time. For instance, before the invention of the motion picture, anyone who wanted to see a play had to attend the theater and see a live performance. Limits on the number of people who could see the best actors and actresses perform created an opportunity for many more people to succeed in the acting profession, and the gap between the salaries earned by the best actors and the salaries earned by average actors was relatively small. Today, when a hit movie starring Julia Roberts appears on DVD, millions of people will buy or rent it, and they will not be forced to spend money to see a lesser actress, as their great-great-grandparents might have been.

*16-3 Making
the Connection*

Why does Julia Roberts earn more today relative to the typical actor than stars did in the 1940s?

Compensating Differentials

Differences in marginal revenue products are the most important factor in explaining differences in wages, but they are not the whole story. To provide a more complete explanation for differences in wages, we must take into account three important aspects of labor markets: compensating differentials, discrimination, and labor unions. We begin with compensating differentials.

Suppose Paul runs a video rental store and acquires a reputation for being a bad boss who yells at his workers and is generally unpleasant. Two blocks away Brendan also runs a video rental store, but Brendan is always very polite to his workers. We would expect in these circumstances that Paul will have to pay a higher wage than Brendan to attract and retain workers. Higher wages that compensate workers for unpleasant aspects of a job are called **compensating differentials.**

If working in a dynamite factory requires the same degree of training and education as working in a semiconductor factory, but is much more dangerous, a larger number of workers will want to work making semiconductors than will want to work making dynamite. As a consequence, the wages of dynamite workers will be higher than the wages of semiconductor workers. We can think of the difference in wages as being the price of risk. As each worker decides on his or her willingness to assume risk and decides how much the higher wage must be to compensate for assuming more risk, wages will adjust so that dynamite factories will end up paying wages that are just high enough to compensate workers who choose to work there for the extra risk they assume. Only when workers in dynamite factories have been fully compensated with higher wages for the additional risk they assume will dynamite companies be able to attract enough workers.

Compensating differentials Higher wages that compensate workers for unpleasant aspects of a job.

Is Job Safety Legislation Good for Workers?

One surprising implication of compensating differentials is that *laws protecting the health and safety of workers may not make workers better off.* To see this, suppose that dynamite factories pay wages of $25 per hour and semiconductor factories pay wages of $20 per hour, with the $5 difference in wages being a compensating differential for the greater risk of working in a dynamite factory. Suppose that the government passes a law regulating the manufacture of dynamite in order to improve safety in dynamite factories. As a result of this law, dynamite factories are no longer any more dangerous than semiconductor factories. Once this happens, the wages in dynamite factories will decline to $20 per hour, the same as in semiconductor factories. Are workers in dynamite factories any better or worse off? Before the law was passed their wages were $25 per hour, but $5 per hour was a compensating differential for the extra risk they were exposed to. Now their wages are only $20 per hour, but the extra risk has been eliminated. The conclusion seems to be that dynamite workers are no better off as a result of the safety legislation.

This conclusion is only true, though, if the compensating differential actually does compensate workers fully for the additional risk. George Akerlof of the University of California, Berkeley and William Dickens of the Brookings Institution have argued that the psychological principle known as *cognitive dissonance* might cause workers to underestimate the true risk of their jobs. According to this principle, people prefer to think of themselves as intelligent and rational and tend to reject evidence that seems to contradict this image. Because working in a very hazardous job may seem irrational, workers in such jobs may refuse to believe that the jobs really are hazardous. Akerlof and Dickens present evidence that workers in chemical plants producing benzene and workers in nuclear power plants underestimate the hazards of their jobs. If this is true, the wages of these workers will not be high enough to compensate them fully for the risk they have assumed. So, in this situation, safety legislation may make workers better off.

Discrimination

Table 16-2 shows that in the United States white males on average earn more than other groups. One possible explanation for this is **economic discrimination,** which involves paying a person a lower wage or excluding a person from an occupation on the basis of an irrelevant characteristic such as race or gender.

Economic discrimination Paying a person a lower wage or excluding a person from an occupation on the basis of an irrelevant characteristic such as race or gender.

TABLE 16-2

Why Do White Males Earn More Than Other Groups?

GROUP	ANNUAL EARNINGS
White males	$41,367
Black males	32,026
White females	31,329
Black females	27,072
Hispanic males	26,014
Hispanic females	22,449

Note: The values are median annual earnings for persons who worked full-time, year-round in 2003. Persons of Hispanic origin can be of any race.

Source: U.S. Bureau of the Census, *Income, Poverty and Health Insurance in the United States: 2003,* Table PINC-10, August 2004. http://pubdb3.census.gov/macro/032004/perinc/new10_000.htm.

If employers discriminate by hiring only white males for high-paying jobs or by paying white males higher wages than other groups working the same jobs, white males would have higher earnings, as Table 16-2 shows. However, excluding groups from certain jobs or paying one group more than another is illegal in the United States since the passage of the Equal Pay Act of 1963 and the Civil Rights Act of 1964. Nevertheless, it is possible that employers are ignoring the law and practicing economic discrimination.

IS IT DISCRIMINATION OR OTHER FACTORS? Most economists, however, believe that only a small amount of the gap between the wages of white males and the wages of other groups is due to discrimination. Instead, most of the gap is explained by three main factors:

1. Differences in education
2. Differences in experience
3. Differing preferences for jobs

DIFFERENCES IN EDUCATION Some of the difference between the incomes of whites and the incomes of blacks can be explained by differences in education. Historically, African Americans have had less schooling than whites. Although the gap has closed significantly over the years, 90 percent of adult non-Hispanic white males in 2004 had graduated from high school, but only 81 percent of adult African American males had. Whereas 33 percent of white males had graduated from college, only 17 percent of African American males had. These statistics understate the true gap in education between blacks and whites because many blacks receive a substandard education in inner-city schools. Not surprisingly, studies have shown that differing levels of education can account for a significant part of the gap between the earnings of white and black males.

DIFFERENCES IN EXPERIENCE Women are much more likely than men to leave their jobs for a period of time after having a child. Women with several children will sometimes have several interruptions in their careers. Some women leave the workforce for several years until their children are of school age. As a result, women with children, on average, have less workforce experience than men of the same age. Because workers with greater experience are, on average, more productive, the difference in levels of experience helps to explain some of the difference in earnings between men and women. One indication of this is that, on average, married women earn about 39 percent less than married men, but women who have never been married—and whose careers are less likely to have been interrupted—earn only about 10 percent less than men who have never been married.

DIFFERING PREFERENCES FOR JOBS Significant differences exist between the types of jobs held by women and men. As Table 16-3 shows, women are overrepresented in some jobs where average weekly earnings are less than $500 per week, and men are overrepresented in some jobs where weekly earnings are greater than $700 per week.

 Although the patterns shown in Table 16-3 could be explained by women being excluded from some occupations, it is likely that they reflect differences in job preferences between men and women. For example, because many women interrupt their careers—at least briefly—when their children are born, they are more likely to take jobs where work experience is less important. Women may also be more likely to take jobs, such as teaching, that allow them to be home in the afternoons when their children return from school.

TABLE 16-3

"Men's Jobs" Often Pay More Than "Women's Jobs"

"WOMEN'S JOBS"			"MEN'S JOBS"		
OCCUPATION	WEEKLY EARNINGS	PERCENTAGE OF WORKERS WHO ARE WOMEN	OCCUPATION	WEEKLY EARNINGS	PERCENTAGE OF WORKERS WHO ARE WOMEN
Preschool and kindergarten teachers	$494	98.3%	Electricians	$748	2.1%
Childcare workers	330	95.2	Aircraft mechanics	821	2.5
Receptionists	449	93.2	Firefighters	816	2.6
Hairdressers	390	93.2	Airline pilots	1,350	4.4
Dental assistants	492	92.9	Aerospace engineers	1,362	9.6
Teacher assistants	351	90.9	Civil engineers	1,150	10.2
Nursing aides	377	89.0	Engineering managers	1,484	10.4
Maids and housekeeping cleaners	323	84.6	Computer software engineers	1,242	22.3
Cashiers	319	75.4	Chief executives	1,558	23.5

Note: Earnings are for both men and women in the occupation and are "median usual weekly earnings of full-time wage and salary workers."

Source: U.S. Department of Labor, Bureau of Labor Statistics, *Highlights of Women's Earnings in 2003,* Report 978, September 2004, Table 2.

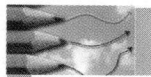

SOLVED PROBLEM 16-2

(4) LEARNING OBJECTIVE

Use demand and supply analysis to explain how compensating differentials, discrimination, and labor unions cause wages to differ.

Is "Comparable Worth" Legislation the Answer to Closing the Gap between Men's and Women's Pay?

As we have seen, either because of discrimination or differing preferences, certain jobs are filled primarily by men and other jobs are filled primarily by women. On average, the "men's jobs" have higher wages than the "women's jobs." Some observers have argued that many "men's jobs" are more highly paid than "women's jobs" despite the jobs being comparable in terms of the education and skills required and the working conditions involved. These observers have argued that the earnings gap between men and women could be closed at least partially if the government required that employers paid the same wages for jobs that have *comparable worth*. Many economists are skeptical of these proposals because they believe allowing markets to determine wages results in a more efficient outcome.

Suppose that electricians are currently being paid a market equilibrium wage of $700 per week and dental technicians are being paid a market equilibrium wage of $400 per week. Comparable worth legislation is passed and a study finds that an electrician and a dental technician are comparable jobs, so employers will now be required to pay workers in both jobs $550 per week. Analyze the effects of this requirement on the market for electricians and on the market for dental technicians. Be sure to use demand and supply graphs.

Solving the Problem:
Step 1: Review the chapter material. This problem is about economic discrimination, so you may want to review the section "Discrimination," which begins on page 514.

Step 2: Draw the graphs. We saw in Chapter 4 that when the government sets the price in a market, the result is a surplus or a shortage, depending on whether the government-mandated price is above or below the competitive market equilibrium. A wage of $550 per week is below the market wage for electricians and above the market wage for dental technicians. Therefore, we expect the requirement to result in a shortage of electricians and a surplus of dental technicians.

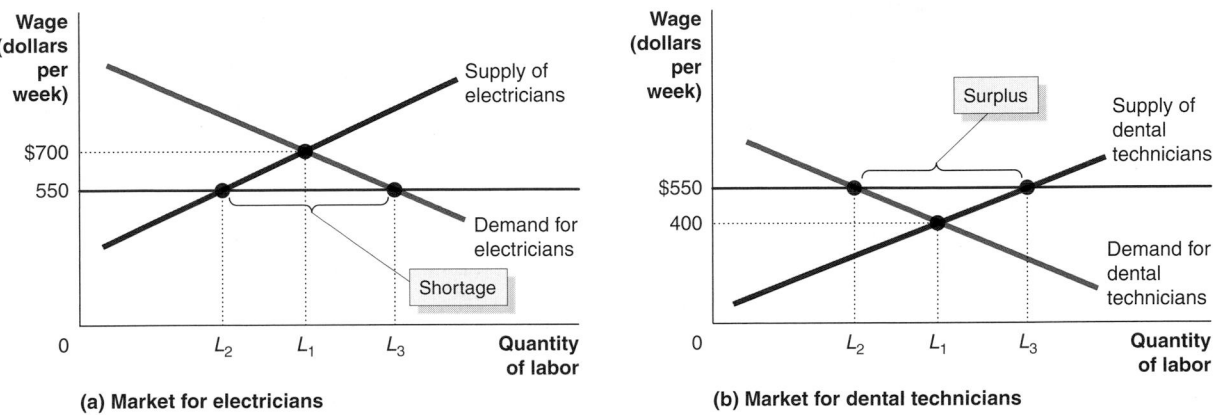

(a) Market for electricians   **(b) Market for dental technicians**

In panel (a), without comparable worth legislation, the equilibrium wage for electricians is $700 and the equilibrium quantity of electricians hired is L_1. Setting the wage for electricians below equilibrium at $550 reduces the quantity of labor supplied in this occupation from L_1 to L_2 but increases the quantity of labor demanded by employers from L_1 to L_3. The result is a shortage of electricians equal to $L_3 - L_2$, as shown by the bracket in the graph.

In panel (b), without comparable worth legislation, the equilibrium wage for dental technicians is $400 and the equilibrium quantity of dental technicians hired is L_1. Setting the wage for dental technicians above equilibrium at $550 increases the quantity of labor supplied in this occupation from L_1 to L_3 but reduces the quantity of labor demanded by employers from L_1 to L_2. The result is a surplus of dental technicians equal to $L_3 - L_2$, as shown by the bracket in the graph.

Extra Credit: Most economists are skeptical of government attempts to set wages and prices, as comparable worth legislation would require. Supporters of comparable worth, by contrast, see differences between men's and women's wages as being mainly due to discrimination and are looking to government legislation as a solution.

YOUR TURN: For more practice, do related problems 15 and 16 on pages 530–531 at the end of this chapter. Visit www.prenhall.com/hubbard for an interactive exercise related to this Solved Problem.

THE DIFFICULTY OF MEASURING DISCRIMINATION When two people are paid different wages, discrimination may be the explanation. The difference in wages also might be explained by differences in productivity or by differences in preferences. Labor economists have attempted to measure what part of differences in wages between blacks and whites and between men and women is due to discrimination and what part is due to other factors. Unfortunately, it is difficult to measure precisely differences in productivity or in worker preferences. As a result, we can't know exactly the extent of economic discrimination in the United States today. Most economists do believe, however, that most of the differences in wages between different groups are due to factors other than discrimination.

DOES IT PAY TO DISCRIMINATE? Many economists argue that economic discrimination is no longer a major factor in labor markets in the United States. One reason is that *employers who discriminate pay an economic penalty.* To see why this is true, let's take a simplified example. Suppose that men and women are equally qualified to be airline pilots and that, initially, airlines do not discriminate. In Figure 16-8, we divide the airlines into two groups: "A" airlines and "B" airlines. If neither group of airlines discriminates, we would expect them to pay an equal wage of $1,100 per week to both men and women pilots. Now suppose that "A" airlines decide to discriminate and to fire all their women pilots. This action will reduce the supply of pilots to these airlines and, as shown in panel (a), that will force up the wage from $1,100 to $1,300. At the same time, as women fired from the jobs with "A" airlines apply for jobs with "B" airlines, the supply of pilots to "B" airlines will increase and the equilibrium wage will fall from $1,100 to $900. All the women pilots will end up being employed at the nondiscriminating airlines and be paid a lower wage than the men who are employed by the discriminating airlines.

But this situation cannot persist for two reasons. First, male pilots employed by "B" airlines will also receive the lower wage. This lower wage gives them an incentive to quit their jobs at "B" airlines and apply at "A" airlines, which will shift the labor supply curve for "B" airlines to the left and the labor supply curve for "A" airlines to the right. Second, "A" airlines are paying $1,300 per week to hire pilots who are no more productive than the pilots being paid $900 per week by "B" airlines. As a result, "B" airlines will have lower costs and will be able to charge lower prices. Eventually, "A" airlines will lose their customers to "B" airlines and be driven out of business. The market will have imposed an economic penalty on the discriminating airlines. So, discrimination will not persist and the wages of men and women pilots will become equal.

Can we conclude from this analysis that competition in markets will eliminate all economic discrimination? Unfortunately, this optimistic conclusion is not completely

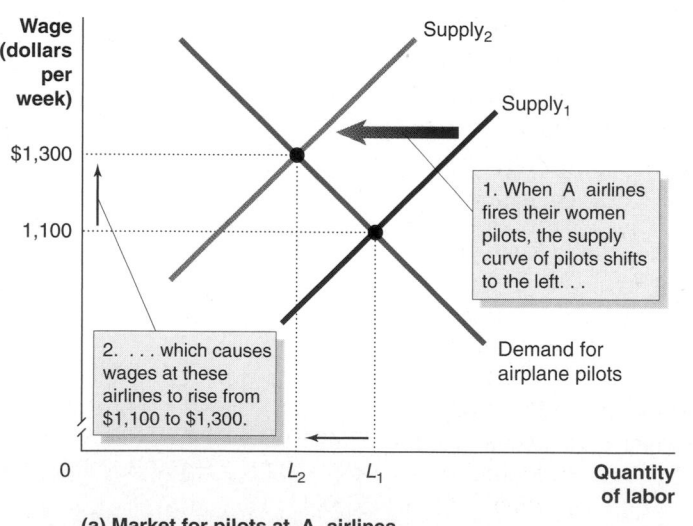

(a) Market for pilots at A airlines

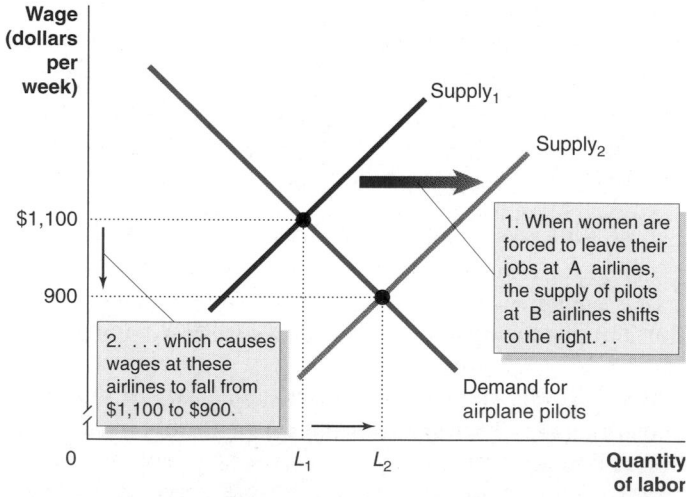

(b) Market for pilots at B airlines

FIGURE 16-8 **Discrimination and Wages**

In this hypothetical example, we assume that initially neither "A" airlines nor "B" airlines discriminates. As a result, men and women pilots receive the same wage of $1,100 per week at both groups of airlines. We then assume that "A" airlines discriminates by firing all their women pilots. Panel (a) shows that this reduces the supply of pilots to "A" airlines and raises the wage paid by these airlines from $1,100 to $1,300. Panel (b) shows that this increases the supply of pilots to "B" airlines and lowers the wage paid by these airlines from $1,100 to $900. All the women pilots will end up being employed at the nondiscriminating airlines and will be paid a lower wage than the men who are employed by the discriminating airlines.

accurate. We know that until the Civil Rights Act of 1964 was passed, many firms in the United States refused to hire blacks. Even though this practice had persisted for decades, nondiscriminating competitors did not drive these firms out of business. Why not? There were three important factors:

1. *Worker discrimination.* In many cases, white workers refused to work alongside blacks. As a result, some industries—such as the important cotton textile industry in the South—were all white. Because of discrimination by white workers, a businessperson who wanted to use low-cost black labor might need to hire an all-black workforce. Some businesspeople tried this, but because blacks had been excluded from these industries, they often lacked the skills and experience to be an effective workforce.

2. *Customer discrimination.* Some white consumers were unwilling to buy from companies in certain industries if they employed black workers. This was not a significant barrier in manufacturing industries, where customers would not know the race of the workers producing the good. It was, however, a problem for firms in industries in which workers came into direct contact with the public.

3. *Negative feedback loops.* Our analysis in Figure 16-8 assumed that men and women pilots were equally qualified. However, if discrimination makes it difficult for a member of a group to find employment in a particular occupation, his or her incentive to be trained to enter that occupation is reduced. Consider the legal profession as an example. In 1952, future Supreme Court Justice Sandra Day O'Connor graduated third in her class at Stanford University Law School and was an editor of the *Stanford Law Review*, but for some time she was unable to find a job as a lawyer because in those years many law firms would not hire women. Facing such bleak jobs prospects, it's not surprising that relatively few women entered law school. As a result, a law firm that did not discriminate would have been unable to act like the nondiscriminating airlines in our example by hiring women lawyers at a lower salary and using this cost advantage to drive discriminating law firms out of business. In this situation, an unfortunate feedback loop was in place: Few women prepared to become lawyers because many law firms discriminated against women and nondiscriminating law firms were unable to drive discriminating law firms out of business because there were too few women lawyers available.

Most economists agree that the market imposes an economic penalty on firms that discriminate, but because of the factors just discussed, it may take the market a very long time to eliminate discrimination entirely. The passage of the Civil Rights Act of 1964, which outlawed hiring discrimination on the basis of race and sex, greatly speeded up the process of reducing economic discrimination in the United States.

Labor Unions

Workers' wages can also differ depending on whether or not they are members of labor unions. **Labor unions** are organizations of employees that have the legal right to bargain with employers about wages and working conditions. If a union is unable to reach an agreement with a company, it has the legal right to call a *strike*, which means its members refuse to work until a satisfactory agreement has been reached. As Figure 16-9 shows, a smaller fraction of the U.S. labor force is unionized than in most other industrial countries.

As Table 16-4 shows, in the United States, workers in unions receive higher wages than workers who are not in unions. Do union members earn more than nonunion members because they are in unions? The answer might seem to be "yes," but many union workers are in industries, such as automobile manufacturing, in which their marginal revenue products are high, so their wages would also be high even if they were not unionized. Economists who have attempted to estimate statistically the impact of unionization on wages have concluded that being in a union increases a worker's wages about 10 percent, holding constant other factors, such as the industry the worker is in. A

Labor union An organization of employees that has the legal right to bargain with employers about wages and working conditions.

FIGURE 16-9

The United States Is Less Unionized Than Most Industrial Countries

The percent of the labor force belonging to unions is lower in the United States than in most other industrial countries.

Source: International Labour Organization.

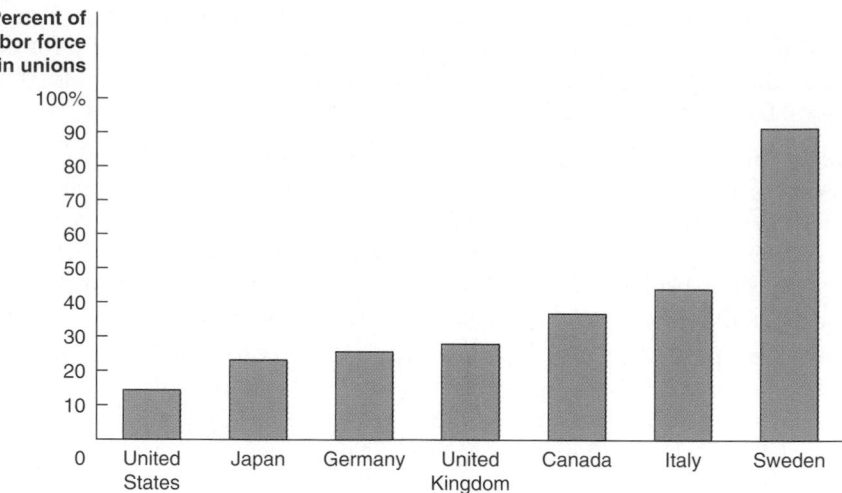

related question is whether unions raise the total amount of wages received by all workers, whether unionized or not. Because the share of national income received by workers has remained roughly constant over many years, most economists do not believe that unions have raised the total amount of wages received by workers.

TABLE 16-4

Union Workers Earn More Than Nonunion Workers

	AVERAGE WEEKLY EARNINGS
Union workers	$781
Nonunion workers	612

Note: "Union workers" includes union members as well as workers who are represented by unions but who are not members of them.

Source: U.S. Bureau of Labor Statistics, "Union Members Summary," January 27, 2005.

⑤ LEARNING OBJECTIVE

Discuss the role personnel economics can play in helping firms deal with human resources issues.

Personnel economics   The application of economic analysis to human resources issues.

Personnel Economics

Traditionally, labor economists have focused on policy issues, such as the effects of labor unions on wages or the determinants of changes in average wages over time. They have spent less time analyzing *human resources issues,* which address how firms hire, train, and promote workers and set their wages and benefits. In recent years, some labor economists, including Edward Lazear of Stanford University and William Neilson of Texas A&M University, have begun exploring the application of economic analysis to human resources issues. This new focus has become known as **personnel economics.**

Personnel economics analyzes the link between differences among jobs and differences in the way workers are paid. Jobs have different skill requirements, require more or less interaction with other workers, have to be performed in more or less unpleasant environments, and so on. Firms need to design compensation policies that take into account these differences. Personnel economics also analyzes policies related to other human resources issues, such as promotions, training, and pensions. In this brief overview, we look only at compensation policies.

Should Workers' Pay Depend on How Much They Work or on How Much They Produce?

One issue personnel economics addresses is when workers should receive *straight-time pay*—a certain wage per hour or salary per week or month—and when they should receive *commission* or *piece-rate pay*—a wage based on how much output they produce.

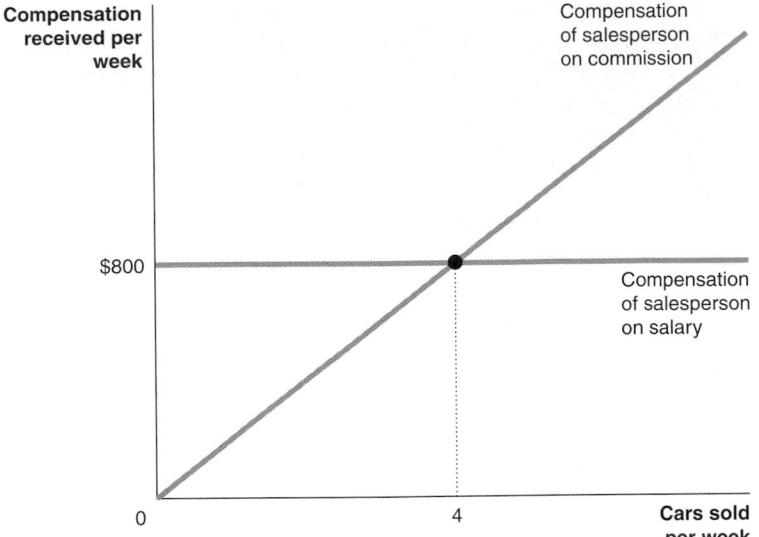

FIGURE 16-10

Paying Car Salespeople by Salary or by Commission

This figure compares the compensation a car salesperson receives if she is on a straight salary of $800 per week or if she receives a commission of $200 for each car she sells. With a straight salary, she receives $800 per week, no matter how many cars she sells. This outcome is shown by the horizontal line in the figure. If she receives a commission of $200 per car, her compensation will increase with every car she sells. This outcome is shown by the upward-sloping line. If she sells fewer than 4 cars per week, she would be better off with the $800 salary. If she sells more than 4 cars per week, she would be better off with the $200 per car commission.

Suppose, for example, that Anne owns a car dealership and is trying to decide whether to pay her salespeople a salary of $800 per week or a commission of $200 on each car they sell. Figure 16-10 compares the compensation a salesperson would receive under the two systems, according to the number of cars the salesperson sells.

With a straight salary, the salesperson receives $800 per week, no matter how many cars she sells. This outcome is shown by the horizontal line in Figure 16-10. If she receives a commission of $200 per car, her compensation will increase with every car she sells. This outcome is shown by the upward-sloping line. A salesperson who sells fewer than 4 cars per week would earn more by receiving a straight salary of $800 per week. A salesperson who sells more than 4 cars per week would be better off receiving the $200 per car commission. We can identify two advantages Anne would receive from paying her salespeople commissions rather than salaries: She would attract and retain the most productive employees, and she would provide an incentive to her employees to sell more cars.

To see why, suppose that other car dealerships were all paying salaries of $800 per week. If Anne pays her employees on commission, any of her employees who are unable to sell at least 4 cars per week can improve their pay by going to work for one of her competitors. By the same token, any salespeople at Anne's competitors who can sell more than 4 cars per week can raise his or her pay by quitting and coming to work for Anne. Over time, Anne will find her least productive employees leaving, while she is able to hire new employees who are more productive.

Paying a commission also increases the incentive Anne's salespeople have to sell more cars. If Anne paid a salary, her employees would receive the same amount no matter how few cars they sold. An employee on salary might decide on a particularly hot or cold day that it was less trouble to stay inside the building than to go out on the car lot to greet potential customers. An employee on commission would know that the additional effort expended on selling more cars would be rewarded with additional compensation.

Raising Pay, Productivity, and Profits at Safelite AutoGlass

16-4 Making the Connection

Safelite Group, headquartered in Columbus, Ohio, is the parent company of Safelite AutoGlass, the nation's largest installer of auto glass, with 600 repair shops. In the mid-1990s, Safelite shifted from paying its glass installers hourly wages to paying them on the basis of how many windows they installed. Safelite already had in place a computer system that allowed it to track easily how many windows each worker installed per day. To make sure

A piece-rate system at Safelite AutoGlass led to increased worker wages and firm profits.

that quality did not suffer, Safelite added a rule that if a workmanship-related defect occurred with the installed windshield, the worker would have to install a new windshield and would not be paid for the additional work.

Edward Lazear analyzed data provided by the firm and discovered that under the new piece-rate system the number of windows installed per worker jumped 44 percent. Lazear estimates that half of this increase was due to increased productivity from workers who continued with the company and half was due to new hires being more productive than the workers they replaced who had left the company. Worker pay rose on average by about 9.9 percent. Ninety-two percent of workers experienced a pay increase and one-quarter received an increase of at least 28 percent. Safelite's profits also increased as the cost to the company per window installed fell from $44.43 under the hourly wage system to $35.24 under the piece-rate system.

Sociologists sometimes question whether worker productivity can be increased through the use of monetary incentives. The experience of Safelite AutoGlass provides a clear example of workers reacting favorably to the opportunity to increase output in exchange for higher compensation.

Source: Edward P. Lazear, "Performance Pay and Productivity," *American Economic Review*, Vol. 90, No. 5, December 2000, pp. 1346–1361.

Other Considerations in Setting Compensation Schemes

The discussion so far indicates that companies will find it more profitable to use a commission or piece-rate system of compensation, rather than a salary system. In fact, many firms continue to pay their workers salaries, which means they are paying their workers on the basis of how long they work, rather than on the basis of how much they produce. Firms may choose a salary system for several good reasons:

➤ *Difficulty in measuring output.* Often it is difficult to attribute output to any particular worker. For example, projects carried out by an engineering firm may involve teams of workers, whose individual contributions are difficult to distinguish. On assembly lines, such as those used in the automobile industry, the amount produced by each worker is determined by the speed of the line, which is set by managers rather than by workers. Managers at many firms perform such a wide variety of tasks that measuring their output would be costly, if it could be done at all.

➤ *Concerns about quality.* If workers are paid on the basis of the number of units produced, they may become less concerned about quality. An office assistant who is paid on the basis of the quantity of letters typed may become careless about how many typos the letters contain. In some cases, there are ways around this problem: for example, the assistant may be required to correct the mistakes on his or her own time without pay.

➤ *Worker dislike of risk.* Piece-rate or commission systems of compensation increase the risk to workers because sometimes output declines for reasons not connected to the worker's effort. For example, if there is a very snowy winter, few customers may show up at Anne's auto dealership. Through no fault of their own, her salespeople may have great difficulty selling any cars. If they are paid a salary, their income will not be affected, but if they are on commission, their incomes may drop to low levels. The flip side of this is that by paying salaries Anne assumes a greater risk. During a snowy winter, her payroll expenses will remain high even though her sales are low. With a commission system of compensation, her payroll expenses will decline along with her sales. But owners of firms are typically better able to bear risk than are workers. As a result, some firms may find that workers who would earn more under a commission system will prefer to receive a salary to reduce their risk. In these situations, paying a lower salary may reduce the firm's payroll expenses, compared with what they would have been under a commission or piece-rate system.

Personnel economics is a relatively new field, but it holds great potential for helping firms deal more efficiently with human relations issues.

The Markets for Capital and Natural Resources

The approach we have used to analyze the market for labor can also be used to analyze the markets for other factors of production. We have seen that the demand for labor is determined by the marginal revenue product of labor because the value to a firm from hiring another worker equals the increase in the firm's revenue from selling the additional output it can produce by hiring the worker. The demand for capital and natural resources is determined in a similar way.

6 LEARNING OBJECTIVE
Show how equilibrium prices are determined in the markets for capital and natural resources.

The Market for Capital

Physical capital includes machines, equipment, and buildings. Firms sometimes buy capital, but we will focus on situations in which firms rent capital. A chocolate manufacturer renting a warehouse or an airline leasing a plane are examples of firms renting capital. Like the demand for labor, the demand for capital is a derived demand. When a firm is considering increasing its capital by, for example, employing another machine, the value it receives equals the increase in the firm's revenue from selling the additional output it can produce by employing the machine. The *marginal revenue product of capital* is the change in the firm's revenue as a result of employing one more unit of capital, such as a machine. We have seen that the marginal revenue product of labor curve is the demand curve for labor. Similarly, the marginal revenue product of capital curve is also the demand curve for capital.

Firms producing capital goods face increasing marginal costs, so the supply curve for capital goods is upward-sloping, as are the supply curves for other goods and services. Figure 16-11 shows equilibrium in the market for capital. In equilibrium, suppliers of capital receive a rental price equal to the marginal revenue product of capital, just as suppliers of labor receive a wage equal to the marginal revenue product of labor.

The Market for Natural Resources

The market for natural resources can be analyzed in the same way as the markets for labor and capital. When a firm is considering employing more natural resources, the value it receives equals the increase in the firm's revenue from selling the additional output it can produce by buying the natural resources. So, the demand for natural resources is also a derived demand. The *marginal revenue product of natural resources* is the change in the firm's revenue as a result of employing one more unit of natural resources, such as a barrel of oil. The marginal revenue product of natural resources curve is also the demand curve for natural resources.

Although the total quantity of most natural resources is ultimately fixed—as the humorist Will Rogers once remarked, "Buy land, they ain't making any more of it"—in many cases the quantity supplied still responds to the price. For example, although the total quantity of oil deposits in the world is fixed, an increase in the price of oil

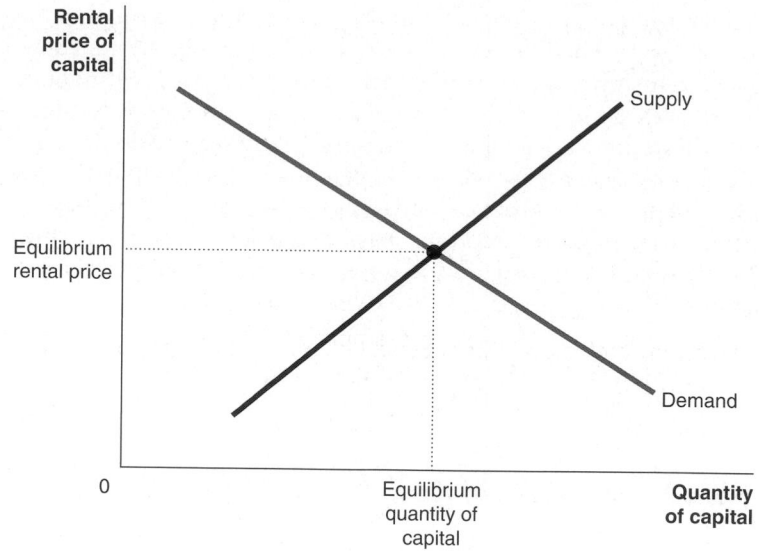

FIGURE 16-11

Equilibrium in the Market for Capital

The rental price of capital is determined by equilibrium in the market for capital. In equilibrium, the rental price of capital is equal to the marginal revenue product of capital.

will result in an increase in the quantity of oil supplied during a particular period. The result, as shown in panel (a) of Figure 16-12, is an upward-sloping supply curve. In some cases, however, the quantity of a natural resource that will be supplied is fixed and will not change as the price changes. The land available at a busy intersection is fixed, for example. In panel (b) of Figure 16-12 we illustrate this situation with a supply curve that is a vertical line, or perfectly inelastic. The price received by a factor of production that is in fixed supply is called an **economic rent** (or **pure rent**). Because in this case, the price of the factor is determined only by demand. For example, if a new highway diverts much of the traffic from a previously busy intersection, the

Economic rent (or **pure rent**) The price of a factor of production that is in fixed supply.

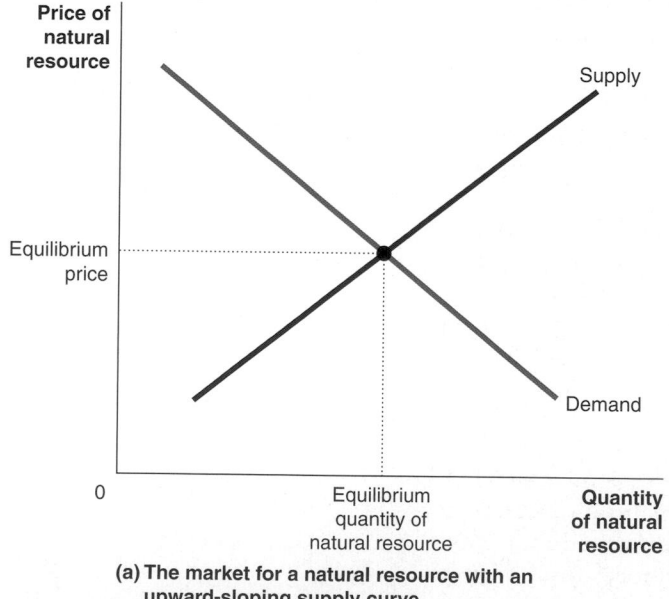

(a) The market for a natural resource with an upward-sloping supply curve

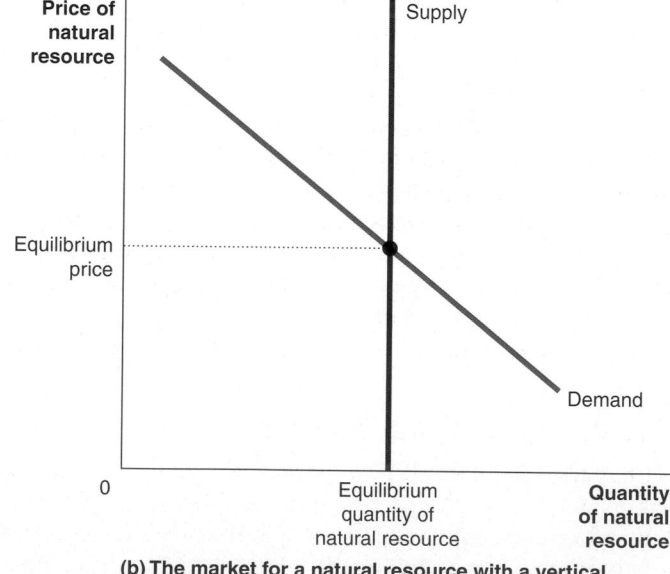

(b) The market for a natural resource with a vertical supply curve

FIGURE 16-12 **Equilibrium in the Market for Natural Resources**

In panel (a), the supply curve for a natural resource is upward-sloping. The price of the natural resource is determined by the interaction of demand and supply. In panel (b), the supply curve for the natural resource is a vertical line, indicating that the quantity supplied does not respond to changes in price. In this case, the price of the natural resource is determined only by demand. The price of a factor of production with a vertical supply curve is called an *economic rent* or a *pure rent*.

demand for the land will decline and the price of the land will fall, but the quantity of the land will not change.

Monopsony

In Chapter 14, we analyzed the case of *monopoly,* where a firm is the sole *seller* of a good or service. What happens if a firm is the sole *buyer* of a factor of production? This case, which is known as **monopsony,** is comparatively rare. An example is a firm in an isolated town—perhaps a lumber mill in a small town in Washington or Oregon—that is the sole employer of labor in that location. We know that a firm with a monopoly in an output market takes advantage of its market power to reduce the quantity supplied to force up the market price and increase its profits. A firm that has a monopsony in a factor market would employ a similar strategy: It would restrict the quantity of the factor demanded to force *down* the price of the factor and increase its profits. A firm with a monopsony in a labor market will hire fewer workers and pay lower wages than would be the case in a competitive market.

Monopsony The sole buyer of a factor of production.

The Marginal Productivity Theory of Income Distribution

We have seen that in equilibrium each factor of production receives a price equal to its marginal revenue product. We can use this fact to explain the distribution of income. Marginal revenue product represents the value of a factor's marginal contribution to producing goods and services. Therefore, individuals will receive income equal to the marginal contributions to production from the factors of production they own, including their labor. The more factors of production an individual owns, and the more productive those factors are, the higher the individual's income will be. This approach to explaining the distribution of income is called the **marginal productivity theory of income distribution.** The marginal productivity theory of income distribution was developed by John Bates Clark, who taught at Columbia University in the late nineteenth and early twentieth centuries.

Marginal productivity theory of income distribution The theory that the distribution of income is determined by the marginal productivity of the factors of production that individuals own.

Conclusion

In this chapter, we used the demand and supply model of Chapter 3 to explain why wages differ among workers. The demand for workers depends on their productivity and on the price that firms receive for the output the workers produce. The supply of workers to an occupation depends on the wages and working conditions offered by employers and on the skills required. The demand and supply for labor can also help us analyze such issues as economic discrimination and the impact of labor unions.

Read *An Inside Look* on the next page to see how demand and supply determine the salaries of college football coaches.

An Inside Look

Is a College Football Coach Worth a $1.1 Million Salary?

WASHINGTON POST, APRIL 28, 2004

Terps' Coaches Have Big Incentives

University of Maryland men's basketball coach Gary Williams and football coach Ralph Friedgen, two of the state's highest-paid employees, earn substantial portions of their incomes through incentive clauses for achievements ranging from winning conference championships to graduating their players and, in Friedgen's case, keeping them out of trouble, according to documents the university released for the first time yesterday.

Williams and Friedgen are each guaranteed more than $1.1 million in annual compensation. The salaries, which include base pay of less than $250,000 per coach, are enhanced by hundreds of thousands of dollars through outside sources such as radio and television appearances, contracts with athletic apparel makers and summer camps each coach hosts on the College Park campus. Each man also can boost his income by hundreds of thousands every year by meeting incentives.

a Such salaries are commensurate with those of other prominent college coaches in those two sports and, according to university officials, have become the cost of competing at college athletics' highest levels.

"It's a goal of Maryland athletics to be competitive in compensation for highly achieving coaches," Maryland Athletic Director Deborah A. Yow said. "In that regard, the compensation that's paid to both Coach Friedgen and Coach Williams is market-driven, and it's within the norm received by their peers. . . ."

"There's a philosophical question: Is any coach worth being paid seven figures? That's a separate conversation than the reality of: Are we or are we not going to be competitive? I'm not mired in that philosophical question."

b Joel Cohen, a mathematics professor and the chair of the faculty senate, said the numbers are not particularly surprising, and the fact that coaches earn far more than professors long predates Williams and Friedgen. Still, he said he occasionally hears the topic discussed in faculty lounges and lunch rooms.

"I think there's still a lot of angst among faculty about what this means," Cohen said. "What does it say about the whole commercialization of the school? I think you'll find a lot of people—not just faculty, but a lot of people, including athletic directors—who would love it somehow if all the coaches got half as much as they're getting. . . . "

University President C. D. Mote Jr. earns $357,000 annually, a university spokesman said.

The money to cover the costs of the coaches' contracts does not come from taxpayers. Rather, the athletic department is financially separate from the university. In 2002–03, it generated more than $39 million in revenue through ticket sales, television contracts, postseason appearances in football and men's basketball, student fees, and private donations. During that year, students poured nearly $6.4 million into the athletic budget through student fees.

According to the university, the athletic department generated $5.7 million in revenue for the campus that year. . . .

Williams earns bonuses of $25,000 for winning either the ACC's regular season or tournament championship. Moreover, he earns $10,000 for advancing to the NCAA tournament, and at least $15,000 for each tournament win. Should the Terps win the national title, Williams would earn a total of $200,000 in bonuses from the school and another $50,000 from athletic apparel maker Nike.

Williams's contract is also laden with bonuses for graduating players. Should between 50 percent and 59 percent of the men's basketball players graduate in a given year, Williams earns $25,000. The bonus increases incrementally, topping out at $150,000 if 75 percent or more graduate.

Friedgen earns a bonus of $75,000 should 75 percent of his players graduate in a given year and $35,000 if between 70 percent and 75 percent graduate.

"It's important for me to reward academic achievement," Yow said. "I think that's essential."

Cohen, the faculty senate chair, said those incentives can be particularly interesting to faculty.

"In principle, I don't like it," Cohen said. "Nobody's going to give me an extra $50,000 if all of my students pass. But if it's able to change the way these kids graduate. . . . Anything that can be done to improve graduation rates is good."

Friedgen also receives a bonus of $50,000 in any year when no player or assistant coach violates school honors codes, is arrested or violates NCAA rules.

Key Points in the Article

This article discusses the high salaries received by the University of Maryland's basketball and football coaches. Both men receive compensation of more than $1.1 million per year, which is about three times as much as the University's president receives. The University's athletic director argues that the University must pay such high salaries to attract and retain coaches capable of developing winning teams in highly competitive sports. The professor who is chair of the faculty senate wonders whether paying such high salaries to athletic coaches "commercializes" the school.

Analyzing the News

a The Maryland athletic director makes the argument that the market determines the salaries of coaches at schools with highly competitive NCAA Division I basketball and football programs. We have seen in this chapter that the marginal revenue product of labor curve is also the demand curve for labor. It seems reasonable to believe that this holds true for basketball and football coaches as well. As the article notes, the coaches are compensated on the basis of their ability to generate revenues for their programs. Just as with the salaries of baseball players, coaches of a given level of ability will be more valuable at some colleges than at others, and their salaries will vary accordingly. The demand for *head coaches* at Division I schools is largely fixed by the total number of positions available. The quantity demanded of all coaches, including assistant coaches, will be more responsive to changes in salaries.

b The University of Maryland mathematics professor remarks that it is not unusual for basketball and football coaches to be paid much higher salaries than those paid to professors. Figure 1 shows that the explanation for the difference in salaries is that the marginal revenue product of coaches is very high and the supply of people with the abilities to coach basketball or football at a Division I school is low, whereas the marginal revenue product of professors is much lower and the supply of people with the ability to be a professor is relatively high. The result is that the equilibrium wage for coaches is $1 million and the equilibrium wage for professors at Division I schools is $85,000.

Thinking Critically
ABOUT POLICY

1. The pay gap between coaches and professors at Division I schools, like the University of Maryland, has widened over time. In the 1920s, for example, Penn State's very successful football coach earned *only* three or four times as much as a typical professor. What could explain the widening of this pay gap over time?

2. The NCAA once placed a cap on the salaries of college basketball assistant coaches, but lost a lawsuit over this. Legal issues aside, would it be a good idea to place caps on the salaries paid to college coaches? What impacts would a cap of, say, $100,000 per year in compensation have?

Source: Barry Svrluga, "Terps' Coaches Have Big Incentives," *Washington Post*, April 28, 2004, p. D01. © 2004, The Washington Post, reprinted with permission.

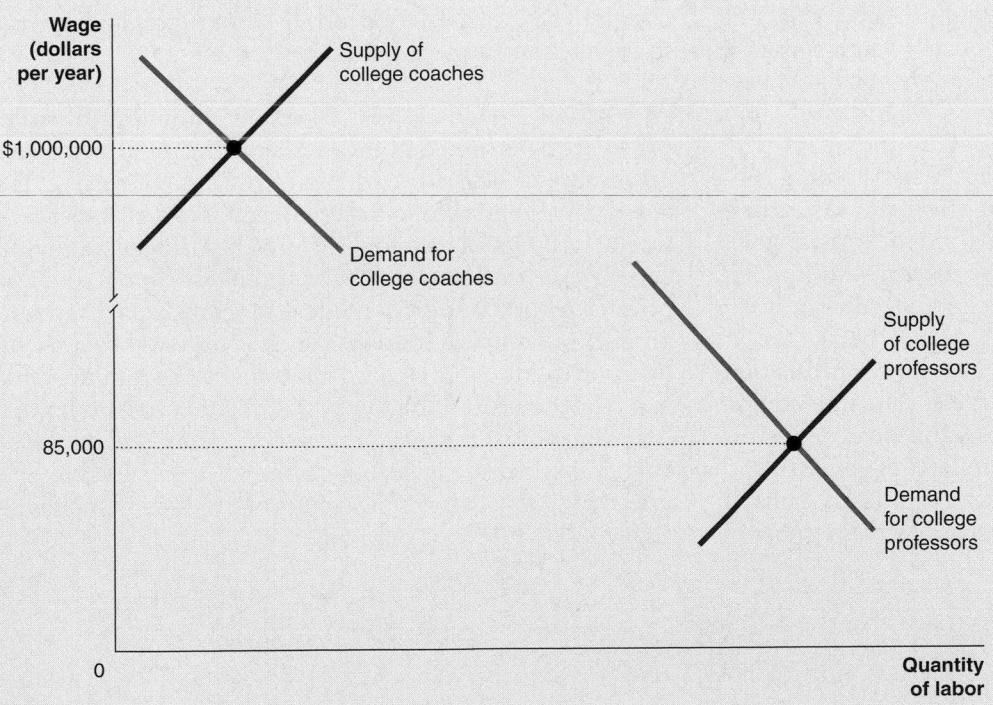

Figure 1: The difference between the salaries of coaches and professors is determined by demand and supply.

SUMMARY

LEARNING OBJECTIVE ① Explain how firms choose the profit-maximizing quantity of workers to employ. The demand for labor is derived from the demand for final goods and services. The additional output produced by a firm as a result of hiring another worker is called the *marginal product of labor*. The amount by which the firm's revenue will increase as a result of hiring one more worker is called the *marginal revenue product of labor*. A firm's marginal revenue product of labor curve is its demand curve for labor. Firms maximize profit by hiring workers up to the point where the wage is equal to the marginal revenue product of labor. The market demand curve for labor is determined by adding up the quantity of labor demanded by each firm at each wage, holding constant all other variables that might affect the willingness of firms to hire workers. The most important variables that shift the labor demand curve are changes in human capital, technology, the price of the product, the quantity of other inputs, and the number of firms in the market.

LEARNING OBJECTIVE ② Explain how people choose the quantity of labor to supply. As the wage increases, the opportunity cost of leisure increases, causing individuals to supply a greater quantity of labor. Normally, the labor supply curve will be upward-sloping, but it is possible that at very high wage levels the supply curve might be backward-bending. This outcome occurs when someone with a high income is willing to accept a somewhat lower income in exchange for more leisure. The market labor supply curve is determined by adding up the quantity of labor supplied by each worker at each wage, holding constant all other variables that might affect the willingness of workers to supply labor. The most important variables that shift the labor supply curve are increases in population, changing demographics, and changing alternatives.

LEARNING OBJECTIVE ③ Explain how equilibrium wages are determined in labor markets. The intersection between labor supply and labor demand determines the equilibrium wage and the equilibrium level of employment. If labor supply is unchanged, an increase in labor demand will increase both the equilibrium wage and the number of workers employed. If labor demand is unchanged, an increase in labor supply will lower the equilibrium wage and increase the number of workers employed.

LEARNING OBJECTIVE ④ Use demand and supply analysis to explain how compensating differentials, discrimination, and labor unions cause wages to differ. The equilibrium wage is determined by the intersection of the labor demand and labor supply curves. Some differences in wages are explained by *compensating differentials*, which are higher wages that compensate workers for unpleasant aspects of a job. Wages can also differ because of *economic discrimination*, which involves paying a person a lower wage or excluding a person from an occupation on the basis of irrelevant characteristics, such as race or gender. *Labor unions* are organizations of employees that have the legal right to bargain with employers about wages and working conditions. Being in a union increases a worker's wages about 10 percent, holding constant other factors, such as the industry in question.

LEARNING OBJECTIVE ⑤ Discuss the role personnel economics can play in helping firms deal with human resources issues. *Personnel economics* is the application of economic analysis to human resources issues. One insight of personnel economics is that the productivity of workers often can be increased if firms move from straight-time pay to commission or piece-rate pay.

LEARNING OBJECTIVE ⑥ Show how equilibrium prices are determined in the markets for capital and natural resources. The approach used to analyze the market for labor can also be used to analyze the markets for other factors of production. In equilibrium the price of capital is equal to the marginal revenue product of capital and the price of natural resources is equal to the marginal revenue product of natural resources. The price received by a factor that is in fixed supply is called an *economic rent* or pure rent. A *monopsony* is the sole buyer of a factor of production. According to the *marginal productivity theory of income distribution*, the distribution of income is determined by the marginal productivity of the factors of production individuals own.

KEY TERMS

Compensating differentials 513

Derived demand 500

Economic discrimination 514

Economic rent (or pure rent) 524

Factors of production 500

Human capital 504

Labor union 519

Marginal product of labor 501

Marginal productivity theory of income distribution 525

Marginal revenue product of labor (MRP) 501

Monopsony 525

Personnel economics 520

REVIEW QUESTIONS

1. What is the difference between the marginal product of labor and the marginal revenue product of labor?

2. Why is the demand curve for labor downward-sloping?

3. How can we measure the opportunity cost of leisure? Why is the supply curve of labor usually upward-sloping?

4. What are the five most important variables that cause the market demand curve for labor to shift?

5. What are the three most important variables that cause the market supply curve of labor to shift?

6. If the labor demand curve shifts to the left and the labor supply curve remains unchanged, what will happen to the equilibrium wage and the equilibrium level of employment? Illustrate your answer with a graph.

7. If the labor supply curve shifts to the left and the labor demand curve remains unchanged, what will happen to the equilibrium wage and the equilibrium level of employment? Illustrate your answer with a graph.

8. What is a compensating differential? Give an example.

9. Define economic discrimination. Is the fact that one group in the population has higher earnings than other groups evidence of economic discrimination? Briefly explain.

10. How does the market undermine economic discrimination?

11. What is personnel economics? If piece-rate or commission systems of compensating workers have important advantages for firms, why don't more firms use them?

12. In equilibrium, what determines the price of capital? What determines the price of natural resources? What is the marginal productivity theory of income distribution?

13. What is an economic rent? What is a monopsony?

PROBLEMS AND APPLICATIONS

Please visit **www.prenhall.com/hubbard** *for solutions to the even-numbered problems as well as multiple-choice and true or false self-assessment quizzes.*

1. Frank Gunter owns an apple orchard. He employs 87 apple pickers and pays them $8 per hour to pick apples, which he sells for $1.60 per box. If Frank is maximizing profits, what is the marginal revenue product of the last worker he hired? What is that worker's marginal product?

2. Most labor economists believe that many adult males are on the vertical section of their labor supply curves. Explain when and why someone's supply of labor curve would be vertical using the concepts of income and substitution effects.
Source: Robert Whaples, ""Is There Consensus among American Labor Economists: Survey Results on Forty Propositions," *Journal of Labor Research*, Vol. 17, No. 4, Fall 1996.

3. Reread the discussion on page 509 of changes in the salaries of film animators. Use a graph to illustrate this situation. Make sure that your graph has labor demand and supply curves for 1994, 1999, and 2002 and that the equilibrium point for each year is clearly indicated.

4. Francis Walker served as commissioner general of the U.S. Immigration Service and as first president of the American Economic Association. In 1896, he wrote the following:

> The question today is protecting the American rate of wages, the American standard of living, and the quality of American citizenship from degradation through the tumultuous access of

> vast throngs of ignorant and brutalized peasantry from the countries of Eastern and Southern Europe.

Why would Walker have feared that immigration to the United States would drive down wages? Did wages, in fact, fall as he predicted? Briefly explain.
Source: Quoted in Julian L. Simon and Rita James Simon, "Do We Really Need All These Immigrants?" in D. N. McCloskey, *Second Thoughts: Myths and Morals of U.S. Economic History*, New York: Oxford University Press, 1993, p. 20.

5. Former presidential candidate Patrick J. Buchanan has argued that "[T]he U.S. labor supply has grown by more tens of millions in the past twenty-five years than in any other period in history. How could the price of labor *not* fall?" Answer Buchanan's question: If there is an increase in labor supply, does the equilibrium wage have to fall?
Source: Patrick J. Buchanan, *The Great Betrayal: How American Sovereignty and Social Justice Are Being Sacrificed to the Gods of the Global Economy*, Boston: Little, Brown, 1998, p. 16.

6. In 541 A.D., an outbreak of bubonic plague hit the Byzantine Empire. Because the plague was spread by flea-infested rats that often lived on ships, ports were hit particularly hard. In some ports, more than 40 percent of the population died. The emperor Justinian was concerned that the wages of sailors were rising very rapidly as a result of the plague. In 544 A.D., he placed a ceiling on the wages of sailors. Use a demand and supply graph of the market for sailors to show the effect of the plague on the wages of sailors. Use this same

graph to show the effect of Justinian's wage ceiling. Briefly explain what is happening in your graph.

Source: Michael McCormick, *The Origins of the European Economy: Communications and Commerce, A.D., 300–900*, New York: Cambridge University Press, 2001, p. 109.

7. The journalist Michael Kinsley has argued, "Free-market capitalism . . . works well for almost all by rewarding some people more than others." Discuss whether or not you agree.

Source: Michael Kinsley, "Curse You, Robert Caro!" *Slate*, November 21, 2002.

8. **[Related to the *Chapter Opener*]** The number of players on each major league baseball team is determined by negotiation between the players' union and the owners of major league teams. How does this fact affect the explanation given in the text of why baseball players are paid more than college professors? Briefly explain.

9. **[Related to the *Chapter Opener*]** A student remarks, "I don't think the idea of marginal revenue product really helps explain differences in wages. After all, a ticket to a baseball game costs much less than college tuition, yet baseball players are paid much more than college professors." Do you agree with the student's reasoning?

10. **[Related to *Don't Let This Happen To You!*]** Joe Morgan is a sportscaster and former baseball player. After he stated that he thought the salaries of major league baseball players were justified, a baseball fan wrote the following to ESPN.com columnist, Rob Neyer:

    Mr. Neyer,

    What are your feelings about Joe Morgan's comment that players are justified in being paid what they're being paid? How is it ok for A-Rod [New York Yankees infielder Alex Rodriguez] to earn $115,000 per GAME while my boss works 80 hour weeks and earns $30,000 per year?

    How would you answer this fan's questions?
    Source: ESPN.com, August 30, 2002.

11. Review Making the Connection 16-3 on superstars, then give an economic explanation of why there are superstar basketball players but no superstar automobile mechanics.

12. Tennis stars Venus Williams and Serena Williams do not play for teams. They enter tennis tournaments as individuals. Is the concept of marginal revenue product as important in explaining their earnings as it is in explaining the earnings of major league baseball players? Briefly explain.

13. Prior to the early twentieth century, a worker who was injured on the job could collect damages only by suing his employer. To sue successfully, the worker—or his family, if the worker had been killed—had to show that the injury was due to the employer's negligence, that the worker did

not know the job was hazardous, and that the worker's own negligence had not contributed to the accident. These lawsuits were difficult for workers to win, and even workers who had been seriously injured on the job often were unable to collect any damages from their employers. Beginning in 1910, most states passed "workers' compensation" laws that required employers to purchase insurance that would compensate workers for injuries suffered on the job. A study by Price Fishback and Shawn Kantor of the University of Arizona shows that after the passage of workers' compensation laws, wages received by workers in the coal and lumber industries fell. Briefly explain why passage of workers' compensation laws would lead to a fall in wages in some industries.

Source: Price V. Fishback and Shawn Everett Kantor, "Did Workers Pay for the Passage of Workers' Compensation Laws?" *Quarterly Journal of Economics*, Vol. 100, No. 3, August 1995, pp. 713–742.

14. The following table is similar to Table 16-2 on page 514, except that it includes the earnings of Asian males and females. Does the fact that Asian males are the highest-earning group in the table affect the likelihood that economic discrimination is the best explanation for why earnings differ among the groups listed in the table? Briefly explain your argument.

GROUP	ANNUAL EARNINGS
Asian males	$45,861
White males	41,367
Asian females	34,794
Black males	32,026
White females	31,329
Black females	27,072
Hispanic males	26,014
Hispanic females	22,449

Source: U.S. Bureau of the Census, *Income, Poverty and Health Insurance in the United States: 2003*, Table PINC-10, August 2004.

15. **[Related to *Solved Problem 16-2*]** Use the following graphs to answer the questions.
    a. What is the equilibrium quantity of sanitary engineers hired, and what is the equilibrium wage?
    b. What is the equilibrium quantity of receptionists hired, and what is the equilibrium wage?
    c. Briefly discuss why sanitary engineers might earn a higher weekly wage than receptionists.
    d. Suppose that comparable worth legislation is passed and the government requires that sanitary engineers and receptionists must be paid the same wage of $500 per week. Now how many sanitary engineers will be hired and how many receptionists will be hired?

Market for sanitary engineers

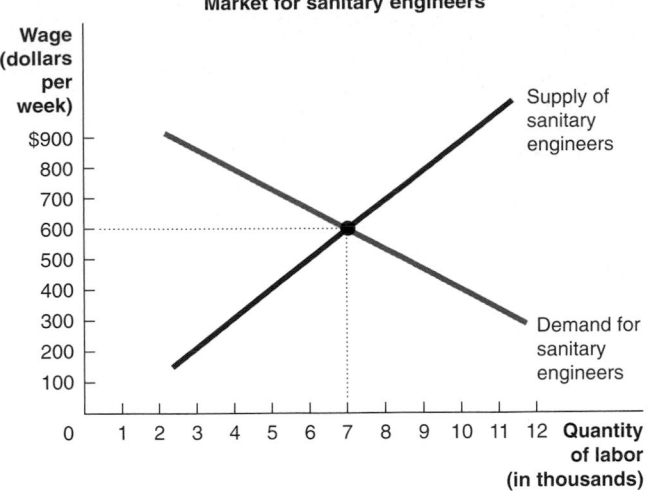

Market for receptionists

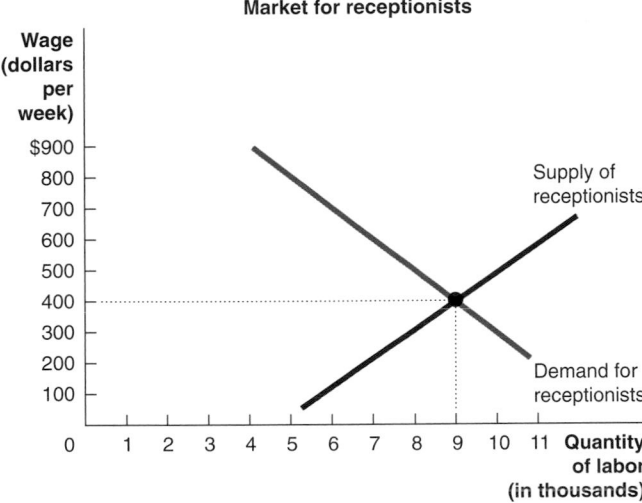

16. **[Related to *Solved Problem 16-2*]** In most universities, economics professors receive larger salaries than English professors. Suppose that the government requires that from now on all universities must pay economics professors the same salaries as English professors. Use demand and supply graphs to analyze the effect of this requirement.

17. During the 1970s, many women changed their minds about whether they would leave the labor force after marrying and having children or whether they would be in the labor force most of their adult lives. In 1968, the National Longitudinal Survey asked a representative sample of women aged 14 to 24 whether they expected to be in the labor force at age 35. Twenty-nine percent of white women and 59 percent of black women responded that they expected to be in the labor force at that age. In fact, when these women were 35, 60 percent of those who were married and 80 percent of those who were unmarried were in the labor force. In other words, many more women ended up being in the labor force than expected to be when they were of high school and college age. What impact did this fact have on the earnings of these women? Briefly explain.
Source: Claudia Goldin, *Explaining the Gender Gap: An Economic History of American Women,* New York: Oxford University Press, 1990, p. 155.

18. In the early twentieth century, blacks in the U.S. South were excluded from some occupations, but in jobs, such as agriculture, that employed both whites and blacks, blacks received about the same wages as whites. Briefly discuss why economic discrimination in the South took this form.

19. Many companies that pay workers an hourly wage require some minimum level of acceptable output. Suppose a company that has been using this system decides to switch to a piece-rate system under which workers are compensated on the basis of how much output they produce, but where they are also free to choose how much to produce. Is it likely that workers under a piece-rate system will end up choosing to produce less than the minimum output that was required under the hourly wage system? Briefly explain.

20. In most jobs, the harder you work, the more you earn. Some workers would rather work harder and earn more, others would rather work less hard, even though as a result they earn less. Suppose, though, that all workers at a company fall into the "work harder and earn more" group. Suppose, also, that the workers all have the same abilities. In these circumstances, would output per worker be the same under an hourly wage compensation system as under a piece-rate system? Briefly explain.

21. For years, the Goodyear Tire & Rubber Company compensated its sales force by paying them a salary plus a bonus based on the number of tires they sold. In early 2002, they made two changes to this policy: (1) The basis for the bonus was changed from the *quantity* of tires sold to the *revenue* from the tires sold, and (2) salespeople were required to get approval from corporate headquarters in Akron, Ohio, before offering to sell tires to customers at reduced prices. Explain why these changes were likely to increase Goodyear's profits.
Source: Timothy Aeppel, "Amid Weak Inflation, Firms Turn Creative to Boost Prices," *Wall Street Journal,* September 18, 2002.

22. **[Related to *Solved Problem 16-1*]** Adam operates a pin factory. Suppose Adam faces the situation shown in the table on the next page and the cost of renting a machine is $550 per week.
    a. Fill in the blanks in the table and determine the profit-maximizing number of machines for Adam to rent. Briefly explain why renting this number of machines is profit-maximizing.
    b. Draw Adam's demand curve for capital.

NUMBER OF MACHINES	OUTPUT OF PINS (BOXES PER WEEK)	MARGINAL PRODUCT OF CAPITAL	PRODUCT PRICE (DOLLARS PER BOX)	TOTAL REVENUE	MARGINAL REVENUE PRODUCT OF CAPITAL	RENTAL COST PER MACHINE	ADDITIONAL PROFIT FROM RENTING ONE ADDITIONAL MACHINE
0	0	—	$100		—	$550	
1	12		100			550	
2	21		100			550	
3	28		100			550	
4	34		100			550	
5	39		100			550	
6	43		100			550	

23. Many people have predicted, using a model like that in Figure 16-12 (b), that the price of natural resources should rise consistently over time in comparison to the price of other goods because the demand curve is rising while the supply curve must be shifting inward as natural resources are used up. However, the relative prices of most natural resources have not been increasing. Draw a graph showing the demand and supply for natural resources that can explain why prices haven't risen, even though demand has.

chapter

seventeen

The Economics of Information

State Farm Experiences the Hazards of Selling Insurance

➤ State Farm Insurance seemed to have a problem during 2004. Some industry analysts believed that the firm was charging the drivers most likely to have accidents too low a price for automobile insurance. If this were true, State Farm was running the risk of paying out more in claims when those drivers had accidents than it was collecting from them in payments on their policies.

With corporate headquarters in Bloomington, Illinois, State Farm is the largest automobile insurance company in the United States, insuring one out of five automobiles. State Farm was founded in 1922 by George J. Mecherle. Mecherle had started life as a farmer, but in his forties he took a job selling insurance. The company he worked for charged the same price for automo-

bile insurance to people living in the city of Bloomington as it did to farmers living outside of town. Mecherle realized that farmers had far fewer accidents than did city drivers. So he started the State Farm Mutual Automobile Insurance Company to offer farmers automobile insurance polices at lower prices.

Mecherle's success highlights the importance to insurance companies of correctly pricing their policies. The difficulty insurance companies have in pricing automobile insurance policies is that drivers know more about how likely they are to have accidents than do insurance companies. As a result, insurance companies may charge safe drivers prices that are too high—causing them to buy their policies from other companies—

and charge risky drivers prices that are too low. The difficulties insurance companies face in pricing their policies are caused by *asymmetric information,* which exists when one party to an economic transaction has less information than the other party. In the market for insurance, asymmetric information leads to two problems: *adverse selection* and *moral hazard.* Adverse selection can result in an insurance company attracting more high-risk drivers than it would like, given the prices of its policies. State Farm faced this problem in 2004. Moral hazard occurs when people change their behavior *after* purchasing insurance. Whether drivers have an accident depends partly on how safely they drive. If drivers did not have insurance to

LEARNING OBJECTIVES

After studying this chapter, you should be able to:

① Define asymmetric information and distinguish between moral hazard and adverse selection.

② Apply the concepts of adverse selection and moral hazard to financial markets.

③ Apply the concepts of adverse selection and moral hazard to labor markets.

④ Explain the winner's curse and why it occurs.

pay for the repairs needed after accidents, they would be likely to drive more cautiously.

In recent years, insurance companies have changed the ways they price their policies. The companies' aim had always been to charge high prices to drivers likely to have more accidents and file more claims and lower prices to safer drivers. Usually, though, companies had divided drivers into just a few categories based on their ages and driving records. Today, many companies use sophisticated models that employ thousands of variables to predict the chance that a driver will have an accident. The result has been an increase in the different prices being charged to drivers. For example, until recently, most companies lumped all drivers aged 21 to 70 into one category. But more sophisticated analysis of accident data shows that more categories would be better. As one executive of an insurance company put it, "Now we know a 22-year-old married woman is not as good a driving risk as a 45-year-old married woman." Some industry analysts believed that State Farm's problems in 2004 were the result of being slow to implement the new pricing models.

An Inside Look on page 548 examines how insurance companies in Florida dealt with huge claims for damage to property following hurricanes.

Source: Christopher Oster, "Auto Insurers Cut Rates—For Some," *Wall Street Journal*, April 22, 2004, p. D1.

➤ In previous chapters, we assumed that buyers and sellers in a market possess the same amount of information. In the market for insurance, as we have seen, buyers often have more information than sellers. Later in this chapter, we will see that the reverse is often true in financial markets: Firms selling stocks and bonds usually have more information than buyers. In other markets, buyers and sellers may both lack complete information. For example, when an oil company bids for the right to drill on tracts of government land, neither the company nor the government has complete information on how much oil the tracts contain. When telecommunications companies bid in U.S. Federal Communications Commission auctions for licenses to provide cellular phone services, they also don't have complete information on how valuable the licenses may be.

In this chapter, we discuss the economics of information and how imperfect information can affect the decisions of both households and firms. After reading this chapter, you will better understand situations, such as auctions and the markets for insurance and stocks and bonds, where the role of imperfect information is particularly important.

---

① **LEARNING OBJECTIVE**

Define asymmetric information and distinguish between moral hazard and adverse selection.

Asymmetric information The situation in which one party to an economic transaction has less information than the other party.

Asymmetric Information

The difficulty in correctly pricing insurance policies arises from the problem of **asymmetric information,** which occurs when one party to an economic transaction has less information than the other party. As we will see, in some markets it is difficult to understand the actions of buyers and sellers without understanding the effects of asymmetric information. In fact, guarding against the effects of asymmetric information is a major objective of sellers in the insurance market and of buyers in financial markets. The market for used automobiles was the first in which economists began to carefully study the problem of asymmetric information.

Adverse Selection and the Market for "Lemons"

The study of asymmetric information began with an analysis of the used car market by George Akerlof, an economist at the University of California, Berkeley. In 2001, Akerlof shared the Nobel Prize in Economics with A. Michael Spence of Stanford University and Joseph Stiglitz of Columbia University. Akerlof pointed out that the seller of a used car will always have more information on the true condition of the car than will potential buyers. A car that has been poorly maintained—by, for instance, not having its oil changed regularly—may have suffered damage that could be difficult to detect even by a trained mechanic.

If potential buyers of used cars know that they will have difficulty separating the good used cars from the bad used cars, or "lemons," they will take this into account in the prices they are willing to pay. Consider the following simple example: Suppose that one-half of the 2003 Volkswagen Golfs offered for sale have been well maintained and are good, reliable used cars. The other half have been poorly maintained and are lemons that will be unreliable. Suppose that potential buyers of 2003 Golfs would be willing to pay $10,000 for a reliable one but only $5,000 for an unreliable one. The sellers know how well they have maintained their cars and whether they are reliable, but the buyers do not have this information and so have no way of telling the reliable cars from the unreliable ones.

In this situation, buyers will generally offer a price somewhere between the price they would be willing to pay for a good car and the price they would be willing to pay for a lemon. In this case, with a 50–50 chance of buying a good car or a lemon, buyers might offer $7,500, which is halfway between the price they would pay if they knew for certain the car was a good one and the price they would pay if they knew it was a lemon.

Unfortunately for used car buyers, a major glitch arises at this point. From the buyers' perspective, given that they don't know whether any particular car offered for sale is a good car or a lemon, an offer of $7,500 seems reasonable. But the sellers *do* know whether the cars they are offering are good cars or lemons. To a seller of a good car, an offer of $7,500 is $2,500 below the true value of the car, and the seller will be reluctant to sell. But to a seller of a lemon, an offer of $7,500 is $2,500 *above* the true value of the car, and the seller will be quite happy to sell. As sellers of lemons take advantage of knowing more about the cars they are selling than buyers do, the used car market will fall victim to **adverse selection:** Most used cars offered for sale will be lemons. In other words, because of asymmetric information, the market has selected adversely the cars that will be offered for sale. Notice as well that the problem of adverse selection reduces the total quantity of used cars bought and sold in the market because few good cars are offered for sale. From this example we can conclude that information problems reduce economic efficiency in a market.

> **Adverse selection** The situation in which one party to a transaction takes advantage of knowing more than the other party to the transaction.

Reducing Adverse Selection in the Car Market

There are ways of reducing the adverse selection problem in the used car market. Car manufacturers provide warranties when cars are sold new. These warranties cover the costs of major repairs and can be transferred to a new owner when a car is resold. Warranties give prospective buyers some assurance that they will not be stuck with all the cost of repairs. In addition, used car dealers take steps to assure buyers that the cars they are selling are not lemons. They do this by building a reputation for selling reliable used cars and by offering their own warranties if the manufacturer's warranty has expired or can't be transferred. If a used car dealer can convince buyers that the dealer is selling reliable cars, then, using the numbers from our earlier example, buyers would be willing to pay $10,000, rather than $7,500, for a used Golf.

Some states have passed "lemon laws" to help reduce information problems in the car market. Most lemon laws have two main provisions:

1. New cars that need several major repairs during the first year or two after the date of the original purchase may be returned to the manufacturer for a full refund.

2. Car manufacturers must indicate whether a used car they are offering for sale was repurchased from the original owner as a lemon.

Although popular with consumers, opposition from manufacturers has resulted in lemon laws being enacted in fewer than 20 states.

Asymmetric Information in the Market for Insurance

Asymmetric information problems are particularly severe in the market for insurance. Buyers of insurance policies will always know more about the likelihood of the event being insured against happening than will insurance companies. For example, buyers of medical insurance policies know more about the state of their health— and, therefore, how likely they are to submit medical bills to the insurance company—than will the insurance company that sells them the policies. Similarly, drivers know more about whether they are reckless drivers, homeowners know more about potential fire hazards in their homes, and so on, than do the insurance companies selling them policies. Insurance companies are able to cover their costs, including the opportunity cost of the funds invested in them by their owners, only if they are able to set the prices—or *premiums*—of their insurance policies at levels that accurately reflect how many claims for payment the people they have insured are likely to submit.

Reducing Adverse Selection in the Insurance Market

Adverse selection problems arise because sick people are more likely to want medical insurance than are healthy people, reckless drivers are more likely to want automobile insurance than are careful drivers, and people living in homes that are fire hazards are more likely to want fire insurance than are people living in safe homes. If insurance companies have trouble determining who is healthy and who is sick or who is a reckless driver and who is a safe driver, they will end up setting their premiums too low and will fail to cover their costs. To reduce the problem of adverse selection, insurance companies gather as much information as they can on people applying for policies. For example, people applying for individual medical insurance policies or life insurance policies usually need to submit their medical records to the insurance company. The insurance company will usually also carry out its own medical examination, including requiring blood tests. People applying for automobile insurance will have their driving record reviewed. People who have caused accidents or who have speeding tickets will be charged higher premiums.

Sometimes the adverse selection problem leads insurance companies simply to refuse to offer insurance policies to certain people at any price. Someone with a terminal or chronic illness, for example, may find it difficult to buy an individual medical insurance or life insurance policy. The owner of a home or warehouse in an area that is prone to arson fires may have difficulty getting fire insurance. An alternative to refusing to sell policies to these people would be for insurance companies to charge very high premiums for coverage. This may make the adverse selection problem worse, however. When premiums are very high, only people who are almost certain to make a claim will purchase a policy.

The adverse selection problem can also be reduced if people are automatically covered by insurance. For example, state governments require that every driver buy automobile insurance. This policy reduces the problem of insurance being purchased primarily by bad drivers. As we saw at the beginning of the chapter, however, insurance companies still face the problem of determining the profit-maximizing prices to charge for their policies.

Insurance companies can reduce adverse selection problems in selling medical insurance and life insurance by offering *group coverage* to large firms—including colleges and universities—or to alliances of smaller firms. With group coverage, everyone employed by a firm is automatically covered. As long as the group is large enough, it is likely to reflect the proportions of healthy and unhealthy people found in the general population. As a result, it is much easier for insurance companies to estimate the average number of claims likely to be filed under a group medical insurance or life insurance policy than it would be to predict the number of claims likely to be filed under an individual policy. Because everyone in the group must pay the premium—or have it paid for them by their employer—the problem of only sick people buying the insurance is avoided. Group coverage that allows healthy people not to participate is still subject to adverse selection problems, however. If healthy people don't participate, the number of claims filed per participating employee is likely to be high. This level of claims may cause the insurance company to raise the price it charges to the firm for the group policy. If the firm then raises the monthly payment required of employees, the higher price will discourage additional numbers of healthy employees from participating.

17-1 Making the Connection

Adverse Selection, Annuities, and Social Security Reform

We have seen that one effect of adverse selection in a market is that the equilibrium quantity of the good or service may be smaller than it would have been if there were no information problems. Several studies have shown that this is true of the market for *annuities* in the United States and other countries. An annuity is a promise by an insurance company to pay a policyholder a certain amount each month or year for as long as the policyholder is alive. Retired people sometimes buy annuities to insure themselves against running out of money before they die. As in other insurance markets, the market for annuities has an asymmetric information problem. Buyers of these policies may have more information on how long they are likely to live, based on their health and their family history, than do insurance companies. Adverse selection, then, can result in more people who expect to be long-lived buying annuities than people who believe they may die early.

In Great Britain, for example, the average 65-year-old man has a 41 percent probability of living until age 82. But 65-year-old men who have purchased annuities have a 56 percent probability of living to the same age. Insurance companies increase the prices they charge for annuities to compensate for the buyers of annuities being longer-lived than the average person. These higher prices deter some buyers from purchasing annuities, reducing the equilibrium quantity below what it would be if asymmetric information were not a problem.

Adverse selection in the market for annuities is important in the debate over reform of the Social Security system in the United States. The Social Security system provides monthly payments to retired workers and is currently financed by a tax on wages. In effect, under the Social Security system the federal government is providing annuities to retirees. Some economists and policymakers have proposed changing the system so that workers would be allowed to invest a portion of the taxes collected from their wages into personal retirement accounts. How retirees would withdraw funds from their retirement accounts is subject to debate. Under a voluntary system of purchasing annuities, adverse selection could be a problem. As we discussed earlier, adverse selection problems in insurance markets are reduced when insurance coverage is made mandatory. If retirees were required to put some specific fraction of the funds in their accounts into annuities, adverse selection would be reduced because those people purchasing annuities would be a cross-section of the population rather than disproportionately people who expected to be long-lived. This would enable insurance companies to sell annuities at a lower price and still cover their costs.

People who buy annuities live longer than people who don't.

Sources: Olivia S. Mitchell, James M. Poterba, Mark J. Warshawsky, and Jeffrey R. Brown, "New Evidence on the Money's Worth of Individual Annuities," *American Economic Review*, Vol. 89. No. 5, December 1999, pp. 1299–1318; and Amy Finkelstein and James M. Poterba, "Selection Effects in the United Kingdom Individual Annuities Market," *Economic Journal*, Vol. 112, January 2002, pp. 28–50.

Moral Hazard

The insurance market is also subject to a second consequence of asymmetric information called *moral hazard*. **Moral hazard** refers to the tendency of people to change their actions because they have insurance. For example, once a firm has taken out a fire insurance policy on a warehouse, it may be a little less careful about avoiding fire hazards. Similarly, someone with medical insurance may visit the doctor for treatment of a cold or other minor illness, when he or she would not do so without the insurance.

Insurance companies can take steps to reduce moral hazard problems. For example, a fire insurance company may insist that a firm install a sprinkler system in a warehouse to offset any increased carelessness once the policy is in place, or it may reserve the right to inspect the warehouse periodically to check for fire hazards. Insurance companies

Moral hazard The tendency of people who have insurance to change their actions because of the insurance, or, more broadly, actions taken by one party to a transaction that are different from what the other party expected at the time of the transaction.

Don't Let This Happen To You!

Don't Confuse Adverse Selection with Moral Hazard

The two key consequences of asymmetric information are adverse selection and moral hazard. It is easy to get these concepts mixed up. One way to keep them straight is to remember that adverse selection refers to what happens *at the time* of entering into the transaction. An example would be an insurance company that sells a life insurance policy to a terminally ill person because the company lacks

full information on the state of the person's health. Moral hazard refers to what happens *after* entering into the transaction. For example, a nonsmoker buys a life insurance policy and then starts smoking four packs of cigarettes a day. (It may help in remembering that *a*dverse selection comes before *m*oral hazard, to notice that *a* comes before *m* in the alphabet.)

YOUR TURN: Test your understanding by doing related problem 11 on page 552 at the end of this chapter.

also use *deductibles* and *co-payments* to reduce moral hazard. A deductible requires the holder of the insurance policy to pay a certain dollar amount of a claim. With a co-payment, the insurance company pays only a percentage of any claim. Suppose you have a medical insurance policy with a $200 deductible and a 20 percent co-payment, and you have a medical bill of $1,000. You must pay the first $200 of the bill and 20 percent of the remaining $800. Deductibles and co-payments give the holders of insurance policies incentives to avoid filing claims.

② **LEARNING OBJECTIVE**

Apply the concepts of adverse selection and moral hazard to financial markets.

Adverse Selection and Moral Hazard in Financial Markets

Adverse selection and moral hazard pose problems for firms and investors in the markets for stocks and bonds. In Chapter 7, we saw that most firms have to raise funds by borrowing from banks. Asymmetric information is a key reason why only large corporations are able to raise funds by selling stocks and bonds. Every firm knows more about its financial situation than does any potential investor. Because investors have trouble distinguishing between well-run and poorly-run firms, they are reluctant to buy the stocks and bonds of firms unless a great deal of public information about these firms is available. As a result, this means only firms that are studied closely by investment analysts working for brokerage firms and investment companies can succeed in selling stocks and bonds to investors. The investment analysts state their opinions of the true financial health of firms in reports that are available to the investing public. A great deal of public information about Microsoft is available, and investment analysts follow the firm closely. Not much public information is available about small firms like Anisul's Software Solutions, and no investment analysts follow the firm. As a result, Microsoft can raise funds by selling stocks and bonds, but Anisul's Software Solutions can't.

Investors also worry about moral hazard. Once a firm has sold stocks and bonds, what will it do with the funds it has raised? Of course, investors expect that the firm will use the funds in ways that will make the firm more profitable. But the possibility exists that the firm will use the funds in ways that actually reduce profits, which is obviously not in the best interests of investors. For instance, the funds might be used to pay higher salaries to the firm's managers or to open an unneeded branch office in Paris, to which the managers can make frequent visits. In the worst case, the firm's managers might actually steal the funds. Once again, the larger the firm is and the more carefully investment analysts follow its activities, the less likely moral hazard is to be a problem. This reason explains, in part, why investors are willing to buy the stocks and bonds of large firms but not of small firms. (You might notice that we are using a broader definition of moral hazard here than we did when discussing insurance. In this case, moral hazard refers to actions taken by one party to a transaction that are different from what the other party expected at the time of the transaction.)

Reducing Adverse Selection and Moral Hazard in Financial Markets

The decline in stock prices that followed the great stock market crash of 1929 wiped out the savings of many investors. Some investors complained that firms had failed to provide them with accurate financial information. Congress responded in 1934 by establishing the *Securities and Exchange Commission* (SEC) to regulate the stock and bond markets. The SEC requires that firms register stocks or bonds they wish to sell with the SEC. The firms must also provide potential investors with a *prospectus* that contains all relevant financial information on the firms. Although investors sometimes complain that a firm's prospectus is difficult to understand, the SEC did succeed in increasing the amount of information available to potential investors. This additional information helped reduce the adverse selection and moral hazard problems in financial markets and increased the number of firms that have been able to raise funds by selling stocks and bonds.

The steep decline in stock prices that occurred from 2000 to 2002 made it clear that information problems still exist in financial markets. During the stock market boom of the late 1990s, many investors became less cautious and more willing to invest in firms about which they had relatively little information. As investors became more focused on stock prices during those years, pressure increased for firms to report that they had earned profits at least as high as investment analysts were forecasting they would. Firms reporting profits that were lower than analysts had forecast could experience a sharp decline in the price of their stock. As we discussed in Chapter 7, the managers of some firms gave in to the temptation to "cook the books" by falsely reporting that their profits were much higher than they really were. This cheating could not be concealed forever. During 2002, a number of scandals involving the reporting of inflated profits came to light. These scandals served as a reminder to investors of the difficulty of overcoming adverse selection and moral hazard problems in financial markets.

Moral Hazard, Big Time: The Accounting Scandals of 2002

17-2 Making the Connection

The basic information on the financial condition of a company is contained in its *financial statements,* particularly its income statement and balance sheet. A firm's income statement reports its profits over a period of time, and its balance sheet shows the net value of the firm, based on the value of everything it owns minus the value of everything it owes. (For more on financial statements, see the Appendix to Chapter 7). Investment analysts at brokerage firms and individual investors rely on this information when evaluating firms. All firms that issue stock to the public have their statements *audited* by a certified public accountant (CPA). The CPA is an employee of an accounting firm, *not* of the company being audited. The audit is intended to provide investors with an independent opinion as to whether the company's financial statements fairly reflect the true financial condition of the firm.

Unfortunately, a series of spectacular scandals during 2002 revealed that the financial statements of even some very large firms were not reliable. In July 2002, WorldCom, the second-largest provider of long-distance telephone service in the United States, filed for bankruptcy. In June, WorldCom executives had admitted to misstating more than $3.8 billion in expenses on its financial statements. As a result, instead of the profit it initially reported earning during 2001 and the first quarter of 2002, it actually had lost $1.2 billion. Investors saw the value of the 3 billion shares of stock issued by WorldCom drop to zero. Enron, an energy trading company, had managed to keep much of its debt from being included on its balance sheet. Eventually, it too had to declare bankruptcy. Members of the Rigas family, which controlled Adelphia Communications, one of the largest cable television companies in the United States, were accused of using more than $250 million of the firm's money for personal expenses—a striking example of moral hazard. The firm also filed for bankruptcy, and two Rigas family members were convicted of looting the company.

The news that these and other firms had "cooked the books" illustrates the difficulty that moral hazard poses for investors. The management of a firm knows far more about the firm's finances than any outside investor can. If investors believe they cannot rely on the firm's financial statements to reflect the true financial condition of the firm, they will be extremely reluctant to invest in the firm.

Former Enron Chairman Kenneth Lay was caught up in the accounting scandals of 2002.

Many observers have argued that a general loss of confidence in the reliability of financial statements was behind the wave of selling that hit U.S. stock markets in the summer of 2002.

To help restore confidence in financial statements, Congress passed and President George W. Bush signed into law the Sarbanes-Oxley Act of 2002, which is aimed at strengthening the country's security laws. The bill authorizes the SEC to set up a government board to oversee the auditing of financial statements. The government board was believed necessary because outside auditors had failed too often in their responsibility to ensure the accuracy of corporate financial statements. Under the provisions of the bill, auditors who willfully violate accounting rules face five-year prison sentences. The bill also requires chief executive officers and chief financial officers to personally certify the accuracy of financial statements. The maximum prison term for violating the securities laws was raised to 25 years.

Adverse Selection and Moral Hazard in Labor Markets

(3) **LEARNING OBJECTIVE**

Apply the concepts of adverse selection and moral hazard to labor markets.

Principal-agent problem Problem caused by an agent pursuing his own interests rather than the interests of the principal who hired him.

We saw in Chapter 7 that economists refer to the conflict between the interests of shareholders and the interests of top management as a **principal-agent problem.** This occurs when agents—in this case, a firm's top management—pursue their own interests rather than the interests of the principal—in this case, the shareholders of the corporation—who hired them. There is also the potential for a principal-agent problem between the managers of a firm and its workers. The moral hazard behind this principal-agent problem is that workers, once hired, may shirk their obligations and not work hard.

Employers can ensure that workers are doing their jobs by closely monitoring them. Telemarketing firms, for example, can monitor their employees electronically to ensure they make the required number of telephone calls per hour. Not all firms, however, can monitor their employees so closely. Often firms must rely on workers being sufficiently motivated so they do not shirk their responsibilities. One way to motivate workers is to increase the value to them of their current jobs, relative to other jobs they might have. If you consider your current job to be more valuable than the alternatives, you will be reluctant to shirk because you won't want to risk being fired. Firms have several ways to make a worker's job seem more valuable:

➤ *Efficiency wages.* There is a market for every kind of labor, just as there is a market for every good and service. A firm's demand for labor is determined by how much output workers can produce for the firm—the workers' *productivity*—and by the price the firm receives when it sells the output the workers produce. The supply of labor is determined by the willingness of workers to supply a given amount of work at a particular wage. The equilibrium wage equates the quantity of labor demanded to the quantity of labor supplied. If a firm offers to pay a wage above the equilibrium wage, a worker will consider the job to be valuable and will be less likely to shirk and risk losing the job. An *efficiency wage* is a higher-than-equilibrium wage used by firms to give workers an incentive to work harder.

➤ *Seniority system.* Many firms use a seniority system under which workers who have been with the firm longer receive higher pay and other benefits, such as the choice of better or more interesting jobs. A worker who early in his career at a firm is fired for shirking will give up the possibility of participating in the benefits of seniority. A seniority system can have an effect similar to an efficiency wage in giving workers an incentive to work harder.

➤ *Profit sharing.* The harder employees work, the more profits a firm makes, but employees don't share in these increased profits if they are paid a fixed wage or salary. Under a profit-sharing plan, employees receive a share of the profits earned by the firm. The harder the employee works, the more profit the firm earns, and the higher the employee's income. Profit sharing increases the incentive of an employee to work hard. One problem with some profit-sharing plans is that they don't increase the incentive very much. For example, suppose you work at a firm with 100 employees and by working harder you can increase the firm's profits by $10,000 per year. If each employee shares equally in the increased profits, your income will rise, but only by $100 per year. This increase is probably not enough to compensate you for the additional effort required. In addition, a firm's profits can be affected by many factors, such as a slowdown in the economy, that are unrelated to how hard a particular employee works. So, you might work very hard during a given period and actually see the profits of the firm fall for reasons you can't control. In that case, your hard work would not have increased your income at all.

SOLVED PROBLEM **17-1**

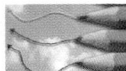

Changing Workers' Compensation to Reduce Adverse Selection and Moral Hazard

③ LEARNING OBJECTIVE

Apply the concepts of adverse selection and moral hazard to labor markets.

Jill runs a clothing store. She is concerned that her salespeople are not making much effort to be friendly to customers or to persuade them to buy more clothes. Because Jill has to be out of the store most of the day, it isn't easy for her to monitor the activities of her salespeople. Jill is paying her workers an hourly wage, but she is considering switching to paying them on commission: They would be compensated on the basis of how much clothing they sold.

a. What effect would this change have on the types of workers Jill attracts?

b. Briefly explain whether this change is likely to increase Jill's profits.

Solving the Problem:
Step 1: Review the chapter material. This problem is about adverse selection and moral hazard in labor markets, so you may want to review the section "Adverse Selection and Moral Hazard in Labor Markets," which begins on page 542.

Step 2: Use the ideas of advsere selection and moral hazard in labor markets to answer question (a). When workers are not monitored, they have an incentive to expend as little effort as possible, which is the moral hazard problem in labor markets. When salespeople are paid an hourly wage, their compensation is determined by how many hours they are at work, rather than how much they sell. If Jill switches to a system in which compensation depends on how much workers sell, she is likely to attract more workers who have the ability and interest to sell clothes. Workers who don't have much interest in selling clothes are unlikely to stay, because their compensation will be reduced. Jill's new compensation scheme will reduce the adverse selection problem she faces when hiring workers.

Step 3: Answer question (b) by analyzing the effect of the new compensation system on Jill's profits. Whether Jill's profits rise under the new compensation system depends on whether she is correct that her workers are not making much effort to sell clothes. If she is correct, switching from paying hourly wages to paying commissions is likely to reduce both the adverse selection and moral hazard problems she faces. She will attract people willing to work harder and she will provide them with an incentive to sell more clothes, so her sales and profits should increase.

YOUR TURN: For more practice, do related problem 12 on page 552 at the end of this chapter. Visit www.prenhall.com/hubbard for an interactive exercise related to this Solved Problem.

The Winner's Curse: When Is It Bad to Win an Auction?

④ LEARNING OBJECTIVE

Explain the winner's curse and why it occurs.

Information problems can also occur in auctions. In some auctions, neither the bidder nor the seller has complete information about what is being auctioned. For example, when the government auctions off land for oil drilling, neither the government nor the oil companies bidding in the auctions know with certainty how much oil is in the land. In the 1950s and 1960s, the oil companies that won bids to drill on the North Slope of

Winner's curse The idea that the winner in certain auctions may have overestimated the value of the good, thus ending up worse off than the losers.

Alaska and in the Gulf of Mexico did not earn the profits they expected. Three engineers with the Atlantic Richfield oil company argued that this was not due to bad luck, but was the result of a general tendency for the winners of auctions, like the ones held for the oil fields, to bid too high. This outcome, called the **winner's curse,** applies to other auctions as well. Knowledge of the winner's curse can make it possible for a savvy firm to win an auction with a high bid that is low enough to be very profitable.

Why were the winning bidders in government auctions of oil fields disappointed with their profits? Three Atlantic Richfield engineers, E. C. Capen, R. V. Clapp, and W. M. Campbell, proposed an explanation. They noted that each firm participating in the auctions used geological data, data on how productive nearby wells had been, and other information to estimate how much oil was likely to be available in each tract of land up for bid. Because of the uncertainty in interpreting the information available, companies made very different bids. Figure 17-1 shows the actual bids made by seven oil companies in 1967 on a tract of land off the Louisiana coast.

Clearly, Company A, with a bid of $32.5 million, was the most optimistic about how much oil the tract contained. Company G, which bid only $3.3 million, was the least optimistic. Who was right? Capen, Clapp, and Campbell argued that as the companies bid on many tracts using the best available information, each company would overestimate the amount of oil in some tracts and underestimate the amount of oil in other tracts. Their mistakes of sometimes being too high would tend to offset their mistakes of sometimes being too low, so *on average their estimates would be correct.* For example, in the case of the tract in Figure 17-1, it was likely that the true amount of oil in the tract was worth about $11.6 million, or the average of the seven bids. The problem for Company A is that it won the auction with a bid of $32.5 million, which was much too high given the amount of oil that was likely to actually be in the tract. Capen, Clapp, and Campbell came to two conclusions:

1. "In competitive bidding, the winner tends to be the player who most overestimates true tract value."

2. "He who bids on a parcel what he thinks it is worth will, in the long run, be taken to the cleaners."

These conclusions became known as the *winner's curse,* because they indicate that the winner of an auction may end up worse off than the losers. In fact, Capen, Clapp, and Campbell concluded that the oil companies would have made a greater return on their investments if they had taken the funds and put them in a savings account in a bank, rather than using them to bid on oil tracts.

FIGURE 17-1

Oil Company Bids to Drill Off the Louisiana Coast, 1967

In 1967, seven oil companies bid to drill on land off the Louisiana coast. Because the amount of oil contained in any particular tract of land up for bid is very uncertain, the bids by oil companies differ widely. The company that has the most optimistic estimate is likely to win the auction. It is also likely to be disappointed in the profits it earns from the tract.

Source: E. C. Capen, R. V. Clapp, and W. M. Campbell, "Competitive Bidding in High-Risk Situations," *Journal of Petroleum Engineering,* June 1971, p. 642.

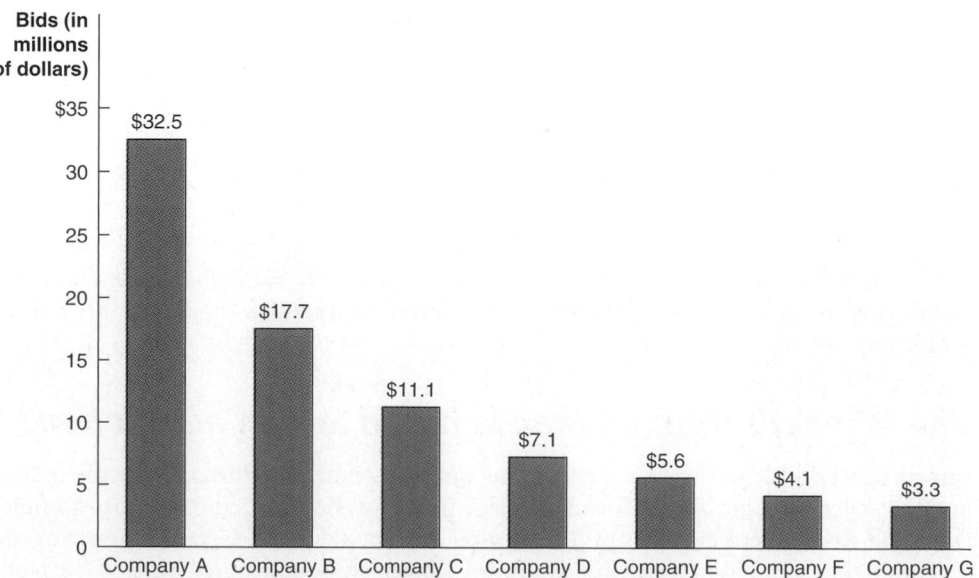

Is There a Winner's Curse in the Marriage Market?

In the United States, about 43 percent of all marriages end in divorce. Why the divorce rate is so high is a complicated question. But economics can provide some insight, even if it can't provide a full explanation. Economists have proposed thinking of the interactions of men and women looking for marriage partners as a *marriage market*. Of course, the marriage market is not a typical market in which a good or service is bought and sold for money. But like participants in other markets, the men and women in the marriage market are trying to make themselves as well off as possible, and they are competing against each other to find the best partners.

It's hard to tell how good a marriage partner someone will make until you are actually married to him or her. Like oil companies trying to estimate the amount of oil in a tract of land, men and women use all the information they can to estimate how good a spouse someone will be. But which potential mate are you likely to pursue most strongly? And which poten- tial mate is most likely to

A life of bliss or the winner's curse?

find your romantic ardor greater than that of other potential marriage partners? The answer to both questions is the person whose value as a marriage partner you have most greatly overestimated. In other words, if your estimate of how desirable someone is as a marriage partner is much higher than other people's estimates, you have a good chance of marrying that person, but also a good chance of discovering later that your estimate was wrong. The idea of the winner's curse can help explain not only why oil companies can be dissatisfied with the profits from winning oil field auctions, but also why many people are apparently dissatisfied with their marriages.

When Does the Winner's Curse Apply?

Does the winner's curse indicate that the winner of every auction would have been better off losing? No, because the winner's curse applies only to auctions of *common-value* assets—such as oil fields—that would be given the same value by all bidders if they had perfect information. The winner's curse does not apply to auctions of *private-value* assets where the value to each bidder depends on the bidder's own preferences. For example, if you win an auction on eBay for a DVD player, you are not subject to the winner's curse if the DVD player is new and the auction described it completely. You had all the informa- tion you needed to evaluate the DVD player, and your bid reflected your preference for a DVD player relative to other things you could have purchased.

SOLVED PROBLEM 17-2

Auctions, Available Information, and the Winner's Curse

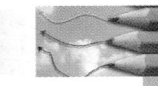

④ LEARNING OBJECTIVE
Explain the winner's curse
and why it occurs.

Suppose that the government has decided to auction off oil fields in Alaska. Suppose, also, that advances in geology have increased the accuracy with which oil companies can predict how much oil will be found in a tract of land. Are these advances likely to increase or decrease the amount of revenue the government receives from the auction?

Solving the Problem:

Step 1: Review the chapter material. This problem is about the winner's curse, so you may want to review the section "The Winner's Curse: When Is It Bad to Win an Auction?" which begins on page 543.

Step 2: Use the information on the winner's curse to answer the problem. This is an example of a common-value auction where the bidders lack full information on what is being auctioned. We've already seen that oil companies run the risk of the winner's curse when they do not know exactly how much oil is in each tract being auctioned. As shown in Figure 17-1, the winning bidder may significantly overestimate the true amount of oil and end up earning little, if any profit, from its investment.

If the oil companies knew with certainty how much oil was in each tract, the bids would all be close together and close to the true value of the tract. The amount of revenue received by the government would be lower in this case, because the highest bid would be lower. In this question, some uncertainty remains about how much oil is in each tract, so the winner's curse may still be a problem for the companies. Because advances in geology have allowed the companies to make more accurate estimates, the highest bid is likely to be lower than it would have been. Therefore, the advances in geology are likely to *decrease* the amount of revenue the government receives from the auction.

YOUR TURN: For more practice, do related problem 20 on page 552 at the end of this chapter. Visit www.prenhall.com/hubbard for an interactive exercise related to this Solved Problem.

Pacific Telesis Uses the Winner's Curse to Its Own Advantage

In late 1994, the Federal Communications Commission began auctioning 99 licenses that would allow firms to operate wireless communication networks—for cell phones and similar devices—in specific geographic areas. Pacific Telesis (now part of SBC Communications) was the local telephone provider in California at that time. It was determined to win the FCC auctions to provide wireless service in California.

Pacific Telesis hired several economists to help plan its bidding strategy. There was no doubt that the licenses being auctioned were valuable, but given the rapid evolution of the market for cell phones and other wireless devices, no firm had enough information to determine exactly how valuable. In these circumstances, Pacific Telesis's economists knew that the problem of the winner's curse meant that the firm ran the risk of either overpaying or losing the auction to another firm that would overpay. To avoid this outcome, Pacific Telesis launched a campaign to warn other firms that it was far more knowledgeable about this market than they were, and that to win the auction another firm would have to pay more than the licenses were worth. Pacific Telesis took out full-page ads in newspapers in the cities where the corporate headquarters of their competitors were located. The ads emphasized that Pacific Telesis had significant cost advantages over its rivals in California and that it was determined to win the licenses there. Lyndon Daniels, president of wireless operations at Pacific Telesis, stated in an interview with the *Wall Street Journal*, "If somebody takes California away from us, they'll never make any money." Finally, in an effort to ensure that other firms understood the potential dangers of overbidding, Pacific Telesis hired a prominent economist to give seminars on the winner's curse to the other telecommunications firms.

Pacific Telesis's strategy proved successful. Most other firms bid very cautiously on the California licenses—at least partly to avoid the winner's curse—and Pacific Telesis won the auctions with relatively low bids. For example, it paid only $437 million—or about $23 per person—for the Los Angeles license. This amount was less than other companies paid for licenses in other U.S. cities where the licenses were thought to be less valuable because of lower incomes, less concentrated populations, and slower population growth than in Los Angeles. Not only had Pacific Telesis avoided the winner's curse, it had used it to help hold down bids from rival companies.

Want to Make Some Money? Try Auctioning a Jar of Coins

A simple experiment illustrates the winner's curse. Fill a jar with coins. Let a group of people—everyone in your economics class?—inspect the jar. Then auction off the jar: Whoever makes the highest bid gets the jar. The winner will, of course, be the person with the highest estimate of how many coins are in the jar. Just as with oil companies bidding on oil fields, the winner is also likely to have *overestimated* the value of the coins in the jar. Because the high bid is likely to be greater than the value of the coins in the jar, you should be left with a profit—equal to the difference between what the high bidder pays and the value of the coins in the jar.

Will the winner's curse really apply in this situation? Max Bazerman of Harvard University and William Samuelson of Boston University tested this possibility using MBA students enrolled in economics classes at Boston University. In each of 12 classes, they auctioned off four jars containing either coins or paper clips. The students were told that large paper clips were worth 4 cents and small paper clips were worth 2 cents. They were also told that the winning bidder would receive the value of the jar minus the value of his bid. For example, if the value of the coins or paper clips in a jar was $20, and the high bid for a jar was $15, the winner would receive $5. In addition, they asked students to submit written estimates of the value of the coins in the jars. They offered a $2 prize for the best estimate of each jar.

Although the students didn't know it, each jar contained exactly $8 worth of coins or paper clips. The students' average estimate of the value of the coins or paper clips in the jar was too low—just $5.13. Despite this, the average of the winning bids in the 48 auctions for the jars was $10.01, so on average the high bidders lost $2.01. These MBA students had fallen victim to the winner's curse.

Sources: Richard H. Thaler, *The Winner's Curse: Paradoxes and Anomalies of Economic Life*, New York: The Free Press, 1992, Chapter 5; and Max Bazerman and William Samuelson, "I Won the Auction but Don't Want the Prize," *Journal of Conflict Resolution*, Vol. 27, December 1983, pp. 618–634.

17-4 *Making the Connection*

The highest bidder on this jar of coins could lose money.

Conclusion

In this chapter, we have looked at situations of asymmetric information, where either the buyer or the seller has information not available to the other. We also looked at situations where both the buyer and the seller lack full information, which can lead to outcomes such as the winner's curse. Markets, including financial markets and labor markets, are more efficient when buyers and sellers have full information. Because information problems are significant in many markets, the economics of information is an important area of study.

Read *An Inside Look* on the next page to learn how insurance companies in Florida dealt with information problems during back-to-back hurricanes in 2004.

WALL STREET JOURNAL, SEPTEMBER 7, 2004

Hurricane Damage

As Floridians begin picking up the pieces from the second devastating hurricane in less than a month, many are also discovering the full effects of a decade of maneuvering by insurance companies and state officials that has dramatically reduced the obligations of private insurers to pay for the impact of catastrophic storms.

Charley and Frances are two of the biggest hurricanes to hit the U.S. since Andrew slammed into southeastern Florida in 1992, wreaking $15.5 billion in insured damage and wiping out every cent of profit insurance companies had ever generated on property policies in the state. The losses forced 11 insurers out of business and triggered a wholesale revamping of Florida's insurance market in a desperate attempt to prevent other carriers from fleeing the state.

Big players such as Allstate Corp. agreed not to abandon a combined 1.2 million policyholders in Florida only after state officials began cooperating in a legislative and regulatory effort to shift from insurance companies to consumers the burden for paying hundreds of millions of future storm-related losses.

As a result, hundreds of thousands of Florida homeowners—including many who have paid for what they believed was "full" property insurance—now find themselves holding the bag for a much bigger portion of the estimated $10 billion to $15 billion in insured damage from Frances and Charley than they would have a decade ago.

Florida regulators and legislators allowed private insurance companies to add hefty new deductibles to homeowners' policies and to raise premium rates in some cases by as much as fourfold. . . .

What has happened in Florida is partly the result of a big shift in the way U.S. insurance companies have operated over the past decade. The industry has adopted increasingly sophisticated underwriting tools to avoid insuring higher-risk homes and has taken steps to lay more of the burden to pay claims on policyholders themselves. California residents who face the threat of storms or wildfires, for example, must choose between sometimes bare-bones coverage offered by insurance pools organized by the state and high-cost policies from niche insurers such as Lloyd's of London. But the shift of responsibility for property losses in Florida—in terms of the number of policyholders pushed into state-backed insurance funds and the hefty increases in premiums and deductibles—far exceeds what has happened in most other states . . .

In 2002, Florida lawmakers combined another insurer of last resort, the Florida Windstorm Underwriters Association, with the other big state-organized insurer, the Joint Underwriting Association, to form the Citizens Property Insurance Corp. Now, about 800,000 coastal homes that private insurers refuse to fully cover are currently insured by Citizens Property. . . .

For homeowners, the biggest change came through dramatically higher premiums and new deductibles that require policyholders to absorb thousand of dollars in costs from wind damage.

A total of 2.5 million Florida homeowners have policies with windstorm deductibles of 2% of their home's policy value. A further 177,000 homeowners have 5% deductibles, meaning a homeowner with a policy value of $300,000 would pay $15,000 to repair hurricane damage before the insurer would pay any part of the claim. . . .

Florida officials say the state's onerous deductibles are simply part of the price residents had to pay to keep private insurers in the state. Insurance generally is regulated on a state level, typically by powerful commissioners who have the authority to block rate increases proposed by companies and to set voluminous rules under which insurers operate. But after Andrew hit, many insurance companies said they would abandon Florida unless the state made radical changes in its regulations and rate structures.

Just months after that hurricane, more than a dozen insurers threatened to dump policyholders, potentially leaving more than one million homeowners without coverage. In April 1993, Allstate alone proposed dropping 300,000 policyholders.

Key Points in the Article

This article describes the insurance market in Florida at the time that hurricanes Charley and Frances hit the state during the summer of 2004. Hurricane Andrew had hit the state in 1992 and caused $15.5 billion in insured damage. This damage was enough to wipe out all of the profits earned by insurance companies on property insurance policies in the history of Florida. As a result, the Florida state government, which regulates the insurance market, allowed insurance companies to increase deductibles—dollar amounts of damage that the insurance policyholders must pay before receiving payments from insurance companies—and to increase the prices, or premiums, charged for the policies. In addition, the state set up the Citizens Property Insurance Corp., which receives state aid to provide insurance to homeowners that no private insurance company is willing to insure.

Analyzing the News

a We saw in this chapter some of the hazards to insurance companies that result from asymmetric information. The people who buy property insurance know more about how likely their homes are to be damaged than do insurance companies. In this market, the adverse selection problem arises because people most likely to buy insurance are the people whose homes are most likely to be damaged. But insurance companies are likely to suffer losses if most of the people they insure are likely to file claims. Companies selling property insurance in Florida also suffer from a moral hazard problem: If homeowners had no insurance, they would be likely to spend more to maintain their houses in a way to minimize damage from hurricanes. For example, the way roofs are constructed can partially determine how vulnerable they are to wind damage. Insurance companies cannot easily gather information on whether the houses they insure are well constructed and maintained.

b If insurance companies had perfect information on how likely people were to file claims, they could adjust the prices they charge accordingly. As we saw at the beginning of this chapter, many insurance companies have begun to use sophisticated models that allow them to better match the prices they charge for insurance with how likely the buyer is to file a claim. Property insurers in Florida faced two problems in pricing their policies: The first was the usual asymmetric information problem of not being able to determine exactly how likely people were to file claims. The other problem was that approval for increases in prices had to be granted by the state government. After hurricane Andrew hit Florida in 1992 and caused heavy losses to insurance companies in the state, the government allowed the companies to begin including high deductibles in their policies and to raise prices.

c Deductibles help to reduce adverse selection and moral hazard problems because they require policyholders to bear some of the costs of claims. In states like Florida that are subject to hard-to-predict but potentially devastating disasters like hurricanes, deductibles also shift some of the risk from the companies to the policyholders. From the insurers' point of view, this reduces the chance that a disaster will force them into bankruptcy. Because hurricanes inflict the most damage to houses built near the coast, after Hurricane Andrew, many insurance companies in Florida refused to insure houses in certain areas. The state government was forced to set up a special insurance corporation to insure these people. A similar approach is used in many states to provide automobile insurance to high-risk drivers that no private company will insure. In both cases, companies are reluctant to insure very high-risk people, even if they are allowed to charge them very high prices, because charging very high prices can make the adverse selection problem even worse. The graph below shows that changes in the Florida insurance market in the 1990s allowed insurance companies to reduce the losses from Hurricane Charley in the summer of 2004 compared with the losses they had suffered from Hurricane Andrew in 1992.

Thinking Critically
ABOUT POLICY

1. A student says to you, "I don't see how the moral hazard problem is an issue when it comes to the hurricane insurance market. After all, how does having insurance affect the odds that your home will get hit by a hurricane?" How do you respond?
2. When a major hurricane strikes, people's lives are thrown into disarray. Some unlucky person may have to evacuate, have his home destroyed, and get laid off by a devastated employer all on the same day. In addition, he is likely to get hit by a hefty insurance deductible. Would you back a policy that requires insurance companies to waive deductibles when such a severe natural disaster hits? Explain.

Source: *Wall Street Journal.* Eastern Edition [Staff Produced Copy Only] by Christopher Oster, Carrick Mollenkamp, C. Copyright 2004 by Dow Jones & Co Inc. Reproduced with permission of Dow Jones & Co Inc. in the format Textbook via Copyright Clearance Center.

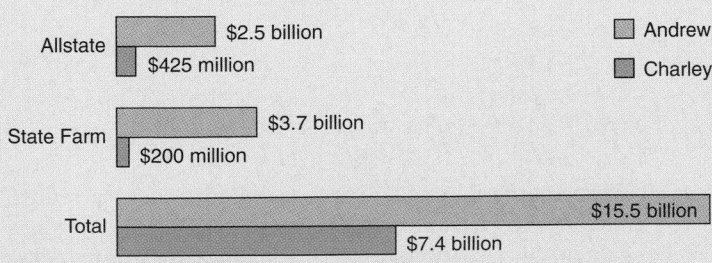

Figure 1: Changes in the Florida insurance market reduced the payout insurance companies made following Hurricane Charley in the summer of 2004.

Sources: Insurance Information Institute; Morgan Stanley

SUMMARY

LEARNING OBJECTIVE ① Define asymmetric information and distinguish between moral hazard and adverse selection. *Asymmetric information* is the situation in which one party to an economic transaction has less information than the other party. Asymmetric information can lead to *adverse selection*, which occurs when one party to a transaction takes advantage of knowing more than the other party to the transaction. An example is the "lemons" problem, where adverse selection may lead to only unreliable used cars being offered for sale. Asymmetric information can also lead to *moral hazard*, which is when one party to a transaction takes actions that are different from what the other party expected at the time of the transaction. For example, a firm that has taken out a fire insurance policy on a warehouse may be less careful in the future about avoiding fire hazards. Information problems result in the equilibrium quantity in markets being smaller than it would be if these problems did not exist. Therefore, there is a reduction in economic efficiency.

LEARNING OBJECTIVE ② Apply the concepts of adverse selection and moral hazard to financial markets. Adverse selection and moral hazard are serious problems in financial markets. When firms sell stocks and bonds, they know much more about their true financial condition than do potential investors. Investors are reluctant to buy stocks and bonds issued by small and medium-sized firms because they lack sufficient information about these firms. Investors also worry about the moral hazard problem of firms misus-

ing the funds they raise through the sale of stocks and bonds. The Securities and Exchange Commission (SEC) has the authority to regulate the stock and bond markets and attempts to reduce adverse selection and moral hazard problems. The scandals of 2002 that involved the top managers in a number of corporations misusing funds and reporting inflated profits indicate the extent of information problems in financial markets.

LEARNING OBJECTIVE ③ Apply the concepts of adverse selection and moral hazard to labor markets. The potential for a *principal-agent problem* exists between employers and workers. This problem is caused by an agent—a worker—pursuing his own interests rather than the interests of the principal who hired him. When workers are not monitored, they may have no incentive to work hard. Employers try to avoid this moral hazard problem by increasing the value to a worker of the worker's current job. Three ways to increase the value of a worker's job are efficiency wages, a seniority system, and profit sharing.

LEARNING OBJECTIVE ④ Explain the winner's curse and why it occurs. In auctions where bidders do not know the true value of what is being auctioned, the winner, by overestimating the value of what is being bid for, can end up worse off than the losers. This is known as the *winner's curse*, and it occurs in auctions of common-value assets that would be given the same value by all bidders if they had perfect information.

KEY TERMS

Adverse selection 537

Asymmetric
  information 536

Moral hazard 539

Principal-agent
  problem 542

Winner's curse 544

REVIEW QUESTIONS

1. What is asymmetric information? How does asymmetric information show up in the market for used cars?

2. What is the difference between adverse selection and moral hazard? Which is a bigger problem for consumers in the market for used cars?

3. Briefly discuss how adverse selection and moral hazard affect the market for insurance.

4. What methods do insurance companies use to reduce adverse selection and moral hazard?

5. Explain why asymmetric information makes it difficult for small firms to sell stocks and bonds.

6. What is the Securities and Exchange Commission? Why was it founded?

7. What additional responsibility did the SEC receive in 2002? Why did Congress and the president decide that the SEC needed to take on this additional responsibility?

8. How do adverse selection and moral hazard affect labor markets? What steps do firms take to deal with these problems?

9. What is the winner's curse? Is it a problem for the winner of every auction? Briefly explain why or why not.

10. Do you agree or disagree with the following statement: "The more information bidders have on the true value of what is being auctioned, the less likely they are to fall victim to the winner's curse." Briefly explain.

PROBLEMS AND APPLICATIONS

Please visit **www.prenhall.com/hubbard** *for solutions to the even-numbered problems as well as multiple-choice and true or false self-assessment quizzes.*

1. Suppose you see a 2001 Volkswagen Jetta advertised in the campus newspaper for $7,500. If you knew it was reliable, you would be willing to pay $10,000 for it. If you knew it was unreliable, you would only be willing to pay $5,000 for it. Under what circumstances should you buy it?

2. Why are there lemon laws for the car market but not for the television market or the toothbrush market?

3. Michael Kinsley, a political columnist, observes that, "The idea of insurance is to share the risks of bad outcomes." In what sense does insurance involve sharing risks? How does the problem of adverse selection affect the ability of insurance to provide the benefit of sharing risk?
Source: Michael Kinsley, "Congress on Drugs," *Slate*, August 1, 2002.

4. Under the Social Security retirement system, the federal government collects a tax on most people's wage income and makes payments to retired workers above a certain age who are covered by the system. (The age to receive full Social Security retirement benefits varies with the year the worker was born.) The Social Security retirement system is sometimes referred to as a program of social insurance. Is Social Security an insurance program in the same sense as a group life insurance or medical insurance policy that is provided by a company to its workers? Briefly explain.

5. There are 10,000 houses in Lawrence. Suppose that houses cost $100,000 and 5 percent of the houses burn down each year. Which 5 percent of houses will burn down in any particular year is impossible for anyone, including the owners, to predict. There is no fire insurance available to Lawrence residents, so you decide to start an insurance company and begin offering policies. Your policy will pay the purchaser $100,000 if his or her house burns down. You charge a premium of $22,000 per year.
   a. Are the residents of Lawrence likely to buy your policies? Briefly explain.

   b. Now suppose that 5 percent of the owners know with certainty that their houses will burn down and that the other 95 percent of the owners know with certainty that their houses will not burn down. You offer everyone the same insurance policy with the same $22,000 premium. What is your accounting profit likely to be for the year? Assume you have no explicit costs except for the payments you make to people who bought your policies and had their houses burn down.

   c. Now suppose people do not know with certainty whether their houses will burn down and that some houses are significantly more likely to burn down than others. Unfortunately, the owners of the houses that are significantly more likely to burn down know it, but you do not. Is it possible for you to restructure the insurance policies you offer—that is, change the terms of how much you pay out and the premium you charge—in order to deal with this problem?

6. Every state requires that drivers have an automobile insurance policy that covers any car they own and operate. Some people have such bad driving records that they are unable to find any insurance company willing to sell them a policy. These drivers are placed in an "assigned risk pool." Every insurance company that sells automobile insurance in the state is required to insure some drivers from the assigned risk pool. The state government usually sets the rates these drivers pay for insurance. Why is this system necessary? Why don't insurance companies voluntarily insure these bad drivers and charge them very high rates? Why does the state government have to force insurance companies to insure bad drivers?

7. An editorial in the *Wall Street Journal* argues that regulations imposed by state governments are responsible for making health insurance "so expensive to buy." The editorial singles out " 'community rating' (insurers can't price based on differing risk factors such as age) and 'guaranteed issue' (you can wait until you're sick to buy insurance)." What problems do these regulations cause for insurance companies? How might insurance companies respond to

these regulations? Do these regulations make consumers better off? The editorial concludes as follows:

> The real scandal in American health insurance isn't that some people lack coverage for this or that treatment, but that tens of millions of Americans risk financial ruin because of [government] policies that make basic insurance difficult or impossible to buy.

Briefly explain whether you agree or disagree with this conclusion.

Source: "Why Can't You Buy Insurance?", *Wall Street Journal*, October 1, 2002.

8. After the countries of Eastern Europe converted from Communism to the market system, they tried to set up stock and bond markets. Most of these markets have remained very small, with few firms being able to find buyers for their stocks or bonds. One economist remarked that the reason these financial markets have been unsuccessful is that, "The lemons problem has been too great." Explain what the economist meant.

9. In an article in the *New York Times*, Warren Buffett, one of the most successful investors of the last 30 years wrote, "For many years, I've had little confidence in the earnings reported by corporations." Why might he be suspicious that firms were not reporting their profits accurately?

Source: Warren Buffett, "Who Really Cooks the Books?", *New York Times*, July 24, 2002.

10. In 2002, Congress prohibited firms from making loans to members of their boards of directors or to their top managers. Do you think that this prohibition is meant to reduce asymmetric information problems? Briefly explain.

11. **[Related to *Don't Let This Happen To You!*]** Briefly explain whether or not you agree with the following: "From an employer's point of view, the moral hazard problem in labor markets is that the potential employees who don't intend to work hard are the ones who are most eager for you to hire them. The adverse selection problem is that once you have hired a worker, he or she has an incentive to work hard only if monitored."

12. **[Related to *Solved Problem 17-1*]** What role do tips play in dealing with the principal-agent problem in the market for restaurant servers? Suppose that a law is passed that outlaws tips, so that now restaurant servers just receive a wage, instead of a wage plus tips. Is the total income of servers likely to rise or fall? Briefly explain.

13. **[Related to the *Chapter Opener*]** Why have auto insurers like State Farm begun collecting more information on drivers and using models that employ thousands of variables to predict the chance that a driver will have an accident? Why didn't it do this sooner if these differences among drivers always existed?

14. Many firms provide information about their plans and financial health to investment analysts who have no stake in the firm. Why would firms divulge such secrets?

15. Colleges and universities grant tenure to many professors, making it virtually impossible to fire them after they've worked there for six or seven years. Analyze this labor market strategy in light of asymmetric information, adverse selection, and moral hazard.

16. The going wage for janitors is $6 per hour. The Executive Building decides to pay its janitors $10 per hour. Will this higher wage increase or decrease the firm's profits—or could it go either way? In your answer, discuss asymmetric information and efficiency wages.

17. Suppose you were advising one of the oil companies involved in the oil field bidding shown in Figure 17-1. What bidding strategy would you have recommended to the company so it could avoid the winner's curse?

18. After playing for six years in the major leagues, baseball players are free to sign a contract to play for any team (before that time they are obligated to play for the team that first signed them). In this situation, players often sign a contract to play for several years with the team that offers them the highest salary. Consider two players: Joe is a minor star who performs at about the same level each year. Sam's performance has been more uneven: Some years he seems like one of the best players in baseball, but in other years his performance has not been very good. Suppose Joe signs with the Cleveland Indians and Sam signs with the Cincinnati Reds. Three years later, is Cleveland or Cincinnati likely to be most satisfied that the player they signed played well enough to justify his salary? Briefly explain.

19. Review Making the Connection 17-4 on page 547. Suppose that a $100 bill is auctioned off instead of a jar containing an unknown number of coins. Will the winner's curse still apply? Briefly explain.

20. **[Related to *Solved Problem 17-2*]** Suppose that everyone in an auction has perfect information about the value of whatever is being auctioned. Will the winner's curse still apply? Briefly explain.

21. A corporate takeover occurs when one firm—or a group of outside investors—buys up a majority of the stock in another firm. The usual aim of a takeover is to take advantage of the efficiencies possible with the newly merged firm or to bring in new management and run the acquired firm more profitably. In either case, the investors taking over the acquired firm are expecting to profit from the takeover. However, studies of corporate takeovers by Richard Roll of UCLA show that although the stockholders of the firm being taken over receive substantial gains—because the acquiring firm or investors bid up the price of the stock of the acquired firm as they try to take it over—the firm or

investors carrying out the takeover earn small gains, if any. Relate Roll's finding to the problem of the winner's curse.
Source: Richard Roll, "The Hubris Hypothesis of Corporate Takeovers," *Journal of Business,* Vol. 59, No. 2, Pt. 1, April 1986, pp. 197–216.

22. Well-known novelists often auction off the rights to publish their latest books. John Dessauer has described the process:

    [M]ajor books are often "auctioned off" among publishers, *i.e.,* literally sold to the highest bidder. . . . The problem is, simply, that most of the auctioned books are not earning [the amounts paid for them]. In fact, very often such books have turned out to be dismal failures whose value was more perceived than real and which benefited from the ability of a plausible agent to sell the big sizzle on a small, tough steak.

    Why do publishers who win auctions for books often end up paying more than the book turns out to be worth?
    Source: John P. Dessauer, *Book Publishing: What It Is, What It Does,* 2nd ed., New York: Bowker, 1981, pp. 34–35.

23. In ancient Rome, the Praetorian Guards were the personal bodyguards of the emperor. The guard was made up of thousands of troops, and occasionally an emperor would lose control over them. In 193 A.D., the Praetorian Guard revolted and murdered Emperor Pertinax. The guard then decided to auction off the office of emperor. The ancient historian Dio described the situation:

    Then ensued a most disgraceful business and one unworthy of Rome. For, just as if it had been in some market or auction-room, both the City and its entire empire were auctioned off. The sellers were the ones who had slain their emperor, and the would-be buyers were Sulpicianus and Julianus.

    Didius Julianus won the auction with a bid that would be the equivalent of more than one billion dollars today. Unfortunately, he greatly overestimated the value of becoming emperor in this way. His reign was very short. The general Septimius Severus brought his army from the Danube to Rome, deposed Didius Julianus, and was proclaimed emperor. In the words of the historian Edward Gibbon, Didius Julianus was "beheaded as a common criminal, after having purchased, with an immense treasure, an anxious and precarious reign of only sixty-six days." Does the analysis in this chapter help you understand what happened to Didius Julianus?
    Source: Paul Klemperer and Peter Temin, "An Early Example of the 'Winner's Curse' in an Auction," *Journal of Political Economy,* December 2001.

24. Making the Connection 17-3 on page 545 shows that the winner's curse may apply to the marriage market. The winner's curse usually applies in markets with common-value assets but not in markets with private-value assets. Discuss whether it is more accurate to think of the marriage market as a market with common-value assets, private-value assets, or some combination of the two.

chapter

eighteen

18

The Tax System and the Distribution of Income

Should the Government Use the Tax System to Reduce Inequality?

> Bob Roth is the president of RoMan Manufacturing Inc. in Grand Rapids, Michigan. RoMan is a family-owned firm that manufactures transformers used in industrial welding. The firm employs about a hundred workers in three facilities in the Grand Rapids area. The profits of large corporations are taxed by the federal government at the corporate income tax rates. The profits of many small businesses, like RoMan, are taxed by the federal government at the individual income tax rates, the same rates that are applied by the federal government to the wages and salaries earned by individuals. Mr.

Roth notes that the federal income tax cuts of 2001 and 2003 helped provide the funds his firm needed to buy three computer-aided machine tools. He was quoted in a newspaper article as saying, "What I can tell you is [the tax cut] allows me to make better investments in our business, allows us to stay competitive and continue to grow our business. . . . Ultimately that is going to increase employment at RoMan."

How should we evaluate proposals to change the tax laws? Tax laws affect economic incentives and economic activity, and can also affect fairness. The questions raised by the

debate over the tax changes of 2001 and 2003 were not new. Presidents John F. Kennedy and Ronald Reagan proposed significant tax cuts that they claimed would enhance economic efficiency, while their opponents claimed that the tax cuts rewarded high-income taxpayers.

The debate over the tax system was particularly heated during 2004. John Kerry, the Democratic nominee for president, argued that major changes were needed in the U.S. tax system. According to Kerry, the tax cuts of 2001 and 2003 had increased the burden on individuals with low and moderate incomes,

After studying this chapter, you should be able to:

① Understand the tax system in the United States, including the principles that governments use to create tax policy.

② Understand the effect of price elasticity on tax incidence.

③ Discuss the distribution of income in the United States, and understand the extent of income mobility.

while the burden on the wealthy had been reduced, and corporations had received "tax giveaways that are nothing more than corporate welfare." He argued that an unfair tax system was contributing to a "widening gap between rich and poor." President George W. Bush argued that, by contrast, the individuals with the highest incomes were paying the majority of the federal individual income tax and that many of those individuals were businesspeople like Mr. Roth. President Bush also argued that changes in taxes had little effect on the distribution of income.

Putting aside the particulars of the political debate of 2004, the design of the tax system and the criteria to use in evaluating it are important questions. Has the tax code improved economic efficiency? Has the government, through its tax and other policies, had much impact on the distribution of income?

Tax policy is the subject of debate in all countries. *An Inside Look* on page 576 examines the effect of tax changes in Great Britain.

Source for quote from Bob Roth: Warren Veith, "The Race for the White House: Are Bush's Tax Cuts Doing the Job?" *Los Angeles Times*, September 29, 2004, p. 22.

> We saw in Chapter 2 that the government plays a significant role in making the market system work efficiently. The government must provide secure rights to private property and an independent court system to enforce contracts among private individuals. We saw in Chapter 5 that the government itself must sometimes supply goods—known as *public goods*—that will not be supplied by private firms. The government pays for its activities by imposing taxes on households, consumers, and firms. In this chapter, we discuss the principles that governments use to create tax policy. In particular, we will see how economists identify which taxes are most economically efficient. At the end of the chapter, we discuss the extent to which government policy—including tax policy—affects the distribution of income. We begin the chapter with an overview of the tax system in the United States.

The Tax System

In previous chapters, we discussed some of the many activities governments engage in, from regulating pollution to providing public goods such as homeland security. To raise the revenue for these activities, federal, state, and local governments in the United States must impose taxes on households, consumers, and firms. Most taxes are used to raise revenue, but some taxes, such as those on cigarettes or alcohol, are intended to discourage what society views as undesirable behavior. The most widely used taxes are these:

> *Individual income taxes.* The federal government, most state governments, and some local governments tax the wages, salaries, and other income of households and the profits of firms. This tax is the second largest source of revenue for the federal government. In 2003, the average U.S. taxpayer earned about $47,583 and paid federal personal income taxes of $6,033.

> *Social insurance taxes.* The federal government taxes wages and salaries to raise revenue for the Social Security and Medicare systems. Social Security makes payments to retired workers and to the disabled. Medicare helps pay the medical expenses of people over age 65. The Social Security and Medicare taxes are often referred to as "payroll taxes." As the U.S. population has aged, payroll taxes have increased. By 2004, 74 percent of taxpayers paid more in payroll taxes than in federal income taxes. Total social insurance tax receipts had grown to be larger than individual income tax receipts. The federal government and state governments also tax wages and salaries to raise revenue for the unemployment insurance system, which makes payments to workers who have lost their jobs.

> *Sales taxes.* Most state and local governments tax retail sales of most products. More than half the states exempt food from the sales tax, and a few states also exempt clothing.

> *Property taxes.* Most local governments tax homes, offices, factories, and the land they are built on. In the United States, the property tax is the largest source of funds for public schools.

> *Excise taxes.* The federal government and some state governments levy excise taxes on specific goods, such as gasoline, cigarettes, and beer.

An Overview of the U.S. Tax System

Panels (a) and (b) of Figure 18-1 show the revenue sources of the federal, state, and local governments. Panel (a) shows that the federal government raises more than 80 percent

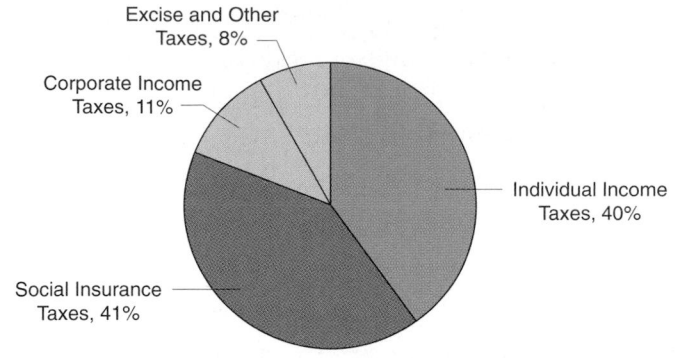

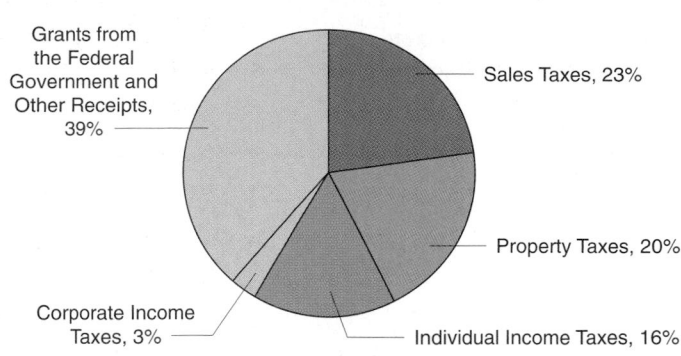

Tax	Amount (billions)	Amount per Person	Percentage of Total Tax Receipts
Social Insurance Taxes	$806	$2,745	41%
Individual Income Taxes	795	2,706	40
Corporate Income Taxes	218	743	11
Excise and Other Taxes	153	521	8
Total	$1,972	$6,715	100%

Tax	Amount (billions)	Amount per Person	Percentage of Total Tax Receipts
Sales Taxes	$364	$1,241	23%
Property Taxes	322	1,095	20
Individual Income Taxes	248	845	16
Corporate Income Taxes	40	137	3
Grants from the Federal Government and Other Receipts	611	2,081	39
Total	$1,585	$5,399	100%

(a) Sources of federal govenment revenue, 2004

(b) Sources of state and local government revenue, 2004

FIGURE 18-1   **Federal, State, and Local Sources of Revenue, 2004**

In recent years, social insurance taxes have passed individual income taxes as the most important source of revenue for the federal government. State and local governments receive large transfers from the federal government, in part to help pay for federally mandated programs. Sales taxes are the largest source of tax revenue for many states. Local governments raise most of their tax revenue from property taxes. (In panel (b), percentages of total tax receipts do not sum to 100 percent precisely due to rounding.)

Source: U.S. Department of Commerce, Bureau of Economic Analysis, *National Income and Product Accounts of the United States*, Tables 3.2 and 3.3, May 26, 2005.

of its revenue from the individual income tax and from social insurance taxes. Corporate income taxes and excise taxes account for much smaller fractions of federal revenues. In 2004, federal revenues of all types amounted to almost $2 trillion, or $6,700 per person. Over the past 40 years, federal revenues as a share of gross domestic product (GDP, the value of all the goods and services produced in the U.S. economy) have remained in a fairly narrow range between 17 and 23 percent.

Panel (b) shows that state and local governments rely on different sources of revenue than does the federal government. In fact, the largest source of revenue for state and local governments is grants from the federal government. These grants are intended in part to pay for programs that the federal government requires states and local governments to carry out. These programs, often called *federal mandates,* include the Medicaid program, which provides health care to poor people, and the Temporary Assistance for Needy Families (TANF) program, which provides financial assistance to poor families. Most states also raise substantial revenue from sales taxes. Local governments depend heavily on property taxes. Many local school districts, in particular, rely almost entirely on revenues from property taxes.

Progressive and Regressive Taxes

Economists often categorize taxes on the basis of how much tax people with different levels of income pay relative to their incomes. A tax is **regressive** if people with lower incomes pay a higher percentage of their income in tax than do people with higher incomes. A tax is **progressive** if people with lower incomes pay a lower percentage of

Regressive tax A tax for which people with lower incomes pay a higher percentage of their income in tax than do people with higher incomes.

Progressive tax A tax for which people with lower incomes pay a lower percentage of their income in tax than do people with higher incomes.

TABLE 18-1

Federal Income Tax Brackets and Tax Rates for Single Taxpayers, 2005

INCOME	TAX RATE
$0 to $7,300	10%
$7,301 to $29,700	15
$29,701 to $71,950	25
$71,951 to $150,150	28
$150,151 to $326,450	33
Over $326,450	35

Source: Internal Revenue Service.

their income in tax than do people with higher incomes. A tax is *proportional* if people with lower incomes pay the same percentage of their income in tax as do people with higher incomes.

The federal income tax is an example of a progressive tax. To see why, we must first consider the important distinction between a tax rate and a tax bracket. A *tax rate* is the percentage of income paid in taxes. A *tax bracket* refers to the income range within which a tax rate applies. Table 18-1 shows the federal income tax brackets and tax rates for single taxpayers in 2005.

We can use the table to calculate the federal income tax paid by Matt, a single taxpayer with an income of $100,000. This example is somewhat simplified because we are ignoring the *exemptions* and *deductions* that taxpayers can use to reduce the amount of income subject to tax. For example, taxpayers are allowed to exclude from taxation a certain amount of income, called the *personal exemption,* that represents very basic living expenses. Ignoring Matt's exemptions and deductions, he will have to make the tax payment to the federal government shown in Table 18-2. Matt's first $7,300 of income is in the 10 percent bracket, so he pays $730. His next $22,400 of income is in the 15 percent bracket, so he pays $3,360. His next $42,250 of income is in the 25 percent bracket, so he pays $10,563. His last $28,050 of income is in the 28 percent bracket, so he pays $7,854, which brings his total federal income tax bill to $22,507.

TABLE 18-2

Federal Income Tax Paid on Taxable Income of $100,000, 2005

ON MATT'S . . .	MATT PAYS TAX OF . . .
First $7,300 of income	$730
Next $22,400 of income	3,360
Next $42,250 of income	10,563
Last $28,050 of income	7,854
His total federal income tax payment	$22,507

18-1 *Making* the *Connection*

Which Groups Pay the Most in Federal Taxes?

At the beginning of this chapter, we mentioned the ongoing debate over whether to increase taxes on people with high incomes. To evaluate this debate, it's useful to know how much each income group pays of the total taxes collected by the federal government. The following table shows projections for 2005 by the Tax Policy Center, with taxpayers divided into quintiles from the 20 percent with the lowest income to the 20 percent with the highest income. The last row also shows taxpayers whose incomes put them in the top 1 percent. Column (1) shows the percentage of total income earned by each income group. Column (2) shows the percentage of total federal individual income tax paid by each income group. Column (3) shows the percentage of all federal taxes—including Social Security and Medicare payroll taxes—paid by each income group.

INCOME CATEGORY	PERCENTAGE OF TOTAL INCOME EARNED (1)	PERCENTAGE OF TOTAL FEDERAL INDIVIDUAL INCOME TAXES PAID (2)	PERCENTAGE OF TOTAL FEDERAL TAXES PAID (3)
Lowest 20%	2.6%	−2.3%	0.3%
Second 20%	6.7	−1.8	2.6
Third 20%	11.4	4.4	8.4
Fourth 20%	18.8	13.8	18.1
Highest 20%	60.7	85.8	70.5
Total	100.0%	100.0%	100.0%
Highest 1%	20.1	37.0	25.9

Federal taxes as a whole are progressive.

Source: Urban Institute and Brookings Institution, Tax Policy Center, www.taxpolicycenter.org. Used with permission. (Columns do not sum to 100 percent precisely due to rounding.)

The data in column (2) show that more than 85 percent of federal individual income taxes are paid by the 20 percent of taxpayers with the highest incomes. This share is more than their share of total income earned, which is about 61 percent, as shown in column (1). Taxpayers whose incomes put them in the top 1 percent pay more than one-third of the individual income tax. Many individuals in the lowest two quintiles of incomes receive tax credits from the federal government, so that they in effect pay negative taxes. Column (3) includes all federal taxes—including the payroll taxes that fund the Social Security and Medicare systems—but does not change the result very much: The 40 percent of taxpayers with the lowest incomes pay only about 3 percent of all federal taxes, while the 20 percent with the highest incomes pay more than two-thirds of all federal taxes. Notice, though, that the distribution of all federal taxes is less progressive than the distribution of income taxes. This outcome occurs because the Social Security and Medicare payroll taxes are less progressive than the federal income tax.

The following table shows taxes paid as a fraction of income by each income group in 2005. Column (1) shows federal income taxes paid as a fraction of income, and column (2) shows all federal taxes paid as a fraction of income. The table shows that as people's incomes rise, they pay a larger fraction of their income in taxes.

INCOME CATEGORY	FEDERAL INCOME TAXES PAID AS A FRACTION OF INCOME (1)	ALL FEDERAL TAXES PAID AS A FRACTION OF INCOME (2)
Lowest 20%	−5.6%	5.5%
Second 20%	0.6	12.0
Third 20%	4.1	15.6
Fourth 20%	7.5	19.6
Highest 20%	15.4	26.3
All income categores	10.0	21.4
Highest 1%	21.4	31.1

Source: Congressional Budget Office, "Effective Federal Tax Rates under Current Law," 2001–2014, http://www.cbo.gov/ftpdocs/57xx/doc5746/08-13-EffectiveFedTaxRates.pdf.

We can conclude that the federal individual income tax and all federal taxes taken together are progressive. Whether the federal tax system should be made more or less progressive is a significant political question.

Marginal tax rate The fraction of each additional dollar of income that must be paid in taxes.

Average tax rate Total tax paid divided by total income.

Marginal and Average Income Tax Rates

The fraction of each additional dollar of income that must be paid in taxes is called the **marginal tax rate.** The **average tax rate** is the total tax paid divided by total income. When a tax is progressive, as is the federal income tax, the marginal and average tax rates will differ. For example, in Table 18-2, Matt had a marginal tax rate of 28 percent because that is the rate he paid on the last dollar of his income. But his average tax rate was

$$\left(\frac{\$22,507}{\$100,000}\right)\times 100 = 22.5\%.$$

His average tax rate was lower than his marginal tax rate because the first $71,950 of his income was taxed at rates below his marginal rate of 28 percent.

When economists consider a change in tax policy, they generally focus on the marginal tax rate rather than the average tax rate because the marginal tax rate is a better indicator of how a change in a tax will affect people's willingness to work, save, and invest. For example, if Matt is considering working longer hours to raise his income, he will use his marginal tax rate to determine how much extra income he will earn after taxes. He will ignore his average tax rate because it does not reflect the taxes he must pay on the *additional* income he earns. The higher the marginal tax rate, the lower the return he receives from working additional hours and the less likely he is to work those additional hours.

The Corporate Income Tax

The federal government taxes the profits earned by corporations under the *corporate income tax.* Like the individual income tax, the corporate income tax is progressive, with the lowest tax rate being 15 percent and the highest being 35 percent. Unlike the personal income tax, however, where relatively few taxpayers are taxed at the highest rate, most corporations are in the 35 percent tax bracket.

Economists debate the costs and benefits of a separate tax on corporate profits. The corporate income tax ultimately must be paid by a corporation's owners—which are its shareholders—or by its employees, in the form of lower wages, or by its customers, in the form of higher prices. Some economists argue that if the purpose of the corporate income tax is to tax the owners of corporations, it would be better to do this directly by taxing the owners' incomes, rather than taxing the owners indirectly through the corporate income tax. Individual taxpayers already pay income taxes on the dividends and capital gains they receive from owning stock in corporations. In effect, the corporate income tax "double taxes" earnings on individual shareholders' investments in corporations. An alternative policy that avoids this double taxation would be for corporations to calculate their total profits each year and send a notice to each shareholder indicating the shareholder's portion of the profits. The shareholder would then be required to include this amount as taxable income on his or her personal income tax. Under another alternative, the federal government could continue to tax corporate income through the corporate income tax but allow individual taxpayers to receive corporate dividends and capital gains tax-free. In 2003, Congress enacted a reduction on dividend and capital gains taxes to reduce double taxation.

Evaluating Taxes

We have seen that to raise revenue, governments have available a variety of taxes. In selecting which taxes to use, governments take into account the following goals and principles:

➤ The goal of economic efficiency
➤ The ability-to-pay principle
➤ The horizontal-equity principle
➤ The benefits-received principle
➤ The goal of attaining social objectives

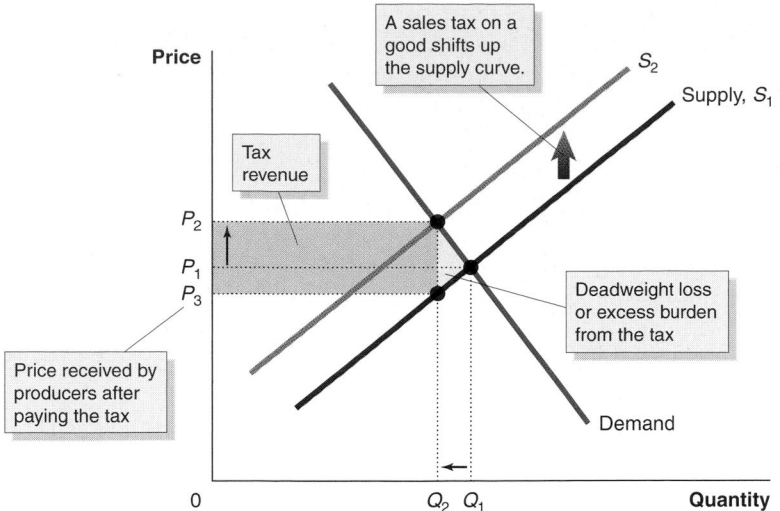

Price

A sales tax on a good shifts up the supply curve.

S_2

Supply, S_1

Tax revenue

P_2

P_1

P_3

Price received by producers after paying the tax

Deadweight loss or excess burden from the tax

Demand

0   Q_2 Q_1 Quantity

FIGURE 18-2

The Efficiency Loss from a Sales Tax

This figure reviews the discussion from Chapter 4 on the efficiency loss from a tax. A sales tax will increase the cost of supplying a good, which causes the supply curve to shift up from S_1 to S_2. Without the tax, the equilibrium price of the good is P_1 and the equilibrium quantity is Q_1. After the tax is imposed, the equilibrium price rises to P_2 and the equilibrium quantity falls to Q_2. After paying the tax, producers receive P_3. The government receives tax revenue equal to the green-shaded rectangle. Some consumer surplus and some producer surplus become tax revenue for the government and some become deadweight loss, shown by the yellow-shaded triangle. The deadweight loss is the *excess burden* of the tax.

THE GOAL OF ECONOMIC EFFICIENCY In Chapter 4, we analyzed the effect taxes have on economic efficiency. We can briefly review that discussion here. Whenever a government taxes an activity, it raises the cost of engaging in that activity, and less of that activity will occur. Figure 18-2 uses a demand and supply graph to illustrate this point for a sales tax. As we saw in Chapter 4, a sales tax will increase the cost of supplying a good, which causes the supply curve to shift up by the amount of the tax. In the graph, the equilibrium price rises from P_1 to P_2, and the equilibrium quantity falls from Q_1 to Q_2. When a good is taxed, less of it will be produced.

The government collects tax revenue equal to the tax per unit multiplied by the number of units sold. The green-shaded rectangle in Figure 18-2 represents the government's tax revenue. Although sellers appear to receive a higher price for the good—P_2— the price they receive after paying the tax falls to P_3. Because the price consumers pay has risen, consumer surplus has fallen. Because the price producers receive also has fallen, producer surplus has fallen. Some of the reduction in consumer surplus and producer surplus becomes tax revenue for the government. The rest of the reduction in consumer surplus and producer surplus is equal to the deadweight loss from the tax and is shown in the figure by the yellow-shaded triangle. The deadweight loss from a tax is known as the **excess burden** of the tax. The excess burden measures the efficiency loss to the economy that results from the tax having reduced the quantity of the good produced. *A tax is efficient if it imposes a small excess burden relative to the tax revenue it raises.*

To improve the economic efficiency of the tax system, economists argue that the government should reduce its reliance on taxes that have a high deadweight loss relative to the revenue raised. The tax on interest earned from saving is an example of a tax with a high deadweight loss because savings often comes from income already taxed once. Therefore, taxing interest earned on savings from income that has already been taxed amounts to double taxation.

There are other examples of significant deadweight losses of taxation. High taxes on work can reduce the number of hours an individual works, as well as how hard the individual works or whether the individual starts a business. In each case, the reduction in the taxed activity—here, work—generates less government revenue, while individuals are worse off because the tax encourages them to change their behavior.

Taxation can have substantial effects on economic efficiency by altering incentives to work, save, or invest. A good illustration of this effect can be seen in the large differences between annual hours worked in Europe and in the United States. It is well known that Europeans now work fewer hours than do Americans. According to a recent analysis by Nobel Prize winner Edward Prescott of Arizona State University, this difference was not always present. In the early 1970s, when European and U.S. tax rates on work were

Excess burden   The efficiency loss to the economy that results from a tax causing a reduction in the quantity of a good produced; also known as the deadweight loss.

comparable, European and U.S. hours worked per employee were also comparable. Prescott finds that virtually all of the difference between labor supply in the United States and labor supply in France and Germany since that time is due to differences in their tax systems.

18-2 *Making the Connection*

Should the United States Shift to a Consumption Tax?

A key issue in the debates over tax policy during 2004 was whether the federal government should shift from relying on an income tax to relying on a *consumption tax*. Under the income tax, households pay taxes on all income earned. Under a consumption tax, households pay taxes only on the part of income they spend. Households would pay taxes on saved income only if they spend the money at a later time.

To see how a shift from an income tax to a consumption tax can affect the economic incentives individuals face, consider the following example: Suppose a 20-year-old is deciding whether to save a $1,000 bonus paid by her employer. If she saves the $1,000 by putting it in a bank certificate of deposit (CD), the $1,000 *and* the interest she earns will both be taxed under the income tax, but neither will be taxed if the income tax is replaced by a consumption tax. Suppose she earns 6 percent per year on the CD and keeps it until she retires at age 70. Fifty years of tax-free interest compounding means that she will have accumulated $18,420 at age 70. Now suppose that under the income tax she is taxed at a rate of 33 percent. As a result, she will only have $670 of her bonus left after paying the tax. In addition, if she saves the money in a CD, her after-tax return each year is only 6 percent × (1 − 0.33) = 4 percent. Now saving her bonus in a CD at age 20 yields only $4,761 at age 70. This big difference in accumulation—$13,659—reflects the tax burden on saving, a burden that makes the saving less attractive.

Many economists argue that a taxpayer's well-being is better measured by his consumption (how much he spends) than by his income (how much he earns). Taxing consumption may therefore be more appropriate than taxing income. Also, because the income tax taxes interest and other returns to saving, it taxes *future* consumption—which is what current saving is for—more heavily than *present* consumption. That is, under an income tax, current consumption is taxed more favorably than future consumption, reducing households' willingness to save, as in the preceding example.

Some economists oppose a shift from an income tax to a consumption tax because they believe a consumption tax will be more regressive than an income tax. These economists argue that people with very low incomes are able to save little or nothing, and so would not be able to benefit from the increased incentives for saving that exist under a consumption tax.

Would a shift to a consumption tax be a radical change in the tax system? For many households, the answer is perhaps surprisingly "no." Most taxpayers can already put part of their savings into accounts where the funds deposited and the interest received are not taxed until the funds are withdrawn for retirement spending—for example, Individual

Would a consumption tax be more efficient than an income tax?

Retirement Accounts (IRAs) or 401(k) plans. In effect, individuals whose savings are mainly in these retirement accounts are already paying a consumption tax rather than an income tax. And recent reductions in tax rates on dividends and capital gains—which are both returns to savings—and proposals to expand saving incentives will further increase the role of consumption taxation.

The administrative burden of a tax represents another example of the deadweight loss of taxation. Individuals spend many hours during the year keeping records for income tax purposes, and many more hours prior to April 15 preparing their tax returns. The opportunity cost of this time is tens of billions of dollars each year, and represents an administrative burden of the federal income tax. For corporations, complexity in tax planning arises in many areas. The federal government also has to devote resources to enforcing the tax laws. Although the government collects the revenue from taxation, the resources spent on administrative burdens benefit neither taxpayers nor the government.

Wouldn't tax simplification reduce the administrative burden and the deadweight loss of taxation? Yes. So why is the tax code complicated? In part, complexity arises because the political process has resulted in different types of income being taxed at different rates, requiring rules to limit taxpayers' ability to avoid taxes. In addition, interest groups seek benefits, while the majority of taxpayers, who do not benefit, find it difficult to organize a drive for a simpler tax system.

THE ABILITY-TO-PAY PRINCIPLE The *ability-to-pay principle* holds that when the government raises revenue through taxes, it is fair to expect a greater share of the tax burden to be borne by people who have a greater ability to pay. Usually this principle means raising more taxes from people with high incomes than from people with low incomes, which is sometimes referred to as *vertical equity*. The federal income tax is consistent with the ability-to-pay principle. The sales tax, in contrast, is not consistent with the ability-to-pay principle because low-income people tend to spend a larger fraction of their income than do high-income people. As a result, low-income people will pay a greater fraction of their income in sales taxes than will high-income people.

THE HORIZONTAL-EQUITY PRINCIPLE The *horizontal-equity principle* states that people in the same economic situation should be treated equally. Although following this principle seems desirable, it is not easy to use in practice because it is sometimes difficult to determine whether two people are in the same economic situation. For example, two people with the same income are not necessarily in the same economic situation. Suppose one person does not work but receives an income of $50,000 per year entirely from interest received on bonds and another person receives an income of $50,000 per year from working at two jobs 16 hours a day. In this case, we could argue that the two people are in different economic situations and should not pay the same tax. Although policymakers and economists usually consider horizontal equity when evaluating proposals to change the tax system, it is not a principle that they can follow easily.

THE BENEFITS-RECEIVED PRINCIPLE According to the *benefits-received principle,* those people who receive the benefits from a government program should pay the taxes that support the program. For example, if a city operates a marina used by private boat owners, the government can raise the revenue to operate the marina by levying a tax on the boat owners. Raising the revenue through a general income tax paid both by boat owners and non–boat owners would be inconsistent with the benefits-received principle. Because the government has many programs, however, it would be impractical to identify and tax the beneficiaries of every program.

ATTAINING SOCIAL OBJECTIVES Taxes are sometimes used to attain social objectives. For example, the government may want to discourage smoking and drinking alcohol. Taxing cigarettes and alcoholic beverages is one way to help achieve this objective. Taxes intended to discourage certain activities are sometimes referred to as "sin taxes."

② LEARNING OBJECTIVE
Understand the effect of price elasticity on tax incidence.

Tax incidence The actual division of the burden of a tax between buyers and sellers in a market.

Tax Incidence Revisited: The Effect of Price Elasticity on Who Actually Bears the Burden of a Tax

In Chapter 4, we saw the difference between who is legally required to send a tax payment to the government and who actually bears the burden of a tax. Recall that the actual division of the burden of a tax between buyers and sellers in a market is known as **tax incidence.** We can go beyond the basic analysis of tax incidence by considering how the price elasticity of demand and price elasticity of supply affect how the burden of a tax is shared between consumers and firms.

In Chapter 4, we discussed whether consumers or firms bear the larger share of a 10-cents-per-gallon federal excise tax on gasoline. We saw that consumers paid the majority of the tax. We can expand on this conclusion to state that consumers of gasoline pay a larger fraction of gasoline taxes than do sellers because the elasticity of demand for gasoline is smaller than the elasticity of supply. In fact, we can draw a general conclusion: *When the demand for a product is less elastic than the supply, consumers pay the majority of the tax on the product. When demand for a product is more elastic than the supply, firms pay the majority of the tax on the product.*

We can see why this conclusion is correct with the aid of Figure 18-3. In Figure 18-3, D_1 is inelastic between points A and B, and D_2 is elastic between points A and C. With demand curve D_1, the 10-cents-per-gallon tax raises the market price of gasoline from \$2.00 (point A) to \$2.08 (point B) per gallon, so consumers pay 8 cents of the tax and firms pay 2 cents. With D_2, the market price rises only to \$2.02 (point C) per gallon, and consumers pay only 2 cents of the tax. With demand curve D_2, sellers of gasoline receive only \$1.92 per gallon after paying the tax. So, the amount they receive per gallon after taxes falls from \$2.00 to \$1.92 per gallon, and they pay 8 cents of the tax.

FIGURE 18-3

The Effect of Elasticity on Tax Incidence

When demand is more elastic than supply, consumers bear less of the burden of a tax. When supply is more elastic than demand, firms bear less of the burden of a tax. D_1 is inelastic between point A and point B, and D_2 is elastic between point A and point C. With demand curve D_1, a 10-cents-per-gallon tax raises the equilibrium price from \$2.00 (point A) to \$2.08 (point B), so consumers pay 8 cents of the tax and firms pay 2 cents. With D_2, a 10-cents-per-gallon tax on gasoline raises the equilibrium price only from \$2.00 (point A) to \$2.02 (point C), so consumers pay 2 cents of the tax. Because in this case producers receive \$1.92 per gallon after paying the tax, their share of the tax is 8 cents per gallon.

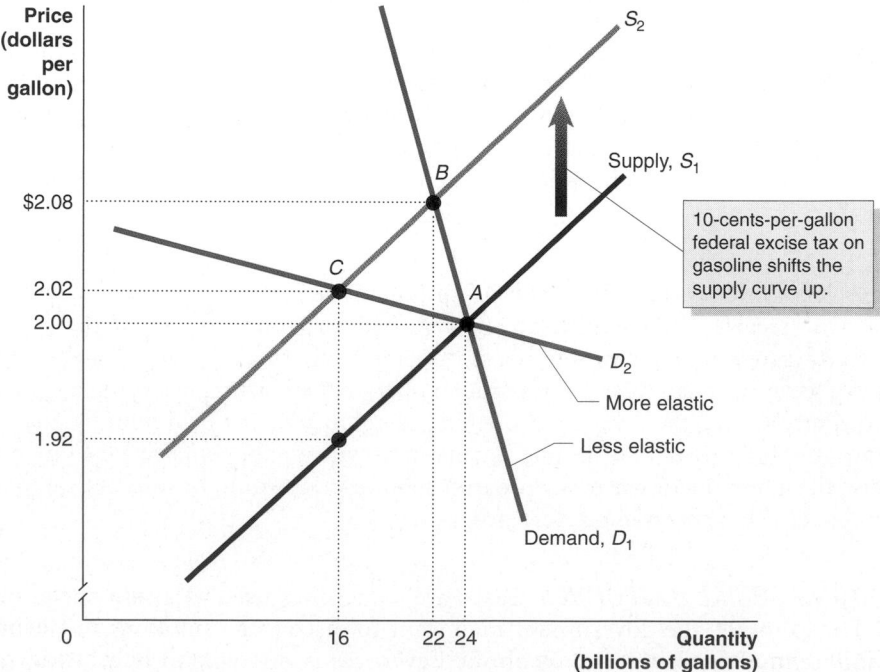

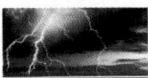

Don't Let This Happen To You!

Remember Not to Confuse Who Pays the Tax with Who Bears the Burden of the Tax

Consider the following statement: "Of course I bear the burden of the sales tax on everything I buy. I can show you my sales receipts with the 6 percent sales tax clearly labeled. The seller doesn't bear that tax. I do."

The statement is incorrect. To understand why it is incorrect, think about what would happen to the price of a product if the sales tax on it were eliminated. Figure 18-3 shows that the price of the product would fall if the sales tax were eliminated because the supply curve would shift down by the amount of the tax. The equilibrium price, however, would fall by less than the amount of the tax. (If you doubt this is true, draw the graph to convince yourself.) So, the gain from eliminating the tax would be received partly by consumers in the form of a lower price but also partly by sellers in the form of a new price that is higher than the amount they received from the old price minus the tax. Therefore, the burden from imposing a sales tax is borne partly by consumers and partly by sellers.

In determining the burden of a tax, what counts is not what is printed on the receipt for a product, but what happens to the price of a product as a result of the tax.

YOUR TURN: Test your understanding by doing related problem 10 on page 580 at the end of this chapter.

Do Corporations Really Bear the Burden of the Federal Corporate Income Tax?

18-3 Making the Connection

The incidence of the corporate income tax is one of the most controversial questions in the economics of tax policy. It is straightforward to determine the incidence of the gasoline tax using demand and supply analysis. Determining the incidence of the corporate income tax is more complicated because economists disagree over how corporations respond to the tax.

As a study by the Congressional Budget Office puts it:

> A corporation may write its check to the Internal Revenue Service for payment of the corporate income tax, but the money must come from somewhere: from reduced returns to investors in the company, lower wages to its workers, or higher prices that consumers pay for the products the company produces.

Most economists agree that some of the burden of the corporate income tax is passed on to consumers in the form of higher prices. There is also some agreement that because the corporate income tax reduces the rates of return received by investors, it results in less investment in corporations. This reduced investment means workers have less capital available to them. As we discussed in Chapter 16, when workers have less capital, their productivity and their wages both fall. In this way, some of the burden of the corporate income tax is shifted from

Who really bears the burden of the taxes paid by Dell?

corporations to workers in the form of lower wages. The deadweight loss or excess burden from the corporate income tax is substantial. A study by the Congressional Budget Office estimated that this excess burden could be equal to more than half of the revenues raised by the tax. This estimate would make the corporate income tax one of the most inefficient taxes imposed by the federal government.

As a consequence, economists have long argued for reform of the system of double taxing income earned on investments that corporations finance by issuing stock. This income is taxed once by the corporate income tax and again by the individual income tax as profits are distributed to shareholders. Tax rates on dividends and capital gains were reduced in 2003, but whether or not to reduce double taxation further remains the subject of a vigorous political debate.

Source: Congressional Budget Office, "The Incidence of the Corporate Income Tax," CBO Paper, March 1996.

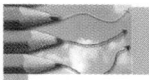

SOLVED PROBLEM   18-1

② **LEARNING OBJECTIVE**

Understand the effect of price elasticity on tax incidence.

The Effect of Price Elasticity on the Excess Burden of a Tax

Explain whether you agree or disagree with the following statement: "For a given supply curve, the excess burden of a tax will be greater when demand is less elastic than when it is more elastic." Illustrate your answer with a demand and supply graph.

Solving the Problem:

Step 1: Review the chapter material. This problem is about both excess burden and tax incidence, so you may want to review the section "Evaluating Taxes," which begins on page 560, and the section "Tax Incidence Revisited: The Effect of Price Elasticity on Who Actually Bears the Burden of a Tax," which begins on page 564.

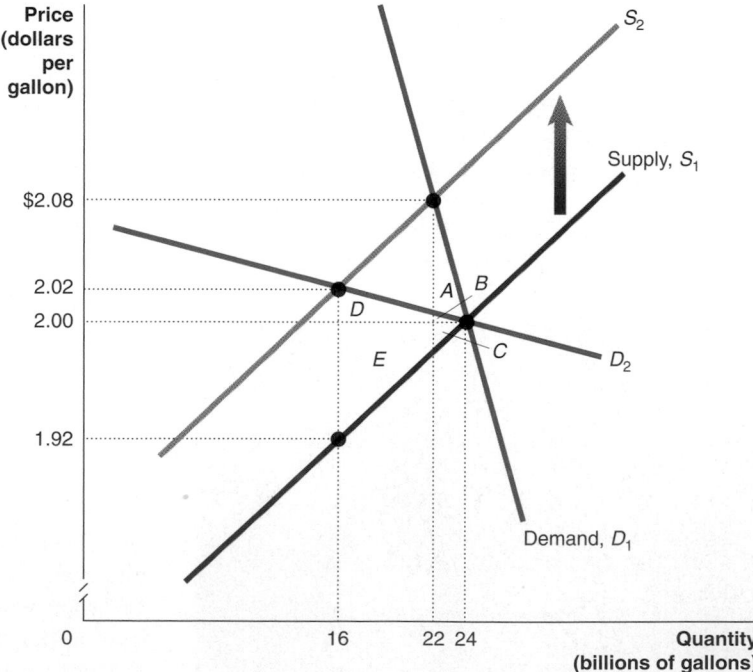

Step 2: Draw a graph to illustrate the relationship between tax incidence and excess burden. Figure 18-3 provides a good example of the type of graph to draw. Be sure to indicate the areas representing excess burden.

Step 3: Use the graph to evaluate the statement. The above graph is the same as Figure 18-3. As we have seen, for a given supply curve, when demand is more elastic, as with demand curve D_2, the fall in equilibrium quantity is greater than when demand is less elastic, as with demand curve D_1. The deadweight loss when demand is less elastic is shown by the area of the triangle made up of A, B, and C. The deadweight loss when demand is more elastic is shown by the area of the triangle made up of B, C, D, and E. The area of the deadweight loss is clearly larger when demand is more elastic than when it is less elastic. Recall that the excess burden of a tax is measured by the deadweight loss. Therefore, when demand is less elastic, the excess burden of a tax is greater than when demand is more elastic. We can conclude that the statement is incorrect.

YOUR TURN: **For more practice do related problem 11 on page 580 at the end of this chapter. Visit www.prenhall.com/hubbard for an interactive exercise related to this Solved Problem.**

The Distribution of Income

(3) LEARNING OBJECTIVE
Discuss the distribution of income in the United States, and understand the extent of income mobility.

In practice, in most economies some individuals will have very high incomes and some individuals will have very low incomes. But how unequal is the distribution of income in the United States today? How does this compare with the distribution of income in the United States in the past or with the distribution of income in other countries today? What determines the distribution of income? And, to return to an issue raised at the beginning of this chapter, what impact does the tax system have on the distribution of income? These are questions we will explore in the remainder of this chapter.

Measuring the Distribution of Income and Poverty

Tables 18-3 and 18-4 show that the distribution of income clearly is unequal. Table 18-3 shows that while about 16 percent of U.S. households have annual incomes of less than $15,000, the top 15 percent of households have incomes of greater than $100,000. Table 18-4 divides the population of the United States into five groups, from the 20 percent with the lowest incomes to the 20 percent with the highest incomes. The fraction of total income received by each of the five groups is shown for selected years. Table 18-4 reinforces the fact that income is unequally distributed in the United States. The first row shows that in 2003 the 20 percent of Americans with the lowest incomes received only 3.4 percent of all income, while the 20 percent with the highest incomes received 49.8 percent of all income.

Table 18-4 also shows that over time there have been some changes in the distribution of income. There was a moderate decline in inequality between 1936 and 1980, followed by some increase in inequality during the 1990s and early 2000s. We will discuss some reasons for the recent increase in income inequality later in this chapter.

THE POVERTY RATE IN THE UNITED STATES Much of the discussion of the distribution of income focuses on poverty. The federal government has a formal definition of poverty that was first developed in the early 1960s. According to this definition, a family

ANNUAL INCOME	PERCENTAGE OF ALL HOUSEHOLDS
$0–$14,999	15.9%
$15,000–$24,999	13.1
$25,000–$34,999	11.9
$35,000–$49,999	15.0
$50,000–$74,999	18.0
$75,000–$99,999	11.0
$100,000 and over	15.1

TABLE 18-3

The Distribution of Household Income in the United States, 2003

Source: U.S. Census Bureau, *Income, Poverty, and Health Insurance Coverage in the United States: 2003*, P60–226, August 2004, www.census.gov/prod/2004pubs/p60–226.pdf.

	YEAR	LOWEST 20%	SECOND 20%	THIRD 20%	FOURTH 20%	HIGHEST 20%
TABLE 18-4	2003	3.4%	8.7%	14.8%	23.4%	49.8%
	1990	3.9	9.6	15.9	24.0	46.6
How Has the Distribution of Income Changed Over Time?	1980	4.3	10.3	16.9	24.9	43.7
	1970	4.1	10.8	17.4	24.5	43.3
	1960	3.2	10.6	17.6	24.7	44.0
	1950	3.1	10.5	17.3	24.1	45.0
	1936	4.1	9.2	14.1	20.9	51.7

Sources: For 2003: U.S. Census Bureau, *Income, Poverty, and Health Insurance Coverage in the United States: 2003*, P60–226, August 2004; for 1970–1990: U.S. Census Bureau, *Income in the United States, 2002*, P60–221, September 2003; for 1936–1960: U.S. Bureau of the Census, *Historical Statistics of the United States, Colonial Times to 1970*, Washington, D.C.: U.S. Government Printing Office, 1975.

Poverty line A level of annual income equal to three times the amount necessary to purchase the minimal quantity of food required for adequate nutrition.

Poverty rate The percentage of the population that is poor according to the federal government's definition.

is below the **poverty line** if its annual income is less than three times the amount necessary to purchase the minimal quantity of food required for adequate nutrition. In 2004, the poverty line was $19,157 for a family of four with two children. Figure 18-4 shows the **poverty rate,** or the percentage of the U.S. population that was poor during each year between 1960 and 2003. Between 1960 and 1973, the poverty rate declined by half, falling from 22 percent of the population to 11 percent. In the past 30 years, however, the poverty rate has declined very little. In 2003, it was actually slightly greater than it had been in 1973.

Different groups in the population have substantially different poverty rates. Table 18-5 shows that whereas the overall poverty rate in 2003 was 12.5 percent, the rate among women who head a family with no husband present, among blacks, and among Hispanics was about twice as high. The poverty rates for whites and Asians were below average.

Explaining Income Inequality

The novelists Ernest Hemingway and F. Scott Fitzgerald supposedly once had a conversation about the rich. Fitzgerald said to Hemingway, "You know, the rich are different from you and me." To which Hemingway replied, "Yes. They have more money." Although witty, Hemingway's reply doesn't help answer the question of why the rich

FIGURE 18-4

Poverty in the United States, 1960–2003

The poverty rate in the United States declined from 22 percent of the population in 1960 to 11 percent in 1973. Over the past 30 years, the poverty rate has fluctuated between 11 percent and 15 percent of the population.

Source: U.S. Census Bureau, *Income, Poverty, and Health Insurance Coverage in the United States: 2003*, P60–226, August 2004.

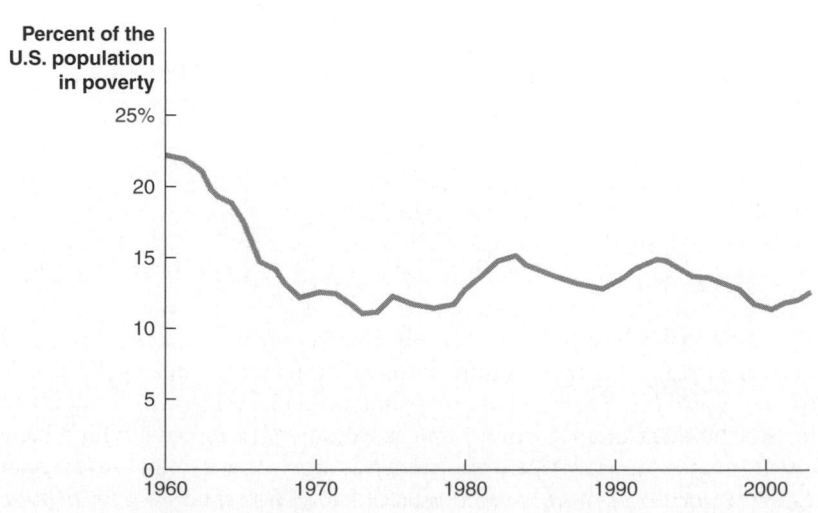

All people	12.5%
Female head of family, no husband present (all races)	28.0
Blacks	24.4
Hispanics	22.5
Asians	11.8
White, not Hispanic	8.2

TABLE 18-5

Poverty Rates Vary across Groups, 2003

Note: Hispanics can be of any race.

Source: U.S. Census Bureau, *Income, Poverty, and Health Insurance Coverage in the United States: 2003*, P60–226, August 2004.

have more money. In Chapter 16, we provided one answer to the question when we discussed the *marginal productivity theory of income distribution.* We saw that in equilibrium each factor of production receives a payment equal to its marginal revenue product. The more factors of production an individual owns, and the more productive those factors are, the higher the individual's income will be.

For most people, of course, the most important factor of production they own is their labor. Therefore, the income they earn will depend on how productive they are and on the prices of the goods and services their labor helps produce. Baseball player Alex Rodriguez earns $25 million per year because he is a very productive player and his employer, the New York Yankees, can sell tickets and television rights to the baseball games A-Rod plays in for a high price. Individuals who help to produce goods and services that can be sold for only a low price, will earn lower incomes.

Many people own other factors of production as well. For example, many people own capital by owning stock in corporations or by owning shares in mutual funds that buy the stock of corporations. Ownership of capital is not equally distributed, and income earned from capital is more unequally distributed than income earned from labor. Some people supply entrepreneurial skills by starting and managing businesses. Their income is increased by the profits from these businesses.

We saw in Table 18-4 that income inequality has increased somewhat during the past 25 years. Two factors that appear to have contributed to this increase are technological change and expanding international trade. Rapid technological change, particularly the development of information technology, has led to the substitution of computers and other machines for unskilled labor. This substitution has caused a decline in the wages of unskilled workers relative to other workers. Expanding international trade has put U.S. workers in competition with foreign workers to a greater extent than in the past. The wages of unskilled workers have been depressed relative to the wages of other workers by this competition.

As noted in the opening to this chapter, the tax system does not seem to have played a major role in recent changes in income inequality. Federal income tax rates have changed dramatically during the years covered in Table 18-4. For example, the top marginal income tax rate was 91 percent in the 1950s, declining to 70 percent in the 1960s, and to 28 percent in the 1980s. It then rose to 39.6 percent in the 1990s, before declining to 35 percent in 2003. Because tax rates changed significantly, but the distribution of income has changed relatively little, it is unlikely that changes in tax rates have had a large impact on the distribution of income.

Finally, like everything else in life, earning an income is also subject to good and bad fortune. The poor person turned instantly into a millionaire by winning the state lottery is an obvious example, as is a person whose earning power drastically declines after a debilitating illness or accident. So, we can say that as a group the people with high incomes are likely to have greater-than-average productivity and own greater-than-average amounts of capital. They are also likely to have experienced good fortune. As a group, poor people are likely to have lower-than-average productivity and own lower-than-average amounts of capital. They are also likely to have been less fortunate.

Showing the Income Distribution with a Lorenz Curve

Lorenz curve A curve showing the distribution of income by arraying incomes from lowest to highest on the horizontal axis and indicating the cumulative fraction of income earned by each fraction of households on the vertical axis.

Figure 18-5 presents the distribution of income using a **Lorenz curve.** A Lorenz curve shows the distribution of income by arraying incomes from lowest to highest on the horizontal axis and indicating the cumulative fraction of income earned by each fraction of households on the vertical axis. If the distribution of income were perfectly equal, the Lorenz curve would be a straight line because the first 20 percent of households would earn 20 percent of total income, the first 40 perent of households would earn 40 percent of total income, and so on. Panel (a) of Figure 18-5 shows a Lorenz curve for the actual distribution of income in the United States in 1980 and another curve for the distribution of income in 2003, reflecting the data in Table 18-4. We know that income was distributed more unequally in 2003 than in 1980 because the Lorenz curve for 2003 is farther away from the line of equal distribution than is the Lorenz curve for 1980.

Panel (b) illustrates how to calculate the *Gini coefficient,* which is one way of summarizing the information provided by a Lorenz curve. The Gini coefficient is equal to the area between the line of perfect income equality and the Lorenz curve—area *A* in panel (b)—divided by the whole area below the line of perfect equality—area *A* plus area *B* in panel (b). Or,

$$\text{Gini coefficient} = \left(\frac{A}{A+B}\right).$$

If the income distribution were completely *equal,* the Lorenz curve would be the same as the line of perfect income equality, area *A* would be zero, and so would the Gini coeffi-

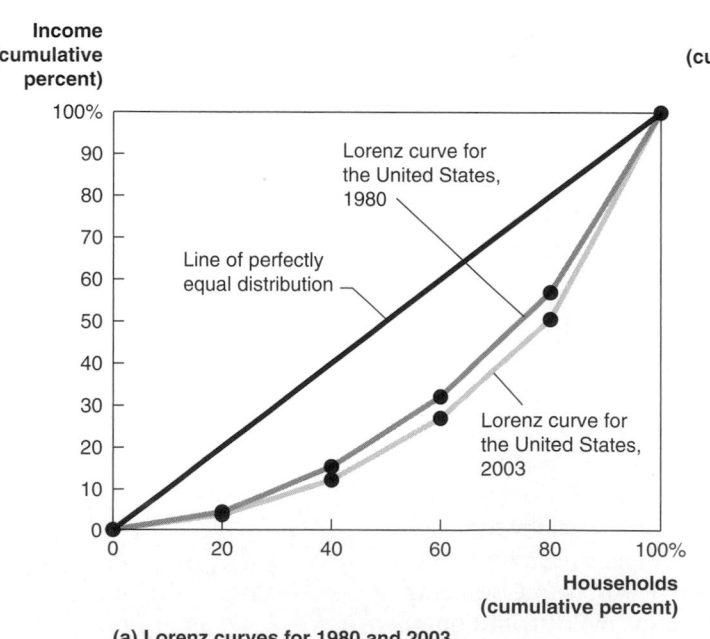

(a) Lorenz curves for 1980 and 2003

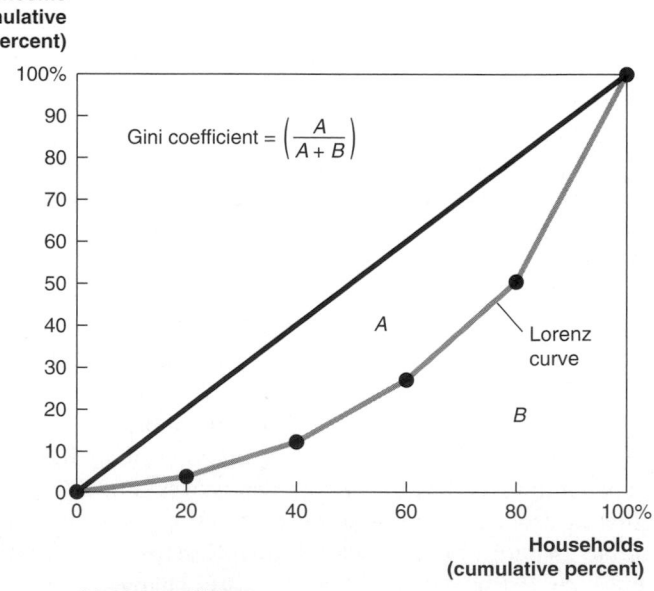

(b) Gini coefficient

FIGURE 18-5   **The Lorenz Curve and Gini Coefficient**

In panel (a), the Lorenz curves show the distribution of income by arraying incomes from the lowest to the highest on the horizontal axis and indicating the cumulative fraction of income by each fraction of households on the vertical axis. The straight line represents perfect income equality. Because the Lorenz curve for 1980 is closer to the line of perfect equality than the Lorenz curve for

2003, we know that income was more equally distributed in 1980 than in 2003. In panel (b), we show the Gini coefficient, which is equal to the area between the line of perfect income equality and the Lorenz curve—area *A*—divided by the whole area below the line of perfect equality—area *A* plus area *B*. The closer the Gini coefficient is to 1, the more unequal the income distribution.

cient. If the income distribution were completely *unequal,* area *B* would be zero and the Gini coefficient would equal 1. Therefore, the greater the degree of income inequality, the greater the value of the Gini coefficient. In 1980, the Gini coefficient for the United States was 0.403. In 2003 it was 0.464, which tells us again that income inequality increased between 1980 and 2003.

Problems in Measuring Poverty and the Distribution of Income

The measures of poverty and the distribution of income that we have discussed to this point may be misleading for two reasons. First, these measures are snapshots in time that do not take into account *income mobility.* Second, they ignore the effects of government programs meant to reduce poverty.

INCOME MOBILITY IN THE UNITED STATES   We expect to see some income mobility. When you graduate from college, your income will rise as you assume a new job. A family may be below the poverty line one year because the main wage earner is unemployed, but may rise well above the poverty line the next year when that wage earner finds a job. A medical student may have a very low income for several years, but a very high income after graduating and establishing a medical practice. It is also true that someone might have a high income one year—perhaps from making a killing on the stock market—and have a much lower income in future years.

Statistics on income mobility—as opposed to statistics on income during a particular year—are more difficult to collect because they involve following the same individuals over a number of years. A study by the U.S. Census Bureau tracked the incomes of the same households for each year from 1996 to 1999. Figure 18-6 shows the results of the study. Each column represents one quintile—or 20 percent—of households arranged by their incomes in 1996. Reading up the column, we can see where the households that started in that quintile in 1996 ended up in 1999. For example, the bottom quintile (the first column) consists of households with incomes of $16,220 or less in 1996 (all values are measured in 1999 dollars to correct for the effects of inflation). Only 62 percent of these households were still in the bottom quintile in 1999. Only a small number—1.2 percent—had moved all the way to the top quintile, but more than

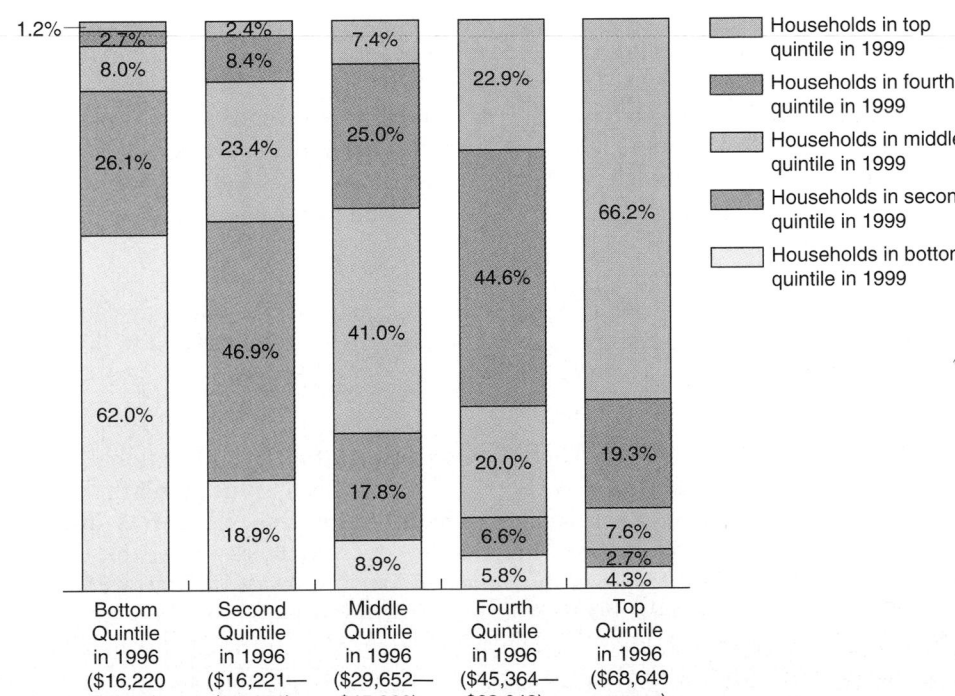

FIGURE 18-6

Income Mobility In the United States, 1996–1999

Each column represents one quintile—or 20 percent—of households arranged by their incomes in 1996. Reading up the column, we can see where the households that started in that quintile in 1996 ended up in 1999. Only 62 percent of the households that were in the bottom quintile of income in 1996 were still in the bottom quintile in 1999. Only 66 percent of the households that were in the top quintile of income in 1996 were still in the top quintile in 1999.

Note: Incomes are in 1999 dollars to correct for the effects of inflation.

Source: U.S. Bureau of the Census, "Dynamics of Economic Well-Being: Movements in the U.S. Income Distribution, 1996–1999," *Current Population Reports,* P70–95, July 2004.

one-third had moved into either the second quintile or the middle quintile. At the other end of the income distribution, of those households in the top income quintile—with incomes of $68,649 or more—in 1996, only two-thirds were still in the top quintile in 1999. Given the relatively short time period involved, this study indicates that there is significant income mobility in the United States over time.

It should be noted that the U.S. economy experienced rapid growth between 1996 and 1999, which may have increased the degree of income mobility. However, an earlier study by Peter Gottschalk of Boston College and Sheldon Danziger of the University of Michigan also provides evidence of significant income mobility. In that study, only 47 percent of those people who were in the lowest 20 percent of incomes in 1968, were still in the lowest bracket in 1991. More than 25 percent had incomes in 1991 that put them in the middle or higher-income brackets. Of those people who were in the highest-income bracket in 1968, only 42 percent were still in the highest bracket in 1991. Almost 8 percent of this group had fallen to the lowest-income bracket.

Another study by the U.S. Census Bureau showed that of the people who were in poverty in 1996, only 50.5 percent remained in poverty in 1999. The same study indicated that of the people who were in poverty at any time during 1996, 51.1 percent were in poverty for four months or less. Only 20.4 percent were in poverty for more than one year.

SOLVED PROBLEM 18-2

③ **LEARNING OBJECTIVE**
Discuss the distribution of income in the United States, and understand the extent of income mobility.

Are Many Individuals Stuck in Poverty?

Evaluate the following statement: "Government statistics indicate that 12 percent of the population is below the poverty line. The fraction of the population in poverty has never dropped below 10 percent. Therefore, more than 10 percent of the population must cope with very low incomes year after year."

Solving the Problem:
Step 1: Review the chapter material. This problem is about income mobility, so you may want to review the section "Income Mobility in the United States," which begins on page 571

Step 2: Use the discussion in this chapter to evaluate the statement. Although it is true that the poverty rate in the United States is never below 10 percent, it is not the same 10 percent of the population that is in poverty each year. This chapter discusses a U.S. Census Bureau study that showed that only about half of the people who were in poverty in 1996 were still in poverty in 1999. Poverty remains a problem in the United States, but fortunately the number of people who remain in poverty for many years is much smaller than the number who are in poverty during any one year.

YOUR TURN: For more practice, do related problem 12 on page 580 at the end of this chapter. Visit www.prenhall.com/hubbard for an interactive exercise related to this Solved Problem.

THE EFFECT OF TAXES AND TRANSFERS A second reason the conventional statistics on poverty and income distribution may be misleading is that they omit the effects of government programs. Because of government programs, there is a difference between the income people earn and the income they actually have available to spend. The data in Tables 18-3 and 18-4 showing the distribution of income are based on income before taxes are paid. We have seen that at the federal level, taxes are progressive, meaning people with high incomes pay a larger share of their incomes in taxes than do people with low incomes. Therefore, income remaining after taxes is more equally distributed than is income before taxes. The tables also did not include income from *transfer payments* individuals receive from the government, such as Social Security payments to retired and disabled people. The Social Security system has been very effective in reducing the poverty rate among people older than 65. In 1960, 35 percent of people in the United States over age 65 had incomes below the poverty line. By 2003, fewer than 11 percent of people over 65 had incomes below the poverty line.

Individuals with low incomes also receive noncash benefits, such as food stamps, free school lunches, and rent subsidies. The *food stamp program* has been a particularly important noncash benefit. Under this program, individuals with low incomes can buy at a discount coupons that can be used to purchase food in supermarkets. During 2004, more than 23 million people participated in this program at a cost to the federal government of $27.2 billion. Because individuals with low incomes are more likely to receive transfer payments and other benefits from the government than are individuals with high incomes, the distribution of income is more equal if we take these benefits into account. For example, in 2002, 12.1 percent of the U.S. population was below the poverty line using the official definition of income. Taking into account taxes paid and benefits received from government programs raises the incomes of enough people to reduce the poverty rate to 10.3 percent.

Poverty and the Distribution of Income around the World

How does income inequality in the United States compare with income inequality in other countries? Table 18-6 compares the ratio of total income received by the 20 percent of the population with the lowest incomes and the 20 percent with the highest incomes in several countries. The countries are ranked from the most unequal to least unequal. In South Africa, for example, the highest-income group has 66.5/2.0 = 33.3 times the income of the lowest-income group. In Japan, by contrast, the highest-income group has only 35.7/10.6 = 3.4 times the income of the lowest-income group. The table shows that the many poor countries, such as South Africa and Botswana,

	LOWEST 20%	HIGHEST 20%	RATIO
South Africa	2.0%	66.5%	33.3
Botswana	2.2	70.3	32.0
Mexico	3.1	59.1	19.1
Chile	3.3	62.2	18.8
United States	5.4	45.8	8.5
Thailand	6.1	50.0	8.2
United Kingdom	6.1	44.0	7.2
Ireland	7.1	43.3	6.1
Canada	7.0	40.4	5.8
France	7.2	40.2	5.6
Germany	8.5	36.9	4.3
Norway	9.6	37.2	3.9
Japan	10.6	35.7	3.4

TABLE 18-6

Income Inequality around the World

Source: Adapted from United Nations, *Human Development Report, 2004*, New York: Oxford University Press, 2005, Table 14. Data for most countries are from 2000.

have more unequal distributions of income than does the United States. The distribution of income in the United States is more equal than some moderate-income countries, such as Chile and Mexico, but less equal than other moderate-income countries, such as Thailand. The United States has the most unequal distribution of income of any high-income country in the world, although it is only moderately less equal than in the United Kingdom. The U.S. distribution of income is significantly less equal than in Germany, Norway, and Japan. Of course, one must be careful with such comparisons because transfer payments are not counted in income. For example, the Social Security and Medicare systems in the United States are much more generous than the corresponding systems in Japan, but less generous than those in France or Germany.

Although poverty remains a problem in high-income countries, it is a much larger problem in poor countries. The level of poverty in much of Africa, in particular, is a human catastrophe. In 2004, the poverty line in the United States for a family of four was an annual income of $19,157, but economists often use a much lower threshold income of $730 per person per year (or $2 per day) when calculating the rate of poverty in poor countries. Figure 18-7 shows the trend in global poverty using this threshold from 1970 to 1998, the most recent year for which statistics are available. In 1970, 41 percent of the world's population existed on $2 or less per day. By 1998, only 19 percent did so.

As Table 18-7 shows, much of this reduction in poverty has taken place in Asia and Latin America. In China, the poverty rate dropped spectacularly from 74.4 percent in 1970 to 18.7 percent in 1998. In the rest of Asia, poverty rates dropped from 49.4 percent to 13.5 percent. In Latin America, the poverty rate dropped from 22.2 percent to 10.5 percent. By contrast, the poverty rate in Africa *increased* from 53 percent in 1970 to 63.6 percent in 1998. Why has poverty fallen dramatically in Asia and Latin America, but risen in Africa? The key explanation is that Asia and Latin America have had higher rates of economic growth than has Africa. Recent economic research demonstrates a positive relationship between economic growth and the incomes of lower-income workers.

FIGURE 18-7

Global Poverty Rates

For poor countries, economists often use a poverty threshold of $730 per year, or $2 per day. Using this threshold, the world poverty rate has declined dramatically over the past 30 years. In 1970, 41 percent of the world's population was in poverty, but by 1998 this rate had fallen by more than half to 19 percent.

Source: Xavier Sala-i-Martin, "The World Distribution of Income," National Bureau of Economic Research, Working Paper 8933, May 2002.

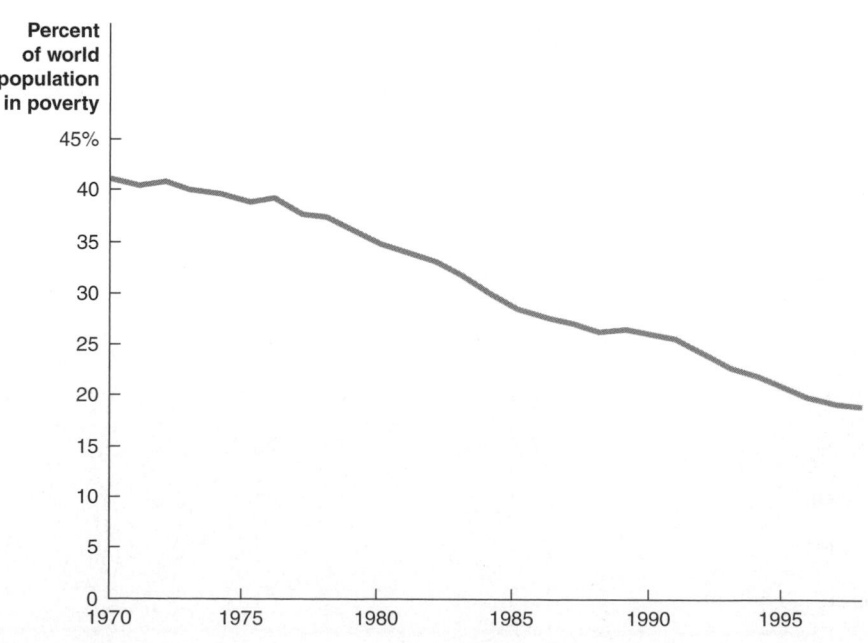

| PERCENTAGE OF THE POPULATION IN POVERTY | | | TABLE 18-7 |
REGION	1970	1998	**Poverty in Africa Is Much Greater Than Elsewhere in the World**
World	41.0%	18.6%	
Asia, minus China	49.4	13.5	
China	74.4	18.7	
Latin America	22.2	10.5	
Africa	53.0	63.6	

Source: Xavier Sala-i-Martin, "The World Distribution of Income," National Bureau of Economic Research, Working Paper 8933, May 2002.

Conclusion

There is an old saying that two things cannot be avoided: death and taxes. But which taxes? As we saw at the beginning of this chapter, politicians continue to debate whether the government should use the tax system and other programs to reduce the level of income inequality in the United States. The tax system represents a balance among objectives of economic efficiency, ability to pay, paying for benefits received, and achieving social objectives. Those favoring government intervention to reduce inequality argue that it is unfair for some people to have much higher incomes than others. Others argue that income inequality largely reflects higher incomes resulting from greater skills and from entrepreneurial ability and that higher taxes reduce work, saving, and investment.

Many economists are skeptical of tax policy proposals to reduce income inequality very significantly. They argue that a market system relies on individuals being willing to work hard and take risks with the promise of high incomes if they are successful. If some of those incomes are taken from them in the name of reducing income inequality, the incentives to work hard and take risks are reduced. Ultimately, whether policies to reduce income inequality should be pursued is a normative question. Economics alone cannot decide the issue.

Read *An Inside Look* on the next page to learn how a tax policy in the United Kingdom had unexpected results.

An Inside Look

Did More Progressive Taxes Make the Distribution of Income More Equal in the United Kingdom?

ECONOMIST, APRIL 3, 2003

The Chancellor's Attempts to Emulate Robin Hood Are Not Working

Gordon Brown has been a highly redistributive chancellor. Income inequality has increased. Which statement is true? No need to ask the audience or to count the coughs: both are.

a The Institute for Fiscal Studies (IFS) has totted up the effects of Mr Brown's six budgets since 1997, including measures that come into effect in the financial year starting this week. Its calculations showed that the chancellor has indeed been playing Robin Hood (see chart). A lone parent, for example, is on average £24 ($38) a week better off in today's money as a result of Mr Brown—an 11% gain.

b Yet overall inequality has risen. A summary measure of the distribution of income is the "Gini coefficient": the higher it is, in a range from 0 to 1, the more unequal income is. It has increased since Labour took office.

Mr Brown has been rowing against a powerful incoming tide. In order to isolate the effect of his measures, the IFS applied his schedules for taxes and benefits—which it assumed are fully claimed—to the latest estimates for underlying income. It then compared the net income of households with their position if Mr Brown had never been chancellor and the taxes and benefits laid down in the last Conservative budget in 1996, uprated with inflation, were still in place.

The chancellor's problem is that the underlying income distribution has not remained frozen. Since 1996–97, for example, there has been a surge in the number of high-earners. According to the Inland Revenue, the number of people paying the top rate of income tax rose from 2.1m in 1996–97 to 3.1m in 2002–03. Furthermore, not everyone claims Mr Brown's new benefits, partly because his enthusiasm for means-testing makes them so complicated. The latest official estimates show that up to £4.5 billion worth of means-tested benefits are going unclaimed.

The chancellor prefers to avoid talking about egalitarianism directly, using phrases about reducing child and pensioner poverty. For example, the government has set a target to cut child poverty from 4.2m in 1998–99 to at least 3.1m in 2004–05. But this, too, is proving an uphill struggle. Figures released last month showed that there were still 3.8m children in poverty in 2001–02, only 100,000 fewer than the year before.

c Progress has been slow mainly because Mr Brown wants to cut relative, rather than absolute, poverty. His aim is to reduce the number of children living in households whose incomes are below 60% of median income—the level that divides the population, when ranked by income, into two. Households on median income will generally have at least one person in work, whereas many poor children live in households where no one works. So the government has been chasing a moving target as earnings have grown and more families have become two-earner households.

Mr Brown may find it easier to reduce inequality and to cut child poverty from now on. The travails of the City and the bursting of the dotcom bubble mean there are fewer high-rollers than before. Employment is likely to stagnate rather than to rise as it did in the late 1990s.

But these are distinctly mixed blessings, since tax revenue will be less buoyant as a result. Whatever his aspirations to combat poverty, he would surely prefer to have the Treasury's coffers clinking than bare. Redistribution may sound like a lovely bit of fair-mindedness, but the only sure way to get there is through more poverty, not more wealth.

Key Points in the Article

The Labour Party in the United Kingdom traditionally has placed a greater emphasis on promoting a more equal distribution of income, even at the expense of some economic efficiency. The Conservative Party, on the other hand, has tended to emphasize economic efficiency, even at the expense of allowing the distribution of income to become more unequal. Therefore, when the Labour Party came to power in 1997, it enacted laws that made the income tax system more progressive and increased government transfer payments to individuals with lower incomes. In this editorial, the *Economist* described the policies of Gordon Brown, the Labour Party's Chancellor of the Exchequer (the equivalent of the Secretary of the Treasury in the United States) as being like Robin Hood—taking from the rich to give to the poor—but notes that they do not seem to have been effective in reducing income inequality in the United Kingdom.

Analyzing the News

a Figure 1 shows that, in fact, the tax and transfer system in the United Kingdom has tended to make the income distribution more equal. Along the horizontal axis, British households are divided into tenths, or deciles. The six poor deciles had their incomes increase as a result of tax cuts or increases in transfers. The increases to the two poorest deciles were greater than 10 percent. The four highest-income deciles had their incomes decrease as a result of the tax increase or decreases in transfers. For the highest-income decile, these changes reduced income by almost 5 percent.

b As we saw in this chapter, the Gini coefficient is a useful way to sum up the distribution of income in a country. The Gini coefficient can have a value between 0 and 1. The closer the Gini coefficient is to 0, the more equal the distribution of income. The closer the Gini coefficient is to 1, the less equal the distribution of income. Figure 2 shows that since the Labour government took office in 1997, the Gini coefficient for the United Kingdom actually has increased, indicating that the distribution of income had become more unequal.

c In the United Kingdom, as in the United States, technological progress and expanding international trade have tended to raise the incomes of more skilled workers relative to less skilled workers. As a consequence, the distribution of income has become more unequal in both countries. The *Economist* editorial argues that because Gordon Brown is attempting to reduce relative poverty, rather than absolute poverty, he is chasing a moving target as average income rises in the United Kingdom.

Thinking Critically
ABOUT POLICY

1. Chancellor Brown's tax and transfer policies have failed to stem the increase in Britain's Gini coefficient. Should Britain adopt other policies that could reduce the Gini coefficient, such as a much higher minimum wage, comparable worth laws, or tariffs to protect low-wage workers competing with imported goods? Discuss the trade-offs involved.

2. Could the Gini coefficient rise while absolute poverty falls? Explain.

Source: "Gordon Hood, The Chancellor's Attempts to Emulate Robin Hood Are Not Working," *Economist*, April 3, 2003. © 2003 The Economist Newspaper ltd. All rights reserved. Reprinted with permission. Further reproduction prohibitied. www.economist.com.

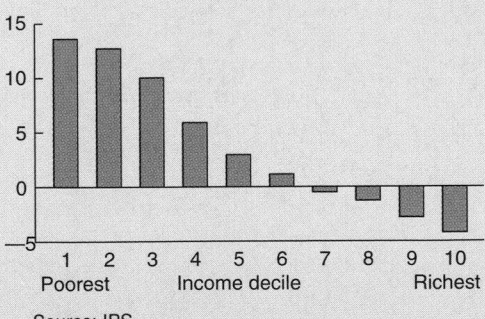

From rich to poor . . .

% change in household net income from tax and benefit measures since 1997

Source: IPS.

Figure 1: Taxes and transfers have made the income distribution more equal in the United Kingdom.

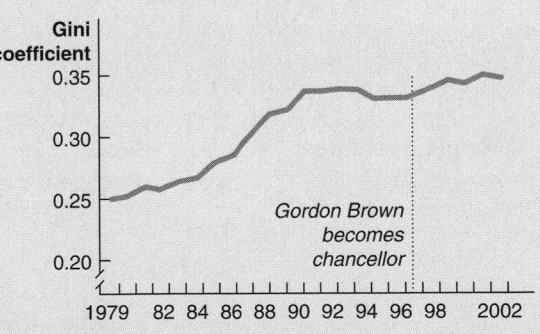

. . . but inequality still rises

Figure 2: The distribution of income in the United Kingdom has become more unequal since the Labour government took office in 1997.

SUMMARY

LEARNING OBJECTIVE ① Understand the tax system in the United States, including the principles of taxation that governments use to create tax policy. Governments raise the funds they need through taxes. The most widely used taxes are income taxes, social insurance taxes, sales taxes, property taxes, and excise taxes. Governments take into account several important objectives when deciding which taxes to use: efficiency, ability to pay, horizontal equity, benefits received, and attaining social objectives. A tax is *regressive* if people with lower incomes pay a higher percentage of their incomes in tax than do people with higher incomes. A tax is *progressive* if people with lower incomes pay a lower percentage of their incomes in tax than do people with higher incomes. The *marginal tax rate* is the fraction of each additional dollar of income that must be paid in taxes. The *average tax rate* is the total tax paid divided by total income. When analyzing the impact of taxes on how much people are willing to work or save or invest, economists focus on the marginal tax rate rather than the average tax rate.

LEARNING OBJECTIVE ② Understand the effect of price elasticity on tax incidence. *Tax incidence* is the actual division of the burden of a tax. In most cases, buyers and sellers share the burden of a tax levied on a good or service. When the elasticity of demand for a product is smaller than the elasticity of supply, consumers pay the majority of the tax on a product. When the elasticity of demand for a product is larger than the elasticity of supply, sellers pay the majority of the tax on a product.

LEARNING OBJECTIVE ③ Discuss the distribution of income in the United States, and understand the extent of income mobility. The distribution of income in the United States is unequal. In 2003, 16 percent of U.S. families had annual incomes of less than $15,000, whereas the top 15 percent of the population had incomes greater than $100,000. No dramatic changes in the distribution of income have occurred over the last 70 years, although there was some decline in inequality between 1936 and 1980, as well as some increase in inequality between 1980 and today. A Lorenz curve shows the distribution of income by arraying incomes from lowest to highest on the horizontal axis and indicating the cumulative fraction of income earned by each fraction of households on the vertical axis. About 12 percent of Americans are below the poverty line. Over time, there has been significant income mobility in the United States. Many people in the lowest-income brackets eventually rise to higher-income brackets, and many people in the highest-income brackets eventually fall to lower-income brackets. Less than one-quarter of the people who are below the poverty line for any time during a year remain in poverty for more than one year. The United States has a more unequal distribution of income than do other high-income countries. Poverty rates have been declining in most countries around the world, with the important exception of Africa. The *marginal productivity theory of income distribution* states that in equilibrium each factor of production receives a payment equal to its marginal revenue product. The more factors of production an individual owns and the more productive those factors are, the higher the individual's income will be.

KEY TERMS

Average tax rate 560	Marginal tax rate 560	Poverty rate 568	Regressive tax 557
Excess burden 561	Poverty line 568	Progressive tax 557	Tax incidence 564
Lorenz curve 570			

REVIEW QUESTIONS

1. Which type of tax raises the most revenue for the federal government?
2. A study showed that on average a family in Pennsylvania earning $40,000 per year paid 6 percent of its income in state taxes. A family earning $100,000 paid 5.6 percent of its income in taxes. Are state taxes in Pennsylvania progressive or regressive? Be sure to explain the difference between a progressive tax and a regressive tax.
3. What is the difference between a marginal tax rate and an average tax rate? Which is more important in determining the impact of the tax system on economic behavior?
4. What is meant by tax incidence? Briefly discuss the effect of price elasticity of supply and demand on tax incidence.
5. Briefly discuss each of the principles governments consider when deciding which taxes to use.

6. Discuss the extent of income inequality in the United States. Has inequality in the distribution of income in the United States increased or decreased over time? Briefly explain.

7. Define the poverty line and the poverty rate. How has the poverty rate changed in the United States since 1960?

8. Describe the extent of income mobility in the United States.

9. Describe the main factors economists believe cause inequality of income.

10. Compare the distribution of income in the United States with the distribution of income in other high-income countries.

11. Describe the trend in global poverty rates.

PROBLEMS AND APPLICATIONS

Please visit **www.prenhall.com/hubbard** *for solutions to the even-numbered problems as well as multiple-choice and true or false self-assessment quizzes.*

1. Why does the federal government raise more tax revenue from taxes on individuals than from taxes on businesses?

2. According to an article in the *New York Times*, "the poor and middle class . . . spend a greater portion of their income on cigarettes than the wealthy do." Assuming this observation is correct, is a sales tax on cigarettes likely to be regressive or progressive? Be sure to define regressive and progressive taxes in your answer.
Source: David Leonhardt, "How a Tax on Cigarettes Can Help the Taxed," *New York Times*, April 14, 2002.

3. Use the information in Table 18-1 to calculate the total federal income tax paid, the marginal tax rate, and the average tax rate for people with the following incomes (for simplicity, assume these people have no exemptions or deductions from their incomes):
   a. $25,000
   b. $125,000
   c. $300,000

4. According to the 2004 *Economic Report of the President*: "The actual incidence of a tax may have little to do with the legal specification of its incidence." Briefly explain what this statement means, and discuss whether you agree or disagree with it.

5. According to the 2004 *Economic Report of the President*: "Another crucial principle [of tax incidence] is that only people can pay taxes. Businesses and other artificial entities cannot pay taxes." Do you agree that businesses cannot pay taxes? Don't businesses pay the federal corporate income tax? Briefly explain.

6. Is the excess burden from a tax likely to be greater if the demand for the product being taxed is elastic or inelastic? Draw a graph to illustrate your answer.

7. Use this graph of the market for cigarettes to answer the following questions:

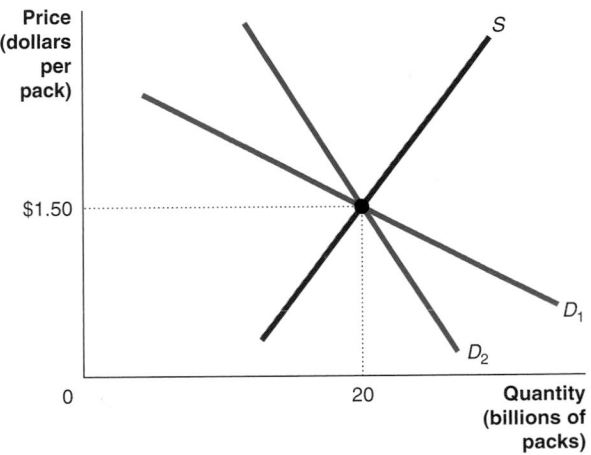

   a. If the government imposes a 10-cents-per-pack tax on cigarettes, will the price consumers pay rise more if the demand curve is D_1 or if the demand curve is D_2? Briefly explain.
   b. If the government imposes a 10-cents-per-pack tax on cigarettes, will the revenue to the government be greater if the demand curve is D_1 or if the demand curve is D_2? Briefly explain.
   c. If the government imposes a 10-cents-per-pack tax on cigarettes, will the excess burden from the tax be greater if the demand curve is D_1 or if the demand curve is D_2? Briefly explain.

8. Governments often have multiple objectives in imposing a tax. In each part of this question, use a demand and supply graph to illustrate your answer.

a. If the government wants to minimize the excess burden from excise taxes, should these taxes be imposed on goods that are elastic or goods that are inelastic?

b. Suppose that rather than minimizing excess burden, the government is most interested in maximizing the revenue it receives from the tax. In this situation, should the government impose excise taxes on goods that are elastic or on goods that are inelastic?

c. Suppose that the government wishes to discourage smoking and drinking alcohol. Will a tax be more effective in achieving this objective if the demand for these goods is elastic or if the demand is inelastic?

9. Many state governments have begun using lotteries to raise revenue. If we think of a lottery as a type of tax, is a lottery likely to be progressive or regressive? What data would you need to determine whether the burden of a lottery is progressive or regressive?

10. [Related to *Don't Let This Happen To You!*] Evaluate the following statement: "I just bought a television set that was priced at $300. Because there was a 5 percent sales tax, the total amount I paid was $315. If only my state didn't have a sales tax, I would only have had to pay $300."

11. [Related to *Solved Problem 18-1*] Explain whether you agree or disagree with the following statement: "For a given demand curve, the excess burden of a tax will be greater when supply is less elastic than when it is more elastic." Illustrate your answer with a demand and supply graph.

12. [Related to *Solved Problem 18-2*] Evaluate the following statement: "Policies to redistribute income are desperately needed in the United States. Without such policies, the more than 12 percent of the population that is currently poor has no hope of ever climbing above the poverty line."

13. Use the following Lorenz curve graph to answer the questions.

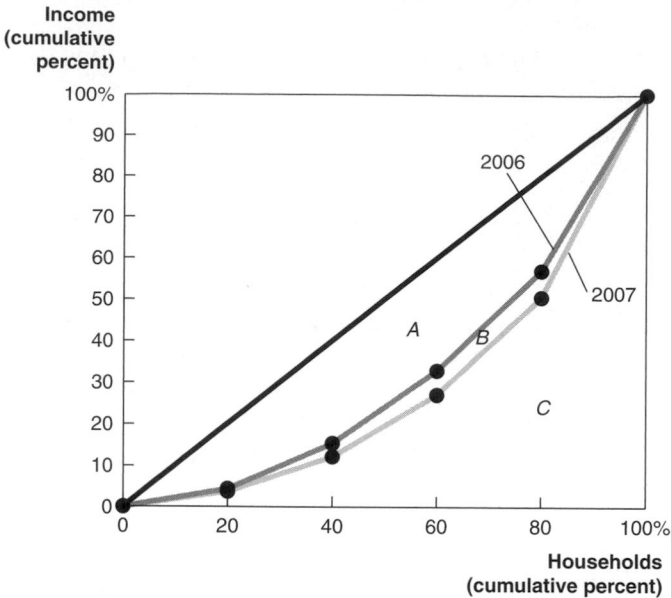

a. Did the distribution become more equal in 2007 than it was in 2006, or less equal? Briefly explain.

b. If area $A = 2,150$, area $B = 250$, and area $C = 2,600$, calculate the Gini coefficient for 2006 and the Gini coefficient for 2007.

14. Draw a Lorenz curve showing the distribution of income for the group of five people in the following table:

NAME	ANNUAL EARNINGS
David	$70,000
Lena	60,000
Sharon	50,000
Robert	40,000
Jeff	30,000

15. Why do economists often use a lower poverty threshold for poor countries than for high-income countries such as the United States? Is there a difference between *relative* poverty and *absolute* poverty?

16. Suppose the Congress and the president decide on a policy of bringing about a perfectly equal distribution of income. What factors might make this policy difficult to achieve? If it were possible to achieve the goal of this policy, would this be desirable?

17. If everyone had the same income, would everyone have the same level of well-being?

18. Almost all states levy sales taxes on retail products, but about half of them exempt purchases of food. In addition, virtually all services are exempt from state sales taxes. Evaluate these tax rate differences using the goals and principles of taxation on pages 560 to 563.

19. Suppose that a country has 20 million households. Ten million are poor households that each have labor market earnings of $20,000 per year and 10 million are rich households that each have labor market earnings of $80,000 per year. If the government enacted a marginal tax of 10 percent on all labor market earnings above $20,000 and transferred this money to households earning $20,000 or less, would the incomes of the poor rise by $6,000 per year? Explain.

20. The Census Bureau reported that 46 percent of households living below the poverty line in 2003 owned their own homes, 76 percent lived in dwellings with air conditioning, about 75 percent owned cars, and 62 percent had cable or satellite TV reception. All these levels are considerably higher than they were for households below the poverty line a generation ago, but the official poverty rate is virtually unchanged over this period, as Figure 18-4 shows. Going back to the official definition of poverty, how could ownership and purchases of these goods by the poor become more common while the poverty rate stayed the same?

A

Absolute advantage The ability of an individual, firm, or country to produce more of a good or service than competitors using the same amount of resources.

Accounting profit A firm's net income measured by revenue less operating expenses and taxes paid.

Adverse selection The situation in which one party to a transaction takes advantage of knowing more than the other party to the transaction.

Allocative efficiency A state of the economy in which production reflects consumer preferences; in particular, every good or service is produced up to the point where the last unit provides a marginal benefit to consumers equal to the marginal cost of producing it.

Antitrust laws Laws aimed at eliminating collusion and promoting competition among firms.

Asset Anything of value owned by a person or a firm.

Asymmetric information The situation in which one party to an economic transaction has less information than the other party.

Autarky A situation in which a country does not trade with other countries.

Average fixed cost Fixed cost divided by the quantity of output produced.

Average product of labor The total output produced by a firm divided by the quantity of workers.

Average revenue (AR) Total revenue divided by the number of units sold.

Average tax rate Total tax paid divided by total income.

Average total cost Total cost divided by the quantity of output produced.

Average variable cost Variable cost divided by the quantity of units produced.

B

Balance sheet A financial statement that sums up a firm's financial position on a particular day, usually the end of a quarter or a year.

Barrier to entry Anything that keeps new firms from entering an industry in which firms are earning economic profits.

Behavioral economics The study of situations in which people act in ways that are not economically rational.

Black market Buying and selling at prices that violate government price regulations.

Bond A financial security that represents a promise to repay a fixed amount of funds.

Brand management The actions of a firm intended to maintain the differentiation of a product over time.

Budget constraint The limited amount of income available to consumers to spend on goods and services.

Business strategy Actions taken by a firm to achieve a goal, such as maximizing profits.

C

Cartel A group of firms that colludes by agreeing to restrict output to increase prices and profits.

Centrally planned economy An economy in which the government decides how economic resources will be allocated.

Ceteris paribus ("all else equal") The requirement that when analyzing the relationship between two variables—such as price and quantity demanded—other variables must be held constant.

Circular-flow diagram A model that illustrates how participants in markets are linked.

Coase theorem The argument of economist Ronald Coase that if transactions costs are low, private bargaining will result in an efficient solution to the problem of externalities.

Collusion An agreement among firms to charge the same price, or otherwise not to compete.

Command and control approach Government-imposed quantitative limits on the amount of pollution firms are allowed to generate, or government-required installation by firms of specific pollution control devices.

Common resource A good that is rival but not excludable.

Comparative advantage The ability of an individual, firm, or country to produce a good or service at a lower opportunity cost than other producers.

Compensating differentials Higher wages that compensate workers for unpleasant aspects of a job.

Competitive market equilibrium A market equilibrium with many buyers and many sellers.

Complements Goods that are used together.

Constant returns to scale Exist when a firm's long-run average costs remain unchanged as it increases output.

Consumer surplus The difference between the highest price a consumer is willing to pay and the price the consumer actually pays.

Cooperative equilibrium An equilibrium in a game in which players cooperate to increase their mutual payoff.

Copyright A government-granted exclusive right to produce and sell a creation.

Corporate governance The way in which a corporation is structured and the impact a corporation's structure has on the firm's behavior.

Corporation A legal form of business that provides the owners with limited liability.

Coupon payment Interest payment on a bond.

Cross-price elasticity of demand The percentage change in quantity demanded of one good divided by the percentage change in the price of another good.

D

Deadweight loss The reduction in economic surplus resulting from a market not being in competitive equilibrium.

Demand curve A curve that shows the relationship between the price of a product and the quantity of the product demanded.

Demand schedule A table showing the relationship between the price of a product and the quantity of the product demanded.

Demographics The characteristics of a population with respect to age, race, and gender.

Derived demand The demand for a factor of production that is derived from the demand for the good the factor produces.

Direct finance A flow of funds from savers to firms through financial markets.

Diseconomies of scale Exist when a firm's long-run average costs rise as it increases output.

Dividends Payments by a corporation to its shareholders.

Dominant strategy A strategy that is the best for a firm, no matter what strategies other firms use.

Dumping Selling a product for a price below its cost of production.

E

Economic discrimination Paying a person a lower wage or excluding a person from an occupation on the basis of an irrelevant characteristic such as race or gender.

Economic efficiency A market outcome in which the marginal benefit to consumers of the last unit produced is equal to its marginal cost of production, and in which the sum of consumer surplus and producer surplus is at a maximum.

Economic growth The ability of the economy to produce increasing quantities of goods and services.

Economic loss The situation in which a firm's total revenue is less than its total cost, including all implicit costs.

Economic model Simplified versions of reality used to analyze real-world economic situations.

Economic profit A firm's revenues minus all its costs, implicit and explicit.

Economic rent (or **pure rent**) The price of a factor of production that is in fixed supply.

Economic surplus The sum of consumer surplus and producer surplus.

Economic variable Something measurable that can have different values, such as the wages of software programmers.

Economics The study of the choices people make to attain their goals, given their scarce resources.

Economies of scale Economies of scale exist when a firm's long-run average costs fall as it increases output.

Elastic demand Demand is elastic when the percentage change in quantity demanded is greater than the percentage change in price, so the price elasticity is greater than 1 in absolute value.

Elasticity A measure of how much one economic variable responds to changes in another economic variable.

Endowment effect The tendency of people to be unwilling to sell something they already own even if they are offered a price that is greater than the price they would be willing to pay to buy the good if they didn't already own it.

Entrepreneur Someone who operates a business, bringing together the factors of production—labor, capital, and natural resources—to produce goods and services.

Equity The fair distribution of economic benefits.

Excess burden The efficiency loss to the economy that results from a tax causing a reduction in the quantity of a good produced; also known as the deadweight loss.

Excludability The situation in which anyone who does not pay for a good cannot consume it.

Expansion path A curve showing a firm's cost-minimizing combination of inputs for every level of output.

Explicit cost A cost that involves spending money.

Exports Goods and services produced domestically but sold to other countries.

External economies Reductions in a firm's costs that result from an expansion in the size of an industry.

Externality A benefit or cost that affects someone who is not directly involved in the production or consumption of a good or service.

F

Factor markets Markets for the factors of production, such as labor, capital, natural resources, and entrepreneurial ability.

Factors of production Labor, capital, natural resources, and other inputs used to produce goods and services.

Fixed costs Costs that remain constant as output changes.

Foreign direct investment The purchase or building by a domestic firm of a facility in a foreign country.

Foreign portfolio investment The purchase by an individual or firm of stocks or bonds issued in another country.

Free market A market with few government restrictions on how a good or service can be produced or sold, or on how a factor of production can be employed.

Free riding Benefiting from a good without paying for it.

Free trade Trade between countries that is without government restrictions.

G

Game theory The study of how people make decisions in situations where attaining their goals depends on their interactions with others; in economics, the study of the decisions of firms in industries where the profits of each firm depend on its interactions with other firms.

Globalization The process of countries becoming more open to foreign trade and investment.

H

Horizontal merger A merger between firms in the same industry.

Human capital The accumulated training and skills that workers possess.

I

Implicit cost A nonmonetary opportunity cost.

Imports Goods and services bought domestically but produced in other countries.

Income effect The change in the quantity demanded of a good that results from the effect of a change in price on consumer purchasing power, holding all other factors constant.

Income elasticity of demand A measure of the responsiveness of quantity demanded to changes in income, measured by the percentage change in quantity demanded divided by the percentage change in income.

Income statement A financial statement that sums up a firm's revenues, costs, and profit over a period of time.

Indifference curve A curve that shows the combinations of consumption bundles that give the consumer the same utility.

Indirect finance A flow of funds from savers to borrowers through financial intermediaries such as banks. Intermediaries raise funds from savers to lend to firms (and other borrowers).

Inelastic demand Demand is inelastic when the percentage change in quantity demanded is less than the percentage change in price, so the price elasticity is less than 1 in absolute value.

Inferior good A good for which the demand increases as income falls, and decreases as income rises.

Interest rate The cost of borrowing funds, usually expressed as a percentage of the amount borrowed.

Isocost line All the combinations of two inputs, such as capital and labor, that have the same total cost.

Isoquant A curve showing all the combinations of two inputs, such as capital and labor, that will produce the same level of output.

Glossary   **G-3**

L

Labor union An organization of employees that has the legal right to bargain with employers about wages and working conditions.

Law of demand Holding everything else constant, when the price of a product falls, the quantity demanded of the product will increase, and when the price of a product rises, the quantity demanded of the product will decrease.

Law of diminishing marginal utility Consumers experience diminishing additional satisfaction as they consume more of a good or service during a given period of time.

Law of diminishing returns The principle that, at some point, adding more of a variable input, such as labor, to the same amount of a fixed input, such as capital, will cause the marginal product of the variable input to decline.

Law of supply Holding everything else constant, increases in price cause increases in the quantity supplied, and decreases in price cause decreases in the quantity supplied.

Liability Anything owed by a person or a firm.

Limited liability The legal provision that shields owners of a corporation from losing more than they have invested in the firm.

Long run A period of time long enough to allow a firm to vary all of its inputs, to adopt new technology, and to increase or decrease the size of its physical plant.

Long-run average cost curve A curve showing the lowest cost at which the firm is able to produce a given quantity of output in the long run, when no inputs are fixed.

Long-run competitive equilibrium The situation in which the entry and exit of firms has resulted in the typical firm breaking even.

Long-run supply curve A curve showing the relationship in the long run between market price and the quantity supplied.

Lorenz curve A curve showing the distribution of income by arraying incomes from lowest to highest on the horizontal axis and indicating the cumulative fraction of income earned by each fraction of households on the vertical axis.

M

Macroeconomics The study of the economy as a whole, including topics such as inflation, unemployment, and economic growth.

Marginal analysis Analysis that involves comparing marginal benefits and marginal costs.

Marginal benefit The additional benefit to a consumer from consuming one more unit of a good or service.

Marginal cost The change in a firm's total cost from producing one more unit of a good or service.

Marginal product of labor The additional output a firm produces as a result of hiring one more worker.

Marginal productivity theory of income distribution The theory that the distribution of income is determined by the marginal productivity of the factors of production that individuals own.

Marginal rate of substitution (MRS) The slope of an indifference curve; represents the rate at which a consumer would be willing to trade off one good for another.

Marginal rate of technical substitution (MRTS) The slope of an isoquant; represents the rate at which a firm is able to substitute one input for another, while keeping the level of output constant.

Marginal revenue (MR) Change in total revenue from selling one more unit.

Marginal revenue product of labor (MRP) The change in the firm's revenue as a result of hiring one more worker.

Marginal tax rate The fraction of each additional dollar of income that must be paid in taxes.

Marginal utility (MU) The change in total utility a person receives from consuming one additional unit of a good or service.

Market A group of buyers and sellers of a good or service and the institution or arrangement by which they come together to trade.

Market demand The demand by all the consumers of a given good or service.

Market economy An economy in which the decisions of households and firms interacting in markets allocate economic resources.

Market equilibrium A situation where quantity demanded equals quantity supplied.

Market failure Situations in which the market fails to produce the efficient level of output.

Market power The ability of a firm to charge a price greater than marginal cost.

Marketing All the activities necessary for a firm to sell a product to a consumer.

Microeconomics The study of how households and firms make choices, how they interact in markets, and how the government attempts to influence their choices.

Minimum efficient scale The level of output at which all economies of scale have been exhausted.

Mixed economy An economy in which most economic decisions result from the interaction of buyers and sellers in markets, but in which the government plays a significant role in the allocation of resources.

Monopolistic competition A market structure in which barriers to entry are low, and many firms compete by selling similar, but not identical, products.

Monopoly The only seller of a good or service that does not have a close substitute.

Monopsony The sole buyer of a factor of production.

Moral hazard The tendency of people who have insurance to change their actions because of the insurance, or, more broadly, actions taken by one party to a transaction that are different from what the other party expected at the time of the transaction.

Multinational enterprise (MNE) A firm that conduct operations in more than one country.

N

Nash equilibrium A situation in which each firm chooses the best strategy, given the strategies chosen by other firms.

Natural monopoly A situation in which economies of scale are so large that one firm can supply the entire market at a lower average total cost than can two or more firms.

Network externalities Network externalities exist when the usefulness of a product increases with the number of consumers who use it.

Noncooperative equilibrium An equilibrium in a game in which players do not cooperate but pursue their own self-interest.

Normal good A good for which the demand increases as income rises and decreases as income falls.

Normative analysis Analysis concerned with what ought to be.

O

Oligopoly A market structure in which a small number of interdependent firms compete.

Opportunity cost The highest-valued alternative that must be given up to engage in an activity.

P

Partnership A firm owned jointly by two or more persons and not organized as a corporation.

Patent The exclusive right to a product for a period of 20 years from the date the product was invented.

Payoff matrix A table that shows the payoffs that each firm earns from every combination of strategies by the firms.

Perfectly competitive market A market that meets the conditions of (1) many buyers and sellers, (2) all firms selling identical products, and (3) no barriers to new firms entering the market.

Perfectly elastic demand Demand is perfectly elastic when a change in price results in an infinite change in quantity demanded.

Perfectly inelastic demand Demand is perfectly inelastic when a change in price results in no change in quantity demanded.

Personnel economics The application of economic analysis to human resources issues.

Pigovian taxes and subsidies Government taxes and subsidies intended to bring about an efficient level of output in the presence of externalities.

Positive analysis Analysis concerned with what is.

Poverty line A level of annual income equal to three times the amount necessary to purchase the minimal quantity of food required for adequate nutrition.

Poverty rate The percentage of the population that is poor according to the federal government's definition.

Present value The value in today's dollars of funds to be paid or received in the future.

Price ceiling A legally determined maximum price that sellers may charge.

Price discrimination Charging different prices to different customers for the same product when the price differences are not due to differences in cost.

Price elasticity of demand The responsiveness of the quantity demanded to a change in price, measured by dividing the percentage change in the quantity demanded of a product by the percentage change in the product's price.

Price elasticity of supply The responsiveness of the quantity supplied to a change in price, measured by dividing the percentage change in the quantity supplied of a product by the percentage change in the product's price.

Price floor A legally determined minimum price that sellers may receive.

Price taker A buyer or seller that is unable to affect the market price.

Principal-agent problem A problem caused by an agent pursuing his own interests rather than the interests of the principal who hired him.

Prisoners' dilemma A game where pursuing dominant strategies results in noncooperation that leaves everyone worse off.

Private benefit The benefit received by the consumer of a good or service.

Private cost The cost borne by the producer of a good or service.

Private good A good that is both rival and excludable.

Producer surplus The difference between the lowest price a firm would have been willing to accept and the price it actually receives.

Product markets Markets for goods—such as computers—and services—such as medical treatment.

Production function The relationship between the inputs employed by the firm and the maximum output it can produce with those inputs.

Production possibilities frontier A curve showing the maximum attainable combinations of two products that may be produced with available resources.

Productive efficiency The situation in which a good or service is produced at the lowest possible cost.

Profit Total revenue minus total cost.

Progressive tax A tax for which people with lower incomes pay a lower percentage of their income in tax than do people with higher incomes.

Property rights The rights individuals or businesses have to the exclusive use of their property, including the right to buy or sell it.

Protectionism The use of trade barriers to shield domestic firms from foreign competition.

Public franchise A designation by the government that a firm is the only legal provider of a good or service.

Public good A good that is both nonrivalrous and nonexcludable.

Q

Quantity demanded The amount of a good or service that a consumer is willing and able to purchase at a given price.

Quantity supplied The amount of a good or service that a firm is willing and able to supply at a given price.

Quota A numerical limit imposed by the government on the quantity of a good that can be imported into a country.

R

Regressive tax A tax for which people with lower incomes pay a higher percentage of their income in tax than do people with higher incomes.

Rivalry The situation that occurs when one person's consuming a unit of a good means no one else can consume it.

S

Scarcity The situation in which unlimited wants exceed the limited resources available to fulfill those wants.

Separation of ownership from control In many large corporations the top management, rather than the shareholders, control day-to-day operations.

Short run The period of time during which at least one of the firm's inputs is fixed.

Shortage A situation in which the quantity demanded is greater than the quantity supplied.

Shutdown point The minimum point on a firm's average variable cost curve; if the price falls below this point, the firm shuts down production in the short run.

Social benefit The total benefit from consuming a good, including both the private benefit and any external benefit.

Social cost The total cost of producing a good, including both the private cost and any external cost.

Sole proprietorship A firm owned by a single individual and not organized as a corporation.

Stock A financial security that represents partial ownership of a firm.

Stockholders' equity The difference between the value of a corporation's assets and the value of its liabilities; also known as net worth.

Substitutes Goods and services that can be used for the same purpose.

Substitution effect The change in the quantity demanded of a good that results from a change in price making the good more or less expensive relative to other goods, holding constant the effect of the price change on consumer purchasing power.

Sunk cost A cost that has already been paid and cannot be recovered.

Supply curve A curve that shows the relationship between the price of a product and the quantity of the product supplied.

Supply schedule A table that shows the relationship between the price of a product and the quantity of the product supplied.

Surplus A situation in which the quantity supplied is greater than the quantity demanded.

T

Tariff A tax imposed by a government on imports.

Tax incidence The actual division of the burden of a tax between buyers and sellers in a market.

Technological change Change in the ability of a firm to produce a given level of output with a given quantity of inputs.

Technology The processes a firm uses to turn inputs into outputs of goods and services.

Terms of trade The ratio at which a country can trade its exports for imports from other countries.

Total cost The cost of all the inputs a firm uses in production.

Total revenue The total amount of funds received by a seller of a good or service, calculated by multiplying price per unit by the number of units sold.

Trade The act of buying or selling.

Trade-off The idea that because of scarcity, producing more of one good or service means producing less of another good or service.

Tragedy of the commons The tendency for a common resource to be overused.

Transactions costs The costs in time and other resources that parties incur in the process of agreeing to and carrying out an exchange of goods or services.

Two-part tariff A situation in which consumers pay one price (or tariff) for the right to buy as much of a related good as they want at a second price.

U

Unit-elastic demand Demand is unit-elastic when the percentage change in quantity demanded is equal to the percentage change in price, so the price elasticity is equal to 1 in absolute value.

Utility The enjoyment or satisfaction people receive from consuming goods and services.

V

Variable costs Costs that change as output changes.

Vertical merger A merger between firms at different stages of production of a good.

Voluntary exchange The situation that occurs in markets when both the buyer and seller of a product are made better off by the transaction.

Voluntary export restraint An agreement negotiated between two countries that places a numerical limit on the quantity of a good that can be imported by one country from the other country.

W

Winner's curse The idea that the winner in certain auctions may have overestimated the value of the good, thus ending up worse off than the losers.

World Trade Organization (WTO) An international organization that enforces international trade agreements.

COMPANY INDEX

Photo

Chapter 1, *page 3,* Michel Setboun, Corbis/Bettmann; *page 12,* Sherwin Castro/Reuters, Landov LLC.

Chapter 2, *page 33,* BMW of North America, LLC; *page 38,* AP Wide World Photos; *page 47,* Corbis/Bettmann; *page 50,* SuperStock, Inc.; *page 52,* S.I.N., Corbis/Bettmann.

Chapter 3, *page 63,* AP Wide World Photos; *page 69,* David Young-Wolff, PhotoEdit; *page 70,* Michael Newman, PhotoEdit; *page 73,* Kathleen Olson; *page 82,* AFP, Getty Images, Inc.-Agence France Presse.

Chapter 4, *page 97,* Rudi Von Briel, PhotoEdit; *page 100,* AP Wide World Photos; *page 107,* Laima Druskis, Pearson Education/PH College; *page 110,* Zefa/N. Guegan, Masterfile Corporation; *page 117,* Bill Aron, PhotoEdit.

Chapter 5, *page 131,* Thomas Kitchin, Tom Stack & Associates, Inc.; *page 137,* Swift, Joe, Index Stock Imagery, Inc.; *page 140,* AP Wide World Photos; *page 146,* Anil Risal Singh/UNEP, Peter Arnold, Inc.; *page 147,* AP Wide World Photos.

Chapter 6, *page 165,* Rune Hellestad, Corbis/Bettmann, *page 173,* Myrleen Ferguson Cate, PhotoEdit; *page 178,* Matthew Staver/Bloomberg News, Landov LLC; *page 180,* Stefko, Bob, Getty Images Inc.-Image Bank; *page 185,* Jim Sulley/Newscast, The Image Works.

Chapter 7, *page 199,* Kim Kulish, Corbis/Bettmann; *page 201,* Ed Pritchard, Getty Images Inc.-Stone Allstock; *page 207,* Jeffrey Brown, Aurora & Quanta Productions Inc.; *page 209,* David McIntyre, Black Star.

Chapter 8, *page 231,* Burke/Triolo, Getty Images, Inc.-Brand X Pictures; *page 234,* Ron Sherman, Corbis/Bettmann; *page 242,* Corbis/Sygma *page 252,* Pallava Bagla, Corbis/Sygma; *page 254,* AP Wide World Photos; *page 266,* The Image Works.

Chapter 9, *page 271,* Corbis/ Bettman; *page 283,* Duomo, Corbis/Bettmann; *page 287,* AP Wide World Photos; *page 290,* Peter Hvizdak, The Image Works; *page 303,* AP Wide World Photos.

Chapter 10, *page 313,* Yoshikazu Tsuno/AFP, Getty Images, Inc.-Agence France Presse; *page 315,* Getty Images, Inc.-Liaison; *page 316,* Stockbyte; *page 320,* AP Wide World Photos; *page 331,* Getty Images Inc.-Hulton Archive Photos; *page 347,* Walt Disney Pictures/Pixar, Picture Desk, Inc./Kobal Collection.

Chapter 11, *page 353,* AP Wide World Photos; *page 365,* Stockbyte; *page 366,* Raymond Forbes, SuperStock, Inc.; *page 375,* Richard Heinzen, SuperStock, Inc.

Chapter 12, *page 387,* AP Wide World Photos; *page 396,* Mario Tama, Getty Images, Inc.-Liaison; *page 399,* Yuriko Nakao/Reuters, Corbis/Reuters America LLC; *page 401,* David Young-Wolff, PhotoEdit.

Chapter 13, *page 413,* Mary Steinbacher, PhotoEdit; *page 419,* Dreamworks/Universal/Eli Reed, Picture Desk, Inc./Kobal Collection; *page 422,* eBay Inc.; *page 424,* KEN REID, Getty Images, Inc.–Taxi; *Page 432,* David Frazier, The Image Works.

Chapter 14, *page 443,* Tom Stewart, Corbis/Bettmann; *page 445,* Tim Boyle, Getty Images; *page 447,* Sean Cayton, The Image Works; *page 448,* Rob Melnychuk, Getty Images, Inc.-Photodisc.; *page 463,* Joe Marquette, AP Wide World Photos.

Chapter 15, *page 475,* John M. Greim, Creative Eye/MIRA.com; *page 482,* David Young-Wolff, PhotoEdit; *page 487,* Spencer Grant, PhotoEdit.

Chapter 16, *page 499,* AP Wide World Photos; *page 508,* Pearson Learning Photo Studio; *page 510,* Archive Holdings, Inc..Levick 03RLEI, Edwin, Getty Images Inc.-Image Bank; *page 513,* Columbia Pictures, Picture Desk, Inc./Kobal Collection; *page 522,* Picturequest-Royalty Free.

Chapter 17, *page 535,* Corbis/Bettmann ; *page 539,* Ronnie Kaufman, Corbis/Bettmann; *page 541,* Stephen Jaffe / AFP, Getty Images, Inc.-Agence France Presse; *page 545,* Stockbyte; *page 547,* Kristen Brochmann, Fundamental Photographs, NYC.

Chapter 18, *page 555,* Chuck Savage, Corbis/Bettmann; *page 559,* Bruce Avery, SuperStock, Inc.; *page 562,* Spencer Grant, PhotoEdit; *page 565,* Dell, Inc.

Text

Chapter 1, *page 84:* Steve W. Martinez, "Vertical Coordination in the Pork and Broiler Industries: Implications for Pork and Chicken Products," Agricultural Economics Report No. 777, April 1999.

Chapter 4, *page 107:* Thomas Sowell, *Applied Economics: Thinking Beyond Stage One,* New York: Basic Books, 2004, page 114.

Chapter 5, *page 137:* Arthur G. Fraas and Vincent G. Munley, "Municipal Wastewater: Treatment and Cost," *Journal of Environmental Economics and Management,* Vol. 11, 1984, pages 28-38.; *page 154:* Paisley Dodds, "Haiti Deforestation Exacerbates Flooding," Associate Press, June 2, 2004.

Chapter 6, *page 179:* Austan Goolsbee and Judith Chevalier, "Price Competition Online: Amazon Versus Barnes and Noble," *Quantitative Marketing and Economics,* Vol. 1, No. 2, June 2003, 203-222; page 181: U.S. Dept. of Commerce, *Historical Statistics of the United States,* Series K507 and K508, and U.S. Department of Agriculture, *Agricultural Statistics, 2004.*

Chapter 7, *page 211:* Deborah Solomon, "WorldCom's Ex-Controller Pleads Guilty to Three Counts," *Wall Street Journal,* September 27, 2002, quoting from Myers's guilty plea; and Sharon Young, "MCI Restates 2001, 2002 Earnings, Cutting Profit by $74.4 Billion," *Wall Street Journal,* March 12, 2004.

Chapter 8, *page 243:* Gary McWilliams, "In Electronics, U.S. Companies Seize Momentum From Japan," *Wall Street Journal,* March 10, 2005, page A1.

Chapter 9, page 282: Gary S. Becker and Kevin M. Murphy, *Social Economics: Market Behavior in a Social Environment,* Cambridge: Harvard University Press, 2000, page 9.

Chapter 9, *page 285:* Richard H. Thaler, *The Winner's Curse: Paradoxes and Anomalies of Economic Life,* New York: Free Press, 1992, page 25; *page 286:* Gary Becker, "A Note on Restaurant Pricing and Other Examples of Social Influences on Prices," *Journal of Political Economy,* Vol. 99, No. 5, October 1991, pages 1109-1116; and Daniel Kahneman, Jack Knetsch, and Richard Thaler, "Fairness as a Constraint on Profit Seeking: Entitlements in the Market," *American Economic Review,* Vol. 76, No. 4, September 1986, pages 728-741; *page 289:* Daniel Kahneman and Amos Tversky, "Choices, Values, and Frames," *American Psychologist,* April 1984.

Chapter 10, *page 329:* Norihiko Shirouzu and Sebastian Moffett,

"As Toyota Closes In on GM, Quality Concerns Also Grow" *Wall Street Journal*, August 4, 2004.

Chapter 11, *page 373:* Sharon M. Oster, *Modern Competitive Analysis*, Third edition, New York: Oxford University Press, 1999, page 11.

Chapter 12, *page 398:* Andy Serwer, "Hot Starbucks to Go," *Fortune*, January 12, 2004; *page 401:* Peter F. Drucker, *Management: Tasks, Responsibilities, Practices*, New York: Harper & Row, 1974, pages 63-64.

Chapter 14, *page 458:* Joseph A. Schumpeter, *Capitalism, Socialism, and Democracy*, New York: Harper & Row, 1975 (first published 1942), page 84.

Chapter 15, *page 487:* Philip Gendall, Judith Holdershaw, and Ron Garland, "The Effect of Odd Pricing on Demand, *European Journal of Marketing*, Vol. 31, No. 11/12, 1997, pages 799-813.

Chapter 16, *page 509:* Bruce Orwall, "Disney Delivers 'Lilo and Stitch' on Competition-Driven Budget," *Wall Street Journal*, June 18, 2002, page A1; *page 514:* George A. Akerlof and William T. Dickens, "The Economic Consequences of Cognitive Dissonance," *American Economic Review*, Vol. 72, No. 3, June 1982, pages 307-319; *page 520:* Edward P. Lazear, *Personnel Economics for Managers*, New York: John Wiley & Sons, 1998, especially Chapter 5; *page 527:* Source of information about Penn State: www.psu.edu/ur/ NEWS/news/flashback4.html.

Chapter 17, *page 546:* Leslie Cauley and Mary Lu Carnevale, "Wireless Giants, Some Surprise Players to Seek New Generation of Licenses," *Wall Street Journal*, October 31, 1994; Rita Koselka, "Playing Poker with Craig McCaw," *Forbes*, July 3, 1995, pages 62-64; Paul Klemperer, "What Really Matters in Auction Design," *Journal of Economic Perspectives*, Vol. 16, No. 1, Winter 2002, pages 169-189.

Chapter 18, *page 571:* Peter Gottschalk and Sheldon Danziger, "Family Income Mobility—How Much Is There, and Has It Changed," in James Auerbach and Richard Belous, eds., *The Inequality Paradox*, Washington, DC: National Policy Association, 1998.

Chapter Title	Chapter Opener	Making the Connection	An Inside Look
CHAPTER 1			
Economics: Foundations and Models	What Happens When U.S. Firms Move to China?	When Economists Disagree: A Debate over Outsourcing	How Does Economic Growth in China Affect Other Countries? Source: Economist
CHAPTER 2			
Trade-offs, Comparative Advantage, and the Market System	Managers Making Choices at BMW	Trade-offs and Tsunami Relief • Story of the Market System in Action, "I, Pencil" • Property Rights in Cyberspace: Napster, Kazaa, and iTunes	Choosing the Production Mix at BMW Source: WSJ
CHAPTER 3			
Where Prices Come From: The Interaction of Demand and Supply	How Hewlett-Packard Manages the Demand for Printers	Why Supermarkets Need to Understand Substitutes and Complements • Companies Respond to a Growing Hispanic Population • Estimating the Demand for Printers at Hewlett-Packard • The Falling Price of Large Flat-Screen Televisions	Hewlett-Packard Cuts PC Prices to Sell More Printers Source: WSJ
CHAPTER 4			
Economic Efficiency, Government Price Setting, and Taxes	Should the Government Control Apartment Rents?	The Consumer Surplus from Satellite Television • Price Floors in Labor Markets: The Minimum Wage • Does Holiday Gift Giving Have a Deadweight Loss? • Is the Burden of the Social Security Tax Really Shared Equally between Workers and Firms?	Dealing with Rent Control Source: Slate
CHAPTER 5			
Externalities, Environmental Policy, and Public Goods	Economic Incentives Spur Duke Energy Corporation to Reduce Pollution	The Reduction in Infant Mortality Due to the Clean Air Act • The Fable of the Bees • Can Tradeable Permits Reduce Global Warming? • Should the Government or the Airlines Screen Luggage at Airports?	Two Approaches to Fighting Global Warming: Kyoto Protocol and the Chicago Climate Exchange Source: NYT
CHAPTER 6			
Elasticity: The Responsiveness of Demand and Supply	Do People Care about the Prices of Books?	The Price Elasticity of Demand for Breakfast Cereal • Determining the Price Elasticity of Demand for DVDs by Market Experiment • Price Elasticity, Cross-Price Elasticity, and Income Elasticity in the Market for Alcoholic Beverages • Why Are Oil Prices So Unstable?	Do People Care about the Prices of Books on Amazon.com? Source: USA Today

We use business examples to explain economic concepts. This table highlights the topic and real-world company introduced in the chapter-opening vignette and revisited throughout the chapter. This table also lists the companies that appear in our *Making the Connection* and *An Inside Look* features.

Chapter Title	Chapter Opener	Making the Connection	An Inside Look
CHAPTER 7			
Firms, the Stock Market, and Corporate Governance	Google: From Dorm Room to Wall Street	What's in a "Name"? Lloyd's of London Learns about Unlimited Liability the Hard Way • Following General Electric's Stock and Bond Prices in the Financial Pages • A Bull in China's Financial Shop	Google's Initial Public Offering Source: WSJ
CHAPTER 8			
Comparative Advantage and the Gains from International Trade	Sugar Quota Drives U.S. Candy Manufacturers Overseas	Has Outsourcing Hurt the U.S. Economy? • Why is Dalton, Georgia the Carpet-Making Capital of the World? • The Unintended Conesquences of Banning Goods Made with Child Labor • Did NAFTA Help or Hurt the U.S. Economy?	The United States and Australia Reduce Trade Barriers Source: San Francisco Chronicle
CHAPTER 9			
Consumer Choice and Economics	Can LeBron James Get You to Drink Powerade?	Network Externalities • Professor Krueger Goes to the Super Bowl • Why Don't Students Study More?	Can Whoopi Goldberg Get You to Buy Slim-Fast? Source: Boston Globe
CHAPTER 10			
Technology, Production, and Costs	Sony Uses a Cost Curve to Determine the Price of Radios	Improving Inventory Control at Wal-Mart • Fixed Costs in the Publishing Industry • Adam Smith's Famous Account of the Division of Labor in a Pin Factory • The Colossal River Rouge: Diseconomies of Scale at the Ford Motor Company	Using Long-Run Average Cost Curves to Analyze Expansion at Sony and Samsung Source: FT
CHAPTER 11			
Firms in Perfectly Competitive Markets	Perfect Competition in the Market for Organic Apples	Losing Money In The Medical Screening Industry • When to Close a Laundry • The Decline of Apple Production in New York State	Firms Crank Out Organic Snacks Source: USA Today
CHAPTER 12			
Monopolistic Competition: The Competitive Model in a More Realistic Setting	Starbucks: Growth through Product Differentiation	The Rise and Fall of Apple's Macintosh Computer • Staying One Step Ahead of the Competition: Eugène Schueller and L'Oréal • Abercrombie and Fitch: Can the Product Be Too Differentiated?	Starbucks and McDonald's Cater to Insomniacs Source: WSJ